Institutional Review Board
Management and Function

Robert J. Amdur, M.D.

University of Florida Health Science Center

Elizabeth A. Bankert, M.A.

Dartmouth College

JONES AND BARTLETT PUBLISHERS

Sudbury, Massachusetts

BOSTON   TORONTO   LONDON   SINGAPORE

World Headquarters
Jones and Bartlett Publishers
40 Tall Pine Drive
Sudbury, MA 01776
978-443-5000
info@jbpub.com
www.jbpub.com

Jones and Bartlett Publishers Canada
2406 Nikanna Road
Mississauga, ON L5C 2W6
CANADA

Jones and Bartlett Publishers International
Barb House, Barb Mews
London, W6 7PA
UK

Library of Congress Cataloging In Publication Data
CIP data unavailable at time of printing

Production Credits
Acquisitions Editor: Penny M. Glynn
Associate Editor: Thomas Prindle
Production Editor: Jon Workman
Marketing Manager: Taryn Wahlquist
Manufacturing Buyer: Amy Duddridge
Cover Design: Philip Regan
Text Design: Anne Spencer
Composition: Carlisle Communications, Ltd.
Printing and Binding: Courier Westford

Printed in the United States of America
05 04 03 02 01   10 9 8 7 6 5 4 3 2 1

We dedicate this book to our friends and colleagues on the Dartmouth Committee for Protection of Human Subjects. Together we have had the energy to handle the challenge of research regulation, the commitment to ask the tough questions, and the courage to make the difficult decisions. You make us proud to be part of the IRB system for protecting the rights and welfare of research subjects.

Robert J. Amdur
Elizabeth A. Bankert

"Let us all remember that a slower progress in the conquest of disease would not threaten society, grievous as it is to those who deplore that particular disease be not yet conquered, but that society would indeed be threatened by the erosion of those moral values whose loss, possibly caused by too ruthless a pursuit of scientific progress, would make its most dazzling triumphs not worth having."

—H. Jonas, in "Philosophical Reflections on Experimenting with Human Subjects." *Experimentation with Human Subjects* (Paul A. Freund, ed.) New York: George Braziller, 1970.

Contents

PART 5 Initial Protocol Review and the Full-Committee Meeting 141

PART 11   Reference Material and Contact Information   487

Acknowledgments

The editors thank Patsy McCarty and Jennifer Brackeen for assistance with formatting and editorial review of the manuscript, and Laura Kendall and Stephanie Hood for checking references. Their expertise and hard work made it feasible to complete the book in a reasonable amount of time.

Jesse's Intent

Paul Gelsinger

Born on June 18, 1981, Jesse Gelsinger was a real character in a lot of ways. Not having picked out a name for him prior to his birth, we decided to name him Jesse three days later. When considering a middle name, we pondered James, but decided that just Jesse was enough for this kid. His infancy was pretty normal. With a brother 13 months his senior, he was not overly spoiled. He crawled and walked at the appropriate ages. When he started talking, it quickly became obvious that this was one kid who would speak his mind and crack everybody up at the same time. He nursed until he was nearly two years old. It wasn't until Jesse was about two years and eight months old that his metabolic disorder reared its ugly head.

Jesse had always been a very picky eater. Since weaning, he would more and more refuse to eat meat and dairy products, focusing instead on potatoes and cereals. After the birth of his sister in late January 1984 and following a mild cold in early March 1984, Jesse's behavior became very erratic over a brief period of time. Because his mother had previously experienced schizophrenic behavior, I was very concerned that Jesse was exhibiting signs of psychoses. His speech was very belligerent—as if possessed. My wife, Pattie, and I took him to see our family doctor. Thinking that Jesse was anemic because of his poor diet and lethargy, the doctor put Jesse on a high protein diet. That was the worst thing for Jesse. Forcing him to eat peanut butter sandwiches, bacon, and to drink milk over the next two days overwhelmed Jesse's system.

On a Saturday in mid-March 1984, Jesse awoke, parked himself in front of the television to watch cartoons, and promptly fell back asleep. When we were unable to rouse him we became alarmed. His mother called the doctor and insisted that we be allowed to take Jesse to Children's Hospital, just across the Delaware River from our home. Upon arrival at the hospital, Jesse was admitted to the emergency room in what they called a "first-stage coma." He responded to stimuli but would not awaken. After several tests indicated high blood ammonia, the doctor told us that Jesse most probably had Reye's syndrome, which upset us very much. Several hours later they told us that other tests indicated that this was not Reye's, and that they would need to run more tests to determine what was wrong with Jesse.

Within a week we had the diagnosis of ornithine transcarbamylase deficiency syndrome (OTC). OTC, we were told, was a very rare metabolic disorder. Jesse's form of the disorder was considered mild and could be controlled by medication and diet.

And so, after eleven days in the hospital, Jesse came home. We hawked everything he ate and made certain he took his medications. From there on Jesse progressed fairly normally, although he remained small for his age. It wasn't until he was ten that he needed to be hospitalized again. Following a weekend of too much protein intake, Jesse's system was unable to rid itself of the ammonia buildup fast enough and he again slipped into a coma. His specialist scrambled to understand how to get him well again, not ever actually having had to treat hyperammonemia. Within five days, Jesse was again well enough to go home, having suffered no apparent neurological damage.

As Jesse entered his teenage years, he resisted taking his medications. He felt that he could control his disorder and only took his meds when he didn't feel well. His mother

Note: This chapter presents an edited transcript of the keynote talk given by Mr. Gelsinger at the meeting of the Applied Research Ethics National Association (ARENA) in San Diego, CA on October 31, 2000.

and I had divorced in 1989, two years after our move to Tucson, Arizona. Jesse was under my care. At age sixteen, Jesse was taking nearly fifty pills a day to control his illness. My new wife, Mickie, and I kept careful watch over Jesse, but as he grew older we expected him to take better care of himself. With six children between us, we had much to consider. Jesse was being seen at a state-funded metabolic clinic in Tucson twice a year to monitor his development and, while not always compliant, he was progressing into adulthood.

In September 1998, Jesse and I were made aware by his specialist of a clinical trial being done at a renowned medical facility in Philadelphia. They were working on what he described as gene therapy for Jesse's disorder. We were instantly interested, but Jesse was told that he could not participate until age eighteen. That fall, Jesse was stressing his metabolism as he had never done before. He had acquired a part time job and an off-road motorcycle, so I saw him only now and then. As a senior in high school, Jesse had a very busy schedule. Unknown to me at the time, he was having symptoms of his disorder but was trying to hide them. He didn't want restrictions placed on him. I knew that he took his medications inconsistently because I rarely had to order them. I spoke with him every other week about his need to take better care of himself. It took his nearly dying to wake him up.

On December 22, 1998, I arrived home in mid-afternoon to find Jesse curled up on the couch. A close friend was with him. Jesse was very frightened. He was vomiting uncontrollably and could not hold down his medications. After about five minutes with him, I determined that I could not manage his recovery. I convinced his pediatrician and specialist that Jesse needed to be hospitalized and placed on intravenous fluids. With his ammonia levels at six times normal, Jesse was in trouble. After no significant changes in his condition by December 24th, the hospital let Jesse go home for Christmas. Listless all day, Jesse crashed Christmas night and was admitted to intensive care, where they discovered hypoglycemia—seriously low blood sugar. His specialist was certain that it was due to one of his medications, l-arginine, and discontinued it. He also decided that Jesse's primary medication, sodium benzoate, was not effective enough and ordered that a newer, better medication be provided.

While awaiting his new medication, Jesse recovered well enough to be placed in a regular room at the hospital, but his ammonia levels refused to drop. I was staying in the hospital at Jesse's side day and night. Two days after Christmas, on a Sunday afternoon, Jesse and I had a conversation about how he was doing. I described to Jess how it seemed that he was stuck up a tree, not knowing whether he was going to climb down or fall out. I went home to be with the rest of my family and sleep in my own bed for one night. Jesse called me at about 11:00 P.M. and said, "Dad, I fell out of the tree." He was again vomiting uncontrollably. I rushed back to the hospital and spent a heart-rending two days trying to help my son through his crisis. On Monday, I discovered that the insurance company was balking at paying for Jesse's new medications and that they had not been shipped. I told the pharmacist to purchase the new medications ($3,300 for one month's supply) with my credit card and that I would deal with the insurance company later. The insurance company relented at that point, authorized the medications, and they were ordered on Tuesday. By Tuesday afternoon, December 29th, Jesse was so listless that I grew very alarmed that he would not get well.

At 5:00 P.M., Jesse's vomiting returned and he became incoherent. I moved into the hall to get help. There I found his pediatrician examining his chart. I summoned him to Jesse's room and, while he called in the intensive care doctor, I called my wife and told her to come immediately. Jesse's aunt and grandmother arrived for a visit only to find Jesse in crisis. Mickie arrived and together we held Jesse while they prepared a bed for him in intensive care. The intensive care doctor, seeing Jesse's deteriorating condition and believing Jesse mentally impaired, inquired if life support would be appropriate. It was then that I realized that these people had not known Jesse well, and I explained that the loss of mental faculties that they were seeing was not Jesse's normal state at all. Jesse developed tremors and began to vomit. Suddenly he just stopped. I whispered to Mickie, "He's still breathing, isn't he?" I asked Jesse's pediatrician to check him. After placing his stethoscope on Jesse's chest for a few moments, he told the nurse to call a code blue. We were whisked from the room while they intubated and manually ventilated Jesse and took him to intensive care. We were distraught, believing Jesse to be near death. After fifteen minutes, they indicated that they were getting him under control and that his heart never stopped.

For two days, Jesse lingered in an induced coma to allow the ventilator to control his breathing. He weighed in at only ninety-seven pounds, down from his healthy weight of one hundred twenty pounds. His old medication only partially lowered his ammonia level.

On Thursday morning, Jesse's new medications arrived. Through a gastrointestinal feed, the doctors gave Jesse a special nutritional formula containing his new medications. Within twenty-four hours, Jesse's ammonia levels started falling. We waited at his side as he began to regain consciousness. His first conscious act was to motion us to change the television station. We knew then that Jesse was back.

Within a day, Jesse was out of intensive care, his ammonia levels normal, something he had never known his entire life. He was ordering and eating food like a teenager—again something he had never experienced. We were ecstatic. When his specialist came to see him, I shook his hand and told him that he had a medical miracle on his hands. One week after nearly dying, Jesse was back in school full time with a newfound zeal for life.

By early February 1999, Jesse had recovered enough strength to consider returning to work, but he came down with a serious case of influenza. Because illness often triggered Jesse's metabolic disorder, I stayed home to keep an eye on his condition. Jesse was kind enough to pass the bug on to me. It was the sickest I'd been in twenty years: a fever for six days and fatigue for four weeks. Jesse recovered within a week and was back in school. I had him tested twice while he was ill and his ammonia level was only slightly elevated. The new medications were working wonderfully.

Near the end of February, Jesse returned to his part-time job as a courtesy clerk at a supermarket three miles from our home. On Saturday the 27th, he called me at 11:00 P.M. for a ride home. I picked him up in my work van, and on the way home we had a fateful conversation. I had been asking Jesse to find out if his job would offer him medical insurance once he graduated from school in May. Being a typical teenager, he had done nothing. I told him in no uncertain terms that he needed medical insurance if he didn't intend to continue his education. At the time, we believed that Jesse would not be covered under our insurance once he left school.

Jesse rarely raged at his illness, but this time he flung a half-full bottle of soda against my windshield while cursing his disorder. In anger, I gave him a backhand punch to the shoulder and chastised him. Only two blocks from home, Jesse flung open the door and told me he was jumping out. I said, "Whoa! Wait until I stop." As I was coming to a stop, he gave me a look like he was jumping and went out the door. All I could envision was Jesse falling under the van and my running him over. Sure enough, even though I had nearly stopped, he fell. As I stopped, I could hear him screaming that I was on his arm. Now, my van is a work van loaded with tools and weighing six thousand pounds. Thinking "Oh, God, no!" I threw the van into park and raced around in back to find Jesse's right arm and elbow pinned under my right rear tire. Making certain that his body was clear; I rolled the van forward off his arm.

The kid was crying in agony. As I cradled him in my arms, I cried, "You idiot! What were you thinking?" and then, "Jesse, I'm sorry." He begged me not to move him, and I knew he would need an ambulance. His arm was a red mess from wrist to upper arm with the elbow area gouged out. The tire print was evident on the underside of his arm.

As I began to think about seeking help, a woman who had witnessed what happened while driving from the other direction asked if she could help. I told her to please call 911 and she drove off to do so. A neighbor, hearing the commotion, came out and offered his help. Another passerby offered me his cell phone and I called my wife. Within minutes the paramedics arrived, strapped Jesse to a gurney, and whisked him off to the hospital. After the police informed me that I had done no wrong, that I could not control his actions, it was all I could do to drive the one block home. I had been there to help Jesse through his near-death experience in December and through a serious bout with the flu only to nearly end his life in an accident.

Shaking and emotional, Mickie drove me to the hospital. Jesse was okay; he hadn't even broken his arm! He had suffered extensive road rash and a serious wound to his elbow, but he recovered full use of his arm following two days in the hospital and a month of physical therapy. I was an emotional wreck for a week following the accident. This kid was something else. His sister told him that if he caused me to have a heart attack she was going to kill him. A month later I got word from our insurance company regarding Jesse's status if he did not continue his education. He was covered until age twenty-five as long as he remained our dependent. I joked with him that I had run him over for nothing. He was proud of his war wound from dad. God, what a relief to see this kid bounce back again.

In early April 1999, Jesse again had an appointment at the metabolic clinic. While there, the subject of gene therapy and the clinical trial at Philadelphia came up again. Jesse and I were both still very interested. I informed the doctor that we were already planning a trip to New Jersey in late June, that Jesse would be eighteen at that time, and to let those running the clinical trial know we were interested. I received a letter from the clinical trial people in late April firming things up. By late May, our visit was set. We would fly in on June 18th and he would be tested on the 22nd. Jesse was none too happy about flying in on the 18th; that was his birthday and he wanted to party with his friends. A few days later he told me it was okay to fly on his birthday. I told him that it was a good thing, since I had already bought the tickets for all six of us a month earlier.

So on Friday, June 18, 1999, Jesse, his three siblings, PJ (19), Mary (15), and Anne (14), and Mickie and I boarded a plane to take us down a path we never imagined. We had a party for Jesse that night at my brother's house. We had a reunion with ten of my fifteen siblings and extended families that Sunday. It was great to see everyone. The kids got to meet cousins they hadn't seen in twelve years. Jesse's cousins nicknamed him Captain Kirk because of the way he struck the volleyball with a two-handed chop. This was turning into a great vacation.

We hung out on Monday, and on Tuesday, June 22nd, we all headed over to Philly to meet with the clinical trial people. We arrived a few minutes late because of a wrong turn on the expressway only to discover that they weren't ready for us. The nurse in charge rounded up the doctor who was the principal investigator, and after a lengthy wait we were all ushered into a hospital room to go over consent forms and discuss the procedures that Jesse would undergo. The doctor described the technique that would be used. Jesse would be sedated and two catheters would be placed into his liver; one in the hepatic artery at the inlet to the liver to inject the viral vector and another to monitor the blood exiting the liver to assure that the vector was all being absorbed by the liver. He explained the dangers associated with this and that Jesse would need to remain immobile for about eight hours after the infusion to minimize the risk of a clot breaking free from the infusion site. The doctor also explained that Jesse would experience flu-like symptoms for a few days. He briefly explained that there was a remote possibility of his contracting hepatitis. When I questioned him on this, he explained that hepatitis was just an inflammation of the liver and that the liver was a remarkable organ, the only organ in the body with the ability to regenerate itself. In reading the consent form, I noticed the possibility of a liver transplant being required if the hepatitis progressed. The hepatitis seemed such a remote possibility and the need for transplant even more remote that no more alarms went off in my head.

The doctor proceeded to the next phase and what appeared the most dangerous aspect of the testing. A needle biopsy was to be performed of Jesse's liver one week after the infusion. Numbers explaining the risks of uncontrolled side effects were included. There was a one in ten thousand chance that Jesse could die from the biopsy! I said to Jesse that he needed to read and understand what he was getting into, that this was serious stuff. The risks seemed very remote, but also very real. Still, one in ten thousand weren't bad odds in my mind. There would be no benefit to Jesse, the doctor explained. Even if the genes worked, the effect would be transient because the body's immune system would attack and kill the virus over a four- to six-week period.

After our forty-five minute conversation with the doctor ended, Jesse consented to undergo the five-hour N15 ammonia study to determine his level of enzyme efficiency. Many vials of blood were taken before Jesse drank a small vial of N15 ammonia. This special isotope of ammonia would then show up in Jesse's blood and urine. The rate at which it was processed out of the body would determine Jesse's efficiency. Going into this study, we were aware that Jesse's efficiency was only six percent of that of a normal person. After waiting with Jesse for two hours, we all decided to head out to Pat's Steaks for lunch and tour South Street for a few hours. On our return to the hospital, Jesse was finished and ready to go.

It was now mid-afternoon and we decided to see the Betsy Ross house and Independence Mall. After we checked out the Liberty Bell, the kids wanted to see the Rocky statue, so we headed over to the Art Museum. Four of us, Jesse, PJ, Mary, and I, raced up the steps Rocky-style (we had watched the movie the night before). Finding only Rocky's footsteps, we learned that the statue had been moved to the Spectrum. So we headed over to Pattison Avenue. A Phillies game was about to start, so I stayed in our rented Durango while the kids had their pictures taken by Mickie. It was a fun time for everyone, especially Jesse. He was starting to feel good about what he was doing. This was his thing and he had a chance to help.

The following day, we toured New York City. Everybody got to pick a place to visit. Jesse chose FAO Schwarz toy store where he bought four pro-wrestling action figures. We all had a great day, finishing with the Empire State Building and the Staten Island Ferry.

Four weeks later, back in Tucson, we received a letter addressed to Mr. Paul Gelsinger and Jesse. It was from another of the principal investigators of the clinical trial, a world-renowned OTC expert, confirming Jesse's six percent efficiency of OTC and stating that they would like to have Jesse in their study. I presented the letter to Jesse and asked him if he still wanted to do this. He hesitated only a moment, then said yes. This same doctor called about a week later to follow up his letter and spoke to Jesse briefly. Jesse told him that he would need to call back and talk to me and explain everything. Jesse was deferring to me to understand this and the doctor was well aware of that.

When I spoke to the OTC expert, we discussed a number of things. Because they had forgotten to include the graph showing Jesse's N15 results, he faxed it to us. I asked if Jesse was the least efficient patient in the study. The doctor explained that he was, and steered the conversation to the results they had experienced to date. He explained that the treatment had worked temporarily in mice, even preventing death in mice exposed to a lethal injection of ammonia. He then explained that the most recent patient had shown a 50% increase in her ability to excrete ammonia following gene therapy. My reaction was to say, "Wow! This really works! So, with Jesse at six percent efficiency, you may be able to show exactly how well this works." His response was that there was hope, and that it would be for these kids. He explained that there were another 25 liver disorders that could be treated with the same technique and that, overall, these disorders affected about one in every 500 people. I did some quick math and figured that's 500,000 people in the U.S.A. alone, 12 million worldwide. I dropped my guard. This doctor and I never discussed the dangerous side of this work. When I presented to Jesse what the OTC specialist had to say, he knew the right thing to do. He signed on to help everybody and, hopefully, himself in the long run. The plan was for him to be the last patient tested. The procedure was tentatively scheduled for mid-October.

By late July 1999, Jesse had a new focus in his life, but he also had other priorities. He had just gotten a tattoo on the back of his right calf. Of course, he didn't discuss it with me first and had used the money he owed me to get it done. I had just bought him a used street motorcycle as a graduation present and he was getting his driver's license. It was great to see him grinning ear to ear as he drove off on his bike for the first time. We saw little of Jesse over the next two weeks. If he wasn't working, he was out riding with his buddy, Gar, or spending the night at a friend's house. He was still living at home and paying $35 a week for rent and $15 a week to pay for the bike insurance that we had fronted for him. This kid was really living and we were so proud of him.

In mid-August, we heard from the clinical trial people that they were having trouble scheduling their next patient and were wondering if Jesse would be available in September. I explained that I would have to check with him. He okayed it and arranged to take an unpaid leave of absence. Most communications with the hospital staff were done via e-mail at this point. The finalized date of admission would be September 9, 1999. I wanted to go with Jesse, but being self-employed and not seeing any great danger, I scheduled to fly in for what I had perceived as the most dangerous aspect of the testing, the liver biopsy. I would fly in on the 18th and return with Jesse on the 21st.

As September 9th approached, we all became more and more focused on Jesse's trip. Mickie bought him some new clothes. Jesse assembled his pro wrestling, Sylvester Stallone, and Adam Sandler videos, and I worked like a dog to get as much done as possible in preparation for my own departure. So with one bag filled with videos and another with clothing, Jesse and I headed off to the airport early on Thursday the 9th. He was both apprehensive and excited. He had to change planes in Phoenix and hail a cab to the hospital once he arrived in Philly. Jesse had never been away from Tucson on his own prior to this trip. Words cannot express how proud I was of this kid. Just eighteen, he was going off to help the world. When we reached his gate, I gave him a big hug. I looked him in the eye and told him he was my hero. As I drove off to work, I thought of him and what he was doing. I started considering how to get him some recognition. Little did I know what effect this kid was going to have.

Jesse called us that night using his phone card. He was well, but had a little mix-up with the cabbie about which hospital to take him to. The cabbie was cool about it though, he said. Reminded him of a scary version of James Earl Jones. Jesse was to have more N15 testing the following day and again on Sunday before the actual gene infusion on Monday, September 13. Saturday was an off day and he would be able to leave the hospital. Two of my brothers had arranged to visit with Jess, and that had put me at ease about not going. Jess had a blast with his uncle and cousins on Saturday and a good visit with his other uncle and aunt on Sunday. Mickie and I spoke with Jesse every day. His spirits were good. He grew apprehensive on Sunday evening. The doctor had put him on intravenous medications because his ammonia was elevated. I reasoned with him that these guys knew what they were doing, that they knew more about OTC than anybody on the planet. I didn't talk with the doctors; it was late.

I received a call from the principal investigator on Monday, just after they infused Jesse. He explained that everything went well and that Jesse would return to his room in a few hours. I discussed the infusion and how the vector did its job. He didn't like the word *invade* when I explained what I thought the virus did to the liver cells. He explained that if they could affect about one percent of Jesse's cells, they would get the results they desired. Mickie and I spoke with Jesse later that evening. He had the expected fever and was not feeling well. I told Jesse to hang in there, that I loved him. He responded, "I love you too, Dad." Mickie got the same kind of goodbye. Little did we know it was our last.

I awoke very early Tuesday morning and went to work. I received a mid-morning call from the doctor, asking if Jesse had a history of jaundice. I told him not since he was first born. He explained that Jesse was jaundiced and a bit disoriented. I said, "That's a liver function, isn't it?" He replied that it was and that they would keep me posted. I was alarmed and worried. My ex-wife, Pattie, happened to call about twenty minutes later, and I told her what was going on. She reminded me that Jesse had jaundice for three weeks at birth. I called the hospital back with that information and got somebody who was apparently typing every word I said. That seemed very unusual to me. I didn't hear from the doctors again until mid-afternoon. The other principal investigator, the OTC expert, called and said Jesse's condition was worsening, that his blood ammonia was rising, and that he was in trouble. When I asked if I should get on a plane, he said to wait, that they were running another test. He called back an hour and a half later. Jesse's ammonia had doubled to 250 micromoles per deciliter. I told him I would be there in the morning.

It's a very helpless feeling, knowing your kid is in serious trouble while you are a continent away. My plane was delayed out of Tucson, but got into Philly at 8:00 A.M. Arriving at the hospital at 8:30 A.M., I immediately went to find Jesse. As I entered through the double doors into surgical intensive care, I noted a lot of activity in the first room I passed. I waited at the nurses' station for perhaps a minute before announcing who I was. Immediately, both principal investigators approached me and asked to talk to me in a private conference room. They explained that Jesse was on a ventilator and in a coma, that his ammonia had peaked at 393 micromoles per deciliter (that's at least ten times a normal reading, but only slightly above the highest reading Jesse had ever had), and that they were just completing dialysis and had his level down under 70. They explained that he was having a blood-clotting problem and that, because he was breathing above the ventilator and hyperventilating, his blood ph was too high. They wanted to induce a deeper coma to allow the ventilator to breathe for him.

I gave my okay and went in to see my son. After dressing in scrubs, gloves, and a mask because of the isolation requirement, I tried to see if I could rouse my boy. Not a twitch, nothing. I was very worried, especially when the neurologist expressed her concern at the way his eyes were downcast. Not a good sign, she said. When the intensivist told me that the clotting problem was going to be a real battle, I grew even more concerned. I called and talked to my wife, crying and afraid for Jesse. It was at least as bad as the previous December, only this time they had been in his liver. I would keep her posted.

They got Jesse's breathing under control and his blood ph returned to normal. The clotting disorder was described as improving, and the OTC expert returned to Washington, D.C. by mid-afternoon. I started relaxing, believing Jesse's condition to be improving. My brother and his wife arrived at the hospital around 5:30 P.M. and we went out to dinner. When I returned, I found Jesse in a different intensive care ward. As I sat watching his monitors, I noted his oxygen content dropping. The nurse saw me noticing and asked me to wait outside, explaining that the doctors were returning to examine Jesse. At 10:30 P.M. the doctor explained to me that Jesse's lungs were failing, that they were unable to oxygenate his blood even on 100% oxygen. I said, "Whoa. Don't you have some sort of artificial lung?" He thought about it for a moment and said yes, that he would need to call in the specialist to see if Jesse was a candidate. I told him to get on it. I called my wife and told her to get on a plane immediately.

At 1:00 A.M., the specialist and the principal investigator indicated that Jesse had about a 10% chance of survival on his own, and a 50% chance with the artificial lung, the ECMO unit. Hooking up the unit would involve inserting a large catheter into the jugular to get a large enough blood supply. I said, "Fifty percent is better than 10. Let's do it." It seemed like forever for them to even get the ECMO unit ready. Jesse's oxygen level was crashing.

At 3:00 A.M., as they were about to hook Jesse up, the specialist rushed into the waiting room to tell me that Jesse was in crisis and rushed back to work on him. The next few hours were really tough. I didn't know anything. Anguish, despair, every emotion imaginable went through me. At 5:00 A.M., the specialist came to see me and said they had the ECMO working, but that they had a major leak, that the doctor literally had his finger on the leak. I quipped that I was a bit of a plumber—maybe that's what they needed. He returned to work on Jesse and I began to worry for my wife. Hurricane Floyd had made landfall in North Carolina at 3:00 A.M. and was heading toward Philly. At 7:00 A.M., I entered through the disabled double doors into the intensive care area and, after noting four people still working on Jesse and another half dozen observing, approached the nurses' station to get them to see if my wife would get in okay. They agreed to check and asked if I would like a chaplain. I'm a pretty tough guy, but it was time for spiritual help. At first they sent a young woman who I think was Jewish. I guess she felt a bit out of place because I am Christian, and another chaplain—a Christian man a few years younger than me—was called in to help me. At this point, I was trying to contact my family—my mother especially—to get emotional support. A hospital staffer was very helpful in that respect.

By mid-morning, six of my siblings and their spouses had arrived. Mickie's plane got in just before they closed the airport, and she arrived by taxi at the hospital in the pouring rain. We weren't able to see Jesse until after noon. The OTC expert was stuck on a train disabled by the hurricane. The two doctors on site described Jesse's condition as very grave; whatever reaction his body was having would have to subside before he could recover. His lungs were severely damaged, and if he survived it would be a very lengthy recovery. They had needed to use more than ten units of blood in hooking him up.

When we finally got to see Jesse, he was bloated beyond recognition. The only way to be sure it was Jesse was the scar from his battle with dad and the tattoo on his right calf. My siblings were shaken to the core. Mickie touched him gently and lovingly. Our hearts were nearly breaking.

Because the hurricane was closing in and threatening to close bridges, my siblings left by late afternoon. My sister and her husband stayed to take us to dinner and drive us to our hotel. Exhausted, I slept for an hour. Then I arose, compelled to return to see Jesse. After leaving Mickie a note, I walked the half-mile back to the hospital in a light rain. Hurricane Floyd had skirted Philly and was heading out to sea. I found Jesse's condition no better. I noted blood in his urine. I thought, "How can anybody survive this?!" I said a quiet goodbye to Jesse and returned to the hotel at about 11:30 P.M. I found Mickie preparing to join me. I described Jesse's condition as unchanged and returned to bed. Mickie went out walking for a couple of hours.

In the morning, we arrived at 8:00 A.M. at Jesse's room. A new nurse indicated that the doctors wished to speak to us in an hour or so about why they should continue with their efforts. We went to have breakfast at the hospital cafeteria. I told Mickie we should be prepared for a funeral. She wanted to believe Jesse would get well.

The principal investigators were with Jesse when we returned. They told us that Jesse had suffered irreparable brain damage and that his vital organs were all shutting down. They wanted to shut off life support. They left us alone for a few minutes, and we collapsed into each other. When they returned, I told them that I wanted to bring my family in and have a brief service for Jesse prior to ending his life. Then I told them that they would be doing a complete autopsy to determine why Jesse had died, that this should not have happened.

While waiting for my siblings, rushes of anger toward the doctors swept over me. Then I said to myself, "No, they couldn't have seen this." I went so far as to tell the OTC expert that I didn't blame them, that I would never file a lawsuit. Little did I know what they really knew.

Seven of my siblings and their spouses and one of my nieces were present for the brief ceremony for Jesse—more for us, at this point. I had all the monitors shut off in his room. Leaning over Jesse, I turned and declared to everyone present that Jesse was a hero. After the chaplain's final prayer, I signaled the doctors. The specialist clamped off Jesse's blood flow to the ECMO machine and shut off the ventilator. After the longest minute of my life, the principal investigator stepped in and I removed my hand from Jesse's chest. After listening with a stethoscope for a moment he said, "Goodbye, Jesse.

We'll figure this out." Not a dry eye all around. This kid died about as pure as it gets. I was humbled beyond words. My kid had just shown me what it was really all about. I still feel that way.

I supported these doctors for months, believing that their intent was nearly as pure as Jesse's. They had promised to tell me everything. Even after the media started exposing the flaws in their work, I continued to support them. I discovered that federal oversight was woefully inadequate, that many researchers were not reporting adverse reactions, and that the FDA was being influenced into inaction by industry. I decided to attend the Recombinant DNA Advisory Committee meeting in December where all the experts were to discuss my son's death. It wasn't until that three-day meeting that I discovered that there was never any efficacy shown in humans. I had believed this procedure was working based on my conversations with the OTC expert, and that is why I defended them and their institution for so long. These men could not go in front of their peers at the RAC meeting in Bethesda and say this was working.

There is so much more to Jesse's story. Please remember Jesse's intent when you review studies or when you make policy. You are professionals and you know the issues. I ask—and life itself demands—that you take the time and energy to review each protocol as if you were going to enroll your own child. Please use Jesse's experience to give you the strength to say no or the courage to ask more questions.

If researchers, industry, and those in government apply Jesse's intent—not for recognition, not for money, but only to help—then they will get all they want and more. They'll get it right.

Biomedical and social science research involving the use of human subjects presents society with a wide range of ethical questions. The defining characteristic of research is that it is designed to develop or contribute to generalizable knowledge. A goal of all research projects is to make discoveries that will benefit future members of society. When research subjects do not benefit from research participation, the welfare of society and the individual may conflict. An additional factor is conflict of interest in which the design or conduct of research may be biased by a researcher's personal incentives. This tension between society, the researcher, and the individual is at the heart of most issues in research ethics. The challenge for society is to develop a system that facilitates the conduct of important research without compromising the rights and welfare of individual research participants.

The development of guidelines related to the ethical conduct of research has paralleled the proliferation of research activity in this country. At the heart of our current system for protecting human research subjects is the Institutional Review Board (IRB). The IRB is a committee made up of a diverse group of individuals who understand the concerns of the local community where research is going to take place. The mission of the IRB is to review research applications and monitor ongoing studies to determine that the conduct of research meets certain ethical standards. In most situations IRB approval of research will require a commitment to obtaining voluntary and informed consent to participate in research, and a study design that minimizes risks to research participants.

The IRB system that we see today evolved from informal committees set up by local researchers who felt that this type of oversight would promote the conduct of research according to the highest of ethical standards. In 1966 the National Institutes of Health (NIH) Policy for the Protection of Human Subjects formalized the ethical review process and established the Institutional Review Board (IRB) as a fundamental component of the system of protection of human research subjects. In 1974 the Department of Health, Education, and Welfare (DHEW) raised NIH's human subject protection policy to regulatory status. In 1991, 16 federal agencies formally adopted the core of these regulations in a common Federal Policy for the Protection of Human Subjects (also known as the "Common Rule"). Parallel requirements have since been established by the Food and Drug Administration (FDA). Today, all federally funded or regulated research must be approved by an IRB that functions as directed by federal regulations.

As many IRBs are not registered with the federal government, the number of active IRBs at any time in the United States is not precisely known. Based on information from the FDA, the number of active IRBs in the United States is likely to exceed 4,000 by the year 2002. IRB issues are a major concern to large numbers of people in all segments of the research community.

The IRB is now part of the fabric of research life and, as such, frequently the focus of criticism when the rights of research participants appear to be violated. With the scope and complexity of research increasing in both the academic and private sector of society, IRBs throughout the country are under pressure to increase the sophistication and effectiveness of their operations in an environment of limited budgetary resources. Educational meeting agendas and IRB Internet forums are filled with questions about the practical aspects of IRB function. For example: What is the role and process of IRB review of adverse event reports from multicenter research trials? What are the requirements when research involves the collection of data by telephone survey? What are the criteria for IRB approval of research involving placebo control? What documents should an IRB maintain to document compliance with federal research regulations? What issues should the IRB consider, and what process of review should the IRB use, when evaluating research with vulnerable populations such as prisoners, children, or the decisionally impaired? What is the role of the IRB in regulating the terms of the investigator/sponsor contract? What is the responsibility of, and process for, IRB evaluation of the quality of informed consent?

The above questions summarize a small fraction of the issues IRBs deal with on a monthly, if not daily, basis. The research community is looking for more information about the basic mechanics of IRB practice. The purpose of this book is to produce an instructional manual that gives Institutional Review Board (IRB) members and administrators the information they need to run an efficient and effective system of protecting human research subjects in compliance with federal research regulations. The impetus to write this book came from our experience directing the IRB at Dartmouth College, interactions with IRB directors from other institutions, and discussion with federal officials at the Food and Drug Administration and Office for Human Research Protections of the Department of Health and Human Services. This book is meant to complement, rather than compete with, existing sources of information about IRB practice. Specifically, the OPRR *Guidebook for Institutional Review Boards* and Robert Levine's *Ethics and Regulation of Clinical Research* will remain the best comprehensive references about the history of and theory behind our current system of regulations related to research involving human subjects. *Institutional Review Board: Management and Function* will differ from these and other excellent references by focusing more extensively on the procedures of IRB practice and the criteria for IRB decisions in specific situations.

To facilitate its use as an instructional manual, this book is divided into a large number of chapters, with each chapter devoted to a relatively narrow topic. A degree of redundancy, especially with respect to administrative procedure and documents, is intentional to make it easier for the reader to locate topics of interest. The basic format for most chapters is for the author(s) to first paraphrase applicable regulations and then explain how and when the IRB should apply the regulations in specific situations. When applicable, authors will discuss how a situation is handled at different institutions and then recommend how they think it should be done. This book is written by IRB people, for IRB people. The contributing authors are chosen to draw on the expertise and perspective from a large segment of the IRB community. To the extent that *Institutional Review Board: Management and Function* improves the effectiveness of IRB function, the goal of protecting human research subjects will be realized.

Robert J. Amdur
Elizabeth A. Bankert

Robert J. Amdur, M.D.
Associate Professor of Radiation Oncology and
    Associate Chair for Clinical Affairs
Radiation Oncology
University of Florida Health Science Center
Gainesville FL

Natalie Bachir
Student
Medicine
Dartmouth College
Hanover, NH

Elizabeth A. Bankert, M.A.
Director
Committee for the Protection of Human Subjects
Dartmouth College
Hanover NH

Deborah L. Barnard, B.A., C.I.P.
Director
Office of Research Affairs
Dana Farber Cancer Institute
Boston MA

C. J. Biddle, CRNA, Ph.D.
Professor
Graduate Program in Anesthesia
Virginia Commonwealth University
Richmond VA

Alan J. Bliss, M.A.
Graduate Research Assistant
Cross-Florida Ship/Barge Canal History Research Team
University of Florida
Gainesville FL

David A. Borasky, B.A.
IRB Representative
Office of International Research Ethics
Family Health International
Research Triangle Park NC

Angela J. Bowen, M.D.
President
Western International Review Board
Olympia WA

Joseph S. Brown, Ph.D.
Associate Professor
Psychology
University of Nebraska at Omaha
Omaha NE

Sherry Bye
Administrator, IRB—Spokane
c/o Washington State University Spokane
Spokane, WA

Timothy Callahan, Ph.D.
Director
Research Integrity
Bastyr University
Kenmore WA

Rebecca Carson Rogers, M.A.
Assistant Director
Institutional Review Board
Dartmouth College
Hanover NH

Gary L. Chadwick, Pharm. D., M.P.H., C.I.P.
Executive Director, Research Subjects Review and
    Clinical Associate
Professor
Division of Medical Humanities
University of Rochester
Rochester NY

Sanford Chodosh, M.D.
President of Board of Directors for Public Responsibility
    in Medicine and Research
Associate Professor in Medicine
Boston University of Medicine in Medicine and Research
Boston MA

Jeffrey M. Cohen, Ph.D.
Director
Division of Education
National Institutes of Health, Office for Human
    Research Protections
Rockville MD

Jeffrey A. Cooper, M.D., M.M.M.
IRB Chair
Nuclear Medicine
Albany Medical Center
Albany NY

Amy L. Davis, J.D., M.P.H.
Public Health Policy and Legal Consultant
Former IRB Vice Chairperson for New England
    Research Institute
Acton MA

Susan J. Delano, C.I.P.
Deputy Managing Director of Clinical Research
  Administration
Research Foundation for Mental Hygiene
Albany NY

Marianne M. Elliott, M.S., C.I.P.
Director
Office for Protection of Research Subjects
University of Illinois at Chicago
Chicago IL

Kevin J. Epperson, B.G.S., R.R.T.
IRB Administrator
Office of Regulatory Affairs
University of Nebraska Medical Center
Omaha NE

Richard B. Ferrell, M.D.
Associate Professor
Psychiatry
Dartmouth Hitchcock Medical Center
Lebanon NH

Susan S. Fish, Pharm. D., M.P.H.
Director of Regulatory Affairs (CareStat, Inc.) and
  Associate Professor
Epidemiology and Biostatistics
Boston University School of Public Health
Boston MA

Ann Barry Flood, Ph.D.
Professor of Community and Family Medicine and
  Sociology, Director of Policy Studies, Chair, Ph.D.
  Program and the NRSA Postdoctoral
  Program Center for the Evaluative Clinical Sciences
  at Dartmouth
Dartmouth Medical School
Hanover NH

David G. Forster, J.D., M.A., C.I.P.
Director, Regulatory Affairs and Auxiliary Faculty
Medical History and Ethics
Western IRB and University of Washington
Olympia WA

William L. Freeman, M.D., M.P.H.
Director of Indian Health Services
  Research Program
Chair, Institutional Review Board
Headquarters Indian Health Services
Rockville MD

Dean R. Gallant, A.B.
Director, Science Center and Executive Officer,
  Committee on the Use of Human Subjects in
  Research
Harvard University
Cambridge MA

Bruce G. Gordon, M.D.
IRB Co-Chair and Associate Professor
Pediatrics
University of Nebraska Medical Center
Omaha NE

Ronald M. Green, Ph.D.
The Eunice and Julian Cohen Professor for the Study of
  Ethics and Human Values
Chair, Department of Religion and Director of Ethics
  Institute
Dartmouth College
Hanover NH

Bambi Grilley, R. Ph., C.C.R.A., C.C.R.C., C.I.P.
Director
Clinical Protocol Research and Regulatory Affairs
Texas Children's Cancer Center for Cell and Gene
  Therapy
Houston TX

Dale E. Hammerschmidt, M.D.
Associate Professor and Editor of J. Lab. Clin. Med
College of Medicine
University of Minnesota
Minneapolis MN

Karen M. Hansen, B.A.
Director
Institutional Review Office
Fred Hutchinson Cancer Research Center
Seattle WA

Erica J. Heath, M.B.A., C.I.P.
President
Independent Review Consulting
San Anselmo CA

Todd F. Heatherton, Ph.D.
Professor
Psychological and Brain Sciences
Dartmouth College
Hanover NH

Sallyann Henry, Ph.D.
President
Professional Testing Corporation
New York NY

Rachel Homer, B.S.
IRB Coordinator
Clinical Investigation
Children's Hospital Boston
Boston MA

Jay G. Hull, Ph.D.
Professor
Psychological and Brain Sciences
Dartmouth College
Hanover NH

Kevin M. Hunt, M.E.D., C.H.F.P.
Director
Patient Financial Services
Dartmouth Hitchcock Medical Center
Lebanon NH

John M. Isidor, J.D.
CEO
Schulman Associates Institutional Review Board, Inc.
Cincinnati OH

Sandra P. Kaltman, R.N., B.S.N., J.D.
Attorney
Sandra P. Kaltman, Attorney at Law
Cincinnati OH

Thomas G. Keens, M.D.
Chair
Committee on Clinical Investigations (IRB)
Children's Hospital
Los Angeles CA

Felix A. Khin-Maung-Gyi, M.B.A., C.I.P.
CEO, Founder
Chesapeake Research Review, Inc.
Columbia, MD

Linda J. Kobokovich, M.Sc.N., R.N.
Director of Nursing Practice
Dartmouth-Hitchcock Medical Center
Lebanon NH

Susan Z. Kornetsky, M.P.H.
Director
Clinical Research Compliance
Children's Hospital
Boston MA

Gail Kotulak, B.S.
IRB Administrator
University of Nebraska Medical Center
Omaha NE

Christopher J. Kratochvil, M.D.
Vice-Chair, IRB and Assistant Professor
Psychiatry
University of Nebraska Medical Center
Omaha NE

Rachel Krebs, B.S.
Senior Coordinator
Clinical Investigations
Children's Hospital, Boston
Boston MA

Eric Larsen, M.D.
Director
Dartmouth Hitchcock Medical Center
Lebanon NH

Robert J. Levine, M.D.
Professor of Medicine and Lecturer in Pharmacology
School of Medicine
Yale University
Woodbridge CT

Sally L. Mann, M.S.
IRB Administrator
Office of Regulatory Affairs
University of Nebraska Medical Center
Omaha NE

Peter Marshall, B.A., C.I.P.
IRB Coordinator
Cleveland Veterans Administration IRB
Cleveland OH

J. Allen McCutchan, M.D.
Professor of Medicine
UCSD School of Medicine—Division of Infectious
    Diseases UCSD Antiviral Research Center
San Diego CA

Helen McGough, M.A.
Director
Human Subjects Division
University of Washington
Seattle WA

Linda Medwar, B.S.
Senior IRB Coordinator
Children's Hospital
Boston MA

Matthew Miller, M.D., M.P.H., Sc.D.
Associate Director
Health Policy and Management
Harvard Injury Control Research Center, Harvard
    School of Public Health
Brookline MA

Daniel K. Nelson, M.S., C.I.P.
Associate Professor and Director
Human Research Studies, School of Medicine
University of North Carolina—Chapel Hill
Chapel Hill NC

Robert M. Nelson, M.D., Ph.D.
Associate Professor
Anesthesia and Pediatrics at The Children's Hospital of
    Philadelphia
University of Pennsylvania School of Medicine
Philadelphia PA

Susan Nicholson, J.D.
Attorney
Ropes and Gray
Boston MA

J. Michael Oakes, Ph.D.
Division of Epidemiology
University of Minnesota
Minneapolis, MN

Gwenn S.F. Oki, M.P.H.
Director
Research Subjects Protection, City of Hope National
    Medical Center
Beckman Research Institute
Duarte CA

Elisabeth A. Smith Parrott, B.A., B.S.
Assistant Director
Institutional Review Board
Dartmouth College
Hanover NH

Lucille Pearson, C.I.P.
Director
Human Subjects Program
University of California
La Jolla CA

Steven Peckman, M.F.A.
Associate Director of Human Subjects Research
Office for the Protection of Research Subjects
University of California
Los Angeles CA

Robin Levin Penslar, J.D.
Legal Researcher
Ogilvy Renault
Toronto ON

Ernest D. Prentice, Ph.D.
Associate Dean of Research, Professor, Co-Chair, IRB
    and Associate Vice-Chancellor for Academic Affairs
    and Regulatory Compliance
Anatomy
University of Nebraska Medical Center
Omaha NE

Thomas Puglisi, Ph.D.
Manager
Healthcare Consulting Team—Healthcare Consulting
    Practice
PricewaterhouseCoopers
Bethesda MD

Joan Rachlin, J.D., M.P.H.
Executive Director
Public Responsibility in Medicine and Research
Boston MA

Francine C. Romero, Ph.D., M.P.H.
Epidemiologist
Northwest Tibal Epidemiology Center
Northwest Portland Area Indian Health Board
Portland OR

Michele Russell-Einhorn, J.D.
PricewaterhouseCoopers LLP
Bethesda MD

Patricia M. Scannell
Director
Human Studies Committee
Washington University School of Medicine
St. Louis MO

Marian Gray Secundy, Ph.D.
Director
National Center for Bioethics in Research and Health
    Care
Tuskegee University
Tuskegee Institute AL

Ada Sue Selwitz, M.A.
Director
Office of Research Integrity
University of Kentucky
Lexington KY

Laurie B. Slone
Graduate Student
Psychologic and Brain Sciences
Dartmouth College
Hanover NH

Marjorie A. Speers, Ph.D.
Senior Consultant
Centers for Disease Control and Prevention
Atlanta GA

Elizabeth Stanton, J.D.
Risk Management Director
Risk Management
Dartmouth-Hitchcock Medical Center
Lebanon NH

Jennifer J. Tickle, B.A.
Graduate Student (Ph.D. candidate)
Psychological and Brain Sciences
Dartmouth College
Hanover NH

Jan L. Trott
Director
Office of Research Affairs
Maine Medical Center Research Institute
Scarborough ME

Pamela Turner, M.A.
IRB Manager
Research Administration
Albany Medical College
Albany NY

Harold Y. Vanderpool, Ph.D., Th.M.
Professor in the History and Philosophy of Medicine
Institute for the Medical Humanities Department of
    Preventive Medicine and Community Health
University of Texas
Galveston TX

Daniel R. Vasgird, Ph.D., C.I.P.
Research Compliance Officer
Office of Research Conduct
City University of New York
New York NY

Cecelia S. Walker, M.A.
Director
Regulatory Compliance
Colorado State University
Fort Collins CO

Matthew D. Whalen, Ph.D.
President, Co-Founder
Chesapeake Research Review, Inc.
Columbia MD

Mark R. Yessian, Ph.D.
Regional Inspector General for Evaluation and Inspections
Office of Inspector General
U.S. Department of Health and Human Services
Boston MA

John A. Zaia, M.D.
Chair of IRB and Director
Virology
City of Hope National Medical Center
Duarte CA

Robert M. Zwolak, M.D., Ph.D.
Professor of Surgery
Section of Vascular Surgery—Dartmouth Medical School
Dartmouth-Hitchcock Medical Center
Lebanon NH

PART 1

Background and Overview Topics

An Ethics Primer for IRBs

Harold Y. Vanderpool

INTRODUCTION

Institutional Review Board (IRB) members and administrators are regularly reminded that ethics is a critical component of the review and approval of research protocols. Ethics training for researchers and IRB members and administrators is required at the federal level. In addition, advisory committees tell us that ethical reasoning is imperative for the protection of human subjects. The Advisory Committee on Human Radiation Experiments, for example, discovered "serious deficiencies" in our present system of protection. To correct these deficiencies, the committee declared that efforts must be "undertaken on a national scale to ensure *the centrality of ethics* in the conduct of scientists whose research involves human subjects"[emphasis added].[1(pp. 817–818)]

Some IRBs can call on the expertise of someone who can describe the nature and content of research ethics in clear, practical, and useful terms. However, many IRB members and administrators remain puzzled and uncertain about how to utilize ethical analysis. Given two notable barriers, this puzzlement is not surprising. Before discussing what ethics is and how and why ethical analysis is necessary for the protection of human subjects, we need to know why ethics has been—and remains—so often neglected.

Barriers to Understanding and Utilizing Ethics

Ethics and Regulations

The first barrier to the utilization of research ethics is erected by two unsuspecting sources. It is created by the two most important documents that IRBs are commissioned to follow: The Code of Federal Regulations Title 45 Part 46: Protection of Human Subjects (the CFR)[2] and *The Belmont Report*[3] (*Belmont*). This assertion is so surprising—and important—that it needs to be carefully explained.

That these critically important documents constitute a barrier to ethical analysis is surprising and disturbing because they were composed for the protection of human subjects and are, in fact, necessary for such protection. Although they share this common goal, their means for accomplishing the goal of protecting research participants are exceedingly different. The problem over ethics occurs because the relationship between the means of protection in the CFR on the one hand and *Belmont* on the other is not mentioned or specified in either document. The CFR hardly mentions ethics, not to speak of the functions of ethics in protecting human research subjects. At the same time, *Belmont* details ethical principles and applications without specifying how they relate to interpreting and applying federal regulatory rules. IRBs need to be aware of this fundamental flaw in our two most important federal documents, and they need to know how to correct this flaw. This chapter will indicate how the right hand of the CFR relates to the left hand of *Belmont's* ethics.

The CFR contains bureaucratic rules that must be followed by IRBs. Many IRBs follow these rules in rote fashion with little attention to ethics. Many CFR rules pertain to organizational and enforcement matters—the necessity and structure of IRBs, the documentation of informed consent, record keeping, and so on. Other rules detail the "general requirements" of informed consent,[2[Sec.111(a)(4)and 116]] factors related to risk/probability of benefit determinations,[2[Sec.111(a)(1)and(2)]] and a few sentences about the "equitable selection" of research subjects.[2[Sec.111(a)(3)]] To apply this last set of rules requires ethical awareness and analysis, but the CFR is virtually silent about the value, not to speak of the necessity, of utilizing ethics.

1. The crucial section in the main body of the CFR that lists what IRBs should utilize—law, institutional regulations, and standards of professional practice—to "ascertain the acceptability of proposed research"[2[107(a)]] does not even mention ethics or ethical reasoning.

2. The CFR mentions ethical standards or principles only twice—both times in its later subparts B[2(Sec.202)] and D[2[Sec.407(b)(1)(ii)]] without any elaboration about what these terms call for.

3. The place where a "statement of ethical principles" is mentioned in the main body of the CFR[2[Sec.103(b)(1)]] pertains to an institution's assurance of compliance agreement. Such a statement is considered optional, and no directions are given as to how any adopted code or ethical statement should be used.

4. The importance of utilizing *Belmont's* three ethical principles (respect for persons, beneficence, and justice) and their respective applications to research (informed consent, risk/benefit assessment, and selection of subjects) is not discussed in the CFR.

These points lead to a disturbing conclusion. Insofar as IRBs follow and focus exclusively on the CFR for research protections (the main, possibly exclusive focus of many IRBs),[1(pp. 697,707–709,817)] they may either neglect ethics altogether or relegate ethical concerns to the periphery of protocol review.

Let us now turn to the main ethical problem arising from *Belmont*. *Belmont* was produced by the National Commission for Protection of Human Subjects of Behavioral and Biomedical Research and was published in *The Federal Register* in 1979. *Belmont* was adopted as an authoritative policy statement by the U.S. Department of Health, Education, and Welfare (now called the Department of Health and Human Services [DHHS]), the National Institutes of Health (NIH), and the Office for Protection from Research Risks (OPRR), now called the Office of Human Research Protections (OHRP).

Does *Belmont* fill the ethical void in the CFR? Assuming the *Belmont* is studied and understood, it can do this, but it fills the void indirectly, not clearly or explicitly.

1. In spite of its official status, the degree to which *Belmont* is actually read, understood, and utilized by IRBs remains an open question.

2. Importantly, *Belmont's* exclusive focus is that moral awareness and reasoning are imperative for strengthening and assuring human subject protection. *Belmont's* stated purposes are, first, to demonstrate to researchers, subjects, IRBs, and interested citizens that ethical issues are "inherent in research involving human subjects." Second, and especially important for IRBs, *Belmont* provides an analytical framework composed of principles and their applications that will help resolve ethical problems arising from research.

3. *Belmont* also asserts that its principles will enable IRB members and others to formulate, criticize, and interpret the regulatory rules of research found in the Nuremberg Code, the Declaration of Helsinki, and the CFR. Unfortunately, *Belmont* never describes or gives examples of how existing regulatory rules can be criticized, interpreted, revised, or supplemented.

4. In short, *Belmont* offers no explicit guidance that will enable IRBs to do what they are precisely responsible for doing as they work with the rules of the CFR.

To summarize these points about the first major barrier to the utilization of ethics in protecting human subjects: The CFR neglects ethics, and *Belmont* does not discuss how its ethical principles and applications relate to interpreting and applying the CFR's rules.

Esoteric Language of Ethics

The second barrier to clarity about how to utilize ethics in IRB deliberations pertains to befuddlement and confusion over ethics itself. Ethics as a discipline of inquiry is readily associated with terminology, assumptions, arguments, and distinctions that seem esoteric and impractical to those who have not studied philosophical ethics. The esoteric nature of ethics reflects the fact that this discipline is explored primarily in elective college courses, graduate schools, and various types of intensive short courses for medical and other professionals. Because traditions of ethical reasoning are very rarely studied in high schools or the earlier years of public and private education, and are not the subject of required courses in college or most professional training programs, the esoteric jargon and concepts of ethics are often not translated into ordinary language and commonly understood categories.

Clarity About Ethical Analysis

A responsible ethical analysis of any proposed action or course of action does not need to be identified with or surrounded by technical and esoteric jargon. Ethical analysis and decision-making involves making judgments that are based on accurate facts, common experience, and coherent and convincing reasons. Ethical judgments or judgment calls pertain to what individuals and groups ought to do and how they/we ought to behave. Ethics focus on what is right or wrong (or something in between), and on what is good and virtuous, or reprehensible.

All of us indulge in ethical thinking and argumentation even if we do not recognize it as ethical reasoning in a formal or academic sense. We use common and shared patterns of reasoning and experience to arrive at what we take to be an acceptable (moral) or unacceptable (immoral) course of action. At times, even extensive and thoughtful ethical analysis will not uncover some clearly "correct" answer to a moral problem. Given the complexities of human life, some problems appear to have equally strong arguments for and against two or more possible solutions—problems that are rightly called *moral dilemmas*. At other times, a clearly correct answer cannot be discovered or agreed upon, but a more or less responsible ethical judgment call can be made. This responsible search for the best possible answer should be distinguished from irresponsible skepticism or laziness.

Ethics as a discipline of reasoning dwells on and wrestles with the many moral beliefs and patterns of thinking that persons in every culture use to make moral assessments and decisions. Over time, ethicists have identified and categorized types of principles and arguments, which they examine to discover which principles and arguments are the most believable and convincing. Disciplined and fully responsible ethical reasoning includes identifying, making explicit, and/or becoming aware of the types and relative strengths of the moral assumptions that we may take for granted. Do we assume that the probable consequences of some action determine its morality? Is this consequentialist assumption sufficient for determining what is moral, or do other assumptions such as freedom of choice (moral autonomy) regardless of the consequences carry more moral weight? And when we appeal to consequences, what do we have in mind—increased pleasure, happiness, or some other valued good such as greater knowledge about the natural world?

Ethical reasoning includes the following factors.

1. Identifying a problem that appears to be morally questionable or troubling
2. Accurately understanding the facts and circumstances pertaining to the problem
3. Identifying common and shared values (including the three principles in *Belmont*) that pertain to the problem
4. Identifying and using tried and true moral arguments
5. Making a considered moral judgment (finding an ethical solution) by relating the moral values, arguments, and pertinent examples to the problem in question

A reasonable and responsible ethical solution to some issue should be viewed as the most convincing answer that an informed and well meaning group of persons can discover. In the process, the group upholds commonly accepted ethical principles and strives to arrive at a sensible and rationally defensible decision.

Because ethical analysis commissions us to make *judgments* based on thoughtful analysis and deliberation, this analysis contrasts with simply *asserting* that something is right or wrong, regardless of the frequency or strength of such assertions.[4(pp. 1–4)] As a form of reasoned discourse based on knowledge and common experience, ethical analysis comes to a halt—sometimes to a screeching halt—when someone in a group asserts that some action is right or wrong based on a personal opinion or the authority of a family member, famous person, or hallowed book or tradition. Such authorities may indeed be wellsprings of moral guidance and insight, but to serve as wellsprings, they must be shown to be relevant and convincing before they can carry ethical weight.

Belmont and the Ethics of Research

These brief points enable us to understand what *research ethics* is. The ethics of research should be defined as the application of the steps and modes of ethical reasoning to the problems and situations arising from research involving human beings.

Belmont is a succinct and compact summary of research ethics that many, if not most, IRB members are unlikely to characterize as easy reading. This is not surprising; *Belmont* traverses a middle road between the somewhat technical (and unquestionably cryptic and compact) concepts and distinctions in its section entitled "Basic Ethical Principles" and its more easily grasped (but still distinction-filled) discussions under the title "Applications." Both sections, especially the first, are like the tips of icebergs that rest on extensive philosophical tradition, the National Commission's deliberations that were predicated on scholarly essays by philosophers and bioethicists, and examples drawn from a number of the reports the Na-

tional Commission had completed before it completed and published *Belmont*.

Nevertheless, *Belmont* discusses ethics in clear, jargon-free terms. It identifies only three of a number of ethical principles because these three principles (beneficence, respect for persons, and justice) are especially applicable to research. Other commonly recognized ethical principles such as the moral duties of gratitude, fidelity (faithfulness to others), promise keeping, and veracity (truth-telling) are also applicable to research, but in less comprehensive ways.

The three principles accented in *Belmont* are set forth as duties that encompass a number of moral concerns and can be readily grasped by persons of varied backgrounds. With respect to the encompassing nature of its principles, *Belmont* includes the far-reaching principle of nonmaleficence (the duty of not harming others) under its principle of beneficence.[5(pp. 189–193)] *Belmont* also includes the duty of protecting vulnerable persons from harm (a dimension of nonmaleficence) under its principle of respect for persons.

With respect to how its principles are generally understandable, *Belmont's* principle of respect for persons, for example, can be understood as crediting human beings of all ages with dignity and worth for a variety of reasons. To the chagrin of many bioethicists, *Belmont's* principle of respect for persons is not merely, nor neatly, drawn from philosophical arguments that speak of the necessity of respecting human autonomy; that is, respecting persons as individuals who are credited with the right to make their own unforced decisions.[6(pp. 2–4)] Instead, the principle of respect for persons in *Belmont* represents a basic moral standard that makes sense to persons with different backgrounds and training. This principle reflects the U.S. Constitution's emphasis on the rights of self-determination and privacy. It emphasizes the sacredness and value of human life in religious traditions as well as basic human dignity in everyday life. It also reflects the moral arguments advanced by philosophers, such as Immanuel Kant, who based morality on the freedom of the will, and John Stuart Mill, who defended the liberty of free choice.[7] This last point enables us to understand how *Belmont's* ethical principles should be understood. They are presented as "an easily grasped set of moral standards" for persons with diverse backgrounds and training.[8(p. 181)] As "the common coin of moral discourse,"[9(p. 333)] these principles constitute condensations or essential elements of morality derived from and generally acceptable within human culture. They are also, as *Belmont* accents, "particularly relevant" to research with human subjects. The sections that follow will indicate how these principles and guidelines can and should be used to interpret, apply, and reformulate the rules in the CFR previously indicated. These essential tasks pertaining to the utilization of ethics by IRBs are not discussed in either the CFR or *Belmont*.

Although the ethical framework of *Belmont* is easily understood, the document itself is intellectually challenging. Members of IRBs should not be discouraged if they do not fully grasp *Belmont's* many messages the first time they read—even carefully read—this historic document. Each time it is studied or discussed, its richness and usefulness are more fully grasped. *Belmont* needs to be discussed, dissected, and reflected upon. Should, for example, its three principles be equally and fully upheld, or can they be "balanced" off of one another in some instances? *Belmont* never indicates whether all of its principles must be upheld for each research protocol (such that fully informed consent is never compromised) or whether one principle (such as respect for a subject's autonomy) can at times be outweighed when another principle (such as beneficence in the form of a favorable benefit-over-harm ratio) appears to warrant protocol approval. This lack of clarity has led to extensive scholarly debate over how *Belmont's* principles should be understood and applied. See, for example, the essays by Veatch, Jonsen, and Ackerman in *The Ethics of Research Involving Human Subjects.*[4(pp. 33–104)]

Ways to Think About and Utilize Ethics to Review Research Protocols

The topics that follow display how members of IRBs and researchers can utilize ethics to protect research subjects/participants. The headings suggest a practical method that can be used to explore some important component of research ethics. The ethical components in these headings represent examples only, not the range, of ethical concerns addressed in *Belmont*. Although an extensive body of literature on research ethics exists, this chapter focuses on *Belmont* as a primary source of ethical insight.

LEARNING SUGGESTION: DWELL ON *BELMONT'S* APPLICATIONS

Research Ethics Topic: The Moral Autonomy of Individuals

Clearly and repeatedly, *Belmont* says that its ethical principles lead to or serve as justifications for its applications. This implies that its principles are primary, while its applications are secondary and inferior because they are derived from its principles. This is deceiving for two reasons. First, both the principles and applications are referred to and viewed as ethical "requirements" and "obligations," which means that they are morally equal, even though the principles are general and the applications are more specific. Second, and of greater practical importance, at critical points, *Belmont's* human subject protections are far greater in the applications than in the principles.

As a historical footnote, it is highly unlikely that the members of the National Commission first determined what their ethical principles should be, then deduced ethically required applications from these principles. They had already published four reports (on research involving prisoners [1976], children [1977], disclosure of information [1977], and IRBs [1978]) filled with applications related to the ethical obligations of informed consent, of protecting vulnerable subjects, and so on. The commissioners appar-

ently chose their three principles because of their reciprocal connections with and support of their applications.

This is illustrated by the way the moral autonomy of each individual is understood under the principle of respect for persons in comparison with the way the autonomy of persons is depicted in *Belmont's* applications. To honor the principle of respect for persons, *Belmont* says that researchers must "give weight" to autonomous persons' considered opinions and choices. This conveys the message that researchers can decide when the subject is to be treated as a free and self-determining agent. This contrasts with *Belmont's* applications, which hold that the subject's choice is free and final. For example, prospective subjects must be granted "the opportunity to choose what shall or shall not happen to them." In addition, they must be given all the information that a "reasonable volunteer" would need to know to decide "whether they wish to participate" in the research or not.

The practical implications of this example are clear. Members of IRBs can profit from *Belmont's* principles, but the ethical strength, specificity, and applicability of the report's research ethics are primarily found in its applications.

LEARNING SUGGESTION: UPHOLD THE DUTY TO SUPPLEMENT CFR'S RULES

Research Ethics Topic: Protecting the Voluntarism of Research Subjects and Other Dimensions of Informed Consent

It is critical for IRB members and investigators to make a fundamental distinction between codified rules and ethical analysis. In its second paragraph, *Belmont* says that the rules found in the Nuremberg Code, the Helsinki Declaration, and the CFR (all of which are specified in its first endnote) "are often inadequate." In addition, they "come into conflict" and "are frequently difficult to interpret or apply." Because *Belmont* never indicates why this is true and what should be done about it, let us explore how ethical analysis exposes the inadequacy and incompleteness of a number of the CFR's rules.

Consider, for example, the rules pertaining to the voluntarism of research subjects, which are given in two places. The introductory paragraph in CFR 46.116 says that investigators should seek consent under circumstances "that minimize the possibility of coercion or undue influence." In 46.116 (a) and 46.116 (a) (8), the CFR holds that one of the "basic elements of informed consent" is "a statement that participation is voluntary." Members of IRBs are very familiar with the boilerplate language in consent forms. These reflect how the rules of the CFR are registered verbatim in most of these forms: "taking part in this study is voluntary . . . you may withdraw from the study at any time without penalty or loss of any benefits to which you are otherwise entitled.[1(p. 708)]

Whether research subjects are indeed approached, recruited, and treated as volunteers is hardly captured by this rote listing of rules in consent forms. Fortunately, *Belmont* contains an excellent discussion of the meaning and ingredients of voluntarism when it summarizes some of the *conditions* voluntarism requires. *Belmont* says that undue influence occurs "through an offer of an excessive, unwarranted, inappropriate, or improper reward or other overture in order to obtain compliance." It also argues that "unjustifiable pressures" occur when "persons in positions of authority . . . urge a course of action for a subject." This includes manipulating a prospective subject's choice by utilizing the "influence of a close relative." *Belmont's* discussion calls ethical reasoning and judgment-making into play because "it is impossible to state precisely where justifiable persuasion ends and undue influence begins." In global terms, IRBs should determine how undue influence (and coercion) should be avoided when they review specific protocols.

When IRBs explore and discuss these issues, they are utilizing ethical reasoning to protect human subjects with the recognition that regulatory rules only touch the hem of the ethical garment. If recruitment strategies are not outlined in the protocol under review, the primary reviewer from the IRB must explore what strategies will be used. This can be done in nonconfrontational ways by asking, for example, "Would you briefly describe how you plan to recruit your research subjects?" Furthermore, IRB members need to be ever alert to the possibility that some subjects are unlikely to receive medical treatment and/or free medical treatment if they do not become enrolled. At times, this requires an awareness of stated or unstated departmental policies that may well have the effect of unduly pressuring patients to enlist in research. This wrestling over issues pertaining to the voluntarism of research subjects supplements the CFR's cryptic references about minimizing coercion or undue influence and its rule that subjects should be told that their participation is voluntary.

These concerns about the voluntarism of research subjects can be extended to the other elements of informed consent registered in the rules of the CFR. As we learned from the analytical framework of *Belmont* previously depicted, informed consent involves adequate information, comprehension, and voluntariness. The first paragraph of CFR 46.116 briefly mentions these three areas of concern, but they are inadequately emphasized. This is true because all the "basic elements of informed consent" in the CFR [2[Sec.116(a)(1)-(8)]] and all the CFR's "additional elements of informed consent"[2[Sec.116(b)(1)-(6)]] deal with only one of *Belmont's* categories: information. This directly encourages IRBs and investigators to equate the basic elements of consent with rules pertaining to the information subjects should receive in consent forms. This links informed consent to information on consent forms, rather than to a process of responsible and ongoing communication between investigators and prospective research subjects.

As a historical footnote, the language and categories pertaining to the "basic elements of informed consent" in the CFR reflect the precise wording of the DHEW/Public Health Service/NIH Yellow Book. The book, entitled *The Institutional Guide to DHEW Policy on Protection of Human Subjects*, was published in 1971. Unfortunately, those who revised the CFR kept the language and cate-

gories of the Yellow Book instead of revising the CFR so that it conforms with the basic elements of informed consent in *Belmont*. *Belmont* has more comprehensive and protective categories of information, comprehension, and voluntariness. To be ethically responsible, IRBs need to recognize this important flaw in the CFR and they need to deal with the informed consent of research subjects in terms of *Belmont's* ethically responsible principles and applications.

LEARNING SUGGESTION: RECOGNIZE THE OPEN ENDEDNESS OF SOME CFR DEFINITIONS

Research Ethics Topic: Definition of "Minimal Risk" in Research with Children

The CFR defines minimal risk as "the probability and magnitude of harm or discomfort. . . not greater . . . than those ordinarily encountered in daily life or during the performance of routine physical or psychological examinations or tests."[Sec.102(i)] This definition is evoked at crucial places in the CFR with respect to the permissibility of expedited review,[2[Sec.110(b)(i)]] research involving prisoners,[2[Sec.306(a)(2)(A)]] and research involving assenting children and/or the permission of their parents or guardians.[2(Sec.404)]

To be ethically responsible, IRBs should recognize that this definition is subject to wide-ranging interpretations that must be made explicit as protocols are analyzed. In research involving children, for example, this minimal risk definition has been taken to mean everything from gently scraping the inside of a child's mouth with a wooden spatula to remove surface cells, to taking fluid from a child's middle ear via a needle passed through the ear drum.[10(pp.343,349-356)] While none would quarrel with the first procedure, the ethical permissibility of the second—even if it is "routine" for children with certain types of ear problems—depends on whose perspective is determining risk and harm.

Should minimal risk be determined by the researcher, by IRB members, by the parents, and/or by prospective child subjects? The subjective nature of this key regulatory concept is not noted in the CFR, but it has become the subject of intense debate in the literature involving research with children.[10(pp. 349-356)] Informed by the section in *Belmont* entitled "The Systematic Assessment of Risks and Benefits," IRBs need to make discriminating judgments about the variables that pertain to this definition. This includes the medical problems children have, the probable responses and feelings of the children, and the benefits they are likely to receive. To refer to the language of *Belmont*, IRBs need to recognize that a number of the definitions and rules in the CFR are "frequently difficult to interpret and apply."

LEARNING SUGGESTION: THINK IN TERMS OF PROBLEMS

Research Ethics Topic: Payments to Research Participants

In keeping with the suggestions made in the section on clarity about ethical analysis, IRBs employ ethical analysis when they identify morally troubling or debatable problems on the basis of a factually accurate understanding of the problem. They identify ethical principles that bear on the problem, then utilize moral arguments to discover a sensible and defensible solution to the problem. In many or most instances, the problem will encompass more than one ethical principle and its respective applications. Sound ethical judgments will arise from an open and informed discussion that takes all of these factors into consideration.

Consider, for example, the increasingly prevalent practice of paying persons who participate in research. Few if any IRBs believe that modest, compensatory payments for transportation, parking, and time commitments by research participants in low-risk protocols pose an ethical problem. However, sizable "salaries" offered to participants who are being asked to participate in invasive protocols (protocols, for example, that require a number of muscle biopsies over the course of several weeks) are another matter. Why? First, these types of protocols can quite easily become coercive for poorer and needy patients—the unemployed, students in need of funds, and so on. Payments of $350 to $600 for, say, six two-hour-long clinical experiments can constitute offers that such populations of prospective subjects find difficult to refuse.

Related to this worry about coercion is the concern that such protocols are unlikely to secure an equitable representation from the general population of prospective subjects.[2][Sec.111(a)(3)] This single reference to equitable selection in the CFR is much more completely and thoughtfully discussed in the "Selection of Subjects" section found under *Belmont's* applications. *Belmont* holds that "the principle of justice gives rise to moral requirements that there be fair *procedures* and *outcomes* in the selection of research subjects." It further argues that "unjust social patterns" contribute to an unjust distribution of the burdens and benefits of research because economically or socially disadvantaged persons are "easy to manipulate as a result of their illness or socioeconomic condition."

These points about coercion, manipulation, and injustice should be taken seriously by IRBs that review invasive or risky protocols with payment scales that are likely to attract needy subjects. These studies are highly unlikely to attract wealthier participants who may, in fact, be the ones who will receive the greatest benefits from the research that is being conducted.

This example demonstrates how problems or possible problems that were never addressed in *Belmont* continue to surface and how their being resolved requires thoughtful ethical scrutiny and analysis based on several ethical principles and arguments.

Taken together, all of the topics and examples in this section illustrate how research subjects are not adequately—much less fully—protected without responsible ethical analysis on the part of IRBs.

Conclusion

Members of IRBs and investigators are faced with the challenge of overcoming the strong and long-standing barriers that block or discourage the use of ethical analysis in the review and submission of research protocols. What ethical analysis entails has been clearly and sensibly described. The topics and examples discussed in this chapter demonstrate that, to protect the rights and well being of human beings who enroll in research, the rules of the CFR must be supplemented and interpreted by the ethical principles and applications of *Belmont*. To protect human subjects, responsible ethical analysis and decision-making by IRBs is an inescapable imperative, not an expendable luxury.

References

1. Advisory Committee on Human Radiation Experiments. *The Human Radiation Experiments: Final Report.* New York: Oxford University Press. 1996. http://tis.eh.doe.gov/ohre/roadmap/achre/report.html (DOE 061-000-00-848-9)

2. Code of Federal Regulations. Title 45A—Department of Health and Human Services; Part 46—Protection of Human Subjects, 1 Oct 1997. Access date 18 Apr 2001. World Wide Web http://www4.law.cornell.edu/cfr/45p46.htm

3. National Commission for the Protection of Human Subjects of Biomedical and Behavioral Research. *The Belmont Report: Ethical Principles and Guidelines for the Protection of Human Subjects of Research.* (DHEW (OS) 78-0013 and (OS) 78-0014.4). Washington DC: U.S. Government Printing Office, 18 Apr 1979. Access date 22 Mar 2001. World Wide Web http://ohsr.od.nih.gov/mpa/belmont.php3

4. Vanderpool HY. Introduction and overview: Ethics, historical case studies, and the research enterprise. In: Vanderpool HY (ed). *The Ethics of Research Involving Human Subjects: Facing the 21st Century.* Frederick, MD: University Publishing Group, Inc. 1996: 1–4.

5. Beauchamp TL, Childress JF. *Principles of Biomedical Ethics,* Ed 4th. New York, NY: Oxford University Press. 1994.

6. Churchill L. R. Disrespect for autonomy: Why the Belmont Report needs revision. Paper presented at "Belmont Revisited," a conference held at the University of Virginia, 16–19 Apr 1999.

7. Vanderpool HY. Unfulfilled promise: How the Belmont Report can amend the Code of Federal Regulations Title 45 Part 46—Protection of Human Subjects. In: National Bioethics Advisory Commission (ed). *Ethical and Policy Issues in Research Involving Human Participants, Volume II. Commissioned Papers and Staff Analysis.* Aug 2001. World Wide Web http://bioethics.gov/human/overvol2.html

8. Beauchamp T. L. Principalism and its alleged competitors. *Kennedy Inst Ethics J* 5:181–198, 1995.

9. Jonsen A. R. *The Birth of Bioethics.* New York: Oxford University Press. 1998:333.

10. Bartholome W. G. Ethical issues in pediatric research. In: Vanderpool HY (ed). *The Ethics of Research Involving Human Subjects: Facing the 21st Century.* Frederick, MD, University Publishing Group, Inc. 1996: 339–370.

Reflections from the Office of the Inspector General

Mark R. Yessian*

INTRODUCTION

I am an outsider because of my job. My role in the Office of the Inspector General is to evaluate how well programs and mandates of the U.S. Department of Health and Human Services are being carried out. I am concerned. After more than four years of evaluating the protections provided to human subjects participating in clinical research, I have found that, even with the good work of so many committed members of Institutional Review Boards (IRBs), there are signs that the long-established system of protections is being undermined. This development could threaten not only human subjects, but the field of clinical research itself.

In this commentary, I will start by quickly reviewing the studies we have conducted that serve as the basis for my reflections and by outlining the dynamics of change that are altering the clinical research landscape so profoundly. These observations will provide the context for the three suggestions I will offer to IRB members.

Four Years of Intensive Review (1996–2000)

During this period, we have visited at least 25 to 30 IRBs of all kinds, talked with representatives of well over 100 IRBs, and immersed ourselves in the literature on IRBs. In addition, we have examined records of all kinds and reviewed all the relevant data we could get our hands on. On the basis of this inquiry, we have produced eight reports, testified at three congressional hearings, and given presentations at 40 to 50 professional meetings. Our style has been not just to issue reports, but to engage the issues with those heavily involved in the work of protecting human subjects. This interaction has deepened our insights and further reinforces the suggestions I will offer in this commentary.

One might say that our involvement in this field began by accident. In a study addressing investigational medical devices, we discovered disturbing inadequacies concerning IRB oversight. These concerned matters such as the implantation of a device in three times the number of human subjects specified in the IRB-approved research protocol. In another instance, a research effort was initiated without the changes the IRB called for in the informed consent document, and another research project was continued even though the IRB suspended it. It was these findings that led us to conduct a more intensive and enduring review of the overall system of human-subject protections.

Reports on IRB

In June 1998, we issued a series of reports on IRBs. The reports, which received considerable national attention, warned that the effectiveness of IRBs was in jeopardy. The reports elaborated that IRBs review too much, too quickly, with too little expertise. They conduct minimal continuing review of approved research; face conflicts that threaten their independence; provide little training to investigators or IRB board members; and devote little emphasis to evaluation of their performance. These findings and our accompanying recommendations struck some in the clinical research field as being alarmist, but they raised awareness among researchers, administrators of academic health centers, and public policy makers. A short time later, the federal Office for Protection from Research Risks (OPRR), which had conducted only one site visit to an IRB in the 11 months preceding the issuance of our report, became much more proactive. The OPRR generated much controversy itself by terminating federally funded research at some institutions because of failures in their protection of human subjects.

*The views expressed in this article are those of the author and do not necessarily represent those of the U.S. Department of Health and Human Services or the Office of the Inspector General.

Congressional Inquiries

Two years later, in response to congressional inquiries, we issued a follow-up report documenting the minimal progress made at the federal level in carrying out our recommendations. This report served as the basis of a congressional hearing. In June 2000, we issued two additional reports drawing attention to many disturbing human-subject recruitment practices, particularly for industry-sponsored clinical trials. These involved the use of financial incentives to investigators, physicians targeting of their own patients as potential subjects, the use of referral fees, and misleading advertisements.[1]

At present, we are working on a report that addresses the significant growth of clinical drug trials conducted in foreign countries and raises concern about the adequacy of the oversight conducted to assure human-subject protection in those trials. This follows extensive attention given to the topic in a series of reports by the *Washington Post*.

A Changed Research Environment

During the 1970s and early 1980s, when federal IRB regulations were formulated, the clinical research environment was much different than it is now. Most research involving human subjects took place with government support in university teaching hospitals with established research-related controls and an underlying culture of professional norms. Trials typically were conducted by a single investigator at a single institution and involved a small cohort of subjects. IRBs had manageable workloads and functioned in an environment where, in the wake of the Tuskegee experiments and other noted abuses, there was heightened awareness of the risks that research could pose for human subjects.

The environment at the beginning of the twenty-first century is vastly different. It is characterized by the increased commercialism of research, the proliferation of multisite trials across the nation and, indeed, around the globe, and a significant expansion of research in many new areas such as gene therapy and xenotransplantation. The heightened cost and pressures make it difficult for IRB members to volunteer their time or to raise questions that could slow down the research process and thereby jeopardize funding for an institution and/or investigator. Not least of all, a rise in patient consumerism has led many potential subjects themselves to worry less about the risks of research than about their rights to gain access to research trials.

In this dramatically altered environment, significant changes must be made in the way that protections are afforded. In my view, there is too little recognition of that. Clearly, IRBs alone cannot do it all. Sponsors, investigators, and government agencies themselves must also assume ongoing responsibilities for ensuring adequate protections. Recently, a number of promising federal initiatives have been taken. Yet, IRBs still have a basic responsibility. IRBs are the only ones in the research process that exist solely to protect human subjects. How best to do that in an environment full of obstacles is a challenge to which all IRB members and others concerned about human-subject protections must devote some attention.

Suggestions

Amid so much change, complexity, and turbulence, it is essential for IRB members to keep an eye on the big picture and to consider their role with some perspective. It is in that context that I offer my three suggestions. Each points to a direction of thought and action that can help make IRBs most relevant in these difficult times.

Sustain a capacity for independent review, in substance and in appearance

I lead with this procedural suggestion deliberately. If the IRBs are not independent of the research enterprise and all the parties and interests associated with it, then they will be hard-pressed to do the job expected of them. Perhaps I have an institutional bias here, because as a representative of the Inspector General's office, I am expected to conduct oversight in an independent manner, separate from the particular interests of programs and their advocates. Our credibility rests on that independence. So, too, I would argue, does that of IRBs. Their job is to ensure the adequacy of protections, even if doing so slows down the research process or adversely affects the immediate interests of an institution, sponsor, or investigator. This does not mean that they should oppose those interests or be unmindful of the abiding societal interest in research, any more than we (in our evaluations) should oppose the interest of a program or fail to be cognizant of its social purposes. But in both cases, our core responsibility requires the capacity and will to act independently. Otherwise our work is likely to be compromised.

This emphasis on independence, I recognize, disturbs many in the IRB community. I have spoken enough with IRB members to know that many (perhaps most) regard their role as a collegial one. They volunteer their time to help fellow investigators ensure that their research plans are in accord with federal and institutional expectations. They speak in terms of a community of interest and an enlightened sense of professionalism rather than an independent role that functions more like that of a gatekeeper or watchdog. They emphasize the importance of trust.

These are important considerations. Certainly, we do not want to establish an adversarial culture that emphasizes confrontation and ignores the importance of professional ethics and sense of responsibility. But it is important to recognize that changes have occurred not only in the research environment but also in our society since the 1970s. We live in an age of increased commercialism and consumerism, where the body politic is not inclined to grant as much discretion to professionals. This is a society where public accountability and disclosure, in all sectors, are increasingly emphasized. Whether we like it or not, we must acknowledge and deal with these realities. So what actions can be taken to sustain a capacity for independent review? Here are three actions that I suggest.

Ensure that the IRB functions with as much organizational independence as possible. For IRBs that are part of an institution, ensure that they are not part of an organizational unit responsible for bringing in research funds. For independent IRBs, ensure that equity owners do not participate in the review process. In themselves, such measures will not guarantee sufficient independence any more than the lack of them necessarily means that IRBs are not functioning independently. However, they reinforce the significance of independent review and public perception of it.

Achieve broad representation on IRBs. IRBs, particularly those in academic health centers and hospitals, are too narrowly focused in their membership. Federal law requires only that they include one noninstitutional and one nonscientific member. Often this requirement is met simply by including a single member who meets both criteria. This deprives the IRB of a valuable counterbalance to pressures that threaten its independence. I would suggest that IRB independence be nourished in important ways by ensuring that its membership includes ample representation from nonscientific members and from scientists who are not part of the institution at which the research is occurring. Again, this is contrary to established norms of collegial review, but better fits the modern environment.

Foster public accountability. IRBs, too, must be accountable to the broader public, not just to an institution, sponsor, or government funder. Public support for clinical research rests in large part on confidence that that research is conducted in ways that protect human subjects. IRBs can foster such confidence by making their activities as transparent as possible. This is difficult given the proprietary nature of much of the research they now review. I suggest that IRBs determine the steps they can take that would contribute to a more open atmosphere, yet are consistent with the reality that certain information must be kept confidential. One element that could help in this regard is to regularly conduct independent, publicly disclosed evaluations of IRB performance.

Strengthen Continuing Review

I recall that when I was first informed about IRBs, an IRB member at an academic health center pulled me aside and counseled me that the job of IRBs is to ensure human subject protections up front, not to serve as an ongoing watchdog. Like so many of his colleagues that we would later meet, he emphasized that the system is based largely on trust, and that any movement toward policing would undermine the credibility that IRBs have developed. Many of the reactions to our first set of reports reiterated that we were pushing IRBs toward an oversight role that was inappropriate.

Yet, as vital as trust is to the effective protection of human subjects, the IRB as a review body must function on the basis of "trust, but verify." This necessity is not just a reflection of the current age, but in fact has been part of the IRB mandate from the very beginning. It was reinforced to me by one of the leading figures who served on the national commission that developed the current system of human-subject protections in the 1970s. In fact, one of the reports of that commission clearly envisioned an active role for IRBs. For instance, it indicated that IRBs may interview human subjects about their research experience or require that investigators provide subjects with a form with which they may report their research experiences to the IRB.

Ironically, the significance of the IRB's initial review of research applications may be decreasing as that of continuing review may be increasing. In the current research environment, where so much research involves sponsor-initiated multisite protocols, the realistic opportunities for IRBs to influence the research design are diminished. Many observers add that the IRB does not have or should not be expected to have the scientific expertise to review many of these designs. In contrast, the continuing review role could become more important as an ongoing check that initial plans and expectations are being met. After all, one of the central notions justifying IRBs in the first place was that they could provide a local presence based on a familiarity with the investigators and with local conditions and norms.

For the skeptical, I would ask that if the IRBs do not assume responsibility for identifying deviations from research plans that threaten human-subject protections (such as those concerning investigational medical devices that I noted at the outset of this commentary), then who should? If IRBs excuse themselves from this oversight role because it violates a tradition of trust and appears too much like policing, or for whatever reason, their inaction could diminish their relevance to human-subject protections. For, surely, some party must play an active part in such monitoring. IRBs, I would submit, are the ones in the best position to play that role and to carry it out in a way that is still respectful of the professionalism that must be part of the research enterprise.

The continuing review role can encompass much more than ensuring that protocols stay on track. Among the key questions that IRBs should address during the course of a trial are the following.

1. How is the human-subject recruitment process working? Is it undermining informed consent? Is it jeopardizing patient confidentiality? Is it fostering the equitable selection of subjects?

2. How is the informed consent process actually working? Is it functioning in a way that fosters human-subject understanding?

3. How is the continuing safety of subjects being ensured? Are reportable adverse events in fact being reported? If so, are they being adequately analyzed and addressed to protect subjects?

These, I recognize, are large questions that overburdened IRBs are hard-pressed to address in a concerted way. However, neither can they ignore them. IRBs must play an ongoing role in raising and addressing such questions and stimulating sufficient attention to them by all those connected with clinical research.

Serve as an Ambassador for Human-Subject Protections

This, I suggest, is a more important role than is generally recognized. When there are disclosures of human subjects being harmed unnecessarily, there tends to be widespread outrage and a call for corrective action. But in a more fundamental way, it seems to me that there is more ongoing societal support (reflected in the actions of elected officials) for the research itself than for ensuring human-subject protections. We are all vitally interested in the search for cures to diseases and seek rapid access to the benefits of effective therapies. In subtle ways, this can translate into more substantial political support for reducing burdens on the research process rather than on conducting reviews to ensure adequate human-subject protections. The latter can readily be demonized as bureaucratic red tape that impedes scientific progress.

This is an ongoing tension that cannot be avoided altogether. IRBs (and the federal officials establishing rules for IRBs) must be attentive to the need to make the review process as efficient as possible, so that it does not unnecessarily delay the research process. Yet, any IRB worth its salt will encounter instances where it must confront powerful research interests and take a stand in support of its consumer protection responsibilities.

IRBs are the players in the research process who have the most singular and focused responsibility to protect human subjects. But if the other parties—sponsors, investigators, government agencies—do not internalize such protective responsibilities in their own spheres as well, then IRBs cannot succeed. IRB members should speak out regularly, reminding all the key parties of their obligations in protecting subjects and of how ongoing societal support for the research depends on carrying out those obligations effectively.

This kind of outreach can be particularly important if it involves drawing attention to troubling developments that warrant greater attention by the research community as a whole. In this context, IRBs—individually and collectively—can provide valuable early warning signals of emerging concerns and help generate greater examination of them. Such concerns include the following:

1. The questionable human-subject oversight for many foreign trials that increasingly serve as a basis for new drug applications
2. The disturbing financial incentives sometimes given to investigators for recruiting human subjects
3. The possible erosion in many settings of meaningful informed consent
4. The uncertainty about how fully sponsors monitor their trials for adherence to human-subject requirements

IRBs should exert more public leadership on these and other such issues. They have a long-established credibility in speaking for human subjects and ought not let their overflowing agendas obscure for them the gains that can be achieved from speaking out more extensively. The issues are too important to be left only to ethicists, academics, and advocacy organizations, or for that matter to oversight bodies such as the Office of the Inspector General.

Acknowledgment

The author thanks Aimee Golbitz, Steven Keenan, and China Eng for their comments on an earlier version of this chapter.

Reference

1. Office of Inspector General. Recruiting human subjects: Pressures in industry-sponsored clinical research (OEI-01-97-00195), June 2000. Access date 12 Apr 2001. World Wide Web http://www.hhs.gov/oig/oei/reports/a459.pdf

A Unified Human-Research Protection Program

Sanford Chodosh

INTRODUCTION

This chapter is intended to relate my personal perspective on the development of systems to protect subjects studied in research while still advocating the advancement of scientific knowledge. I have had the unusual opportunity to observe and participate in this process over the past 40 years. This included involvement with IRBs and active membership in Public Responsibility in Medicine and Research (PRIM&R) for 30 years. When I began my career as a clinical investigator in the early 1960s, investigators almost universally developed their own protocols, and the majority were based at academic institutions. The IRB did not exist, and the consent process was primitive at best. When I was asked to become a member of our Human Studies Committee in the late 1960s, the system had minimal guidelines and little institutional support. I became the chair of the committee in 1971 at a time when the institution and the statewide research community were in the midst of a crisis over an approved study at my institution that had utilized fetal tissue. This was in addition to other problems with investigations at state psychiatric hospitals. I was asked to join a group of fellow scientists and lawyers in devising a plan to defuse proposed restrictive state legislation that would have made research in my state difficult. This group eventually became incorporated in 1974 as PRIM&R, with the intent of being a not-for-profit organization that could promote the ethical conduct of human research through education of the scientific community and the public. We began by organizing meetings of local IRB chairs and administrators to discuss common problems and soon found that we also could play a role in the federal regulations that were being developed. By 1977, PRIM&R initiated annual national conferences to meet the need for a forum for those involved with the protection of human subjects. The growth of attendance at these conferences reflects that IRBs were eager for guidance to deal with the routine issues and increasing complexity of regulatory requirements.

Standards for IRBs

Since those early days, much has changed in terms of where and by whom human research is conducted. Institutionally based IRBs are no longer the only game in town. In addition, the progressive increase in research funds, the increased numbers and complexity of protocols, and the burden of regulatory requirements have all compromised the ability of the IRB to properly carry out its responsibility to protect the individuals studied in research. There is a sense that IRBs have become so involved with the workload of properly reviewing protocols and complying with regulatory details that providing systems that actually protect the individuals studied has slipped from the IRB's primary function to a secondary role.

Since 1999, PRIM&R has recognized the problems related to these changes and has been developing performance standards that should apply to the variety of IRBs that now exist, many of which are outside the governance of academically oriented institutions. The shutdown of a number of major institutions' research programs due to noncompliance was one manifestation of the pressures these problems created. It also became evident that the IRB should not be expected to fulfill the role of the sole protector of human subjects. The PRIM&R performance standards propose that the responsibility should be vested in the governing organization, the investigator, and the IRB all working together as a unified human-research protection program (HRPP). From the perspective of past experience, it is important to review why such protection programs are necessary. What current problems exist that need to be resolved so that meaningful and effective systems can be established to truly protect those individuals studied in research?

When studying humans in research, a basic tenet is to respect the dignity of such individuals and to minimize the possibility of harm. *The Belmont Report* restated the basic ethical principles that should guide all of us in our interactions with all humans, whether in the context of research or everyday living. Unfortunately, the history of research has become marked with terrible examples of how these basic ethical principles have been ignored. Although the majority of scientists have followed these principles, the exceptions created a need for legal measures in an attempt to avoid future problems. These steps were not taken in the Western world until long after the World War II Nazi experiments became known. The assumption was that, in a civilized society, scientists abided by ethical standards that would not permit such atrocities. This was true in the majority of cases. In the academic world, most risky research was biomedical, and clinician–investigators had a background of training to do no harm to their patients that carried over to how they dealt with their research subjects. In those early days, additional assurance came from the oversight by clinical service chiefs, who provided guidance to the investigators in their departments. This oversight became more tenuous as clinical services grew in size and complexity and research generated more and more of the operating funds of services and institutions.

After Tuskegee and other ethical failures in research, the public and the scientific community realized that a better means of protecting subjects in research needed to be implemented. These misadventures led to distrust by the public of the ethical behavior of those responsible for the conduct of research. Federal agencies that had initially recommended simple peer review of research now promulgated regulations requiring a review of protocols and developed an assurance process in which institutions receiving federal funds promised to comply with the new rules. Most of these assurances also promised coverage of non–federally funded human research. Institutional Review Boards were established wherever federal funds were received or research involving investigational drugs and devices was carried out. Institutions depended on their IRBs to provide a mantle of ethical credibility to the conduct of their research. The IRB was clearly identified as the central focus of an institution's program for the protection of human subjects. As research increased in volume and complexity, and as regulatory demands increased, IRBs found themselves inundated with work. However, increased resources did not always follow. The IRB's primary role in protecting human subjects often became secondary to meeting regulatory requirements. The institution's need to meet the conditions of their assurances, and continue the income and prestige of the institution's research program, became the primary need for IRBs to fulfill.

IRBs also had less time and resources to devote to their vital role to investigators in the protection of those individuals studied in research. Institution-based scientists were assumed to be qualified to do research because of their staff appointments. Investigators were under pressure to do productive research in terms of their academic advancement and funding. Investigators, and sometimes institution officials, began to view the IRB as an adversary that obstructed opportunities to do research. Often, IRBs would become wary of making mistakes in judgment for which they and their institutions could be held accountable. Delays in approving protocols would reinforce the sense that the IRB worked against the best interests of the institution and investigators. Conversely, because most research was funded by federal agencies or under federal regulations, lack of compliance could result in funding cutbacks. Consequently, if the IRB did not review and approve protocols in a timely fashion, they could not be sent forward to be considered for approval by funding agencies. While trying to meet these conflicting demands, it was not uncommon for IRB members to lose the respect of their peers and superiors. Service on the IRB frequently meant less time for teaching, research, and practice with little recognition for performing a difficult job.

New problems arose in the 1980s. Federal and foundation research support increased progressively, leading to more investigators and investigations. Budgetary pressures caused institutions to expect more from their clinicians and teachers. Concomitantly, there was a huge increase in industry-sponsored research in both drugs and devices. Congressional laws now pressed the Food and Drug Administration (FDA) to act in a timely manner to approve investigational products, and industry was allowed to help fund the FDA so they could comply. Industry, realizing the financial rewards of obtaining earlier approval for marketing, pressed investigators to complete studies as rapidly as possible. It soon became clear that academic institutions could not supply the numbers of subjects fast enough to meet this demand. Institution-based IRBs were also viewed as being too slow or too demanding of changes to their multicenter designed protocols. Industry was allowed by the FDA to develop a non–institutional-based source of subjects—namely, practicing physicians—to meet their requirements. Research increasingly took place in foreign countries. A new industry developed to provide IRB approval for these multicenter protocols for each of the geographically diverse practitioner–investigators. These new central and independent review boards supplied the "peer" review for the practicing clinician who was not affiliated with an institution. This became a big business enterprise; 60% to 70% of pharmaceutical research is now accomplished in this setting. These significant financial rewards led to the development of large central and independent IRBs, as well as the incorporation of practicing clinicians into business units to facilitate managing more protocols. This new paradigm resulted in a different set of relationships than existed when the institution, IRB, and investigator were all part of a single organization. Because the noninstitutional IRB is usually geographically separate from the investigator, IRB members are unlikely to know the investigators personally. The sponsoring pharmaceutical or device company generally selects the investigators. These investigators often do not answer to a professional peer organization other than their state licensure agency. The sponsor, rather than the investigator, usually submits the protocol and consent form to these noninstitutional IRBs.

There is little question that this revolutionary change has increased the speed with which new drugs and devices have been approved. However, there are questions concerning the protection of the subjects in this new system. Although there are conflicts of interest in academia, they are not as blatantly financial as they can be in the noninstitutional setting. The inducement to enter as many subjects as possible is overtly evident because the funds often go directly to the investigator rather than to an institution that can control the investigator's income.

The logistical needs for review by IRBs of multicenter and cooperative studies have not been limited to industry-sponsored research. Increasing numbers of National Institutes of Health (NIH), VA, and oncology studies require access to numbers of subjects rarely available at a single site. Besides the requirement for significant numbers of subjects for scientific validity, it is often important to include subjects from diverse geographic or demographic population bases. The use of multiple centers may be the only way of recruiting sufficient numbers of subjects to study diseases that occur infrequently. Obviously, the protocols used for multicenter or cooperative studies must be scientifically uniform or the data cannot be combined. It seems logical that central review of such protocols can be more scientifically rigorous and more timely. However, the issue of the responsibility for the protection of subjects must also be considered, and local review is more likely to be able to take into account special circumstances that could influence the risk/benefit assessment. Currently, how the investigator relates in the setting of central review is not always clearly defined, and the chain of responsibility for protecting the individual subject may also be vague. Guidelines need to be developed that more clearly define the responsibilities of the various components in these circumstances so that the best elements of central and local review are preserved.

IRBs, whether they are institutionally based, central, or independent, face problems that clearly can undermine the ethical standards that are essential to scientific investigations and that protect subjects from risks when benefits are not honestly expected. The common problems are (a) the lack of efficient methods or resources to oversee/monitor ongoing approved studies; (b) pressures by the organization, sponsors, and investigators to approve studies for financial or prestige reasons; and, in a similar vein, (c) pressure to look sideways at the questionable scientific values of a study in order to gain financial support. Additional problems primarily affect institution-based IRBs. There is much evidence that institutions often supply inadequate support. IRB chairs and members often are not given appropriate recognition for serving. With increasing pressures to bring in income from managed-care practice and research, the time devoted to IRB work is of-ten not counted in the balance as valued time and effort. Large institutions with very large research programs require very efficient management to accomplish their responsibilities. Institutions that do only a small volume of research often do not have enough workload to justify the required administrative expertise and may even lack the scientific review capability in their professional staff. A possible solution would be to utilize an independent IRB or join with other small institutions to support an IRB that would have appropriate resources.

What is clear is that IRBs cannot be expected to continue to be the prime element in the protection of humans studied in research. That responsibility must be broadened to stress the role of the governance of the organization in setting high ethical standards and to emphasize the critical role that the investigator and the research team must play. These three components of the HRPP can no longer be adversarial, but must operate as a single entity whose basic value is the ethical treatment of all individuals studied in research. Even when the components of an HRPP are not institutionally based, there should be a clear plan for how it will function and who is responsible for the various aspects required for the protection of subjects, regardless of where the various components are physically located. The specific conditions of how the triad is organized should determine how the HRPP will operate. Multicenter and cooperative studies must designate how the responsibility for the subjects' protection will be assigned.

An integrated HRPP must establish policies and procedures to support the role played by each component. The investigator is the key element in the responsible conduct of the research and for the protection of the subjects recruited into studies. The investigator and the research team are perfectly positioned to accept this responsibility. This team must be sufficiently knowledgeable to implement the scientific aspects of the investigation in an ethical manner. It is likely that measures of competency for the research team will become accepted practice.

Whatever measures are implemented, the intent to do the right thing must remain the driving ethical principle. The governance of the HRPP must establish and maintain high ethical standards that are clearly disseminated to the IRB, investigators, and the community they serve. There should be appropriate support of the IRB and investigators so that their responsibilities can be carried out appropriately and expeditiously. Meaningful conflict-of-interest policies must be established and implemented for all components of the HRPP. Visible recognition of the contribution made by IRB members and staff helps to promote respect for the IRB function and for the organization's commitment to ethical research.

Adequate functioning of the IRB requires the support of a trained staff with access to needed resources. The governance should select an IRB chair who can be a leader with stature and credibility in the organization. Chairs should not be rotated on a short-term basis, as stability of IRB functions is more likely to be maintained when there is continuity of leadership. IRB members should be selected with the understanding that this is an important organizational function and should be given the same recognition as research, teaching, or clinical activities.

I am hopeful that the evolution of the system to protect humans studied in research will again become the organization's primary goal by returning to simple humane and ethical principles. There is a need to refocus the primary effort to strengthening the front line of this endeavor, namely, the investigator/subject interface.

Any actual or perceived conflicts of interest cannot be allowed to interfere with the protective role of the HRPP. Although the system has a great need to evolve to correct the past problems in research involving humans, we must nevertheless always return to the basic ethical principles in dealing with our fellow human beings. Simply stated, "Do unto others as you would have others do unto you."

A Shared Responsibility for Protecting Human Subjects

Steven Peckman

INTRODUCTION

This chapter will address the importance of the shared responsibility for creating an institutional culture of respect and trust in the protection of the rights and welfare of human research subjects. It will outline the separate responsibilities of the institution, as represented through the institutional official, investigators, and the institutional review board (IRB), in promoting an ethical and safe research environment. The chapter will also highlight the collective responsibility for building the culture of respect and trust through education and support.

A Culture of Respect for the Mission of the IRB

The Department of Health and Human Services/Office for Human Research Protections (DHHS/OHRP) defines an IRB as "an administrative body" composed of scientists and nonscientists "established to protect the rights and welfare of human research subjects recruited to participate in research activities conducted under the auspices of the institution with which it is affiliated."[1(Chap. IA)] The IRB conducts a prospective review of proposed research and monitors continuing research in order to safeguard the rights and welfare of the participants. Although the IRB is responsible for the review and approval of proposed research, the institutional official is responsible for all parties engaged in the review or conduct of research under the auspices of the institution. Thus, the institutional official should have the "legal authority to act and speak for the institution, and should be someone who can ensure that the institution will effectively fulfill its research oversight function."[1(Chap.IB)]

The requirement that each federally funded institution engaged in human experimentation must constitute a local IRB encourages the institution to promote an environment that supports the highest ethical standards for the review and conduct of its research. Moore[2(P. 375)] highlighted the importance of "the intellectual and ethical climate of the institution. Such a climate is difficult to regulate or standardize, at times even to recognize or describe. Yet it is more important than any other single consideration in protecting the willing patient from unwise, inexpert, or ill-advised therapeutic innovation." Moore's 1969 comments on the importance of institutional culture remain largely true today. Most importantly, the imprimatur of the institution makes the local IRB an agent of the highest ethical standards embraced by the institution itself, rather than a foreign agent of the government or an adversary of research, and creates a community that supports such standards.

The research institution is uniquely situated to create a culture in which ethics are valued and the importance of IRB review is honored. Levine[3(p. 342)] noted that "to function most effectively, the IRB must not only be, but also must be perceived to be, an agent of its own institution." To achieve Levine's goal, it is incumbent on the institutional official to use his or her moral and academic authority to require the highest ethical conduct from the faculty and staff. The institution should develop and implement local policies and procedures that reflect the ethical principles of *The Belmont Report*[4] and the federal regulations to create an internal standard of acceptable behavior. Institutional policies and procedures translate into a demonstration of philosophical and practical support for the autonomy and authority of the IRB, while facilitating a fair, timely, and collegial review of proposed research. An institutional ethos that highlights the importance of ethical principles will also insist on well-conceived and properly executed research. The requirement should be evident in written institutional policies, the actions and communications of institutional officials, and the IRB. Research that is designed or conducted so poorly as to be unethical or invalid exposes subjects and the institution to unnecessary risk. The institutional standard for well-conceived and properly conducted research minimizes the potential for conflicts between the IRB and the research community, facilitates local review, and assures the protection of the rights and welfare of the human subjects.

Investigators will perceive such internal standards as an expression of a communal commitment to ethical behavior rather than as an intrusion into academic research by a colonizing federal authority. The IRB is thus perceived by the research community as an expression of its own commitment to human subjects' protection and the expression of an institutional mandate and policy, rather than an alien and disembodied review process. As noted by the National Commission for the Protection of Human Subjects in Biomedical and Behavioral Research, such an environment demystifies the review process and builds the trust of the research community and the public.[5]

The institution underscores the importance of ethical conduct by convening IRBs with a respected membership that reflects the highest level of scientific expertise and community participation and support. An IRB that has the respect of the research community is better able to fulfill its principal charge as outlined by the National Commission: education of the research community.

> The Commission believes that the rights of subjects should be protected by local review committees operating pursuant to federal regulations and located in institutions where research involving human subjects is conducted. Compared to the possible alternatives of a regional or national review process, local committees have the advantage of greater familiarity with the actual conditions surrounding the conduct of research. Such committees can work closely with investigators to assure that the rights and welfare of human subjects are protected and, at the same time, that the application of policies is fair to the investigators. They can contribute to the education of the research community and the public regarding the ethical conduct of research. The committees can become resource centers for information concerning ethical standards and federal requirements and can communicate with federal officials and with other local committees about matters of common concerns.[5]

The institutional official recognizes that the board can only carry out its regulatory, educational, and ethical functions when there are sufficient resources and high-level support staff to communicate effectively with the research community and to ensure adequate protections of subjects through oversight, including continuing review and monitoring of approved research.

The Belmont Circle

Human research is based on trust. The biomedical and social/behavioral investigator must build a relationship of trust with the subject in order to obtain information that will help answer a scientific question. All parties are entrusted with the responsibility to ensure the rights and welfare of research participants through IRB review and compliance with the federal regulations. This means they are *allowed* to perform human research only after demonstrating an understanding of the responsibility by obtaining an IRB approval. Therefore, human-subjects research is a *privilege* and not a *right*. A federal court determined that human research is not a right, such as the right of intellectual inquiry embodied in academic freedom. Rather, it is a privilege given by the institution to individuals who have assured their willingness to work within the federal guidelines and state law.[6]

The National Commission outlined three ethical principles in *The Belmont Report* to guide research with human subjects and ensure the maintenance of a culture of trust: respect for persons/autonomy, beneficence, and justice.[4] The ethical principles of *The Belmont Report* and the federal regulations are applied through the creation of an institutional culture that honors and demonstrates respect for human subjects through the process of IRB review of research protocols, as well as the conduct of research by investigators and support by institutional officials. Successful IRB review balances the interests of three distinct but interrelated social and political entities: scientists, society, and the individual human subject.

The IRB, however, does not balance these interests alone. The IRB functions in a dynamic relationship with federal agencies, research sponsors, institutions hosting research, investigators, and the public. The dynamic relationship balances the competing interests of all parties and facilitates the continued conduct of human research in an ethical and collegial environment. Ultimately, an effective system of protections is a collective responsibility that requires a collaborative effort. When all parties acknowledge their shared ethical responsibilities at both the local and national level and a balance of interests is met, they create a culture of trust. This allows for their effective collaboration with the public and research subjects.

An institution's assurance of compliance with the federal government outlines the responsibilities of the institutional administration, IRB, and scientists. This allows an institution to demonstrate responsibility for the ethical conduct of research by creating a culture that respects and endorses the imperative of IRB review, approval, and oversight. Additionally, the assurance stipulates that local IRB review of human research will comply with federal regulations and the ethical principles outlined in *The Belmont Report*.

The system of assurances for local IRB review is based on trust. The public has entrusted the federal government with its well-being as it relates to human-subject research. The federal government trusts the research institution through the assurance of compliance to impanel an appropriate IRB to review its own research. The trust is based on the acknowledged institutional responsibility for instituting effective mechanisms for the protection of human research subjects. The IRB is entrusted to review research responsibly according to the federal regulations, community standards, and ethical guidelines in order to maximize the protection of the subjects and to collegially negotiate the conditions of approval with investigators. The local IRB review engages the scientist in a dialogue that ensures that the conduct of research is in compliance with federal regulations and ethical guidelines and is performed according to the agreed-upon IRB conditions of approval. The subject entrusts the investigator through the process of informed consent with the protection of his or her rights and welfare beyond any research objectives, and the investigator trusts the subject to be truthful. The collective trust is built through institutional support of local IRB review and compliance with federal regulations.

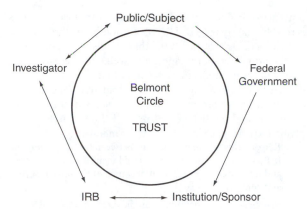

Figure 1.4.1 The Belmont Circle

Thus, the ability to conduct ethical human research is predicated on an ability to create a system where many levels of trust are seamlessly woven together.

The creation of a supportive institutional culture is based on the ability of all parties to apply the concepts of trust embraced by *The Belmont Report* and the federal regulations through successful working relationships with their colleagues. In other words, to effectively apply the principles of *Belmont*, respect for persons, beneficence, and justice to human research subjects, they must first share a common goal: the application of these same principles, not in a hierarchical way but in a circular fashion, to interactions with IRBs, support staff, investigators, sponsors, and federal agencies. This is called the Belmont circle (Figure 1.4.1). A circle is created that links all parties equally, and each party demonstrates dedication, both individually and collectively, through education and cooperation, to upholding human dignity through the application of the letter and spirit of the National Commission's report. Using various ethical codes and regulations, they create an environment that ensures the protection of human subjects as well as the advancement of science. The collaboration must exist in a culture of trust, complete openness, and honesty. By upholding the highest ethical principles and standards, they build public support for the pursuit of greater knowledge in a safe research environment.

The Three Levels of Accountability or Compliance

The circle of trust remains whole only when all responsible entities within the institution dedicate themselves to upholding the federal assurance and the concepts within *The Belmont Report*. The responsibility of ensuring accountability or compliance for human research is often placed solely on the shoulders of the IRB and the IRB administrator. The creation of a successful local human-subject protection system, however, is predicated on the interlinking relationship of the three institutional levels of responsibility as outlined in the regulations and guidelines: institution, investigator, and IRB.[1(Chap. ID)]

Each party—investigator, IRB, and institutional official—holds the responsibility for ensuring respect and collegiality in the IRB review process. We should understand the role each of the participants is expected to play in order to ensure accountability.

The federal regulations embody a self-regulating system that depends on the honesty and integrity of the participants, namely, the institutions, the researchers, and the IRBs. The efficacy of the system is predicated on the ability of the institutions, IRBs, and investigators to work together in a supportive environment of mutual trust toward a common goal: the safe and ethical conduct of research. The systems will not work unless the three levels of accountability reflect and enhance each other. History has shown that a breakdown in any level of compliance will weaken the protection of human subjects, erode the public's trust in scientific research, and result in a demand for broader and stronger regulation and oversight.

Institutional Accountability

Active institutional support is the foundation for a successful, ethical human-research program. The institutional official is responsible for upholding the assurance and is accountable for the actions of investigators and the IRB. Institutional noncompliance is defined as a systemic failure of the institution to implement practices and procedures contained in the institution's assurance. The institution must ensure that (a) the IRB is properly constituted and functions in accordance with the regulations; (b) the IRB receives appropriate institutional support and adequate staffing; and (c) the investigators meet their obligations to the IRB.[7(Sec. 103)] Systemic failure to abide by the terms and conditions of an institution's assurance may result in withdrawal of approval of the assurance.[1] Such an action could effectively result in the suspension of all human research at the institution and the requirement that each investigator apply directly to the DHHS/OHRP for the review and approval of each protocol.

The institution ensures that the IRB retains the ultimate authority for the approval of research with human subjects and has the authority to approve, to require modification of, and disapprove proposed human research.[7(Sec. 109)] The IRB also has the authority to suspend or revoke its approval of ongoing research.[7(Sec. 113)] It is, therefore, the institution's obligation and responsibility to support IRB decisions made within the course and scope of its charge. Institutional support, however, does not absolve the IRB from the responsibility of working collegially with investigators, nor does it make the IRB the federal police. Rather, it requires that the board serve as an educational resource for the local research community. The Advisory Committee on Human Radiation Experiments highlighted the importance of education: "The historical record makes clear that the rights and interests of research subjects cannot be protected if researchers fail to appreciate sufficiently the moral aspects of human subject research and the value of institutional oversight."[8] The institutional official, therefore, should set the highest ethical standards for the research community and insist upon an institutional culture that demonstrates support for the charge of the IRB, namely respect for human dignity.

The institution, therefore, is uniquely situated to take responsibility for various aspects of human research, such as the following:

1. It should create an institutional culture that promotes and upholds the highest ethical standards in the conduct of human research.

2. It should educate and mentor the research community and provide sufficient resources and staff to support the educational mandate of the IRB.

3. It should create an IRB with sufficient scientific expertise and community representation to assess proposed research projects.

4. It should involve all interested parties in the review process, emphasizing open communication and interaction with the community (the source of potential research subjects).

5. It should oversee research.

6. It should be aware of local resources and standards that may impact proposed research.

Investigator Accountability

Investigators are required to submit research for prospective IRB review. They must comply with all IRB conditions of approval, institutional policy, and federal and state regulations and laws. The OHRP notes the most common lapses in compliance include (a) unreported changes in the protocol; (b) misuse or non-use of the informed consent document; and (c) failure to submit protocols to the IRB in a timely fashion.

"Occasionally, an investigator will either avoid or ignore the IRB. Such cases present a more serious challenge to the systems of human subject protection. Regardless of intent, investigators initiating unapproved research involving human subjects place those subjects as well as the institution at an unacceptable risk."[1(Chap. ID)]

IRB Accountability

The IRB must ensure that all appropriate review procedures are followed. Noncompliance occurs whenever the IRB deviates from the duties required of it by federal regulations. The deviations may include (a) inadequate review of research protocols; (b) failure to ensure the consent document and process provide sufficient information to allow prospective subjects to make an informed decision whether to participate in the research; (c) failure to ensure the research design includes adequate monitoring of the data and any additional safeguards necessary to protect the welfare of particularly vulnerable subjects; and (d) failure to conduct continuing review of research at intervals appropriate to the degree of risk. IRBs must also uphold their regulatory recordkeeping responsibilities[1(Chap. IB)] and only make research-related decisions with appropriate quorum and attendance of sufficient nonscientific and nonaffiliated members.[7(Sec. 107)]

If the three partners—institutional official, investigator, and IRB—embrace and express *The Belmont Report*, they will create a culture that is free of hostility and where the importance of IRB review and compliance with the regulations is readily acknowledged. The integration of the three ethical principles of *Belmont* with the three levels of responsibility for the protection of the rights and welfare of research subjects will result in program accountability as well as commitment to the federal assurance, ultimately benefiting all stakeholders and promoting justice. The institution, the investigator, and the IRB complete the Belmont circle by applying the principles in the following manner.

1. *Respect.* Respectful interactions between the institution, the IRB, and the investigator will build a culture of respect for, and understanding of, the importance of the ethical review and conduct of research.

2. *Beneficence.* It is incumbent on the institution, the IRB, and the investigator to apply the concept of beneficence to their relationships with each other. Ineffective accountability harms the institution and fellow researchers and puts research at risk. Additionally, maximizing benefit through acknowledgment of institutional accountability will help create a culture of understanding and trust. In other words, all parties should agree that minimizing the risk of noncompliance and maximizing the benefits of collegial interactions will lead to a common goal: an environment that ensures continued research through the protection of the rights and welfare of human subjects. To build a program that upholds respect for human dignity, the concept of beneficence must have primacy, even if that means deciding that the potential risk of the institution's participation in a project outweighs the possible benefits in academic promotion, extramural funds, etc. Ultimately, a lack of unity in the acknowledgement of the importance of the letter and spirit of *Belmont* and the federal regulations poses great risk to the success of the IRB process and the general research program.

3. *Justice.* The application of justice requires that no single party carries an unfair burden and that there is an equal distribution of responsibility. The IRB cannot ensure compliance alone. The function and support of the IRB and membership on the IRB should not be an "unfunded mandate." The IRB and investigators should be supported through appropriate education regarding their responsibilities and obligations. Without appropriate education, it is impossible to ensure a respectful research environment. Furthermore, all members of the institution's human research community should actively participate in the IRB process through revolving membership that will act as an educational tool and allow for an equitable distribution of the burden of membership.

Conclusion

In spite of past and recent problems in the conduct of human-subject research, society continues to allow investigators to engage in human experimentation because specific parameters are in place to ensure the protection of the participants. An institution that takes responsibility for the review and conduct of human research positions itself to engage the trust and support of the scientific community. In addition, it attracts additional financial support for research because it can assure ethical conduct and safety, and it creates an environment for successful collaboration with the community of potential research subjects. The responsibility of local review obliges all institutional parties to acknowledge a collective responsibility for the creation of a culture of intramural and extramural community participation, mentoring, and accountability. The local system of review is most effective when the institutional official sets the highest ethical standards for the research community and insists on an institutional culture that demonstrates support for the charge of the IRB, namely, respect for human dignity.

Acknowledgment

Sections of this chapter were adapted from Steven Peckman, *Local Institutional Review Boards,* National Bioethics Advisory Commission, 2001, as well as from "Developing a Program of Human Subject Protection Before an FDA Inspection or OPRR Site Visit," *Balancing the Belmont: Human Subjects and Future Research,* Wayne State University/OPRR/FDA Conference, Keynote Address, September 16, 1999.

References

1. Penslar RL, Porter J. P., Office for Human Research Protections. *Institutional Review Board Guidebook.* Updated 6 Feb 2001. Access date 29 Mar 2001. World Wide Web http://ohrp.osophs.dhhs.gov/irb/irb_guidebook.htm

2. Moore F. D. Therapeutic innovation: Ethical boundaries in the initial clinical trials of new drugs and surgical procedures. In: Freund PA (ed). *Experimentation With Human Subjects.* New York: George Braziller. 1970: 375.

3. Levine R. J. *Ethics and Regulation of Clinical Research,* Ed 2. Baltimore, MD: Urban and Schwarzenberg. 1986.

4. National Commission for the Protection of Human Subjects of Biomedical and Behavioral Research. *The Belmont Report: Ethical Principles and Guidelines for the Protection of Human Subjects of Research.* In DHEW Publication No. (OS) 78-0013 and (OS) 78-0014.4, 18 Apr 1979. Access date 22 Mar 2001. World Wide Web http://ohsr.od.nih.gov/mpa/belmont.php3

5. National Commission for the Protection of Human Subjects of Biomedical and Behavioral Research. *Report and Recommendations: Institutional Review Boards* (DHEW report No. OS 78-0008). 1978. Washington, DC: Department of Health, Education, and Welfare.

6. Hammerschmidt D. "There is no substantive due process right to conduct human subject research": The saga of the Minnesota Gamma Hydroxybutyrate Study. *IRB: A Review of Human Subjects Research* 19(3, 4):13–15, 1997.

7. Code of Federal Regulations. Title 45A—Department of Health and Human Services; Part 46—Protection of Human Subjects. Updated 1 Oct 1997. Access date 18 Apr 2001. World Wide Web http://www4.law.cornell.edu/cfr/45p46.htm

8. Advisory Committee on Human Radiation Experiments. *The Human Radiation Experiments: Final Report.* New York: Oxford University Press. 1996. http://tis.eh.doe.gov/ohre/roadmap/achre/report.html (DOE 061-000-00-848-9)

The Tension Between Science and Ethics

Marian G. Secundy

INTRODUCTION

The historical record within the United States and the shameful memories of the Holocaust are critical to an understanding of the development of federal guidelines, rules, regulations, and legislation governing the conduct of Institutional Review Boards (IRBs). All have been put into place as mechanisms for the protection of persons who might become participants in scientific research. The reality of past exploitation and callous disregard for the personhood of vulnerable, unempowered, frail, poor persons and persons of color has resulted in the IRB system to regulate research conduct. Although regulations have been in place for over 25 years, inherent and inevitable tensions exist between the scientists and the regulators who claim an ethical responsibility to protect participants in research from harm. Those tensions, very simply, are between science and ethics. Science is rational and has noble objectives; for example, advancing knowledge, eradicating disease, and forever moving in a forward direction for the good of all people. Although those claiming an ethical responsibility also believe themselves rational, their concerns are for individuals in the final analysis. Advancing knowledge is a good, but not the primary good, as it often seems to be with scientists who do not appear to pay equal attention to the inherent value of the persons who might be negatively affected by the specific methods of the scientific inquiry under consideration. It is in the traditions and worldview of Western philosophical thought that the pursuit of knowledge and ethical responsibility have come into conflict. It is out of that situation that we have IRBs and the federal guidelines under which they operate.

Mechanisms of Oversight

The Belmont Report of 1979, the Common Rule, and the federal guidelines have informed scientific investigations of federally funded projects involving human subjects. Researchers receiving such funds have been charged with conducting their investigations with careful attention to the risks and benefits to individuals who are to be involved in moving that research forward. The national agenda, while clearly valuing the advancement of science, has attempted to acknowledge and incorporate protections for persons in order to avoid repetition of violations and exploitation like the Tuskegee Study, Willowbrook, Jewish Chronic Hospital, and the experiments conducted during the period of the Holocaust in Nazi Germany.

Mechanisms of oversight, peer review, and checks and balances have been put into place largely through requirements for IRBs at those places where federal funding supports the work of investigators. These mechanisms have not been fully effective because of the inherent tensions mentioned above regarding differing priorities and have, in part, been responsible for what many consider a failure to sufficiently support, implement, and enforce existing research in accordance with the rules, regulations, and guidelines.

Recent reports from the Government Accounting Office have spoken to the deficits and gaps to be found in the work of IRBs. Clarification of roles, inadequate budgeting, and the lack of uniform standards and criteria are problematic. Insufficient staffing to maximize the possibility of adequate compliance has often provided a convenient and very real excuse for some IRBs to cut corners regarding documentation of protocol reviews, or an excuse not to follow the required review process in its entirety.

The Principle of Justice

In the past, national focus on obligations not to exploit or harm others has resulted in decisions not to involve women, prisoners, and ethnic minorities—particularly African Americans—in research studies, even though they might have been beneficial. The existing knowledge available from studies conducted without a truly representative population is by definition flawed, incomplete, and misleading. Today, an inevitable and ongoing tension exists relative to when or if to include or exclude certain groups or individuals. Despite that tension, federal guidelines now require that women and minorities are included in research activities or that justification for their exclusion is provided.

Few federal mechanisms exist for monitoring or follow-up once research is funded. Researchers are not required to give a detailed plan for compliance monitoring. This is especially true regarding the selection of subjects. Researchers do not usually report how well they have been able to recruit minorities. Strategies that successfully recruit minorities are critical elements of the armamentarium of researchers. Retention strategies and methods are equally important. Both recruitment and retention ought to be addressed by IRBs in their initial assessment of the researcher's plan and need careful review during the life of the protocol.

Therein lies another inevitable tension, for appropriate and successful recruitment and retention require cultural competence of the researcher or someone designated as a member of the research team. Researchers are usually scientists without exposure to the social sciences or humanities that might have allowed them to develop a mastery of the cultural variations among diverse groups and individuals within this pluralistic society. There is continuing resistance by many scientists to an expectation of such mastery. The very undefined and vague definitions of what cultural competence entails and the problems of demonstrating, making operational, and measuring such competence also present a challenge to those who claim such competence is necessary. Becoming culturally competent requires an appreciation for the knowledge base of other disciplines, particularly those generally believed to be "soft." Openness to collaboration and teamwork is also necessary. Once again, an inevitable tension surfaces within the culture of traditional academic scientific research that is competitive, often isolated, and closed as it becomes necessary to be more open, flexible, collaborative, and appreciative of difference. The challenge to the IRB is to include voices from both worlds.

The Challenge for IRBs

Clearly, inclusion of persons from groups with historical baggage places significant responsibilities on IRBs to be protective. The informed consent document and process are essential elements for such protections. Unfortunately, some IRBs do not appear to value or appreciate the critical importance of the informed consent process to their central mission of protecting human subjects and minimizing harms. Not enough attention is given to this document or to the process that the investigator intends to use. Emphasis is on the scientific merit of the proposed investigation and its methodologies. There are inadequate mechanisms at the federal level to influence or provide any real sanctions regarding the informed consent process. If the informed consent document or process is inadequate or flawed, but has been described to the satisfaction of the IRB, little authority exists at the federal level to override approvals given to proceed with the research. The lack of uniform criteria and the reality that there are great variations in competency of IRB members to assess and understand the relationship of informed consent to protection of persons are perhaps the most problematic aspects of the entire effort.

All of the tensions described above converge around the problem of inadequate attention to the informed consent process. To summarize, these tensions include the following:

1. The tension between science and its goals, and the goals of ethics to protect persons from harm

2. The charge to investigators to include participants without exploitation and harm

3. The lack of assessment tools to determine competency and capacity of researchers to fulfill that charge

4. The historical and social climate that continues to shape the response and behavior of investigators and potential participants. Uncertainty, ambivalence, and resistance from both are elements of today's requirement for inclusion of women and minorities.

Conclusion

The tension between science and ethics makes it necessary to focus attention on the need to establish an oversight system to protect the rights and welfare of research subjects. IRBs are called on to respond to these tensions and turn them from insurmountable challenges into opportunities to demonstrate respect for all persons and a capacity to protect even the least of these, and to not allow intentional or unintentional harms. Of the utmost importance is the selection of diverse members, with appropriate competencies to address science and culture, who fully understand and appreciate the critical importance of attending to informed consent as process and event.

A Brief History of PRIM&R and IRB Education

Joan Rachlin

INTRODUCTION

As the long-time executive director of the nonprofit organization Public Responsibility in Medicine and Research (PRIM&R), I am one of a small but stalwart group of IRB "lifers," or at least a member of the "Quarter Century Club!" Over the past 25 years, there has been tremendous change in the world of research regulation, and particularly in the IRB system. I am not a historian, but I am—and have always been—an avid IRB-watcher, and therefore my perspective may be of interest to IRB newcomers and may evoke warm memories in IRB veterans.

Beginnings of PRIM&R

PRIM&R and IRBs grew up together, and therefore the history of one is a window on the history of the other. When I first came to work at PRIM&R, I was an idealistic young law student working part-time for a firm specializing in health care law. I began working in the law firm in late 1974, just as PRIM&R was being incorporated. As I was the low person on the firm's totem pole, the tasks associated with this pro bono effort were left to me. PRIM&R's initial mission was to improve, and proactively influence, the level of both governmental and public understanding on issues relating to research. Another objective was to improve the general image of and climate for research, but in truth, none of us knew how to approach either of those very theoretical goals.

One of the hot research topics in the 1970s was the growth of IRBs and federal involvement in their regulation. Federal funding of clinical research had grown exponentially after World War II, and the National Institutes of Health (NIH) opened their Clinical Center in 1953 to accommodate that growth. The NIH Clinical Center insisted on committee review of all proposed research protocols in its intramural program but, along with a handful of teaching hospitals, was unusual in this practice.

Then, in 1966, the U.S. Surgeon General required prior local review of all clinical research involving human subjects funded by the U.S. Public Health Service. This review was to take into account the rights and welfare of subjects and the potential risks and medical benefits of the research. In 1974, these policies and guidelines were revised and issued as regulations mandating that institutions establish diversely constituted review boards consisting of at least five members. So, 1974 was a milestone year in IRB history! The IRB regulations were first issued, and both the National Commission (a federal advisory committee) and PRIM&R were born.

One of the key missions of the National Commission was to consider procedures for evaluating and monitoring the performance of the above-described IRBs following their establishment by the National Research Act of 1974, and to recommend appropriate enforcement mechanisms. The Commission issued a report and recommendations on IRBs in 1978, and, along with the *Belmont Report* and Jay Katz's seminal work, *Experimentation in Human Beings*, it became one of our three early bibles. It is haunting to note that the question Jay Katz articulated in the early 1970s—"When may a society expose some of its members to harm in order to seek benefits for others?"—is still the fundamental question that researchers and IRBs struggle with today.

I remember hearing many observers predict back in the mid-1970s that IRBs, once widely adopted and well developed, would solve many, if not most, of the ethical and "public perception" problems in research. *Would that it were so easy.* I recently heard a talk by Jeremy Sugarman of Duke University in which he humorously referred to a scene from the movie *Pulp Fiction* when describing the situations in which IRBs often find themselves today. The analogy Sugarman invoked described the plight of the "clean-up crew" called to the scene after a significant amount of blood had already been shed. The leader of the clean-up crew said to his would-be employer: "We don't DO the cleaning; we show YOU how to do it," or words to that effect. So, too, with IRBs: A small, often underfunded, and always overworked committee, no matter how dedicated and competent, cannot "clean up" the problems that plague the research programs and cultures at many institutions. But that reality did not stop many of us idealists from having high hopes when the IRB system was young. And so the journey began.

Administering the IRB

The task of administering IRBs fell to an early collection of mostly unwitting individuals who answered job descriptions that plunged them down the rabbit hole quickly and deeply. The IRB professionals who have endured and established credible programs are an intelligent, patient, well-organized, and committed lot, who are also (a) able to keep many balls in the air without missing a beat, (b) determined to keep many investigators and institutional officials grounded without their feeling attacked and unappreciated, (c) capable of keeping many protocols moving without incurring the wrath of the investigators on the one hand and the sponsors on the other, and (d) willing to, in her/his "spare" time, read, read, read, and then read some more, because there is always so much to learn.

In the hope of improving the quality of research by protecting the rights of those who participate as subjects, a core group of people did meet these criteria and have dedicated themselves to building effective IRBs at their institutions. These are people of remarkable character, competence, and personal courage who have made the IRB community what it is today. This is an unusual group of professionals, and it is one of the main reasons that I, and so many others, have remained connected to the IRB world for as long as we have.

Developments in the Late 1970s

On to more history! In the early days of the IRB system, no one knew how to establish an IRB, whom to recruit, how to structure IRB reviews, and most urgently, how to interpret and apply the regulations. Recognizing the need for education in basic aspects of IRB function, PRIM&R decided to launch an educational campaign with its first IRB conference—for that matter, the first IRB conference anywhere—in April 1977. The meeting was held in the Suffolk Law School auditorium, and lunch cost $3.75 per person. We had no idea how many people would attend the conference because we had no idea if anyone was interested enough in IRB issues to travel to Boston. We invited Donald Chalkley, the first director of the Office for Protection from Research Risks (OPRR), to be one of the speakers, and he obliged. We sent out our very primitive brochures and waited. Hoping for 75-100 attendees, we were delighted to welcome 175, and the PRIM&R IRB conference tradition was launched.

Shortly after this first PRIM&R conference in 1977, what has fondly become known as the "Charlie Mc-Carthy" era arrived. Dr. Charles McCarthy took over from Don Chalkley in 1978 and led OPRR for the next 14 years with a thoroughly enchanting and effective blend of wit, warmth, determination, and wisdom. Dr. McCarthy was an ideal leader of OPRR during its formative years. He was one part ethicist, one part federal emissary, one part negotiator, and one part educator. He filled each role with competence and grace, and both the promulgation and widespread adoption of 45 CFR 46 in 1981 are rightly credited to him. Dr. McCarthy not only mediated the many battles that raged when the proposed regulations were first published in 1979, but he implicitly understood the need for community buy-in and worked tirelessly to achieve that through education and ready access to his office.

The next hallmark on our timeline was 1980, when the President's Commission was empaneled. Although it was the federal successor to the National Commission, it had an expanded mandate to look at issues outside the NIH. The President's Commission portfolio included reporting on the adequacy of human-subjects regulations, gene transfer, compensation for research-related injuries, and whistleblowing. Its recommendations include these requests.

1. All federal agencies should adopt common regulations.

2. The DHHS Secretary should establish an office to coordinate and monitor implementation of the human-subject protection regulations.

3. Each federal agency should apply one set of rules consistently to all of its subunits.

4. Principal investigators should be required to submit annual data on the number of subjects in their research and on the number and nature of adverse events.

5. Action should be taken on the National Commission's recommendations for added protections in research with children and mentally disabled persons.

6. Institutions should be free to handle misconduct through mechanisms other than IRBs.

7. A procedure should be adopted for debarring grantees found guilty of serious misconduct and for sharing each agency's results.

Sound familiar? The more things change, the more they stay the same! Perhaps the most directly relevant connection between the work of the President's Commission and this book is that the Commission contracted with PRIM&R to develop a Guidebook for IRBs, which we did with gusto and pride in 1979. The Official IRB Guidebook took many of you far and served many of you well, but its time had long since come, and this book is a welcome and long overdue successor to that groundbreaking volume.

The 1980s and Beyond

In 1986, one of the most significant events on the timeline occurred when PRIM&R formed its membership affiliate, Applied Research Ethics National Association (ARENA), which has filled a huge void in the leadership and information vacuum for the IRB community. I know that many of the chapters in this book are the result of ARENA initiatives and have been penned by ARENA leaders and members. The formation of ARENA and the subsequent achievements of this organization are PRIM&R's greatest "reflected" accomplishments.

In 1994, Dr. Gary Ellis assumed the leadership of OPRR upon Dr. McCarthy's retirement, and he built on the foundation of outreach and education with his own brand of activism and unswerving principle. Dr. Ellis understood that OPRR's stewardship had entered a new era, owing in part to the growing complexity of research itself and to the financial ties between researchers and sponsors. He was a courageous and tireless leader of the office as it sought to reform, correct, revise, and improve the dynamic system that keeps those who are enrolled in research out of harm's way. Like Dr. McCarthy, his belief in the value of and need for education was fierce. He preached his own version of the "trickle-down" theory in which conscientious and committed institutional leaders set the tone for the ethical conduct of research at their respective facilities. Under Dr. Ellis's direction, OPRR's compliance site visits increased despite acute staffing shortages and increased workload. The results of those site visits are widely credited with improving the research community's willingness to more adequately staff and otherwise fund IRBs.

Conclusion

We now find ourselves in the twenty-first century, with the conversion of an NIH-based OPRR to a DHHS-based OHRP, ably headed by Dr. Greg Koski. The new office possesses broader authority, a larger budget, and a strong public mandate to improve the protection of research subjects. But, despite the passage of time, the problems that led to the formation of IRBs almost 30 years ago are still among the main issues with which IRBs struggle today.

As we all know, progress never comes easily, but as I look back on the past 27 years I am proud of everything that has been accomplished and excited about the possibilities for the future. Today the opportunity has never been greater for IRBs to impact the conduct of research in a way that we only imagined could be possible in the early days of this field. As I look around the room at the meetings and other discussion forums I attend and/or organize around the country, I see nothing but good things: energy, determination, and commitment to the fundamental ideals of research ethics. The protection of research subjects has never been in better hands owing to the coming of age of a community of committed and principled IRB professionals. Thank you for keeping the flame burning, and for caring enough to never stop learning, to never stop teaching, to never stop asking! May it always be so, for your vigilance ensures "their" protection, and no one could ask for anything more.

The IRB: Definition and Federal Oversight

Robert J. Amdur and Elizabeth A. Bankert

INTRODUCTION

An Institutional Review Board (IRB) is a committee whose primary responsibility is to protect the rights and welfare of human research participants. Currently, no law or national directive defines an IRB or requires research to be reviewed in a uniform way regardless of researcher affiliation or funding source. In situations where research is subject to federal regulation, the definition of an IRB and the procedures for research review are described in detail in the Code of Federal Regulations (see subsequent chapters). When research is not subject to federal regulation, research directors are under no formal obligation to monitor the ethical aspects of research, but many elect to do so with a system modeled after the federal IRB system. In this setting, research review committees are often called IRBs regardless of their connection to federal authority.

The distinction between a federally regulated and non-federally regulated IRB is important because the purpose of this book is to explain how an IRB should function. One could argue that the standards or procedures described in federal IRB regulations are not the best way to monitor the ethical aspects of research. As many IRBs operate in an environment where they are free to customize their policy and procedures independent of federal regulations, a discussion of alternative research review options would be of interest to a segment of the research community. However, in an effort to focus the discussions presented in this book, a decision has been made to use federal research regulations as the reference standard for IRB practice. This book will not attempt to explore alternatives to the federal IRB system. All explanations and recommendations about IRB policy are organized for readers who want to understand how to conduct IRB activities in compliance with federal research regulations.

The two segments of the federal government that tell the IRB what to do and how to do it are the Office for Human Research Protections (OHRP) and the Food and Drug Administration (FDA). It is important to understand when and how these agencies interface with the IRB. These are the federal authorities that determine performance standards and enforce compliance with federal research regulations.

Office for Human Research Protections (OHRP)

The mission of the OHRP is to monitor and promote compliance with regulations promulgated by the U.S. Department of Health and Human Services (HHS) that relate to the ethical standards of research involving human subjects (45 CFR 46).[1] The OHRP currently has about 25 full-time staff members who deal with research involving human subjects. OHRP offices are currently located in an office complex in Bethesda, Maryland. The OHRP Web site is listed in Chapter 11-3.

The administrative reporting structure for OHRP within HHS has recently changed. Before 2000, this office was called the Office for Protection from Research Risks (OPRR) and administratively was located in the Office of Extramural Research in the National Institutes of Health (NIH). However, in September 2000 the office was reconstituted as OHRP and moved from NIH to the Office of Public Health and Science within the Office of the Secretary of HHS. The administrative location of OHRP was changed to eliminate the situation where a research regulatory office reported to the director of an agency whose primary mission is to conduct research (NIH). In addition to changing the administrative location so that the OHRP's viewpoint can now be communicated directly within the highest levels of HHS, the status of the OHRP director was upgraded to the Senior Executive Service, which is the highest level of nonpolitical civil servant.

Compliance Monitoring

The OHRP monitors compliance with HHS research regulations by establishing a type of contract called an *assurance* with institutions that conduct research that is funded by, or otherwise subject to, HHS regulation. OHRP assurances are explained in detail in Chapter 8-1. For the purpose of this discussion, it is sufficient to understand that an OHRP assurance is a document that is signed by a high-level representative of a research institution. The assurance is a type of contract between the institution and OHRP that specifies when and how the institution will comply with HHS research regulations. IRB leadership should understand any assurances that the institution has with OHRP.

OHRP site visits and FDA audits are the subjects of Chapters 8-14 and 8-15. Unlike some other federal agencies such as the Internal Revenue Service, the OHRP does not routinely audit institutions for compliance purposes. OHRP usually does not audit IRB activities without provocation. With most institutions, OHRP documents compliance by recording the assurance agreements previously mentioned. In other words, OHRP's basic approach to monitoring compliance is simply to ask an institution for a formal pledge (an assurance) that it will comply with HHS research regulations.

OHRP Investigations

OHRP site visits are discussed in detail in Chapter 8-14. It is important to note that the indications for an investigation of noncompliance by OHRP are not discussed in any detail in the federal regulations. If your institution has an OHRP assurance, OHRP needs no justification for investigating your institution's research program for the purpose of evaluating compliance with HHS regulations. Common examples of events that trigger an OHRP investigation include an adverse event that receives national publicity, a complaint by a research subject or someone connected with the research program, and review of publications that describe research that is of concern to OHRP officials.

Federal regulations do not explain the process of an OHRP compliance investigation. OHRP has the final word on when an institution is not complying with HHS regulations and what the institution must do to correct the problem. An OHRP contact may range anywhere from a simple phone call seeking clarification about a specific issue to a comprehensive, formal investigation, including a site visit. Any time that OHRP launches an official investigation, the institution is notified in writing and given the full opportunity to respond.

When OHRP determines that an institution has not complied with the terms of its assurance, OHRP officials present a representative from the institution (usually the OHRP assurance signatory) with a list of corrective actions that must be followed to maintain an approved OHRP assurance of compliance with HHS regulations. The threat to restrict or suspend approval of an OHRP assurance is a powerful motivation for an institution to change its research review program. A restricted OHRP assurance can dramatically increase the administrative work associated with the review of research (for example, when an assurance is restricted such that the IRB may not use the expedited process to approve research). Suspension of HHS approval of an institution's OHRP assurance means that, with the stroke of a pen, HHS funding for ongoing or previously approved research is suspended.

Food and Drug Administration (FDA)

To understand the authority of the FDA over IRBs, it is important to realize that although the FDA is an agency within HHS, FDA and HHS have separate regulations that apply to research involving human subjects and the IRB function. OHRP is the office within HHS responsible for overseeing the implementation of HHS research regulations.

HHS and FDA regulations related to IRB responsibility are presented in the Federal Code of Regulations at 45 CFR 46[1] and 21 CFR 50,[2] 56,[3] respectively. Fortunately, the regulations that concern the IRB are similar for HHS and FDA, but they are not identical. The important differences that the IRB should be aware of between HHS and FDA regulations are discussed in Chapter 8-5. For the purposes of this chapter, the point is that when research is subject to both HHS and FDA regulation, an institution has two masters to satisfy when considering the need for, and process of, IRB review. In this situation, IRB review must be done in compliance with the regulations of both of these federal authorities.

The factors that determine HHS authority over an IRB have been discussed above and basically consist of an assurance of compliance with OHRP. FDA regulations are cited in the reference section of this book. Basically, any research involving a drug, a biologic, or a medical device is subject to FDA regulation. In many situations, research that is not funded by a federal agency is subject to FDA regulation.

The FDA system of compliance evaluation differs in several ways from that of OHRP. First, the FDA compliance program includes a plan to audit the IRBs at all institutions that conduct FDA-regulated research at regular intervals. Although an FDA investigation may be triggered by a concern about noncompliance, most FDA audits are done for routine evaluation. The standard program is for the FDA to audit each IRB that is subject to FDA regulation approximately once every four years. A second difference between the FDA and OHRP is that with the FDA, the processes for determining noncompliance and penalties are specified in some detail by the regulations.[3(Sec. 121-124)] As is true with OHRP, FDA compliance officials have a wide range of options when directing a change in an institution's regulatory program.

With the FDA, the leverage to change institutional behavior comes from FDA authority under the Food, Drug, and Cosmetic Act to impose civil penalties on an institution that does not comply with FDA regulations.

References

1. Code of Federal Regulations. Title 45A—Department of Health and Human Services; Part 46—Protection of Human Subjects. Updated 1 Oct 1997. Access date 18 Apr 2001. World Wide Web http://www4.law.cornell.edu/cfr/45p46.htm

2. Code of Federal Regulations. Title 21, Chapter 1—Food and Drug Administration, DHHS; Part 50—Protection of Human Subjects. Updated 1 Apr 1999. Access date 18 Apr 2001. World Wide Web http://www4.law.cornell.edu/cfr/21p50.htm

3. Code of Federal Regulations. Title 21, Chapter 1—Food and Drug Administration, DHHS; Part 56—Institutional Review Boards. Updated 1 Apr 1999. Access date 27 Mar 2001. World Wide Web http://www4.law.cornell.edu/cfr/21p56.htm

The Limits of IRB Authority

Robert J. Amdur

INTRODUCTION

The mission of an IRB is to protect the rights and welfare of human research participants. Such a mission makes it difficult to limit the scope of IRB activities. In the world of research ethics, there is no finish line when it comes to quality improvement. There is no limit to the amount of time and energy an IRB could spend on protocol review, research monitoring, continuing education, and the process of informed consent. Federal regulations require that an institution provide for "meeting space and sufficient staff to support the IRB's review and record-keeping duties."[1][Sec.103(b)(2)] Few IRBs operate in an environment without pressure to improve efficiency and prioritize the allocation of limited resources. Several recent reports have been critical of the IRB function in important aspects of research review (e.g., monitoring of ongoing studies) and the ability to manage heavy workloads.[2] These realities make it important for institutional and IRB leadership to realize that the IRB cannot afford to spend time on activities not required for protection of human research subjects in compliance with federal research regulations.

At most institutions, anything that distracts the IRB from its fundamental responsibilities will compromise the IRB function. Although this concept may seem straightforward, in practice it is often difficult to apply. IRBs often find themselves in the position of being the most convenient or qualified group to take responsibility for important administrative responsibilities that, from the regulatory standpoint, could be handled by another administrative body. Most of this book is devoted to helping the IRB understand what it must do to comply with federal regulations. However, at some institutions, understanding what the IRB does *not* have to do is a critical factor in improving IRB function.

The IRB Is Not an Editorial Service

The IRB reviews the consent document to see that it clearly and accurately describes the essential elements of informed consent in language appropriate for the study population. When the IRB thinks it is important to revise the consent document, such changes are made a requirement for approval of the study. Some IRB members are extremely demanding about the wording of the consent document, while others have a high threshold for requiring editorial changes. The amount of time and energy that the IRB spends on the consent document is an important issue because it may limit the thoroughness of review of other components of the research process. This topic is discussed in Chapter 6-2.

When the IRB requires a change in the consent document, a decision has to be made about the role of the IRB in drafting the revision. Whenever possible, the IRB should be as explicit as possible about required changes, but the IRB is under no regulatory obligation to direct the revision process. When problems with the consent document are extensive or complex, it is appropriate for the IRB to simply describe the problems in a general sense and then require the investigator to figure out the details of the revision. A researcher who is not motivated to improve the consent document, or who does not understand the basic goal of the consent document, should not be doing research. The IRB should help the researcher whenever possible, but it is important for everyone to understand that it is not a productive use of institutional resources for the IRB to function as an editorial service for investigators or protocol managers.

Example: Revise the consent document so that it is in "lay language." It is not unusual to see language used throughout a consent document that is too complex for the target population. The meaning of "too complex" and "lay language" will vary with the IRB and study population and need not be formally defined. When complex language is used throughout a consent document, the IRB should instruct the investigator to revise the document. This is to present complex terms and explanations in "lay language," meaning in a manner that is likely to be understood by the general public. The IRB need not be more explicit.

The IRB Is Not the Office of the Medical Director

At most medical centers, the medical director is the administrative authority responsible for making the rules of medical practice. When the IRB identifies the need for guidelines regarding activities that involve both research and nonresearch practice, the IRB may be asked or encouraged to administer policy that is more appropriately handled by the office of the medical director. An example of a situation that recently occurred at a major U.S. medical center will aid in understanding this issue.

Example: The IRB reviews a research protocol involving genetic testing.   *Study procedures do not specify whether genetic test results will, or will not, be recorded in the hospital medical record. Before approving the protocol, the IRB requires that the investigator establish a clear policy regarding the reporting of test results. In addition, if genetic results are going to be recorded in the medical record, they need to provide for genetic counseling and explanation of risks in the initial consent process.*

As part of the process of evaluating this study, the IRB learns that no institutional policy exists regarding the reporting of genetic test results. Several members of the IRB believe strongly that patients who undergo genetic testing outside the setting of a research protocol should have the same protections as research participants. They recommend that the establishment of institutional policy on genetic testing be made a requirement for IRB approval of the research protocol.

If the IRB follows this recommendation, it will be in the position of forcing the institution to make policy for nonresearch activity. The IRB will be committed to spending time and energy directing or critiquing such policy as part of the research approval process. The IRB does not want to take responsibility for something that would distract it from the mission of protecting the rights of human research subjects. Recognizing the limits of IRB authority in this setting, the IRB approves the protocol with the appropriate changes. IRB approval is not made contingent on the development of an institutional policy on genetic testing. In an effort to improve patient care at their medical center, the IRB sends an unsolicited letter to the office of the medical director. The letter explains the issues related to the reporting of genetic test results and recommends that institutional policy on this subject be established.

The IRB Is Not the Medical Records Department or Confidentiality Committee

The problem of determining the need for, and process of, IRB review of projects that involve analysis of confidential information from the medical record is discussed in detail in Chapter 4-4 and Chapter 5-6. The bottom line for this discussion is that it is important for the IRB to recognize that (a) many projects that involve a systematic investigation of medical records are appropriately classified as something other than research (for example, quality assessment, education, outcome evaluation, or utilization review); and (b) recording private information from the medical record with linkage to personal identifiers puts people at risk for the problems associated with a breach in confidentiality, regardless of whether medical information is collected for research or nonresearch purposes.

When data from the medical record are being collected for research purposes, federal regulations unquestionably require that the IRB approve the conditions for access to the medical record and the procedures for protecting confidentiality. However, when medical record review is being done for something other than research, the IRB has no regulatory authority over the activity. To avoid distracting the IRB from its mission of research regulation, a division of the medical records department or a separate "confidentiality committee" should oversee the use of confidential information from the medical record. The IRB and other segments of the medical center will need to work together to make medical record policy uniform throughout the medical center. Procedures for screening and triaging projects that require access to the medical record are discussed in the chapters mentioned earlier.

The IRB Is Not the Risk-Management Department

The term *risk-management department* is used in this section to describe the institutional authority responsible for advising institutional leadership on ways to avoid or minimize problems that could lead to charges of criminal activity, civil misconduct, or regulatory noncompliance. Risk-management advisors are usually lawyers who are familiar with the laws and regulations that apply to the activities that go on at their institution. At some institutions, a member of the risk-management team advises or serves on the IRB. (See Chapter 3-4.)

When an institution conducts research regulated by the federal government, some overlap occurs between the risk-management department and the IRB because the penalties may be significant if the IRB process does not comply with applicable federal regulations. The purpose of this section is to clarify the distinction between the IRB and an institution's risk-management department. This distinction is important when situations occur where IRB review of a research protocol identifies a practice pattern that could represent a legal liability for the institution. In many of these cases, the problematic activity is not limited to research; simply modifying or not approving the research study will not eliminate liability exposure for the institution. In this setting, there may be a tendency to use the IRB as a tool to draw attention to the problem or to advance the policy agenda of the risk-management department. The IRB should avoid this position because it does not support the IRB mission of protecting the rights and welfare of human research subjects. An example will help to illustrate the issue of IRB versus the risk-management department.

Example: An IRB reviews a research protocol involving an investigational medical treatment for patients in a coma after brain injury.   *Because eligible patients are in critical but stable condition, this is not an emergency research situation. However, the subjects of research will not be competent to give informed consent to study participation.*

State law is not definitive about who may or may not serve as a surrogate decision-maker in this setting.

The IRB consults the risk-management department for help in understanding who qualifies as a legally authorized representative for an incompetent patient when it comes to enrolling in a research study. The risk-management advisor explains that the surrogate decision-maker issue is one that raises a concern about legal liability for the institution regardless of whether patients are involved in research. The risk-management department would like to see an internal institutional policy on the hierarchy of people (spouse, adult child, parent, sibling, etc.) who may serve as a surrogate decision-maker when a patient is not competent to give informed consent for medical treatment. The risk-management representative advises the IRB to make IRB approval of the research protocol contingent on the establishment of institutional policy on this subject.

The IRB should not make modification of general institutional policy a condition for IRB approval of a research study. As discussed previously, such a decision puts the IRB in the position of directing or critiquing policy that is primarily aimed at nonresearch activity. The IRB does not need an institutional policy to decide on conditions for approval of the research project in question. In the example described above, the IRB approves the project with changes suggested by the risk-management consultant. The IRB leaves it to the risk-management department to establish institutional policy regarding surrogate consent as they think appropriate.

The IRB Is Not the Office of Patient Financial Services

The role of the IRB in evaluating the explanation of the costs of medical treatment delivered on a research protocol is currently not well defined. In Chapter 6-11 this issue is discussed in detail. The reason to mention it here is that few IRBs have the resources to administer a system that documents research versus nonresearch costs to the degree that may soon be required by federal health insurance programs. IRBs are struggling with this issue because federal regulations require the investigator to explain "any additional costs to the subject that may result from participation in the research"[1][Sec.116(b)(3)] as part of the consent process. How the IRB interprets this regulation will determine if the IRB has time to focus on other aspects of the research process.

The IRB Is Not a Data Safety Monitoring Board

A problem for many IRBs is the management of adverse event (AE) reports for multicenter medical research studies. In Chapter 7-3 and 7-4, this issue is discussed in detail. The reason to mention AE reporting in this section is to remind readers that the IRB cannot, and should not, attempt to function as a data safety monitoring board (DSMB). During initial review of a protocol, DHHS regulations require that the IRB determine that the study design provides for an appropriate system for monitoring the study from the point of view of reacting to unexpected reports of inefficacy or toxicity. The role of the IRB is to document that an appropriate monitoring system is in place, but the IRB is not required to oversee the monitoring process.

Conclusion

At most institutions anything that distracts the IRB from its fundamental responsibilities will compromise IRB function. IRBs often find themselves in the position of being the most convenient or qualified group to take responsibility for important administrative responsibilities that, from the regulatory standpoint, could be handled by another administrative body. At some institutions, understanding what the IRB does not have to do is a critical factor in improving IRB function. To this end, it may be useful for some IRBs to recognize that:

1. The IRB is not an editorial service
2. The IRB is not the office of the medical director
3. The IRB is not the medical records department or confidentiality committee
4. The IRB is not the risk management department
5. The IRB is not the office of patient financial services
6. The IRB is not a data safety monitoring board

References

1. Code of Federal Regulations. Title 45A—Department of Health and Human Services; Part 46—Protection of Human Subjects. Updated 1 Oct 1997. Access date 18 Apr 2001. World Wide Web http://www4.law.cornell.edu/cfr/45p46.htm
2. Office of Inspector General. Institutional review boards: A time for reform (OEI-01-97-00193). Dept of Health and Human Services, June 1998. Access date 27 Mar 2001. World Wide Web http://www.dhhs.gov/progorg/oei/reportindex.html

PART 2

Organizing the Office

Administrative Reporting Structure for the IRB

Ernest D. Prentice, Sally L. Mann, and Bruce G. Gordon

INTRODUCTION

The purpose of this chapter is to discuss the reporting structure of the IRB. In this context, *reporting structure* refers to the administrative home of the IRB, the administrative superiors of the IRB Chair and administrative director, and the position(s) in the organization that control IRB resources. The reporting structure of the IRB is important because it may have significant influence on the quality and efficiency of IRB function. The reporting structure of the IRB is related to the topic of conflict of interest, which is discussed in detail in Part 5 of this book.

Tension Between Conflicting Goals

Some IRBs function well with a reporting structure where the IRB is a division of an office that is organized for the primary purpose of promoting research at the IRB's institution. The criticism that has been raised to this kind of organization is that it creates the potential for conflict between the mission of the IRB and the mission of the IRB's administrative superiors. For an IRB to function effectively, it is essential that the IRB have adequate resources and work in an environment where there is support for the IRB to make independent decisions related to the protection of research subjects. IRB leaders who function well in organizations where the IRB is administratively housed in a grants and contracts or sponsored research office explain that the primary goals of their administrative superiors are not only to increase research volume, but, more importantly, to manage the overall research enterprise according to the highest of ethical and regulatory standards.

Federal regulations do not address the reporting structure of the IRB to a degree that answers the question of whether it is acceptable for the IRB to be part of the grants and contracts or sponsored research office. Regardless of the name of the office that administers the IRB, the important thing is that the IRB reporting structure must be organized so that no real or perceived conflict of interest compromises IRB function or credibility. In the absence of definitive federal guidance, it is our recommendation that the IRB be administratively independent from offices that have any direct responsibility for the recruitment of research to the institution.

Institutional Official

Each institution should appoint a high-ranking administrative officer who is authorized to act for the institution and assume overall responsibility, for compliance with the federal regulations for the protection of human subjects. This individual is designated as the "Institutional Official" (IO) and is the person who signs the Office for Human Research Protections (OHRP) assurance of compliance. In many small to medium-sized institutions, the chief executive officer (CEO) serves as the IO. Large institutions usually assign administrators such as a vice-president, vice-chancellor, associate dean, or other senior administrator. Regardless of who is chosen to serve as the IO, it is of paramount importance that he or she has the knowledge, authority, and ability to commit the resources needed by the IRB.

As alluded to earlier, we think that problems are more likely to occur if the sponsored programs or grants and contracts director serves as the IO. Many perceive these departments to have an unacceptable conflict of interest because the primary role of the IRB is to protect research subjects. In contrast, the major role of any office that deals with funding programs is necessarily focused on increasing the amount of research funds awarded to the institution and its investigators. Although a vice-president or vice-chancellor for research may also be involved in obtaining grant funds, such individuals usually have broad-based responsibility for many aspects of the research infrastructure, such as chemical safety, radiation safety, and the animal facilities. Thus, any potential conflict of interest should effectively be reduced to an acceptable level. The rights and welfare of human subjects must always take precedence over the needs of science or fiscal considerations. All IOs should recognize this ethics-based mandate and take all necessary steps to ensure the integrity and functionality of the institution's program for the protection of human subjects.

Lines of Authority

IRB Chair

Although in many organizations, the IRB Chair currently reports to a subordinate of the IO, in our opinion this is not the optimal arrangement. The IRB Chair acts on behalf of the IRB and the IO acts on behalf of the institution. It is, therefore, essential that there be direct reporting and regular communication between these two individuals. For this reason, we recommend that the IRB Chair report directly to the IO. The IRB Chair should not report to a committee such as the "executive committee of the medical staff" or the "dean's council" except to provide information and respond to questions. It is important to preserve the autonomy of the IRB and insulate it from pressure exerted by individuals or groups with special interests that are inconsistent with the mission of the IRB. The IRB must be able to act as an independent and objective body without answering to multiple masters who may have different agendas.

Reporting Line for the Chief IRB Administrator

The chief administrator of the IRB is usually the director of the IRB's support office. He or she should report to the IO or other high-level officer who can act on behalf of the IO on matters related to the administrative operation and support of the IRB. Normally, the director should not report to the IRB Chair. This is because the IRB chair is usually a faculty member who serves as the Chair on a voluntary and part-time basis. Thus, the Chair usually is not in a position to deal with personnel issues, budgets, and other administrative matters. The director and IRB Chair must obviously work closely together on policy development, protocol reviews, and other activities of the IRB. The effectiveness of this interaction, however, is not dependent on a direct reporting relationship. Indeed, quite the opposite may be true. When the IRB Chair is not re-

sponsible for potentially contentious personnel decisions like promotions, salary increases, and budgets, the Chair and administrators are able to focus their efforts on protecting research subjects without the interpersonal tension that often accompanies a supervisor–subordinate relationship.

Reporting Line(s) for the IRB Staff

The volume and nature of research requiring IRB review should determine the number of IRBs required by a given institution and the size of the IRB staff. A small institution may have only one IRB and one or two IRB staff persons, whereas a large institution may have four or more IRBs and 30 or more IRB staff. The administrative reporting structure and IRB personnel classifications obviously vary among institutions. Regardless of the size of the institution, however, all IRBs should employ a management system that allows the IRB to perform quality reviews that are both efficient and consistent.

The IRB management systems adopted by large institutions with multiple IRBs are usually more complex than the systems utilized by smaller institutions. One common model employed by large institutions is to provide each IRB with its own designated staff. For example, an institution with four IRBs may have a support office with a director, associate director, and four assistant directors. Each assistant director would report to the associate director and be responsible for one of the four IRBs. Each IRB, in turn, would have three protocol analysts and one secretary. Thus, each of the four IRBs would have five staff. The IRB support office would have a total of 22 personnel. To promote consistency and common standards of review, the director and/or associate director would normally attend all IRB meetings.

Conclusion

The IRB should occupy a highly visible and elevated position within the administrative structure of the institution. A culture of compliance is best established from the top down, and ideally, the CEO or other high-ranking official should serve as the IO and play an active role in fostering the important work of the IRB. When an institution's IRB does not command the respect and support of the highest administrative officials, its effectiveness and credibility are jeopardized. Thus, it is incumbent on the institution to establish an administrative reporting structure for the IRB that will allow it to operate in a highly functional manner that best serves the institution, its investigators, and research participants.

Documenting Compliance with Federal Regulations

Deborah L. Barnard

INTRODUCTION

"If it's not written down, it didn't happen."

How many times have we heard this in the past few years? This is really what we do in IRB offices: We document. We are archivists. We create paper and track it. We prove that something happened.

Policy regarding what, when, and how to document things is often something that the IRB has to establish without formal directives. The regulations give us bare-bones guidance. This chapter will provide guidance on how to document compliance with federal research regulations. When presenting these guidelines, I will attempt to distinguish between documentation that is required and that which is recommended. Throughout the chapter, I will summarize recommendations from the federal agencies that regulate IRB activity: the Office for Human Research Protections (OHRP)[1] and the Food and Drug Administration (FDA). The OHRP opinions on compliance documentation come from either the OHRP/OPRR "Dear Colleague" letters[2] or a document called "OHRP Compliance Activities: Common Findings and Guidance."[3] The FDA guidance comes from the regulations and the FDA Information Sheets.

Federal Regulations

The regulations require that IRBs have written policies and follow them. Just because you might have a multiple project assurance (MPA) (or now a federal-wide assurance [FWA]) does not necessarily mean that you have written procedures. An MPA/FWA is a promise to follow the rules, but generally does not include the level of detail that is required by the regulators for written procedures or guidelines.

The specific federal regulations that discuss documentation requirements that IRBs must comply with are 45 CFR 46[4][Sec.103(a),108(a)] and 21 CFR 50[5] and 56.[6][Sec.108(a)] The few differences between these regulations are discussed elsewhere in this book.

Getting Started

When you begin writing policies, keep things simple. Do not create a document that is so cumbersome that it will be impossible for you to stay in compliance with your own policies. Review the requirements. Consider how you do things or how you want to start doing things, and then start writing.

Before you start to review research, your IRB must be established. OHRP requires that you have an updated list of IRB members on file with its office. In the written procedures, there must be a statement acknowledging the IRB's authority to approve, modify, or disapprove proposed human research studies.[4][Sec.103(b)(1)] This statement must also acknowledge the IRB's authority to modify or disapprove ongoing studies. There must also be a clear statement that no one in the institution can approve a project that the IRB has disapproved. These statements can be copied from the MPA, if your institution has one.

Membership

There is a minimum requirement of five members for an IRB.[4][Sec.103(2)] You can have more than one IRB if you like. Each IRB must include at least one member who is not otherwise affiliated with the institution and who is not part of the immediate family of a person who is affiliated with the institution. The IRB should be as diverse a group as possible. You should try to recruit members of both sexes and various professional specialties.

In your written procedures, define your membership; remember to include the nonscientific member. The nonaffiliated member and the nonscientist can be the same person, but this can hamper your meeting. You absolutely cannot have a meeting without the nonscientific member present. If you are unable to have your community member present every single time, the regulators do not like it, but the meeting can still go on. Concerns about meeting your quorum are a good argument against having your community member and nonscientist be the same individual. OHRP has recently cited IRBs when they appear to lack diversity. This includes considerations of race, sex, and cultural background.

A record in your IRB file must document who is on the committee, what their specialties are, and what their relationships are with the institution. This must be updated with OHRP anytime you change membership. The FDA does not require that you file your IRB membership information with them.

If your IRB includes alternate members, they should be listed on the roster in such a way that it is easy to tell whom they are assigned to as alternates.

Your IRB may, at its discretion, invite individuals with special expertise (consultants) to assist in the review of issues that require expertise beyond or in addition to that available on the IRB. A simple statement in your written procedures will cover this issue.

Meeting Schedule

Determine your meeting schedule, remembering that your IRB must meet, at a minimum, once each year. The regulations require that IRBs have a meeting space and sufficient staff to support the IRB's review and record-keeping duties. A statement acknowledging this should be placed in your written procedures. When you have determined the meeting schedule, document it in your policies and procedures.

Written Policies and Procedures

The regulations require that IRBs have written policies and procedures.[4][Sec.103(b)(4),(b)(5) and 108],6 The following items must be addressed in the written procedures:

1. Conducting initial and continuing review of research

2. Reporting IRB findings and actions to the investigator and the institution

3. Determining which projects require IRB review more often than annually

4. Determining which projects need verification from sources other than the investigators that no material changes have occurred since previous IRB review

5. Ensuring prompt reporting to the IRB of proposed changes in a research activity. In addition, ensuring that such changes in approved research, during the period for which IRB approval has already been given, may not be initiated without IRB review and approval except when necessary to eliminate apparent immediate hazards to the subject.

6. Ensuring prompt reporting to the IRB, appropriate institutional officials, and the federal department or agency head of any unanticipated problems involving risks to subjects or others

7. Reporting any serious or continuing noncompliance with these federal regulations or the requirements or determinations of the IRB

8. Reporting any suspension or termination of IRB approval to the appropriate person or persons

Types of Review

The regulations recognize three levels or categories of review. The first is the review conducted at a fully convened meeting of the IRB, which most of us refer to as a "full-committee review." The second is the expedited review, which allows the IRB Chair or one or more experienced members designated by the Chair to perform the review of appropriate projects. Finally, some projects might be exempt from IRB review. OHRP now recommends that investigators should not make the determination of whether a project can be exempt from IRB review. OHRP recommends that, at minimum, an administrative review in the IRB office should take place to determine whether a project is exempt.

There is more to review than just making a determination as to whether a project can be approved. Written procedures should include details such as the method for receiving paperwork from investigators and then distributing these materials to IRB members for review. You must define this process for both full reviews and expedited reviews, as well as define who has the authority to perform expedited review and who can determine exemption from review. You should address such things as how soon materials will be distributed before an IRB meeting and how you will determine that you have quorum with the appropriate members in attendance. If your IRB office uses an electronic database, include its function in the written policies and procedures.

Full-Committee Review

The following is considered an acceptable package of documents for review at a fully convened meeting of the IRB.

1. The proposed protocol outlined or summarized in whatever application is used

2. A copy of the protocol, grant, study proposal, or any other written document that defines the work to be done

3. Any consent documents to be used

4. for a study sponsored by a drug company or device company, the drug or device brochure

5. any advertisements to be used in recruitment

6. if non-English versions of the consent will be used, these must be submitted in the translated language

7. surveys, questionnaires, or other such research tools

Remember to document that alternate members receive the same information that regular members receive for any meeting when they are present at the meeting.

Reviewer Systems If your IRB uses the primary reviewer system, provide an explanation of how this system will be used. In many IRB systems, the primary reviewer provides an in-depth review of the proposal, consent document, and any supporting documentation. Therefore, the primary reviewer is the only person receiving all of the materials submitted. If this system is used, then your written procedures must include a clear statement that, at minimum, the rest of the members receive a copy of the consent document and a summary of the protocol and any advertisements. Make it clear in the written procedures that IRB members at the convened meeting have access to all project materials to be reviewed. If everyone gets everything, then explain how the review takes place during the meeting. Whatever system you choose, you must explain this system and how it will work.

Quorum   Your written procedures must explain how you will determine that quorum is met for convened meetings and that the appropriate members were at the meeting.

Member Conflict of Interest   IRB members present at a given meeting cannot take part in the IRB's initial or continuing review of any project in which the member has a conflicting interest. This means that you must define what conflict of interest is to an IRB member. Common indicators of conflict of interest from the standpoint of participating in IRB decisions are that the IRB member is a principal or co-investigator for the project, a member of the project's support staff, or has a major financial interest in the conduct of the project. When an IRB member thinks that he or she has a conflict of interest with IRB evaluation of a project, this should be documented in the IRB minutes. OHRP recommends that an IRB member with a conflict of interest be excused from the room after he or she has provided any necessary information to the IRB. The minutes should then reflect that the IRB member was out of the room for the discussion and vote for the project. Conflict of interest is discussed in more detail in Part 5 of this book.

Investigational Devices Reviews   IRBs that review projects involving investigational devices must have written procedures that explain how they determine which devices are considered nonsignificant risk devices and which are significant risk devices requiring an investigational device exemption. The FDA's Web page[7,8] offers definitions for these two classes of devices and some practical help in documenting this information in written procedures. IRB review of medical devices is the subject of Chapter 10-7 in this book. In the written procedures, include an explanation as to what documentation your IRB will expect to receive and review in order to determine which devices are significant risk devices and which are nonsignificant risk devices.

If Revisions Are Requested   When a request to the investigator for revisions or more information is made by the IRB at a full meeting, the process for assuring that these changes take place must be in your written procedures. How will the IRB follow up? Who will follow up? These issues need to be addressed. OHRP has cited IRBs for approving research contingent on "substantive modifications or clarifications without requiring additional review by the convened IRB." OHRP recommends that when substantive changes are required, the IRB must review

these changes at a convened meeting, but when the revisions require only "simple concurrence by the investigator," the IRB Chair or designated reviewer may approve the research on behalf of the IRB. Be very clear what you are going to do and how you are going to do it. Then follow your own rules.

Model Consent Documents for Cooperative Group Studies   IRBs that review projects involving national cooperative group studies should receive a copy of the cooperative group's model consent. This document is the basis for the consent document that will be used locally. A copy of the model consent should be maintained in the IRB's files and should be provided to the IRB when the project is under review.

Reporting IRB Findings   Your written procedures must include an explanation as to how investigators will be notified of the outcome of the IRB reviews. In your procedures, you might describe time frames for notification and how it will be managed. Your written procedures must include a statement as to how the institution will be notified of IRB decisions and issues of concern.

Continuing Review
Part 7 of this book is devoted to continuing review. Briefly, you are required to have written procedures for ongoing or continuing review. Written procedures should include the following:

1. The method or manner in which investigators will be notified regarding the continuing review of their projects
2. When the project will be re-reviewed
3. A statement that all IRB members have access to all pertinent information for the continuing review
4. How the IRB determines when a project should be amended, terminated, or allowed to continue as originally approved

You are also required to have written procedures for determining which projects might require review more often than every 12 months. OHRP recommends that the minutes clearly reflect the IRB's determination that the review interval is appropriate to the degree of risk.

When IRB Approval Has Expired   OHRP recommends that if the IRB does not re-approve a research project by the specified review date, subject accrual should be suspended pending re-review by the IRB. Continuations of research interventions or interactions in already-enrolled subjects should only occur when the IRB finds that continuation is in the best interest of individual subjects. Situations should be addressed on a case-by-case basis in those very rare instances where failure to enroll would seriously jeopardize the safety or well-being of an individual prospective subject.[3,8]

Expedited Review
The IRB must have written procedures for managing the expedited review mechanism. It is very important that expedited review is used only as listed in the regulations.[4(Sec.110),6(Sec.110)]

In your written procedures, define who will be doing the expedited reviewing. Explain how the other members of the IRB are notified that these reviews and approvals have taken place. It is also important to emphasize that, when conducting an expedited review, the reviewer may have all the rights and privileges of the full IRB except that the single reviewer cannot disapprove the research. If there is a question about disapproval, the project must be referred to the full IRB.

Regulators will review the written procedures for using expedited review in part to determine that the process is *not* being used inappropriately. Examples of inappropriate use include single-patient-use reviews, expedited review of more than minor changes to approved research, and expedited approval based on IRB approval of the protocol at another institution for which no cooperative agreement exists.

Amendments or Modifications to Existing Protocols
Major changes must be reviewed by the full IRB. However, the regulations allow expedited review of minor changes to previously approved research. You must define "minor changes" in your written procedures. You must also explain how amendments not meeting the definition of minor changes will be sent to a fully convened meeting of the IRB. For example, a minor change might be revisions to the existing protocol based on numerous typographical errors that were found in the text of the protocol or changes in research study staff who have been listed as contact people on the consent form. Changes that are not minor might be changes in exclusion and inclusion criteria, changes in the study design, or major changes to the information in the existing consent document.

Exemption From IRB Review

What must be reviewed and what is considered exempt from IRB review is defined in 45 CFR46 [4][Sec.101(b)] Many institutions require that investigators submit their projects for a determination of exemption. Your procedures for determining exemption must be clearly documented.

Emergency Review

Compassionate use and emergency research are discussed in Chapter 4–5 in this book. The reason to mention these issues here is to emphasize that a medical emergency does not make a research activity exempt from IRB review or eligible for expedited IRB review when it otherwise would require full-committee review. OHRP has provided the following guidance for IRBs, institutions, and investigators regarding this issue: "Whenever emergency care is initiated without prior IRB review and approval, the patient may not be considered to be a research subject. Such emergency care may not be claimed as research, nor may the outcome of such care be included in any report of a research activity."[3(p.7)] Simply stated: HHS regulations for the protection of human subjects do not permit *research* activities to be started, even in emergency, without prior IRB review and approval. The FDA defines *emergency use* as the use of an investigational drug or biological product with a human subject in a life-threatening situation in which no standard acceptable treatment is available and in which there is not sufficient time to obtain IRB approval.[6][Sec. 102(d)] The FDA has very specific

guidelines for this use. You will need to review them carefully and document how your IRB will manage this issue.

In the IRB Minutes

One of the most important things the IRB must do is create minutes of its meetings. The regulators require the following to be included in the minutes.

1. Attendance at the meetings.
2. Actions taken by the IRB.
3. The vote on these actions, including the number of members voting for, voting against, and abstaining. The OHRP recommends that you list the names of those abstaining and why they voted to abstain.
4. The basis for requiring changes in or disapproving research.
5. A written summary of the discussion of controverted issues and their resolution.

The IRB must provide the above documentation for each project considered.

Quality of IRB Review

OHRP has cited IRBs for "inadequate review at convened meetings." Specifically, inspections have found little evidence that the IRB approval of research is consistently based on consideration of the criteria found at 45 CFR 46.111. When reviewing a project, the IRB must find and document, usually in the minutes, the following issues.

1. Risks to the subjects are minimized.
2. Risks to the subjects are reasonable in relation to anticipated benefits, if any, and the importance of the knowledge that may reasonably be expected to result.
3. Selection of subjects is equitable.
4. Informed consent will be sought from each prospective subject or the subject's legally authorized representative, in accordance with and to the extent required by the regulations.
5. Informed consent will be appropriately documented, in accordance with and to the extent required in the section of the regulations that explains documentation of informed consent.
6. When appropriate, the research plan makes adequate provision for monitoring the data collected to ensure the safety of subjects.
7. When appropriate, there are adequate provisions to protect the privacy of subjects and to maintain the confidentiality of data.
8. When some or all of the subjects are likely to be vulnerable to coercion or undue influence, such as children, prisoners, pregnant women, mentally disabled persons, or economically or educationally disadvantaged persons, additional safeguards have been included in the study to protect the rights and welfare of these subjects.

The criteria for approval are discussed in Chapter 5-2 of this book. Your IRB's policies should reflect the criteria the IRB will consider during review and how the IRB will determine that the criteria are met.

Attendees at the Meeting

Attendance can be documented in a number of ways. Perhaps the most common way is to list those IRB members present at the meeting. It is a good idea to include any special function that the member serves, such as pediatrician, behavior specialist, or prisoner advocate. Nonvoting members of the IRB should be designated and listed as well. Any guests at the meeting must be listed.

Actions Taken

What courses of action does your IRB take? The IRB may approve, disapprove, approve with contingencies, provisionally approve, table, or make a vote of no decision. You should define the IRB's actions and include the steps taken after the action is made. For example, you might define a vote of approval as "The IRB accepts the project as presented." The investigator will be notified of this action in writing. This written communication will include the period of approval. The OHRP has determined that the date of a vote to provisionally approve a project sets the clock ticking for the re-review period. For example, say that your IRB approves with contingencies or provisionally approves a project at a meeting on January 1, 2001, with a period for review of one year. The investigator takes two months to respond to the contingencies. After meeting the IRB's requirements, the investigator only has ten months until the IRB approval for the project expires.

The Vote

Recording the vote is easy. You simply document in the minutes how many people voted for each action. Your written policies and procedures should explain whether this was a hand vote, written ballot, or count of "yeas and nays." OHRP strongly recommends that the vote be recorded in the following manner: Total: 15; For - 14, Opposed - 0, Abstained - 1 (the name of the person abstaining).

Basis for Requiring Changes in the Research

The minutes must reflect the reasoning of the IRB and its deliberations. If the IRB had concerns about the safety of subjects and wanted more information on how specific safety issues were going to be monitored, this should be reflected in the minutes. If, upon review of the consent document, the IRB found that certain phrases or sections in the consent document required rewriting to help assure accuracy or clarity of the protocol, this should be documented in the minutes. The minutes must clearly state why changes are being requested.

Summary of Controverted Issues

When IRB members debate or discuss an issue related to a protocol, summarize this discussion in the minutes. It is important to record the resolution of this debate. For example, if several members debated whether consent could be waived for a project, summarize the discussion in the minutes, state what issues or regulations were considered, and give the outcome of the discussion. The minutes should be in sufficient detail that someone who did not attend the meeting could review this summary and understand what took place.

For Investigational Devices Reviews

The FDA expects the IRB to consider whether an investigational device is of significant or nonsignificant risk to the subjects to be studied. Based on the FDA's definition

of "significant risk," your policies and procedures must state how this determination will be made. The discussion and decision must be reflected in the minutes.

For Vulnerable Populations

OHRP has cited institutions during their reviews when "the IRB appears not to consider systematically and rigorously such issues as equitable selection of subjects and subject recruitment, privacy and confidentiality protections, and special protections required for vulnerable subjects." [3]

Special populations must be addressed in the IRB policies and procedures and also documented in the IRB minutes during a review. Sections in 45 CFR 46 specifically discuss children,[4(Sec.405)] prisoners,[4(Sec.301)] and women and fetuses[4(Sec.201)] (this has recently been updated). These regulations must be reviewed carefully and the implications of each action considered. It is not enough to cite or quote the regulations. The minutes must include the IRB's review and determination that the proper criteria are met for these groups to be included. The IRB is required to document in the minutes that it considered and ensured any additional safeguards that are needed to protect the rights and welfare of vulnerable subjects.

Waiving or Altering Informed Consent

Whenever the IRB approves a procedure that alters or waives the requirements for informed consent, or approves a procedure that waives the requirement for obtaining signed consent, these decisions and the relevant regulations must be documented in the minutes. OHRP recommends that protocol-specific information is cited as the justification for waiving any of these requirements. When you cite the protocol, you provide the rationale for the IRB's decision.

Documentation of Problems

Adverse Event Reports

The reporting and review of adverse events (AEs) is a tremendous task. Chapter 7-3 focuses on AE reporting. Briefly, the written procedures should define what the IRB expects to be reported and when. Determine and document who will receive this information and who will review it. Finally, document the procedures for sharing the information with institutional officials, any sponsor, and the OHRP and FDA.

On page 22 of the FDA information sheet entitled, "Continuing Review after Study Approval,"[7] the role of the IRB in monitoring AEs is discussed. The FDA advises that promptness and level of review may vary, depending on such things as the seriousness of the event and whether it occurred at a location for which your IRB is the IRB of record. IRB review of AEs is discussed in item 3, "Process for Dealing with Reports of Adverse Reactions and Unexpected Events."

Both the FDA and OHRP are actively reviewing the present requirements in the hope of giving IRBs some relief from the heavy burden of reviewing AEs. The NIH now has guidelines in place for (data safety monitoring boards). In cases where a DSMB is reviewing AEs, the IRB should consider how it will use this information in its reviews.

Two pertinent NIH guidance documents are posted on the Web.[9,10]

Serious or Continuing Noncompliance

Your written procedures should define investigator noncompliance and explain how the IRB will address this situation. Include actions the IRB will consider in its review of such an allegation and what action will be taken. If there is a separate committee that reviews these issues, explain how this committee interacts with the IRB. It is important to document what determinations are used to report noncompliance to the OHRP and/or FDA.

Suspension or Termination of Approval

Your written procedures should describe situations in which the IRB will suspend or terminate IRB approvals. This could include causes such as subject safety concerns or investigator noncompliance.

Communicating with the Investigator

Once you have created the IRB's operating procedures, it is easy to adapt them to an "investigator's guide."

Whether a guidance document, letter, memo, or a Web site is used, the investigators must be notified of their duties and obligations. OHRP strongly recommends that institutions develop and distribute a handbook of IRB guidelines for investigators. This handbook should include detailed information concerning the following:

1. Federal and institutional requirements for the protection of human research subjects

2. The IRB's roles and responsibilities

3. Requirements and procedures for the initial and continuing IRB review and approval of research

4. Rationale and procedures for proposing that the research may meet the criteria for expedited review

5. Requirements and procedures for verifying that research is exempt from IRB review

6. Responsibilities of investigators during the review of the conduct of research

7. Requirements and procedures for notifying the IRB of unanticipated problems or events involving risks to the subjects, as well as any other expected or unexpected adverse event

8. Explanation of the distinction between FDA requirements for emergency use of test articles versus HHS regulations for the conduct of human subjects research

9. Relevant examples of user-friendly forms for providing information to the IRB

10. A copy of the institution's MPA (assuming there is one), the human subjects regulations, and the *Belmont Report*

Conclusion

Documenting compliance with federal regulations is an essential part of the IRB process. When it comes to com-

pliance documentation, the mantra of the IRB administrator should be "If it's not written down, it didn't happen." This chapter has reviewed the main steps and procedures in IRB review that require written documentation. Specific recommendations are made regarding the method for documentation of these important aspects of IRB function. Procedures for documenting compliance with federal regulations are an evolving area that requires constant attention on the part of the IRB leadership.

References

1. Office for Human Research Protections. Policy Guidance. Updated 2001. World Wide Web http://ohrp.osophs.dhhs.gov/g-topics.htm

2. Office for Human Research Protections. Dear Colleague Letters. 20 Mar 2001. Access date 30 Mar 2001. World Wide Web http://ohrp.osophs.dhhs.gov/dearcoll.htm

3. Office for Human Research Protection. Common Findings and Guidance. 21 Jun 2001. Access date 2 Aug 2001. World Wide Web http://ohrp.osophs.dhhs.gov/compovr.htm.

4. Code of Federal Regulations. Title 45A—Department of Health and Human Services; Part 46—Protection of Human Subjects. Updated 1 Oct 1997. Access date 18 Apr 2001. World Wide Web http://www4.law.cornell.edu/cfr/45p46.htm

5. Code of Federal Regulations. Title 21, Chapter 1—Food and Drug Administration, DHHS; Part 50—Protection of Human Subjects. Updated 1 Apr 1999. Access date 18 Apr 2001. World Wide Web http://www4.law.cornell.edu/cfr/21p50.htm

6. Code of Federal Regulations. Title 21, Chapter 1—Food and Drug Administration, DHHS; Part 56—Institutional Review Boards. Updated 1 Apr 1999. Access date 27 Mar 2001. World Wide Web http://www4.law.cornell.edu/cfr/21p56.htm

7. Food and Drug Administration. Information Sheets: Guidance for Institutional Review Boards and Clinical Investigators. Sept 1998. Access date 9 Apr 2001. World Wide Web http://www.fda.gov/oc/oha/IRB/toc.html

8. Food and Drug Administration. A Self-Evaluation Checklist for IRBs. Updated 12 Mar 2001. World Wide Web www.fda.gov/oc/oha/IRB/toc11.html

9. National Institutes of Health. Guidance on Reporting Adverse Events to Institutional Review Boards for NIH-Supported Multicenter Clinical Trials (from NIH Guide for June 11, 1999). Updated 11 Jun 1999. Access date 29 Mar 29 Mar 2001. World Wide Web http://grants.nih.gov/grants/guide/notice-files/not99-107.html

10. National Institutes of Health. Implementation of Policies for Human Intervention Studies (draft). 8 Jun 1999. Access date 2 Aug 2001. World Wide Web http://www.nih.gov/nia/funding/policy/humint.htm

IRB Policies and Procedures

Celia S. Walker

INTRODUCTION

This chapter focuses on IRB policies and procedures. Procedures are differentiated from policies and suggestions are offered about how to produce written procedures. Most importantly, however, the chapter emphasizes the importance of creating and using written procedures in IRB administration.

Differentiating Procedures from Policies

Policies and procedures is such a stock phrase we might not stop to discriminate between the two or consider what they are. In general, they are explanations of why and how matters are handled a specific way. They describe how the IRB operates.

Policies tend to be general statements of broad principles, strategies, and philosophical guides.

Procedures, on the other hand, are practical, specific, step-by-step tactics and detailed directives about how to implement a policy.

Policies provide overall guidance, but procedures are what an IRB, its administrative staff, and the institution's researchers consult every day (Table 2.3.1).

This chapter will concentrate on procedures instead of policy, but many institutions promulgate both, either separate or combined. The University of Minnesota's Web-based policy library exemplifies broad policy dissemination at an institutional level.[1] The policies typically refer to more complete sets of procedures that are more likely to be developed at the unit level, rather than the institution. Another format would entail an integrated document, with the policy as opening paragraph, followed by higher-level procedures that implement the policy. Consult *The Handbook Handbook* for a more detailed discussion of the interplay between policies and procedures.[2]

Why Have Written Procedures?

There are two responses to this question. First, written procedures are required by federal regulation and the anticipated accreditation process. Second, and more importantly, written procedures are required because of what they accomplish.

Federal Requirements

"Written procedures" are what the federal regulations require. Written procedures for the IRB's functioning and for reporting unanticipated problems are listed in Common Rule sections 103(b)(4) and (b)(5) among the minimal requirements for a federal assurance. While the process for obtaining a federal-wide assurance is changing, this core requirement will not change. Among the Office for Human Research Protections (OHRP) Common Findings,[3] the list of deficiencies commonly found in audits, appears No. 67:

Written IRB Guidelines and Procedures. OHRP strongly recommends that institutions develop and distribute a handbook of IRB guidelines for research investigators. The handbook should include detailed information concerning (a) federal and institutional requirements for the protection of human research subjects; (b) the IRB's role and responsibilities; (c) the requirements and procedures for initial and continuing IRB review and approval of research; (d) the rationale and procedures for proposing that the research may meet the criteria for expedited review; (e) the requirements and procedures for verifying that research is exempt from IRB review; (f) the responsibilities of investigators during the review and conduct of research; (g) requirements and procedures for notifying the IRB of unanticipated problems or events involving risks to the subjects, as well as any other expected or unexpected adverse events; (h) an explanation of the distinction between FDA requirements for emergency use of test articles versus HHS regulations for the conduct of human subjects research; (i) relevant examples and user-friendly forms for providing information to the IRB; and (j) a copy of the institution's MPA, the HHS humans subjects regulations (45 CFR Part 46), and the Belmont Report. Where appropriate, OHRP also recommends that IRBs develop written operating procedures to supplement its guidelines for investigators.

The proposed accreditation standards likewise insist that an institution have developed written procedures for IRB functioning. Standard 1.7, currently a draft, requires written procedures: "The organization must follow written policies and procedures governing all research involving human subjects. The policies and procedures specify to whom they apply and how they are disseminated. The policies and procedures must be reviewed periodically and updated as necessary." Subsequent sections refer to a variety of situations for which the institution must have and follow procedures, such as addressing allegations of noncompliance.

Table 2.3.1   Policies versus Procedures

	Cooking	IRB
Policy	Create meringue	Decisions are made at properly constituted meeting.
Procedure	Beat two egg whites in a bowl with a mixer until stiff. Be sure there is no grease in the bowl. Add two tablespoons of sugar slowly when the egg whites have begun to stiffen.	An IRB quorum consists of one half of the regular membership plus one person. If a quorum is present, and a nonscientific member is in attendance as a part of the quorum, a meeting is considered properly constituted.

The Food and Drug Administration's (FDA's) regulations mirror the Common Rule requirements, but with a critical difference in interpretation. While OHRP in the past has accepted the written procedures appearing in a multiple project assurance (MPA) as being adequate in the past, the FDA has a record of requiring a separate document of written procedures when it audits programs. A survey of recent FDA audit-finding letters sent to sanctioned IRBs shows almost every one with a finding of "Failure to have and follow written procedures for IRB functions and operations in accordance with 21 CFR 56.108 and 812.66."

Likewise, the terms of a federal-wide assurance include a requirement to establish within 90 days, and provide OHRP upon request, written procedures including specific items.[3] In light of the emphasis in the proposed accreditation standards and changes in the assurance process, the distinction becomes moot, and a separate set of written procedures will be required by both the FDA and OHRP.

The FDA additionally provides a checklist for evaluating procedures. This allows an institution to assess the completeness of its procedures before any kind of audit or accreditation visit. The entire list can be obtained from the FDA's Web site,[4] and will be discussed below.

In summation: Institutions should have been using written procedures for a variety of audiences because they are required by federal regulation, and that requirement does not appear likely to change.

What Written Procedures Accomplish

Although we all use *unwritten* procedures to some degree, they are not as effective or desirable as written ones. Institutions operating solely with unwritten procedures may be viewed as unorganized, understaffed, unknowledgeable, or inconsistent, and certainly would not be viewed by federal oversight agencies as adequate. Unwritten procedures should be formalized into written ones as soon as possible for use.

It might be tempting to maintain that the singular goal of written procedures is to maintain institutional compliance with federal regulations: "Written procedures are required, and we have them." However, just having them is not sufficient to constitute compliance. Having, but not following, those written procedures will be cited as a deficit by federal audit agencies every bit as quickly as not having written procedures in the first place. The procedures are not a mantelpiece just for display; they should become an integral, practical description of the various IRB functions. Finally, they engender many positive outcomes.

1. They will establish consistency in how situations are handled. This is especially valuable for instances that may not occur frequently enough for the handling to become a well-learned pattern. Researchers appreciate greater consistency and view IRB decisions as more credible.

2. They result in an overall reduction in errors. It is harder to overlook critical procedural aspects if they are in writing.

3. They provide clarity about who is responsible for what. For those tasks that are left undone because neither the Chair nor the administrator realizes it is his or her responsibility, the written procedures explicitly address responsibilities.

4. They lead to faster and improved training for new faculty, IRB members, and IRB staff. New staff has a reference manual, and new IRB members have a complete procedural framework upon which to structure their experiences in reviewing protocols.

5. They provide a partial defense against complaints, grievances, or lawsuits about inequitable treatment with respect to IRB determinations.

Policies and Procedures for Whom?

The federal regulations tend to be interpreted as requiring written procedures for researchers. In fact, there are three sets of interlocking procedures that need to be developed, including those for the IRB itself.

IRB Administrative Office

This set is an expanded "desk reference" for all staff serving the IRB. In it might appear application intake procedures, schedules, contacts, application routings, procedures for operating and maintaining any database, the protocol for assigning approval numbers, and a catalog of applicable document files. It can even include procedures for producing procedure manuals, with the frequency and method for revising them. The administrative manual is useful for training new staff and is critical for maintaining consistency in handling protocols.

Researchers

Often called an *institutional handbook* or *manual,* it informs researchers about the application process, researcher responsibilities, and specific techniques such as obtaining a child's assent. It would be useful to include the location of core resources such as the *Belmont Report,* the federal regulations, and other institutional procedures (such as for graduate advisors). The Web is generally an effective way of distributing such a handbook, in part because the Web is so widely available, and in part because changes can be made centrally so that any subsequent access shows the new information.

The IRB

The IRB's procedures will begin with the governing federal regulations. However, they will be expanded to include the institutional and committee interpretations and implementations of those regulations.

How to Produce Written Procedures

It is rarely necessary to start from scratch. It is almost always easier to begin with some existing written procedures, then modify them for your purposes. Contact IRB administrators at other institutions similar to yours and ask if you could receive a copy of their written procedures to adapt. Likewise, consult the Web for the procedures of other institutions to see what topics they include. IRB administrators are typically quite generous in allowing use or adaptation of their documents; it is a courtesy to acknowledge the source in your finished product.

The FDA self-evaluation checklist, available from their Web page, offers a good start with respect to topics that might be covered.[4] For institutions not engaged in FDA-regulated research, there are obviously sections that would not need to be covered in your procedures (such as provisions for emergency use at X.C.3), as well as institution-specific processes that differ. In addition, FDA references would need to be converted to Common Rule references. Nonetheless, the outline affords a workable map for comprehensive IRB procedures. The following is a comprehensive outline of policies and procedures related to IRB function. Use this list to create a procedures manual applicable to your organization.[4]

I. The institutional authority under which the IRB is established and empowered.

II. The definition of the purpose of the IRB, i.e., the protection of human subjects of research.

III. The principles which govern the IRB in assuring that the rights and welfare of subjects are protected.

IV. The authority of the IRB.
   A. The scope of authority is defined, i.e., what types of studies must be reviewed.
   B. Authority to disapprove, modify, or approve studies based upon consideration of human subject protection aspects.
   C. Authority to require progress reports from the investigators and oversee the conduct of the study.
   D. Authority to suspend or terminate approval of a study.
   E. Authority to place restrictions on a study.

V. The IRB's relationships to
   A. The top administration of the institution.
   B. The other committees and department chairpersons within the institution.
   C. The research investigators.
   D. Other institutions.
   E. Regulatory agencies.

VI. The membership of the IRB.
   A. Number of members.
   B. Qualification of members.
   C. Diversity of members (for example, representation from the community, and minority groups), including representation by:
      1. both men and women
      2. multiple professions
      3. scientific and nonscientific member(s)
      4. not otherwise affiliated member(s)
   D. Alternate members (if used).

VII. Management of the IRB.
   A. The Chairperson.
      1. selection and appointment
      2. length of term/service
      3. duties
      4. removal
   B. The IRB members.
      1. selection and appointment
      2. length of term/service and description of staggered rotation or overlapping of terms, if used
      3. duties
      4. attendance requirements
      5. removal
   C. Training of IRB Chair and members.
      1. orientation
      2. continuing education
      3. reference materials (IRB library)
   D. Compensation of IRB members.
   E. Liability coverage for IRB members.
   F. Use of consultants.
   G. Secretarial/administrative support staff (duties).
   H. Resources (for example, meeting area, filing space, reproduction equipment, computers).

VIII. Conflict of interest policy.
   A. No selection of IRB members by investigators.
   B. Prohibition of participation in IRB deliberations and voting by investigators.

IX. Functions of the IRB.
   A. Conducting initial and continuing review.
   B. Reporting, in writing, findings and actions of the IRB to the investigator and the institution.
   C. Determining which studies require review more often than annually.
   D. Determining which studies need verification from sources other than the investigators that no material changes have occurred since previous IRB review.
   E. Ensuring prompt reporting to the IRB of changes in research activities.
   F. Ensuring that changes in approved research are not initiated without IRB review and approval except where necessary to eliminate apparent immediate hazards.
   G. Ensuring prompt reporting to the IRB, appropriate institutional officials, and the FDA of:

1. unanticipated problems involving risks to subjects or others
2. serious or continuing noncompliance with 21 CFR parts 50 and 56 or the requirements of the IRB
3. suspension or termination of IRB approval

H. Determining which device studies pose significant or nonsignificant risk.

X. Operations of the IRB.
   A. Scheduling of meetings.
   B. Pre-meeting distribution to members, of, for example, place and time of meeting, agenda, and study material to be reviewed.
   C. The review process.
      1. Description of the review process ensuring that:
         a. all members receive complete study documentation for review (see XI.B);
         b. *or one or more "primary reviewers"/ "secondary reviewers"* receives the complete study documentation for review, reports to IRB and leads discussion; if other members review summary information only, these members must have access to complete study documentation
      2. role of any subcommittees of the IRB
      3. emergency use notification and reporting procedures
      4. expedited review procedure
         a. for approval of studies that are both minimal risk *and* on the FDA-approved list
         b. for approval of modifications to ongoing studies involving no more than minimal risk
   D. Criteria for IRB approval contain all requirements of 21 CFR 56.111.
   E. Voting requirements.
      1. quorum required to transact business
      2. diversity requirements of quorum (for example requiring at least one physician member when reviewing studies of FDA-regulated articles)
      3. percent needed to approve or disapprove a study
      4. full voting rights of all reviewing members
      5. no proxy votes (written or telephone)
      6. prohibition against conflict-of-interest voting
   F. Further review/approval of IRB actions by others within the institution. (Override of disapproval is prohibited.)
   G. Communication from the IRB.
      1. to the investigator for additional information
      2. to the investigator conveying IRB decision
      3. to institution administration conveying IRB decision
      4. to sponsor of research conveying IRB decision
   H. Appeal of IRB decisions.
      1. criteria for appeal
      2. to whom appeal is addressed
      3. how appeal is resolved (Override of IRB disapprovals by external body/official is prohibited.)

XI. IRB record requirements.
   A. IRB membership roster showing qualifications.
   B. Written procedures and guidelines.

C. Minutes of meetings.
   1. members present (any consultants/guests/ others shown separately)
   2. summary of discussion on debated issues
   3. record of IRB decisions
   4. record of voting (showing votes for, against and abstentions)
D. Retention of protocols reviewed and approved consent documents.
E. Communications to and from the IRB.
F. Adverse reactions reports, and
G. Documentation that the IRB reviews adverse reaction reports.
H. Records of continuing review.
I. Record retention requirements (at least three years after completion for FDA studies).
J. Budget and accounting records.
K. Emergency use reports.
L. Statements of significant new findings provided to subjects.

XII. Information the investigator provides to the IRB.
   A. Professional qualifications to do the research (including a description of necessary support services and facilities)
   B. Study protocol that includes/addresses
      1. title of the study
      2. purpose of the study (including the expected benefits obtained by doing the study)
      3. sponsor of the study
      4. results of previous related research
      5. subject inclusion/exclusion criteria
      6. justification for use of any special/vulnerable subject populations (for example, the decisionally impaired, children)
      7. study design (including as needed, a discussion of the appropriateness of research methods)
      8. description of procedures to be performed
      9. provisions for managing adverse reactions
      10. the circumstances surrounding consent procedure, including setting, subject autonomy concerns, language difficulties, vulnerable populations
      11. the procedures for documentation of informed consent, including any procedures for obtaining assent from minors, using witnesses, translators and document storage
      12. compensation to subjects for their participation
      13. any compensation for injured research subjects
      14. provisions for protection of subject's privacy
      15. extra costs to subjects for their participation in the study
      16. extra costs to third party payers because of subject's participation
   C. Investigator's brochure (when one exists)
   D. The case report form (when one exists)
   E. The proposed informed consent document.
      1. containing all requirements of 21 CFR 50.25(a)
      2. containing requirements of 21 CFR 50.25(b) that are appropriate to the study
      3. meeting all requirements of 21 CFR 50.20
      4. translated consent documents, as necessary, considering likely subject population(s)
   F. Requests for changes in study after initiation.
   G. Reports of unexpected adverse events.
   H. Progress reports.

I. Final report.

J. Institutional forms/reports.

XIII. Exemption from prospective IRB review.

A. Notify IRB within 5 working days.

B. Emergency use.

C. Review protocol and consent when subsequent use is anticipated.

XIV. Emergency research consent exception.

A. The IRB may find that the 50.24 requirements are met.

B. The IRB shall promptly notify in writing the investigator and the sponsor when it determines it cannot approve a 50.24 study.

C. The IRB shall provide in writing to the sponsor a copy of the information that has been publicly disclosed under 50.24(a)(7)(ii) and (a)(7)(iii).

D. In order to approve an emergency research consent waiver study, the IRB must find and document:

1. Subjects are in a life-threatening situation, available treatments are unproven or unsatisfactory and collection of scientific evidence is necessary

2. Obtaining informed consent is not feasible because:

a. medical condition precludes consent

b. no time to get consent from legally authorized representative

c. prospective identity of likely subjects not reasonable

3. Prospect of direct benefits to study subjects because:

a. life-threatening situation that necessitates treatment

b. data support potential for direct benefit to individual subjects

c. risk/benefit of both standard and proposed treatments reasonable

4. Waiver needed to carry out study

5. Plan defines therapeutic window, during which investigator will seek consent rather than starting without consent. Summary of efforts will be given to IRB at time of continuing review.

6. IRB reviews and approves consent procedures and document. IRB reviews and approves family member objection procedures.

7. Additional protections, including at least:

a. consultation with community representatives

b. public disclosure of plans, risks, and expected benefits

c. public disclosure of study results

d. assure an independent Data Monitoring Committee established

e. objection of family member summarized for continuing review

8. Ensure procedures in place to inform at earliest feasible opportunity of subject's inclusion in the study, participation may be discontinued. Procedures to inform family the subject was in the study if subject dies.

9. Separate IND or IDE required, even for marketed products.

10. IRB disapproval must be documented in writing and sent to the clinical investigator and the sponsor of the clinical investigation. Sponsor must promptly disclose to FDA, other investigators and other IRBs.

How to Create Written Procedures

One of the largest hurdles faced by an IRB administrator in writing procedures is simply getting started. The task seems insurmountable, the necessary "handle" missing. Once one has broken into the assignment, it will begin to seem much more manageable. Adapting another institution's procedures to make them complete and pertinent to your institution is one expedient way of beginning. There are several resources available to help.[5-7]

It is likely, though, that some sections will need to be written from "scratch." To get started, use the guidelines that follow.

1. Brainstorm a list of all the topics that need to be covered. Pay no attention to order. Do not worry about including too much; extraneous topics can be weeded out later. Attempt to capture every related aspect.

EXAMPLE

Appointing new members. Should not be appointed by researchers. Authorized institutional official (IO) makes final decision. Existing IRB makes recommendations. Involve deans. New members need to train. Need to represent research areas reviewed by IRB. Pay attention to diversity (gender, ethnicity). Watch balances on IRB (longevity, scientist/nonscientist, physicians, prisoner representative, community membership). Have an order in which various bodies are consulted. Make the appointment in writing from IO. Get current curriculum vitae. IRB administrative office provides instructional materials and basic orientation.

2. Order the topics by grouping them into logical relationships, chronological sequence, or some other system.

EXAMPLE

Selecting → Appointing → Finalizing the appointment

3. Create an outline of the topics that is a further refinement of the grouping.

EXAMPLE

1.0 Procedure for Appointing New IRB Members

1.1 Selecting candidates

1.1.1 Timing

1.1.2 IRB starts process

1.1.3 Get Deans' input

1.1.4 Can the IRB propose? Can researchers select?

1.1.5 Prioritizing and getting list to authorized institutional official (IO)

1.1.6 The appointment

1.1.7 Communicating to new member and IRB

4. Then, finalize and "polish" each procedure.

a. Assess the situation needing a written procedure. Think through the variations and exceptions that can occur.

b. Gather and review background material: existing procedures, laws and regulations from federal, state, and local sources; previous IRB actions (both those that worked and those that did not).

c. Draft the procedure. Write rapidly and do not worry about grammatical precision. Get it down in a train of thought. Organize by introductory paragraph containing policy, description of procedure, summary of main points. Depending on the ultimate audience and use of the procedures, you may wish to cite pertinent regulations.

d. Let the draft procedures rest at least 24 hours. When you return to them, you will see them with new eyes and are likely to see aspects you missed in the first draft.

e. Test the procedure. "Drop" actual situations through the procedure to see if it works. You may identify gaps or needed variations or additions, some of which may require IRB action to rectify processes or approve new ones.

f. Revise procedures as necessary.

EXAMPLE OF RESULT
1.0 Procedure for Appointing New IRB Members

Members shall be appointed to the IRB such that requirements of Common Rule § 107 are met.

1.1 Selecting candidates

1.1.1 The selection process for routine appointments shall begin approximately three months before the appointment date; *ad hoc* appointments needed to fill unanticipated vacancies shall begin as soon as possible after the announcement is given.

1.1.2 The IRB shall ascertain what attributes a new member needs to possess (community member, scientist/nonscientist, duration of term, diversity, representation for vulnerable populations, academic standing, research arena).

1.1.3 The IRB administrator will communicate these attributes to the college deans either by memo or e-mail, asking on behalf of the IRB for suggested candidates. A response date needs to be stipulated.

1.1.4 The IRB shall likewise suggest candidates.

1.1.5 At a convened meeting, or using an appointed subcommittee process, the IRB shall prioritize the list of candidates generated by deans and the IRB, listing briefly the reasons for the priority ranking. The IRB administrator will communicate the listing to the authorized Institutional Official (IO) within three working days of receiving the list.

1.1.6 The IO shall appoint the new member. The IO retains this responsibility exclusively; researchers may not appoint new members; the IRB and college deans may recommend, but may not appoint.

1.1.7 The IO shall convey in memo or e-mail his/her appointments to the IRB administrator, who shall

1.1.7.1 Notify the IRB Chair of the selection.

1.1.7.2 Prepare the official appointment letter to the new member, using the model retained electronically at c:/appointments/ appointment memo, with alterations as needed to fit the circumstances.

5. Have others review the procedures. You may wish to use several reviewers, including a "typical user" as well as a knowledgeable colleague.

6. Determine a workable layout: numbering system; format (outline, paragraph, play script); fonts; headings; how to handle graphics and appendices; issue and revision numbers and/or dates; pagination scheme; logo/institutional name; how new material will be inserted; front and back matter such as preface, table of contents, index, glossary, appendix; headers and footers; justification style. Be sure the format accommodates revisions, additions, and withdrawn procedures. (Be sure there is a procedure for making these changes as well.)

7. Produce final version. Consider whether multiple venues are necessary: Web, printed, office manual.

8. Promulgate the procedures among the target audience.

9. Follow procedures.

10. Revisit procedures on schedule to ascertain if they continue to be current.

11. Revise procedures as needed.

What Contributes to Good Procedures

Simply *having* procedures—meeting the letter of the law— is not adequate. Unduly complex or unrealistic procedures are difficult to follow. They may actually misinform or introduce ambiguity. High-quality written procedures will have several characteristics.

1. They will be appropriate to the audience, in terms of content, detail, and tone.

2. They will be concise: Users do not get lost in verbiage or unnecessary detail.

3. They will be clear: "10 days" raises the question of working days or calendar days, and 10 days from what event?

4. They will use the active voice: "Mail the approval letter" instead of "The approval letter is mailed." The active voice is more dynamic and readable, and reduces ambiguity surrounding who does what.

5. They will be coherent. The organization needs to be obvious, complete, and typically sequential.

6. They will be factual. The procedures reflect what is accurate and actually will be implemented.

7. They will avoid vague, superfluous words such as superlatives, "really," and "actually."

8. They will explain acronyms, slang, special terms, and shortcuts to the reader before using them. A glossary and index may be in order.

9. They will avoid repetition unless necessary.

10. They will use a positive rather than a negative tone. ("Use the provided form," instead of "Do not use forms other than the provided one.")

11. They will use bullets, numbers, flow-charts, or formatting to increase readability. For printed formats, wider margins allow for notes. On-line venues can effectively use embedded links to provide additional details, cross-references, and immediate definitions.

12. They will judiciously employ cross-referencing to place the procedures in a broader context and reduce repetition. Overuse of cross-referencing may make the procedures difficult to follow.

Conclusion

Producing, maintaining, and using written procedures for the IRB, its administrative staff, and researchers are obligatory. While the task may seem daunting, its alternatives are distinctly unappealing, and could culminate in federal sanctions against the institution. A methodological approach is available that, although time-consuming, has a high probability of generating workable procedures. Once developed, the procedures must be followed, revisited on a regular basis, and revised as necessary.

Reference List

1. University of Minnesota. University of Minnesota Web-based policy library. Access date 22 Mar 2001. World Wide Web
   www.fpd.finop.umn.edu

2. Travis AB. *The Handbook Handbook: The Complete How-To Guide to Publishing Policies and Procedures.* New York, NY: R.R. Bowker Company. 1984.

3. Office for Human Research Protections. Compliance Oversight, 12 Dec 2000. Access date 20 Mar 2001. World Wide Web
   http://ohrp.osophs.dhhs.gov/compovr.htm

4. Food and Drug Administration. A Self-Evaluation Checklist for IRBs (1998), 16 Apr 2001. World Wide Web
   www.fda.gov/oc/ohrt/irbs/irbchecklist.html

5. Campbell NJ. *Writing Effective Policies and Procedures: A Step-by-Step Resource for Clear Communication.* New York, NY: Amacom. 1998.

6. Lunine LR. *How to Research, Write, and Package Administrative Manuals.* New York, NY: American Management Association. 1985.

7. Page SB. *Business Policies and Procedures Handbook: How to Create Professional Policy and Procedure Publications.* Englewood Cliffs, NJ: Prentice-Hall, Inc. 1984.

Tracking Systems

Patricia M. Scannell

INTRODUCTION

This chapter looks at one of the many ways to track protocols within an IRB office. At the Washington University Medical Center IRB, we custom-designed a computer program to track all activities taking place on research submissions. There are, however, commercially available products and other IRB software programs (often available as collegial gifts) that can be modified to meet one's own IRB specifications.

Whatever your institution's decision, an efficient system to track protocol submissions is essential. The WUMC IRB uses the program described here to oversee more than 3,000 active protocols and all ancillary reports associated with these protocols (e.g., serious adverse events (SAEs), revisions, and amendments).

The application program consists of two parts: front end and back end. The front end of the application—the part that allows data entry and runs reports—was developed in Microsoft Access. The back end holds the actual data, ensures data integrity, and also does some data processing; it was developed using Microsoft SQL Server.

Data Entry

Protocol files and specific data in these files can be tracked in direct relation to the fields populated in the database. The protocol coordinator who is responsible for a particular committee or subcommittee meeting enters the required data (investigators' demographics, protocol-specific information such as key words, investigational drugs or devices, etc.) into the database. When the information is for a new protocol, the computer assigns it a unique IRB number.

Whenever possible, fields self-populate with minimal keystrokes, and protocol coordinators are required to use pull-down lists of options to avoid inaccurate data entry. For example, a new investigator is entered one time, and in the future, his or her protocols are located by entering only the first few letters of the investigator's name.

Data entered for a new protocol are principal investigator (PI) name, department/division, credentials, address, and phone number. For the protocol, we enter the protocol title, population (adult or pediatric), methodology, treatment, keywords, funding source, and the number of subjects anticipated to attain the accrual goal. Additional data are entered for research involving an investigational drug or device, radioactive drug, fee for review of industry-sponsored research, etc.

When all data are entered and the protocol coordinator clicks "SAVE," the protocol is assigned a unique IRB number. This designates the year and sequence in which it was received in the IRB for its initial review; i.e., 01-0122 means this is the 122nd protocol received for review in 2001.

Tracking Options

The following is a brief overview of a number of different mechanisms that can be used to locate a protocol within the WUMC IRB office. Examples of data screens are appended to this chapter.

Tracking via Type of Submission

Renewals, serious adverse events, revisions, and amendments must be submitted to the IRB and appropriate data entered into the database for subsequent tracking. Based on the type of submission, the protocol coordinator selects the meeting to which the protocol will be assigned (new protocol committee, continuing review committee, or subcommittee). When preparing the meeting materials, the protocol coordinator selects the type of meeting, and the computer generates an agenda designed to meet the needs of the designated committee. All agendas list the protocols in alphabetical order. In addition, the continuing review committee meeting agendas segregate protocols into minimal and greater than minimal risks.

Because all activities (including administrative actions) are reported to a committee, all activities can ultimately be tracked by going to the "reviews and events" screen. To locate a protocol, the protocol coordinator looks to see if an activity is currently scheduled. If it is, the protocol coordinator knows where the file is located within the IRB office. If, for example, the screen shows a revision/amendment is pending approval, the protocol coordinator can see when it will be reviewed, or when it was reviewed, at a subcommittee meeting. Protocols awaiting a response from an investigator are held in a designated section of the IRB mobile filing cabinet and filed according to the terminal digit filing system explained later.

Locating a Protocol File via Its IRB Number/Other Data

If the protocol coordinator knows the unique protocol number, he or she can quickly determine its location by typing in the IRB number. From the computer, the protocol coordinator can see if the protocol is currently scheduled for review at a new protocol committee, continuing review committee, or SAE or revision/amendment subcommittee.

By referencing the information shown on the "reviews and events" screen, the protocol coordinator can see whether the protocol is awaiting a response from an investigator to an IRB request for protocol modifications or additional information. If it is, it can be located in the pending section of the filing cabinet.

The pending section of the IRB mobile filing cabinet is divided into categories in which files are held pending a response from the principal investigator. These categories include the following:

1. New protocol committees
2. Continuing review committees
3. SAE, revision/amendment subcommittees
4. Certificates of confidentiality

The protocols are filed in the section designated for the type of committee that reviewed their most recent submission or under the certificate of confidentiality section. Within the designated section, protocols are filed according to the terminal digit filing system.

If the protocol is a new submission that was not approved at the reviewing committee, the protocol coordinator can look in the computer to see which research review specialist wrote to the investigator to request clarifications or modifications. The file may then be located in that particular research review specialist's office.

The protocol coordinator can select all open and/or closed studies for any particular investigator. By putting in keywords such as breast cancer, diabetes, or schizophrenia, the protocol coordinator can generate a list of all protocols involving those diagnoses. Likewise, if a person from the community calls to inquire as to whether we have a protocol using a specific investigational drug, we can search the database and find every protocol using the investigational drug. We can then give the person inquiring the name(s) of the investigator(s).

The protocol coordinator can track protocols and generate reports according to the type of submission (i.e., full board, expedited, exempt, emergency, identical to, inconcept). Many different kinds of reports can be generated according to the fields within the database.

Tracking All Activities from Initiation to Closure

A report on all activities that have taken place on a protocol can be generated at any time to show what activities have taken place and the dates of all such activities. A history report is always generated when a protocol is closed and is the first document that the protocol coordinator will see when accessing it from the computer disk on which it is archived.

Terminal Digit Filing System

The WUMC IRB uses the terminal digit filing system. The file clerk files and locates files first by the last two digits, working his or her way toward the first two digits. For example, the unique number assigned by the database is 01-0138. The numerals 01- represent the year that the protocol was first approved by the IRB (i.e., 2001). The numerals 0138 represent the sequence in which the protocol was received for review within the IRB office (i.e., it was the 138th protocol).

The protocol coordinator determines the status of the protocol from the database (e.g., new or continuing submission; pending a response from an investigator, etc.) With this information, the file clerk can quickly locate the file by looking under 0138 and then the first two numbers that represent the year of its initial review.

Using the terminal digit file system distributes the files evenly and thus decreases the need to redistribute files. We have found this to be an excellent system that provides us with efficient, reliable access to our protocol files.

Looking to the Future

This brief description reflects how one IRB tracks protocols within its office. We have found it efficient and effective to meet the needs of our IRB. The next step to which we aspire is electronic submission in which the database automatically assigns protocols to the appropriate meeting on the designated deadline and then makes the information immediately available to the reviewers.

Commercial Vendors and Other Institutions

To help you determine what is best for your IRB, information on how other IRBs track protocols can be obtained by contacting commercial vendors and other institutions listed below.

Disclaimer: This is information for your institution to explore and it is not intended to endorse any company, vendor, or institution's product. Cost issues will need to be discussed individually with each company, vendor, or institution.

Commercial Products

Academic Performance Institute, Inc.
Biomedical Research and Assurances Information
    Network (BRAIN)
Contact: Greg Schulmeier
Phone: 601-948-0940
E-mail: gschulme@jam.rr.com

BRAIN is a Web-based package that has been developed by Baylor College of Medicine to manage research oppor-

tunity data as well as to facilitate proposal and protocol submissions.

Data Doctor Office Technology Systems (DDOTS)
Institutional Review Board Activity Negotiation
　　Accountability (IRBANA) Software
4571 Ellsworth Road
Ypsilanti, MI
Contact: Stephen W. Burke, President
Phone: 734-434-7734
E-mail: Stephen.Burke@ddots.com
Web address: 222.ddots.com

IRBANA is a comprehensive Web-based data management system for Institutional Review Boards. A complete protocol database (SQL) (protocol title, investigators, date of IRB approval) provides the information for the extensive reports function including dates for continuing reviews, protocol status. IRBANA records and tracks revisions, amendments, and adverse events. From this information, the IRB meeting agenda is automatically generated.

InfoEd International
2301 Western Avenue
Guiderland, NY 12084
Contact: Ed Johnson, President
Phone: 800-727-6427
Fax: 518-464-0695
E-mail: Ejohnson@infoed.org
Web address: http://www.infoed.org

Totally Web-based, integrated suite of electronic research administration applications serves the needs of sponsored funds, compliance, and technology transfer offices at institutions, small and large, world-wide.

PRO_IRB Plus, Inc.
6020 44th Avenue North
St. Petersburg, FL 33709
Contact: Dick
E-mail: Dick@proirb.com
Phone: 727-545-5314
FAX: 727-541-2433
E-mail: info@proirb.com
Web site: http://www.proirb.com

ProIRB Plus, Inc. is a Microsoft Access-based Institutional Review Board software application providing productivity and compliance assurance tools for managing the Institutional Review Board process. You can test a free trial-version CD.

West Beach Software
P.O. Box 6009
Santa Barbara, CA 93160
Contact: Alison Wollitzer
Phone: 805-692-0089
Fax: 805-692-0079
E-mail: Awollitzer@wbeachsoftware
Web address: http://www.wbeachsoftware.com

IRB Navigator is a full-featured database and document management system for administration and support of In-

stitutional Review Board activities. It tracks all studies and events that take place on studies plus data on conflict of interest and training.

Custom-Designed Institution Databases
Center for Clinical Research Practice
40 Washington Street, Suite 130
Wellesley, MA 02481
Contact: James Saunders
Phone: 781-431-7577
Fax: 781-237-0330

Create and customize comprehensive programs to improve compliance communication, communication, and interdependence throughout the institution and across the facilities and communities that it serves.

Children's Hospital of Cincinnati, Ohio
Cincinnati, Ohio
Contact: Jan McGrath
E-mail: McGrj0@chmcc.org
Phone: 513-636-8039
Fax: 513-636-3959

Developed their own database using Access.

Fred Hutchinson Cancer Research Center, Seattle, WA
Contact: Karen Hansen, Director, Institutional Review
　　Office, 1100 Fairview Ave, N., Mailstop DS-100, PO
　　Box 19024, Seattle, WA 98109-1024
Phone: 206-667-4867
Fax: 206-667-6831
E-mail: khansen@fhcrc.org

Uses a custom-designed Access database to track protocols.

Lovelace Institutional Review Board
2441 Ridgecrest Drive, SE
Albuquerque, NM 87108
Contact: Charlotte E. Pacheco, CIM
Director, Administrator
Phone: 505-348-9395
Fax: 505-348-8546
E-mail: cpacheco@Lrri.org

Designed a database using Access (Microsoft) relational database that has been "awesome."

St. Joseph's Hospital & Medical Center
Barbara Brown, IRB Coordinator
350 W. Thomas Road
Phoenix, AZ 85013
Phone: 602-406-3195
Fax: 602-406-7197
E-mail: b2brown@chw.edu

Currently using IRB! Info IRB information system, but in the future would like to transfer information into an Access database.

University of California, Los Angeles
Contact: Steve Peckman
Associate Director-Human Subjects Research
Phone: 310-825-5344

Fax: 310-794-9565
E-mail: speckman@oprs.ucla.edu

Uses a database developed by UCLA that is extensive in its ability to track protocols and related actions, remind PIs and IRB staff regarding outstanding activities, continuing review, and link FDA products, IRB actions, etc.

Wright State University
3640 Col. Glenn Hwy.
201J University Hall
Dayton, OH 45435-0001
Contact: William Sellers
Phone: 937-775-2709
Fax: 937-775-3781
E-mail: william.sellers@wright.edu

Uses Filemaker Pro. They have had to create numerous scripts and layouts, but it works very well for them.

IRB – Spokane
Contact: Sherry Bye, Administrator
c/o WSU Spokane
601 West First Avenue
Spokane, WA 99201-3899
Phone: 509-358-7627
Fax: 509-358-7627

E-mail: byes@wsu.edu
Web site: http://www.irb.spokane.wsu.edu

Uses a database on Access that they developed.

Conclusion

This chapter has explained the importance of setting up a system for tracking protocols within the IRB office. While there are many different tracking systems available, the chapter has focused on the system that is currently used by the Washington University Medical Center IRB. Tracking systems should be user friendly but sophisticated enough to give the IRB all the information that it needs to manage all aspects of protocol review. A high quality tracking system will increase the productivity of the IRB administrative team and facilitate compliance with federal research regulations. A list of sophisticated IRB tracking systems from commercial vendors and other institutions is provided.

Appendix

Examples of Data Screens

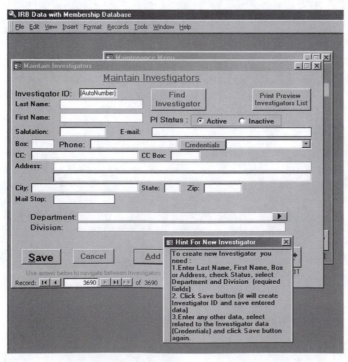

Figure 2.4.1   New Protocol—This screen is used when entering a new protocol; the highlighted areas will pop up after you click on "Add" to show what is required to be filled in before saving. (Used with permission of Washington University, St. Louis, Mo.)

Figure 2.4.2   New Investigator—This screen allows you to enter a new principal investigator's existing information. (Used with permission of Washington University, St. Louis, Mo.)

Figure 2.4.3 Agenda Reports—This screen allows you to run a specific agenda for a meeting. (Used with permission of Washington University, St. Louis, Mo.)

Figure 2.4.4 Maintain Protocol—This screen allows you to look at existing protocols or add a new protocol into the database. (Used with permission of Washington University, St. Louis, Mo.)

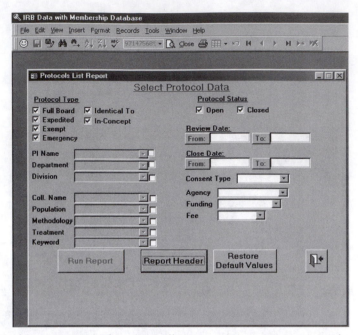

Figure 2.4.5 Select Protocol Data Report—This screen allows you to run various protocol reports. Type in the principal investigator and click "Run." The database generates a report of all protocols with that investigator. Do the same for department, methodology, population, and so on. (Used with permission of Washington University, St. Louis, Mo.)

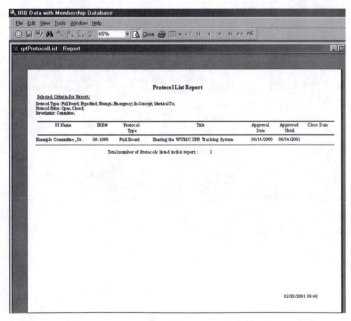

Figure 2.4.6 Protocol List Report—This is an example of the report of all protocols for a particular principal investigator. (Used with permission of Washington University, St. Louis, Mo.)

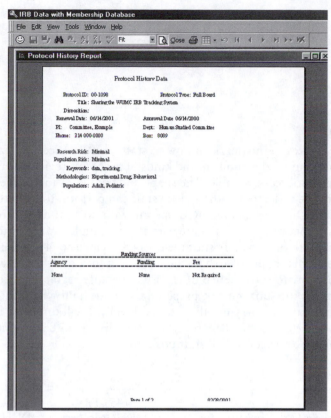

Figure 2.4.7   Protocol History Report—This screen gives a report showing all the events that have been entered into the database for a certain protocol. (Used with permission of Washington University, St. Louis, Mo.)

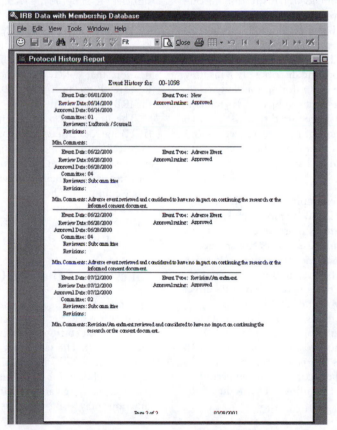

Figure 2.4.8   This screen is another example of a history report showing all the events entered into the database for a certain protocol. (Used with permission of Washington University, St. Louis, Mo.)

Support Staff

Helen McGough

INTRODUCTION

There are many pieces to the puzzle of how to staff an IRB office: the size, nature, and culture of the institution; the numbers and kinds of protocols reviewed; and the budget, space, and other resources available. The shape and configuration of these pieces must be matched with the tasks that an IRB office staff can perform to keep the IRB operating efficiently and effectively. Some IRBs operate with no staff at all, some with part-time staff whose other responsibilities are partially or completely separate from the IRB office, and some with one or more staff members dedicated solely to the IRB.

The purpose of this chapter is to help the reader put the puzzle together and come up with answers on how to staff an IRB office. I will identify regulatory requirements for support, what tasks the staff must be prepared to handle, and what kinds of qualifications staff should have to carry out these tasks. Finally, I will outline a number of different strategies for staffing the IRB office. An appendix to this chapter includes sample job descriptions for a variety of IRB staff positions.

Why Is Staffing Important?

Proper staffing is crucial to the effective operation of an IRB. In most cases, IRB members and Chairs are volunteers from within and from outside the institution hosting the IRB. The time they have to devote to the everyday functions required of the IRB is quite limited. It is unrealistic to expect that members and Chairs will have the time and resources to prepare and distribute IRB protocol materials before the meeting, take and distribute IRB meeting minutes, and provide advice and information daily to researchers, sponsors, and research subjects. To manage these and the many other tasks required to assist the IRB in its mission of the protection of human subjects, an institution hosting an IRB must be prepared to devote sufficient resources to hiring qualified staff.

Federal Regulations

All the regulatory authorities imply that an IRB is supported by an infrastructure. IRB members must be appointed; policies and procedures must be developed and disseminated; members and researchers must receive training and education about the protection of human subjects; and records must be prepared and maintained. Beyond these general rules, there is relatively little direct regulatory guidance on how to staff the IRB office.

In 21 CFR 56, which addresses the U.S. Food and Drug Administration (FDA) regulations pertaining to IRBs, there are no specific references to the staffing of the IRB office. One section mandates the records that an IRB or its institution must maintain, the records retention period required, and the requirement to allow FDA audit of the IRB records.[1(Sec. 115)]

In 45 CFR 46, which includes the Department of Health and Human Services (DHHS) regulations pertaining to IRBs, the regulations state that resources and space must be sufficient to support the IRB, but do not specify staffing in particular. In 1993, Dr. Gary B. Ellis, then director of the Office for Protection from Research Risks (OPRR), stated his opinion that the ratio of support staff to number of protocols reviewed should be 1:300. It is also clear in its investigations that OPRR, now known as the Office for Human Research Protections (OHRP), regards adequate staffing of the IRB office as a necessary condition.

The International Commission on Harmonisation (ICH) has developed a set of guidelines for the conduct of research involving human subjects. This is to be used by those agencies that are not regulated by the FDA, but wish to market their products in the United States and other countries. These guidelines have been accepted by the FDA and also underscore the importance of adequate staffing for the IRB office. ICH guidelines are the subject of Chapter 8-2.

Functions of the IRB Office

The staff of an IRB, as opposed to its Chair and members, can perform a variety of functions. The assumption in this section is that staff members will not hold membership on the IRB itself. The tasks that follow, therefore, do not include those for which formal IRB action is required. This section will describe each function and illustrate how appropriate staffing can facilitate the work of the IRB. These functions may also be used as job descriptions for the various staff positions an IRB might consider incorporating into its structure.

Screening Protocols Before IRB Review

Most IRBs require that researchers complete application forms or follow fairly specific instructions about what information the IRB will need to complete its review. An important staff function that can improve the efficiency of IRB review is screening the applications or submissions for completeness and accuracy before review. This screening process can be as rudimentary as making sure that the forms have been completed and the appropriate attachments are in place. More sophisticated screening responsibilities can include reviewing the consent forms to make sure that the required elements have been addressed and the language level is appropriate for the intended research population. Experienced staff members can review the actual content of the submissions to make sure they provide enough detail to allow adequate review. For example, most applications ask the researcher to identify the background and purpose of the review. If a researcher answers, "The purpose of this study is to test X drug for safety and efficacy," a competent screener can recognize that this is not an adequate answer and can request a more detailed description from the researcher before the protocol goes to the board for review.

Agenda Preparation

IRB members must be provided sufficient time to review the submissions before the meeting actually takes place. This means that the applications must be made available to them, whether electronically through secure e-mail attachments or a secure Web site, or on paper through the mail system or via messenger. An agenda for the meeting must be prepared and the submissions copied and sent to each member. In some cases, the staff may assign primary and secondary reviewers to each submission. If this is the case, the staff must be familiar enough with the expertise of each member to make appropriate assignments.

Taking Minutes

Minutes in sufficient detail to provide information about the number of members present at the review of each submission, the vote, and a description of any controverted issues are required by the regulations. Usually, this responsibility is assigned to an IRB staff person. The staff member must be sufficiently skilled to take notes that reflect the discussion and disposition of each submission reviewed. An alternative is to make an audio recording of the meeting and have it transcribed afterwards. Although this method would appear to require less skill on the part of the staff member, it requires transcription time, a transcriptionist who is at least familiar with the functions of an IRB, and staff and IRB member time to review the transcript for accuracy. The transcript will usually not include the number of members who voted for and against the submission, the number of abstentions, and who was actually present.

Drafting Correspondence

After the meeting, correspondence must be sent to the researchers to inform them of the IRB's disposition. Ideally, the IRB Chair prepares this correspondence. In many cases, however, the Chair does not have the time to perform this task, which then falls to a staff person. This responsibility requires that the staff person either attends the IRB meetings or has immediate access to detailed meeting minutes. It also requires that the staff person has sufficient experience with biomedical or behavioral research to draft correspondence that describes the IRB's concerns correctly.

Triage of Amendments and Modifications

Unless the IRB is a fairly small operation, the Chair and members will not have time to review requests to amend or modify approved protocols. IRB staff can assist in this process by making determinations about which requests require full IRB review and which can be reviewed using the expedited process.

Mail and Reception

These information-flow management functions may be handled at a simple level (office hours, contact information, and meeting dates) by IRB staff, or may involve transmission of more complex advice about submission preparation, status of review, and regulatory information.

Database and Information Management

As with any regulatory and compliance function, much of the success of the operation depends on managing information flow. The IRB office requires a staff person who can establish and maintain a database, and staff to make sure that documents coming to and from the IRB can be tracked and located. Even if construction of a database is contracted out, a staff member must be able to troubleshoot and correct minor problems.

Triage of Adverse Event and Safety Reports

As with amendments and modifications, the IRB staff can simply transmit the information to the IRB Chair and members. In addition, it can be assigned the task of triaging these reports for presentation to the IRB Chair or full board. At the very least, the staff can assist the IRB by separating reports into "on-site" and "off-site." Staff can also pull relevant files, flag consent forms, and generally make the IRB's huge task a little more manageable.

Staff Supervision

In an IRB office with more than one person, one or more of the staff will have to assume supervisory responsibilities over the others. This may include recruitment and hiring of new staff, training, on-going evaluation, maintaining time records, and other personnel issues. A well staffed IRB office may require that more than one person assume some or all of these responsibilities.

Responding to Subject Concerns

Most commonly, research subjects are directed during the consent process to contact the IRB office if they have questions about their rights. The IRB office may be assigned the responsibility of answering participants' questions about the research, about whom to call in case of an adverse event, and who will provide treatment for adverse events. The assumption of one or more of these responsibilities requires IRB staff members who are able to respond quickly and appropriately to these inquiries. Staff may be required to negotiate a research subject's concerns with a billing department, with risk management, with the researcher or the researcher's staff, and with legal counsel.

Triage of Protocol Violations

Reports of protocol violations may come directly to the IRB Chair or to its members. However, if the IRB staff has high visibility within the institution, these problems may be directed first to the IRB office. Staff members must be able to determine what the violation consists of and how it should be directed for consideration. Reports of noncompliance within the institution may come from research and other staff who feel more at ease making their reports to IRB staff rather than to the IRB Chair and members. At a minimum, IRB staff must be trained to handle these reports appropriately.

Office Procedures

Many of the procedures that the OHRP, FDA, and research sponsors are concerned about are directed at how the IRB accomplishes its work. However, some ancillary procedures are also auditable and are more appropriate to the staff than to the IRB Chair and members. These may include establishing procedures for putting an agenda together, entering protocol data into a database, establishing a filing system, a file purging system, protocols for security, information referral, and for all the other tasks listed in this chapter. IRB staff should be able to develop office procedures and train other staff members in their application.

IRB Policy and Procedures

Every IRB operates according to policy consistent with its regulations and must make its procedures available to researchers. When regulations and policies outside the IRB change, the IRB must be able to respond to those changes promptly and appropriately. An institution may want to consider using its IRB office staff to develop and recommend policy and procedures with regard to IRB operations. Often IRB chairs and members rotate frequently enough that there is relatively little "institutional memory" located in the IRB itself. However, long-term staff may understand both the implications of regulatory changes and the culture of the institution in which the IRB functions and, therefore, be in a good position to recommend policies that satisfy both. For example, when a regulatory agency issues new guidance information, someone knowledgeable about the IRB must be able to analyze the guidance and explain how it differs from current policy and procedures. He or she can recommend changes that must be made to bring the IRB into compliance with the new guidance.

Education and Training

At a minimum, each institution conducting research with humans must also make sure that its IRB members and researchers (from principal investigators to research administrators to research staff) are knowledgeable about the ethics and regulations pertaining to this kind of research. Although a few external sources exist for this kind of education and training, the responsibility for training researchers and their staffs often falls to the IRB members and office staff. If staff exercise this responsibility, they should have the necessary skills and credibility to do the job well. Even if the staff do not actually deliver education and training, they can be responsible for organizing events and providing the infrastructure for training and education within and outside the institution.

Intrainstitutional Relations

An IRB cannot operate in isolation. The IRB must coordinate its activities with a variety of other compliance and management groups and individuals within the institution. These include the institutional official, risk managers, researchers, grants and contracts management, and other regulatory committees such as biohazards, radiation safety, and recombinant DNA committees. The IRB office staff can take responsibility for maintaining relations between the IRB and appropriate persons within the institution. This is to make sure that the IRB is aware of and acts in accord with the actions and policies of these other groups, and to make its own policies and procedures known as appropriate.

External Relations

IRBs must maintain positive and productive relationships with a variety of agencies and individuals outside of as well as within the institution. These may include regulatory agencies, research sponsors, other IRBs with which it has review relationships, local and state legislators, and community and special-interest advocacy groups. Staff can be assigned tasks such as acting as legislative liaison, drafting assurance documents, negotiating reviews between IRBs, and communicating with non-affiliated research and advocacy groups.

Meeting Logistics

IRBs have basic needs: a meeting place, transportation and parking, food and beverages, and other support. If the meeting will incorporate members by tele- or video conference, arrangements for these technologies must be made before each meeting. Non-affiliated members may require transportation to meetings. IRB staff can be assigned to carry out support activities ranging from reserving meeting space to ordering pizza to washing the coffee cups after the meeting.

Number of Staff Members Needed

There is considerable controversy and a serious lack of reliable information on how many staff members should support an IRB. The following are some options for determining the number of staff members that are necessary to serve the needs of the IRB.

Ratios of Staff to Volume

Although some data show that the ratio of IRB administrators to number of new applications is about 1:300, it is dangerous to leap to the conclusion that this ratio is appropriate for all situations. For example, it might be tempting to assume that an IRB reviewing only 150 protocols per year could manage adequately with only a half-time IRB staff person. However, there appears to be an economy of scale that kicks in only after a certain volume of protocols is reached. As with almost any other activity, one achieves excellence only with practice. It will take a part-time IRB staff member longer to learn the regulations and procedures and longer to achieve an appropriate comfort level with the work. At the other end of the spectrum, certain IRB office activities can be streamlined to some extent through automation, and the ratio of staff to protocols may be higher without ill effect. Even at this end, however, the drafting of correspondence and negotiations with researchers cannot be streamlined.

Number and Type of IRBs

It is recommended that if an institution hosts more than one IRB panel, it should have IRB staff dedicated to each board. This is especially true if the IRBs operate in different spheres within the institution. For example, in a college or university setting, one IRB may be dedicated to the review of biomedical research and one to the review of behavioral research. The skills required to support these two kinds of IRBs may be quite different in terms of the protocols reviewed and the culture of the community of researchers. IRB staff who have familiarity with the subject matter and the subject populations may ease the path for the IRB in carrying out its responsibilities.

Time Allocation for Chair and Other IRB Members

IRB Chairs and members who are paid for their services will need less support than those who are volunteers. Given the relative costs of staff versus faculty, most institutions will make the choice to hire dedicated staff rather than to pay faculty or researchers for the time they devote to the IRB. A volunteer Chair and members will not have the time to draft IRB correspondence, prepare and distribute agendas, take and prepare minutes, maintain a database, maintain intra/interinstitutional relations, and keep up on regulatory changes. A qualified dedicated staff can perform these functions at less cost to the institution than if faculty were paid to do them.

Expertise of Investigators

If an institution's researchers demonstrate a high level of expertise in the area of research ethics, and if an effective training system and a good mentoring program for new members of the institution exist, then the IRB will need fewer staff. In addition, if the institution is young, lacks experience, or has a culture of noncompliance, the IRB will (at least initially) require more staff support. This will help create a culture in which the ethical conduct of research is valued and the training and advising requirements are more limited.

Resources Available

Although it is clearly not reasonable to deprive research subjects of adequate protections because of lack of resources, it is also clear that some institutions are better endowed than others to be able to absorb the costs of running a protection program. Institutions with lower levels of funding available for the IRB will have to resort to

other sources of support for the IRB staff: work-study students, hospital volunteers, retired staff members, and community volunteers, for example.

Turnover

A higher rate of staff turnover places increased demands on existing staff to hire and train replacements. An institution having high turnover will have to consider a higher staffing ratio. An institution in which IRB staff turnover is low will be able to use the experience of its staff more effectively and may be able to employ fewer staff members.

Staff Qualifications

Another controversial area is what characteristics IRB staff should have. Requirements for assessing staff fall into several areas.

Educational Requirements

The qualifications of IRB staff depend largely on the level of responsibility they are expected to assume. It is clear that what is important in good IRB staff are personality characteristics as well as areas of expertise. Candidates for IRB staff positions should demonstrate high levels of skill in the following areas:

1. Oral and written communication
2. Interactions with people from a wide variety of educational, occupational, and ethnic backgrounds
3. Management of high volumes of work with limited turn-around time
4. Ability to learn complex concepts (regulatory, ethical, and scientific)

In an IRB office in which staff are expected to operate at a high level of interaction with researchers and board members, a Ph.D. or M.D. may be required. However, an individual with a bachelor's degree or even a high school diploma plus years of regulatory and management experience can also function effectively.

Certification

Several certification programs are available for IRB office staff. The institution may want to investigate these programs to evaluate their suitability for a particular IRB's needs. Certification is one way to measure the qualifications of new staff and to provide on-going assurance that existing staff is knowledgeable about current regulations and IRB office management.

Conflict of Interest

IRB staff should understand the principles of conflict of interest so that they can assist the IRB in determining when such a conflict exists for themselves as well as for the IRB members.

Models for Staffing

A variety of models may be used to staff an IRB office.

Team Model

This staffing model may work very well in an institution in which more than one IRB panel functions. In this case, each IRB panel has its own IRB coordinator and one or more clerical support persons. The advantages of this model are that the IRB staff has a smaller number of protocols to work with and can share the tasks associated with supporting the IRB and facilitating the review of proposals more effectively. Members of one team can substitute for equivalent members of another team in an emergency. The teams could be located in one office, or could be located where the IRB is housed. This model can be decentralized in a situation in which, for example, a school of medicine has an IRB that operates independently of the IRB for a school of social work. The disadvantage of the team model is that consistency between IRBs may decrease. It is, therefore, appropriate to include an overall administrator in the team model whose responsibilities include maintaining consistency.

Traditional Model

The more traditional model of staffing an IRB office is stratified and hierarchical. In this model, there is usually an administrator whose responsibilities include managing the IRB office, one or more IRB coordinators (depending on how many IRBs there are), and clerical staff who func-tion to support all of the IRBs within an institution. Some economy of scale is achieved with this kind of staffing model, and it is easier to maintain consistency if there is more than one IRB. The disadvantage of this model is that functions become more discrete, cross-training becomes more time-consuming, and it is not as easy to ask one staff member to take over the functions of another in an emergency situation.

Conclusion

An appropriately qualified and trained IRB staff can reduce the burden of review for both researchers and the IRB Chair and members. The more responsibility staff members assume, the more responsibility the institution assumes for making sure that they are qualified and able. A high-functioning IRB staff increases the ability of the IRB Chair and members to focus their attention on the business of protecting human research subjects.

Reference

1. Code of Federal Regulations. Title 21, Chapter 1—Food and Drug Administration, DHHS; Part 56—Institutional Review Boards. Updated 1 Apr 1999. Access date 25 Apr 2001. World Wide Web http://www4.law.cornell.edu/cfr/21p56.htm

Appendix: Sample Job Descriptions

Job Description: IRB Administrative Assistant

This position will share responsibility for the administration of the operation of the IRB program with the director. Primary administrative responsibilities include assisting the director and IRB coordinators with implementation of the program to researchers, external researchers, and sponsors.

Job responsibilities include assisting the director and coordinators with the following:

1. Interview, hire, train and supervise IRB staff.

2. Negotiate administrative modifications to existing IRB applications.

3. Perform ethical and technical review of IRB applications meeting criteria for exempt review.

4. Provide consultation, assistance and dissemination of information regarding the review process.

5. Provide information on technical and ethical requirements for conducting research involving human subjects.

6. Provide assistance to researchers to bring proposals into compliance with minimum review standards (screening).

7. Provide assistance with development of written guidelines to improve communication and understanding of human research requirements.

8. Provide assistance with development of written office procedures.

9. Prepare certification of compliance with review requirements for funding agencies.

10. Assist with review of IRB applications eligible for expedited review.

11. Receive adverse effect reports and forward to director and coordinators.

12. Receive close-out reports and review for signature by director.

13. Other duties as requested.

This job requires a person able to learn the program function, skilled in interpersonal relationships, oral and written communication and able to deal with seasonal high volume and rigid deadlines. Computer skills required include data entry, word processing and database management. Attention to detail and research experience are all valuable assets.

Job Description: IRB Administrator

This position will manage the privileged and confidential institutional review and approval process of all proposed research activities involving human subjects to protect their safety, rights, and welfare.

Under administrative direction, the IRB coordinator will serve as a member, with vote, on the Institutional Review Board; will perform highly complex duties to facilitate the review and approval process, such as use of independent judgment in interpreting and applying relevant federal and state laws, regulations, and institutional policies and guidelines; conduct literature reviews and prepare reports on scientific topics and on regulatory precedent and changes; instruct IRB chairs, members, and researchers on the regulations and ethical principles essential to the review process; provide training and advice to faculty, staff, and student researchers on the regulations and on preparation of applications and consent forms; and review and approve administrative and procedural modifications of applications.

Typical Work

1. Serve as ex-officio member, with vote, on IRB(s).

2. Interpret and apply federal and state laws, regulations, institutional policies and guidelines to protect human subjects and to ensure institutional compliance.

3. Conduct literature reviews and prepare reports for the IRBs on scientific, ethical, and existing and proposed regulatory topics.

4. Draft correspondence that conveys IRB deliberations and contingencies for approval of research activities involving human subjects.

5. Signatory authority for certifications documenting IRB approval for funding agencies (federal and non-federal).

6. Independently review correspondence to the IRB; review and approve administrative and procedural modifications; reconcile proposals for funding with approved IRB applications; and facilitate approval for emergency or unique research opportunities.

7. Provide regulatory, ethical, and methodological advice to individual faculty, staff, and students in preparation of applications for research proposals involving human subjects and consent documents.

8. Direct the work of others.

9. Develop and present materials and training programs for faculty, staff, and students on the ethical conduct of research involving human subjects.

10. Provide orientation and training to IRB members.

11. Assist in program development, implementation, and evaluation.

12. Act in the absence of the director.

13. Perform related duties as required.

This job requires a person who can learn the program function, who is skilled in interpersonal relationships and in oral and written communication, and who is able to deal with high volumes and rigid deadlines. Familiarity with research ethics and methodologies and the ability to conduct independent literature research (including Internet-based research) are required. Computer literacy is a necessary skill. A Master's degree and two years applicable work experience or a Bachelor's degree and equivalent education/experience are required. Previous research experience is desirable.

Job Description: IRB Program Coordinator

This position will share responsibility for the coordination of the operation of the IRB program. Primary coordination responsibilities include representation and assistance with implementation of the program to researchers and external researchers and sponsors. Based on experience and knowledge of the program, the incumbent will disseminate information about and assist investigators in the preparation of IRB applications. The incumbent will coordinate the preparation of applications for presentation to the IRBs and will independently determine adequacy of the application and level of review required.

This job requires a flexible person with experience in IRB review, skilled in interpersonal relationships and able to deal with seasonal high volume and rigid deadlines. Computer literacy, word processing, and computer entry skills are required. Attention to detail is a valuable asset. Specific job tasks include:

1. Log in and complete new and renewal applications: computer entry; hard copy entry.

2. Screen new and renewal applications: contact and advise investigators in preparation and completion of application process.

3. Prepare meeting agendas: assign applications to committees; prepare agenda; prepare member packets.

4. Maintain renewal system: prepare tickler report; prepare and mail reminders, forms.

5. Close out applications: prepare final reports for closure.

6. Withdraw applications: prepare applications at several stages of withdrawal.

7. Prepare finalized applications for filing: prepare applications, certifications.

8. Enter information into the computer for: modified applications, adverse effect reports.

9. Prepare subcommittee (biomedical and behavioral) agendas.

10. Prepare final meeting reports for biomedical and behavioral IRBs and subcommittees.

11. Maintain record and filing system: paper and computer-based files.

12. Assist internal and external sponsors to assure human subjects compliance.

13. Provide lead for office assistant, hourly; assign work when necessary.

14. Assist other program coordinators when necessary.

15. Assist IRB coordinators with modifications when requested.

16. Open, date stamp, and sort mail.

17. Answer and refer telephone calls.

18. Filing and copying as requested.

19. Proof and edit IRB correspondence as requested.

20. Coordinate supply orders, physical plant, and other on-campus coordination.

21. Other duties as requested.

Job Description: IRB Director

Has responsibility for implementing university policy and procedures, federal and state statutes and regulations on the protection of human subjects for the university and several of its affiliates. In this capacity, the following duties are performed:

1. Functions as chief administrative and programmatic support for the IRB.

   • Administers policy on the protection of human subjects.
   • Recruits and interviews prospective IRB Chairs and members; makes recommendations to the appropriate department chair for appointments; supervises training and orientation of new members to the technical and ethical literature, appropriate policy, statutes and regulations, and duties as IRB members.
   • Provides technical consultation to IRBs concerning review of ethically and scientifically complex research involving vulnerable client and patient populations and sensitive research.
   • Advises IRB members of review requirements based on policy, regulation, statute, and legal precedent; monitors changes and recommends appropriate revisions in policy and procedures.
   • Represents the university in audits and deliberations with federal, state, and local agencies and organizations.
   • Advises on handling of subpoenas for the release of study data filed against researchers.
   • Supervises ethical and technical review of proposals meeting criteria for exempt and expedited review.
   • Coordinates with grant and contract services regarding compliance on new, continuing, and competing proposals with human subjects regulations and policy.
   • Provides advice on regulatory compliance to deans, directors, chairs, and to the office of the president within the university and to federal regulatory agencies as requested.
   • Maintains liaison with federal regulators.
   • Serves on university-level committees and task forces as required.

2. Provides consultation, assistance, and dissemination of information regarding the review process:

   • Provides information on technical and ethical requirements for conducting research involving human subjects to faculty, staff, and students at all three campuses and affiliate institutions.
   • Provides advice and assistance to researchers to bring proposals into compliance with minimum review standards.
   • Develops written guidelines to improve communication and understanding of human research requirements.
   • Develops and presents formal and informal workshops upon request on the review process in general and on topics of particular interest to university and non-university audiences.
   • Provides liaison with the state legislature and other community agencies on human subjects issues such as privacy and genetic research.
   • Participates in professional conferences and training opportunities to improve knowledge of technical and ethical aspects of research with human subjects.
3. Directs, coordinates, and supervises the administrative and clerical functions of IRB office.

   • Supervises maintenance and updating of database.
   • Prepares annual reports on IRB office activities.
   • Prepares budget recommendations for IRB office; approves expenditures, requisitions, vouchers.
   • Prepares certification of compliance with review requirements for funding agencies.
   • Responsible for hiring, training, evaluating, disciplining support staff; establishes work priorities and deadlines.
   • Provides technical and ethical information to staff members responsible for screening and reviewing applications.
   • Receives and triages adverse effect reports and complaints from subjects and researchers.
   • Attends IRB meetings as necessary.

Minimum requirements: Bachelor's degree in relevant field, Master's degree preferred. At least two years of experience in program administration and personnel management. Computer literacy and word processing skills required. Experience in the conduct of basic or applied health, social, or behavioral research preferred. Demonstrated ability in effective oral and written communication.

Audit Systems

Ernest D. Prentice, Ada Sue Selwitz, and Gwenn S. F. Oki

INTRODUCTION

One strategy for improving the quality of a human subjects protection program is to implement an internal audit process. An audit process can heighten investigator and Institutional Review Board (IRB) awareness of regulatory requirements and improve the ethical conduct of research. Traditionally, IRBs have not had a structured research audit program in place, largely because IRBs were and still are overloaded with work and underresourced. There is now, however, an enhanced Office for Human Research Protections (OHRP) and Food and Drug Administration (FDA) emphasis on maintaining compliance, which has pressured more IRBs to engage in auditing functions. Auditing of research can be a key component of an institution's program for the protection of human subjects.

The purpose of this chapter is to discuss quality improvement in human subject protection through the audit of research and to describe the basic components of a successful audit program. The focus will be on the audit of investigator research records and the corresponding IRB files. This chapter does not describe the procedures for assessing an institution's total human subject protection program, which could include an evaluation of the organization and reporting structure, the infrastructure, written policies, procedures, training, data bases, file records, and overall efficiency. All IRBs, however, can benefit from routine general audits that can be performed using the 1998 *FDA Information Sheets* as a guide.[1] In addition, IRBs may wish to consult the OHRP[2] and FDA[3] Web sites to review citation letters, which can be very instructive.

Regulatory-Based Authority for the Research Audit Program

In 1991, 15 federal agencies and departments adopted the Federal Policy for the Protection of Human Subjects (Federal Policy, also known as the Common Rule). The FDA adopted a modified version of the Common Rule, codified at 21 CFR 50 and 56. For the purpose of avoiding multiple but equivalent regulatory citations, only Department of Health and Human Services (DHHS) and FDA regulations for the protection of human subjects will be referred to in this chapter.

DHHS regulations at 45 CFR 46[4][Sec.109(e)] and FDA regulations at 21 CFR 56[5][Sec.109(f)] state, "An IRB shall conduct continuing review of research covered by this policy [regulation] at intervals appropriate to the degree of risk, but not less than once per year, and shall have authority to observe or have a third party observe the consent process and the research." The IRB is also required by 45 CFR 46[4][Sec.111(a)(6)] and 21 CFR 56[5][Sec.111(a)(6)] to ensure that "when appropriate, the research plan makes adequate provision for monitoring the data collected to ensure the safety of subjects." These provisions grant the institution, the IRB, and/or its representative(s) the authority to audit research.

Institutions that hold an approved OHRP federal-wide assurance (FWA) are required to assure that they have procedures that "include formal mechanisms for monitoring compliance with human subject protection requirements." Research audit programs provide one mechanism for ensuring compliance with this requirement.

Characteristics of a Sound Research Audit Program

A research audit program might include any or all of the following: review of investigator records; monitoring of ongoing research on site; observation of the consent process from initiation to documentation of the subject's consent; and interview of investigators, staff, or subjects. A research audit program should be proactive, nonpunitive, and focused on educating investigators about their ethical and regulatory responsibilities in the conduct of research. It should be designed to promote the institution's research within the current legal, ethical, and regulatory framework. Ideally, the audit program should be accepted, if not embraced, by investigators and their research coordinators. The program should also be as comprehensive as possible, given any limitations imposed by the available staff and resources that can be devoted to audit functions.

Research audit responsibilities may be delegated to the IRB staff and/or IRB members, or a separate but linked office can be set up solely for assessment of the institution's human subject protection program, including the audit of research. The decision about the appropriate assignment of the audit function depends on a number of variables such as the size and nature of the research program, organizational structure of the institution, resources available, and the goals/objectives of the audit program. The focus of the research audit should encompass not only the investigator's research, but also the corresponding IRB records. In other words, every time an investigator's protocol is selected for audit, the IRB's record of the review of that protocol should also be audited. In this way, quality improvement will likely occur across the board.

The Administrative Structure

The administrative structure of a research audit program is obviously dependent on the needs and the nature of the institution itself. Nevertheless, aside from which administrative entity is assigned audit responsibilities, there are certain characteristics that successful research audit programs display. Based on the experience of institutions or IRBs that have initiated research audit mechanisms, the following six principles have proved to be critical to the success of the programs.

1. Develop an organized audit research plan based on immediate objectives and long-term goals that fit the institution and its needs.

2. Obtain administrative endorsement of the research audit program by senior institutional officials, which would include allocation of adequate resources.

3. Ensure that the program is adequately staffed and that personnel involved in the research audit have the requisite scientific and regulatory experience as well as the necessary interpersonal skills.

4. Ensure that the research audit program is proactive and educational in nature. To facilitate this, the audit program should use a positive title, such as "Quality Improvement Program for Human Subjects Research."

5. Ensure that all investigators and their staff are educated about the goals of the research audit program and that they do not feel disenfranchised or disengaged from the audit process. Input from key investigators should be obtained during the development of the audit program.

6. Perform an on-going quality control assessment of the research audit program and make changes as necessary.

The Research Audit Program

In developing a research audit program, institutions or IRBs should consider the following procedures that can be adapted or modified to suit the specific needs of the institution or the IRB.

1. The program should establish the criteria for selecting the studies to be audited. The selection criteria will be impacted by resources available to conduct audits and the nature of the research conducted at the institution or reviewed by the IRB. For example, audit personnel could select categories of research from which a specified number of studies would be audited. Categories that should be considered given the institution's research portfolio include investigational new drug (IND) studies; investigational device exemption (IDE) studies; research involving children, decisionally impaired subjects, or prisoners; research conducted under an emergency waiver of informed consent; research approved by expedited review; and exempt research. Additional examples of criteria that could be used include the following: number of subjects enrolled (e.g., select only studies that have enrolled four or more subjects); IRB approval status (e.g., select only studies that are currently active and received approval during the past three years); and the funding status (e.g., select federally funded studies and drug company–sponsored studies).

2. The audit personnel should carefully review, in advance, the entire IRB file for each protocol selected for audit.

3. The audit should be scheduled at a time convenient for the investigator and his or her research staff. Unannounced audits are generally counterproductive.

4. Investigators should be informed in writing about the research audit including the date, time, place, and protocol(s) selected for audit. They also should be given a description of the audit process and criteria. A comprehensive research audit would normally include a review of the investigator's study records, observation of the consent process, and interviews with both the investigator and his or her research coordinators. Although less typical, some programs even include an interview or survey of research subjects to determine if they understood that they were actually participating in research. If the audit program includes either observation of the consent process or an interview with the subject, procedures should be developed to address protection of privacy and confidentiality. Certainly, the consent form should disclose the possibility of a requested interview as well as IRB and auditor access to the subject's research record and/or medical record.

5. A reasonable time frame should be established for completing the audit and producing the audit report.

6. The role of the institution and/or the IRB in reviewing, approving, or taking further action on the final audit report should be delineated and included in the IRB written procedures.

Mechanics of the Research Audit

The mechanics of a research audit are critical to a successful quality improvement program. The following questions address the criteria that should be used in evaluating compliance. The criteria are based upon the FDA and DHHS regulations that focus the audit on goals of increasing investigator and IRB awareness of regulatory requirements.

Audit of IRB Records

1. Does the IRB file contain all the records required by 45 CFR 46[4(Sec.115)] and 21 CFR 56[5(Sec.115)] in sufficient detail

to demonstrate compliance and performance of a substantive review(s)? These records include the following: IRB application; detailed protocol; investigator's brochure, if applicable; DHHS grant application, if applicable; informed consent/assent forms; consent addenda (e.g., significant new findings); amendments; adverse event or unanticipated problem(s) reports; continuing review reports; all correspondence between the IRB and the investigator; and the relevant IRB minutes.

2. Are the IRB minutes pertaining to the protocol(s) in question sufficiently detailed per 45 CFR 46[4][Sec.115(a)(2)] and 21 CFR 56[5][Sec.115(a)(2)]? For example, the IRB meeting attendance is recorded; the vote on the protocol is recorded (number for, against, and abstaining); and nonparticipation of IRB members with a conflict of interest is documented. The basis for the board's action(s) is recorded, where appropriate. Additional protections for vulnerable subjects are documented as well in accordance with 45 CFR 46,[4][Subparts B, C, D] and there is a reasonably detailed summary of the IRB's discussion of any controverted issues and their resolution.

3. Is the consent form approved by the IRB in compliance with 45 CFR 46[4][Sec.116(a),(b)] and 21 CFR 50?[6][Sec.25(a),(b)]

4. Were the IRB's initial review and subsequent reviews (e.g., amendments and adverse events) and the IRB office's handling of the review timely and efficient?

5. Was continuing review substantive per the requirements of OPRR Report 95-01[7] and the 1998 *FDA Information Sheets*?[1] Was the continuing review conducted within the annual time limit or earlier, as required by the IRB?

6. Were adverse events or other unanticipated problems involving risk to the subject or others promptly reported to OHRP and/or the FDA per the requirements of 45 CFR 46[4][Sec.103(b)(5)] and 21 CFR 56?[5][Sec.108(b)(1)]

7. Was serious or continuing noncompliance promptly reported to OHRP and/or FDA per the requirements of 45 CFR 46[4][Sec.103(b)(5)] and 21 CFR 56?[5][Sec.108(b)(2)]

8. Were IRB review activities conducted under expedited review processes permissible under 45 CFR 46?[4][Sec.110)] Is the expedited review category documented?

9. Was research that was exempted permissible under 45 CFR 46?[4][Sec.101(b)] Is the applicable exempt category documented?

Audit of Study Records

Does the investigator have a comprehensive and secured file containing the following records?

1. The IRB-approved application and detailed protocol

2. The investigator's brochure, if applicable, and the IRB-approved amendments

3. Current IRB-approved stamped copy of the consent form and copies of all IND safety reports, adverse event reports, and other relevant safety information

4. Records of continuing reviews and copies of all correspondence between the investigator and the IRB (e.g., IRB review and approval letters)

Note that all of the above records should also be present in the IRB file.

Did the investigator implement the protocol as approved by the IRB according to the following criteria?

1. The current, IRB-approved version of the consent form was used.

2. The consent form(s) were signed and dated by the subject and by a person authorized to obtain consent.

3. IRB-approved inclusion and exclusion criteria for subject accrual were met.

4. The date of the first intervention(s) is consistent with the date the consent form was signed.

5. All research-related procedures performed are described in the IRB-approved protocol.

6. Subjects received only the approved dose range(s) of the study drug(s), and all adverse events were promptly reported to the IRB.

7. All protocol modifications were implemented only after IRB approval, except when in the immediate medical interest of the subject.

8. The number of evaluable subjects accrued to date is within the IRB approved limit; and the procedures for ensuring confidentiality of data were implemented as approved by the IRB.

Note that the number of individual subject records that should ultimately be audited can vary. If four to six subject records are audited and no major problems are identified, this would normally be sufficient. However, if problems are identified, it would be prudent for the auditors to review additional and perhaps even all the study records. Review of records may include case report forms used in FDA regulated research, original data, and/or pertinent portions of the medical records.

Observation of the Consent Process

1. Was the environment in which the consent process took place conducive to rational and thoughtful decision-making on the part of the subject?

2. Was the length of time devoted to the consent process sufficient?

3. Was the subject given adequate opportunity to ask questions?

4. Was the subject given an adequate explanation of the research using appropriate simplified language?

5. Did the subject demonstrate an acceptable understanding of the research before signing the consent form?

Interviews with the Investigator and Research Personnel

1. Did the investigator encounter any problems in recruitment, subject retention, or other areas? If so, what was the nature of the problem and how was it addressed?

2. Did any subject suffer a serious, unanticipated adverse event? If so, what was the nature of the event and how was the subject treated?

3. Do the investigator and/or research coordinator(s) have any problems with the IRB, IRB staff, or IRB reviews? If so, what are the problems and proposed solutions?

Note: The interview is a time when problems identified during the records review can be discussed and any neces-

sary clarifications obtained. It is also an ideal time to educate the investigator and his or her staff.

Preparation of the Audit Report and Follow-up

The audit personnel should utilize institution-specific forms to record audit findings. (A copy of the forms currently used at the University of Kentucky is presented at the end of this chapter.) After the audit is complete and all findings are analyzed and determined to be valid, a written report should be developed. It should be structured to be proactive and educational in nature by providing comments concerning strengths and recommendations on how deficiencies can best be corrected, with appropriate citations of the federal regulations and institutional policies. The report should be completed in a timely manner, and a copy of the report should be provided to the IRB and/or the institution for review, approval, or initiation of additional action. If evidence of serious or continuing noncompliance is found, this must be promptly reported to the appropriate institutional official and the OHRP per the requirements of 45 CFR 46.[4][Sec.103(b)(5)] Noncompliance must also be reported to the FDA per the requirements of 21 CFR 56.[5][Sec.108(b)(2)] Obviously, such a report will likely be viewed by the investigator with a certain degree of concern and alarm that may interfere with the intended collegiality of the audit. Nevertheless, if such deficiencies are identified, they must be corrected immediately and reported as required.

The audit program should include appropriate follow-up to ensure that deficiencies are corrected in a timely manner. This follow-up may include only a written report of corrective action(s) implemented by the investigator, or it may require additional auditing or monitoring by the IRB. In some cases, it may be appropriate to require the investigator to undergo specific training in order to help him or her achieve the desired level of compliance.

Conclusion

Quality improvement in an institution's program for the protection of human subjects can be achieved through a variety of mechanisms, including audit of research. A research audit program can be an integral component of an institution's efforts to enhance the ethical quality of its research. It can also ensure that compliance with applicable federal and state regulations is maintained. Considering the evolving nature of the ethics and regulation of research, however, the audit program must be progressive, up-to-date, and educational in nature. Indeed, education of the investigator and the IRB with a resultant enhancement of the quality of human subjects protection is the most important product of a research audit program.

Acknowledgment

The authors thank Steve Hansen, Ph.D., for his help in editing this chapter.

References

1. Food and Drug Administration. Information Sheets: Guidance for Institutional Review Boards and Clinical Investigators, Sept 1998. Access date 9 Apr 2001. World Wide Web http://www.fda.gov/oc/oha/IRB/toc.html

2. Office for Human Research Protections. Dear Colleague Letters, 20 Mar 2001. Access date 30 Mar 2001. World Wide Web http://ohrp.osophs.dhhs.gov/dearcoll.htm

3. Food and Drug Administration. A Self-Evaluation Checklist for IRBs, 16 Apr 2001. Access date 2 Aug 2001. World Wide Web www.fda.gov/oc/ohrt/irbs/irbchecklist.html

4. Code of Federal Regulations. Title 45A—Department of Health and Human Services; Part 46—Protection of Human Subjects. Updated 1 Oct 1997. Access date 18 Apr 2001. World Wide Web http://www4.law.cornell.edu/cfr/45p46.htm

5. Code of Federal Regulations. Title 21, Chapter 1—Food and Drug Administration, DHHS; Part 56—Institutional Review Boards. Updated 1 Apr 1999. Access date 27 Mar 2001. World Wide Web http://www4.law.cornell.edu/cfr/21p56.htm

6. Code of Federal Regulations. Title 21, Chapter 1—Food and Drug Administration, DHHS; Part 50—Protection of Human Subjects. Updated 1 Apr 1999. Access date 18 Apr 2001. World Wide Web http://www4.law.cornell.edu/cfr/21p50.htm

7. Office for Protection from Research Risks. Continuing Review—Institutional and Institutional Review Board Responsibilities. Updated 10 Jan 1995. Access date 2 Aug 2001. World Wide Web http://ohrp.osophs.dhhs.gov/humansubjects/guidance/hsdc95-01.htm

University of Kentucky IRB Quality Improvement Program

Objectives

1. Determine if investigators implement protocols as approved

2. Evaluate whether the IRB adequately addressed applicable ethical and compliance issues

3. Identify issues to be addressed in IRB educational/training initiatives

4. Examine the informed consent process to determine if it can be improved (e.g., contact subjects and observe consent process) [To be implemented, 3rd year of project]

Mechanics of Program

Selection Criteria for Identifying Protocols to Be Reviewed
- Federal, state, or industry funded project
- Approved IRB protocol active for more than two years
- Protocol in which subjects have been enrolled
- Exclude exempt IRB protocols
- Ensure one of 12 from nonmedical IRB
- May exclude protocols that are subject to ongoing agency audits (other than FDA)

Frequency/Number per Year: One per month

Personnel: To be conducted with one IRB member and one ORI staff member
- ORI and IRB member conduct PI record review and interview
- ORI and IRB member review IRB minutes
- ORI reviews IRB and Sponsored Projects records
- ORI prepares summary report; reviewed by IRB and PI

Data to Be Reviewed to Meet Each Objective

Objective One: Determine if investigators implement protocols as approved
- Randomly select four subjects (or all of the subjects if less than four subjects were enrolled). For each subject, review the following:
  - Determine whether the approved inclusion/exclusion criteria were met
  - Determine whether the signed consent forms were current
  - Compare date of informed consent with date of first procedure
  - Determine whether the approved dose ranges of the study drug were administered
  - Review procedures to determine if consistent with protocol
- Discuss recruitment procedures with Investigator
- Compare list of subjects from Investigator with continuation review report for consistency
- Determine whether all of the amendments were reported before change implemented
- Determine whether adverse reactions were reported in a timely manner
- Determine how many subjects were screened

Objective Two: Evaluate whether the IRB addressed the appropriate regulatory and ethical issues
- Review meeting minutes to assess ethical issues raised by IRB and compliance requirements
- Review consent form to determine whether it complies with federal regulations
- Determine whether ORI file contains all amendments and adverse reactions the investigator submitted
- Determine whether IRB review was timely and ORI met Customer Service Standards
- Determine whether continuation review was completed within 365 days (or more often if appropriate)
- Compare grant submissions and progress reports/research descriptions and continuation review reports in ORI and Sponsored Projects files for consistency

Objective Three: Identify issues to be addressed in IRB educational initiatives
- Review findings based on PI and IRB inspections

Form included by permission from the University of Kentucky Office of Research Integrity.

University of Kentucky IRB Inspection Forms

Date of Inspection: _____

Reviewer(s) : _____   _____

IRB #: _____ PI: _____

Title of Study: _____

Funding Source: _____ Grant/Award # _____

A. Study Progress

Are all the study records available for review?   YES _____   NO _____

Do the study records appear to be in order and up-to-date?   YES _____   NO _____

Comments: _____

Do the study records reflect the protocol was followed?   YES _____   NO _____

Comments: _____

Is there documentation to support PI/Co-PI involvement in approved
procedures?   YES _____   NO _____

Comments: _____

_____

Research conducted at any other sites?   YES _____   NO _____

Study currently closed to enrollment?   YES _____   NO _____

Have there been deviations during the course of the study?   YES _____   NO _____

Have these deviations been reported to the IRB appropriately?   YES _____   NO _____

Any complaints noted in study documents or subject patient records
that pertain to study implementation?   YES _____   NO _____

If YES, describe below:

_____

_____

B. Modification Review Process

Number of modifications listed in Investigator's records: _____

Does this match the IRB file?   YES _____   NO _____

Modifications submitted and approved before implementation?   YES _____   NO _____

If NO for either question, explain findings:

_____

_____

(Continued)

C. Continuation Review Process

Date of last CR: _____ # Subjects approved for enrollment: _____ # Enrolled: _____

Reported number of subjects consistent with last CR report?   YES _____   NO _____

Of subjects screened: _____ # Of subjects withdrawn: _____

Rationale for subject withdrawal:

_____

_____

Do amendments to study protocol & consent listed on last CR match
investigator study records?   YES _____   NO _____

If NO, comment:

_____

_____

D. Reporting of Adverse Events

Of AEs: _____   # Matches IRB file: YES _____   NO _____

Were the AEs submitted in a timely fashion?   YES _____   NO _____

Is there a Data Safety Monitoring Board for this study?   YES _____   NO _____

SUBJECT RECORDS

Date of inspection: _____   Subject #_____

IRB #:_____   PI:_____

Subject Enrollment

Does the subject meet inclusion/exclusion criteria?   YES _____   NO _____

If NO, describe discrepancy between approved I/E criteria and subject: _____

_____

Consent Process

Who obtained informed consent? _____

Were these individuals of the study team approved by the IRB?   YES _____   NO _____

What is the date the initial consent form was signed?   _____

What is the date of the first research procedure?   _____

Dates of any additional reconsent(s)?   _____

                _____

Is the consent process documented in the research records?   YES _____   NO _____

Is there documentation to support PI / Co-PI involvement in the   YES _____   NO _____
consent process?

Is there a consent form for the subject enrolled?   YES _____ NO _____

Was the IRB-approved form used?   YES _____ NO _____

Is the consent form appropriately signed and dated?   YES _____ NO _____

Is there any indication in the study records that a copy of the
consent document was provided to the subject?   YES _____ NO _____
Comments on any observed deviations:

Research Procedures

Is the date of the first procedure after the date the consent form
was signed?   YES _____ NO _____

Were the procedures implemented as approved by the IRB?   YES _____ NO _____

Were the procedures for this subject documented in the study records?   YES _____ NO _____

Is there documentation that either the PI or Co-PI saw the subject
during the scheduled visits or reviewed the study records for the visits?   YES _____ NO _____

Reviewers' comments:

_____

_____

_____

_____

_____

_____

_____

_____

_____

Reviewers' Signature(s):

_____

Reviewers' names typed: _____

_____

University of Kentucky Office of Research Integrity

ORI CHECKLIST: [Form Used in Reviewing IRB and Sponsored Project Files]	
IRB MINUTES:	
Appropriate ethical issues addressed?	
Appropriate "special findings" documented?	
Quorum?	
Necessary members (lay, M.D., etc.)	
Vote?	
IRB FILE:	
Investigator brochure/detailed protocol included?	
Funded? By whom?	
Consent forms were stamped with the correct dates?	
IRB file contains all amendments that occurred?	
ORI and PI sides correspond?	
ORI responded in a timely manner?	
ADRS submitted in a timely manner?	
All modifications affecting GIS were entered?	
All requested revisions were addressed by PI?	
CR - Number of subjects enrolled ≤ approved?	
CRs consistent with each other? (i.e., earlier CR does not indicate more subjects enrolled than a later CR)	
CR timely?	
Modifications to CF remained in later submissions when appropriate?	
Sponsored Projects file consistent with IRB file? (compare the initial submissions for both files)	
Consent form contains all necessary elements?	

Timeliness of Review Record Form

A =   Amendment
ADR = Adverse Reaction
CR =   Continuation Review
IDB = Investigator Drug Brochure
CF =   Consent Form

TYPE: A, ADR, or CR REQS CHANGE OF CF? CF CHANGED AS NEC?	ORI: Action date (letter)	PI: 1st date stamp (letter)	COMMENTS:

Form included by permission from the University of Kentucky Office of Research Integrity.

Charging for IRB Review

Ernest D. Prentice, Sally L. Mann, and Bruce G. Gordon

INTRODUCTION

This chapter will explore the issue of charging a fee for local Institutional Review Board (IRB) review. Concern has often been expressed that if IRBs are not adequately funded, these institution-based oversight boards will be unable to successfully carry out their federally mandated responsibility to protect the rights and welfare of research participants. In 1978, the National Commission for the Protection of Human Subjects of Biomedical and Behavioral Research recommended that IRBs receive direct funding as opposed to relying on support from indirect cost mechanisms.[1] Unfortunately, the commission's recommendation was not implemented.

In the 1980s, many academic medical center (AMC) IRBs began to experience problems related to inadequate staffing and operational budgets. Institutions, however, were generally not very sympathetic to the needs of the IRB, which largely remained unmet. Consequently, the possibility of charging an IRB review fee for commercially sponsored research was explored by an increasing number of IRBs. After consideration of a review fee as a form of supplemental funding for their IRBs, some AMCs then decided to implement such a fee. The common prevailing concern at the time, however, was one of fear that institutions that charged for IRB review would be less competitive for award of commercial contracts than those that did not charge. In addition, some IRB members expressed concern that charging an IRB review fee would create a conflict of interest that, in turn, could bias IRB reviews at worst and raise questions about the board's objectivity and independence at best. Thus, during the decade of the 1980s, there was little movement in the direction of charging for IRB review.

As the clinical research enterprise moved into the 1990s, most AMCs experienced a significant increase in their research volume. This, in turn, exerted even more pressure on IRBs, which found themselves without the necessary staffing and resources to effectively handle the workload. IRB review turn-around times were often inordinately slow, and protocol reviews were all too often characterized as overly cumbersome. It was, therefore, not surprising when commercial sponsors began relying, more than ever before, on physicians in the private sector to conduct many of their clinical trials. This, in turn, created an increased demand for the services of independent IRBs, which operated in an efficient business mode and, obviously, charged for their reviews. Questions about conflict of interest were invariably raised, but no data were ever presented to substantiate such concerns.

By the mid-1990s, many AMCs were suffering from the budgetary throes of managed care. The Balanced Budget Act of 1997 generally resulted in reductions in net clinical income.[2] AMCs struggled to remain fiscally sound, and downsizing or mergers were common. At the same time, the workload of their IRBs grew because of increased research and escalating compliance requirements from the Office for Protection from Research Risks (OPRR) and the Food and Drug Administration (FDA). In the face of restricted budgets and inadequate resources, AMC IRBs across the country began to examine or reexamine the issue of charging for IRB review. Support for initiating such a fee was indirectly provided by the Office of the Inspector General (OIG), which called attention to the critical shortage of IRB resources.[3] While the same concerns expressed previously about charging for IRB review were still present, opposition was clearly not as strong. Many IRB members, research administrators, and investigators began to realize that when an IRB charges a review fee, the quality and integrity of its review are not compromised, commercial sponsors do not object to paying a reasonable review fee, and institutions that charge for review are no less competitive. Indeed, charging commercial sponsors for IRB review has become the norm and is no longer the exception. Although there are no data to indicate the percentage of IRBs that charge a review fee, it is reasonable to suggest that most AMC IRBs either currently charge a review fee or will do so in the near future.

The IRB Review Fee

A number of limited and unpublished surveys of IRB review fees have been conducted during the past five years. Data obtained in a 2000 survey indicate that AMC IRBs typically charge between $500 and $2000 for initial review with an average fee of $1,130.[4] Most IRBs charge only for initial review, although some IRBs also charge a fee for continuing review and amendments. The data also indicate that IRB review fees are routinely increased over time. For example, the University of Nebraska Medical Center (UNMC) IRB began charging a review fee of $650 in 1995, which was increased to $700 in 1998 and to $1250 in 2001. Finally, it should be noted that it is not uncommon for institutions with a clinical trials office (CTO) to charge a fee to offset the costs of reviewing and processing the contract. An unpublished survey of 32 institutions conducted by the UNMC CTO in 2000 indicates that 50% of institutions surveyed have a CTO fee and the average fee is $1500.

Collection of Fees

It is not surprising that institutions employ various methods of collecting IRB review fees. For example, some institutions collect fees from investigators up front, before IRB review, whereas other institutions bill the investigator on completion of the initial review but before final approval is granted. In the latter case, final approval may be contingent on actual receipt of the fee or receipt of a promissory note from the investigator payable on establishment of the research account. Some institutions, however, bypass the investigator and directly bill the commercial sponsor, either up front or on completion of the IRB review. Other institutions rely on the investigator to directly bill the sponsor. Regardless of which collection method an institution chooses to use, it is imperative that if a review fee is assessed, it should be collected routinely, even when an IRB chooses to disapprove a protocol. It is obviously inappropriate to collect a fee only if the protocol is ultimately approved. However, it is also desirable for institutions to allow a waiver of the IRB review fee for studies funded by small contracts or grants or when there are extenuating circumstances. The point is that the IRB fee should never be an obstacle to the conduct of important research. IRB policy regarding the IRB review fee should clearly provide for waiving of the fee when it would create a meaningful obstacle to research conduct.

Preservation of the IRB Budget

Budget cutting is a way of life at many institutions. The IRBs that generate revenue by charging for reviews should be wary of the possibility that the administration of the institution may find it easier to cut its support of the IRB during financially hard times. This, in turn, may ultimately force an IRB to rely too much on the money generated from review fees to carry out little more than the basics of its daily operation. Therefore, it is extremely important for the IRB to have an adequate and ongoing budgetary commitment from the institution without excessive reliance on review fees. In this age of enhanced emphasis on maintaining compliance, no institution can afford to underfund its IRB.

Conclusion

Charging an IRB review fee for commercially sponsored research is a common way for an IRB to supplement the operating budget provided by the institution. Sponsors do not object to paying reasonable IRB review fees, and the additional revenue can be used by the IRB to improve the quality and efficiency of its service. Clearly, an adequately resourced IRB is a benefit to the sponsor as well as to the institution, its investigators, and, most importantly, the subjects who participate in research.

References

1. National Commission for the Protection of Human Subjects of Biomedical and Behavioral Research. Report and Recommendations: Institutional Review Boards. (OS)78-0008. 1978. Washington, D.C., Department of Health, Education, and Welfare.

2. 105th Congress. Balanced Budget Act of 1997. Public Law 105-33. 5 Aug 1997. Access date 2 Aug 2001. http://www.access.gpo.gov/nara/publaw/105publ.html

3. Office of Inspector General. Institutional Review Boards: A Time for Reform (OEI-01-97-00193), June 1998. Access date 27 Mar 2001. World Wide Web http://www.dhhs.gov/progorg/oei/reportindex.html

4. Office of Research. Fees for IRB Review—Baylor College of Medicine. Access date 2 Aug 2001. World Wide Web http://research.bcm.tmc.edu/Whats_New/whats_new.html

PART 3

Organizing the
IRB Committee

Reflections on Chairing an IRB

Robert J. Levine

INTRODUCTION

In 1961 I accepted the invitation of Dr. Paul Beeson, Chair of the Department of Medicine at Yale University School of Medicine, to leave the National Institutes of Health (NIH) to be chief resident at the Yale-affiliated Veterans Administration Hospital in West Haven, CT. About eight months later, when I was preparing to move to West Haven, I was stricken with anxiety. I did not have the slightest idea of how to be a good chief resident. My principal role model was Dr. Buris Boshell, who had been chief resident in medicine at the Peter Bent Brigham Hospital when I served on that service as an intern. (Actually, in those days we were called "house officers.") He gave me much good advice. I will now adapt the advice he gave me on being a good chief resident to make it fit the job of IRB Chair. In principle, it is almost the same. Most importantly, he said that I should always strive to "make molehills out of mountains."

Solve Problems When They Are Small

Always be alert to detect problems when they are so small that almost nobody else has noticed them. Small problems that are not satisfactorily dealt with have a tendency to become larger problems. When they get large enough that many others can recognize them, the range of options available to the Chair for their resolution is often diminished.

Handle each problem at the lowest permissible level in the administration of your institution. The regulations require that you report serious or continuing noncompliance by investigators to appropriate institutional officials and to the federal government. After you have detected a problem early—one hopes before it becomes serious—you should try to resolve it before it becomes necessary to report it. If it is necessary to report it, you should send a letter to the deviant investigator with a copy to his or her immediate supervisor. With physician–investigators, this usually means the section or division chief. Your letter should state why the copy is being sent to the section chief and that, if it is necessary to send another to the same investigator, a copy of that one will go to the next level, usually the department chair. Now you have two individuals working with you to prevent future noncompliance. Also, by limiting the scope of the embarrassing exposure, you preserve the possibility that these two people—the investigator and the section chief—will be motivated in the future to work with you as colleagues.

Assemble the Right Team

Surround yourself with people who are highly intelligent and devoted to doing the work of the IRB. This, of course, includes a high quality staff and IRB members. It also should include many other members of the institution's faculty, staff, and students. When an IRB has a high degree of credibility within its community, one sees the development of rather extensive *informal monitoring systems* in the form of unsolicited reports by students, physicians, nurses, and others. An IRB without credibility is not likely to have this large network of volunteers assisting it. Payment of equally efficient and effective replacements, if such could be found, would be very expensive.

The IRB chair should see to it that the IRB staff and its members have an adequate degree of familiarity with the applicable federal, state, and local laws and regulations. While they should be conversant with the major themes in the regulations, they should be allowed to rely on one or two of their fellow members to provide the detailed knowledge needed to resolve some difficult issues. There is no need to make the cardiologist–member an expert on the law. By the same token, the lawyer does not need to have an intimate knowledge of cardiac electrophysiology. The layperson–members should be assured that each and every IRB member is a part of the laity with regard to the specialties of some or all others. They should work together in a climate of trust that each will contribute according to his or her abilities to the overall function of the IRB.

The IRB Is an Agent of Its Own Institution

Even though it is necessary to be sufficiently familiar with relevant law to avoid inadvertent violations, an effort should be made to promote within the institution the attitude that the IRB is an agent of its own institution; its purpose is to uphold the value system of the institution. Respect for persons, beneficence, and justice are (or should be) principles that your institution values greatly and not just because they were once published in the *Federal Register*. IRBs began to function in most institutions before the *Belmont Report* was published in 1978 by the National Commission for the Protection of Human Subjects of Biomedical and Behavioral Research.[1] Historical evidence suggests that in the 1960s (even earlier in many institutions), the forerunners of IRBs were conducting their business as if they were being responsive to basic ethical principles. In passing, it is worth recalling that Congress instructed the National Commission to identify the ethical principles that should underlie the conduct of research involving human subjects—identify, not invent.

Don't Blame the Feds for IRB Policy and Practices

IRB personnel should scrupulously avoid saying, in effect, "Don't blame us for enforcing these rules; it's all the feds' fault." Such statements diminish the credibility of the entire system. The IRB that relies on this "justification" for its decisions loses its ability to make decisions that are not explicitly required by federal regulations. IRBs have the authority and responsibility to be able to exercise judgment in making their decisions; they should exercise this authority wisely and be willing to be held accountable for their decisions.

Treat Researchers as Trusted Colleagues

The authority of the IRB to monitor the activities of investigators should be exercised with great caution. There is generally not much of a problem with conducting "for-cause" audits. An effort should be made to bring "whistle-blowers" into the process of investigating the complaint; in this way, they can be satisfied that you are taking their complaints seriously. For-cause audits should begin with an assumption that there is a misunderstanding, perhaps a miscommunication, and not that someone has violated institutional policy. Every aspect of the IRB's interaction with its community should be grounded in the belief that all participants in the research process can be trusted—at least until the accuracy of any contrary evidence is confirmed.

Routine audits are more problematic. It is very difficult to avoid projecting an attitude of distrust in the investigator. To the extent that such audits are perceived in the community as similar to the audits of the Internal Revenue

Service, there is an increasing probability that the IRB will be treated like the IRS in its dealings with the investigators. This would essentially close down the informal monitoring system.

Continuing Education

IRB chairs and members should be conversant with the major themes in the current commentary on research ethics, particularly those that have a bearing on the interpretation and revision of the policies and practices of IRBs. There are some concepts in the field that do not have precise definitions. For example, what is a "minor increase over minimal risk?" Even though there is no clear definition of this standard, we can learn by reading reports of actual decisions reached by IRBs in their consideration of actual cases. By reading such cases, we learn that IRBs consider as a minor increase the risk attached to such procedures as lumbar punctures and bone marrow biopsies; it is less than the risk presented by liver biopsies.

I suppose you are thinking, "How can I possibly keep up with the current deluge of information?" You cannot. It is necessary to be selective. The most reliable sources of information on the policies and practices of IRBs and the underlying rationale for them are peer-reviewed periodicals. Authoritative sources of current policies and practices of federal regulators are the information sheets and other documents prepared by the federal regulators for the guidance of IRB members. Some books are very helpful and some are not. Those that are well documented by references to peer-reviewed literature tend to be more reliable than the others.

The spontaneous contributions of individuals in such places as Internet chat groups tend, in general, to be less reliable. While some good information is made available in such forums, many Internet offerings are incorrect facts or idiosyncratic opinions. One needs a high level of expertise to distinguish the wheat from the chaff.

What about going to conferences designed for the continuing education of IRB members? Again, there are good ones and bad ones. I think those presented by PRIM&R are clearly the best. But as I am a member of its Board of Directors, what else would you expect me to say?

Conclusion

Chairing an IRB is a demanding job. To function optimally, an IRB chair should focus on achieving six fundamental goals:

1. Solve problems when they are small.
2. Assemble the right team.
3. Support the concept that the IRB is an agent of its own institution.
4. Don't blame the federal government for IRB policy and practices.
5. Treat researchers as trusted colleagues.
6. Make continuing education a priority.

Reference

1. National Commission for the Protection of Human Subjects of Biomedical and Behavioral Research. *The Belmont Report: Ethical Principles and Guidelines for the Protection of Human Subjects of Research.* (DHEW (OS) 78-0012. Washington DC: U.S. Government Printing Office, 1978. Access date 22 Mar 2001. World Wide Web http://ohsr.od.nih.gov/mpa/belmont.php3

The IRB Chair

Robert J. Amdur and Robert M. Nelson

INTRODUCTION

The person who directs the proceedings of an organized meeting is referred to as the *Chair, Chairman,* or *Chairperson.* The word *Chair* may be used as a noun or a verb. When used as a noun, the words *Chair, Chairman,* and *Chairperson* are synonyms. Therefore, it is correct to say either "The Chair called the meeting to order" or "The Chairperson called the meeting to order." *Chair* may also be used as a verb to describe the act of directing the meeting process: "Dr. Jones chaired the IRB meeting." The purpose of this chapter is to discuss the role and responsibilities of the IRB Chair in the overall IRB organization.

Different Models for the IRB Chair

The roles and responsibilities of the IRB Chair vary widely across the IRB community. Some IRB Chairs direct every important aspect of the IRB process, many share decision-making responsibility with other members of the leadership team, and some view their job to be limited to directing the full IRB committee meeting. Recognizing that many different options are possible, it is conceptually useful to discuss the role of the IRB Chair in terms of two basic models.

Director of the Full-Committee Meeting

An important responsibility of an IRB Chair is to direct the full-committee meeting. Specific tasks are discussed below. The job of directing meeting discussions, keeping the membership focused on the established agenda, and reminding IRB members of the basic guidelines for the IRB meeting procedure is critical to the process of full-committee protocol review. Although all IRB Chairs take primary responsibility for directing discussion at the full-committee meeting, some view this as the only absolute requirement of the Chair position. In our view, it will be difficult for an IRB to function optimally without additional leadership from its Chair.

An IRB may function well with a Chair whose role is limited to that of a meeting director if other members of the organization provide expertise in, and take responsibility for, the other activities that are required for the IRB to function properly. IRB members may understand the ethical issues associated with the studies they review well enough to make excellent decisions without insight from the IRB Chair. In some organizations, the IRB administrative director is the best person to direct the overall IRB process, establish IRB policy, evaluate compliance with federal research regulations, and interact with other segments of the research and administrative community. Some organizations employ an attorney (separate from the IRB administrative director) specifically to instruct the IRB about federal research regulations and to represent the IRB in policy decisions that involve other segments of the organization. At some institutions, administrators—such as the director of sponsored research, vice president for research administration, or dean of research—make decisions about the process of research regulation with or without input from the IRB and IRB Chair. Within this model, an IRB Chair does little more than direct the full-committee meeting.

Comprehensive IRB Professional

All IRB Chairs are expected to direct the full-committee IRB meeting. In many organizations, the IRB Chair also is expected to play a major role in other areas of the IRB system. For the sake of this discussion, the term *comprehensive IRB professional* is used to describe the model where the IRB Chair is expected to provide expertise and leadership in a wide range of areas related to IRB function. Discussion with IRB Chairs and administrative directors at several busy research organizations suggests a similar group of expectations for the IRB Chair.

Responsibilities of the IRB Chair

1. The Chair should play a leadership role in establishing and implementing IRB policy. As a primary representative of IRB decisions, the IRB Chair should have shared authority over all IRB policy and procedures in collaboration with the institutional official and/or IRB administrative director.

2. The Chair should represent the IRB in discussions with other segments of the organization.

3. The Chair should represent the organization in discussions with federal authorities.

4. The Chair should review all protocols presented to the full-committee. The IRB Chair is expected to have read each full-committee protocol and to communicate with other reviewers so that important IRB issues are resolved or identified before the full-committee meeting. For example, at the University of Washington, the IRB Chair is formally listed

as the primary or secondary reviewer for all full-committee protocols.

5. The Chair should direct the proceedings and discussion of the full-committee meeting. This includes keeping the discussion focused on important IRB issues and seeing that the full-committee meeting process is both efficient and effective.

6. The Chair should vote at the full-committee meeting. Most IRB Chairs routinely vote on protocols at the full-committee meeting. However, there are experienced IRBs that use a process where the IRB Chair serves as a full-committee IRB member, but does not vote at the full-committee meeting (personal communication with Ernest Prentice, University of Nebraska, November 2000). This is discussed in more detail in Chapter 5-15.

7. The Chair should have an in-depth understanding of the ethical issues, state law, institutional policy, and federal research regulations that are applicable to studies that are reviewed by the IRB. The IRB Chair is not expected to be the only, or ultimate, authority on compliance issues. The IRB administrative director or other members of the IRB organization also take responsibility for compliance verification, but the IRB Chair is expected to be an active and knowledgeable partner in this aspect of the IRB system.

8. The Chair should assist IRB administration in the drafting of letters from the IRB to researchers regarding IRB decisions.

9. The Chair should review and sign IRB response letters in a timely fashion.

10. The Chair should review and make decisions about responses to conditions for IRB approval of research in a timely fashion. In some situations, this task is shared with the IRB administrative director.

11. The Chair should serve as the reviewer for research that is reviewed by an expedited process. This task is often shared with other members of the IRB, depending on expertise.

12. The Chair should represent the IRB in defending or discussing IRB decisions with researchers.

Skills, Qualifications, and Time Commitment

Meeting Skills
At a minimum, the IRB Chair should have the leadership and management skills to direct discussion at the full-committee meeting. Ideally, the IRB Chair would have experience chairing similar kinds of meetings, but this should not be an absolute requirement. The ability to foster open and collaborative discussion among IRB members while maintaining a directed focus on the issues at hand is an important skill for the IRB Chair.

Interpersonal Skills
To be effective, an IRB Chair should be able to interact under difficult circumstances with people from many different backgrounds and levels of experience. In most settings, the IRB functions with the culture of a volunteer committee such that it will not be productive for the IRB Chair to force the membership into functioning a certain way. Making good IRB decisions in an efficient time frame requires that IRB members discuss issues in an atmos-

phere that encourages new insights and trust. It is not easy to maintain an atmosphere that promotes consensus on the issues that are critical for the IRB to evaluate. An IRB Chair whose interpersonal style leads to tension or disorganization will inhibit the IRB review process.

An IRB Chair must work closely with the IRB administrative director and other administrative staff under conditions that involve time pressure and other stressful influences. Each group will have its own dynamics, but optimal IRB function requires that all members of the IRB leadership work as a team to improve the protection of human research subjects and operate the IRB in compliance with all applicable laws and regulations. It will be difficult for the IRB to function well if the IRB Chair and administrative director do not work well together.

Another challenge to the IRB Chair's interpersonal skills lies in his or her interactions with researchers. In many organizations, the IRB Chair is expected to discuss IRB concerns with protocol directors in moderately contentious situations that may develop between the IRB and the research community. This is often a difficult job under the best of circumstances, and an IRB Chair with the wrong background or weak interpersonal skills will not be able to manage things in a way that leads to an environment that promotes the conduct of ethical research.

Leadership and Respect
It is important for the IRB Chair to have a background and reputation that encourage respect from both the IRB membership, the administration, and local researchers. The respect of the IRB membership is a precondition of the role of the IRB Chair in directing the full-committee meeting, but the respect of administration and researchers is also extremely important. To have a meaningful impact on the protection of human subjects, the IRB must promote a culture of respect for the IRB process and for issues related to research ethics. It is difficult to do this if researchers do not respect the IRB leadership, especially the IRB Chair. For this reason, it is important for the IRB Chair to be a person who is able to command the respect of most of the research community. The IRB Chair should be recognized as an authority on the protection of human research subjects. To this end, it is highly desirable for the IRB Chair to have a strong background, knowledge, and expertise in research involving human subjects.

An IRB Chair who is familiar with the practical aspects of the type of research that the IRB will be reviewing will be able to focus the IRB on the important ethical issues and support the view of the IRB as a respected member of the peer-review process. Although there are other attributes that engender respect, it may be helpful if the IRB Chair is or has been actively involved in clinical research in the community where the IRB reviews research. While this is not the case with many respected IRBs, it is a factor that will tend to improve the effectiveness of an IRB. While having a researcher in a leadership position on the IRB may appear to create a conflict of interest, the rote application of this line of thinking fails to appreciate the importance of an IRB Chair's reputation to the effectiveness of an IRB. An IRB Chair who is a respected colleague of local researchers is likely to facilitate the ability of the IRB to make difficult decisions and will enhance respect for the IRB within the research community.

Profession

For the IRB Chair to possess the requisite knowledge and expertise, it may be desirable to have the IRB Chair be from the same profession as the majority of researchers who will interact with the IRB. If the IRB reviews only social science research, the IRB Chair should be an accomplished social scientist. Similarly, if the great majority of full-committee reviews involve psychology research, then it will be useful for the IRB Chair to be a psychologist. If the IRB mainly reviews nursing research, then it would be ideal to recruit an accomplished nurse–researcher to be the IRB Chair. For IRBs that review a large volume of biomedical research conducted by physicians, it is important to appoint a physician as the IRB Chair. As discussed in other chapters, the situation where a single IRB reviews both social and biomedical research may present some challenges related to respect for the IRB process. In this situation, it may be desirable to have an individual IRB member, or subcommittee of IRB members, from the appropriate field of expertise as the primary reviewers for research protocols that are directed by investigators who are from a field of research that is very different from that of the IRB Chair. Whether the focus is the IRB Chair or the overall IRB committee, everyone must possess sufficient knowledge and expertise either individually or as a group to be able to conduct an effective protocol review and to communicate that review to researchers in a manner that engenders respect for the IRB process and decisions.

Time Commitment

The time commitment required to serve as an IRB Chair will depend on the volume of IRB activity that the Chair is responsible for and the model of responsibility of the Chair position. Reliable data on IRB staff-volume relationships are not available for the IRB Chair (or support staff). Based on the experience of the authors and conversations with Chairs and administrators of IRBs that operate in a variety of research environments, it is possible to make some general statements about the time commitment that is required for an IRB Chair to function as a comprehensive IRB professional.

A minimum of five hours per week is required for an IRB Chair to direct an IRB that conducts a full-committee review of approximately 200 new protocols per year. This volume of full-committee reviews (~200/year) usually means that there are approximately 25 full-committee meetings per year and approximately 1000 active full-committee protocols in the IRB office at any time. Depending on the process for expedited reviews and IRB correspondence, an IRB Chair of such a committee would likely spend one full day per week on IRB business. In addition, the IRB Chair may serve on other committees in the organization that serve to coordinate the various activities that fall under the more general human subjects

protection program, such as clinical trials support, compliance oversight, and other research administration.

It is common for university faculty to discuss professional commitments in terms of a unit called an FTE, which stands for "full time equivalent." IRB Chairs in charge of IRBs that review approximately 200 new protocols per year likely spend 0.15–0.25 FTE on work directly related to their role as IRB Chair. At institutions where the IRB Chair receives salary support for IRB service, salary support at the 0.15–0.3 FTE level is not unusual.

Continuing Education

For IRB Chairs who are expected to function as comprehensive IRB professionals, continuing education will be a requirement of the job. Federal research regulations are constantly being revised, and the interpretation of existing regulations is a rapidly evolving process. Most IRBs review research that presents a wide range of complex ethical issues. IRBs are under increasing demand to function more efficiently in an environment of limited resources. All of these factors require that the Chair of the IRB attend to the disciplines of research ethics and research regulation as to his or her other fields of work. To stay informed, most IRB Chairs need to read journals and reference books that specifically deal with IRB issues. Another important source of information is discussion with other members of the IRB community, especially other IRB Chairs. IRB Chairs should plan to attend a national IRB-related meeting at least once every two years. The IRB Forum (known as MCWIRB) is useful for exchanging ideas and understanding norms of IRB practice. Contact information for organizations that have information about IRB meetings and the IRB Forum (MCWIRB) Web site are presented in Part 11 of this book.

Academic Rank

An institution must assure that the IRB is able to function in an independent and credible manner. As such, at some academic institutions, professorial rank may be an important factor to consider when choosing or accepting the position of an IRB Chair. (The standard categories in ascending order of accomplishment are assistant professor, associate professor, and professor.) Another factor to consider is whether a faculty member's appointment is tenured. In the standard academic model, tenure is given with the appointment to associate professor.

Academic rank may be important for the IRB Chair for two reasons. First is the issue of respect, as previously discussed. Academic rank usually parallels seniority and academic accomplishment. In general, therefore, a full professor will have an easier time than an assistant professor in gaining the respect of local researchers and IRB colleagues.

A related, but different, issue is job security. When an IRB is functioning properly, it is not unusual for the IRB to make decisions that are unpopular with powerful researchers or upper-level administrators. An IRB Chair with a junior or intermediate academic rank may be concerned that unpopular IRB decisions will compromise chances for promotion in the future. If this is an important factor, an institution should consider whether high academic rank—preferably full professorship with tenure—should be a requirement for the IRB Chair.

There are no data on the influence of academic rank on the behavior of IRB Chairs. In the authors' experience, most junior IRB Chairs are not concerned that unpopular IRB decisions will negatively impact the chance that they will be promoted in the future. IRB Chairs from every academic rank explain that the most important factor is to have support for the IRB process from upper-level administrators and a culture of respect for the IRB process. There are IRB Chairs at the assistant or associate professor level who routinely support unpopular IRB decisions and policy that may increase the protection of human research subjects.

Another aspect of the academic rank is the negative effect that serving as IRB Chair may have on academic productivity. As discussed above, serving as an IRB Chair is likely to require a major time commitment, on the order of 0.2–0.3 FTE. For many faculty members, a commitment of this magnitude will come at the expense of teaching, research, or other activities that have traditionally been required for academic promotion. In our opinion, performing well as the IRB Chair should be viewed as an important academic accomplishment on par with getting a major research grant, publishing important papers, or directing an innovative education program. However, it is important to recognize that many promotion committees currently do not give much weight to committee service, including chairing the IRB.

Therefore, when a junior or mid-level faculty member is a candidate for chair of the IRB, it is important to consider the effect that the time commitment associated with this service will have on the chance of academic promotion in the future.

Conclusion

The IRB Chair is responsible for ensuring protection of human research subjects through the appropriate development and implementation of IRB policy and procedure. In addition, the IRB Chair must engender respect for the IRB process by possessing the necessary knowledge and expertise about research practices, ethics, and regulations. The leadership role of the IRB Chair within an institution thus requires that the IRB Chair has at least shared authority over IRB policy and procedure in collaboration with other institutional officials. Some institutions limit the IRB Chair to the role of directing the full IRB committee meeting, with other functions divided among different administrative positions. Although such a system can function effectively in protecting human research subjects, the lack of a strong institutional leadership role for the IRB Chair is likely to reduce the overall effectiveness of the IRB in promoting a culture of respect for and compliance with human subject protections. The IRB Chair, like the position of the IRB administrative director, should be considered a professional position that requires a comprehensive set of knowledge, skills, and expertise as outlined in this chapter.

The IRB Administrative Director

Elizabeth A. Bankert and Robert J. Amdur

INTRODUCTION

From discussions at national IRB meetings and Internet forums, it is clear that the responsibilities of the IRB administrative director are currently not uniform throughout the country. At one end of the spectrum, the IRB administrative director is expected to function as a comprehensive IRB professional with an in-depth understanding of federal research regulations and the ability to direct or manage all aspects of the IRB process. At the other end of the spectrum are organizations where the IRB administrator acts more as an executive secretary with a limited scope of responsibilities that focus on procedural aspects of IRB work. Specific recommendations are made throughout this chapter. The role of the IRB administrator should be that of a knowledgeable and respected partner in the leadership of an organization's overall system for regulating research. In the past few years, the organization ARENA (Applied Research Ethics National Association) has established a national certification program for IRB administrators. This certification effort requires that an IRB professional master a core knowledge base that includes a detailed understanding of federal research regulations and accepted ethical standards (see Chapter 8-13). In this chapter, we discuss specific responsibilities that IRB administrators have in organizations where the IRB administrator is expected to function as a comprehensive IRB professional.

Partnership with the IRB Chair

The role of the IRB Chair was discussed in Chapter 3-2. In most organizations, the responsibilities of the IRB Chair and administrator will overlap in important areas. For an IRB to function optimally, the IRB Chair and administrative director(s) must be able to work well together on issues ranging from policy creation to the management of routine committee functions. Open communication between the Chair and administrator must exist in an atmosphere of mutual respect and support that facilitates productive leadership. In some situations, the IRB administrative director will have a better understanding of the issue, while in others the IRB Chair will be more experienced. The ability of IRB leadership to work together as an administrative team will determine the efficiency and effectiveness of the IRB process. Each relationship will have its own chemistry. The important thing is that both IRB administrators and the IRB Chair understand the importance of a partnership in advancing the mission of the IRB.

Establish Compliance with Federal Research Regulations

In organizations that are committed to operating in compliance with federal regulations, the IRB administrative director should be an expert in all regulations that apply to the IRB review of research conducted by the organizations with which the IRB works. Federal regulations that apply to most of the settings in which IRBs function are promulgated by the Department of Health and Human Services (DHHS) and the Food and Drug Administration (FDA). Other agency regulations also apply in some instances. DHHS regulations related to the IRB are described in 45 CFR 46[1] and a National Institutes of Health (NIH) guidance document.[2] FDA regulations related to the IRB are found in four areas: 21 CFR 50,[3] 56,[4] 312,[5] and 812.[6] These regulations are discussed in more detail throughout this book, and some are reproduced or referenced in Part 11.

Understanding, interpreting, and documenting compliance with research regulations are extremely complex and important responsibilities of the IRB leadership. Many IRB administrative directors are expected to be the organization's main authority on the regulations pertinent to the IRB and to be sure that the IRB is operating in full compliance with them. This is certainly the case at most of the institutions that direct IRB educational programs and play a leadership role in establishing IRB policy at the national level.

Regulatory Issues

At the other end of the spectrum is the situation where regulatory issues are primarily the responsibility of someone other than the IRB administrative director. Organizations that do not expect the IRB administrative director to be an authority on the regulations may turn to the IRB Chair for this function. However, they more commonly hire an attorney with specialized expertise in this area (see Chapter 3-4, The Role of an Attorney). In some organizations, an attorney who is not a member of the IRB committee or administrative office directs IRB policy, procedure, and important aspects of the full-committee meeting. There are organizations that require a consultant attorney to attend each IRB meeting to help the Chair identify important ethical issues for discussion. In addition, the attorney instructs the IRB on the criteria for approving research in specific situations and directs the administrative staff (including the IRB administrative director) on how to document things appropriately. With this kind of authority structure, the role of the IRB administrative director is similar to that of an executive secretary. It is certainly possible for multiple people connected with the IRB to understand pertinent research regulations. However, we do not know of IRB administrators with an in-depth understanding of research standards who operate in an organization where they are not responsible for regulatory issues every day.

We strongly endorse an organization where the IRB administrative director is an expert on policy and regulations that relate to the details of IRB function. In our experience, it often is not possible to correctly apply research standards without an in-depth understanding of the practical aspects of the process of research review for a specific IRB. The IRB administrative director is likely to understand the operational issues the IRB faces better than someone who is peripherally associated with the IRB. In addition, it is the IRB administrator who must manage operational issues every day. An organization in which the IRB administrative director is not an expert in the federal regulations that direct the IRB process is likely to be without the kind of leadership that all IRBs need to function optimally. Educational resources for IRB administrative directors are discussed later in this chapter.

Promote the Image of the IRB as a Partner in the Research Process

As discussed in Part 1 of this book, the best systems for protecting the rights and welfare of research subjects include a culture of respect for the IRB process. Our current IRB system is a direct extension of the review committees that were organized throughout the country by local investigators in an effort to evaluate ethical aspects of their research. The relationship between the IRB and local researchers was never meant to be adversarial, and it is important to recognize that the ability of the IRB to influence the conduct of research will be limited if this is the case.

It is desirable to have members of the local research community on the IRB so that the IRB understands local research standards and has the necessary expertise to evaluate research in specific areas. For a regulatory system to be productive, the IRB must understand the practical aspects of research conduct, and local researchers must understand the operational process of the IRB. Having local researchers on the IRB facilitates this kind of information transfer and helps to solidify the connection between the IRB and the research community. An organization where the IRB is viewed as a bureaucratic obstacle to the advancement of science has a problem with its system for protecting research subjects. Both researchers and the IRB must approach their work from the point of view that the role of the IRB is to facilitate the conduct of important research according to the highest of ethical standards.

The Importance of Functioning as a Partner

An IRB that understands the importance of functioning as a partner in the research process will interact very differently with researchers, unlike the IRB that views itself as an obstacle that researchers should overcome if they want to conduct research. An IRB that is trying to facilitate research will be as "user friendly" as possible from the administrative standpoint. To emphasize the attitude that should drive the way the IRB interacts with researchers, prominent IRB administrators have urged the IRB office to view itself as a "research service center," which actively assists the researcher in going through the IRB review process. Some IRB offices routinely help the research team write the consent document and prepare the IRB application package. Some IRB administrators spend an enormous amount of time and energy in the days before each full-committee meeting, relaying concerns of IRB members to researchers in an effort to resolve issues that could lead to a delay in protocol approval. Recommendations along these lines were published in the spring 2000 issue of the ARENA newsletter. The section is titled *Twelve Practical Hints for IRB Administrators*.[7] Nine of these points address the way the

IRB administrative office should interface with the research community.

1. It should promote an environment that fosters honest feedback from investigators and research staff about the IRB at the institution. Can the office provide better service in accordance with federal regulations?

2. It should ask the investigators to consider the IRB as a collaborator in the research.

3. It should remain flexible. Each protocol may be slightly different. Policies and procedures need to be adaptable.

4. It should let investigators know when an IRB policy changes. It should not wait until it reviews a specific protocol to advise the investigator that a policy has changed or been implemented.

5. It should consider involving investigators in discussions about establishing new policies and procedures.

6. It should be available and encourage an open-door policy. It should work with investigators, not against them.

7. It should offer to attend departmental meetings for question-and-answer sessions.

8. It should discuss IRB issues with other areas of the institution (like pathology or medical records) in a joint effort.

9. When referencing a policy or practice to investigators, it should help them understand the rationale behind the policy. This helps eliminate the stereotype of a "bureaucratic, paper-pushing office."

Later in this chapter, we discuss the factors to consider when deciding if the IRB administrative director, or other members of the IRB administrative staff, should serve as a voting member of the IRB. The reason to mention this issue here is that a main argument against an IRB administrator's serving on the IRB is that it may compromise his or her ability to assist researchers in preparing IRB applications.

Develop and Implement IRB Policy

The IRB administrative director should play a major role in establishing or modifying IRB policies and procedures. In most situations, the IRB administrator will work with the IRB chair and/or other members of the organization on policy issues. A good IRB administrator will constantly be looking for ways to improve IRB function and therefore will frequently be the one to suggest policy changes. Examples of situations where the IRB administrative director should play an important role in establishing policy include staffing requirements of the IRB office, criteria for classifying a project as research, the format of the IRB minutes, the forms required for documentation of IRB activities, management of adverse event reports, and standard wording in the consent document.

Provide Expertise to Other Segments of the Organization

The IRB is not the only segment of an organization that affects research conduct. In most situations it will be desirable to have close communication between the IRB leadership and other segments of the organization that make policy that may influence research conduct or regulation. In many situations it will be important for the IRB administrative director to be part of interdepartmental policy discussions. In some cases the IRB administrative director should provide expertise in the capacity of a consultant, whereas in others it will be appropriate for the IRB administrator to serve on committees that evaluate issues that may affect the IRB. Interdepartmental responsibilities that IRB administrators have at many university-based organizations include the following:

1. Advise the medical director's office regarding policy related to professional credentials and research activity

2. Advise risk management and compliance officials regarding institutional policies related to research

3. Advise the medical records department or information services on issues related to privacy and confidentiality of health information

4. Serve as a member of the confidentiality committee

5. Serve as a member of the hospital or university ethics committee

6. Advise the clinical trials office on a wide range of policy issues

7. Advise undergraduate and graduate course directors on standards for research conducted by students

8. Advise the hospital tumor registry on issues related to access to information for research

9. Advise the cancer center data monitoring committee on the IRB requirements for approval of research

10. Advise the grants and contracts office regarding issues related to payment for research services and conflicts of interest

11. Advise the department of pathology on standards and procedures for access to tissue specimens for research

Represent the Organization in Discussions with Federal Authorities

Federal authorities may evaluate an organization's research program in response to concern about a specific issue or as part of a routine compliance audit. When a federal regulatory agency has questions about research, it is common for the IRB to be a focus of the discussion. In responding to questions related to the IRB, the IRB administrative director commonly plays a major role in drafting the response and assists another member of the organization (the IRB chair, an institutional official, etc.) with this process. In some interactions, the IRB administrative director will be required to speak to federal officials to explain aspects of the IRB system. For all of these reasons, it is important for the IRB administrative director to understand how to document compliance with the regulations related to the IRB. In addition, documentation must be to a degree that allows the organization to demonstrate a high level of competence in interactions with federal authorities.

Administration of the IRB Office and IRB Meetings
The IRB administrative director is the primary person responsible for managing the IRB office and many of the administrative aspects of IRB meetings. These responsibilities are discussed in detail in separate chapters.

Triaging Research Between IRB Review Categories

In many organizations, the IRB administrative director and the IRB Chair share the responsibility for determining when a project should be classified as research, when new research projects should be considered exempt from further IRB review, or when research may be reviewed by the expedited versus full-committee process. Similarly, the IRB administrative director frequently shares the responsibility for determining when it is appropriate to use an expedited procedure to review a revision to an approved protocol. When triaging projects, the IRB administrator should always act within the limits of his or her expertise. In view of the complexity of many medical and social science protocols, it will frequently be necessary for the IRB administrator to refer triage decisions to the Chair or other designated IRB member.

Approving Research with Expedited Review

In addition to the responsibility for determining the appropriate mechanism for IRB review of research, IRB administrators may have the authority to approve certain kinds of revisions. These are for approved protocols that meet the regulatory criteria for expedited review.[2] To approve research by the expedited procedure, the IRB administrator must be designated to function in this capacity by the IRB Chair. In addition, the administrator must be an experienced IRB reviewer and a current member of the IRB committee.[1][Sec.110(b)(2)] For IRBs that use a subcommittee for the expedited review procedure, it is not usual for the IRB administrator to be a member of this group.

Serving as a Voting Member of the Full Committee

Experienced IRB administrators disagree on whether the IRB administrators should serve as voting members of the full committee. When experienced IRB administrators, including several who have directed IRBs at multiple different institutions, were asked for their recommendation on this subject, half of the administrators believed strongly that IRB administrators should serve as voting members for two main reasons. First, an IRB administrator is extremely knowledgeable about research regulation. This expertise is of value to the IRB in making decisions about specific research projects. Second, not serving on the IRB decreases the respect that IRB members have for the IRB staff, especially when it comes to suggesting ways to improve IRB function: "If you don't play the game, you can't make the rules."

Other experienced administrators strongly believed that IRB administrators should not serve on the full committee, also for two main reasons. First, a major role of the IRB administrative staff should be to help the research team prepare its application for IRB review. The IRB administrator should be viewed as an important member of the research team, and to some degree must be an advocate for its proposal. By clearly separating the role of the IRB office from the role of the IRB committee, the IRB can be user-friendly from the administrative standpoint without compromising the ethical standards for approving re-

search conduct. Second, administering the IRB and working with researchers is a full-time job. Serving on the IRB demands a considerable amount of time and energy. The mission of the IRB is compromised by anything that distracts IRB administrators from their core responsibilities.

Oversee IRB and Researcher Education Programs

Federal regulations require a structured educational program for IRB members regarding ethical standards and fundamental guidelines for IRB approval of research. In many settings, federal regulations and/or local policy requires similar instruction for researchers and upper-level administrators who are responsible for research conduct. Educational requirements and programs related to the IRB are discussed in Part 8 of this book.

In many organizations, the IRB administrative director is responsible for organizing educational programs related to research regulation. In some cases, IRB administrators teach the sessions, while in others the administrator arranges for someone else (the IRB chair, an outside consultant, etc.) to lead the program. In most organizations, the IRB office is responsible for documenting compliance with educational requirements for IRB members. To accomplish this task it is important that the IRB administrative director understands the expectations of the federal agencies—mainly the DHHS Office for Human Research Protections—that establish the standards for IRB compliance in this setting.

Continuing Education for the Administrative Director

The scope and complexity of the job of an IRB administrative director require that the person in this position devote a considerable amount of time to continuing education. The standards for efficient and effective IRB function are rapidly evolving. New regulations are being promulgated and existing regulations are constantly being interpreted in new ways by oversight agencies. A comprehensive list of reference material and contact information related to IRB issues is provided in Part 11 of this book. The form and frequency of education should vary with the individual IRB administrator and the research environment in which the administrator works. Many accomplished IRB administrators consider the following four measures foundational to their continuing education program:

1. Membership in an organization specifically geared to the operational aspects of the IRB process. We recommend the organization called Applied Research Ethics National Association (ARENA). The ARENA newsletter is particularly useful for learning about practical aspects of IRB administration.[8]

2. A subscription to the journal *IRB: A Review of Human Subjects Research*.[9]

3. Attendance, at least once every two years, at the annual meeting organized by the organizations Public Responsibility in Medicine and Research (PRIM&R) and ARENA. This joint meeting is specifically geared to IRB administrative directors and IRB Chairs.[10]

4. Some administrators find that the Internet service MCWIRB is a useful way to discuss ideas with experienced colleagues.[11] However, as Levine emphasized in Chapter 3-1 of this book, users of MCWIRB should understand that there is no organized quality control regarding the accuracy of the

advice given in this setting. IRB administrators should discuss their situation with experienced IRB authorities before making important changes in their work habits based on MCWIRB advice.

Conclusion

The responsibilities of the IRB administrative director are currently not uniform throughout the country. At one end of the spectrum, the IRB administrative director is expected to function as a comprehensive IRB professional with an in-depth understanding of the federal research regulations and the ability to direct or manage all aspects of the IRB process. At the other end of the spectrum are organizations where the IRB administrator acts more as an executive secretary with a limited scope of responsibilities that focus on procedural aspects of IRB work. This chapter has explained the responsibilities that it is appropriate for the IRB administrative director to assume. In the authors' opinion, the role of the IRB administrator should be that of a knowledgeable and respected partner in the leadership of an organization's overall system for regulating research.

References

1. Code of Federal Regulations. Title 45A—Department of Health and Human Services; Part 46—Protection of Human Subjects. Updated 1 Oct 1997. Access date 18 Apr 2001. World Wide Web http://www4.law.cornell.edu/cfr/45p46.htm

2. Office for Protection from Research Risks, NIH, DHHS. Protection of human subjects: categories of research that may be reviewed by the Institutional Review Board (IRB) through an expedited review procedure. *Fed Register* 63(216):60353, 9 Nov 1998. Access date 3 Aug 2001.World Wide Web http://frwebgate.access.gpo.gov/ cgi-bin/getdoc.cgi? dbname=1998-register=&docid= fr09no98-109

3. Code of Federal Regulations. Title 21, Chapter 1—Food and Drug Administration, DHHS; Part 50—Protection of Human Subjects. Updated 1 Apr 1999. Access date 18 Apr 2001. World Wide Web http://www4.law.cornell.edu/cfr/21p50.htm

4. Code of Federal Regulations. Title 21, Chapter 1—Food and Drug Administration, DHHS; Part 56—Institutional Review Boards. Updated 1 Apr 1999. Access date 27 Mar 2001. World Wide Web http://www4.law.cornell.edu/cfr/21p56.htm

5. Code of Federal Regulations. Title 21, Chapter 1—Food and Drug Administration, DHHS; Part 312—Investigational New Drug Application. Updated 1 Apr 1999. Access date 18 Apr 2001. World Wide Web http://www4.law.cornell.edu/cfr/21p312.htm

6. Code of Federal Regulations. Title 21, Chapter 1—Food and Drug Administration, DHHS; Subchapter H—Medical Devices; Parts 800 through 898. Updated 1 Apr 1999. Access date 18 Apr 2001. World Wide Web http://www4.law.cornell.edu/cfr/21p800.htm

7. Twelve practical hints for IRB administrators. *ARENA Newsletter.* Spring 2000. Boston, MA, ARENA.

8. Applied Research Ethics National Association (ARENA). Updated 25 Jul 2001. Access date 3 Aug 2001. World Wide Web http://www.primr.org/arena.html

9. The Hastings Center. IRB: *A Review of Human Subjects Research.* Updated May 2000. Access date 3 Aug 2001. World Wide Web http://www.thehastingscenter.org/irbindex.htm

10. Public Responsibility in Medicine and Research (PRIM&R). Updated 18 Jul 2001. Access date 3 Aug 2001. World Wide Web http://www.primr.org

11. The IRB Discussion Forum (MCWIRB). Updated 21 Feb 2001. Access date 3 Aug 2001. World Wide Web http://www.mcwirb.org/

The Role of an Attorney

Susan Nicholson

INTRODUCTION

When organizing a new Institutional Review Board (IRB) or evaluating the operation of an existing one, the following question may arise: Does this committee need an attorney? Assuming that question is answered in the affirmative, further questions may follow: Should the attorney attend the meetings of the committee, or simply serve as a resource to the committee? If the attorney attends the meetings, should he or she do so as a voting member of the committee? Does it matter whether the attorney is employed by the organization that operates the IRB or by another organization, such as an independent law firm?

There is no regulatory requirement that IRB membership include an attorney. Thus, an IRB that lacks an attorney is not out of compliance with the federal regulations for the protection of human subjects as it would be, for example, if the committee lacked a scientist or a nonaffiliated member. Nonetheless, an attorney can play a key role in helping an IRB stay in compliance with all applicable laws and regulations.

The section that follows sets out three different models of how an attorney might function in this regard. Because the choice of model may affect whether an attorney should be a committee member or should be employed by the institution that operates the IRB, these issues also are discussed briefly.

Three Models of the Role of an Attorney

The three models described below differ with respect to the manner in which the specialized skills and knowledge of an attorney are utilized and relied upon by an IRB.

Model 1—The Analytical Attorney

Legal education and training are designed to equip attorneys with certain analytical skills and habits of mind. Ideally, an attorney is able to construct logical arguments, identify hidden assumptions, apply principles to complex fact patterns, evaluate opposing arguments in an objective manner, summarize and weigh evidence, and express findings and conclusions in a cogent manner. These skills are content-neutral. Consequently, they can be applied in a variety of contexts, even when the attorney has limited knowledge of the underlying science or applicable regulatory framework.

A few examples may serve to illustrate how these skills can be helpful in an IRB context. In a committee discussion of whether a particular protocol presents more than minimal risk, an attorney might be helpful in reminding the committee to refer back to the language of the regulatory definition of minimal risk. The attorney can also summarize the evidence for the conclusion that the study does, or does not, exceed minimal risk. An attorney who participates over time in a committee's risk/benefit analysis might help ensure that the analysis takes place within a consistent framework. For example, if the committee excludes indirect benefits from the risk/benefit analysis on some occasions but includes them on others, an attorney may press for a more consistent treatment or may suggest a principled distinction between different types of indirect benefits. In a discussion of possible investigator noncompliance, an attorney might be helpful to the committee in avoiding a precipitous judgment and in suggesting a reasonable process for gathering the relevant evidence for subsequent consideration by the committee.

Because the analytical skills involved are content-neutral, the functions previously described can be performed by an attorney even if the attorney practices in a specialized area of the law—such as tax or trusts and estates—that has little substantive relevance to IRB operations. To apply these skills effectively, the attorney should possess a genuine interest in research and human subject protections. He or she must be willing to spend the time required of every committee member to acquire a basic familiarity with relevant ethical principles and federal regulations. Obviously, not every attorney possesses the analytical skills in question, together with an interest in human subject protections. Conversely, many individuals—including scientist–members of the committee—who possess such skills and interest are not attorneys. Consequently, a committee does not have to have an attorney in order to bring analytical rigor to its deliberations. Nonetheless, this is one area in which attorneys frequently make a valuable contribution.

Model 2—The Attorney as Advisor on Ancillary Legal Matters

In Model 1, an attorney contributes content-neutral skills to assist the committee in making reasoned judgments. In Models 2 and 3, an attorney contributes substantive knowledge in areas relevant to the operation of the IRB.

It can reasonably be expected that the administrator and Chair of the IRB and, to a lesser extent, IRB members will be familiar with the core federal regulations. The regulations specify the responsibilities of an IRB for protecting human subjects of research. These core regulations consist of the federal Common Rule (45 CFR 46)[1] and the related regulations issued by the federal Food and Drug Administration (FDA) at 21 CFR 50 and 56.[2,3] To implement these core regulations, however, it is necessary to understand certain other laws and regulations with which IRB leadership and members may not be familiar. IRBs frequently rely on an attorney for guidance on these ancillary legal matters. Several examples follow.

To apply the federal regulations protecting children involved as subjects in research, the IRB must know who is considered a child. This is a matter of state law and varies from state to state. Moreover, a person who is below the general age of majority in a particular state may nonetheless be considered by that state to be an adult for certain purposes. In some states, for example, a person below the age of majority can admit himself or herself to a mental health facility for treatment. In the state of Massachusetts, although 18 years is the age of majority, a drug-dependent minor, 12 years of age or older, may consent to treatment for drug dependency (except for methadone maintenance therapy). In addition, a person of any age is considered to be an adult in respect to consenting to a treatment, should he or she be the parent of a child (in which case he or she may also consent to medical care of the child). An IRB may rely on an attorney to know these laws and provide guidance on the extent to which they apply in a research context.

The federal regulations provide that research may not begin until consent has been obtained from the research subject or the subject's "legally authorized representative." The question of who is legally authorized to consent to treatment of persons unable to consent for themselves—for example, a legal guardian, health care attorney, conservator, or next-of-kin—is again a matter of state law. In some states, moreover, there is no single answer to the question, as the appropriate legal representative may depend on the type of treatment proposed. In the state of Massachusetts, for instance, a legal guardian cannot consent to administration of antipsychotic drugs to an incompetent patient unless there has first been a judicial hearing to evaluate the risks and benefits of the proposed treatment. Once it has been determined who the legally authorized representative is for purposes of consent to treatment, the question remains as to whether this representative is also authorized under state law to consent to investigational treatment or to nontherapeutic interventions for research purposes.

The two previous examples illustrate situations in which the IRB needs an understanding of state law in order to make an appropriate application of the core federal regulations for the protection of human subjects. State laws and regulations may themselves contain human subject protections that go beyond those found in the core federal regulations.

For example, the laws of several states, including Massachusetts, prohibit or limit research on fetuses. Because of the way in which the Massachusetts legislature defines the term *fetus,* the prohibition also limits neonatal research. State laws or regulations may also place special limits on, or prescribe special procedures that must be followed before, conducting research on certain classes of subjects, such as persons who are mentally ill, mentally disabled, or incarcerated. To discharge its responsibility to protect human subjects of research, an IRB must be aware of these state laws and regulations as well.

Still other state laws that do not address research directly may have an indirect impact on it. State laws may, for example, limit the circumstances in which a hospital is permitted to disclose medical record information outside the institution, or prescribe the content of a consent form for the performance of genetic testing. IRBs considering research projects that involve the collection of medical record information or the collection of human tissues for genetic testing may need legal guidance as to the content of these laws and their application to research. Massachusetts has a statute that strictly protects the confidentiality of HIV test information. This law has been interpreted by the relevant state agency as prohibiting access by researchers to HIV records without explicit patient consent, even if the researcher is on the medical staff of the hospital that maintains the records.

Finally, certain federal laws and regulations contain human subject protections that go beyond those found in the core federal regulations. The new federal privacy regulations issued under the Health Insurance Portability and Accountability Act (HIPAA) of 1996 are a case in point. The privacy rule specifies the information that must be included in any informed consent for the use or disclosure of protected health information for research purposes, and the criteria that must be satisfied in order for an IRB to waive the requirement to obtain an informed consent. These topics are, of course, also addressed by the Common Rule. In both respects, the privacy regulations go beyond the Common Rule, requiring the disclosure of additional information and the satisfaction of additional criteria. Consequently, when reviewing medical records research, the IRB must have knowledge of and meet two separate sets of regulatory requirements.

All of the examples given above involve state and federal laws and regulations that are ancillary to the core federal regulations. To reach appropriate judgments about particular protocols, IRBs need reliable advice about these ancillary laws and regulations. To the extent that an IRB relies on an attorney to provide this advice, the attorney is functioning under Model 2.

The attorney's role in Model 1 can be performed by an attorney from any practice area. Model 2 requires substantive legal knowledge and is best performed by an attorney who practices in a specialized area, such as health law.

Model 3—The Attorney as Advisor on the Core Federal Regulations

In Model 1, an attorney contributes content-neutral skills to the committee's deliberations. In Models 2 and 3, the attorney contributes substantive knowledge in particular areas of the law relevant to those deliberations. The distinction between the latter two models is that in Model 2, the committee relies on the attorney's knowledge of federal and state laws and regulations that are ancillary to the core federal regulations. In Model 3, the committee relies on the attorney's specialized expertise with regard to the core regulations themselves.

Because the core federal regulations are not lengthy or complex, one may ask why any specialized expertise is necessary. The answer is that the federal regulations are not self-interpreting. Accordingly, the federal government has issued interpretations of the regulations in the form of guidances or guidelines covering a wide range of topics with which IRBs are expected to be familiar.

To take a simple and straightforward example, anyone reading the Common Rule knows that IRBs are required to conduct continuing review of research not less than once a year. Unless one has also read the guidances on continuing review, issued by the FDA and by the federal Office for Protection from Research Risks (OPRR) (the predecessor agency to the Office for Human Research Protections [OHRP]), one would not be aware of the information that the government expects IRBs to review in order for continuing review to be considered substantive and meaningful. Nor would one know that OHRP interprets the one-year approval period as beginning on the date the research is reviewed by the convened IRB, not the subsequent date on which the IRB Chair determines that the research, having met IRB-specified conditions of approval, can begin.

Because the government's interpretations are issued in the form of guidelines, IRBs are not legally bound by them. Nonetheless, an IRB that is unaware of the guidelines and thus unable to provide a reasoned explanation for deviating from them risks being found to be out of compliance with the core federal regulations for the protection of human subjects. See "OHRP Compliance Activities: Common Findings and Guidance."[4(findings 5,7)]

Another example comes from innovative research involving xenotransplantation, the transplantation or implantation into a human subject of live cells, tissues, or organs from a nonhuman animal source. Because the core federal regulations were issued before the development of xenotransplantation, they make no mention of it. Consequently, one must be familiar with the detailed guideline on infectious disease issues in xenotransplantation issued on March 12, 2001, by the federal Public Health Service (PHS).[5] One would otherwise be unaware

of the additional elements of informed consent that are, in the opinion of the PHS, required to obtain an adequate informed consent from research subjects undergoing xenotransplantation. (The PHS is, like the FDA, part of the federal DHHS.) More importantly, one would be unaware that in the view of the PHS, an institution conducting xenotransplantation research cannot adequately protect human subjects unless the institution's biosafety committee and animal care and use committee, as well as the IRB, review and approve the research. In light of the PHS guidelines, an IRB reviewing xenotransplantation research would be well advised to condition final approval on receipt of the necessary additional committee approvals.

Similar guidelines, imposing additional IRB and institutional responsibilities, have been issued with respect to certain categories of human gene-therapy research. (See "NIH guidelines for recombinant DNA and gene transfer," October 2000.[6]) As new areas of research are developed, one can expect the federal government to address the human subject protection issues they raise not by amending the Common Rule, but by issuing specialized guidances.

An IRB reviewing a moderate to high volume of research will regularly encounter protocols involving the federal guidances listed above. For such an IRB, consequently, a thorough understanding of the broad range of government guidances is a necessity. An attorney who provides specialized expertise to an IRB in this regard is functioning under Model 3.

To be effective in this role, an attorney should have experience in advising IRBs as well as comprehensive knowledge of the relevant literature. One need not be an attorney to have this specialized expertise. Rather than relying on an attorney, an IRB might look to its Chair or administrator for the necessary expertise. What is important is not who fills this role, but that someone does.

The discussion above addresses an IRB's need for specialized expertise with respect to the government's interpretations of the Common Rule as reflected in published guidances. Not all provisions of the Common Rule requiring interpretation are the subject of federal guidances. The Common Rule gives rise to a number of interpretative questions that remain the topic of considerable controversy and discussion, and about which the government has not yet formulated any guidance.

An example is the question discussed in the most recent report of the National Bioethics Advisory Commission (NBAC) entitled *Ethical and Policy Issues in Research Involving Human Participants*.[7] The NBAC asks whether an IRB should analyze study risks in relation to the study benefits of a study as a whole, or whether they should analyze separately the therapeutic and nontherapeutic components of the study. Another example is the question of how an IRB should conceptualize the possibility of benefit in Phase 1 studies. A related question is whether, under the Common Rule, an IRB can approve Phase 1 research on children where the research involves more than a minor increase over minimal risk.

An attorney who is functioning under Model 3 may be helpful in developing best practices for the IRB in such controversial areas. An attorney who serves in this capacity should be familiar with the recommendations contained in the various reports on IRBs and human subject protections that have been issued by the DHHS Office of Inspector General (OIG) and the NBAC.

Finally, an attorney who functions under Model 3 should also be familiar with the recent government suspensions of IRB activity at certain major academic institutions. The attorney will be able to assist the IRB in assessing its own performance against the shortcomings identified at those institutions.

Structuring the Attorney's Role

The three models just described are not meant to be mutually exclusive. An attorney whose knowledge of ancillary legal issues enables him or her to function under Model 2 can also be helpful to the committee by applying analytical skills to the committee's deliberations (the role of an attorney under Model 1). A health law attorney who has developed the specialized expertise in the core federal regulations necessary to function under Model 3 is likely also to be knowledgeable about state and federal law matters that are ancillary to those regulations (Model 2). Consequently, an IRB that wants an attorney in all three roles does not need three attorneys.

Assuming an IRB has decided that it wants one or more of the three roles described above to be filled by an attorney, further questions arise.

Should the Attorney Attend the Committee Meetings?

An attorney cannot contribute analytical skills to a committee's discussions unless the attorney is present to hear them. Under Model 1, then, the attorney should attend committee meetings.

If the attorney's primary contribution is knowledge of ancillary legal matters as described in Model 2, it is preferable, but not essential, that the attorney attends committee meetings. If the attorney does not attend, some issues will possibly be missed. If, for example, no one on the committee is aware that a state law limits fetal experimentation, no one will know to ask if a particular protocol falls under an exemption to that law. An experienced committee, on the other hand, may be able to recognize the protocols that raise ancillary legal issues. In these circumstances, it may be sufficient to have an attorney available outside the meeting for consultation when necessary.

For IRBs reviewing a moderate to high volume of research, every committee meeting will involve some protocols to which specialized expertise on the core federal regulations is directly relevant. Generally speaking, an IRB that relies on an attorney to provide the specialized expertise described in Model 3 will need that attorney to be present at meetings.

Should the Attorney Be a Voting Member of the IRB?

The lawyer's role in Model 1 is consistent with the ordinary functions of a committee member. Lawyers who function in this capacity frequently serve as nonscientific or nonaffiliated voting members of the IRB. In Models 2 and 3, the IRB relies on the professional advice of a lawyer with regard to the interpretation of laws and regulations. Consequently, the relationship is usually structured as an attorney/client relationship, in which case the lawyer represents, but is not a member of, the IRB.

Should the Attorney Be an In-House or Outside Attorney?

If the attorney's role is limited to the functions described in Model 1, it would probably not be an efficient use of the time of an in-house counsel. Such roles are usually filled by volunteer lawyers from the community who, while practicing in other areas of the law, have a special interest in research and human subject protections.

The lawyer's role in Models 2 or 3 could be filled equally well by an attorney employed by the institution that operates the IRB (an in-house attorney) or by a paid lawyer from outside the institution. Some commentators have suggested that the use of outside counsel is preferable, as in-house attorneys might identify too closely with the institution's financial interest in having research go forward or, conversely, may be unduly concerned with protecting the institution from potential liability. Outside counsel, however, are retained by the institution and so are not ultimately immune from these same pressures. To the extent that the institution's priorities are properly aligned to promote research that protects the rights of research subjects, it should not matter whether the IRB is represented by in-house or outside counsel.

Conclusion

The expertise of an attorney is an important resource for the IRB. There are three basic models of the role of an attorney with the IRB. In Model 1 the attorney provides an analytical perspective on IRB issues that other committee members may lack. In Model 2 the attorney acts as an advisor on ancillary legal matters such as the legal definition of a child or the definition of a legally authorized representative from the standpoint of surrogate decision making. In Model 3 the attorney acts as an advisor on the core federal regulations. For an IRB to function optimally, it is important that the committee understand the potential value of input from an attorney and that an attorney assigned to the IRB understand the role that it is expected to play in the review of research involving human subjects.

References

1. Code of Federal Regulations. Title 45A—Department of Health and Human Services; Part 46—Protection of Human Subjects. Updated 1 Oct 1997. Access date 18 Apr 2001. World Wide Web http://www4.law.cornell.edu/cfr/45p46.htm

2. Code of Federal Regulations. Title 21, Chapter 1—Food and Drug Administration, DHHS; Part 50—Protection of Human Subjects. Updated 1 Apr 1999. Access date 18 Apr 2001. World Wide Web http://www4.law.cornell.edu/cfr/21p50.htm

3. Code of Federal Regulations. Title 21, Chapter 1—Food and Drug Administration, DHHS; Part 56—Institutional Review Boards. Updated 1 Apr 1999. Access date 27 Mar 2001. World Wide Web http://www4.law.cornell.edu/cfr/21p56.htm

4. Office of Human Research Protections. OHRP compliance activities: Common findings and guidance. Updated 1 Sep 2000. Access date 20 Apr 2001. World Wide Web http://ohrp.osophs.dhhs.gov/nhrpac/mtg12-00/finguid.htm

5. Public Health Service. PHS guideline on infectious disease issues in xenotransplantation. Updated 12 Mar 2001. Access date 8 Aug 2001. World Wide Web http://www.fda.gov/cber/gdlns/xenophs0101.htm

6. National Institutes of Health. NIH guidelines for research involving recombinant DNA molecules. *Fed Regist* 65(196):60327-60332, 2000. Access date 14 Sep 2001. World Wide Web http://www4.od.nih.gov/oba/rac/guidelines.html

7. National Bioethics Advisory Commission. Ethical and policy issues in research involving human participants: Report and recommendations. Bethesda, MD, U.S. Government Printing Office. Updated 20 Aug 2001. Access date 31 Aug 2001. World Wide Web http://bioethics.gov/human/overvol1.html

Committee Size, Alternates, and Consultants

Robert J. Amdur and Elizabeth A. Bankert

INTRODUCTION

It is often necessary for IRB leadership to make decisions that affect the size of the IRB. When establishing a new IRB, the size of the committee is an initial step in the organization process. For established IRBs, the question of adding or removing positions from the membership roster is an ongoing issue. Members rotate off the IRB at regular intervals, people with an interest in research regulation ask to join the IRB, and the nature or scope of research changes over time. The need for expertise in the wide range of studies that most IRBs review creates pressure to add additional members to the IRB and to ask for help from people not affiliated with the committee. Often a complicating factor is the desire to improve the efficiency of the IRB meeting. The purpose of this chapter is to discuss factors that are important to consider when making decisions that affect the size of the IRB.

Size of the IRB

The only direct reference to the size of the IRB in the Department of Health and Human Services (DHHS) regulations is the requirement that the IRB consist of at least five members: "Each IRB shall have at least five members...."[1][Sec.107(a)] In addition to this regulatory minimum, four main factors are important to consider when making decisions about the size of the IRB.

An Odd Number of IRB Members Makes It Easier to Get a Quorum

Federal Regulation [1][Sec.108(b)] requires attendance by a majority of IRB members to conduct a full-committee meeting: "In order to fulfill the requirements of this policy each IRB shall. . . (except when an expedited review procedure is used). . . review proposed research at convened meetings at which a majority of the members of the IRB are present."

The more positions on the IRB full-committee roster, the more people will be available to attend the IRB meeting. However, the larger the committee, the more people who have to attend the meeting to make a quorum. Majority means "more than half." An odd number of positions on the membership roster maximizes the number of IRB members for a given quorum requirement. For example, if the IRB has 10 full-committee positions, it takes six people to make a quorum. By increasing the IRB membership to 11 positions, the IRB increases the membership workforce without increasing the quorum because six is more than half of both 10 and 11. When the schedule of IRB members is such that it may be difficult to make a quorum, the IRB will find it useful to have an odd number of voting positions on the IRB roster.

Adequate Expertise and Diversity

The regulatory requirements for IRB membership are discussed in detail in the next chapter. Basically, the federal regulations[1][Sec.107] require that an IRB include at least one scientist, one nonscientist, and one person not affiliated with the institution, and that the IRB have sufficient expertise and diversity to evaluate ethical issues involved in protocols that are sent for IRB review.

Because the regulations go into considerable detail about required areas of expertise and diversity of the IRB membership, these factors often create pressure to add more positions to the IRB roster. Most IRBs review research that may recruit subjects from heterogeneous backgrounds in terms of racial, ethnic, gender, educational, and socioeconomic factors. It becomes difficult for the IRB to know when to stop adding members to comply with this section of the regulations. Similarly, for IRBs that review technically complex protocols from a wide range of medical or behavioral research specialties, the IRB sometimes needs more expertise to evaluate a specific research study. Clearly, the composition of the IRB is an area that requires a high degree of judgment on the part of IRB leadership. An alternative to adding new members to the IRB is to use consultants to advise the IRB on specific issues.

Workload Issues Affect the Size of the IRB

The volume and complexity of the studies that an IRB monitors will be a major factor in determining the size of the IRB. There is no regulatory guideline on appropriate workload. This is the subject of a separate chapter in Part 2. Ideally, we would have benchmark data from "best practice" IRBs to define national guidelines on the volume of studies per meeting time per IRB member for different research environments (biomedical, social science, etc.). At present there are no formal data of this kind.

Logistics of the Full-Committee Meeting

The larger the IRB, the more difficult it will be to support full-committee meetings from the administrative standpoint. Large meeting rooms may be difficult to reserve at a time and location that is convenient for IRB members. When the IRB committee is spread around a large meeting area, it may be difficult for IRB members and support staff to hear what is going on without a sound amplification system. Ideally, the full-committee meeting is a discussion in which people feel comfortable disagreeing with their colleagues or expressing their confusion about an important issue. When a meeting is so large that the members have trouble seeing or hearing their colleagues, it will be difficult for the IRB to function optimally.

The administrative work that must be done to prepare for the full-committee meeting is directly related to the size of the IRB. For most agenda items, each committee member will be given a copy of the IRB forms and supporting documents sometime (usually days) before the meeting. The time that it takes to photocopy, collate, and organize study material will be extensive for large IRBs.

A related issue is the transportation of IRB material to the home or office of committee members in time for them to review it before the meeting. Large IRBs usually have heavy meeting agendas, and getting the necessary documents to members in a timely fashion may require special transportation equipment and full time employees specifically for this task.

Consultants to the IRB

From the administrative standpoint, consultants have the advantage of providing the IRB with additional expertise or cultural diversity without increasing the requirement for quorum or other factors that are associated with adding additional members to the IRB. There is no standard procedure or published guideline regarding the use of consultants to assist the IRB with the review of specific protocols. An informal survey of IRB directors around the country suggests that this is not a common practice. In our opinion, the use of consultants to help the IRB review a project that the IRB is not comfortable with is an underutilized procedure that has the potential to increase both the efficiency and efficacy of IRB review.

At Dartmouth, we have used consultants many times to help the IRB evaluate issues like the value of alternative therapy, the choice of the control group, and the potential for coercion in the proposed study population. The procedure is simple. The IRB Chair simply calls a person who is likely to be both unbiased and knowledgeable about the issue in question and asks him or her to provide an opinion to the IRB. The consultant may be a local colleague or may work at another institution. The consultant is given the relevant protocol materials and asked to submit a brief (one-half to one page) opinion in writing (e-mail is acceptable). The consultant's opinion is shown to all IRB members who will be voting on the protocol, and the issue is discussed at the full-committee meeting.

It is best to remove the consultants name and other identifying information if there is any question that there could be problems if the investigator knows the identity of the consultant. The identity of the consultant may be kept separately in the IRB files. In some cases, it will be appropriate to ask the consultant to attend the IRB meeting, but in our experience this is rarely necessary.

Administrative Cost

Most IRBs operate in an environment where there is pressure to limit administrative cost. As discussed above, the cost of copying and transporting documents related to the full-committee meeting is directly related to IRB size. Similarly, for IRBs that provide meals during regularly scheduled meetings, the cost of food and beverages will be a considerable expense for large IRBs.

When the IRB pays members for the time they spend participating in IRB-related activities, each addition to the IRB roster may have a large impact on the IRB budget. This will be especially true when reimbursement is based on a percentage of the member's salary and high-paid members of society (like physicians) are recruited for IRB service.

Alternate IRB Members

Federal regulations contain specific instructions on the size and composition of the IRB full committee. The purpose of this section is to explain the use of alternate IRB members. To follow the alternate member discussion, it is important to understand the difference between the IRB membership roster and the IRB membership list. The term *IRB membership roster* refers to the number of voting member positions on the IRB. In federal regulations, instructions about the number and characteristics of the IRB membership refer to voting member positions. For example, when the regulations require that "each IRB shall have at least five members," it means five voting member positions. When the regulations require a majority of IRB members for a meeting quorum, it means that more than half of the number of voting member positions must be represented at an IRB meeting.

The difference between the IRB membership roster and the IRB membership list is the use of alternate IRB members where *alternate* refers to the situation where there is more than one member for an IRB roster position. The Office of Human Research Protection (OHRP) must approve all appointments to the IRB (including alternate members) before their service as voting members.[1][Sec.103(b)(3)]

Most IRBs will find it useful to have alternate members for at least some IRB roster positions because the use of alternate members increases the functional capacity and administrative flexibility of the committee. As discussed in other chapters, federal regulations require an approval vote by a majority of the IRB and that the IRB be composed of people with specific characteristics in terms of cultural and professional experience.[1][Sec.108(b)] These constraints often create a situation of competing objectives when selecting the IRB membership. The goal of diverse representation creates pressure to increase the size of the IRB, while the majority quorum requirement creates an incentive to keep the IRB as small as possible. The use of alternate IRB members makes it easier for the IRB to satisfy diversity requirements without increasing the number of voting members that must be present to have a full-committee meeting quorum.

Federal regulations and OHRP policy do not limit the overall number of alternate members on an IRB or the number of alternates for any given IRB position. While most IRBs have only two members for a given roster position (a single alternate member), in some cases it may be desirable to have more than two people who alternate in providing the IRB with a specific type of representation.

The Nonscientific Member   To approve research at a full-committee IRB meeting, federal regulations require at least one voting member whose primary concerns are in nonscientific areas.[1][Sec.107(c)] If the IRB membership list has only one nonscientific member, the full committee cannot meet if this person is not available for the duration of the meeting. However, if the IRB recruits several people to serve as alternates for the nonscientific voting member position, the IRB has the flexibility to conduct a full-committee meeting anytime that any one of the nonscientific members is available.

Diversity and Issue-Specific Representation   Members who have issue-specific knowledge are required to provide cultural diversity when the IRB routinely reviews research involving diverse populations or populations that are especially vulnerable (e.g., children, prisoners, or persons with mental disabilities).[1][Sec.107(a)] As with the requirement for a nonscience member, the IRB will find it useful to have multiple members for each voting-member roster position that represents important dimensions of the IRB committee.

Alternate Member-at-Large   It is not unusual for IRBs to receive approval from OHRP to add an "alternate member-

at-large" to the membership list. An alternate-at-large position does not change the requirement for quorum because it is not viewed as a regular voting member position. The alternate-at-large only votes at the full-committee meeting when he or she is filling in for another member position. For example, if the IRB roster lists two people in a certain membership position (a regular and one alternate) and neither of these people attends the meeting, then the alternate-at-large may be able to vote in place of these members (and count toward quorum).

The only limitation in terms of the use of an alternate-at-large is that the member-at-large and the voting member for whom he or she is substituting must have the same issue-specific knowledge when such knowledge is required for research review. For example, when reviewing a protocol involving research with autistic children, an alternate-at-large who is not familiar with autistic children is not permitted to substitute for an IRB member who was appointed to provide the IRB with expertise in this area.

Most IRBs that include a member-at-large appoint a person whose primary concerns are in nonscience areas to this position so that there is additional backup for this critical position at the full-committee meeting. Some IRBs appoint an experienced member of the IRB administrative staff as the alternate-at-large so they know that there will always be a nonscientific member available if there are last minute or unexpected problems with the members who usually bring this required perspective to the IRB meeting.

Conclusion

The optimal size of an IRB is determined by the following factors:

1. An odd number of members makes it easier to get a quorum
2. The need for adequate expertise and diversity
3. The use of alternate IRB members and IRB consultants
4. IRB workload
5. Logistics of the full-committee meeting
6. Administrative cost

Reference

1. Code of Federal Regulations. Title 45A—Department of Health and Human Services; Part 46—Protection of Human Subjects. Updated 1 Oct 1997. Access date 18 Apr 2001. World Wide Web http://www4.law.cornell.edu/cfr/45p46.htm

Length, Frequency, and Time of IRB Meetings

Robert J. Amdur and Elizabeth A. Bankert

INTRODUCTION

Should the full-committee meeting be scheduled for eight hours once a month or four hours every other week? Should a four-hour meeting be scheduled from 8 AM to noon or from 10 AM to 2 PM? The schedule of IRB meetings may seem like a minor detail, but it may have an important influence on the efficiency and effectiveness of IRB function. An informal survey of university-based IRBs suggests that there is no standard template regarding the schedule of IRB meetings. For some IRBs, the meeting schedule has been developed in response to objective constraints, whereas in others it is "just the way we have always done it." Recognizing that the schedule of IRB meetings is something that should be customized to meet the specific needs of each institution, there are some basic principles to consider when evaluating this aspect of the IRB organization.

Federal Regulations

There is no information in DHHS or FDA regulations about the length, frequency, or time of IRB meetings with the exception of the requirement that continuing review of an approved protocol take place at least once a year.

Length of the IRB Meeting

The IRB meeting should last only as long as necessary to carry out important IRB business and education that require the presence of the full committee. An inefficient IRB meeting wastes committee members' time and creates a situation where it is difficult to recruit and retain high quality people for IRB service.

Assuming IRB meeting time is used productively, the main argument in favor of long IRB meetings (as opposed to shorter meetings at more frequent intervals) is an increase in administrative efficiency. This advantage must be weighed against the tendency for people to lose their ability to concentrate on meeting discussion after an extended time. IRB decisions often require an understanding of complex and controversial ethical or regulatory issues such that even for experienced IRB members the full-committee meeting is usually an intellectually demanding experience. As the integrity of the IRB system depends on an educated opinion from all committee members, it is important that members pay attention throughout the meeting. When the IRB meeting lasts too long, the efficiency and effectiveness of IRB review is likely to be compromised. Although some members may

be able to concentrate for lengthy IRB meetings on a regular basis, in our experience IRB function clearly deteriorates when the meeting lasts more than four or five hours. For this reason, we recommend scheduling regular full-committee meetings for no more than four hours per session.

Frequency of IRB Meetings

After an IRB determines the maximum meeting duration that is appropriate for their membership and agenda, the minimum frequency of full-committee meetings will be determined by IRB workload and the efficiency of the review process. All segments of the research community benefit when research review is completed in a timely fashion. An IRB that is consistently unable to complete a review of all agenda items assigned to a given meeting session will need to improve the efficiency of IRB review or meet more frequently.

For many IRBs, the question is whether the IRB should meet for the maximum time as infrequently as possible or for a shorter period of time at more frequent intervals. For example, many IRBs can effectively manage research review at their institution with a single half-day meeting every four weeks (one meeting per month). IRBs in this situation may want to consider changing the meeting schedule so that the IRB meets for a few hours every other week. Similarly, an IRB that is reviewing all submitted review items with a half-day meeting every two weeks may consider a shorter meeting every week. Several factors must be considered when determining meeting frequency in this setting.

Research Review Interval

The review interval is the time between the date that a protocol is submitted for IRB review and the date that the investigator is informed of the IRB's final decision (approval or disapproval). This may have important implications for an institution's research program. Excessive IRB turnaround time will compromise an investigator's ability to secure research contracts that benefit both the institution and research subjects, decrease investigator enthusiasm for doing research, and compromise respect for the local IRB system. Although multiple factors may influence the research review interval, it is important for an IRB to recognize when the frequency of IRB meetings is a problem for the research enterprise. When more frequent IRB meetings will meaningfully decrease the time between submission and approval of IRB applications, the IRB should consider changing the IRB meeting schedule accordingly.

Member Availability

The availability of IRB members may determine the frequency of the full-committee meeting. For some IRBs it will be easier to retain a quorum with high quality members if the IRB meets frequently for short periods of time, whereas for others a less frequent but longer meeting will be preferable. An IRB that is having trouble with meeting attendance should consider the possibility that meeting frequency is a source of the problem.

Administrative Efficiency

The main argument in favor of less frequent full-committee meetings is administrative efficiency. The amount of work involved with reserving meeting space, confirming attendance, preparing and delivering information to each member, interacting with IRB members and investigators immediately before the meeting, providing administrative support during the meeting, and generating the postmeeting letters and documentation is such that there is a net loss in administrative productivity with more frequent full-committee meetings.

Alternate Reviewer System

The alternate reviewer system is discussed in Chapter 3-5. The use of alternate IRB members may make it possible to have IRB meetings more frequently than would otherwise be possible. For example, an IRB that would like to meet every week may find it difficult to recruit qualified members who can meet that frequently. If the IRB has two members for each IRB roster position, each member can attend every other IRB meeting, and the IRB will have full-committee attendance at each meeting without increasing the requirement for quorum.

The Time of Day for the IRB Meeting

Factors to consider when deciding on the time of day for the IRB full-committee meetings include several mentioned in the discussions of meeting duration and frequency.

Member Availability

When IRB members are unable to attend the meetings because they are scheduled at a time when the member has an important conflict, it may be advantageous for IRB leadership to move the IRB meeting to a more convenient time. IRBs that are having trouble with meeting attendance should determine if the time of day of the meeting is part of the problem.

Ability of IRB Members to Concentrate

As discussed earlier, it is essential that all committee members stay alert during the entire full-committee meeting. Some IRBs, especially those with light agendas, seem to function well with late afternoon or evening meetings. However, in our experience, IRB review is more thorough and conducted more efficiently when the IRB meeting takes place at the beginning of the work day. Similarly, meeting times that straddle a major mealtime are likely to be problematic. For example, it is likely to be difficult to keep the committee focused on IRB business in a meeting that goes from 10 AM to 2 PM, especially if a formal lunch is provided at noon. Most people have trouble concentrating on a technical discussion when they are hungry, waiting for food, or recovering from a large meal. When productivity changes during the IRB meeting seem to be related to issues related to the focus and concentration of IRB members, IRB leadership should consider changing the time of day of the IRB meeting.

Conclusion

There is no information in DHHS or FDA regulations about the length, frequency, or time of IRB meetings with the exception of the requirement that continuing review of an approved protocol take place at least once a year. In our experience, IRB function deteriorates when meetings last more than four hours. The frequency of IRB meetings should be determined by the research review interval, member availability, and the need to improve administrative efficiency.

IRB Subcommittees

Robert J. Amdur and Elizabeth A. Bankert

INTRODUCTION

The term *subcommittee* is used in this chapter to refer to a group of IRB members organized for the purpose of managing a specific task, or making a specific type of decision, related to IRB function.

The use of subcommittees is extremely variable across the IRB community. Some IRB offices rely on the full committee for essentially all decisions and reviews. Some advocate subcommittees for a fraction of these decisions, and other IRB offices make decisions based solely on the expertise of the IRB chair, IRB administrative director, and/or one other IRB member. In this chapter, we will discuss the use of these three options for making IRB decisions and establishing IRB policy and procedure in a variety of areas.

Federal Research Regulations

The Department of Health and Human Services (DHHS) and the Food and Drug Administration (FDA) regulations related to human research do not contain the term *subcommittee*. The DHHS regulations indirectly address the subcommittee issue in the section on review of research using an *expedited review* procedure. [1(Sec.110)] Under an expedited review procedure, "The review may be carried out by the IRB chairperson or by one or more experienced reviewers designated by the chairperson from among members of the IRB." [1[Sec.110(b)(2)]] The regulations therefore allow for an IRB to form a subcommittee consisting of one *or more* experienced reviewers, but the regulations do not imply that multiple reviewers are an important aspect of the expedited review procedure. The regulations stress the importance of *experience*, which implies knowledge of IRB issues and the ability to make decisive judgments in this setting.

Models for Making IRB Decisions

No organizational structure will guarantee efficient, high-quality decision making. Some IRBs function best by assigning decision-making authority to groups of people (subcommittees), whereas others find the group model counterproductive. The alternative to an IRB subcommittee is to have IRB decisions (those that do not require review by the full committee) made by the IRB Chair, the IRB administrative director (assuming she or he is an IRB member), or an appropriately qualified IRB member (other than the Chair or administrative director). Recognizing that optimal IRB function will require that each IRB customize its organization, there are several points to consider when deciding about the use of a subcommittee.

Efficiency

Scheduling and conducting a meeting that involves several people is usually a process that requires considerable time and energy on the part of the committee members and IRB administration. For this reason, a subcommittee is likely to be less efficient than a decision-making process based on an individual such as the IRB Chair, IRB administrative director, or an experienced IRB member.

Workload Distribution

Some IRBs may create subcommittees to improve workload distribution. Although an organization that involves subcommittees may achieve this goal, it is important to understand that workload distribution and subcommittee meetings are two different issues. From the administrative standpoint, it may be easier to distribute IRB work by dividing a specific IRB task among different IRB members, each working independently from the others.

Better Decisions

The main advantage of group decisions is the potential to draw on the experience and expertise of a number of people. A subcommittee creates a forum for ideas to be exchanged, opinions to be challenged, and alternate points of view to be considered. Under ideal conditions, a subcommittee increases the chance that decisions will be free from personal bias and based on sound logic after consideration of all the important issues. However, in many settings, more people does not translate into a more thorough analysis, better judgment, or other factors that contribute to sound decision making. When one person has the necessary experience and decision-making skills, a subcommittee process is not likely to improve the quality of IRB decisions.

Possible Subcommittees for an IRB

Expedited Review

When specific criteria are met, IRB review may be accomplished with an expedited procedure[2(pp.60364–60367)] (see Chapter 4-2). However, for the purposes of this discussion, it is important to remember that the regulations do not permit research to be *disapproved* by an expedited procedure.[1[Sec.110(b)(2)]] Expedited review of research should be done with the understanding that the reviewers should only approve research when there is no concern that an approval decision will meaningfully compromise the protection of research subjects. When a reviewer is uncomfortable with approving research by the expedited procedure, he or she should ask for advice from other IRB members or outside consultants, or refer the decision to the full IRB committee.

An IRB may elect to establish one or more subcommittees specifically for the expedited review of research. In our experience, an individual IRB member with expertise in the area of research in question is sufficient for the expedited review procedure, but some IRBs may prefer a group decision in this setting. A situation where review by a subcommittee or individual specialist may be especially useful is the expedited review of a particular type of research that routinely raises issues that are beyond the expertise of the IRB Chair or administrative director. For example, at institutions that manage both social science and biomedical research with a single IRB committee, it may be useful to designate an individual or subcommittee for expedited review of each of these general classes of research.

A format that has worked well at Dartmouth College is that a single IRB reviews both social science and biomedical research, but the IRB designates a member with social science expertise to be the initial review mechanism for all issues involving social science research. This social science research specialist either approves qualified research by the expedited procedure or refers it to the full IRB committee. The IRB Chair (a physician) or a member of the IRB with biomedical research expertise (who has been specifically educated about the regulatory guidelines for expedited review) handles the expedited review of biomedical research. To minimize the full-committee workload, we recommend using the expedited review process in all situations permitted by federal regulations.

Determination of Research Versus Nonresearch

In some situations it is difficult to decide if a project that uses scientific methodology to collect private, identifiable health information should be classified as research or as some form of nonresearch activity (student survey assignments, medical record reviews, etc.). The classification of a project as research is obviously important because the IRB system is designed and authorized—from the standpoint of federal research regulations—only to oversee research. Our recommendation is for the IRB administrator and Chair to interact with appropriate departments at the institution (e.g., research administration, medical records,

risk management) to generate an institutional policy for classifying projects as research. After guidelines are developed, the decision for each specific project can be made by the IRB Chair or administrative director.

Determination of Review Category

The three main categories of initial protocol review are full committee, expedited, or exempt (from further IRB review). The regulatory criteria for each of these procedures are discussed in separate chapters. The regulations do not explain where the decision regarding the procedure for review should be made in the IRB organization. It is our impression that in most organizations the IRB administrative director and/or IRB Chair decides on the procedure for initial protocol review. However, some IRBs prefer to have this important triage decision made by a subcommittee of IRB members. For this decision, we believe the use of a subcommittee is not an efficient or effective use of time. To streamline this process, our recommendation is to give the responsibility of determination of review category to the IRB administrative director or IRB Chair.

Primary Reviewer Subcommittees

Although not described in the federal regulations, OHRP has approved a process known as the *primary reviewer system* (see Chapter 5-15). The primary reviewer system involves one, two, or three full-committee members taking responsibility for a detailed review of a research study. At the time of the full-committee meeting, the primary reviewer(s) provide comments and recommendations to the full committee.

Some institutions have taken the primary reviewer model one step further by designating subcommittees to review each protocol before the full-committee meeting. As in the primary reviewer system, the primary review subcommittee is responsible for analyzing the protocol and IRB application in detail and discussing any unanswered questions with consultants or the researchers before the full-committee meeting. At the full-committee meeting, a representative from the subcommittee presents the final recommendation regarding IRB approval, often with a brief explanation of the important issues that were evaluated. Like the primary reviewer system, the potential advantage of a primary review subcommittee is that it may help the IRB conduct a high quality review without a lengthy discussion at the full-committee meeting. However, it is important to remember that *all* members of the full committee must receive the consent form and enough information about the protocol to conduct a substantive review.

Adverse Event Reports

The role of the IRB in reviewing adverse event reports (AERs), especially from multicenter trials, is one of the most controversial issues in the field of research regulation. Chapter 7-3 is devoted to this topic. For this discussion, it is sufficient to understand that federal regulations are not specific about the procedure for IRB review of AERs from ongoing research. Specifically, the IRB does not have clear guidance on the procedure for review or criteria for approval of an AER. In view of this uncertainty, it is not surprising that the procedure for reviewing AERs is extremely variable within the IRB community.

In some organizations, all AERs are reviewed as separate agenda items at full-committee meetings. Some IRBs designate a subcommittee to review AERs with the understanding that only those AERs that raise concern are forwarded to the full committee. Our recommendation is for each AER to be reviewed first by the principal investigator (who must complete a questionnaire indicating his or her assessment of the AER) and then the IRB Chair. If the IRB Chair decides that the AER may indicate a meaningful change in the risk to research subjects, the Chair forwards the AER for review at the next full-committee meeting. This may suspend IRB approval of the research protocol in the interim. However, when the IRB Chair does not have further inquiries about the AER, then no further IRB review is done until the regularly scheduled time of continuing protocol review, when all AERs are included in the renewal materials.

Revision Requests

Federal research regulations provide for the use of an expedited procedure to review minor changes to research that has been previously approved.[1(Sec.110)] The use of a subcommittee in this type of review is likely to be less efficient than a review by the IRB Chair or designee, without a difference in quality. We also note here that the definition of *minor change* is an opportunity for the institution to carefully review the federal regulations (OHRP and FDA) and document their interpretation in an internal policy document. For example, at Dartmouth College, after reviewing federal regulations, a definition of *minor change* was established that focuses on whether risks to subjects are increased as a result of the revision. Specifically, if risks to subjects are not increased, then the revision is reviewed only by the IRB Chair or designee, using an expedited procedure. However, if risks to subjects are increased, then full-committee review is required.

Continuing Review

In 1988, the categories of research that could be reviewed with an expedited process were revised to include continuing review of some studies that were initially reviewed by a full IRB committee.[2(pp.60364–60367)] Expedited review in this setting by an IRB subcommittee, the IRB Chair, administrative director, or designated IRB member will increase IRB efficiency and decrease waiting time for ongoing IRB approval.

Compliance Audits

An issue that is receiving increased attention is the need to establish a formal mechanism to audit research records or research practice for compliance with federal regulations and internal IRB policy. Federal research regulations do not require that the IRB conduct an audit outside the scope of the procedures that make up the standard IRB review. However, there are two settings in which an audit system may improve IRB function: the audit of IRB records as well as the audit of the conduct of research (evaluating the quality of informed consent, verifying that current participants meet the approved inclusion criteria, etc.). Both of these topics are the subjects of Chapters 2-6 and 6-13.

For the purpose of this discussion, the point is that auditing IRB records or the conduct of research is a specialized function that goes on outside the framework of other IRB activities. An IRB that wants to make an audit an effective part of its routine procedures must establish audit guidelines and designate people who will manage audit tasks. At many organizations, the IRB administrative director and administrative staff conduct the audits that are limited to the review of IRB records, but some IRBs assign this task to a subcommittee of IRB members or even the full IRB committee.

Because few institutions routinely audit research conduct, it is difficult to make generalizations about the process for this practice. As with other specialized activities, some IRBs will find it useful to audit the conduct of research with a subcommittee, while others will assign this job to individual IRB members. In this instance, a subcommittee could serve a useful role in establishing an audit process at your institution. For example, an audit subcommittee could assist in establishing the policy, parameters, and schedule of routine audits as well as to perform the actual audit reviews. As in other settings where subcommittees are used, an audit subcommittee should forward reports and problematic cases to the full committee for evaluation.

IRB Policy and Procedures

IRB work is a dynamic and evolving process. Although some aspects of the IRB function are required to be the same for all IRBs that operate in compliance with federal regulations, in many situations each individual IRB will need or want to establish its own policy. For example, should the IRB establish subcommittees to perform a preliminary review of research that will be reviewed by the full IRB committee? Should an IRB voting option include *table*? How should the IRB manage AERs? Should there be standard wording in the consent document when the research involves storage of tissue for future research?

Some IRBs will choose to make decisions about IRB policy and procedure with a subcommittee composed of the IRB Chair, IRB administrative director, and other experienced IRB members. IRBs that use this organization often give this type of committee a title like *executive committee*. Certainly the subcommittee approach makes sense in this setting, but many IRBs appear to function extremely well where all decisions related to IRB policy and procedure are made by the IRB Chair and administrative director.

Conclusion

Throughout this book, authors are encouraged to analyze a topic and then make recommendations based on their experience managing human research protection programs. In preparing this chapter, we discussed the use of subcommittees with IRB directors at several large commercial and university-based IRBs. As stated in the initial section of this chapter, there is no right or wrong way to use subcommittees in the overall IRB organization. Some institutions function well with subcommittees and others function well without them. With this in mind, it is the recommendation of the authors of this chapter to use subcommittees as little as possible to distribute workload, establish IRB policy, or make important IRB decisions.

References

1. Code of Federal Regulations. Title 45A—Department of Health and Human Services; Part 46—Protection of Human Subjects. Updated 1 Oct 1997. Access date 18 Apr 2001. World Wide Web http://www4.law.cornell.edu/cfr/45p46.htm

2. National Institutes of Health. Protection of human subjects: Categories of research that may be reviewed by the Institutional Review Board (IRB) through an expedited review procedure. *Fed Regist* 63(216):60364-60367, 1998. World Wide Web http://ohrp.osophs.dhhs.gov/humansubjects/guidance/63fr60364.htm

Social Science Versus Biomedical IRBs

Robert J. Amdur and Elizabeth A. Bankert

INTRODUCTION

A frequent request at national IRB meetings is to spend more time on topics related to social science research. At many institutions that conduct both social science and biomedical research, IRB review of these two general categories of research is assigned to separate IRB committees. This organizational structure may suggest that there is a fundamental difference between social science and biomedical research in terms of ethical issues and the process of IRB review. The purpose of this chapter is to challenge this concept. There is no question that many biomedical research issues are not applicable to social science. However, the quality of research review will be enhanced by requiring that members of both disciplines contribute their expertise and unique perspective on research involving human subjects, rather than segregating the discussion of social science and biomedical issues.

Definitions

Social science is "the study of human society and of individual relationships in, and to, society." Academic disciplines that usually conduct social science research include sociology, psychology, anthropology, economics, political science, and history. The terms *behavioral science* and *social science* are used interchangeably.

In contrast to the social science focus on interpersonal relationships, biomedical scientists study human physiology and the treatment or understanding of disease. A dictionary definition of *biomedical science* is "the application of the principles of the natural sciences to medicine."

Why Distinguish Between Social Science and Biomedical Research?

The use of topic-specific IRB committees may be a convenient way to divide the workload at institutions that handle a large volume of research protocols. This section will review the limitations to a conceptual framework that focuses on the distinction between social science and biomedical research.

Research Regulations Hold Research from All Disciplines to the Same Standards

There is no legal or regulatory basis for making a distinction between social science and biomedical research from the IRB standpoint. Specifically, the U.S. Department of Health and Human Services (DHHS) regulations that focus on the IRB do not mention the terms *social science, behavioral science,* or *biomedical research*.[1] The regulations describe ethical standards for research based on the specific characteristic of the risk to research participants, not on the academic field in which research may be classified. The section of these regulations that describes IRB membership requirements[1[sec.107(a)]] requires that the IRB "have at least five members with varying backgrounds to promote complete and adequate review of research activities commonly conducted by the institution" and "In addition to . . . professional competence . . . , the IRB shall be able to ascertain the acceptability of proposed research in terms of institutional commitments . . . and standards of professional conduct and practice." Clearly, this means that if an institution conducts social science and/or biomedical research, then it must have individuals with social science and/or biomedical research expertise on the IRB.

Other sections of the regulations go into detail to clarify IRB procedures and approval criteria when research is conducted in a setting with distinguishing ethical characteristics—for example, research involving certain kinds of educational testing, research involving children, research involving prisoners, etc.—but nothing implies a general distinction between social science and biomedical research. The fact that the regulations do not distinguish between social science and biomedical research emphasizes the similarities between these two general types of research in terms of ethical standards and research regulation.

Understanding the Importance of Social Harm

Historically, research regulations and ethical codes were developed in response to situations that resulted in physical harm to research subjects. As social science research usually does not involve a risk of physical harm, some members of the research community may misunderstand the applicability of research standards to both biomedical and social science research. It is still not unusual to read research proposals in which the investigator limits the discussion of risk to the physical harm that may result from research participation. The problem with situations like this, as well as many of the discussions that imply that there are important differences between the ethical standards of social science and biomedical research, is that they ignore the potential impact of social harm on the lives of research participants.

Social harm refers to decreases in quality of life that result from information being created or used in a way that is damaging to the individual in question. Social harm may result in well-defined events such as loss of employability, loss of insurability, and criminal or civil litigation, but more commonly it disrupts interpersonal relationships by causing embarrassment, humiliation, discrimination, or stigmatization. Social harms are real harms that are just as much a threat to the rights and welfare of research participants as physical harms. To identify the risks of research participation, as well as to structure research to minimize such risk, it may be important to understand the difference between social and physical harm. However, from the standpoint of a conceptual model for thinking about the ethics of research and research regulation, there is no reason to make a distinction between social and physical risks of research participation.

Privacy and Confidentiality

Social science research rarely involves a risk of serious physical harm, but biomedical research often involves an important risk of social harm, either as the primary risk of research participation or in addition to the risk of physical harm. This latter point deserves some emphasis. For those who find it useful to use a social science versus biomedical approach to thinking about research regulation, it is important to understand that modern biomedical research often involves a risk of both social and physical harm. This is especially true with studies that evaluate a condition that is socially stigmatizing, for example, sexually transmitted disease, sexual dysfunction, and psychiatric disorders. A wide range of other aspects of biomedical research impose a risk of social harm for research participants. Advances in the understanding of the genetic basis of human physiology and disease have been a major factor in focusing attention on the social risk associated with participation in biomedical research. The importance of this aspect of biomedical research will certainly increase in the future.

Social harm is a result of the creation or transfer of information in a way that may negatively affect the research subject. Whenever the risk of research is related to access to information, IRB review will focus on the protection of privacy and confidentiality. It is for this reason that a major focus of the IRB review of social science research usually involves evaluation of things like the nature of the information being collected, the mechanism of identifying potential subjects, and the implications of a breach in confidentiality. Other areas of emphasis are the plans for protecting privacy and confidentiality, and the likelihood that potential subjects will understand the nature of the social risks associated with research participation. Privacy and confidentiality are also important in biomedical research projects, and IRB review of both social science and biomedical research should consider these important issues.

Considering Separate Social Science and Biomedical IRBs

What specific issues should the IRB leadership consider when deciding if social science and biomedical research should be reviewed by separate IRB committees? Although we hope that our treatment of this issue is balanced, it is important to recognize that all authors write from a perspective that has been shaped by their experience and training. With this in mind, it may be useful for the reader to understand that the authors of this chapter directed the IRB at Dartmouth College. Dartmouth used a single IRB to monitor a wide range, and moderately large volume, of both social science and biomedical research. In our experience, the single committee approach worked well. Indeed, most members of the Dartmouth research community, IRB, and research administration see important advantages to organizing the IRB review in a way that focuses on the similarities between social science and biomedical research.

Specialization

The main argument one hears for separate IRB review of social science and biomedical research is that this type of specialization increases the quality and efficiency of issue specialization by the IRB. Social scientists are intimately familiar with the techniques, theory, and standards of social science research. Similarly, an IRB composed of physicians is more likely to understand the issues pertinent to biomedical research. In theory, organizing an IRB in a way that concentrates issue-specific expertise could increase the efficiency and effectiveness of IRB review. However, given the increasing complexity of both social science and biomedical research, and the increased awareness of the importance of the risk of social harm in biomedical studies, the segregation of IRB expertise may be counterproductive. There is now a large degree of overlap in the issues that the IRB must consider when reviewing social science or biomedical research projects. Our current IRB system is based on the concept that input from people with a wide range of expertise and perspective will improve the ethical standards of research. In our experience, an IRB with the expertise to review both social science and biomedical research functions more effectively than either group alone.

Workload

A factor that may influence the decision to use separate IRBs is workload distribution. At institutions where the workload is too high for a single IRB, it will be desirable to divide the work of research regulation between multiple separate IRB committees. When workload requires multiple IRBs, and segregating IRB work based on a social science versus biomedical model would result in an acceptable work distribution, then the simplest way to triage protocols may be with a social science versus biomedical approach. However, segregating IRB review based on research type may limit flexibility from the administrative standpoint. The trade off between these factors at any given institution will depend on the characteristics of IRB members and the scope of the research that is presented for IRB review. In our opinion, the optimal model is to structure all IRBs so that they have the expertise to review both social science and biomedical research.

Conclusion

At many institutions that conduct both social science and biomedical research, IRB review of these two general categories of research is assigned to separate IRB committees. This organizational structure may suggest that there is a fundamental difference between social science and biomedical research in terms of ethical issues and the process of IRB review. There is no question that many biomedical research issues are not applicable to social science. However, the quality of research review will be enhanced by requiring that members of both disciplines contribute their expertise and unique perspective on research involving human subjects, rather than segregating the discussion of social science and biomedical issues. In most situations the quality of IRB review of research will be enhanced by constructing IRBs so that both social science and biomedical research may be reviewed by the same committee.

Reference

1. Code of Federal Regulations. Title 45A—Department of Health and Human Services; Part 46—Protection of Human Subjects. Updated 1 Oct 1997. Access date 18 Apr 2001. World Wide Web http://www4.law.cornell.edu/cfr/45p46.htm

PART 4

Review Categories Other Than Full Board Review

Exempt from IRB Review

Ernest D. Prentice and Gwenn S. F. Oki

INTRODUCTION

Many educational, behavioral, and social science studies present little or no risk to the participants. Likewise, research involving existing data, medical records, and pathological specimens usually has little, if any, associated risk, particularly if subject identifiers are removed from the data. Thus, although the rights and welfare of subjects in those studies still require protection, there is usually no need for a detailed Institutional Review Board (IRB) review, the equivalent of the kind performed at a convened meeting of the IRB. Accordingly, certain research activities are exempt from compliance with Department of Health and Human Services (DHHS) regulations for the protection of human subjects.[1] The purpose of this chapter is to assist IRBs in understanding what exempt research means and how to determine what types of research qualify for exempt status.

What Is Exempt Research?

DHHS regulations[1[Sec.101(b)]] describe six categories of research that may qualify for exempt status. Although the regulations do not address a maximum risk level, it is implicit within the concept of exempt research that there must be very little, if any, associated risk. Therefore, research that qualifies for exemption from the requirements of 45 CFR 46 must meet the aforementioned risk threshold and fall within one or more of the six exempt categories. Research involving prisoners, pregnant women, fetuses, and human in vitro fertilization (IVF) is, however, not exempt from the federal regulations because these classes of subjects are considered vulnerable.[1[Sec.101(i)]] Survey research involving children is also not exempt, nor is observation of a minor's public behavior unless the investigator does not participate in the activities being observed.[1[Sec.401(b)]] In addition, some IRBs exclude research involving the decisionally impaired from exempt status as well as other subjects considered vulnerable, such as the homeless or nursing home residents.

Who Determines That a Protocol Is Exempt?

The regulations do not specify who has or does not have the authority to decide if a research project is exempt. At many institutions, a member of the IRB or administrative staff makes this determination. In other organizations, it is permissible for the researcher, department directors, or others to triage a project to the exempt category. Recognizing that this is an area where federal regulations are silent, the Office of Human Research Protection (OHRP) recommends that the decision to exempt a study from IRB review is made by someone other than a research investigator associated with the project. Many investigators do not have sufficient knowledge of the federal regulations to properly determine, in all cases, whether research is ex-

empt. In addition, they have an obvious conflict of interest. To avoid the confusion that may be associated with determining which studies are exempt from IRB review, some organizations choose not to exempt any projects, and use either expedited review or review by the full IRB for all human subjects research.

Written Policy Regarding Exempt Status

If an institution allows research to be exempt under the provisions of 45 CFR 46,[1[Sec.101(b)]] it is important for the IRB to have a clear policy that allows for research that is technically exempt to be referred for further review or even be disqualified from exempt status altogether. Accordingly, any research project submitted by an investigator who requests an exemption should be carefully reviewed to determine if the project ought to qualify for exempt status. This review should be designed to identify any potential problems or ethical considerations that may impact the subjects. Appropriate clarifications or modifications of the protocol should be obtained from the investigator. A determination should also be made concerning whether informed consent is necessary. No regulation requires consent for exempt research, but there may be an ethical imperative for full disclosure, even including utilization of a written consent form that should be submitted to the appropriate IRB representative(s) for approval. Depending on the nature of the research, the consent form may include most of the elements of consent prescribed by 45 CFR 46.[1(Sec.116)]

FDA Regulations Do Not Exempt Research from IRB Review

It is important to understand that Food and Drug Administration (FDA) regulations for the protection of human subjects[2] do not have categories of research that qualify for exempt status like those listed by DHHS.[1][Sec.101(b)] The FDA does not exempt any research under its jurisdiction from IRB review except in emergency circumstances[2][Sec.104(c)] and taste and food quality studies[2][Sec.104(d)] (the same as exemption category 6 under the DHHS regulations). Because the FDA primarily regulates clinical trials involving investigational drugs, biologics, and medical devices, there is no need for expanded exemptions.

Categories of Exempt Research

The following are the six categories of exempt research specified by DHHS.[1][Sec.101(b)] Because all of the categories can be problematic in terms of interpretation and application, the authors have included notes that we hope will assist both IRBs and investigators in decisions concerning research activities that qualify for exempt status.

Exemption 1: Normal Educational Practices and Settings

Research conducted in established or commonly accepted educational settings, involving normal educational practices, such as (i) research on regular and special education instructional strategies, or (ii) research on the effectiveness of or the comparison among instructional techniques, curricula, or classroom management methods.

Exemption 1 should be limited to the study of normal educational practices and be conducted in commonly accepted settings such as elementary, secondary, or postsecondary schools. Thus, a study that involves evaluation of a radical new instructional strategy or use of random assignment of subjects to different instructional methods should usually not be exempt, because the methodologies employed in the studies deviate from normal educational practices. Certainly, educational research that involves deception or withholding of information from subjects should not be exempt. Exemptions should also not be routinely granted for research on physical education that involves exercise, if the activity is altered in a significant way for the purposes of the research. Even though the exercise may still be considered normal educational practice, an element of risk is associated with physical activity, particularly if it is intense.

Exemption 2: Anonymous Educational Tests, Surveys, Interviews, or Observations

Research involving the use of educational tests (cognitive, diagnostic, aptitude, achievement), survey procedures, interview procedures, or observations of public behavior, unless: (i) information obtained is recorded in such a manner that human subjects can be identified, directly or through identifiers linked to the subjects; and (ii) any disclosure of the human subjects' responses outside the research could reasonably place the subjects at risk of criminal or civil liability or be damaging to the subjects' financial standing, employability, or reputation.

Exemption 2 clearly reflects concern about protecting the subject's privacy and avoiding any risks associated with breach of confidentiality. Thus, if the research data contain any subject identifiers and if disclosure of data to unauthorized persons could harm the subject in any way, then the research is not exempt. For example, survey research that deals with sensitive and private aspects of the subject's behavior, such as sexual preferences, substance abuse, or illegal conduct, should obviously not be exempt if the data are linked to individual subjects. If there are no subject identifiers, then the research is technically exempt. The IRB, however, should consider all potential risks associated with this kind of research in deciding the criteria for exemption. In the example previously given, there may be more than minimal risk involved even in the absence of subject identifiers. Such surveys often contain invasive questions that may cause the subject to experience emotional distress or discomfort while answering them. Thus, although the research technically qualifies for exempt status because there are no subject identifiers, the potential risks of the research should negate exemption. Indeed, such research should utilize an unsigned consent form that clearly describes the nature and possible risks of the research.

Research involving cognitive or diagnostic testing should not normally be exempt if the testing is psychologically invasive in nature (e.g., detailed personality inventory) and could potentially cause the subject some discomfort or distress. Again, although the research is technically exempt if there are no subject identifiers, it should be considered as nonexempt research because of the risk level. Also, IRBs should guard against the possibility that an investigator may inappropriately characterize testing as normal educational practice and apply for exempt status under Exemption 1, which is less stringent in its requirements than Exemption 2.

Exemption 3: Identifiable Subjects in Special Circumstances

Research involving the use of educational tests (cognitive, diagnostic, aptitude, achievement), survey procedures, interview procedures, or observation of public behavior that is not exempt under paragraph (b)(2) of this section, if: (i) the human subjects are elected or appointed public officials or candidates for public office; or (ii) Federal statute(s) require(s) without exception that the confidentiality of the personally identifiable information will be maintained throughout the research and thereafter.

Exemption 3 represents an extension of Exemption 2, but without the same level of oversight of the subject's right to privacy. Personal identifiers can be maintained if there is a federal statute that protects confidentiality or if the subject is either a public official or a candidate for public office. Exemption 3 effectively holds public officials who become research subjects to a different standard by providing less protection of their rights than we do for other members of society. Nevertheless, despite the loophole created by this exemption, the rights of individuals who hold public office should obviously be protected by conducting a thorough review of the proposed research as previously addressed.

Exemption 4: Collection or Study of Existing Data

Research involving the collection or study of existing data, documents, records, pathological specimens, or diagnostic specimens, if these sources are publicly available or if the information is recorded by the investigator in such a manner that subjects cannot be identified, directly or through identifiers linked to the subjects.

Exemption 4 is the most used and often the most problematic category of exempt research conducted at academic medical centers. For research to qualify for exemption under Exemption 4, the information derived from use of the data, records, or biological specimens must be recorded so that subjects cannot be identified. This means there must be no direct or indirect subject identifiers (e.g., demographic information) that can be linked to the subjects. Some investigators erroneously assume that if they do not have access to the subject's name, which is, however, linked to the data or specimen, the research is exempt. However, the existence of even a one-way identifier, such as a code that can then be used by anyone to identify a subject, disqualifies the research from exemption under Category 4. It should also be noted that the research material must be existent at the time the research begins. Any use of additional research material collected after the research is initiated will disqualify the study from exempt status. In other words, exempt research under Exemption 4 must be totally retrospective in nature.

Exemption 5: Public Benefit or Service Programs

Research and demonstration projects that are conducted by or subject to the approval of department or agency heads, and which are designed to study, evaluate, or otherwise examine: (i) public benefit or service programs; (ii) procedures for obtaining benefits or services under those programs; (iii) possible changes in or alternatives to those programs or procedures; (iv) possible changes in methods or levels of payment for benefits or services under those programs.

Exemption 5 allows research on public benefit or service programs, such as welfare, Medicaid, unemployment, and Social Security. This research may involve vulnerable subjects such as economically disadvantaged persons or elderly individuals who are decisionally impaired. Research under Exemption 5 may also involve analysis of data that are routinely compiled by the public office that administers the program, but which would be considered private by the subject. Again, a thorough review of the research project can help protect the rights and welfare of the participants.

Exemption 6: Taste and Food Evaluation and Acceptance Studies

Taste and food quality evaluation and consumer acceptance studies, (i) if wholesome foods without additives are consumed or (ii) if a food is consumed that contains a food ingredient at or below the level for a use found to be safe, or agricultural chemical or environmental contaminant at or below the level found to be safe, by the Food and Drug Administration or approved by the Environmental Protection Agency or the Food Safety and Inspection Service of the U.S. Department of Agriculture.

Exemption 6 should be limited to taste and food quality evaluation studies that do not involve consumption by the subject of any type or volume of food that has any potential risks such as indigestion or vitamin deficiencies. Clearly, the food consumed by the subject and the time frame in which this is accomplished should constitute reasonable eating behaviors. Studies that involve consumption of alcohol, vitamins, or supplements like protein power, creatine, and glucosamine chondroitin sulfate should not qualify for exempt status.

Conclusion

Correct application of the exempt categories at 45 CFR 46.101(b) can be one of the most difficult tasks facing the IRB staff and/or IRB Chair. On the one hand, some investigators regard exempt research as being more or less exempt from any kind of substantive review because DHHS regulations in 45 CFR 46 do not apply. On the other hand, the participants in exempt research are, in fact, human subjects who have rights that must be fully protected. In some cases, research that is technically exempt has associated risk. Clearly, such research presents a compelling ethical argument for performing a thorough review and possibly disqualifying the research project from exempt status altogether. IRBs, therefore, should have a well-thought-out policy concerning exempt research and should remember that 45 CFR 46 sets the minimum standard. Institutions are expected to adopt more stringent requirements for the protection of human subjects as the need arises. Certainly, the area of exempt research is a case in point where IRBs should, at times, look beyond the regulations.

References

1. Code of Federal Regulations. Title 45A—Department of Health and Human Services; Part 46—Protection of Human Subjects. Updated 1 Oct 1997. Access date 18 Apr 2001. World Wide Web http://www4.law.cornell.edu/cfr/45p46.htm
2. Code of Federal Regulations. Title 21, Chapter 1—Food and Drug Administration, DHHS; Part 56—Institutional Review Boards. Updated 1 Apr 1999. Access date 27 Mar 2001. World Wide Web http://www4.law.cornell.edu/cfr/21p56.htm

Expedited IRB Review

Gwenn S. F. Oki and John Zaia

INTRODUCTION

The Department of Health and Human Services (DHHS) and the Food and Drug Administration (FDA) regulations for the protection of human subjects[1,2] recognize that not all research warrants review by the full IRB at a convened meeting. Accordingly, DHHS regulations at 45 CFR 46[1] and FDA regulations at 21 CFR 56[2(Sec.110)] permit certain types of research to be reviewed and approved by expedited review. The purpose of this chapter is to assist IRBs in understanding what expedited review means and, in addition, how this type of review should be effected.

Definition of Expedited Review

Expedited review is a type of review that can be conducted by the IRB Chair, other IRB members designated by the Chair, or a subcommittee of the IRB.[1[Sec.110(b)],2] The IRB members designated to conduct expedited review must be experienced reviewers who are also voting members. Reviewers are empowered by the regulations to approve research qualifying for expedited review, or to require modifications of a study to gain approval. The regulations, however, prohibit disapproval of any research reviewed by the expedited method, and require that such "proposed disapprovals" be referred to the full board for review and disposition. Therefore, the IRB Chair or Chair designee(s) may exercise all of the authority of the IRB to review research qualifying for expedited review, but does not have the authority to disapprove such research. The full IRB must be notified of all research projects ultimately approved using the expedited review process. While the regulations are silent on the rationale for this notification, it is clear that the full IRB has the authority to question any approval granted through expedited review.

General Eligibility Criteria for Expedited Review

DHHS regulations[1[Sec.110(b)]] and [2[Sec.110(b)]] refer to two general categories that can qualify for expedited review. The categories are: (1) Research activities that present no more than minimal risk and are listed in a National Institutes of Health guidance document[3] as an "adjunct" to the DHHS and FDA regulations; and (2) "minor changes in previously approved research during the period (of one year or less) for which approval is granted." In contrast to research activities that can be initially reviewed and approved by the expedited method, a risk threshold for expedited review of minor changes is not specified. The concept of *minor,* however, implies that the allowable risk associated with the change is either no more than minimum, or the risk-benefit relationship of the research is not altered in a way that makes it less favorable.

A major criterion for research that can be initially reviewed through the expedited process is that it must involve no more than minimal risk. Therefore, a review of the definition of *minimal risk* is warranted. The DHHS regulations[1[Sec.102(i)]] and FDA regulations[2] define *minimal risk* to mean that "the probability and magnitude of harm or discomfort anticipated in the research are not greater in and of themselves than those ordinarily encountered in the daily life or during performance of routine physical or psychological examinations or tests." Based on the interpretation by the Office for Human Research Protections (OHRP), minimal risk is determined to be relative to the daily life of a normal, healthy person. Therefore, the risk threshold of what constitutes minimal risk cannot increase just because the subject is sick and faces greater risks because of the illness, or because of the medical or psychological interventions that would be expected. In fact, just the opposite may be true, and even the normal, healthy person standard of minimal risk may be too high in certain circumstances. For example, a study involving a relatively minor procedure such as a venipuncture, considered to be minimal risk in the life of a normal, healthy individual, would constitute more than minimal risk in the hemophilia population. Therefore, IRBs need to be cognizant of the restrictions and considerations related to determining whether a research project actually is associated with no more than minimal risk.

As mentioned previously, a minor modification of a currently approved protocol can be reviewed by the expedited process. Although the regulations do not specify what types of modifications would qualify as minor changes, common sense dictates that expedited review could be used to approve administrative changes such as routine closure of a study to new subject accrual. In addition, minor clarification of eligibility criteria, consent form clarifications, changes in advertisements, addition of monitoring procedures that are on the adjunct list, and other, no more than minimal-risk changes would qualify. Any change that includes an intervention that is greater than minimal risk or negatively impacts the risk-benefit relationship of the research should normally be referred to the full board for review.

Criteria for Approval of Research Using Expedited Review

In addition to meeting the general eligibility criteria previously indicated, research qualifying for expedited review must also meet the approval criteria defined by DHHS.[1(Sec.111),2(Sec.111)] These are briefly summarized as follows:

1. The proposed procedures must be consistent with sound research design, and when possible, procedures already being performed on subjects should be utilized. For example, obtaining an additional amount of blood at the time of routine venipuncture is preferred rather than doing an additional needle stick to obtain the research sample.

2. The risks of the research must be reasonable in relation to the anticipated benefits, if any, to the subjects and the importance of the knowledge that may be gained.

3. Subject selection must be equitable.

4. Informed consent should be sought and documented unless a waiver of consent and/or documentation of consent has met the waiver criteria at 45 CFR 46.[1[Sec.116(d),117(c)]] It should be noted that the requirements for informed consent found at 45 CFR 46[1(Sec.116)] and 21 CFR 50[4(Sec.20,25,27)] have been reviewed extensively in Part 6 of this book.

5. Where appropriate, there is a plan to collect and monitor data to ensure subject safety.

6. The privacy of subjects and maintenance of confidentiality of data is protected.

7. Where necessary, additional safeguards have been included to protect vulnerable subjects.

Finally, as mentioned previously, research approved by the expedited method must be communicated to the full board. This should be accomplished by providing a list of all such approved studies accompanied by a brief synopsis of the nature of the research and the expedited category under which the research qualifies for review. All IRB members will then have the opportunity to review the list and ask questions. Thus, all are kept informed of the activities of the IRB outside of the full-board deliberations.

Adjunct List of Categories Qualifying for Expedited Review

The "applicability" standards that preface the nine categories of research indicate a strong warning regarding potential risks to research subjects who can be identified. In addition, subjects whose responses could reasonably place them at risk for criminal or civil liability, be damaging to their financial standing, insurability, reputation, or be stigmatizing may be at risk, unless appropriate mechanisms to prevent breaches of confidentiality or privacy are in place. Studies that have this potential may best be reviewed by the full board, rather than by a designated reviewer.

In consideration of the applicability standards for expedited review and because some of the activities listed could raise issues and problems related to interpretation, the authors have provided relevant examples and guidance under each of the nine categories on the adjunct list that qualify for expedited review.[3(p.60364)] The examples and guidance are not meant to be comprehensive.

Category 1

Clinical studies of drugs and medical devices only when condition (a) or (b) is met. (a) Research on drugs for which an investigational new drug application (21 CFR Part 312) is not required. (b) Research on medical devices for which (i) an investigational device exemption application (21 CFR Part 812) is not required; or (ii) the medical device is cleared/approved for marketing and the medical device is being used in accordance with its cleared/approved labeling.

Although this may be an allowable category of expedited review, the authors are hard pressed to find an applicable example. It appears that the minimal risk threshold would be exceeded by the very nature of studies involving drugs and/or devices. Indeed, of the IRB administrators canvassed, none have utilized this category as justification for conducting expedited review.

Category 2

Collection of blood samples by finger stick, heel stick, ear stick, or venipuncture as follows: (a) from healthy, nonpregnant adults who weigh at least 110 pounds. For these subjects, the amounts drawn may not exceed 550 ml in an 8 week period and collection may not occur more frequently than 2 times per week; or (b) from other adults and children, considering the age, weight, and health of the subjects, the collection procedure, the amount of blood to be collected, and the frequency with which it will be collected. For these subjects, the amount drawn may not exceed the lesser of 50 ml or 3 ml per kg in an 8 week period and collection may not occur more frequently than 2 times per week.

This category description is very detailed and does not appear to require any examples to facilitate understanding. However, expedited review of research that fits this category that involves very small children and infants warrants a cautionary approach based on health status, frequency of venipuncture, and blood volumes. Although the physical risks in the pediatric population may be very low when the blood volumes to be drawn are safe and appropriate for age and weight, consideration should be given to needle phobia associated with children's real and perceived fear of a venipuncture. Indeed, where minors are concerned, all efforts should be made to obtain the additional research sample at the time of routine venipuncture, rather than necessitate a separate, additional needle stick. Some IRBs have gone so far as to prohibit research venipuncture in minors unless it is done at the time of routine blood draw, thereby completely avoiding an extra needle stick.

Category 3

Prospective collection of biological specimens for research purposes by noninvasive means. Examples: (a) Hair and nail clippings in a nondisfiguring manner; (b) Deciduous teeth at time of exfoliation or if routine patient care indicates a need for extraction; (c) Permanent teeth if routine patient care indicates a need for extraction; (d) Excreta and external secretions (including sweat); and (e) uncannulated saliva collected either in an unstimulated fashion or stimulated by chewing gumbase or wax or by applying a dilute citric solution to the tongue; (f) Placenta removal at delivery; (g) Amniotic fluid obtained at the time of rupture of the membrane prior to or during labor; (h) Supra- and subgingival dental plaque and calculus, provided the collection procedure is not more invasive than routine prophylactic scaling of the teeth and the process is accomplished in accordance with accepted prophylactic techniques; (i) Mucosal and skin cells collected by buccal scraping or swab, skin swab, or mouth washings; (j) Sputum collected after saline mist nebulization.

This category description is also very detailed and does not appear to require examples to facilitate understanding. However, it should be noted that any specimens collected for use in research involving DNA testing or searching for a new way to test for pathogenic organisms that could be deemed potentially sensitive should be carefully reviewed. Such studies may ultimately require referral of the study to the full IRB. Clearly, such research may present more than minimal risk to subjects.

Category 4

Collection of data through noninvasive procedures (not involving general anesthesia or sedation) routinely employed in clinical practice, excluding procedures involving x-rays or microwaves. Where medical devices are employed, they must be cleared/approved for marketing. (Studies intended to evaluate the safety and effectiveness of the medical device are not generally eligible for expedited review, including studies of cleared medical devices for new indications.) Examples: (a) physical sensors that are applied either to the surface of the body or at a distance and do not involve input of significant amounts of energy into the subject or an invasion of the subject's privacy. (b) weighing or testing sensory acuity; (c) magnetic resonance imaging; (d) electrocardiography, electroencephalography, thermography, detection of naturally occurring radioactivity, electroretinoraphy, ultrasound, diagnostic infrared imaging, doppler blood flow, and echocardiography; (e) moderate exercise, muscular strength testing, body composition assessment, and flexibility testing where appropriate given the age, weight and health of the individual.

This category contains a number of routine clinical tests that present no more than minimal risk and would routinely qualify for expedited review. Possible exceptions are exercise, strength testing, and flexibility testing. For example, a study on the health effects of moderate exercise over a six-month period on the overall well-being of senior citizens with mild arthritis, which involves strength testing, noninvasive cardiac monitoring, and use of quality-of-life questionnaires, is research that would qualify for expedited review in Category 4. On the other hand, the same study using a more debilitated subject population would likely not qualify for expedited review because the risks associated with the exercise and strength testing would pose more than minimal risk.

Category 5

Research involving materials (data, documents, records, or specimens) that have been collected for any reason or will be collected solely for nonresearch purposes (such as medical treatment or diagnosis).

Research utilizing retrospectively or prospectively collected, routine medical record information or leftover specimens collected at the time of clinical care would qualify in this category of expedited review if the information is not considered sensitive and any potential breach of confidentiality would not be damaging to the subject. Research using the medical records of HIV-positive patients is an example of a study that should not be reviewed by the expedited method.

Category 6

Collection of data from voice, video, digital, or image recordings made for research purposes.

Depending on the nature of the study, the IRB must carefully review the types of information that will be recorded. The IRB must determine whether the study would involve information considered sensitive or potentially damaging to the subject's financial standing, employability, insurability, reputation, etc., if his or her voice or image (still or moving) could be identified. The IRB must ensure that appropriate safeguards are in place to prevent any potential harm that may be associated with a breach of confidentiality. For example, if the subject is asked to verbally describe his or her working conditions in a sweatshop, and his or her voice could be recognized, appropriate mechanisms should be used to disguise the subject's voice to prevent any potential harm such as loss of employment. Such a study should not be reviewed by the expedited method.

Category 7

Research on group characteristics or behavior (including, but not limited to, research on perception, cognition, motivation, identity, language, communication, cultural beliefs or practices, and social behavior) or research employing survey, interview, oral history, focus group, program evaluation, human factors evaluation, or quality assurance methodologies.

Survey research studies on intelligence or other traits involving specific populations require careful analysis because this type of research, depending on the nature of the survey questions, could result in stigmatization of a segment of society. For example, the results of research involving standardized IQ scores of a particular ethnic group correlated with their socioeconomic status and the educational levels of their parents may potentially be stigmatizing. This is particularly true if the group identified or the general cultural background of the subjects becomes known. Although research of this nature clearly fits this expeditable category, many issues, particularly the potential for stigmatization of a class of individuals and issues related to privacy and confidentiality, must be considered so that the subjects are protected. Thus, such research should be reviewed by the full IRB.

Category 8

> Continuing review of research previously approved by a convened IRB as follows: (a) where (i) the research is permanently closed to the enrollment of new subjects; (ii) all subjects have completed all research-related interventions; and (iii) the research remains active only for the long term follow-up of subjects; or (b) where no subjects have been enrolled and no additional risks have been identified or (c) where the remaining research activities are limited to data analysis.

An example of 8(a) would be a cooperative group clinical trial when the study is closed to new accrual. All subjects have completed active treatment and are in routine clinical follow-up with only the data used for research. Item 8(b) is somewhat more complex. Although subjects may not have been enrolled during the time period that the study has been open to accrual, the IRB is charged with ensuring that there is no new information about risk. If new risks have been identified, the full IRB must perform continuing review.

Category 9

> Continuing review of research not conducted under an investigational new drug application or investigational drug exemption where categories 2 through 8 do not apply but the IRB has determined and documented at a convened meeting that the research involves no greater than minimal risk and no additional risks have been identified.

As mentioned previously, initial review of research by the expedited method is limited to only those activities that fall within one or more of the categories specified on the adjunct list. However, at the time of full-board review, the IRB may decide that although the research did not qualify for expedited review initially, it is, nevertheless, no more than minimal risk. Therefore, it can be reviewed at the time of continuing review using the expedited method. This decision must be documented at the time of initial review and can be implemented if no additional risks are identified during the conduct of the research.

Conclusion

Some research projects simply do not warrant review by the full IRB in order to protect the rights and welfare of the subjects. Thus, appropriate use of expedited review helps reduce the workload of the full IRB and, ideally, decreases IRB turnaround time. However, whether expedited review actually results in a faster review and turnaround time is, in reality, dependent on the IRB administrative workload and/or the availability of the IRB Chair or his or her designee. Nonetheless, it must be stressed that regardless of whether a research proposal is reviewed by the expedited method or by the full IRB, the same regulatory and ethically based standards apply.

References

1. Code of Federal Regulations. Title 45A—Department of Health and Human Services; Part 46—Protection of Human Subjects. Updated 1 Oct 1997. Access date 18 Apr 2001. World Wide Web http://www4.law.cornell.edu/cfr/45p46.htm

2. Code of Federal Regulations. Title 21, Chapter 1—Food and Drug Administration, DHHS; Part 56—Institutional Review Boards. Updated 1 Apr 1999. Access date 27 Mar 2001. World Wide Web http://www4.law.cornell.edu/cfr/21p56.htm

3. National Institutes of Health. Protection of human subjects: Categories of research that may be reviewed by the Institutional Review Board (IRB) through an expedited review procedure. *Fed Regist* 63(216):60364-60367, 1998. World Wide Web http://ohrp.osophs.dhhs.gov/humansubjects/guidance/63fr60364.htm

4. Code of Federal Regulations. Title 21, Chapter 1—Food and Drug Administration, DHHS; Part 50—Protection of Human Subjects. Updated 1 Apr 1999. Access date 18 Apr 2001. World Wide Web http://www4.law.cornell.edu/cfr/21p50.htm

Identifying Research Intent

Robert J. Amdur and Marjorie A. Speers

*"It is impossible to avoid slippery slopes in medicine (or in any other aspect of life).
The issue is how and where to find a purchase."* **Marcia Angell, MD, 1997**

INTRODUCTION

Protecting the privacy and confidentiality of health information is a topic of national interest.[1] Unauthorized access to a person's medical record may result in psychological distress, disruption in interpersonal relationships, social stigmatization, discrimination, compromise in employability or insurability, and other undesirable consequences. The ethical basis for limiting access to private, identifiable medical information is the principle of *respect for persons*. This means that individuals should be treated as autonomous agents with the right to make choices and take actions based on their personal values.[2,3]

Regulating access to medical records has been the subject of recent articles in both the academic and lay press.[4,5] A major branchpoint in the thinking on this subject is whether private information will be collected for research or nonresearch purposes. At institutions that operate in compliance with federal regulations, the collection of private, identifiable medical information for research must be reviewed and monitored by an institutional review board (IRB) according to a detailed set of standards listed in the *Federal Register.*[6] Some state laws require informed consent to review a person's medical record for research purposes.[7] The U.S. Department of Health and Human Services is currently finalizing regulations under the authority of the 1996 Health Insurance Portability Protection Act (HIPPA). This will require all American health-care providers to comply with a restrictive system of oversight and documentation to release private health information without patient authorization.[8] HIPPA requirements are different for research versus nonresearch activity.

A problem with discussing privacy protection in terms of a research versus nonresearch model is that it is difficult to make this distinction for many of the activities that are now part of the fabric of our modern health-care system. Should retrospective medical record review by a qualified physician be classified as research or a nonresearch outcome analysis? Is a program that prospectively tracks the cost of therapy for patients with a given diagnosis research or a nonresearch evaluation of resource utilization? Is an analysis of the association between a hospital's nurse staffing model and the length of hospital stay following a given surgical procedure health services research or quality assessment? Is review of the medical records of all patients at a given hospital with an antibiotic-resistant bacterial infection research or a public health intervention?

To those not familiar with health-care regulation, the above questions may seem like an academic exercise about semantics. However, to IRB directors and other people who make important decisions based on research-specific standards, the classification of projects as *research* is serious business. Specifically, medical journal editors use a formal list of ethical standards as criteria for publication of research results.[9] Federal regulatory officials, medical center compliance officers, risk-management advisors, and IRB directors determine when access to the medical record must comply with laws and regulations that apply only to research activity.[6,7] As a wide range of activities currently collect medical information in a manner that does not comply with standards that are required for research, criteria for classifying an activity as research will affect a large segment of the medical community.[7,10,11]

Research versus Nonresearch

The next chapter explains how the IRB should triage projects that involve medical record review. Fundamental to the IRB process is the ability to distinguish research from nonresearch activity. As this is one of the most complex issues in research ethics, IRBs, research investigators, and regulatory officials will often struggle with the need for IRB review of projects that analyze health information. To address this fundamental aspect of the IRB review process, the purpose of this chapter is to discuss the factors that are important to consider when deciding if a project that involves the analysis of private, identifiable medical information should be considered research from the regulatory standpoint. After reviewing terminology and accepted definitions, we suggest a paradigm for identifying research intent that will facilitate the application of ethical standards. When reviewing this topic, it is important to understand that many activities that collect private, identifiable medical information are near the conceptual boundary between research and nonresearch such that there are no definitive classification criteria.[3,9] Reasonable people will disagree about how to apply the principles discussed in this chapter.

Related to the research versus nonresearch issue are the nature of the information that is being collected (private versus nonprivate information) and the ease with which health information can be tracked back to individual patients (linkage of information to personal identifiers).[9] While the definitions of *private information* and *personally identifiable information* are critical to evaluation of the ethics of medical record review, these topics do not inform the research versus nonresearch decision and therefore are considered to be beyond the scope of this paper. See the next chapter for an explanation of these concepts.

Terminology

To understand when a project that uses private, identifiable medical information should be classified as research, it is important to understand the major categories of activities that may be appropriately classified as something other than research (nonresearch).

Medical Practice   A commonly cited definition of *medical practice* describes an activity that is designed solely to enhance the well being of an individual patient.[12] A type of medical practice that is often confused with research is a class of activities that has been called *innovative therapy*.[13] Basically, innovative therapy describes an activity that is designed solely to benefit individual patient(s), but in which the ability of the activity to result in the desired outcome is to some degree unproven. Levine has explained that a better term for this class of activity is *nonvalidated practice*.[12]

Medical Practice for the Benefit of Others   In some situations, the goal of medical practice is to benefit people other than those directly affected by the health-care intervention. Examples of medical practice for the benefit of others include blood donation and some vaccination programs. In terms of the research/nonresearch issue, the critical feature of this form of medical practice is that the goal of the activity is to benefit a well-defined group of people in a predictable way.

Public Health Practice   Public health practice is similar to medical practice for the benefit of others in that the activity involves people who do not directly benefit from the intervention. Examples of public health practices that require the review of private, identifiable information about health status include surveillance (e.g., monitoring of diseases) and program evaluation (e.g., immunization coverage or use of clinical preventive services such as mammography).

Quality Assessment or Improvement   Activities that are designed to determine if aspects of medical practice are being performed in line with established standards are called *quality assessment* (QA). When an activity is specifically initiated with a goal of improving the performance of medical practice in relation to an established standard, the activity is called *quality improvement* (QI). Although it is possible for research to involve QA and QI activities, these terms usually refer to nonresearch activities.

Outcome Analysis   *Outcome analysis* is a nonspecific term that may be used to describe a variety of projects in which medical records are reviewed to evaluate the outcome of medical treatment or the course of patients with a specific medical condition.[7,10,11,14] Because medical research usually involves a formal analysis of outcome, use of the term *outcome analysis* to describe a nonresearch activity is confusing. Nevertheless, it is common practice for physicians, nurses, and other health care providers to perform descriptive analyses of medical outcomes that are appropriately described as something other than research but do not clearly fall into a better-defined category. Recognizing that there is no accepted definition of *outcome analysis* in the context of health-care evaluation, the main difference between a nonresearch outcome analysis and a quality-assessment project is that comparison of results to an established standard is not a defining feature of outcome analysis.

Resource Utilization Review   Medical record review is often conducted to evaluate the use of resources in a specific health-care activity. Terms like *cost control* are used to describe this class of activity,[4] but the terms *utilization review* or *resource utilization review* are more general and often more accurately reflect the fundamental goal of projects in this category. While a research project may involve review of resource utilization, the term *resource utilization review* usually refers to a nonresearch activity.

Investigational   *Investigational* is the term used by the Food and Drug Administration (FDA) for test articles (drugs and medical devices) that have not yet been approved for marketing.[12] Medications and devices may be used in situations other than those for which the FDA has approved marketing. *Off-label use of an approved medication* is an example of a nonresearch situation where medical practice involves the use of a medication in a setting that has not been approved by the FDA.

Experimental   Although research on human subjects may have a study design that involves an experiment, the meaning of the term *experimental* in the context of a discussion of research standards is so unclear that it is usually serves to confuse rather than enlighten the reader.[3] Some experts consider *experimental* to be unacceptable terminology.[12]

Distinguishing Research from Practice

The published literature on the distinction between research and nonresearch activity initially focused on the difference between research and medical practice. In 1974, the National Research Act established the National Commission for the Protection of Human Subjects of Biomedical and Behavioral Research and directed it to identify the basic ethical principles underlying the conduct of biomedical and behavioral research involving human subjects.[15] The first portion of this assignment was to consider "the boundaries between biomedical and behavioral research and the accepted and routine practice of medicine."[3] The fact that the commission was directed to evaluate the research versus nonresearch issue indicates both the importance of, and the difficulty in, separating these concepts from the standpoint of establishing ethical standards for the protection of human research subjects. As bioethicist Jay Katz stated, "Drawing the line between research and accepted practice . . . [is] . . . the most difficult and complex problem facing the commission."[12]

In April 1979, the commission issued a report on ethical principles and guidelines for the protection of human subjects of research entitled *The Belmont Report*.[3] Section A of *The Belmont Report* is labeled "Boundaries Between Practice and Research." The text of this section is reproduced here because it presents an authoritative and articulate explanation of this fundamental issue.

It is important to distinguish between biomedical and behavioral research, on the one hand, and the practice of accepted therapy on the other, in order to know what activities ought to undergo review for the protection of human subjects of research. The distinction between research and practice is blurred partly because both often occur together (as in research designed to evaluate a therapy) and partly because notable departures from standard practice are often called experimental when the terms *experimental* and *research* are not carefully defined.

For the most part, the term *practice* refers to interventions that are designed solely to enhance the well being of an individual patient or client and that have a reasonable expectation of success. The purpose of medical or behavioral practice is to provide diagnosis, preventive treatment, or therapy to particular individuals. By contrast, the term *research* designates an activity designed to test a hypothesis, permit conclusions to be drawn, and thereby develop or contribute to generalizable knowledge (expressed, for example, in theories, principles, and statements of relationships). Research is usually described in a formal protocol that sets forth an objective and a set of procedures designed to reach that objective.

When a clinician departs in a significant way from standard or accepted practice, the innovation does not, in and of itself, constitute research. The fact that a procedure is experimental, in the sense of new, untested, or different, does not automatically place it in the category of research. Radically new procedures of this description should, however, be made the object of formal research at an early stage in order to determine whether they are safe and effective. Thus, it is the responsibility of medical practice committees, for example, to insist that a major innovation be incorporated into a formal research project.

Research and practice may be carried on together when research is designed to evaluate the safety and efficacy of a therapy. This need not cause any confusion regarding whether or not the activity requires review; the general rule is that if there is any element of research in an activity, that activity should undergo review for the protection of human subjects.[3(Sec.A)]

Identifying Research Intent

Federal research regulations and the proposed HIPPA privacy law define *research* as "a systematic investigation, including research development, testing, and evaluation, designed to develop or contribute to generalizable knowledge."[6,8] When evaluating a specific project, it is useful to think of this definition as a requirement for two key elements: (1) the project involves a *systematic investigation* and (2) the *design*—meaning goal, purpose, or intent—of the investigation is to develop or contribute to generalizable knowledge.

The first of these two elements—the use of a systematic investigation—may be a characteristic of both research and nonresearch projects. Public health practice, QA and QI programs, resource utilization review, and outcome analyses are examples of nonresearch activities that frequently use scientific methodology to collect and analyze data from the medical record in a manner identical to that of research studies. All well-designed medical research involves a systematic approach to investigate a scientific hypothesis, but a systematic investigation is not synonymous with research intent.

Defining *Research*

The defining characteristic of research is that a fundamental goal of the activity is to learn something (test a hypothesis) that may benefit people other than research subjects. In some classes of research, the research subjects may directly benefit from research participation, but that is not the primary goal of a research effort. In the language of the federal regulations, the *design*—meaning primary goal, purpose, or intent—of a research investigation is to develop or contribute to generalizable knowledge.[6] When discussing standards for protecting the confidentiality of health information, the conceptual basis for the research/nonresearch distinction is that additional protections are needed when direct benefit is not the primary intent of the activity that involves an invasion of privacy or potential breach in confidentiality.

In the proposed HIPPA standards, *generalizable knowledge* is knowledge related to health that can be applied to populations outside of the population served by entities covered by the HIPPA legislation.[8] It is important to recognize that, just as scientific methodology may be used in nonresearch activities, research intent is not defined by the generalizability of a project's results. It is not unusual in medicine and other sectors of society for information that was collected for a nonresearch purpose to be in some way applicable, of value, and/or of interest to society in general or to an audience beyond that for which the activity was designed. Research is not required for one organization or segment of society to learn something from the experience of another. Medical education programs exist to disseminate (generalize) important information throughout the medical community.

To see how society currently evaluates research intent with projects that collect private, identifiable medical information, it is useful to look at IRBs. Because most academic medical centers are required to conduct research in compliance with federal regulations, IRBs routinely make important decisions about research intent with projects that collect private, identifiable medical information.[9] Based on discussions at the 1999 Public Responsibility in Medicine and Research (PRIM&R) meeting (December 6, 1999, Boston, MA), it is clear that some IRBs currently base institutional policy on the assumption that publication of results in a scientific journal defines a project as research. Project investigators are told that if they "hope to" or "might want to" publish results of their project in a medical journal or present some aspect of the project at an academic meeting, then the project involves research and should not be done without IRB approval. At some institutions, project investigators are told that if a project involving medical record review is, or was, done without IRB approval, then institutional policy prohibits them from publishing project results as this would document noncompliance with federal research regulations. An information document from the U.S. Food and Drug Administration on Humanitarian Use Devices suggests that this approach to identifying research intent is not unique to the IRB community.[16]

Several things must be considered when applying research standards to all activities that may produce results that are suitable for publication in a medical journal or presentation at a national meeting.

1. Medical journals often contain articles that discuss information that is not the result of research activity.[7,11,17,18] The same is true with medical meeting agendas. Specific examples are discussed in the next section of this chapter. The assumption that academic publication or presentation equals research is incorrect.

2. Ethical standards that are designed for research may not apply to nonresearch activity. As explained above, federal regulations and proposed national legislation related to the privacy of health information make a major distinction between research and nonresearch activity. One could argue that the fundamental issue—namely, respect for persons—is

the same regardless of the motive for invading privacy. This issue is the subject of other papers.[4,14] The purpose of mentioning ethical standards here is to point out that if research intent is important, then it is a mistake to establish policy that applies research standards to nonresearch activities. For example, in the field of public health, it is not unusual to conduct projects, such as outbreak investigations, where the application of research standards would be inappropriate and associated with administrative obstacles that would likely compromise the public's health.

3. A major difference currently exists in the processes of regulating research and nonresearch activity. Federal regulations require IRB approval to conduct most types of research that involve collection of private, identifiable medical information. Nonresearch activities often proceed with no formal review or oversight. Federal legislation will soon require a different process for evaluating research versus nonresearch access to most versions of the medical record.[8] Extending the authority of research regulations to nonresearch activity will discourage many projects that make important contributions to our society.[4,10]

Evaluating Research Intent

As previously discussed, the use of a systematic investigation and the potential generalizability of results are not unique identifiers of research intent. To accurately classify projects as either research or nonresearch, the critical factor is the primary intent (design) of the activity. In our experience, questions about publication or presentation of results in an academic forum are the most useful way to evaluate research intent, but the focus of the question should be different than as described above. The important question is not if the project investigator might want to publish or present results in the future, but rather if the project would be done as planned if academic recognition is definitely not a possibility. When a project involves the use of private, identifiable medical information, the following question is useful in identifying research intent: Would the project be conducted as proposed if the project investigator knew that he or she would never receive any form of academic recognition for the project, including publication of results in a medical journal or presentation of the project at an academic meeting?

Answering this question usually requires input from the project investigator. When evaluating projects to determine the need for IRB review, research authorities (usually the IRB director) should ask the project investigator to answer the above question. If the lack of academic recognition would affect the conduct of the project, then research intent is a primary motive for the activity.

For projects where the only ethical issues are the privacy and confidentiality of private, identifiable medical information, it is often difficult to evaluate research intent without trusting the project investigator to be truthful when discussing the role of academic recognition. As our system for protecting the rights and welfare of patients and research subjects depends on the integrity of the individuals conducting the activity, it is both necessary and appropriate to make decisions based on the project investigator's response in this setting. To understand how to evaluate research intent for the wide range of projects that use private, identifiable medical information, it is useful to discuss specific examples.

Case Discussions

The Case Report

A medical student requests access to a patient's medical record to prepare a "case report" for publication in a medical journal.

Question: Would the project be conducted as proposed if the student knew that he or she would never receive any form of academic recognition for the project? The answer is no. The goal of this activity is to produce a paper that will be accepted for publication in a medical journal. The medical student would not conduct this project as planned if he or she knew that this case report would not be accepted for publication.

Informal discussions with multiple experts in research regulation and research ethics at the December 6, 1999, PRIM&R meeting (Boston, MA) suggest that there is presently a lack of consensus on the classification of case reports as research. Federal regulations define research as "a systematic investigation, including research development, testing, and evaluation, designed to develop or contribute to generalizable knowledge." [19] One could argue that the preparation of a case report for publication does not constitute research because the activity does not involve a systematic investigation. There are no hypotheses to be tested, no study design, and no structured method of data analysis. However, there is no question that the primary intent of the activity is to contribute to generalizable knowledge that will benefit persons other than the patient who is the subject of the case report. In our opinion, the collection of private, identifiable medical information to prepare a case report for academic publication should be classified as research from the regulatory standpoint.

Modification of Standard Practice

An internal medicine physician plans to treat her next 50 patients with bacterial endocarditis with an antibiotic program that has not been previously used in this setting. All medications are FDA-approved for the treatment of bacterial infections in humans. Results of treatment will be compared to historical controls in an attempt to determine if the new schedule improves survival or decreases toxicity. The physician in charge of the project plans to submit a report of the project for publication in a medical journal.

Question: Would the project be conducted as proposed if the internist knew that she would never receive any form of academic recognition for the project? Based on the above information, this project could be classified as nonvalidated practice, quality improvement, outcome analysis, or research. The only way to identify research intent is to ask the internist about her motivation for using this

nonvalidated treatment program in this group of patients. It may be that the primary intent of this activity is to improve the care of her patients. If the project investigator will proceed with treatment and data analysis as planned, even if she were prohibited from publishing or presenting the project in an academic forum, then the primary intent of the project is not to "develop or contribute to generalizable knowledge." However, if the project would be changed because there is no prospect of academic recognition, then research intent is an important goal of this activity. Federal research regulations require IRB approval to review medical records in this situation.

Retrospective Evaluation of Outcome

A radiation oncologist plans to review the medical records of patients who have been treated at his institution over the past 30 years with radiation therapy for cancer of the larynx. Scientific methodology will be used to evaluate the probability of the tumor cure and treatment-related complications. Approximately 500 cases will be analyzed. When necessary, patients or their families will be called at home to provide follow-up information. The project investigator hopes the project will be suitable for publication in a medical journal.

Outcome evaluations similar to what is described in this example are common in both academic and community medical practice. Peer-reviewed medical journals publish "retrospective chart-review" studies on a regular basis.[7] Based on the above information, this project could be classified as either an outcome analysis, quality assessment, or research.

Question: Would the project be conducted as proposed if the project investigator knew that he would never receive any form of academic recognition for the project? The goal of this project may be to provide a specific group of physicians with the information they need to make treatment decisions for future patients with larynx cancer. As in the preceding example, the only way to evaluate research intent in this type of project is to ask the oncologist about his motivation for conducting the activity. If there are meaningful changes in the way the project would be conducted if the oncologist knew that this activity would not result in an academic publication, then the project should be classified as research.

Case-Controlled Evaluation of Disease Incidence

An epidemiologist wishes to review all the medical records at a hospital to evaluate risk factors for patients with vancomycin-resistant enterococcus and matched controls. Medical information will be collected with linkage to personal identifiers. The epidemiologist may try to publish the results of this project in a medical journal.

Question: Would the project be conducted as proposed if the epidemiologist knew that she would never receive any form of academic recognition for the project? We need more information to answer this question. If the epidemiologist is a public health official or part of a hospital infection-control program, the primary intent of the activity may be to provide the information needed to make decisions related to decreasing antibiotic-resistant infections. If it is clear that the project would be done as planned in the absence of academic recognition, then the project is best classified as a public health practice rather than research. If important aspects of the design or conduct of this project would change if the epidemiologist knew that the project would not result in a publication or other form of academic recognition, then it should be classified as research.

The Prospective Randomized Trial

A urologist plans to conduct a randomized trial to evaluate the value of prophylactic antibiotics to prevent urinary tract infection after cystoscopy. The two study groups include no treatment versus prophylactic treatment using an antibiotic that is commonly used for this purpose. The urologist claims that the goal of this project is to generate the information he needs to decide how to treat future patients. The project investigator claims that the project will be conducted as planned regardless of the prospect for academic recognition.

The type of situation described in this example is unlikely, but not unheard of.[20] It is presented here to illustrate the point that extreme examples stretch the applicability of any guideline. One could argue that the design of an investigation does not define a project as research. Although this could be viewed as a logical extension of the ideas we have presented in this paper, at some point the design of an investigation makes it unreasonable to classify the project as a nonresearch activity. In our opinion, the use of a prospective randomized study design defines a project as research, regardless of the stated intent regarding academic recognition.

Data Collection to Support an Application to the Food and Drug Administration (FDA)

A physician plans to collect private, identifiable medical information to assess the efficacy of a medication as part of an FDA-regulated new drug application effort. The project clearly involves a systematic investigation, but the project investigator has no plans to publish or present the results of the project in an academic forum.

A large volume of industry-sponsored research is done for the sole purpose of supporting an FDA application to market a product for a specific purpose. Investigations associated with FDA applications may or may not result in academic publications. For this reason, it may be difficult to use the guidelines discussed in this paper to evaluate the research intent in this class of activity. The reason for mentioning this example is to point out that the question of research intent in this context is moot because federal regulations require all FDA-regulated investigations to be classified as research from the regulatory standpoint.[19]

Conclusion

Inappropriate use of private, identifiable medical information may result in psychological distress, disruption of interpersonal relationships, social stigmatization, discrimination, compromise of employability or insurability, and other undesirable consequences. Protecting the confidentiality of information about a person's health status is currently the subject of federal law, federal regulations, ethical codes, and local medical center policy. A major branchpoint in the regulation of access to medical information is whether information is being collected for research or nonresearch purposes.

To identify research intent, it is important to understand that nonresearch activities may use scientific methodology and produce results that are suitable for publication in a medical journal. The defining characteristic of research is that a fundamental goal of the activity is to learn something (test a hypothesis) that will benefit people other than today's research subjects. To accurately classify projects as either research or nonresearch, the critical factor is the primary intent (design) of the activity. The following question facilitates the evaluation of research intent with projects that use private, identifiable medical information: Would the project be conducted as planned if the project investigators knew that they would never receive any form of academic recognition for the project, including publication of results in a medical journal or presentation of the project at an academic meeting?

References

1. General Accounting Office. Medical record privacy: Access needed for health research, but oversight of privacy protections is limited. (GAO/HEHS-99-55). Updated 25 Feb 1999. Access date 24 Apr 2001. World Wide Web http://www.epic.org/privacy/medical/gao-medical-privacy-399.pdf

2. Beauchamp TLCJF. *Principles of Biomedical Ethics,* Ed 4. New York: Oxford University Press. 1994.

3. National Commission for the Protection of Human Subjects of Biomedical and Behavioral Research. *The Belmont Report: Ethical Principles and Guidelines for the Protection of Human Subjects of Research.* (DHEW Publication No.(OS) 78-0012, 18 Apr 1979. Access date 22 Mar 2001. World Wide Web http://ohsr.od.nih.gov/mpa/belmont.php3

4. Etzioni A. Medical records: Enhancing privacy, preserving the common good. *Hastings Cent Rep* 29(2):14-23, 1999.

5. Where's the privacy? *Gainesville Sun.* 1G. 2000.

6. Code of Federal Regulations. Title 45A—Department of Health and Human Services; Part 46—Protection of Human Subjects. Updated 1 Oct 1997. Access date 18 Apr 2001. World Wide Web http://www4.law.cornell.edu/cfr/45p46.htm

7. Office for Human Research Protections. Compliance oversight. Updated 12 Dec 2000. Access date 20 Mar 2001. World Wide Web http:// ohrp.osophs.dhhs.gov/compovr.htm

8. Office of the Secretary of the Department of Health and Human Services. Standards for privacy of individually identifiable health information: Proposed rule. *Federal Register* 64(212):59918-60064, 1999.

9. Amdur RJ, Speers MA, Bankert EA. IRB triage of projects that involve medical record review. *IRB: A Review of Human Subjects Research* 22:4-7, 2000.

10. Lynn J, Johnson J, Levine RJ. The ethical conduct of health services research: A case study of 55 institutions' applications to the SUPPORT project. *Clin Res* 42(1):3-10, 1994.

11. Bull AR. Audit and research: Complementary but distinct. *Ann R Coll Surg Engl* 75(5):308-311, 1993.

12. Levine RJ. *Ethics and Regulation of Clinical Research,* Ed 2. Baltimore, MD: Urban and Schwarzenberg. 1986.

13. Levine RJ. The impact on fetal research of the report of the National Commission for the Protection of Human Subjects of Biomedical and Behavioral Research. *Villanova Law Rev* 22:367-383, 1977.

14. Casarett D, Karlawish JH, Sugarman J. Determining when quality improvement initiatives should be considered research: Proposed criteria and potential implications. *JAMA* 283(17):2275-2280, 2000.

15. 93rd Congress. National Research Act of 1974. PL93-348. 1974.

16. Center for Devices and Radiological Health. Humanitarian device exemption regulation questions and answers. Updated 4 Jan 2000. Access date 26 Mar 2001. World Wide Web http://www.fda.gov/cdrh/ode/hdeqna.html

17. Amdur RJ, Biddle C. Institutional review board approval and publication of human research results. *JAMA* 277(11):909-914, 1997.

18. Choo V. Thin line between research and audit. *Lancet* 352(9125):337-338, 1998.

19. Code of Federal Regulations. Title 21, Chapter 1—Food and Drug Administration, DHHS; Part 50—Protection of Human Subjects. Updated 1 Apr 1999. Access date 18 Apr 2001. World Wide Web http://www4.law.cornell.edu/cfr/21p50.htm

20. Berwick DM. Developing and testing changes in delivery of care. *Ann Intern Med* 128(8):651-656, 1998.

IRB Triage of Projects That Involve Medical Record Review

Robert J. Amdur, Marjorie A. Speers, and Elizabeth A. Bankert

INTRODUCTION

A medical student wants to review a medical record to prepare a "case report" for publication. An orthopedic surgeon wants to review hundreds of medical records to determine patients' outcome after hip replacement surgery. The ICU director wants to track resource utilization and patient outcome with the two treatment protocols that are currently being used to manage patients with acute respiratory distress syndrome. An epidemiologist wishes to review all the medical records at a hospital to evaluate risk factors in patients with vancomycin-resistant enterococcus and matched controls.

Medical records departments, hospital tumor registries, and directors of other medical databases frequently receive requests for access to confidential information for projects that could be defined as research. Over the past few years, a number of factors have resulted in an increased awareness about issues related to confidentiality of an individual's medical record.[1] At our medical centers, clinical faculty call the Institutional Review Board (IRB) frequently with questions about the need for IRB review of projects that collect data from medical records. Based on national meeting discussions and prior publications, it is clear that this is an important issue at other institutions.[1-6] This chapter will review the factors that determine the need for IRB review of projects that involve collection of data from medical records. A related topic is the potential need for informed consent to conduct medical record research. Informed consent and other criteria for IRB approval of medical record research will not be discussed in this chapter.

Regulatory Requirements for IRB Review

From the IRB standpoint, there are four main questions that must be answered when deciding how to apply the federal regulations to a project that involves collection of information from medical records.

Is the Project Research? [45 CFR 46.101(a)]

Authors from a wide range of scientific backgrounds have discussed the complexity of classifying a project as research.[4-8] In 45 CFR 46,[9[Sec.102(d)]] research is defined as "a systematic investigation designed to develop or contribute to generalizable knowledge." When evaluating a specific project, it is useful to think of this definition as a requirement for two key elements: (1) the project involves a systematic investigation, and (2) the design—meaning goal, purpose, or intent—of the investigation is to develop or contribute to generalizable knowledge.

It is important for IRBs to recognize that the first of these two elements (the use of a systematic investigation) may be a characteristic of both research and nonresearch projects. Public health interventions, quality assessment efforts, resource utilization review, and programs that evaluate medication side-effects after Food and Drug Administration licensure are examples of nonresearch activities. These activities frequently use scientific methodology to collect and analyze data from the medical record in a manner identical to that of research studies.

The defining characteristic of research is that the primary intent of the investigation is to develop or contribute to generalizable knowledge. Nonresearch activities may have the potential to produce results that are generalizable

Note: An abbreviated version of this chapter is published in *IRB: A Review of Human Subjects Research* 2000; 22(1):4-7. Used with permission.

beyond the population from which data are collected, but only a research project is designed with this as the primary goal. Similarly, results from both research and nonresearch activities may be worthy of publication in a medical journal or presentation at a national meeting; thus, discussion of a project in a public forum does not define a project as research.

Identifying the boundary between research and nonresearch activity is one of the most difficult issues in research ethics. This distinction becomes especially ambiguous when the only activity that could potentially be classified as research is the analysis or review of information that was, or will be, collected during the routine delivery of medical care. As the classification of a project as research is fundamental to the IRB review process, Chapter 4–3 is devoted entirely to the identification of research intent with projects that involve the collection of private, identifiable health information.

If the Project Is Research, Does It Involve Human Subjects? [45 CFR 46.101(a)]

In 45 CFR 46,[9[Sec.102(f)]] human subject is defined as "a living individual." Therefore, research that involves collection of data from the medical records of patients no longer living does not require IRB approval. The possible exception to this would be the situation where reviewing the medical history of a deceased person would put a living person at risk. This situation does exist in certain types of infectious disease or genetics research.

If the Project Is Research Involving Human Subjects, May It Be Exempt from IRB Review? [45 CFR 46.101(b)(4)]

Understanding when it is appropriate to exempt medical records research from IRB review will benefit IRBs and research investigators. To exempt research involving the collection or study of existing data, documents, or records from IRB review, these sources must be publicly available or recorded by the investigator. They must be recorded in such a manner that subjects cannot be identified, directly or through identifiers linked to the subjects. As there is no question that a person's medical record is not a publicly available source of information,[9[Sec.101(b)(4)]] the criterion for exempting research review of information from medical records is a lack of linkage to subject identifiers.

Identifying Information At 45 CFR 46,[9[Sec.102(f)(2)]] the regulations explain that information recorded for research purposes is individually identifiable when "the identity of the subject is or may readily be ascertained by the investigator or associated with the information." Therefore, research may not be exempt from IRB review if information is recorded in a form that identifies the subject by name or through a code. In our experience, some investigators are under the impression that the issue of identifiers applies only to data that are presented or published in a public forum. We have had investigators tell us that IRB approval is not required because "data will be published without patient names." To address this misunderstanding, it is important to point out that federal regulations require IRB approval when identifiers are present at any point in records created by the researcher, not just at the time of study presentation. Even when study data are recorded without subject identifiers, IRB approval may be required if the researcher takes medical records out of the medical record room as part of the research process.

The rationale for requiring IRB approval in this setting is that improper use of confidential medical information may harm a person in the form of psychological trauma, social stigmatization, or discrimination. IRB review may identify situations where a potential breach in confidentiality may harm human research subjects. The IRB may protect subjects by not approving a research project or, more commonly, by decreasing the risks of a study by educating research personnel about the importance of protecting confidentiality. The IRB can assist them in implementing safeguards to protect the rights and welfare of study participants.

If the Research Project Is Not Exempt from IRB Review, Is Expedited Review an Option? [63FR60364 and 60353]

On November 9, 1998, the list of categories of research that may be reviewed by an IRB with an expedited review procedure was revised in a National Institutes of Health (NIH) guidance document.[10] Two sections of the 1998 NIH regulations clarify issues related to medical record research.

Applicability (C): The expedited review procedure may not be used when identification of research subjects would reasonably place them at risk of damage to their financial standing, employability, insurability, or reputation, or when identification would be stigmatizing. If reasonable and appropriate protections are implemented so that risks related to invasion of privacy and breach of confidentiality are no greater than minimal, expedited review may be appropriate.

Applicability (F), category (5): To be eligible for expedited review, participation in research must present no more than minimal risk to human subjects. The research must be limited to the review of data, documents, or records that have been, or will be, collected solely for nonresearch purposes (such as medical treatment or diagnosis).

IRB Evaluation Process

Therefore, to decide whether expedited IRB review is appropriate for a study in which confidential information will be collected from medical records, the IRB must consider the risk of harm due to a breach in confidentiality. We structure this evaluation by asking ourselves two questions.

First, could identifying the person as a participant in this study, or linking the person with the information that is going to be recorded in this study, result in meaningful harm to him or her? For example, would the information lead to social stigmatization or damage to the person's financial standing, employability, insurability, or reputation?

There is no simple algorithm, guideline, or list that tells an IRB when a breach in confidentiality will result in meaningful harm. This is a decision that must be based on subjective criteria using the personal judgment of the IRB representative(s) making the decision. Factors that guide the assessment of risk in this setting are the nature of the information being recorded and the people who are expected to review study data. Examples of situations in which a breach in confidentiality is likely to result in more than minimal risk of harm include studies involving sensitive information, such as neurologic or psychiatric disorders that affect cognition and judgment, testing for genetic markers that are known to predict the development of serious medical illnesses (e.g., Huntington's chorea), sexually transmitted diseases, and medical issues that involve criminal behavior (e.g., child abuse, rape, illegal drug use).

Second, when information regarding study participation may result in meaningful harm to a participant, are there adequate safeguards to protect against a breach in confidentiality?

Investigators have multiple options for decreasing the chance that a participant will be harmed from participating in a medical record study involving linkage of study data to personal identifiers. For example, to decrease the range of people who know that a person is participating in a research study, the study can be administered so that references to, and documentation of, study participation do not appear in the medical record. To decrease the likelihood that study data can be connected to individual identifiers, the study can be set up so that identifiers are encoded or encrypted with a level of complexity that is appropriate for the degree of sensitivity of the information being recorded. To control access to study data, it may be desirable to use and store study records in an area with special security procedures, such as locked file storage and personalized access codes.

Conclusion

The IRB Should Review All Requests for Access to Medical Records for Research

Hospitals and clinics that maintain medical records should establish a policy that requires the medical records department, the tumor registry, computer services, and any other department that maintains records or a database containing confidential medical information to ask about research intent before giving out patient lists or allowing access to information from medical records. We think it appropriate to ask project directors to play a major role in identifying investigations that may need IRB review. Database administrators should not be in the position of deciding how to apply research regulations. A useful way to screen requests for medical information is to have a "request for medical records," a "request for patient list," and a "request for tumor registry information" form. It asks the person requesting access to medical information to indicate if research is the primary goal of the investigation. We suggest that the form read something like: "You are requesting access to confidential medical information. Please indicate if your review of medical records is being done for research or nonresearch purposes. Common nonresearch reasons for reviewing medical records include patient care, a public health intervention, quality assessment, evaluation of resource utilization, and adverse event monitoring after FDA licensure." The applicants are asked to circle the response that best describes the main purpose of their review of medical information.

Medical records departments, tumor registries, and other medical database directors should refer all projects that could be considered research to the IRB before giving access to confidential medical information.

If medical record review is being done for research, or if applicants are unsure about the role of research in their project, the request should be forwarded to the IRB. This is to determine the need for, and format of, IRB review. The criteria for considering a project as research from the regulatory standpoint and for exempting a study from IRB review are best evaluated by the IRB rather than a member of the medical records department or other institutional authority.

IRBs Should Review the Sections of 45 CFR 46 Relevant to Medical Record Research

In 45 CFR 46, subparts 101(a), 101(b)(4), and 102(f) require that research involving a human subject must be reviewed by an IRB if private information is recorded in a manner that is individually identifiable with specific research subjects. The regulations are clear that information from the medical record is private information. Research should not be exempt from IRB review if study data are linked to identifying information at any point in records created by the researcher.

IRB Should Use Primary Intent Rather Than Methodology to Distinguish Research from Nonresearch Activity

The distinguishing feature of research is that the primary intent of the investigation is to develop or contribute to generalizable knowledge. Investigations that are being done for purposes that are appropriately classified as something other than research may use scientific methodology to collect and analyze data from the medical record in a manner identical to that of research studies. Therefore, when faced with a situation where there is uncertainty about how to classify a project that involves a systematic investigation of data from the medical record, the IRB and project director should work to identify the primary intent of medical record review. As most people are not familiar with the concept of "generalizable knowledge," it may be useful to ask the project director to identify changes that might result from the proposed investigation. Research projects are done to change the way the medical community thinks about a specific issue. Nonresearch investigations are done to give a specific group the information needed to make a specific decision. When a project director considers his or her work to be research, the project should be handled as such, even if it could appropriately be classified otherwise from the IRB standpoint.

IRBs Should Understand How to Apply Recently Revised Requirements for Expedited Review of Medical Record Research

The decision to use the expedited process for IRB review of medical record research should be based on three factors: the degree of harm that would result from a breach in confidentiality, the likelihood that such a breach would occur, and the feasibility of establishing safeguards to maximally protect patient privacy. When there is concern that a breach in confidentiality regarding study participation may result in meaningful harm to a study participant, the study should be evaluated by full-committee IRB review.

References

1. Melton LJ. The threat to medical-records research. *N Engl J Med* 337(20):1466-1470, 1997.

2. Norsigian J, Whelan S, Billings P. Privacy and medical-records research. Correspondence. *N Engl J Med* 338(15):1076, 1998.

3. Public Responsibility in Medicine and Research. IRBs in the Shifting Sands of Public Opinion, San Diego, CA, 8-9 Nov. 1998.

4. Prentice ED, Gordon BG, Lin MH. Determining when a clinical activity should be classified as research requiring institutional review board review. *J Extra Corpor Technol* 29(2):89-91, 1997.

5. Bull AR. Audit and research: Complementary but distinct. *Ann R Coll Surg Engl* 75(5):308-311, 1993.

6. Choo V. Thin line between research and audit. *Lancet* 352(9125):337-338, 1998.

7. Levine RJ. *Ethics and Regulation of Clinical Research*, Ed 2. Baltimore, MD: Urban and Schwarzenberg. 1986.

8. Eddy DM. Investigational treatments: How strict should we be? *JAMA* 278(3):179-185, 1997.

9. Code of Federal Regulations. Title 45A—Department of Health and Human Services; Part 46—Protection of Human Subjects. Updated 1 Oct 1997. Access date 18 Apr 2001. World Wide Web http://www4.law.cornell.edu/cfr/45p46.htm

10. National Institutes of Health. Protection of human subjects: Categories of research that may be reviewed by the Institutional Review Board (IRB) through an expedited review procedure. *Fed Regist* 63(216):60364-60367, 1998. World Wide Web http://ohrp.osophs.dhhs.gov/humansubjects/guidance/63fr60364.htm

"Compassionate Use" and Emergency Exemption from IRB Approval

Elizabeth A. Bankert and Robert J. Amdur

INTRODUCTION

Institutional Review Boards (IRBs) that review biomedical research may be asked to approve the use of an investigational drug on a so-called compassionate-use basis. There is no way to know what an investigator means by *compassionate use* without evaluating the details of each individual request. It may be surprising for some IRBs or investigators to learn that there is no such thing as "compassionate use" from the standpoint of research regulation. The term *compassionate use* does not appear in either the Department of Health and Human Services (DHHS) or the Food and Drug Administration (FDA) regulations. The *IRB Guidebook*[1] states that the research community should not use this term because it serves to confuse discussions of access mechanisms. The purpose of this chapter is to clarify the role of the IRB in situations where the IRB may encounter the terms *compassionate use* or *emergency exemption*.

The Term *Compassionate Use*

Historically, the term *compassionate use* has been used to describe a situation where an investigational drug is being used outside the setting of a clinical trial. The use is in a small number of extremely ill patients for whom standard therapy is unlikely to be effective. The following scenario describes a situation that leads to a request for IRB approval of research on a compassionate-use basis.

Example

A physician has a patient with a condition for which an investigational drug may offer an advantage to all current FDA-approved treatments. The investigational drug is currently only available to patients enrolled in a clinical trial. The patient cannot receive the drug as part of a clinical trial because the trial is not being conducted in the medical system where the patient is being cared for or because the patient is ineligible for the trial. To treat the patient with the investigational drug, the physician must have the sponsor's permission to use the drug outside the setting of a clinical trial. The physician asks the IRB to approve the use of the investigational agent on a compassionate-use basis.

The sponsor will be violating FDA regulations and/or federal law if it releases the investigational drug under circumstances that are not specifically approved by the FDA. FDA regulations provide for the use of investigational drugs in research that is approved by an appropriately constituted IRB. Otherwise, FDA regulations provide for the use of investigational drugs outside the standard research setting in three circumstances: emergency exemption from prospective IRB approval, treatment investigational new drug application (IND), and the parallel track mechanism. Treatment INDs and parallel track programs are discussed in the *IRB Guidebook*.[1] The rest of this chapter will focus on the FDA's emergency exemption option.

Federal Regulation (FDA)

Federal regulations related to emergency exemption from prospective IRB approval include 21 CFR 56,[2][Sec.102 (d), 104(c)] 21 CFR 50,[3(Sec.23)] and 21 CFR 312.[4(Sec.36)] A description of the process can also be found in the FDA Information Sheets.[5] The FDA definition of *emergency use* makes reference to two essential components: (1) a life-threatening situation in which no standard acceptable treatment is available, and (2) insufficient time to convene a quorum for full-board IRB approval. In an emergency situation as described above, prior IRB approval is not required for provision of the test article to one patient. Rather, the FDA requirement is that the IRB is notified before or within five days of the emergency use of the test article. It is important to understand that there is no type of expedited or subcommittee process allowed for IRB review and approval of the emergency use of a test article according to federal regulations.

Processing a Request for "Compassionate Use" (FDA Rules)

This algorithm may help you when you receive the next phone call from an investigator at your institution requesting compassionate-use approval:

1. First, determine if the compassionate-use request fulfills the FDA criteria for emergency use. Do not assume the investigator knows the FDA definition of emergency use: (a) a life-threatening situation exists in which no standard acceptable treatment is available, and (b) there is not sufficient time to convene a quorum for full-board IRB review and approval.

2. If the situation satisfies the FDA criteria for emergency use, the next step is to determine if an IRB acknowledgment letter (versus an IRB approval letter) is what the sponsor requires. In some cases, the investigator misunderstands the sponsor's requirements for access to the test article. Explain to the investigator that the sponsor may actually be requesting IRB acknowledgment of emergency use prior to or within five days of use of the test article. It is unusual for a sponsor to require full-board IRB approval to release medication for emergency use in a single patient.

3. If the situation fits the criteria for emergency use *and* the sponsor requires an acknowledgment letter, follow the procedures for emergency exemption from IRB approval described below.

4. If the situation does not meet FDA criteria for emergency use, a convened full-board IRB review and approval of the protocol and consent form per standard IRB review procedure must be completed before release of the test article.

5. If the sponsor requires IRB approval before release of the test article, an IRB approval letter may only be written after a convened full-board review and approval of the protocol and the consent form according to standard IRB procedure. Remember, there is no type of expedited or subcommittee process allowed for IRB review and approval of the emergency use of a test article, according to federal regulations.

IRB Procedure for FDA Emergency Exemption

Instruct the investigator to generate a letter to the IRB Chair describing the emergency-use situation. The letter must document compliance with specific FDA requirements for emergency use, indicating (a) a life-threatening situation exists in which no standard acceptable treatment is available, *and* (b) the test article must be used expeditiously, meaning insufficient time is available to convene a quorum for full-board IRB approval. The notification to the IRB must occur prior to or within five days of use of the test article.

The IRB Chair or appropriate designee (IRB member with appropriate medical knowledge) reviews the investigator's letter and confirms that (a) an emergency situation

exists, and (b) there is not sufficient time to convene a full-board IRB meeting.

The IRB office generates a letter to be signed by the IRB Chair acknowledging notification of emergency use of the test article.

Example

Dear Dr. Smith,

The office of the Institutional Review Board (IRB) has received your written notification of the request for emergency use of the investigational drug, xxxx, for one patient, initials A.A.

Prior IRB review and approval are not required for the emergency use of a test article as described in 21 CFR 56.102(d) and 21 CFR 56.104(c). This memo is not a notification of IRB review or approval.

The notification you have provided to the IRB meets the requirements of our IRB office and federal regulations. Please note, if subsequent use of drug xxxx is anticipated, please submit an application for review by the full IRB before its next use.

Thank you,

IRB Chair signature

The IRB letter should indicate only knowledge of, acknowledgement of, or appropriate notification of the use of the test article. The IRB letter should not indicate IRB review or approval.

All subsequent uses of the test article should be reviewed using the standard full-board IRB review process. If an investigator believes another request for the use of this test article is forthcoming, the full IRB review process should be initiated. Note that the FDA acknowledges that subsequent uses should not be denied because the IRB could not convene in a timely manner. The IRB letter to the investigator should also describe the FDA subsequent-use requirement.

Informed Consent

The patient must understand the investigational nature of the test article. Informed consent must be obtained; however, the consent form is not a standard research consent form. In most cases, the sponsor will supply a consent form. The IRB is not involved in the review or approval of the consent form if the situation meets the criteria for emergency use. The FDA describes the "Exception from informed consent requirements" in 21 CFR 50.[3][Sec.24(a)]

Written Policy and Procedures

There should be a description of the policy for emergency exemption from IRB approval. This should be located in the IRB internal procedure manual at your IRB office. The information in this chapter will be sufficient to write this section. We also recommend that your office create an internal procedure document for emergency use that can readily be sent to an investigator upon request. Again, this chapter contains the necessary information for this document. The requesting physician can send the document describing your emergency-use procedure to the sponsor, which ensures that all interested parties are aware of the appropriate procedures. Because time is often of the essence in these situations, having a description of the process ready to send out is very useful.

DHHS Rules

Please note that the procedures described in this chapter pertain only to FDA-regulated research. The FDA elected to make some changes in the DHHS federal policy (Common Rule). DHHS does not provide for an emergency exception to IRB review. However, DHHS allows physicians to provide emergency medical treatment to their patients.[6][Sec.116(f)] The difference between research conducted through the DHHS and research regulated through the FDA is that in an emergency-use situation, the DHHS does not consider the patient a research participant. Thus, the data are not allowed as part of a research study. The FDA does allow the data from an emergency-use situation to be used as part of a research study.

If the research is funded by the DHHS and/or your organization has agreed to abide by DHHS regulations, and the research involves the use of a drug, biologic, or device, the research also falls under the jurisdiction of the FDA. Consequently, both sets of regulations must be followed. In this instance, a sentence may be added to the IRB acknowledgment letter: *The data obtained from the emergency use of this investigational drug may not be used as part of a research study.*

Conclusion

Guidance from federal regulatory authorities makes it clear that "compassionate use" is a term that should not be used to direct the process of research regulation. From the standpoint of IRB review of research, the term "com-passionate use" has no meaning. This chapter has explained the situations where the IRB will be asked to approve a study on a "compassionate use" basis. Federal regulations related to approval of research by an expedited process and FDA rules related to emergency use of an investigational agent will direct the IRB in this setting. A step-by-step explanation of how an IRB should manage the compassionate use situation is presented.

References

1. Penslar RL, Porter JP, Office for Human Research Protections (DHHS). Chapter II, Part A, Section ii, Question 22. In: *Institutional Review Board Guidebook,* ed 2. Updated 27 Jun 2000. Access date 9 Aug 2001. World Wide Web
http://ohrp.osophs.dhhs.gov/irb/irb_chapter2.htm

2. Code of Federal Regulations. Title 21, Chapter 1—Food and Drug Administration, DHHS; Part 56—Institutional Review Boards. Updated 1 Apr 1999. Access date 27 Mar 2001. World Wide Web
http://www4.law.cornell.edu/cfr/21p56.htm

3. Code of Federal Regulations. Title 21, Chapter 1—Food and Drug Administration, DHHS; Part 50—Protection of Human Subjects. Updated 1 Apr 1999. Access date 18 Apr 2001. World Wide Web
http://www4.law.cornell.edu/cfr/21p50.htm

4. Code of Federal Regulations. Title 21, Chapter 1—Food and Drug Administration, DHHS; Part 312—Investigational New Drug Application. Updated 1 Apr 1999. Access date 18 Apr 2001. World Wide Web
http://www4.law.cornell.edu/cfr/21p312.htm

5. Food and Drug Administration. Information sheets: Guidance for Institutional Review Boards and clinical investigators, Sept 1998. Access date 9 Apr 2001. World Wide Web
http://www.fda.gov/oc/oha/IRB/toc.html

6. Code of Federal Regulations. Title 45A—Department of Health and Human Services; Part 46—Protection of Human Subjects. Updated 1 Oct 1997. Access date 18 Apr 2001. World Wide Web
http://www4.law.cornell.edu/cfr/45p46.htm

Waiver of Consent in Emergency Medicine Research

Helen McGough

INTRODUCTION

In 1996, both the Food and Drug Administration (FDA) and the Office for Protection from Research Risks (OPRR; now Office for Human Research Protections, OHRP) issued regulations permitting a waiver of the general requirements for informed consent for certain research settings involving risks to subjects that are greater than minimal. The intent of the regulations is to allow research on life-threatening conditions for which available treatments are unproven or unsatisfactory and when it is not possible to obtain informed consent. The regulations establish additional protections to make sure the studies are safe and ethical. The situations to which the regulations apply are limited to cases in which subjects cannot give consent, and for whom a legally authorized representative cannot be located by the time the intervention must be used to be effective. The underlying assumption is that these subjects, because they cannot either consent or refuse to consent, are a vulnerable population worthy of additional protections provided by the regulations. The complete text of this regulation is included as the Appendix to this chapter. Sufficient controversy surrounds the ethics of these regulations that an IRB should be wary about venturing into this arena.[1] The committee should discuss the issues in the abstract before an actual case is presented to it for consideration. The intent of this chapter is not to debate the ethics of the regulation, but to assist the IRB in complying with it.

Applicability

The regulations allowing waiver of consent in emergency medicine research are limited to two kinds of situations. The first is when the research involves an investigational intervention that comes under FDA regulation. This includes drugs, devices, and biologics that are not approved for the conditions in which the researcher proposes to use them. For example, a researcher may wish to test an investigational drug to reduce brain swelling after closed head injury, or to test an investigational defibrillator to resuscitate people who suffer cardiac arrest. The second is when the research is either sponsored by a federal agency or conducted by an institution that has chosen to apply the federal regulations to all its research activities. Examples of this second area of applicability might include research that evaluates an innovative surgical procedure or evaluates approved treatments in a research setting.

Implementing the Regulations

Implementing these regulations requires extensive time and effort by the IRB and by the researchers and the research sponsors. The remainder of this chapter breaks down the regulation (97-01[2]) into sections and addresses the points to consider from each section.

Section 1

> The human subjects are in a life-threatening situation, available treatments are unproven or unsatisfactory. In addition, the collection of valid scientific evidence, which may include evidence obtained through randomized placebo-controlled investigations, is necessary to determine the safety and effectiveness of particular interventions.

The points to be considered through the IRB review process include the following:

1. Are the subjects in a life-threatening condition? To answer this question, the IRB must have a fairly clear notion of how

it is willing to define *life-threatening*. Generally speaking, the determination is made within the context of the research protocol. The question to be asked and answered is: "Are the potential subjects in an emergent situation in which survival without the intervention is in question?"

2. Are there no other treatments that could be used to save the lives of these subjects? The IRB must require the researchers to demonstrate (usually through a literature review) that there are no acceptable treatments for the condition under consideration or that the relative benefits and risks of the proposed intervention, as compared with standard therapy, are thought to be equivalent ("clinical equipoise") or better.

3. Is a placebo control allowed? An algorithm for evaluating the ethics of placebo control is presented in a Chapter 10-10 of this book. The IRB should ensure that when a placebo is used, standard care, if any, will be provided to all subjects. Subjects would then be randomized to receive, in addition to standard care, the study intervention or placebo. The IRB should use the same standards it uses with nonemergency research to determine if the use of placebo is ethically acceptable.

4. Is it necessary to experiment on human subjects to test the safety and effectiveness of the proposed intervention? The IRB may answer this question by requesting the researcher to describe research on the intervention already conducted using animal or other models, or on consenting subjects who are in less serious condition.

Section 2

Obtaining informed consent is not feasible because: (i) the subjects will not be able to give their informed consent as a result of their medical condition, (ii) the intervention involved in the research must be administered before consent from the subjects' legally authorized representatives is feasible, and (iii) there is no reasonable way to identify prospectively the individuals likely to become eligible for participation in the research.

The IRB must ask the following questions:

1. Are the subjects incompetent to provide informed consent? The researcher must describe the general condition of the prospective subjects and describe why they are not in a position to provide consent.

2. Must the experimental intervention be initiated before it is possible to obtain consent from the subjects' legally authorized guardians? Generally, the experimental intervention should be one that must be implemented within a narrow window of time, making it impossible to either wait until the subjects become able to provide consent or to arrange court appointment of a guardian. The researcher should document to the IRB's satisfaction that this is the case.

3. Is it possible to identify (and somehow obtain prospective consent from) the people who are likely to become subjects in this research? The researchers must document that it would not be possible to identify the proposed subject population beforehand and get prospective consent from them. For example, if a group of patients is at high risk for developing a condition for which there is no standard treatment, could the researcher obtain consent from the subjects to undergo the experimental intervention should they develop that condition? If the answer is yes, then a waiver of consent may not be necessary. However, the use of prospective consent involves its own ethical dilemmas. Unless the community of

interest and the IRB are willing to accept the concept of a "Ulysses contract," the concept of prospective consent may be difficult to justify. Basically, a Ulysses contract says to ignore any future objections to the terms of the contract.[3]

Section 3

Participation in the research holds out the prospect of direct benefit to the subjects because: (i) subjects are facing a life-threatening situation that necessitates intervention; (ii) appropriate animal and other preclinical studies have been conducted, and the information derived from those studies, and related evidence, supports the potential for the intervention to provide a direct benefit to the individual subjects; (iii) risks associated with the research are reasonable in relation to what is known about the medical condition of the potential class of subjects, and the risks and benefits of standard therapy, if any, of what is known about the risks and benefits of the proposed intervention or activity.

This criterion requires the IRB to ask the following questions:

1. Is there no other effective treatment available for the condition without which the subjects will die or will be seriously disabled? Most IRBs will rely on either the researchers themselves or special consultants to the IRB to answer this question. One of the difficult parts of making this determination is that the request for a waiver often involves situations in which the study intervention may save the person's life. However, it is difficult for the researcher to determine what the subject's quality of life will be following the intervention. Secondly, there is usually no way of determining, in emergency medicine research, whether the subject has a "living will" or a "do not resuscitate" order that might prohibit life-saving efforts.

2. Is there good scientific evidence that the study intervention will have a beneficial effect on the proposed subject population?

3. Are the known risks of the study intervention reasonable when the IRB considers the risks the subjects face as a result of their life-threatening condition and the risks of available standard treatments? This is a difficult determination for the IRB in that the risks of the study intervention are often not well known and the risks of the condition are not known for individual subjects. IRBs should use expert consultants if their membership does not have the expertise to make these decisions.

Section 4

The research could not practicably be carried out without the waiver.

IRBs are often asked to consider the practicability of obtaining consent, particularly in research eligible for the expedited review procedure. In the case of emergency research, practicability usually means determining that the research goals could not be met if the study population was limited to those able to provide consent, either personally or through a legal representative. If the IRB cannot make this determination, there is no need to allow a waiver. The IRB may wish to consider the following:

1. Would it take an unreasonable length of time to accrue a sufficient number of subjects from whom consent could be obtained?

2. Does the context of the research (head trauma from vehicle crashes, for example) make it highly unlikely that consent can be obtained from the subjects, or that a legally authorized representative will be available?

3. Is the window of opportunity so short that the possibility of identifying or contacting legal representatives is small?

Section 5

The proposed research protocol defines the length of the potential therapeutic window based on scientific evidence. The investigator has committed to attempting to contact a legally authorized representative for each subject within that window of time and, if feasible, to asking the legally authorized representative contacted for consent within that window rather than proceeding without consent. The investigator will summarize efforts made to contact representatives and make this information available to the IRB at the time of continuing review.

This criterion requires the IRB to document the following:

1. Has the researcher presented solid scientific evidence to document the period of time within which the experimental intervention must be used? The IRB may wish to use the services of a consultant to assist in evaluating this information.

2. Has the researcher outlined what steps will be taken to learn the subjects' identity and to contact their legal representatives before implementing a waiver? For subjects who are already in a medical setting at the time they are considered to be eligible as research subjects, identities are usually known and legal representatives are available, making a waiver unnecessary. However, when subjects are brought to a medical setting *in extremis,* or are treated by emergency personnel away from their homes, it may be impossible to get consent or to identify a legal guardian. Nonetheless, the researchers must document to the IRB that they are prepared to take all steps necessary to obtain consent from the subject or from a subject's legal representative. This may include locating legal representatives by telephone and obtaining oral consent or consent by facsimile if the legal representative is not available to read and sign a consent form. The researchers should present the IRB with a written protocol documenting the steps they will take to identify the subject, identify the subject's legal representative, contact and identify the representative, and obtain oral or facsimile consent from the legal representative.

3. At the time of continuing review, has the researcher summarized, on a case-by-case basis, the efforts that have been made to identify the subject and locate a legally authorized representative? The IRB has an obligation to make sure that the researcher is aware of this requirement at the time of initial approval. This permits the data to be collected in a systematic way that is easy for the IRB to review.

Section 6

The IRB has reviewed and approved informed consent procedures and an informed consent document in accord with Sections 46.116 and 46.117 of 45 CFR Part 46. These procedures and the informed consent document are to be used with subjects or their legally authorized representatives in situations where use of such procedures and documents is feasible. The IRB has reviewed and approved procedures and information to be used when providing an opportunity for a family member to object to a subject's participation in the research consistent with paragraph (b)(7)(v) of this waiver.

This criterion emphasizes that consent must be obtained from the subject or the subject's legal representative whenever possible, **even if the IRB has approved a waiver of consent.** This means that the IRB must review and approve the following:

1. Written consent documents for the subject or the subject's legal representative

2. Oral consent scripts for the subject or the subject's legal representative

3. The researcher's protocol for identifying the subject and locating the subject's legally authorized representative

4. The researcher's protocol for contacting family members to obtain their permission for the subject to be in the research when it is not possible to contact the legally authorized representative

The IRB must be familiar with the laws pertaining to consent in the location where the study will take place. Generally speaking, the laws that determine who may give consent for health-care treatment are used to determine who may give consent for participation in medical research. However, if an IRB has questions about this, it should consult an expert in the governing statutes.

Section 7

Additional protections of the rights and welfare of the subjects will be provided, including, at least: (i) Consultation (including, where appropriate, consultation carried out by the IRB) with representatives of the communities in which the research will be conducted, as well as communities from which the subjects will be drawn; (ii) Public disclosure to the communities in which the research will be conducted and from which the subjects will be drawn, prior to initiation of the research, in addition to the plans for the research and its risks and expected benefits; (iii) Public disclosure of sufficient information following completion of the research to apprise the community and researchers of the study, including the demographic characteristics of the research population, and its results; (iv) Establishment of an independent data monitoring committee to exercise oversight of the research; and (v) If obtaining informed consent is not feasible and a legally authorized representative is not reasonably available, the investigator has committed, if feasible, to attempting to contact within the therapeutic window the subject's family member who is not a legally authorized representative, and asking whether he or she objects to the subject's participation in the research. The investigator will summarize efforts made to contact family members and make this information available to the IRB at the time of continuing review.

This criterion is perhaps the most difficult for an IRB to interpret and implement.[4] To meet this criterion, the IRB must do the following.

Community Consultation   The IRB must consult with, or have the investigator consult with, representatives of the communities in which the research will be conducted and from which the subjects will be drawn. Typically, IRBs request researchers to conduct and document this consultation process in accord with IRB direction.[5]

a. The researchers and the IRB must first define the "community" in which the research will be conducted. Then it must determine if there is a "community" of research subjects. For example, if the research is to be conducted by emergency medical personnel within a certain geographic catchment area, that area becomes the community. Likewise, if the research is to provide an experimental intervention to scuba divers who experience decompression, the community is "scuba divers."

b. The researchers and the IRB must determine the best way of "consulting" with these communities. In the examples given above, consulting with the geographic catchment area of a hospital might include conducting random surveys of residents with area codes within the area or consulting with the local political organizations (city, town, or neighborhood councils, legislatures) and civic groups (business, church, or advocacy organizations). Consulting with the community of subjects in the second case cited above might include meeting with scuba diving organizations and schools, and conducting surveys with divers at popular scuba diving sites. Care must be taken to consider the special community's characteristics (age, gender, ethnicity, cultural values, etc.) in designing and implementing community consultation. As with any information-gathering effort, the questions to be asked must be framed in a way that is value-neutral and sensitive to community values.

c. The researchers and the IRB must agree about the goals of community consultation and how the results of the consultation efforts are to be used. The regulation does not include an explanation of the purpose of consulting with the community. There are at least two possibilities: allowing the community to determine whether a study should be conducted and gathering information from the community on how to design and implement the study. The regulation also does not state how the consultation effort should be used. For example, suppose the researcher conducts a survey of community residents to ask their opinions about the conduct of a study. The results show that 45% of respondents reply that the study is ethical and should be conducted, 45% respond that the study is not ethical and should not be conducted, and 10% are undecided. The IRB and the researcher will have to agree on how the survey will be designed and implemented and how the results will be used *before* the survey is conducted.

Public Disclosure Before the Research Is Conducted

The IRB must work with the investigators to make the communities aware of the purpose of the research and its possible risks and benefits before the research begins. A wide range of possibilities may be considered in meeting this obligation, ranging from radio and television announcements, newspaper articles and press releases from the research site, to announcements on billboards and public transportation. Disclosure of the study should also offer those who see the announcements an opportunity to provide comments on the proposed study. This may be achieved by use of a toll-free telephone number, mailing address, or Web site.

Public Disclosure After the Research is Completed

The IRB must work with the investigators to make the communities aware of the results of the research (including the characteristics of the subject population) after the research has been completed. The same kinds of mechanisms that were used to notify the communities about the research be-

fore it was undertaken may also be used to publicize the results of the study. In addition, if the results of the study were positive, there is an ethical obligation on the part of the researchers to make sure that the study interventions are implemented as standard care when this is reasonable and appropriate.

Independent Data-Monitoring Committee The IRB must require that the research protocol include a data safety and monitoring board (DSMB) that is independent of the research to provide oversight and to make sure that the study continues to be conducted safely and ethically. The DSMB has the authority to stop the study if the risks are greater than the anticipated benefits or if the study design must be changed to minimize risks. The board may also stop the study if the benefits of the intervention are clear. Membership on the DSMB should not include representatives from the research team, and should include experts in the field, ethicists, and statisticians experienced in research data analysis. Often the research sponsor establishes the independent DSMB. The IRB must request that the results of the DSMB meetings are forwarded to the IRB in a timely fashion.

Authorization from Family Members The IRB should request from the researcher a protocol for identifying and contacting family members in the event that the subject cannot consent and the subject's legally authorized representative cannot be located. The protocol should include a script that requests identification of the family members, explains the study to the family members, and asks if the family members object to the subject's participation in the research. At the time of continuing review, the researcher should summarize these attempts to contact family members.[6]

Section 8

The IRB is responsible for ensuring that procedures are in place to inform, at the earliest feasible opportunity, each subject, or if the subject remains incapacitated, a legally authorized representative of the subject, or if such a representative is not reasonably available, a family member, of the subject's inclusion in the clinical investigation, the details of the investigation and other information contained in the informed consent document. The IRB shall also ensure that there is a procedure to inform the subject, or if the subject remains incapacitated, a legally authorized representative of the subject, or if such a representative is not reasonably available, a family member, that he or she may discontinue the subject's participation at any time without penalty or loss of benefits to which the subject is otherwise entitled. If a legally authorized representative or family member is told about the clinical investigation and the subject's condition improves, the subject is also to be informed as soon as feasible. If a subject is entered into a clinical investigation with waived consent and the subject dies before a legally authorized representative or family member can be contacted, information about the clinical investigation is to be provided to the subject's legally authorized representative or family member, if feasible.

The IRB should request the following from the investigator.

1. A procedure for informing the subject at the earliest possible opportunity that he or she has been included in a research activity. This procedure should include as many of the elements of informed consent as are appropriate for consent to *continue* participation in the study.

2. A procedure for informing the subject's legally authorized representative or family member—whichever becomes available soonest—that the subject has been included in a research activity. The information must provide a description of the research activity, a request to allow the subject to continue to participate in the research activity, and an opportunity to discontinue participation in the research activity without penalty or loss of benefits to which the subject might otherwise be entitled. The regulation does not determine whether permission to continue or authorization to discontinue participation should be obtained in writing. It may be difficult for the researcher to develop a written template for the procedure. This is because it is not possible to determine in advance at what point in the protocol it will be possible to interview the subject or the subject's legal representative or family member.

3. A procedure for documenting, on a case-by-case basis at continuing review (or whenever requested by the IRB), that these protocols were followed.

It is important to note that this procedure does not constitute requesting permission for what has already happened to the subject, but only permission to either continue or discontinue participation.

Additional FDA Requirements

If the research involves a test article (drug, device, or biologic) regulated by the FDA, additional requirements must be met before the IRB may approve a waiver of consent. The IRB must determine that the researcher or the research sponsor has obtained an investigational new drug application (IND) or an investigational device exemption (IDE) from the FDA before implementing the research. The application to the FDA must include a protocol that clearly states that it will include subjects who are unable to consent. This requirement must be met even if there is an existing IND or IDE for the use of the test article in a protocol not requiring a waiver of consent.[7]

The IRB must document that a licensed physician "who is a member of or consultant to the IRB and who is not otherwise participating in the clinical investigation" concurs that the waiver of consent is allowable. IRBs should ensure that meeting minutes specifically record this affirmative vote.

If the IRB determines that it cannot approve a protocol involving a waiver of consent either because it does not meet the requirements of the regulations or because of other relevant ethical concerns, it must provide documentation of this decision promptly to the researcher and to the sponsor of the research. The sponsor must promptly disclose this information to the FDA and to other researchers who are conducting or have been asked to conduct this or similar protocols, and to other IRBs that have been, or are, asked to review this or similar protocols by that sponsor.

Important Exceptions to the Waiver for Emergency Research

The waiver is explicitly excluded when the research involves certain protected research populations. These include fetuses, pregnant women, and human in vitro fertilization (Subpart B of 45 CFR 46), and prisoners (Subpart C of 45 CFR 46).

Conclusion

This chapter has reviewed the criteria for waiver of consent in emergency medicine research. This is a relatively new class of regulatory guidelines that requires a list of specific activities on the part of the IRB and research team. It is important that the IRB understand that these regulations are applicable to only a narrow class of activities. This chapter discusses each section of the regulations with the goal of clarifying the things that researchers and the IRB must document to protect the rights and welfare of this extremely vulnerable research population.

References

1. Adams JG, Wegener J. Acting without asking: an ethical analysis of the Food and Drug Administration waiver of informed consent for emergency research. *Ann Emerg Med* 33(2):218-223, 1999.

2. Office for Human Research Protections. Human Subject—Dear Colleague Letters, 31 Oct 1996 (No. 97-01). Access date 9 Aug 2001. World Wide Web http://ohrp.osophs.dhhs.gov/humansubjects/guidance/hsdc97-01.htm

3. Annas GJ. Ulysses and the fate of frozen embryos—reproduction, research, or destruction? *N Engl J Med* 343(5):373-376, 2000.

4. Biros MH, Fish SS, Lewis RJ. Implementing the Food and Drug Administration's final rule for waiver of informed consent in certain emergency research circumstances. *Acad Emerg Med* 6(12):1272-1282, 1999.

5. Baren JM, Anicetti JP, Ledesma S, Biros MH, Mahabee-Gittens M, Lewis RJ. An approach to community consultation prior to initiating an emergency research study incorporating a waiver of informed consent. *Acad Emerg Med* 6(12):1210-1215, 1999.

6. Smithline HA, Gerstle ML. Waiver of informed consent: a survey of emergency medicine patients. *Am J Emerg Med* 16(1):90-91, 1998.

7. Kremers MS, Whisnant DR, Lowder LS, Gregg L. Initial experience using the Food and Drug Administration guidelines for emergency research without consent. *Ann Emerg Med* 33(2):224-229, 1999.

Appendix

OPRR Reports

October 31, 1996

Subject: Informed Consent Requirements in Emergency Research

Dear Colleague:

This letter advises Institutional Officials and Institutional Review Board (IRB) Chairs of responsibilities related to informed consent when research subjects are enrolled in emergent circumstances.

As in the past, the regulations for protection of human subjects of the Department of Health and Human Services (HHS) at 45 CFR Part 46 stipulate requirements for obtaining (Section 46.116) and documenting (Section 46.117) informed consent. And, the regulations give IRBs authority to alter or waive the required consent in certain circumstances (Sections 46.116(c)-(d)).[1] These provisions of HHS regulations remain unchanged and in full force.

On October 2, 1996 (*Federal Register*, Vol. 61, pp. 51531-51533), the Secretary, HHS, announced under Section 46.101(i), a waiver of the applicability of the 45 CFR Part 46 requirement for obtaining and documenting informed consent for a strictly limited class of research, involving research activities that may be carried out in human subjects who are in need of emergency therapy and for whom, because of the subjects' medical condition and the unavailability of legally authorized representatives of the subjects, no legally effective informed consent can be obtained. This waiver, which provides a third route through which IRBs may approve research in this class, takes effect November 1, 1996.

This waiver applies to the Basic HHS Policy for Protection of Human Research Subjects (Subpart A of 45 CFR Part 46) and to research involving children (Subpart D of 45 CFR Part 46). However, because of special regulatory limitations relating to research involving fetuses, pregnant women, and human in vitro fertilization (Subpart B of 45 CFR 46), and research involving prisoners (Subpart C of 45 CFR Part 46), this waiver is inapplicable to these categories of research.

Emergency Research Consent Waiver

Pursuant to Section 46.101(i), the Secretary, HHS, has waived the general requirements for informed consent at 45 CFR46.116(a) and (b) and 46.408, to be referred to as the "Emergency Research Consent Waiver" for a class of research consisting of activities, each of which has met the following strictly limited conditions detailed under either A or B below:

a. **Research subject to FDA regulations**
   The IRB responsible for the review, approval, and continuing review of the research activity has approved both the activity and a waiver of informed consent and found and documented:
   1. that the research activity is subject to regulations codified by the Food and Drug Administration (FDA) (see *Federal Register,* Vol. 61, pp. 51498-51531) at Title 21 CFR Part 50 and will be carried out under an FDA investigational new drug application (IND) or an FDA investigational device exemption (IDE), the application for which has clearly identified the protocols that would include subjects who are unable to consent, and
   2. that the requirements for exception from informed consent for emergency research detailed in 21 CFR Section 50.24 have been met relative to those protocols, **or**

b. **Research not subject to FDA regulations**
   The IRB responsible for the review, approval, and continuing review of the research has approved both the research and a waiver of informed consent and has (i) found and documented that the research is not subject to regulations codified by the FDA at 21 CFR Part 50, and (ii) found and documented and reported to the OPRR that the following conditions have been met relative to the research:
   1. The human subjects are in a life-threatening situation, available treatments are unproven or unsatisfactory. In addition, the collection of valid scientific evidence, which may include evidence obtained through randomized placebo-controlled investigations, is necessary to determine the safety and effectiveness of particular interventions.
   2. Obtaining informed consent is not feasible because:
      i. the subjects will not be able to give their informed consent as a result of their medical condition;

ii. the intervention involved in the research must be administered before consent from the subjects' legally authorized representatives is feasible; and

iii. there is no reasonable way to identify prospectively the individuals likely to become eligible for participation in the research.

3. Participation in the research holds out the prospect of direct benefit to the subjects because:

i. subjects are facing a life-threatening situation that necessitates intervention;

ii. appropriate animal and other preclinical studies have been conducted, and the information derived from those studies and related evidence support the potential for the intervention to provide a direct benefit to the individual subjects; and

iii. risks associated with the research are reasonable in relation to what is known about the medical condition of the potential class of subjects, the risks and benefits of standard therapy, if any, and what is known about the risks and benefits of the proposed intervention or activity.

4. The research could not practicably be carried out without the waiver.

5. The proposed research protocol defines the length of the potential therapeutic window based on scientific evidence, and the investigator has committed to attempting to contact a legally authorized representative for each subject within that window of time and, if feasible, to the asking of the legally authorized representative contacted for consent within that window rather than proceeding without consent. The investigator will summarize efforts made to contact representatives and make this information available to the IRB at the time of continuing review.

6. The IRB has reviewed and approved informed consent procedures and an informed consent document in accord with Sections 46.116 and 46.117 of 45 CFR Part 46. These procedures and the informed consent document are to be used with subjects or their legally authorized representatives in situations where use of such procedures and documents is feasible. The IRB has reviewed and approved procedures and information to be used when providing an opportunity for a family member to object to a subject's participation in the research consistent with paragraph (b)(7)(v) of this waiver.

7. Additional protections of the rights and welfare of the subjects will be provided, including, at least:

i. consultation (including, where appropriate, consultation carried out by the IRB) with representatives of the communities in which the research will be conducted and from which the subjects will be drawn;

ii. public disclosure to the communities in which the research will be conducted and from which the subjects will be drawn, prior to initiation of the research, of plans for the research and its risks and expected benefits;

iii. public disclosure of sufficient information following completion of the research to apprise the community and researchers of the study, including the demographic characteristics of the research population, and its results;

iv. establishment of an independent data monitoring committee to exercise oversight of the research; and

v. if obtaining informed consent is not feasible and a legally authorized representative is not reasonably available, the investigator has committed, if feasible, to attempting to contact within the therapeutic window the subject's family member who is not a legally authorized representative, and asking whether he or she objects to the subject's participation in the research. The investigator will summarize efforts made to contact family members and make this information available to the IRB at the time of continuing review.

In addition, the IRB is responsible for ensuring that procedures are in place to inform, at the earliest feasible opportunity, each subject, or if the subject remains incapacitated, a legally authorized representative of the subject, or if such a representative is not reasonably available, a family member, of the subject's inclusion in the research, the details of the research and other information contained in the informed consent document. The IRB shall also ensure that there is a procedure to inform the subject, or if the subject remains incapacitated, a legally authorized representative of the subject, or if such a representative is not reasonably available, a family member, that he or she may discontinue the subject's participation at any time without penalty or loss of benefits to which the subject is otherwise entitled. If a legally authorized representative or family member is told about the research and the subject's condition improves, the subject is also to be informed as soon as feasible. If a subject is entered into research with waived consent and the subject dies before a legally authorized representative or family member can be contacted, information about the research is to be provided to the subject's legally authorized representative or family member, if feasible.

For the purposes of this waiver, "family member" means any one of the following legally competent persons: spouses; parents; children (including adopted children); brothers, sisters, and spouses of brothers and sisters; and any individual related by blood or affinity whose close association with the subject is the equivalent of a family relationship.

On October 2, 1996 (*Federal Register*, Vol. 61, pp. 51498-51531), the FDA published a final rule which amends FDA regulations to authorize a waiver of informed consent in research which is regulated by the FDA. The joint publication of these actions permit harmonization of the HHS and FDA regulations regarding research in emergency circumstances. The HHS waiver, just as the FDA regulatory change, provides a narrow exception to the requirement for obtaining and documenting informed consent from each human subject or his or her legally authorized representative prior to initiation of research if the waiver of informed consent is approved by an IRB. The waiver authorization applies to a limited class of research activities involving human subjects who are in need of emergency medical intervention but who cannot give informed consent because of their life-threatening medical condition, and who do not have available a legally authorized person to represent them. The Secretary of the HHS, is authorizing this waiver in response to growing concerns that current regulations, absent this waiver, are making high quality research in emergency circumstances difficult or impossible to carry out at a time when the need for such research is increasingly recognized.

Sincerely,

/s/
Gary B. Ellis, Ph.D.
Director
Office for Protection
from Research Risks

/s/
Melody H. Lin, Ph.D.
Deputy Director
Office for Protection from
Research Risks

PART 5

Initial Protocol Review and the Full-Committee Meeting

Overview of Initial Protocol Review

Susan Z. Kornetsky

INTRODUCTION

The purpose of this chapter is to provide an overview of the process for initial Institutional Review Board (IRB) review of human subject protocols. The overview focuses on the administrative and logistical methods for performing initial IRB review, and suggests criteria for the administrative staff and IRB members to use to complete initial review. Many of the topics included in this chapter are also discussed in greater detail in other chapters. The chapter will describe methods that may be used for receipt of protocol applications, prereview mechanisms, preparation of protocols for IRB members, and criteria for the initial evaluation of research protocols. The ideas presented in this chapter are not meant to be an exhaustive list of policies and procedures for initial submission and review, but rather to present some potential possible mechanisms for this process. The intent of the author is to provoke thought and consideration as to what policies and procedures for initial review work best within individual institutions. Answers to all of the issues will not be provided. Some examples will be described. Most importantly, questions that an IRB administrator should consider when establishing policies and procedures are provided. Implementation and the establishment of policies and procedures will depend on the size and culture of the institution as well as the resources and staffing available. For each section, an overview of the responsibilities and process is provided, followed by a list of individual issues and questions to take into consideration when establishing procedures to best meet the needs of your institution.

The Protocol Application

Federal regulations [1(Sec.111)] specify criteria that IRBs must consider in order to approve a human subject research protocol. IRBs must receive the information in an organized and comprehensive way to determine whether the criteria have been met. Most often, investigators are required to submit the required information in a format specified by the IRB. This is commonly referred to as a *protocol application*. Sample forms are presented in Chapter 11-9 and elsewhere in this book.

The protocol application is developed to take into consideration federally mandated criteria as well as local institutional policies and practices. The form requires that investigators respond to questions and issues that are pertinent to making a risk/benefit determination. The protocol application also includes the opportunity to address institution-specific requirements. The development of a comprehensive protocol application by an investigator is essential.

Often, as new regulatory and ethical issues arise, it becomes necessary to modify the protocol application form. IRBs need to develop a continuous process by which questions within a protocol application form are reviewed and modified to meet the current regulatory environment. For example, many institutions have developed separate questions that are to be addressed for genetic research. The use of biological specimens for genetic research has raised a series of ethical concerns (dissemination of research results, consent from family members, and social and economic risks to subjects who participate). To be certain they respond to the many ethical concerns, investigators are asked to address these issues within the protocol application. The need for separate questions may also apply to the inclusion of women, minorities, and children. A good indicator that a protocol application requires revision is when the IRB finds itself repetitively asking the same question during review. This may signify that questions need to be revised or added to the form to assure complete information is provided for the initial review process.

Types of Applications

Cooperative Groups Protocols If a cooperative group such as ECOG or ACTG sponsors a protocol, a copy of the protocol is prepared by the cooperative group of investigators and then is submitted to cooperating institutions for review. Investigators based at the cooperating institutions may also need to complete institutional forms to be submitted with the cooperative protocol. The protocol material prepared by the cooperative group typically includes background information and preliminary studies, specific aims, eligibility criteria, procedures and evaluations, procedures for handling and reporting adverse events, and data analysis. A suggested version of the informed consent is also provided. However, institution-specific issues, such as recruitment practices, are not included. Individual investigators are usually not permitted to modify the body of the protocol; however, they may submit supplementary information to their IRB. Informed consents should be modified to meet institutional standards.

Industry-Sponsored Protocols   A drug or device company sponsoring the research may also prepare protocols. The company prepares the research proposal as well as an investigational brochure. This information is then forwarded to the institutions participating in the trial. The same type of information as listed for the cooperative-groups protocols is provided. In addition, the same policies regarding modification of the protocol exist. The informed consent remains the responsibility of the institution and may be modified. Frequently, institutional forms also accompany a protocol to request information on who may administer the drug. Other institution-specific information is usually requested in addition to the protocol prepared by the sponsor.

Investigator-Initiated Protocols   Investigators often propose original research. In this situation, it is the investigator's responsibility to prepare a clear discussion of the research plan in addition to supporting background information, data analysis, eligibility, adverse event monitoring, discussion of risks, benefits, and alternatives, and informed consent documents. Therefore, it is important that all institutions specify in detail their expectations for protocol content.

Information Required in Applications

Regardless of where and by whom the protocol application is prepared, the following information must be included in each protocol application in order for an initial review to occur: background, discussion of preliminary studies, specific aims, recruitment practices, eligibility criteria (inclusion/exclusion criteria), proposed plan of research, plans for data analysis, adverse event reporting and monitoring, risks, benefits, and alternatives.

Each application must also contain informed consent/assent forms and recruitment materials such as advertisements and postings, if desired. Many IRBs also request copies of actual assessment tools and measurements.

Institutions are responsible for developing, maintaining, and disseminating appropriate policies and procedures for the submission of research protocols to the IRB. Investigators must understand the IRB's expectations. When possible, it is recommended that the policies, instructions, and actual protocol application forms be placed on a Web site. Written policy and procedure booklets are also encouraged. Clear instructions and expectations are essential for the initiation of an initial review by the IRB.

Submission Process for Protocol Applications

This section describes the initial steps needed to prepare and submit a protocol application for IRB review. Timing of meetings and deadlines, protocol application materials, and signature requirements need to be carefully considered and planned. The receipt of a protocol is the first step in IRB review. The IRB must receive all materials the committee needs to perform a meaningful and comprehensive initial review.

IRB Issues To Be Considered

Is there an established deadline for protocol application submissions? Deadlines may be used when there are established meeting dates. However, consideration should be given as to whether all protocols and materials that are submitted for a particular deadline are guaranteed review at the next meeting. Some institutions that meet more frequently do not work with deadlines but rather on a "first come, first served" basis. Protocols are triaged to the next meeting that has an open agenda. Limits are set as to the number of protocols reviewed per meeting. Some institutions also maintain IRBs with expertise in specific areas: for example, behavioral and social science IRBs.

Where is the best location to submit protocol applications? Is this an administrative office or another location? Protocol applications including any supplementary information should be submitted to a central location when possible. This is usually the IRB administrative office. Some institutions have developed electronic submission of protocol applications. The electronic submission goes to a central location as well.

How long before the meeting do you require protocols to be submitted? IRB members need to be given ample time to review protocols before the IRB meeting. Timing of protocol submission will depend on the number of protocols, number of committee members reviewing the protocols, and the IRB meeting dates. It is recommended that protocols be distributed to IRB members at least one week in advance of the meeting. The time required for preparation of protocol materials before distribution to members will determine how much in advance protocol applications need to be received in the IRB administrative office.

Is a staff member available at all times to answer questions about protocol submissions? An IRB administrator should be available at all times to answer questions regarding protocol submissions.

How often and for how long does the IRB meet? Does this influence how many protocols are submitted to the IRB for review at a meeting? Many IRBs have moved to limiting the number of protocols reviewed per meeting.

IRBs have been criticized for reviewing protocols too quickly and in a cursory manner. For this reason, IRBs want to allow ample time for discussion. The ability to limit the number of protocols per meeting will depend on the frequency of the meetings. It is not always possible to limit the number of protocols. This needs to be an institution-specific decision based on resources, staffing, and frequency of meetings.

How many copies of a protocol application should an investigator submit? Who will do the photocopying and with what does each member need to be supplied? The answers to these questions depend on factors such as whether all members are to receive a full copy of every protocol or if only reviewers receive complete copies of protocols. In addition, whether the IRB office has a budget to copy protocols will influence the decision about whether copying is a responsibility of the investigator or the IRB.

Instructions and policies for applications should be available on a Web site, if possible. The possibility of electronic submissions is worth considering if resources are available. IRB application materials and instructions must be reviewed and updated on an ongoing basis.

Required Signature on Applications

It is common for a protocol to require a variety of signatures or sign-offs before it is submitted to the IRB for review. This is the beginning of initial IRB review. The signatures designate that other departments or individuals within the institution have initially approved the protocol application for submission to the IRB. At a minimum, the signature of the principal investigator is usually required. Often the signature section includes a declaration by the investigator that he or she assumes responsibility for the conduct of the research and conformance with human-subject protection regulations.

Signatures are also requested from department chairpersons, institutional officials of several ranks, and study personnel who conduct or are responsible for some component of the research activity. Signature requirements are often used to assist investigators in communicating to other individuals or departments that a specific research activity is planned. The department head or other individuals asked to sign the application now have a mechanism to indicate their willingness to assume responsibility for their role and for support of the research activities. For example, in a hospital setting, it is common to require signatures from co-investigators, from pharmacy, nursing, and other support services, and possibly from scientific review committees before submission to the IRB. All expectations of signature requirements must be specified and communicated to investigators to ensure a thorough and timely initial review. Questions to consider in requiring signatures for protocol applications include the following: (a) What signatures does the IRB determine are necessary before it can review the protocol? (b) Is it the investigator's responsibility to obtain the required signatures? (c) Will the IRB accept protocols if the signatures are not obtained or the individuals are not available? (d) Are electronic signatures acceptable?

Prereview and Distribution of Applications

IRB administrative staff often receive protocol applications, prepare the materials for IRB members, and track the protocol application through the review process. IRBs often identify each new protocol submission with a unique identification number. This number is assigned at the time the protocol application is received and is used to track the protocol through the review process. Often protocol review numbers reflect the time and sequence of the submission.

Example
If the protocol review number is 01-03-045, the numerals represent the year of submission (2001), the month of submission (March), and the sequence of submission (the 45th protocol submitted that year).

Many other mechanisms for identifying protocol applications exist.

Prereview Mechanisms

If it is determined that a protocol requires full IRB review, there should be a process by which the protocol undergoes preliminary review prior to formal review by the IRB at a convened meeting. Any type of preliminary review should help investigators focus on what may be problematic or sensitive issues pertinent to the research protocol. The following are some examples of different mechanisms for prereview.

No or Limited Prereview by the Administrative Staff
The protocol materials are received, immediately copied, and distributed to IRB members or selected individuals for review. Although this method is the quickest up front, it has the potential for distributing incomplete or poorly constructed protocols to IRB members. Significant additional time may be required after the meeting to adequately address all questions and concerns.

Prereview by a Designated IRB Member The IRB designates an IRB member to perform a prereview of the protocol and question the investigator on any issue, question, or concern before the meeting. The investigator is then required to respond to the comments before the protocol is distributed and reviewed by IRB members. The breadth and scope of this type of review depend on the definition of the role of the prereviewer, including his or her level of expertise and understanding. The benefit of this type of system is that the actual IRB meeting time can be reduced because information gathering and questioning is done outside the IRB meeting. The IRB can concentrate its discussion on more substantial issues. However, in some institutions, IRB members would rather not have direct communication with investigators regarding review of their protocol. Members would rather have comments go to the investigator anonymously after review by the entire IRB.

Prereview by Administrative Staff Depending on the experience and training of the IRB administrative staff, it is also possible for administrative staff members to perform a preliminary review. Administrative staff may be able to review issues related to human subject protection, such as recruitment practices and informed consent methods, as well as carry out the general preparation of the protocol materials. However, they may not be able to review scientific issues such as preliminary data, specific aims, and data analysis. If administrative staff perform prereview, the scope of prereview must depend on the training and background of the administrative staff.

Continuing Prereview or Consultative Discussions Prereview or consultative discussions may be offered at any time before submission to the IRB. At Children's Hospital in Boston, investigators are encouraged to seek advice and consultation from IRB administrative staff in planning their research protocol and for a preliminary review of the protocol application. The researchers are encouraged to seek consultation even before a protocol is prepared. Consultation at the earliest time may provide investigators with guidance as to what human subject issues are likely to be of concern and suggestions for addressing them within the protocol application. This type of consultation helps an investigator develop a protocol application that incorporates responses to potential human subject concerns.

For example, a protocol that has to recruit subjects in the emergency room would require particular attention to the recruitment and informed consent process during a stressful period. The protocol application must address precautions and steps that have to be taken to assure voluntary consent and informed decision-making and issues related to who has jurisdiction to consent for an emergency patient to enter into a research protocol. Investigators may not automatically consider these issues in preparing the protocol application.

A second example is when a protocol involves schoolchildren in a classroom. Recruitment of subjects in school raises issues about how to obtain consent from the parents and the need to obtain approval from the school or school system. An administrative person could advise investigators about these issues to be sure they are adequately addressed in the protocol application.

Offering this type of service within an IRB office requires that staff have in-depth knowledge and experience. It also requires adequate staffing and resources because this type of consultation takes time. This consultative system has worked well at Children's Hospital, Boston, and is well appreciated by the investigator community. It helps promote the image of an IRB that is customer-service oriented and proactive in trying to address human subject concerns. This process may also save time during the review process.

The previously mentioned examples suggest several mechanisms for a prereview system. An institution will need to ask several questions in determining what type of prereview should be offered, including: (a) How should protocols be tracked once they are received in an administrative office? (b) Does the IRB find value in a prereview process? If so, who is appropriately experienced to perform this prereview? (c) At what level should a prereview occur? (d) How long does it take to perform a preliminary review and how does this impact an IRB's time schedule? (e) Does the institution have appropriate staffing to perform prereview?

Expedited Review

The full IRB must receive protocol applications after the completion of any prereview process. IRBs establish procedures to determine which protocols require full-committee review and which protocols may be expedited. This determination is an important consideration and therefore must be the responsibility of either the Chair or an IRB member who is familiar with the federal regulations pertaining to expedited review. IRB administrators often serve as a first screen for determining what may be eligible for expedited review. Some institutions have developed a checklist that asks investigators to specify which, if any, expedited review category the protocol falls within. In other institutions, such as Children's Hospital, Boston, administrative staff bring to the attention of the Chair protocols that seem to fall within the regulated criteria for expedited review. The Chair is responsible for making this final determination in accordance with the regulations.[1(Sec.110),2(Sec.110)] The Chair may perform the review or assign one or several IRB members to perform the review. Administrative IRB staff members track and administer this process. Further details about expedited review and the criteria for allowing expedited review are found in Chapter 4-2 in this book.

If a protocol does not meet the criteria for expedited review, it is forwarded to the full IRB for review at a convened meeting.

Assignment of Primary and Secondary Reviewers

Each institution has different methods for distributing and reviewing research protocols. IRB procedures must address the following question: Should all IRB members assume responsibility for reviewing each protocol in detail, or are primary reviewers and possibly secondary reviewers assigned? Whether all members are responsible for reviewing each protocol depends on the size of the IRB and the number of protocols undergoing review. In general, larger institutions have relied on a primary and secondary reviewer system. In this manner, two members review the protocol in detail and present the protocol, including their questions and concerns, to the full IRB. After this presentation, the full IRB discusses the protocol and takes final action. The more a committee member has to review, the less time he or she may put into each individual review. The benefit of this method is assurance that at least two IRB members conduct an in-depth review. The risk is that the remaining members may be less likely to review all protocols even on a limited basis.

A member's expertise should be used to determine which protocols he or she is assigned to review. However, careful attention should be given to ensure that protocols are not assigned to reviewers who may have a real or perceived potential conflict of interest. IRB administrators and/or the IRB Chair often assign reviewers.

Should all IRB members be expected to review each protocol in detail, and should all IRB members receive copies of all sections of all protocol applications? Ideally, it would be best if all members received all protocol materials. This practice must be implemented if all members are expected to review all protocol applications. However, if a primary and secondary reviewer system is used, you may want to consider providing a full copy of protocol application materials to the primary and secondary reviewers and limited information to the remainder of the IRB. It is not recommended that only the primary and secondary reviewers receive protocol materials.

Initial Review

The regulations specify criteria for IRB review and approval. IRB members must apply these criteria during the review process and have appropriate knowledge and understanding of the regulations. These criteria are specified in 45 CFR 46.[1(Sec.111)]

A tool to assist investigators in performing an in-depth and thorough review is a reviewer worksheet. Use of a worksheet promotes consistency of the IRB review process. Many IRBs provide worksheets or guidelines for their IRB members to use when reviewing research protocols. In some institutions, use of a worksheet is suggested; in other institutions, use of the worksheet is mandatory. The remainder of this chapter describes and explains the worksheet that is currently in use at Children's Hospital, Boston. It was developed after reviewing many other institutions' IRB worksheets. IRB members are required to complete a worksheet for each protocol assigned. The worksheet is broken up into 12 sections; each addresses one of the criteria for IRB approval as specified in the regulations. Each section has specific questions and criteria to be considered. In addition, in some sections members can write questions or concerns that an investigator needs to address. The worksheet sections are written to prompt IRB members to make specific determinations for an individual protocol.

Introduction, Specific Aims, and Background

Review of any research protocol must begin by the IRB member's asking and answering the question, "Why this research?" IRB members should be provided with adequate data regarding earlier related studies and associated references. Applications must reveal the objectives of the research through the statement of a hypothesis. In short, the question "What will be learned from the proposed study?" should be addressed. For each objective, the protocol should adequately address how answers will be obtained.

Worksheet Questions
1. Are the aims clearly specified?
2. Are there adequate preliminary data to justify the research?
3. Is there appropriate justification for this research protocol?

Scientific Design

Institutions have varying policies and practices for reviewing and approving the scientific design and merit of a research protocol. Some institutions have a separate scientific review committee; at others, scientific review is conducted at the departmental level. Other IRBs assume full responsibility for scientific review. Even when scientific review is not designated as an institutional IRB responsibility, IRBs must feel confident that the scientific merit of the protocol justifies a risk/benefit determination. IRBs are required to determine that use of study procedures consistent with sound research design minimizes the risks to the subject. It may not be within the purview of the IRB to resolve scientific merit issues that are raised. However, it would be impossible for an IRB to approve a protocol if these issues are not adequately addressed. At a minimum, to conduct an initial review of a protocol, IRB members should consider the following questions.

Worksheet Questions
1. Is the scientific design adequate to answer the question?
2. Are the objectives likely to be achievable within a given time period?
3. Is the scientific design (i.e., randomization; placebo controls; phase I, II, or III) described and adequately justified?

Inclusion/Exclusion Criteria for Subjects

Appropriate inclusion and exclusion criteria for research participants are essential in order to ethically justify human subject research. Criteria for inclusion may consist of a combination of biomedical and behavioral characteristics. Poorly specified inclusion and exclusion criteria may be the basis for misinterpretation of eligible research subjects and inappropriate enrollment of research subjects. In addition, IRBs are mandated to assure that specific classes of subjects (i.e., women, minorities, and children) are included.

Worksheet Questions
1. Are inclusion and exclusion criteria clearly specified and appropriate?
2. If women, minorities, or children are included or excluded, is this justified?
3. Is the choice of subjects appropriate for the question being asked?
4. Is the principle of distributive justice adequately incorporated into the inclusion and exclusion criteria for the research protocol? Is subject selection equitable?

Recruitment of Subjects

IRB members must consider how and when participants are to be identified and approached for recruitment. Reviewers must consider methods for recruiting subjects (advertisements, World Wide Web sites, medical records, databases, newsletters, letters, referrals, etc.). In addition, it is important to consider who will approach potential research subjects, when subjects will be contacted, where they will be approached, and the amount of time provided for potential subjects to consider participation. All recruitment materials and practices must be reviewed and approved by the IRB. The IRB must be assured that the recruitment process promotes voluntary participation and is not coercive.

Worksheet Questions

1. Are the methods for recruiting potential subjects well defined?
2. Are the location and timing of the recruitment process acceptable?
3. Is the individual performing the recruitment appropriate for the process?
4. Are all recruitment materials submitted and appropriate?
5. Are there acceptable methods for screening subjects before recruitment?

Research Procedures

IRB reviewers must fully consider the procedures involved in research. Reviewers should ask, "How is the participant to be treated? What procedures will they undergo for the purposes of research?" Reviewers must differentiate those procedures that are performed for research purposes from those that are performed for routine care or evaluation. Reviewers are responsible for understanding the actual studies, including the timing, the setting, and the qualifications of those conducting the procedures or evaluations. Procedures for monitoring the subject during the research must be evaluated. When questionnaires and behavioral or psychological assessments are to be included as part of the research evaluation, the reviewer should review copies of the assessment instruments. IRB members should review what would happen to the study results. If there are flow charts or schemas, it is important that they be consistent with the text of the protocol and the informed consent document.

Worksheet Questions

1. Are the rationale and details of the research procedures accurately described and acceptable?
2. Is there a clear differentiation between research procedures and standard care and evaluation?
3. Are the individuals performing the procedures appropriately trained, and is the location for performing the procedure acceptable?
4. Are there adequate plans to inform subjects about specific research results if necessary (clinically relevant results, risk of depression, suicidality, incidental findings, etc.)?

Drugs, Biologics, and Devices

IRB members have additional responsibilities when considering research protocols that include the use of drugs, devices, and biologics. The reviewer must apply the regulations of the Food and Drug Administration (FDA). If drugs or biologics are to be administered as part of a research protocol, their investigational new drug application (IND) or investigational device exemption (IDE) status should be specified. Information including the dosage, route of administration, previous use, and safety and efficacy data need to be evaluated. Reviewers need to take into consideration the phase of drug/biologic testing as it relates to risks and benefits.

IRB members also have additional responsibilities for reviewing research proposing the use of investigational devices. The reviewer must apply the FDA regulations. The reviewer must consider the definitions of *nonsignificant risk* and *significant risk* as applied to devices. This determination has implications for the sponsor of the device and the requirements for filing with the FDA. Details regarding the determination of significant risk versus nonsignificant risk are provided in Chapter 10-7.

Worksheet Questions

1. Is the status of the drug described and appropriate (investigational, new use of an FDA-approved drug, or an FDA-approved drug within approved indications)?
2. Are the drug dosage and route of administration appropriate?
3. Are the drug or device safety and efficacy data sufficient to warrant the proposed phase of testing?
4. Is the significant risk or nonsignificant risk status of the device described and appropriate?

Data Analysis and Statistical Analysis

Research protocols must contain well conceived and appropriate sections on interpretation of data and statistics. The interpretation of data should summarize the proposal design, the reasoning for the design, and plans for analysis of results. This section should provide enough evidence to convince a reviewer that the proposed design has a reasonable chance of achieving the principal objectives of the research. IRB members should determine that the sample size and statistical power or precision associated with the sample size are adequate. In addition, there must be a sound method of data and statistical analysis, with adequate stratification factors and treatment allocation plans for the study design. When appropriate, IRB members must be adequately informed about plans to monitor the data, including the description of early stopping rules if necessary and the proposed use and necessity of a Data Safety Monitoring Board (DSMB).

Worksheet Questions

1. Is the rationale for the proposed number of subjects reasonable?
2. Are the plans for data and statistical analysis defined and justified, including the use of stopping rules and endpoints?
3. Are there adequate provisions for monitoring data (DSMB)?

Potential Risks, Discomforts, and Benefits for Subjects

IRB members are charged with the responsibility of reviewing the potential risks, discomforts, hazards, or inconveniences of a research protocol. This includes the probability, magnitude, and duration of the risks. IRB members must identify the physical pain or discomfort as well as the psychological, emotional, or sociological harm, including invasion of privacy, loss of confidentiality, harassment, and lessening of an individual's dignity. Inconveniences such as loss of time or pay are also included in this category. Risk to a community or a group of individuals must also be considered. The initial reviewer must consider the potential risks as well as the precautions that will be taken to avoid or minimize potential risks.

Potential benefits can apply directly to the subject or to the advancement of scientific knowledge. IRBs must consider the magnitude and probability of direct benefit to a subject to be certain the research protocol does not overstate the benefits or potentially raise false expectations in the participants. It is important for the IRB to evaluate the risk/benefit ratio and to understand the rationale for believing the risk/benefit ratio is acceptable.

The IRB must give special consideration to risks and benefits for research involving children and other vulnerable populations such as the mentally impaired and prisoners. The details of these determinations are included in other chapters of this book. It is strongly recommended that the reviewer worksheet include specific questions about the special assessments to be made if vulnerable populations are part of the potential research population.

Worksheet Questions

1. Are the risks and benefits adequately identified, evaluated, and described?
2. Are the potential risks minimized and likelihood of benefits maximized?
3. Is the risk/benefit ratio acceptable for proceeding with the research?
4. Example of more specific questions for a vulnerable population: If children are involved, within which category of risk/benefit does the protocol fall? Are all criteria within the category adequately addressed?
5. Institution-specific questions should also be listed.

Compensation and Costs for Subjects

IRB members are charged with the responsibility for reviewing and approving compensation or reimbursement provided to research subjects. Such compensation may take the form of reimbursement for expenses associated with research participation such as travel expenses, lost wages, parking costs, etc. At times, it may also be appropriate to offer incentives for participation. In all instances, the IRB must be certain that the compensation or reimbursement offered is not so large as to be coercive. The form of compensation and the timing of offering the compensation also become part of the review process. When children are the research subjects, IRB members have to consider who receives the compensation.

The IRB also must consider any costs associated with participation in the research and expenses that may occur as a result of research participation. If the subject's medical expenses are covered by health insurance, it is important to indicate who is responsible for any study expenses, especially if the research is not covered by the health insurance or the insurance company refuses to pay. Plans for compensation and treatment in the event of an injury that results from participation must also be addressed.

Worksheet Questions

1. Is the amount or type of compensation or reimbursement reasonable?
2. Are there adequate provisions to avoid out-of-pocket expenses by the research subject, or is there sufficient justification to allow subjects to pay?
3. If children or adolescents are involved, who receives the compensation, and is this appropriate?

Privacy and Confidentiality

Reviewers must consider the possibility of a research protocol's invading the privacy of a research subject or breaching confidentiality. These possibilities present a risk of harm to the subject. IRBs must consider the type and sensitivity of the information sought, how the information will be recorded, precautions taken to protect confidentiality, and who has access to the research records. Precautions can and should be taken, depending on the nature of the research. This may include the possibility of applying for a certificate of confidentiality.

Worksheet Questions

1. Are there adequate provisions to protect the privacy and assure the confidentiality of the research subject?
2. Are there adequate plans to store and code the data?
3. Is the use of identifiers or links to identifiers necessary, and how is this information protected?

Other Issues

Other issues may have to be considered for a particular investigation, topic of research, or institution conducting research. This will depend on the nature of the research being performed. It is also the IRB's responsibility to determine when the next continuing review should occur. At a maximum, this must occur one year after IRB review. This decision must be made on an individualized, per-protocol basis, taking into consideration the degree of risk associated with the research. More frequent review may be recommended in high-risk protocols.

Worksheet Questions

1. Are adequate references provided?
2. When should the next review occur? If frequent reviews are necessary, how should the interval be determined?
3. Institution-specific questions should also be listed.

Informed Consent/Assent

The consent and assent sections of the reviewer worksheet are divided into three sections: the consent document, the consent process, and any waivers or alterations of informed consent requirements.

The Consent Document   A checklist is provided of all of the federally mandated elements of informed consent. The checklist combines the requirements of the Department of Health and Human Services and the FDA. Reviewers are responsible for reviewing the informed consent and determining whether each element is present, absent, or not applicable. IRB members are encouraged to "mark up" a copy of the proposed consent with any additions, deletions, comments, suggestions, or rewording necessary. A marked-up version of the informed consent, which combines all comments, is forwarded to the investigator after the meeting along with any other questions and concerns raised regarding the protocol application.

Checklist of Informed Consent Elements

1. Consent/assent form checklist
2. Statement that the study involves research
3. Purpose of research stated in lay language
4. Reason subject is asked to participate
5. Expected duration of study
6. Study design described in lay language (number of groups, randomization, use of placebo)
7. Study procedures or treatments
8. Description of drug or device (if applicable); state whether it is investigational
9. Compensation or reimbursement
10. Number of subjects in the trial
11. Potential risks or discomforts to the subject
12. Potential direct benefits or benefits to society
13. Alternatives available (indicate if none)
14. Statement that participation is voluntary and subject may withdraw
15. Additional costs associated with participating—who will pay for what
16. How confidentiality will be protected; who has access to the data

If applicable:

17. Anticipated circumstances under which a subject's participation may be terminated
18. Statement that significant new findings will be disclosed
19. Consequences of withdrawal
20. If greater than minimal risk, statement included regarding compensation in event of injury

Process of Obtaining Informed Consent/Assent

Worksheet Questions

1. Is the process well defined?
2. Is the individual obtaining consent appropriate?

3. Are the issues of subject's comprehension and autonomy considered?

Assent from Children   For protocols that involve children, the IRB is required to determine whether assent is required and, if so, determine an appropriate mechanism to obtain and document assent. The reviewer worksheet contains questions that will prompt the IRB members to make this special determination as required. There is no federal regulation for an assent document or form. Many institutions require separate documentation, whereas others require a child's cosignature on the parental permission form.

Worksheet Questions

Note: Assent is required unless the child in not capable (age, psychological state, sedation) or the research holds out the prospect of direct benefit that is only available within the context of the research.

1. Is assent required?
2. Are the children who are potential subjects all capable of providing assent?
3. Is the method of obtaining assent appropriate?

Waiver or Modification of Informed Consent   The federal regulations also permit the waiver or alteration of informed consent in protocols that meet very specific criteria. This determination has to be made and documented by the IRB. It is essential that investigators seeking a waiver or alteration of informed consent provide adequate justification for the IRB to be able to make its final determinations. Other sections of this book discuss the criteria for waivers or alterations. The reviewer worksheet generally prompts IRB reviewers to look for the appropriate justification if a waiver or alteration in the written consent or consent process is suggested.

Worksheet Questions

Consider as appropriate:

1. Are criteria for waiver of parental consent provided and acceptable?
2. Are criteria for waiver of written informed consent criteria provided and acceptable?
3. Are procedures for modification or alteration of written consent provided and acceptable?

How the Reviewer Worksheet Is Used

Depending on IRB policies and practices for initial review of research protocols, the reviewer checklist may be used at different times during the initial review process. The time at which the checklist is used is not important as long as the criteria listed on the worksheet are considered during the review process. However, in general, the earlier in the review process these criteria can be evaluated, the better the outcome is for the investigator and the IRB. One example of how the worksheet is used is provided here.

At Children's Hospital in Boston, each research protocol submission is assigned a primary and secondary IRB reviewer. Although all members of the IRB receive a copy of the protocol application and are encouraged to comment on each protocol, it is the responsibility of the primary and secondary reviewers to review the protocol in detail and to be certain all of the issues included on the reviewer worksheet are addressed. Both the primary and secondary reviewers independently complete a reviewer worksheet for each protocol they are assigned. Completion and return of the checklist is mandatory. Additional materials such as investigational brochures and other appendix materials are distributed to the primary and secondary reviewers only. At Children's Hospital, the investigator is not asked to attend the IRB committee meeting. The primary reviewer gives a brief summary of the protocol and then discusses comments, concerns, and questions. The secondary reviewer then provides comments, concerns, and questions. After the meeting, these are transcribed into a written report of action and sent to the investigator. The reviewer worksheet serves as a constant reminder that IRB reviewers must consider each of the mandated criteria for approval. It becomes a convenient and organized way to assist IRB reviewers in discussing their critique of the protocol. It also assists the IRB administrative staff in documenting the IRB review process and reporting the IRB's findings back to the investigator.

It is important to emphasize that complete initial review of a research protocol is an essential process for any IRB. It is the basis for further discussion and dialogue between the IRB and investigators. The IRB reviewer worksheet can be used at any time during the initial review process. The major advantages that it brings to the IRB review process follow:

1. The reviewer worksheet is a mechanism to help IRB reviewers organize their critique of a research protocol.

2. The reviewer worksheet is a quality-control mechanism that ensures that reviewers have considered all of the regulatory and institutional criteria for review and approval.

3. The reviewer worksheet encourages and provides a level of consistency in the IRB review process.

4. Written comments from the worksheet may assist administrative staff in preparing follow-up summaries to investigators after the meeting and in preparing minutes of the IRB meeting.

5. The reviewer worksheet can serve as written documentation for the initial review process.

Conclusion

IRB administrators play an important role in coordinating and performing the initial review of human subject protocols. IRB administrators assist in the development of the protocol application. The protocol application is the first step in obtaining the information necessary to perform an initial review. Mechanisms must be established to receive the protocol applications and prepare them for IRB review. When resources and staffing permit, IRB administrators can play an essential role in the initial review of the protocol and can advise investigators about their applications before the IRB review. This often saves time once a protocol is submitted to the full IRB. IRB administrators and Chairs are responsible for assuring that members perform a complete and thorough initial review. The use of a worksheet is strongly suggested. Initial review is an essential process that helps ensure human subject protection and regulatory compliance. Institutions must designate appropriate staff and resources for this critical function.

References

1. Code of Federal Regulations. Title 45A—Department of Health and Human Services; Part 46—Protection of Human Subjects. Updated 1 Oct 1997. Access date 18 Apr 2001. World Wide Web http://www4.law.cornell.edu/cfr/45p46.htm

2. Code of Federal Regulations. Title 21, Chapter 1—Food and Drug Administration, DHHS; Part 56—Institutional Review Boards. Updated 1 Apr 1999. Access date 27 Mar 2001. World Wide Web http://www4.law.cornell.edu/cfr/21p56.htm

Evaluating Study Design and Quality

Robert J. Amdur

INTRODUCTION

It is not unusual for IRB members, institutional officials, and researchers to debate the role of the IRB in evaluating study design or other aspects that affect the fundamental quality of the science of research. For example, is it appropriate for IRB members to vote not to approve a study because they believe study results would be more persuasive if a different control group were used, or because previously completed research has already answered the study question? Is it appropriate for the IRB to question the validity of the statistical power calculation used to determine the number of subjects in a study? Some members of the research community are under the impression that it is not the role of the IRB to routinely evaluate the quality of the science of a protocol. Many IRB Chairs have been confronted with statements like "The IRB's job is to evaluate ethics. The IRB has no business commenting on the science of a study." In most cases this view will be presented by a researcher who has been criticized by the IRB, but in some situations the argument will come from IRB members or institutional officials. The purpose of this chapter is to explain the role of the IRB in evaluating study design and the other features of a study that may affect scientific quality. The bottom line is that there is no question that the IRB not only has the authority to evaluate scientific quality, but it has the obligation to do so if it is to function in compliance with accepted ethical codes and federal research regulations.

Ethical Codes

Nuremberg Code (1949)

Several sections of the Nuremberg code address scientific quality and the risk/benefit profile. Point 3 is representative: "The experiment should be so designed and based on the results of animal experimentation and a knowledge of the natural history of the disease or other problem under study that the anticipated results will justify the performance of the experiment."

Declaration of Helsinki (2000)

Multiple sections of the latest version of this ethical code address specific aspects of study design. Sections 11, 18, and 29 are especially relevant to the question of IRB review of scientific quality.

11. Medical research involving human subjects must conform to generally accepted scientific principles, be based on a thorough knowledge of the scientific literature, other relevant sources of information, and on adequate laboratory and, where appropriate, animal experimentation.
18. Medical research involving human subjects should only be conducted if the importance of the objective outweighs the in-
herent risks and burdens to the subject. This is especially important when the human subjects are healthy volunteers.
29. The benefits, risks, burdens, and effectiveness of a new method should be tested against those of the best current prophylactic, diagnostic, and therapeutic methods. This does not exclude the use of placebo, or no treatment, in studies where no proven prophylactic, diagnostic, or therapeutic method exists.

Federal Research Regulations

Department of Health and Human Services and corresponding Food and Drug Administration regulations require the IRB to determine that the study is designed so that risks to subjects are minimized and justified by potential benefits. This excerpt is from 45 CFR 46.[1][Sec.111(a)]

(a). Criteria for IRB approval of Research:
(1) Risks to subjects are minimized: (i) by using procedures which are consistent with sound research design, and which do not unnecessarily expose subjects to risk.
(2) Risks to subjects are reasonable in relation to anticipated benefits, if any, to subjects, and the importance of the knowledge that may reasonably be expected to result. In evaluating risks

and benefits, the IRB should consider only those risks and benefits that may result from the research (as distinguished from risks and benefits of therapies subjects would receive even if not participating in the research).

The IRB's Responsibility to Evaluate Scientific Quality

The IRB is supposed to act in compliance with federal research regulations and make decisions that support the ethical principles in accepted ethical codes like the Nuremberg Code and the Declaration of Helsinki. The sections from these guidance documents reproduced above emphasize that a characteristic of ethical research is that (a) the study is designed so that the risks to subjects are minimized, and (b) the potential benefits of the research justify the potential risks. It is these two directives that establish the obligation of the IRB to carefully consider the study design and overall scientific quality of each study.

The Study Design

If revising the study design will meaningfully decrease the risk to subjects without a major compromise in the persuasiveness of the study results, then the IRB should not approve the protocol. There are also situations where the IRB should not approve research because the study design is so flawed that the value of the study results will be almost zero. In this setting, risks may be low, but the potential benefit is zero, so the overall risk/benefit profile of the study is unacceptable. Similarly, when a study that involves risk is set up to ask a question that is not important or has already been answered by previous research, the risk/benefit profile is likely to be unfavorable. The point is that the IRB is obligated to evaluate the study design and other aspects of scientific quality because these are ethical issues that affect the rights and welfare of research participants.

Having stressed the importance of evaluating the scientific quality of research, it is important to remember that, as with all ethical principles, the IRB should use individual judgment and common sense when considering not approving a study because of the study design. In organizations where a large volume of social science research is done by students, it is not unusual for the IRB to review protocols where the scientific design is not optimal, but the risk to subjects is virtually zero. An example would be a survey study that attempts to correlate the attitudes of college students about globalization of the economy with their decision to apply to graduate school.

Although one could argue that many of these student projects could legitimately be classified as educational exercises rather than research, that is a separate issue. The point is that there are projects where the study design is flawed, but the risk is basically zero. Certainly, it makes sense for IRB members who are knowledgeable in this type of research to recommend revisions to the study plan. However, in the absence of meaningful risk, there is really no ethical justification for the IRB to make such revisions a condition for IRB approval. Each case must be evaluated independently.

Departmental Scientific Review Before IRB Review

Given that scientific quality is a criterion for IRB approval of research, the next question is the process of IRB review of scientific aspects of specific studies. Tasks such as evaluating the details of study design, the qualifications of the investigator, and the value of a proposed study in the context of what is already known require specialized expertise in the area that is being evaluated in the study. Many IRBs will find that the background of their membership is such that it is difficult for the committee to effectively evaluate scientific issues for the wide range of protocols that the committee reviews. One solution is to request a consultant who is expert in the area in question to comment on scientific issues. However, when scientific evaluations outside the IRB are needed on a regular basis, asking for consultant opinions on a case-by-case basis is likely to be awkward and inefficient.

To facilitate the evaluation of scientific quality in research, some organizations establish policy that requires a formal review of scientific issues by a representative of the investigator's department (or other relevant group) before the protocol is forwarded to the IRB. A system that works well for both researchers and the IRB has been in place for over 10 years at Dartmouth College and Dartmouth Medical School. The requirement for review of scientific quality prior to IRB review was established at the level of the Office of the Dean of the School of Medicine and is called "departmental scientific review." In most departments, a committee—usually consisting of three to six individuals with research experience—reviews each protocol that is to be submitted to the IRB from a member of that department. In small departments or departments with limited research experience, the departmental scientific review is handled by a single individual (possibly from another department) who is not a collaborator on the research under review. As the system has evolved, the IRB has found it useful to use an issue-specific form to guide and document evaluation of the scientific issues that are especially important to the IRB. This departmental scientific review form is attached as an appendix to this chapter. Notice that the Dartmouth IRB asks for the name of a representative from the group conducting the scientific review who will be available to attend an IRB meeting to explain the protocol if this is considered necessary. This is a unique aspect of the Dartmouth system compared with that used at most other centers. Because the review form emphasizes that a member of the reviewing team may be expected to defend the science of the study to the IRB, there is a level of accountability that is not present when the scientific review committee knows that it is the principal investigator who will be discussing any contentious issues.

Conclusion

This chapter has explained the role of the IRB in evaluating study design and the other features of a study that may affect scientific quality. There is no question that the IRB not only has the authority to evaluate scientific quality, but it has the obligation to do so if it is to function in compliance with accepted ethical codes and federal research regulations. The Nuremberg Code, the Declaration of Helsinki, and federal research regulations contain sections that highlight the importance of study design and scientific quality as standards for ethical research. In most organizations it will be useful to establish scientific review committees to comment on study design and scientific quality before the proposal goes to the IRB.

References

1. Code of Federal Regulations. Title 45A—Department of Health and Human Services; Part 46—Protection of Human Subjects. Updated 1 Oct 1997. Access date 18 Apr 2001. World Wide Web http:www4.law.cornell.edu/cfr/45p46.htm

---

Departmental Scientific Review of Research Protocols Involving Human Subjects

Principal Investigator _____

Project Title _____

_____

_____

     All protocols must undergo scientific review by a departmental research group or other designated authority prior to submission to the IRB. The review must involve individuals qualified to evaluate the scientific merit of the study being proposed. If the departmental research review group does not include individuals who are capable of evaluating the scientific merit of a particular proposal, it is the responsibility of the department Chair or designated representative to have the protocol reviewed by an appropriate authority not involved in the study in question.

<u>Approval Checklist</u>

This protocol has been reviewed by the departmental research group . . . .**YES**   **NO**

        Other (specify) _____

        _____

        _____

a. The scientific questions addressed in this protocol have adequate merit to justify experimentation involving human subjects . . . .**YES**   **NO**

b. The potential risks of this study have been accurately and fully described . . . .**YES**   **NO**

c. The study design is adequate to answer the questions being asked . . . .**YES**   **NO**

(Please attach a brief summary of the discussion of the study design including issues that you think could be raised by the IRB.)

d. Prior animal or *in vitro* studies are adequate to support human trials . . . .**YES**   **NO**

e. Is there a method to investigate this scientific problem without human subjects? . . . .**YES**   **NO**

    (If **YES**, then please explain, on the back of this form, why human subjects are to be employed.)

f. The principal investigator and co-investigator(s) have adequate experience to conduct the study . . . .**YES**   **NO**

Please identify a member of the review team (NOT an investigator involved in the study) who will be responsible for discussing this protocol with members of the IRB if necessary:

Name _____ Phone _____

_____ Date _____

Signature of Departmental Research Group Chair or other cognizant authority

---

The Study Population: Women, Minorities, and Children

Amy L. Davis

INTRODUCTION

This chapter will introduce the ethical issues related to the selection of human research populations for behavioral/biomedical research studies. Federal regulations require the equitable selection of research subjects. To meet this mandate requires consideration of several questions: What constitutes equitable selection? Who is included in the study cohort? What are the inclusion/exclusion criteria? Do any of the criteria relate to sex, race, or age? Are the inclusion/exclusion criteria reasonably related to the purpose of the research? Are the criteria related to the study issue, or are they based on the convenience of the researcher? These are some critical questions an IRB must consider at the outset of the protocol review.

The purpose of this chapter should be distinguished from that of other chapters in this book that discuss specific regulatory requirements for IRB review of protocols involving special populations. The questions answered in this chapter precede those addressed in later chapters. This chapter relates to study design and the ethics of initial subject selection. Initially, the IRB must determine that the target population is appropriate for the research project under the guidelines discussed in this chapter. Should the target population be considered vulnerable, the IRB must then consider the additional protections, discussed in later chapters, applicable to the special population that is the subject of the research protocol. This chapter will review the current regulations and related policy on the selection of human subjects. It will cover the historical bases for the policy, its practical application, and finally implementation issues that arise in the equitable selection of human research subjects.

The Regulations

Federal regulations set forth at 45 CFR 46 [1][Sec.111(a)(3)] and at 21 CFR 56 [2][Sec.111(a)(3)] state simply that "in order to approve research covered by this policy, the IRB shall determine that . . . selection of subjects is equitable." The regulation specifies three criteria that the IRB should consider in making this assessment:

1. The purpose of the research
2. The setting in which the research will be conducted
3. The special problems of research involving vulnerable populations

The regulation is based on the *Belmont Report's* principle of justice, which requires the fair distribution of both the benefits and risks of research.[3] The *IRB Guidebook*[4(Chap.III)] explains the purpose and application of this requirement as follows: "The requirement for an equitable selection of subjects helps ensure that the burdens and benefits of research will be fairly distributed." In evaluating the potential *benefits* of proposed research, the IRB must consider the purpose of the research and whether the subjects selected to participate in the research will be among the population most likely to benefit from the research. In considering the *burdens* associated with the research, the IRB must consider whether the selected group of subjects is already burdened by poverty, illness, or institutionalization and whether asking them to assume the additional burdens associated with participating in research is justified. Accordingly, the equitable-selection-of-subjects criterion requires a preliminary assessment of risks and benefits of research in the context of the particular characteristics of the research subjects.

Historical Basis

The National Commission for the Protection of Human Subjects, which developed the *Belmont Report*, was created to identify the basic ethical principles that should be followed in conducting human subjects research.[3] In establishing the principle of justice and its corollary doctrine of equitable selection of human subjects, the Commission was responding to certain historical examples of discriminatory practices in human subjects research.[3] The most egregious examples are the Nazi experiments with concentration camp victims. The Tuskegee experiments, where poor, black men from the rural South were recruited to participate in a study of the course of syphilis as it progressed untreated, form another example. Researchers have even exploited children confined to mental hospitals. In experiments conducted during the mid-1950s at the Willowbrook State Institution for "mentally defective children" in New York, for example, researchers deliberately infected newly admitted patients with the hepatitis virus to watch the course of the disease. At the Fernald School in Massachusetts, children with mental impairments confined to an institution were given cereal containing minute amounts of radioactive materials. The purpose of the study was to examine mineral uptake in the body. In this example, there was no scientific reason related to the purpose of the research that would justify the selection of this group of subjects. The only reason for selecting this group of children was for the convenience of the researchers.[5] These were the kinds of abuses that the *Belmont Report* aimed at preventing.

This history demonstrates that, before the writing of the *Belmont Report*, the burdens of human subjects research fell largely on poor and vulnerable populations while the benefits of such research were enjoyed by the wealthy and powerful segments of societies. Today such blatant examples of unjust research practices are rare. Nevertheless, inequities in subject selection can occur, and IRBs must be sensitive to the more subtle variations.

Recent Policy Developments: Inclusion of Women, Minorities, and Children

Since the publication of the *Belmont Report* and the human subjects protection regulations in the early 1970s, there have been several refinements to the general principle that research subjects be equitably selected. These developments reflect the intrinsic conflict between ensuring that research benefits are equitably distributed and protecting vulnerable populations. The *IRB Guidebook* instructs IRBs not to overprotect vulnerable populations to the extent that they are systematically excluded from the benefits of research.[4(Chap.III)] The

challenge is determining the level of risk to which vulnerable subjects may be exposed.

The struggle to balance the interest in fairly distributing the benefits of research with the interest in protecting the vulnerable is particularly evident in the development of regulations pertaining to the inclusion of women and children in research studies. In 1977, the Food and Drug Administration (FDA) issued guidance that excluded women of childbearing potential from participation in early studies of new drugs.[6] The rationale was to protect the fetus from unknown risks of unapproved, experimental drugs. This policy was developed in part in response to the tragic effects associated with two drugs: thalidomide and diethylstilbestrol (DES).[7] Thalidomide, used to treat nausea in pregnant women, was found to cause deformed limbs in newborns.[7] DES, prescribed to prevent miscarriage, was later associated with a rare form of cancer of the vagina in the daughters of women who had taken the drug.[7]

As a result of the 1977 regulation, little scientific information was collected about the effect of many therapies and drugs in women. For example, studies done to evaluate the effect of aspirin on cardiovascular disease excluded women.[6] Therefore, in 1993, the FDA revised its policy to withdraw this restriction on the participation of women of childbearing age in early clinical trials including pharmacology studies.[6] The revised policy was based on the expectation that women could be relied on to take appropriate measures against becoming pregnant while enrolled in a research trial. In addition, testing could be done to ensure that pregnant women were not enrolled in a drug trial.[6]

Less than a year later, the National Institutes of Health (NIH) issued a new policy requiring the inclusion of women and minorities in clinical research.[8] The new policy prohibited the routine exclusion of women of childbearing potential from NIH-funded research. Specifically, the policy states

> . . . women and members of minority groups and their subpopulations must be included in all NIH-supported biomedical and behavioral research projects involving human subjects, unless a clear and compelling rationale and justification establishes to the satisfaction of the relevant Institute/Center Director that inclusion is inappropriate with respect to the health of the subjects or the purpose of the research.[8]

The policy explicitly eliminates financial cost as an acceptable justification for the exclusion of any group.[8] Under this new policy, the protocol must describe the sexual and racial/ethnic composition of the proposed study population. It also must provide a rationale for the selection of these subjects.[8]

In January 2001, the human subjects protection regulations were revised again to create a presumption of inclusion for pregnant women to participate in research. These regulations revise the policy that had presumptively excluded pregnant women from research. The August 1975 regulations stated, "(a) No pregnant woman may be involved as a subject in an activity covered by this subpart unless . . ."[1(Sec. 207)] Under the new regulations, a pregnant woman is the sole decision-maker on whether to participate in research. Even when the research relates to the health of the fetus, the mother alone—without consultation with the father—may consent to participate in the study. This policy resolves a longstanding weakness in federal policy that suggested that pregnant women were less autonomous than nonpregnant women as research subjects.[9]

Policy development related to the inclusion of children in research reflects a similar debate. In response to what policy makers perceived to be overprotective research practices in connection with children, NIH issued a new policy in 1998 to encourage the enrollment of children in research studies.[10] The NIH policy was a deliberate application of the regulation to select subjects equitably and addressed the potential risks of treating children with medications that receive FDA approval based on research done on adults.[10] Like the policies requiring the inclusion of women and minority groups in research studies, this policy is based on the assumption that children may experience discrete biologic responses to new treatments or drugs. Notwithstanding these regulations, the wisdom of including children in clinical trials is still vigorously debated among members of The IRB Forum (formerly MCWIRB), an on-line discussion forum. (See discussion listed under "Inclusion of Children" on Web site http://www.mcwirb.org/index.html.)

IRB Review and the Principle of Equitable Subject Selection

The goal of the equitable selection policy is to fairly distribute the risks and benefits of research among the populations that stand to benefit from it. The IRB has the authority and the responsibility to examine the extent to which this goal is achieved or impeded in each protocol it reviews. Obviously, the goal cannot be achieved or impeded by any individual protocol, but every protocol has an impact on the ultimate distribution of benefits and risks.

The IRB is in the best position in any given institution to assess that institution's overall performance on this criterion of ethical research. This section will outline a strategy for conducting IRB review of compliance with the equitable selection criterion. It is intended to break down the IRB analysis of equitable selection into discrete questions listed below.

What Is the Study Population?
First, the IRB must review a description of the study population. Every study should provide a thorough description of the study population in terms of sex, race, ethnicity, and age. Is the study limited to a certain sex, a certain age group, certain racial or ethnic categories, or certain socioeconomic categories? If some of this information is missing, the IRB must request it and evaluate it before approving the protocol.

To answer some of these questions it may not be sufficient to merely examine the protocol description of the target population. It may also be necessary to examine the

methods and manner of recruitment. If, for example, the study intends to target a representative population of men and women of multiple races and ethnic backgrounds, but recruitment will only take place through suburban hospitals located in mostly white neighborhoods, the IRB may be justified in challenging the recruitment methodology as inadequate to meet the goal of enrolling a representative group of human subjects.

Is the Description of the Study Population Reasonably Related to the Purpose of the Research?
The IRB should be sure that criteria for selecting certain groups or individuals to participate in a study are scientifically related to the goals of the research and not based merely on criteria of convenience, such as where the researchers or the subjects live or work. For example, an IRB should question the ethics of a study in which the researcher from a medical school targets medical students to study the efficacy and safety of a new drug to treat diabetes. In such a case, there would be no research-related reason for targeting medical students. Medical students do not share unique biologic characteristics that might affect the pharmacokinetics of the new drug. Moreover, the convenience of recruiting human subjects from the same institution in which the researcher works is not sufficient justification for selecting this group. In addition, there may be a risk that the medical students could feel some pressure to enroll in a study conducted by a person of authority and influence over them. Similarly, it would probably be unethical to conduct a clinical study of a new drug to treat AIDS using a prison population because prisoners do not share biological characteristics that differ from other populations. Therefore, the selection of prisoner subjects would have no scientific relevance to the drug's effects.

What Are the Inclusion/Exclusion Criteria for the Study Population?
A related principle is that the target population should be representative of the population that stands to potentially benefit from the research. Research that has the potential to benefit men, women, and children or different races should target study subjects that reflect this diversity in sufficient numbers to distinguish differing effects, risks, and benefits.[8] No group or individual should be categorically *excluded* from the research without a good scientific reason to do so.[11]

An example of unethical exclusion may be a study of the effectiveness of a new drug for hypertension using a male-only cohort. It may be difficult to justify such a study because women also suffer from hypertension and, therefore, could potentially benefit from a new drug for treating the condition. In such a case, both men and women should either be represented in a single study cohort or be represented in two separate studies of the same drug. In this manner, data are collected on the efficacy and safety of the drug in men and women.

To merely include men and women, or subjects of different races or ethnic backgrounds, may not be sufficient to meet the federal standards. Researchers must be sensitive to the possibility that variations in data may be based on sex, race, or ethnicity. The 1994 NIH Guidelines specifically require investigators planning Phase III clinical trials to examine data from prior studies to determine whether significant differences exist in intervention effect among sexual or ethnic groups.[8] If such differences are detected, then the Phase III trial must be designed to study the effect separately for each group.[8] In evaluating a Phase III trial protocol, the IRB must assess whether the investigator has met this obligation.

IRBs should also be sensitive to the potential for indirect exclusion of certain groups. A study that includes men and women may still enroll a disproportionate number of one sex. For example, a study of cardiovascular disease that has an exclusion criterion related to age could indirectly exclude women, who contract heart diseases at older ages than men.[12]

The requirement that the study population be representative of the population that may benefit from the research does not mean that it is unethical to study the effect of a drug or intervention on one sex. Because there is less research information on the effects of certain drugs or treatments in women, it may be ethical to conduct "catch-up" research with an all-female cohort. Moreover, there may be gender-specific research questions that might justify a single sex research study. For example, a study of a drug's effect in menopausal women would most likely satisfy this ethical standard.[6]

What Is the Rationale for Inclusion/Exclusion Criteria?

Since the early 1990s, awareness has grown that research findings ought to be generalizable to individuals outside the study population, and that IRBs should not overprotect vulnerable populations. Routine exclusion of certain populations based on sex, race, or age results in a disparity of information about treatment options for the excluded groups and unequal distribution of the risks and benefits of research.[12]

An IRB should review the inclusion/exclusion criteria for the study population and determine whether any group that could be affected by the research is excluded. If such a group is excluded, the IRB should determine whether there is a justification in the proposal for the exclusion and whether that justification is reasonable in relation to the risks, benefits, and purpose of the research. For example, a study of risk factors for breast cancer could justifiably exclude men, and probably children, but most likely could not justify the exclusion of minority women.

This requirement that groups not be excluded without adequate justification does not mean that it is never appropriate for exclusion criteria to be based on race, sex, or age. If there is evidence from prior research that men and women, for example, experience a particular condition disproportionately, then it may be appropriate to conduct separate studies of a particular treatment for that condition using different study populations. For example, because women are affected by osteoporosis in far greater numbers than men, it would be appropriate to study the effects of a new treatment for the condition using an all-female study population.[7(p. 89)] In another, less obvious example, it may

be appropriate to study the effectiveness of an intervention to prevent HIV infection in a study population of women only. Such a study may be justified by data produced in previous studies that demonstrate that unprotected, heterosexual intercourse poses greater risk to women than men.

To assess the rationale for selecting certain subject groups, IRBs will need to review information on the distribution of the health condition in the general population.[9] If the IRB is not satisfied with the justification for excluding a certain group, the IRB may decide to ask for additional justification from the investigator, condition its approval on the removal of the exclusion criterion, or disapprove the research.

Conclusion

IRBs may be reluctant to demand additional information on the justification for subject selection. Limited resources and excessive demands force IRBs to focus on other approval criteria, such as the balance of risks and benefits and the effectiveness of the informed consent document. Moreover, IRBs are often concerned about maintaining positive relations with the researchers with whom they work.[9]

In assuming the awesome responsibility for assessing equity in subject selection, IRBs should be aware that the responsibility is shared with research sponsors. The distribution of research funds nationally determines the ultimate justice of subject selection. An individual study is unlikely to affect the overall equality of the distribution of research risks and benefits.[7(p. 89)] Researchers and IRBs should also remember that the equitable selection of research subjects is directly linked to the generalizability of research. Research that is broadly generalizable has greater value than other research.[12]

As with so many challenges of human subjects research, the most effective solution may be training. Education of researchers that heightens sensitivity to the equitable selection of subjects may be the most effective method of realizing the goal.

References

1. Code of Federal Regulations. Title 45A—Department of Health and Human Services; Part 46—Protection of Human Subjects. Updated 1 Oct 1997. Access date 18 Apr 2001. World Wide Web http://www4.law.cornell.edu/cfr/45p46.htm

2. Code of Federal Regulations. Title 21, Chapter 1—Food and Drug Administration, DHHS; Part 56—Institutional Review Boards. Updated 1 Apr 1999. Access date 27 Mar 2001. World Wide Web http://www4.law.cornell.edu/cfr/21p56.htm

3. National Commission for the Protection of Human Subjects of Biomedical and Behavioral Research. *The Belmont Report: Ethical principles and guidelines for the protection of human subjects of research.* Updated 1979. Access date 22 Mar 2001. World Wide Web http://ohsr.od.nih.gov/mpa/belmont.php3

4. Penslar R. L, Porter JP, Office for Human Research Protections. *Institutional Review Board Guidebook.* Updated 6 Feb 2001. Access date 29 Mar 2001. World Wide Web http://ohrp.osophs.dhhs.gov/irb/irb_guidebook.htm

5. Advisory Committee on Human Radiation Experiments. *The Human Radiation Experiments: Final Report.* New York: Oxford University Press. 1996. World Wide Web http://tis.eh.doe.gov/ohre/roadmap/achre/report.html (DOE 061-000-00-848-9)

6. Food and Drug Administration. Guidelines for the study and evaluation of gender differences in the clinical evaluation of drugs. *Fed Regist* 58(139):39406–39416, 1993.

7. Mastroianni A. C, Faden R, Federman D, (editors); Committee on the Ethical and Legal Issues Relating to the Inclusion of Women in Clinical Studies, Div . of Health Sciences Policy, Institute of Medicine. *Women and Health Research: Ethical and Legal Issues of Including Women in Clinical Studies,* Vol 1. Washington, DC: National Academy Press. 1994. World Wide Web http://search.nap.edu/books/030904992X/html/

8. National Institutes of Health. NIH Guidelines on the Inclusion of Women and Minorities as Subjects in Clinical Research (RIN 0905-ZA18). *Fed Regist* 59:14508–14513, 1994.

9. Rothenberg K. H. The Institute of Medicine's report on women and health research: Implications for IRBs and the research community. *IRB: A Review of Human Subjects Research* 18(2):1–3, 1996.

10. National Institutes of Health. NIH Policy and Guidelines on the Inclusion of Children as Participants in Research Involving Human Subjects, 6 Mar 1998. Access date 13 Aug 2001. World Wide Web http://grants.nih.gov/grants/guide/notice-files/not98-024.html

11. Emanuel E. J., Wendler D, Grady C. What makes clinical research ethical? *JAMA* 283(20:2701–2711, 2000.

12. Weijer C. The IRB's role in assessing the generalizability of non-NIH-funded clinical trials. *IRB: A Review of Human Subjects Research* 20(2,3): 1–5, 1998.

Community Consultation to Evaluate Group Risk

William L. Freeman and Francine C. Romero

INTRODUCTION

The primary goal of this chapter is to explain the importance of community consultation in evaluating and conducting research that targets a distinct and vulnerable population. The recommendations made in this chapter should be considered to represent the best practices for human research protection because there is little detailed guidance from federal authorities on this subject. This chapter will focus on research involving American Indian or Alaska Native (AI/AN) as well as Canadian First Nation and Inuit peoples and tribes, but the principles discussed will apply to any vulnerable group in our society.

A Hypothetical Research Protocol

Consider the following hypothetical research protocol involving an Indian reservation that has two distinct subgroups derived from different tribes that had been enemies in the 19th century. One subgroup has a more traditional lifestyle and lives primarily in an eastern enclave of the reservation; the other has a more acculturated lifestyle and lives primarily in a western enclave. The research hypotheses are that the average stress level will be less in the group with a more traditional lifestyle, but the expression of genes that have been linked to the stress response will be similar in each group. The methods include qualitative ethnography; quantitative surveys of traditional beliefs and of likely confounding factors (alcoholism, substance abuse, history of being sexually or physically abused in childhood or as a spouse); and blood draws both for levels of stress-related hormones and testing for variants of stress-related genes.

When evaluating the ethics of this research, the IRB should evaluate the risk to individual participants as well as the risks to community subgroups. What are the potential harms of this research to the *groups* that may be affected by it? For example, what are the risks of this research to the tribe that is the focus of the research, subgroups of the tribe currently living on the reservation, and native people from other tribes? At this point, please STOP READING. Please WRITE on a sheet of paper all of the group harms that you think are important to consider with this kind of research. After you have completed your list, continue reading the chapter.

Historical Examples of Group Harms

Research projects that caused great harm to individual participants are well known and frequently cited.[1] An example of ethically questionable research that involved many IA/AN people is the Public Health Service (PHS) longitudinal study of the health of uranium miners.[2] A large percentage of the participants in this study were Navajo and Pueblo miners. The purpose of the study was to document the lung cancer death risk. At the time of the study, there was no question that uranium exposure was a risk factor for lung cancer. Participants in this study were not counseled on the risk of lung cancer as part of the study.

The risk of research to groups of people other than the individual research participants is a factor that is complex to evaluate and often overlooked by IRBs and researchers. Examples of research that caused group harm were the many studies comparing the average IQ of various racial groups, especially of African-American people. The science of education, on which many educators relied in making decisions about students, was riddled with racist assumptions. Culturally biased IQ tests, whose defects were magnified by racist interpretations, seemed to prove the mental inferiority of African-Americans and to justify relegating them to nonacademic ranks.[3] As recently as 1996, a popular book claimed the results of IQ research as scientific evidence that African-Americans had less intellectual capacity than European-Americans.[4]

Some AI/AN tribes have also experienced group harms due to research. For instance, researchers announced the bleak results of their study on alcoholism in an identified far-northwestern native community at a news conference held in Pennsylvania. The publicity had immediate adverse effects on the community that had been the subject of this research. The most striking result was the difficulty raising investment capital on Wall Street.[5] Other examples of group harm done by research include studies of an outbreak of congenital syphilis and of the first known epidemic of Hantavirus pulmonary syndrome.[6]

Please STOP READING. If you have not done so already, or if you have thought of new potential group harms, please add them to the list you made at the beginning of this chapter. Then read the rest of the chapter.

Potential Group Harms to Consider

We compiled the following list of group harms from recent reports and articles about the actual experiences of vulnerable groups involved in research. Many reports and articles concerned AI/AN or Canadian First Nations and Inuit tribes and bands; a few concerned other groups, primarily African-Americans, Jews, and groups with Mendelian (single gene, recessive or dominant, or sex-linked) diseases. Note that the potential harm most commonly thought of by ethicists and IRBs—discrimination in health and other insurance—is not listed; we are not aware of a group experiencing loss of insurability, although it is possible. Observed group harms from research were the following:

1. **External genetic determinism and stigmatization of the group.** Stereotypic conclusions in which genes predict outcomes; absolutist statements are based on a partial statistical association such that they are actually value statements, e.g., "Ashkenazi Jews are genetically prone to cancer," or "American/Canadian Natives are genetically prone to alcoholism."

2. **Internal genetic determinism and self-stigmatization of the group.** "We Jews are defective because our genes make us prone to cancer" or "We American Indians are defective because our genes make us prone to alcoholism."

3. **Public policy genetic determinism.** A federal agency or state or tribal government determines group membership by presence or absence of genetic markers for being a native person or tribal/band member.[7]

4. **Fostering discrimination and stigmatization.** Revealing the identity of the tribe in socially undesirable and stigmatizing situations, such as investigation of congenital syphilis.

5. **Disruption of the tribe's values.** The research makes public to the outside world what is private tribal knowledge, without the tribe's permission.

6. **Loss of status in the majority society.** An editorial in a Tulsa, Oklahoma, newspaper asserted that because science proved that Indians are immigrants to the North American continent, just like Europeans, Indians should not have special treaty rights or benefits.

7. **Disruption of the tribe's self-understanding.** The origins of North American tribes, as understood by them, does not

include ancestral migration from Siberia over the Bering Strait.

8. **Raised expectations that lead to disappointment.** Services that are started as part of a research program are discontinued when the research is completed.

9. **"Dignitary harms"—insult to the community's respect or control.** A study recruits tribal members living in a city distant from the reservation that had rejected the study. A researcher has a public affair with a married community person, violating community norms.

10. **Increased distrust of health care.** A bad experience with a genetics research study leads to general distrust of all genetic medicine and care.

How many of these potential harms did you have on your list? If you know of other group harms from research that were not described above, please e-mail them to us. In our discussions with IRBs, researchers, and ethicists about group harms, it is unusual for someone to identify all 10 of the potential problems listed above.

Do you know how to protect participant individuals and communities from the group harms listed earlier? This is a difficult issue. In our experience there is no consensus on how to prevent potential group harms with many of the kinds of research that are important to advance the understanding of life or improve medical care in minority segments of our society.

Community Consultation Will Improve IRB Review

The Common Rule [8][Sec.107(a)] requires that "If an IRB regularly reviews research that involves a vulnerable category of subjects, consideration shall be given to the inclusion of one or more individuals who are knowledgeable about and experienced in working with these subjects." While such inclusion is necessary and important, it may not be sufficient to minimize harms.

Our experience, as cochairs of the Indian Health Service (IHS) IRB, is instructive. Its membership is more than 70% native, including AI/AN MDs, Ph.D.s (including one of the only two native Ph.D. geneticists), RNs, MSWs, and several nonscientist tribal members. In spite of this depth of AI/AN membership, we and the IRB have not always recognized important group harms that would likely be associated with research proposals that we reviewed. We have observed many situations in which community consultation outside the formal membership of the IRB identified research risks related to group harm that the IRB had missed. In our experience, community consultation improves the quality of IRB review when research involves vulnerable and/or minority populations. The IHS IRB appreciates and relies on community consultation with the tribe(s) involved as a supplement to our review, to ensure that all serious potential harms are recognized and minimized.

Can your IRB and researchers fully recognize and minimize potential harms involving vulnerable groups in research? Because the IHS IRB (with 70% membership from the vulnerable group being researched) needs tribal review to promote best outcomes, we believe that community consultation is a best practice for all IRBs. For instance, community consultation with people with HIV/AIDS helped improve the ethics of AIDS clinical trials.[9,10] The terms *community review, communal discourse,* and *communal review* have been used for community consultation with leaders and members of AI/AN communities "to identify and minimize research-related risks posed by genetic research."[11] The FDA has mandated "community consultation" for emergency research in which consent by the individual and his/her legal representative may not be possible (See Chapter 4-6).

Community consultation is useful to identify not only potential harms but also potential benefits. "Failure to consider prospective participants' point of view. . . . can lead to acceptance of research procedures causing significant participant distress or to rejection of potentially worthwhile scientific procedures that subjects and their families would perceive as benign and/or worthwhile."[12] For instance, Fisher[12] consulted with teenagers about their desires concerning confidentiality when a researcher finds a teenager is a victim or behaving in ways teens themselves perceive as serious problems. Teens did not want researchers to maintain absolute confidentiality, but instead preferred that researchers inform a concerned parent or adult about potentially dangerous behavior. That is, teens considered the best research ethics to be proactive and paternalistic rather than based on the type of self-determination that guide IRB decisions in most situations.

The Common Rule and Group Harms

Some people interpret the Common Rule[8[Sec.111(a)(2)]] to prohibit IRBs from considering group harms resulting from research; they think, for example, that the IRB should not consider possible long-range effects of applying knowledge gained in the research (for example, the possible effects of the research on public policy) as among those research risks that fall within the purview of its responsibility.

We disagree with that interpretation. All 10 group harms previously listed occurred soon after the research and were not long-range effects. With the possible exception of "loss of status in the dominant society," none involved effects on public policy. Even without a definitive interpretation by federal authorities to settle the issue, the spirit of the federal regulations demands that whenever possible, research should be conducted in a way that does not harm groups or individuals. We thus urge IRBs to be meticulous in their consideration of potential social harms that may result to groups of people other than the current participants. This risk of group harm is especially important when research involves a vulnerable population or minority community in our society.

How to Consult the Community

Researchers and IRBs may be intimidated by community consultation because they are unable to identify who is the community. Many vulnerable groups are heterogeneous and, except for native tribes/bands, do not have recognized formal government. One option is to consider the community stakeholders to be people who would be likely to experience the most negative adverse consequences of research. In many situations, the lack of a well-defined community governance structure has not prevented researchers from seeking community consultation. For instance, as two coauthors personally know, the Jewish community is fractionated, with multiple leaders with different perspectives. Yet the National Human Genome Research Institute (NHGRI) representatives consulted with the Jewish community at a meeting organized by Hadassah that included leaders of most national Jewish organizations. Even though differences were expressed, the representatives heard widespread concern about possible economic and social discrimination that could result from the genetic research being considered.[13] Similarly, HIV/AIDS clinical trial researchers routinely engage in community consultation by having discussions with the many local HIV/AIDS advocacy groups.[9,10] An Institute of Medicine (IOM) committee recommended that "even if there are multiple overlapping groups involved, the IRB could ensure that the investigator had consulted several representatives and at least had some input even if it is not possible to have a definitive or comprehensive statement."[14]

If one already has an ongoing relationship with subgroups and leaders in a community, community consultation means discussing the research with individuals, in groups, and in other ways that will become apparent from these initial discussions (such as public meetings in the community). If one does not have such an ongoing relationship, one can start the process by asking people from, or knowledgeable about, the community for names of people to discuss community consultation regarding the research. IRBs and researchers should not shy away from community consultation simply because it may be an unfamiliar process or because there is no standard way of getting this kind of input.

Community Consultation with Native People in the United States and Canada

Community consultation with AI/AN and Canadian First Nations and Inuit tribes, bands, and communities includes the process just described, and then a process of formal approval by the government or council for the tribe or band. In the United States, the legal basis for tribal approval and disapproval of research within the reservation is the treaty-based jurisdiction of tribal governments to regulate societal activities within their reservation, recognized by the U.S. Supreme Court. "The Supreme Court recognized that tribal power can extend to activities of [non-Indians] . . . if there is a tribal interest sufficient to justify tribal regulation. . . .Tribal jurisdiction within reservations can also be based on transactions between non-Indians or tribes or on non-Indian activities that directly affect Indians or their property."[15] Research falls within what the tribal government can regulate.

In Canada, the latest Tri-Council Policy mandates that researchers consult with the band government and obtain its approval before the research can start.[16] The Tri-Council Policy in Canada has a functional equivalence of both an updated *Belmont Report* and federal regulations in the United States.

The process of tribal review and approval often takes several months. Many tribal/band councils meet monthly; the researcher must ask beforehand to be put on the agenda. Tribal sovereignty and economic survival have higher priority in many tribal/band council meetings than health-related research; thus, discussion about the research may be postponed until the next meeting.

Review and approval (or disapproval) of the research by the tribal/band council is not review by the tribal IRB, although some people use that label; IRB review, therefore, is still required, by at least the IRB of the researcher's institution. As of this writing, two tribes have formal IRBs: Cherokee Nation of Oklahoma and Navajo Nation. For both, the tribal council delegated to its IRB the combined authority of both tribal and IRB review. If the IHS is involved in the research (e.g., IHS staff as coinvestigators, use of IHS charts or other resources, or funding by IHS), the IHS IRB system must also review the research; the tribe may also ask the IHS IRB to review it. The IHS IRB system is two-tiered: the IHS area (i.e., region) IRB reviews the research, as does the IHS headquarters (i.e., national) IRB.

Three recommendations will help facilitate the processes of tribal/band and IRB review of research. By extension, they also help promote research partnerships and ethical research with all communities.

1. Develop a working research-team relationship with colleagues in the tribe/band before finalizing the protocol, and certainly before meeting with its council.[17]

2. Discuss the protocol with all IRBs involved before finalizing the protocol; even if the IHS IRB does not have jurisdiction, voluntary consultation with it may be quite helpful.

3. Apply for review and approval by, and send the protocol to, all IRBs and tribe(s) concurrently, not sequentially. Because so many different reviews are involved, sequential reviews (i.e., first one IRB, then another, then the tribal/band council) may consume a year or more; concurrent reviews may shorten the process to six months.

Conclusion

When research targets a distinct and vulnerable population, it is important for the IRB to consider the risk of research to population groups in addition to the risk of research to individual research participants. This chapter has explained 10 group risks that are often overlooked when evaluating research proposals involving specific populations. In our experience, community consultation usually helps the IRB evaluate group risk and identify ways to minimize potential group harm from research. Community consultation is practicable in most of the situations for which IRBs need to evaluate group risk and should be used routinely in a wide range of research settings.

Acknowledgments
We wish to thank the members of the IHS IRBs for their wise teachings. The views expressed in this chapter do not necessarily represent the views of the IHS.

References

1. Levine R J. *Ethics and Regulation of Clinical Research,* Ed 2. Baltimore, MD: Urban and Schwarzenberg. 1986.

2. Advisory Committee on Human Radiation Experiments. *The Human Radiation Experiments: Final Report.* New York: Oxford University Press. 1996.

3. Tyack D. Schooling and Social Diversity: Historical Reflections. In: Hawley W D, Jackson A W (eds). *Toward a Common Destiny.* San Francisco: Jossey-Bass. 1995: 3–38.

4. Hernstein R J, Murray C. *The Bell Curve: Intelligence and Class Structure in American Life.* New York, NY: Free Press. 1994.

5. *American Indian and Alaskan Native Mental Health Research* 3(2), Spring 1989.

6. Freeman W L. The Role of Community in Research with Stored Tissue Samples. In: Weir R. F. (ed). *Stored Tissue Samples: Ethical, Legal, and Public Policy Implications.* Iowa City, IA: University Iowa Press. 1998: 267–301.

7. Vermont General Assembly Committee on Health and Welfare. An Act Relating to DNA Testing and Native Americans. Proposed bill H-809. 2000.

8. Code of Federal Regulations. Title 45A—Department of Health and Human Services; Part 46—Protection of Human Subjects. Updated 1 Oct 1997. Access date 18 Apr 2001. World Wide Web http://www4.law.cornell.edu/cfr/45p46.htm

9. Melton G B, Levine R J, Koocher G P, Rosenthal R, Thompson W C. Community consultation in socially sensitive research: Lessons from clinical trials of treatments for AIDS. *Am Psychol* 43(7):573–581, 1988.

10. Levine C, Dubler N N, Levine R J. Building a new consensus: Ethical principles and policies for clinical research on HIV/AIDS. *IRB: A Review of Human Subjects Research* 13(1-2):1–17, 1991.

11. Foster M W, Sharp R R, Freeman W L, Chino M, Bernsten D, Carter T H. The role of community review in evaluating the risks of human genetic variation research. *Am J Hum Genet* 64(6):1719–1727, 1999.

12. Fisher C B. A relational perspective on ethics-in-science decision making for research with vulnerable populations. *IRB: A Review of Human Subjects Research* 19(5):1–4, 1997.

13. Stolberg S G. Concern among Jews is heightened as scientists deepen gene studies. *New York Times,* Section A Ed. A:24. 1998.

14. *Committee on the Role of Institutional Review Boards in Health Services Research Data Privacy Protection,* Institute of Medicine. Protecting Data Privacy in Health Services Research. Washington, DC, National Academy Press, 2000. Access date 20 Mar 2001. World Wide Web http://www.nap.edu/html/data_privacy/

15. Strickland R, Wilkinson C F, et al. (eds.) *Felix S. Cohen's Handbook of Federal Indian Law.* Charlottesville, VA: Michie Bobbs-Merril. 1982:256–257.

16. Tri-Council Policy Statement: Ethical Conduct for Research Involving Humans. Updated 21 Nov 2000. Access date 17 Apr 2001. World Wide Web http://www.nserc.ca/programs/ethics/english/policy.htm

17. Freeman W L. Making research consent forms informative and understandable: The experience of the Indian Health Service. *Cambr Q Healthcare Ethics* 3(4):510–521, 1994.

Requiring Birth Control to Participate in Research

Bruce G. Gordon and Ernest D. Prentice

INTRODUCTION

The inclusion of women in clinical research has been the source of much heated debate over the past 20 years, with legal (if not moral) consensus changing dramatically over this time. The specific regulations currently governing the inclusion of women (and in particular pregnant women) are discussed elsewhere in this book. In this chapter, we take as a truth that inclusion of women in clinical research is both morally and scientifically justified. With this as background, we will briefly examine the ethical justification and the practical ramifications for requiring the use of contraception as a precondition for participation in clinical research.

Federal Regulations and Guidelines

The regulations pertinent to the inclusion of pregnant women in biomedical and behavioral research have been described in detail in other sections of this book. However, a brief reiteration is appropriate to understand the ethical and pragmatic basis for the following discussion of the requirement for contraception.

The mid 1970s saw a backlash against the biomedical research community, justified by the excesses of Tuskegee, Willowbrook, and other research misadventures and by the tragedy of thalidomide and diethylstilbestrol (DES). In 1975, the Department of Health, Education, and Welfare (DHEW) published regulations pertaining to research involving pregnant women.[1(subpart B)] This was consistent with the recommendations of the National Commission for the Protection of Human Subjects of Biomedical and Behavioral Research. These regulations were based on a presumption of exclusion of pregnant women from research. This was followed in 1977 by Food and Drug Administration (FDA) guidelines for drug development. The guidelines recommended that women of child-bearing potential be excluded from phase I (toxicity) and early phase II (efficacy) trials of new drugs.[2] Although not mandated by these guidelines, investigators, sponsors, and IRBs tended to extend this policy to include all phases of drug development. There was little discussion at the time about potential benefits that might accrue to these women from participating, nor to the potential greater harm of subsequent use of these approved drugs in women on whom they had never been tested.

In the 1980s, attitudes began changing, in some measure owing to the rise of AIDS and the benefits received by participants in trials of new antiviral drugs. Research began to be seen less as a burden and more as a benefit, and advocates for women's health lobbied vigorously for a relaxing of the protectionist rules and attitudes. In 1984, a Public Health Service (PHS) task force found that the longstanding lack of research in women's health had compromised the quality of available information on diseases affecting women.[3] In 1994, the Institute of Medicine (IOM) Committee on Ethical and Legal Issues Related to Inclusion of Women in Clinical Studies recommended that women should be enrolled as participants in clinical studies, "in a manner that ensures research yields scientifically generalizable results applicable to both genders. . . ."[4]

In 1993, the FDA issued "Guideline for Study and Evaluation of Gender Differences in the Clinical Evaluation of Drugs." This articulated the agency's decision to reverse the 1977 policy that had barred most women from participating in the early phases of clinical trials.[5] In 1994, the National Institutes of Health (NIH) issued "Guidelines on Inclusion of Women and Minorities as Subjects in Clinical Research," which stated that "women . . . must be included in all NIH-supported biomedical and behavioral research projects involving human subjects unless a clear and compelling rationale and justification establishes . . . that inclusion is inappropriate . . . ."[6]

Inclusion of Pregnant Women in Research

In 1998, the Department of Health and Human Services (DHHS) published a proposed rule that would amend subpart B.[7] Among the many changes to this regulation, the proposed rule "institutes a policy of presumed opportunity for inclusion of pregnant women in research . . . ." This proposed rule was approved by DHHS Secretary Donna Shalala, but subsequent enactment was delayed by President Bush.

Ethical Rationale for Requirement of Contraception

Ethical Arguments

The ethical arguments regarding the requirement of contraception mirror in part those used as justification for exclusion or inclusion of women from research; therefore, a review of these arguments is in order.

The most commonly cited rationale for exclusion of women is the moral duty to avoid infliction of harm to a fetus. As Merton[8] states, the view is "All women are always pregnable and therefore always pregnant." Therefore, inclusion of women of childbearing potential carries a risk of causing fetal harm that should preclude the inclusion of these women.

A counterargument is that this view is overly paternalistic. Researchers do not have the right to arrogate to themselves the determination of when participation in a protocol may create a greater risk of harm to the fetus than chance of benefit. The judgment should be made by the pregnant (or potentially pregnant) woman. The principle of respect for persons would seem to demand that a woman of childbearing potential should be allowed to make her own decision regarding participation. Nonetheless, there is precedent (in law, regulations, and ethics) for protecting vulnerable populations, like children, even when other parties (like parents) are and should be responsible for this protection. The principle of respect for persons requires this protection, and the principle of nonmaleficence further impels us to at least "do no harm" to the fetus.

To a certain extent, the requirement for contraception can be seen as a compromise, allowing practical (if not philosophic) resolution of this dilemma. The requirement for contraception serves to eliminate (or at least attenuate) the link between "pregnable" and "pregnant" and thereby eliminates (or reduces) the risk of fetal damage.

Scientific Rigor

Another argument cited for exclusion of women is one of scientific rigor. Because women and men are physiologically different, it is difficult or impossible to obtain "clean" data from gender-integrated trials. A similar argument can be made for excluding pregnant (and by implication, pregnable) women in that these women are physiologically different from women who are not of childbearing potential. The argument refutes itself. If the data obtained from a mixed population (men and women, or nonpregnant women and pregnant women) is so different from that generated by studying only one population, then how can it later be extrapolated to a real world with multiple populations? From the point of view of the women (or the pregnant women) excluded, the data are not "cleaner," they are irrelevant.[8]

With the requirement for adequate contraception, pregnable women are no longer pregnant women, and the need to exclude them to enhance scientific rigor is reduced. However, this solution is still not satisfactory because it skirts the issue of the scientific need to obtain data

from pregnant women. This need was acknowledged in both the PHS[3] and the IOM reports.[4] Indeed, Hall[9] has argued that it is not only unethical but illegal to exclude pregnant women from clinical research. Therefore, is contraception unethical because it leads to the exclusion of pregnant women?

Nonetheless, the requirement for contraception can be seen as a (partial) solution to the two main objections for inclusion of women in clinical research. This is a way to minimize the risk to a fetus (and thereby satisfy the investigator's moral requirement for nonmaleficence). However, practical concerns remain, some of which will be addressed below.

Practical Issues with Requiring Contraception

Consideration of "Risk" in Determining the Need for Contraception

As discussed above, we find the "scientific rigor" argument not compelling. The nonmaleficence argument is stronger, but still impacts on the autonomy of the women subjects. This impact is balanced in most cases by the need to protect the fetus from risk, but what if there is no risk to the fetus associated with a research protocol? Clearly, most studies involving therapeutic interventions like drugs and medical devices carry some risk to the fetus, even if the magnitude of the risk is unknown. Still, there are drugs that are not shown to cause harm to the fetus (FDA category A drugs and some category B drugs). It would be difficult to make a strong case based on the nonmaleficence argument to require a woman of child-bearing potential to utilize contraception if participating in a clinical trial where the only intervention is a drug of these classes. Similarly, it would be hard to justify requirement for contraception for many nondrug studies if the interventions themselves are not risky to the fetus. Therefore, we suggest that each study should be assessed individually, and contraception required only on a case-by-case basis where there is defined or truly unknown risk to the fetus.

Adequacy of Birth Control

If there is adequate ethical justification for requiring contraception, then there appears an equivalent ethical requirement to assure that contraception is adequate, and that it truly will eliminate or reduce the risk of fetal damage by eliminating or reducing the risk of pregnancy.

Various contraceptive methods have different failure rates, and these rates tend to vary according to age, race, ethnicity, marital status, and socioeconomic status.[4,10] Therefore, adequate contraception may be an elusive target, varying from population to population. Hormonal methods offer the advantage of low failure rate, without the need to apply the technique prior to every episode of intercourse. However, hormonal contraceptives may interact with drugs being studied in clinical trials by affecting the pharmacokinetics or pharmacodynamics of the test drug. Alternately, and perhaps of more concern, is the possibility that the drug being studied may interact in a manner that makes the hormonal contraception less effective. Barrier methods of contraception (especially multiple barrier methods, such as condom or diaphragm with spermicidal jelly) may be a better choice for drug studies, but compliance may be inferior.

Abstinence

Abstinence may be the ideal form of contraception, but it is probably only reasonable for very short-term studies. Yet, many studies specifically exclude abstinence as an "adequate" form of birth control. Such an exclusion is ethically problematic, particularly among certain populations, like nuns and lesbians (in the latter case, "abstinence" meaning refraining from sexual intercourse with men). Bush insists that "enrolling someone in a trial as a condition of their current sexual or religious belief is wrong. . . . If the [research] program treated nuns or lesbians differently from other women of childbearing potential, it would be invading their privacy and their right to change their minds."[11]

In contrast, VandenBosch et al. argue forcibly that "the criteria that exclude women who are not on birth control clearly fail to recognize and respect the values and personal choices of the female . . . who has chosen abstinence. To include a [woman] who is taking oral contraceptives on the assumption that she can be relied upon to take that medication regularly to avoid pregnancy . . . but, to exclude [one] who has chosen to abstain from sexual intercourse on the assumption that she cannot be relied upon to continue that behavior violates . . . [the principle of respect for persons]. It states 'to respect autonomy is to give weight to autonomous persons' considered opinions and choices. . . .' "[12]

Termination of Pregnancy

The Institute of Medicine report recommends that pregnancy termination options be discussed as a part of the consent process in clinical studies that have unknown or foreseeable risks to potential offspring.[4] We concur with this recommendation in principle, though, clearly, implementation is difficult. Subjects and investigators alike are likely to have strong feelings regarding abortion, and state statutes may limit the subject's options. Nonetheless, a neutral, nonjudgmental discussion of this option is indicated at the time of initial consent to participate in the study.

Discussion of termination options at the time of enrollment in the research does not, however, imply that women should be asked if they would terminate if they became pregnant. The asking of such a question might be (erroneously) taken to be a suggestion on the part of the investigator or a requirement for participation in the research. Further, and more importantly, we do not believe that a subject's stated intent to terminate a pregnancy is adequate justification to dispense with a requirement for contraception, and therefore the answer is irrelevant. An intent to terminate is changeable and unenforceable (as it should be) and therefore does not serve to minimize risks to the fetus the way contraception would.

Adolescents as Research Subjects

Additional concerns arise when the participants in research are adolescents, some of which are discussed nicely by VandenBosch and colleagues.[12] Investigators must be particularly sensitive in discussions of sexual activity. Issues previously described with regard to abstinence as a form of contraception are pertinent to this group. VandenBosch et al. make an interesting point that "if the physician says the adolescent must be on 'acceptable' birth control to be in the study, the message may be interpreted as approval of sexual activity and disapproval of abstinence . . . as 'unacceptable.' "

Investigators and IRBs must be alert to the risks of loss of confidentiality, particularly when discussing sexual activity and performing pregnancy tests. If this information is to be shared with parents (especially if required by state statute), this should be stated clearly in the consent document and stressed to the adolescent before her enrollment in the trial. If the information is not to be shared with parents, Levine[13] raises the concern that it might appear that the institution not only approves of deception, but also collaborates with the adolescent in this deception, thus setting a poor example for the adolescent.

Consent Issues

Several authors have discussed the information that should be present in the consent for women of childbearing potential who are involved in clinical trials. The IOM report[4] recommends that "the informed consent process [should include] an adequate discussion of the risks to reproduction and potential offspring and, where appropriate, an adequate discussion of relevant considerations of birth control." These discussions should, of course, include information regarding the risk of failure of various forms of birth control, though the IOM report further recommends that "the participant be permitted to select voluntarily the contraceptive method of his or her choice . . . ." Finally, the IOM report advises "pregnancy termination options be discussed as part of the consent process in clinical studies that pose unknown or foreseeable risks to potential offspring."

Among other things, Halbreich and Carson[14] suggest that the consent process include instructions for advising the investigator if pregnancy is suspected. We concur although we have been noting an increase in the number of clinical studies that include the "requirement" that women who become pregnant during a clinical trial are removed from the study. In addition, they must have follow-up to determine the outcome of the pregnancy (often including assessment of the baby's health up to one year of age). Although the scientific rationale for this provision is clear and justifiable (though perhaps tainted by fears of litigation), we object strongly to this requirement as a violation of the subject's right to withdraw from or cease participating in the research. Our investigators and sponsors are informed that agreeing to this provision may not be an inclusion criterion for the study. Also, women who become pregnant and are withdrawn from the study may be asked to allow this follow-up. But they are under no obligation to agree to it, and this follow-up information may not be obtained without their express consent.

The extent to which consent forms actually include the information previously described is unclear. Nolan and colleagues[15] recently reported a survey of consent documents for studies conducted between 1994 and 1998 that involved drugs or radiation. They examined discussion of four broad categories of reproductive risk or fetal risk information: (1) reproductive/fetal risk, (2) mandatory pregnancy-related exclusion, (3) pregnancy prevention advice, and (4) pregnancy testing. They found that, although many consent forms contained pregnancy related-exclusions (including anticipated pregnancy and breast feeding), fewer contained information regarding the specific reproductive risk. Only a minority of consent forms mentioned methods to prevent pregnancy or pregnancy testing, or what subjects should do if they became pregnant during the study.

Conclusion

In summary, requirement for contraception is probably justified (in many cases) as a compromise between the conflicting principles of autonomy and nonmaleficence. If contraception is required, there is an equivalent requirement for it to be effective, though the definition of *effective* varies between populations and studies. The informed consent process should address issues related to reproductive and fetal risk, contraception, and pregnancy testing.

References

1. Code of Federal Regulations. Title 45A—Department of Health and Human Services; Part 46—Protection of Human Subjects. Updated 1 Oct 1997. Access date 18 Apr 2001. World Wide Web http://www4.law.cornell.edu/cfr/45p46.htm

2. Food and Drug Administration. General considerations for clinical evaluation of drugs. HEW (FDA) 77-3040. 1977. Washington DC.

3. Public Health Service. Report of the Public Health Service Task Force on Women's Health Issues. DHHS publication no. 85-50206. 1985. Washington, DC.

4. Mastroianni A C, Faden R, Federman D, (editors); Committee on the Ethical and Legal Issues Relating to the Inclusion of Women in Clinical Studies, Div of Health Sciences Policy, Institute of Medicine. *Women and Health Research: Ethical and Legal Issues of Including Women in Clinical Studies,* Vol 1. Washington, DC: National Academy Press. 1994. http://search.nap.edu/books/030904992X/html/

5. Food and Drug Administration. Guidelines for the study and evaluation of gender differences in the clinical evaluation of drugs. *Fed Regist* 58(139):39406–39416, 1993.

6. National Institutes of Health. NIH Guidelines on the Inclusion of Women and Minorities as Subjects in Clinical Research. *Fed Regist* 59(59):14508–14513, 1994.

7. Department of Health and Human Services. Protection of Human Subjects, Proposed Rule (RIN 0925-AA14). *Fed Regist* 63(97):27794–27804, 1998.

8. Merton V. The exclusion of pregnant, pregnable, and once-pregnable people (aka women) from biomedical research. *Am J Law Med* 19(4):369–451, 1993.

9. Hall J K. Exclusion of pregnant women from research protocols: Unethical and illegal. *IRB: A Review of Human Subjects Research* 17(2):1–3, 1995.

10. Potter L S. How effective are contraceptives? The determination and measurement of pregnancy rates. *Obstet Gynecol* 88:13S–23S, 1996.

11. Bush J K. The industry perspective on the inclusion of women in clinical trials. *Acad Med* 69(9):708–715, 1994.

12. VandenBosch T M, Ward B G, Mattison D. A reappraisal of female adolescent participation in drug clinical trials. *IRB: A Review of Human Subjects Research* 21(1):1–5, 1999.

13. Levine C. Commentary: Teenagers, research and family involvement. *IRB: A Review of Human Subjects Research* 3(9):8, 1981.

14. Halbreich U, Carson S W. Drug studies in women of childbearing age: Ethical and methodological considerations. *J Clin Psychopharmacol* 9(328), 1989.

15. Nolan M T, Pressman E K, Starklauf B L, Gregory R E. Consent documents, reproductive issues, and the inclusion of women in clinical trials. *Acad Med* 74(3):275–281, 1999.

Privacy and Confidentiality

David G. Forster

INTRODUCTION

This chapter addresses the role of privacy and confidentiality in the IRB review of human subject research. Subjects benefit from having privacy and confidentiality protected when appropriate, and subjects need to be informed of the extent to which they can expect that their privacy and the confidentiality of information identifying them will be maintained.

Both privacy and confidentiality are complex concepts with a multitude of facets and potential definitions. For the purposes of this chapter, the definitions of "privacy" and "confidentiality" presented in the 1993 OPRR IRB Guidebook[1] will be used:

Privacy can be defined in terms of having control over the extent, timing, and circumstances of sharing oneself (physically, behaviorally, or intellectually) with others. *Confidentiality* pertains to the treatment of information that an individual has disclosed in a relationship of trust and with the expectation that it will not be divulged to others in ways that are inconsistent with the understanding of the original disclosure without permission.

Relationship of Privacy and Confidentiality to the *Belmont* Principles

Privacy and confidentiality are supported by two of the three principles of research ethics identified by the National Commission for the Protection of Human Subjects of Biomedical and Behavioral Research in the *Belmont Report*[2]: respect for persons and beneficence. Respect for persons requires that subjects be allowed to exercise their autonomy to the fullest extent possible, including the autonomy to maintain their privacy and to have private information identifying them kept confidential. Beneficence requires that risks to subjects are minimized, benefits are maximized, and risks to subjects do not outweigh the benefits to subjects and others. The maintenance of privacy and confidentiality helps to protect subjects from a variety of potential harms, including psychological distress, loss of insurance, loss of employment, or damage to social standing, that could occur as the result of an invasion of privacy or a breach of confidentiality.

Federal Guidance and Regulations

The Common Rule and the Food and Drug Administration (FDA) regulations address the issues of privacy and confidentiality in several places. Furthermore, both the Office for Human Research Protections (OHRP) (formerly the Office for Protection from Research Risks, OPRR) and the FDA have issued valuable guidance on the topic. This section will review human subject protection regulations and guidance that require the IRB to consider privacy and confidentiality, and discuss issues on which there is disagreement among IRBs.

Criteria for Approval of Research

Both the Common Rule and the FDA regulations require the IRB to determine, as part of the IRB review of research, that privacy and confidentiality are protected when appropriate. The wording used in the two regulations is slightly different, but identical in meaning.

Common Rule, 45 CFR § 46.111, Criteria for IRB Approval of Research

(a) In order to approve research covered by this policy the IRB shall determine that all of the following requirements are satisfied. . . . (7) When appropriate, there are adequate provisions to protect the privacy of subjects and to maintain the confidentiality of data.

FDA, 21 CFR § 56.111, Criteria for IRB Approval of Research

(a) In order to approve research covered by these regulations the IRB shall determine that all of the following requirements are satisfied. . . . (7) Where appropriate, there are adequate provisions to protect the privacy of subjects and to maintain the confidentiality of data.

In fulfilling the regulatory requirements,[3][Sec.111(a)(7)], [4][Sec.111(a)(7)] the IRB should consider the degree of privacy of the information being collected and the measures that have been established to protect the confidentiality of the information. In determining the degree of privacy of the information, the IRB should use the standard of a reasonable member of the research population, and consider whether such a reasonable member would consider the information collected in the research to be private. In addition, the IRB should consider whether the reasonable member would consider the release of the information without permission to be an invasion of privacy. However, views on privacy vary greatly within and across cultures and research populations, and information that is not considered particularly sensitive by one individual may be very sensitive to another individual. For research involving unique cultures, the IRB should consider having a representative of the culture on the IRB or consulting with individuals knowledgeable of feelings about privacy within the culture.

The IRB should require the investigator or other relevant parties to explain how privacy and the confidentiality of the information obtained in the course of the study will be maintained. This is most easily accomplished by requiring investigators to provide this information on the IRB submission form. There are several methods that investigators may employ to protect privacy, particularly in research involving questionnaires. In a face-to-face interview, investigators can allow subjects to provide information in writing or by using a computer keyboard, instead of orally. With the availability of laptop computers, the investigator can allow subjects to provide answers to some or all questions on the computer in a field setting. For research conducted by telephone, subjects can answer using the touch tones. For clinical research, the IRB may wish to consider privacy protections that go beyond those available in traditional clinical care.

Common measures employed by investigators to protect confidentiality include storage of records in locked file cabinets, in locked offices, on computers protected by a password, or on computers that are not linked into a network. Another common protection is to code the data with an identifier, and keep the key to the code located in another physical location or on a separate computer. Destruction of the research records also provides protection by eliminating the potential for inadvertent disclosure. Many IRBs require the investigator to state on the submission form how long the records will be kept. Some IRBs require the data to be destroyed once the research is finished unless the investigator provides a compelling reason for maintaining the records.

Subject Recruitment and Long-Term Follow-Up

The IRB must also consider the protection of privacy and confidentiality during the subject recruitment process. The manner in which subjects are identified and approached for participation in research may constitute an invasion of privacy or confidentiality. For instance, it has not been uncommon in the past for research staff to search medical records to which they do not have clinical access. This constitutes a breach of confidentiality of the patients' medical records. If potential subjects are identified in this manner, and the individuals are contacted by research staff with whom they have had no previous contact, these individuals may rightly feel that their privacy has been vi-

olated. Similar concerns arise with any search of a database conducted to identify potential subjects. Examples of databases include disease registries, non-public state records, insurance records, and pharmacy records.

Issues of confidentiality should be particularly scrutinized in research conducted over an extended period of time. Some longitudinal studies extend for periods of 10 or more years. Likewise, many cancer studies can include subject follow-up until death. During the course of such a study, the subjects' values and circumstances can change greatly, causing changes in the importance of privacy and the confidentiality of the records. For instance, subjects may not have informed spouses or other family members of their past participation in research. A poorly conducted follow-up call could create severe family disruption and psychological harm in such a case.

Another potential breach of privacy is the collection of sensitive information during the screening period, and subsequent retention of the information without consent from the subject. This is particularly troubling if the information is maintained even though the potential subject declines to participate in or does not qualify for the research. Some pharmaceutical sponsors and contract research organizations (CROs) have created databases of potential subjects based on these recruitment procedures. The FDA offers the following guidance on privacy and confidentiality during the screening process in the FDA Information Sheet, "Recruiting Study Subjects."[5]

> The first contact prospective study subjects make is often with a receptionist who follows a script to determine basic eligibility for the specific study. The IRB should assure that the procedures followed adequately protect the rights and welfare of the prospective subjects. In some cases personal and sensitive information is gathered about the individual. The IRB should have assurance that the information will be appropriately handled. A simple statement such as "confidentiality will be maintained" does not adequately inform the IRB of the procedures that will be used.
>
> The following issues are appropriate for IRB review: What happens to personal information if the caller ends the interview or simply hangs up? Are the data gathered by a marketing company? If so, are names, etc., sold to others? Are names of noneligibles maintained in case they would qualify for another study? Are paper copies of records shredded, or are readable copies put out as trash? The acceptability of the procedures would depend on the sensitivity of the data gathered, including personal, medical, and financial.[5]

IRBs can ask for this information on the IRB submission form. If IRBs do not ask, they may not receive the information in the submitted study documents such as the protocol. This is particularly true for large, multisite research projects that often have centralized subject recruitment procedures.

For research involving particularly sensitive information, such as drug abuse, the IRB may also require that the investigator obtains a Federal Certificate of Confidentiality to protect the research records from release. Release could be in any federal, state, or local civil, criminal, administrative, legislative, or other proceeding. Certificates of Confidentiality are the subject of Chapter 8-9.

The IRB must decide on a case-by-case basis whether there are adequate provisions to protect the privacy of subjects and to maintain the confidentiality of data. The committee must take into account the degree of sensitivity of the information obtained in the research and the protections offered. As with other aspects of IRB review, these determinations will be dependent on the factual circumstances.

Confidentiality in the Consent Form

After the IRB has decided that there are adequate provisions in the research plan to protect the privacy and confidentiality of the subjects, it must also ensure that the consent form accurately provides the subject with information concerning the confidentiality of the research records. This allows the subject to make his or her own determination of whether the provisions for protecting privacy and confidentiality are adequate. The Common Rule and the FDA regulations differ in regard to the requirements for the consent form.

Common Rule, 45 CFR § 46.116, General Requirements for Informed Consent

(a) Basic elements of informed consent. Except as provided in paragraph (c) or (d) of this section, in seeking informed consent the following information shall be provided to each subject. . . . (5) A statement describing the extent, if any, to which confidentiality of records identifying the subject will be maintained.

FDA, 21 CFR § 50.25, Elements of Informed Consent

(a) Basic elements of informed consent. In seeking informed consent, the following information shall be provided to each subject. . . . (5) A statement describing the extent, if any, to which confidentiality of records identifying the subject will be maintained and that notes the possibility that the Food and Drug Administration may inspect the records.

The essential difference between the Common Rule[3][sec.116(a)] and the FDA regulations[6][sec.25(a)] is that the FDA regulations require that subjects are informed of the possibility that the FDA may inspect the records of the study. The Common Rule regulations do not impose a similar requirement for the consent form. However, many of the agencies that have adopted the Common Rule do have the authority to investigate the misconduct of research and/or human subject protection violations, and in the process confidential subject records could be reviewed.

IRBs across the country have taken very different approaches to satisfying the requirements of these regulations. At one end of the spectrum, some IRBs have adopted a standard statement to the effect that "research records will be kept confidential," and also include a statement that "the FDA may inspect the research

records" for research under FDA jurisdiction. At the other end of the spectrum, some IRBs have taken the position that it is overly reassuring to subjects to promise confidentiality. Instead, they state that confidentiality cannot be guaranteed, and then list the parties who may have access to research records, including government agencies, sponsors, sponsor contractors, the IRB, and the institution.

The best practice is to address both sides of the issue in two paragraphs. First, the consent form should present the procedures that are in place to protect the confidentiality of data, such as the use of coding systems and locked file cabinets. Second, the form should disclose those parties who could potentially have access to the research data. This dual approach provides the subjects with the material information about the confidentiality of their research records, allowing them to make their own choice about the adequacy of the protections and the acceptability of the possible release of private information to the listed parties.

The FDA has issued the following guidance to clarify its interpretation of 21 CFR 50[6][Sec.(a)(5)] in the FDA Information Sheet, "Informed Consent."[5]

Study subjects should be informed of the extent to which the institution intends to maintain confidentiality of records identifying the subjects. In addition, they should be informed that the FDA may inspect study records (which include individual medical records). If any other entity, such as the sponsor of the study, may gain access to the study records, the subjects should be so informed. The consent document may, at the option of the IRB, state that subjects' names are not routinely required to be divulged to the FDA. When the FDA requires subject names, it will treat such information as confidential, but on rare occasions, disclosure to third parties may be required. Therefore, absolute protection of confidentiality by the FDA should not be promised or implied. Also, consent documents should not state or imply that the FDA needs clearance or permission from the subject for access. When clinical investigators conduct a study for submission to the FDA, they agree to allow FDA access to the study records. Informed consent documents should make it clear that when a subject participates in research, the subject's records automatically become part of the research database. Subjects do not have the option to keep their records from being audited/reviewed by the FDA.[5]

In addition, the FDA has issued the guidance to clarify its interpretation of access by other third parties to research records in the FDA Information Sheet, "Sponsor—Investigator—IRB Relationship."[5]

Sponsor–Investigator–IRB Relationship

The IRB is responsible for ensuring that informed consent documents include the extent to which the confidentiality of medical records will be maintained.[6][Sec.25(a)(5)] The FDA requires sponsors (or research monitors hired by them) to monitor the accuracy of the data submitted to the FDA in accordance with regulatory requirements. These data are generally in the possession of the clinical investigator. Each subject must be advised during the informed consent process of the extent to which confidentiality of records identifying the subject will be maintained and of the possibility that the FDA may inspect the records. Although FDA access to medical records is a regulatory requirement, subject names are not usually requested by the FDA unless the records of particular individuals require a more detailed study of the cases or unless there is reason to believe that the records do not represent actual cases studied or actual results obtained. The consent document should list all other entities (e.g., the sponsor) who will have access to records identifying the subject. The extent to which confidentiality will be maintained may affect a subject's decision to participate in a clinical investigation.[5]

Privacy Considerations in the Definition of *Human Subject*

Under the Common Rule, the definition of *human subject* involves as one of the criteria an analysis of whether information is private.[3[Sec.102(f)]]

Human subject means a living individual about whom an investigator (whether professional or student) conducting research obtains (1) data through intervention or interaction with the individual, or (2) identifiable private information.

When an IRB is considering whether an individual is a subject because of the collection of information about that individual (without direct intervention or interaction), it must necessarily consider whether the information obtained is private or not. One situation in which this regulatory definition[3[Sec.102(f)(2)]] applies is the collection of information about "secondary subjects." Secondary subjects exist when an investigator asks a primary subject, with whom the investigator is directly interacting, to provide information about other individuals, often family members. For example, in a well-publicized case, a father opened a research questionnaire sent to his daughter, who was away at college. The questionnaire contained several very personal questions to be asked of the daughter about her father and other family members, covering topics such as abnormal genitalia, mental illness, and substance abuse. In reviewing such research, the IRB must consider whether the information collected about the secondary subjects is private.

An important factor in this consideration is the relationship between privacy and confidentiality. If the information is clearly private in nature, but the confidentiality protections are adequate to ensure against all but the most unlikely sources of improper breach, is this information still private? Some have argued that the protection of the confidentiality of the information curtails the private nature of the information. However, many individuals will feel that the release of this type of information without their consent is an invasion of privacy, regardless of whether there are confidentiality protections in place. If privacy is defined as "having control over the extent, timing, and circumstances of sharing oneself (physically, behaviorally, or intellectually) with

others,"[1] then the collection of sensitive information about secondary subjects without their consent clearly involves a breach of privacy.

Confidentiality Requirements for Research Exempt from IRB Review

Confidentiality is explicitly addressed in the Common Rule,[3[Sec.101(b)(3)(ii)]] which allows certain research to be exempt from IRB review if there are federal statutes that require that the confidentiality of the personally identifiable information will be maintained. However, this is not an exemption that is used on a regular basis by most IRBs.

Title §46.101 To what does this policy apply?

. . . (b) Unless otherwise required by Department or Agency heads, research activities in which the only involvement of human subjects will be in one or more of the following categories are exempt from this policy. . . .(2) Research involving the use of educational tests (cognitive, diagnostic, aptitude, achievement), survey procedures, interview procedures or observation of public behavior, unless:
(i) information obtained is recorded in such a manner that human subjects can be identified, directly or through identifiers linked to the subjects; and
(ii) any disclosure of the human subjects' responses outside the research could reasonably place the subjects at risk of criminal or civil liability or be damaging to the subjects' financial standing, employability, or reputation.
(3) Research involving the use of educational tests (cognitive, diagnostic, aptitude, achievement), survey procedures, interview procedures, or observation of public behavior that is not exempt under paragraph (b)(2) of this section, if:
(i) the human subjects are elected or appointed public officials or candidates for public office; or
(ii) Federal statute(s) require(s) without exception that the confidentiality of the personally identifiable information will be maintained throughout the research and thereafter.[3Sec.(101)]

The fourth category of exempt research also brings up questions about privacy and confidentiality. The following class of research is exempt from IRB review:[3[Sec.101(b)(4)]]

Research involving the collection or study of existing data, documents, records, pathological specimens, or diagnostic specimens. If these sources are publicly available or if the information is recorded by the investigator in such a manner that subjects cannot be identified, directly or through identifiers linked to the subjects.

There is a great deal of confusion and disagreement over the meaning of the phrase "if the information is recorded by the investigator in such a manner that subjects cannot be identified, directly or through identifiers linked to the subjects." Many people have interpreted this to mean that the existing information can be used for research without IRB review as long as the person conducting the research cannot identify the subjects. However, others have argued that if anyone has access to an identifier linking the identity of the information to the individual subject, then there is not true anonymity and there should be IRB review. This has become a particularly common topic in the use of human tissues for research purposes. In at least one context regarding tissue research, OHRP (then OPRR) stated that if there is an existing link between the information and the identity of the subject, then there must be IRB review.[7]

Interestingly, this memorandum relies on the definition of human subject at 45 CFR 46.102(f) for support, rather than 45 CFR 46.101(b)(4). Therefore, if a link is being maintained anywhere between the identity of the subject and the information, as a best practice, the IRB should review the research. This is to determine if the privacy and confidentiality of the subjects are adequately protected in light of the potential risks of disclosure of the information.

Confidentiality in the Waiver of Documentation of Informed Consent

Another regulatory section specifically requiring the IRB to address the issue of confidentiality is 45 CFR 46[3][sec.117(c)(1)] which allows for a waiver of documentation of consent.

Title §46.117 Documentation of Informed Consent

(c) An IRB may waive the requirement for the investigator to obtain a signed consent form for some or all subjects if it finds either:
(1) That the only record linking the subject and the research would be the consent document and the principal risk would be potential harm resulting from a breach of confidentiality. Each subject will be asked whether the subject wants documentation linking the subject with the research, and the subject's wishes will govern; or
(2) That the research presents no more than minimal risk of harm to subjects and involves no procedures for which written consent is normally required outside of the research context. In cases in which the documentation requirement is waived, the IRB may require the investigator to provide subjects with a written statement regarding the research.

An example of research that fits under the waiver of documentation of consent would be an anonymous questionnaire on risk factors for HIV conducted at a public free-needle-exchange table. Because the questionnaire is anonymous and does not include names, the only way to link subjects to the research would be the name on the consent form. In this case, the main risk of harm is the breach of confidentiality that could occur if individual subjects were linked to receiving free needles, indicating that they are using illegal drugs. The subjects must be asked if they want to be linked to the information, and the subjects' wishes govern. This waiver from documentation of consent does not exist under the FDA regulations, and cannot be used for any research falling under FDA oversight.

Waiver of Consent Under Common Rule

Under the Common Rule, an IRB may allow an investigator to conduct research without consent of the subjects if four criteria are met.[3][Sec.116(d)]

An IRB may approve a consent procedure which does not include, or which alters, some or all of the elements of informed consent set forth in this section, or waive the requirements to obtain informed consent provided the IRB finds and documents that
(1) the research involves no more than minimal risk to the subjects;
(2) the waiver or alteration will not adversely affect the rights and welfare of the subjects;
(3) the research could not practicably be carried out without the waiver or alteration; and
(4) whenever appropriate, the subjects will be provided with additional pertinent information after participation.

The IRB must consider privacy and confidentiality in its analysis of criteria (1) and (2). Under criterion (1), the IRB must decide whether the research under consideration represents a minimal risk to the study subjects. Some research that involves no physical risk may still represent more than minimal risk because of potential breaches of privacy and confidentiality. For example, genetic research concerning a chronic or fatal disease could lead to loss of insurance, employment, or social standing or to psychological distress if there were a breach of identifiable information. This type of harm is more likely if the research records are kept with medical records and are thereby accessible to insurers or employers, whether intentionally or accidentally. There have been reported cases of genetic discrimination in the past few years, making this a very real concern.

Under criterion (2), the IRB must consider whether the waiver or alteration will adversely affect the rights and welfare of the subjects. One of the central rights to be considered in this analysis is privacy. Subjects should not have their reasonable expectations about privacy violated without their permission. Even if the release of identifiable information is not likely to cause economic or other harm to the subjects, such as loss of insurance, an IRB should still consider whether the collection of the information, even with reasonable protections on confidentiality, may still constitute an invasion of privacy.

The International Conference on Harmonisation Consent Form Requirements Regarding Confidentiality

The International Conference on Harmonisation (ICH) is an international agreement allowing drug research results to be submitted to drug approval agencies of many countries if the research is conducted in accordance with ICH requirements. The ICH is discussed in detail in Chapter 8-2. The ICH has been adopted by the FDA only as guidance in the United States, and therefore compliance is not mandatory for IRBs in the United States. However, many sponsors request that IRBs state that they are compliant with ICH. In comparison with FDA and Common Rule requirements, compliance with ICH requires that the subject is informed of and authorizes much broader access to research records by third parties. The relevant sections of the ICH regarding the information presented in the consent form are as follows.

> **ICH § 4.8.10** Both the informed consent discussion and the written informed consent form and any other written information to be provided to subjects should include explanations of the following:
> That the monitor(s), the auditor(s), the IRB/IEC, and the regulatory authority(ies) will be granted direct access to the subject's original medical records for verification of clinical trial procedures and/or data, without violating the confidentiality of the subject, to the extent permitted by the applicable laws and regulations and that, by signing a written informed consent form, the subject or the subject's legally acceptable representative is authorizing such access.
> That records identifying the subject will be kept confidential and, to the extent permitted by the applicable laws and/or regulations, will not be made publicly available. If the results of the trial are published, the subject's identity will remain confidential.

The ICH also requires the sponsors to ensure that there is access to identifiable subject information.

> **ICH § 5.15.1** The sponsor should ensure that it is specified in the protocol or other written agreement that the investigator(s)/institution(s) provide direct access to source data/documents for trial-related monitoring, audits, IRB/IEC review, and regulatory inspection.
> **ICH § 5.15.2** The sponsor should verify that each subject has consented, in writing, to direct access to his/her original medical records for trial-related monitoring, audit, IRB/IEC review, and regulatory inspection.

Because ICH is an international agreement, "regulatory inspection" as used in §§ 5.15.1 and 5.15.2 covers the drug approval agencies of many countries. Subjects who enroll in research complying with ICH need to be clearly told about the ramifications to confidentiality and privacy. Several IRBs have received complaints from subjects regarding the consent form sections regarding potential access of personal medical records by agencies of other countries. Some subjects have refused to participate in research being conducted in compliance with ICH requirements because of this confidentiality issue. Similarly, many IRB members are uncomfortable with this international access to identifiable research data. Each IRB, investigator, and institution must decide if it truly wishes to comply with ICH requirements, including the broad potential access to identifiable research data.

Other Federal Regulations and Laws Addressing Privacy and Confidentiality

A variety of federal regulations and laws address privacy and confidentiality in addition to those previously described that are not specific to research but could affect the conduct of research. The Health Insurance Portability and Accountability Act of 1996 (HIPAA) required the passage of regulations providing privacy and confidentiality protections for electronic medical records. If, or when, HIPAA regulations are activated, IRBs will need to be aware of these regulations and the institution's procedures for their implementation.

The Freedom of Information Act of 1966[8] allows public access to many records maintained or created by the federal government. One of the categories of records exempt from disclosure under the Freedom of Information Act is "personnel and medical files, and similar files the disclosure of which would constitute a clearly unwarranted invasion of personal privacy."[8[Sec.(b)(6)]] The Federal Privacy Act of 1974[9] provides individuals with some control over personal information maintained or created by the federal government. Both DHHS and FDA have enacted regulations implementing the Freedom of Information Act and the Federal Privacy Act.

Two Public Health Service acts also deal with the protection of confidential information regarding patients in drug and alcohol treatment programs at federally funded clinics.[10[Sec.dd-3],10[Sec.ee-3]] Many additional federal laws exist that could affect privacy and confidentiality of research subjects, but an inclusion of all of them is beyond the scope of this work.

State Laws Addressing Privacy and Confidentiality

IRBs must consider state laws concerning privacy and confidentiality when reviewing research. These may take the form of either statute or case law. The Common Rule and FDA regulations[3[Sec.107(a)],4[Sec.107(a)]] require the IRB to be able to ascertain the acceptability of proposed research in terms of "applicable law," which includes state law. The Common Rule and FDA regulations also clearly state that other laws are not preempted by the federal regulations and continue to apply.[3[Sec.101(f)],4[Sec.103(c)]] Therefore, any state laws that require greater protections for subjects than the Common Rule and FDA regulations continue to apply.

A variety of state laws address privacy and confidentiality. These laws generally can be grouped under broad categories. The first category is laws allowing patients to have access to their own medical records. Many states provide detailed requirements for patient access to their medical records, but many states do not have statutes addressing this issue.

The second category is laws that require various third parties, such as physicians, hospitals, and HMOs, to maintain the confidentiality of patient medical records. These laws do not exist in all states, and where they do exist they vary greatly in scope and the identity of the restricted parties. Often states have different laws addressing specific medical conditions. For instance, there are often stricter confidentiality protections in place for drug abuse or mental health records than for other types of medical records.

The third category is laws that require informed consent from patients before medical information is released to third parties. Again, these do not exist in all states, and vary greatly in those states where they do exist.

A fourth category is laws that allow the disclosure of patient records for research purposes. Such laws have not been adopted in all states. Sometimes they require patient consent, other times they do not. Many of them are limited to certain types of records, such as cancer or mental health.

A fifth category of state laws comprises mandatory reporting laws of various types. Many types of medical conditions must be reported to the state, such as sexually transmitted diseases and cancer. Evidence suggesting child abuse, and often elder or other population abuse, must also be reported by physicians and other professionals. IRBs across the country are very inconsistent in their approach to child-abuse reporting requirements. Some IRBs require that information regarding this requirement be included in every consent form involving a medical procedure or an interview that could elicit information regarding child abuse. Other IRBs only require such consent form disclosure when the research is very likely to elicit this type of information. Many IRBs rarely or never disclose the existence of these laws.

Finally, many state laws affecting medical privacy and confidentiality do not fit into neat categories. For instance, some states such as Arizona prohibit genetic testing without specific, written informed consent. This would potentially affect the conduct of research involving genetic testing on stored tissue samples in Arizona, and would be important for IRB consideration.

In addition, many state laws potentially could affect research but do not specifically address medicine or research. These include privacy provisions of state constitutions, state freedom of information acts (often known as sunshine laws) that control access to records maintained or created by the state government, and common law actions regarding the right to privacy.

Conclusion

IRBs must consider the protection of privacy and confidentiality as part of their ethical and regulatory duty to protect the rights and welfare of human subjects. While privacy and confidentiality are difficult to define and are viewed differently by different individuals, IRBs can successfully apply them to research projects on a case-by-case basis. The IRB must consider both privacy and confidentiality for each segment of the research, from subject recruitment through follow-up and maintenance of the research records after the study has finished. Oftentimes, particularly in behavioral research, the main risk to subjects will be the possibility of an invasion of privacy or a breach of confidentiality. In the consent process, subjects

must be informed of the precautions that will be taken to protect the confidentiality of the subjects' information, and also be informed of the parties who will or may have access to the information. This will allow the subjects to decide if they agree with the IRB's assessment that the human-subjects protections are adequate.

References

1. Office for Protection From Research Risks. *OPRR Guidebook* (1993). Updated 23 Jun 2000. Access date 3 Apr 2001. World Wide Web http://ohrp.osophs.dhhs.gov/irb/irb_guidebook.htm

2. National Commission for the Protection of Human Subjects of Biomedical and Behavioral Research. *The Belmont Report: Ethical principles and guidelines for the protection of human subjects of research.* 1979. Access date 22 Mar 2001. World Wide Web http://ohsr.od.nih.gov/mpa/belmont.php3

3. Code of Federal Regulations. Title 45A—Department of Health and Human Services; Part 46—Protection of Human Subjects. Updated 1 Oct 1997. Access date 18 Apr 2001. World Wide Web http://www4.law.cornell.edu/cfr/45p46.htm

4. Code of Federal Regulations. Title 21, Chapter 1—Food and Drug Administration, DHHS; Part 56—Institutional Review Boards. Updated 1 Apr 1999. Access date 27 Mar 2001. World Wide Web http://www4.law.cornell.edu/cfr/21p56.htm

5. Food and Drug Administration. Information Sheets: Guidance for Institutional Review Boards and Clinical Investigators. Sept 1998. Access date 9 Apr 2001. World Wide Web http://www.fda.gov/oc/oha/IRB/toc.html

6. Code of Federal Regulations. Title 21, Chapter 1—Food and Drug Administration, DHHS; Part 50—Protection of Human Subjects. Updated 1 Apr 1999. Access date 18 Apr 2001. World Wide Web http://www4.law.cornell.edu/cfr/21p50.htm

7. Office for Protection From Research Risks. Protections for Human Subjects in the NIGMS Human Genetic Mutant Cell Repository: Submission of Non-Identifiable Materials for the Repository, 22 May 1997. Access date 14 Aug 2001. World Wide Web http://ohrp.osophs.dhhs.gov/humansubjectsguidance/reposit.htm

8. 104th Congress. The Freedom of Information Act. 5 U.S.C. § 552. 1996. amended by public law No. 104-231, 110 Stat. 3048. http://www.usdoj.gov/oip/foia_updates/Vol_XVII_4/page2.htm

9. 104th Congress. The Federal Privacy Act of 1974. 5 U.S.C. § 552a. 1996.

10. 103rd Congress. Public Health Service Act (§290)—Title 42 US Code, 1 Jan 2001. World Wide Web http://frwebgate2.access.gpo.gov/cgi-bin/waisgate.cgi?waisdocid=2637221675+0+0+0&waisaction=retrieve

Recruitment of Research Subjects

Felix A. Khin-Maung-Gyi and Matthew D. Whalen

INTRODUCTION

Certain critical topics related to human participant recruitment in clinical trials serve as focal points for this chapter, including the following:

1. Recruitment of subjects as the beginning of the informed consent process
2. Principles of information, comprehension, and voluntariness: what the IRB will especially attend to in the course of its deliberations, which also provides the underpinning of this discussion
3. The Office of the Inspector General (OIG) reports of June 2000; what the OIG is, what their reports are, and why they are important for those involved in clinical research
4. Facing the reality of recruitment in a world of e-trials and e-IRBs; emerging technologies and their impact on the recruitment process

Recruitment of Subjects: The Beginning of the Informed Consent Process

By regulations and common sense, involvement of a person considering participating in a clinical trial begins with his or her obtaining information on a specific clinical trial for which he or she may be eligible. This is distinct from an individual's learning about clinical research and what a trial is in general. The sponsor of the research, its agents involved in implementing certain aspects of a trial, the investigator, the study coordinator, and the IRB are all intimately involved in the recruitment of subjects. Their interactions ought to be as proactive and collaborative as possible, because each brings a different, perspective and set of concerns in developing, reviewing, and/or implementing recruitment efforts.

From the perspective of those most directly involved in recruiting subjects—sponsors and investigators, including their agents, such as clinical research organizations (CROs), communications firms, and study coordinators— this means that information they are providing and information they are obtaining has human-subject protection ramifications.

Overall, from an IRB perspective, early interaction with those involved in developing any recruitment effort is paramount in importance to the effort. Indeed, submission of the full recruitment plan to the IRB before any initiation efforts is appropriate to meet regulatory and ethical as well as business objectives. Principles of information, comprehension, and voluntariness are what the IRB will especially attend to in the course of its deliberations. Accordingly, these principles will provide the underpinning of the discussion throughout this chapter.

For some trials and sites, recruitment efforts are centralized; for others, they are highly localized. The responsibility for taking human-subject protection seriously does not change. From the perspective of the individual being recruited, the need for clear and accurate information is essential. What kind of information this is has been outlined in the regulations (the elements of informed consent, both required and optional) and discussed in Part 6.

However, is information that is clear and accurate also sufficient? The answer is no, as reemphasized by the recent Office of the Inspector General reports on patient recruitment. Informed consent is a process—a communications process. Possibilities for misinforming or disinforming potential subjects abound, whether in overly enthusiastic public relations material or by an overly zealous study coordinator. Indeed, the possibilities for inadvertent, even intentional, coercion or undue influence are also high. Solutions of separating the investigator from the potential subject's physician and having third-party auditing of the process have been offered as remedies. Their usefulness in all cases, or even most, is unclear. Certainly, IRB review authority over recruitment efforts (from fundamental advertising through screening scripts and Web sites) appears a meaningful step in the right direction.

Regarding truly informed subjects, inevitably the conclusion to be reached is that it depends on the individual and those involved in communicating the information. Given the enormous variability in comprehension of potential subjects for clinical trials and the impracticality of monitoring (regardless of monitor) each consent process, elaborate regulations or guidance is not possible. Equally inevitably, as in so much of clinical research, trust and integrity become both minimum and maximum criteria.

The tension, of course, is between creating trust and creating a dependant relationship in which the potential subject yields control of his or her decision to the expert (advertiser, physician, study coordinator; even IRB). "Undue influence" is one factor potentially at work here, in addition to the prospect of subject's minimizing his or her own responsibilities as trial participants, as the National Bioethics Advisory Commission has noted in a draft report, referred to later in this chapter. Both coercion and undue influence can be at play throughout a trial, not only during initial recruitment. In the case of coercion, for example, special or added inducements to maintain a subject in a trial run into the same ethical and regulatory difficulties as do incentives offered for participation in the trial in the first place.

The moral imperative here is that the informed consent process is a continuing one, not simply a one-time occurrence of first consent. It certainly also applies in the case of the ongoing undue influence of, for example, a study coordinator or investigator whose relationship with the subject itself may be powerful encouragement to stay in the trial or not report accurately if some event is occurring in order to remain in the trial.

The OIG Reports of June 2000

The Office of the Inspector General (OIG) of the Department of Health and Human Services (DHHS) has been releasing reports of great interest to IRB participants and professionals since June 1998 in particular. Three OIG reports were released in June 2000, two related to recruiting subjects and one regarded regulatory oversight of clinical investigators, as well as providing a foundation for discussion of subject recruitment and how far-reaching its implications are.

By way of background, OIG is a part of the DHHS, the agency that contains both the National Institutes of Health (NIH) and the Food and Drug Administration (FDA), including the units of both of those agencies that oversee various aspects of human subject protection, such as the Office for Human Research Protections (OHRP). OIG's primary role is to oversee the overseers, like NIH and FDA. As a result, their reports carry particular importance for professionals in the clinical research community to review and understand.

The first report relating to subject recruitment, entitled "Recruiting Human Subjects: Pressures in Industry-Sponsored Clinical Research,"[1] notes that reviewing recruitment methods provides "additional opportunity for oversight bodies to monitor the actual content of the consent process." Herein lies the importance of recruitment. For IRBs, this is a clear indication of the significance of their involvement with subject recruitment, whether in e-commerce or paper flyer media, because recruitment is tied intimately to the consent process itself.

From an ethical and regulatory perspective, the OIG reports specifically refer to issues of information, comprehension, and voluntariness. These *Belmont Report*-based cornerstones of good clinical practice are then related specifically to recruitment practices. Dr. Bert Spilker, of the trade association of major drug manufacturers (PhRMA), simplifies what these practices are in his commentary on the draft of the first report. He suggests that there are basically three primary forms of recruiting:

1. An investigator's own patients
2. A physician referring patients to an investigator
3. Advertising (a more anonymous form of recruitment; that is, obtaining potential subjects via means less personal than preestablished relationships)

When IRBs attend to recruitment, one way to do so is to consider the ethical issues of information, comprehension, and voluntariness in each setting of recruitment (the investigator's own patients, the referring physician, and advertising). Briefly, information focuses on disinformation or misinformation as much as accurate information; comprehension has to do with presentation and communication; and voluntariness has to do with coercion and undue influence as well as freedom of choice.

In the new millennium, both ethical issues and recruitment settings have become far more complicated in comparison with when the IRB system first evolved three decades or so ago. Indeed, simply to invoke the image of international clinical trials can send IRB administrators and IRB participants into a frenzy of review activities, not to mention lengthy deliberations and formal communications among various segments of the clinical research enterprise, including sponsors, CROs, and academic or hospital administrators. It is "this market-driven research environment" and contemporary global society that provided the rationale for the OIG reports.

Recruitment in a World of E-Trials and E-IRBs

Far from the early history of research volunteers' self-referral (and self-experimentation in the case of the physician–researcher), contemporary subject recruitment has become an industry. In an age of multimedia and technology, the range of avenues for recruiting has expanded exponentially, not to mention the advent of e-trials and e-IRBs. Major public relations, marketing, and advertising firms construct entire mass-media campaigns to support clinical research studies, whether enabled by the Web or not. Innovative technology companies either assist these firms or create their own proprietary approaches to accelerate enrollment. Fulfillment centers stand ready to accompany any of these efforts to enhance retention of subjects in recognition of the reality that speedy recruitment is one thing, maintaining subjects in the study is quite another—and necessary to obtaining data to be submitted for FDA approval of the test drug, device, or biologic. Aside from the mass media and e-commerce business dimensions of recruitment, inherent ethical issues must be considered. The point of intersection of both business and ethical issues is the conference table of the IRB. There are two perspectives to be considered in this regard. First, perhaps foremost, is that of the IRB's basic identity and role. The second is that of the deliberation process of the IRB.

An IRB is not intended to be a scientific review body, like an NIH study section or other body with specialized expertise. Neither is the IRB supposed to be an apologist for the clinical research enterprise, or an advocate (in the public policy or political senses) for the patient. Rather, it is a gathering of individuals with various backgrounds and experience deliberating appropriate human-subject protections using regulations, guidance, and ethical principles to frame its discussions and decisions. Indeed, the OIG reports on recruitment offer unambiguous statements in regard to an IRB's membership, certainly one component of its basic identity. The recommendations are made to "require more extensive representation on IRBs of nonscientific and noninstitutional members," and acknowledge that "the perspectives of independent lay members are of particular importance".

Clearly, whether the issues are subject protection or otherwise, lay and unaffiliated representation is essential, emphasizing that the voice of the IRB is a social and cultural one, not exclusively one of technical (scientific, public policy, legal, public relations, political, or economic) expertise.

Beyond the fundamental identity of the IRB, another perspective to be considered is that of the IRB deliberative process. In criticizing the standard audit model of the FDA, the OIG reports point to a focus on *how* an IRB deliberates, not only that it does so in an administratively compliant way. One approach to deliberating subject recruitment issues has been suggested earlier: creating a matrix to consider the ethical issues of information, comprehension, and voluntariness in each setting of recruitment (the investigator's own patients; the referring physician, and advertising). But another issue for deliberation is *how much* the IRB should know, ranging from reviewing advertising budgets and plans for nationwide public relations campaigns to wireframes of Web sites, in order to assure lack of coercion and maintenance of confidentiality.

The Four Cs of Recruitment from an IRB Perspective

The issues of greatest concern for IRBs and for IRB staffs relating to recruitment campaigns are as follows:
1. Consent (on-going, or continuing)
2. Coercion (of medium and message)
3. Confidentiality (and privacy)
4. Completeness (accuracy as well as truthfulness vs. deception)

In a wired world where there can be very few guarantees of absolute confidentiality—much less privacy—without extraordinary efforts, protecting confidentiality involves a number of measures.

1. The subject, or potential subject, is given frequent opportunity to reassert his or her consent to providing the information requested, conforming nicely with the regulatory and ethical reality that consent is an on-going or continual process. An illustration is potential subjects being screened via an interactive Web site.

2. Either data that are obtained are eliminated from a database at regular intervals, or the subject is told that data will be maintained up to a year without additional consent.

3. Unblinded information and data obtained are not provided to any third party without the subject's permission, along with disclosure about financial gains to be achieved by the providing party, which may impact the subject's willingness to continue to have it released.

Another challenge for recruitment design (and review by an IRB) is completeness. A principle to invoke, of course, would be to "make the material as accurate as possible." Yet, this can create significant problems if one is also trying to be clear, understandable, and concise—hallmarks for informed consent. In addition, being accurate in a way that encourages comprehension may be at odds with being scientifically accurate, at least in the study design and procedure details.

One approach is to be as general as possible with information intended simply to introduce the clinical trial to a prospective participant, irrespective of media. Discussion of details can be left to other parts of the informed consent process, including especially the dialog between the site personnel and the individual. What confounds this approach are screening processes that continue to get more and more elaborate, especially as administered remotely, for example, by a call center. In these cases, using highly qualified screening personnel conducting the process as one would do face-to-face at the site provides a solution. A separate issue is deception. As related to completeness, deception is the equivalent of undue influence because an underlying factor of undue influence is that it encourages incomplete information exchange.

For example, because of the research professional's role in the potential subject's life, the potential subject does not ask additional questions or seek clarification. In essence, the person says, "I trust you" or "I trust the system." In media presentations, a spokesperson for a trial may be of such public or local visibility that virtually the same thing occurs. Granting that influence is one thing and undue influence another, drawing the line can be a frustrating matter. This is one of the reasons there is so much discussion among regulators regarding separating clinical research roles from clinical practice roles, as well as encouraging more rather than less IRB scrutiny of advertising campaigns and screening processes.

Another dimension of deception involves the nature of marketing, advertising, and public relations, which have as a goal promoting a product, service, or idea. In the case of clinical research, where is the meaningful distinction to be made between informing and enticing a prospective subject? The situation of the study coordinator serves as an important illustration of this dimension.

The role of the study coordinator requires communications skills. A good communicator is naturally also gifted at promoting. The alternative of being bound regulatorily to following a script while being overseen by a third party does not appear either viable or practical. As a result, the conscientious coordinator is constantly facing the issue of undue influence, even in situations where she or he has not interacted with the prospective subject in the past. As a research professional (often also as a health care professional), he or she has more medical knowledge than most individuals and, if a strong communicator in addition, can certainly influence decisions. Overtly deceptive are instances of clinical research professionals' making promises to a prospective subject that are not verifiable through the research, not the least of which is conveying to possible participants that the trial is nontherapeutic. These deceptions cannot be countenanced ethically or regulatorily, and do not appear to make good business sense either.

Conclusion

Sites and sponsors need to communicate directly, indicating any and all forms of recruitment, from mining databases through centralized media campaigns, that are either going to be used or may be used. Discussions between sites and sponsors result in what the IRB will review.

The IRB oversees both sponsor and site by way of direct communications; that is, the IRB receives full documentation on all aspects of the recruitment campaign as planned or envisioned by the investigator or site as well as the sponsor. Such disclosure is to be thorough; that is, the IRB can extract the size, scope, and dimensions of how subjects will be enlisted; and IRB, sponsor, and site have the exact same information, assured by copying communications to each.

References

1. Office of Inspector General D. Recruiting Human Subjects: Pressures in Industry-Sponsored Clinical Research (OEI-01-97-00195). Department of Health and Human Services, June 2000. Access date 12 Apr 2001. World Wide Web http://www.hhs.gov/oig/oei/reports/a459.pdf

Advertisements for Research

Rachel Homer, Rachel Krebs, and Linda Medwar

INTRODUCTION

The purpose of this chapter is to explain the role of the IRB in evaluating the practices used to recruit subjects for research participation. Federal Regulations (45 CFR 46.111) state that selection of subjects must be equitable. In making this assessment, the Institutional Review Board (IRB) should take into account the purposes of the research and the setting in which the study will be conducted. The IRB should be particularly cognizant of the special problems of research involving vulnerable populations, such as children, prisoners, pregnant women, mentally disabled persons, or economically or educationally disadvantaged persons. The IRB must determine that the procedure for recruitment is not coercive and accurately describes the likely risks and benefits of study participation.

Recruitment of subjects is considered the start of the consent/assent process. Recruitment of subjects and feasibility of recruiting must be considered and planned before initiation of a study and must continue throughout the study.[1] For this reason, the IRB must review the methods, materials, procedures, and tools used to recruit potential research subjects before they are implemented. Some of the more commonly used tools of recruitment include direct advertising (flyers, posters, press releases, brochures), media advertisements (newspaper, TV, radio, websites), recruitment letters, and presentations at community meeting places. Each of these recruitment methods presents different ethical issues for an IRB to consider, and will be discussed in the following sections.

Direct Advertising

Direct advertising refers to any activity that solicits research participation directly from potential subjects. All direct advertising must have IRB approval before being used. The information contained in the advertisement and the mode of communication must also be reviewed by the IRB. The IRB should determine that the advertisement is not coercive and accurately describes the potential risks and benefits of study participation. A 1998 update of the FDA Information Sheet: Recruiting Study Subjects presents guidelines for the format of study advertisement.[2]

1. Name and address of the investigator and/or research facility/institution
2. Condition under study and/or purpose of the research
3. Inclusion/exclusion criteria in summary form
4. A brief list of procedures involved
5. Time or other commitment required (number of visits, total duration including follow-up visits, etc.)
6. Compensation/reimbursement
7. Location of research and contact person for further information

Flyers, Posters, Brochures

Flyers, posters, and brochures are often used to solicit potential research subjects. These types of advertisements are typically placed in strategic locations in hopes of targeting the population being studied. Some of these locations may include bulletin boards, professional offices/businesses, schools, public transportation (buses, subways, trains), and at other public areas such as restaurants. Although it is mandatory to obtain IRB approval for use of such advertisements, it may also be necessary for an investigator to obtain approval from the various sites where the flyer, poster, and/or brochure will be placed. This should also be done before posting or distribution of the advertisement, and evidence of this approval may be required by the IRB. Because these types of advertisements are visible tools of recruitment, they must present information that is adequate, accurate, and balanced so that potential subjects can make an informed decision about possible participation. The decision to include compensation and/or reimbursement in the advertisement may be made on a case-by-case basis, depending on the study itself and the particular policies and guidelines of the IRB. Although compensation or reimbursement may factor into one's decision to participate in a study, the offer must be carefully thought out and worded appropriately so as not to coerce a subject's willingness to participate. Acceptable and unacceptable research advertisements will clarify these issues.

Example #1: Unapproved advertisement

Lose Weight Fast and Receive Cash!!!
Join an Exciting Weight Loss Study

• Are you a teenager?

• Are you fat and want to lose weight?

If you answered **YES** to these questions, you may qualify to participate in a weight loss study.

You will receive a <u>free</u> medical evaluation and participate in a cutting-edge nutrition program.

You will also receive $$$ money $$$ and parking vouchers. No medications will be given.

Call (213) 456-9870 for more information.

This advertisement should not be approved by the IRB for several reasons.
1. There is an emphasis on monetary compensation.
2. The advertisement uses catchy words such as *exciting, fast, cutting-edge,* and *free.*
3. Ages for eligibility are not specified.
4. The purpose of the study is not specified.
5. No mention is made that this study is "research."
6. Terms such as *fat* may be insulting.
7. The name of contact person is not included.
8. The study location is not included.
9. The advertisement is misleading concerning its purpose.

Example #2: Revised advertisement

Weight Loss and Diabetes Prevention Study

Be part of an important Nutrition Research Study

• Are you between 13 and 21 years of age?

• Do you want to change your eating habits in order to lose weight?

If you answered **YES** to these questions, you may be eligible to participate in a nutrition research study.

The purpose of this research study is to compare the effectiveness of different diets in preventing type 2 diabetes. Benefits include a comprehensive medical evaluation and nutrition program. Par-

ticipants also will receive monetary compensation and parking vouchers. No medications will be given.

Both **adolescents** (13 years of age and older) and **adults** (21 years of age and younger) are eligible. The study is being conducted at Central Hospital.

Please call John Smith at (555) 123-4567
for more information.

This is an example of an advertisement that meets the basic guidelines for IRB approval.
1. The approach is straightforward and honest.
2. "Research" is specified.
3. The ages for eligibility are included.
4. The purpose is clearly stated.
5. The benefits are included.
6. The contact person's name is included.
7. The institution is identified.

Media Advertisements (Newspaper, TV, Radio, Internet)

As a result of the increasing complexity and number of research studies, investigators have recently become interested in the use of recruitment tools that reach a large number of potential research subjects. Media advertisements serve this role, as newspapers, television and radio communication, and Internet advertisements allow for the dissemination of research information to many people over the course of their daily lives. In these situations, individuals are not necessarily searching for such advertisements, but an individual who is interested in an advertised research study may nonetheless pursue contacting the research site for further information. All media research advertisements must be reviewed and approved by the IRB prior to use.

Coercion in Media Advertising
One of the key issues an IRB will focus upon in reviewing media advertisements is the elimination of coercion. Subtle forms of coercion may appear in media advertisements without an investigator's awareness. Coercion that is subtle could be apparent in the tone of voice used, the speed of speech, and/or the inclusion of soothing background music. The guidelines for the development of flyers, posters, and brochures, as discussed earlier in this chapter, should be adhered to in creating media advertisements. In general, media advertisements should be straightforward and honest in order to target the appropriate audience and elicit the desired response from potential research subjects.

IRB Approval of Media Advertisements
For radio advertisements, a recording must first be approved by the IRB. It is recommended that the IRB's review and approval of the radio advertisement be obtained be-

fore the final taping, as the IRB may require changes. This process is also recommended for the development and implementation of television advertisements. An institutional policy may be developed in which the IRB Chair reviews television and radio advertisements and then determines whether the entire IRB should review the advertisement prior to approval. Newspaper advertisements must also be approved by the IRB before publication.[1]

Internet Advertising

Another recruitment tool to consider is the Internet. As the Internet has become more widely used by patients and patient advocacy groups, it has also become a popular method for recruiting research subjects. The Internet may be used as a recruitment tool by adding the study to a listing of research studies or by the posting of research advertisements. For example, specific clinical trial listings include http://www.clinicaltrials.gov, a Web site that is maintained by the NIH that lists both government and industry-sponsored clinical trials. The NIH requires evidence of IRB approval before listing a clinical trial on the Web site, as does the commercial site *Centerwatch*, http://www.centerwatch.com. Institutional policies may indicate that advertisements and listings of research studies require IRB approval, even though this is not a federal regulatory requirement.

The FDA has provided guidance regarding the use of the Internet for recruiting research subjects. As stated in the FDA Information Sheets, "IRB review and approval of listings of clinical trials on the Internet would provide no additional safeguard and is not required when the system format limits the information provided to basic trial information, such as the title; purpose of the study; protocol summary; basic eligibility criteria; study site location(s); and how to contact the site for further information."[2]

Depending on the target population, the Internet may be the most effective recruitment tool. Some individuals may use the Internet as a source of information and support. For this reason, advertising on the Internet for research studies is sometimes cost-effective and is, therefore, a popular method of recruitment for research studies.[3] An additional issue to consider regarding Internet listings of research studies is the method by which interested individuals should contact a research site. Certain populations may prefer calling a research center instead of sending an e-mail response, as their anonymity may not be assured with an e-mail response.

Another electronic method for advertising research studies is the use of an internal intranet system within an institution. This method may be used for two purposes: to inform employees of studies they may consider for participation, such as occupational health studies, or to inform employees of studies for particular patient populations. In an effort to minimize coercion and allow employees to decide whether they would like to view the research studies, it is preferred to have the option of clicking into a listing of research studies as opposed to sending a broadcast e-mail message to all employees. An internal intranet system also allows research investigators to become familiar with studies being conducted by other physicians and researchers at their institution.

Recruitment Letters

Many investigators use recruitment letters as the first step in the recruitment process. Depending on the nature of the research, the recruitment letter may or may not need to include all of the elements normally disclosed in an informed consent document. The investigator may choose to explain the purpose of the research, what participation will involve, the risks and benefits associated with subject participation, whether any compensation will be offered, and the fact that participation is voluntary. On the other hand, if the research study involves sensitive material, the investigator may choose to keep the recruitment letter vague. For example, in an effort to protect the privacy of a potential subject, an investigator may decide not to disclose many details of the study in case the letter gets into the hands of someone other than the potential subject for whom it was intended. Regardless of what the research involves, the recruitment letter should explain how the investigator got the potential subjects' names to contact.

One key factor that will influence the content of a recruitment letter is the intended audience. The following sections will outline some of the issues that investigators must consider when they wish to send recruitment letters to potential subjects who are patients, students in schools, and employers and employees.

Patients

Certain factors must be considered when the research involves recruiting patients. Some research studies will seek the enrollment of patients who were previously seen by the investigator, whereas other studies will seek potential new patients for the research. If it is the case that an investigator has received a list of potential research subjects from another investigator, this should be disclosed in the recruitment letter. Other points to consider mentioning in the recruitment letter include whether the subjects' participation will affect their current or future care and whether results of the research will be released to the subjects.

Schools/Students

Investigators who conduct research in schools should be aware of federal laws that govern the conduct of these research studies and disclosure of information. The Family Educational Rights and Privacy Act (FERPA) and the Protection of Pupil Rights Amendment (PPRA) are two laws that directly address the conduct of research involving school children. Unfortunately, at the time of this writing, these two laws have not been implemented to the point that we can say exactly what they will require. FERPA defines the rights of students and parents concerning reviewing, amending, and disclosing education records. Current drafts of this law require written permission to disclose personally identifiable information from a student's education record, except under certain circumstances such as an order of subpoena. If a student's school record is to be reviewed by an investigator and identifiers are to be maintained, the investigator must obtain parental permission to inspect the records of students.

PPRA applies to survey research conducted in schools. The current draft of PPRA states that parents and/or guardians have the right to inspect surveys and questionnaires distributed within schools. This draft also specifies that parental permission must be obtained to have minors participate in surveys that disclose information regarding political affiliations; mental and psychological problems; income; sex behavior and attitudes; illegal, antisocial, self-incriminating, and demeaning behavior; critical appraisals of other individuals with close family relationships; and legally recognized, privileged relationships.

Employers/Employees

When research studies are intended for businesses and their employees or employers, the investigator should consider the following factors when sending recruitment letters to such businesses. The potential subject (employer/employee) should not be pressured into participating in the research for fear of job loss, delayed promotion, or other influences from the supervisor or superior. An investigator should make it clear that information disclosed will remain confidential. Employees will obviously be reluctant to participate in a research study if they know that their confidentiality cannot be guaranteed. The investigator should consider whether the employer needs to be aware that employees are being recruited for research. If the research is to be conducted at the place of employment during the course of a regular business day, the employer may need to be notified. It is important to remember that the investigator may need to obtain permission from the employer before approaching or sending a recruitment letter to the employees.

Postcards and Phone Calls

Aside from considering the types of subjects that will be recruited and the timing for sending the recruitment letter to potential subjects, an investigator should consider what the next course of action will be if subjects do not respond to the recruitment letter. Many investigators choose to resend the recruitment letter and questionnaire or survey to those individuals who did not respond to the initial mailing. If the investigator plans to send a second mailing, he or she may wish to state this in the recruitment letter. Some investigators choose to include return postcards with the mailing of their recruitment letters. Subjects could then indicate their desire to participate in the research or not. In this case, the investigator will know whom to contact for further discussion and clarification about the research study. If the study involves a sensitive subject, the investigator may opt to have the postcard be vague in its identification of the study, or the investigator may include an envelope in which subjects can return the postcard so as to secure privacy and confidentiality. It is important that the investigator state the appropriate response instructions in the recruitment letter in order to generate the greatest response rate.

If an investigator wishes to contact potential subjects by telephone, several considerations should be kept in mind during the development of the recruitment letter. It may be necessary for the recruitment letter to state that the investigator will be telephoning potential subjects. An investigator should outline the conditions under which subjects will be contacted. If a postcard is included with the recruitment letter, it may ask interested subjects to include their telephone number and the appropriate times that the investigator may reach them. Again, subjects may also have the choice to indicate that they do not want to participate in the research. An investigator who will be contacting subjects by telephone should be conscious of the privacy and confidentiality of these subjects and should also consider appropriate times to contact potential subjects.

Certainly, individual IRBs may have their own requirements regarding the use of recruitment letters. The above-mentioned information should serve merely as a guide for what investigators should consider when developing recruitment letters. An investigator should consult with the IRB office to inquire about specific guidelines and policies relevant to the particular study in mind.

Advertising and Recruiting Through Word of Mouth

Subjects may be drawn to participation in a research protocol simply through word of mouth. Information about research studies is often disseminated to appropriate target audiences at organized meetings such as advocacy groups and business workshops. For example, physicians often inform their peers about their need for research subjects within their community or area of expertise. Another example is the formation of social networks among individuals who share a common concern or interest. Through these social networks, people will exchange information pertinent to their needs, including their health. For example, if an individual with a rare form of cancer chooses to participate in an investigational treatment protocol, he or she may inform others with the same cancer about this research protocol. If investigators consider information disclosed through word of mouth to be among their recruitment tools, then this should be acknowledged and mentioned in the written protocol. The investigator should submit any written materials that may be discussed or given out at such advocacy groups, business workshops, or peer meetings to the IRB for review and approval.

In-Person Recruitment

The first step of the recruitment process often occurs through the efforts of research personnel approaching potential research subjects in person. There are many issues to consider when directly approaching individuals for possible inclusion in a research study. The time at which an individual is approached is of particular importance; it should be a time that is convenient and should not increase a person's anxiety level. Sometimes it is helpful to present a research study to individuals in advance so that they can take the consent form and other recruitment materials home to review with family members. This approach would also provide potential research subjects with ample time to consider whether or not participation is of interest to them.

The location of recruitment should also be considered. Research studies of a more sensitive nature, such as some survey questionnaires, may require privacy, in which case an individual examination room or office may be the most appropriate environment for discussing or completing the questionnaire.

It is also important that the person recruiting is known to the subjects and is qualified to recruit them. In certain situations, the investigator may not be the best person to recruit, as he or she may unduly influence the potential research subject.[4] For example, in a patient–physician relationship, a patient may confuse the physician's role as a clinician with the role as a researcher. The issue of who is identifying potential research subjects is also important to consider when an investigator is recruiting a control population for a research study. An institutional policy may indicate that researchers are not allowed to recruit employees whom they directly supervise, as these individuals may feel coerced to participate in their supervisors' research studies.

Conclusion

IRB members and staff play an important role in ensuring that investigators are informed of the process for the review and approval of recruitment materials. Educational sessions provide an opportunity for stressing the review process, as does the protocol application itself. Within the protocol application, it may be helpful to include information concerning the materials that must be submitted for review and approval along with specific recruitment questions. Such questions may inquire as to how potential research subject names are obtained before contact is made, who recruits potential subjects for the study, where potential subjects will be recruited from, and what process will be used to recruit potential subjects.

Direct advertising (flyers, posters, press releases, brochures), media advertisements (newspapers, TV, radio, and Web sites), recruitment letters, word of mouth, and in-person recruiting represent the majority of recruitment tools used by investigators to identify potential research subjects. It is important to remain mindful of the fact that recruitment methods are, many times, the first step in the consent process. Every aspect of research should adhere to the guidelines set forth in the *Belmont Report* and the Code of Federal Regulations. Furthermore, individual IRBs can establish more rigorous guidelines for the review and approval of recruitment materials than those contained in the federal regulations. Individual institutional policies should outline the circumstances under which recruitment tools require expedited or full IRB review and approval. With increased awareness of human subject protection issues, the interpretation and implementation of the federal regulations and institutional policies have evolved to ensure more appropriate protection of research subjects. As better protection methods are developed and secured, better recruitment methods will evolve. Potential subjects need to be given sufficient information that is accurate and balanced in order to make an informed decision about their participation in a research study.[3]

We end with a final list of recommendations regarding the recruitment of subjects for research.

1. Clearly state that the project is research.

2. Err on the side of underestimating benefits and overestimating risks.

3. Do not make claims of safety, equivalence, or superiority.

4. Avoid phrases like "new treatment," "new medicine," or "new drug."

5. Avoid using the term *free* in reference to treatment procedures.

6. Do not use dollar signs or focus on monetary issues.

7. Obtain approval from all applicable groups to post advertisements.

References

1. Dunn C., Chadwick G., Allen W. (Eds.) Protecting Study Volunteers in Clinical Research. Center Watch, Inc. Sept. 1999.

2. Food and Drug Administration. Information Sheets: Guidance for Institutional Review Boards and Clinical Investigators. Sep 1998. Access date 9 Apr 2001. World Wide Web http://www.fda.gov/oc/oha/IRB/toc.html

3. Office of Inspector General. Recruiting Human Subjects: Pressures in Industry-Sponsored Clinical Research (OEI-01-97-00195). June 2000. Access date 12 Apr 2001. World Wide Web http://www.hhs.gov/oig/oei/reports/a459.pdf

4. Office of Inspector General. Recruiting Human Subjects: Sample Guidelines for Practice (OEI-01-97-00196). June 2000. Access date 6 Apr 2001. World Wide Web http://www.hhs.gov/oig/oei/reports/a458.pdf

Paying Research Subjects

Bruce G. Gordon, Joseph Brown, Christopher Kratochvil, and Ernest D. Prentice

INTRODUCTION

Payment of human subjects to participate in research remains one of the most contentious ethical problems facing Institutional Review Boards (IRBs). Although concerns over this practice have existed for many years, there are few regulatory guidelines, nor indeed any consensus, to shape institutional and individual IRB policy. In this chapter, we will briefly review the ethical arguments pertaining to this practice, the federal regulations and guidance, and some of the models proposed to standardize the practice.

In this chapter, we have deliberately avoided providing the opinion of the authors regarding the "optimal" compensation scheme or specific recommendations addressing the other issues described below. This is a conscious decision, which is grounded in the understanding that the relative weight of ethical arguments may vary from institution to institution and from IRB to IRB.

Ethical Arguments

It has been suggested that the payment of subjects represents "undue inducement" that influences potential subjects to do something they would not ordinarily have done.[1-4] One may argue that research participation should be based on a risk/benefit relationship in which the benefits are those inherently present in the research itself. For "therapeutic research," these potential benefits may include relief from disease, diminished suffering, or the provision of diagnostic information. For nontherapeutic research, ideally, subjects participate for entirely altruistic reasons, principally to benefit society. In exchange for these benefits, subjects accept a certain degree of risk, the acceptability of which reflects each subject's weighing and calculation. In the case of either therapeutic or nontherapeutic research, but more obviously in the latter case, payment may influence this calculation. Now risk is balanced against health or societal benefit and financial reward, and the scale is shifted, however slightly. Hence, subjects no longer act solely for the benefit of their health or for altruism, but for some other (financial) reason.

On the other hand, it may be just as cogently argued that financial reward is a benefit no more or less valid than altruism or relief from illness. In addition, there is not *a priori* reason to exclude it from the risk/benefit analysis. Indeed, for an IRB to do so may represent excessive paternalism in presuming that it can determine what benefits ought to be important to a person. The ethical principle of autonomy might be invoked to allow an informed, reasoning person to decide what value he or she places on money, and what risks he or she is willing to undertake in exchange for that value.

A second argument against payment of research subjects is that such payment may result in economically disadvantaged persons bearing a disproportionately large share of the risks of research.[1,4] Such a policy would thus appear to contravene the principle of justice. However, it has been asserted that this view is rather one sided: it considers research solely as a "burden." To the extent that the benefits of research are distributed primarily to participants, one might argue that any procedure such as payment of subjects that encourages recruitment of populations that have traditionally not participated in clinical research—like African Americans—is ethically acceptable and appropriate. Of course, this argument is based on the assumption that participation in the research is undoubtedly beneficial. Members of minority populations clearly disagree with that assumption or they would participate without inducement. Certainly, historical abuses such as the Tuskegee Study suggest that a certain suspicion of the research community is not without foundation.

In addition, this counterargument is not compelling from a utilitarian standpoint. Certainly, if there are features of the underserved population that can only be assessed by their direct participation in research, benefits to that population as a whole may outweigh risks to the individuals participating in the research. In a drug study, for example, different physiologic populations such as children, pregnant women, or the elderly may require participation from these groups to assess how a specific medication is metabolized in these subgroups. However, in the absence of a reason to believe economically disadvantaged persons metabolize a drug differently than more affluent persons do, the "benefit" of enrolling those economically disadvantaged persons accrues only to the subjects themselves (not the population) and only if the subjects have the disease being treated by the drug, only to the subjects randomized to receive the drug, and only for the duration of the trial. Moreover, if the eventual cost of the new drug under study will be significant, as is often the case, the population who undertook the risks to test the drug may not be able to afford the benefits of its use. Taken together, the limited benefits make it unlikely that the assumption that research participation is "undoubtedly beneficial" would be met.

A third argument against paying research subjects is that payment dehumanizes the subject and, by making him or her a "salaried worker," potentially alters the relationship between the subject and the investigator. Payment for participation in research amounts to selling the services of one's body, often at some significant risk.[4]

However, payment for labor is not fundamentally unethical; one's services or capacities are commodities that, in our free-market social and economic system, are regularly exchanged for wages. Nor would it generally be considered unethical to pay wages for work that is inherently risky; police officers, firefighters, and commercial fishermen regularly experience risk in their jobs. One might note that many would be uncomfortable with the notion of paying for the risk per se. That is, though the job is risky, we pay for the job, not the risk. In research, we must be very careful that we are not crossing this ethical line by using compensation to induce others to take certain risks on our behalf.

Wartofsky[4] eloquently compares the extent to which prostitution is like wage labor, involving, as it were, the sale of a disposition over one's body for a certain purpose, at a certain rate, and for a certain time. The relevance of the inquiry lies in the fact that what is being bought and sold in prostitution, just as in participation in research, is something that is "so intimate to one's person that there is something disturbing in the notion that it is alienable, as a commodity." In his view, the ethical objections to prostitution, and to being a paid-research subject, derive from the translation of relations that are supposed to express fundamental aspects of humanity into an economic exchange. In the paid research context, both the investigator and the subject are reducing an essential human capacity (putting oneself at risk for others) to a commodity. In so doing, they may dehumanize each other.

Empiric Data

Data regarding the importance of payment in the decision of research subjects to participate support the notion that financial compensation is an important motivator, at least among healthy volunteers. Payment was cited as the most important reason to participate in subjects undergoing pharmacologic studies[5,6] or physiology studies,[7] among participants in private or university-based research projects,[5] and among new participants as well as experienced volunteers.[8,9]

There are fewer data regarding participants in so-called "therapeutic research," as payment is less common in these trials. Among patients with asthma and allergies enrolled in therapy trials, health improvement was the primary motivator, but financial reward was still cited as a reason, especially among experienced participants.[10]

These studies all looked at research subjects' reasons for participating. Russell and colleagues[11] took a different approach, surveying a group of unpaid participants in a vaccine trial, seeking information not on why they participated, but on their opinions as to whether compensation was ethical. A majority of respondents disagreed with the payment of research subjects regardless of whether the subjects were healthy volunteers (76%) or patients (73%). In their comments, respondents identified potential problems with payment, including undue pressure to participate and impact on costs.

Respondents recognized that payment could improve recruitment, and many thought it appropriate if recruitment was a problem. Also of interest, some commented that payment may be justified to obtain more equitable representation across social strata, so that poorer persons could have a chance to benefit from the research. This is in contrast to most traditional ethical arguments that focus on the burdens of research rather than the potential benefits. Respondents distinguished between payment as incentive, payment of expenses, compensation for injury, and payment as recognition for time and effort. The latter three were judged more acceptable than the first.

Although these data are interesting, it is important to consider that the respondents were already self-selected as being, perhaps, more altruistic than others in that they had all agreed to participate in a trial with some risk, with no direct benefit to them, and with no monetary compensation. Therefore, results from this study may be difficult to extrapolate to other populations.

Regulations and Guidelines

Neither the Department of Health and Human Services (DHHS)[12] nor the Food and Drug Administration (FDA)[13,14] regulations offer specific limitations on the payment of research subjects. DHHS regulations state only that "an investigator shall seek such consent only under circumstances . . . that minimize the possibility of coercion or undue influence."[12(Sec.116)] The Office for Human Research Protections (OHRP) has issued no guidance on the definition of "undue influence," and it has been widely and variously interpreted. As previously described, some have argued that any financial remuneration, over and above reimbursement of direct costs to the subject, represents "undue inducement." A more temperate interpretation would require examination of the amount of payment in relation to the risks and burdens of the research before deciding influence is "undue."

FDA guidance on the payment of research subjects is no more informative.[15] The FDA Information Sheets[15] state, "It is not uncommon for subjects to be paid for their participation in research, especially in the early phases of investigational drug, biologic, or device development." The FDA neither endorses nor prohibits payment to subjects, but charges IRBs with the responsibility to "review both the amount of payment and the proposed method and timing of disbursement to assure that neither are coercive or present undue influence."[13(Sec.20)] The FDA does, however, assert that "payment to research subjects for participation in studies is not considered a benefit, it is a recruitment incentive." This statement implies that IRBs ought not to consider payment in their assessment of the risk/benefit relationship, but it does not suggest subjects should not use payment as a benefit in their own calculation.

The OHRP *IRB Guidebook*[16] acknowledges the differing opinions regarding the ethics of payment of research subjects, but neither endorses nor condemns the practice. It does point out appropriately, "Free health care for persons with limited resources and major medical problems may be a significant inducement to participate in research (even if the research activity is nontherapeutic)." But the guidebook goes on to say, "There is no consensus as to whether this kind of inducement is unacceptable." The guidebook offers several models for payment, including compensation "according to an established fee schedule, based upon the complexity of the study, the type and number of procedures to be performed, the time involved, and the anticipated discomfort or inconvenience." The other option is "an hourly rate or a fixed amount, depending on the duration of the study and whether the study requires admission to research ward [with] extra payments . . . provided for a variety of additional inconveniences."

Most international codes provide no firm guidance. The International Conference on Harmonisation (ICH) does not address the issue at all. In addition, the 2000 revision of the World Medical Association Declaration of Helsinki states only that "the researcher should also submit to the [ethical review] committee . . . information regarding . . . incentives for subjects."[17] Only the Council for International Organizations of Medical Sciences (CIOMS) offers a more definitive answer. Guideline 4 (Inducement to Participate) of the "International Ethical Guidelines for Biomedical Research Involving Human Subjects," states:

> Subjects may be paid for inconvenience and time spent, and should be reimbursed for expenses incurred, in connection with their participation in research; they may also receive free medical services. However, the payments should not be so large or the medical services so extensive as to induce prospective subjects to consent to participate in the research against their better judgment ("undue inducement").[18]

Thus, it would appear that CIOMS is of the opinion that at least reimbursement is not only ethical but is an obligation to the subject.

Models for Payment

IRBs that ultimately decide to allow payment to research subjects must decide what level of compensation is appropriate. Dickert and Grady[19] have proposed various models of payment, which we describe below.

Market Model

In this model, the laws of supply and demand determine how much a subject should be paid for participating in a given trial. Payment is a "benefit" to offset risks associated with a particular trial. Studies that involve greater risk (or have no other benefit) would likely have the highest rate of compensation. Studies in which subjects stand to gain a significant health benefit (i.e., therapeutic studies) would likely have minimal or no monetary payment. This model also allows for higher compensation to speed recruitment and bonuses to assure subjects complete the study.

The advantages of the market model are obvious: recruitment for high risk (or low benefit) studies would be augmented, and completion bonuses would help ensure that subjects finish the research. The market model is not unlike wage payment for a dangerous job: the laborer is compensated for services despite risk, and society benefits.

The major disadvantage of the market model is that payment may be so high that potential subjects enroll and remain on the study against their own best interests. Potential subjects may also conceal important health information in order to remain eligible, and thus place themselves (and the research protocol) at even higher risk. Finally, economically vulnerable groups are most likely to be attracted by this model, thereby inequitably distributing risks of research.

Wage Payment Model

In this second model proposed by Dickert and Grady, and based on previous work by Ackerman,[1] payment is made based on the premise that participation in research is unskilled labor that requires little training and some risk. Thus, subjects are compensated "on a scale commensurate with that of other unskilled but essential jobs;"[19] that is, a fairly low, standardized hourly wage, with bonuses for hazardous procedures.

The wage-payment model appears less likely to present undue inducement to subjects because the "wages" they would earn from participation would be no more than they could earn in other unskilled labor. Further, the standardization of payment would reduce competition for subjects between studies (which would be expected to drive up "prices" on the market model).

On the other hand, the wage payment model reduces but does not eliminate the potential for inequitable distribution of the risks of research to economically vulnerable groups. Though there is less undue incentive than with the market model, the wage model still presents a source of income to persons who may be unemployed and having difficulty finding jobs. Potential subjects with higher income are more likely to avoid studies that compensate using this model because participation may entail a loss of income if time has to be taken off from work. This is particularly problematic, as the bonuses for hazardous procedures will, once again, place the risks of research predominantly on the backs of the economically disadvantaged. Finally, from a more philosophic point of view, as Dickert and Grady[19] and others[20–22] suggest, "treating the subject's role as an unskilled job may be seen as inappropriately commercializing participation in research."[19]

Reimbursement Model

In this model, payment is provided to cover the subject's expenses (travel, food, gasoline). The definition of "expenses" may be somewhat flexible and can, at one end of the spectrum, be considered to include lost wages resulting from time taken off from work without pay. This model is based on the view that "research participation should not require financial sacrifice, but should be revenue neutral for participants."[19]

The reimbursement model notably eliminates the risk of undue inducement to participate in research. It also reduces the likelihood that potential subjects will withhold medical information so as not be to excluded from a study, although it does not eliminate the possibility that subjects will withhold information for some other benefit, such as access to a new treatment or free medical exams. Finally, it is not likely that financially disadvantaged potential subjects will be attracted inappropriately to these studies.

On the other hand, studies that reimburse using this model will be more apt to accrue subjects slowly, particularly if other competing studies utilize a different model. Accrual will be slower still if compensation does not include lost wages. For those studies that do include compensation for lost wages, the reimbursement model could paradoxically lead to targeting low-income populations by the sponsors in order to reduce costs.

Fair Share Model

Saunders and Sugar[23] propose a fourth model of payment. In this schema, the subject is treated like a partner in the research enterprise rather than a commodity or a wage laborer. Investigators are typically reimbursed a certain amount of money per patient. This is then used by the investigator to pay the direct (e.g., lab fees, IV tubing) and indirect (e.g., salaries, overhead) costs associated with performance of the study at his or her location. Utilizing this model, subjects would be compensated a fixed proportion of the per-subject reimbursement. Because investigator reimbursement per patient is based, in part, on whether a subject completes the trial, so would subjects' compensation be prorated depending on the duration of their participation.

This model unfortunately suffers from all the disadvantages of the market model, though the amount of compensation seems somewhat more equitable in that subjects are compensated more for studies that are more "profitable" to researchers. However, it is still likely to unduly induce subjects, especially financially disadvantaged ones, and may also lead to competitions among studies for the highest "cut" and the most lucrative "per patient" payment. Finally, it does not address payment in studies that are not reimbursed using a "per patient" system.

Prorating Payment

The FDA clearly requires prorating payments based on the duration of participation of the subject in the research. The FDA Information Sheets state, "Any credit for payment should accrue as the study progresses and not be contingent upon the subject completing the entire study."[15] Prorated payment should be made regardless of whether withdrawal was voluntary or involuntary; that is, whether the withdrawal was based on the decision of the subject to discontinue or based on some withdrawal criterion of the research protocol.

Protocols submitted to the IRB should clearly define the scheme for payment of subjects who withdraw from a study, and this scheme should be described in the consent documents. Often, payment is awarded based on a fixed-fee-per-clinic-visit or per intervention. The amount paid for each visit or intervention must be examined by the IRB in consideration of the ethical issues raised above, such that subjects are not unduly induced to continue when they would otherwise not have done so. The FDA does allow for the payment of "a small proportion as an incentive for completion of the study," provided that such incentive is not coercive.[15]

Payment to Minors

The ethical concerns regarding payment of subjects are magnified when the subjects are minors. Children and adolescents may be more or less prone to being unduly influenced by financial reward depending on their age and maturity. To a 10-year-old, a five dollar payment is a fortune; to a three-year-old, it may be irrelevant. Although the monetary benefits may appear especially clear, children and younger adolescents often have a limited capability to understand the risks, and therefore are not likely to perform an adequate assessment of the risk/benefit relationship. This may be especially true for adolescents, who feel invulnerable and indestructible, and therefore may be especially prey to monetary inducements. It may be difficult to determine "appropriate" compensation, even based on the models previously described.

Payment directed, then, to the minor himself or herself is probably inappropriate. It could be argued that payment to the parent is preferable because the parent (rather than the child) incurs the financial costs of participating in research (e.g., loss of wages, car expenses, food). However, payment beyond reimbursement to a parent, who is also making the legal decision to allow the child to participate, is also problematic. Certainly, it appears a conflict of interest, although it would be a reasonable presumption that parents have their children's best interest at heart. Further, not directly compensating the child appears not to respect the child as a developing, autonomous person.

One potential approach to the problem is to offer the child some age-appropriate token for participation, such as a small toy, a gift certificate, or a fast-food lunch. Reimbursement for the parents would be only for their time and expenses (e.g., the reimbursement model previously described). This approach would probably carry the smallest risk of undue inducement, while still recognizing the developing autonomy of the child.

IRB Responsibilities

As the proportion of studies offering payment for participation shows no evidence of decreasing, it is essential that IRBs develop guidelines to judge the appropriateness of payment schemes. Such guidelines require consensus within the board and within the community of stakeholders. This is especially difficult considering the multiplicity of ethical arguments for and against each payment model (and indeed, for and against payment per se).

Nonetheless, at a minimum, guidelines developed by IRBs should require that compensation is not of a nature that it interferes with the ability of the potential subject to give informed consent. This is without the possibility of coercion or undue influence (understanding, of course, that the meaning of this is nebulous at best). IRB guidelines should also stress the need for prorating compensation and define the limited situations under which such proration is not needed. Finally, guidelines should address the particularly sensitive issues related to direct compensation of minors.

Conclusion

Paying people to participate in research is one of the most contentious issues that IRBs deal with on a regular basis. This chapter has reviewed the regulations applicable to the payment issue and the ethical arguments both for and against monetary rewards for research participation. When an IRB does permit payment to participate in research, the IRB will need to establish criteria that define the characteristics of an acceptable payment structure. Four basic payment models have been discussed in the literature on this subject: the market model, the wage payment model, the reimbursement model, and the fair share model. The goal of this chapter is to give IRB members the information they need to evaluate research payment programs in a way that is consistent with the appropriate ethical standards.

References

1. Ackerman T. An ethical framework for the practice of paying research subjects. *IRB: A Review of Human Subjects Research* 11(4):1–4, 1989.
2. McGee G. A piece of my mind: Subject to payment? *JAMA* 278(3):199–200, 1997.
3. Macklin R. Due and undue inducements: On paying money to research subjects. *IRB: A Review of Human Subjects Research* 3(5):1–6, 1981.
4. Wartofsky M. On doing it for money. In: *Research involving prisoners: report and recommendations*. 1976. Washington, DC, National Commission for the Protection of Human Subjects of Biomedical and Behavioral Research.
5. Hassar M, Pocelinko R, Weintraub M, Nelson D, Thomas G, Lasagna L. Free-living volunteer's motivations and attitudes toward pharmacologic studies in man. *Clin Pharmacol Ther* 21(5):515–519, 1977.
6. Van Gelderen C E, Savelkoul T J, Van Dokkum W, Meulenbelt J. Motives and perception of healthy volunteers who participate in experiments. *Eur J Clin Pharmacol* 45(1):15–21, 1993.
7. Whinnery J E. Motivational analysis of human volunteers for centrifuge acceleration research. *Aviat Space Environ Med* 53(10):1017–1020, 1982.
8. Bigorra J, Banos J E. Weight of financial reward in the decision by medical students and experienced healthy volunteers to participate in clinical trials. *Eur J Clin Pharmacol* 38(5):443–446, 1990.
9. Novak E, Seckman C E, Stewart R D. Motivations for volunteering as research subjects. *J Clin Pharmacol* 17(7):365–371, 1977.
10. Aby J S, Pheley A M, Steinberg P. Motivation for participation in clinical trials of drugs for the treatment of asthma, seasonal allergic rhinitis, and perennial nonallergic rhinitis. *Ann Allergy Asthma Immunol* 76(4):348–354, 1996.
11. Russell M L, Moralejo D G, Burgess E D. Paying research subjects: Participants' perspectives. *J Med Ethics* 26:126–130, 2000.
12. Code of Federal Regulations. Title 45A—Department of Health and Human Services; Part 46—Protection of Human Subjects. Updated 1 Oct 1997. Access date 18 Apr 2001. World Wide Web http://www4.law.cornell.edu/cfr/45p46.htm
13. Code of Federal Regulations. Title 21, Chapter 1—Food and Drug Administration, DHHS; Part 50—Protection of Human Subjects. Updated 1 Apr 1999. Access date 18 Apr 2001. World Wide Web http://www4.law.cornell.edu/cfr/21p50.htm
14. Code of Federal Regulations. Title 21, Chapter 1—Food and Drug Administration, DHHS; Part 56—Institutional Review Boards. Updated 1 Apr 1999. Access date 27 Mar 2001. World Wide Web http://www4.law.cornell.edu/cfr/21p56.htm
15. Food and Drug Administration. Information Sheets: Guidance for Institutional Review Boards and Clinical Investigators, Sept 1998. Access date 9 Apr 2001. World Wide Web http://www.fda.gov/oc/oha/IRB/toc.html
16. Penslar R L, Porter J P, Office for Human Research Protections. Institutional Review Board Guidebook, ed. 2. 6 Feb 2001. Access date 29 Mar 2001. World Wide Web http://ohrp.osophs.dhhs.gov/irb/irb_guidebook.htm

17. Office for Human Research Protections. Compliance Oversight, 12 Dec 2000. Access date 20 Mar 2001. World Wide Web http://ohrp.osophs.dhhs.gov/compovr.htm

18. World Medical Association. *Declaration of Helsinki: Ethical Principles for Medical Research Involving Human Subjects.* World Medical Association, Inc.: WMA Policy. First adopted in Helsinki, Finland, in 1964. Updated 10 Jul 2000. Access date 20 Mar 2001. World Wide Web http://www.wma.net/e/policy/17-c_e.html

19. Council for International Organizations of Medical Sciences. *International Ethical Guidelines for Biomedical Research Involving Human Subjects.* 1993. Geneva.

20. Dickert N, Grady C. What's the price of a research subject? Approaches to payment for research participation. *N Engl J Med* 341(3):198–203, 1999.

21. Titmuss R. *The Gift Relationship: From Human Blood to Social Policy.* New York: New Press. 1997.

22. Murray T H. Gifts of the body and needs of strangers. *Hastings Cent Rep* 17(2):30–38, 1987.

23. Saunders C A, Sugar A M. What's the price of a research subject? *N Engl J Med* 341(20):1550–1551, 1999.

Provisions for Data Monitoring

Robert J. Amdur

INTRODUCTION

One criterion for IRB approval of research at the time of initial protocol review is that the study plan makes adequate provisions for the ongoing monitoring of data throughout the life of the study. Ongoing data monitoring is important because study results may differ from what was predicted prior to starting the study. The purpose of this chapter is to explain the responsibilities of the IRB at the time of initial protocol review related to the plan for data monitoring. As data-monitoring procedures are important to the IRB throughout the course of a study, there is overlap of this chapter with those in the continuing review section of this book.

Federal Regulations

Federal regulations and guidance documents make it clear that the IRB has a responsibility to determine that the research plan provides for the ongoing monitoring of data in a way that is sufficient to protect the welfare of research participants: DHHS regulations[1][Sec.111(a)(6)] and FDA regulations[2][Sec.111(a)(6)] state a criterion for IRB approval of research is that "when appropriate, the research plan makes adequate provisions for monitoring the data collected to ensure the safety of subjects."

The OPRR *IRB Guidebook*[3(pp3-9)] states, "At the time of initial review, the IRB should determine whether an independent data and safety monitoring board or committee is required, and should also set a date for reevaluating the research."

Limitations of the IRB

In many situations, it will be appropriate to have an individual or group other than the IRB take primary responsibility for data and safety monitoring throughout the course of a study. The three main options that the IRB will need to consider in this regard are discussed in the next section. First, however, it is important to understand a basic controversy that may affect the standards that the IRB should use to approve a data-monitoring plan at the time of initial protocol review. This controversy concerns the role of the IRB in analyzing individual adverse data events, particularly adverse events from multicenter trials.[4] Basically, an IRB must decide if it is going to take responsibility for analyzing individual event reports from the standpoint of making aggregate comparisons.

The role of the IRB in evaluating individual adverse event reports (AERs) is discussed in detail in several other sections of this book. The IRB's job is to protect the rights and welfare of research participants. Theoretically, IRB review of AERs from an ongoing clinical trial might result in study modification or the notification of participants about new findings that may affect their decision to continue research participation. However, for review to be meaningful, the IRB must be able to recognize when an event is in some way unexpected for the study population. When the study population is small and the adverse event is exotic in nature, or being reported at an extremely high frequency, a local IRB might be able to recognize an important pattern simply by reviewing AERs that are forwarded from the investigator. However, when the study population is large and diverse, as is the case with most multicenter clinical trials, a local IRB does not have access to the information it needs to evaluate the importance of AERs in the overall context of the trial. The problem is best illustrated with an example.

Example

An IRB receives four AERs of fatal stroke from a large multicenter trial of a new chemotherapy regimen for breast cancer. To make a decision about the importance of these AERs, the IRB needs to know if the observed incidence of stroke exceeds what is expected to occur in this study population independent of research participation. This type of evaluation requires sophisticated information about the number of participants at risk for stroke and the distribution of stroke risk factors in the study population. If the observed exceeds the expected incidence of stroke, the IRB will need to know if this difference is statistically significant and clinically meaningful in the context of the other medical problems in this population. As the IRB does not have the data base, administrative support, or expertise to evaluate these parameters, it is impossible for the IRB to make even a rough estimate about how these or other AERs might affect the rights and welfare of study participants.

For many kinds of studies, meaningful evaluation of study events requires a group of experts with the resources to monitor data in an ongoing fashion and to compare event data with predetermined stopping or modification rules. Sophisticated statistical analyses are often essential for meaningful ongoing monitoring from the standpoint of protecting research participants. The IRB cannot function as a data-monitoring committee for studies when sophisticated data monitoring is required.[4] A panel of experts convened to evaluate the issue of data monitoring in clinical research concluded: "Institutional review boards should not be forced to function as data-monitoring committees, and there should be no overlap of their functions."[5]

Federal Policy Statements

It is reasonable to interpret federal regulations to mean that the IRB is responsible for being sure that there is a mechanism in place to perform a high-quality evaluation of study data throughout the course of the study, but the IRB need not be that mechanism. In the past few years, multiple federal policy statements have supported this view.

1998 National Institutes of Health (NIH) Policy Statement "Data and safety monitoring is required for all types of clinical trials, including physiologic, toxicity, and dose finding studies (Phase I); efficacy studies (Phase II); efficacy, effectiveness and comparative trials (Phase III); etc.... The data and safety monitoring functions and oversight of such activities are distinct from the requirement for study review and approval by an Institutional Review Board."[6]

2000 NIH Policy Statement This statement discusses data monitoring requirements in Phase I and Phase II trials.

For Phase I and Phase II clinical trials, investigators must submit a general description of the data and safety monitoring plan as part of the research application. A detailed monitoring plan . . . must be included as part of the protocol and submitted to the local IRB and reviewed and approved by the funding Institute and Center (IC) before the trial begins. We strongly encourage the IRB to review the plan. Each IC should have a system for appropriate oversight and monitoring of the conduct of clinical trials to ensure the safety of participants and validity and integrity of the data. IC oversight of the monitoring activities is distinct from the monitoring itself . . . ICs have the flexibility to determine the reporting requirements of adverse events.[7]

2000 OPRR Clarification Letter OPRR guidance in the form of a letter dated May 22, 2000, indicated the following.

. . . continuing review of research by the IRB should include consideration of adverse events, interim findings, and any recent literature that may be relevant to the research. OPRR recognizes that

such information may not be readily available to local investigators participating in multicenter clinical trials or their local IRBs. However, OPRR notes that such trials are often subject to oversight by a Data Safety and Monitoring Board (DSMB) . . . operating in accordance with the National Cancer Institute (NCI) policy . . . . In such circumstances, IRBs conducting continuing review of research may rely on a current statement from the DSMB indicating that it has reviewed study-wide adverse events, interim findings, and any recent literature that may be relevant to the research, in lieu of requiring that this information be submitted directly to the IRB.[8]

Three Basic Options for Data Monitoring

As previously explained, federal regulations require that the IRB determine that "the research plan makes adequate provisions for monitoring the data collected to ensure the safety of subjects."[1[sec.111(a)(6)]] When evaluating provisions for data monitoring, the first thing that the IRB should do is to determine whether the formal process of data and safety monitoring will be performed by an individual investigator, an internal monitoring group employed by the study sponsor, or an independent data and safety monitoring board (DSMB).

An Individual Investigator

When the study population is small and the range of study events that could have an important impact on the risks and benefits of research participation is narrow, it may be appropriate for the principal investigator to manage the data and safety monitoring. As stated in the 1998 NIH policy statement, "Every clinical trial should have provision for data and safety monitoring. A variety of types of monitoring may be anticipated depending on the nature, size, and complexity of the clinical trial. In many cases, the principal investigator would be expected to perform the monitoring function."[6] Subsequent guidance from the NIH discusses data monitoring by an individual investigator based on study design and risk level: "For many Phase I and Phase II trails, independent DSMBs may not be necessary or appropriate when the intervention is low risk. Continuous, close monitoring by the study investigator may be an adequate and appropriate format for monitoring, with prompt reporting of toxicity to the IRB, FDA, and/or NIH. In studies of small numbers of subjects, toxicity may more readily become apparent through close monitoring of individual patients, while in larger studies risk may better be assessed through statistical comparisons of treatment groups."[7]

A Group Representing the Study Sponsor

There is no formal term for this class of programs for data and safety monitoring. Some discussions simply refer to a "data-monitoring committee." The reason to define this general category is that with industry-sponsored research, the research plan may explain that data and safety monitoring will be performed "by the sponsor." What this usually means is that employees of the organization that is funding or directing the study will be responsible for analyzing study information to evaluate data integrity and the risk/benefit profile of research participation for current and future subjects. There are no federal standards that describe the composition of, or procedures for, monitoring groups other than DSMBs (discussed below). Conflict of interest is an important consideration when employees of the study sponsor have the primary responsibility for monitoring data from the standpoint of scientific integrity and participant safety.

Federal guidance statements do not directly explain when it is or is not acceptable for data monitoring to be done by the study sponsor. Guidance documents exist that explain the general conditions under which it is acceptable for an individual investigator to monitor study data, and others that suggest criteria for requiring an independent DSMB. But there is no federal guidance that provides definitive advice for the IRB when data and safety monitoring is too complex for a single investigator but may not meet the criteria that demand an independent DSMB. This middle ground is a confusing area for the IRB because it describes many industry-sponsored multicenter trials.

In the absence of published guidance, it is appropriate to consider oral recommendations that have been made in national forums. For example, at the October 30, 2000, meeting sponsored by the Public Responsibility in Medicine and Research (San Diego, CA), FDA representative Susan Ellenberg, MD, directed a workshop on data monitoring in clinical research. In this forum, Dr. Ellenberg explained that the type of sponsor-controlled monitoring systems that are routinely used in industry-sponsored multicenter trials are appropriate for studies in which death or severe disability is not a major risk of research participation. Dr. Ellenberg also explained that requiring independent DSMBs for such studies would have a negative impact on the progress of research in this country. She urged the IRB community to approve low- and moderate-risk research based on a plan whereby the study sponsor is responsible for data and safety monitoring. The 1998 NIH policy statement supports this message: "All clinical trials require monitoring. Monitoring should be commensurate with risks. Monitoring may be conducted in various ways or by various individuals or groups. These exist on a continuum from monitoring by the principal investigator . . . to the establishment of an independent data and safety monitoring board for a large phase III clinical trial."[6]

A Data and Safety Monitoring Board (DSMB)

In a discussion of clinical trial monitoring, the terms *DSMB* and *independent DSMB* are used interchangeably. A DSMB is a committee that is established specifically to monitor data throughout the life of a study to determine if it is appropriate, from both scientific and ethical standpoints, to continue the study as planned. In 1999, the National Cancer Institute established formal standards for DSMB composition and procedures.[9] Other federal agencies have referred to these standards when discussing criteria for IRB approval of research.

Basically, a DSMB is made up of an eclectic group of experts in the fields of medicine and science that are applicable to the study, individuals with statistical expertise, lay representatives, often administrators, and people from other backgrounds that are likely to help the committee make an unbiased assessment of study progress. In most cases, the DSMB is funded by the study sponsor, but the funding is independent of committee determinations, and DSMB members are not permitted to have affiliations or interests that could be affected by study outcome. DSMBs usually meet several times a year, but the frequency of discussion depends on the nature of the study. It is both complex and expensive to use a DSMB to monitor a study; therefore, a DSMB should only be required when it is unreasonable to consider other options.

Guidance Documents

Three federal guidance documents and one panel statement describe situations when data should be monitored by a DSMB. The statements differ in their recommendations. Several statements suggest that study design (Phase III versus I or II) is the critical factor for requiring a DSMB. Other statements suggest that risk level and the number of study sites should determine the need for a DSMB, independent of study design. The latest NIH statement introduces additional factors such as blinding and the vulnerability of the study population.

The Duke Working Group   "In definitive Phase III trials, we recommend that the sponsor allocate responsibility for safety evaluation to an independent data monitoring committee to minimize conflicts of interest among those making the necessary judgments during the trial."[5]

1998 NIH Policy Statement   "The establishment of data safety monitoring boards (DSMBs) is required for multisite clinical trials involving interventions that entail potential risk to the participants."[6] However, a later statement in this document suggests that DSMBs should be required in all Phase III trials, regardless of risk: "In 1994 the Committee on Clinical Trial Monitoring [presented] a strong recommendation that all [Phase III] clinical trials, even those that pose little likelihood of harm, should consider an external monitoring body. This policy affirms the Committee's recommendations concerning DSMBs."[6]

1999 NCI Policy Statement   "Phase I and Phase II studies may be monitored by the principal investigator/project manager, by NCI program staff or designee, or jointly. . . . All phase III randomized clinical trials supported by NCI require monitoring by a DSMB."[9]

2000 NIH Policy Statement   "The NIH already requires data and safety monitoring, generally in the form of DSMBs for Phase III clinical trials. For earlier trials (Phases I and II), a DSMB may be appropriate if the studies have multiple clinical sites, are blinded (masked), or employ particularly high-risk interventions or vulnerable populations."[7]

Communication Between the IRB and DSMBs

At the time of initial protocol review, the IRB should evaluate not only the provisions for data and safety monitoring, but also the plan to communicate the findings of the monitoring activity to the IRB. Several reports from the Office of the Inspector General have explained that a major problem with current monitoring programs is that IRB review of the activities of DSMBs and other monitoring groups is neither timely or substantive.[10] Many IRBs are unable to get access to DSMB or sponsor-run monitoring committee reports even when they formally request them.

Federal Policy Statements

To respond to this problem, several federal agencies have released policy statements that address the issue of IRB access to information about data and safety monitoring activities. These statements are presented below. The bottom line is that the 1999 NIH policy statement makes it clear that the IRB is expected to review a detailed plan for data and safety monitoring at the time of initial protocol review and to review interim reports from the DSMB during continuing review. The main focus of these statements is to require the study directors to make DSMB summary reports related to toxicity available to the IRB.

It is also important to note that these policy documents show that federal authorities expect the line of communication to be between the IRB and local investigators. It appears that the IRB is not supposed to speak directly to study directors or to the DSMB. This is spelled out most clearly by NCI policy in which the DSMB is instructed to send reports to the study leadership, who are in turn instructed to forward it to local investigators, who are then supposed to share it with the IRB. Note that the DSMB does not release outcome data before the general dissemination of final recommendations except under specific conditions, none of which involve the IRB. None of the statements specify how long an IRB should expect to wait to receive a DSMB report following a DSMB meeting.

1999 NIH policy statement Effective July 1, 1999, all multisite trials with DSMBs are expected to forward summary reports of adverse events to each IRB involved in the study. . . . Once a DSMB is established, each IRB should be informed of the operating procedures with regard to data and safety monitoring (e.g., who, what, when, where, and how monitoring will take place). If the IRB is not satisfied with the monitoring procedures, it should request modifications. . . . The DSMB's summary report should provide feedback at regular and defined intervals to the IRBs. The Institutes and Centers should assure that there is a mechanism in place to distribute the report to all participating investigators for submission to their local IRB. For example, after each meeting of the DSMB, the executive secretary should send a brief summary report to each investigator. The report should. . . . summarize the Board's review of the cumulative toxicities reported from all participating sites without specific disclosure by treatment arm. It should also inform investigators of the Board's conclusion with respect to progress or need for modifications of the protocol. The investigator is required to transmit the report to the local IRB.[9]

1999 NCI policy Statement responsibilities of the DSMB Following each DSMB meeting, provide the study leadership with written information concerning findings for the trial as a whole related to cumulative toxicities observed and any relevant recommendations related to continuing, changing, or terminating the trial. The study leadership will provide information on cumulative toxicities and relevant recommendations to the local principal investigators to be shared with their IRBs. . . . In general, outcome data should not be made available to individuals outside the DSMB until accrual has been completed and all patients have completed their treatment. At this time the DSMB may approve the release of outcome data on a confidential basis to the trial principal investigator for planning the preparation of manuscripts or to a small number of other investigators for purposes of planning future trials.[11]

Stopping Rules

This chapter began by reviewing federal regulations at §46.111(a)(6) that require the IRB to determine that "the research plan makes adequate provision for monitoring the data collected to ensure the safety of subjects." The first step in responding to this directive is to decide who—meaning what individual or group—should take primary responsibility for analyzing individual events to determine if the study should be modified to minimize risk to current or future research subjects. The basic options of an individual investigator, a group representing the study sponsor, or an independent DSMB are discussed above along with published guidance on standards the IRB should consider when making this decision. A level of detail that is not addressed in any of the regulations or guidance documents pertaining to this subject is the question of stopping rules. *Stopping rules* is the general term for specific and predetermined parameters that guide the data monitoring process. These parameters specify when and how research is revised, including the criteria for terminating the study, in response to interim data analysis. Some people may prefer to call these guidelines "revision rules." However, to simplify this discussion, the term *stopping rules* will be used to refer to any guideline that is established for the specific purpose of forcing a revision of the study protocol based on review of events that occur during the conduct of the study. Stopping rules are presented in a variety of ways depending on the nature of the study. Stopping rules should be specific about the endpoints that will be used and the decisions that will be made. The following example is instructive.

Example

A multicenter, industry-sponsored, single-arm phase II study of an investigational antifungal agent in patients with serious fungal infections that are refractory to first line standard therapy is proposed. The IRB application explains that the sponsor will perform the data and safety monitoring. The data-monitoring section of the protocol contains a detailed list of stopping rules based on statistical evaluation of aggregate data: "This multicen-

ter trial will be monitored after every 12th patient, with a recommendation for termination if the accumulating data provide evidence that the conventional response rate does not exceed the 17% rate observed in historical experience by at least 13%, that is, an increase to a 30% conventional response rate. A Bayesian monitoring scheme will be used, comparing data to the prior response experience of 192 patients treated on a variety of protocols at MDACC. The trial will be recommended for termination if the probability is less than 5% that the new target response level of 30% is achieved, based on data accumulated after every 12th patient."

The reason to discuss stopping rules in this chapter is that these guidelines establish the critical parameters of the data-monitoring process. Every study that involves significant risk to the participants should include a clear description of the endpoints that are going to be evaluated as part of the data-monitoring process and the decisions that are going to be made if these endpoints are reached. Stopping rules are a fundamental part of the research methods. These guidelines should be presented as part of the research plan at the time of initial protocol review.

When the protocol application describes stopping rules, then, clearly, IRB approval of the study requires that the IRB approve these guidelines. However, many study applications do not describe stopping rules, or at least do not describe them in much detail. In this situation, the IRB must operate without guidance from federal authorities. Is it acceptable for the IRB to approve a study application that explains that data will be monitored by an investigator, the sponsor, or a DSMB, but does not describe the stopping rules that will guide protocol revision? In my opinion, the answer is no. Stopping rules are an essential feature of ethical research. A study plan that does not describe guidelines that are appropriate in detail and content does not give the IRB the information it needs to conclude that the research plan makes "adequate provision for monitoring the data collected to ensure the safety of subjects" as required by federal regulations. IRB policy should require a careful review and approval of stopping rules at the time of initial protocol review.

Conclusion

1. *The research plan should provide for data and safety monitoring.* The IRB should understand that federal regulations require that the IRB determine that the research plan makes provisions for data and safety monitoring that are sufficient to protect the rights and welfare of research participants.

2. *The IRB should not be the primary mechanism for data and safety monitoring.* The IRB should interpret federal research regulations to mean that the IRB is required to determine that an appropriate monitoring mechanism is in place prior to starting the study, but the IRB need not be that mechanism.

3. *The IRB should not attempt to function as a data monitoring committee.* When a study involves a large number of subjects and multiple study sites, the IRB will not be capable of performing the type of data comparisons and analyses

that are required to make the data-monitoring process meaningful from the standpoint of protecting research subjects.

4. *The research plan should describe the basic parameters of the data monitoring process.* All IRB applications should include a section that describes a plan for data and safety monitoring. The information in this section should permit the IRB to determine that the plan is adequate to protect research participants.

   a. The IRB should be told whether the plan is to assign the responsibility for data and safety monitoring to an individual investigator, the sponsor, or a DSMB.

   b. If the study sponsor will be responsible for data and safety monitoring, the IRB application should explain the number of people who will be responsible for this task and their qualifications to function in this capacity.

   c. The IRB application should describe the planned frequency of data analysis. Will data be analyzed on a per time basis (e.g., every six months), on a per subject basis (e.g., after every 10 subjects), or in response to specific events (e.g., after any fatality)?

   d. The IRB should require a description of stopping rules regarding the potential outcomes of the study that are likely to have a major impact on the rights or welfare of research participants.

5. *The IRB should establish criteria for requiring a DSMB.* The IRB should understand that federal guidance statements do not establish unambiguous criteria that the IRB can use to determine when an independent DSMB should be a requirement for approval of research. The following guidelines may be useful when evaluating a plan for data and safety monitoring.

   a. Do not require a DSMB if it is reasonable to accept an alternative option. An independent DSMB is complicated and expensive to assemble. The IRB should require a DSMB only in those situations where there is no other reasonable alternative.

   b. First, decide if data monitoring requires sophisticated capabilities. The first thing to decide is if a committee with the resources to perform sophisticated statistical comparisons or aggregate data analyses is required to make data monitoring meaningful from the standpoint of protecting research participants. If this is the case, then it is not acceptable for data monitoring to be done by an individual investigator, and it is unlikely that it would be acceptable to approve a plan where data monitoring would be done by a small group of employees of the sponsor. When data monitoring requires sophisticated capabilities, then the IRB should require an independent DSMB or an appropriately constructed data-monitoring committee that is employed by the study sponsor. The IRB should understand that commercial sponsors have a long track record of administering complex data-monitoring programs with good results in terms of the protection of research participants.

   c. Decide if conflict of interest is likely to bias the data-monitoring process. Conflict of interest is discussed in other chapters in the book. There are no absolute guidelines for making this determination. The NIH, NCI, and Duke Working Group statements presented above all require DSMBs for Phase III trials. IRBs should follow this recommendation with the understanding that a Phase III trial refers to a large multicenter trial that is being done to make a definitive determination about the efficacy of a study agent, usually to support an application for FDA approval. There are prospective, randomized trials that do not present the same issues regarding potential bias and conflict of interest. These trials would not be considered Phase III by FDA criteria and may not require DSMBs.

With single arm studies (including FDA categories Phase I and II), the IRB must evaluate the potential for bias on a case-by-case basis. It is appropriate for an individual investigator or the study sponsor to monitor data in many of the trials in this category. The most recent NIH policy statement implies that multiple clinical sites, blinding, high-risk interventions, or vulnerable populations should be considered as absolute indicators for the need for data monitoring by an independent DSMB. The IRB should consider these factors carefully when evaluating the potential for bias that might result from a sponsor-directed monitoring system.

References

1. Code of Federal Regulations. Title 45A—Department of Health and Human Services; Part 46—Protection of Human Subjects. Updated 1 Oct 1997. Access date 18 Apr 2001. World Wide Web http://www4.law.cornell.edu/cfr/45p46.htm

2. Code of Federal Regulations. Title 21, Chapter 1—Food and Drug Administration. Part 56—Institutional Review Boards. Updated 1 Apr 1999. Access date 27 Mar 2001. World Wide Web http://www4.law.cornell.edu/cfr/21p56.htm

3. Penslar R L, Porter J P, Office for Human Research Protections. *Institutional Review Board Guidebook.* Updated 6 Feb 2001. Access date 29 Mar 2001. World Wide Web http://ohrp.osophs.dhhs.gov/irb/irb_guidebook.htm

4. Bankert E, Amdur R J. The IRB is not a data and safety monitoring committee. *IRB: A Review of Human Subjects Research* 22(6):9–10, 2000.

5. Morse M A, Califf R M, Sugarman J. Monitoring and ensuring safety during clinical research. *JAMA* 285(9):1201–1205, 2001.

6. National Institutes of Health. NIH Policy for Data and Safety Monitoring. Updated 10 Jun 1998. Access date 29 Mar 2001. World Wide Web http://www.nih.gov/grants/ guide/notice-files/not98-084.html

7. National Institutes of Health. Further Guidance on a Data and Safety Monitoring for Phase I and Phase II Trials. Updated 5 Jun 2000. Access date 29 Mar 2001. World Wide Web http://grants.nih.gov/grants/guide/notice-files/ NOT-OD-00-038.html

8. Director Division of Human Subjects Protection, DHHS. Continuing Review of DSMB-Monitored Clinical Trials. Updated 22 May 2000. Access date 18 Apr 2001. World Wide Web http://ohrp.osophs. dhhs.gov/humansubjects/guidance/ dsmb.htm

9. National Institutes of Health. Guidance on Reporting Adverse Events to Institutional Review Boards for NIH-Supported Multicenter Clinical Trials (from *NIH Guide* for June 11, 1999). Access date 29 Mar 2001. World Wide Web http://grants.nih.gov/grants/guide/notice-files/ not99-107.html

10. Office of Inspector General D. Protecting Human Research Subjects: Status of Recommendations (OEI-01-97-00197). Department of Health and Human Services. Apr 2000. Access date 9 Apr 2001. World Wide Web http://oig.hhs.gov/oei/reports/a447.pdf

11. National Cancer Institute. Policy of the National Cancer Institute for Data and Safety Monitoring of Clinical Trials, 22 Jun 1999. Access date 9 Apr 2001. World Wide Web http://deainfo/nci/nih.gov/grantspolicies/ datasafety.htm

Conflict of Interest: Researchers

Daniel K. Nelson

"If you have no conflict of interest, then you would stand out like a sore thumb."
Clinical trials investigator, 1999

INTRODUCTION

Conflicts of interest are inherent to the conduct of research. This was recognized in 1978 by the National Commission for the Protection of Human Subjects of Biomedical and Behavioral Research, which wrote that ". . . investigators are always in positions of potential conflict by virtue of their concern with the pursuit of knowledge as well as the welfare of the human subjects of their research."[1] The Commission echoed earlier reports by the National Institutes of Health (NIH) and the Surgeon General in viewing investigators as poorly positioned to reconcile these competing interests on their own, and in calling for a shared responsibility that incorporated independent review (e.g., the Institutional Review Board [IRB]). The National Bioethics Advisory Commission (NBAC) reiterated this fundamental observation over 20 years later in their current examination of our system of protections, noting that research "necessarily creates a conflict of interest for investigators" through their use of fellow humans to obtain knowledge.[2] Note that neither commission held these conflicts to be irreconcilable, nor did they link conflict of interest to character flaws of investigators as individuals or as a class.

Notwithstanding this prior recognition, several factors have converged to propel conflict of interest to the forefront as one of the major concerns facing IRBs at the turn of the 21st century. These factors include increased funding of research, increased competition, greater involvement of commercial interests, larger payoffs for successful outcomes, more direct participation of investigators and institutions in those rewards, and a shift in the settings where research is performed. Against that background, several recent events have lent credence to the growing sense of concern. The tragic death of Jesse Gelsinger in a gene transfer study in 1999 has prompted a reexamination of many aspects of human subjects research, but perhaps no single aspect more than conflict of interest.[3-7] The goals of this chapter are to define conflict of interest and provide examples, to describe how the research environment has evolved in ways that increase the opportunity for conflicts, to review existing regulations, and to discuss possible management strategies.

Definitions

Before considering conflicts of interest as they relate to research involving human subjects, it is important to establish a working definition. Explaining what we mean by *conflict of interest* is not straightforward because it is difficult to apply this concept to the situations that we encounter in research or in many other areas of modern life.[8] One source of confusion lies in the semantics of the discussion.[9] The problem that we are trying to avoid is bias in judgment. We are looking for a term to describe situations where the potential for bias is such that decisions may be called into question. This is of particular concern in relation to professional roles or obligations, especially those that come with positions of trust.

One of the most misunderstood aspects of conflict of interest is that the problem may exist in the absence of documentation of bias or improper decisions. Saying that a conflict of interest exists does not mean that somebody made the wrong decision. It means that people who evaluate the situation may reasonably conclude that the potential for bias is such that improper decisions are possible. In other words, it is the people who evaluate the decision who determine if a conflict of interest exists, not the person making the decisions. As Friedman explains, ". . . a conflict exists whether or not decisions are affected by the personal interest; a conflict of interest implies only the potential for bias or wrongdoing, not a certainty or likelihood."[9]

For the purposes of this chapter, a *conflict of interest* can be defined[5,8,10,11] as a set of conditions in which an investigator's judgment concerning a primary interest (e.g., subject's welfare, integrity of research) may be biased by a secondary interest (e.g., personal gain).

With regard to financial relationships, Angell[5] has defined conflict of interest as "any financial association that would cause an investigator to prefer one outcome . . . to another." Angell goes on to argue that there is no such thing as "potential" conflict of interest because conflict is a function of the situation, and not of the investigator's response to that situation. Thus, the opportunity need not be acted on to represent a conflict of interest and a situation worthy of concern.

Sources of Conflict of Interest in Research

Although the following discussion will largely focus on financial incentives, it is important to recognize that there are many rewards associated with research that are not directly linked to money. Clearly, many investigators are driven by pursuit of knowledge in its purest sense. The altruistic desires to advance scientific frontiers, contribute to society, alleviate suffering, and improve lives are powerful motivators. So, too, are more personal goals that become important to many investigators, including respect of peers, appointments, promotions, tenure, grants, fame, prizes, and the publications that support all of the above. Some have argued that these academic pressures present greater conflicts than the prospect for material gain. Anyone who has observed the battles that can be waged over authorship or tenure may be hard-pressed to disagree. But these academic incentives are embedded within the fabric of research. They are widely recognized and broadly shared, and therefore tend to be viewed with less concern.[5,6,12,13]

Most recently, attention has been focused on financial conflict of interest in clinical research, where both the risks and the rewards are potentially the greatest. Examples of such interests include equity holdings in commercial sponsors, consulting fees, royalties, patent rights, and honoraria for serving on advisory boards or for giving lectures. Any of these may be problematic if linked to the sponsor of research or the product under study. Also of concern are scenarios where faculty may assign students or trainees to work on projects from which the investigator stands to benefit financially. Even the negotiated budgets to compensate investigators and institutions for conducting research may represent sizable conflicts of interest, depending on how they are structured and how the resulting revenues are handled.[14–17]

There is ample evidence that health care providers preferentially refer patients to facilities in which they hold a personal financial stake.[5,8] Given incentive, investigators might similarly be inclined to enroll as many subjects as possible, push the limits on entry criteria, promote research participation when other alternatives might be preferable, or report positive findings when results are equivocal. At a minimum, even the appearance of conflict calls into question the judgment of the investigator and the integrity of the process. This is no small matter if it jeopardizes the trust and confidence of the public. At its worst, conflict of interest may endanger lives—not only those of the immediate subjects under study, but those of future patients treated on the basis of biased results.[5,14,18] To understand why conditions today create increased opportunities for conflict, both real and apparent, requires an understanding of how clinical research has evolved.

Evolution of the Clinical Research Enterprise

"The modern investigator must be just as good a business person as a scientist."
Inaugural issue of Clinical Researcher, 2001

Once upon a time, most biomedical research was funded by the government and conducted in academic centers. The rewards were primarily related to advancement of knowledge. To be sure, advancement of careers and reputations was also a motivator, albeit of a different nature than the current focus on advancement of wealth. Clinical studies tended to be small in scale, observational, investigator-initiated, and relatively inexpensive.[8]

This began to change in the decades after World War II as both federal and industrial funding of research increased. The nature of clinical research also evolved, with large-scale, multicenter, randomized trials providing the safety and efficacy testing that society demanded before new products were brought to market.

This growth has continued to the present, with research-and-development investments by pharmaceutical companies increasing from $2 billion to $30 billion over the past 20 years (See "Industry Serves Through Innovation" in the Annual Report 2001-2002 of the Pharmaceutical Research and Manufacturers of America at http://www.pharma.org/publications/publications/annual2001.) The return on this investment for the manufacturers is also considerable, with many drugs now exceeding $1 billion per year in sales. Total spending on clinical trials by government and industry reached $4.5 billion in 2000 in the United States alone, and rapid expansion is now occurring in the international arena. Of this amount, only 20% is now funded by the government, with 80% coming from industry.[19]

In the 1990s, managed care influenced the clinical trial environment at several levels. At the corporate level, the economics of drug development changed such that companies could no longer increase their prices, as they had previously, to recoup costs and generate profits. This brought pressure to cut costs, move more drugs through the pipeline, and reduce time to market in order to beat competitors and maximize their time under patent protections. These pressures forced sponsors to reevaluate every aspect of drug development, including the sites they used to conduct their clinical trials. Academic medical centers were traditionally a locale of choice for conducting clinical trials, owing to their expertise, prestige, and access to large numbers of patients. As pressures mounted, however, sponsors came to view academic centers as "slow, inefficient, expensive, not always top-quality, and sometimes exasperating to work with."[20]

While IRBs were often identified as a bottleneck in this process, other institution-based entities (e.g., contracts and grants, office, sponsored programs, other peer-review committees) contributed to this perception of a clogged bureaucracy. Faced with a competitive, market-driven environment, sponsors were free to take their business where they pleased, and they did this by actively avoiding academic centers when selecting sites to conduct their trials. Filling the niche were independent sites, private-practice or hospital-based physicians not affiliated with academic centers, perhaps gathered into networks by site management organizations (SMOs). Contract research organizations (CROs) became a major force, allowing companies to outsource much of the work of managing their trials.[18,20]

As managed care exerted pressures on industry, it also created difficulties and opportunities for physicians at an individual level.[4,12,14,15,20,21] The difficulties came in the form of declining reimbursements by third-party payers as the costs of delivering care and maintaining practices continued to rise. But as managed care closed the door on fee-for-service reimbursement on the clinical side, many saw the opportunity to replace lost revenues by conducting industry-sponsored research studies. Clinical trials are now reimbursed on what amounts to a fee-for-service basis, presenting lucrative alternatives for physicians who were frustrated with HMOs and capitated payments. While some physicians incorporated research as a supplement to clinical practice, others effectively transferred their focus to conducting clinical trials. Thus was born a new player in this enterprise: the independent, for-profit investigative site.

With physicians based outside of academic centers looking to increase their involvement, sponsors were happy to engage this emerging workforce, which came unencumbered with the unwieldy bureaucracies of more traditional sites. As the number of sites conducting studies tripled during the mid 1990s, most of that growth occurred in office-based settings. The number of private-practice physicians involved in drug studies increased by 60% over a five-year span. Conversely, the proportion of trials conducted in academic medical centers dropped from 80% to 40% over the same period of time, during which the industry as a whole was enjoying steady growth. From a business perspective, academic centers lost market share.[14,20–23]

This migration of clinical trials away from academic medical centers has not gone unnoticed by those centers, which are facing many of the same financial pressures as community-based practices. A growing number have established clinical trials offices to centralize administrative processes, streamline IRB submissions and contract negotiations, and facilitate interactions with industrial sponsors.[22,23] Fewer than 10% of academic centers had such centralized structures as recently as 1997. Within three years, that number had increased to over 50% as academic sites regrouped to make themselves more competitive in the modern environment.[19] Some are also forming networks with community-based practices, to provide broader access to potential subjects. This effort is having the desired effect, and industry has begun to return to this traditional base. For the first time in a decade, academic centers are reporting increases in revenue from industry grants.[19]

As a backdrop to the economic pressures driving change at corporate, individual, and institutional levels, a change in federal law signaled a shift in the government's approach to the proceeds of research. In 1980, Congress passed the Bayh-Dole Act, which provided universities with incentives to move research results into commercial applications. Before Bayh-Dole, the government retained the intellectual property rights to technology developed through federal support. It was observed, however, that only a tiny fraction of publicly funded technology ever made it to the marketplace. The 1980 legislation encouraged academic institutions to patent new products, to license these products to industry, and to share resulting royalties with their faculty. This technology transfer paved the way for productive joint ventures between the nonprofit and for-profit sectors. It also, however, paralleled the evolution described previously in creating new and unanticipated opportunities for conflict of interest.[4,10,24,25]

The preceding discussion is intended neither to defend nor criticize the various players in this enterprise, but to describe its evolution and current state for readers expected to oversee research conduct. That growth and restructuring are occurring, driven by real-world market forces, is undeniable. Whether it can occur in a way that optimizes the safety and well-being of subjects is the question, and it represents a challenge for all involved.

Regulations and Guidance

Reflecting the increased attention to conflict of interest, the October 2000 revision of the Declaration of Helsinki contains guidance for physician–investigators and IRBs in this area.[26] Researchers are instructed to disclose "any possible conflicts of interest" (including sources of funding) to independent ethical review committees, to subjects, and in publications resulting from the research. There is no guidance as to what constitutes an inappropriate interest from the standpoint of IRB review.

With regard to U.S. federal regulations directed at IRBs, specific guidance is limited to removing members from review of projects in which they have a conflicting interest (e.g., as an investigator). Beyond that, there is little to guide IRBs in considering investigator conflict of interest. Conflict of interest for IRBs and their members is discussed in Chapter 5-13. The requirements for informed consent[27(Sec.116),28(Sec.20)] instruct: "An investigator shall seek consent only under circumstances that . . . minimize the possibility of coercion or undue influence." It can be argued that investigators who hold a significant conflict of interest in relation to a given study will be inclined, even if only subconsciously, to exert influence on subjects to enroll.[12] Similarly, IRBs must determine that risks are minimized, reasonable in relation to benefits, and disclosed to subjects. Conflict of interest can be viewed as one such risk.[27(Sec.111),29(Sec.111)] Although the regulations empower IRBs to act at their discretion, these readings require broad interpretations, and specific guidance is needed.[6,30]

Only recently have regulations begun to address investigator conflicts of interest. In July 1995, the Public Health Service (PHS, which includes NIH) and the National Science Foundation (NSF) issued guidelines that required disclosure and peer review of any "significant financial interests" held by investigators applying for federal funds.[3,4,31] NIH had first proposed guidelines in 1989 suggesting that conflicts should be prohibited, but these were viewed as overly restrictive by the research community and were withdrawn. The final rule[32(Sec.604)] gave research institutions discretion in how they would manage conflicts at the local level, and they are not required to report details to the government. The threshold for disclosure is $10,000 in income, $10,000 in equity, or 5% ownership in a company, if these might be affected by the investigator's research. Institutions receiving federal funds were charged with establishing and enforcing policies to "manage, reduce, or eliminate" the conflict of interest, once disclosed. With much discretion given to institutions, it is not surprising that considerable variability exists in implementation of these policies.[10,33,34]

In February 1998, the FDA issued a final rule[35] that required sponsors to certify the absence of financial interests of investigators who conducted their studies, or to disclose those interests. Such interests include patents, equity, or payments of $25,000 or more to support investigator activities outside of conducting the clinical study (e.g., equipment, honoraria, or consulting fees). This disclosure is tied to the submission of a marketing application to the FDA, and the intent is to protect the integrity of supporting data.

Beyond federal regulations, an increasing number of professional organizations have begun to establish policies to guide their members. For example, the American Society of Gene Therapy recommends that ". . . investiga-tors and team members directly responsible for patient selection, the informed consent process and/or clinical management in a trial must not have equity, stock options or comparable arrangements in companies sponsoring the trial."[36] Although this policy was prompted by problems in gene transfer trials, conflicts of interest are by no means limited to this small field, and it is hoped that other professional groups will take equally strong positions.

Managing Conflict of Interest

"Publicity is justly commended as a remedy for social and industrial diseases. Sunlight is said to be the best of disinfectants. . . ."
Supreme Court Justice Louis Brandeis, 1914

Disclosure

Disclosure to the Government Identification of conflicts is an important first step in managing them, and disclosure might occur at one or more levels. As previously explained above, disclosure to the government of investigator conflicts is required by federal agencies (e.g., FDA, PHS, NSF). In the case of grant awards, institutions are expected to manage the conflicts, and reporting of details to the granting agency is not required. In the case of marketing applications to the FDA, disclosure of investigator interests that might affect the reliability of submissions is made through the sponsor. Disclosure occurs at the time of submission to the FDA, after the study is completed, and does not apply to practices that might affect subjects (e.g., recruitment incentives; see Chapter 5-12). For these reasons, disclosure to the government does not impact the protection of research subjects in a substantive way.

Disclosure to the Institution Disclosure to the institution is mandatory for those investigators receiving federal funds, with their institutions given discretion in how they manage any conflicts. Predictably, there is considerable variability in how institutions handle this process.[10,33,34] Many, including the author's home institution, have established policies requiring disclosure by all faculty members. However, few institutions have linked this process to protection of human subjects, as suggested by the fact that none of 235 institutions recently surveyed incorporated disclosure to either IRBs or subjects as a management strategy in their conflict of interest policies.[34]

Several universities are currently working to strengthen the link between conflict of interest mechanisms and human subjects protections. A complete review of issues that institutions should address in their policies is outside the scope of this chapter, and perhaps outside the scope of IRB purview, but several recent reports provide guidance.[2,5,6,10,13,30,33,34,37] With regard to the broader goal of protecting all subjects, however, we must remember that a majority of industry-sponsored studies are now conducted at sites where there may be no institutional policies. That is,

Conflict of Interest: Researchers 201

there may be no "institution" beyond the investigator or research team, and therefore no local oversight.

Disclosure to the IRB Disclosure to the IRB is increasingly advocated as a routine part of protocol review. OHRP has strongly recommended that financial relationships are described when investigators submit IRB applications, and that IRBs should take into consideration the funding arrangements between sponsor and investigator institution.[30] A recent survey of 200 IRBs that oversee clinical trials suggests that only 25% review such financial matters.[37] These have tended to be regarded, by both investigators and IRBs, as "none of our business." IRBs should be aware of any interests on the part of investigators that are likely to bias their judgment or actions in areas that affect the rights and welfare of research participants.

Disclosure to Subjects Disclosure via the informed consent process is at once the most direct and ethically intuitive route of disclosure, but also the most difficult to accomplish in a meaningful way. At the very least, subjects should be aware that the study is sponsored by outside entities, be they commercial or governmental. The consent form might include a lay definition of what this means (e.g., ". . . investigators/institution are compensated for the costs of conducting this research . . ."), as sponsorship may not be understood by the public in terms we take for granted. As to the level of detail provided, I would stop short of advocating that consent forms include dollar amounts from routine study budgets, even when paid on a per capita basis. Although there may be a temptation, in the spirit of full disclosure, to suggest language like ". . . your study doctor will receive $7800 for enrolling you in this study," this begs additional clarification and may only confuse what is already a complicated process. Placing this statement in perspective demands that subjects also understand that (from this seemingly large amount) X goes to pay for the extra MRI scan done for research purposes only, Y goes to hire the study nurse who is attending to their needs, Z goes to institutional overhead, and so on. Thus, dollar amounts may be misleading because some may represent justifiable expenses, some may represent inappropriate incentives, and some may be both at the same time.

Subjects should certainly be made aware of any conflicts of interest on the part of investigators or institution that might affect their decision to participate. We should not take it upon ourselves to make that decision for them. On the other hand, IRBs should avoid "passing the buck" to subjects, who may not be in a position to fully integrate the information provided. An analogy might be drawn to disclosure of physical risks associated with the study. We routinely describe every possible adverse event, even though many are no more likely to occur than the chance that enrollment is swayed by financial incentives. If we accept conflict of interest as yet another risk, it is relevant to inform subjects, but disclosure alone is not sufficient.[2,24]

Managing Beyond Disclosure

Management strategies should be aimed at eliminating or minimizing conflict of interest. Some have argued that the only acceptable solution is a complete prohibition of interests that could potentially influence the research in an adverse manner. These observers would ban any institution or investigator from conducting research from which they stood to benefit. Others view that as an unattainable—perhaps even undesirable—goal in the modern environment. They advocate mechanisms to manage the conflict while still permitting what they perceive to be vital relationships to exist. This debate is ongoing,[3,5,13,24] and will not be resolved by this chapter. OHRP has, however, issued interim draft guidance that provides useful concepts to consider.[30] While IRBs may not be well situated or equipped to directly oversee this process, they should establish open lines of communication with those institutional bodies that are (e.g., conflict of interest committee). IRBs should then consider the mechanisms proposed to manage the identified conflict, with a particular eye for aspects that could affect research subjects. This could include removing the conflicted investigator from designing the study, obtaining informed consent, performing procedures, monitoring or reporting adverse events, or analyzing data. Readers may surmise that excluding investigators from any or all of these aspects of the study is tantamount to removing them altogether, and that remains an option if the IRB (with or without input from other entities) determines that a given conflict is unmanageable.

Simply put, the conflicted person should not be involved in any aspect of the research that could be influenced by that conflict. In some cases, the only way to accomplish that may be for investigators to divest themselves of their conflicting interest or identify someone else to conduct the research. If the latter approach is taken, the IRB should ensure that the substituted investigator is not subordinate to the conflicted investigator or otherwise situated so that this becomes a meaningless exercise, with the "real" investigator still controlling the study. The same rationale may be extended to institutional interests in a given line of research. If institutional holdings (e.g., major ownership in a start-up company) are such that the integrity of the research can be called into question, it may be preferable to perform the study elsewhere.

Given that even the appearance of impropriety is enough to damage individual careers and institutional reputations, it can truly be said that a cautious approach to these issues is in everyone's mutual interest. IRBs may first need to overcome the perception that managing conflict of interest is reliant on their trust of the investigator in question. Management should not hinge on anyone's perception of an individual, but on an objective assessment of situations in which people have placed themselves. All parties involved in this process should be clear that managing conflict of interest has everything to do with the situation, and nothing to do with the character or honesty of the individual. Here is another area where proactive education can be helpful by creating a culture of compliance that promotes self-identification and cooperative resolution of conflicts before they become problems.

Much of the foregoing presumes involvement of an institution, with institution-based mechanisms in place. Managing conflicts of interest in the extra-institutional settings where the majority of clinical trials are now performed presents an even greater challenge for the central IRBs that oversee these sites, for sponsors (who are themselves conflicted, by definition), and for the public at large.

Conclusion

At the time of this writing, initiatives are underway that may have a substantial impact on our thinking about and management of conflict of interest. Several groups, including the Association of American Medical Colleges, Institute of Medicine, NIH, NBAC, OHRP, and Congress have turned their attention to financial interests in research. The recommendations and policies that come out of these deliberations promise to provide guidance more in keeping with the modern research environment. Whatever form these guidelines take, they will represent a minimum floor, and IRBs would be well advised to establish policies in anticipation. It is difficult to imagine that local efforts could be overprotective of subjects in addressing conflict of interest, whether that protection is grounded in ethics, regulations, or common sense.

References

1. National Commission for the Protection of Human Subjects of Biomedical and Behavioral Research. Report and recommendations: Institutional review boards (DHEW (OS) 78-0008). 1978. Washington, D.C., Department of Health, Education, and Welfare.

2. National Bioethics Advisory Commission. Ethical and policy issues in research involving human participants (draft report). Bethesda, MD, U.S. Government Printing Office, 19 Dec 2000. Access date 20 Mar 2001. World Wide Web http://bioethics.gov/pubs.html

3. Agnew B. Bioethics: Financial conflicts get more scrutiny in clinical trials. *Science* 289(5483):1266–1267, 2000.

4. Andrews L B. Money is putting people at risk in biomedical research. *The Chronicle of Higher Education.* Washington DC, 10 Mar 2000, p. B4-B5.

5. National Institutes of Health. *Conference on Human Subject Protection and Financial Conflicts of Interest,* 15–16 Aug 2000 (transcript).

6. National Institutes of Health. Financial conflicts of interest and research objectivity: Issues for investigators and institutional review boards, June 2000. World Wide Web http://grants.nih.gov/grants/guide/notice-files/NOT-OD-00-040.html

7. Shalala D E. Protecting research subjects—What must be done. *N Engl J Med* 343(11):808–810, 2000.

8. Spece R G, Jr., Shimm D S, Buchanan A E. *Conflicts of Interest in Clinical Practice and Research.* New York: Oxford University Press. 1996.

9. Friedman P J. The troublesome semantics of conflict of interest. *Ethics and Behavior* 2(4):245–251, 1992.

10. Cho M K, Shohara R, Schissel A, Rennie D. Policies on faculty conflicts of interest at US universities. *JAMA* 284(17):2203–2208, 2000.

11. Thompson D F. Understanding financial conflicts of interest. *N Engl J Med* 329(8):573–576, 1993.

12. DeRenzo E G. Coercion of the recruitment and retention of human research subjects, pharmaceutical industry payments to physician-investigators, and the moral courage of the IRB. *IRB: A Review of Human Subjects Research* 22(2):1–5, 2000.

13. Korn D. Conflicts of interest in biomedical research. *JAMA* 284(17):2234–2237, 2000.

14. Eichenwald K, Kolata G. Drug trials hide conflicts for doctors. *The New York Times,* May 16, 1999.

15. Eichenwald K, Kolata G. A doctor's drug studies turn into fraud. *The New York Times.* May 17, 1999.

16. LaPuma J, Kraut J. How much do you get paid if I volunteer? Suggested institutional policy on reward, consent, and research. *Hospital and Health Services Administration* 39(2):193–203, 1994.

17. Shimm D S, Spece R G, Jr. Conflict of interest and informed consent in industry-sponsored clinical trials. *J Leg Med* 12(4):477–513, 1991.

18. Bodenheimer T. Uneasy alliance: Clinical investigators and the pharmaceutical industry. *N Engl J Med* 342(20):1539–1544, 2000.

19. CenterWatch Clinical Trials Listing Service. Home Page. Updated 2001. Access date 25 Apr 2001. World Wide Web http://www.centerwatch.com/

20. Lightfoot G, Getz K A, Harwood F, Hovde M, Rauscher S M, Reilly P, Vogel J R. Faster Time to Market, 1998. Access date 20 Apr 2001. Association of Clinical Research Professionals. World Wide Web http://www.acrpnet.org/whitepaper2/white_paper-home.html

21. Hovde M, Seskin R. Selecting U.S. clinical investigators. *Appl Clin Trials* 8:34–42, 1997.

22. Kowalczyk L. Drug trials branch from teaching hospitals: Suburban doctors answer call to help. *The Boston Globe.* Aug 16, 2000, p. C01

23. Maguire P. Marriage of town and gown brings clinical research to busy practices. *ACP-ASIM Observer* 21(1):1,14–16, 2001.

24. Angell M. Is academic medicine for sale? *N Engl J Med* 342(20):1516–1518, 2000.

25. Boyd E A, Bero L A. Assessing faculty financial relationships with industry: A case study. *JAMA* 284(17):2209–2214, 2000.

26. World Medical Association. *Declaration of Helsinki: Ethical Principles for Medical Research Involving Human Subjects.* World Medical Association, Inc.: WMA Policy. First adopted in Helsinki, Finland, in 1964. Updated 10 Jul 2000. Access date 20 Mar 2001. World Wide Web http://www.wma.net/e/policy/17-c_e.html

27. Code of Federal Regulations. Title 45A—Department of Health and Human Services; Part 46—Protection of Human Subjects. Updated 1 Oct 1997. Access date

18 Apr 2001. World Wide Web
http://www4.law.cornell.edu/cfr/45p46.htm

28. Code of Federal Regulations. Title 21, Chapter 1—Food and Drug Administration, DHHS; Part 50—Protection of Human Subjects. Updated 1 Apr 1999. Access date 18 Apr 2001. World Wide Web http://www4.law.cornell.edu/cfr/21p50.htm

29. Code of Federal Regulations. Title 21, Chapter 1—Food and Drug Administration, DHHS; Part 56—Institutional Review Boards. Updated 1 Apr 1999. Access date 27 Mar 2001. World Wide Web http://www4.law.cornell.edu/cfr/21p56.htm

30. Office of Human Research Protections. Draft interim guidance: Financial relationships in clinical research: Issues for institutions, clinical investigators, and IRBs to consider when dealing with issues of financial interests and human subject protection, 24 Jan 2001. Access date 20 Apr 2001. World Wide Web http://ohrp.osophs.dhhs.gov/nhrpac/mtg12-00/finguid.htm

31. Mervis J. Conflict of interest: Final rules put universities in charge. *Science* 269(5222):294, 1995.

32. Code of Federal Regulations. Title 42, Chapter 1—Public Health Service, DHHS; Part 50—Policies of General Applicability. Updated 2001. World Wide Web http://www4.law.cornell.edu/cfr/42p50.htm

33. Lo B, Wolf L, Berkeley A. Conflict-of-interest policies for investigators in clinical trials. *N Engl J Med* 343(22):1616–1620, 2000.

34. McCrary S V, Anderson C B, Jakovljevic J, Khan T, McCullough L B, Wray N P, Brody B A. A national survey of policies on disclosure of conflicts of interest in biomedical research. *N Engl J Med* 343(22):1621–1625, 2000.

35. Code of Federal Regulations. Title 21, Chapter 1—Food and Drug Administration, DHHS; Part 54—Financial Disclosure by Clinical Investigators. Updated 1 Apr 1999. Access date 25 Apr 2001. World Wide Web http://www4.law.cornell.edu/cfr/21p54.htm

36. American Society of Gene Therapy. Policy on financial conflict of interest in clinical research. Updated 5 Apr 2000. Access date 25 Apr 2001. World Wide Web http://www.asgt.org/policy/index.html

37. Office of Inspector General. *Recruiting human subjects: Pressures in industry-sponsored clinical research* (OEI-01-97-00195), June 2000. Access date 12 Apr 2001. World Wide Web http://www.hhs.gov/oig/oei/reports/a459.pdf

Conflict of Interest: Recruitment Incentives

Daniel K. Nelson

> *"When there is a possibility that you are going to get a car, you're going to do whatever you can."*
> **A Study coordinator offered a Honda Accord as an enrollment bonus**

INTRODUCTION

This chapter will focus on the various incentives that are offered to promote enrollment of subjects in clinical research. These include payments and other inducements to investigators, research staff, or referring physicians, but do not include payments to subjects themselves. Recruitment incentives may come in several forms, including enrollment bonuses, referral or finder's fees, and nonmonetary "perks" or rewards. For the purposes of this discussion, the distinguishing feature of these incentives is that they occur outside of the negotiated payments that represent compensation for work performed. Although budgeted payments may also represent considerable conflicts of interest, many ethicists find these additional incentives to be particularly troubling.

As discussed in other chapters, the clinical research environment has changed dramatically, and the resulting competition has placed sponsors under pressure to move new drugs through the development pipeline and get them to market faster than ever before. This pressure has translated into increasingly aggressive practices to recruit subjects into clinical trials. Thus, another distinguishing feature of these incentives is their intended purpose of spurring investigators to enroll as many subjects as possible, as quickly as possible.

Financial Incentives

Enrollment Bonuses

In keeping with the competitive nature of the clinical trials environment, a reward system has developed so that study sites are effectively penalized for enrollment that falls short of projected targets or proceeds more slowly than anticipated.[1-3] Conversely, faster-enrolling sites are rewarded. As an aside, this also explains why investigators are often frustrated with the pace of IRB review; they may be facing "competitive enrollment," which means that subjects are accepted on a first-come, first-served basis. Sites that are too slow in securing the necessary approvals from the IRB and other institutional entities (offices of research services, contracts and grants, etc.) may find all available slots filled and the study completed before they enroll their first subject. Once those approvals are obtained and enrollment begins, this time pressure remains and converts into yet another source for conflict of interest in recruiting subjects.

Because sponsors typically reimburse sites on a per capita basis, this reward system is, in one sense, embedded within the normal contractual process. However, it has now become commonplace that "bonuses" are offered outside of the negotiated budget. For example, investigators or study coordinators may receive a letter from the contract research organization (CRO) managing the study, urging them to find the last few subjects needed to meet the predetermined enrollment goals and offering additional payments for each subject. This typically occurs late in a trial when a deadline is looming, and is meant to stimulate what may be flagging interest on the part of study staff to find those last few patients. Depending on the study, these bonuses may range from a few hundred to several thousand dollars per subject. The CRO may itself be eligible for a bonus if enrollment targets are met by sponsor-imposed deadlines, so it becomes natural in this market-driven environment for the CRO to provide "trickle-down" incentives to their study sites. These sites are, after all, helping them to achieve their goals. From the

CRO and/or sponsor's perspective, this will be money well spent if it helps them retain the millions of dollars that may be lost with a delayed marketing approval.

While it can be argued that extra costs will be incurred in identifying these last few subjects, the amounts offered typically far exceed those costs, even if advertising is involved. Moreover, the budget negotiated to cover the actual cost of conducting the research often includes amounts for advertising or recruitment efforts. Thus, enrollment bonuses must be considered to be over and above actual costs, and may represent something approaching pure profit for the investigator. Sponsors may also approach study coordinators directly with these offers, recognizing that these staff are often the first points of contact with potential subjects. Whether investigators or study coordinators can accept these bonus payments may depend on institutional policies. Remember, however, that clinical trials are increasingly conducted in more entrepreneurial settings where profit-taking may not only be allowed, but encouraged. This stands in contrast to more traditional settings, where investigators are more likely to be prohibited from profiting personally.

Implications for IRBs There are few empirical data to document the prevalence of this practice, but what there are suggest that the use of bonuses is on the rise, tracking with the heightened economic pressures driving clinical trials. Ironically, there is also some suggestion that these financial incentives may be ineffective in accomplishing their intended purpose.[2,3] Nevertheless, the offering of enrollment bonuses is a feature of many clinical trials, and IRBs should be aware of the practice.

As with any study-related payments to investigator and/or institution, enrollment bonuses represent a potential conflict of interest. However, because the costs of conducting the study have already been covered in the initial budget, it can be argued that enrollment bonuses constitute an even bigger conflict. There is an inherent risk that such incentives might lead an investigator or study coordinator to inappropriately influence a potential subject's decision to participate. This might occur though downplaying the risks of a study, overselling the possible benefits, ignoring alternatives that might be available, overlooking medical history that might exclude a patient, or otherwise pushing the limits on entry criteria. The odds that members of the research team would consciously subvert the process in these ways may be quite small, but there is ample opportunity for subconscious influence. Recruitment, screening, and enrollment of subjects in a clinical trial is a complex, multistep process, involving subjective determinations that might be swayed by financial incentives.

At least two factors call into question the ability of IRBs to oversee this aspect of subject recruitment. First, IRBs have not traditionally had access to financial information regarding the studies they review, although this is now changing. Even when they do request budgetary information, IRBs may not be privy to bonuses offered after a trial is approved and running. Second, a recent survey suggests that the great majority of IRBs are uncertain about their authority to review financial incentives offered to investigators.[3] This may explain why so few IRBs evaluate this aspect of research in any detail.

This author's personal opinion is that IRBs hold regulatory and ethical imperatives to review any aspect of a clinical trial that might influence the enrollment or well-being of subjects, and that recruitment incentives are one such aspect. IRBs are encouraged to develop policies that require the disclosure of enrollment bonuses, including those offered as a trial progresses, so that all incentives might be reviewed in the context of subject recruitment. In general, IRBs should not approve a study in which investigators or their staff will receive an enrollment bonus.

Referral Fees

Referral fees, also called "finder's fees" or "bounties," are payments offered to physicians or other primary caregivers for identifying patients who may be eligible study subjects.[3,4] These might be offered at the suggestion of the sponsor or CRO but, unlike enrollment bonuses, would typically be offered indirectly, by or through the principal investigator. Like enrollment bonuses, referral fees are intended to promote identification and recruitment of subjects.

In one scenario, a specialist conducting a trial might send out "Dear Colleague" letters to primary care physicians who are more likely to come across patients fitting a certain profile, offering them $100 for every patient referred to the study. In another scenario, residents at a hospital might be offered certificates for textbooks or meals at a fine restaurant for identifying potential subjects. At some level, it might be argued that these amount to token gestures, particularly if the referring party performs any work in screening patients for eligibility criteria. In this case, the referring physician may actually be serving as an extension of the research team, and compensation of some sort may be appropriate. At another level, however, the payment of referral fees interjects an influence that may run counter to the fiduciary obligation of a primary caregiver. That is, the physician or nurse may be motivated by financial interests to refer a patient when such referral might not be of any benefit to the patient. There may, of course, be circumstances when research participation holds the potential for direct medical benefit and represents an option that the primary caregiver cannot offer. This might especially be true for patients with life-threatening illnesses such as cancer or AIDS, when trials are designed with therapeutic intent. These may also, however, be among the studies least likely to offer finder's fees to referring physicians.

The act of referring may also influence the potential subject's decision making if participation in research is perceived to be the recommendation of a trusted caregiver. Thus, referral could effectively translate into diminished autonomy for the patient considering participation. This is not an abstract possibility, given the difficulty many patients (and physicians) have in recognizing that research studies are not designed to treat each subject for his or her individual benefit (i.e., the "therapeutic misconception").

Implications for IRBs For the reasons previously discussed, many institutions have taken a stand against the practice of referral fees. For example, this author's home institution established a policy in 1990 that the IRB should "not approve of finder's fees being paid to physicians, nurses, and others who have a treating and/or counseling relationship to the patient being referred for enrollment in a clinical trial." This policy has support from the American Medical Association's Code of Medical Ethics, which states: "A physician may not accept payment of any kind, in any form, from any source, such as a pharmaceutical company . . . for prescribing or referring a patient to said source," and that "Offering or accepting payment for referring patients to research studies (finder's fees) is also unethical."[5(Sec.6.02,6.03)] Indeed, other authors have equated referral or finder's fees with fee splitting by physicians, which is prohibited in the clinical practice setting. The American College of Physicians has also taken a stand against this practice, holding that: "Giving finder's fees to individual physicians for referring patients to a research project generates an unethical conflict of interest."[6]

There would not appear to be any federal guidelines that specifically address referral fees, other than what might be extrapolated from requirements that promote a subject's voluntary and informed choice in a setting free from undue influence.[7(Sec.20),8(Sec.116)] The DHHS Office of the Inspector General, in its recent report on recruitment practices, identified referral fees as one of several questionable practices,[3] but this has yet to translate into regulatory requirements. Nevertheless, IRBs may wish to draft local policies and should, at the very least, establish mechanisms to screen for referral fees being offered by or through investigators under their jurisdiction. The acceptability of such offers can then be assessed on a case-by-case basis, with a particular eye toward potentially negative influences on subject recruitment.

Nonmonetary Perquisites or Rewards

A "bonus" of another kind involves nonfinancial incentives given as a study progresses or after its completion. As discussed in the preceding chapter, there are many rewards or outcomes associated with research that are not linked directly to money. Some have argued that concerns for promotions, tenure, publications, and grants provide motives more powerful than cash, but these tend to be linked to research productivity in a more global sense. That is, these rewards accrue to the study as a whole or, more likely, to a collective body of investigator-initiated work. In the present context, let us consider nonmonetary rewards that are linked more directly to the number of subjects enrolled, much like financial recruitment incentives.

Token Gifts

Token gifts might include lunches during sponsor site visits, gift certificates, baseball caps, coffee mugs, sweatshirts, or other articles of clothing. Emblazoned with the sponsor's logo, or perhaps even the study logo if the trial is large enough to warrant its own, these gifts may represent nothing more than token gestures of the sponsor's appreciation for the team's hard work. As such, they are often neither solicited nor offered, but simply arrive after the first subject is enrolled, perhaps increasing in value with subsequent subjects. Sponsors doubtless view these as innocuous gifts and/or subliminal reminders to keep the study in mind, and few could argue that a sweatshirt is likely to unduly influence an investigator's behavior.

Poststudy

Of greater concern are goal-oriented awards intended to stoke competition and interest, again serving much the same purpose as monetary bonuses. One of the most extravagant vacations this author ever took was an all-expenses-paid trip to Cancun, as a poststudy reward for having enrolled five subjects in a rather ordinary clinical trial. In return, the sponsor flew three members of our research team (plus spouses) to a luxury resort, where we joined similar groups from other sites that had also hit their enrollment targets. Ostensibly at an "investigator's meeting," we spent 30 minutes reviewing the results of the trial, and three days on the beach. Was this enjoyable? Absolutely. Did the prospect of being rewarded in this manner, advertised through periodic newsletters showing our enrollment in relation to other sites, color our judgment in recruiting subjects? I don't think so, and certainly hope not. But we had already been adequately reimbursed for the costs of conducting the study through the negotiated budget, with some profit built in. Given that I was serving as an IRB chair at the time, should I have recognized the conflict of interest and rejected this "perk"? Perhaps so, but neither I nor my colleagues nor several hundred honorable investigators perceived this as inappropriate. Am I being hypocritical in telling this story now, as an example of conflict of interest? Again, perhaps so. But I hope it illustrates the insidious nature of this reward system, and the very human response we can expect when investigators are offered what might be judged in hindsight to be a conflict. For me, this personal experience confirms yet again the fundamental observation that investigators are not always in a position to critically assess their own circumstances, despite the best of intentions.

Authorships

For some investigators, poststudy rewards may also come in the form of authorship on publications reporting a clinical trial.[1,9] In the past, papers were authored by the lead investigators who designed and conducted the study, analyzed the resulting data, and wrote the manuscript. This remains the case for "homegrown" protocols, but authorship on industry-sponsored research has evolved into yet another recruitment incentive. Manuscripts are increasingly drafted by the sponsor's medical writers, with authorship on the final publication offered to investigators who enrolled the most subjects, or to "names" in the field who may not have been involved in the actual research. Such "gift authorships" lend credibility to the resulting publication and constitute another element in the evolving reward system. These rewards may be especially important to those investigators from the academic sector, where publications represent a valuable form of compensation.

Future Participation

One final example in this category of rewards is the cultivation of high-enrolling sites as members of a pool from which the sponsor or CRO will draw in the future. Top-performing sites that meet (or exceed) their enrollment targets in a timely manner take on "most-favored site" status and will be invited to participate in future studies. Conversely, low-enrolling sites will be dropped. Again, this is a very logical approach in a market-driven environment, but the linkage to number of subjects enrolled makes this another form of recruitment incentive.

Implications for IRBs

Of the types of incentives discussed in this chapter, non-monetary perks or rewards may be hardest for IRBs to identify or assess. As with monetary bonuses, they may arise as a study progresses or after a study is complete, at which point the IRB may be removed from the process. Even if review is ongoing, disclosure is unlikely. Few institutions and even fewer investigators or sponsors are likely to regard these incentives as legitimate causes for concern. At some level, however, these rewards hold enough intrinsic value (e.g., cars, vacations) that its non-monetary nature becomes irrelevant. Something valued at several thousand dollars provides incentive as great as an equivalent amount of cash, perhaps greater if the cash is taxed in ways the gift is not. Tied as they are to number of subjects enrolled, these are recruitment incentives in their own right, and warrant consideration as potential conflicts of interest.

Conclusion

Recruitment incentives are a particularly direct expression of the pressures inherent to the current research environment. For all intents and purposes, this phenomenon is limited to the setting of industry-sponsored clinical trials. Whether these incentives come in the form of financial bonuses or referral fees, or as nonmonetary rewards that may include trips, gifts, or authorships, they represent sources for conflict of interest. As discussed in Chapter 5-11,

such incentives need not impact negatively on subjects to be a legitimate concern. That is, the potential for bias in judgment exists, even if conflicting motivations are not acted upon. IRBs should establish mechanisms to monitor recruitment incentives that may be offered in the studies under their purview.

References

1. Eichenwald K, Kolata G. Drug trials hide conflicts for doctors. *The New York Times.* 16 May 1999.

2. Harper B D. The effectiveness of sponsor/CRO-site performance incentives. *The Monitor (Association of Clinical Research Professionals)*:9–18, 1997.

3. Office of Inspector General. Recruiting human subjects: Pressures in industry-sponsored clinical research (OEI-01-97-00195). Department of Health and Human Services, June 2000. Access date 12 Apr 2001. World Wide Web http://www.hhs.gov/oig/oei/reports/a459.pdf

4. Lind S E. Financial issues and incentives related to clinical research and innovative therapies. In: Vanderpool H (ed). *The Ethics of Research Involving Human Subjects* (Chapter 8). Frederick, MD: University Publishing Group. 1996: 185–202.

5. American Medical Association. *American Medical Association's Code of Ethics.* Access date 7 May 2001. World Wide Web http://www.ama-assn.org/meetings/public/interim99/reports/bot/rtf/bot5i.rtf

6. American College of Physicians. *American College of Physicians Ethics Manual,* 4th edition: "The Ethics of Practice," and "The Changing Practice Environment." Access date 7 May 2001. World Wide Web http://www.acponline.org/journals/annals/01apr98/ethicman.htm

7. Code of Federal Regulations. Title 21, Chapter 1—Food and Drug Administration, DHHS; Part 50—Protection of Human Subjects. Updated 1 Apr 1999. Access date 18 Apr 2001. World Wide Web http://www4.law.cornell.edu/cfr/21p50.htm

8. Code of Federal Regulations. Title 45A—Department of Health and Human Services; Part 46—Protection of Human Subjects. Updated 1 Oct 1997. Access date 18 Apr 2001. World Wide Web http://www4.law.cornell.edu/cfr/45p46.htm

9. Bodenheimer T. Uneasy alliance: Clinical investigators and the pharmaceutical industry. *N Engl J Med* 342(20):1539–1544, 2000.

Conflict of Interest: IRBs

Daniel K. Nelson

INTRODUCTION

This chapter will review conflicts of interest that may face either the IRB as an entity or the individuals that contribute to the IRB's mission. Given the central role of IRBs in overseeing the ethical conduct of research involving human subjects, it is critical that they operate free from inappropriate influence. Accordingly, IRB members, Chairs, and staff should follow policies and procedures similar to those of investigators to eliminate or minimize any conflicts of interest. In this context, a *conflict of interest* could be defined as any situation or relationship that biases, or has the potential to bias, the conduct of IRB review.

Possible sources of conflict of interest for IRBs are listed as an appendix to this chapter. These might originate or be felt at individual or institutional levels. None of these scenarios or factors, in and of themselves, may represent unmanageable conflicts. But any of these could exert inappropriate influence on the IRB and should be considered.

Sources of IRB Conflict of Interest: Individual Level

Research by Members

Perhaps the most widely recognized conflict of interest for IRBs is when research conducted by one of the members comes up for review. The investigator–member has an obvious interest in seeing the research approved for a number of personal and professional reasons. Because this type of conflict is usually apparent, proper management is largely a procedural matter. Beyond this direct conflict involving review of members' own research, there are multiple sources for indirect conflict of interest. These may be harder to discern and, therefore, harder to manage.

Members' Financial Interests

One example of these less apparent conflicts would be situations where IRB members or staff hold significant equity or other financial interests in the research itself or in the sponsors of research. These might include equity holdings, consulting arrangements, or patent rights—in short, the same types of financial conflicts that investigators might hold. Although the majority of academic research institutions have policies governing financial conflicts of interest,[1] these invariably focus on faculty serving as investigators and not as IRB members. The same concerns would apply, however, regarding the objectivity of individuals who stand to gain financially from research they are being asked to review and approve.

Loyalty to Colleagues

Another potential source of conflict is loyalty to colleagues submitting research for IRB review, be they peers, subordinates, or superiors. Members might logically be inclined to support the work of departmental colleagues with whom they interact every day (i.e., more directly than with other IRB members). Beyond mere camaraderie, members may sense a need to promote the work of subordinates or to avoid antagonizing their chief with a critical review. At a practical level, this potential conflict may be impossible to avoid because few institutions are large enough to assemble a panel of individuals with sufficient insight who do not also have overlapping interactions with colleagues submitting research.

Members' Areas of Expertise

Selection of members with sufficient expertise to comprehend the complexities of the research under review presents another potential problem. Members whose training or own area of research is closely tied to the studies under review may tend to show more leniency than they might to other areas with which they are less familiar. That is, it may be natural for them to take novel issues or procedures for granted. Conversely, this familiarity might work in the opposite direction if reviewers regard submitting investigators as competitors or rivals and are more critical than they might be otherwise. Members in this position might also find themselves with access to proprietary information when reviewing protocols, providing tempting insight to ongoing research in their personal area of interest (i.e., "insider trading"). Whether overly lenient or overly critical, neither tendency is conducive to the objective review that the IRB should strive to achieve.

As an aside, the potential for biased reviews may be something for institutions to consider before establishing "specialty boards" as a means of focusing expertise in a given area. The increased insight that comes with this structure must be viewed as a trade-off for decreased diversity of perspectives.

Impact of Decisions

IRB members might also be mindful of the possible impact of IRB decisions on their own work. For example, an IRB member who does clinical outcome studies may be reluctant to support IRB decisions that strengthen privacy protection if these lead to policies that restrict his or her own access to medical records for research.

Personal Agendas

Personal agendas of members may also interfere with the review process. For example, members of an advocacy group for a given disease or disorder can yield valuable insight as community representatives, but can represent a negative influence if they see their role as promotion of a certain agenda.

Non-IRB Roles

The institutional roles filled by members in their daily work outside the IRB may carry inherent conflicts of interest. For example, the director of a university contracts and grants office, whose primary duties revolve around bringing more research support into the institution, may not be an appropriate individual to serve on the IRB. The same could be said for any institutional official charged with promoting or supporting the research enterprise if that obligation might run counter to a critical assessment of protocols. Indeed, reliance on individuals with these types of positional conflicts has been cited as an unacceptable situation in recent federal compliance actions.[2] Another institutional role that may exclude a person from IRB service is that of the legal counsel. Although legal counsel can be extremely helpful in an advisory capacity, a primary role of protecting the institution may run counter to the IRB's mission of protecting the subject. It can be argued that these goals are not incompatible to the extent that "a happy subject is a happy institution," but care must be exercised to avoid conflicting objectives.

The preceding discussion should not detract from the clear benefit of having IRB members with legal training, which is increasingly important for interpreting and applying regulations, interdigitating with state laws, and multiple other functions. Similarly, members with insight on the financing of research can provide valuable input to IRB deliberations. Nevertheless, care should be taken when appointing members who will be forced to wear too many institutional hats in serving the IRB.

Sources of IRB Conflict of Interest: Institutional Level

Protecting the Institution

Apart from any internal desire to protect the institution on the part of individual members, the institution must also avoid placing external pressure on the IRB to serve in this capacity. This may be a natural expectation for deans, provosts, presidents, and other officials and, again, is not necessarily incompatible with the role of the IRB, but should never be confused with its primary role. This separation of roles will be especially important to bear in mind as the penalties for noncompliance increase and institutions come to view their IRBs as a chief means of preventing regulatory sanctions.

Enhancing the Institution

In a more positive direction, a related source of conflict could arise from members' innate concerns for their institution's reputation or prestige, to the extent that it is enhanced through an active research portfolio. Once again, this desire is not incompatible with sound IRB review, but should never be an excuse for relaxing standards in the review of research.

Promoting Research

Yet another related concern is the desire on the part of individual members—and on the part of the IRB as an agent of the institution—to promote research in general. This is a laudable goal, but should never be pursued to the extent that it detracts from the IRB's reason for being, which is to protect the rights and welfare of human subjects.

Value of Membership

Undervaluation of service to the IRB is another factor that could translate into a conflict of interest. If members do not believe that their work on the IRB is appreciated or valued by their superiors, they may not believe that they can or should devote the time necessary to do the job well. Department chairs, deans, and other institutional officials should send a clear signal to their subordinates that IRB membership is a necessary and important activity, and recognize such service when considering promotions, tenure, and clinical work schedules. Some institutions are going beyond this by purchasing or "protecting" a percentage of faculty effort for IRB service.

Liability

The potential for legal liability is another factor that could influence an IRB's decision making. Although lawsuits implicating the IRB have been few in number and most institutions are likely to indemnify IRB members in the performance of their professional duties, the threat of lawsuit is an ever-present possibility in our litigious society. Possible sources of lawsuits include not only subjects who have been injured in research, but also investigators who believe their research has been unfairly hindered by an IRB. Liability of IRB members is the subject of Chapter 8-8.

Institutional or Community Values

Institutional or community values are another source of possible conflict to the extent they may be reflected in reviews by individual members or the IRB as a whole. Clearly there is a regulatory mandate[3[Sec.107(a)],4[Sec.107(a)]] that the IRB do exactly that (reflect community attitudes), but there may be times when these values run counter to the mission of the IRB. For example, some institutions may be particularly sensitive to social or political issues (e.g., abortion) in ways that run counter to regulatory guidance that IRBs should not consider the long-range public policy implications of research under review.[3(Sec.111)] This separation from institutional values may admittedly be difficult to achieve when beliefs are deeply held.

Pressure for Speed

IRB members or staff often come under pressure from individual investigators or from the institution to conduct speedy review. Although it may be in everyone's best interest to establish systems for review that are both effective and efficient, the process should not be hastened to the point that important issues are overlooked.

Institutional Holdings or Interests

Institutions are increasingly entering agreements with industry that may create conflict of interest for the institution itself. These arrangements might include patent rights for new innovations, spin-off companies, technology licensing, or equity holdings. (See Chapter 5-11.) If an institution will be conducting research in which it bears a direct financial interest, appropriate firewalls should be in place to ensure that ethical oversight (i.e., the IRB) is not subject to influence from the institution. If the independence of the IRB cannot be assured, it may be preferable to solicit the services of another IRB or to conduct the research at other institutions.

Review Fees

Finally, the charging of review fees may create a conflict of interest that biases IRB review. Institutions that compete successfully for federal grant support receive a sizable percentage in the form of indirect costs, which are intended to support a variety of functions necessary to conduct research. In a sense, these indirects have been subsidizing the handling of industry protocols, which did not generate the same kind of indirect pool. Many institutions, perhaps now the majority, have begun charging review fees for industry-sponsored protocols as a means of generating support for the IRB. These fees, ranging from a few hundred to a few thousand dollars, are legitimate sources of revenue for work performed. All parties should be clear, however, that the fees are linked to protocol submissions and are not contingent on approval by the IRB. It is also highly advisable that the fees be administered through mechanisms separate from the IRB (e.g., contracts and grants office, billing department, or other administrative entities), so that the IRB is not placed in the position of bill collector. Ideally, the IRB should operate in complete ignorance of the billing status of any individual protocol.

This also presents a conflict for independent, for-profit IRBs, which may derive their entire revenue from such fees. There is nothing inherently improper in this arrangement, and many independent IRBs conduct credible, ethical review. They are, however, subject to an added element of conflict because they are businesses in their own right. This makes them dependent on the good will and satisfaction of their clients (e.g., pharmaceutical companies or contract research organizations), who are free to take their business elsewhere. This might logically occur if reviews were consistently perceived as being nit-picky, unfavorable, or slow. Thus, independent IRBs may be subject to conflict of interest pressures over and above those facing institution-based IRBs. Conversely, it can be argued that independent IRBs are free from many of the influences discussed previously because they are not subject to institutional expectations and pressures. By definition, each setting will have its own particular set of motivating factors, and neither is free from potential conflicts of interest.

Regulatory Guidance

If the IRB is to function in an independent, unbiased manner, it must not be subject to inappropriate pressures. Recognizing this, federal regulations specifically addressed IRB conflict of interest long before investigator conflict of interest became a focus of regulatory guidance. Both DHHS[3(Sec.107(e))] and FDA[4(Sec.107(e))] regulations instruct that:

> No IRB may have a member participate in the IRB's initial or continuing review of any project in which the member has a conflicting interest, except to provide information requested by the IRB.

This means that each IRB should have clearly defined mechanisms for identifying conflicts among its members and for excluding conflicted members from a situation where review may be compromised.

Management of IRB Conflicts of Interest

In contrast to the enormous attention paid to investigator conflicts of interest in recent years, very little has been paid to similar conflicts on the part of IRBs. This may be partly because IRBs are not involved hands-on with the actual conduct of the study, and partly because those involved with ethical review are seen as somehow immune to baser instincts. For whatever reason, few authors or policy makers have specifically addressed the conflicts that might be faced by IRBs, or their resolution.[5] As with conflicts for investigators, the first (and perhaps most difficult) task is to recognize that a conflict exists. Once this potential is identified and acknowledged, steps should be taken to eliminate or minimize its impact.

For the purpose of discussion, let us consider the fairly routine scenario where an IRB member is involved as an investigator on the research under review, recognizing that many of the conflicts described above might be addressed through similar mechanisms. As with identification of conflicts for the larger pool of investigators outside the IRB, this process would typically rely on self-identification by the investigator–member. Once identified, written policies and procedures should describe how the conflicted member will be removed from deliberations on the protocol for which they hold the conflict.

Recusal of Members From Meetings

In the setting of a convened meeting, the most obvious solution is that the member in question should physically leave the room during consideration of that protocol. This approach minimizes two sources of influence, neither of them desirable. First, the investigator–member would naturally be inclined to give the protocol preferential treatment. Second, other members may not feel completely free to discuss openly or to criticize out of deference to their fellow board member. Thus, removal from the meeting is the clearest means by which to manage that member's conflict. Some IRBs, however, may wish the member to remain present for initial discussion to answer any questions, as they would any other investigator. As noted above, this is expressly allowed by the regulations. If an IRB chooses to adopt this as local policy, remaining members should be given further opportunity for discussion once the conflicted member eventually does leave the meeting.

In some circumstances, the IRB may be placed in an untenable position if the physical absence of a conflicted member would force the loss of quorum, thereby halting the meeting. This creates a catch-22 of sorts if the IRB would really prefer that any conflicted member leave the room, yet needs that member present in order to meet regulatory requirements for quorum. Under these circumstances, one would hope that the valid concept of having sufficient numbers present to conduct business (i.e., quorum) would give way to the intent behind these regulatory requirements, namely, to ensure that research undergoes review by an unbiased, independent body.

This author's personal opinion is that we may be missing the forest for the trees if it means compromising review by keeping a conflicted member present only to preserve an arbitrary quorum. This argument gains more credence when we remember that the minimum quorum under existing regulations only requires that three members be present (of the minimum five total members), and that most IRBs are much larger than that in practice, even at half strength. That is, one could envision a situation where an IRB with 20 members had 11 members in attendance, and wished to temporarily excuse a conflicted member. It is difficult to accept that the remaining 10 members are insufficient to conduct review, when 10 still represents thrice the number required for a duly constituted quorum under regulatory requirements.

All that said, the regulations do require the presence of a quorum,[3(Sec.108),4(Sec.108)] and the foregoing is not an argument to disregard that requirement. The best approach is to ensure that adequate numbers of members will be present so that quorum is never endangered. This can be accomplished through the use of alternates to cover absences, reminders on the days of meetings, and selection of members who will take seriously their commitment to attend.

Regulatory Guidance   Regulatory guidance on the question of conflicted members leaving the room is vague and subject to interpretation. As previously noted, the regulations themselves only state that the conflicted member should not "participate" in the review of a given project. The FDA has both clarified and reversed its position on this question. In the 1998 update of its Information Sheets, the FDA indicated that an IRB could lose quorum when members with a conflict of interest leave the room for deliberation and voting on a study[6] In a subsequent addendum, published February 1999, the FDA clarified that:

> The quorum is the count of the number of [voting] members present. If the number present falls below majority, the quorum fails. The regulations only require that a member who is conflicted not participate in the deliberations and voting on a study on which he or she is conflicted. The IRB may decide whether an individual should remain in the room.

Through still further clarifications, the FDA took an interim position that members who abstain from the vote are still counted as present even if they are required to leave the room for voting, so that an IRB would not lose quorum through conflicted members' abstentions. Most recently, however, the FDA has agreed with the Office for Human Research Protections (OHRP) that quorum may be lost through the recusal of conflicted members (Paul Goebel, personal communication, 2001), and OHRP has cited this as a finding of noncompliance.[2]

However the recusal of conflicted members is handled, study files and minutes of IRB meetings should reflect the identity of members recused for deliberations or voting. Given the increasing attention to detail in minutes, it may be advisable to also note the nature of the member's conflict that led to recusal.

IRB Reporting Structure

Beyond the recusal of investigator–members for deliberations or voting on their own protocols, the more systemic forms of conflict may be more difficult to manage, but no less important. Attention should be paid to the placement of the IRB within the institution and resulting reporting relationships, as well as to institutional policies that might negate some of the influences already discussed. The reporting structure of the IRB is the subject of Chapter 2-1 in this book.

Selection of Members

One of the most effective mechanisms to manage or avoid IRB conflict of interest lies in the appointment of a diverse membership.[7] This would include, but not be limited to, recruitment of unaffiliated members not beholden to the host institution.[3(Sec.107(d)),4(Sec.107(d))] Consideration to potential conflict of interest should be given when selecting members from inside the institution. Involvement in research gives valuable and necessary insight, and should not exclude a potential member from serving on an IRB. However, if circumstances would lead a member to be recused from a majority of protocols considered, he or she may not be a good choice. This might occur in settings where a single investigator or department accounts for a disproportionate amount of the institution's total research portfolio. This creates a dilemma in populating the IRB with sufficient expertise to review studies while simultaneously avoiding conflicts of interest, as the individuals with the greatest insight into scientific aspects of studies under review may also be conflicted. The potential for problems when institutional roles outside of service to the IRB run counter to a primary focus on protecting subjects has already been discussed. This may especially be true in smaller institutions, where individuals are more likely to wear multiple hats.

Education

As with every other aspect of human subjects protection, proactive education is another important component of an effective management strategy. Investigators, IRB members and staff, and institutional officials should all be made aware of existing policies and of potential for conflicts of interest in their own activities. This may be especially relevant for IRB Chairs, members, and staff, who may be accustomed to looking for conflicts in the investigators they oversee but not in themselves. OHRP included a section on IRB members and staff in its recent draft interim guidance on financial relationships in clinical research,[7] providing perhaps the first federal guidance directed at this group of individuals. Along with reiterating the need for education and training activities in this area, OHRP added financial interests to the conflicts Chairs and members should be mindful of during meetings. This guidance suggests that IRBs remind their members of policies at the outset of each meeting, providing members with the opportunity to consider any personal conflicts relating to the protocols they are about to review. They should then follow clear procedures for recusal from deliberations and voting, as previously discussed.

Conclusion

Any conflicts of interest on the part of the IRB would seriously undermine the credibility of the process and must be avoided at all costs. Whether a particular influence is real or perceived, originates from within or without, or is felt consciously or subconsciously, IRBs are not immune from conflicts of interest. No one doubts the integrity or motivation of those serving to protect human subjects, but we are no more or less human than the investigators we oversee and can only benefit from self-awareness in areas that might impact our effectiveness.

References

1. McCrary S V, Anderson C B, Jakovljevic J, Khan T, McCullough L B, Wray NP, Brody BA. A national survey of policies on disclosure of conflicts of interest in biomedical research. *N Engl J Med* 343(22):1621–1626, 2000.

2. Office for Human Research Protections COB. *OHRP Compliance activities: Common findings and guidance.* 2000. World Wide Web http://ohrp.osophs.dhhs.gov/references/findings.pdf

3. Code of Federal Regulations. Title 45A—Department of Health and Human Services; Part 46—Protection of Human Subjects. Updated 1 Oct 1997. Access date 18 Apr 2001. World Wide Web http://www4.law.cornell.edu/cfr/45p46.htm

4. Code of Federal Regulations. Title 21, Chapter 1—Food and Drug Administration, DHHS; Part 56—Institutional Review Boards. Updated 1 Apr 1999. Access date 27 Mar 2001. World Wide Web http://www4.law.cornell.edu/cfr/21p56.htm

5. Spece R G, Jr., Shimm D S, Buchanan A E. *Conflicts of Interest in Clinical Practice and Research.* New York: Oxford University Press. 1996.

6. Food and Drug Administration. Information sheets: Guidance for institutional review boards and clinical investigators, Sep 1998. Access date 9 Apr 2001. World Wide Web http://www.fda.gov/oc/oha/IRB/toc.html

7. Office for Human Research Protections. Draft interim guidance: Financial relationships in clinical research: Issues for institutions, clinical investigators, and IRBs to consider when dealing with issues of financial interests and human subject protection, 10 Jan 2001. Date of access 25 Apr 2001. World Wide Web http://ohrp.osophs.dhhs.gov/humansubjects/finreltn/finguid.htm

Appendix: Possible Sources of Conflict of Interest for IRBs

Individual Level

Member is investigator on research under review
Members or staff hold significant financial interest in sponsor of research
Loyalty to colleagues submitting for review
Members closely tied to area of research under review
    Familiar = too lenient
    Competitor = too critical
Possible impact of decisions on member's own work (e.g., policy changes)
Personal agendas
Non-IRB roles of members
    Contracts and grants office
    Legal counsel

Institutional Level

Pressure or desire to protect institution
Concern for institution's reputation or prestige
Promoting research vs. protecting subjects
Undervaluation of IRB service
Potential liability
Institutional or community values
Pressure for speedy reviews
Institutional equity or ownership
Review fees

Administrative Tasks Before the Meeting

Rebecca Carson Rogers and Elizabeth A. Bankert

INTRODUCTION

A successful full-committee IRB meeting is largely dependent on the comprehensiveness of the administrative details completed *before* the meeting. The variety and number of these tasks are considerable, and all are critical; but when done efficiently, they will be virtually inconspicuous to committee members. The purpose of this chapter is to discuss the administrative tasks that should be done in preparation for the full-committee meeting.

General Administrative Tasks

Each organization must develop internal office processes dependent on many variables (number of IRBs, how often IRBs meet, number of IRB office staff). This chapter will discuss the processes we have developed at Dartmouth where we have two IRBs (one devoted exclusively to oncology studies). Each IRB meets on the same day, once per month. Our IRBs together review approximately 15 to 20 new protocols each month, with approximately 30 renewals each month. We have four staff persons in our IRB office: a director, assistant director, education specialist, and office manager.

To start, we strongly endorse the development of good will and mutual respect with the research community. Time spent in reaching out to researchers in a comprehensive manner, before a study is even submitted, will save the IRB office time in the long run. Provide as much administrative assistance as possible to researchers and their staff. Names, e-mail addresses, and phone numbers of staff who can answer questions should be listed. If the IRB office has resources to review all or parts of a protocol before submission, this should be communicated. Researchers may be directed to any other on-line examples of protocols or consent forms, as well as workshops that cover these topics.

Materials Submission Deadline

The deadline for submitting materials must be set by the IRB office and communicated to researchers. This date must allow time for the IRB office to prepare and distribute materials to each IRB member. IRB members need to receive these materials with adequate time for review before the meeting. The number of office work days this process will take depends on the amount of IRB office staff and specific details of copying and distributing materials to members. It is advisable for this submission date to be a fixed amount of time before the IRB meeting; for example, a materials deadline date is the first Thursday of the month for a full-committee meeting to be held on the third Thursday of the month. Utilize all resources possible (Web sites, education sessions, electronic lists, investigator's guidelines) to ensure researchers are aware of the most current IRB forms, deadline dates, and other concerns.

Determine Attendance for the Upcoming Meeting

IRB members and alternates must be canvassed regarding their attendance at the upcoming IRB meeting. Be sure a "majority of the members of the IRB are present, including at least one member whose primary concerns are in nonscientific areas."[1][Sec.108(b)]

IRB Meeting Space

Once attendance is determined, meeting room reservations should be confirmed and any refreshments ordered. We have morning IRB meetings and thus provide a buffet breakfast to our IRB members. We suggest a comfortable, quiet location, slightly removed from the hustle and bustle of daily work life, for your IRB meetings. IRB members should feel relaxed and able to concentrate on the important task at hand.

Administrative Check of Submitted Materials

The IRB office should check new protocol, renewal, and revision submission materials for completeness and consistency between all documents and with the existing file (if applicable). All required signatures must be included. An IRB office may encourage the electronic submission of materials to meet a deadline, with a signed hard copy to follow in the mail. Hard copies must be matched with the copy printed from the electronic submission. Whenever possible, before materials are copied and distributed to the IRB members, the administrator communicates with the investigator or the research contact person to clarify any issues that may arise from the review of the new protocol, renewal, or revision submission. After every new protocol, renewal, or revision is prereviewed, it is added to the IRB meeting agenda (see agenda section).

New Study Submission

For tracking purposes, a study number should be assigned to each new protocol. Each IRB office will establish a procedure for identifying every study that is reviewed. This number, as well as a variety of other information, must be entered into the IRB database or record-keeping system. A file folder must also be created for hard copy storage related to that study. Our hard copy filing system consists of hanging file folders in file cabinets. The IRB number and investigator name are typed on the folder for easy readability when searching for a file. Our files are primarily in alphabetical order by investigator and the materials are kept in chronological order, with the exception of adverse event reports, which are separated into one section of the file.

At our institution, a new submission requires the following materials:

1. Human subject review form
2. Departmental scientific review form
3. IRB summary protocol
4. Consent form
5. Full sponsor protocol (if applicable)
6. Sponsor contract (if applicable)
7. All other relevant materials

These forms are presented in Chapter 11-9, devoted exclusively to IRB forms and documents. Other relevant materials may include recruitment letters, advertisements, examples of survey questions, patient diaries, etc. All IRB office forms should be easily accessible (posted on Web sites and available electronically via e-mail).

Checklist A checklist of materials needed for a new protocol submission is helpful to researchers and their staff as well as to the IRB office. This will increase the percentage of studies submitted to the IRB office with all required forms and attachments. It is best if this document can be a single specific and clear page, including deadline dates, location where materials are submitted, and resources for questions or concerns.

Human Subjects Review Form The human subjects review form is a single-page form that outlines the basic information and issues of the study. This form is also the main source of information we input into our database. The IRB office reviews the submission materials to be sure that all supporting materials are consistent with the information on the human subjects review form. For instance, the ages and number of participants listed on the human subjects review form must correspond with the numbers in the summary protocol and consent forms. If the submission includes any

category of vulnerable participants, the summary protocol must include the appropriate attachment. We use the bottom of this form for each IRB member to record his or her vote for each study.

Departmental Scientific Review Form At our institution, we require a scientific peer review within the submitting department to be conducted before review by the IRB. This form documents that review by asking specific questions related to the science of the study. A signature by a departmental authority is required with submission of the form.

IRB Summary Protocol and Attachments We have spent a considerable amount of time developing our summary protocol, which guides the researcher and (subsequently) the IRB members through the project with a specific focus on human subject issues. Also note the myriad of attachments we have developed (see Chapter 11-9). For example, if a project involves minors, the minors attachment must be submitted with the summary protocol. Other examples include attachments required for medical devices, use of placebo, genetic research, employee and student participants, illiterate subjects, incompetent participants, waiver of participant consent, and waiver of signed consent form. This format has been very useful for IRB members as it assists us in the review process by ensuring all appropriate issues are covered. The IRB office checks the summary protocol to determine if all appropriate attachments are included in the submission. If not, the IRB office will follow up with the research team to ensure a complete application is submitted to IRB members.

Consent Form Researchers are provided electronically with a consent form template. The consent form must be submitted in this template format. The IRB office conducts a prereview of the consent form for conformity to the template and for the use of any institutionally required language (e.g., institutional policy regarding research-related injury or contact information). The consent form is also reviewed for inclusion of any special issues that are noted in the summary protocol: for example, if the study includes a placebo arm, consent must include the risks of being in the placebo arm; if minors are participants, a parental consent and a minor's assent form may be needed. An experienced IRB administrator may also provide improvements to the consent form through simplifications and clarifications. A thorough review of the consent form before distribution to IRB members may save time and increase efficiency during the IRB meeting.

Other Relevant Materials Based on the information in the summary protocol, the IRB administrator will check for inclusion of all other relevant material. These may include the following:

1. Sponsor materials, such as protocols, investigator's brochures, clinical trial agreements, and site agreements
2. NIH protocols
3. Responses to concerns raised in the scientific review of the study

4. Survey questions and questionnaires

5. Other institutional consent forms, registration forms, or medical history forms that will be used in the study

6. Participant diaries

7. Information sheets

8. All recruitment materials including print, radio, television, and on-line advertisements, telephone scripts, statements read to participants, posters, or letters to potential participants

Renewal Submission

Renewal Notification   Protocol renewal is discussed in detail in Chapter 7-2. Researchers should be notified of the date that full IRB renewal of their study is required if they wish to proceed with uninterrupted participant enrollment. We provide renewal notification six weeks before the deadline of material submission, and again two weeks before the deadline. The renewal notice should include the title and number of the study, the material submission deadline date, the continuing review form that is needed for renewal, and information about where to submit materials.

The IRB office will function more efficiently if the renewal notifications can be generated from the database and sent electronically to researchers with the continuing review form sent as an attachment. Even with the best of database systems, it is still important to check the renewal list against the minutes of the meeting from the previous year. All new protocols and renewals that were reviewed at the corresponding meeting in the previous year should be on the renewal notification list, unless they have been terminated within the year. As renewal applications are submitted to the IRB office, they are checked off the list of expected renewals. This will assure that the office is able to notify any researchers whose studies are not reviewed by their renewal date that their study is suspended for further enrollment.

Materials to Be Submitted   At our institution, a renewal for full-committee review requires the following materials.

1. Human subject review form

2. Continuing review form

3. IRB summary protocol

4. Consent form

5. Full sponsor protocol (if applicable)

6. All other relevant materials including data safety monitoring report

The IRB office provides all original adverse event forms found in the IRB office file to the primary reviewer.

Revision Submission

Protocol revisions are discussed in detail in Chapter 7-1. Depending on the nature of the revision, a full-committee review may be required. At our institution, each revision is required to be accompanied by our revision request form (see Chapter 11-9) and any relevant attachments. In addition, all study materials that require changes based on the revision of the project must accompany the revision submission. For example, when protocol changes affect the wording of the consent form, the IRB administrator checks for the required revised protocol and consent. Changes in recruitment strategy or inclusion criteria often mean revised copies of telephone scripts or advertisements, which must also be included.

Primary Reviewer Systems

Our primary reviewer systems for new protocols, renewals, and revisions are described below. Please note that these systems make it a bit tricky for the IRB office to track which member receives what. Thus, planning and strict attention to detail are required to use the systems successfully. One intent of the primary reviewer systems is to reduce the paperwork burden while ensuring that appropriate, complete reviews are conducted.

New Protocols

From our researchers, we require one copy of items 1–4, 6, and 7 as listed in the "new protocol submission" section. Once the application is reviewed and determined to be in final form, the IRB office copies the forms for the IRB members—in our case, approximately 12 copies for IRB No. 1 and five copies for IRB No. 2. In our IRB No. 1, we utilize the primary reviewer system; thus, we also require three (double-sided, three-hole punched) copies of the full study sponsor protocol (item 5 from the "new protocol submission" section). Although we call it the primary reviewer system, we actually assign two reviewers to each protocol. Thus, each primary reviewer receives a copy of the full study sponsor protocol. In addition, the IRB Chair receives a copy of each full protocol. All IRB members receive all other items in our checklist of submission requirements, with the exception of "other relevant materials," which, depending on the content, may only be sent to the primary reviewers.

Renewals

We also utilize the primary reviewer system for renewals; however, in the case of renewals, there is only one primary reviewer assigned (versus two primary reviewers for new study submissions). At a minimum, all IRB members receive items 1–4 listed in the "renewal submission" section; however, all materials are available for all members. In addition, although a summary of adverse events is required in the continuing review form, if a summary report is submitted, each IRB member may receive it as well. At a minimum, the primary reviewer will receive items 5–7. The primary reviewer will also receive copies of all the above material plus any other materials that have been submitted to the IRB office since the last review of the study. This includes revised protocols, amendments, investigator's brochures, and adverse event reports.

Administrative Tasks Before the Meeting **217**

Revisions

Similarly, we utilize the single primary reviewer system for revision requests. All members of the IRB receive a copy of the revision request form. This form must be signed by each member at the meeting to document his or her vote on the revision submission, and this form is placed before all other materials associated with the revision. Following the revision request form, members will find the appropriate revised documents such as the protocol, consent, or advertising material. The primary reviewer receives copies of all the above materials plus any multipage attachments such as sponsor amendments. Depending on the nature of the study revision, the primary reviewer may need to receive a copy of the original study protocol or consent form. Adverse event reports may have to be included if the study revision addresses those issues.

Assigning Reviewers

The primary reviewer system requires the assignment of IRB members to specific studies. It is expected that all IRB members review all the studies. However, we rely on the primary reviewers to conduct a particularly detailed analysis of their assigned studies and to provide a verbal summary of potential issues at the IRB meeting. We tend to assign IRB members who have expertise in the area of the study being reviewed. For example, in our biomedical IRB, we assign an oncologist as one of the three reviewers for all cancer studies. However, our psychiatrist–member recently exclaimed, "I am only assigned to psychiatric studies." At the next meeting, we assigned him to a cardiology study, at which he exclaimed, "I don't know anything about cardiology." It is a bit of an art to make appropriate assignments. We try to be fair, and all members clearly realize that their comments, whether as primary reviewer or not, are important and listened to at the meeting. Work with your IRB members to obtain feedback and establish an assignment system with which everyone is comfortable.

Preparing the Agenda

There are no federal regulations to guide us in the development of an IRB meeting agenda. We have found the order of items on the agenda plays an important role in the efficiency and effectiveness of the IRB meeting. After trying several different formats, we have settled on the following agenda outline.

1. Continuing education

(This is an important feature of the IRB meeting. Topics and articles to be included are determined by the IRB director or Chair.)

2. Review of minutes from the previous month
3. Announcements
4. Studies to be reviewed, which are broken down into the following categories:
   a. Studies previously voted "not approved"
   b. Studies previously voted "conditionally approved"

In most instances, a study voted "conditionally approved" is not required to be re-reviewed by the full committee because the conditions of approval are such that simple concurrence by the researcher is all that is required to receive final approval. Usually this is accomplished by the review of revised materials by the IRB Chair. However, on occasion, the researcher does not provide simple concurrence; in that case, the study is re-reviewed by the full committee.

   c. New protocols
   d. Revisions to previously approved studies

At our institution, the full committee must review all study revisions that increase the risk to participants.

   e. Renewals with revisions

This category is for studies that are being renewed and also includes revision requests.

   f. Renewals
   g. Adverse events

On occasion, we receive an adverse event report that merits a review by the full committee as per our adverse event reporting procedure.

Studies in each category are listed alphabetically by primary investigator. The IRB file number, study title, and sponsor are included for all studies. To aid in the administrative work after the meeting, it is helpful for the agenda to include more information for the revision and renewal studies. Listing a brief revision description and all document names and version dates to be approved will eliminate a later search in the file for this information when writing study approval letters. After all studies are on the agenda, IRB reviewers are selected and their names added to the respective studies on the agenda.

Presenting and Distributing Materials to IRB Members

We have a saying: "The only thing more important than IRB members are the research participants." It is important to make IRB members understand that they are highly appreciated and respected. Presenting the meeting materials in a way that simplifies IRB review for the members improves IRB function in many ways.

We have found that three-ring binders are an excellent way to present IRB meeting materials to the members. Yes, it is a lot of work for our office staff. Before each meeting we create one notebook per member. Each notebook is organized in the order of the meeting agenda. Dividers are used to separate each agenda item. Each notebook contains the agenda, continuing education materials, and study submission materials that are copied for every member. By identifying each notebook with a member's name, the binder can be individualized to include the primary reviewer materials needed by that particular IRB member. Standardizing the order that submission materials are placed in the notebook for each study aids the members and the office staff. Certain reference documents may stay in the notebooks permanently (e.g., a copy of the *Belmont Report*, federal regulations, or selections from the institution's internal guidelines).

After the permanent section, each study is presented in the same manner. First is placed the document that members will use to record their vote and signature; this helps to ensure that this will not be forgotten during the course of the meeting (human subjects review form). Thereafter, materials follow in the order as listed in the "new protocol submission" and "renewal submission" sections.

Completed notebooks should be delivered to IRB members early enough to allow review before the full-committee meeting. We hand-deliver his or her notebook to each IRB member on the Friday prior to a Thursday meeting.

Late Submissions

Despite an IRB office's best attempt to include everything needed for a meeting in the members' notebooks, there may be documents or information that must be distributed to members after the notebooks have been delivered but before the meeting date. Information that is important for all members to receive is usually best communicated through e-mail. Actual documents for primary reviewer(s) may need to be delivered. Rarely, a document will need to be distributed at the IRB meeting itself.

We may also receive a special last-minute request to include a new protocol, renewal, or revision on the agenda after the IRB deadline has passed. As we strive to promote goodwill between the IRB and researchers, we do try to accommodate late submissions. However, the tasks required of the IRB office staff must also be taken into consideration. If the IRB office accepts a late submission, we suggest this generous act *not* be made widely known. We recently included a late submission on our agenda under the heading "late submission." The IRB office subsequently received a tongue-in-cheek message from a senior IRB member (who is also a clinical investigator) inquiring, "Just how late was this study? I want to plan my next submission accordingly." So remember, if you do not adhere to your own deadlines, they will soon be rendered meaningless!

Communicating with Researchers

Some IRBs require each researcher either to attend the IRB meeting or to be available for questions during the IRB meeting time. We have found it very effective to contact researchers with questions related to their study *before* the IRB meeting. All IRB members, and primary reviewers in particular, are encouraged to either contact the researcher directly with questions prior to the meeting or to contact the IRB office with a request to obtain further information from the researcher. During the days immediately before the meeting, the IRB administrative staff at our institution expects to spend hours relaying information back and forth between reviewers and researchers. There is no substitute for trying to solve problems and clarify issues before the full committee is assembled. In most cases, questions that would have consumed considerable full-committee time are answered during the premeeting dialogue. When a reviewer thinks that there are likely to be questions for the researcher or objections to approving the protocol, then this perspective is relayed to the researcher by the IRB staff before the meeting. The researcher is asked either to attend the meeting or, more frequently, to be available by pager to answer questions by telephone or to come to the meeting on short notice.

Of course, there are times when important issues are not brought out until the discussions at the IRB meeting. But the attempt to solve problems and clarify issues before the meeting promotes a positive rapport with researchers and dramatically improves the efficiency and effectiveness of the full-committee meeting. It is very satisfying when an IRB member says, "I had a question about aspect X of the study; however, I contacted the researcher and she explained it to me. Thus, from my perspective on this issue, we just need 'simple concurrence' in a revised consent form."

Meeting Minutes

The ability to take the minutes of the meeting directly on a computer is a great advantage (see Chapter 5-16). In any case, the meeting agenda can be used as the outline for the minutes. After copying the meeting agenda, the following changes will prepare it to be the outline for the meeting minutes.

1. Change the title to "Minutes (notes)."

2. Below the title, add "Members Present," "Staff Present," and "Guests" sections. Input names of those expected to attend.

3. Delete the names of reviewers for each study, as this information is not appropriate for the permanent record of the IRB Committee meeting.

4. Add "Discussion Items" and "Conditions for Approval" sections under each study entry.

5. Add a section to record the vote for each study.

Conclusion

For an IRB meeting to be productive and efficient, it is essential to complete a wide range of administrative tasks before the meeting begins. This chapter lists the tasks that are most important to perform and explains how IRB administrators should go about getting them done. In our experience, it is especially important to establish the practice of routinely contacting researchers before the meeting to discuss areas of confusion or potential problem issues. Whenever possible, the IRB staff should help IRB members and researchers prepare the research proposal so that the IRB will have the information it needs to make a definitive determination the first time the protocol is discussed.

Reference

1. Code of Federal Regulations. Title 45A—Department of Health and Human Services; Part 46—Protection of Human Subjects. Updated 1 Oct 1997. Access date 18 Apr 2001. World Wide Web http://www4.law.cornell.edu/cfr/45p46.htm

Guidelines for Review, Discussion, and Voting

Robert J. Amdur and Elizabeth A. Bankert

INTRODUCTION

Other chapters in this part of the book discuss administrative aspects of the full-committee meeting. The purpose of this chapter is to discuss some of these issues in further detail or from a different perspective. This chapter will suggest guidelines regarding three aspects of the process of full-committee review: (1) what IRB members should do to prepare for the meeting, (2) the format for presenting and discussing each study, and (3) the voting options.

What IRB Members Should Do to Prepare for the Meeting

Conduct a Systematic Review of the Application Material

As discussed in other chapters, most IRBs find that the primary reviewer system improves the quality and efficiency of IRB review. The primary reviewer system means that a limited number of IRB members—usually two or three—are assigned to each protocol to be reviewed at the full-committee meeting. We have found it to be efficient and effective for the reviewers to develop a structured approach to reviewing a study prior to the full committee meeting. What works well for one reviewer, however, may not be the best system for another. Some experienced IRB reviewers favor the following approach.

1. **Read the consent document.** Read the consent document first. Because the purpose of the document is to explain the important aspects of the study to potential subjects in lay language, it should give the reviewer a good introduction to the protocol. At this initial reading, the reviewer should not take notes or attempt to correct the wording of the document. The purpose of this reading is to orient the reviewer to the overall design of the study.

2. **Read the IRB summary protocol.** After completing an overview of the study based on the consent form, review the summary of the protocol submitted as part of the IRB application. IRB summary protocols are discussed in other chapters and presented in the reference section of this book. The IRB summary protocol is the part of the application where the investigator summarizes the important aspects of the study in a way that facilitates IRB review.

3. **Read the supporting material.** Next, read the supporting material that completes the information presented in the IRB application form. For example, primary reviewers receive the full sponsor protocol from the study sponsor. This will provide the reviewer with detailed information such as prior studies applicable to the study treatment or that validate study procedures, statistical power analysis, detailed inclusion/exclusion requirements, recruitment advertisements, etc.

4. **Read the consent document again.** This time, record suggested corrections or questions for the investigator.

5. **Use a review template.** When completing the review process, it may be helpful to use a review template to take notes while reading the IRB application form, supporting material, and consent document. A template helps to organize the review, reminds the reviewer what issues have and have not been addressed, is useful for presenting the review at the full-committee meeting, and can be kept in the IRB file as documentation that a detailed review was performed. Some reviewers create their own templates according to the format that works best for them. Some IRB offices ask every reviewer to use the same template. Some IRBs use review forms that are lengthy and extremely detailed. In organizations that view the primary purpose of the reviewer template as a mechanism for documenting compliance with federal regulations, the template may contain legalistic wording.

In our opinion, the primary purpose of the reviewer template is to help the reviewer evaluate the protocol and explain it to other IRB members. For this reason, it is useful to keep the reviewer template as short and simple as possible. Examples of reviewer templates are presented in other chapters in this book. The template that the authors use is included as an appendix to this chapter.

Answer as Many Questions as Possible Before the Meeting

A hallmark of effective and efficient IRBs is the extent to which IRB reviewers and support staff work to prepare the protocol application, answer questions, and resolve potentially controversial issues before the full-committee meeting. Clearly, it is an enormous task to ask IRB members to conduct a thorough protocol review *and* to find answers to unresolved issues before the meeting, but in the long run this approach will pay large dividends for both the IRB and research community.

As emphasized in Chapter 6-2, an IRB reviewer should revise the consent document as needed before the full-committee meeting. It is undesirable, for many reasons, to routinely use the full-committee meeting to clarify issues and identify questions to discuss with the investigator. The efficiency and effectiveness of IRB review is important for the IRB, the research community, the institution, and society in general. Delaying study approval time may have a negative effect on the progress of research or the welfare of the individuals who may benefit from research participation. For these reasons, it is useful to structure the review process so that the full-committee IRB meeting is primarily a place to make decisions rather than gather information.

Several other chapters in this book stress that it is important for the IRB to work closely with the research team before the full-committee meeting to maximize the possibility that the full committee will be able to make a definitive and informed decision the first time the protocol is reviewed. Not approving a protocol, or tabling it, at the full-committee meeting because the IRB needs clarification on basic issues or revisions that could have been addressed before the meeting decreases the efficiency of IRB review. Efficiency and quality are related because anything that decreases respect for the IRB process compromises the ability of the IRB to protect the rights and welfare of research participants. Several other chapters in this book explain how the IRB administrative staff should function as a colleague of the researcher prior to the meeting by helping the research team revise the consent document or application material in a way that will facilitate IRB review.

Specific Recommendations for IRB Reviewers

1. **Review study information before the meeting.** Most IRB members receive materials at least a week in advance of the IRB meeting. Although the IRB office should ensure materials are complete, in some instances a thorough evaluation of IRB issues requires information that was not included in the application package. After reading the protocol application, the reviewer may need to discuss the protocol with a colleague, IRB staff, or investigator. It is essential to give the evaluation process the time that it deserves in advance of the IRB meeting.

2. **Try to get your questions answered before the meeting.** This is a restatement of the fundamental message of this section.

3. **Do not hesitate to discuss the protocol with the investigator.** Collegial interaction between the investigator and primary IRB reviewer will facilitate the IRB review and promote respect for the local IRB system. The IRB Chair or administrative director should encourage members to directly contact investigators for further information or clarification. However, the IRB office also should serve as an intermediary for any IRB member who may wish to obtain further information but does not have time to (or prefers not to) personally follow up with the investigator. Investigators who resist talking with IRB reviewers or insult them for requesting clarification or justification of important ethical issues demonstrate a lack of respect for the system of

protecting research subjects that has been mandated by the organization for which the IRB serves. The commitment of the investigator to conducting research according to the highest of ethical standards is an important criterion for IRB approval of research. We have found that open discussion between the IRB office, IRB members, and investigators has improved the review process, and we rarely encounter an investigator who is not supportive of efforts to help with this process.

4. **Decide if the investigator should attend the meeting.** When an investigator cannot be contacted or an issue cannot be resolved before the meeting, the reviewer should inform the IRB administrator or Chair of the details of the situation. Reviewers should indicate if they think it will be important for the investigator to attend the IRB meeting. The most common reason that the IRB should ask an investigator to attend the IRB meeting (if he or she otherwise was not planning to) is to discuss an important issue that could not be resolved before the meeting. However, in some situations a reviewer may believe it will be important for other IRB members to hear an investigator explain something personally rather than to have the reviewer explain to the committee that there is no reason to be concerned.

Format of Discussion at the Meeting

Federal regulations and guidance documents do not discuss the format for discussion of protocols at the full-committee meeting. In talking with experienced IRB Chairs around the country, it appears that a variety of routines work well. Each IRB should use the approach that fits best with the personalities and interpersonal styles of the committee. The important thing is to use a system that promotes an efficient discussion of important IRB issues in an atmosphere that encourages all members to express their views. The following is the basic routine that has worked well for several experienced IRBs.

1. The first primary reviewer presents the protocol. There are no questions or interruptions until this presentation is completed.

2. The first primary reviewer uses an organized format to summarize the important issues that the IRB should consider. The reviewer does not explain the background or study methods in detail. All IRB members (not just the assigned reviewers) are expected to have read the condensed summary of the protocol in the IRB application package. A template like the one included at the end of this chapter will simplify both the processes of review and the presentation. The presentation should end with a summary of any issues that are unresolved in the mind of the reviewer or issues that require revision in the reviewer's opinion. The reviewer should be encouraged to make a recommendation regarding how the committee should vote on the protocol.

This format may seem time-consuming or complex, but it works well after everyone gets in the habit of preparing an organized presentation before the meeting. This should be a bottom-line summary of the reviewer's assessment of the protocol. Routine presentations should be short and to the point.

3. The second primary reviewer comments on the protocol. The second reviewer does not repeat the information pre-

sented by the first reviewer, but rather indicates where he or she agrees or disagrees with the assessments of the first reviewer with a brief explanation of the rationale for any disagreements. The second reviewer adds or clarifies information as considered appropriate. The second reviewer ends these comments with a vote recommendation that may or may not be the same as the first reviewer's.

4. If there are three (or more) assigned reviewers, they present their comments according to the same guidelines as described for the second reviewer. In general, the Chair should discourage questions or comments until all of the assigned reviewers have had a chance to complete their initial presentations.

5. The Chair opens the discussion up to the full committee. IRB members should raise their hands or in some other way indicate that they have a question or comment. The Chair should control the discussion by calling on people in turn. The Chair may ask the primary reviewers to respond to questions or comments of other IRB members, but in many cases it will be more appropriate for the Chair or a member other than one of the primary reviewers to respond.

Under the best of circumstances, it may be difficult to manage the full-committee discussion of a controversial protocol. The goal is to discuss the protocol in a way that encourages all IRB members to express their views and identifies the issues that are important for the IRB to consider. There is no formula for this process, but it is essential that the Chair is able to manage this aspect of the meeting if the IRB is to function effectively. There must be a mechanism to terminate discussion so that the committee can turn its attention to voting on the protocol. Some IRBs let the discussion continue until an IRB member seconds a motion for a vote. In other committees, the Chair determines when all of the important issues have been raised, declares the discussion over, and calls for the vote.

The Voting Options

The only section of federal research regulations that addresses the different determinations that the IRB may make regarding a research protocol (voting options) is 45 CFR 46[1][Sec.109(a)] and analogous FDA regulations that say "An IRB shall review and have authority to approve, require modifications in (to secure approval), or disapprove all research activities covered by this policy." Some IRBs use the term *conditional approval* to refer to the situation where specific modifications are required to secure approval. Some IRBs prefer the term *not approve* to *disapprove*.

Approval Pending Specific Modification (Conditional Approval)

There is considerable variation in the way IRBs handle a protocol that has been approved by the full committee pending specific modifications. Aspects of this controversy are discussed in other chapters in this book. Basically there is confusion or a lack of consensus on when federal regulations permit the expedited review procedure to determine that the investigator has made the modifications that were required by the full committee. Federal regulations do not inform this question. Guidance on this subject may be found in the list of common findings of noncompliance by the OHRP.[2]

In this and other forums, OHRP has advised IRBs that the expedited procedure may only be used to approve modifications required by the full committee when the modifications are such that they require only "simple concurrence" by investigators. Interpretation of the term "simple concurrence" is variable across the IRB community. A more detailed discussion of this issue is beyond the scope of this chapter.

Semantics: Table, Disapprove, and Not Approve

Many IRBs include "table" as a voting option. "Table" is not mentioned in federal research regulations or guidance documents. In the setting of an IRB meeting, a vote to table a protocol means that the committee requests additional information from the investigator. From the functional standpoint, a table determination means that the investigator is prohibited from starting the study. Common reasons to table a protocol include the need to review the answers to questions raised by IRB members or the need to review the investigator's response to requested modifications.

Because the procedural implications, in terms of starting or not starting the study, are the same for both the IRB and investigator, some IRBs prefer to simplify the decision process at the IRB meeting by deleting "table" as a determination option. IRBs that do not give the committee the option of tabling a protocol simply determine if the protocol is approved, approved pending specific modifications (conditional approval), or not approved (disapproved). When a protocol is not approved, a letter to the investigator summarizes the reasons that the committee did not approve the protocol at the current meeting. The point is that the IRB does not need a "table" option to convey determinations to investigators or to administer the voting process. So, why do IRBs table protocols instead of not approving or disapproving them?

IRB Chairs who prefer to table rather than not approve a protocol explain that they are concerned about the psychological impact a "not approved" or "disapproved" determination may have on the investigator. The thinking is that "table" more clearly indicates that the protocol is still under evaluation by the IRB, whereas "not approve" or "disapprove" implies that the IRB objects to a fundamental aspect of the study. There is no limit to the extent one could debate this question of psychological impact. In our experience, investigators do not care about the label of the IRB determination. Investigators want to know if the protocol is or is not approved by the IRB, because this determines if they can start the study. When they are not permitted to start the study after the IRB meeting, the investigator wants to know why the study was not approved and what should be done to have the protocol reconsidered as soon as possible.

Is there a reason that an IRB might want to delete "table" from the determination options? In our experience, removing "table" from the list of potential IRB determinations simplifies the voting process and helps to clarify the functional implications of an IRB decision. The phrase "not approve" or "disapprove" tends to focus the committee on the next step in the dialogue with the investigator. When the IRB is unable to approve a study, it is essential that the committee articulate the reasons for this determination in a way that clearly indicates the information the IRB needs to reconsider in the study or the items to be addressed if the investigator wishes to appeal the determination.

Majority Requirement and the "Abstain" Controversy

As discussed in other chapters, federal regulation[1][Sec.108(b)] requires a majority of IRB members to convene a full-committee meeting. The second part of this regulation gives the requirement for an approval determination: "In order for the research to be approved, it shall receive the approval of the majority of those members present at the meeting." In other words, a majority of IRB members (or their alternates) must be present for quorum, and a majority of the members at the meeting must agree to approve a study. *Majority* means more than half.

Presently, no definitive guidance exists on whether an IRB member who abstains from voting may nevertheless count toward the quorum. For IRBs that have never thought about this issue, consider the following scenario: The IRB has 10 full-committee positions. Only six members are able to attend the meeting. Six is a quorum, so the meeting is held. During the meeting the chair is informed that an IRB member prefers to abstain from voting on a study that is on the agenda because he has a major financial holding in the company sponsoring the research. There is another study on the agenda for which a second IRB member must abstain from voting because she is listed as the coinvestigator of the protocol. The problem here is that for each of the studies in question, one of the six members present for the meeting will abstain from voting. If a member who abstains from voting is not counted toward the quorum, the committee will not have sufficient people to vote on the study in compliance with federal regulations.

The question of including an IRB member who abstains from voting in the quorum count has been discussed at length at national IRB meetings. Federal regulations and guidance documents do not definitively answer this question. It seems logical to require that all members who are counted for quorum participate in the vote. This means that a member who abstains from voting is considered to be absent from the meeting from the standpoint of the quorum count. In terms of the above example, it means that the committee would not be able to make a determination on the two studies in which one of the six IRB members abstained from the vote.

Presenting the Vote Options

There are two basic ways to present the vote options to the committee. One approach is to call for an "in favor" or "opposed" vote on a single determination option. For example, the Chair (or another IRB member with the motion seconded) calls for a vote to approve a protocol pending specific modifications (conditional approval). The vote is taken by first asking for a show of hands of members who are in favor of this determination and then asking for a show of hands of members who are opposed to this determination. If a majority of the members vote in favor of the conditional approval decision, then this will be the determination of the IRB on this study. If a vote in favor is recorded from less than a majority of the members present at the meeting, then the study has not been approved by the IRB. At this point, the IRB Chair or membership may suggest another determination, possibly changing the modification requirements, and a second vote can be taken. This procedure can be repeated as many times as the committee wants to consider additional determinations.

Another approach to the vote procedure is to call for a vote and give each member the option of voting for the determination that he or she prefers. This approach has worked well at Dartmouth for many years. Basically, the IRB Chair calls for a vote after all relevant issues have been discussed and all members have had a chance to express their views. The Chair announces all of the potential IRB determinations (approve, conditionally approve, not approve, and abstain), pausing after each one long enough to record the number of members who raise a hand to indicate that this is the determination for which they are voting. Each IRB member is only permitted to vote for one option per voting session.

It usually takes only one round of voting to identify the determination favored by the majority of the committee. However, like the approve-or-oppose approach previously described, there are situations where multiple vote sessions are required to refine the committee's determination. For example, if 50% of the members vote to approve the study as submitted, 40% vote to approve it with a requirement for certain revisions, and 10% vote to not approve it, then there is not a clear majority for any single determination. To manage all the various scenarios that could occur, a policy statement was prepared that describes the process for determining the IRB determination that will be recorded in the IRB minutes and communicated to the investigator. The policy currently in use at Dartmouth is presented as a general model for other IRBs who want to establish a policy statement on this subject.

IRB Voting Procedure

After appropriate study discussion, the chairperson will call for a vote. The chairperson will then announce each vote option; each member will vote in one category only.

Approved
Conditionally approved
Not approved
Abstain

Vote outcome: Per federal regulations, for a study to receive approval, it must obtain an approval vote from a majority of the members attending the meeting. The vote for each category will be tabulated. If there is not a majority vote in one category, the following process will occur.

1. Approved (A) and Conditionally Approved (CA) Versus Not Approved (NA):

   The NA vote will be compared with the sum of the A and CA vote. If the sum (A+CA) is greater than the NA votes, the conditions of approval must be refined using the approach described in No. 2.

   If the NA vote is greater than the sum (A+CA), the study will be not approved.

   If the NA vote and the (A+CA) vote are tied, the study will be not approved.

2. Approved (A) Versus Conditionally Approved (CA):

   If the CA vote is greater than (A+NA), the study will be conditionally approved.

   If the CA vote is less than or equal to (A+NA), a second vote will be taken with the choices limited to approved, conditionally approved, and abstain.

   If the A vote and CA votes are tied, the study will be conditionally approved.

3. Description of Vote Categories:

Approved—The study has been approved as submitted. The investigator is not required to change any aspect of the protocol or consent document. The approval date is the date of the IRB meeting. The approval is valid for one year unless the committee designates a shorter period based on the risk of the study. An approval letter will be sent to the investigator.

Conditionally Approved—There are no structural problems with the study. Simple concurrence of listed items is required prior to final approval. A letter describing the concerns of the committee will be sent to the investigator. The letter will make it clear that the study may not begin until the IRB issues a letter of approval. The investigator's response will be reviewed for appropriateness by the chairperson or designated IRB member(s). A final approval letter from the IRB will be sent to the investigator once the response has been approved. At that time, the study may begin. The approval date is the date of the original IRB meeting at which the conditional approval determination was made. IRB approval is valid for one year unless the committee designates a shorter period based on the risk of the study.

Not Approved—The magnitude and/or number of concerns, questions, and /or problems is such that "conditional approval" is not appropriate. A letter describing the concerns of the committee will be sent to the investigator. A designation of "not approved" indicates that resubmission of the study must be reviewed by the full committee. The investigator will be notified of the opportunity to respond to the IRB in writing or in person with regard to the IRB determination.

Abstain—If an IRB member is helping to direct the study, is an investigator or coinvestigator of the study, has any significant financial interest in the outcome of the study, or has what he, she, or the IRB considers to be an unacceptable conflict of interest for other reasons, the member shall declare an "abstain" vote. The minutes of the IRB meeting will reflect a vote of abstention. In addition to abstaining from voting on the study, an IRB member with a conflict of interest related to a study will not participate in the discussion of the study by the committee except as requested to answer specific questions. This will be reflected in the IRB minutes.

Conclusion

For an IRB to function optimally, it is important to establish a routine for reviewing research proposals prior to the meeting, discussing protocols at the meeting, and voting on the final determination. This chapter suggests a formal approach to these functions that will facilitate effective and efficient IRB function. We cannot emphasize enough the importance of getting questions answered before the meeting whenever this is possible. The IRB meeting should be viewed as a place to make decisions, not identify issues.

References

1. Code of Federal Regulations. Title 45A—Department of Health and Human Services; Part 46—Protection of Human Subjects. Updated 1 Oct 1997. Access date 18 Apr 2001. World Wide Web http://www4.law.cornell.edu/cfr/45p46.htm

2. Office for Human Research Protections. OHRP compliance activities: Common findings and guidance, 1 Sep 2000. Date of access 18 Aug 2001. World Wide Web http://ohrp.osophs.dhhs.gov/references/findings.pdf

Appendix

Study # _____

(Write on the other side of page as needed.)

The purpose of the study is to:

Study population:

Summary (background, number of arms, controls, different from nonresearch alternative, IND/IDE):

Sponsor:

Investigator: (Name, department, qualified?, COI)

Vulnerability: (Children, incompetent adults, employees, students, prisoners)

Informed consent: (Required, written, surrogate)

Birth control:

Subject recruitment? (Who, where, how, advertise?) Is subject selection likely to be equitable?

IRB Primary Reviewer Template—continued

Genetic testing/tissue repository:

Cost relative to nonresearch cost:

Payment or reimbursements: (Coercive?)

Risks (relative to nonresearch alternative):

Potential benefit: (Direct for subject, altruism, what is benefit to sponsor/PI)

Risk/Benefit analysis: Are risks minimized by study design and reasonable in view of potential benefits?

Confidentiality: Are provisions to protect the privacy of subjects and the confidentiality of data adequate?

Data oversight: (DSMB?, stopping rules)

Consent document:

Administrative Tasks After Each IRB Meeting

Jan Trott and Elizabeth A. Bankert

INTRODUCTION

"The IRB shall prepare and maintain adequate documentation of IRB activities."[1(Sec.115), 2(Sec.115)] Please read this section of the federal regulations carefully to ensure your office is maintaining all required documentation. Many of the administrative tasks that take place directly after the IRB meeting must be done in order to comply with these regulations, but of equal importance is that these tasks need to be done efficiently and accurately to track the evolution of approved studies. This chapter will provide you with a list of tasks that will help you with these endeavors. The individual responsible for these administrative duties must have organized work habits that include attention to detail.

Adequate Documentation

What to Collect and Retain After the Meeting

In most cases, the IRB meeting will not take place in your office. After the meeting, it is very important to remove from the meeting room any agenda packets or member notebooks that may contain confidential information. Everything that was distributed should be collected for proper maintenance or disposal.

It is important to keep any forms used by the members to record their vote and signatures. Keep any forms that were given to the primary and/or secondary reviewers for their initial review and comment. If any articles or informational documents were distributed to the members for educational purposes, keep these articles on file. Keep a copy of the agenda also. In other words, any documents that support the determinations or activities of the meeting should be adequately maintained and retained.

Importance of Documentation

Over the past few years, it has become clear that documentation and maintenance of IRB records is very important. Audits conducted by sponsors and federal agencies rely exclusively on what is written down. Gary Ellis, past director of the Office of Protection from Research Risks, summarized the attitude of his office's compliance officials as "If it isn't documented, then it wasn't done."

Even if we know that the IRB discusses all the important ethical aspects of each study, unless it is written down, we have no way to show the discussions occurred. There are several ways to document IRB discussions. Some organizations have a primary reviewer checklist that documents the issues required for regulatory compliance.

The reviewer checklist is saved in the IRB file (see Chapter 5-1). Other organizations require the submission of a protocol summary in which the investigator responds to a checklist similar to the one just described. However, a potential problem with these checklist systems is that they rely on the reviewer to document all of the essential issues. Another approach is to use the meeting minutes to document that IRB review was in compliance with regulatory standards. Other organizations use the minutes to document discussions of important ethical aspects of the project. A template for recording minutes from the full-committee meeting is appended to this chapter.

Preparation of Minutes

Title 45 CFR 46.115 (2):

> Minutes of IRB meetings which shall be in sufficient detail to show attendance at the meetings; actions taken by the IRB; the vote on these actions including the number of members voting for, against, and abstaining; the basis for requiring changes in or disapproving research; and a written summary of the discussion of controverted issues and their resolution.

This regulation lists the items that must be documented in the IRB minutes for every study. There is no reason to recount actual conversations. The template included as an appendix to this chapter allows the person taking the minutes to fill in the appropriate areas with a few words that summarize the result of IRB deliberations. We strongly advise against including information such as "Dr. Smith said, 'The study is unethical.'" In our opinion, it is a mistake to match any statement with a member's name in the minutes. The minutes should be a brief summary of "the basis for requiring changes in or disapproving research" and "of the discussion of controverted issues and their resolutions."

In other sections of the regulations, the words "the IRB finds and documents that. . ." or "the IRB finds. . ." or ". . .the IRB shall determine. . ." indicate specific issues that should be addressed in the minutes if they are not documented elsewhere.

Examples (emphasis added)
Title 45 CFR 46.405

DHHS will conduct or fund research in which the IRB finds that more than minimal risk to children is presented by an intervention or procedure that holds out the prospect of direct benefit for the individual subject or by a monitoring procedure that is likely to contribute to the subject's well being, only **if the IRB finds that.** . . .

45 CFR 46.111 Criteria for IRB approval of research

(a) In order to approve research covered by this policy the **IRB shall determine** that all of the following requirements are satisfied. . . .

45 CFR 46.116(d)

An IRB may approve a consent procedure which does not include, or which alters, some or all of the elements of informed consent set forth in this section, or waive the requirements to obtain informed consent provided the **IRB finds and documents that.** . . .

45 CFR 46.117(c)

An IRB may waive the requirement for the investigator to obtain a signed consent form for some or all subjects **if it finds** either. . . .

In addition, if the research involves one of the special classes of subjects requiring additional protections (fetuses, pregnant women, human in vitro fertilization [Subpart B], prisoners [Subpart C], or children [Subpart D]), a description that the appropriate regulations and requirements have been met, such as assent, should be recorded in the minutes and/or study file.

As mentioned in Chapter 5-15, the ability to take the minutes of the meeting directly on a computer during the meeting proceedings is a great advantage. Even if that is not possible at your site, using the agenda outline for the preparation of the minutes is very helpful.

After the minutes have been reviewed and signed by the Chair, the original should be filed appropriately. In many cases, there are other boards within your institution that will review these minutes, and copies should be distributed as needed. Copies of the minutes should be filed in a way that will ensure that a copy is included in each member's agenda packet at the next meeting.

Communicating Meeting Results to the Researcher

Title 45 CFR 46.109

(d): An IRB shall notify investigators and the institution in writing of its decision to approve or disapprove the proposed research activity, or of modifications required to secure IRB approval of the research activity. If the IRB decides to disapprove a research activity, it shall include in its written notification, a statement of the reasons for its decision and give the investigator an opportunity to respond in person or in writing.

The IRB office must notify each investigator in a timely fashion, in writing, of the outcome of the IRB's review specific to their study. The determination of the IRB, including any conditions of approval, should be clearly stated. This applies to letters of approval for new proposals, full-board approval of revisions, and full-board approval of study renewals.

Letters to Investigators

The letter informing the principal investigator of the result of IRB review should include the following information:

1. The identification number given to the study
2. The title of the study
3. If commercially sponsored, the version date of the protocol and consent document
4. The name of the IRB
5. The IRB determination: unconditional, conditional, tabled, disapproved
6. The date of the determination
7. If approved, the duration of approval and date of re-review by the board
8. If conditionally approved, a list of conditions and a statement that the study should not begin until the investigator receives formal notification of IRB approval following review of the response to the approval conditions
9. If tabled or disapproved, the basis for the determination and a statement that the investigator is welcome to resubmit the proposal

In final approval letters, additional standard approval conditions should be outlined.

1. Research must be conducted according to the proposal that was approved by the IRB.
2. Changes to the protocol or its related consent document must be approved by the IRB prior to implementation.
3. Adverse events must be reported promptly to the IRB.
4. Each subject should receive a copy of the consent document, if appropriate.
5. Records must be retained for at least three years.
6. Any future correspondence should include the IRB identification number provided and the study title.

Remember, you must follow up with the principal investigator regarding any outstanding conditions of the approval before final unconditional approval can be granted. The IRB office may contact the principal investigator at regular intervals as a reminder and to offer assistance, if appropriate.

On occasion, you may receive an inquiry from a researcher about a vote by a specific IRB member. At no time is it appropriate for an IRB member or staff person to discuss votes by individual members of the committee.

Consent Document

The final draft of the consent document for an approved project should be stamped or somehow flagged as "IRB Approved" with the date of final approval indicated. If an electronic version of the consent document is available, the footer of the document may include the version date. Some organizations require that the correct version date appear on every page of the consent document and the expiration date is also contained in the document. To complete the documentation procedure, some organizations send the "stamped" consent to the investigator as an enclosure with the approval letter. Other organizations e-mail the final consent document but reference the date of the final approved version in the approval letter.

What to Save for Each Proposed Study

At this point, a study number has probably already been assigned and a folder made for each proposed study. To begin with, each study folder should include the following.

1. The completed and signed application to the IRB
2. The IRB application form that summarizes the research plan
3. The stamped, approved consent document, if appropriate
4. Scientific reviews or opinions of consultants
5. Approval letters from other committees (e.g., the radiation safety committee)
6. Recruitment forms or advertisements for the study
7. The sponsor protocol or grant proposal
8. Attachments specific to the protocol (articles, surveys, questionnaires, etc.)
9. The IRB determination letter

This is the beginning of the folder of information that should be kept on each study. Through the life of a study, many adverse events can be reported, advertisements submitted for approval, changes or amendments submitted for approval, reapprovals granted, and so forth. Everything that the IRB receives should be kept together in one folder, preferably in chronological order, the most recent information on top.

Tracking a Study

Tracking systems are discussed in detail in Chapter 2-4. Most organizations that conduct a large volume of research will track the status of each study with an electronic database system. If you are a small institution and do not have a database, you should at least keep a record of each study, its IRB number, the approval date, title, principal investigator, review determination, and date when the study should be re-reviewed. You must be reminded by either a computer-generated or a manual flagging system so you will know when to notify investigators of their renewals within a sufficient timeframe for them to respond before the study renewal date.

Closed Studies
45 CFR 46.115 (b)

The records required by this policy shall be retained for at least 3 years, and records relating to research which is conducted shall be retained for at least 3 years after completion of the research. . . .

If an investigator notifies the IRB of the completion of a study and the final summary has been received and accepted by the board, the file for this study should either be flagged somehow as closed or be removed from the active study file section. Remember that the documents have to be retained for at least three years. It may be helpful to flag the chart with the date three years from completion just for recordkeeping purposes.

IRB Fee Invoicing

An administrative task that is often done immediately after the full-committee meeting is the generation of the list of studies that should be associated with a fee for IRB review. Organizations that charge for IRB review must set up a system to track this aspect of the process. Each institution will have a different system. In some cases, a financial person or department will need a list of studies to generate the appropriate invoices. In most cases, simply generating a list of the studies according to review category (full board versus expedited) will be sufficient.

Conclusion

This chapter has explained the administrative tasks that should be accomplished after a full-committee IRB meeting. The need to document IRB activities in compliance with federal research regulation drives much of the process. The minutes of the IRB meeting must include specific wording and information. A template for recording the meeting minutes is presented. The list of items that must be included in the letter that the IRB must send to the researcher after the meeting should be used as a checklist when evaluating the quality of the IRB administrative process.

References

1. Code of Federal Regulations. Title 45A—Department of Health and Human Services; Part 46—Protection of Human Subjects. Updated 1 Oct 1997. Access date 18 Apr 2001. World Wide Web http://www4.law.cornell.edu/cfr/45p46.htm
2. Code of Federal Regulations. Title 21, Chapter 1—Food and Drug Administration, DHHS; Part 56—Institutional Review Boards. Updated 1 Apr 1999. Access date 27 Mar 2001. World Wide Web http://www4.law.cornell.edu/cfr/21p56.htm

Appendix

IRB Full-Committee Minutes Template

Date:

Minutes from last month's meeting: The minutes from last month's meeting (or give date) were reviewed. There were no controversial entries or objections. The committee voted unanimously to approve the minutes.

Continuing education: The following items were distributed to all committee members before the meeting:. . . . The committee discussed these items with specific emphasis on the implications for future IRB practice.

Announcements:

Individual protocol reviews:
Protocol number and title
Type of review: Initial, Continuing, Revision, Adverse Event

For each initial protocol review:
Committee review included, but was not limited to, evaluation of the following issues:

The investigator: The investigator in charge of this project is qualified to conduct this study and there are no conflicts of interest that would be expected to compromise the integrity of the study.

Vulnerable populations: The study does not specifically target people who have traditionally been considered "vulnerable" from the standpoint of needing additional protection from the risks associated with research participation.

The study specifically targets people who have traditionally been considered "vulnerable" from the standpoint of needing additional protection from the risks associated with research participation: children, adults who are not competent to give informed consent, pregnant women, prisoners, the mentally disabled, educationally or economically disadvantaged persons.

In this study, the investigator is sensitive to the ethical issues involved with research involving vulnerable subjects and is committed to conducting the research according to the highest of ethical standards. Specific safeguards include:

Informed consent: Written informed consent will be obtained from the subject.

This study may enroll children: written informed consent will be obtained from the child's parent or guardian / both parents. When appropriate, verbal assent will be obtained from the subjects.

This study may enroll adult subjects who are not competent to give informed consent: Written informed consent will be obtained from the subjects legally authorized representative.

Birth control: Pregnancy is an exclusion criterion for this study. Women of childbearing potential may participate in this study. A pregnancy test is/ is not required to participate in the study. Subjects are instructed not to become pregnant during this study. Birth control is recommended. This study may involve men who may be sexually active. Sexually active men are advised to use a condom during sexual intercourse.

Subject recruitment: Subjects will be recruited from the ____(example: cardiology clinic). The person recruiting subjects may be/will not be the subject's health-care provider. A research advertisement will/will not be used. The method and form of advertisement are acceptable.

Genetic testing: This study involves/does not involve testing for genetic markers that are known to predict for the development of disease.

Tissue repository: This study involves/does not involve the storage of tissue for future research. Tissue samples are/are not linked to personal identifiers. *If yes*. . . The procedures for collecting, storing, and controlling access to tissue samples appear to be adequate to protect the rights of research participants.

Cost of research participation relative to the nonresearch alternative: This study does/does not involve increased costs to participants relative to a research alternative. *If yes*. . . The increase in cost is ethical in this situation and adequately explained in the consent document.

Payment or reimbursements to research participants: This study does/does not reimburse or pay subjects for their participation in the study. *If yes*. . . . The level and schedule of reimbursement/payment is reasonable in relation to study procedures. The investigators are sensitive to the issue of coercion and undue influence. Subjects for whom the payment is likely to be coercive will be excluded from the study.

Risks (relative to nonresearch alternative): The risks and discomforts of research participation were thoroughly evaluated. Risks are minimized by study design. The main risks of research participation are adequately summarized in the consent document.

Potential benefits: The committee determined that participation in this study
　　Will not directly benefit research participants
　　May directly benefit research participants
The study may benefit people in the future.
Altruism is the main reason that someone would participate in this study.

Risk/Benefit ratio: Risks of research participation are reasonable in view of potential benefits.

Confidentiality: Provisions to protect the privacy of subjects and the confidentiality of data are adequate

Data oversight: Study design provides for ongoing monitoring for the purpose of identifying unexpected results that would indicate a need for study revision. Data oversight will be performed by the principle investigator, the study sponsor, a formal Data Safety and Monitoring Board.

Consent document: The consent document accurately describes the important aspects of this study. Recognizing that participants are expected to discuss the details of the study with members of the research team, the consent document is likely to be understood by study participants. Revisions in the consent document that are required before final study approval can be granted include:

Vote (quorum:): approve, conditionally approve, not approve, abstain.

Interval of IRB approval: The study was approved for 12 months. The committee specifically addressed the issue of the degree of risk of the study when determining the approval interval.

PART 6
Informed Consent

The IRB's Role in Editing the Consent Document

Robin L. Penslar

INTRODUCTION

The consent document has been seen to absorb an inordinate amount of an IRB's time and resources. But in my view, the time IRBs spend on consent documents is not misplaced. They are not more important than the assessment of risk and ensuring that risks are minimized, but the consent materials submitted to IRBs are often of such a poor quality that they require considerable time and effort to ensure that subjects are properly informed and that their consent is appropriately documented. IRBs must not be bullied into accepting poorly constructed consent documents. If investigators cannot or will not generate consent documents that communicate clearly the necessary information, IRBs must do so. The way they go about ensuring that the final product is appropriate may vary, and I hope to offer here some advice about how they might do that. But first, I want to provide IRBs support for their efforts.

Importance of the Consent Document

The fact that IRBs spend so much time on the informed consent document has drawn a certain amount of criticism, with critics implying that the IRB has become no more than a high-powered editing team. And yet, because informed consent forms one of the cornerstones of the ethical conduct of research involving humans, it is imperative that IRBs ensure that participants are *informed about* and *voluntarily consent* to participation. That means that the study must not go forward until the IRB is assured that the consent *process* will take place in a way that ensures that prospective subjects' informed, voluntary decision to participate is not compromised, and the informed consent *document* communicates the necessary information in a meaningful, understandable way.

Document Versus Process

While I am going to focus here on the consent document, I also want to stress that IRBs must insist that investigators not refer to the consent document as "the consent." I am not saying that investigators do not, on some level, recognize the difference, but the language that is used is important, and IRBs must insist that the difference is acknowledged. Investigators must understand the difference between the presentation of information, and even the signing of a consent document, and bona fide consent as such. The document is not consent; it is only the record of what was supposed to have been communicated—

something for participants or prospective participants to take home to help them remember what they have agreed to do or think about doing. (It is not, however, proof of what participants actually understood or proof that they voluntarily consented, even it if says "I understand that . . ." and "I voluntarily consent. . . .") But for many subjects, it is also the primary means through which they learn the details of the study. For many studies, the consent process is as follows:

1. Tell the prospective subject there is a study in which he or she might want to participate.
2. Give the prospective subject a consent form to read.
3. Ask the prospective subject if he or she has any questions.
4. Ask the prospective subject to sign the form.

To be fair, I think that some of the confusion may have developed because the consent document has become the means through which investigators tell the IRB what they will tell subjects about the study, that is, the contents of the informed consent process. In that sense, then, the consent document and the consent process overlap. But they are conceptually distinct, and, in my opinion, IRBs must be vigilant in ensuring that the distinction is recognized. That said, the consent document is the only means IRBs have for determining what subjects will be told about the study and the language that will be used to provide that information.

The Importance of Grammar and Punctuation

Although they have to take care that the changes requested of consent documents are meaningful, IRBs must not blindly accept criticism that they are just nit-picking at the grammar or punctuation of the consent form. Consent documents often do not clearly communicate that the addressee is being invited to participate in research, what the study is trying to discover, what the procedures are, what the material risks are, and so forth. Even when all the relevant information is in the document (comments regarding the length of consent documents will be left to another day), it may be scattered, use lingo, not make sense, have mistakes (e.g., information in the protocol does not match information in the consent document), or provide contradictory information. If the document is ungrammatical, it does not communicate; if it does not communicate, it cannot serve its purpose. If the investigator cannot produce a proper consent document, then the IRB must do it, and the investigator must wait for study approval until the document satisfies the IRB.

Education of Investigators

IRBs should not give up on investigators. They can learn to prepare proper consents—I have seen them. An IRB that invests time in an educational effort can train its investigators and sponsors, and this investment of time will reduce review time in the long run.

Although IRB members may be frustrated with the quality of consent materials, simply sending materials back with the directive to "rewrite this" is not helpful. A great deal of literature on consent and drafting consent documents is not heeded; the question is how best to serve prospective subjects while providing timely reviews. I am arguing here that IRBs, who understand the issues the best, should accept the role of editor for projects submitted to them, while working to improve the quality of consents-as-submitted for future projects. Investigators are so overwhelmed by the size of submission packets and instructional materials that they simply shut down, unable to absorb what they perceive as an unwarrantedly complex review process. They learn best from being given exemplary material to use in guiding the preparation of their submission together with the changes that are requested during the review. Often, subsequent submissions improve as the investigator implements in the first instance things that were changed in the earlier review. I would suggest, then, that educational efforts take place at two points in time: before the review and during the review.

As Part of the Presubmission Process

1. Prepare template consent materials and make them available to investigators.

2. Distinguish between "required" language and "suggested" language.

3. If the IRB has decided that only certain language is acceptable, say so and provide it as part of the application packet.

4. If the IRB can provide suggested approaches to express various issues, provide several examples. Make it clear that the IRB will consider alternative language, but that the examples provided have been determined to be acceptable ways to handle an issue.

5. Do not try to force investigators to use specific language unless it truly is necessary. However, at times there are good reasons for insisting on certain language. Do not be intimidated by investigators who are anxious to begin the project and insist (for example) that the IRB is costing the university thousands of dollars by holding up their enrollments.

6. Remind investigators to review the consent to make sure that it addresses issues in the investigator's brochure or IRB application where risks, benefits, and procedures are described to make sure that there are not any contradictions and that all relevant risks are described. As a reviewer, I have often observed that the consent seems to be written from memory rather than from reference to the study documents.

7. Provide investigators a comprehensive list of the information that must go into a consent, with contingencies for various kinds of activities (e.g., videotaping, pregnancy testing, placebos).

8. Prepare advice for submitting investigators that addresses various issues that arise repeatedly. For example, warn investigators that if a study involves minors, they need to prepare an assent document as well as a parental permission document. Advise them to take care in the permission and assent documents' language regarding who is signing the document. Often, the language used in the parental permission confuses the parent's actions as opposed to the child's; keep clear what the parent is doing (allowing his child to do [X] if the child agrees plus any activities that the parent is specifically required to do) and what the child is doing (the study procedures).

9. Prepare information about the consent issues in research in various settings (e.g., schools, workplaces), or when various relationships require special handling (e.g., a teacher who wants to do research in his or her own classroom).

10. Provide examples of what is meant by sixth- to eighth-grade reading level. One way to do this might be to provide an example of typical consent language describing a procedure alongside a second version written in simpler language.

In Response to the Investigator During the Review

1. Tell the investigator exactly what you want, and where possible provide the exact language you want to be used, or give sufficient, well-worded instructions about the issue and options for handling it. It is not sufficient to simply say, "The risks are not clear" or "Include a statement about voluntariness." As advised earlier, be prepared to accept alternative wording if it satisfies the IRB's concerns.

2. Designate a single member of the IRB to be the primary consent editor. If your IRB charges for reviews, include a charge for consent editing and pay a member a stipend for editing to cover the additional time editing takes.

3. Make clear to investigators that the final step before approval of the study will be a thorough edit of the consent document for readability. They will be forewarned that there will likely be more than one set of revisions to the consent document.

4. When communicating with the investigator about the approved consent document, suggest that he or she refer to the requested changes when preparing future submissions; this can reduce the review time that will be required. In other words, suggest that investigators use the approved consent as a kind of template for future submissions, taking into account differences in the study design and special aspects of the studies (e.g., involvement of children or persons of child-bearing capacity, special confidentiality issues, etc.).

Conclusion

The time IRBs spend reviewing and editing consent documents is not misplaced. The consent document is one of the most important elements of the informed consent process. IRBs should not be bullied into accepting documents that fail to communicate the necessary information in language that is likely to be understood by potential research subjects. In my opinion, it is the responsibility of the IRB to revise the consent document as needed when the researcher is unable or unwilling to do so.

The Consent Document

Angela J. Bowen

INTRODUCTION

IRB members always hope that the consent document is only one step in the consent process. We know from experience, however, that it is not always so. The consent document should be clear and descriptive enough to stand alone in describing the essential elements of informed consent. This is not to say that the consent document should describe every event or potential risk that might be encountered by a study participant. Excessive detail may actually compromise the effectiveness of the consent document as an educational tool. As a basic guideline, the consent document should explain all of the information that a reasonable person would want to know to decide about research participation. The written format provides the subject with a continuing reference to the details of the research project and a historical reference, if needed. The review and processing of the document itself is often the most time-consuming part of the entire review process. While some of this is inevitable, there are economies of time that can be built into the system.

Processing the Document

As in most IRB staff work, there is no substitute for a well-trained staff member who knows the regulations and can write simple, declarative sentences. Most IRBs receive consent forms in a "finished" condition. That is to say, the sender thinks the document is finished. This is rarely the case. If the consent comes from the sponsor, it is likely to be too technical for the average reader. If the investigator has written it, expect the language to be on the reassuring side.

Have a seasoned staff member read the consent document before the full-committee meeting to be sure it contains all of the required elements of informed consent. These are listed here.

1. Informed consent shall include the following elements

   a. Statement that the study involves research (DHHS 45 CFR § 46.116(a)(1); FDA 21 CFR § 50.23(a)(1); ICH E6 § 4.8.10(a)).

   b. Explanation of the purposes of the research (DHHS 45 CFR § 46.116(a)(1); FDA 21 CFR § 50.23(a)(1); ICH E6 § 4.8.10(b)).

   c. Expected duration of the subject's participation in the research (DHHS 45 CFR § 46.116(a)(1); FDA 21 CFR § 50.23(a)(1); ICH E6 § 4.8.10(s)).

   d. Description of the procedures to be followed (DHHS 45 CFR § 46.116(a)(1); FDA 21 CFR § 50.23(a)(1); ICH E6 § 4.8.10(d)).

   e. Identification of any procedures that are experimental (DHHS 45 CFR § 46.116(a)(1); FDA 21 CFR § 50.25(a)(1); ICH E6 § 4.8.10(f)).

   f. Description of any reasonably foreseeable risks or discomforts to the subject (DHHS 45 CFR § 46.116(a)(2); FDA 21 CFR § 50.25(a)(2); ICH E6 § 4.8.10(g)).

   g. Description of any benefits to the subject or to others that may reasonably be expected from the research (DHHS 45 CFR § 46.116(a)(3); FDA 21 CFR § 50.25(a)(3); ICH E6 § 4.8.10(h)).

   h. Disclosure of appropriate alternative procedures or courses of treatment, if any, that might be advantageous to the subject (DHHS 45 CFR § 46.116(a)(4); FDA 21 CFR § 50.25(a)(4); ICH E6 § 4.8.10(i)).

   i. Statement describing the extent, if any, to which confidentiality of records identifying the subject will be maintained, and if applicable, a statement of the possibility that the Food and Drug Administration may inspect the records (DHHS 45 CFR § 46.116(a)(5); FDA 21 CFR § 50.25(a)(5); ICH E6 § 4.8.10(n) and (o)).

   j. For research involving more than minimal risk, an explanation as to whether any compensation is available if injury occurs, whether any medical treatments are available if injury occurs, and if so, what they consist of, or where further information can be obtained (DHHS 45 CFR § 46.116(a)(6); FDA 21 CFR § 50.25(a)(6); ICH E6 § 4.8.10(j)).

   k. Explanation of whom to contact for answers to pertinent questions about the research, research subject's rights, and whom to contact in the event of a research-related injury to the subject (DHHS 45 CFR § 46.116(a)(7); FDA 21 CFR § 50.25(a)(7); ICH E6 § 4.8.10(q)).

   l. Statement that participation is voluntary, that refusal to participate involves no penalty or loss of benefits to which the subject is otherwise entitled, and that the subject may discontinue participation at any time without penalty or loss of benefits to which the subject is otherwise entitled (DHHS 45 CFR § 46.116(a)(8); FDA 21 CFR § 50.25(a)(8); ICH E6 § 4.8.10(m)).

2. When appropriate, one or more of the following elements of information shall also be provided to each subject

   a. Statement that the particular treatment or procedure may involve risks to the subject (or to the embryo or fetus, if the subject is or may become pregnant) that are currently unforeseeable (DHHS 45 CFR § 46.116(b)(1); FDA 21 CFR § 50.25(b)(1)).

   b. Anticipated circumstances under which the subject's participation may be terminated by the investigator without regard to the subject's consent (DHHS 45 CFR § 46.116(b)(2); FDA 21 CFR § 50.25(b)(2); ICH E6 § 4.8.10(r)).

   c. Any additional costs to the subject that may result from participation in the research (DHHS 45 CFR § 46.116(b)(3); FDA 21 CFR § 50.25(b)(3); ICH E6 § 4.8.10(l)).

   d. Consequence of a subject's decision to withdraw from the research and procedures for orderly termination of participation by the subject (DHHS 45 CFR § 46.116(b)(4); FDA 21 CFR § 50.25(b)(4)).

   e. Statement that significant new findings developed during the course of the research, which may relate to the subject's willingness to continue, will be provided to the subject (DHHS 45 CFR § 46.116(b)(5); FDA 21 CFR § 50.25(b)(5); ICH E6 § 4.8.10(p)).

   f. Approximate number of subjects involved in the study (DHHS 45 CFR § 46.116(b)(6); FDA 21 CFR § 50.25(b)(6); ICH E6 § 4.8.10(t)).

   g. Study treatment(s) and the probability of random assignment to placebo or to each treatment (ICH E6 § 4.8.10(c)).

   h. The IRB may require that information, in addition to that required in Federal Regulations (DHHS 45 CFR Part 46; FDA 21 CFR Part 50) and ICH § 4.8, be given to research subjects when in its judgment the information would meaningfully add to the protection of the rights and welfare of subjects (DHHS 45 CFR § 46.109(b); FDA 21 CFR § 56.109(b); ICH E6 § 3.1.5).

If there are missing elements, staff can prepare a "redlined" version to go to the IRB, using autotext that has been previously approved by the IRB for use in such cases, or request such language from the investigator. In no case should an incomplete document be sent to the IRB for review, as this only wastes precious IRB time. I cannot emphasize enough the importance of using a system whereby an experienced reviewer revises the consent document as needed before the full-committee meeting. The IRB system was not set up with the idea that the full committee would spend time polishing the wording of the consent document. Most institutions have drafted certain stock language for confidentiality, compensation for injury, etc. These are acceptable practices that save considerable time during review.

Reviewing the Document

The IRB as a whole may review the proposed consent document, or the primary reviewer system can be used. In the latter case, the consent document is assigned to a nonphysician IRB member who recommends to the IRB necessary changes to make the final version readable at an elementary level. IRB members may then comment and discuss until consensus is reached.

Some IRBs make the necessary changes and send the approved version to the investigator, along with notice of what changes have been made and why. If the investigator does not accept all of the changes made by the IRB, it will be necessary to resubmit and await further review. I recommend this type of system because it saves the IRB time and energy, improves the efficiency of the IRB process, and creates good will between the IRB and research community. However, some IRBs view this process as unacceptable because they do not like the idea of "doing work that the investigator should do." There are IRBs that use the full-board meeting to identify changes that should be made to the consent document, then send the submitted document back unapproved, and request that the investigator try again. The belief, apparently, is that this exercise will provide engagement of the investigator into the consent process and provide needed instruction, as well. This may be a useful approach in institutions where teaching young investigators is a part of the IRB's responsibility, but it certainly decreases IRB efficiency and is likely to compromise respect for the IRB process within the institution.

Whatever procedure is employed, careful review by a convened IRB must occur. Following this review, the document must be approved and the pertinent discussions captured in the minutes. If the IRB has required additional changes, the reasons for these changes must be noted as well.

Finally, the document should be stamped "approved" on each page. This detail will prevent unauthorized changes, or at least render them easier to detect. The approval stamp should also include the date of approval and the designation of the approving IRB. Some boards include an expiration date, usually one year after initial approval.

If the board is making the required changes and sending out finished work, careful proofing must be included in the process. The Chair, or designee, should assure that all IRB-directed changes were captured in the final version.

If the investigator is making the IRB-directed changes and preparing the final document, there must be included in the process some procedure for assuring that all of the IRB's directed changes have been carried out. Note that this will require resubmission of the prepared final consent document for comparison with the original and the IRB-recommended changes. The final, complete version can then be stamped with the IRB's imprimatur as described above.

A copy of the final, approved version should be retained in the IRB's file for the study. The form, as submitted, should also be retained in the official study record.

Much has been written about the readability of consent forms. In the evaluation of this important element, the IRB should take into account the demographics of the population likely to be recruited into the research and make adjustments accordingly.

Conclusion

The consent document must be clear and descriptive enough to stand alone in describing the essential elements of informed consent. As a basic guideline, the consent document should explain all the information that a reasonable person would want to know to decide about research participation. Information beyond this simple standard is likely to compromise the consent process. This chapter presents recommendations for processing the consent document prior to the IRB meeting and reviewing the document at the meeting.

Regulation Resources
Sections of several documents were cited in the text in abbreviated form.

DHHS 45 CFR 46
Code of Federal Regulations. Title 45A—Department of Health and Human Services; Part 46—Protection of Human Subjects.
Updated 1 Oct 1997. Access date 18 Apr 2001.
World Wide Web
http://www4law.cornell.edu/cfr/45p46.htm

FDA 21 CFR 50
Code of Federal Regulations. Title 21, Chapter 1—Food and Drug Administration, DHHS; Part 50—Protection of Human Subjects.
Updated 1 Apr 1999. Access date 18 Apr 2001.
World Wide Web
http://www4.law.cornell.edu/cfr/21p50.htm

FDA 21 CFR 56
Code of Federal Regulations. Title 21, Chapter 1—Food and Drug Administration, DHHS; Part 56—Institutional Review Boards.
Updated 1 Apr 1999. Access date 27 Mar 2001
World Wide Web
http://www4.law.cornell.edu/cfr/21p56.htm

ICH E6 Sections 3.1 and 4.8
Food and Drug Administration. International Conference on Harmonisation: Good clinical practice. Published in the *Federal Register,* Vol. 62, No. 90, May 9, 1997, pages 25691–25709
World Wide Web
http://www.ifpma.org/ich5e.html

Exculpatory Language in Informed Consent Documents

Michele Russell-Einhorn and Thomas Puglisi

INTRODUCTION

Investigators are frequently admonished by their Institutional Review Boards (IRBs) to refrain from using exculpatory language in their informed consent documents. Almost as frequently, this admonishment comes with little or no explanation of what constitutes "exculpatory language." Indeed, many IRBs seem confused about where to draw the line in determining whether a proposed statement is exculpatory. The purpose of this chapter is to explain how IRB members and researchers can identify and avoid the use of exculpatory language in the consent document.

Federal Regulations

Whenever there is doubt about a regulatory requirement, a careful reading of the regulatory language itself is an important starting point. Federal policy (the Common Rule) for the protection of human subjects in research sets forth the following prohibition.

> No informed consent, whether oral or written, may include any exculpatory language through which the subject or the representative is made to waive or appear to waive any of the subject's legal rights or releases or appears to release the investigator, the sponsor, the institution or its agents from liability for negligence.[1]

This prohibition is codified in exactly the same language in regulations of the Department of Health and Human Services (DHHS) [2(Sec.116)] and the Food and Drug Administration (FDA).[3(Sec.20)]

The Narrow (But Incorrect) Interpretation

A narrow interpretation of the regulatory language would limit the prohibition to statements involving a release from liability for negligence. Those who argue in favor of the narrow interpretation point out that in common usage (as verified by any current dictionary), the word *exculpatory* relates to lack of guilt. This is also the case relative to its usage in law. According to Black's Law Dictionary,[4] *exculpatory* involves clearing "from alleged fault or guilt" or releasing "from liability" for "wrongful acts."

The Broad (Correct) Interpretation

These arguments notwithstanding, the DHHS, through the Office for Protection from Research Risks (OPRR), its successor Office for Human Research Protections (OHRP), and the FDA, has a long history of applying a much broader interpretation of the exculpatory language prohibition. A careful reading of the regulatory language reveals that, in this context, the meaning of the phrase *exculpatory language* is expanded to include any language "through which the subject or the representative is made to waive or appear to waive *any* of the subject's legal rights." Thus, any language waiving or appearing to waive any legal right (regardless of the nature of that right) is prohibited.

Practical Applications

In a practical sense, exculpatory statements tend to be statements in which a subject in a research protocol is asked to agree to or accept something, usually something unfavorable to the subject. A statement that sets forth simple facts, on the other hand, is usually not likely to be viewed as exculpatory.

In the following examples, the institution simply sets forth the facts describing the institution's intent and policy. These statements would not be considered exculpatory under the regulations, and would be permissible.

Examples

1. The University Medical School has no policy or plan to pay for any injuries you might receive as a result of participating in this research protocol.
2. As part of the research protocol, the investigators will extract some cells from the blood you have donated. The university may commercialize some of these cells that derive from the research. The university does not plan to share any profits with the subject from whom the cells were obtained.

The following examples, however, would be considered exculpatory and are prohibited under the regulations. Note that in these examples, subjects are being asked to make a statement that they agree with and accept the actions of the institution as a condition for participation in the research.

Examples

1. I agree that the medical center will not pay me for any injuries that I might sustain as a result of participating in this research.

2. I understand that the institution will not share with me any profits received from the sale or commercialization of any cells developed in this research.

3. I agree that everything in this consent form is adequate and complies with the regulations.

4. I understand that I will not sue the sponsor or the investigator for any negligence.

5. Subjects agree to hold harmless all institutions, investigators, or sponsors affiliated with or in any way a part of this research protocol.

Again, a good rule of thumb is to state simply the factual situation and avoid any statement that requires the agreement or concurrence of the subject.

OHRP Guidance

The Office for Human Research Protections (OHRP) (formerly the Office of Protection from Research Risks, OPRR) maintains a Web site that includes guidance on various topics relevant to the protection of human subjects in research. The OHRP's Web site includes the appended document on exculpatory language from the 1996 Cooperative Oncology Group Chairpersons Meeting.[5]

References

1. Federal Policy for Protection of Human Subjects (Common Rule). Source: *Fed Regist* 56:28003, June 18, 1991 (Final Rule). Effective date: August 19, 1991. Posted on University of Michigan IRB Web site. Access date 19 Aug 2001. World Wide Web http://www.med.umich.edu/irbined/FederalDocuments/FedPolicy/FederalPolicy.html

2. Code of Federal Regulations. Title 45A—Department of Health and Human Services; Part 46—Protection of Human Subjects. Updated 1 Oct 1997. Access date 18 Apr 2001. World Wide Web http://www4.law.cornell.edu/cfr/45p46.htm

3. Code of Federal Regulations. Title 21, Chapter 1—Food and Drug Administration, DHHS; Part 50—Protection of Human Subjects. Updated 1 Apr 1999. Access date 18 Apr 2001. World Wide Web http://www4.law.cornell.edu/cfr/21p50.htm

4. Black HC. Black's Law Dictionary: Definitions of the Terms and Phrases of American and English Jurisprudence, Ancient and Modern, 6th ed. Nolan JR, Nolan-Haley JM (editors). St. Paul, MN, West Publishing Co., 1990.

5. Office for Protection from Research Risks. "Exculpatory language" in informed consent. Cooperative Oncology Group Chairpersons Meeting, November 15, 1996. Access date 19 Aug 2001. World Wide Web http://ohrp.osophs.dhhs.gov/humansubjects/guidance/exculp.htm

Appendix

Office for Protection from Research Risks (OPRR)

**Cooperative Oncology Group Chairpersons Meeting[5]
November 15, 1996**

"Exculpatory Language" in Informed Consent

No informed consent, whether oral or written, may include any exculpatory language through which the subject is made to waive or appear to waive any of the subject's legal rights, or releases or appears to release the investigator, the sponsor, the institution, or its agents from liability for negligence. — *45 CFR 46.116*

Examples of Exculpatory Language:
- By agreeing to this use, you should understand that you will give up all claim to personal benefit from commercial or other use of these substances.
- I voluntarily and freely donate any and all blood, urine, and tissue samples to the U.S. Government and hereby relinquish all right, title, and interest to said items.

- By consent to participate in this research, I give up any property rights I may have in bodily fluids or tissue samples obtained in the course of the research.
- I waive any possibility of compensation for injuries that I may receive as a result of participation in this research.

Examples of Acceptable Language:
- Tissue obtained from you in this research may be used to establish a cell line that could be patented and licensed. There are no plans to provide financial compensation to you should this occur.
- By consenting to participate, you authorize the use of your bodily fluids and tissue samples for the research described above.
- This hospital is not able to offer financial compensation nor to absorb the costs of medical treatment should you be injured as a result of participating in this research.
- This hospital makes no commitment to provide free medical care or payment for any unfavorable outcomes resulting from participation in this research. Medical services will be offered at the usual charge.

Requiring a Witness Signature on the Consent Form

Michele Russell-Einhorn and Thomas Puglisi

INTRODUCTION

Some Institutional Review Boards (IRBs) require the signature of a witness on informed consent documents. The requirement for a witness signature could derive from four possible sources: (1) the Federal Policy (Common Rule) for the Protection of Human Subjects; (2) Food and Drug Administration (FDA) regulations; (3) state law; or (4) IRB or institutional policy.

Federal Requirements

The Federal Policy (Common Rule) for the Protection of Human Subjects does not require a witness signature when the research utilizes a standard informed consent document that embodies all of the required elements of informed consent codified by the Department of Health and Human Services (DHHS) at 45 CFR 46.[1][Sec.116(a),(b)] Nor do the regulations require the investigator's signature when a standard consent document is used. In this situation, federal policy only requires that the consent document is signed by the subject or the subject's legally authorized representative.[1][Sec.117(b)(1)]

The signature of a witness is required under federal policy only when the IRB authorizes the use of a "short form written consent document."[1][Sec.117(b)(2)] In this situation, federal policy requires that the witness (a) observe the oral presentation of informed consent information to the subject; (b) sign the short form written consent document; and (c) sign a copy of the summary of the oral presentation approved by the IRB. In addition, the summary must also be signed by the person obtaining consent, and the short form consent document must also be signed by the subject or the subject's legally authorized representative.

FDA regulations contain these same provisions.[2][Sec.26], [2][Sec.27(b)(1),(2)]

State and Institutional Requirements

Although federal regulations require a witness signature on the informed consent document only in the circumstances described above, state laws regarding informed consent for research may require the signature of a witness in additional circumstances. It is important to understand that when state requirements provide protections for human subjects beyond those required under federal regulations, the more protective state requirements must be observed.

State laws vary widely as to the specificity of requirements for informed consent in research contexts. Consequently, IRBs have a responsibility to educate themselves thoroughly as to state law requirements.

In addition, an institution or an IRB may require the signature of a witness on informed consent documents as a matter of policy. Institutions and IRBs always have the authority to require protections for human subjects that exceed the minimum standards required under federal regulations.

The Purpose of Witness Signatures

It is important that investigators and IRBs understand the purpose of requiring witness signatures on informed consent documents. There are two key issues to be considered: (1) to what is the witness attesting, i.e., what does the signature mean? and (2) under what circumstances should the witness refrain from signing the document?

Requiring that a witness merely observe the subject signing the consent document without witnessing any part of the consent process adds little or nothing to the goal of protecting human subjects. Such a requirement may serve to protect the investigator or the institution from liability, but it contributes nothing to the quality of the information exchange between investigator and subject.

On the other hand, a witness who observes the dialogue between the investigator and the human subject can qualitatively enhance the informed consent process. The mere presence of a witness–observer during the consent conference should motivate the investigator to ensure a complete and meaningful disclosure of information. The witness can then attest that the informed consent process included all required elements, that the subject appeared to be capable of making an informed decision, and that an opportunity was provided for the subject to ask questions of the investigator. In this situation, the witness signature means that the witness has observed a consent process that appeared to satisfy regulatory requirements.

Conclusion

To make the requirement for a witness signature meaningful, witnesses should be instructed about what to look for in observing the informed consent process and the circumstances under which they should decline to sign the informed consent document. If the witness observes any indication of coercion by the investigator or lack of understanding on the part of the subject, it would be appropriate for the witness to refrain from signing the informed consent document.

Finally, whether or not the signature of a witness is required, the fundamental purpose of informed consent must be honored. By whatever means, the subject must be provided with sufficient information to make a truly informed, voluntary decision free from coercion or undue influence. Regardless of the circumstances, any witness signature requirement should be made with the goal of serving this fundamental purpose.

References

1. Code of Federal Regulations. Title 45A—Department of Health and Human Services; Part 46—Protection of Human Subjects. Updated 1 Oct 1997. Access date 18 Apr 2001. World Wide Web http://www4.law.cornell.edu/cfr/45p46.htm

2. Code of Federal Regulations. Title 21, Chapter 1—Food and Drug Administration, DHHS; Part 50—Protection of Human Subjects. Updated 1 Apr 1999. Access date 18 Apr 2001. World Wide Web http://www4.law.cornell.edu/cfr/21p50.htm

Deception of Research Subjects

Laurie Slone and Jay Hull

INTRODUCTION

The purpose of this chapter is to discuss research in which the subject is intentionally deceived about research participation. Deception is common in studies that evaluate fundamental aspects of human behavior. The rationale for deception in this setting is that it is not possible to obtain accurate information about how people behave when they know that they are being observed or evaluated.

Despite its possible justification, the use of deception creates ethical problems for researchers. Although many would argue that some forms of deception can be justified, most would also argue that those who would use deception in their research must explicitly justify its use in their particular case. The very practice of deception may create harm, exacerbate harm created in other ways, and raise difficult issues regarding the nature and meaning of informed consent. Arguments against the use of deception are usually weighed against arguments in favor of the benefits of gaining knowledge about the causes of human behavior. This chapter explores both the costs and the benefits of the use of deception in psychological research for the purpose of outlining specific issues with which Institutional Review Boards (IRBs) need to be concerned. The goal of this chapter is to describe when the use of deception may be considered justifiable as well as to indicate what forms of deception should not be tolerated.

Background

The use of deception in research on human behavior has been debated extensively over the past 35 years. Ironically, much of this debate was initially triggered by what many consider one of the most important sets of social psychological experiments ever conducted: research on obedience by Stanley Milgram (1963). In the Milgram studies, participants were recruited to participate in a "teacher-learner experiment." When they arrived, they were told that they were to play the role of the teacher. The other "participant" in the study was to play the role of the learner and was taken to a room next door. The "teacher" was told that the study concerned the effects of punishment on learning and that each time the "learner" made a mistake, he or she was to administer an electric shock. Shocks started at 15 volts, and for each mistake the subsequent shock was to be increased by 15 volts. The maximum shock was labeled 450 volts and was two steps beyond the designation "Danger: Severe Shock." If at any time the "teacher" balked at administering the shocks, the experimenter adhered to a script that basically told the participant to continue and that the experimenter would take responsibility for any consequences of the participant's action.

In actuality, (a) the study did not concern learning but rather concerned the causes of obedience; (b) the "student" was a confederate of the experimenter and did not receive any shocks, and (c) the behavior of interest was not the ability of the student to learn but rather the amount of shock that the participant would administer. As reported by Milgram,[1] independent judges estimated that very few people (1%) would go all the way to the end of the shock scale. In fact, the majority of participants (65%) administered shocks up to and including the highest levels possible.

The Milgram experiment includes classic elements of many social psychological experiments that use deception: a "cover story" providing a plausible but inaccurate account of the purpose of the study, a "confederate" pretending to be another participant in the study, and misdirection regarding the particular behaviors of interest to the researchers. The Milgram experiments are also widely cited as some of the most important ever conducted in social psychology. This is because they provide striking insights into an aspect of human behavior held to be responsible for some of the worst atrocities of the twentieth century: unquestioned obedience to authority, as witnessed in the horrors of the Holocaust. As a consequence, these obedience studies place, in stark contrast, arguments for and against the use of deception in research on human behavior.

One of the most vocal early critics of the Milgram studies was Herbert Kelman. Kelman[2] argued that deception in psychological experimentation generally — and in the Milgram studies specifically — is unethical, potentially harmful to the research participant, harmful to the profession, and ultimately harmful to society. There is no denying that participants in Milgram's research were distressed by the experience. They were visibly upset during the experiment and some were upset at the conclusion of the experiment when they realized the implications of their actions. They realized their own capacity to do harm to others — a lesson that was unaffected when they subsequently learned that no one was actually shocked. Kelman's other argument — that the use of deceptive research is harmful to the reputation of the profession and to society as a whole — appears to be less persuasive.

In counterpoint to Kelman's and others' critiques,[3] many have argued[4] that social psychological research often *requires* deceptive techniques. The argument for the selective use of deception in research is essentially twofold. First, it is important to understand the causes of human behavior (e.g., why and when people conform, what conditions facilitate and impede helping behavior, why people are aggressive, and the causes of prejudiced behavior). Second, to discern the true causes of such behavior, research at a minimum requires that the participant does not know the topic under investigation. Thus, for example, it is argued that one cannot study the dynamics of conformity by asking participants whether they would or would not go along with the majority when the latter was obviously wrong. Rather, one must lead a participant to believe that he or she is the only individual in a group to hold a particular opinion.[5] Similarly, one cannot study helping behavior by having people imagine how they would behave if they heard another person cry for help. Rather, one must lead them to believe that another person actually needs help, and observe what they do.[6] According to a review by Gross and Fleming,[7] 90% of the studies on compliance/conformity, altruism, and aggression use deceptive techniques. In addition, 50% or more of the studies on attribution processes, achievement motivation, attraction/affiliation, attitude formation/consistency/change, nonverbal communication, bargaining, self-disclosure, self-awareness, and interpersonal equity use deceptive techniques. In essence, then, "experimenters often find themselves in the troublesome position of concealing the truth from their subjects in order to *reveal* a truth about human behavior."[8]

Milgram's research is itself a good example that a person's response to a hypothetical situation cannot be taken as representative of how that person would actually act. Although a small minority of individuals were thought to be capable of administering extreme shocks, in point of fact, a majority of people actually did. Multiple well-established lines of research provide support for the claim that individuals do not actually know why they do what they do, but this does not stop them from making up coherent accounts of their actions. These accounts are often at odds with the actual causes of their behavior in such circumstances.[9] Thus, simply asking participants to "role play" how they would act in a particular situation does not produce the same behavior as that actually observed by "naive" participants.[10] Some researchers *are* interested in studying such "as if" behaviors in the sense that the stories people tell about how they would act and the theories they have about themselves and others are themselves interesting objects of study. However, few would claim that these behaviors are governed by the same processes that yield spontaneous behavior when confronting actual situations.

Thus, the argument is made that to build a base of knowledge on what causes people to act certain ways, one must examine their behavior in situations they regard as "real." This often requires deception.

Guidelines for Research Involving Deception

If one grants that it is impossible to study certain aspects of human behavior without adopting deceptive techniques, then the justification of such research evolves into a question of costs and benefits: the benefits gained by knowledge relative to the potential harm caused by deception. To some extent, this is a question of personal values. However, it also suggests that specific codes of conduct should be developed that serve to minimize the negative impact of deceptive techniques. The American Psychological Association (APA) has developed just such a code.[11] The two sections relevant to deception in research are presented here.

6.15 Deception in Research

(a) Psychologists do not conduct studies involving deception unless they have determined that the use of deceptive techniques is justified by the study's prospective scientific, educational, or applied value and that equally effective alternative procedures that do not use deception are not feasible.

(b) Psychologists never deceive research participants about significant aspects that would affect their willingness to participate, such as physical risks, discomfort, or unpleasant emotional experiences.

(c) Any other deception that is an integral feature of the design and conduct of an experiment must be explained to participants as early as is feasible. Preferably, at the conclusion of their participation, but no later than at the conclusion of the research.

6.18 Providing Participants with Information About the Study

(a) Psychologists provide a prompt opportunity for participants to obtain appropriate information about the nature, results, and conclusions of the research, and psychologists attempt to correct any misconceptions that participants may have.

(b) If scientific or humane values justify delaying or withholding this information, psychologists take reasonable measures to reduce the risk of harm.

Basically, according to the APA, deception in research requires that the researcher (a) apply a cost-benefit analysis that explicitly considers the potential for harm created and/or exacerbated by the use of deception; (b) consider alternative methodologies; and (c) fully explain the nature of the deception at the conclusion of the study or explicitly justify withholding such information. In all cases, the safety and comfort of the participant should be of paramount concern.

Issues When Evaluating the Use of Deception in Research

As we have seen in the Milgram study, deception in an experimental setting can take many forms, as can subterfuge regarding the specific behaviors that are the subject of study. For example, a "cover story" can provide an alternate account of the true nature of the experiment, and experimental "confederates" can be used to enact a particular role for the sake of the experimental design. A review by Gross and Fleming[7] found that, among studies using deceptive techniques, 82% of the deceptions involved a cover story or false statements regarding the purpose of the research. In addition, 42% involved incorrect information concerning the stimulus materials. In addition, 29% involved the use of a confederate or actor, 18% involved false feedback to the participant, and 14% involved unawareness on the part of the participant that he or she was even in a study. Additionally, 9% involved two related experiments being presented as if they were unrelated, 5% involved false feedback about a confederate or another person, and 4% involved unawareness that the study was in progress at the time of the manipulation.

As implied in the APA code, when evaluating the use of any of these deceptive techniques, IRB members should consider the following:

1. The scientific value and validity of the research

2. The efficacy of alternative procedures

3. The certainty that deception does not extend to influence participants' willingness to participate

4. The possibility of experimentally induced harm and the ability of the proposed procedures to remove such harm through debriefing

5. The potential of deception to facilitate unwanted and inappropriate invasions of privacy

Validity of the Research

Deciding that the proposed research is a valid and worthwhile undertaking is a mainstay of the scientific review process. Thoughtful planning, solid empirical background research, precedent, and a determination of the potential benefits of the proposed research all need to be considered.

Alternative Methodologies

Having made the decision that an experimental design is valid and potentially worthwhile, the researcher must consider alternative procedures before concluding that the knowledge sought by the study requires the use of deception. From a methodological perspective, deception is used on the premise that it is important to keep participants naive about the purpose of the study so that they can respond to experimental manipulations spontaneously. According to this view, deception is an essential methodology because it enables researchers to obtain adequate experimental control and to observe behavior of participants that would be qualitatively altered if nondeceptive techniques were used. Researchers must make the case that these arguments are in fact applicable to their specific hypotheses.

Limits

As stated in the APA code, the researcher cannot deceive participants regarding "significant aspects that would affect their willingness to participate."[11][Sec.6.15(b)] One limit to be considered is the compatibility of deceptive practices with participants' moral values. The characteristics, values, and morals of the experimental sample must be carefully considered. A group of senior citizens will undoubtedly have quite a different reaction to talking about sex than will a group of 20-year-old college students. Deception on specific topics should be reviewed with the target group in mind.

Potential Harm

Deception is rarely used when physical harm is a possibility. Deception *is* sometimes used when the experimental procedures may result in temporary psychological discomfort including stress, loss in self-esteem in response to experimental manipulations, embarrassment at being deceived, and guilt at having been induced to commit regretted acts. For example, false feedback about task performance is often intended to induce a temporary loss of self-esteem, and regret can occur when participants are induced to present themselves in a manner that is inconsistent with their own personal beliefs. Negative responses can occur even when the deceptive techniques appear relatively innocuous. Imagine, for example, a case in which participants are told they are being recruited for participation in a study in which they will receive electric shocks. Imagine further that they never receive any shocks but are simply observed for their anticipatory reaction. In this case, the participants obviously receive less physical pain than they expected and agreed to undergo. Yet once they are told of the ruse, they also may feel a sense of embarrassment over allowing themselves to be duped by the experimenter.

Researchers conducting studies in which temporary psychological discomfort may be created often follow two guidelines. First, an attempt is made to limit such discomfort to a level that is normally encountered in everyday life. Second, at the end of the study an attempt is made to eliminate any discomfort through a thorough and sensitive "debriefing." As stated in the APA code, such postexperimental debriefings involve a complete disclosure as to any deceptions or misconceptions that the participant may have about the purpose of the experiment, the nature of the manipulations, the role of confederates, the fact that they were randomly assigned to receive particular forms of feedback, etc. In addition, the experimenter should make explicit attempts to relieve any negative reactions that the participant may have experienced. How this is accomplished obviously depends on the nature of the experimental procedures and the particular experiences of the participants. However, in most cases in which deception is used as a technique, the experimenter must make sure that the participant understands the nature of the deception, the care with which it was designed to ensure that all participants would actually be deceived, and the necessity of its use to properly test the hypotheses of interest. Experimenters should especially be aware of the possibility of embarrassment at having been deceived. Additionally, they must go to some lengths to emphasize that it is not the gullibility of the participant but rather the skill of the experimenter that is responsible for the success of the deception.

Privacy and Confidentiality

Finally, the use of deception raises potential issues regarding unwanted invasions of privacy. Particularly with the advent and widespread availability of sophisticated surveillance technology, care must be taken either to obtain in advance the participants' approval to record their behavior for research purposes, or in cases where they believed that they were not being recorded to allow them the opportunity to deny the use of such information after it has been acquired. Specific procedures are often used by researchers that require a separate signature of the participant on the debriefing form giving explicit permission to use video or audio tapes of the participant's behaviors. On a related issue, participants should never be deceived regarding the confidentiality of the information they provide. Experimental data and results should be kept confidential, and if possible, the participants' identity should be kept anonymous, especially if the acquired information is of a sensitive nature.

Informed Consent

By definition, deceptive procedures eliminate the possibility of fully informed consent. As a consequence, the APA code explicitly states: "Psychologists never deceive research participants about significant aspects that would affect their willingness to participate."[11] Obviously, this places the researcher and the IRB in the position of determining whether the procedures are potentially of a nature such that they would cause discomfort sufficient to cause a participant to withdraw from the study if they were known in advance. The fact that all participants are informed that they may choose to withdraw from a study at any time for any reason does not reduce the responsibilities of the researcher in this regard. Furthermore, as stated earlier, at the conclusion of the experiment it is the researcher's responsibility to institute explicit procedures to alleviate any discomfort that was experienced during the course of the study.

Although participants may not be fully informed, obviously they should be informed of as much as possible without threatening the ability of the researcher to test the true hypothesis of the study. Our recommendation is that the consent form (a) should *never* be used as part of the deception and thus should not include anything that is untrue, and (b) should reveal as much as possible to the participant regarding the procedures in the study. However, the consent form does not need to detail specific elements of the study if this will eliminate the capability of the study to inform the process under investigation. A useful guideline to keep in mind is that the experimenter—subject relationship is a real relationship "in which we have responsibility toward the subject as another human being whose dignity we must preserve."[12]

Research on Participants' Reactions to Experiments Involving Deception

The relative incidence and psychological consequences of deceptive research have actually been examined empirically. According to reviews by Gross and Fleming[7] and Sieber et al. (as cited by Cozby[13]), for selected years between 1959 and 1992, between one third (32%) and two thirds (69%) of the articles published in the premier social psychological journal (*Journal of Personality and Social Psychology*) have involved deception. Most recently (1992), 47% of articles in this journal were observed to use some form of deception.

The fact that rates have remained relatively stable for over 30 years despite the advent of IRBs and changes in the APA standards for research suggests that the typical use of deception is seen as warranted and justified. Most deception in social psychological research involves laboratory research in which a cover story is constructed to lead the participant to believe that a particular set of circumstances exists. The deceptions are relatively innocuous, do not involve harm to the subject, and are clearly justified given the nature of the processes the researchers are interested in investigating and the procedures adopted to circumvent any negative consequences that may be caused or worsened by the deception. Support for this point of view comes from research that has directly examined participants' responses to their experiences in deceptive research.

Multiple studies that have examined the effects of deception on participants' perceptions have found that the vast majority of participants (90%) perceive social psychological experiments as valuable and valid. In addition, the use of deception is seen as necessary to examine the behavior of interest.[14] In one study, Gerdes[15] randomly assigned participants to one of 15 different experiments that used a range of deceptive techniques. It was found that participants reported virtually no annoyance (.42 on a 5-point [0 – 4] scale, "not at all to very much") and stated they did not mind being misled (.61 on the same scale). Indeed, Smith and Richardson[16] actually found that participants in deception experiments found the experience more enjoyable and reported more educational benefit than those in nondeception experiments, presumably because the former were less boring.

As noted earlier, Kelman[2] expressed concern over the potential harm of deceptive research to the reputation of the profession ("our potential subjects will become increasingly distrustful of us and our future relations with them are likely to be undermined"). In fact, a study by Sharpe et al.[17] compared ratings from 1970 and 1990 of participants' favorability toward psychological research. They concluded their results "do not support the proposition that introductory psychology students . . . have become more negative toward psychological research over the last two decades."

Although empirical evidence does seem to support the continued use of deception in psychological research, we should not use this evidence to lull us into the complacent belief that deception is an acceptable procedure for use in all studies. Christensen[18] reports that although subjects do not appear to object to the use of deception in general, if deception is used as a means of invading their privacy, it is viewed less positively. If nonprivate behaviors are being investigated (as is typical in laboratory studies), deception is viewed as a rather innocuous experimental procedure. If behaviors are investigated where participants had a reasonable expectation of privacy, however, the use of deception serves to enhance the participants' perception that their privacy has been invaded. A study by Tanke[19] makes a related point. This study revealed that the inclusion of deception is not independently correlated with the perception of ethicality: as long as the experimental procedure itself runs little risk in harming the research participant, deception is viewed as innocuous. However, perceived harm *is* correlated with the perception of ethicality of the study and interacts with deception such that if the experimental procedure has a significant potential for harming the research participant, then deception is viewed as ethically less acceptable than a nondeceptive design.

Conclusion

As previously noted, most forms of deception encountered by IRB members involve the creation of plausible but inaccurate cover stories and procedures designed to misdirect the participant's attention for the sake of examining spontaneous behavior. As long as the main procedures used in the study are judged to be innocuous, such deception is not typically viewed as objectionable. If the main procedures do engender temporary negative reactions of a nature typically experienced in the course of everyday life, the use of deception need not be viewed as objectionable as long as it is scientifically justified and the researcher uses procedures specifically designed to alleviate such re-

actions. If the procedures cause negative reactions that could plausibly affect the participant's willingness to take part in the study, that are outside the range of everyday experience, or that are not amenable to alleviation through debriefing, then deception is in all likelihood inappropriate. IRBs and researchers must continue to work together to ensure proper and appropriate research procedures that protect experimental participants while supporting the pursuit of scientific knowledge.

References

1. Milgram S. Behavioral study of obedience. *J Abnorm Soc Psychol* 67:371–378, 1963.

2. Kelman HC. Human use of human subjects: The problem of deception in social psychological experiments. *Psychological Bulletin* 67:1–11, 1967.

3. Baumrind D. Some thoughts on ethics research: After reading Milgram's "Behavioral Study of Obedience." *Am Psychol* 19:421–423, 1964.

4. Aronson E, Carlsmith JM. Experimentation in social psychology. In: Lindzey G, Aronson E (eds). *The Handbook of Social Psychology*, Ed. 2 (Chapter 2). Reading,MA: Addison-Wesley. 1968: 1–79.

5. Asch S. Effects of group pressure upon the modification and distortion of judgements. In: Swanson GE, Newcomb TM, Hartley EL (eds). *Readings in Social Psychology*. New York: Holt, Rhinehart and Winston. 1952.

6. Latane B, Darley JM. Group inhibition of bystander intervention in emergencies. *J Person Soc Psychol* 10:215–221, 1968.

7. Gross AE, Fleming I. Twenty years of deception in social psychology. *Personality and Social Psychology Bulletin* 8:402–408, 1982.

8. Aronson E, Ellsworth PC, Carlsmith JM, Gonzales MH. *Methods of Research in Social Psychology*. New York: McGraw-Hill. 1990.

9. Nisbett RE, Wilson TD. Telling more than we can know: Verbal reports on mental processes. *Psychological Review* 84:231–259, 1977.

10. Freedman JL. Role playing: Psychology by consensus. *J Person Soc Psychol* 13:107–114, 1969.

11. American Psychological Association. Ethical principles of psychologists and code of conduct. Updated 1992. Access date 22 Mar 2001. World Wide Web http://www.apa.org/ethics/code.html

12. Kelman HC. The rights of the subject in social research: An analysis in terms of relative power and legitimacy. *Am Psychol* 27:989–1016, 1972.

13. Cozby PC. *Methods in Behavioral Research*, Ed 6. Mountain View, CA: Mayfield Publishing Co. 1997.

14. Fisher CB, Fyrberg D. Participant partners: College students weigh the costs and benefits of deceptive research. *Am Psychol* 49:417–427, 1994.

15. Gerdes EP. College students' reactions to social psychological experiments involving deception. *J Soc Psychol* 107:99–110, 1979.

16. Smith SS, Richardson D. Amelioration of deception and harm in psychological research: The important role of debriefing. *J Person Soc Psychol* 44:1075–1082, 1983.

17. Sharpe D, Adair JG, Roese NJ. Twenty years of deception research: A decline in subjects' trust? *Personality and Social Psychology Bulletin* 18:585–590, 1992.

18. Christensen L. Deception in psychological research: When is its use justified? *Personality and Social Psychology Bulletin* 14:664–675, 1988.

19. Tanke ED. Perceptions of ethicality of psychological research: Effects of experiment status, experimenter outcome, and authoritarianism. *Personality and Social Psychology Bulletin* 5:164–168, 1979.

Research Without Consent or Documentation Thereof

Marianne M. Elliott

INTRODUCTION

The purpose of this chapter is to explain the situations wherein federal regulations permit the Institutional Review Board (IRB) to approve research and waive the requirement for informed consent or the requirement for documentation of informed consent. A special case of the waiver-of-consent issue is the situation wherein research is conducted in the setting of medical emergency. Emergency medical research without consent is discussed in Chapter 4-6.

Respect for Persons

The principle of respect for persons described in the *Belmont Report* notes that individuals must be autonomous in their decisions about whether to participate in research. For individuals to make an informed decision, the researcher must provide specific information about the research to potential subjects. The Department of Health and Human Services (DHHS) human subject protections regulations[1(Sec.116)] and the Food and Drug Administration (FDA) regulations[2] describe the specific context of the consent process and the required elements of a consent. Researchers must present this information to individuals in language understandable to them and assess that individuals have comprehended the information for them to make an informed decision. Researchers must also ensure that the consent process and the consent document affirm that each individual's decision to participate in research is voluntary and free from undue influence. In general, the researcher documents the consent process, while the individuals who decide to participate document their agreement to participate in the research by signing and dating the consent document.

In some instances, the IRB has authority based on federal regulations to waive the requirement to obtain informed consent from subjects and/or the requirement to have subjects sign a consent document. In these instances, the IRB determines that, before his or her participation in the research, the individual's informed consent, or elements of the process and document, can be waived. The IRB may also decide that the documentation of the consent from the individual subject can be waived. The regulations provide specific criteria that the IRB must consider before making a decision to waive or alter either informed consent or documentation of informed consent (obtaining the individual's signature on a consent document).

These two types of waiver are separate and distinct, yet researchers, IRB members, and IRB administrators frequently confuse the two different types. Each type of waiver must satisfy specific criteria before the IRB can grant the waiver. The IRB and IRB administrators must be aware of the limited instances where the IRB may waive these requirements.

Risk Assessment

To grant a waiver of informed consent, an alteration of the consent elements or procedures, or the requirement to obtain a signed consent document, the IRB must assess and evaluate the potential risks and expected benefits associated with participation in the research and the consent process. In evaluating the risk, the IRB must assess the risk or harms inherent in the informed consent process or documentation of informed consent. In some circumstances, the consent process and existence of a signed consent document may involve more risk or potentially more harm to subjects than participating in the research itself. Thus, the first step in determining whether a waiver is appropriate is the IRB's evaluation of the risks.

When the IRB approves a waiver of the requirement for informed consent or a procedure that does not include or alters elements of informed consent, the IRB must determine that the research meets the definition of minimal risk. The determination that the research involves minimal risk allows the IRB, if appropriate, to waive the requirement for obtaining informed consent from subjects. In essence, the IRB has acted under the principles of respect for persons, as an autonomous committee, and provided informed consent on behalf of the subject for the research to be conducted. The waiver or alteration is based on the determination of minimal risk to subjects.

In contrast, when the IRB waives the documentation of informed consent (that is, the requirement to obtain a signed consent form), the IRB must determine that the principal risk is the potential harm from a breach of confidentiality of the signed consent forms while held by the researcher. Both the risks associated with participating in the research and the risks associated with a breach of confidentiality may be greater than minimal risk. In this instance, the IRB demonstrates respect for persons and their autonomy in allowing subjects to decide whether or not they wish to sign a consent document that identifies them as research subjects. By granting the waiver of the documentation of consent, the IRB minimizes potential harm to subjects from a confidentiality breach.

Waiver of Informed Consent

DHHS regulations [1][Sec.116(d)] describe the criteria for waiving the requirement for informed consent. A form that guides the IRB through these criteria is appended to this chapter.

An IRB may approve a consent procedure which does not include, or which alters, some or all of the elements of informed consent set forth in this section, or waive the requirement to obtain informed consent provided the IRB finds and documents that:

(1) The research involves no more than minimal risk to the subjects;

(2) The waiver or alteration will not adversely affect the rights and welfare of the subjects;

(3) The research could not practicably be carried out without the waiver or alteration; and

(4) Whenever appropriate, the subjects will be provided with additional pertinent information after participation. [1][Sec.116(d)]

Example

The researcher plans to determine how mood and perception of one's body image may be related. Initially, student subjects complete a series of written questionnaires and scales about their body image. After the subjects are presented with visual images intended to evoke a negative mood, the subjects are asked to complete the same questionnaires and scales. The effect of evoking a negative mood is evaluated.

Although the actual purpose of the research is to determine how mood may be related to body image, subjects are informed that the research is actually two separate research projects, one related to moods and how they may change and the other related to body image. This deception is part of the research design, and the student subjects are not fully informed about the purpose of the research.

In this example, the IRB may find that an alteration of informed consent is appropriate and that the criteria from 45 CFR 46 [1][Sec.116(d)] have been met based on the following.

1. The research involves minimal risk. The visual images are similar to those that the subjects might see in magazines or films about health and exercise. There are no provocative images. The questionnaires and scales are valid and reliable and are used in standard psychosocial testing.

2. The rights and welfare of subjects are not adversely affected because subjects are informed about the actual procedures, questionnaires, scales, and visual images involved in the research; the risks of feeling uncomfortable or upset with the questions or visual images; that there are no anticipated benefits from participating in the research; and that they may choose not to answer any questions that may cause them to be uncomfortable and they may stop their participation at any time without affecting their status as a student or their grades. Subjects are not informed that the research actually has one purpose and that the data will be evaluated for that intent.

3. The research could not practicably be carried out without the alteration in the informed consent process. The research design is intended to minimize the subject's preconceived thoughts or feelings by presenting visual images and measuring subject's responses before and after being exposed to those specific visual images resulting in a mood change.

4. In this research, it is appropriate to provide subjects with additional pertinent information after participation. The researcher debriefs the subjects after their participation to explain the actual purpose of the research and why the research design was appropriate. The researcher also offers to be available for any questions subjects may have, and provides information about appropriate services if subjects experience distress or anxiety about their participation in the research.

Example

The researcher plans to determine whether some specific blood chemistry values change in individuals undergoing clinically indicated abdominal surgery and if there is a correlation of changes with the increased incidence of complications after surgery. The researcher plans to review the medical records of all individuals who have undergone abdominal surgery in the past two years. From a preliminary estimate, there are about 5,000 abdominal surgeries performed per year at the hospital. The researcher will collect limited data for this research. The types of data to be collected include such items as the diagnosis before surgery, the type of abdominal surgery, specific blood chemistry values before the surgery, the same specific blood chemistry values after the surgery, a description of problems after surgery, and the age ranges of the individuals. The researcher will double-code the data so that the link is known only to the researcher and no others in the unlikely event the data must be verified for accuracy. The results of the research will not affect the clinical care of the individuals, as the information will not be examined until after subjects leave the hospital.

In this example, the IRB may find that a waiver of informed consent is appropriate and that the criteria from 45 CFR 46 [1][Sec.116(d)] have been met based on the following.

1. The research involves minimal risk, as the review of subjects' medical records is for limited information, the information is not sensitive in nature, and the data are derived from clinically indicated procedures. There is an extremely low probability of harm to subjects' status, employment, or insurability. The precautions taken to limit the record review to specified data and the double coding of the data further minimize the major risk, which is a breach of confidentiality. Contacting subjects to obtain their consent could be considered an invasion of privacy and cause subjects undue anxiety.

2. The rights and welfare of the individual would not be adversely affected because the clinically indicated surgical procedure and the associated blood chemistry values were already completed, or would be completed, regardless of the research. None of the results of the research would affect the clinical decisions about the individual's care because the results are analyzed after the fact. Subjects are not being deprived of clinical care to which they would normally be entitled.

3. The research could not be practically carried out without the waiver. Identifying and contacting the thousands of potential subjects, while not impossible, would not be feasible for a review of their medical records for information that would not change the care they would already have received.

4. It would not be appropriate to provide these subjects with additional pertinent information about the results of the research as the results would have no effect on the subjects. The surgical procedure and care afterwards have both been completed for these subjects. There is no anticipated benefit to subjects that would change what has already occurred.

Example

A researcher plans to review the medical records using the same procedures as previously described. However, in this research the hypothesis is that there is a correlation between a particular drug intervention and development of neurological problems several years later.

In this example, the IRB may find that a waiver of informed consent is appropriate and that the criteria 1, 2, and 3 from 45 CFR 46[1][Sec.116(d)] have been met based on the same basic reasons. There is one potential difference.

Under criterion 4, it may be appropriate to provide these subjects with additional pertinent information about the results of the research. In this case, the IRB may not be able to determine whether the results of the research would, or would not, provide information that may be pertinent to those subjects. To make this determination, the IRB may require the researcher to submit the results of the research, along with an assessment of whether subjects should be provided additional pertinent information, to the IRB for review. If the results of the research submitted to the IRB indicate that no additional pertinent information should be provided to subjects (e.g., there was no statistical significance to support the research question), the IRB may determine that it is not appropriate to provide these subjects with additional information. In contrast, if the results of the research submitted to the IRB indicate that there is additional pertinent information that should be provided to subjects (e.g., there is a high probability that subjects who received the drug may experience late negative effects), the IRB may determine that the researcher should provide subjects with this information.

The IRB should work with the researcher to determine what pertinent information should be provided to subjects and how this information would be provided. For example, the IRB may require the researcher to outline a process that would include how the information about results of the research would be communicated to subjects, what the results might mean to subjects, and what to do if there are any ques-

tions. The IRB would review the process and perhaps a document, such as an information letter to subjects, much the way the IRB reviews the informed consent process and the consent document to ensure that the pertinent information is communicated clearly and in language understandable to subjects. The IRB may require the researcher to include a statement noting that subjects should or may wish to share this information with their primary care physicians.

Waiver of the Requirement to Obtain Documentation of Consent

DHHS regulations[1][Sec.117(c)] describe two circumstances when an IRB may waive the requirement to obtain a signed consent form. A form that guides the IRB through these criteria is appended to the end of this chapter.

An IRB may waive the requirement for the investigator to obtain a signed consent form for some or all subjects if it finds either: (1) That the only record linking the subject and the research would be the consent document and the principal risk would be potential harm resulting from a breach of confidentiality. Each subject will be asked whether the subject wants documentation linking the subject with the research, and the subject's wishes will govern; or (2) That the research presents no more than minimal risk of harm to subjects and involves no procedures for which written consent is normally required outside of the research context.
In cases in which the documentation requirement is waived, the IRB may require the investigator to provide subjects with a written statement regarding the research.[1][Sec.117(c)]

Example

A researcher plans to evaluate the effectiveness of a smoking cessation program with women who are receiving prenatal care at the local health clinic. During a prenatal visit, any women who are already participating in the smoking cessation program will be asked to complete a written questionnaire about the program. The one-time written questionnaire includes questions about how well the women are complying with the program and how they feel about their progress. There is no identifying information about subjects on the questionnaire, and whether the subjects complete the questionnaire has no effect on the care they may receive at the clinic.

In this example, the IRB may waive the requirement to obtain a signed consent form because the research presents no more than minimal risk of harm to subjects. The questionnaire has no identifying information about the subject, and the purpose of the research is to evaluate the effectiveness of the program itself. Normally, there is no requirement for written consent for completion of written questionnaires outside the research context. By virtue of completing the questionnaire, subjects have consented to participate in the research. In this case, the IRB may require the researcher to provide subjects with a written summary or an information sheet about the research. The IRB may further require that the information contain all the relevant elements of informed consent outlined in 45 CFR 46.[1][Sec.116] At a minimum, the IRB may require that the information sheets include the purpose of the research, the procedure, how much time is involved, the assessment of minimal risk, a statement that there is no benefit to subjects for completing the questionnaire, whom to contact for questions about the research, and whom to contact for questions about their rights as research subjects.

Example

A researcher plans face-to-face interviews with university students who belong to a support group on campus for transgendered, gay, lesbian, and bisexual individuals. The purpose of the research is to evaluate the quality of health care services for these individuals. The researcher plans to recruit subjects through flyers and information distributed at support group meetings. Potential subjects will contact the researcher directly. The researcher plans to conduct two face-to-face interviews six months apart. The interviews will be audiotaped, and the researcher will ask subjects to use a pseudonym during the interviews. Also, each subject will be assigned a coded number on the audiotape.

In this example, the IRB determines that the only record linking the subject and the research would be the consent document. The principal risk would be potential harm resulting from a breach of confidentiality if the consent documents were disclosed, purposefully or inadvertently. To minimize the potential harm to subjects, the IRB may permit the informed consent process to be conducted orally and have the researcher document, perhaps in a research note, the circumstances of the consent process. The IRB may also require the researcher to provide each subject with a written summary or information sheet about the research. However, in this example, even having an information sheet about the research could be potentially harmful to subjects who may already suffer from social stigma, embarrassment, or ostracism. The IRB may suggest providing subjects with a card that lists only the name and phone number of the researcher in the event they have any questions or concerns.

The IRB may then request that the researcher ask subjects whether they want documentation linking them with the research, and each subject's wishes will be honored. The IRB may ask the researcher to inform each subject about the temporal aspects of the risks associated with the signed consent document as the only link between the subject and the research. Subjects, as students or activists, might believe that the immediate potential harm from having a document with their signature confirming their participation in the research is minimal and a potential breach of confidentiality is not relevant. In contrast, the same subjects may find that the harm caused by an inadvertent breach of confidentiality perhaps 5 to 10 years later during a job interview to be greater.

Documentation of Waiver Determinations by the IRB

When the IRB approves a consent procedure that does not include, or alters, some or all of the elements of informed consent, or waives the requirement to obtain informed consent, the IRB must both make the specific findings required by the regulations and document those determinations.

If the IRB approves a waiver of informed consent or waiver of the requirement to obtain a signed consent form for research reviewed during a convened IRB meeting, the IRB meeting minutes must document the IRB's findings regarding their decision to grant the waiver.

However, when a research protocol meets the criteria for review under expedited procedures, [1(Sec.110(b))] the review is conducted by the IRB Chair or designated IRB members outside of a convened meeting. In this case, the IRB member's review must document the decision. There is the same documentation requirement regardless of whether the waiver is granted by the convened IRB or by the IRB member–reviewers through expedited review procedures.

Appended to this chapter are examples from IRB member review guides for determining and documenting whether a waiver of informed consent or waiver of documentation of informed consent may be granted. The IRB member–reviewers use the review guide regardless of whether the review of the research protocol and determination of a waiver are granted by the convened IRB or by IRB member–reviewers through expedited review procedures. If the determinations and decisions are documented in the convened IRB's meeting minutes, the IRB member–reviewer guide serves as additional documentation for the determination. When the IRB member–reviewer grants a waiver for a research protocol reviewed under expedited procedures, the IRB member–reviewer guide is the only documentation for the determination and decision.

Conclusion

The IRB may waive or alter the requirement for informed consent or waive the requirement to document informed consent from subjects if certain criteria from the federal regulations[1(Secs.116,117)] are satisfied. The IRB must always consider the principle of respect for persons and allow individuals autonomy with regard to their decisions about research participation. In some instances, the IRB waives informed consent and provides consent on behalf of subjects for the research to be conducted. The IRB must always determine the risks and potential harms involved in the research and the consent process before granting a waiver. The same standard of documentation is required regardless of whether the waiver is granted by the convened IRB or by the IRB members reviewing research through expedited review procedures.

References

1. Code of Federal Regulations. Title 45A—Department of Health and Human Services; Part 46—Protection of Human Subjects. Updated 1 Oct 1997. Access date 18 Apr 2001. World Wide Web http://www4.law.cornell.edu/cfr/45p46.htm

2. Code of Federal Regulations. Title 21, Chapter 1—Food and Drug Administration, DHHS; Part 50—Protection of Human Subjects. Updated 1 Apr 1999. Access date 18 Apr 2001. World Wide Web http://www4.law.cornell.edu/cfr/21p50.htm

Appendix

Used with permission from the University of Illinois at Chicago Office for Protection of Research Subjects (OPRS).

Appendix

IRB REVIEWER GUIDE: Waiver of Documentation of Consent

If you are granting a waiver of the requirement to obtain a signed consent form for some or all subjects [45 CFR 46.117(c)], you must document responses to each of the following statements.

1. The entire consent (or elements thereof) was waived under 45 CFR 46.116(d).   Yes   No

2. The only record linking the subject and the research is the consent document, and the principal risk is potential harm resulting from a breach of confidentiality. Subjects are asked whether they want documentation linking them to the research, and their wishes will govern.   Yes   No

3. The research involves no more than minimal risk of harm *and* involves no procedure for which written consent is normally required outside of the research context.   Yes   No

If you have circled the "yes" response to at least *one* of the questions above, in order to grant the waiver you must describe the reason(s) the waiver is necessary. _____

_____

_____

NOTE: Even if the waiver is granted, the IRB may require other conditions. The IRB may require the researcher to provide subjects with an information sheet (written summary) about the research.

Used with permission from the University of Illinois at Chicago Office for Protection of Research Subjects (OPRS).

Active Versus Passive Consent

Linda J. Kobokovich, Robert J. Amdur, and Elizabeth A. Bankert

INTRODUCTION

In organizations that conduct research involving survey interviews, the collection of information from the medical record, or the study of children at school, the Institutional Review Board (IRB) may encounter the situation where the investigator requests that the study be conducted based on the use of passive consent. For the purposes of this discussion, *passive consent* is defined as a situation where the lack of an objection to research participation is considered to be an affirmative declaration of informed consent. This is a complicated way of saying that passive consent means that if you do not say "no," it means that you say "yes."

Request to Use a Passive Consent Process

An example will help illustrate the most common scenario where the IRB encounters the passive consent issue.

Example

A research study involves a survey that evaluates alcoholic beverage consumption in junior high school students. The survey will be administered in the school cafeteria during the student lunch break. The researchers will explain the essential elements of informed consent to potential subjects, and that their assent is a requirement for study participation. The researchers have permission to conduct the study from the school principal. The researchers plan to inform parents of the study by sending them a letter that explains the study in detail. The letter explains that students will not be approached about the study if parents send in a "refusal to participate" card; the stamped, self-addressed card is included with the letter. The letter explains that if parents do not register an objection to the study, it will be assumed that they are giving the researchers permission to ask their child to participate.

In this example, the researchers are asking the IRB to approve the study with the understanding that parental permission will be obtained using a passive procedure. To evaluate this issue, it is important that the IRB understand several important points.

1. Federal regulations do not support the concept of passive consent. At national IRB meetings, OHRP officials have repeatedly emphasized that there is no such thing as passive consent from the regulatory standpoint. There is only one form of valid consent, and that involves the type of active process described in federal regulations and accepted ethical codes.

2. To approve the use of a passive consent procedure, an IRB that operates in compliance with federal regulations must determine that the study meets either the criteria to waive the requirement for informed consent[1][Sec.116(d)] or the criteria to waive the requirement for documentation of informed consent.[1][Sec.117(c)] These regulations are discussed in detail in Chapter 6-6.

In terms of the example previously presented, the ability of the IRB to approve the use of passive consent in this setting would depend on the individual judgment of the IRB members who evaluate the study. Criteria for waiving the requirement for informed consent are that the study involves no more than minimal risk and could not practicably be carried out without the waiver. If survey responses may be linked to individual identifiers, then it would be difficult to consider this as a minimal-risk study. Aggregate information about an illegal behavior like alcohol consumption in minors may put students and parents at risk even without individual identifiers. For this reason, we would not consider waiving the requirement for informed consent in this setting.

However, to demonstrate the decision process that the IRB should follow, let us consider the situation where an IRB decides that the study does not meet the criteria for waiver of informed consent. Then the next issue would be the waiver of the requirement for documentation of informed consent. Again, this would be a judgment call on the part of the IRB related to the risk of the study. In our opinion, the IRB should not approve the study described in the previous example. The study involves more than minimal risk for a variety of reasons, the study could be done with written documentation of active consent from the parents, and the potential benefit of the study does not justify the potential compromise in ethical standards with which the waiver of standard consent procedures is likely to be associated.

Reasons to Use a Passive Consent Process

Active consent generally yields response rates that many consider unacceptably low (40%–60%), with underrepresentation of important groups such as minorities, low achievers, children with less educated parents, and those at risk for engaging in problem behaviors.[2-4] Passive consent for participation tends to yield higher response rates of 80%–100%.[2,4,5] The low response rate of active consent procedures thus limits scientific validity and generalizability of survey and evaluation research. Reduced sample size can make it difficult to detect all but the most powerful treatment effects when conducting prevention and evaluation research.

When looking specifically at research conducted with minors, selection bias is introduced by the active consent procedure.[3] Parents of at-risk youth are less likely to respond. Passive consent procedures are more likely to include youth with parents who are less educated, who are members of minority ethnic groups, who are more likely to be disenchanted with school, and who are more likely to participate in risky behaviors.[6]

These factors affect the external validity of the research. Studies employing passive consent procedures usually target low-frequency behaviors; therefore, large numbers of participants are needed and usually the research is conducted at multiple sites. This makes the use of active consent extremely costly and requires extensive follow-up, which is time-consuming for large projects. Active consent requires overly stringent informed consent procedures, especially when applied to programs that offer benefits and have minimal risk. It is estimated that it costs $25 per participant to achieve high response rates in active-consent research.[5,7]

For the great majority of participants, including parents, failure to return a consent form appears to reflect latent consent combined with apathy or inertia.[2,7,8] Equating nonresponse with permission accurately reflected the wishes of 96% of a group of nonresponding parents who were reached by telephone.[2] Therefore, nonresponse is not synonymous with refusal, and apathy and inertia are usually at the core of a parent's failure to respond to a request to participate in survey research.[8]

Conclusion

IRBs should recognize when they are being presented with a request to approve research based on a passive rather than active consent process. From the practical stand-point, passive consent describes a situation where the researcher is saying that when a person does not say "no" to a request to participate in research it means that they are saying "yes." As federal research regulations do not provide for the approval of research based on passive consent, IRBs should hold all research to the same standards when evaluating the need to obtain and document the informed consent of research participants.

References

1. Code of Federal Regulations. Title 45A—Department of Health and Human Services; Part 46—Protection of Human Subjects. Updated 1 Oct 1997. Access date 18 Apr 2001. World Wide Web http://www4.law.cornell.edu/cfr/45p46.htm

2. Ellickson PL, Hawes JP. An assessment of active versus passive methods for obtaining parental consent. *Evaluation Review* 13(1):45–55, 1989.

3. Severson H, Ary D. Sampling bias due to consent procedures with adolescents. *Addictive Behaviors* 8(4):433–437, 1983.

4. Severson H, Biglan A. Rationale for the use of passive consent in smoking prevention research: Politics, policy, and pragmatics. *Preventive Medicine* 18(1):267–279, 1989.

5. Esbensen FA, Deschenes EP, Vogel RE, West J, Arboit K, Harris L. Active parental consent in school-based research: An examination of ethical and methodological issues. *Evaluation Review* 20(6):737–753, 1996.

6. Dent CW, Galaif J, Sussman S, Stacey A, Burton F, Flay BR. Demographic, psychosocial, and behavioral differences in samples of actively and passively consented adolescents. *Addictive Behaviors* 18(1):51–56, 1993.

7. Esbensen FA, Miller MA, Taylor TJ, He N, Frena A. Differential attrition rates and active parental consent. *Evaluation Research* 23(3):316–335, 1999.

8. Lueptow L, Mueller SA, Hammes RR, Master LS. The impact of informed consent regulations on response rate and response bias. *Sociological Methods and Research* 6:183–204, 1977.

Selecting a Surrogate to Consent to Medical Research

Robert J. Amdur, Natalie Bachir, and Elizabeth Stanton

INTRODUCTION

A clinical investigator requested permission from the Dartmouth College institutional review board (IRB) to initiate a research study to evaluate the effect of a new medication for the treatment of patients with bacterial sepsis. Only patients who were both critically ill from sepsis and already had failed to respond to standard therapies were eligible for the study. Given their medical condition, most subjects would not be clinically competent to give informed consent to medical treatment. Historical evidence suggested that most of the patients eligible for the study would die of sepsis-related problems unless a new treatment proved to be effective. Preliminary data indicated a favorable risk/benefit profile for the experimental medication in this setting.

The IRB's concern was whether an informally appointed surrogate decision-maker could legally consent to an incompetent patient's participation in the research. To be effective, the medication had to be administered within hours of the patient's eligibility. Formal court appointment of a guardian was impractical, if not impossible, within that time frame. Furthermore, the expectation was that only a small percentage of patients would have formally preappointed a surrogate by a durable power of attorney for health care (DPAHC). Presenting even greater difficulty, New Hampshire did not have a law delineating a hierarchy of surrogate decision-makers. After much deliberation, the IRB approved the study under the condition that consent would come from a well-informed and properly motivated family member when a formally appointed surrogate was not available.

When state law does not provide guidance on health care consent by a surrogate, research institutions should establish a policy and procedure to address this issue. In this process, institutions should consider the principles underlying the informed consent doctrine and the application of those principles when a surrogate is to give consent. Additionally, institutions should examine existing state law for any limitations on the consent power of the legal guardian or agent under DPAHC, and standards for surrogate decision-making recognized by the state. Finally, institutions should review the public policy of family and friends as informally appointed surrogates. The following discussion presents such an analysis.

Informed Consent

The legal doctrine of informed consent embodies some of the most important ethical and legal principles guiding the conduct of research involving human subjects. In 1914, Justice Cardozo articulated the basic principle of informed consent in medical care when he wrote, "Every human being of adult years and sound mind has a right to determine what shall be done with his own body."[1] Since

Note: An abbreviated version of this chapter is published in *IRB: A Review of Human Subjects Research* 22(4): 7–11, 2000. Used with permission.

then, the doctrine has come to include much more. Today, the informed consent doctrine provides recognition of individual autonomy and imposes on the physician a duty to disclose information to a patient in a way the patient understands so that he or she may make an informed decision about care.[2(Sec.6-9,6-11)]

The Commission for the Protection of Human Subjects of Biomedical and Behavioral Research (Commission) addressed informed consent in human subject research.[3] The Commission identified the basic ethical principles of such research and provided guidelines for the federal law governing that research.[4(A6-8)] Human subject research posed concerns that therapeutic practice did not. These concerns are notoriously recognized in the conduct of the Nazi physicians in World War II and the conduct of the physicians of the Tuskegee study. Design differences between therapeutic practice and research practice summarize the concern. The physician designs a therapeutic practice, the Commission explained, to enhance the well-being of a particular patient, whereas the physician–researcher designs a research practice to test a hypothesis for generalizable knowledge.[4(A6-11,6-12)] Though the research subject may benefit from the research practice, the physician–researcher has a dual interest and thus, to some degree, a conflict of interest in regard to the patient. The work of the Commission was to create protections against this conflict for the human research subject.

In 1979, the Commission presented the ethical foundation for the federal rules on human subject research in the *Belmont Report*.[4(A6-8)] The Commission established respect for persons as a fundamental principle in human subject research and as the principle underlying the doctrine of informed consent.[4(A6-10)] Respect for persons, the Commission elaborated, requires (a) recognition of the individual as an autonomous agent, and (b) protection of the individual with diminished autonomy.[4(A6-10)] To recognize the individual's autonomy is to recognize the individual's ability to deliberate choices and then to act on that deliberation.[4(A6-10)] To protect the individual with diminished autonomy is to assess both the risk of harm and the likelihood of benefit to the individual from the research and to afford protection accordingly.[4(A6-10)]

The concept of providing protection to the person with diminished autonomy incorporates and heightens another fundamental principle of human subject research identified by the Commission: beneficence. Beneficence, the doing of good, obligates the researcher to secure the individual's well-being by maximizing benefits and minimizing harms to the individual.[4(A6-10)] Beneficence requires that the researcher perform a risk/ benefit analysis, examining the probability and magnitude of possible harms and anticipated benefits to the individual.[4(A6-12,6-13)] In the case of a research subject with diminished autonomy, beneficence is enhanced through protections proportional to risks and harms.

The Commission applied the principles of respect and beneficence to obtaining informed consent in the conduct of research. First, the Commission explained, inform the individual of the benefits, risks, and the voluntariness of the research participation.[4(A6-12)] Second, convey the information in such a manner that it will be understood by the individual and ascertain that understanding.[4(A6-12)] Third, do not coerce, unduly influence, or induce the individual to consent to participation. Lastly, when the individual is of diminished autonomy, provide added protection to the individual that is reflective of the risk of harm and the likelihood of benefit.[4(A6-12)]

The federal rules on human subject research reflect the Commission's work with varying degrees of success. Although federal protections are fairly straightforward for the competent research subject, they fall short for the incompetent subject, leaving research institutions to devise policy and procedure to deal with the latter situation. As the principles and guidelines defined by the Commission remain the foundation for legal analysis today,[5(pp. 88–90),][6(n.2)] states and research institutions should incorporate them into the laws and policies on surrogate decision-making for the incompetent research subject.

Federal Law

Under the guidance of the Commission's work, the United States Department of Health and Human Services (DHHS) promulgated rules that define protections for human research subjects.[7(Sec.101 et seq.)] Institutions must comply with these rules when research is federally funded.[7[Sec.101(a)]] Most institutions, however, also apply the policy of the federal rules to privately funded research to avoid the difficulty of administering two different sets of administrative rules for research.[2(Sec.23-2)]

In recognition of the Commission's enunciation, DHHS established the requirement of a participant's informed consent as an important criterion for research approval. DHHS requires that each prospective research subject, or a subject's legally authorized representative, provide a legally effective informed consent to participation in the project.[7[Sec.111(a)(4),116]] To be legally effective, the consent must meet both federal and state requirements for informed consent and, when applicable, for surrogate decision-making.[7[Sec.102(d),116(e)]] The federal law provides basic procedural protections and defers to more restrictive state procedure.[7[Sec.116(e)]] State law provides the substantive law of informed consent and the law governing surrogate decision-making.

Although the federal law details the essential elements of informed consent, including those elements that must be explained to a research subject or representative,[7[Sec.116(a)]] the law falls short in defining the "surrogate decision-maker" and the protections that researchers should afford the incompetent patient. The law recognizes and allows the participation of a surrogate decision-maker in the informed consent process but defers to state law to define the "legally authorized representative."[7(Sec.102)] Problematically, state law may or may not more fully define either the doctrine of informed consent or the surrogate decision-maker.

Federal law also requires that the IRB approve and oversee human subject research through a process that reflects local conditions and values.[2(Sec.23-3)] The law requires that the board include sufficient scientific and nonscientific expertise, but also diversity in race, gender, and cultural backgrounds and sensitivity to issues such as community attitudes.[7[Sec.107(a)=(c)]] As such, the IRB policy and procedure on informed consent or the incompetent research subject should reflect both the law and public policy of the state in which it operates.

State Law

Most states have legislatively addressed health care consent by one individual on behalf of another. States have most commonly enacted laws addressing guardianship, durable power of attorney for health care, or surrogate consent. Many states, however, do not address all three, and most fail to address surrogate consent in medical research, leaving research institutions in these states to structure policies and procedures without the benefit of legislative guidance.

To establish institutional principles and procedures that reflect local conditions and values and to provide liability protection to the institution and to the researcher, institutions should look to the laws of the state for guidance. Specifically, the institution should look for (a) a specific prohibition of the informal appointment of a surrogate, such as a family member or close friend, (b) limitations on the consent power of the formally appointed surrogate, and (c) prescribed standards for the decision-making process.

A comprehensive review of legislation from each state concerning surrogate decision-making is beyond the scope of this chapter. New Hampshire is an example of a state without statutory law that specifically addresses the role of surrogate decision-makers in medical research. New Hampshire state law is reviewed here as a model for the type of analysis that interested parties in other states will need to conduct when establishing research policy.

Guardianship

A court-appointed guardian is a surrogate decision-maker appointed by a court to protect the interests of, and make decisions for, a person who is not legally competent to make such decisions on his/her own. In many cases, a concerned family member may serve as guardian, but in situations where a qualified and properly motivated relative does not exist, a nonrelative may be appointed.

From the standpoint of a clinical investigator who is interested in enrolling an incompetent patient in a research study, there are two main problems with establishing a court-appointed guardian. First, although it is possible to establish temporary guardianship in a few days, it often takes much longer. For example, in New Hampshire, the guardianship process usually takes at least a month. Second, establishing a legal guardianship may be a complicated and expensive process. In most cases, the party wanting to establish guardianship must hire a lawyer to direct the appointment process. In 1999, the legal fees associated with an uncomplicated guardianship appointment in New Hampshire were approximately $1,500.

The New Hampshire court appoints a guardian to a person only after finding all of the following: (a) the person is incapacitated; (b) guardianship is necessary to provide continuing care, supervision, and rehabilitation; (c) there are no available alternative resources suitable to the welfare, safety, and rehabilitation of the person; and (d) guardianship is the least restrictive form of intervention consistent with preserving the civil liberties of the person.[8[Sec.9 III(1992)]] The court determines incapacity through a measure of a person's functional limitations.[8[Sec.2 XI(1992)]] Finally, because courts seek the least restrictive form of intervention, the guardianship imposes only the limitations necessary to provide needed care and rehabilitative services.[8[Sec.2 XIV(1992)]]

The purpose and limited scope of the New Hampshire guardianship law suggests an intent to provide due process protections when needed and guardianship only as a last resort, allowing the coexistence of the law with, for example, the practice of family consent.[9] In its purpose statement, the law clearly is intended to "provide procedural and substantive safeguards for civil liberties."[8[Sec.1(1992)]] The nature of the court's inquiry, however, suggests that guardianship is a last remedial resort.

A New Hampshire court-appointed guardian probably does not have the authority to consent to medical research participation on behalf of a ward. A purpose of the guardianship law in New Hampshire is "to encourage rehabilitative care" for incapacitated individuals.[8[Sec.1(1992)]] If authorized by the court, the New Hampshire guardian may give or withhold consent to health care on behalf of the ward.[8[Sec.25I(c)(Supp.1997)]] No guardian, however, may consent to psychosurgery, electroconvulsive therapy, sterilization, or *experimental treatment* without prior court approval [emphasis added].[8[Sec.25I(c)(Supp.1997)]] Although the guardianship law does not define "experimental treatment," a plain language and conservative interpretation of the term suggests the guardian may not consent to research participation without judicial approval.

Additionally, guardians must adhere to the terms of a valid living will or durable power of attorney for health care.[8[Sec.25I(d)(Supp.1997)]] The guardian must adhere to any express wishes of the executor, including wishes made in regard to research participation. This requirement demonstrates state deference to the express wishes of the executor of the document, the patient for whom the court appoints a guardian. The wishes of the patient, expressed when competent, override even court-appointed authority.

The New Hampshire guardianship law indirectly reflects the state's policy on the informally appointed surrogate in medical research consent. The law does not prohibit the appointment of a family member or close friend. Guardianship law, however, does prohibit consent to experimental treatment without judicial approval, reflecting heightened state concern in such matters. The law is silent on the process by which the guardian decides about routine health care matters. The exception is that the guardian must defer to the express wishes of the patient as stated in a valid living will or durable power of attorney for health care.

Durable Power of Attorney for Health Care

A durable power of attorney for health care (DPAHC) is a document executed by a competent person (principal) delegating decision-making authority to another person (agent) in the event the principal becomes incapacitated. The principal may limit durable powers in time, scope, or method of decision-making.[2(p.17–22)] State statutes regulating the DPAHC vary in scope and often expressly provide immunity to the institution and physician that rely in good faith on the consent of the DPAHC agent.

The New Hampshire DPAHC statute reads:

> The durable power of attorney shall be in substantially the following form:
> I, ____, hereby appoint ____ of ____ as my agent to make any and all health care decisions for me, except to the extent I state otherwise in this document or as prohibited by law.[10[Sec.15(1996)]]

Researchers encounter two difficulties in regard to the DPAHC. First, most people do not establish a DPAHC. A DPAHC is an advance directive, which means that it must be executed before the principal is either clinically or legally incompetent. Although the need for an advance directive is receiving increased attention nationwide, most patients will not have executed a DPAHC before becoming incapacitated.

Second, most DPAHC agreements do not mention research. Standard DPAHC language does not include reference to medical research consent as a health care decision, and unless the principal has the foresight to include such direction, difficulties in obtaining consent may ensue.

In the event an incompetent person is without a DPAHC, New Hampshire law does not prohibit other forms of surrogate consent. New Hampshire enacted the DPAHC law "to enable adults to retain control over their own medical care during periods of incapacity," authority becoming effective only in that event.[10[Sec.2III(1996)]] Legislative notes caution that the law "is not to be construed to reflect any legislative intent or public policy either in favor of or opposed to the ability of an appropriate surrogate to render health-care decisions on behalf of a person who has not executed, when competent, a power of attorney or who was not formally competent to execute a power of attorney."[10[Sec.J.History;Construction(1996)]]

The New Hampshire DPAHC agent may make any health care decision the principal could make, with some exceptions.[10[Sec.2I(1996)]] "'Health-care decision' means consent, refusal to consent, or withdrawal of consent to any care, treatment, admission to a health-care facility, any service or procedure to maintain, diagnose, or treat an individual's physical or mental condition except as prohibited in this chapter or otherwise by law."[10[Sec.1VI(1996)]] The agent may not make decisions expressly prohibited in the DPAHC or the principal's living will.[10[Sec.2I(1996)]] In addition, the agent may not consent to a voluntary admission to a state institution, voluntary sterilization, or, with some exceptions, to withholding life-sustaining treatment from a pregnant patient.[10[Sec.2V(1996)]] Overall, however, the agent may exercise broad power in health care decision-making. The law further grants immunity from civil or criminal liability to the agent or health-care provider who acts in good faith and in accordance with the DPAHC and the law.[10[Sec.J:11(1996)]]

Despite the agent's broad decision-making power, the law prescribes the manner in which the agent should make that decision.[10[Sec.J:2II]] The law requires that the agent make health-care decisions in consultation with the principal's health-care provider, as well as "in accordance with the agent's knowledge of the principal's wishes and religious or moral beliefs, as stated orally or otherwise by [the] principal to [the] agent."[10[J:2II]] When the principal's wishes are not known, the agent must decide in accordance with accepted medical practice and an assessment of the principal's best interest.[10[J:2II]]

As does the guardianship law, the New Hampshire DPAHC law indirectly reflects the state's policy on the informally appointed surrogate in medical research consent. The law does not prohibit the appointment of a family member or close friend. Nor does the law prohibit consent to experimental treatment. Notably, the DPAHC law prescribes the process by which the agent should consent to health care matters: either by substituted judgment, when the principal's wishes and beliefs are known, or by a best-interest standard in conjunction with accepted medical practice when the principal's wishes are not known.

Family or Friend as Surrogate

In the absence of a formally designated surrogate, researchers may wish to seek consent for research participation from a family member. Although it has long been standard medical practice to seek consent to health care from family, there is no basis for this practice in common law. Policy arguments exist for and against the practice. Some states have clarified the allowance through "family consent laws" or "surrogate laws" that include relatives or friends in a hierarchical list of allowable health-care decision-makers for the incompetent patient. The statute may or may not specifically mention medical research. When a state has not enacted such a law, institutions must decide if and when it is acceptable to allow an informally appointed decision-maker to consent to a clinically incompetent person's participation in a medical research study.

The Commission for the Protection of Human Subjects of Biomedical and Behavioral Research, in a 1983 report, proposed reasons for the legal deference to family consent to health care for the incompetent patient.

1. The family is generally most concerned about the good of the patient.

2. The family will also usually be most knowledgeable about the patient's goals, preferences, and values.

3. The family deserves recognition as an important social unit that ought to be treated, within limits, as a responsible decision-maker in matters that intimately affect its members.

4. Especially in a society in which many other traditional forms of community have eroded, participation in a family is often an important dimension of personal fulfillment.

5. Since a protected sphere of privacy and autonomy is required for the flourishing of this interpersonal union, institutions and the state should be reluctant to intrude, particularly regarding matters that are personal and on which there is a wide range of opinion in society.[11(pp. 127–128)]

Even if family members are somehow disqualified as decision-makers, the Commission continued, it may be appropriate to consult with them in the decision-making process.[11(pp. 128–129)]

James Bopp, president of the National Legal Center for the Medically Dependent and Disabled, recently listed eight reasons why family members may not always appropriately make health care decisions for incompetent relatives.[12(pp. 133, 141–151)]

1. Family may lack information in the decision-making process due to an inability to obtain or assimilate the information.

2. Family decisions may be influenced by emotional reactions, such as shock, denial, anger, or guilt.

3. Family members may be unable to separate their interests from the interests of the patient.

4. Family financial interests may present a conflict of interest in the decision-making process.

5. Family may inaccurately predict the patient's wishes because of lack of discussion on these topics, difficulty assessing the patient's quality of life, or an inability to predict the wishes of an elder.

6. Family decisions may fail to recognize the changing interests of patients.

7. Family health-care decision-making may be emotionally burdensome, more so when there is disagreement in the family on the decision.

8. Deference to family may falsely assume a familial bond when there is none.

A balancing of the arguments for and against the family as a surrogate health-care decision-maker presents no obvious test for the appointment of a surrogate. The familiar and beneficent family, a critical social unit essential to the personal fulfillment of many, deserves the respect and deference of the state and the medical profession. Yet, even the Commission recognized the necessity of limits to the deference. In difficult and emotional times, family must seek out and assimilate technical information and disregard personal or conflicting interests in order to decide, with questionable predictive accuracy, what their incompetent relative would want. Deference to that decision may arise out of a false presumption of familial bond. In the interest of all parties concerned, a structured policy that promotes the proper selection of a surrogate, specific standards of decision-making, and limitations on consent power seems appropriate to support and maximize appropriate decision-making.

A Decision-Maker Who Is Not Family

The person closest to the patient and most knowledgeable about the patient's wishes may not be a "family member" in the traditional sense. As the law generally lags behind societal changes, it often fails to recognize the evolution of new and different units of family.

Unmarried domestic partners or an individual with whom the patient has a long-term, committed relationship may, though not commonly, appear on the priority list of surrogate consent laws.[13,14] Some states recognize the close friend as a possible surrogate in health-care decision-making, although this person is usually at the bottom of the priority list.[13-19] The non–family member is often described as an adult who has exhibited special care and concern for the patient, is familiar with the patient's values and desires, and is reasonably available.

Surrogate Decision-Maker Hierarchies

Some states have codified their policy for acceptable, informally appointed surrogates through family consent laws or surrogate laws.[13-21] These laws establish a hierarchy of acceptable surrogate decision-makers.

1. Spouse
2. Adult children
3. Parents
4. Adult siblings
5. Grandparents
6. Close friend

Although the establishment of formal legal ranks may be useful from the point of view of a physician who is concerned about obtaining consent from the "wrong" surrogate decision-maker, legislation of this kind may create more problems than it solves. The presence of a surrogate decision-maker hierarchy means that the law, not the patient's physician, decides who is best qualified to make decisions in a given situation. Some would argue that this is as it should be. To those who think the choice of a surrogate decision-maker is best left to a managing physician, surrogate decision-maker hierarchies may be undesirable.

Recommendations

1. IRB members and research investigators should understand the legal and ethical controversies associated with choosing a surrogate decision-maker when medical research involves participants who are not competent to give informed consent.

2. Institutions responsible for formulating research policy should review state law on guardianship, informed consent, surrogate decision-making, and advance directives to understand which agents are legally authorized to make health care decisions for incompetent patients. Important questions to answer include the following.

   a. *May a court-appointed guardian consent to research-related activities, or must the guardian refer such decisions to probate court?*

   Some states include "experimental treatment" in the list of activities that are beyond the authority of a guardian. While one may argue that medical therapy should not be considered experimental simply because it is delivered as part of a research protocol, there is no recognition of a distinction between "experimental" and "research" therapy in federal or state law. Therefore, states like New Hampshire, that clearly do not give a guardian the authority to consent to experimental therapy and do not define "experimental," as a conservative interpretation of state law, require a guardian to obtain permission from the court to enroll an incompetent patient in a medical research study.

   b. *Is there legislation on the durable power of attorney for health care? If so, does it address participation in experimental therapy or medical research?*

Researchers should examine the DPAHC document to determine the situations in which a DPAHC agent is not authorized to consent to research participation. For example, in New Hampshire, DPAHC authority would not extend to consent for participation in medical research under two circumstances: (1) when the executor of the DPAHC has added a statement that specifically limits the agent's authority to consent to participation in medical research, and (2) when research involves an activity that is prohibited by law (psychosurgery, sterilization, commitment to a state institution, or termination of treatment under certain well-defined circumstances when the principal is pregnant).

In the absence of any of these situations and if not defined otherwise, the phrase "any and all health care decisions" gives the DPAHC agent legal authority to consent to participation in any type of medical research study, including research that involves the use of experimental therapy.

c. *Is there legislation that authorizes health-care providers to act upon consent of a family member or friend not formally appointed by a court or DPAHC?*

In states with surrogate decision-maker hierarchies, the argument that designated surrogates are legally authorized to consent to participation in medical research may be easier to support. However, as discussed earlier, in addition to defining who is legally authorized to make health care decisions for incompetent patients, it is important to know whether the law prohibits certain decisions made by these agents. For example, in New Hampshire an agent with DPAHC is not authorized to consent to psychosurgery. In states with surrogate decision-maker statutes, it is likely that the law will limit the authority of informally appointed surrogates in similarly sensitive situations.

3. Research policy should recognize the authority of a family or friend to participate in health care decisions, including participation in medical research. The pros and cons of family involvement in health-care decisions were discussed earlier. Local policy should embrace the growing national acceptance of the family-centered philosophy of care by recognizing the right of a properly motivated relative or close friend to participate in the full range of health-care decisions in the absence of a formal legal appointment.

4. Institutional policy regarding the use of consent from surrogate decision-makers should hold research to a higher standard than general medical practice. In the *Belmont Report,* the Commission for the Protection of Human Subjects of Biomedical and Behavioral Research argues that the ethical conduct of research requires that individuals with diminished autonomy be given added protection under the law to help protect their rights and welfare. In New Hampshire, state law places limitations on consent that reflect heightened standards for research and the primacy of self-determination. The New Hampshire guardian may not consent to experimental treatment without court approval, demonstrating the legislature's recognition of heightened standards specific to the research setting. The guardian's power of consent is further limited by a valid DPAHC, establishing the primacy of self-determination.

5. The decision to use consent from an informally appointed surrogate to enroll a clinically incompetent person in a medical research study should be based on three factors: the risk of harm, the probability of direct benefit, and the implications of delaying study participation for the time it would take to appoint a legal guardian. IRBs and research investigators need unambiguous criteria that define the circumstances under which consent from a person who is not a court-appointed guardian or agent under a DPAHC may be used to enroll a clinically incompetent patient in a medical research study. For example, the Dartmouth College IRB requires that all investigators who want to enroll incompetent patients in research answer a series of questions that evaluate the issues critical to the choice of surrogate decision-makers.

a. *Will participation in the study increase the risk of harm or discomfort compared with what would be expected if the subject were managed outside the setting of a research protocol?*

The distinction between absolute and relative risk is critical when evaluating medical research that involves surrogate consent. The absolute risk of a given form of medical treatment is irrelevant. The important factor to evaluate is the difference in risk associated with research participation. The goal of research laws and regulations is to protect research subjects from harm. When there is no risk differential, a liberal interpretation of legal limits on surrogate decision-maker authority is appropriate. When research participation is associated with a meaningful increase in risk, maximum ethical safeguards should be required for the incompetent patient.

b. *Will participation in the study increase the chance of a favorable outcome compared with what would be expected if the subject were managed outside the setting of a research protocol?*

As with risk, when evaluating the potential benefits of research participation, it is important to look at relative rather than absolute outcome. In some situations, research therapy is likely to be better than what would be obtained outside the research setting. Denying patients access to beneficial treatment is harmful.

c. *The process of appointing a legal guardian may take months. Would this type of delay compromise patient care?*

When there is a meaningful chance of direct benefit to the research subject, over and above what could be obtained outside the setting of a research protocol, a requirement that consent be obtained from a formally appointed surrogate may limit access to potentially beneficial therapy. In this situation, IRB members must use their judgment to decide whether to allow consent from an informal surrogate.

When a study is likely to have a favorable risk/benefit ratio (compared with standard therapy), and it would be detrimental to delay for the time it takes to appoint a guardian, the Dartmouth IRB accepts consent from a family member.

d. *What benefit will future patients experience as a result of the subject's participating in this study?*

This question is only important when research participation does not have a chance of increasing direct benefit for the participant. The Dartmouth policy is that it is never acceptable to conduct research on a clinically incompetent patient when research participation increases risk and there is no chance of direct benefit for the participant. Regardless of how strongly a surrogate believes the incompetent person would wish to participate in research for the benefit of future patients, the presence of increased risk establishes an ethical boundary to surrogate authority that should not be crossed.

There are acceptable situations where participation in research does not increase risk or offer the potential for direct benefit. Studies that involve the prospective collection of data from routine medical care frequently fall into this category. When a study does not increase risk, the Dartmouth IRB will approve the involvement of incompetent subjects based on consent from a family member.

Conclusion

It is frequently difficult to determine which surrogate decision-makers are legally authorized to consent for an incompetent patient to participate in medical research. Some states have surrogate decision-maker statutes that clearly define the role of a surrogate in general medical practice, but it may be difficult to decide how such laws apply to medical research. As most states will not have legislation on this point, institutions in these states must establish a policy that defines the "legally authorized representative." Such policy should be rooted in the principles enunciated by the Commission and in the institution's state law and state public policy.

Acknowledgment
The authors thank Michelle Winchester for extensive legal research and editorial revision.

References

1. Mary E. Schloendorff, Appellant, v. The Society of the New York Hospital, Respondent. *Schloendorff v. Society of New York Hospital.* (105 N.E. 92, 93). 1914. Court of Appeals of New York. Affirmed.

2. Furrow BR, Greaney TL, Johnson SH, Jost TS, Schwartz R. L. *Health Law,* Volumes 1 and 2. St. Paul, MN: West Publishing Co. Hornbook Series. 1995.

3. 93rd Congress. National Research Act of 1974. PL93-348. 1974.

4. National Commission for the Protection of Human Subjects of Biomedical and Behavioral Research. *The Belmont Report: Ethical principles and guidelines for the protection of human subjects of research.* DHEW Publication No. (OS) 78-0013 and (OS) 78-0014.4. Washington, DC, U.S. Government Printing Office, 18 Apr 1979. Access date 22 Mar 2001. World Wide Web http://ohsr.od.nih.gov/mpa/belmont.php3

5. Wichman A. Protecting vulnerable research subjects: Practical realities of institutional review board review and approval. *Journal of Health Care and Policy* 1(1):88-104, 1998.

6. Busby-Mott S. The trend towards enlightenment: Health care decisionmaking in Lawrance and Doe. *Conn L Rev* 25(4):1159-1225, 1993.

7. Code of Federal Regulations. Title 45A—Department of Health and Human Services; Part 46—Protection of Human Subjects. Updated 1 Oct 1997. Access date 18 Apr 2001. World Wide Web http: www4.law.cornell.edu/cfr/45p46.htm

8. New Hampshire Revised Statutes Annotated. Title XLIV. Guardians and Conservators. Chapter 464-A. Guardians and Conservators. RSA 464-A (2000), 1-25. 2001.

9. Simon MM, Blais VL. The role of family in health care decisions: NH law. *New Hampshire Bar Journal* 36:34-37, 1995.

10. New Hampshire Revised Statutes Annotated. Title X. Public Health. Chapter 137-J. Durable Power of Attorney for Health Care. RSA 137-J, 1-15. 2000.

11. President's Commission for the Study of Ethical Problems in Medicine and Biomedical and Behavioral Research. *Deciding to Forego Life-Sustaining Treatment: A Report on the Ethical, Medical, and Legal Issues in Treatment Decisions.* Washington, D.C.: Superintendent of Documents. 1983, 554 pages.

12. Bopp J Jr, Coleson RE. A critique of family members as proxy decisionmakers without legal limits. *Issues Law Med* 12(2):133-165, 1996.

13. Arizona Revised Statutes. Title 36. Public Health and Safety. Chapter 32. Living Wills and Health Care Directives. Article 3. Surrogate Decision Makers. A.R.S. 36-3231 (2000) (Supp. 1997). 2000.

14. New Mexico Statutes Annotated. Chapter 24. Health and Safety. Article 7A. Uniform Health-Care Decisions. Section 24-7A-5. Decisions by surrogate. N.M. Stat. Ann. 24-7A-5 (2000). 2000.

15. Delaware Code Annotated. Title 16. Health and Safety. Part II. Regulatory Provisions Concerning Public Health. Chapter 25. Health-Care Decisions. Section 2507. Surrogates. 16 Del. C. 2507 (2000) (Suppl. 1996). 2001.

16. Florida Statutes 2000. Title XLIV Civil Rights. Chapter 765 Health Care Advance Directives. Part IV Absence of Advance Directive. Section 401 The Proxy. Fla. Stat. 765.401 (2000) (West 1997). 2000.

17. Illinois Compiled Statutes Annotated. Chapter 755. Estates. Health Care Surrogate Act. Section 40/25. Surrogate decision making. 755 ILCS 40/25 (2000) (Smith-Hurd Supp. 1998). 2000.

18. Maine Revised Statutes. Title 18-A. Probate Code. Article V. Protection of Persons Under Disability and Their Property. Part 8. Uniform Health-Care Decisions Act. Section 5-805. Decisions by surrogate. 18-A M.R.S. 5-805 (2000). 2000.

19. Maryland Annotated Code. Health-General. Title 5. Death. Subtitle 6. Health Care Decisions Act. Section 5-605. Surrogate decision making. Md. Health-General Code Ann. 5-605 (2001). 2001.

20. Connecticut General Statutes. Title 19A. Public Health and Well-Being. Chapter 368W. Removal of Life Support Systems. Section 19a-570. Definitions. Conn. Gen. Stat. 19a-570 (1999) (West 1997). 2000.

21. Kentucky Revised Statutes Annotated. Title XXVI. Occupations and Professions. Chapter 311. Physicians, Osteopaths, and Podiatrists. Kentucky Living Will Directive Act. Section 631. Responsible Parties Authorized to Make Health Care Decisions. KRS 311-631 (Michie/Bobbs-Merrill 1995). 2001.

Research-Related Injuries

Daniel R. Vasgird

INTRODUCTION

Currently, research institutions are not mandated to provide free medical care or compensation to research participants for research-induced injuries. The Code of Federal Regulations addresses the issue of the medical liability of research institutions to their subjects.[1][Sec.116(a)(6)] Under the regulations, research institutions are only responsible for explaining whether medical treatments are available and whether any compensation will be provided to the research subject in the event that the individual should sustain an injury as a result of his or her participation in the study. In essence, the clause does not require research institutions to provide free medical care to research subjects for research-related injuries.

From a practical standpoint, there are two points for Institutional Review Board (IRB) members and administrators to keep in mind related to this issue. First, IRBs have the ethical responsibility to raise the bar when necessary to ensure the adequate provision of free or compensated medical care for research-related injury; and second, they have the regulatory authority to enact these provisions as they see fit.

Ongoing Debate

National commissions of bioethics have debated this issue for decades and have even gone so far as to endorse a recommendation that compensation should be provided to research subjects for injuries that include harm, disability, or death directly and proximately caused by their participation in a research study.[2,3] This has all been to no avail, though, with the past 20 years marked by increasing responsiveness to the research needs of business and industry and less focus on the concerns of the research subject.[4–6]

Vulnerability

Study subjects often do not understand the full implications of the decision to participate in research.[7] Informed consent forms are often abstract and filled with medical and scientific jargon that is confusing to many research subjects. At the same time, it is evident that a growing number of research subjects in high-risk studies are drawn from lower socioeconomic status groups.[8] Therefore, the issue of whether these individuals understand when they will not receive compensated or free medical care for injuries sustained as a result of their participation in a study is of great importance if we are to safeguard their rights.

Case in Point

To illustrate how important this topic is, let me recount an incident that happened about 10 years ago. I had just begun a decade-long tenure as chairperson of the New York City Department of Health's IRB. About the same time I started as Chair, a series of quinalone antibiotic studies were submitted for IRB review. The principal investigator (PI) was a well-known researcher who had received funding from a pharmaceutical company and wanted to use departmental clinics for tuberculosis and sexually transmitted diseases to recruit subjects for his studies, something he had done a number of times in the past. When I read through the first protocol, I noted that everything seemed to be in order. However, when I reached the end of the informed consent form, I noticed a clause that essentially stated that should anything go wrong, the research subject was responsible for the costs of any required medical care in the event he or she was not insured.

This struck an immediate chord of sensibility, so I looked into past studies and made some inquiries. What I found out was not reassuring. Federal regulations were minimal in this area, requiring only that the subject be told that he or she would not receive free medical care or be compensated for research-related injuries or problems. *On the other hand, OHRP (formerly OPRR) was clear that we were entitled to be more exacting if necessary.* Further inquiry within our department revealed that over 70% of individuals using our clinical services had no health insurance whatsoever, as opposed to roughly 20% of the population in general. In addition, a careful reading of the risk section of the consent document made it obvious that the side-effects from the proposed drugs could be serious enough to necessitate seeking medical care. When we broached this with the PI, insisting that he provide free medical care in the event of problems, he was insistent that this was standard operating procedure for all medical research and argued that our IRB was overstepping its bounds in making these demands. After prolonged and sometimes heated discussion, the PI ultimately had the pharmaceutical company agree to pay any medical costs stemming from the research, and this was included in the consent form.

The Nuremberg Code and the *Belmont Report*

The fourth provision of the Nuremberg Code addresses the issue of compensation for research-related injuries: "The experiment should be so conducted as to avoid all unnecessary physical and mental suffering and injury."[9] Drawn from the Nuremberg Code, the *Belmont Report* explicitly supports the view that its three ethical principles should serve as the criteria by which decisions on changes in policy governing human research can be justified. These principles of respect for persons, beneficence, and justice were constructed to "provide a basis on which specific rules may be formulated, criticized, and interpreted."[10] Specifically, the principles of beneficence and justice inform us of our responsibility to address the issue of medical liability. In my opinion, they provide grounds for requiring research institutions to provide free medical coverage to human subjects.

Beneficence

The principle of beneficence calls on us to secure the well-being of human subjects by reducing the risks involved in studies. These efforts are not simply acts of kindness or charity, as the word *beneficence* might suggest, but rather an expression of our moral obligation. If we fail to respond to an opportunity that would reduce the involved risks without compromising the potential benefits that are likely to be generated by research, we have violated the principle of beneficence at the outset. In some situations, mandating free medical coverage for research-related injuries would limit study accrual and thereby decrease societal benefit. Such a compromise is justified in deference to the protection of individual welfare in this setting. The ethical mandate to require coverage of medical care related to research injury is particularly strong when research is conducted in a setting with a high potential for coercion resulting from the lack of access to comparable care outside the setting of a research protocol.

Justice

In its most simple terms, the lack of compensation for medical care to individuals who are injured as a result of their involvement in a research study is ethically indefensible because it is unjust. There is a matter of relativity in this issue, though, and those who are financially most vulnerable among us run the greatest risks. In its *IRB Guidebook*, OHRP's interpretation of the *Belmont* principle of justice explicitly states that "considerations (of the principle of justice) may be appropriate to avoid the injustice that arises from social, racial, sexual, and cultural biases institutionalized in society."[11] As is often mentioned when this matter is discussed, if we had national health insur-

ance, this would be a nonissue. However, we do not, and the present does not bode well for such an initiative in the near future. Injustice related to a lack of coverage for research-related injury can be prevented by IRBs' accepting ethical responsibility and understanding their authority in this regard.

Sample IRB Policy Statement for Researchers Regarding Research-Related Injury

The following statement (or one similar) might be adopted as a component of IRB policy.

Investigators must include a statement in the consent document explaining that medical treatment will be provided free of charge to research subjects should they sustain any injury as a consequence of their participation in the study. Any statements that waive or appear to waive the subject's rights and release the investigator from any liability should not be included in the informed consent form.

By federal regulation 45 CFR 46Sec.116(a)(6), research institutions are only responsible for providing "an explanation as to whether any compensation and an explanation as to whether any medical treatments are available if injury occurs, and, if so, what they consist of, or where information may be obtained for research involving more than minimal risk."

This clause outlines only a minimum federal standard that must be met by research institutions. It is federal policy that individual IRBs can exceed that standard as they deem appropriate. The IRB of [name of institution] requires all research involving human subjects to provide medical treatment to subjects who are injured as a result of participation in that research, regardless of the risk involved. Consent forms lacking this requirement will be denied approval from this IRB.

Sample Wording for Informed Consent Form

Wording suggested for use in the consent document follows.

What will it cost me to participate?
There is no cost to you for participating in this study. Medical treatment will be provided free of charge should you sustain an injury as a consequence of your participation in the study.

Conclusion

As the research industry continues to proliferate and the proportion of uninsured and underinsured individuals in the United States population remains a growing problem, the only practical approach is to educate our colleagues and encourage individual institutions to realistically appraise the potential for injury, insisting that researchers make provisions for free care in circumstances that dictate as much. By necessity, it is a decentralized approach, allowing for flexibility and discretion on the one hand but unfortunately, self-serving or uninformed disregard on the other. Certainly, this is such a fundamental and extraordinarily important ethical requirement that it should be federally mandated and not left to the inconsistent discretion of individual IRBs. However, present circumstances dictate a more singular approach. There certainly is precedent now for institutions to rectify this ethical lapse. The University of Washington in Seattle has had such a policy in place for a number of years, and in 1998 the Department of Veterans Affairs (VA) amended its medical regulations to provide free medical treatment to human subjects injured as a result of their participating in VA clinical research projects.[12]

In conclusion, this chapter presents the view that research subjects should receive free medical treatment if their participation in the research results in adverse health effects. The benefits that result from a study often are indirect and are primarily for the good and benefit of society. Thus, society has a responsibility to subjects who suffer research-related injuries, especially those in vulnerable population subgroups, who face an additional—and heavier—burden of research risk because they lack adequate health insurance. It is unlikely that these truly vulnerable groups would have the skills to negotiate the legal pathways to obtain reimbursement for medical care for research-related injuries. While the debate over universal health care—that is, health care as a right versus health care as privilege—will continue, the question of providing free medical care for research-related injuries is an issue of present social and moral responsibility. It is the obligation and right of IRBs to seize opportunities in which they can minimize these inequities and prevent additional burdens.

References

1. Code of Federal Regulations. Title 45A—Department of Health and Human Services; Part 46—Protection of Human Subjects. Updated 1 Oct 1997. Access date 18 Apr 2001. World Wide Web http://www4.law.cornell.edu/cfr/45p46.htm

2. President's Commission for the Study of Ethical Problems in Medicine and Biomedical and Behavioral Research. *Compensating for Research Injuries*, Vol 1 and 2. Buffalo, NY: William S. Hein & Co. 1982.

3. McCarthy CR. Challenges to IRB's in the coming decades. In: Vanderpool HY (ed). *The Ethics of Research Involving Human Subjects: Facing the 21st Century.* Frederick,MD: University Publishing Group, Inc.. 1996: 140–141.

4. Havighurst C. Compensating persons injured in human experimentation. *Science* 169:154–155, 1970.

5. Vasgird DR. Protecting the uninsured human research subject. *Journal of Public Health Management and Practice* 6(6):37–47, 2000.

6. Anna GJ. *The Rights of Patients: The Basic ACLU Guide to Patient Rights*, Ed 2. Carbondale, IL: Southern Illinois University Press. 1989:154.

7. Pullman D. General provisional proxy consent to research: Redefining the role of the local research ethics board. *IRB: A Review of Human Subjects Research* 21(3):1–9, 1999.

8. Darity WA. Ethics in human experimentation in health care delivery. In: National Commission for the Protection of Human Subjects of Biomedical and Behavioral Research. *Ethical Guidelines for the Delivery of Health Services.* Washington, DC: Government Printing Office. 1978.

9. The Nuremberg Code. Chapter 12: Permissible medical experiments. *Trials of War Criminals Before the Nuernberg Military Tribunals Under Control Council Law No. 10, Vol. 2.* Washington, D.C.: U.S. Government Printing Office. 1949: 181–182. Access date 20 Aug 2001. World Wide Web http://www.ushmm.org/research/doctors/Nuremberg_Code.htm

10. National Commission for the Protection of Human Subjects of Biomedical and Behavioral Research. *The Belmont Report: Ethical Principles and Guidelines for the Protection of Human Subjects of Research*, 18 Apr 1979. Access date 22 Mar 2001. World Wide Web http://ohsr.od.nih.gov/mpa/belmont.php3

11. Penslar RL, Porter JP, Office for Human Research Protections. *Institutional Review Board Guidebook*, ed. 2, 6 Feb 2001. Access date 29 Mar 2001. World Wide Web http://ohrp.osophs.dhhs.gov/irb/irb_guidebook.htm

12. Department of Veterans Affairs. Treatment of research-related injuries to human subjects (38 CFR Part 17). *Fed Regist* 63(44):11123–11124, 1998. www.access.gpo.gov/nara/cfr/cfrhtml_00/Title_38/38cfr17_main_00.html

Informing Subjects About Research Results

Thomas G. Keens

INTRODUCTION

To explain the decisions Institutional Review Boards (IRBs) face regarding informing subjects of study results, it is best to start with case discussions.

CASE 1

Investigators wish to determine whether a specific genetic mutation is associated with an increased risk for heart disease. To do this, they will sample blood from a large number of normal individuals. They will then wait to see who develops heart disease, and correlate the information with the genetic finding. It is not now known if this gene is related to heart disease, though the investigators have some reason to believe that this might be true.

Should the subjects in the study be told whether or not they have the gene mutation? On the one hand, informing subjects that they have the mutation might motivate them to do things to decrease their risk of heart disease, such as stop cigarette smoking, eat less fat, and exercise more. However, informing subjects that they do not have the genetic mutation may lull some into complacency in the belief that they will not get heart disease. On the other hand, it is not known if the genetic mutation is truly associated with a higher risk of heart disease. Therefore, the implications of having the genetic mutation are not known, but knowledge that one has the mutation might cause undue anxiety or distress in subjects who would then believe they are destined to die of heart disease.

Should the research subjects be told whether or not they have the genetic mutation? Do the subjects have a right to know? Do the investigators have an obligation to tell the subjects? Do the investigators have a right to withhold this information?

CASE 2

Urinary tract infections in newborn infants are a known cause of neonatal jaundice. Investigators wish to determine how often undetected urinary tract infections are present in otherwise asymptomatic infants who are seen in the emergency department for persistent neonatal jaundice in the first week of life. They will perform urinalyses and urine cultures on all such infants seen in the emergency department. This testing is not the clinical standard of care in this setting. The urine culture will accurately determine whether an infant has a urinary tract infection. Current medical practice would recommend that such urinary tract infections should be treated with antibiotics.

Should the investigators be required to inform the parents of the research subject, or their doctor, if the subject has a urinary tract infection? Informing them will give subjects the opportunity to receive treatment. Do the parents of the subjects have a right to know? Do the investigators have a right to withhold this information?

CASE 3

Infants born to mothers who used cocaine during pregnancy have an increased risk of dying of sudden infant death syndrome (SIDS). Some researchers believe that SIDS may be related to abnormal breathing patterns or pauses in breathing during sleep, but this is not proven. The investigators wish to record breathing patterns in infants born to mothers who used cocaine during pregnancy to see if they are abnormal. These investigators do not believe that clinical care should be changed based on breathing pattern results. However, other experts would put babies with abnormal breathing patterns on electronic monitors or alarm systems when they sleep.

The investigators inform the IRB that they will not disclose the results of these recordings to the families. Should the families be told the results of these research tests? If the parents are told the results of the research study, some may monitor their infants. Some may needlessly worry about information that the researchers do not believe has any predictive value. If these recordings are ultimately shown to relate to the risk for SIDS, not being told the information may deprive families of the opportunity to do something to prevent SIDS. Should the families be told the research results? Do the parents have a right to be told? Do the investigators have an obligation to tell the parents? Do the investigators have a right to withhold the results?

Clinical Care Versus Research

In clinical care, physicians and health-care professionals have a primary obligation to place the interests of their patient foremost. All diagnostic tests and therapeutic procedures are performed with the best interests of the patient in mind. Although medicine is not an exact science with predictable laws like physics, patients believe to some degree that they can rely on medical knowledge to guide their medical care. For most medical conditions, diagnostic tests are performed because the results will have an impact on the patient's situation. The information derived from these tests may allow a physician to select the most appropriate therapy, to guide treatment, or to give a prognosis. Because diagnostic tests in medicine are being performed to benefit the patient, physicians generally have an obligation to inform patients about the results of these tests.

Research, by its very nature, deals with the unknown. There is less certainty. Research information is more speculative than information derived from medical tests performed for clinical care. A primary goal of research is always to benefit society in general. Although some studies have the potential to directly benefit current subjects, in many situations altruism is the main reason to participate in research. Thus, tests and procedures may be performed primarily to benefit the research study, and not because the results will have an impact on the patient's disease. The information derived from these tests will not allow a physician to select the most appropriate therapy, to guide treatment, or to give a prognosis. When diagnostic tests in research are not being performed to benefit the subject, it is reasonable to suggest that researchers do not have an obligation to inform subjects about the results of these tests. A more difficult issue is the ethics of refusing to give research results to subjects who understand the uncertainty involved.

Federal Regulations

Federal regulations on protecting human subjects are silent on the issue of whether or not subjects should be given research results.[1] International codes on the ethical conduct of human research similarly do not comment on whether research subjects should be told research results.[2–4] These codes do indicate information that subjects should be given before consenting to participation in a research study. In some cases, the regulations require that the investigators explicitly tell potential subjects whether or not they will be given the research results, and if so, how and by whom.[1] However, the regulations do not say that research subjects are always entitled to receive such results. They do not say that investigators are always ob-

ligated to communicate such results, nor that they are entitled to withhold such results.

The one situation in which federal regulations require that subjects are informed about research results is when the new findings developed in the course of the study may change the balance of risks versus benefits to the subject.[1][Sec.116(b)(5)] In this case, the following information shall be provided to research subjects:

> ...significant new findings developed during the course of the research which may relate to the subject's willingness to continue participation will be provided to the subject; ...

Thus, investigators have an obligation to inform subjects about results from the study that may change their decision to participate. However, this is a different issue than whether or not to inform a research subject about test results performed on him or her as part of research. Therefore, regulations on protecting human research subjects do not guide the IRB in deciding which research information, if any, should be communicated to subjects.

Other Legal Requirements in Specific Cases

There are situations where state law requires the reporting of information whether it is collected for research or nonresearch purposes. There are limits to confidentiality. For example, if a research study determines that child abuse has occurred, or that a subject may be a danger to himself or others, or that reportable communicable diseases are present, the investigator has a legal obligation to report such findings to appropriate authorities. It is important to note that in situations where the law requires the reporting of test results or evaluations, the information carries the same degree of certainty as information obtained as part of medical care. Disclosure of this type of information will benefit the subject and/or others. Therefore, disclosing this type of information is analogous to informing patients about their own medical test results.

Ethical Principles

The *Belmont Report* is the classic reference for the three basic principles underlying the ethical conduct of human research and the protection of human research subjects.[5] Of these principles, respect for persons and beneficence address the issue of informing subjects about research results. At first glance, these principles appear to present competing obligations.

Respect for Persons
The principle of respect for persons acknowledges the freedom and dignity of every person. A person should be able to choose what will and will not happen to him or her. Respect for persons motivates ethical research to require that subjects understand the full implications of their decision to participate in research. There are two ways one could apply the principle of respect for persons

to the question of informing subjects of research results. One might argue that respect for persons requires that researchers give each subject the option of being informed of research results, with a full explanation of the potential implications of this decision. From this perspective, researchers would be ethically obligated to report research results to any subject who wants them.

The alternative view interprets the principle of respect for persons to mean that informed consent requires the potential subjects to understand if they will or will not be informed of research results. However, there is no ethical justification for requiring result disclosure per se. Subjects are not required to participate in research. It is perfectly ethical to allow people to exercise their right as autonomous agents to decline to participate in a research study because they do not agree with the plan to limit access to research results.

Beneficence

Beneficence recognizes the obligation to maximize potential benefits and minimize potential risks. One should not injure a person despite the possibility of benefit to others, such as to society. Research-related risks to subjects must be reasonable in light of expected benefits to the subject or to society. Risks to subjects should be minimized. This principle argues that investigators should do what is best for the subject. Beneficence dictates that an investigator is obligated to provide a subject with research information if that information will maximize benefits or minimize risks to the subject. However, beneficence also argues that the investigator should not inform the subject about research results if that information will cause harm. If we apply this argument to the three case studies at the beginning of this chapter, the outcome is not definitive. One can support an argument that it is ethical to not inform subjects of research results in cases where there is uncertainty about the validity of these results to issues that would affect the welfare of the subject. In Case 1, the research results are not known to maximize benefits, and they may be harmful, so the investigator should not inform the subject. In Case 2, informing the subject would clearly maximize benefits and minimize harm, so the investigator would be obligated to inform the subject. In Case 3, the interpretation of these research results differs according to different experts. Therefore, the investigator may be obligated to inform or not inform subjects, depending on the investigator's bias. The take-home message from this analysis is that the critical issue in evaluating the ethics of a study that plans to withhold information about research results from subjects is the level of confidence in the accuracy of the information at the time that the study is being conducted.

Research Information: Knowledge or Speculation

Information derived from subjects through research may constitute knowledge or potentially relevant information, or it may constitute speculative data of little relevance to the subject. In Case 1, the information derived about each subject is speculative at best. It is not known if this information truly predicts any clinical outcome. Further, there may be harm in providing this information to subjects if they are misled to believe that they are at risk. Therefore, as a generalization, for speculative information, not proven to have clinical relevance to the subject, the investigator is not obligated to inform the research subject. In addition, because providing subjects with this information may cause harm, one can make a strong argument that the investigator has an ethical obligation to withhold such information from the research subject.

In Case 2, the information has direct clinical implications for the subject. The information is not speculative, but has specific and agreed-upon clinical implications. Therefore, it is likely to be in the best interest of research subjects to have research results disclosed to the parents of the subjects or their physicians. In general, the investigator is obligated to inform the subject of research results when there is little or no question that access to the information could benefit the subject.

Case 3 provides an example where there is more ambiguity. Some experts believe that the research information has clinically relevant predictive value and that treatment may be implemented based on this information. Other experts believe this information has no clinical relevance and that treatment should not be based on this information. This study was actually performed by investigators at two institutions, and therefore the study was reviewed by two IRBs. Both IRBs approved the study. At Institution A, the IRB agreed with the investigators' assessment that the research information had no clinical utility and that it might worry some parents. Therefore, the study was approved at Institution A, provided parents were not given the results of the research study, and the parents were informed that they would not receive the research results. At Institution B, the IRB sided with experts who believed the research results might have potential predictive value and/or clinical relevance. Therefore, the study was approved at Institution B, provided that parents were given the results of the research study, and the parents were informed that they would receive these results. Both IRB decisions were correct. Both IRBs acted on their views of the strength of the research information and its relevance to the subjects' clinical care.

The bottom line is that subjects should always understand if they or their physicians will or will not be informed of research results. Sometimes it may be appropriate to offer subjects a choice about whether they wish to have the information disclosed after they have been informed about the nature of the information. An example of this would be a population study on the incidence of the Huntington's disease gene. Huntington's disease is an incurable, degenerative neurologic disorder, which is inherited and ultimately fatal. If a subject has the gene, he or she will develop Huntington's disease in middle age. Some subjects want to know this information in young adult life, when they are still asymptomatic. Other subjects do not want to know such information. Although the information is certain (correlates absolutely with the development of Huntington's disease), there is nothing subjects can do to prevent or modify the fact that they will develop this fatal disease if they have the gene. In such a study, the IRB could permit the subjects to decide whether or not they want to have the information disclosed after informing them of the implications.

Conclusion

As part of their review of human research protocols, IRBs must decide whether or not research information should be given to subjects. To help in this determination, the IRB should consider the following.

1. A complete understanding of the extent to which research results will be disclosed to the subjects and/or their physicians is an absolute requirement of ethical research.

2. When considering the ethics of withholding research results from study subjects, an important consideration is the level of certainty that this information will impact the diagnosis, management, or prognosis of the subject.

3. Disclosing research results to subjects may harm research subjects. Risks may be the dominant factor when the accuracy of research results are in question.

4. In some situations it is appropriate for the research plan to allow the subjects to choose whether research results will be given to them or their physician.

5. When research results are disclosed to subjects, the process should always be structured in a way that respects privacy, offers appropriate support when news is bad, and involves

persons knowledgeable about all of the implications of the information with respect to the subject's disease or disorder.

References

1. Code of Federal Regulations. Title 45A—Department of Health and Human Services; Part 46—Protection of Human Subjects. Updated 1 Oct 1997. Access date 18 Apr 2001. World Wide Web http://www4.law.cornell.edu/cfr/45p46.htm

2. US Supreme Court. Order denying writ of habeas corpus, October 20, 1947. *Trials of War Criminals Before the Nuremburg Military Tribunals Under Control Council Law, Volume 2, Chapter 10.* 1949: 888.

3. World Medical Association. *Declaration of Helsinki: Ethical Principles for Medical Research Involving Human Subjects.* First adopted in Helsinki, Finland, in 1964. Updated 10 Jul 2000. Access date 20 Mar 2001. World Wide Web http://www.wma.net/e/policy/17-c_e.html

4. Council for International Organizations of Medical Sciences, World Health Organization. International ethical guidelines for biomedical research involving human subjects. In: Vanderpool HY (ed). *The Ethics of Research Involving Human Subjects: Facing the 21st Century.* Frederick, Maryland: University Publishing Group. 1996: 501–510.

5. National Commission for the Protection of Human Subjects of Biomedical and Behavioral Research. *The Belmont Report: Ethical Principles and Guidelines for the Protection of Human Subjects of Research*, 18 Apr 1979. Access date 22 Mar 2001. World Wide Web http://ohsr.od.nih.gov/mpa/belmont.php3

Explaining the Cost of Research Participation

Kevin M. Hunt

INTRODUCTION

Just after my first IRB meeting, I was attempting to describe to a colleague what had happened there. I related the efforts required for reading copious amounts of esoteric research and the nature of the debates at the meeting. I questioned how my financial focus intersected with this process. My colleague's response to my doubts was to declare, "This is where the rubber meets the blue sky."

As the Director of Patient Financial Services at a prestigious academic medical center, I have spent more than three years participating with the Committee for the Protection of Human Subjects (IRB). I have found the work involved with the IRB to be both very rewarding and extremely meaningful. Furthermore, in contrast to the doubts that characterized my earlier participation with the IRB, I am now convinced that the complete and accurate disclosure of research-related costs is critical to the essential protections that must be offered to all human subjects. I further believe this same level of disclosure of research-related costs is critical to the compliance protections that need to be in place for the medical organizations where the research is taking place. Lastly, the complete disclosure of research-related costs will help minimize any possible potential conflict of interest issues that could adversely impact the research participant.

Over the past several years, I have witnessed a dramatic evolution in the collective thinking of IRB members regarding the numerous issues related to explaining research-related costs. Literally, the progression in member thinking has gone from considering the issues of research-related costs as being little more than an administrative burden, demanding only the slightest attention, to being an essential component of every deliberation on every protocol submitted to the IRB. The purpose of this chapter is to review and examine the IRB's responsibility to extend protections regarding research-related costs to human subjects. I will also discuss the role the IRB must play in protecting the institution's exposure as it pertains to research-related costs.

Disclosure of Research-Related Costs to Human Subjects

The cost associated with research participation directly impacts every human subject enrolling in a research study. Research-related costs are all potential out-of-pocket expenses participants are likely to experience as a result of their participation in a research protocol. Typically, these costs include greater and more frequent coinsurance and deductible payments, and potentially the costs of noncovered services as defined by the participant's insurance carrier. In addition, other first-dollar expenses may be associated with their participation in a protocol, such as travel or payment for an explicit research service or item. For participants who are uninsured, all costs will be first-dollar expenses for all care being rendered during the course of a study. Most studies provide varying degrees of financial coverage from the industrial sponsor for those drugs or procedures being studied within the research design. However, studies that do not clearly distinguish services that are medically necessary from those services being provided to advance research objectives can result in another set of cost exposures being shifted to the research participants. These are services that may be denied for payment by the insurance carrier and ultimately passed on and billed to the participant.

On occasion, there are studies in which participants may incur substantial research-related costs. For example, a recent Phase I cancer drug trial was proposed to our IRB that required both inpatient hospitalization as well as extensive outpatient follow-up, testing, and monitoring. The study was well received by the scientific community, but had no corporate or industrial sponsor. Furthermore, the protocol consent documents did not address the research-related costs, as it was the principal investigator's intention to find a sponsor. What should an IRB do in such a case? Given that the scientific merits of the investigation were recognized, and that adequate safety monitoring was available to the human subjects, should the IRB act to approve the study? Should the IRB table consideration of the protocol until a sponsor is found? Or might the IRB approve the study because its first mission to protect human subjects had been met, and let the individual research participant make the final determination as to his or her enrollment in the study? There may be more than one right answer to these questions, but this protocol, as presented, placed the research participant at significant financial risk. The total research-related costs in this study were estimated to be in the range of $10,000 to $20,000. The financial impacts on the participants were simply too great; the total expenses, in my opinion, clearly crossed a reasonableness threshold. However, what should a reasonable cost threshold be? IRBs easily recognize when research stipends are too high and border on being an inappropriate inducement or even coercion. However, IRBs have not really evolved similar policy or practice for reasonableness standards as they apply to deferring research-related costs to participants. Perhaps we want to believe that if the research participant has insurance, then all research-related expenses are covered. I would argue that this point of view is no longer sufficient if we want to provide reasonable protections to human subjects, as well as to the institution where the research is taking place. Unfortunately, the devil is in the details, and although it is difficult to know how all insurance plans will provide coverage, we need to do a better job than we are doing today.

Informed Consent Language

It is my view that research participants should be routinely informed that their participation in a clinical trial may result in the refusal of their insurance company to pay any costs of their medical care. Ironically, Medicare has the most comprehensive coverage policy for beneficiaries who participate in research. Most commercial carrier insurance policies typically extricate the plan from providing any coverage for any investigational, experimental, or research-related services. However, a recent United States GAO report to Congress indicated, "insurers may unknowingly pay for trial-related care for patients who enroll without the insurer's explicit approval."[1] Having insurance plans unwittingly pay for research-related costs is definitely not the correct approach for providing protections to human subjects. The informed consent language from the "financial consideration" section a few years ago was very clear. At that time, the consent document stated: "All costs associated with this study will be billed to you or your insurance carrier. Your insurance company may not pay the costs for medical treatment as a result of your enrollment in a research study."

It is remarkable that anybody sought to enroll in a research protocol when statements such as these were included in the informed consent language. Clearly, human subjects are willing to risk a great deal if they believe their health or their life may hang in the balance. Participants may even have a subconscious belief that the services being provided to them while being enrolled in a research protocol are superior to the standard of care. Clearly that is not the case, and this is where a participant's altruism, health care needs, and hopes make him or her part of a very vulnerable population. Routinely, IRBs approve studies where research participants must be willing to incur research-related costs in order to receive placebo.

IRB members must begin to question whether human subjects in research protocols are being adequately protected if the protocols include exposures to unreasonable research-related costs. Each IRB needs to articulate its own financial reasonableness standards for research-related costs in order to evaluate when this line has been crossed. Evidence that IRBs are moving in this positive direction may be found in the wording of a current "financial considerations" section of the informed consent when it paraphrases the following statement.

> You will not be charged, nor will your insurance carrier be charged, for any test or visit that is completed solely for the purpose of this study. The sponsor of the study will pay for all costs associated with the research component of this study. The tests you will not be charged for include . . . . The parts of your care that would normally be done as standard treatment, such as . . ., will be billed to your insurance company.

This type of explicit disclosure may place a greater burden on the sponsor, the principal investigator, or perhaps even the research participant. However, the specificity of the wording, as to who will be paying for what, is essential if the IRB is to evaluate the reasonableness of research-related costs before they are passed along to the participant.

Supporting the explicit disclosure of research-related costs to research participants is one thing, whereas actually getting to a detailed and explicit accounting of these costs has proven to be even more difficult. In most medical centers, if the concept of providing explicit disclosure is not still open to controversy, it certainly is still open to noncompliance.

When an individual either elects, or considers, enrollment in a research protocol that his or her physician is helping to direct, the relationship between patient and physician changes. The relationship is now not doctor-patient, but is more accurately described from the ethical standpoint as researcher-participant. Researcher and participant need to fully and collaboratively discuss all financial concepts: incentives to the researcher, complex billing issues, conflicts of interests, and so forth. Although these discussions do form the basis of responsible patient advocacy, they may not, in and of themselves, be sufficient to fulfill the IRB's mandates for protecting human subjects. I would argue that explicit disclosures that are discussed must also be in writing, be easily understood, and be incorporated into the informed consent process as overseen by the IRB. The principal investigator/researcher (PI) is in the best position for crafting such an explicit disclosure. The PI can distinguish services that are routinely part of the standard of care for the patient population being studied and those services and procedures in the trial that are solely conducted to advance research objectives. The PI can also reveal all financial incentives to the researcher or the institution, as well as any potential conflicts of interest. Without this explicit and detailed input to the IRB from the PI, the IRB will be hampered in determining if its reasonableness standard for incurring research-related costs has been eclipsed.

Disclosure in the Informed Consent

Should this information be explicitly detailed in the study's informed consent document? Could the financial disclosure information be an addendum to the consent, but reviewed by the IRB? Should all disclosures be reconciled against the research grant or contract? Are these administrative tasks more appropriately handled by a group other than the IRB? Each of these questions must be answered in order to strengthen the IRB process and to ensure the protection of human subjects as it pertains to research-related costs. Failure to meet these new and emerging standards for financial disclosure could ultimately jeopardize enrollment in future clinical trials, especially if the public believes researchers and research institutions are not forthcoming with full and complete financial disclosures.

An illustration of this is found in a recent national investigational product study that moved from the clinical trial status to a procedure (and implant) approved by the federal government. Clearly, this type of outcome and approval is the goal of many—if not most—clinical trials being reviewed by IRBs. However, the original protocol in this study provided a five-year follow-up period in which a greater number of MRI scans would be performed than was the standard of care. Now that the procedure has been approved, the greater number of MRI scans has become the new standard of care. Consequently, even though no new participants were being enrolled in these studies, the sponsor and the PI sought to have patients sign a new consent allowing the patient's insurance to be billed for all subsequent MRI scans. The reaction from the research participants/patients resulted in a significant number of withdrawals from the studies. Participants were angry they were suddenly going to incur greater out-of-pocket costs. One participant agreed to sign the new consent, but explicitly demanded that none of his follow-up data be forwarded to the industrial sponsor. Other participants refused to sign the new consent and to comply with the new standard of care because they could not afford the extra MRI procedures.

This example raises some very important and potentially troublesome disclosure issues. What financial and clinical obligations does a sponsor have to its original participants if the product or procedure is subsequently approved for commercial use or becomes the new standard of care? Do the original consent and its care provisions remain in effect if the participant refuses to sign the new consent? What provisions should there be in this process for participants who no longer have insurance and are medically indigent?

These questions may assist IRBs in evolving their policy positions regarding research-related costs, as well as in preparing revisions to the "financial considerations" section of the informed consent. My recommendation is that the consent document contain language that reflects the principles which follow. Note that reasonable people will disagree with some of these statements. Every IRB must make its own decisions.

1. Patients should be charged only for medically necessary services or for services for which they agreed in advance to incur the direct cost.

2. The cost of services solely for advancing the objectives of the research should be borne by the research sponsor. There is a legitimate argument against this point of view. People are not required to participate in research. As long as a person understands the implications of the decision to participate in a study, one can argue that it is ethically sound to charge participants for research costs.

3. Enrollment in a study protocol should never be exclusionary based on a person's ability to pay. Wealth should not be a defining issue in gaining access to needed care, including research. The principle of justice is my rationale for this recommendation.

4. It should always be clearly and simply stated, down to a visit/charge level of detail, which services are part of a patient's standard of care and which services are necessary to advance the research objectives.

5. Research participants should be reassured that sufficient research dollars are available to cover all research-related costs, and that the research protocol will not be curtailed for financial reasons.

6. Research participants should be informed about any financial incentives being provided to the researcher or the research institution from the industrial sponsor or the grant. This includes per capita payments to researchers for subject enrollment.

7. Participants should be explicitly informed of any and all potential conflicts of interest as identified under the institution's policies.

8. Research participants should have access to financial counselors who are able to advise them, based on the explicit disclosure, about the extent of their financial exposure. Financial counseling is an essential part of the consent process in many studies and therefore should be available both before the initial decision to participate in research and during the course of the study.

Protecting the Institutions

Several years ago, I received a compelling memo from the Medicare fiscal intermediary (FI) demanding a complete listing of all Medicare beneficiaries actively enrolled in research protocols taking place at the medical center. This request raised some institutional consciousness because it required a mandated response from every PI on campus. In general, and by statute, Medicare reimburses only items and services that are medically necessary and reasonable, especially excluding payment for research-related costs. Section 1862(a)(1)(A)[2] of the Medicare regulations states:

> Notwithstanding any other provision of this title, no payment may be made under Part A or Part B for any expenses incurred for items or services which are not reasonable and necessary for the diagnosis and treatment of illness or injury or to improve the functioning of a malformed body member.

Medicare interprets "reasonable and necessary" to mean "safe, effective, and not experimental," as noted in the presentation by S.T. Nicholson entitled "Medicare Reimbursement for Research-Related Activities" given to the Dartmouth Hitchcock Medical Center Hematology/ Oncology section retreat on September 3, 1998.

By now, most people are aware of Medicare compliance initiatives from the Office of the Inspector General since research-related prosecutions and settlements under the Federal False Claims Act have appeared as unfortunate headlines on a regular basis. However, my focus in this section is only to convey how these emerging legal and ethical realities should be influencing the IRB to take steps to protect the institution as it protects human subjects.

The IRB must not assume the financial and administrative requirements to assure compliance with federal regulations, local medical review policies (LMRPs), third-party contracts, and appropriate state laws are automatically happening within its institution. Although the IRB may decide to delegate these responsibilities to other administrative units within the organization, it must be sure that the division of responsibilities is clear, well-coordinated, and integrated with each operational unit. IRBs may, at times, be appropriately risk-averse to taking a leadership role in advancing a new administrative standard or advocating for a new regulatory mandate, but it must be understood that avoiding or ignoring these mandates is not an option. Because the IRB is in a position to meld patient interests, public interests, clinical interests, research interests, and financial interests, it must become an essential voice in bringing about institutional change.

IRB Review

It is probably safe to say that the IRB, most of the time, does not know the capacity of its institution's health information system for carrying out its emerging and changing policies having to do with research-related costs. This gap in understanding can adversely impact billing compliance and potentially place the institution's entire research program at risk. Medical centers are typically large, complex organizations, some with decentralized administration. Compliance exposures can occur if management controls are not sufficient or properly monitored. The IRB can be integral in examining these types of issues by exercising its prerogative to conduct reviews of approved protocols. These reviews might include a review of claims to ascertain if human subjects are being charged in a manner prescribed by the protocol. Other reviews might involve extended interviews with research participants regarding how clearly they were informed about research-related costs. Although the complexity of the role of the PI is extended by these audits, all functions in the continuum of patient care as it relates to research should be monitored if the numerous and burgeoning compliance demands are going to be met by our institutions.

Once again, an illustration of the above may include a review of approved protocols where FDA-approved class B investigational devices/implants were employed. Use of investigational implants invariably requires IRB approval.

Even though the FDA has approved class B implants and has issued a corresponding IDE number, local FIs maintain the prerogative to approve, or disapprove, payment for these devices. Furthermore, LMRPs issued by the Medicare FI may prescribe numerous steps to be taken subsequent to IRB approval if a patient claim is to be submitted for payment. It is essential that the IRB find a means to assure, when it approves a research protocol, that the protocol is not only suitable and safe to be pursued with human subjects, but also is coordinated with the administrative and regulatory processes that are downstream from its approval.

In August 2000, the government published the National Coverage Decision for Medicare Coverage of Clinical Trials.[3] These new regulations provide the framework that institutions must use to integrate all of their research-related activities, including the activities of the IRB. No longer will the lack of administrative rules be a haven from compliance demands. All patients enrolled in research protocols have to be tracked through the institution's health information system (HIS). Financial coverage decisions must be rendered for each Medicare patient visit and each patient service provided during the course of a clinical trial. Billing modifiers must be attached to all routine medically necessary services provided during the course of a clinical trial. Although IRBs have been typically removed from these bureaucratic burdens, research participants will now be entitled to a new level of information. From increased levels of information, new advocacy rights will also emerge requiring an improved informed consent process.

Conclusion

In this chapter, I have attempted to make a case to expand the IRB's patient advocacy role in closely looking at research-related costs routinely passed along to participants. The same level of diligence that an IRB applies to assuring the safety monitoring of a clinical trial must be applied to all potential financial impacts. Overlooking or not thoroughly examining research-related costs would be to short-circuit a very critical step of the continuum of patient care. The examination of research-related costs is not entirely new territory for IRBs, but there are newly added regulatory and compliance reasons to elevate the need for explicit and detailed financial disclosures. Furthermore, improved disclosures are not only the best steps to take for extending protections to human subjects, but the same practices required to craft more complete disclosures should also extend added protections to research institutions. New administrative or policy burdens may be placed on the IRB when fulfilling these mandates, but it is not an option to ignore the numerous issues associated with research-related costs.

To the average person, health care billing is virtually unintelligible. Adding a dash of research-related costs to routine health care claims is to take an already confusing situation and make it worse. It is therefore recommended the IRB have a knowledgeable member from the patient financial services department join the committee. This will provide a means for extending important patient/participant advocacy discussions of research-related costs. Most organizations have a very long way to go to improve and to make understandable the cost, reimbursement, and billing of research-related services.

References

1. General Accounting Office. NIH clinical trials: Various factors affect patient participation (report No. GAO/HEHS-99-182), Sept 1999. Access date 21 Aug 2001. World Wide Web http:frwebgate.access.gpo.gov/cgi-bin/useftp.cgi?IPaddress=162.140.64.21&filename=he99182.pdf&directory=/diskb/wais/data/gao

2. United States Code. Social Security Act. Title XVIII—Health Insurance for Aged and Disabled; Part D—Miscellaneous Provisions; Sec. 1862(a)(1)(A) Exclusions from coverage and Medicare as secondary payer. Updated 1 Jan 1999. Access date 22 Aug 2001. World Wide Web http://www.ssa.gov/OP_Home ssact/title18/1862.htm

3. Health Care Financing Administration. Medicare coverage policy—Clinical trials. Final national coverage decision, 19 Sept 2000. Access date 22 Aug 2001. World Wide Web http://www.hcfa.gov/coverage/8d2.htm

Improving Informed Consent

Jeffrey A. Cooper and Pamela Turner

INTRODUCTION

The quality of informed consent can be improved by following the four basic steps that would be used to improve the quality of any process.

1. Establish a baseline measurement for the quality of informed consent and determine a hypothesis by which informed consent can be improved.
2. Implement an intervention designed to improve informed consent.
3. Monitor the effectiveness of that intervention by continuously measuring the quality of informed consent and evaluating for any changes from the baseline.
4. Act on the results of measurements and standardize the plan if successful. Continue the cycle for further improvement. This is commonly referred to as the Plan-Do-Check-Act cycle (Figure 6.12.1).[1]

Elements of Informed Consent Quality

In evaluating the quality of informed consent, three areas should be considered: structure, process, and outcome. These three items have a serial relationship, where process depends on structure and outcome depends on process (Figure 6.12.2).[2]

Structure

Structure refers to the tangible elements required to have a good informed consent. Such tangible elements would include recruitment materials, consent documents, addenda to consents, and any other written or visual information used to convey information and understanding to subjects about the research. The regulations define a specific structure for informed consent documentation.[3(Sec.117),4(Sec.27)] The regulatory mandated structure should be considered a minimum standard, and additional structural features may be required for a high-quality informed consent. The relationship of the informed consent documentation and the quality of the informed consent process is controversial.

Process

Process refers to the actions necessary to obtain a high-quality informed consent. These actions include recruitment, the presentation of the study, and the provision of additional information about the research. In evaluating these actions, one needs to consider the five questions of "who," "what," "where," "when," and "how" applied to a quality informed consent. Who should provide information to the subject? What information should be presented? Where should the information be given? In what time sequence should the research staff present the information? How should the information be presented? The answers to these questions are much debated.

Outcome

Outcome refers to the actual results of a high-quality informed consent. It is the answer to the question: "How do you know a subject had a good informed consent?" This question can be evaluated several different ways. For example, did the subject gain adequate knowledge and

Figure 6.12.1 Four Basic Steps to Improve the Quality of Any Process
Source: Data from Graham N.D.[1]

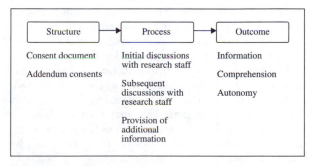

Figure 6.12.2 Serial Relationship of the Basic Elements of the Informed Consent Process
Source: Data from Donabedian A.[2]

comprehension of the research because of the informed consent process? Was the subject satisfied that all questions were answered during the informed consent process? Did the subject's experiences in the research match the information provided during the informed consent process?

In the final analysis, the outcome of the informed consent is more important than the structure or process of informed consent.[5] However, the outcome of informed consent is difficult to define and measure. For example, it is easier to determine whether the risks of a research project are listed in the consent documentation or conveyed orally to a prospective subject than it is to determine if the subject understood the risks and used the information to make a knowledgeable decision about participation in the research. Unfortunately, the regulations focus on the structure of informed consent (the requirements of consent documentation) and the process for approval of the structure (IRB review of the protocol and consent document), but have no requirements for the outcome of informed consent. If we wish to improve informed consent, then we will have to define the desired outcomes of informed consent and learn how to reliably measure the presence or absence of these desired outcomes. We can use that metric to determine the structure and process that result in the desired outcomes and assess the quality of the necessary structure or process as a proxy for the quality of the outcome.

We know very little about the structure and process that lead to the desired outcome of informed consent. Interventions that manipulate the structure or process without measuring outcome should be avoided.

The *Belmont Report*

The *Belmont Report* clearly articulates the desired outcome of informed consent: "Respect for persons requires that subjects, to the degree that they are capable, be given the opportunity to choose what shall or shall not happen to them."[6] Subjects should be provided information, understand the information, and based on their comprehension of the information make a voluntary decision to participate in research.[7–9]

The consent process includes communication of information to the subject, which the subject should take away in the form of knowledge. The ideal state might be that all subjects know everything in the consent document; however, this is clearly an unrealistic expectation. Few investigators or IRB members can recite all knowledge contained in any arbitrary consent document. Knowledge may also be time-limited. Subjects may know at the time of a decision the specific information provided to them, but after the decision has been made they may readily forget that information. As Levine[7] has pointed out, when we make decisions about which car to buy or college to attend, we may do a great deal of in-depth research and gain a large amount of knowledge that allows us to make an informed decision. However, after the decision is made, we may forget the specific knowledge that we used to make such a decision. On the other hand, there are some items of knowledge that subjects should know throughout a research study. For example, we expect subjects to know that they are participating in research, that they made a choice to participate, and that they may withdraw from the research at any time without penalty. Therefore, we need to be circumspect about what kind of knowledge subjects should be expected to recollect after agreeing to participate in a research study.

Comprehension of Consent Process

As part of the consent process, subjects should comprehend important elements of the information provided. Comprehension is more than just knowledge. Memorization of knowledge does not equate with comprehension. Comprehension requires an ability to interpret the knowledge imparted in the consent process and it requires subjects to be able to perceive meaning and ascribe significance to the knowledge that they have gained.[7]

Another desired outcome of the consent process is the autonomy of the subject in making a free choice regarding participation in a research study. This requires a subject to exercise his or her free will. Subjects must choose freely for themselves with no restraint or coercion.

The autonomy of the subject's informed consent can also be evaluated in terms of the subject's satisfaction with specific elements of the process. The evaluation of satisfaction examines the outcomes of the research experience relative to the subject's expectations, as well as the information and understanding by the subject during the consent process. Satisfaction with the consent process does not mean that the subject's expectations of the research were fulfilled, such as expecting a cure of one's cancer. Instead, satisfaction with the consent process means that the subject believes that the consent process provided adequate explanation and preparation for the eventual research experience. An important limitation of the use of satisfaction measurements is the difficulty of assessing satisfaction with rare events. For example, there may be a rare, but serious, adverse event in a research study, and the research staff may poorly communicate the possibility of that event to subjects. However, measurement of satisfaction may not detect that limitation of the informed consent process, if none of the subjects in that research study experienced the rare event.

To improve the quality of informed consent, the IRB should focus on strategies that improve the outcome of informed consent and manipulate the structure and process to improve the outcome. An IRB must assess and improve the structure and process of informed consent mandated by the regulations, but should not make the assumption that meeting the regulatory standards guarantees the desired outcome of informed consent.

Measurement of Consent Quality

The quality of the structure of informed consent is generally measured through audits and inspections. The IRB can audit the informed consent documents of subjects who have agreed to participate in research and measure how often the consent has the appropriate signatures, how often the approved consent was used, and how often the date of the consent precedes the date of research procedures. The IRB can also re-review a sample of approved consent documents and measure how often the IRB approves a consent document with a missing element, overly technical language, absence of relevant risks, exculpatory language, or other deficiencies. Similar data can be collected during the process of continuation review. The IRB can also assess the structural quality of the consent document by measuring the reading level using several commercially available tools.

The measurement of process quality can be performed through audits, monitoring, interviews, or surveys. The IRB can audit protocols to determine how often additional information discovered during the course of research that might have influenced subjects' willingness to continue participation was presented to subjects. The IRB can use a consent monitor to determine that all elements of informed consent were provided to prospective subjects, that prospective subjects were given the opportunity to ask questions, the prospective subjects' questions were answered correctly and appropriately, and that consenting subjects made an autonomous decision. The IRB can also conduct a postconsent survey or interview with subjects. The survey or interview can be used to measure the amount of time allocated to the informed consent process. It can also determine if the subject had any unanswered questions about the research and if specific elements of consent were discussed with the subject.

The quality of the outcome of informed consent can be measured with retrospective surveys and interviews of subjects. The surveys can focus on knowledge, understanding, autonomy, and satisfaction. The literature contains validated surveys that IRBs can use to measure the outcome of informed consent.[5,10] IRBs should have a clear understanding of survey development before developing their own tools.[11,12]

Throughout the course of a research study, one can evaluate the subject's knowledge of his or her rights as a research subject. Does the subject know that he or she took part in a research study? Does the subject know that he or she gave voluntary consent to take part in a research study? Does the subject know that he or she has the right to withdraw from the research at any time without penalty or loss of benefits?

Other issues to evaluate after informed consent include the subject's knowledge of the research protocol itself. Does the subject understand the research purpose of the procedures being performed? Does the subject know the duration of his or her participation? Does the subject know that some procedures are being performed solely for research? Does the subject know that taking part in the research entails risk or potential benefits? Does the subject know that detailed information about the research is contained in the informed consent document? Again, subjects are unlikely to remember specific details about the research. Therefore, the best knowledge issues to evaluate are likely those that are quite general.

Several elements of subject comprehension may be useful to evaluate immediately after informed consent or at any time during or after the subject's participation in research. Does the subject understand the concept of research? Does the subject understand his or her rights as a research subject? Does the subject understand the elements of consent? The measurement of understanding independent of knowledge is difficult, and likely involves the assistance of a knowledgeable educator.

Various elements of the subject's autonomy might be useful to evaluate either immediately after informed consent or at any time during or after participation in the research. Did the subject agree to take part in the research? Who, according to the subject, made the decision to take part in the research? Did the subject make the decision for himself or herself? Because subjects may express their autonomy through delegation, the IRB should also ask if the subject freely delegated the decision to take part in research to a third party.

The information, knowledge, and autonomy of subjects can be evaluated in part through questions directed at their satisfaction with the consent process. Was the subject satisfied with the information that was provided during the informed consent process about what would happen during the research? Was the subject satisfied with the information provided about the risks or potential benefits of the research? Was the subject satisfied with the information provided about the alternative to participation in the research? The IRB can ask subjects how well their experiences in the research met their expectations and if there were any surprises during the research.

Benchmarking

Once the IRB has developed baseline measurements, it can use benchmarking to generate hypotheses about how the outcome of informed consent could be improved and to implement interventions in the structure or process of consent based on those hypotheses.[1,13] In benchmarking, the IRB measures the outcome of informed consent against other institutions and determines a structure or process associated with better outcomes. The interventions can be stratified according to those related to structure, process, and outcome. The five strategies for implementing interventions, in order from greatest to least effectiveness, include peer-based feedback, rewards and punishments, involving people in the change process, administrative rules, and education.[14,15] Generally, providing IRB members or research staff with a scorecard that allows them to compare their quality outcomes relative to their peers' is most effective in changing behavior. Administrative rules and education, despite their popularity among IRBs, are the two least effective methods for changing behavior.

Structural Interventions

Structural interventions change the tangible aspects of informed consent. Examples of structural interventions include the development of a consent template, standardized consent language, or a glossary of lay definitions; increasing or decreasing the amount of information in the consent document; and lowering the reading level of the consent document. With each of these interventions, the IRB can assess the impact on outcome by measuring subject knowledge, comprehension, autonomy, and satisfaction. The IRB can provide feedback to committee members on deficiencies observed in audits of approved consent documents. The IRB can also develop other promising structural interventions by measuring outcomes across a variety of research studies.

Process interventions include requiring that qualified personnel conduct the informed consent process, that subjects are given a minimum amount of time to make a decision regarding participation, that information is repeated to subjects, or that subjects discuss the research with their primary care physician. The IRB can involve investigators and research staff to develop strategies to improve informed consent and can also develop other promising process interventions by measuring outcomes across a variety of research studies. For example, IRBs can evaluate the influence of repetition of information given by research coordinators and principal investigators to subjects on the retention of knowledge or comprehension.

When the IRB implements an intervention, it must reevaluate the outcome of informed consent and look for changes from the baseline measurement. Statistical process control charts represent a statistically valid technique for determining changes in a baseline[16,17] and are beyond the scope of this chapter. Many institutions have quality improvement departments that can provide support for statistical process control charts, and the reader should refer to the references for further assistance.

When evaluating the effect of structure and process on outcome, many structures or processes will vary without a clear or known effect on outcome. This is referred to as *unexplained variation*[18] and is common among IRBs. For example, IRBs have different requirements for boilerplate language and the format of consent documents. Researchers have different methods of obtaining informed consent, none of which have been demonstrated to have advantageous effects on outcome. Unexplained variation has several negative side-effects and can cause researchers and sponsors to lose respect for the authority of the IRB when a structure or process acceptable to one IRB is not acceptable to another. Unexplained variation also minimizes the likelihood that IRBs or researchers will adhere to effective procedures. When the IRB detects variability

in its structure or process, the IRB should determine whether the variability is explainable in terms of outcome or represents unexplained variation. In the case of unexplained variation, the IRB should measure the outcome and choose the structure and process that leads to the best outcome. If two or more structures or processes lead to equivalent outcomes, the IRB should choose one to maximize compliance and therefore maximize outcome.

The Environment of Quality

When improving any function, several recurring themes emerge as key elements to success.[19] The IRB and the institution must be committed to quality improvement. Front-line research personnel must be involved in the change process and have ownership of the process. Measurements should be kept simple and reliable to maximize the validity of the measurement and to maximize the likelihood that the measurement will be performed consistently. In general, 80% of the improvement can be achieved with 20% of all possible changes that can be made.

Conclusion

In summary, the quality of informed consent can be measured by considering the structure, process, and outcome of informed consent. IRBs tend to focus on structure and process because that is the focus of the federal regulations. However, to improve the informed consent structure and process, we must develop measurements of the outcome of informed consent as defined in the *Belmont Report*.[6] From those outcome measurements, we can implement interventions that will allow us to discover the ideal structure and process of informed consent.

References

1. Graham ND, editor. *Quality in Health Care: Theory, Application, and Evolution.* Gaithersberg, Maryland: Aspen Publications, Inc. 1995.

2. Donabedian A. The role of outcomes in quality assessment and assurance. *QRB Quality Review Bulletin* 18(11):356–360, 1992.

3. Code of Federal Regulations. Title 45A—Department of Health and Human Services; Part 46—Protection of Human Subjects. Updated 1 Oct 1997. Access date 18 Apr 2001. World Wide Web http://www4.law.cornell.edu/cfr/45p46.htm

4. Code of Federal Regulations. Title 21, Chapter 1—Food and Drug Administration, DHHS; Part 50—Protection of Human Subjects. Updated 1 Apr 1999. Access date 18 Apr 2001. World Wide Web http://www4.law.cornell.edu/cfr/21p50.htm

5. Joffe S, Cook EF, Cleary PD, Clark JW, Weeks JC. Quality of informed consent: A new measure of understanding among research subjects. *J Natl Cancer Inst* 93(2):139–147, 2001.

6. National Commission for the Protection of Human Subjects of Biomedical and Behavioral Research. *The*

Belmont Report: Ethical Principles and Guidelines for the Protection of Human Subjects of Research, 18 Apr. 1979. Access date 22 Mar 2001. World Wide Web http://ohsr.od.nih.gov/mpa/belmont.php3

7. Levine RJ. *Ethics and Regulation of Clinical Research,* Ed 2. Baltimore, MD: Urban and Schwarzenberg. 1986.

8. Beauchamp TL, Childress JF. *Principles of Biomedical Ethics,* Ed 4. New York, NY: Oxford University Press. 1994.

9. Meisel A, Roth LH, Lidz CW. Toward a model of the legal doctrine of informed consent. *Am J Psychiatry* 134(3):285–289, 1977.

10. Miller CK, O'Donnell DC, Searight HR, Barbarash RA. The Deaconess Informed Consent Comprehension Test: An assessment tool for clinical research subjects. *Pharmacotherapy* 16(5):872–878, 1996.

11. Alreck PL, Settle RB. *The Survey Research Handbook: Guidelines and Strategies for Conducting a Survey,* Ed 2. Chicago, Illinois: Richard D. Irwin, Co. 1995.

12. Sudman S, Bradburn NM. *Asking Questions.* San Francisco, California: Jossey-Bass Publishers. 1982.

13. Lenz S, Myers S, Nordlund S, Sullivan D, Vasista V. Benchmarking: Finding ways to improve. *Jt Comm J Qual Improv* 20(5):250–259, 1994.

14. Greco PJ, Eisenberg JM. Changing physicians' practices. *N Engl J Med* 329(17):1271–1273, 1993.

15. Oxman AD, Thomson MA, Davis DA, Haynes RB. No magic bullet: A systematic review of 102 trials of interventions to improve professional practice. *Can Med Assoc J* 153(10):1423–1431, 1995.

16. Wheeler DJ, Chambers DS. *Understanding Statistical Process Control,* Ed 2. Knoxville, Tennessee: SPC Press. 1992.

17. Plesk PE. Tutorial: Introduction to control charts. *Quality Management in Health Care* 1(1):65–74, 1992.

18. Berwick DM. Controlling variation in health care: A consultation from Walter Shewhart. *Med Care* 29(12):1212–1225, 1991.

19. Carman JM, Shortell SM, Foster RW, Hughes EF, Boerstler H, O'Brien JL, O'Conner EJ. Keys for successful implementation of total quality management in hospitals. *Health Care Management Review* 21(1):48–60, 1996.

Informed Consent Evaluation Feedback Tool

Elizabeth A. Bankert and Robert J. Amdur

"Most codes dealing with human experimentation start out with the bland assumption that consent is ours for the asking. This is a myth. The reality is that informed consent is often exceedingly difficult to obtain in any complete sense. . . . Nevertheless, it remains a goal toward which one must strive for sociological, ethical, and legal reasons." —Henry Beecher, MD, 1966

INTRODUCTION

In 1998, we started an interview process to determine how well participants understand what they are supposed to understand about research. Our goal was to find a simple and user-friendly way to evaluate the quality of informed consent of people who had recently decided to participate in a research project. Our motivation for doing this was more operational than academic. Our IRB was spending considerable time and energy evaluating and revising the consent document as part of the process of initial protocol review. The experience of many of the clinician–investigators at our medical center suggested that we were overestimating the importance of the consent document in the consent process. Research participants often told us that they obtained important information about the study from sources other than the consent document. Detailed interview studies at other institutions suggested that, in spite of detailed consent documents, many research participants do not understand the essential elements of informed consent to the degree that we would like.

To get the information that we needed to direct our process of IRB review, as well as to find ways to improve the quality of informed consent in research participants, we focused our attention on developing a survey tool that would evaluate comprehension of research issues. Our efforts evolved through several stages. We worked with educational psychologists and piloted several different evaluation tools. We started with a very detailed and complex survey that covered many aspects of informed consent in detail. This proved to be both difficult to administer and poorly accepted by research subjects. As the program evolved, the survey instrument became progressively simpler and shorter.

The first phase of the project included the use of an informed consent evaluation (ICE) form with approximately 75 research participants. We asked individuals who had recently enrolled in a research project to respond to a one-page survey that tested comprehension of the eight basic elements of informed consent as described in the federal regulations. These initial surveys convinced us that many of the people who participate in biomedical research do not understand the essential elements of informed consent. The structure of our interview system did not involve research methodology, so it would not be appropriate to present quantitative results here.

The reason to mention this qualitative experience is that it was a turning point in the direction of our project. We decided that a program that focused on the comprehension of subjects after they had made the decision to enroll in a study was of limited value. We already know that informed consent is suboptimal in many settings. In our minds, the more important question is how to improve the consent process so that subjects do not enroll until they are well informed. To this end, we directed our attention to developing a program that could be used by members of the research team as a routine part of the consent process to evaluate and improve the quality of informed consent before participant enrollment. This is still a work in progress, but at this point we have enough experience with a particular survey instrument to be optimistic.

Informed Consent Evaluation Feedback Tool

For the past year, we have been using a survey instrument that we call the Informed Consent Evaluation Feedback Tool (ICE FT), which is appended to this chapter. We pronounce this acronym "ice foot." The primary goal of the ICE FT is to focus the attention of potential research participants on the basic elements of informed consent as described in the federal regulations. The ICE FT is a simple list of questions the researcher uses to obtain information during the consent process about the level of comprehension of the potential research participant. The main purpose of the ICE FT is to guide the dialogue between the researcher and potential participant. It is not a test to be taken and then graded by the researcher. There are two basic ways to use the ICE FT to evaluate and improve the quality of informed consent.

Use the ICE FT to Guide the Initial Discussion During the Consent Process

The ICE FT is given to the potential participant before discussing the details of the research study with a statement such as, "We are about to discuss a research project. There are good reasons to participate in this research study, but the study is not right for everyone. It is not the kind of situation where we can just tell you what you should do. It is important that you make the final decision about taking part in this study, and that means you need to understand what the study is all about. We know this is new information for you, and people often need to ask questions and hear things explained more than once before they feel like they understand what they want to know. I am going to go over a list of questions with you. This list of questions will help us discuss the study. Please take a look at the questions before we get started."

The researcher then uses the ICE FT tool throughout the consent process as a prompt to encourage an interactive dialogue. The intent is to create an atmosphere where the potential participant is comfortable asking questions and interacting verbally about the study. The subject's questions and responses are used to determine the general level of comprehension of specific issues. There is no refined grading system. The researcher should think in terms of a pass/fail model for evaluating comprehension in this setting.

The session begins with the researcher's asking the participant to explain the purpose of the study. In most cases, the researcher and potential subject will need to discuss possible answers before the potential participant will be able to demonstrate that he or she understands the study well enough to go on to the next question.

Use the ICE FT After the Initial Study Discussion

Without mentioning or showing the potential subject the ICE FT, the researcher explains the study, including the essential elements of informed consent. Questions are answered and comments are discussed. After the researcher is satisfied that the potential subject is adequately informed, the researcher explains the ICE FT. At this point, the basic format for the discussion is as described in the previous example. The researcher asks the potential participant to answer each of the ICE FT questions either verbally or in writing (researcher preference). It may be desirable for the potential participant to take the ICE FT home to think about the questions and discuss them with family members. Before enrolling a person in the study, the researcher reviews the potential subject's answers to the ICE FT. This review is an interactive dialogue that further educates the potential participant and allows the researcher to determine if the person is informed to the point that it is ethically acceptable to allow enrollment in the study.

The primary purpose of the ICE FT is to evaluate and improve the level of comprehension of potential research subjects. A secondary function of this tool is that it may be used as a form of documentation of the consent process. We do not recommend asking research subjects to sign the ICE FT, as this gives people the impression that its purpose is to help defend the researcher or organization from legal liability. The consent document already suffers from this problem, and it will compromise the effectiveness of the ICE FT to have it viewed as anything other than a tool to promote subject education. However, it is certainly appropriate for the researcher to make notes on the ICE FT and to record a copy of the document in the research file. We recommend giving a copy of the ICE FT to research participants so they can review it as often as they like throughout the course of the study.

Our Experience With the ICE FT

The ICE FT has been used by protocol nurses in the oncology, cardiology, and psychiatric departments at the Dartmouth Hitchcock Medical Center in Lebanon, New Hampshire. We appreciate and acknowledge the time and effort these research teams have contributed to all phases of the ICE FT project. To date, the feedback we have received has been extremely positive. Most of the protocol nurses say that it facilitates the informed consent discussion from their standpoint in terms of saving time as well as identifying people who are not good candidates for the study under consideration.

As previously mentioned, the ICE FT project has never been pursued as a research effort, so we have no control group for comparison or outcome measurements. The potential participants seem to like it based on the positive comments that have been written at the bottom of the ICE FT form: "I would not have known what to ask if it was not for the list of questions" and "If you have to answer questions, it forces you to read what you are signing." This kind of feedback is enough for us to continue working with the ICE FT at Dartmouth. We are currently in the process of educating all of the research groups at our institution about the need to evaluate the quality of informed consent during the initial consent process. We present the ICE FT as a way to help researchers accomplish this goal.

Conclusion

Major improvements in the protection of research subjects will require the evaluation of the endpoints of ethical behavior. As informed consent is one of the most important requirements for ethical research, it is important to develop tools that allow both researchers and the IRB to evaluate the quality of the informed consent process prior to starting research procedures. The Informed Consent Evaluation Feedback Tool described in this chapter is a simple set of questions that helps direct and evaluate the informed consent process. Our initial experience with it suggests that it is useful for both research investigators and research subjects.

Appendix

Informed Consent Evaluation Feedback Tool (ICE FT)

IRB #   **Title of the study**

1. The purpose of this study is to: **or I am not sure**

2. The treatment that I will receive in this study will be chosen by one of my doctors.
         True   **False**   **Not Sure**

3. I hope to benefit from participating in this study by: **or I am not sure**

4. There is almost no chance that I will directly benefit from being in this study.
         True   **False**   **Not Sure**

5. The main risks of this study are: **or I am not sure**

6. My alternatives to participating in this study are to: **or I am not sure**

7. If I do decide to participate in this study, I can change my mind and withdraw from the study at any time without any kind of penalty:
         True   **False**   **Not Sure**

8. It will end up costing my insurance company, or me, more if I participate in this study than if I choose another alternative.
         True   **False**   **Not Sure**

9. The people who are directing this study and people from the government who are responsible for being sure that research is done correctly have the right to review my records from this study whenever they want to.
         True   **False**   **Not Sure**

10. I have these questions for the research team:

PART 7

Continuing Review

Revisions of an Approved Protocol

Sherry Bye

INTRODUCTION

It would be a perfect world for Institutional Review Board (IRB) administrators if, after a research protocol and a consent form were reviewed and approved by the IRB, they were never revised throughout the lifetime of the research study. However, this hardly ever occurs, and perhaps a good research protocol should be revised to respond to periodic data analysis. This chapter will address the IRB requirement to review revisions, types of revisions, the level of review required by the IRB based on the risk to the study participants, the submission of a revision to an IRB, and the review process by the IRB. Amendments, modifications, revisions, addenda, updates, administrative changes, and a long list of other labels are identified with protocol and/or consent form changes. Throughout this chapter, the term *revision* will be used to refer to all of these changes.

The research protocols reviewed by IRBs may be prepared and submitted by individual researchers or by a sponsor such as a pharmaceutical company. Federal agencies like the National Cancer Institute issue research studies that are monitored by cooperative groups such as Southwest Oncology Group and Children's Oncology Group. Consequently, revisions appear in different formats and with different labels.

After a study is reviewed and approved by the IRB, a lengthy list of revisions often is submitted to the IRB for review within weeks of the original submission. Perhaps all of the typographical errors and inconsistencies that were not caught during the original proofing are now visible because the study has started and study participants are enrolled. The recruitment of study participants may be delayed until revisions have been reviewed and approved by the IRB. Therefore, researchers should submit revisions in a timely manner, allowing the IRB the opportunity to review the revisions according to appropriate guidelines.

Federal Regulations

Why do protocol revisions have to be approved by the IRB? Food and Drug Administration (FDA) guidelines[1][Sec.108(a)(3)] state that the IRB shall follow written procedures "for ensuring prompt reporting to the IRB of changes in research activity; and for ensuring that changes in approved research, during the period for which IRB approval has already been given may not be initiated without IRB review and approval except where necessary to eliminate apparent immediate hazards to the human subjects." The Department of Health and Human Services (DHHS) regulation has similar wording.[2][Sec.102(b)(4)(iii)] In addition, the FDA information sheet for IRBs and clinical investigators, "Continuing Review After Study Approval," item 4, "Process for Reviewing Changes in Ongoing Research During the Approval Period," provides further guidance.[3]

To comply with these regulations, the IRB operating manual should include a written procedure for submitting, reviewing, and approving revisions in an approved protocol. The IRB approval letter should include a statement that IRB approval is required before implementing a revision in a protocol. A sample statement for inclusion in an approval letter is "Procedural changes or amendments must be reported to the IRB, and no changes may be made without IRB approval except to eliminate apparent immediate hazards."

Types of Revisions

Revisions are usually of three types: informational revisions, minor revisions, and major revisions.

Informational revisions involve changes in the protocol with no potential impact on the risks for human subjects. Many of these changes are editorial changes within the protocol. Examples include changes in telephone numbers, the addition or deletion of associates or staff, the reduction in the number of research participants, or the deletion of questions in a questionnaire.

Minor revisions include changes in the protocol that may impact the research participants, but do not significantly affect the risks to the participants. Examples of these changes include adding to the population, changing the amount of blood that is drawn or the frequency, adding nonsensitive questions to a questionnaire, revising the format of the consent form, changing telephone numbers or contact persons on the consent form, or other minor revisions to the consent form.

Major revisions can be divided into two subtypes: minimal risks revisions and major risks revisions. *Minimal risk*[2[Sec.102(I)]] means that the probability and magnitude of harm or discomfort anticipated in the research are not greater in and of themselves than those ordinarily encountered in daily life or during the performance of routine physical or psychological examinations or tests.

Minimal risks revisions are those changes that can be identified as minimal risks to the research participant. Examples include the following: adding a standardized test, changing the treatment, decreasing the drug dosage or the frequency of drug administration, changing the recruitment plan, adding a standard quality-of-life questionnaire, extending the time period of the study to include follow-up with the research participants, revising eligibility to include or exclude study participants, adding a research site, changing the principal investigator, or changing the consent form to include a newly identified side-effect or adverse event related to the study drug. The key determining factor is the amount of risk to the study participant based on the definition of minimal risk. This determination must be made by the IRB administrator and/or IRB Chair or designated IRB member.

Major risks revisions involve more than minimal risk to research participants. Examples of a major change include a change of the study drug or the addition of a research arm to the study. These changes reflect a major-risk change in the direction of the study that may substantially change the purpose or goals of the study.

Submission of Revision Requests

The request for revision to an approved protocol may be prepared in a letter addressed to the IRB Chair or the IRB administrator. The IRB may have a prepared form to use for submitting the request. A copy of the revision form used at Dartmouth College is presented as an appendix to this chapter. In all cases, the revision request should identify the principal investigator, the title of the study, and the IRB number (if numbers are assigned by the IRB to approved research protocols). In addition, it must include a description and justification for the requested revision(s) and information on the change in level of risk to the study participants, if any. In addition, copies of the protocol pages where the revisions appear should be attached to the letter or form. To clearly identify the changes, it is helpful to highlight the specific revisions.

Revisions to a protocol often require revisions in the approved consent form. These changes should be described and justified, and a copy of the revised consent form should be attached. Again, to clearly identify the changes, the specific revisions should be highlighted. The complete consent form—not just the affected pages—should be attached. It is suggested that the latest revision date be inserted at the bottom of each page of the consent form. This can be as a footer in tiny font to assure that the most recently approved consent form is currently being used.

Providing clearly identified information with an easily understood description and justification assists the IRB in conducting a timely review and approval. This will permit the principal investigator to continue enrolling study participants after the revision has been approved by the IRB.

Review Procedures

The IRB staff should review protocol revisions to determine the level of review required. To determine the appropriate level of review, the IRB staff and the IRB Chair must be familiar with the federal guidelines related to the review of revisions.

Acknowledgment and File

It is important to understand that all changes to a protocol, regardless of how minor, must be approved according to either the expedited or full-board process as specified in the regulations. Informational changes that qualify for expedited review may be approved by an IRB staff member, provided that this person is a voting member of the IRB and designated by the Chair to perform this function.[2[Sec.110(b)(2)]] After approval, informational revisions should be recorded and placed in the study file. An acknowledgment of receipt of the informational revisions may be sent to the researcher.

Expedited Review and Approval

Federal guidelines [1[Sec.110(b)],2[Sec.110(b)]] state "An IRB may use the expedited review procedure to review. . .(2) minor changes in previously approved research during the period (of one year or less) for which approval is authorized."

In compliance with federal guidelines, minor revisions and major revisions with minimal risks to research participants may be reviewed and approved by expedited review procedures. The expedited review procedure allows the IRB Chair and/or a qualified member of the IRB to review the revision and determine approval. A revision cannot be disapproved by expedited review; however, the Chair or IRB member may recommend that the revision be reviewed by the full IRB.

All members of the IRB must be informed of revisions to study protocols approved by the expedited review procedures. These revisions should be included in the IRB agenda and minutes. An IRB revision approval document should be sent to the researcher indicating the expedited review and approval by the IRB. The revision approval is only effective until the expiration date of the most recent continuation review. A copy of this document should be placed in the study file.

Full-Board Approval

When the revision is a major risks revision to the protocol that increases the risks to the research participant, the revision should be reviewed by the full IRB. This review should follow the IRB's procedure for full-board review for any research protocol. For example, the revision should be included on the agenda. The researcher should provide written documentation of the reason for the revision, how it will change the protocol, how it will impact the risks to the study participant, and what safeguards will be implemented to protect the study participant from the additional risks. The document should include information about how the revision will impact the currently enrolled study participants. If appropriate, the researcher should provide references to support the revision. If it is the policy of the IRB, the researcher should present the revision to the members during the IRB meeting and provide answers to questions from IRB members.

If the revision involves a change in the consent form, a revised consent form should be submitted with the revision to the full IRB. The IRB should determine if the revision impacts previously enrolled study participants and might affect their willingness to continue in the study. In this case, study participants should be contacted and presented with a revised consent form.

After the IRB review, members will determine by vote if the revision is approved, if the revision requires additional revisions and possibly resubmission to the IRB, or if it is disapproved. The discussion and the vote should be included in the IRB minutes. If additional revisions are required, the researcher should be notified in writing what the additional revisions are, whether the IRB expects the researcher to resubmit in writing, and whether the researcher must reappear at an IRB meeting. When the revision has been approved by the IRB, an IRB revision approval document should be sent to the researcher indicating the revision has been reviewed and approved by the full board. A copy of this document should be placed in the study file.

Continued Enrollment During IRB Review of Protocol Revision

When the researcher has a currently approved protocol, enrollment may continue under the protocol as approved by the IRB. However, the revisions cannot be made in the protocol or the consent form until the IRB approves them. An exception to this would be if there were an apparent, immediate hazard to the participant. In this case, the change must be made without waiting for IRB approval.

Revised Informed Consent Forms

Protocol revisions may require the consent form to be revised to reflect protocol changes. Submission of a revised consent form can be simplified in order to assist the IRB in a timely review. Provide a copy of the consent form with the changes highlighted for easy identification. Include all pages of the revised consent form, not just the page where the revisions appear. Insert a footer on the bottom of each page of the consent form that includes the latest revision date. This can appear in a tiny font. Provide a clean copy of the consent form that can be stamped with an IRB approval stamp including the IRB approval date. This IRB-stamped, approved consent form can be machine copied, which assures that the most recently approved consent form is used for enrolling patients.

Conclusion

It is important for IRBs and researchers to understand that federal regulations require IRB approval *prior to* changing a research procedure or deviating from the IRB-approved protocol unless waiting for an IRB determination could jeopardize subject welfare. A common area of misunderstanding is the situation where a researcher wants to enroll a subject who does not meet all of the inclusion criteria stated in the IRB-approved protocol. Some researchers think that it is acceptable to waive certain inclusion criteria based only on approval of the study sponsor. From the regulatory standpoint, the act of waiving an inclusion criterion without prior IRB approval is no different than ignoring IRB-approved conditions. Revising inclusion criteria, or any other aspect of the protocol, even for a single subject, requires prospective IRB approval.

References

1. Code of Federal Regulations. Title 21, Chapter 1—Food and Drug Administration, DHHS; Part 56—Institutional Review Boards. Updated 1 Apr 1999. Access date 27 Mar 2001. World Wide Web http://www4.law.cornell.edu/cfr/21p56.htm

2. Code of Federal Regulations. Title 45A—Department of Health and Human Services; Part 46—Protection of Human Subjects, 1 Oct 1997. Access date 18 Apr 2001. World Wide Web http://www4.law.cornell.edu/cfr/45p46.htm

3. Food and Drug Administration. Information Sheets: Guidance for Institutional Review Boards and Clinical Investigators. Updated Sep 1998. Access date 9 Apr 2001. World Wide Web http://www.fda.gov/oc/oha/IRB/toc.html

Appendix

Institution Name
IRB
Request for Revision

Principal Investigator: _____ IRB #: _____

Study Title: _____

1. Revision description (check all as appropriate).
_____ Revision to currently approved *protocol*
_____ Revision to currently approved *consent*
_____ Other (e.g., advertisement)

2. Check one.
_____ This revision *does not* increase risks to participants enrolled in the study.
_____ This revision *does* increase risks to participants enrolled in the study (include explanation in revision description, and department chairperson signature is required).

3. Describe revision request.

4. Attach *revised* protocol and/or consent (HIGHLIGHT all revisions).

Signature of PI _____ Date: _____

Signature of section chief or department chairperson _____
(Required if risks to patients are *increased*.)

TO:

[ ] Approved: <u>**This signifies notification of IRB APPROVAL of the revision described above.**</u>
Note to IRB reviewer(s): Please contact the IRB office with comments for follow-up on other options.
[ ] Not Approved [ ] Abstain [ ] Conditionally Approved

IRB REVIEWER'S SIGNATURE: _____ DATE: _____
RfRv.9/98

Used with permission from the Dartmouth College Office of Grants and Contracts.

Protocol Renewal

Karen M. Hansen

INTRODUCTION

An Institutional Review Board's (IRB's) review and approval of a new study is intended to ensure that, where appropriate, ethical principles and safeguards for research participants are considered and applied. These initial steps are only the first in a series of shared, ongoing monitoring activities extending throughout the life of a study.

The research investigator's and/or participant's experience(s) inevitably reshape and change the course of a study. Feedback from participants, adverse event reports, drug toxicities, or preliminary findings may alter the study's design and/or methods. Each new study requires ongoing monitoring by the investigator and the IRB. Renewal of protocols through the IRB occurs at intervals specified by the IRB and no less than annually. It is an inherently sound, ethical process that is also federally mandated.

What Is Protocol Renewal?

Protocol renewal is a form of *continuation review*. At IRB-defined time intervals, the investigator reports the study's progress and findings to date. It is a monitoring mechanism that assures continuing safeguards are in place to protect the rights and welfare of study participants. It is often not possible to predict the complex interactions and evolution of a study solely at the development stage. Periodic review of findings allows the IRB and investigator to determine if the benefits and risks of the research have changed as the study has progressed. Simply put, it is an opportunity to revisit and reapply the ethical principles and norms[1] (p. 326) outlined in the *Belmont Report*[2] and federal regulations for the protection of human subjects. As noted by Levine,[1] (p. 342) each IRB is an agent of its own institution. Therefore, IRBs should specify their own requirements while factoring in the regulatory or policy requirements and other issues necessary to safeguard the rights and welfare of human subjects.

Federal Regulations and International Guidelines

Office for Human Research Protection

The United States Department of Health and Human Services (DHHS) Office for Human Research Protections (OHRP; formerly known as the Office for Protection from Research Risks [OPRR]) offers guidance[3] about their continuing review expectations. Federal regulations outline initial IRB review criteria that include determinations regarding risks, potential benefits, informed consent, and safeguards for human subjects. OHRP has stated that the same review criteria are required during continuing review as well. OHRP specifies the following review parameters.

In conducting continuing review, the IRB should review, at a minimum, the protocol and any amendments as well as a status report on the progress of the research, including (a) the number of subjects accrued; (b) a description of any: adverse events or unanticipated problems involving risks to subjects or others, withdrawal of subjects from the research, or complaints about the research; (c) a summary of any recent literature, findings, or other relevant information, especially information about risks associated with the research; and (d) a copy of the current informed consent document. Primary reviewer systems may be employed, so long as the full IRB receives the above information. Primary reviewers should also receive a copy of the complete protocol including any modifications previously approved by the IRB.[3]

Food and Drug Administration

The Food and Drug Administration (FDA) provides the following guidance.

Routine continuing review should include IRB review of a written progress report(s) from the clinical investigator. Progress reports include information such as the number of subjects entering the research study and a summary description of subject experiences (benefits, adverse reactions); numbers of withdrawals from the research; reasons for withdrawals; the research results obtained thus far; a current risk-benefit assessment based on study results; and any new information since the IRB's last review. Special attention should be paid to determining whether new information or unanticipated risks were discovered during the research. Any significant new findings that may relate to the subjects' willingness to continue participation should be provided to the subjects in accordance with 21 CFR 50.25(b)(5). The IRB should obtain a copy of the consent document currently in use and determine whether the information contained in it is still accurate and complete, including whether new information that may have been obtained during the course of the study needs to be added."[4]

Frequency of Protocol Renewal

The OHRP, FDA, and International Conference on Harmonisation (ICH) guidance reiterate the expectation that IRB review occur at least once every 365 days, or more frequently, if specified by the IRB. ICH guidelines are discussed in detail in Chapter 8-2.

Both OHRP and FDA regulations describe timing for continuation review. Specifically, human subject studies funded by the NIH or regulated by the FDA must undergo continuation review after approval by the IRB in compliance with regulations[5(Sec.109(e)),6(Sec.109(f))] that state: "An IRB shall conduct continuing review of research covered by this policy at intervals appropriate to the degree of risk, but not less than once per year, . . ."

Furthermore, the ICH guidelines require IRB review of progress reports in a report[7(Sec.4.10.1)] that states "The investigator shall submit written summaries of the trial status to the IRB/IEC annually, or more frequently, if requested by the IRB."

Administering Protocol Renewal

Timing of IRB Review

Send timely renewal notices to the investigator. Some IRBs meet weekly, whereas others may meet quarterly. Thus, the timing of the continuation reviews may cycle differently at each organization/institution. It is up to your institutional infrastructure and operations to assure that protocol renewal review occurs annually. The IRB's administrative office must have an operating system in place for tracking time frames of protocol approvals and ensuring that renewal notices are sent out to investigators on time.

Deadlines for Renewal

Advance notices may be sent to investigators two and three months before the expected IRB review date for the protocol renewal. It is important to anticipate your investigators' real-time response rates and office staff needed to track renewal notices and their receipt for IRB review.

Specify the documents to be submitted for protocol renewal review. Request the research study documents (i.e., current protocol, consent form, questionnaire, or survey instrument) and, if applicable, completed protocol renewal form. Protocol renewal forms are an efficient way for the investigator and IRB to evaluate data from the study and make determinations about the study's continued approval through the IRB.

State the consequences of failing to comply with protocol renewal requirements. The renewal notice letter can help inform and educate the investigator about the importance of complying with the protocol renewal request. Failure to provide a continuation review report could lead to study suspension, a loss of funding and/or publication possibilities, or reporting of noncompliance to sponsors or funding agencies.

Issues to Evaluate at Protocol Renewal

It is useful for the IRB to have an institution-specific form to facilitate the protocol renewal process. A copy of a form that has been useful to experienced IRB staff and members is included as an appendix to this chapter.

Accrual

1. Has accrual progressed as planned? If not, will this impact the ability of the researcher to complete the study?
2. If the study objectives cannot be met, and the study involves more than minimal-risk interventions, is it reasonable to continue accrual?
3. If the study is a multisite trial, has the investigator provided you with trial-wide accrual data in addition to local accrual data?

Revisions

1. Are new revisions being submitted at the time of continuation review/protocol renewal?
2. Will each committee member get a full copy of the revised protocol, or is the revision a minor change in previously approved research?

Unanticipated Toxicity

1. How many serious and unexpected toxicities have occurred since the trial's initiation?
2. If the toxicities (in type or number) are linked to the study intervention, are new toxicity risks described in the consent form?
3. Will the information about unanticipated toxicity(ies) impact the risk/benefit ratio and continued study approval?

Subject Complaints

1. Were there concerns about approach or contact for the study?
2. Have subjects withdrawn because of disappointing interactions with the study team?
3. Is there a need to modify procedures or reeducate staff because of these concerns?
4. Do study team members know whom to contact with questions about the rights of research participants?

New Information or Findings Relating to Risk/Benefit Assessment

1. Are safety and risk factors for participants adequately described in the consent form based on findings to date? If not, is the informed consent process or document still acceptable or does it require revision?
2. Has any new institutional policy or regulation been instituted since the last IRB review? If so, does this influence the future conduct of the study?

Interval of Renewal

Should renewal review be done annually or more frequently? The risk to subjects determines the renewal interval.

Other Continuation Review Considerations

Each institution's infrastructure, history, policy development, and state law may impact the process of protocol renewal and the information requested. For example, comprehensive cancer center grants require clinical trial review by a scientific review committee as well as a protocol data and monitoring committee separate from the IRB. Collectively, these committees conduct continuation review in addition to the IRB. A dual system of protection is in place.

Coordinating centers for multisite trials also provide IRBs with reports from data safety monitoring boards (DSMBs) and/or statistical centers at the time of continuation review. These reports enable the IRB review process and provide trial-wide data findings that may impact the risk/benefits assessment at the local IRB level. For this reason, IRBs request both local and trial-wide data on continuation review report forms.

A private hospital may not be involved in multisite trials or rely on a separate protocol monitoring committee within the institution. In this situation, careful reassessment at continuation review hinges primarily on the investigator and the IRB.

Full-Board or Expedited Review?

Initial Full-Board Review

Studies that initially went through a convened meeting of the IRB will continue with full-board review at the time of protocol renewal. However, *expedited review may be used for continuation review of studies that initially underwent full review in the following circumstances*[8]:

1. (a) Research is permanently closed to the enrollment of new subjects; all subjects have completed all research-related interventions; and research remains active only for long-term follow-up of subjects; or (b) no subjects have been enrolled and no additional risks have been identified; or (c) the remaining research activities are limited to data analysis.

2. Protocol renewals may also undergo expedited continuation review in specific circumstances. The following categories of research qualify for expedited review unless the IRB, sponsor, or other study-related party requires full review: continuing review of research not conducted under an investigational new drug application or investigational device exemption where categories 2 through 8 of the expedited review categories[8] do not apply; however, the IRB has determined and documented at a convened meeting that the research involves no greater than minimal risk and no additional risks have been identified.

Initial Expedited Review

Research activities that initially qualified as minimal risk and underwent initial expedited review and approval can continue as expedited review activities at protocol renewal unless changes in procedures or intervention cause the activity to be more than minimal risk. A more detailed discussion of expedited review categories is the subject of Chapter 4-2.

Conclusion

Ongoing protocol review is an important—some would say the most important—aspect of the IRB's role in protecting the rights and welfare of research participants. Guidelines for protocol renewal by IRBs are presented in this chapter with an emphasis on the administration of the renewal process. By establishing standard operating procedures that focus attention on evaluating study progress in view of the major ethical standards, the IRB will comply with federal regulations and fulfill its institutional commitments. The documentation of the continuation review process is a complex task that requires attention to the details of several different sections of the federal regulations that apply to the IRB review process.

References

1. Levine RJ. *Ethics and Regulation of Clinical Research*, Ed 2. Baltimore, MD: Urban and Schwarzenberg. 1986.

2. National Commission for the Protection of Human Subjects of Biomedical and Behavioral Research. *The Belmont Report: Ethical Principles and Guidelines for the Protection of Human Subjects of Research*, 18 Apr 1979. Access date 22 Mar 2001. World Wide Web http://ohsr.od.nih.gov/mpa/belmont.php3

3. Office for Protection From Research Risks. *Continuing Review—Institutional and Institutional Review Board Responsibilities*. Report no. 95-01, 1995. Access date 27 Mar 2001. World Wide Web http://ohrp.osophs.dhhs.gov/humansubjects/guidance/hsdc95-01.htm

4. Food and Drug Administration. Information Sheets: Guidance for Institutional Review Boards and Clinical Investigators, Sept 1998. Access date 9 Apr 2001. World Wide Web http://www.fda.gov/oc/oha/IRB/toc.html

5. Code of Federal Regulations. Title 45A—Department of Health and Human Services; Part 46—Protection of Human Subjects. Updated 1 Oct 1997. Access date 18 Apr 2001. World Wide Web http://www4.law.cornell.edu/cfr/45p46.htm

6. Code of Federal Regulations. Title 21, Chapter 1—Food and Drug Administration, DHHS; Part 56—Institutional Review Boards. Updated 1 Apr 1999. Access date 27 Mar 2001. World Wide Web http://www4.law.cornell.edu/cfr/21p56.htm

7. Food and Drug Administration. International Conference on Harmonisation: Choice of control group in clinical trials. Docket No. 99D-3082. *Fed Regist* 64(185), 51767-51780. 1999. World Wide Web http://www.fda.gov/OHRMS/DOCKETS/98fr/092499a.pdf

8. Department of Health and Human Services. Protection of human subjects: Categories of research that may be reviewed by the Institutional Review Board (IRB) through an expedited review procedure. *Fed Regist* 63(216):60364-60367, 1998. World Wide Web http://www.os.dhhs.gov/topics/humanresearch.html

Appendix

IRB Review of Adverse Events

Ernest D. Prentice, Kevin J. Epperson, Christopher J. Kratochvil, and Bruce G. Gordon

INTRODUCTION

Department of Health and Human Services (DHHS) regulations for the protection of human subjects[1][Sec.109(e)] and the corollary Food and Drug Administration (FDA) regulations[2][Sec.109(f)] require the Institutional Review Board (IRB) to conduct "continuing review of research . . . at intervals appropriate to the degree of risk but not less than once per year." The IRB is also required[1][Sec.111(a)(6)],[2][Sec.111(a)(6)] to ensure that "when appropriate, the research plan makes adequate provision for monitoring the data collected to ensure the safety of subjects." Depending on the size and nature of the research, monitoring may be performed by the investigator, a Data and Safety Monitoring Board (DSMB), or even the IRB itself.

The purpose of continuing to review and monitoring on-going studies is to ensure that the research remains justified and that the rights and welfare of the participants continue to be fully protected. Accordingly, it is of paramount importance that the IRB is assured as the study progresses that the risks are minimized, the benefits are maximized, and the risk/benefit relationship of the research continues to be acceptable. Indeed, these are the cardinal responsibilities of the IRB.

From a practical standpoint, the risk/benefit relationship of on-going research, particularly in the early stages, is most affected by the occurrence of adverse events (AEs) that impact subject morbidity and mortality. Thus, it is important for the IRB to be able to perform a valid review of AEs and determine their impact on continuation of the research, whether the informed consent form requires revision, and whether subjects already enrolled in the research should be re-consented. All IRBs recognize and acknowledge this responsibility, but IRBs are generally not equipped to deal effectively with the current avalanche of adverse event reports (AERs) sent by study sponsors via the investigator. This chapter will address the DHHS and FDA regulations that apply to AE reporting and the IRB review of AEs. Inconsistencies and problems in interpreting the federal regulations are discussed, and practical suggestions are offered on how IRBs should review AERs.

Federal Regulations

The institution is required by the DHHS[1][Sec.103(b)(5)] and the FDA[2][Sec.108(b)(1)] to establish written procedures for ensuring "prompt reporting" to the IRB and appropriate institutional officials about "any unanticipated problems involving risks to subjects or others. . . ." This reporting requirement is unclear, however. The meaning of *prompt* is not clarified, and there is also no minimum risk threshold for reporting a problem. Also, the term *any* implies that all unanticipated problems involving risk must be reported to the IRB regardless of the level of risk and irrespective of any causal relationship between the problem and the research.

Thus, using a literal but clearly impractical interpretation of the federal regulations, even a minor unanticipated AE should be reported regardless of its relationship to the research. Few IRBs, however, require either minor or unrelated AEs to be reported. Although this position may not be totally consistent with the written requirements of the regulations, it is a practical approach, and there is little danger that the rights and welfare of research subjects would be compromised. For example, if a subject suffered an unanticipated, transient, minor headache in a drug study, the investigator should certainly evaluate this AE, but it is not necessary from a subject safety standpoint to report the event to the IRB.

It should also be noted that the aforementioned sections of the DHHS and FDA regulations do not use the term *adverse event*. Instead, the broader phrase *problems involving risks* is used. Clearly, any unanticipated problem involving "risk" that ultimately results in harm to the subject and is related to a research intervention encompasses a reportable AE. For example, an unexpected cardiac arrest in an exercise study or a corneal ulcer in a glaucoma study is obviously reportable to the IRB. The term *problems involving risk*, however, can also be construed to mean a problem involving risk to the subject that does not actually result in any harm. Indeed, the word *risk* literally means only the possibility of harm occurring, as opposed to the actual occurrence of a harm. For example, the loss of a subject's research records that contain identifiable private information would be a reportable event. There is a risk of a breach of confidentiality, which may or may not occur. Thus, IRBs should be aware of the fact that, technically, under the federal regulations, an unanticipated risk to which a subject is exposed is a reportable event, and actual harm is not required.

Risk to "Others"

The regulations also require that unanticipated problems involving risk to "others" must be promptly reported. For example, if a research technician is inadvertently exposed to a low level of radiation during a study, this would be a reportable event. The term "others" can also be interpreted to mean other subjects enrolled in the same clinical trial or receiving the same drug or device at another study site. The implementation of this interpretation by pharmaceutical companies and device manufacturers, however, has been problematic. Without objection or clarification by federal regulators, a massive number of AERs are being sent to IRBs across the nation, even though it is generally acknowledged that IRBs cannot effectively review these AERs, particularly in the context of a multicenter clinical trial. Individual AERs seldom contain sufficient information about the AE to allow the IRB to make an informed assessment of its significance. An AER without a denominator and unblinding of its study arm assignment handicaps the IRB and can lead to errors in judgment that can either affect subject safety or unnecessarily impede the progress of the research.

On the other hand, even in the absence of clinically meaningful data, certainly an unanticipated, serious AE that "may" be related to the drug or device that occurs at an external site cannot be ignored by the IRB. This is obviously for subject safety as well as legal reasons. It is entirely possible that prompt review of an AER by the IRB could prevent other subjects from suffering the same AE and make the investigator more aware of the need for surveillance for a particular problem. If changes to the consent form result, it may also help new subjects make a more informed decision regarding participation. Disclosure in the consent document of a previously unidentified risk will also help protect the investigator against liability for breach of fiduciary duty, i.e., failure to disclose all known risks. Thus, whenever the IRB receives a safety report or other information about an AE that occurred in a multicenter trial, the board is obligated under the current interpretation of the regulations to perform the best review possible even when the data are not yet complete or statistically valid. This is a difficult situation plaguing every IRB that reviews AERs from multicenter trials. The problem is obviously very significant at large institutions, which commonly receive 3000–5000 AERs annually. It is reasonable to speculate that pharmaceutical companies are asking IRBs to review AERs for primarily liability reasons as opposed to any real expectation that the IRB can actually perform a consistently valid review of the AE.[3]

AE Reporting by the Institution to Federal Agencies

AE reporting requirements extend beyond the IRB and institutional officials. DHHS regulations[1][Sec.103(b)(5)] and FDA regulations[2][Sec.108(b)(1)] also require the institution to have a procedure in place for prompt reporting of any unanticipated problems involving risk to the subject or others to the appropriate "department or agency head." In the case of research that is subject to DHHS regulations, the AE must be reported to the Office for Human Research Protections (OHRP), which acts on behalf of the Secretary of DHHS. AEs must also be reported to federally funded cooperative research groups in accordance with their requirements. For example, the National Cancer Institute (NCI) Cancer Therapy Evaluation Program (CTEP) has comprehensive guidelines on AE reporting.[4] AEs that occur in research regulated by the FDA must be reported to the FDA. This reporting is normally accomplished through established reporting channels from investigator to sponsor to FDA. If, however, the investigator holds the investigational new drug (IND) application or investigational device exemption (IDE), he or she should report the AE directly to the FDA or to the FDA through their IRB.

As mentioned previously, federal regulations for the protection of human subjects do not base reporting requirements on a risk threshold. Theoretically, this should result in a tremendous number of AERs being sent to the FDA and OHRP. However, with the exception of any sponsor requirements to the contrary, institutions in general do not routinely submit AERs or reports of unexpected problems involving risk to federal authorities unless the event is serious and related to the research. As a matter of fact, very few IRBs ever report problems involving risk where there is no concomitant harm to the subjects. Clearly, neither OHRP nor the FDA has the resources to review all AEs or problems that occur during the conduct of research. It is equally clear that comprehensive review of AEs at the federal compliance oversight level is neither warranted nor cost-effective. Thus, it is not surprising that OHRP and the FDA have never enforced the "letter of the law."

AE Reporting by the Sponsor

As previously pointed out by Gordon and Prentice,[5] sponsors of FDA-regulated research involving drugs or biologics are required[6][Sec.32(c)] to notify the FDA and all participating investigators in a written IND safety report of any AEs associated with the use of the drug/biologic that are both serious and unexpected. Although this regulation does not require the sponsor to notify IRBs at participating study sites, it is nevertheless routine to do so. Sponsors instruct investigators to provide a copy of the safety report to the IRB or to send a copy of the report directly to the IRB.

It should be noted that, contrary to the FDA regulations for the protection of human subjects,[2][Sec.108(b)(1)] the FDA IND regulations[6][Sec.32(c)] include a risk-reporting threshold. That is, the AE must be serious and unexpected, and must be associated with the use of the drug/biologic, all as defined in 21 CFR 312.[6][Sec.32(a)] It is also interesting to note that the FDA requirements for AE reporting in device studies are similar to 21 CFR 56[2][Sec.108(b)(1)] but differ from 21 CFR 312[6][Sec.32(c)] in terms of reporting criteria. The FDA IDE regulations[7][Sec.150(b)(1)] require the sponsor to report any unanticipated adverse device effects (i.e., an AE that occurs in a device study, to all reviewing IRBs and participating investigators). This more comprehensive AE reporting requirement is undoubtedly because many medical devices are implanted and, thus, the risk remains relatively constant over time.

IRB Policies and Procedures for Review of AEs

Every IRB should have written policies and procedures concerning review of AERs. Given the impracticalities and inconsistencies in the applicable DHHS and FDA regulations as well as a distinct lack of written guidance from OHRP and FDA, many IRBs are struggling to deal with an overwhelming number of AERs. It is, therefore, not surprising that there is little consistency in the way IRBs review AERs. The remainder of this chapter provides general guidance, which will, we hope, help IRBs in their review of AEs. This guidance is based on the University of Nebraska Medical Center IRB's policies and procedures for review of AERs.[3,5]

The IRB should develop separate and specific review forms for AEs: one for AEs that occur at institution(s) served by the IRB and another for those that occur at external unaffiliated study sites. For convenience, these IRB AER forms are referred to as "internal" and "external." The internal and external IRB AER forms should be designed so that the investigator provides the IRB with a reasonably detailed analysis of the AE. Clearly, the investigator, as opposed to the IRB, is usually in a better position to assess the significance of the AE in terms of whether the protocol requires modification to minimize risk, whether the consent form should be revised, or if subjects should be re-consented. Thus, an IRB should utilize the expertise of its investigators, particularly in cases where there is little available information concerning the AE.

Internal Events

The IRB should require investigators to submit an AER form for internal AEs or problems involving risks that are unanticipated and related or possibly related to the drug, biologic, device, or other research intervention. A sample form is presented as an appendix to this chapter. The risk-reporting threshold should probably be set at a level equivalent to "greater than minimal risk," but this is up to the judgment of individual IRBs, which may adopt a more stringent standard in consideration of the federal regulations.[1][Sec.103(b)(5)],[2][Sec.108(b)(1)] AEs that are expected and, therefore, described in the protocol as well as the consent document should normally not be reviewed by the IRB unless an expected AE occurs more frequently than anticipated or is more serious than expected. One possible

exception to this rule is in the case of a death. Some IRBs review all deaths that occur on protocol, regardless of whether the death was related to the research.

External Events

The IRB should require investigators to submit an AER form for external AEs or problems involving risk that are unanticipated and related (or possibly related) to the drug, biologic, device, or other research intervention. The IRB should not routinely review external AEs that occur in studies of drugs or biologics unless the event is serious. The difference in the risk-reporting threshold for internal versus external AEs in such studies is based on the premise that an IRB should have greater responsibility for the review of internal AEs than external AEs. As mentioned, the sponsor's FDA-reporting requirements are limited to AEs that are serious, related, and unexpected. Indeed, as will be addressed shortly, IRBs should not be required to routinely review individual external AEs except under unusual circumstances where the sponsor has determined that immediate IRB review is necessary.

Finally, it should be reiterated that the AE reporting requirements for device studies are different from the requirements for studies that involve investigational drugs or biologics. FDA regulations[7][Sec.150(b)(1)] require the sponsor to report any AEs that occur during device studies to all reviewing IRBs. Thus, the IRB cannot review only serious, unanticipated adverse device effects.

The Role of the Data Safety Monitoring Board

The DHHS and FDA regulations that require the reporting and IRB review of AEs are complex, inconsistent, and out of touch with the realities of modern-day clinical research. Perhaps this is in part because the regulations for the protection of human subjects were issued in 1980 and have never been revised to accommodate the nature of multicenter clinical trials. Even if local IRBs received complete information about every AE in a timely fashion and the board possessed the required expertise, it is both unrealistic and inefficient to expect each IRB to perform this time-consuming task. Although IRBs should perform a thorough review of all unanticipated AEs that are more than minor in terms of health-related significance and occur at the institution(s) under their jurisdiction, this responsibility should not be extended to AEs that occur at other institutions.

The responsibility for safety monitoring in a multicenter clinical trial should rest with a DSMB. As Bankert and Amdur point out, "the IRB is not a data and safety monitoring committee."[8] To attempt to put an IRB in this role is inappropriate. DSMBs should be required to provide IRBs with safety information in a digestible format, at appropriate intervals that will allow IRBs, together with their investigators, to perform a more reliable assessment of the significance of AE data in terms of the protection of human subjects. The DSMBs have all of the available data, including the treatment arm in blinded studies, which helps them make an informed decision, as opposed to local IRBs who are forced to make decisions based on limited and often anecdotal information. The National Institutes of Health (NIH) have taken a step in this direction by requiring that a DSMB be in place for multicenter clinical trials and that DSMB reports be given to the IRBs with ongoing oversight responsibilities.[9] It should, however, be emphasized that while the DSMB and the sponsor clearly have the authority to amend or halt a study, the reviewing IRB that approved the protocol bears the ultimate responsibility for ensuring that the rights and welfare of subjects at their institution are fully protected. Thus, IRBs need to communicate with investigators, DSMBs, other IRBs, and federal regulators as the need arises.

Conclusion

Clearly, there are significant regulatory inconsistencies related to the reporting and IRB review of AEs in studies regulated by the FDA and DHHS. These inconsistencies are confusing for investigators and troubling to IRBs. Additionally, the requirements for reporting AEs as the regulations are currently written are so burdensome—particularly in the current era of large multisite trials—that they have become extremely impractical. Therefore, both harmonization and modification of regulatory requirements are needed. In the meantime, IRBs should utilize a rational approach to the review of AEs that is based upon a reasonable interpretation and application of the federal regulations.

References

1. Code of Federal Regulations. Title 45A—Department of Health and Human Services; Part 46—Protection of Human Subjects. Updated 1 Oct 1997. Access date 18 Apr 2001. World Wide Web http://www4.law.cornell.edu/cfr/45p46.htm

2. Code of Federal Regulations. Title 21, Chapter 1—Food and Drug Administration, DHHS; Part 56—Institutional Review Boards. Updated 1 Apr 1999. Access date 27 Mar 2001. World Wide Web http://www4.law.cornell.edu/cfr/21p56.htm

3. Prentice ED, Gordon B. IRB review of adverse events in investigational drug studies. *IRB: A Review of Human Subjects Research* 19(6):1–4, 1997.

4. National Cancer Institute Cancer Therapy Evaluation Program. National Cancer Institute guidelines: Expedited adverse event reporting requirements for National Cancer Institute investigational agents. Access date 1 Apr 2001. World Wide Web http://ctep.info.nih.gov/handbook/handbook/Part_F_main.HTM

5. Gordon B, Prentice E. Selective review of external adverse events: One IRB's response to the avalanche of IND safety reports. *IRB: A Review of Human Subjects Research* 21(3):10–11, 1999.

6. Code of Federal Regulations. Title 21, Chapter 1—Food and Drug Administration, DHHS; Part 312—Investigational New Drug Application. Updated 1 Apr 1999. Access date 18 Apr 2001. World Wide Web http://www4.law.cornell.edu/cfr/21p312.htm

7. Code of Federal Regulations. Title 21, Chapter 1—Food and Drug Administration, DHHS; Subchapter H—Medical Devices; Parts 800 through 898. Updated 1 Apr 1999. Access date 18 Apr 2001. World Wide Web http://www4.law.cornell.edu/cfr/21p800.htm

8. Bankert E, Amdur RJ. The IRB is not a data and safety monitoring committee. *IRB: A Review of Human Subjects Research* 22(6):9–10, 2000.

9. National Institutes of Health. NIH Policy for Data and Safety Monitoring, 10 Jun 1998. Access date 29 Mar 2001. World Wide Web http://www.nih.gov/grants/guide/notice-files/not98-084.html

Appendix

IRB Report of Unexpected Internal Adverse Event
Section I
Protocol Information

IRB# _____ Title of Protocol _____

_____

_____

Principal Investigator: _____ E-mail: _____

Department: _____ Campus ZIP: _____ Phone: _____

SECTION II
Nature of the Adverse Event

Only submit this form if a box in each row is checked. That is, the AE is both (1) unexpected and (2) related or possibly related, and (3) either serious or not serious.

☐ UNEXPECTED
the specificity or severity of the AE is **not** consistent with the current investigator's brochure or with other current risk information

---

☐ RELATED **OR** POSSIBLE RELATED
there is a reasonable possibility the AE may have been caused by the drug or intervention **OR** it is possible that the AE may have been caused by the drug or intervention, but there is insufficient information to determine the likelihood of this possibility

---

☐ SERIOUS
(1) results in death, or (2) is life-threatening, or (3) requires inpatient hospitalization or prolongation of existing hospitalization, or (4) results in persistent or significant disability or incapacity, or (5) results in a congenital anomaly or birth defect, or (6) causes cancer, or (7) is an overdose, or (8) is any medical event which requires treatment to prevent one of the medical outcomes listed above.

☐ NOT SERIOUS
Does not meet the criteria for classification as serious.

SECTION III
Certification of Principal Investigator

My signature certifies the following

☐   All necessary information has been assessed and Section IV completed in sufficient detail to facilitate IRB review.
☐   The risks of the research are minimized to the greatest extent possible.
☐   The risk-benefit relationship of the research continues to be acceptable.
☐   The consent form does not require revision. A copy of the current consent form is attached.
☐   The consent form requires revision. An underlined copy and **two clean** originals per Section IV (7) are attached.

_____   _____
Signature of Principal Investigator   Date
Internal AE (09-18-01)

SECTION IV

INSTRUCTIONS: Please respond to each of the following questions in sequence. Each part must be titled using **boldface sub-headings** as described below and addressed independently without reliance on information covered under other parts.

1. **Subject Identifier:** Identify the subject using their patient ID number.
2. **Description:** Describe the medical nature of the adverse event.
3. **Date and Time of the Adverse Event:** State the date and time the subject suffered the adverse event.
4. **Location of the Adverse Event:** State the location where the subject suffered the adverse event.
5. **Treatment of the Subject:** Describe the medical treatment of the subject who suffered the adverse event.
6. **Prognosis:** Describe the subject's prognosis.
7. **Explanation of AE Classification:**
   a. Explain your assessment of causality
   b. Explain your assessment of the severity of the AE
8. **Risk-Benefit Analysis Update:** Explain why the overall risk-benefit relationship of the research is still acceptable in light of the information concerning this adverse event report.
9. **Changes in Protocol:** In your judgement, is a change in protocol necessary to reduce or eliminate risk? If **NO**, provide a brief rationale. If **YES**, then attach a description of the changes. Describe **each** proposed change in protocol separately in numbered sequence. The justification or rationale for each change must be included, and the investigator must advise the IRB in this subpart whether or not **each** proposed change that directly affects the subject requires revision of the consent/assent document(s). *Note: if the investigator completes this section, no additional IRB Change in Protocol Form is required for these changes.*
10. **Informed Consent/Assent Document:** Are any changes required in the informed consent/assent document(s) to better inform and protect the rights of subjects? If **YES,** then attach one copy of the **revised consent/assent form(s)** with the changes highlighted/marked and two clean (unhighlighted, unmarked) originals suitable for reproduction (printed single sided using a 12-point font) for use during the IRB approval period. Upon IRB re-approval this form will be <u>stamped</u> with the date of the valid approval period. If **NO,** then provide a brief rationale and attach one copy of the **current IRB approved consent form(s).**
11. **Re-consent/Assent:** Is it necessary to inform subjects (or their legally authorized representatives) who have already consented to participate in the study of the adverse event with either an amendment to or a revision of the consent/assent form? If **YES,** then attach one copy of the **amendment and/or revised consent/assent form(s)** with the changes highlighted/marked and two clean (unhighlighted, unmarked) originals suitable for reproduction (printed single sided using a 12-point font) for use during the IRB approval period. Upon IRB re-approval this form will be <u>stamped</u> with the date of the valid approval period. If **NO,** then provide a brief rationale.
12. **Report Requirements.** Have you complied with all applicable reporting requirements of the sponsor, NCI, or FDA?

Data and Safety Monitoring

J. Allen McCutchan

INTRODUCTION

IRBs are tasked with the "continuing review" of research (i.e., monitoring studies after their initial approval), but face a multitude of problems in trying to do so. This chapter attempts to clarify the responsibility of investigators, sponsors, and Institutional Review Boards (IRBs) for monitoring the conduct of studies after their initial approval. It advocates a central role for data safety monitoring boards (DSMBs) in the monitoring of complex or potentially risky studies.

Data and Safety Monitoring Boards

A DSMB is a multidisciplinary group, usually composed of three to six experts in at least two areas: (1) medical issues (the disease, drug, device, procedure, or outcome measures), and (2) methodological issues (clinical trials design, data management, and statistical analysis). For some studies, expertise in research and biomedical ethics is also required. DSMBs can monitor the timeliness of accrual, the quality of data collection and management, and the accumulating outcomes to assure the safety of participants and the scientific integrity of the study.

The terms *DSMB* and *independent DSMB* are used interchangeably because a criterion for serving on a DSMB is a lack of ties, affiliations, or interests that might create bias when evaluating data or making recommendations. The independence of the DSMB requires that its members have no professional or financial interest in the outcome of the studies it monitors. On the other hand, the sponsors or investigators convene and support the DSMB, selecting and compensating its members for their services. Moreover, the data that the DSMB reviews are usually processed and presented by data managers who are employees or contractors of the sponsors or investigators. Thus, the DSMB depends on the professional integrity of the data managers for the accuracy of data it reviews.

When Is a DSMB Needed?

IRBs are currently without meaningful guidance on when to require a DSMB as opposed to other models of data oversight. A definitive evaluation of this issue is beyond the scope of this chapter. In general, the factors that suggest that a DSMB is the most appropriate way to monitor data include these.

1. *A large study population.* Many persons may be harmed before problems are recognized.

2. *Multiple study sites.* When no investigator treats more than a fraction of the participants, it is difficult to recognize a pattern of increased or unusual problems.

3. *Highly toxic therapies or dangerous procedures.* This is a critical determinant of how frequently and intensely participants should be monitored for adverse effects.

4. *High expected rates of morbidity or mortality in the study population.* Problems related to the natural history of disease or aging may obscure adverse events caused by the intervention.

5. *High chance of early termination.* There is a reasonable likelihood that the study may be terminated early for reasons of safety, futility, or efficacy.

What Does a DSMB Do?

DSMBs usually review data at predetermined intervals during the study, sometimes operating under protocol-specified rules for considering whether or not the study should continue. The DSMB may specify the type and form of data presented, examine the blinded data by group (without being told which group is which), and/or completely unblind the study. Their decisions are rendered as suggestions to the sponsors or investigators and are subject to review and negotiation before their implementation.

Meetings of a DSMB are often divided into an open session attended by the investigators and sponsors and a closed session limited to the members of the DSMB. During the open period, issues of data quality may be discussed. In addition, the rates of accrual of participants, outcomes (such as deaths, relapses, or responses), and adverse events may be reviewed for the study as a whole. In a closed session, the DSMB may see the rates of these events in each study arm and discuss the issues of modifying or stopping the study.

DSMBs may conclude that the study should be stopped for one of several reasons.

1. **Efficacy**—With high certainty, the study question has been answered. For example, one group is doing better than the others, or no group is likely to do better than any other.

2. **Futility**—The study question will not be answered when the study is completed, for example, because too many of the patients have been lost to follow-up or stopped the intervention.

3. **Safety**—Risks to patients are too high.

Most investigators and sponsors immediately accept and implement the conclusions of the DSMB, but occasional disagreements require negotiation. The IRB should insist that it be notified immediately of the DSMB's recommendations to modify or stop a study.

DSMBs and the IRB

DSMBs can monitor the safety of study participants more rigorously and more easily than IRBs and should routinely communicate their findings and recommendations to all the IRBs involved in multisite studies. The frequency and content of the reports will vary depending on the safety issues and specific monitoring plan proposed for each study. IRB members and administrators have persuasively advocated this approach in several recent articles.[1,2] Moreover, the NIH has adopted this policy.[3]

DSMBs can assist IRBs in their oversight of studies because DSMBs have greater access to the accumulating data than IRBs and can unblind the treatment assignments of either individuals or groups of participants. Because unblinding can be independent of the investigators or sponsors of the study, safety issues may be addressed without compromising the objectivity of the investigators. Knowing the group assignment of individuals in blinded treatment studies is often invaluable for assessing an individual adverse event. DSMBs can make informed decisions that the IRB could not attempt. For example, review of unblinded data by a DSMB can detect excess morbidity or mortality in one arm of a large trial that is not apparent to the IRB or investigators. As discussed earlier, DSMBs may also terminate a study earlier than scheduled because the study has already reached a clear outcome or is very unlikely to do so even if completed. This unique insight of the DSMB contributes to safety because it minimizes the exposure of patients to more risky or less effective therapies.

DSMBs have become standard in the monitoring of most NIH-sponsored and many industry-sponsored Phase III clinical trials over the past decade. Large, multisite clinical trials groups such as the AIDS Clinical Trials Group (ACTG) of the National Institute of Allergy and Infectious Diseases (NIAID) routinely review their interventional studies.[4] Guidelines for monitoring of Phase I, II, and III studies are available on the Web.[5,6] Despite this widespread appreciation of their usefulness by the NIH, their DSMBs do not routinely communicate with local IRBs, and many IRBs are unaware of their existence.

How Can DSMBs Be Integrated into IRB Procedures?

The time to deal with the DSMB issue is at the time of initial protocol review. This is the subject of other chapters in this book. Initially, IRB members and administra-tors may be unfamiliar with the functions of DSMBs and their advantages for investigators and the IRB. Data-monitoring plans including consideration of the need for a DSMB should be a routine part of evaluating the data management and statistical section of protocols. This may require that the IRB sponsor training, for both investigators and IRB members, addressing the need for DSMBs, and that reminders be added to the instructions for protocol submission and review.

Negotiations with the sponsors of studies to establish a DSMB, ask for reports on their reviews, or request unblinded reviews of SAEs are usually conducted via the principal investigator (PI) of the study at the IRB's institution. The PI may not be able to convey the rationale for the IRB's request to the sponsor without help. IRBs should provide explicit reasons for requesting establishment of or action by a DSMB in writing to the PI. These requests may explain (1) the features of the study that require establishment of a DSMB, (2) the specific reports required from the DSMB, (3) the reason that SAEs need to be evaluated by the DSMB, or (4) additional information required by the IRB, such as "stopping rules" for the study.

For example, the letter to an investigator might contain remarks like the following.

"The plan and resources for data collection and monitoring were not adequately outlined in your submission. Please indicate the personnel, site, computer resources, and monitoring procedures you will employ as required in the data and monitoring section of the outline for submission of protocols to the IRB. Your submission indicates that (DRUG X) has been associated with (SEVERE TOXICITY) in a substantial proportion of patients in prior studies and that you intend to treat patients at a more advanced stage of disease than in prior studies. For these reasons, the board suggests that you convene a DSMB to review the safety of the study. Specifically, after treating the first 50 patients and after each group of 50 patients thereafter, the DSMB should assess and compare the accumulating rates of (SEVERE TOXICITY) in the two arms of your study and communicate to the IRB that continuation is appropriate. Also indicate and justify in the protocol what rate of toxicity in the DRUG X arm would trigger the DSMB to stop enrollment and reevaluate the safety of the study."

Approval or continuation of the protocol should depend on an adequate response to the IRB's requests for better definition of the monitoring plan. Investigators at cautious institutions may be unable to participate in the study if the sponsor or DSMB is unwilling to respond to such requests. Because individual IRBs require that DSMBs be convened and communicate regularly with IRBs, they may be perceived initially as "difficult" by study sponsors or local investigators. This may appear to place local investigators in an awkward position, especially if they have no control over the content of the study protocol. However, the protections afforded to the research subjects, the investigators, and the institution greatly outweigh this disadvantage. Moreover, as multiple IRBs make similar requests, investigators and sponsors will understand that, for many studies, regular monitoring by a DSMB is the standard of practice.

Conclusion

Data and safety monitoring is one of the most complex and important aspects of the process of protecting human research subjects. The role of the IRB in the data safety monitoring process is discussed in detail in several other chapters in this book. This chapter has focused on the most rigorous approach to on-going data monitoring, the data and safety monitoring board (DSMB). For IRBs to function optimally from the standpoint of protecting research participants in compliance with federal regulations, it is important for the IRB to understand when it is appropriate to require a DSMB as part of the initial research plan and how the IRB and DSMB should interact during the life of the study.

References

1. Gordon V M, Sugarman J, Kass N. Toward a more comprehensive approach to protecting human subjects: The interface of data safety monitoring boards and institutional review boards in randomized clinical trials. *IRB: A Review of Human Subjects Research* 20(1):1–5, 1998.

2. Bankert E, Amdur RJ. The IRB is not a data and safety monitoring committee. *IRB: A Review of Human Subjects Research* 22(6):9–10, 2000.

3. National Institutes of Health. Guidance on reporting adverse events to institutional review boards for NIH-supported multicenter clinical trials (from NIH Guide for June 11, 1999). Access date 29 Mar 2001. World Wide Web http://grants.nih.gov/grants/guide/notice-files/not99-107.html

4. Ellenberg SS, Myers MW, Blackwelder WC, Hoth DF. The use of external monitoring committees in clinical trials of the National Institute of Allergy and Infectious Diseases. *Stat Med* 12(5–6):461–467, 1993.

5. National Institutes of Health. NIH policy for data and safety monitoring, 10 Jun 1998. Access date 29 Mar 2001. World Wide Web http://www.grants.nih/gov/grants/guide/notice-files/not98-084.html

6. National Institutes of Health. Further guidance on a data and safety monitoring for Phase I and Phase II trials, 5 Jun 2000. Access date 29 Mar 2001. World Wide Web http://grants.nih.gov/grants/guide/notice-files/NOT-OD-00-038.html

Noncompliance/Complaint Procedure

Lucille Pearson

INTRODUCTION

The purpose of this chapter is to explain how the IRB should follow up a complaint or a report of noncompliance with research regulations. Reports of noncompliance may come to the IRB from a wide range of sources. A whistleblower may call the IRB, a participant or family member may complain, or noncompliance may be suspected as a result of an internal IRB audit. This chapter will not specifically address the issue of the origin of the noncompliance. It is also important to mention that the process described in this chapter is not applicable to the process for responding to an adverse event report, which is discussed in detail in Chapter 7-4.

Federal Regulations Related to IRB Response to Noncompliance

Title 45 CFR 46.103 (b)(5)

Written procedures for ensuring prompt reporting to the IRB, appropriate institutional officials, and the Department or Agency head of (i) any unanticipated problems involving risks to subjects or others, as well as any serious or continuing noncompliance with this policy or the requirements or determinations of the IRB, and (ii) any suspension or termination of IRB approval.

Title 45 CFR 46.113

Suspension or termination of IRB approval of research. An IRB shall have the authority to suspend or terminate approval of research that is not being conducted in accordance with the IRB's requirements or that has been associated with unexpected serious harm to subjects. Any suspension or termination of approval shall include a statement of the reasons for the IRB's action, and shall be reported promptly to the investigator, appropriate institutional officials, and the Department or Agency head.

Title 21 CFR 56.113

Suspension or termination of IRB approval of research. An IRB shall have authority to suspend or terminate approval of research that is not being conducted in accordance with the IRB's requirements, or that has been associated with unexpected serious harm to subjects. Any suspension or termination of approval shall include a statement of the reasons for the IRB's action and shall be reported promptly to the investigator, appropriate institutional officials, and the Food and Drug Administration.

IRB Written Policy for Noncompliance

How do you go about adhering to these regulations? The first step is to write clear, concise procedures describing your institution's policy regarding noncompliance and complaints. This task can be delegated to the IRB Chair, administrator, or the IRB itself. Many institutions use a combination of methods, starting by assigning the initial draft to the IRB administrator. When the draft is completed, it is forwarded to the IRB for corrections, additions, and final approval. Other institutions use a subcommittee of IRB members to draft the initial policy. There is no one right method. The important component is that the process results in a written policy.

The policy should outline the procedures that the IRB will follow when it receives the following types of complaints.

1. Verbal or written complaints from subjects in research
2. Reports that the investigator is not following the protocol as approved by the IRB
3. Repeated failure of the investigator to report required or requested information to the IRB
4. Research publication written by investigators at your institution for which there is not an approved protocol
5. Whistleblower information
6. An FDA audit report regarding an investigator or a study

Please note that these are some elements that can be included in your policy—not necessarily *all* of the elements. Each institution must decide what is important to ensure the proper protection of human subjects within its own organization. One day you may receive a phone call from a research participant indicating her privacy was invaded by a survey in the mail. The next day, you may receive a report indicating an investigator used an incorrect consent form. In addition, the next day you may receive a report indicating improper eligibility criteria were used to enroll a participant in a research study. Each report is important to review, and follow-up must be documented. Every complaint or comment should be addressed in a consistent, professional, prompt manner through a qualified individual (IRB director, IRB Chair, ombsudperson, etc.). No complaint should be dismissed or viewed as unimportant. However, each instance need not be subjected to the same level of scrutiny. Some reports will be more serious than others. Thus, it is appropriate to investigate the complaint or report of noncompliance relative to its level of seriousness.

Template for an IRB Noncompliance/Complaint Procedure

Determine If It Is Necessary to Suspend the Study

The first step in this noncompliance/complaint procedure is to make a determination of suspension or nonsuspension. A sample policy statement follows.

The IRB will determine if immediate suspension of participant enrollment is required for the project in question as well as for other projects with the same PI. This initial decision will be based on preliminary information and the seriousness of the situation. Consultations and/or receipt of further information in conjunction with continuation of the noncompliance process will determine the length of suspension (no further participant enrollment). If applicable, the sponsor contract or grant award notice will be reviewed to determine requirements for notification of the sponsor.

Once the initial decision of suspension versus nonsuspension is completed, subsequent steps follow accordingly. We found it would be impractical to follow a complex and extensive procedure for *each* situation that could raise a question of noncompliance. For example, forming a subcommittee and conducting an extensive audit may not be appropriate for the isolated use of an outdated consent form. The initial inquiry requires information such as the nature of the study or whether or not the consent form contained inappropriate information. From this inquiry, a determination of continued inquiry (e.g., suspension) is merited.

When Suspension Is Not Necessary

If the situation does not merit suspension of the research study, a summary of the report is completed and a noncompliance/complaint form is attached. The letter "a" is circled, dated, and initialed by the IRB administrator, IRB Chair, or designee. The form is filed in the study folder and in a noncompliance/complaint notebook in the IRB office. A sample statement follows.

a. Suspension not merited: If IRB director and IRB Chair agree suspension is not merited, the issue will be resolved between any combination of the following individuals: IRB director, IRB Chair, PI, PI department Chair. All communication will be documented.

When It Is Necessary to Suspend the Study

If the report does merit suspension of the research study, further steps are required. The letter "b" is circled on the noncompliance/complaint form, dated, and initialed by the IRB administrator, IRB Chair, or designee. The steps are followed as described here.

b. Notice of suspension effective immediately will be sent: To the PI, co-PIs, department Chair, grants and contracts department, IRB institutional official, and IRB Chair. The notification includes the requirement to halt further participant enrollment.

Within two days, a meeting will be called of any combination of the following individuals: IRB director, IRB Chair, PI, PI department Chair. This will be to discuss the nature of the situation and to determine if the situation merits a designation of serious or continuing noncompliance.

To make the determination of serious or continuing noncompliance, it may be necessary to perform an audit of study records. The PI will be required to produce, at a minimum, (1) all signed consent forms and (2) all data related to the study project.

Study Suspended: Determine If the Event Is Serious or Continuing

The results of the review of study records and discussions with the PI will determine whether the situation is of a nonserious and noncontinuing nature.

i. Nonserious and Noncontinuing: If the incident appears to be isolated and, in essence, a miscommunication or misunderstanding of a nonserious and noncontinuing nature, the incident will remain internal. A letter from the IRB office to the PI describing a summary of the audit will be written. A response from the PI describing corrective actions is also required. This will be considered the final step if the incident is considered nonserious and continuing noncompliance was not determined. Suspension of patient enrollment will be lifted.

If a designation of "nonserious and noncontinuing" is found to be applicable, a summary of the proceedings must be added to the noncompliance/complaint form. The letter "i" must be circled, dated, and initialed by the IRB administrator and IRB Chair (or designee). The IRB office should feel confident in requiring any further type of increased overview of the research if deemed necessary.

ii. Serious or Continuing: If the audit indicates noncompliance that is serious or continuing, the Office for Human Research Protections (OHRP) will be notified within 48 hours—regardless of the funding source. If applicable, the Food and Drug Administration (FDA) will be notified. This will be a phone call to OHRP (or FDA) to apprise the office of the incident of serious, continuing noncompliance and will be followed with a letter within 48 hours. The initial letter will briefly describe the incident, the preliminary steps, and an indication of the time frame for full audit and full report to follow, including corrective actions for this specific incident as well as for the research program in general at [name of institution] to ensure incidents will not occur again.

a. An audit will be performed of all research conducted by the PI.

> **b.** Communication with PI, OHRP, FDA will occur.
>
> **c.** Notice to the internal committee for misconduct in science will be given.
>
> **d.** Suspension of patient enrollment will be lifted once the audit process and communication process are completed to the satisfaction of the IRB.

If a designation of serious or continuing noncompliance is found to be applicable, the steps previously described must be initiated. The letters "ii" should be circled, dated, and initialed by the IRB administrator and the IRB Chair or her/his designee.

Research Audit

A determination is made by the IRB that an audit is necessary. What mechanism will the IRB use to conduct an audit? This may depend on the size of your organization. In a large institution with the responsibility of monitoring thousands of protocols, this task cannot be accomplished by a single individual. In a small community hospital setting, it is not unusual for the IRB administrator to be given the task of auditing the researcher/study and reporting the findings to the IRB. Some organizations have a regulatory compliance officer whose job is to investigate issues of noncompliance. This individual reports his or her findings to the IRB.

Audit Subcommittee

In a large institution, the IRB often appoints an audit subcommittee consisting of IRB members and nonmembers, if appropriate, to ensure fairness and expertise. Many institutions have found it helpful to include an non-IRB-affiliated (community) member as part of the audit subcommittee. The perspective of such an individual can play a critical role in ensuring a fair and equitable process that is free from institutional political pressures.

At times, there may not be sufficient technical knowledge among the IRB members or even the institution to guarantee the required expertise in the investigator's field to compose the audit subcommittee. In that case, the IRB has the right—and the duty—to appoint an individual or individuals from outside the institution with specific expertise in the discipline in which the investigator is doing research. This could be an expert from another institution in your city, or even from another part of the country. Caution must also be taken when naming individuals to the subcommittee that there is not even the appearance of impropriety or politics in its makeup. For example, in an audit that we are aware of, in order to ensure fairness, the investigator being audited was asked to send the IRB names of three individuals whom he considered experts in his field. The IRB then chose one individual from that list to possibly serve as part of the subcommittee. The only caveat that the IRB made was that the individuals on that list could not be the investigator's subordinates.

The subcommittee, once formed, is given the charge by the IRB that may include any or all of the following.

1. Review protocol(s) in question.
2. Review FDA audit report of the investigator/study, if appropriate.
3. Review any relevant documentation, including consent documents, case report forms, subjects' investigational and/or medical files, etc., as they relate to the investigator's execution of his or her study involving human subjects.
4. Interview subject(s) involved in the study, if appropriate.
5. Interview appropriate study or hospital personnel, if necessary.
6. Prepare either a written or oral report of the subcommittee's findings that is presented to the full IRB at its next convened meeting.
7. Recommend actions to the full IRB, if appropriate, based on its findings.

The IRB then makes the final determination of the appropriate action(s) to be taken in the case based on its own knowledge of the facts and the additional facts gathered by the subcommittee during the course of its audit/investigation.

Reporting Audit Results

Once the final determination is made by the IRB, the investigator is informed in writing. If the determination includes suspension of an investigator because the research was not conducted in accordance with the IRB's requirements or has been associated with unexpected serious harm to subjects, the IRB under federal regulations[1][Sec.113] has the responsibility to report that suspension promptly to the Office for Human Research Protections (OHRP). If the study in question involves an investigational drug, biologic, or device, regulations[2][Sec.113] also require a report to the Food and Drug Administration (FDA).

When reporting the suspension to either OHRP or FDA, you must include your reasons for the IRB's action. You also have the regulatory responsibility to report the IRB actions to the appropriate institutional officials. In an academic medical setting, this would include the institutional official for human subjects, the chancellor or president of the institution, the dean of the medical school, and the investigator's department Chair. In a community hospital setting, it could include the chief executive officer (CEO), the president of the hospital, the hospital's medical director, and, in some institutions, the hospital's board of directors.

Conclusion

You now have a written process. A copy of the noncompliance/complaint form used at Dartmouth College is presented in Chapter 11-9. There are still two important issues outstanding. The first is that you must have a mechanism to disseminate these written standards to all the investigators within your institution. You can do this by producing written copies that are sent to all investigators, or you can place them on your Web site, if you have one. The second step is to ensure that the process is included in your internal IRB procedure manual. Some institutions include a brief reference to this process in all final approval letters. Also refer to the noncompliance/complaint process in your educational outreach activities so that all are aware of these procedures.

References

1. Code of Federal Regulations. Title 45A—Department of Health and Human Services; Part 46—Protection of Human Subjects. Updated 1 Oct 1997. Access date 18 Apr 2001. World Wide Web http://www4.law.cornell.edu/cfr/45p46.htm

2. Code of Federal Regulations. Title 21, Chapter 1—Food and Drug Administration, DHHS; Part 56—Institutional Review Boards. Updated 1 Apr 1999. Access date 27 Mar 2001. World Wide Web http://www4.law.cornell.edu/cfr/21p56.htm

PART 8

Administrative and Regulatory Issues

OHRP Federal-Wide Assurance

Jeffrey M. Cohen

INTRODUCTION

An assurance is a type of contract that an institution or project director has with a federal agency that establishes standards for research conduct. In the past, there were many different kinds of assurances related to IRB overview of research (e.g., single project assurance, multiple project assurance, etc). In an effort to simplify the assurance system related to research, the Department of Health and Human Services (DHHS) has recently revised the assurance program so that there is only one kind of assurance document. The purpose of this chapter is to explain the current assurance program.

An Assurance Is Required for DHHS-Funded Research

Each institution engaged in research which is covered by this policy and which is conducted or supported by a Federal Department or Agency shall provide written assurance satisfactory to the Department or Agency head that it will comply with the requirements set forth in this policy. In lieu of requiring submission of an assurance, individual Department or Agency heads shall accept the existence of a current assurance, appropriate for the research in question, on file with the Office for Protection from Research Risks, National Institutes Health, DHHS, and approved for Federalwide use by that office. . . . [1][Sec.103(a)]

Departments and agencies will conduct or support research covered by this policy only if the institution has an assurance approved as provided in this section, and only if the institution has certified to the Department or Agency head that the research has been reviewed and approved by an IRB provided for in the assurance, and will be subject to continuing review by the IRB. . . . [1][Sec.103(b)]

As the above quotations from 45 CFR 46 indicate, in order for institutions to receive federal funding for research involving human subjects, the institutions must have an approved assurance of compliance on file with the Office for Human Research Protections (OHRP) (previously known as the Office for Protection from Research Risks [OPRR]).

Research Not Funded by a Federal Agency

An assurance is not required to conduct research that is not funded by a federal agency. Many institutions that conduct both federally and privately funded research elect to structure their assurance so that they commit to holding all research that is conducted under their authority to the same standards. Although there are multiple reasons for an institution to extend its federal assurance to privately funded research, it is important to understand that this is purely an elective move. Currently, federal regulations do not require an institution that receives federal funds to establish an assurance that includes privately funded research. The implications of this option for the IRB may be profound. Federal regulations give the IRB authority to regulate research under two conditions: (1) the research is subject to FDA regulations that require IRB review, or (2) the research is subject to IRB authority based on a federal assurance. Therefore, an IRB that serves an organization that does not have a federal assurance, or that has not extended their assurance to privately funded research, has no authority to regulate research that is not subject to FDA regulation.

What Is an Assurance of Compliance?

Basically, an assurance is written documentation of an institution's commitment to comply with the federal regulations governing human subjects research. In December 2000, OHRP established a new format for the assurance of compliance entitled the "federalwide assurance of protection for human subjects" (FWA). The FWA replaced the previous format, which involved considerable paperwork and was labor-intensive, with a simplified document in which the institution stipulates that it will comply with appropriate ethical standards and procedural standards rather than spelling them out in a written document. Another change from the previous assurance is that international institutions have more flexibility in substituting international ethical codes and standards for U.S. codes and standards.

Although the terms of the FWA must be met for all federally sponsored research, OHRP strongly encourages institutions to comply with the terms for all of its human-subjects research, regardless of funding source, and to indicate this in its FWA.

As the title indicates, the FWA covers all federally supported or conducted research involving human subjects. However, some federal agencies or departments other than the DHHS may have additional requirements or may require additional documentation along with the FWA. Institutions conducting human subjects research supported by another federal agency or department should contact the sponsor for details on its assurance policies.

What Is Included in an FWA?

Statement of Ethical Principles Governing the Institution

For most domestic institutions, this will be *The Ethical Principles and Guidelines for the Protection of Human Subjects (The Belmont Report)* prepared by the National Commission for the Protection of Human Subjects of Biomedical and Behavioral Research in 1979. International institutions may choose to apply "Recommendations Guiding Medical Doctors in Biomedical Research Involving Human Subjects" (*The Declaration of Helsinki*), prepared by the World Medical Assembly, which was revised in October 2000.

An Assurance of Compliance with Procedural Standards

For domestic institutions, this will be 45 CFR 46,[1] while international institutions can commit to international standards such as the Canadian Tri-Council Policy, Council for International Organizations of Medical Sciences (CIOMS) International Ethical Guidelines, International Conference on Harmonisation,[2][Sec.E6(1-4)] the guidelines from the Indian Council of Medical Research,[3] or another equivalent international standard.

An Assurance of Compliance with the Terms of the Assurance

In addition to the above, the terms of the assurance include a commitment to do the following:

1. Provide IRB review of nonexempt research covered by the FWA
2. Obtain written informed consent unless otherwise waived in accordance with the regulations
3. Have written IRB procedures
4. Provide appropriate training of the institutional signatory official, the IRB Chair, and the human protections administrator
5. Establish educational and oversight mechanisms and a procedure for documenting the training of investigators
6. Verify that its designated IRB(s) will comply with the above and have adequate knowledge of the local context for research reviewed
7. Ensure that all collaborating institutions operate under an approved FWA

8. Provide IRBs operated by the institution with sufficient resources
9. Have a formal written agreement of compliance from all nonaffiliated investigators
10. Designate one or more IRBs responsible for reviewing research under the FWA

All IRBs designated in an FWA must be registered with the DHHS. To register an IRB, an institution simply completes the form available on the OHRP Web site and submits it to OHRP. The registration process does not involve formal commitments or evaluation; the information about the IRB is simply entered into the IRB registration database.

An institution may rely on another IRB, either from another institution or an independent IRB, as long as the other IRB agrees to the arrangement, the head of the organization or the IRB Chair signs the FWA, and the guidelines for satisfactory knowledge of the local research context are met. (See the OHRP Web site for this guidance.[4])

Institutions may, on an occasional or ad hoc basis, choose to rely on an IRB operating under another institution's assurance. Such occasional reliance must be documented in writing and provided to OHRP upon request, but need not be listed in the FWA. OHRP's sample IRB authorization agreement may be used for this purpose, or institutions may develop their own agreement.

Designation of a Human Protections Administrator

The *human protections administrator* is an employee or agent of the FWA institution who exercises day-to-day operational responsibility for the institution's program for protecting human subjects. This individual's title and position within the institutional structure will vary from institution to institution. What is important is the individual's comprehensive knowledge of all aspects of the institution's systematic protections for human subjects. Every domestic FWA institution should have a human protections administrator, even if the institution relies totally on IRBs from other organizations.

Signature of the Institutional Signatory Official

The FWA signatory must be a high institutional official who has the legal authority to represent the institution named in the FWA, as well as all the institutional components listed in the FWA. Entities that the signatory official is not legally authorized to represent may not be covered under the FWA.

Who Must Submit an FWA?

Each legally separate entity needs its own FWA. An institution's FWA can only cover components of that institution that are legally part of its corporate structure. Institutions that are affiliated solely through professional or collaborative arrangements must provide a separate FWA.

Questions often arise concerning performance sites and collaborating institutions. The regulations require that each institution that is "engaged" in covered research must have an FWA. Therefore, the question is whether the performance site is engaged in the research. OHRP has guidance on when institutions are engaged in research on its Web site. In general, institutions become "engaged" in human subject research whenever their employees or agents do the following:

1. Intervene or interact with living individuals for research purposes

2. Obtain or access individually identifiable private information for research purposes

3. Release individually identifiable private information, or permit investigators to obtain individually identifiable private information, without subjects' explicit written permission

Awardee institutions are automatically considered to be engaged in human subject research, even if all activities involving human subjects are carried out by a subcontractor or collaborator.

Educational Requirements

The FWA has two educational requirements. It is important that institutions applying for an FWA understand the difference between these two requirements.

Completion of the OHRP Assurance Training Modules Completion of the OHRP assurance training modules is intended to ensure that the key individuals at an institution (the institutional signatory official, the IRB Chair, and the human protections administrator) understand the roles and responsibilities involved in an institutional human research protections program. An application for an FWA will not be approved unless each of these individuals completes the online assurance training module or training certified to OHRP by the institution as equivalent to the OHRP modules.

Establishment of an Institutional Human Protections Education Program This program is intended to ensure that research investigators, IRB members and staff, and other relevant personnel maintain continuing knowledge of basic ethical principles, relevant federal regulations, OHRP guidance, other applicable guidance, state and local law, and institutional policies for the protection of human subjects. Institutions have considerable flexibility in designing a program to meet their specific needs. In addition to establishing an education program, the terms of the FWA require institutions to document that research investigators have completed such training as a condition for conducting human subjects research.

Conclusion

The FWA formalizes an institution's commitment to protect human subjects. OHRP holds institutions responsible for all research involving human subjects covered under their assurance. The FWA makes these responsibilities clear and serves as OHRP's primary mechanism for compliance oversight. When problems arise at an institution, OHRP determines whether the institution is complying with the commitments it made in the FWA. If it is not, OHRP may restrict or suspend an institution's FWA, thus limiting or prohibiting human subjects research at the institution. Therefore, it is essential that institutions ensure that everyone involved in human subjects research is knowledgeable about and understands the commitments made in the FWA.

Additional information and guidance on the FWA may be found on the OHRP Web site.[4]

References

1. Code of Federal Regulations. Title 45A—Department of Health and Human Services; Part 46—Protection of Human Subjects. Updated 1 Oct 1997. Access date 18 Apr 2001. World Wide Web http://www4.law.cornell.edu/cfr/45p46.htm

2. International Conference on Harmonisation. E6 Good Clinical Practice. ICH harmonised tripartite guidelines: Guideline for a good clinical practice, 1 May 1996. Access date 23 Aug 2001. World Wide Web http://www.ifpma.org/pdfifpma/e6.pdf

3. Indian Council of Medical Research, New Delhi, Chairperson MN Venkatachaliah. Ethical Guidelines for Biomedical Research on Human Subjects, 6 Sep 2000. Access date 24 Sep 2001. World Wide Web http://www.icmr.nic.in/ethical.pdf

4. Office for Human Research Protections. OHRP compliance activities: Common findings and guidance, 1 Sep 2000. Access date 7 May 2001. World Wide Web http://ohrp.osophs.dhhs.gov/references/findings.pdf

International Conference on Harmonisation

David G. Forster and Gary L. Chadwick

INTRODUCTION

The International Conference on Harmonisation of Technical Requirements for the Registration of Pharmaceuticals for Human Use, commonly referred to as the International Conference on Harmonisation, or ICH, is an attempt to streamline the process for developing and marketing new drugs internationally. As stated on the ICH Web site[1]: "Harmonisation of regulatory requirements was pioneered by the European Community, in the 1980s, as the EC (now the European Union) moved towards the development of a single market for pharmaceuticals. The success achieved in Europe demonstrated that harmonisation was feasible."

The birth of ICH took place at a meeting in April 1990, hosted by the European Federation of Pharmaceutical Industries and Associations (EFPIA) in Brussels. Representatives of the regulatory agencies and industry associations of Europe, Japan, and the United States met primarily to plan an international conference, but the meeting also discussed the wider implications and terms of reference of ICH.

The ICH is composed of representatives from the pharmaceutical industry and the regulatory bodies of the United States, Japan, and the European Union. In addition, observers to the process include Canada, the European Free Trade Area, and the World Health Organization.

The ICH has established several international standards of good clinical practice for the development of pharmaceutical products. The guideline that primarily affects IRBs is E6, "ICH harmonized tripartite guideline: Guideline for good clinical practice."[2] The E6 guideline has eight parts: (1) glossary, (2) principles, (3) IRBs, (4) investigator, (5) sponsor, (6) protocol and amendments, (7) investigator's brochure, and (8) essential documents. The drafting of E6, like other guidelines, took years and several rewrites. The initial basis for drafting the E6 guidelines was the U.S. FDA regulations for the protection of human subjects.[3,4]

Legal Status and Compliance

After the guidelines were finalized, several countries adopted them as law. In the United States, however, the FDA adopted the ICH only as guidance.[5] Therefore, the ICH guidelines do not have the force of law in the United States and are not even regulation. In the *Federal Register* notice, the FDA stated that the ICH guideline "does not create or confer any rights for or on any person and does not operate to bind the FDA or the public. An alternative approach may be used if such approach satisfies the requirements of the applicable statutes, regulations, or both." Therefore, compliance is voluntary, but, as with any published FDA guideline, compliance is considered part of good clinical practice.

The FDA regulations[3,4] do have full legal effect in the United States, and compliance is mandatory. The FDA regulations apply to all research with human subjects that uses products regulated by the FDA.

For drug manufacturers/sponsors, the advantage of complying with the ICH guidelines is that the FDA and equivalent government agencies in other countries will consider studies conducted in accordance with the ICH guidelines as meeting the regulatory requirements of the drug approval processes for all of these countries. Therefore, sponsors increasingly want to use IRBs that meet the ICH requirements. One of the requirements of the ICH guidelines is that "the sponsor obtain from the investigator/ institution . . . [a] statement obtained from the IRB/IEC that it is organized and operates according to GCP and the applicable laws and regulations."[2(Sec.5.11)] Based on this requirement, several sponsors have issued letters to IRBs asking them to state that they comply with ICH.

Some have suggested that in response to this question, IRBs can answer that inasmuch as the ICH guidelines mirror the FDA regulations, then the IRB complies with ICH. There are, however, certain requirements of ICH that are not included in FDA or DHHS regulations. A sponsor could be adversely affected if a drug agency, in a country that has adopted ICH as law, refuses to accept data in an application because the IRB that oversaw the research was not fully in compliance with the ICH requirements.

Each IRB needs to review the ICH guidelines and either adopt them, not adopt them, or adopt those parts that require minimal changes and provide an increase in human subject protection.

Differences Between ICH Guidelines and U.S. Regulations

As stated previously, the ICH E6 guidelines generally agree with the FDA regulations for IRBs and informed consent. However, in a few areas, the ICH guidelines have requirements that go beyond either FDA or DHHS (Common Rule) requirements. It is important to know what these differences are because full compliance with ICH requires some changes in IRB operations. If the written procedures include—as they should—how the IRB complies with the various requirements of the ICH guidelines, they must be followed by the IRB. The FDA only inspects IRBs to the standards of the FDA regulations, not ICH; but the FDA can cite an IRB for not following its own written procedures. References below are either to the ICH E6 guidelines[2] or to the FDA regulations.[3,4]

Definition of Vulnerable Subjects

ICH provides the following definition of vulnerable subjects.[2(Sec.1.61)]

Vulnerable Subjects: Individuals whose willingness to volunteer in a clinical trial may be unduly influenced by the expectation, whether justified or not, of benefits associated with participation; or of a retaliatory response from senior members of a hierarchy in case of refusal to participate. Examples are members of a group with a hierarchical structure, such as medical, pharmacy, dental, and nursing students, subordinate hospital and laboratory personnel, employees of the pharmaceutical industry, members of the armed forces, and persons kept in detention. Other vulnerable subjects include patients with incurable diseases, and persons in nursing homes, unemployed or impoverished persons, patients in emergency situations, ethnic minority groups, homeless persons, nomads, refugees, minors, and those incapable of giving consent.

The FDA describes vulnerable subjects as individuals "such as children, prisoners, pregnant women, handicapped, or mentally disabled persons, or economically or educationally disadvantaged persons."[4(Sec.111(b))]

Neither the FDA nor the ICH definition provides a complete list of vulnerable subjects, and the examples of vulnerable subjects provided in each are somewhat differ-

ent. Because both definitions do rely on the ethical principle of respect for persons, the central criterion for IRBs and investigators to consider is whether the potential subject's ability to exercise free choice (autonomy) is limited in some way. Special DHHS regulations exist for children, prisoners, pregnant women, and fetuses. IRBs must decide what types of special protections are required for these and other vulnerable populations, as well as whether to extend protections to those not specifically named in the regulations or the ICH guidelines.

Confidentiality of Medical Records

ICH has broader requirements than the FDA or DHHS concerning notice to subjects about potential access to identifiable research records by third parties. The informed consent should include the following information.

That the monitor(s), the auditor(s), the IRB/IEC, and the regulatory authority(ies) will be granted direct access to the subject's original medical records for verification of clinical trial procedures and/or data, without violating the confidentiality of the subject, to the extent permitted by the applicable laws and regulations and that, by signing a written informed consent form, the subject or the subject's legally acceptable representative is authorizing such access.[2(Sec.4.8.10(n))]
The sponsor should verify that each subject has consented, in writing, to direct access to his/her original medical records for trial-related monitoring, audit, IRB/IEC review, and regulatory inspection.[2(Sec.5.15.2)]

FDA regulations state only the following.

In seeking informed consent, the following information shall be provided to each subject. (5) A statement describing the extent, if any, to which confidentiality of records identifying the subject will be maintained and that notes the possibility that the Food and Drug Administration may inspect the records.[3(Sec.25(a)(5))]

Thus, ICH allows a much broader access to research records and to otherwise confidential medical records. Many IRBs have received complaints from subjects about the extent of this access. Most consent forms approved by IRBs now permit access to research records by sponsors. Access of foreign regulatory agencies to research records is not troubling. However, access for these entities to subjects' medical records is problematic for both IRBs and subjects. For the sake of compliance, it is an easy matter to change the wording in a consent form from *research records* to *research and medical records*, but philosophically it is quite a leap.

Signature by Person Conducting the Consent Discussion

The ICH guidelines[2(Sec.4.8.8)] state, "Prior to a subject's participation in the trial, the written informed consent form should be signed and personally dated by the subject or by the subject's legally acceptable representative, and by the person who conducted the informed consent discussion." The FDA regulations only require the signature of the subject and the date the subject signed the consent form.[3(Sec.27(a))]

Many IRBs already require the signature of the person obtaining consent on consent forms, especially for greater-than-minimal-risk research. This means that many IRBs already meet this ICH requirement. If not, it is easy to include a signature line labeled "Person Conducting Informed Consent Discussion." This line should not be labeled "Investigator's Signature," as the investigator is not always the person who obtains consent.

Subject Receipt of a Signed and Dated Copy of the Consent Form

The ICH guidelines[2][Sec.4.8.11] require that the subject or the legally authorized representative receive a copy of the signed and dated written informed consent form.

FDA regulations allow subjects to receive either a signed or unsigned copy.[6(p.11)] To be in compliance with ICH guidelines, the IRB should include notice in the consent form that the subject will receive a signed and dated copy of the consent form. Persons obtaining consent must then ensure that this procedure is followed.

Assent of Children and Mentally Disabled Adults

The ICH guidelines[2][Sec.4.8.12] require that

When a clinical trial (therapeutic or nontherapeutic) includes subjects who can only be enrolled in the trial with the consent of the subject's legally acceptable representative (e.g., minors, or patients with severe dementia), the subject should be informed about the trial to the extent compatible with the subject's understanding and, if capable, the subject should sign and personally date the written informed consent.

The FDA regulations do not require the assent of children; however, the National Children's Protection Act of 2000 requires the FDA to adopt regulations for enrollment of children. It is expected that FDA regulations will mirror DHHS regulations on the inclusion of children in research[7(Subpart D)] and require the assent of children for clinical research.

Neither FDA nor DHHS regulations, however, specifically require that incapacitated adults assent to research participation. Most IRBs have considered this mechanism to be an additional protection, which they have required for this vulnerable population. To meet the ICH requirement, the IRB would have to institute a policy for formally considering assent whenever a protocol allows decisionally impaired adult subjects to be enrolled. This policy can easily be based on DHHS regulations,[7 (subpart D)] with similar risk/benefit considerations.

Impartial Witness for Illiterate Subjects

The ICH guidelines[2][Sec.4.8.9] state:

If a subject is unable to read or if a legally acceptable representative is unable to read, an impartial witness should be present during the entire informed consent discussion. After the written informed consent form and any other written information to be provided to subjects, is read and explained to the subject or the subject's legally acceptable representative, and after the subject or the subject's legally acceptable representative has orally consented to the subject's participation in the trial and, if capable of doing so, has signed and personally dated the informed consent form, the witness should sign and personally date the consent form. By signing the consent form, the witness attests that the information in the consent form and any other written information was accurately explained to, and apparently understood by, the subject or the subject's legally acceptable representative, and that informed consent was freely given by the subject or the subject's legally acceptable representative.

The FDA addresses the documentation of informed consent for illiterate subjects by allowing the use of a short form consent document and a written summary for oral presentation.[3][Sec.27(b)(2)] The ICH guideline goes beyond the FDA regulations in requiring that the witness be impartial and specifying to what the witness should attest.

Most IRBs define impartial as not being connected with the study team. This allows relatives, nonstudy employees, and similar persons to fill this role. Whatever the definition, it should be included in the IRB written procedures, and investigators must know who qualifies as impartial.

Once the problem of who can be a witness has been solved, the IRB must figure out how to provide for documentation of the signature. One approach that some IRBs have taken is to provide investigators with an IRB-approved addendum that can be used with any consent form. This approach creates some logistical problems in supplying the form or having it readily available and known to the investigator. A second approach is to have an impartial witness signature block at the end of every consent form intended to comply with ICH, with clear instructions regarding the use of the signature block. A disadvantage to this approach is that consent forms are already too long and often have a confusing array of signature blocks. Other IRBs have advised having the witness sign on a signature line drawn onto the consent form, but this creates a problem by allowing a change to the consent form without prior IRB approval. Investigators might get the mistaken impression that ad hoc changes to the consent form are acceptable. Also, ensuring that the wording of the attestation is correctly inserted can be a problem with this method.

It must be pointed out here that both FDA and DHHS regulations require that no change be made to the study without prior IRB approval.[4][Sec.108(a)(4)] The ICH guidelines, in contrast, allow the investigator to make some changes to the protocol without prior IRB approval, as stated in the ICH guidelines.[2(Sec.4.5.2)]

The investigator should not implement any deviation from, or changes of, the protocol without agreement by the sponsor and prior review and documented approval/favorable opinion from the IRB/IEC of an amendment, except where necessary to eliminate an immediate hazard(s) to trial subjects, or when the change(s) involves only logistical or administrative aspects of the trial (e.g., change of monitor(s), change of telephone number(s)).

IRBs in the United States must continue to meet FDA and DHHS requirements in this situation because they are more stringent.

Elements of Consent

A few of the ICH guideline requirements for elements of informed consent go beyond the FDA requirements and must be included by the IRB for studies that are intended to meet ICH requirements.

Alternative Treatments

The ICH guidelines[2[Sec.4.8.10(i)]] require an explanation of "the alternative procedure(s) or course(s) of treatment that may be available to the subject, and their important potential benefits and risks." Most IRBs have not included the benefits and risks of alternative treatments, as consent forms are already long and difficult to understand. This is an area where many IRBs decide to limit their compliance with ICH. The IRB should consider whether the addition of these risks and benefits in consent forms will be useful to the subject, or if their inclusion will make the consent form less effective.

Probability of Assignment to Each Study Arm in a Study

The FDA regulations[3[Sec.25(a)(1)]] state that the consent form must include "a statement that the study involves research, an explanation of the purposes of the research, and the expected duration of the subject's participation, as well as a description of the procedures to be followed, and identification of any procedures which are experimental."

The ICH guidelines[2[Sec.4.8.10(c)]] state that, in addition, the informed consent should include "the trial treatment(s) and the probability for random assignment to each treatment."

This difference can be addressed by including a description of each arm of the study in the consent form, and including a statement about the likelihood of receiving each of the study arms.

Compensation for Injury

The ICH guidelines[2[Sec.4.8.10(j)]] require an explanation of "the compensation and/or treatment available to the subject in the event of trial-related injury" in all consent forms. The FDA only requires this information for research involving more than minimal risk.[3[Sec.25(a)(6)]] In actuality, this difference is not that large, as most drug studies are, in fact, greater than minimal risk and therefore require a compensation-for-injury clause.

Description of Subject's Responsibilities

The ICH guidelines[2[Sec.4.8.10(e)]] require an explanation of "the subject's responsibilities." Some IRBs include this information as part of their procedures. One of the unintended consequences of this requirement is to make the consent form look more like a contract between two parties, and it may confuse subjects about their right to withdraw.

Statement of No Benefit

The ICH guidelines[2[Sec.4.8.10(h)]] require an explanation of "the reasonably expected benefits. When there is no intended clinical benefit to the subject, the subject should be made aware of this." Many IRBs also customarily include this information, so compliance with this requirement should not pose any problems.

Prorated Payment in the Consent Form

The ICH guidelines[2[Sec.4.8.10(k)]] state that "anticipated prorated payment, if any, to the subject for participating in the trial" must be included in the consent form.

Although not an FDA requirement, prorated payment is addressed in the FDA information sheet entitled "Payment to research subjects,"[6] and it is common practice for IRBs in the United States to include this in consent forms.

Nontherapeutic Trials

The following ICH sections address nontherapeutic research and the requirements for consent. This is not specifically addressed in the FDA regulations.

Except as described in 4.8.14, a non-therapeutic trial (i.e., a trial in which there is no anticipated direct clinical benefit to the subject), should be conducted in subjects who personally give consent and who sign and date the written informed consent form.[2[Sec.4.8.13]]

Non-therapeutic trials may be conducted in subjects with consent of a legally acceptable representative provided the following conditions are fulfilled:

(a) The objectives of the trial can not be met by means of a trial in subjects who can give informed consent personally.

(b) The foreseeable risks to the subjects are low.

(c) The negative impact on the subject's well-being is minimized and low.

(d) The trial is not prohibited by law.

(e) The approval/favorable opinion of the IRB/IEC is expressly sought on the inclusion of such subjects, and the written approval/favorable opinion covers this aspect.

Such trials, unless an exception is justified, should be conducted in patients having a disease or condition for which the investigational product is intended. Subjects in these trials should be particularly closely monitored and should be withdrawn if they appear to be unduly distressed.[2[Sec.4.8.14]]

The ICH requirements for inclusion of subjects in nontherapeutic trials are straightforward. To comply with ICH requirements, IRBs should ensure that subjects without the capacity to consent are not used for nontherapeutic trials, except as described above.

IRB Responsibilities

There are several differences between the FDA and ICH regarding the responsibilities and duties of the IRB.

Documents the IRB Must Review

The ICH provides a list of documents that the IRB should review, and IRBs routinely review most of the materials listed. Compliance with ICH requires reviewing all the listed materials.

The IRB/IEC should obtain the following documents: trial protocol(s)/amendment(s), written informed consent form(s) and consent form updates that the investigator proposes for use in the trial, subject recruitment procedures (e.g., advertisements), and written information to be provided to subjects, investigator's brochure (IB), available safety information, information about payments and compensation available to subjects, the investigator's current curriculum vitae and/or other documentation evidencing qualifications, as well as any other documents that the IRB/IEC may require to fulfill its responsibilities.[2[Sec.3.1.2]]

The FDA regulations do not specifically list in one place what documents an IRB should review. The FDA requires the IRB to review the consent form[4[Sec.109(b)]] and "copies of all research proposals reviewed, scientific evaluations, if any, that accompany the proposals, and approved sample consent documents."[4[Sec.115(a)]]

Review of Changes in Research

The ICH guidelines[2[Sec.3.3.7]] state, "The IRB/IEC should [specify] that no deviations from, or changes of, the protocol should be initiated without prior written IRB/IEC approval" and[2[Sec.4.5.3]] "Investigators . . . should document and explain any deviations from the approved protocol." Review of changes in research is already required by the FDA regulations;[4[Sec.108(a)(4)]] however, review of deviations is not required by the FDA and could be quite burdensome if applied literally. IRBs intending to comply with this ICH requirement would be well advised to define the word *deviation* as a permanent change in a protocol. Thus, they avoid the need to report and review each minor departure from the protocol (e.g., a missed dose).

Availability of Written Procedures

The ICH guidelines[2[Sec.3.4]] state, "The IRB/IEC may be asked by investigators, sponsors, or regulatory authorities to provide copies of its written procedures and membership lists."

FDA regulations do not contain a similar disclosure provision. Many IRBs consider their membership roster as private information and are concerned that disclosure to sponsors may encourage attempts at inappropriate influence. Some IRBs have addressed this concern by disclosing the roster with the names deleted. Some IRBs also consider their written procedures as proprietary information; however, even the National Bioethics Advisory Commission has suggested a greater openness and public sharing of the procedures used by IRBs to review and approve research. Perhaps more IRBs will be willing to provide this information to sponsors.

IRB Appeals Process

Although FDA regulations do not require an appeals process, the ICH requires it[2[Sec.3.3.9]] by stating that "the IRB/IEC [will have] procedures for appeal of its decisions/opinions." A written appeals process is a good practice as long as it does not violate the FDA regulation that states that no other body may approve a study that the IRB has disapproved.[4(Sec.112)]

Conclusion

In the United States, compliance with the ICH E6 guidelines is voluntary for IRBs in that it is not a federal regulation. For research institutions that conduct clinical trials of drugs, however, pharmaceutical sponsors often insist that the ICH requirements be met. IRBs have to assess their level of compliance and decide if the changes in operations can be made without compromising subject protections or institutional values.

Investigators and institutions also must review the applicable sections of the ICH guidelines for duties and responsibilities required of them to be compliant. IRBs and institutions seeking compliance with ICH requirements also need to define what the scope of applicability is for their policies intended to address ICH requirements (i.e., if they apply only to clinical trials of drugs, to all studies, or some subset of studies).

References

1. International Conference on Harmonisation. A brief history of ICH. Updated Jul 1997. Access date 23 Aug 2001. World Wide Web http://www.pharmweb.net/pwmirror/pw9/ifpma/ich8.html

2. International Conference on Harmonisation. ICH harmonised tripartite guidelines: E6 Guideline for good clinical practice, 1 May 1996. Access date 23 Aug 2001. World Wide Web http://www.ifpma.org/pdfifpma/e6.pdf

3. Code of Federal Regulations. Title 21, Chapter 1—Food and Drug Administration, DHHS; Part 50—Protection of Human Subjects. Updated 1 Apr 1999. Access date 18 Apr 2001. World Wide Web http://www4.law.cornell.edu/cfr/21p50.htm

4. Code of Federal Regulations. Title 21, Chapter 1—Food and Drug Administration, DHHS; Part 56—Institutional Review Boards. Updated 1 Apr 1999. Access date 27 Mar 2001. World Wide Web http://www4.law.cornell.edu/cfr/21p56.htm

5. Food and Drug Administration, DHHS. Good clinical practice: Consolidated guideline. *Fed Regist* 62(90):25691-25709, 1997. http://frwebgate.access.gpo.gov/cgi-bin/getdoc.cgi?dbname=1997_register&docid=fr09my97-190

6. Food and Drug Administration. Information sheets: Guidance for institutional review boards and clinical investigators, Sep 1998. Access date 9 Apr 2001. World Wide Web http://www.fda.gov/oc/oha/IRB/toc.html

7. Code of Federal Regulations. Title 45A—Department of Health and Human Services; Part 46—Protection of Human Subjects. Updated 1 Oct 1997. Access date 18 Apr 2001. World Wide Web http://www4.law.cornell.edu/cfr/45p46.htm

Gene Therapy Oversight

Bambi Grilley

INTRODUCTION

Review of gene therapy protocols (including both gene replacement and gene marking protocols) presents unique challenges to IRBs. Originally touted as a miracle cure and more recently demonized in the press as the ultimate example of patient deception, gene therapy has been high profile and controversial since its origins in the 1980s.

Federal Regulations

From a regulatory standpoint, review of gene therapy protocols is very complex. Gene therapy protocols are subject to review by four different agencies and review committees. Those agencies/committees include the Food and Drug Administration (FDA), the Recombinant DNA Advisory Committee (RAC), local institutional biosafety committees (IBCs), and local institutional review boards (IRBs). Each of these agencies/committees brings a different perspective to the review process. Thus, each of these agencies/committees serves a different purpose in the review of gene therapy protocols.

Food and Drug Administration (FDA)

The role of the FDA in the review of gene therapy protocols mirrors their role in the review of other protocols utilizing devices, drugs, and biologics. Primarily, they ensure that medicines and medical devices sold in this country are safe and effective. For investigational drugs and biologics (including gene therapy), submissions to the FDA are referred to as "investigational new drug applications" (INDs). The requirements for IND submissions are codified in 21 CFR 312.[1] There are currently no licensed gene therapy products available in the United States; therefore, IRBs should require the submission of proof of an FDA-approved IND prior to allowing a gene therapy protocol to accrue patients.[1]

Recombinant DNA Advisory Committee (RAC)

The role of the RAC in the review of gene therapy protocols is to consider the current state of knowledge of technology regarding DNA recombinants, their survival in nature, their transferability to other organisms, and their societal impact. RAC review is public and includes an evaluation of the scientific, medical, legal, and ethical components of research. Submission requirements to the RAC are set forth in Appendix M (Points to consider in the design and submission of protocols for the transfer of recombinant DNA molecules into one or more human research participants) of the NIH Guidelines for research involving recombinant DNA molecules.[2] Again, IRBs should require submission of proof of RAC approval be-

fore allowing a gene therapy protocol to accrue patients. Ideally, both the IRB and the IBC may want to review the Appendix M response that was submitted to the RAC, any RAC recommendations to the principal investigator, and the investigator's response to those recommendations.

Institutional BioSafety Committee

The role of the IBC is to review recombinant DNA research conducted at or sponsored by the institution to ensure compliance with NIH guidelines. Equally important, the IBC should assess the safety of recombinant DNA research and identify any potential risk to the public health or the environment.[2] Submission requirements to local IBCs are defined by the local committees. In October 2000, the Office of Biotechnology Activities (the branch of the NIH that oversees the function of both the RAC and the local IBC) released new guidelines related to research involving recombinant DNA molecules. As a result of these guidelines, gene therapy protocols must be submitted to the RAC before submission to the local IBC.[3]

Institutional Review Board (IRB)

As stated elsewhere in this book, the IRB is responsible for reviewing and approving all human subject research. Consideration must be given to the risks to the subjects and the benefits to the subjects and others as well as the importance of the knowledge that may be reasonably expected to result from the research and the informed consent form to be utilized in the research. Again, submission requirements to local IRBs are defined by the local committees.[4]

Gene Therapy

What is different about gene therapy protocols as compared to other interventions? Gene therapy protocols present risks to the subject, the subject's progeny, and potentially society as a whole. These risks, whether known or postulated, need to be transmitted to the study subject. The subject should be made aware that it will remain unknown for many years whether long-term risks exist or will occur.

Gene therapy protocols are primarily conducted in critically ill patients. As with other research conducted in this patient population, there is some evidence that such patients are motivated to participate in research by the hope of therapeutic benefit.[5] It is therefore necessary for the investigator to emphasize the experimental nature of the research and to realistically present any potential for benefit, including any available outcome data from ongoing or completed gene therapy protocols.

Gene therapy is a scientifically complex intervention that is difficult to describe in lay terms. When one considers that recent reports on the readability of consent forms for cancer research protocols indicate that only 1% – 6% of the consent forms were readable at the eighth grade level, it is easy to see how adding a discussion of gene therapy could overwhelm a potential study subject.[6] It is therefore imperative that the IRB reviews consent forms for gene therapy carefully for readability.

Additionally, gene therapy protocols present unique responsibilities to the subjects. It is expected that subjects enrolling in gene therapy protocols will be available for long-term follow-up and that autopsies of these subjects will be requested when they die. Again, these responsibilities should be clearly explained to the study subject.

Because of the complexity of the intervention, the responsibilities of the subjects, and the unknown risks, it can be beneficial to have a patient advocate available during the consent process. This individual should preferably be someone who is not associated with the study but understands the patient's condition. A social worker is a good example of someone who could act as a patient advocate during the consent process for a gene therapy protocol.

Finally, issues such as germ cell modification and fetal gene replacement present unique ethical challenges to all reviewers. Currently, gene therapy efforts have concentrated on gene replacement or gene marking of somatic cells in nonfetal subjects. However, as advances are made in the gene therapy field, the likelihood of germ cell modification and/or fetal gene replacement will increase.

Conclusion

As originally stated, the review of gene therapy protocols poses unique challenges to IRBs. IRBs should take full advantage of available resources such as the FDA and the RAC. Additionally, when reviewing gene therapy studies for the first time or reviewing novel gene therapy studies, IRBs may want to consult with other institutions conducting gene therapy studies and with their local IBC.

References

1. Code of Federal Regulations. Title 21, Chapter 1—Food and Drug Administration, DHHS; Part 312—Investigational New Drug Application. Updated 1 Apr 1999. Access date 18 Apr 2001. World Wide Web http://www4.law.cornell.edu/cfr/21p312.htm

2. National Institutes of Health. NIH Guidelines for research involving recombinant DNA molecules. *Fed Regist* 63(90): 26017–26019, 11 May 1998. Access date 24 Aug 2001. World Wide Web http://frwebgate.access.gpo.gov/cgi-bin/getdoc.cgi?dbname=1998_register&docid=fr11my98-123

3. Department of Health and Human Services. Recombinant DNA research: Action under the guidelines. *Fed Regist* 65(196): 60327–60332, 10 Oct 2000. Access date 24 Aug 2001. World Wide Web http://frwebgate.access.gpo.gov/cgi-bin/getdoc.cgi?dbname=2000_register&docid=fr10oc00-162

4. Code of Federal Regulations. Title 45A—Department of Health and Human Services; Part 46—Protection of Human Subjects. Updated 1 Oct 1997. Access date 18 Apr 2001. World Wide Web http://www4.law.cornell.edu/cfr/45p46.htm

5. Daugherty C. Ethical issues in the development of new agents. *Investigational New Drugs* 17(2):145–153, 1999.

6. Grossman SA, Piantadosi S, Covahey C. Are informed consent forms that describe clinical oncology research protocols readable by most patients and their families? *J Clin Oncol* 12(10):2211–2215, 1994.

Understanding the FDA's IND Process

Dale E. Hammerschmidt

INTRODUCTION

In 1962, the United States narrowly avoided a public health disaster when it failed to license a new drug, thalidomide, which had been on the market for several years in Europe, Britain, and Canada. By all reports, it was a wonderful sedative, with strong antinausea properties and almost no respiratory depression. It was finding wide use in treating "morning sickness" and pregnancy-related sleep disturbance, and its clearance in the United States would have been all but automatic. An FDA official (herself ironically a Canadian) was unsatisfied that all was yet in order and delayed approval; in the time that followed, reports appeared of serious birth defects, most striking among them phocomelia ("flipper limbs"). The drug was not licensed in the United States; its marketing approval in other countries was withdrawn, and we now know it to be an inhibitor of the formation of new blood vessels. This near miss called attention to the lack of stringent protections against the potential dangers of new drugs, and the Food, Drug, and Cosmetic Act was amended to require evidence of efficacy and safety—as well as systematic reporting of adverse events and the informed consent of persons in studies of new drugs—before marketing approval could be granted. There have been numerous refinements to the process in the last four decades, and the current requirements are codified at 21 CFR 50,[1] 21 CFR 56,[2] and 21 CFR 312.[3]

The fundamental ideas underlying this process are straightforward, even if the details might sometimes be complex or confusing. In order that drugs being introduced to market are indeed acceptably safe and effective for their claimed indications, their evaluation must be carried out according to generally accepted principles of ethical propriety and scientific rigor; the evaluation must be overseen and be subject to the scrutiny of the licensing agency; and on successful licensure, the advertising claims made for the drug must be limited to those that have actually been supported by data. The regulatory process for achieving these goals is a permitting system in which a sponsor planning to study a drug receives permission to do so after filing an investigational new drug application with the Food and Drug Administration; the application, the process, and the resulting permit are often known by the acronym IND. The permission granted is limited to the specific drug, the specific uses (indications) for which licensure is to be sought, and the specific evaluative study to be performed.

What Requires an IND?

The simplest example is that for which the process is named. An IND application must be filed when a sponsor wishes to test a newly developed drug to see if its safety and efficacy are such that it can be approved for marketing. Remember, however, that the permission granted a successful IND applicant is very specific, as is the licensing approval that results. Thus, an IND is also required for studies of drugs that are already licensed if the intent of the study is to generate data that will lead to approval of a new advertising claim, a new clinical indication, or a new formulation of the product. Similarly, an IND (or an amendment to an existing IND) is required to add a new study design, a new patient group, or a new clinical indication to the evaluation of a product that is under study but not yet marketed.[3[Sec.2(a)]]

What Does *Not* Require an IND?

If a drug is already licensed and approved by the FDA for marketing in the United States, it may be studied without an IND. However, there are conditions that must be met for this exemption to apply, some of which were previously implied.[3[Sec.(2b)]] The study must not be one that is designed to change the approved indications, advertising claims, or labeling of the product. The study must not be one that changes dose, route of administration, or target population in a way that is likely to increase risk. The study is still subject to all of the usual requirements for IRB oversight, and the study must not violate any of the FDA's rules about advertising and promotion of drugs.[3[Sec. 7]] A simple example of an allowable study would be a postmarketing evaluation of a licensed drug to test whether its efficacy in ordinary clinical use is similar to that which had been found in carefully selected subject groups in Phase III trials.

Drug studies being done in animals do not ordinarily require an IND; however, if the results are to be used in support of the design of subsequent studies in humans, their quality and verifiability are important, and it is wise to follow the applicable FDA guidances.

Areas Where It Is Not Always Clear

Particular difficulty may be encountered when a drug is to be used on a single-patient basis, and there is no intent to develop the drug commercially. The wording of the context-setting regulation provides that the IND rules apply ". . . to all clinical investigations of products that are subject to section 505 or 507 of the Federal Food, Drug, and Cosmetic Act or to the licensing provisions of the Public Health Service Act."[3[Sec. 2], 4 [Sec. 201 et seq.]] Single-patient use will usually not satisfy the regulatory definition of "research"[5[Sec.102(d)]] or of "clinical investigation,"[1[Sec. 3(c)]] so it would appear to fail the applicability criterion. However, the specific definition of "clinical investigation" within the IND regulations is broader, including ". . . any experiment in which a drug is administered or dispensed to, or used involving, one or more human subjects. For the purposes of this part, an experiment is any use of a drug except for the use of a marketed drug in the course of medical practice."[3[Sec. 3(b)]] A use of a nonmarketed drug in the course of medical practice would satisfy this definition of "experiment" and of "clinical investigation."

That creates several tensions, for which the resolution may be difficult or even contentious. Once such single-patient use expands to multiple patients, the likelihood of organized data-gathering and contribution to generalizable knowledge increases. Thus, the activity creeps through a gray zone in the direction of research. Opinions (investigator, manufacturer, IRB, federal regulators) are likely to differ as to just when the line has been crossed. Moreover, there has been disagreement about the need for an IND for a use that is clearly research but does not have product licensure as a goal. Because the exemptions[3[2(b)(1)]] specifically refer to a drug that is "lawfully marketed in the United States," they cannot be invoked for an unlicensed product. On the other hand, it is not clear that a drug not intended for marketing is subject to §505 or §507 of the Food, Drug, and Cosmetic Act.

An additional tension relates to quality control. When a formal study is carried out under an IND, certain assurances are given, and there is a mechanism for the central reporting of adverse events. When an unlicensed agent is used on a single-patient basis and no IND application is filed, there is no mechanism for centralized adverse event reporting, and quality control may not be assured. IRBs have occasionally asked that investigators file IND applications specifically to bring an activity under federal scrutiny. This is an imperfect response, as the FDA may simply opine that an IND is not necessary, or an IND may be granted without careful examination of the quality controls that are in place.

In institutions where such issues arise with any frequency, it is wise to establish institutional policies and procedures for dealing with them. For example, many academic centers now have research drug pharmacists and GLP (good laboratory practices) facilities that can help a physician–investigator assure that the product being prepared meets the conventional standards for purity, stability, nonpyrogenicity, etc. Central data and safety monitoring may also be imposed for a center, even if it is not provided for on a national basis.

In circumstances where it has been impossible to reach a confident decision as to the need for an IND, the FDA may be consulted directly.[3[Sec. 2(e)]]

"Off-Label" Use of Drugs

It is important to recognize that the approved labeling indications for a drug are marketing constructs as well as scientific ones. That is, a drug manufacturer must ask, "Is the market potential for this indication sufficient to justify the studies that would be necessary to obtain the corresponding approval?" From a business perspective, this decision must consider the size of the potential market, the quality of other competing drugs in that market, the advantages of the new product in that context, the likely profit per unit sold, the length of patent protection remaining to the new product, and the time and expense required to gain marketing approval for the proposed indication. Often, even if the drug is a very good one for the indication under discussion, the answer will be, "No. We'll never recover our R&D costs before the patent runs out." In a more general sense, this type of consideration encourages a manufacturer to seek first the marketing approval that best combines ease of study and initial yield, then to be very selective in seeking additional approvals. Even if a drug is the best possible therapy for a rare disorder, the profit potential may not be sufficient to make the manufacturer seek specific labeling approval for that use.

Often, it rapidly becomes clear that a drug has valuable uses beyond its approved indications. A treating physician may administer a drug for an indication other than the approved ones ("off-label use") without regulatory barrier. That is, one may consider preliminary reports or the mechanism of action of a drug and decide that it is likely to work in a given situation—then go ahead and try it. Such use is specifically allowed without an IND;[3[Sec. 2(d)]] an IND is only required if such use is carried out in a systematic way with the intention of generating information of use in a licensing application.

Confusion may arise because the question "Is this research?" is distinct from the question "Is an IND required?" If a clinician uses a drug off-label, in a systematic way, with the intent to generate or contribute to generalizable knowledge, the regulatory definition of research with human subjects has been satisfied.[5][Sec.102(d)] Thus, IRB oversight and other protections will be required, even though an IND may not be. As a simple example, an allergist or pulmonologist may wish to compare two licensed drugs for their efficacy and ease of use in asthmatic patients. A prospective, randomized, crossover trial is to be carried out. Publication is likely, but no drug company is involved, and use of the results in support of an advertising claim is unlikely. This is unambiguously research involving human subjects, but nothing about the study brings it under IND rules.

These distinctions are very important because they preserve the ability to use drugs clinically in difficult situations. If every off-label use were to be construed as research, or if every off-label use were to require an IND, only patients with common and well-studied conditions would be candidates for treatment.

Outline of the Process

The overarching purposes of the IND process are to ensure the rights and welfare of study subjects and to ensure the quality and integrity of the data on which licensing applications are to be based. The former dominates the process in consideration of Phase I trials, whereas data quality questions become more important in later trials.[3][Sec.22(a)]

The process begins with the submission of a "Notice of claimed investigational exemption for a new drug" by the sponsor. Typically, the sponsor is the drug manufacturer; it may be the clinician–investigator. Sometimes the manufacturer *is* the clinician–investigator, as when an intramurally developed drug enters clinical trials on its home turf. This application sets forth the background information establishing that the time is right to move into human studies, and it sets forth a fair amount of detail about the plan of investigation in humans. A detailed protocol for the first human studies and a complete investigators' brochure for them are typically made part of the initial application. Specific content guidelines are provided at 21 CFR 312.[3][Sec.23]

The FDA then has 30 days to respond. For commercial IND applications, the response is typically a beginning of the dialogue to agree on what additional information may be needed, or what modifications may be required in the plan of investigation or the information for researchers. In investigator-initiated INDs involving products of low risk, the response is often simply granting the request.

After approval has been secured, the described investigations may begin, but only in strict accordance with the protocols that have been accepted by the FDA. The approval is for a very specific course of study, and is not a more general permission to study the drug. Carefully following the approved protocol is often one of the most important safety provisions of research. Individual study sites may not begin to enter subjects until appropriate local approvals are in place (including IRB approval).

The investigator and sponsor then have a number of recordkeeping and reporting obligations that must be satisfied. Data must be kept secure, and must be verifiable. Data must be monitored for safety issues as well as for study quality. Adverse events must be reported, both to the FDA and to IRBs. Changes in protocols must be submitted for approval, both to the FDA and to IRBs, and may not be implemented until approved by the IRB and reported to FDA, unless their purpose is to protect subjects from serious harm (for example, by removing a newly recognized substantive risk). Annual progress reports must be submitted to the FDA, as must continuing review applications/reports to the IRBs.

Exactly how these responsibilities are divided depends a bit upon the nature of the study. If it is a multicenter study with a commercial sponsor, the sponsor deals with the FDA and the local investigator deals with local regulatory matters, such as IRB oversight. If it is a single-site study and the investigator has been involved in developing the product, the same person may be dealing with both local and federal concerns.

Special Types of IND

There are two special categories of IND of which IRBs should be aware, even though neither is very common.

The first is what is known as a "treatment" IND.[3(Sec.34)] When antiretroviral drugs were first being developed, there was great concern (fueled by advocacy from groups of HIV-infected persons) that they be made available for treatment use as early as was feasible—recognizing that no therapy existed for HIV infection. Special rules were adopted to facilitate this, allowing the drugs to be used for treatment while Phase II studies were still underway. After initial enthusiasm, the use of such INDs has declined because most of the need is satisfied by the inclusion of compassionate-use arms in Phase III studies.

The second is a special class of IND for studies invoking the special waiver of consent for treatment studies in an emergency setting. Recognizing that "retrospective consent" and "passive consent" are oxymoronic, the Office for Protection from Research Risks and the FDA developed a set of rules under which therapeutic trials in an emergency setting could be done.[1(Sec.24)] These rules provided for "community consultation" in lieu of individualized consent and restricted the research to a very narrow context involving attempts to improve the care of very serious conditions under circumstances that precluded getting surrogate consent in a timely manner. One of the procedural safeguards put in place for such research was to require a special IND, even if the product under study were covered by another IND or were even licensed.[3(Sec.54)] In effect, it created a mechanism for the FDA to always have oversight authority for such research.

IRBs should be aware that any time they are considering an application under subsection 24 of 21 CFR 50, a special IND application will be required.

Another Special Case—IND: Yes; IRB: No!
More common than the special provisions for waiving consent in the emergency-care setting is the circumstance in which a treating physician wishes to use an experimental drug (or device) in a life-threatening situation and does not have time to get prospective IRB approval. The IND regulations provide an exception to the requirement for prospective approval for this scenario. To use an experimental agent under such circumstances, the following conditions must be met.[2(Sec. 102(d))]

1. It must be a life-and-limb-threatening situation. Although the regulation says "life-threatening," the interpretation has generally been given that this may be limb-threatening, or merely likely to become life-threatening if the customary delay for IRB approval were interposed.

2. There must be no standard therapy available. This may be true in an absolute sense, or standard therapy may be failing in this patient, or there may be contraindications to standard therapy, or there may be reason to believe that standard therapy will be ineffective or excessively dangerous.

3. There must be insufficient time for prospective IRB review. Typically, such requests involve drugs that must be started within hours or, at most, a couple of days. If more time is available, full IRB review — even if it means a special quorum call—is a better option.

4. There must be no preclusive regulatory barriers. This is seldom a limiting factor. Many of the drugs for which such requests are made are ones that are in Phase III trials and for which the manufacturer has a compassionate-use IND provision already in place. Moreover, in a genuine emergency, the FDA will often authorize release of the drug while an application for such an IND provision is still in preparation.[3(Sec. 36)]

5. The concurrence of a physician uninvolved in the patient's care is often added to the list. This is a requirement for the waiver of consent in such situations, but it is not a strict requirement if the patient can give consent or if an appropriate surrogate consent giver is available.[1(Sec. 23(a))] Nonetheless, it is a useful additional safeguard.

Such an exception may only be invoked once for a given drug at a given site[2(Sec. 104(c))] (although operationally the possibility of an unexpected second need is recognized). The physician (now also an investigator) must report the use in writing to the IRB of local jurisdiction within five working days,[2(Sec. 104(c))] and all of the recordkeeping and reporting obligations of an investigator accrue to him or her. The physician also must be aware of the fact that this drug use is occurring in the absence of IRB approval; this may have implications for use of any data that result.

If the drug is a product of a commercial supplier, that supplier/sponsor will want assurance that the regulatory obligations will be complied with. That request often comes in the form of a request for an "emergency IRB approval" (an unfortunate misnomer). Many institutions therefore have a local policy that clinicians screen such requests with an IRB officer. That provides some assurance that the rules will in fact be satisfied, provides an entrée into the required oversight process, and allows the IRB to generate a letter to the sponsor indicating that the request has been screened and found to meet the regulatory criteria for exemption from the requirement for prior IRB review.

When Things Go Really Wrong

A sponsor may withdraw an IND at any time, with or without cause. The FDA may also terminate an IND under a number of circumstances. A *clinical hold* is a suspension of an IND, during which no new subjects may be enrolled, and subjects who have already been enrolled may only continue the study drug if it is clinically necessary for them to do so.[3(Sec. 42)] This action may be taken when it appears that subjects are being exposed to greater risk than had originally been recognized; the IND—and the studies—are then often reactivated when appropriate adjustments in study design have been made. A clinical hold may also result if the researchers' qualifications are called into serious question or if the study design proves flawed in a way that precludes meaningful results.

More serious deficiencies may lead to termination of an IND. In that case, reactivation is not foreseen and the project is shut down.[3(Sec. 44)] If the cause is clear and compelling danger to research subjects, this may be a rather precipitous action. If it is for problems in study conduct that do not place subjects at increased risk, the FDA will ordinarily notify the sponsor of the intent to terminate the IND and give the sponsor an opportunity to respond.

Tensions

The IND process often creates problems because it involves interface between groups of people who tend to be intelligent and sophisticated, but whose areas of sophistication and expertise may not agree. A few are important enough to mention here.

Local investigators often expect to be able to submit their manufacturer-sponsored protocols to their local IRBs and have smooth sailing. This is often not the case. Sponsors vary widely (and protocols from a single sponsor vary widely) in the quality and organization of the information they provide in the investigators' brochures. The quality of consent forms is also quite variable. Thus, it is sometimes easy and sometimes difficult to craft a successful IRB application from the materials provided.

It is often the local investigator's understanding that the protocol cannot be changed in response to IRB concerns, as it is often understood that the protocol provisions have been mandated by the FDA. Far more commonly, the IRB's concerns address something that the FDA has not mandated, but has merely failed to disallow. In fact, the FDA depends on IRB review and is usually receptive to protocol amendments made in response to IRB concerns. The sponsor, of course, does not want to have 25 slightly different protocols in effect at its 25 active sites, so it is in the sponsor's best interest to resist trivial changes and to try to implement uniformly those that address an important issue. The weaknesses in this part of the process are several. First, many protocols are not "vetted" by a demanding IRB before they go out. As a result, the process of critical IRB review is done piecemeal; the result may be non-uniform, and consensus about what is important builds agonizingly slowly. Second, the IRB's primary interaction is with the submitting local investigator. This is often someone who is clinically busy and does not want to spend a lot of time with administrative issues. It is also often someone who is not particularly knowledgeable about the regulations or FDA process, and who knows little about the sponsor's actual reasons for any provisions that might be problematic for the IRB. IRBs, for their part, may or may not have expertise pertaining to an individual protocol before them, and thus may or may not be able to help the local investigator find a resolution. The institutions where the research is to be conducted may see the whole issue primarily in terms of revenue flow, and may try to encourage prompt IRB acceptance of sponsored research without carefully examining other dimensions.

A common example of this is the exclusion of women of childbearing potential from clinical trials of potential benefit to individual participants. Federal guidelines since 1994 have identified this as a justice concern that IRBs must address,[6] but many sponsors continue to have such exclusions in their protocols—presumably out of concern for liability risk exposure. Many investigators' brochures also do not have the necessary information to explain and defend such exclusions to an IRB (which is ironic, as many of them, in fact, turn out to be allowable). The local investigator may then go before the IRB, armed only with his or her understanding that the FDA has probably required the exclusion. Unfortunately, it may take several exchanges before the truth is known and avoidable delay has been substantial.

Another common example is the inclusion in sample consent documents of language that seems to set sponsor's liability limits. This is not allowable under FDA rules,[1(Sec.20)] DHHS rules,[5(Sec.116)] or International Conference on Harmonisation guidelines.[7(Sec.4.8.4)] Again, the poor local investigator is caught in the middle, as the IRB and the sponsor disagree about the allowability of a specific wording.

A major set of tensions centers about privacy and confidentiality with respect to study subjects and their medical records. The FDA has the authority to compare primary sources with case report forms to establish that the data on the case report forms are or are not correct (in the worst case, that the study subject does or does not exist). In clinical studies, such primary sources are often medical records. FDA regulations, in fact, require that consent forms for FDA-scrutinized research include the information that identifiable records may be audited.[1[25(a)(5)]] The sponsor does not have audit authority *per se,* but has the obligation to guarantee the integrity of data submitted to the FDA in a licensing application.[3[Secs.58(a), 62(b)]] Therefore, the sponsor has a major interest in access to medical records, but the legal and ethical authority for such access is not automatically present. This tension is best resolved by a clear disclosure in the consent process that the quality assessment/assurance activities of the sponsor may include checking the subject's medical record to make sure that the tabulated data are correct. The details of this agreement may be problematic, as the easiest thing for the sponsor is to seek unfettered access or to seek study sites where few questions will be asked.

Conclusion

The ethical conduct of research with human subjects requires that the science be meritorious, that subject selection be equitable, that unnecessary risks be avoided, that risks and benefits be in reasonable balance, that those risks and benefits be examined independently by someone without a stake in the process, and that an information and consent process appropriate to the circumstance be employed. The IND process—supported by the more general FDA regulations for human subjects' protection—is an attempt to put those principles into practical (and auditable) form.

A fair number of rough spots exist, quite a few of which derive from something I like to term "regulatory autism." Autistic children find it difficult to imagine what another person may be thinking, even at the most basic level. That may be perceived as an exaggeration of a normal trait when one reflects on the difficulties in regulatory process. Sponsors may have trouble figuring out what is in the minds of their local investigators, the IRBs, and federal regulators. IRBs may have trouble figuring out what is in the minds of investigators, sponsors, regulators, and so on.

That being said, the regulations provide a framework in which compliance yields research that is usually credible and usually ethical. Better education of all parties to the process, and more open exchange and dialogue among them, could help ease or eliminate many of the tensions that persist.

References

1. Code of Federal Regulations. Title 21, Chapter 1—Food and Drug Administration, DHHS; Part 50—Protection of Human Subjects. Updated 1 Apr 1999. Access date 18 Apr 2001. World Wide Web http://www4.law.cornell.edu/cfr/21p50.htm

2. Code of Federal Regulations. Title 21, Chapter 1—Food and Drug Administration, DHHS; Part 56—Institutional Review Boards. Updated 1 Apr 1999. Access date 27 Mar 2001. World Wide Web http://www4.law.cornell.edu/cfr/21p56.htm

3. Code of Federal Regulations. Title 21, Chapter 1—Food and Drug Administration, DHHS; Part 312—Investigational New Drug Application. Updated 1 Apr 1999. Access date 18 Apr 2001. World Wide Web http://www4.law.cornell.edu/cfr/21p312.htm

4. 103rd Congress. Public Health Service Act (§201)—Title 42 US Code. Updated 1 Jan 2001. World Wide Web http://frwebgate2.access.gpo.gov/cgi-bin/waisgate.cgi?WAISdocID=2637221675+0+0+0&WAISaction=retrieve

5. Code of Federal Regulations. Title 45A—Department of Health and Human Services; Part 46—Protection of Human Subjects. Updated 1 Oct 1997. Access date 18 Apr 2001. World Wide Web http://www4.law.cornell.edu/cfr/45p46.htm

6. Mastroianni AC, Faden R, Federman D, (editors), Committee on the Ethical and Legal Issues Relating to the Inclusion of Women in Clinical Studies, Div of Health Sciences Policy, Institute of Medicine. *Women and Health Research: Ethical and Legal Issues of Including Women in Clinical Studies,* Vol 1. Washington, DC: National Academy Press. 1994. http://search.nap.edu/books/030904992X/html/

7. International Conference on Harmonisation. E6 Good Clinical Practice. ICH harmonised tripartite guidelines: Guideline for good clinical practice. Updated 1 May 1996. Access date 23 Aug 2001. World Wide Web http://www.ifpma.org/pdfifpma/e6.pdf

Differences Between DHHS and FDA Regulations

Robert J. Amdur

INTRODUCTION

As discussed in Chapter 1-7, the Department of Health and Human Services (DHHS) and the Food and Drug Administration (FDA) have separate regulations related to research involving human subjects.[1-3] From the standpoint of IRB policy and procedure, the two sets of regulations are similar such that in most situations an IRB that is in compliance with DHHS regulations will also be in compliance with those of the FDA, and vice versa. However, regulations from these two agencies are not identical, and in some settings there are important differences with which the IRB needs to be familiar.

Institutions that do not have an assurance of compliance with the Office for Human Research Protections (OHRP) must comply with FDA regulations when research involves the investigational use of drugs, biologics, or devices, regardless of the source of research funding. When an institution conducts research that is subject to both DHHS and FDA regulations, the process of IRB review must comply with both sets of regulations. For more information on when research is regulated by the DHHS or the FDA, see Chapter 1-7. A copy of DHHS and FDA regulations for protection of human subjects is presented in Chapter 11-2.

A comprehensive review of the differences between DHHS and FDA research regulations is presented in the OPRR Guidebook[4(Chap.IIB)] and in appendix E of the FDA Information Sheets.[5] In this chapter, discussion will be limited to three areas that frequently generate discussion in the IRB community.

Emergency Use of a Test Article

In contrast to DHHS regulations,[1(Sec.116)] FDA regulations[3(Sec.104)] do *not* require prospective IRB approval for "emergency use" of a test article in specific situations. The DHHS requires IRB approval for all research that does not meet the regulatory criteria to be exempt from IRB review (see Chapter 4-3). DHHS regulations do not explicitly address the emergency use of an investigational article without IRB approval other than to say that they are not intended to limit access to emergency medical care.

IRBs at institutions with an OHRP assurance (see Chapter 8-1) frequently encounter the situation where a physician wants IRB approval to use an investigational medication or device in a "compassionate use" situation that does not constitute research. The usual scenario involves (a) a patient with a serious medical problem that is unlikely to respond to standard therapy, (b) a promising treatment involving a drug that is being studied at another institution under IND with the FDA, and (c) it is not desirable to transfer medical care to an institution where the investigational treatment is available. In this situation, a physician who does not have access to the desired treatment at his or her institution will call the study sponsor and ask for use of the investigational medication outside the study setting. The sponsor will tell the physician that it will not provide the medication in question because FDA regulations do not permit the use of an investigational drug without IRB approval. The physician then asks their IRB to approve the use of the investigational medication on a "compassionate use" basis—meaning in a manner that does not constitute research. The request for IRB approval is usually made on short notice because these situations usually involve an emergent or semi-emergent medical condition.

A discussion of how an IRB should handle the above situation is discussed in detail in Chapter 4-5. The bottom line is that there is a mechanism for managing this situation in a way that usually satisfies all concerned parties: the FDA, the DHHS, the study sponsor, the local physician, and the IRB. For the purpose of this discussion, it is sufficient to recognize that use of an investigational agent without IRB approval identifies a situation where DHHS and FDA regulations may differ.

IRB Management of Adverse Event Reports

The management of adverse event (AE) reports from multicenter clinical trials is one of the most important and controversial issues facing IRBs today. Most IRBs cannot afford to waste time with activities that do not meaningfully affect the protection of human research subjects. IRBs are confused about the regulatory definition of an AE. They are unsure of when an investigator is required to report an AE to the IRB, the timing of AE reporting, the procedure for IRB review of an AE report, and the relationship between the IRB and a data and safety monitoring board. Part of the problem is differences between DHHS[1][Secs.103(5),108,111(a)(6),116(b)(5)] and FDA[2][Sec.108(b)(1)] regulations related to the various components of this topic. A comprehensive discussion of the AE reporting issue is presented in Chapter 7-3.

Explaining Access to Study Records in the Consent Document

An issue that is frequently overlooked by institutions that focus on DHHS regulations[1][Sec.116(a)(5)] is the requirement by the FDA[2][Sec.25(a)(5)] to include in the consent document a statement that the FDA may inspect a subject's medical record as part of a review of information pertaining to the research study. Although the DHHS has the right to inspect the records of studies that are subject to DHHS regulation, DHHS regulations do not require an explicit statement regarding review of study records in the consent document.

Conclusion

The DHHS and the FDA have separate regulations related to research involving human subjects. The two sets of regulations are similar such that in most settings the IRB that is in compliance with the DHHS regulations will also be in compliance with those of the FDA, and visa versa. However, there are three main situations where the regulations differ in a way that affects IRB policy. These situations are the emergency use of a test article (the compassionate use situation), the management of adverse event reports, and the explanation of access to study records in the consent document.

References

1. Code of Federal Regulations. Title 45A—Department of Health and Human Services; Part 46—Protection of Human Subjects. Updated 1 Oct 1997. Access date 18 Apr 2001. World Wide Web http://www4.law.cornell.edu/cfr/45p46.htm

2. Code of Federal Regulations. Title 21, Chapter 1—Food and Drug Administration, DHHS; Part 50—Protection of Human Subjects. Updated 1 Apr 1999. Access date 18 Apr 2001. World Wide Web http://www4.law.cornell.edu/cfr/21p50.htm

3. Code of Federal Regulations. Title 21, Chapter 1—Food and Drug Administration, DHHS; Part 56—Institutional Review Boards. Updated 1 Apr 1999. Access date 27 Mar 2001. World Wide Web http://www4.law.cornell.edu/cfr/21p56.htm

4. Penslar RL, Porter JP, Office for Human Research Protections. *Institutional Review Board Guidebook,* ed. 2, 6 Feb 2001. Access date 29 Mar 2001. World Wide Web http://ohrp.osophs.dhhs.gov/irb/irb_guidebook.htm

5. Food and Drug Administration. Information sheets: Guidance for institutional review boards and clinical investigators, Sept 1998. Access date 9 Apr 2001. World Wide Web http://www.fda.gov/oc/oha/IRB/toc.html

Veterans Administration Research Guidelines

Peter Marshall

INTRODUCTION

The purpose of this chapter is to describe the additional regulatory and policy requirements that institutional review boards (IRBs) in the Department of Veterans Affairs (VA) must follow. The information provided in this chapter applies to both a VA IRB (referred to in the VA as "Subcommittee on Human Studies") and an affiliated-university IRB that serves as the IRB of record for a VA medical center.

Regulatory Differences

The Common Rule

The Common Rule is a set of human subject research regulations. The purpose of the Common Rule is to standardize the rules for human subject research among federal departments and agencies.[1] Since 1991, the Common Rule has been adopted by 17 federal departments and agencies. For the Department of Veterans Affairs, the Common Rule is codified in 38 CFR 16, Protection of Human Subjects.[2]

Differences exist between the Common Rule and the Department of Health and Human Services (DHHS) human subjects research regulations in that the DHHS regulations are found in 45 CFR 46, Subparts A–D, whereas the Common Rule is codified by DHHS at 45 CFR 46, Subpart A only.[1(Secs.101-124)] In other words, for the DHHS, the Common Rule is a subset of the DHHS human subjects research regulations. The Common Rule does not include DHHS regulations 45 CFR 46, Subparts B–D, which describe additional protections for fetuses, pregnant women, human *in vitro* fertilization, prisoners, and children. However, the Common Rule does require additional protections for vulnerable groups. In 45 CFR 46.111(b), the criteria for IRB approval of research specify that whenever a study involves vulnerable subjects, "additional safeguards have been included in the study to protect the rights and welfare of these subjects." The difference is that the Common Rule does not

Disclaimer: Peter Marshall is with the Louis Stokes Cleveland Department of Veterans Affairs Medical Center, Cleveland, Ohio. However, this chapter was written by Peter Marshall in his private capacity. No official support or endorsement by the Department of Veterans Affairs or the Louis Stokes Cleveland Department of Veterans Affairs Medical Center is intended or should be inferred.

have specific criteria required for the approval of research involving certain vulnerable subjects. VA medical centers are required to follow all subparts of 45 CFR 46 only if they have signed a contract (e.g., a DHHS multiple-project assurance, single-project assurance, interinstitutional amendment, etc.) stating such.

VA Guidance Differences

The primary source of guidance from the VA concerning its interpretation of the Common Rule for human subjects protection is defined in the VA Manual M-3, Part I, Chapter 9, which was last revised on October 30, 1992.[3] At the time of this writing, the VA headquarters is preparing a new handbook, which will be available shortly. For purposes of VA Manual M-3, Part I, Chapter 9, the Subcommittee on Human Studies of the Research & Development (R&D) Committee constitutes an IRB. Thus, in the VA Manual M-3, Part I, Chapter 9, the term *IRB* refers to either the Subcommittee on Human Studies or any affiliated-university IRB that serves as the IRB of record for a VA medical center.

The definition of *legally authorized representative* is expanded beyond that provided for in the Common Rule.[1(Sec.102(c))] In VA Manual M-3, Part I, Chapter 9,[3] a *legally authorized representative* includes not only persons appointed as health care agents under durable powers of attorney for health care (DPAHCs) and court-appointed guardians of the person but also next of kin in the following order of priority: (1) spouse; (2) adult child (18 years of age or older); (3) parent; and (4) adult sibling (18 years of age or older).

The definition of *human subject* also differs from that defined in the Common Rule.[1(Sec.102(f))] In VA Manual M-3, Part I, Chapter 9,[3] *human subject* is expanded to include "investigators, technicians, and other assisting investigators, when they serve in a 'subject' role by being observed, manipulated, or sampled."

Certain members of the community are recommended to serve on an IRB. According to VA Manual M-3, Part I, Chapter 9, clergy, attorneys, representatives of legally recognized veterans organizations, and practicing physicians are types of individuals recommended to represent the local community on the IRB.

Surrogate Consent

Surrogate consent is permission to enroll a subject that is obtained from a research subject's legally authorized representative under appropriate conditions. A hierarchy of surrogate consent is specified among next of kin for the VA. Surrogate consent may be obtained not only from the health care agent appointed by the patient in a DPAHC or similar document, and from court-appointed guardians of the person, but also from next of kin in the following order of priority: spouse; adult child (18 years of age or older); parent; adult sibling (18 years of age or older).[3[Sec.9.12a(1)]] What requirements must be met for surrogate consent? Surrogate consent may be requested and accepted only when (a) the prospective research participant is incompetent as determined by two VA physicians, after appropriate medical evaluation; (b) there is little or no likelihood that the patient will regain competence within a reasonable period of time; or (c) as established by a legal determination.[3[Sec.9.12a(2)]]

Before incompetent persons may be considered for participation in any VA research, the IRB must find that the proposed research meets all of the following conditions and record in writing a determination of each of the following:[3[Sec.9.12b,c]]

1. Only incompetent patients are suitable.

2. Incompetent people will not be subjects of research that imposes a risk of injury unless that research is intended to benefit the subject and the probability of benefit is greater than the probability of harm.

3. Some patients may resist participating in a research protocol approved by their representatives. Under no circumstances may subjects be forced or coerced to participate.

4. Procedures have been devised to assure that participants' representatives are well informed regarding their roles and obligations to protect incompetent subjects. Health care agents (appointed under DPAHCs), next of kin, or guardians must be given descriptions of both the proposed research studies and the obligations of patients' representatives. They must be told that their obligation is to try to determine what the subject would do if competent or, if the subject's wishes cannot be determined, what they think is in the incompetent person's best interests.

Payment of Research Subjects

VA policy prohibits paying patients to participate in research when the research is an integral part of a patient's medical care and when it makes no special demands on the patient beyond those of medical care. Payment may be permitted with prior approval of the IRB in the following circumstances:[3[Sec.9.13a]]

1. The study to be performed is not directly intended to enhance the diagnosis or treatment of the medical condition for which the volunteer subject is being treated, and the standard of practice in affiliated non-VA institutions is to pay patients in this situation.

2. In multi-institution studies, patients at a collaborating non-VA institution are to be paid for the same participation in the same study at the same rate proposed.

3. In other comparable situations in which, in the opinion of the IRB, payment of patient volunteers is appropriate.

Investigators who wish to pay research subjects shall indicate in their proposal the justification for such payment with reference to the criteria previously listed and do the following:[3[Sec.9.13b]]

1. They must substantiate that proposed payments are reasonable and commensurate with the expected contributions of the subjects.

2. They must state the terms of the subject participation agreement and the amount of payment in the informed consent form.

3. They must substantiate that subject payments are fair and appropriate, and that they do not constitute (or appear to constitute) undue pressure on the veteran patient to volunteer for the research study.

Investigational New Drugs

According to the Food and Drug Administration (FDA) regulations,[4[Sec.3(b)]] an investigational new drug is a new drug, antibiotic drug, or biological drug that is used in a clinical investigation. The term also includes a biological product that is used in vitro for diagnostic purposes. The terms *investigational drug* and *investigational new drug* are deemed to be synonymous for the FDA regulations. An FDA investigational new drug application is known as an IND. The FDA has specific regulations for INDs.[4] Whoever sponsors a study that requires an IND must submit the IND application to the FDA. Studies that require INDs may not proceed until both the FDA has cleared the use of an IND and a local IRB has approved the study. Typically, IRBs request the FDA-assigned IND number as proof that an IND has been submitted to the FDA.

Certain procedures must be followed with a pharmacy service in a VA medical center when a research study has an IND. A VA Form 10-9012, Investigational Drug Information Record, must be completed by the principal investigator and monitored by the R&D Committee. The data contained in VA Form 10-9012 will serve as a protocol abstract. The original of this form will be kept on file by the pharmacy service as part of the study protocol. A copy of VA Form 10-9012 for each patient, with the appropriate patient identification, will be filed in the patient's medical record. The principal investigator will provide a copy of the approved protocol to the chief of the pharmacy service of the VA medical center involved in the study.[3[Sec.9.15]] When the Subcommittee on Human Studies and the R&D Committee approve the research study employing an investigational drug, VA Form 10-1223, Report of Subcommittee on Human Studies, will be completed with copies forwarded to the investigator and to the chief of the pharmacy service. The original will be placed in the protocol file in the medical center's research office.

The principal investigator will obtain the investigational drug from the manufacturer and deliver it or have it delivered, with proper identification, in accordance with FDA regulations,[4] to the custody of the chief of the pharmacy service. The investigational drug will be ordered from the pharmacy service on a properly completed VA Form 10-2577f, Prescription Form, signed by an authorized prescriber registered with the chief of the pharmacy service.

The principal investigator will send the pharmacy service a copy of the signed informed consent form, VA Form 10-1086, for each patient entered into the study. Before dispensing an investigational drug, the pharmacy service will verify that the informed consent form has been signed. Each time an investigational drug is issued to laboratory personnel for use in laboratory studies, the principal investigator must provide written authorization for such use. The principal investigator will inform the chief of the pharmacy service and the R&D Committee when a study involving investigational drugs has been terminated and will direct in writing the disposition of any remaining drug.

One of the advantages of keeping a copy of VA Form 10-9012, Investigational Drug Information Record, in the research subject's medical record is that this form provides information about potential side-effects that are not otherwise available because side-effects of new investigational drugs are not publicly available. In addition, VA Form 10-9012 alerts medical providers of the patient–subject's use of the study drug(s) in case such information may influence subsequent clinical decisions.

Informed Consent

Per VA policies, veteran patient–subjects' original signed written informed consent forms must be filed in the patient–subjects' medical records.[3][Sec.9.11b(1)] Investigators can only avoid storing the signed written informed consent form in the research subject's medical record if the subject is a nonveteran subject. However, written informed consent forms signed by nonveteran subjects are supposed to be stored in the investigator's files.

For studies regulated by the FDA, a special statement should be included in the written informed consent form. For a study that involves investigational drugs, biologics, or devices, the VA Manual M-3, Part I, Chapter 9, requires the following statement in the written informed consent form: "I have been informed that because this study involves articles regulated by the FDA (Food and Drug Administration), the FDA may choose to inspect research identifying me as a subject of this investigation."[3][App.9C Sec.2b(9)]

Research-Related Injury Policy

The VA policy regarding treatment of research-related injuries to human subjects is defined in 38 CFR 17.85 and was published in the Friday, March 6, 1998, *Federal Register* on page 11123. The conditions for receiving treat-

ment for a research-related injury according to this VA policy are that the research study must have been approved by both the VA R&D Committee and the Subcommittee on Human Studies/IRB, and conducted under the supervision of one or more VA employees (i.e., investigators). For this purpose, a *VA employee* (i.e., investigator) means any person appointed by the VA as an officer or employee and acting within the scope of his or her appointment.[5]

Research-related injuries not covered by this VA policy include injuries due to noncompliance with study procedures by a subject or injuries that occur during research conducted for the VA under a contract with an individual or a non-VA institution. Veteran subjects not covered by this policy may still be eligible for care from the VA.[5] The law requires, however, that if VA medical care funds pay for the care of research subjects who are not otherwise eligible for VA care, the VA research appropriation must reimburse the VA medical care appropriation.[5]

One possible statement to describe this VA research-related injury policy in consent forms is "If you sustain injury as a direct result of your study participation, medical care will be provided by the {fill in name of VA medical center} VA Medical Center at no cost to you."

VA IRB (Human Studies Subcommittee) Relationships

Office of Research and Development

The Office of Research and Development (ORD) is located at VA headquarters in Washington, DC. The ORD is headed by the chief R&D officer (CRADO), who is responsible for the overall policy, planning, coordination, and direction of R&D activities within the Veterans Health Administration (VHA).[6] ORD oversees all VA R&D Committees that are located within VA medical centers. Each VA Human Studies Subcommittee is a Subcommittee of an R&D Committee. The CRADO has the authority to disapprove or add stipulations to research that has been approved by local R&D Committees and VA Subcommittees on Human Studies/IRBs.

Office of Research Compliance and Assurance

The primary mission of the VA Office of Research Compliance and Assurance (ORCA) with respect to Human Studies Subcommittees is advising the VA undersecretary for health on all matters affecting the integrity of human subject research, promoting enhancements in the ethical conduct of research, and investigating any allegations of research improprieties and scientific misconduct.[7]

ORCA provides five product lines that affect VA Subcommittees on Human Studies and affiliated-university IRBs that serve VA medical centers: (a) conduct annual comprehensive oversight site-visits of human subjects protections at each VA medical center; (b) serve as participant/observer at external "accreditation" site visits for human subjects; (c) oversee investigations of allegations of research improprieties and research misconduct; (d) support training, education, and development activities in conjunction with the Veterans Integrated Systems Networks (VISNs); and (e) develop and maintain areas of emphasis and expertise in conjunction with established affiliation arrangements and advance "the state of the art" of research assurance and compliance activities.[8] The five ORCA regional offices are located in Atlanta, Boston, Chicago, Los Angeles, and Washington, DC.[9]

VHA National Center for Ethics

The National Center for Ethics is VHA's primary office for addressing the complex ethical issues that arise in patient care, health care management, and research. The center is a field-based national program that is administratively located in the office of the VA undersecretary for health.[10]

The center supports the development of integrated ethics programs at the local, regional, and national levels. The center addresses research ethics issues (e.g., adequacy of informed consent for clinical trials, use of placebos, research on patients who lack decision-making capacity). Each VA medical center has an ethics advisory committee (EAC) that offers assistance in resolving ethical dilemmas at the local level. The EAC is the best place to start when looking for advice about ethics problems. On request, the VHA National Center for Ethics will advise VA Subcommittees on Human Studies on issues that remain unclear and will serve as an educational resource for VA Subcommittees on Human Studies in collaboration with ORD and ORCA. This topic was covered in a presentation by Robert A. Pearlman, MD, MPH, of the VA National Center for Ethics at "VA Day at PRIM&R," San Diego, CA, October 28, 2000.

Food and Drug Administration

The Food and Drug Administration (FDA) may audit VA Subcommittees on Human Studies and VA investigators. In the event that the FDA intends to audit a VA clinical investigator or Human Studies Subcommittee, the FDA will notify the medical center director so that suitable arrangements for the inspection may be made.[3(Sec.9.16)]

VA Subcommittees on Human Studies must follow FDA informed consent (21 CFR 50) and IRB regulations (21 CFR 56) whenever FDA-regulated products (drugs, biologics, and devices) are the focus of a research study. VA Subcommittees on Human Studies must follow the same FDA regulations as do all other IRBs in the United States.

Office for Human Research Protections

The Office for Human Research Protections (OHRP) has no jurisdiction over VA Subcommittees on Human Studies unless their VA medical center has signed a contract (a multiple-project assurance, single-project assurance, interinstitutional amendment, etc.) with OHRP. If such a contract is in place, the affected VA Subcommittee on Human Studies must follow Department of Health and Human Services IRB regulations and OHRP guidance in addition to VA regulations and guidance.

What is the relationship between OHRP's federal-wide assurance (FWA) and the VA's multiple-project assurance (MPA)? ORCA and OHRP are collaborating on the implementation of the FWA. The FWA is accepted by the VA and will replace both the OHRP MPA and VA MPA contracts.[11] The FWA has an extra page to be completed by VA medical centers and approved by ORCA, even if the VA medical center's IRB of record is the affiliated university's IRB(s) or another acceptable IRB(s).[12]

Under OHRP assurances, VA Subcommittees on Human Studies, just like other IRBs with OHRP assurances, must report serious or continuing noncompliance with the IRB regulations or the local IRB requirements to OHRP. VA Subcommittees on Human Studies must report the same to ORCA.

VA Cooperative Studies Program

The VA Cooperative Studies Program (CSP) enables investigators from two or more VA (or non-VA, as appropriate) medical centers to collectively study a selected problem in a uniform manner, using a common protocol with central coordination.[13(p.1)] Each cooperative study is managed by a Cooperative Studies Program Coordinating Center (CSPCC). The four CSPCCs are located in Hines, Illinois; Palo Alto, California; Perry Point, Maryland; and West Haven, Connecticut.[13(p.1)]

Each CSPCC has a Human Rights Committee that is responsible for the protection of the rights and welfare of Human Subjects in cooperative studies trials. The CSP will not implement a study until a Human Rights Committee has approved it. The Human Rights Committee provides a general assessment of the human rights aspects of the proposal. Review by the Human Rights Committee is not a substitute for review by the Subcommittees on Human Studies or local IRBs.[13(p.25)]

According to the CSP guidelines dated January 2001, although it is the preference of the CSP that a single standard consent procedure is used at all participating centers, the ultimate responsibility for the welfare of the patient resides at the individual center. The consent form developed by the principal proponent and approved by the CSPCC Human Rights Committee should be considered a prototype. If the Subcommittee on Human Studies/IRB from a participating medical center makes suggestions for changes, they will be seriously considered by the corresponding CSPCC. Similarly, local variations can be incorporated into a standard document for use in all or most medical centers. When necessary and appropriate, variations across centers will be permitted with the approval of the director of the CSPCC. Major changes must have the approval of the corresponding CSPCC Human Rights Committee.[13(p.30)]

Veterans Integrated Service Network

The VA system is geographically and organizationally divided into 22 Veterans Integrated Service Networks, or VISNs. Each VISN contains one or more VA medical centers. Responsibility of VA Subcommittees on Human Studies flows from the VA medical center to the corresponding VISN. Some VISNs have employed research compliance and assurance officers (RACOs) that oversee the conduct of research offices within the entire VISN. Some individual VA medical centers have hired research compliance officers (RCOs) to oversee the conduct of the individual VA medical center's research office. The VISN director is a signatory official of the OHRP FWA that is issued to each VA medical center. The VISN director is ultimately responsible for the VISN's human subjects protection program, including the corresponding VA Subcommittees on Human Studies and affiliated-university IRBs (when such IRBs serve as the IRB of record for a VA medical center).

Affiliated-University IRBs

If a VA medical center relies on its affiliated university for IRB services, VA interests will be represented usually by the inclusion of at least one VA employee with scientific expertise on the IRB.[3(Sec.9.07a(3)(a))]

R&D Committees

The R&D Committee review differs from IRB review. The R&D Committee assesses the scientific quality of R&D projects and investigator's qualifications; recommends the distribution of R&D funds, space, personnel, equipment, supplies, and other common resources; reviews and approves R&D budgetary requests of the facility; and recommends policies for the recruitment and development of personnel supported by R&D funds.[14(Sec.3.01b(1))] The VA Subcommittee on Human Studies is a subcommittee of the R&D Committee. VA regulations require that no human subject research be initiated until it is approved by both the Subcommittee on Human Studies or affiliated-university IRB, and the R&D Committee. R&D Committee review should follow VA a Subcommittee on Human Studies/IRB review. One of the R&D Committee's responsibilities is to assure the scientific quality of research studies. However, one of the criteria for IRB approval is that the risks to subjects are reasonable in relation to anticipated benefits to subjects and the importance of the knowledge that may reasonably be expected to result.[2(Sec.111(a)(2)), 15(Sec.111(a)(2))] If a study is unlikely to produce generalizable knowledge, then this criterion of IRB approval is not met because the study has no benefit to society; therefore, the study cannot be approved. Although the IRB may rely on other groups, including the R&D Committee, to determine the scientific validity of a study, the IRB alone is responsible for determining this IRB approval criterion.

The R&D Committee cannot approve research that has not been approved by a Subcommittee on Human Studies or affiliated-university IRB.[2(Sec.112), 15(Sec.112)] In addition, the R&D Committee cannot alter an adverse report or recommendation (e.g., disapproval for ethical or legal reasons) by the Subcommittee on Human Studies.[14(Sec.3.01e)] However, the R&D Committee may always disapprove research that has been approved by a Subcommittee on Human Studies or affiliated-university IRB. Approval by a Subcommittee on Human Studies or affiliated-university IRB does not force a VA medical center or the R&D Committee to undertake a study.

VA Research Corporations (Nonprofit Corporations)

Before 1987, nonappropriated funds available for support of VA-approved research could be administered through the General Post Fund, the affiliated medical school, and occasionally other ill-suited mechanisms.[16(Sec.17.02)] In 1987, Congress authorized the creation of VA nonprofit research corporations to administer research funds received from non-VA sources. The primary statutory purpose of VA research corporations is to be a flexible funding mechanism for the conduct of peer-reviewed and approved research activities.[16(Sec.17.03)] VA research corporations are connected to an affiliated VA medical center. It is required that the board of directors of each VA research corporation includes the corresponding VA medical center's director, chief of staff, and associate chief of staff for R&D.[16(Sec.17.04)]

Some VA research corporations financially support the staff of their corresponding VA subcommittee on human studies.

VA Associate Chief of Staff for R&D and Research Administrative Officer

The Associate Chief of Staff (ACOS) for R&D is established in the office of the chief of staff when authorized by the chief medical director (i.e., the undersecretary for health) at VA headquarters.[17(Sec.2.03a)] The director of each health care facility, advised and assisted by an R&D Committee, is responsible for the R&D program of that institution. Ordinarily, the director delegates authority to administer the R&D program to an appropriately designated executive, typically the ACOS/R&D through the chief of staff.[17(Sec.2.02a)]

The VA Research Administrative Officer (AO) typically manages the research office and supports the ACOS for R&D in overseeing the multiple functions of the VA medical center's research service.

Because of the appearance of a conflict of interest with VA research protocols, neither the ACOS for R&D nor the research AO can vote with his or her VA Subcommittee on Human Studies or affiliated IRB. The OHRP states that individuals who work for the office of research support (sponsored programs) or office of grants and contracts cannot serve as voting IRB members because such individuals have duties that create a real or apparent conflicting interest. Individuals whose duties involve bringing research funds to the institution cannot be voting IRB members. An ACOS for R&D is rated on the ability to increase research funding, and an AO typically is expected to help investigators successfully compete for research funding.[18(p.2,item #4),19(item #47)]

VA Implementation Differences

All VA medical centers involved in human subject research are required to hold a VA multiple-project assurance (MPA) contract. In the future, all VA medical centers involved in human subject research must hold an OHRP federal-wide assurance (FWA) negotiated through ORCA. The FWA will replace the VA MPA contract.[20]

The VA Merit Review Program is an intramural program designed to provide funding for VA staff members for biomedical, behavioral, rehabilitation, and health services research.[21(Sec.4.01)] VA investigators may apply to VA headquarters for funding for a specifically defined study falling within their area of interests and competence. All merit review applications must first be evaluated by the corresponding VA medical center R&D Committee and approved by the director of the medical center before submission to VA headquarters.[21(Sec.4.01a)]

Merit review applications involving human subjects will not be reviewed by a VA-headquarters constituted merit review board unless such applications have been approved by the corresponding VA medical center Subcommittee on Human Studies or affiliated-university IRB before their submission. A completed and current VA Form 10-1223, Report of Subcommittee on Human Studies, dated no earlier than one year before the receipt date for the application, must be submitted with the merit review application and must be accompanied by the consent form, VA Form 10-1086.[21(Sec.4.01k)]

Vulnerable Subjects

VA medical centers often treat veterans who have no health insurance and cannot afford medical care outside the VA. Such veteran patients may feel constrained to join a research study out of fear of losing their medical coverage. As many as 37% of VA patients have reading skills below the ninth grade level; some have reading skills below the sixth grade level.[22] In addition, many veteran patients are elderly and frequently are cognitively impaired. For these reasons, many veteran subjects are considered vulnerable subjects. VA Subcommittees on Human Studies or affiliated-university IRBs must take such vulnerabilities into consideration during their review and approval of research involving veteran patients.

In addition, the VA patient population is at risk for a type of vulnerability that differs from the general population. Veteran patients are current and former military personnel. Some veterans mistake requests to join a VA research study as requests to serve their country. This point was addressed by a presentation given by John Mather, MD, VA Office of Research Compliance and Assurance at VA day at PRIM&R, San Diego, CA, October 28, 2000. As much as possible, veteran subjects should not feel compelled to join research studies for any reason, including beliefs that they are following orders or that joining a study is part of their patriotic duty. Veteran subjects, as is the case for nonveteran subjects, must make their own individual informed decision to participate in a research study without coercion or undue influence.

Independent (Commercial) Institutional Review Boards

Independent (commercial) institutional review boards are not part of any organization in which research is conducted. They are hired by research sponsors (most often pharmaceutical and device manufacturers) and investigators to review research plans. Most are for-profit entities. Some are owned by other organizations, such as contract research organizations that place clinical studies for re-search sponsors. Board members are paid for their work, either on a per-meeting basis, an hourly basis, a per-protocol-reviewed basis, or some combination thereof.[23] The VA Office of Research and Development does not approve of VA medical centers' relying on IRB services provided by an independent (commercial) IRB. This was another issue covered by Dr. Mather at the VA day at PRIM&R in October 2000.

Special Format for VA Research Consent Forms

The special format for VA research consent forms is defined in VA Form 10-1086.[3[Sec.9.11b(2)(a)]] VA Form 10-1086 has specific formatting for headers, footers, and the last page; it contains eight specific section headings that must be addressed.

Educational Requirements for VA Investigators

As of January 1, 2001, all active VA investigators involved in human subject research must provide documentation of completion of an appropriate educational program designed for investigators conducting research involving human subjects. The VA Subcommittee on Human Studies/IRB and the R&D Committee will not review any of the corresponding investigators' new or continuing review proposals unless this documentation is on file in the corresponding local R&D office. This documentation must also be included with proposals sent to ORD. This is in accordance with a memorandum from the Chief Research and Development Officer (12), "Required Education for Investigators," dated August 15, 2000. Appropriate educational programs include Web-based courses, seminars, and lectures. ORD is not mandating a specific educational course. To avoid duplication of effort, ORD accepts academic affiliates' educational programs that meet the requirements of this policy. Completion of the educational program must be within three years of submission of any new or continuing review proposal. All active VA investigators involved in human subject research must recertify every three years. This is in accordance with a memorandum from the Chief Research and Development Officer (12), "Submission of Research Proposals," dated March 14, 2001.

All principal investigators, co-principal investigators, and co-investigators involved in human subject research are required to fulfill the educational requirements. This is in accordance with a memorandum from the Chief Research and Development Officer (12), "Required Education for Investigators," dated on August 15, 2000. This requirement applies to all investigators involved in human subject research, independent of the funding status or funding sponsor of their research proposals. The educational requirements do not change if the investigators' studies are unfunded or funded by any specific entity.

The educational requirements changed after June 1, 2001. A March 14, 2001, memorandum titled "Submission of Research Proposals" from the chief R&D officer stated that, effective June 1, 2001, appropriate educational programs must require investigators to pass a test after completing the program. The investigator must receive a passing grade as defined by the educational program. Receiving a passing grade for the educational program will be verified by the receipt of a certificate from the program. In addition, appropriate educational programs must contain required course elements.

Tissue and Blood Specimen Banking

In November 2000, the VA ORD released VHA Directive 2000-043 entitled "Banking of human research subjects' specimens."[24] One of the key aspects of this policy is that all human biological specimens and linked clinical data collected as part of research projects conducted by VA investigators in VA facilities or approved off-site locations will be maintained at either VA-sponsored tissue banks or VA-approved tissue banks. Non-VA sites that may not be acceptable for storage of tissue specimens include nonacademic, for-profit institutions, such as pharmaceutical companies. At the time of this writing, a handbook providing more guidance is in the process of being completed.

Under this directive, a "VA-sponsored tissue bank" means a tissue repository or storage facility at a VA facility or approved off-site location that operates in accordance with VA regulations. It contains human biological specimens collected under VA-approved research protocols that are under both VA ownership and VA control. Under this directive, "VA-approved tissue bank" differs from a "VA-sponsored tissue bank" in that a VA-approved tissue bank is located at a non-VA facility and has the appropriate approval from the chief R&D officer of the ORD.

Conclusion

This chapter has presented a detailed explanation of current VA research guidelines. Areas where future developments are likely to affect IRB policy involve accreditation programs and an updated VA manual.

Accreditation Program

The Department of Veterans Affairs (VA) has awarded a five-year contract to the National Council of Quality Assurance (NCQA) to operate an accreditation program to ensure that VA medical centers comply with VA and other relevant federal regulations designed to protect human research subjects. NCQA is a private, nonprofit organization dedicated to improving health care quality.[25]

An affiliated-university IRB that serves as the IRB of record for its corresponding VA medical center is expected to undergo the NCQA accreditation process.

ORCA representatives will accompany site visitors from NCQA.[8]

Updated Manual

The VA Manual M-3, Part I, Chapter 9, was last updated in 1992. At the time of this writing, the replacement for VA Manual M-3, Part I, Chapter 9, which is entitled VHA Handbook 1200.5, is being completed. It is difficult to anticipate the date of the official version. Given the number of changes introduced in the draft version, the new manual is expected to be substantially different and more detailed in some areas.

References

1. Department of Health and Human Services. Federal policy for the protection of human subjects. *Fed Regist* 56(117):28003–28018, 1991.

2. Code of Federal Regulations. Title 38, Chapter 1—Department of Veterans Affairs; Part 16—Protection of Human Subjects, 1 July 1997. Access date 17 Mar 2001. World Wide Web http://www4.law.cornell.edu/cfr/38p16.htm

3. Veterans Health Administration. Chapter 9. Requirements for the protection of human subjects in research. In *Manual M-3, Research and Development in Medicine*; Part I, General, 30 Oct 1992. Access date 10 Apr 2001. World Wide Web http://www.va.gov/resdev/fr/manualM3.htm

4. Code of Federal Regulations. Title 21, Chapter 1—Food and Drug Administration, DHHS; Part 312—Investigational New Drug Application. Updated 1 Apr 1999. Access date 18 Apr 2001. World Wide Web http://www4.law.cornell.edu/cfr/21p312.htm

5. Department of Veterans Affairs. Treatment of research-related injuries to human subjects (38 CFR Part 17). *Fed Regist* 63(44):11123–11124, 1998. World Wide Web www.access.gpo.gov/nara/cfr/cfrhtml_00/Title_38/38cfr17_main_00.html

6. Veterans Health Administration. VHA directive 1200, Draft, VHA research and development, Sep 2000. Access date 10 Apr 2001. World Wide Web http://www.va.gov/resdev/directive/Instruct1a.htm

7. VA Office of Research Compliance and Assurance (ORCA). Mission statement. Updated 29 Oct 2000. World Wide Web www.va.gov/orca/mission/

8. VA Office of Research Compliance and Assurance (ORCA). Product lines. Access date 12 April 2001. World Wide Web www.va.gov/orca/mission/product_lines.cfm

9. VA Office of Research Compliance and Assurance (ORCA). Regional offices. Access date 12 Apr 2001. World Wide Web www.va.gov/orca/org/field_sites.cfm

10. Veterans Health Administration National Center for Ethics. What we do. Access date 12 Apr 2001. World Wide Web http://www.va.gov/vhaethics/about_5.cfm

11. VA Office of Research Compliance and Assurance (ORCA). Meeting Minutes: Bimonthly Teleconference, Monday, February 12, 2001. Access date 12 Apr 2001. World Wide Web http://www.va.gov/orca/docs/hq_minutes.cfm

12. Department of Health and Human Services. Additional page required for Department of Veterans Affairs Veterans Health Administration facilities. Updated Feb 2001. World Wide Web http://ohrp.osophs.dhhs.gov/humansubjects/assurance/vasup.rtf

13. VA Cooperative Studies Program. *Guidelines,* Jan 2001. World Wide Web http://www.va.gov/resdev/csp.htm

14. Veterans Health Administration. Chapter 3. Functions. In *Manual M-3, Research and Development in Medicine*; Part I, General. Updated 25 Oct 1985. Access date 10 Apr 2001. World Wide Web http://www.va.gov/publ/direc/health/manual/030103.pdf

15. Code of Federal Regulations. Title 45A—Department of Health and Human Services; Part 46—Protection of Human Subjects. Updated 1 Oct 1997. Access date 18 Apr 2001. World Wide Web http://www4.law.cornell.edu/cfr/45p46.htm

16. Veterans Health Administration. Chapter 17. VA research corporations authorized by Title 38 United States Code (U.S.C.) sections 7361 through 7368. In *Manual M-3, Research and Development in Medicine*; Part I, General. Updated 20 May 1994. Access date 10 Apr 2001. World Wide Web http://www.va.gov/publ/direc/health/manual/M-3Part_IChapter_17.DOC

17. Veterans Health Administration. Chapter 2. Organizational structure. In *Manual M-3, Research and Development in Medicine*; Part I, General. Updated 5 Mar 1985. Access date 10 Apr 2001. World Wide Web http://www.va.gov/publ/direc/health/manual/030102.DOC

18. VA Office of Research Compliance and Assurance (ORCA). Human subjects checklist. Updated 10 Jan 2001. Access date 13 Apr 2001. World Wide Web http://www.va.gov/orca/docs/Human_Subjects_Checklist.doc

19. Office for Human Research Protections. OHRP compliance activities: Common findings and guidance, 1 Sep 2000. Access date 7 May 2001. World Wide Web http://ohrp.osophs.dhhs.gov/references/findings.pdf

20. VA Office of Research and Development. Memorandum from Chief Research and Development Officer (12), VA multiple project assurance contract, 30 Jun 1999. Access date 13 Apr 2001. World Wide Web http://www.va.gov/resdev/fr/nompa.doc

21. Veterans Health Administration. Chapter 4, Merit review program. In *Manual M-3, Research and Development in Medicine*; Part II, Medical Research Program. Updated 25 Oct 1985. Access date 10 Apr 2001. World Wide Web http://www.va.gov/publ/direc/health/manual/030204.DOC

22. Collins E, Pauliks S, McShane A, Drysch M, Lawson L. Reading levels of VA patients. In *VA Practitioner* 11(1): 15–16, Jan 1994.

23. Office of Inspector General. Institutional review boards: The emergence of independent boards (OEI-01-97-00192). Dept of Health and Human Services, June 1998. Access date 27 Mar 2001. World Wide Web http://www.dhhs.gov/progorg/oei/reportindex.html

24. VA Office of Research and Development. VHA Directive 2000-043: Banking of human research subjects' specimens, 6 Nov 2000. Access date 27 Aug 2001. World Wide Web http://www.va.gov/publ/direc/health/direct/12000043.pdf

25. National Committee for Quality Assurance (NCQA). VA human research protection accreditation program. Updated 8 May 2000. Access date 13 Apr 2001. World Wide Web http://www.ncqa.org/pages/programs/qsg/announcement.htm

State Law

Sandra P. Kaltman and John M. Isidor

INTRODUCTION

The Code of Federal Regulations charges IRBs with the responsibility of evaluating proposed research in light of applicable law.[1][Sec.107(a)],[2][Sec.107] Understanding federal laws, regulations, and guidelines is not enough to satisfy that responsibility. Every state has its own statutes, regulations, and case law that may impose requirements on the research process that add to or are different from what federal law requires. A wide range of issues may be affected:

1. Age of consent
2. Capacity to consent/legally authorized representative
3. Children's assent
4. Informed consent
5. Genetic research
6. Confidentiality of medical records
7. HIV/STD reporting requirements
8. Laws about referral fees and recruitment methods
9. Laws governing clinical research
10. Laws governing IRBs
11. Laws about investigational drugs
12. Laws about vulnerable patients
13. Laws about medical practice and delegation of authority to perform procedures

Although some federal laws in essence "overrule" conflicting state laws, that is generally not the case with state laws relating to the research process. Those laws vary considerably from state to state. Here are some examples.

Age of Consent

Federal law defers to state law in determining the age of consent for participation in research.[2][Sec.402(a)] In most states, a subject who is eighteen years old is considered to have reached the age of majority, and, as an adult, may give consent on his or her own behalf to participate in research. However, this is not the case in every state. In Nebraska, the age of majority is nineteen years old.[3] In Alabama, while the age of majority is also nineteen, state law permits a fourteen-year-old to give consent for medical treatment.[4] In Rhode Island and South Carolina, a 16-year-old can give consent for most kinds of medical treatment.[5,6] Therefore, in order to determine whether research sites are properly obtaining consent in studies involving teenagers, the IRB must be aware of the relevant state law.

Surrogate Decision Makers

Every IRB reviewing studies involving elderly patients needs to know who is legally authorized to give consent for an incapacitated adult patient to participate in research. Unless a potential subject has signed a durable power of attorney for health care designating someone to make health care decisions on his or her behalf, there is surprisingly little uniformity in state laws regarding who may make such decisions.

In some states, such as Kentucky and Arizona, the statute describes a hierarchy of people who can make health care decisions. However, the hierarchies are not identical. In Kentucky, decisions can be made by a court appointed guardian, a spouse, an adult child, a parent, or the nearest living relative, in that order.[7] In Arizona, the hierarchy also includes the domestic partner of an unmarried person, a sibling, and a close friend.[8] Other states, such as Ohio, have no provisions at all for alternate decision makers. Thus, in order to determine whether a site is obtaining consents from those who are legally authorized to give it, the IRB must know the applicable state law.

Genetic Testing

When reviewing studies that include genetic testing, the IRB must be aware of state law relating to such testing. Most states have specific laws about informed consent and genetic research. Most require written consent and some, such as Louisiana and Nevada, require the use of a specific consent form whenever genetic testing is performed.[9,10] Some states give the subject the right to be informed of the results of genetic testing.[11]

The Importance of Court Cases

Besides determining which state statutes and regulations are applicable, the IRB must also be aware of court decisions that have an impact on research. Although there have not been many court cases involving clinical research, those that do exist shape the law in the geographic area they come from and can be used as examples in other geographic areas as well. They also demonstrate how a failure to understand the law can expose those involved in research to liability.

Intraocular Lens in Illinois

In an Illinois case, a court of appeals found failure to inform a patient that an intraocular lens that was being implanted was investigational and therefore a failure to obtain informed consent. The investigator had altered the IRB-approved informed consent to delete any reference to the study as "investigational." The court noted the breach of the IRB's obligation to compare the consent signed by the subject with the IRB-approved consent. The court further found that a failure to obtain proper consent could be a "medical battery," meaning a wrongful use of force, or negligence under state law, entitling the patient to receive compensation for injury.[12]

The Moore Case in California

A leukemia patient in a study claimed that he was harmed when the investigator failed to disclose his financial interest in using the subject's cells to develop an extremely valuable cell line. The California Supreme Court found that, in order to obtain proper consent, an investigator must disclose personal and economic interests unrelated to the subject's health that might affect the investigator's medical judgment. The court found that failure to make such disclosures could entitle the subject to compensation.[13]

A Promise of Free Medication

A U.S. Court of Appeals has found that an informed consent document is a contract that can require a sponsor to perform services for study subjects even after a clinical trial ends.[14] In this case, the informed consent stated that subjects would receive the study drug free for one year after the conclusion of the double-blind phase of the study if the study drug appeared to be effective. When the sponsor did not provide the free study drug, eighteen subjects filed suit. The court found that the sponsor could be forced to provide the study drug because the informed consent was considered to be a binding contract between the sponsor and subjects.

As these cases illustrate, state law can provide the legal basis for litigation against parties involved in research. IRBs and their members could be named in lawsuits. The liability of IRBs and their members is the subject of a separate chapter in this book.

Sources of Information About State Laws

Unfortunately, there is no Web site you can check for a comprehensive listing of all applicable state laws, although some of the federal government Web sites have information about federal law.[15,16] Possible resources about state law include attorneys experienced in health care law, the state department of health, the risk-management department of the institution where the research is being performed, or the sponsor or contract organization's legal department. It is risky for an IRB to assume that it is someone else's job to know the law applicable to the studies it reviews. Unless the IRB is aware of and understands relevant law, it cannot discharge its responsibility under the federal regulations to evaluate research in light of that law.

Conclusion

Federal regulations require the IRB to conduct research in compliance with applicable state law. In some situations, federal laws overrule conflicting state laws, but this is generally not the case with state laws relating to the research process. The range of situations in which state law has important implications for local IRB procedures and determinations is wide and constantly evolving. This chapter explains the main areas where state law is likely to impose restrictions on research conduct that go beyond those discussed in federal research regulations. Understanding how and when to apply state law to the local IRB process will be an ongoing challenge for the IRB and research community.

References

1. Code of Federal Regulations. Title 21, Chapter 1—Food and Drug Administration, DHHS; Part 56—Institutional Review Boards. Updated 1 Apr 1999. Access date 27 Mar 2001. World Wide Web http://www4.law.cornell.edu/cfr/21p56.htm

2. Code of Federal Regulations. Title 45A—Department of Health and Human Services; Part 46—Protection of Human Subjects. Updated 1 Oct 1997. Access date 18 Apr 2001. World Wide Web http://www4.law.cornell.edu/cfr/45p46.htm

3. Rev. Stat. of Neb. Ann. Chapter 43. Infants and Juveniles-Article 2-Juvenile Code-(b) General Provisions. §43-245-terms, defined. 2000.

4. Alabama Code. Title 22. Health, Mental and Environmental Control-Subtitle 1-Health and Environmental Control Generally-Chapter 8-Consent for Health Services. §22-8-4-Minors; consent for self. 2000.

5. S.C. Code Ann. Title 20. Domestic Relations-Chapter 7-Children's Code -Article 3-Legal Status of Children-Subarticle 7-Legal Capacity of Minors. §20-7-280-Minor sixteen years old or over may consent to health services other than operations. 2000.

6. R.I. Gen. Laws. Title 23. Health and Safety-Chapter4.6- Consent to Medical and Surgical Care. §23-4.6-1: Consent to medical and surgical care. 2001.

7. Ky. Rev. Stat. Title XXVI. Occupations and Professions-Chapter 311-Physicians, Osteopaths, and Podiatrists Kentucky Living Will Directive Act. §311.631-Responsible parties authorized to make health care decisions, 2000.

8. Ariz. Rev. Stat. Title 36. Public Health and Safety-Chapter 32-Living Wills and Health Care Directives-Article 3-Surrogate Decison Makers. §36-3231 - Surrogate decision makers; priorities, limitations. 2000.

9. Nev. Rev. Stat. Ann. Title 54. Professions, Occupations and Businesses-Chapter 629-Healing Arts Generally, Genetic Information. §629.171-Disclosure of genetic information of person without consent unlawful; exceptions. §629. 181-Procedure for obtaining consent of person. 2000.

10. La. Rev. Stat. Title 22. Insurance -Chapter 1-Insurance Code-Part VI-Health and Accident Insurance. §213.7 - Prohibited discrimination; genetic information; disclosure requirements; definitions. 2000.

11. Tex. Rev. Civ. Stat. Title 132. Occupational and Business Regulation. Art. 9031-Prohibited use of genetic information. Added by Acts 1997, 75th Leg., ch.1215, §2, eff. Sept. 1, 1997. Access date 11 May 2001. World Wide Web http://www.capitol.state.tx.us.statutes/vntoc.html

12. U.S. Appellate Court of Illinois, 2nd District. *Richard Kus v. Sherman Hospital.* 644 N.E. 2d 1214(No. 2-94-0156). 5 Jan 1995. Appeal from the Circuit Court of Kane County. Nos. 8-L-33, 91-L-43.

13. Supreme Court of California. *John Moore v. the Regents of the University of California.* 51 Cal. 3d 120 (No.S006987). 9 Jul 1990.

14. U.S. Court of Appeals, 9th Circuit. *Kristina Anne Dahl, et al., v. HEM Pharmaceuticals Corporation and HEM Research, Inc..* 7 F. 3d 1399 (Case Nos. 91-16897, 92-15093, 92-15117). 13 Oct 1993. Appeal from the United States District Court for the District of Nevada (D.C. No. CV-91-00459-ECR).

15. National Bioethics Advisory Commission. Publications. Updated 21 Aug 2001. Access date 27 Aug 2001. World Wide Web http://bioethics.gov/pubs.html

16. General Services Administration. FedLaw. Updated 31 Jul 2001. Access date 27 Aug 2001. World Wide Web http://www.legal.gsa.gov/

IRB Member Liability

Sandra P. Kaltman and John M. Isidor

INTRODUCTION

In these litigious times, IRBs may find their members or potential members concerned about being sued as a result of their board service. While this concern may have seemed far-fetched five years ago, today it not unreasonable. Growing media attention and public concern about protection for subjects participating in clinical research are making it more likely that IRBs and their members could be named as defendants in lawsuits relating to clinical research. The purpose of this chapter is to explain the liability issue as it pertains to individual IRB members and IRBs as an entity within an organization.

Potential Plaintiffs

Research Subjects

Who might bring such lawsuits against IRB members? The most obvious potential plaintiff is a subject alleging injury as a result of participation in a study. In such a case filed in federal court in the Northern District of Oklahoma in 2000, eight subjects (or their estates) sued all the IRB members of the University of Oklahoma Health Sciences Center in Tulsa as well as other IRB and university officials and investigators.[1]

The research study at issue involved an investigational vaccine for melanoma skin cancer. All of the study subjects had melanoma. They alleged that they were not informed about the risks of their participation, that the vaccine was unsafe, and the study design unsound. Regarding the IRB members, the plaintiffs alleged that they neglected their duties by failing to (a) examine the protocol design; (b) examine the qualifications of the investigator; (c) review the operation of the clinical trial; (d) assure the protection of the participants; (e) review proposed amendments; (f) approve advertisements; (g) ensure proper reporting; and (h) make sure the clinical trial comported with ethical standards. They also alleged that the conduct of the study violated the subjects' right to "be treated with dignity in the conduct of a clinical trial." The case is still pending in court.

In a similar high-profile case, the family of Jesse Gelsinger filed suit against the University of Pennsylvania after the 18-year-old subject died several days after beginning a gene transfer study at the University of Pennsylvania.[2] The case was settled before trial. The lawsuit alleged that the defendants failed to give Mr. Gelsinger the opportunity to give informed consent by failing to describe adequately the risks of the study and overstating the potential benefits. Although the IRB members were not sued, the bioethics advisor to the IRB was included as a defendant in the lawsuit.

In another noteworthy case in which the adequacy of informed consent was a major issue, a class action suit was filed in federal court in Florida on behalf of thousands of pregnant women who had agreed to participate in various research studies.[3] Although the IRB was not named, the institution was. The lawsuit alleged that the written consent documents were too difficult for the subjects to understand. There was no dispute that the subjects had signed the appropriate consent documents or that the documents presented accurate information. The subjects did not claim that they or their babies suffered any physical harm. After 10 years of litigation, and without the defendant hospital or investigators admitting any liability, the case was settled in 2000 for $3.8 million.

As part of the settlement, the University of South Florida agreed to require researchers to ask all pregnant women who are potential study patients about their highest level of education. The university also agreed to use standard readability tests when designing consent forms for studies involving pregnant women before submission of such consents to the IRB. These cases show how important a clear and readable consent form becomes if a lawsuit is filed.

People Denied Access to Research

Another type of possible plaintiff is a person who wants to participate in a trial but is excluded, or whose participation is limited in some way. In one such case that was decided by the United States Court of Appeals for the Ninth Circuit, the plaintiffs alleged that the sponsor of the fibromyalgia study should be forced to provide the subjects with the study drug at no cost for one year after the study ended.[4]

The consent document stated that after the completion of the study, the subjects would receive the study drug for one year at no cost if statistical analysis showed efficacy compared with placebo. The sponsor tried to back out of the arrangement on the basis that the FDA had rejected the investigational new device (IND) application, although allowing the next phase of the trial, an open label study, to go forward. The Court of Appeals found that the consent document created a binding contract and ordered the sponsor to provide the drug at no cost. Although the IRB was not sued, the case shows that dissatisfied subjects can use the courts to achieve their aims, and IRBs and their members could be included as defendants along with sponsors and investigators.

Investigators

Investigators could also bring suit against IRBs and their members on a number of bases. Investigators who are not approved to conduct studies or whose approval is withdrawn by an IRB could allege that the IRB interfered with their business opportunities with sponsors or deprived them of their right to appeal their exclusion. If any information about denial of approval or withdrawal of approval is disseminated to others, except as part of a public record, the investigators could claim that they have been slandered or libeled.

In a Minnesota case, an investigator sued the University of Minnesota, its IRB, and the IRB members.[5] He sought to prevent them from disseminating information about the IRB's investigation into his conduct of a study in which questions had been raised by another faculty member as to whether consent had been properly obtained from non–English-speaking subjects. As a result of the controversy about the study, the investigator terminated it.

The IRB started an investigation, suspended the investigator's research privileges, and notified the FDA, which initiated its own investigation. The Federal District Court for the District of Minnesota found that barring the IRB from transmitting the results of its investigation would endanger the public, as well as hinder the IRB in its essential function of maintaining the integrity of institutional research on human subjects. The IRB was permitted to fulfill its own obligations in reporting the results of its investigation to the University and the FDA pursuant to the 21 CFR 56.[6]

The investigator also alleged that he should have had the opportunity to be present when the IRB took testimony from witnesses who criticized him and to cross-examine those witnesses who testified against him in the IRB investigation. The court held that the IRB had followed its own procedures in conducting the investigation. In addition, the investigator, unlike a defendant in a criminal case, did not have the right to be involved in all aspects of the IRB's investigation. As this case shows, it is important for an IRB to have procedures that comply with the federal regulations for handling problem investigators and to follow them.

Minimizing Exposure to Liability

In addition to following all the regulatory requirements, IRBs and their members can take a preventive approach to limiting liability by using two methods: making certain they have adequate general liability insurance and obtaining written indemnification from sponsors and consultant research organizations (CROs) with whom they work.

Every private IRB or institution should attempt to obtain general liability insurance that specifically covers all the functions of an IRB. The insurance should cover all IRB members and employees for all the work they do for the IRB. If such coverage is in place at the time a claim is made or a lawsuit is filed against the IRB or its members, the insurance company should take over the defense of the case for the IRB. In addition, if a judgment is entered against the IRB or its members, or a settlement is reached, the insurance company should pay the amount of the judgment or settlement up to the amount of the policy limits of the insurance.

Conclusion

IRB members should inquire about their IRB's insurance coverage and make certain they are covered for their IRB activities. In addition, members who have their own professional malpractice insurance, such as physicians, attorneys, and nurses, should check with their own carriers to see whether the scope of their own insurance includes their actions as IRB members. IRB administrators should be prepared for these questions and can seek assistance from legal counsel or a risk-management department in answering them.

The IRB should also ask all sponsors, CROs, and investigators involved in the protocols they work with to sign a written agreement to indemnify the IRB from all claims arising out of the IRB's work. This means that the sponsor, CRO, or investigator will assume responsibility for defending all claims and paying all costs, including judgments or settlements and attorney fees, connected with reviewing studies. In addition, IRB members can ask their IRBs and institutions to indemnify them from all claims arising out of their work as IRB members.

Although insurance and indemnity agreements cannot eliminate the threat of being sued, they can minimize the extent of exposure to potential liability. Indemnity agreements and insurance policies are critical protections. Legal counsel or a risk-management department can help by reviewing the agreements to make certain they are suitable for use in clinical studies.

References

1. U.S. District Court for the Northern District of Oklahoma. *Robertson, et al. v. McGee, et al.* (CV00G0H(M)). Filed 2000.

2. Pennsylvania District Court. *Gelsinger v. Trustees of the University of Pennsylvania, et al.* Filed 18 Sept 2000. Case No. 000901885.

3. U.S. District Court for the Middle District of Florida TD. *Flora Diaz, et al., v. Tampa General Hospital, et al.* (Case No. 90-120-CIV-T-25B). Filed 27 March 1996.

4. U.S. Court of Appeals, 9th Circuit. *Kristina Anne Dahl, et al., v. HEM Pharmaceuticals Corporation and HEM Research, Inc.* 7 F. 3d 1399(Case Nos. 91-16897,92-15093). Filed 13 Oct 1993. Appeal from the United States District Court for the District of Nevada (D.C. No. CV-91-00459-ECR).

5. U.S. District Court for the District of Minnesota, 4th Division. *James A. Halikas, M.D., v. the University of Minnesota; the Institutional Review Board-Human Subjects Committee, of the University of Minnesota; and its members. 856 F. Supp. 1331* (Case No. 4-94-CV-448). Filed 8 Jul 1994.

6. Code of Federal Regulations. Title 21, Chapter 1—Food and Drug Administration, DHHS; Part 56—Institutional Review Boards. Updated 1 Apr 1999. Access date 25 Apr 2001. World Wide Web http://www4.law.cornell.edu/cfr/21p56.htm

Certificates of Confidentiality

Sandra P. Kaltman and John M. Isidor

INTRODUCTION

Although researchers generally do not disclose identifying information about subjects who participate in clinical research studies, there are circumstances under which investigators are required to make such disclosures. For example, if an investigator receives a valid subpoena from a court or administrative agency, he or she could be required to disclose records of a subject's participation in a study. Such records could include the subject's full name, address, and medical history.

In the 1970s, Congress realized that people were unwilling to participate in research involving certain sensitive issues, such as illegal drug use, unless their privacy was protected. This would mean that they could not be identified or possibly prosecuted as a result of participating in studies. As a result, Congress enacted a law allowing researchers to obtain certificates of confidentiality. These permitted them to protect the privacy of subjects by refusing to disclose their names or other identifying characteristics, even if asked to do so by courts or governmental agencies.[1] At least one court has upheld the validity of such certificates.[2]

How Do You Get a Certificate of Confidentiality?

Applications for federally funded research must be made to the agencies responsible for the funding. However, certificates of confidentiality are not limited to use in federally funded studies. The FDA accepts applications for certificates of confidentiality for research requiring an investigational new drug exemption.

Researchers may obtain certificates of confidentiality only if a determination is made that the research is of a sensitive nature and protection is necessary to reach the objectives of the research. The Office of Human Research Protections (OHRP) finds research to be sensitive if it involves collecting any of the following types of information:

1. Information relating to sexual attitudes, preferences, or practices

2. Information relating to the use of alcohol, drugs, or other addictive products

3. Information pertaining to illegal conduct

4. Information that, if released, could reasonably be damaging to an individual's financial standing, employability, or reputation in the community

5. Information that would normally be recorded in a patient's medical record, and the disclosure of which could reasonably lead to social stigmatization or discrimination

6. Information pertaining to an individual's psychological well being or mental health

7. Genetic information

Other agencies may evaluate applications using different criteria.

Limitations on Certificates of Confidentiality

The certificate of confidentiality does not apply to voluntary disclosure of identifying information by either a subject or an investigator. Therefore, even if a study is covered by a certificate of confidentiality, the subject may voluntarily disclose information about himself or herself. The investigator may also voluntarily disclose issues such as child abuse involving a subject or a subject's threats of violence to self or others. Subjects should be advised about the existence of a certificate of confidentiality and the exceptions to the protection it offers.

In addition, DHHS personnel may request identifying information for purposes of performing audits, carrying out investigations of DHHS grant recipients, or evaluating DHHS-funded research projects.[3]

Mechanics of Certificates of Confidentiality

Applications must be made for particular research projects. Once obtained, a certificate of confidentiality is not transferable from one study to another.[3] In addition, if there are major changes in the protocol, the personnel responsible for the study, or the drugs to be administered, the issuing agency must be notified by the submission of an amended application.[3]

Confidentiality certificates are effective from the date they are issued until the date of their termination. If the research will not be completed before the date the certificate expires, the recipient of the certificate must make a written application for an extension.[3]

Conclusion

Certificates of confidentiality can serve to promote recruitment in studies requiring disclosures of sensitive personal information, and IRBs can suggest that investigators apply for them when appropriate. The Web site of the OHRP contains a list of contacts at different agencies for information about obtaining certificates of confidentiality.[4] As long as a certificate is in place when a subject enrolls in a study, the protection provided by the certificate is permanent. Information identifying that subject will never be disclosed unless it is volunteered by the subject or investigator.[3]

References

1. 103rd Congress. Public Health Service Act (§301(d))—Title 42 US Code, 1 Jan 1994. Access date 25 Apr 2001. World Wide Web http://frwebgate2.access.gpo.gov/cgi-bin/waisgate.cgi?WAISdocID=2637221675+0+0+0&WAISaction=retrieve

2. Court of Appeals of New York. *People of the State of New York, Respondent, v. Robert Newman, Apellant.* (40 A D 2d 633, 672; 32 NY 2d 379; 298 NE2d 651; 1973 NY LEXIS 1211; 345 NYS2d 502). 23 Mar 1973. Reversed.

3. Code of Federal Regulations. Title 42, Chapter 1—Public Health Service, DHHS; Part 2A—Protection of Identity. Research Subjects. Updated 2001. World Wide Web http://www4.law.cornell.edu/cfr/42p2A.htm

4. Office of Human Research Protections. Certificates of confidentiality. Updated 2001. World Wide Web http://ohrp.osops.dhhs.gov/jan2001bu/humansubjects/guidance/cert-con.htm

Educating IRB Members

Jeffrey A. Cooper and Pamela Turner

INTRODUCTION

The Common Rule and FDA regulations require that an IRB "be sufficiently qualified through the experience and expertise of its members . . . to promote respect for its advice and counsel in safeguarding the rights and welfare of human subjects."[1][Sec.107(a)] Meeting this regulatory requirement requires initial and continuous training of IRB members. Institutions have been criticized for failing to provide training adequate to meet the needs of the IRB.

The IRB functions as a committee with a fund of communal knowledge. The regulatory requirement for IRB expertise applies to the entire IRB, not to each individual member. The regulations also note the requirement for experience, which in part can only be gained by serving on an IRB. Novice IRB members need to have a core understanding before participating in IRB functions, whereas more experienced members are expected to have a greater depth of knowledge. The regulations cited above also require that the IRB "shall be able to ascertain the acceptability of proposed research in terms of institutional commitments and regulations, applicable law, and standards of professional conduct and practice . . . if an IRB regularly reviews research that involves a vulnerable category of subjects, such as children, prisoners, pregnant women, or handicapped or mentally disabled persons, consideration shall be given to the inclusion of one or more individuals who are knowledgeable about and experienced in working with these subjects." Considering these requirements, three aspects of IRB-member training need to be considered: (1) core knowledge required of all IRB members, (2) in-depth knowledge required of experienced IRB members, and (3) specialized knowledge required by specific IRB members.

Training for Core Knowledge Required of All IRB Members

Before participation in IRB review, IRB members should have an understanding of basic ethical principles, the regulatory requirements, and the mechanics of serving on the IRB. IRB staff may provide new IRB members with an orientation, may link new IRB members with an experienced IRB member as a mentor, or both. Regardless of the training method, all new IRB members should be provided with basic reference materials. Sources for these materials are listed and some are reprinted in Chapter 11. All IRB members should receive and be familiar with a core list of guidance material. The following list should be modified to create a list of reference materials that matches the focus and scope of research reviewed by each IRB:

1. **Ethical Principles:** Nuremburg Code, Declaration of Helsinki, *The Belmont Report*
2. **Local Policies:** Federal-wide assurances, IRB bylaws, institutional policies relevant to research, IRB standard operating procedures, investigator's manual
3. **DHHS Documents:** 45 CFR 46 DHHS Regulations, NIH Policy on Inclusion of Women and Minorities, OPRR Report on Inclusion of Women and Minorities, NIH Policy on Inclusion of Children, OPRR Report on Inclusion of Children, OPRR Compliance Activities: Common Findings and Guidance, OHRP IRB Guidebook, Research That May Be Reviewed Through an Expedited Review Procedure
4. **FDA Documents:** 21 CFR 50 and 56 (Basic FDA Regulations), 21 CFR 312 (FDA Drug Regulations), 21 CFR 812 (FDA Device Regulations), 21 CFR 10, 310, 314, and 320, FDA Information Sheets, Significant Differences in FDA and DHHS Regulations for Protection of Human Subjects, Acute Care Waiver of Informed Consent reference, FDA Investigational Devices Exemption Manual
5. **Other Documents:** International Conference on Harmonisation Guidelines to Good Clinical Practice

At a minimum, all new IRB members should read *The Belmont Report* and be familiar with the basic applicable regulations governing the review of research by their IRB. Basic orientation can be conducted in one-on-one sessions, or by videotape, Web-based presentations, or other formats. IRBs may also find it useful to use review checklists to guide new or experienced members in the review process.

Training for In-Depth Knowledge Required of Experienced IRB Members

All IRB members should have in-depth knowledge of the history and ethics of human subject protections and the regulations governing research in human subjects. A list of recommended topics follows:

History and Ethics

1. Ethical decision making (ethical theory, ethical principles, ethical rules, deductive and case-based reasoning, conflict and incoherence)

2. History of research ethics (Nuremberg Code, Declaration of Helsinki, PHS policy, scandals such as the study of untreated syphilis in Negro men, The National Commission on Biomedical and Behavioral Research, *The Belmont Report*)

3. *Belmont* principles (beneficence, respect for persons, and justice and derivative rules)

4. Applying research ethics to protocol review

5. Investigator–subject relationship (primary responsibility of investigator to protect rights, welfare, and safety of subjects)

6. Investigator–staff relationship (use of team management to maximize protection of subjects)

7. Current events (deaths of research subjects, recent research studies with questionable ethical basis, federal shutdowns of research, "hot topics")

8. IRB decision-making (need for members to speak up and listen to minority views)

Regulations

1. DHHS regulations

2. FDA regulations

3. State and local regulations

Training Methods and Resources

IRB members can be provided with such training through a combination of resources. Less experienced members can be teamed with more experienced members in a mentor–trainee relationship. Information can be provided during a formal lecture series in an all-day session, distributed in small seg-

ments as part of each IRB meeting, or as part of a self-directed Web-based, computer-based, or video-based teaching program. Members can participate in mock IRB review of hypothetical cases or actual papers with ethical issues. Members can be provided with articles from the literature relevant to IRB review. These articles can commonly be found in journals devoted to research ethics such as *IRB: A Review of Human Subjects Research* published by the Hastings Center, and medical journals like the *New England Journal of Medicine,* the *Journal of the American Medical Association,* and the *British Medical Journal.* Over time, IRB members should be required to read all of the items in the reference materials.

Specialized Knowledge

Certain IRB members require specialized training. These members include the IRB Chair and vice-Chair, legal specialists, and advocates for populations served by the IRB such as prisoners, children, minority groups, non-English speaking subjects, etc. These individuals should develop and maintain expertise beyond that of experienced IRB members. This expertise can be maintained through participation in regional or national meetings, participation in national discussion groups such as The IRB Forum (formerly MCWIRB), and review of publications. Publications with relevant literature include governmental publications such as OHRP and FDA guidance, reports of the National Bioethics Advisory Commission, books, and peer-reviewed literature.

Conclusion

IRB committee members must be trained to effectively conduct review of human subject research and protect the rights and welfare of human subjects. IRBs should consider training each member, appropriate to his or her level of expertise and experience, as a novice, experienced, or specialized member. Such training requires a multi-pronged approach that emphasizes initial and continuous training of all members.

Reference

1. Code of Federal Regulations. Title 45A—Department of Health and Human Services; Part 46—Protection of Human Subjects. Updated 1 Oct 1997. Access date 18 Apr 2001. World Wide Web http://www4.law.cornell.edu/cfr/45p46.htm

Investigator Training

Jeffrey A. Cooper and Pamela Turner

INTRODUCTION

The need for investigator training has become more apparent over the past several years, as indicated in a 1998 report published by the Office of the Inspector General. Investigators were found to have inadequate knowledge of their responsibilities in human subject research. Rules, based on the ethical principles of *The Belmont Report*, have been developed to guide investigators conducting human subject research.[1] The basic principles of *Belmont* include beneficence, respect for persons, and justice. The principle of beneficence requires that competent investigators design ethical research, protect human subjects from risk, and make continuing assessments of the risk/benefit ratio. The principle of respect for persons requires that researchers carry out the process of informed consent and protect subject privacy. The current DHHS regulations[2(Sec.103)] imply the need for investigator training by requiring that institutions assure the protection of human subjects in part through having competent investigators. Under FDA regulations,[3(Sec.50)] sponsors are responsible for selecting qualified investigators and providing them with the information they need to conduct an investigation properly. However, there has been no uniform definition of the term *qualified,* and the process by which sponsors select and train investigators is highly variable. Because of the significance of the investigator's role in protecting human subjects, all IRBs are obligated to ensure that investigators conducting a research study are qualified to conduct the study, to uphold *Belmont* principles, and ensure compliance with the regulations and the requirements of the IRB in the approved protocol. The IRB may or may not need to conduct the actual training; however, in the current environment, investigator training commonly falls to the IRB. In this chapter, we will outline the goals of training, discuss the methods available for training, summarize available resources, and provide information on how to implement investigator training.

Goals of Investigator Training

The ultimate goal of investigator training is to impart knowledge and understanding to an investigator that will result in behavior that protects the rights and welfare of research subjects. Proper training requires that investigators master four main objectives: (1) understand and apply the ethical principles underlying research; (2) put the rights, welfare, and safety of each individual enrolled in the research ahead of their professional, academic, financial, personal, or other interests; (3) meet organizational requirements and comply with all applicable federal, state, and local regulations; and (4) responsibly manage personnel involved in the research.

Understand and Apply the Ethical Principles Underlying Research

The *Belmont* principles form the basis for the protection of human subjects of research.[1] The first objective states that investigators should understand and apply these basic principles in research. Investigators should know what is involved within the study of ethics and see the ethical conduct of research as a virtue. They should be able to (a) carry out principle-based and case-based ethical decision-making; (b) examine conflict and incoherence in research; (c) know the history leading to the formulation of the principles; (d) understand the relationship between the regulations and *Belmont* principles; and (e) apply those principles to protocol design and day-to-day practice of research.

Investigators should also be knowledgeable about recent history regarding subject deaths in research and unethical research.

Put the Rights, Welfare, and Safety of Each Individual Enrolled in the Research Ahead of Professional, Academic, Financial, Personal, or Other Interests

This is a corollary of the *Belmont* principle of beneficence and is described by some ethicists as a "moral fiduciary relationship."[4] Many investigators mistakenly consider their primary goal to be the execution of the protocol rather than the protection of their subjects. This objective identifies the need to manage conflict of interest and is required to maintain trust between investigators and subjects. We emphasize this objective because it has been neglected in the past.

Meet Organizational Requirements and Comply with All Applicable Federal, State, and Local Regulations

As part of this objective, IRBs should train investigators to do the following:

1. Design ethical research
2. Comply with federal regulations
3. Obtain prior IRB approval
4. Comply with IRB requirements
5. Implement approved research and obtain prior approval for modifications before implementing the change
6. Obtain and document informed consent/assent
7. Submit progress reports
8. Report unanticipated problems, injuries, and events
9. Retain records for required intervals

These obligations should be combined with other elements of appropriate data collection, documentation, and monitoring subsumed under the body of knowledge commonly referred to as "good clinical practice."

Responsibly Manage Personnel Involved in the Research

This objective requires that investigators understand that they are the leaders of a team of individuals responsible for the conduct of research. Investigators should ensure that the staff understands and acts according to the ethical principles governing research. As a team, it is paramount that they protect the rights and safety of research subjects, and know and follow the policies and laws governing research. Investigators should ensure that the research team has adequate resources to carry out the research and that all personnel function as a team to ensure subject protection and regulatory compliance.

The issue of team management in research is important, yet often overlooked. We and several other IRB administrators have found that many noncompliance investigations uncover a participant in the research, usually a research coordinator, who recognized the noncompliance issue, brought the information forward to the investigator, and was either brushed off or incorrectly assured that procedures were compliant. This is a well described psychological phenomenon known as the "response to authority" described in the ethically infamous Milgram Studies.[5] In the Milgram Studies, a principal investigator coaxed a participant to administer lethal electric shocks to a research subject, who was actually a member of the research staff (a confederate). Approximately two thirds of the participants delivered what they believed to be potentially lethal shocks to the confederate subject.

These authority relationships are common in research. They do not imply an authoritarian nature in the investigator, but rather an authoritative nature, or someone who is a respected leader with superior knowledge whom the staff looks to for guidance. The airline industry recognized in the mid 1980s that the authority position of the captain of the flight crew interfered with the functioning of the flight crew as a team to protect passenger safety. The airline responded with the implementation of crew training in "crew resource management."[6] This program is in part responsible for the dramatic improvement in airline safety in the past 15 years. The lessons of this program should be applied to the management of the research team and the leadership skills of investigators.

Training Methods

IRBs often view investigator training as an educational process wherein investigators gain knowledge from didactic teaching methods such as lectures, books, or computer-based training. However, this approach often overlooks two important issues. First, the goal of training should be to influence investigator behavior. In fact, the fundamental question of research ethics is "How ought researchers to behave?" Second, it is important to recognize that when it comes to professionals, education is often a relatively ineffective way to influence behavior. Therefore, in designing a training program, IRBs should consider a portfolio approach to improving investigator behavior and use multiple methods rather than relying on one particular method. There are five main methods for changing the behavior of professionals: performance feedback, rewards and penalties, participation in improving the process, administrative rules, and education. These methods are listed and discussed in decreasing order of effectiveness.[7]

Performance Feedback

The most effective way to influence a professional's behavior is through performance feedback. Auditing and monitoring are two methods of performance feedback commonly used by industry. We have implemented auditing and monitoring through a research quality assurance unit separate from the IRB. This separates the deliberative role of the IRB from its investigative functions, which may be perceived by investigators as intrusive. Auditing and monitoring are most effective when conducted as a collaborative learning experience. Generally, investigators want to be ethical and compliant, but often lack the objectivity to see their own shortcomings. When specific actions of noncompliance are pointed out and suggestions made for improvement of research operations, investigators are often very responsive.

Another form of performance feedback is to use monitored role-playing and problem-solving with group discussion, self-criticism, and feedback. This is the main method used for teaching crew resource management to commercial airline flight crews. Adding peer-based comparisons to performance feedback is often extremely helpful. Most investigators have a natural desire to excel, and when presented with data that show other investigators that have better outcomes, they often become highly motivated to improve their own practice. Peer-based feedback should be anonymous to protect the privacy of investigators.

Rewards and Penalties

The second most effective form of modifying investigator behavior is the use of administrative rewards and penalties. Recent FDA and OHRP shutdowns of research represent an administrative penalty that has probably been a major influence on changing investigator behavior in the past two years. The IRB's ability to bestow the right to conduct human subject research represents a powerful reward for investigators to participate in other training projects.

Participation in Improving the Process

The third most effective form of modifying investigator behavior is to involve investigators in improving the research process. To ensure built-in acceptance, whenever possible, encourage the input of investigators when planning any training program. They will often have specific needs, such as flexibility, or specific educational goals that can be accommodated in the design of the program.

Administrative Rules

Administrative rules, the mainstay of most IRB programs, do influence investigator behavior. Federal regulations, combined with local institutional policy, form the mainstay of these rules. Specific rules can be helpful in situations where issues of judgment or regulatory clarity arise. For example, institutions often develop administrative rules to determine what type of research is exempt from regulation or for prior clearance of emergency research, even though it is not required by regulation. Because investigators have different levels of knowledge, this is generally done to assure regulatory compliance. Institutions also will develop administrative rules for reporting adverse events because of the inconsistency and difficulty in interpreting various regulations. These administrative rules change behavior without the need to impart a high degree of knowledge and understanding on the part of investigators.

Education

Education represents the least effective method for changing physician behavior. Nonetheless, in many cases, education remains unavoidable in an effective training program. Investigators should have a core knowledge learned before conducting research. Even the implementation of administrative rules requires education to communicate the rules to all affected investigators.

Resources for Training

Numerous resources are currently available for training. These include books,[8] Web-based training programs,[9] computer-based training programs,[10] lecture programs,[10] and independent consultants.[11,12] Each of these may need some customization to the needs of each IRB or institution. Most of these resources are educational, although independent consultants can provide help with perform-

ance feedback and establishing administrative rewards and punishments. The exact resources required will depend on an assessment of the internal strengths and weaknesses of each institution.

How to Implement Investigator Training

Successful implementation of an investigator training program requires more than having effective methods that lead to the desired behavioral objectives. For most investigators, the implementation of the training program represents a change from previous methods of doing business. Many investigators believe they are too busy for further training, or they think they do not need it because they already have the knowledge required to conduct research. To change the mindset of these investigators requires understanding the principles of change management.[13] Effective change management involves three main steps. These steps will be required to implement a training program for research investigators.

Principles of Change Management

1. **Where and Why?** Create a compelling vision for the training program. Where will the training program lead? Why is it imperative that the training program be undertaken?

2. **Who and What?** Whom will the training program involve? What are the options for implementing the training program, and what are the preferences of the investigators?

3. **How and When?** What are the mechanics of the program? How will the training be conducted? What is the timeline for implementation?

Each step is best implemented with aggressive and repeated communication with investigators. We found that small, frequent "town meetings" with investigators in which a 10-minute presentation was made, followed by questions and answers, were very effective. The presentation was designed to explain the "where and why" of mandatory investigator training. The presentation explained the system of federal regulation of research, reviewed the recent enforcement actions of the DHHS and the FDA, explained our current training program, and emphasized that improved training was now an obligation of our DHHS assurance. We also acknowledged the negative perceptions of investigators and responded in order to minimize the impact of those negatives.

Investigators' Negative Perceptions of Training

1. **Unnecessary for Me.** We respond to the perception that training is "unnecessary for me" by emphasizing that the training actually is useful for every investigator.

2. **Not Enough Time.** Some investigators say that they do not have enough time to fulfill training requirements. We explain that training can be accomplished with a flexible time commitment.

3. **Unfunded Mandate.** Institutional officials and investigators may be concerned that ethical training is an unfunded mandate by the federal government. We explain that the recommended training program is inexpensive.

4. **Evaluations Are Unfair.** Investigators may be concerned that the focus of the training program or the evaluation of their performance in the training program is unfair. We respond that it is a self-directed training program that allows each investigator to focus on the areas that he or she is deficient in and to track progress personally.

Investigators' Positive Feedback

The town meetings were also an opportunity to explain to investigators the types of training programs initiated by other institutions, the options available to our institution, and to solicit feedback from investigators. This began the process of determining the "who and how" in step 2. Several positive suggestions came out of those meetings and influenced the structure of the final program. For example, based on investigator suggestions we applied for and received Category 1 AMA continuing education credit. Several investigators believed it was unfair to have to undergo training that would not be required of IRB members; in response, we asked IRB members to undergo the same training.

Notification of Investigators

Once investigators are on board and accept the need for training and the method of training, final details need to be communicated clearly regarding the "how and when" step. We sent several direct communications to investigators; we also posted announcements in the medical center's weekly one page newsletter. This step is important to minimize the number of investigators who claim they were never notified about the training program or the implications associated with not completing the program.

Result of Change Program

In the end, our change program was very successful. We received many compliments from investigators about establishing a program that helped to educate them about the conduct of human subject research. The program has also increased the number of inquiries to the research office regarding regulatory compliance.

Conclusion

IRBs are now under a clear mandate from federal regulators to provide investigator training. Training currently focuses on education, but IRBs need to understand that the goal of training must be about behavior rather than just knowledge. Education is the least effective method to improve the behavior of investigators. IRBs have many resources available to them to accomplish training. However, IRBs should also understand that the greatest impediment to an effective training program is resistance on the part of investigators. They have to apply change management techniques in order to maximize the success of current and future training programs.

References

1. National Commission for the Protection of Human Subjects of Biomedical and Behavioral Research. *The Belmont Report: Ethical principles and guidelines for the protection of human subjects of research,* 18 Apr 1979. Access date 22 Mar 2001. World Wide Web http://ohsr.od.nih.gov/mpa/belmont.php3

2. Code of Federal Regulations. Title 45A—Department of Health and Human Services; Part 46—Protection of Human Subjects. Updated 1 Oct 1997. Access date 18 Apr 2001. World Wide Web http://www4.law.cornell.edu/cfr/45p46.htm

3. Code of Federal Regulations. Title 21, Chapter 1—Food and Drug Administration, DHHS; Part 312—Investigational New Drug Application. Updated 1 Apr 1999. Access date 18 Apr 2001. World Wide Web http://www4.law.cornell.edu/cfr/21p312.htm

4. McCullough L B John Gregory (1724–1773) and the intervention of professional relationships in medicine. *J Clin Ethics* 8(1):11–21, 1997.

5. Milgram S. *Obedience to Authority.* New York, NY: Harper Collins Publishers. 1983.

6. Industry Crew Resource Management. (CRM) Developers Group Web site, 2000. Access date 16 Apr 2001. World Wide Web http://www.crm-devel.org/

7. Greco P J, Eisenberg J M Changing physicians' practices. *N Engl J Med* 329(17):1271–1273, 1993.

8. Dunn C M, Chadwick G. *Protecting Study Volunteers in Research: A Manual for Investigative Sites.* Boston: CenterWatch Inc. 1999.

9. The Collaborative IRB Training Initiative (CITI) and The University of Miami. The Human Subjects Research Education Registration. Access date 16 Apr 2001. World Wide Web http://www.miami.edu/UMH/CDA/UMH_Main/1,1770,4706-3,00.html

10. IRB 101 and Investigator 101 Training Programs. Boston, MA, Public Responsibility in Medicine and Research, 1999. Access date 17 Apr 2001. World Wide Web http://www.uic.edu/depts/ovcr/oprs/Education/policy.html

11. Impact Consulting Group. Access date 17 Apr 2001. World Wide Web http://www.impactcg.com/info/pres.htm

12. Price-Waterhouse-Cooper. Access date 16 Apr 2001. World Wide Web http://www.pricewaterhouse.com/

13. O'Connor E J, Fiol C M A road map for leading change: Energizers, barriers, and action steps. *Culture Clash.* Chicago, Ill.: American Hospital Publishing, Inc. 1997.

Accreditation of an IRB

Susan S. Fish

INTRODUCTION

The ethics organization Public Responsibility in Medicine and Research (PRIM&R) has committed to developing a voluntary accreditation system to assess the protection of human subjects in research. To accomplish this task, an independent organization, the Association for the Accreditation of Human Research Protection Programs (AAHRPP), has been formed and incorporated. This chapter will discuss the history and reasons for accreditation in the human subjects protection field, describe the current status of AAHRPP and accreditation, describe plans for the future, and discuss the implications for IRBs.

Background

Although protection of human subjects has been a keystone of clinical research for the past 50 years, thoughts of accreditation are just now reaching maturity. However, there have been calls for accreditation for more than 20 years. In 1978, the National Commission for the Protection of Human Subjects of Biomedical and Behavioral Research did more than issue *The Belmont Report* that gives us our ethical underpinnings for the conduct of clinical research. In their report, they also mentioned concern about requirements for the review of federally funded studies and the lack of requirements for review of all other studies. Such a double standard might suggest that IRBs are important only for meeting federal requirements rather than because of the nature of their work. Concerned about this apparent double standard, the National Commission in 1978 recommended that a program of peer-based site visits be undertaken.[1] They concluded that a full assessment of an IRB should be based on an examination of that IRB's performance in its particular institutional context and with its particular workload, membership, and procedures. The National Commission disbanded after its report was issued, and the President's Commission for the Study of Ethical Problems in Medicine and Biomedical and Behavioral Research was appointed. In 1981, the President's Commission decided to explore the possible benefits of IRB site visits to assess the qualitative aspects of the functioning of IRBs, suggesting that the site visits would be collegial and more educational in orientation than is typical of inspections or investigations. Two years later, the 1983 President's Commission Report included a chapter describing a study of IRBs, with the data having been gathered through peer-based site visits.[2] The report stated that site visits and a review process stimulate improvements at the institutional level. The Commission's site visitors were oriented more toward the goals and purposes of IRB review than toward technical conformity with regulatory requirements. The report then spent 12 pages discussing an accreditation model—in 1983, almost 20 years ago!

The Need for Accreditation

More recent reports from the General Accounting Office and the Inspector General's Office have also contained references to accreditation. The General Accounting Office in its 1996 report, *Scientific Research: Continued Vigilance Critical to Protecting Human Subjects,* stated that "little data exists that directly measures the effectiveness of human subject protection regulations." Thus, they suggested that protection of human subjects might be more than simply abiding by the regulations.[3] The Office of the Inspector General in 1998 issued a report entitled *IRBs— A Time for Reform* that recommended all IRBs under the purview of NIH or OPRR (now OHRP) and the FDA undergo regular performance-based evaluations. In addition, the evaluations were to be carried out in accord with the federal regulations.[4]

The lay press has had an equally important effect, continuing to highlight research activities as it has been doing for the past 20 or 30 years. For example, the cover story in the October 11, 1999, issue of the magazine *U.S. News and World Report* describes studies showing what appears to be a lack of informed consent by patients enrolled in cancer trials. This type of coverage in the lay press adds to the deterioration of the public's confidence and trust in the research effort. We must assure the public that their rights and welfare as research subjects are being protected, while we further the development of new diagnostic and therapeutic approaches to disease.

An Accreditation System

After more than 20 years of recommendations, why is now the right time? First, the protection of human subjects has become a profession over the past 25 or so years. Public Responsibility in Medicine and Research (PRIM&R) is almost 27 years old, and Applied Research Ethics National Association (ARENA) is about 17 years old. ARENA has developed a certification program for IRB professionals. Second, research has become more complex, and thus it is more difficult to review studies and more difficult to design studies with risks minimized. In addition, it is more difficult to explain such complex studies to potential participants and, thus, more difficult for us to protect human subjects. Third, the patient empowerment movement has dramatically changed research. This movement is led mostly by HIV and cancer patient groups, and in some situations, subjects have become more like research partners than traditional research subjects. Finally, George Lundberg, the previous editor of *JAMA,* suggested "self-governance prevents legislation." There is some suggestion that if we within the profession do not move forward on accreditation, then Congress may legislate such activities. For all of these reasons, and in order to help restore the trust of the public in the research effort, now is the right time to develop an accreditation system for programs of protection of human research subjects.

The Accreditation Program

To implement the accreditation program, a new organization, the Association for the Accreditation of Human Research Protection Programs (AAHRPP) has been incorporated. The mission of AAHRPP is "to provide a process of voluntary peer review and education among organizations concerned with research involving humans, in order to promote preservation of the rights and welfare of subjects in research and compliance with relevant ethical and regulatory standards."[5]

Because there are at least three points in the research process where human subjects can be protected, the accreditation process will focus on all three points. Those points are in the design of the study to assure that risks are minimized; in the IRB review process, particularly of the consent form; and finally in the consent process itself. In addition, to encourage protection of human subjects, this must be an important value within the organizational or institutional culture. Thus, accreditation will encompass not just IRBs but "human research protection programs," which include the institution or organization, the IRB, and the investigators.

The accreditation process will consist of a self-assessment step and a peer-review site visit step. These site visits will be educational, using a collegial rather than punitive approach. This collegial approach is intended to encourage sharing of solutions to the challenges many IRBs and human subject protection programs face. Both the self-assessment and the site visit may use a set of performance standards that will look beyond the federal regulations, using them as a base and moving on to describe best practice. The performance standards will provide guidance to institutions that seek to meet contemporary standards of research ethics and federal oversight. Programs of human research protection will use the performance standards to self-assess their programs, and AAHRPP reviewers will use the same standards to perform site-visit assessments. The standards will address the fundamental structure and processes of the program and provide goals for targeted intervention to address deficiencies identified either by self-assessment or by the outside reviewers.

Performance Standards

Performance standards have been developed by PRIM&R, under contract from the National Academy of Sciences' Institute of Medicine. Although not yet final, they will cover areas that affect the protection of human subjects in research. There will be standards addressing the institution, the IRB, and the investigators. The standards will examine the institution's culture, the position of the IRB within the institution, and the value of protecting human subjects within that institution or organization. Obviously, there will be a number of standards to assess many aspects of IRBs. In addition, standards will look at the education and actions of investigators, IRB members, and staff as demonstrated by their knowledge and their behaviors. The performance standards will include those that are generally applicable to all human subject protection programs and may include some that are narrowly applicable to particular areas of research. Some of the criteria will include outcome measures to be used, similar to a continuous quality improvement system, which would be customized to the needs of each program.

Site Visits

Along with self-assessment, site visits will be conducted by trained site visiting teams composed of members of the IRB community, the research community, and others. The site visits will be conducted as an educational tool rather than as an audit. The length of the site visit will vary depending on the issues to be reviewed and the size and complexity of the facility's program of human research protections. The number of site visitors will also depend on the complexity of issues to be reviewed, type of research conducted at the institution, location of the institution, and size of the human subject protection program.

One goal of the AAHRPP site visit is to collect qualitative as well as quantitative data on the functioning of the human subject protection program. Another goal is to provide useful guidance on how to improve the program.

Exit Interview

At the conclusion of the site visit, the team will conduct an exit briefing with the institutional official and other appropriate personnel to provide the program with early feedback of preliminary findings and impressions. Based on the findings of the site visit, appropriate referrals to educational resources will be made by site visitors.

After the exit interview, the site visit team will prepare a site visit report. This report will summarize the program's strengths and weaknesses and present the team's findings, as well as their recommendation on conferring accreditation. Reports will be submitted to the Committee on Accreditation by the site-visit team. The Committee will determine its recommendation concerning accreditation and will then forward its recommendation to the Board, which will issue its decision on accreditation. The Board of Directors will make all final decisions on accreditation status and will serve as an appeals board when necessary. AAHRPP will provide a final report to the institutional official, and if the institution is accredited, a certificate will follow. The current plan is for accreditation to be valid for three years.

Implementation of Accreditation Program

To implement this accreditation program, AAHRPP has been developed as an independent, nonprofit organization. The AAHRPP Board of Directors is responsible for all of the activities of AAHRPP. An Advisory Committee will include a variety of stakeholders, including professional organizations and patient advocacy groups, all of which are concerned with clinical research and the protection of human subjects. An Executive Director will be responsible for overseeing the work of two important working committees. The Committee on Accreditation, which will be made up of the site visitors, will make recommendations to the Board of Directors concerning the accreditation of applicant programs. The Committee on Revisions will look continuously at the performance standards and assess which ones need to be revised and where we need new standards.

The Future

At the time of this writing, the performance standards are in development. Once final, the standards will be pilot tested to make sure that they have relevance in the real world. There will be a small but varied set of pilot sites representing the diversity of IRBs and programs in the United States that are willing to participate in this pilot testing. This will lead to another revision of the standards. The Institute of Medicine is expected to issue a final set of performance standards. The accreditation system will begin in full force once a set of performance standards is approved, site visitors are trained, and AAHRPP staff is in place.

Conclusion

By developing a set of performance standards and making these available to IRBs and human subject protection programs, the intent of the AAHRPP is to help IRBs do what they do better. The accreditation process is voluntary. An IRB, in conjunction with its institution and its researchers (its human subject protection program), will have access to these performance standards. Self-assessment alone will be a useful exercise and will provide a framework to allow IRBs to determine where their strengths and weaknesses lie. If an IRB's self-assessment is a positive one, it may decide that its program should apply for accreditation. The subsequent site visit will provide peer review and potential external validation of the self-assessment. In addition, the site visit will provide an outside source of new ideas for improvement and referral to other resources. If accredited, the IRB and its human research protection program can be identified to others as going beyond the federal regulations in protecting the rights and welfare of research subjects. It is hoped that this process of review—both self-assessment and peer review—will help to assure that the institutional value of protection of human subjects is instilled by the institutional official into all researchers and research staff. In addition, the IRB will have external, objective support for justifying the resources it needs to perform its important work.

References

1. National Commission for the Protection of Human Subjects of Biomedical and Behavioral Research. *The Belmont Report: Ethical Principles and Guidelines for the Protection of Human Subjects of Research,* 18 Apr 1979. Access date 22 Mar 2001. World Wide Web http://ohsr.od.nih.gov/mpa/belmont.php3

2. President's Commission for the Study of Ethical Problems in Medicine and Biomedical and Behavioral Research. *Implementing Human Research Regulations: Second Biennial Report on the Adequacy and Uniformity of Federal Rules and Policies, and of Their Implementation, for the Protection of Human Subjects.* Mar 1983.

3. General Accounting Office. *Scientific Research: Continued Vigilance Critical to Protecting Human Subjects.* GAO/HEHS-96-72. Mar 1996.

4. Office of Inspector General. *Institutional Review Boards: A Time for Reform* (OEI-01-97-00193). Dept of Health and Human Services, June 1998. Access date 27 Mar 2001. World Wide Web http://www.dhhs.gov/progorg/oei/reportindex.html

5. Public Responsibility in Medicine and Research. *What is AAHRPP (Association for the Accreditation of Human Research Protection Programs)?* Updated 13 Sep 2001. Access date 24 Sep 2001. World Wide Web http://www.primr.org/aahrpp.html

Certification of IRB Professionals

Susan J. Delano, Sallyann Henry, and Gary L. Chadwick

INTRODUCTION

Certification is one part of a process called *credentialing*. It focuses on the individual and is an indication of that individual's current proficiency in a specialized field. It is a formal recognition that an individual has met the professional experience requirements and demonstrated understanding of a specific body of knowledge at a level sufficient to meet established standards. Certification is usually granted by a professional group and is a form of peer recognition rather than registration or licensure, which are legally mandated. Certification is not, however, an endorsement of particular individuals by the professional group, nor is it a guarantee of qualification to do a particular job.

Certification of persons who conduct research and are responsible for its review and monitoring have been discussed and supported at the national level by groups including the National Bioethics Advisory Commission.[1] In addition to Institutional Review Board (IRB) professionals, research administrators and research monitors have well established certification programs. Certification is increasingly being recognized as an important part of an effective human subjects protection program.

What Are the Benefits of Certification?

National certification of professionals involved in research assists the public, legislators, and sponsors by offering a standard for professional practice. It helps assure adherence to regulatory requirements, good clinical practices, and ethical principles.

For the individual, certification can provide a sense of professional accomplishment, enhancement of professional standing, and peer recognition. It identifies the individual as possessing technical expertise and demonstrates a commitment to professionalism. Certification may also serve as a valuable career tool by confirming value to current employers and by making one's resume more appealing to a prospective employer. In addition to personal satisfaction, national certification enhances the employer's program and recognition for support of professional programs.

For a profession, certification can help to raise competency through the education and training in which individuals participate while preparing for initial testing and for recertification. It can also help set national standards of performance within the profession by analyzing the functions performed by professionals in the field, creating a "body of knowledge" based on these functions, and setting expectations for proficiency.

How a Certification Program Is Developed

In the early stages of a credentialing process, many issues must be addressed, including who are the people that should be credentialed, what experience and qualifications are required, and what methods of credentialing and recredentialing will be used. Examinations can provide an objective measure of candidates' knowledge. Creating a valid examination process that will be respected by those in the profession and also by the community they serve is complex and includes a number of important steps.

Administrative details also require attention. Information about the test, including the required body of knowledge and test application forms, have to be distributed. Applications and fees must be processed and checked. Testing centers must be identified and carefully supervised. Processes for scoring examinations, retaining records, and reporting results to candidates have to be developed.

The following is a description of an approach that has been used by diverse professional groups across the country. Among the groups that have applied this process is the Applied Research Ethics National Association (ARENA) in its development of the Certified IRB Professional (CIP) program. The CIP program is designed for individuals who have experience participating in and overseeing the daily activities associated with an IRB.

1. The first step in the process is the establishment of a credentialing board or council to oversee and develop the credentialing program. Typically six to 10 experienced practitioners from different locations and with different areas of specialization are chosen. This council may then collaborate with a testing company to provide professional and technical assistance. The council develops examinations from a pool of test items, which are also developed under the authority of the council. Ongoing meetings are required for test development and maintenance.

2. Second, it is necessary to develop the body of knowledge essential to competent practice and practitioner roles and functions. The council develops this outline of the knowledge based on the skills and abilities needed for competent performance.

3. Based on the body of knowledge, the content to be covered in the examination is identified, and the council establishes the emphasis or weight to be assigned to each section.

4. The format of the examination is chosen. For examinations given over a period of only a few hours, the most practical and efficient format for determining competence is multiple-choice. This allows a wide coverage of content in the time allowable, thus increasing the reliability of the resultant measurement.

5. Preliminary examination questions are written by a broad group of practitioners to ensure input by persons with different levels of expertise, background, and specialization and from different geographic locations. Included in this group are experienced practitioners who are most likely to be familiar with appropriate practices as well as common misconceptions.

6. Test-item development is an ongoing activity with new items continually required to ensure currency and the quality of examinations. Questions are designed to test candidates' understanding of the concepts and principles as well as their application to the profession.

7. To help ensure validity, test questions should be edited by psychometric specialists. In this process, items are revised to make them conform to testing standards; spelling and use of standard abbreviations are checked. Grammatical correctness and conciseness of presentation are reviewed so that each item tests for knowledge and application of content, not for reading skills.

8. Test questions are then subject to item review by small groups of six to eight certified practitioners from different regions of the country. One or two members of the council also attend. In the item review sessions, each question is considered to assess its accuracy, the correctness of the designated right answer, the incorrectness of the other answers (called distracters), and the clarity of the meaning of the question. Most importantly, the item review group evaluates whether each question deals with something that is directly relevant to the practice of the profession. Items are also coded in relation to the body of knowledge. This information is used to ensure that the appropriate number of questions is assigned to each content area based on the weights determined by the council.

9. Items that survive the item-review process are then placed in an item bank. As items are used in examinations, statistics regarding the performance of the item are developed. These include the date used, percentage of high-scoring candidates answering correctly, and percentage of low-scoring candidates answering correctly.

10. An examination based on the weighting of the content areas is developed using items that have gone through the item-review process. Some items that have never been used before are included with items that have been used in prior examinations. The draft examination is reviewed by the council. All items are again reviewed to ensure that they are currently relevant and appropriate. The overall content of the examination is reviewed to ensure that it covers the material specified in the body of knowledge.

11. At the time the council reviews the draft test, the standards for passing the examination are discussed and set. Established approaches to setting passing scores are used. A passing score is established based on sound psychometric practice and theory; it is realistic and appropriate in terms of setting standards for evaluating the knowledge required for competent practice.

12. Test security is a vitally important consideration. Security encompasses many issues including the item bank, printed test booklets, and all item materials provided to item reviewers and council members. A professional testing company can greatly assist in this endeavor.

13. Standards for recertification by examination, continuing education, or some combination of these also must be established by the council and made known to the profession.

How Do You Prepare for the Certification Examination?

As with any examination, awareness of the content areas that will be covered is essential. The certifying organization provides a handbook for candidates that includes the body of knowledge that will be covered and suggested references. For the CIP exam, it may be helpful to begin your review with basic regulatory documents and federal guidance documents. Other standard references and texts that are usually found in the IRB library and Internet sources can be very useful. References that provide background and context to the subject area should be reviewed. For example, for IRB professionals, the history and the development of codes of ethics for human subjects research provide important background. Of course, consultation with professionals who are currently certified can be helpful for advice on how to prepare.

Conclusion

A defining characteristic of a profession is a system of credentialing that indicates proficiency in a specialized field. The administration of an IRB has now reached a level of complexity and sophistication that it is necessary and appropriate to have a meaningful certification process to establish the credentials of an IRB professional. This chapter describes the general characteristics of a credentialing process and the details of the process that is currently used by the ARENA CIP program. Completing a high-quality credentialing program ensures that IRB professionals will share a core body of knowledge in a way that will improve the protection of research participants and facilitate productive interaction between all segments of the IRB community.

Reference

1. National Bioethics Advisory Commission. *Ethical and Policy Issues in Research Involving Human Participants*. Draft report. Bethesda, MD, U.S. Government Printing Office, 19 Dec 2000. Access date 20 Mar 2001. World Wide Web http://bioethics.gov

Preparing for an FDA Audit

Gary L. Chadwick

INTRODUCTION

The focus of this chapter is on Food and Drug Administration (FDA) inspections. The FDA has a program of routine audits for IRBs, so IRBs are more likely to experience an FDA audit than one from other agencies. However, there are commonalities between audits whether they are conducted by the FDA, the National Cancer Institute (NCI), the Joint Commission on Accreditation of Health Care Organizations (JCAHO), or any other entity.

Inspections by regulatory agencies do tend to be more stressful and do not have the primary intent to be educational, although one can always learn from them. Audits from sponsors tend to be more collegial and focus on ensuring that all the necessary documentation is in place and that required procedures are being followed.

The Audit Process

The FDA conducts audits of research studies to determine compliance with regulations and to verify the integrity of the data. Audits of IRBs are intended to determine compliance with the human-subject protection regulations. The Bioresearch Monitoring Program of the FDA is charged with conducting audits. Inspections are assigned by the Center for Drug Evaluation and Research (CDER), the Center for Biologics Evaluation and Research (CBER), or the Center for Devices and Radiological Health (CDRH). Assignments to inspect IRBs are made for routine surveillance, for follow-up of complaints or concerns, and as part of the approval process when new products are submitted for approval. The actual audit is generally conducted by one or more field personnel from the local district office. Sometimes, experts from FDA headquarters will accompany the field inspectors.

Ongoing Preparations

If the first time you have thought about an audit is when the inspector calls and says he or she is arriving tomorrow, it may already be too late. Preparedness and readiness are valuable military concepts that apply to audits, and they are the key to a good outcome. A phrase that you may hear at health care facilities is "survey-ready every day," referring to JCAHO audits. Because this phrase indicates that your policies and procedures are in order, an audit is likely to show that you are operating correctly and that no major problems exist. It is toward this state of continual readiness that research institutions should strive.

Conduct Internal Audits

A good way to assess readiness for an external audit is to conduct self-audits looking at the same areas. The FDA has published a useful checklist in the FDA Information Sheets[1] that can be used for this purpose (available from the FDA Web site). Targeted audits are very helpful, especially if you think you may have vulnerability in specific areas. It is always better to find something wrong yourself and fix it than to have someone else find it and put it in a report as a deficiency. A random audit of files to ensure completeness and availability for review is a good routine check. When conducting self-audits, always document the audit activity both in the files reviewed and in a final report. This is true even if you find things wrong. The report should state what you have done, are doing, or are recommending to correct the problem. The report should be a useful tool both for the IRB and for the institutional officials who have responsibility for the IRB. Again, it is better to try to fix the system and improve it than to ignore problems and hope for the best.

Review FDA and OHRP Letters to Other Institutions

One of the best things you can do to anticipate inspection findings is to get copies of warning letters issued to other facilities. These letters are available to the public on the FDA's Web page.[2] These letters contain guidance about what needs to be in place and operating at your facility if it is to be "in compliance" with regulations. These letters also show what types of deficiencies are of concern. The Office for Human Research Protections (OHRP) also displays letters and cited deficiencies on its Web page.[3]

Maintain Adequate IRB Staffing

One of the major keys to a successful audit is adequate IRB staffing. The IRB function requires sufficient numbers of qualified personnel so that the review process operates in compliance, the necessary documentation is maintained, and the research is adequately tracked through the review cycle. One of the major root causes for failure to pass an IRB audit is lack of staff and/or lack of qualified staff.

Keep Records Up to Date

IRB records and documents should always be kept up to date, especially IRB written procedures. The written procedure manual is the key document that the FDA will review to assess the operation of the IRB. The FDA expects this document to describe how the institution complies with the regulations. Therefore, your written procedures along with the federal regulations will drive the inspection. The written procedures should be reviewed annually and must be updated as procedures and policies change. A revision log page or at least a record of the revision dates on the title page is recommended. Again, this shows that you are keeping current and in control of your program.

Notification and Preparation for Audit

What do you do when the FDA notifies you that it wants to conduct an inspection? Although the FDA may conduct an unannounced IRB inspection, usually they notify the institution by telephone in advance. By law, the FDA has the right to inspect at reasonable times with reasonable notice. For IRBs, reasonable notice is generally two to three days. Clinical investigators often get a week's notice because the FDA does not expect that the investigator's office will be staffed and organized at the same level as is an administrative office such as the IRB.

FDA field inspectors will try to accommodate legitimate requests to postpone an audit (for example, if the IRB Chair and administrator are both away at a training conference). Usually, only a couple of days' reprieve is acceptable. Beyond that, suspicions are raised. The FDA inspector also has deadlines and work plans that must be accomplished.

Ask About Special Materials and Contact Numbers

After you confirm when the inspection will start (day and hour), ask how long the audit is anticipated to take so that you can make appropriate arrangements. It is also a good idea to ask if there are any special materials or specific files the inspectors would like to have available. Be sure to obtain the telephone number of the inspector, in case it becomes necessary to contact him or her, before the audit starts.

Alert Appropriate Institutional Authorities

As soon as possible after the FDA inspector's call, you should alert the appropriate institutional authorities. Obviously, other IRB office staff, the IRB Chair, and board members need to be alerted, as do the institutional official (IO) (who signed the institutional assurance document) and the chain of command. Collateral offices, such as the legal office and the grants management office, also need to be informed.

Have Senior Officials Available

Any audit is important, but inspections from federal or state regulators are doubly so. The institution should prepare and respond as if the audit could shut down research at the institution. Senior officials should be available for interviews with the inspectors as well as quick consultations with the IRB staff during the audit. These senior officials need to understand and be able to articulate the importance of the IRB and the operation of the IRB within the institutional structure.

Have Files Organized and Readily Available

FDA audits are often linked to a specific study or studies. If you know in advance that a specific study is to be reviewed, be sure the clinical investigator and the sponsor are aware of the audit. They should ensure that their study files agree with the IRB files and that they are organized for the audit. Be sure that all the paperwork is in both files. Be sure you can find all your study files. You may need to get them back from reviewers or at least know who has the files and where they are. It is not acceptable to have files that you cannot retrieve because someone is on vacation or off doing six weeks of field research.

Organize IRB Office Documents

The next thing to do is organize your IRB office documents. The inspector will want to review the IRB written procedures, so put them on a special shelf in the room that the inspector will be using or on a cart if you will be using a shared conference room. If you have not done so recently, it is a good idea to give the procedures a quick review just to be sure that nothing is out of date or missing. It is always a good idea to review copies of manuals and other documents that you will give to the investigator to make sure they are up to date and complete, with no pages or sections missing.

Prepare an Organizational and Personnel Chart

A table of organization (personnel chart) is very helpful for auditors. If the staffing pattern of the IRB and how the function fits into the institution's overall operations (reporting lines, etc.) are not part of the written procedures, this information should be provided as a separate document. Also, print out the IRB membership rosters for the past three or four years. The inspector will need these rosters to check against meeting attendance to ensure that a quorum was maintained at all meetings.

Prepare a Notebook with IRB Minutes

Gather the meeting minutes in a notebook or file and put them on the shelf or cart. Most auditors will want to see at least one year's minutes. Sometimes two or three years are asked for, so be prepared. Again, check to be sure that the minutes are up to date. If the minutes are a couple of meetings behind, get them typed up. If you have some that need to be approved and they will not be before the inspection, label them as "draft."

Prepare a Workspace for the Auditor

When selecting a work area, do not put the inspector in the IRB workflow area. It is disruptive both for him or her and for you. In addition, the inspector may see you doing something that raises questions; problems have the tendency to crop up at the most inopportune moments. A private office or conference room is best. If you need to schedule an off-site room, keep it reasonably close to the IRB offices, as the inspector will want and need close contact with the IRB staff. For security, the space should be lockable, or the files and materials will have to be returned to the IRB office whenever the room is not occupied.

The work area should be available for the full inspection time. Although most inspectors will accommodate some moving around because of a meeting or other need for the room, it is an inconvenience for them and it should be avoided if possible. The room you choose should have a table and comfortable chairs. Office supplies (e.g., stapler and paper clips) are not required, but are appreciated. The room should have space for three or four people to comfortably meet with the inspector.

Access to a Copy Machine

Access to a copy machine can be dealt with in two ways. You may give the inspectors unrestricted access to a copier if they will agree to make you copies of whatever they copy, or you can make the copies they request and make copies for yourself, too. Either of these methods is usually acceptable to inspectors and should be agreed upon at the beginning of the audit.

Access to a Telephone

Give the inspectors access to a telephone. If they have a question and want to call someone about it, it is usually to your advantage for them to do so. FDA field inspectors are generally not IRB experts, so they may need to call headquarters to check on something unique to your site or to a study they are reviewing.

Commit Staff to Facilitate the Audit Visit

The time necessary for these preparations will be significant, and additional help may be needed to get things in order before the inspection starts. Everyone in the institution should realize the importance of having a good outcome, so you should be able to draw on institutional resources. If you need to delay the protocol review process a couple of days to focus on the inspection, your investigators should understand. If you need to hire some temporary employees or reassign some personnel to help, your administration should support the expenditure and the conscription, although this may be a sign that the IRB is understaffed.

During the inspection itself, the IRB staff and Chair should plan on spending additional hours in the office. Time will be needed to prepare before the inspectors arrive each day, and time will be needed at the end of each day for debriefing, finding requested information, and preparing notes, reports, or briefings. A short meeting with key institutional officials for debriefing and planning should be scheduled after the inspector leaves each day.

One person should be designated as the key contact for the FDA inspector. This person will answer the inspector's questions and respond for the institution. Usually, this is the senior IRB administrator or the IRB Chair.

The Inspection

Notice of Inspection (FDA Form 482)

When the inspector arrives, a "Notice of Inspection" will be given to the institution's representative (FDA Form 482). It contains the name of the inspector and the address of the inspector's district office. It also contains the preprinted standard terms of inspection. This form should be the first piece of paper in the audit file, which is your record of the inspection.

Prepare a Notebook Containing FDA Correspondence

You should store your notes on the inspection and copies of all documents that the FDA inspector has copied in the audit file, folder, or notebook. It is very important to have exactly the same records that the FDA has so that you can accurately respond to any further queries the FDA might have. When notified by letter regarding a specific memo, it is more useful to have it in hand rather than to try to guess which one it might have been.

Review Documentation of the Auditor's Credentials

Along with presenting the Form 482, the inspectors will show you their credentials verifying that they are from the FDA and that they have a legal right to have access to your records. In the unlikely event that the inspectors forget to show you credentials, you should ask to see them. Remember, you are responsible for maintaining the security of your records. If you have any doubt about the legitimacy of the inspector's credentials or questions about the inspection procedures, you should call the district office listed on the Form 482.

The Orientation Presentation

After the inspector completes this identification and notification step and makes any introductory remarks about the audit, usually a brief orientation to your system is requested. This overview is given to the inspector by the most knowledgeable person or persons, usually the IRB administrator and/or the IRB Chair. If there are unique aspects of your system or in how things are done, this is the time to explain them. This is also a good time to point out where the restrooms are and where the cafeteria and/or vending machines are located. Unless you normally have coffee or drinks and food available to staff, you do not need to provide it for the inspectors. In fact, FDA's conflict of interest rules prohibit acceptance of anything but light refreshments.

Request a "Mini Exit Review" at the End of Each Day

In the orientation presentation, you should ask the inspectors to update you at the end of each day. This "mini exit review" helps to ensure that there are no surprises. Often, if an inspector has not been able to find some item during the day, you can find that document and provide it to her or him the next day. This strategy often prevents being cited for something that was easily remediable. Some inspectors are uncomfortable with daily updates and if so, do not push—they are not required to provide this service. Most will, however, and they usually appreciate the chance to clear their questions and problem areas. This also provides an opportunity for them to set the next day's agenda to facilitate gathering documents and scheduling people and rooms. It is a good idea to brief senior management after the daily exit interview and begin the planning for any necessary institutional corrective actions.

IRB Procedures, Membership Roster, and Minutes

Inspectors will always ask for the IRB written procedures, the IRB membership roster, and the IRB meeting minutes, so these should be ready beforehand. These documents will be reviewed and copied for forwarding to FDA headquarters. Note that the FDA does not accept an assurance of compliance document in place of written procedures. They are looking for your standard operating procedures, which are explanations of how you carry out the obligations and promises made in the assurance.

Study Files

Specific study files will usually be requested, and often the inspector may request a file or two meeting a specified requirement; for example, the last file that had an adverse event to a study drug or the file of a study that has been open for at least three years. These are the types of files you may wish to select for the targeted self-audits mentioned earlier.

The study files will be read by the inspector, and portions will be copied for later analysis. The review of study files usually comprises the majority of the audit. One of the best protective mechanisms for the site, if time permits, is to preview the requested study files and mark (with tape flags or stickers) critical letters and reports. This would include items such as the initial approval letter, continuing review approval letters, the current approved consent form, the protocol, adverse event reports, progress reports, and communications with the investigator. This advance organization is intended to make it easier for the inspector to find what he or she is looking for, and to be sure the file is complete.

Record a List of Audit Interviews

At some point during the audit, the inspector will usually interview the IRB staff and the IRB Chair to see how things actually work. They will compare the verbal explanations with how the functions are described in the written procedures. It is a good idea to keep a list of who meets with the inspector so that if questions arise later, you can go back to the source. Some institutions even keep notes on such interviews or conduct a debriefing. These lists and notes should go into the audit file so that they are available when responding to postaudit inquiries.

Observation of an IRB Meeting

If your IRB is scheduled to meet during the inspection, members should be prepared to have the inspector sit in. Not all inspectors will ask to sit in on an IRB meeting, but some will. General wisdom is not to offer if you are not asked, but some institutions may want to showcase their IRB if it is truly first-rate. Just remember the adage, "Whatever can go wrong, will go wrong — and at the worst possible time."

The Exit Interview

At the conclusion of the inspection, an exit interview will be conducted by the inspectors. The inspectors usually schedule these in advance. You should gather the appropriate persons to participate. Such people would include at least the IRB administrator, the IRB Chair, and the in-stitutional official (IO) and should include the person that the IRB reports to if it is not the IO. Who attends should be guided by the tone of the daily summaries and by the scope of the responses that may be needed.

The inspector will tell you what deficiencies were found. This may be just an oral summary, or the inspector may issue these observations in writing on FDA Form 483. Form 483, called the "Statement of Findings," is basically a blank page. The inspector can write anything down and can put it in any order. Often, serious violations will be mixed in with lesser infractions. If a Form 483 is issued, usually the inspector will review each item that is listed. It is inappropriate, not to mention foolish, to argue with the inspector. It is appropriate, however, to request clarifications of items that you do not understand, and the inspectors should correct factual errors. Remember that inspectors may not be IRB experts, and sometimes they do misinterpret what they see.

If there has been an earlier indication from the daily summaries that a major problem exists, and if a preliminary plan for correction has been developed (as it should be), it can be offered. Remember, the Form 483 is only a preliminary finding—do not overreact. You should understand, however, what each observation that the inspector has listed means. Unless no Form 483 is issued, tell the inspector that you *will* send a written response in seven to ten days. This allows them to expect it, so that they can include your response with their report.

The Establishment Inspection Report

After returning to the District Office, the inspector will write an "Establishment Inspection Report" (EIR). The EIR contains both positive and negative observations. The inspector may consult with other district office personnel and/or FDA headquarters staff during the write-up. The EIR with all the documentation collected from your site is sent to headquarters. If you have sent a letter in response to the audit, it will also be included. The EIR will go to the FDA Center that assigned the audit for review and comment.

Postinspection Activities

After the inspector leaves, collect, in the audit notebook or file, all the copies of documents that the inspector made and any staff notes that were taken. Write up the exit interview. (You can assign someone to take notes during the exit interview.) You should have a meeting with the appropriate institutional people to discuss the audit and to decide what needs to be corrected immediately.

The institution should develop a plan of correction and send it to the inspector's district office. Again, do not overreact, but be sure to respond in the seven to ten day window. The letter you write to the district office should be focused on those items that you can fix or have fixed. Send along any missing documents that you have found. You may dispute regulatory interpretations, especially if you know the inspector's interpretation is in conflict with agency guidance or even general wisdom. You can point out items cited on a Form 483 that are not based on regulations. (Here is where having someone on staff who is an expert on the regulations is helpful.) Keep the tone of the letter respectful and factual.

Postinspection Letters and Response
Approximately six weeks to six months after an inspection, you will receive a letter from the FDA headquarters. Usually, the greater the FDA's concern (i.e., the longer the list on the Form 483), the faster the letter will arrive. The exit interview usually gives you some indication of the potential level of concern.

You should have immediately begun working on corrections, especially if a Form 483 was issued at the close of the inspection. The FDA will expect the institution to have made progress on any major deficiencies by the time that you receive the postinspection letter from their headquarters.

The FDA's experts at the Centers write the follow-up letters, so argument about regulatory interpretation is rarely successful. Be very careful and sure of your position if you do choose to dispute items in these letters. Although there is increasing coordination between the Centers, there is some variation in the emphasis and interpretation of the regulations. Remember that everyone's goal is to ensure compliance and protection of human subjects, and teamwork is preferable to antagonism.

A Voluntary Action Letter Versus a Warning Letter
The FDA issues two types of letters when deviations are found. The preferred kind, *voluntary action letters,* simply ask for the correction of minor deficiencies found. If you receive a voluntary correction letter, respond by explaining what you have done and/or what you are doing to fix the problem. Keep it short and address all concerns raised in the FDA letter. This will usually close the process as far as the FDA is concerned.

The other kind of letter demands correction of what the FDA believes to be serious deficiencies and/or violations of the regulations. These letters are called *warning letters.* Often, they carry some type of sanction for the institution and its investigators.

Warning Letters

Warning letters must be taken very seriously. Explain how you have or will comply with any sanction. Explain what you have done and what you are going to do immediately to address the identified problems. Explain your long-range plans for ensuring that the problems stay fixed. Remember that the institution has had notice of the deficiencies since the time the Form 483 was issued, so the FDA's letter should not be a complete surprise. Therefore, only having plans is not as acceptable as demonstrating progress. For example, if the Form 483 listed a shortage of IRB staff, instead of writing that you are planning to hire additional staff, the institution should have the vacancy announcements out. An even better response is to have the selections made and people on board. The institution needs to show reasonable action to correct defi-

ciencies. The FDA will remain in contact with the institution until corrections are satisfactory.

After the deficiencies have been corrected and the case is closed, it is time to start preparing for the next audit. Keep the files and records up-to-date. Look for ways to improve IRB practices. Keep the staff and IRB members current by sending them to conferences and meetings.

Investigator Inspections

Investigator inspections are similar in format to IRB inspections. The FDA conducts two types of investigator inspections. These are called *study-oriented* and *investigator-oriented* inspections. (They used to be called *routine* and *for-cause* inspections.)

Study-Oriented Inspections
Study-oriented inspections are done at study sites that have participated in pivotal clinical trials. *Pivotal trials* are those that the FDA uses to approve drugs and devices for marketing. Obviously, the FDA must ensure that data from these studies support the sponsor's claim of safety and efficacy. It is important that investigators let IRBs know when they are to be inspected because normally both the investigator and the IRB will be audited.

Investigator-Oriented Inspections
Inspections that are investigator-oriented are usually the result of one or more reports of questionable behavior or of suspicions that have been raised. The FDA's suspicion index is raised for investigators who conduct studies outside of their specialty areas, conduct a large number of studies, enroll large numbers of subjects (especially in a short time), or have results that differ from everyone else's. Complaints from research subjects are taken very seriously by the FDA, and they usually result in at least a written inquiry if not a full audit.

Recently, an increasing number of investigator inspections have been triggered by sponsors reporting that they have had difficulty with an investigator on their trials. Generally, this is because the sponsor is concerned about the quality of the data received, or because the information flow is not sufficient for the sponsor to meet its obligations for reporting to the FDA.

Investigator inspections of either type usually focus on the review of research records for one or more specific studies. These records include source documents such as medical records, laboratory results, and tracings; case report forms (CRFs); signed consent forms; IRB approvals; and other communications and correspondence. The FDA's watchwords for clinical investigators are "If it isn't documented, it didn't happen."

Inspection Activities
The actions that an investigator should take when notified of an FDA inspection are similar to those described above for an IRB audit. That is, the sponsor, institutional officials, and institutional offices—especially the IRB—should be notified. The investigator should ensure that records are complete and accessible. Again, a reasonable

workspace should be provided, and key team members who participated in the research study should be available. It is critical for the investigator to be available during the inspection.

Resources

There are some resources available to IRBs and investigators to prepare for audits. The FDA publishes two documents as part of its *Compliance Program Guidance Manual*. One, for use in IRB audits, is entitled "Compliance Program 7348.809."[4] The other is for clinical investigator inspections and is entitled "Compliance Program 7348.811."[4] Both are available by writing the FDA or visiting the FDA Web site. Guidance on operating an IRB and investigator responsibilities is available in the FDA Information Sheets.[5]

Conclusion

Although audits may not be fun, they need not be dreaded, especially if you are ready for them and know what to expect. Preparation and constant fine-tuning are keys to hav-

ing a successful audit and a program that truly protects the rights and welfare of human subjects of research.

References

1. Food and Drug Administration. A self-evaluation checklist for IRBs. Updated 12 Mar 2001. Access date 9 Apr 2001. World Wide Web www.fda.gov/oc/oha/IRB/toc11.html

2. Food and Drug Administration. Electronic freedom of information reading room, 12 Mar 2001. Access date 9 Apr 2001. World Wide Web http://www.fda.gov/foi/warning.htm

3. Office for Human Research Protections. OHRP compliance activities: Common findings and guidance, 1 Sep 2000. Access date 7 May 2001. World Wide Web http://ohrp.osophs.dhhs.gov/references/findings.pdf

4. Food and Drug Administration. Office of Regulatory Affairs compliance references: Bioresearch monitoring, 21 Feb 2001. Access date 11 May 2001. World Wide Web http://www.fda.gov/ora/compliance_ref/bimo/7348_810/default.htm

5. Food and Drug Administration. Information sheets: Guidance for institutional review boards and clinical investigators, Sep 1998. Access date 9 Apr 2001. World Wide Web http://www.fda.gov/oc/oha/IRB/toc.html

Preparing for an OHRP Site Visit

Thomas Puglisi and Michele Russell-Einhorn

INTRODUCTION

The Office for Human Research Protections (OHRP) conducts several different types of visits to institutions that it regulates under an assurance of protection for human subjects. Every institution wishing to conduct human subject research supported by the Department of Health and Human Services (DHHS) must file an assurance acceptable to, and approved by, OHRP. OHRP site visits include technical assistance site visits, educational site visits, and compliance oversight site visits.

Technical Assistance and Educational Site Visits

Technical assistance site visits are designed to be non-threatening and collegial in nature. They offer the opportunity for an OHRP professional to spend a full day at a single institution in order to provide information and assistance to the institution in developing and strengthening its program for protecting human subjects. They also promote good will between OHRP and the institution in the hope that the institution will build stronger contacts with OHRP professionals and feel comfortable approaching OHRP when questions arise and problems are identified.

Although the OHRP visitor may review the IRB's written policies and procedures, as well as other written information about the institution's systemic protections for human subjects, an in-depth review of IRB and research records is not typically conducted during technical assistance site visits. The purpose of the visit is not to ferret out deficiencies, and the OHRP visitor will not go out of the way to discover and document institutional shortcomings.

Rather, the OHRP visitor will spend time discussing the principles of human subject protection with various members of the institution, usually including a brief meeting with the assurance signatory official and longer meetings with the IRB Chair and IRB administrator. An open question-and-answer session with IRB members and investigators is usually a highlight of the visit. Overall, the goal is to increase institutional awareness of the importance of human subject protections and to assist the institution in developing a stronger program. A follow-up letter to the institution may suggest specific areas in which the institution should consider improvements.

Educational visits are often directed toward several institutions located in close proximity to each other. The visit usually consists of a formal presentation by an OHRP professional at a central location, with plenty of time for questions and answers afterward. Informal discussion with representatives of the participating institutions is also encouraged. Again, the goal is to raise awareness about human subject protections and to build collegial relationships between OHRP professionals and institutional representatives.

OHRP Compliance Oversight Activities

OHRP has three statutory responsibilities: education, the administration of assurances, and compliance oversight. OHRP exercises its *compliance oversight* responsibility by conducting investigations of all credible allegations or indications of noncompliance that come to its attention. Corrective actions may be required under the OHRP-approved institutional assurance that each institution must maintain in order to conduct DHHS-supported human subject research.

OHRP may receive information about possible noncompliance from a research subject or family member who has complaints about a research project, from a whistleblower who alleges noncompliance, from the funding agency, from institutional self-reports, via the media, or through review of the published literature.

In most cases, OHRP is able to reach determinations regarding the alleged noncompliance and the institution's systemic protections for human subjects through an exchange of correspondence and review of relevant materials and records. Corrective actions may or may not be required of the institution in connection with OHRP's determinations. In certain cases, however, OHRP may need to conduct an on-site review to determine whether noncompliance has occurred and whether specific or systemic corrective actions are warranted.

Most OHRP compliance oversight site visits occur within the context of an on-going compliance investigation. It is rare for OHRP to conduct an unannounced site visit or a site visit that has not been preceded by a complaint or a report of possible noncompliance. However, nothing prohibits the OHRP from conducting such an unannounced or "not-for-cause" site visit, and it has occasionally done so in the past. For example, OHRP's site visit to Duke University in the late 1990s was not precipitated by a prior complaint.

The Importance of Prevention

Any institution with a significant volume of DHHS-sponsored human-subjects research will sooner or later experience an OHRP investigation or site visit. The best strategy in preparing for such an event is to invest in long-term prevention. If the institution has maintained a strong, well-resourced human-subjects protection program, it should be in a good position to deal with any compliance oversight investigation or site visit. Proactive audits, adequate resources, and well-designed training programs all contribute to a strong system of protections capable of withstanding close scrutiny.

Thus, the preparation for an OHRP compliance investigation or site visit begins long before the investigation or site visit is announced. Perhaps the most common source of problems in the protection of human subjects is the institutional failure to maintain a well-resourced and well-trained IRB and to establish a culture in which all research investigators understand and take seriously their responsibilities for protecting human subjects.

The era is long past in which an institution can rely on an occasional memorandum to investigators about human subject protections and populate its IRB with untrained members supported by a clerical assistant. In today's world, it is critically important for the IRB to be supported by one or more certified IRB professionals who can provide expert advice and guidance to IRB members and investigators. Sufficient support staff must be provided to fulfill the IRB's growing recordkeeping responsibilities. IRB members and research investigators must be well trained on a continuing basis.

One cannot overemphasize the importance of maintaining the knowledge and expertise of IRB members and staff through continuing education. The IRB Chair, members, and professional staff should participate regularly in human-subjects conferences sponsored by Public Responsibility in Medicine & Research (PRIM&R) and the Applied Research Ethics National Association (ARENA), as well as in the regional workshops sponsored by OHRP and the local, regional, and national meetings sponsored by other groups. The IRB listserve is also an important resource for staying up-to-date. Any institution whose IRB members and support professionals become isolated from the national IRB community runs the risk of maintaining an outdated program that will eventually get into regulatory trouble.

Responding to OHRP Compliance Oversight Investigations

The typical OHRP compliance site visit takes place within a compliance oversight investigation. It follows an OHRP inquiry to an institution concerning an allegation of noncompliance, and receipt by OHRP of the institution's response to the allegation. It is not uncommon for this initial exchange to be followed by additional questions from OHRP and additional responses from the institution. OHRP will schedule a compliance site visit if concerns about the allegation, and especially about the institution's systemic protections for human subjects, cannot be resolved through correspondence.

Just as the best strategy for avoiding an OHRP compliance investigation is to maintain a vigorous and well-resourced institutional program for protecting human subjects, the best strategy for avoiding an OHRP compliance site visit is to respond candidly and constructively to any OHRP compliance investigation.

OHRP's first step in investigating an allegation of noncompliance is to present the allegation to the institution, and request that the institution investigate the allegation and provide OHRP with a detailed report on its investigation, including appropriate documentation such as the IRB protocol file and other relevant records. At this time, OHRP will also request copies of institutional policies and procedures for protecting human subjects.

Upon receipt of such a request, the institution should investigate the alleged noncompliance as thoroughly and objectively as possible. If the allegation is complicated or sensitive, it may be important to obtain the assistance of one or more external consultants in obtaining an objective analysis of the situation. At the same time, the institution should complete a self-assessment of its systemic protections for human subjects. Again, the assistance of external consults is often helpful in ensuring an objective assessment.

Once the institution has obtained an objective understanding of the circumstances relevant to the allegation and an objective assessment of the adequacy of its systemic human-subjects protections, it should report its findings to OHRP in a straightforward and honest manner. If the allegation has been substantiated and/or if systemic deficiencies have been identified, the institution should present OHRP with a detailed corrective action plan to address any shortcomings.

OHRP's response to a candid and complete report of deficiencies accompanied by a substantive and detailed corrective action plan is inevitably positive. OHRP has no authority to impose civil or criminal penalties for past noncompliance (although it will refer findings to other government agencies with such authority where appropriate). Rather, OHRP's mission and authority focus on ensuring satisfactory protections for present and future human subjects. An institutional response that acknowledges past deficiencies and outlines a rigorous timetable for appropriate corrective action permits OHRP to move on to other investigations at institutions where subjects may be at greater risk.

The Format for OHRP Compliance Site Visits

OHRP's compliance site visits are usually conducted by a team of three to five OHRP professionals and two to four external consultants. Consultants typically include at least one IRB expert (often an IRB Chair and/or an experienced IRB administrator) and may include experts in particular scientific areas, depending on the nature of the allegation involved.

OHRP compliance site visits are usually announced to the assurance signatory official both orally (by telephone) and in writing (by letter) about three to four weeks in advance of the visit. If logistics permit, OHRP occasionally invites the institution to choose from two sets of possible dates. More often, however, competing OHRP priorities and the limited availability of consultants preclude much flexibility as to the timing of the visit, and the institution must adapt to the dates announced by OHRP.

When the site visit is announced, OHRP will provide the institution with a tentative agenda and will request a complete list of all of the institution's human-subjects research. This includes identification of the funding agency (if any), the initial IRB approval date, and the most recent date of continuing IRB review and approval. Three to five days before arrival, OHRP will request that the institution make available for on-site review the complete IRB files for 50 to 100 specific protocols that OHRP has identified. In addition, the institution should be prepared for OHRP to request additional files once the on-site record review has begun.

OHRP will also request files for research that has been approved by the IRB under expedited procedures, and for research determined by the institution to be exempt from IRB review requirements. OHRP routinely requests the minutes for all IRB meetings held within three years before the site visit. In addition to IRB records, OHRP may also wish to review specific research records, sometimes including relevant medical records of individual subjects involved in federally supported research. If such records are needed, OHRP almost always notifies the institution in advance of its arrival on site.

The typical OHRP compliance site visit begins with a five to eight hour day devoted entirely to on-site review of IRB and research records. The second day usually begins with an introductory meeting with the assurance signatory official and any other officials deemed appropriate by the institution. During the remainder of the second day and on the morning of the third, the OHRP team will hold individual and/or group meetings with the IRB Chair(s), members, administrator, and staff as well as selected federally supported research investigators and individuals relevant to any specific allegations that are under investigation. The goal of these meetings is to address both the allegations that precipitated the investigation and, more broadly, to achieve a thorough understanding of the institution's systemic protections for human subjects.

Except for the entrance and exit interviews, at which the assurance signatory official may include any number of appropriate individuals, the OHRP prefers that institutional observers are not present during its interviews with institutional personnel. Should institutional counsel wish to be present during these interviews, the institution should inform the ORHP before the site visit so that the OHRP can make the necessary arrangements with its own counsel.

The afternoon and evening of the third day are generally spent in executive session, during which the OHRP will reach and document its determinations, including any corrective actions that may be necessary to ensure present and future protections for human subjects under the assurance. The determinations and required corrective actions may be formalized in a letter to be presented to the assurance signatory official during the exit interview on the morning of the fourth day. Alternatively, issuance of the determination letter may be delayed for several days and presented to the institution after the ORHP team has returned to its office in Rockville, MD.

In either case, however, the OHRP's determinations are presented orally and explained thoroughly during the exit interview with the institution's assurance signatory official before the OHRP's departure at the end of the site visit. Although the OHRP does not go out of its way to announce its determination, institutions should understand that the OHRP determination letters are available to the public under the Freedom of Information Act (FOIA) and are routinely posted on the OHRP Web site.[1] The OHRP will not comment to the media before issuing the determination letter. Once the determination letter is released, the OHRP's comments are generally limited to explaining the meaning and significance of its determinations and any required corrective actions.

Surviving an OHRP Compliance Site Visit

An institution's first step upon receiving notice of an impending compliance site visit is to achieve an objective understanding of the quality of its institutional program for the protection of human subjects in research. One effective strategy is to create a small but diversified task force, including individuals with authority to make decisions on behalf of the institution. The task force should develop the set of procedures that it will follow in reviewing the institution's system for protecting human subjects and, if appropriate, the specific allegation that precipitated the OHRP's investigation.

The OHRP has prepared and published on its Web site a document entitled "Compliance activities: Common findings and guidance."[2] Institutions should review the 74 issues described in this document and critically apply them to their own system as a tool to identify systemic weaknesses and deficiencies. As indicated previously, it is often extremely beneficial to obtain the assistance of outside IRB experts to assist in this type of assessment. An assessment conducted solely by institutional personnel often lacks objectivity and exposes the institution to unrecognized risks that could be identified through a more unbiased assessment by recognized experts.

One important element that is often overlooked during institutional self-assessments is the existence of previous reports from government agencies that may be relevant to the institution's system for protecting human subjects. Many such agencies conduct audits or inspections of various aspects of federally supported or federally regulated research. Examples include Food and Drug Administration (FDA) inspections of clinical investigators; FDA IRB inspections; site visits to Department of Veterans Affairs (VA) facilities from the Office of Research Compliance and Assurance (ORCA); site visits to Department of Energy (DOE) facilities by the DOE Human Subject Protection Program; peer review evaluations from the National Institutes of Health (NIH) funding components; and audits by National Cancer Institute (NCI) Cooperative Groups.

Unfortunately, appropriate institutional officials are often not informed about the results of such evaluations. The institution should be certain to gather from all of its personnel and components every piece of correspondence and every report from every relevant government agency. Far too many institutional officials find out about such materials during the exit interview at the conclusion of an OHRP site visit. At that point, it is too late for the institution to implement proactive, self-initiated corrective actions.

Once the institution has conducted its own assessment, it should develop solutions and a detailed corrective action plan with timelines to implement those solutions. This kind of information can sometimes avert an extended shutdown of the institution's human subject research and can be incorporated directly into any required corrective action plan mandated by OHRP.

Managing the Logistics for an OHRP Site Visit

Many of the strategies suggested in Chapter 8-14 on FDA site visits are equally applicable to managing the logistics for an OHRP site visit. In addition, it is important for the institution to identify a responsible individual to assist the OHRP on administrative and logistical matters for the visit. The following are of particular importance.

Selecting a Work Site and Interview Rooms The OHRP prefers that a single, large conference room is reserved for its entire visit, including all meetings, interviews, and onsite executive sessions. The room should have a conference table and be large enough to accommodate the OHRP team and the largest institutional group to be interviewed.

Selecting Individuals to Be Interviewed The OHRP will provide a list of requested individuals, but with the OHRP's concurrence, the institution can sometimes add or substitute individuals of its own choosing.

Selecting Materials for Review The OHRP will provide a list of requested documents, but will be happy to review additional documents or materials that the institution wishes to provide.

Organizing Files The OHRP prefers that files are clearly labeled by IRB protocol number and the name of the principal investigator, and that file contents are logically organized. Because the OHRP will request additional files

after arriving, it is important that files are properly labeled, organized, and up to date on an on-going basis.

Making Institutional Officials Available The assurance signatory official and other institutional officials who have authority for the institution's system for the protection of human subjects (including those to whom the IRB reports) should be informed on a timely basis of all aspects of the site visit. In addition, they should be prepared to be available during the site visit as needed. If the assurance signatory official is not the institution's highest official, that official should be prepared to meet with the OHRP on request. The OHRP often requests such a meeting if serious deficiencies are determined to be jeopardizing the institution's systemic protections for human subjects.

Preparing Interviewees The institution should make sure that the institutional officials, IRB members and staff, investigators, study coordinators, and others who are going to be interviewed recognize the importance of their interviews. They should be instructed to be on time, but should be warned that meetings often run late, and they may need to stay later than anticipated. Institutions may assist interviewees in preparing for their meetings with the OHRP team, but they should never be coached in such a way as to provide less than accurate information. It is our experience that honesty and openness with the OHRP site visit team is in the long-term best interest not only of human subjects, but also of the institution itself.

Corrective Action Plans

As indicated previously, OHRP looks to the development of an institutional corrective action plan to resolve any weaknesses or deficiencies in the institution's system for protecting human subjects. A corrective action plan may be mandated by the OHRP after a compliance oversight investigation or compliance site visit in order to ensure protections for human subjects under an OHRP-approved assurance; or an institution may voluntarily present a corrective action plan to the OHRP in response to self-identified problems or deficiencies.

In any event, a corrective action plan should be clear and succinct, and should squarely address all identified deficiencies. It should make clear how the institution proposes to rectify any weakness and include a specific timetable for implementing each proposed action. Depending on the situation, corrective action plans often include bringing in outside expert consultants to help assess the effectiveness of existing human protection mechanisms, developing and conducting educational or training programs for IRB members or investigators, and/or assisting in designing and implementing improved policies and procedures.

The institution should consider the timetable for implementing proposed corrective actions very carefully. The OHRP is more interested in the quality and effectiveness of implemented corrective actions than in the speed of implementation. Once convinced that subjects are not routinely being exposed to unacceptable levels of risk, the OHRP often accepts corrective action plans that propose as long as 12 months for full implementation. However, the OHRP expects the institution to report and document meaningful progress at periodic intervals through the implementation period.

Finally, it is important to remember that the OHRP does not take actions for punitive purposes. Rather, the OHRP concentrates on ensuring present and future protections for human subjects. Indeed, the OHRP prides itself on assisting institutions that are genuinely concerned about strengthening their human subjects protection programs, and the OHRP professionals are always available to help institutions that self-identify problems and sincerely want to correct them.

Conclusion

Institutions that want to conduct research supported by the DHHS must file an assurance that is acceptable to, and approved by the OHRP. Institutions with OHRP assur-

ances may be the focus of an OHRP site visit for the purpose of technical assistance, education, or compliance oversight. This chapter has explained the mechanics of OHRP site visits with the emphasis on the things an IRB should do to avoid compliance problems. Preparing for and managing an OHRP site visit that is being done for compliance oversight requires planning, resources, and an understanding of specific steps to follow. This chapter provides IRBs with the information they need to interface with OHRP officials in a way that is likely to be productive from the standpoint of institutional function and research conduct.

References

1. Office for Human Research Protections. Compliance determination letters, 20 Mar 2001. Access date 30 Mar 2001. World Wide Web http://ohrp.osophs.dhhs.gov/detrm_letrs/jan2001.htm

2. Office for Human Research Protections. OHRP compliance activities: Common findings and guidance, 1 Sept 2000. Access date 7 May 2001. World Wide Web http://ohrp.osophs.dhhs.gov/references/findings.pdf

PART 9

Issues Based on Study Population

Research Involving Fetuses and In Vitro Fertilization

Ronald M. Green

INTRODUCTION

Biomedical research involving the human embryo or fetus raises a host of special concerns for institutional review board (IRB) reviewers. The embryo or fetus cannot consent to be a research subject. The fetus has a unique and inextricable relationship to the mother. The moral status of the embryo or fetus is a source of widespread disagreement. All these considerations make embryo and fetal research one of the most controversial issues in our society.

Since the mid-1970s, beginning with the work of the National Commission for the Protection of Human Subjects of Biomedical and Behavioral Research, federal bioethics advisory groups have recommended a variety of regulations for the conduct of federally funded research affecting prenatal human life.[1] Many of these recommendations have attained the status of law and now form part of a complex body of regulations that must be taken into account by investigators working in this area as well as the IRBs that must approve and review their research. Many of these regulations have a sound moral basis. Others require IRB members to make difficult and controversial moral decisions. Some appear to be inconsistent with regulations in related research areas. This reflects the fact that regulations often incorporate one or another contested points of view from our ongoing social debates about the moral claims of embryos or fetuses.

Federal Regulations

Regulations governing research on embryos or fetuses can be classed into four broad categories: (1) research on the fetus itself; (2) research directed toward pregnant women or the condition of pregnancy (for which the embryo or fetus is an indirect subject of research); (3) fetal tissue transplantation research; and (4) research on the ex utero preimplantation human embryo, or that utilizes human pluripotential stem cells (hPSCs) derived from such embryos.

These classes of research share at least five common features. First, they all presume some common definitions. The *fetus* itself is defined as "the product of conception from the time of implantation until delivery."[2[Sec.203(c)]] Implantation is confirmed through a presumptive sign of pregnancy such as missed menses or a positive pregnancy test.[2[Sec.203(b)]] *Pregnancy* is defined as encompassing "the period of time from confirmation of implantation (through any of the presumptive signs of pregnancy, such as missed menses, or by a medically acceptable pregnancy test) until expulsion or extraction of the fetus."[2[Sec.403(b)]]

Because implantation normally occurs before the end of the first week after fertilization, this definition differs from standard medical ones, which usually term the earliest product of conception as an *embryo* and define the fetus as coming into being only at the eighth week of pregnancy. It follows from the regulatory definition that the ex utero preimplantation human embryo (i.e., the embryo conceived through in vitro fertilization but not yet or never transferred to a womb) is not covered by regulations pertaining to federally funded fetal research. In 1996, this perceived gap in regulations was closed when Congress adopted language found in the Dickey-Wicker Amendment to the Department of Health and Human Services (DHHS) budget bill.[3,4] This amendment, which has been reenacted in each subsequent year, prohibits federal funding of any "research in which a human embryo or embryos are destroyed, discarded, or knowingly subjected to risk of injury or death greater than that allowed for research on fetuses in utero" under existing federal regulations. Dickey-Wicker also offers a wide-ranging definition of the human embryo as "any organism . . . that is derived by fertilization, parthenogenesis, cloning, or any other means from one or more human gametes." Many individuals will have moral difficulties with a definition that affords parthenotes—egg cells that have been artificially stimulated to divide and cannot possibly develop beyond a few cell divisions—the same degree of research protection given to later fetuses. This is one consequence of the highly politicized process that has led to current regulations.

A second feature common to federal regulations in this area is the complexity of consent requirements. Because embryos and fetuses normally have male and female progenitors, the consent of both progenitors for any research is normally required. (Exceptions are embryos produced by somatic cell nuclear transfer [cloning] technology or parthenogenesis. Both types of organisms are defined as embryos under the provisions of current U.S. law.) However, the fact that the fetus resides inside the mother's body makes her position special. Not only is she often the most proximate individual to the fetus, her health or life can be affected by decisions in this research area. Federal regulations reflect this in their complex provisions for bypassing paternal consent in the case of some research protocols.

A third feature common to all regulations in this area is the effort to separate embryo or fetal progenitors from any medical or pecuniary advantages that research may offer. Donors of embryos or fetal tissues for research are prohibited from directing these cells or tissues to recipients (including relatives) who may benefit from transplants using them. Regulations also prohibit the provision of monetary or other inducements (such as free or discounted medical services) to embryo or fetal tissue donors or suppliers. This is consistent with the general discouragement of the sale of organs or body parts in this country, but it also reflects a special concern to prevent research from becoming an inducement to abortion or embryo destruction.

Fourth, constraints in current regulations seek to remove inducements to abortion or involvement in abortion procedures on the part of researchers. Regulations specify that individuals engaged in the research will have no part in any decisions as to the timing, method, and procedures used to terminate the pregnancy or in determining the viability of the fetus at the termination of the pregnancy. They also specify that "no procedural changes which may cause greater than minimal risk to the fetus or the pregnant woman will be introduced into the procedure for terminating the pregnancy solely in the interest of the (research) activity."[2(Sec.208)]

Fifth, and finally, there is a requirement pertaining to all this research that appropriate studies on animals and nonpregnant individuals have been completed. This provision reflects the seriousness with which interventions affecting the human fetus or embryo are taken. It also poses an ongoing challenge to members of IRBs. Biological differences between animals or other human beings and developing human embryos or fetuses often recommend specific types of fetal or embryo research. Members of IRBs must determine when all "appropriate" alternative studies have been completed and when the step to fetal or embryo research may be taken.

Research Directed at the Fetus Itself

An IRB may approve research directed at the fetus in utero if (a) the purpose of the activity is to meet the health needs of the particular fetus and the fetus will be placed at risk only to the minimum extent necessary to meet such needs, or (b) the risk to the fetus imposed by the research is minimal and the purpose of the activity is the development of important biomedical knowledge that cannot be obtained by other means.[2(Sec.208)] An example of the first purpose is the use of a new technique for fetal transfusion for Rh incompatibility; an example of the second is minor change in maternal diet or use of ultrasonography. As in pediatric and other human subjects research, *minimal* means that "the probability and magnitude of harm or discomfort anticipated in the research are not greater in and of themselves than those ordinarily encountered in daily life or during the performance of routine physical or psychological examinations or tests."[2(Sec.102)]

It is noteworthy that this standard for research on the fetus in utero is somewhat stricter than that which applies to research on children. Regulations permit research on children that represents no prospect of direct benefit to individual subjects and a minor increase over minimal risk if the intervention or procedure is likely to yield "generalizable knowledge about the subjects' disorder or condition which is of vital importance for the understanding or amelioration of the subjects' disorder or condition."[2(Sec.406)] Unless the mother's health is at issue, no such permission for a minor increase over minimal risk exists where research on the fetus is concerned.

Implicit in this strict standard is a refusal to distinguish between a fetus destined for abortion and one intended to be carried to term. At first sight, one might think it reasonable to permit some degree of increased risk to the fetus when pregnancy termination is in prospect and the fetus will die in any event. For example, the preabortion fetus might seem a suitable subject for research on whether a teratogenic drug passes through the placenta. However, endangering the fetus in such cases will either limit a woman's freedom to change her mind about abortion or will result in harm to the child if she should choose to continue the pregnancy to term. The unacceptability of both these alternatives commends a standard of equal treatment of all fetuses with regard to risk. It is important to note, however, that once this standard has been met, nothing prevents preferential use of fetuses intended for abortion in minimal-risk research.

The process of consent to such research is complex and may involve the IRB in difficult determinations and judgments. In all such research, the consent of the mother on behalf of the fetus is required. As a general rule, the father, as coprogenitor, is also required to consent on behalf of the fetus. However, there are three exceptions to this rule: (1) if the father's identity or whereabouts cannot reasonably be ascertained; (2) if he is not reasonably available; or (3) if the pregnancy resulted from rape.[2[Sec.208(b),209(d)]] The IRB has a limited role to play here in assisting investigators in determining when these conditions are met. It is usually sufficient for the IRB to ensure that the investigator obtains a statement about the applicability of one or another of these exceptions from the mother. No further assessment of the facts is required.

Research can also take place on the fetus ex utero after a spontaneous or induced abortion. In such cases, the fetus is judged to be viable if it is able to survive (given the benefit of available medical therapy) to the point of independently maintaining heartbeat and respiration. A viable fetus is treated by existing regulations as a premature infant and comes under the protections of regulations governing research on children. In general, a fetus that has not attained a gestational age of 20 weeks and does not exceed 400 g in weight is judged to be nonviable. Independent medical assessment of nonviability is required when these limits have been exceeded. A nonviable fetus may be involved in research only if (a) its vital functions are not artificially maintained; (b) experimental activities which of themselves would terminate its heartbeat or respiration are not employed; and (c) the purpose of the activity is the development of important biomedical knowledge that cannot be obtained by other means. Until it is ascertained whether or not a fetus ex utero is viable, it may not be involved in research unless there will be no added risk to the fetus resulting from the activity, and the purpose of the activity is the development of important biomedical knowledge that cannot be obtained by other means; or the purpose of the activity is to enhance the possibility of survival of the particular fetus to the point of viability.[2(Sec.209)]

The Fetus as an Indirect Subject of Research

Research on women who are pregnant necessarily implicates the fetus. Federal regulations specify that no pregnant woman may be involved as a subject unless either (1) the purpose of the activity is to meet the health needs of the mother, and the fetus will be placed at risk only to the minimum extent necessary to meet such needs; or (2) the risk to the fetus is minimal.[2(Sec.207)] In such cases, research may proceed only if the mother and father are legally competent and have given their informed consent. The father's consent is not required, however, if the purpose of the activity is to meet the health needs of the mother or if the three exceptions to paternal consent mentioned in connection with research directed at the fetus apply. In research undertaken to meet the health problems of a pregnant woman, her needs generally take precedence over those of the fetus,[2(Sec.207)] except, perhaps, where the health benefit to her is minimal and risk to the fetus is high.

Regulatory protections also apply to nonpregnant women of childbearing age. These regulations require that, when appropriate, subjects be provided "a statement that the particular treatment or procedure may involve risks to the subject (or to the embryo or fetus, if the subject is or may become pregnant) which are currently unforeseeable" as part of the informed consent process.[2[Sec.116(b)(1)]] In such cases, IRBs may need to ensure that nonpregnant subjects are advised to avoid pregnancy or nursing for a time during or following the research. Furthermore, where appropriate, subjects should be advised to notify the investigator immediately should they become pregnant. In some

instances, the potential risk may be sufficient to justify requiring that pregnant or fertile women either be specifically excluded from the research or studied separately.

These regulations raise several ethical questions for IRBs and for society as a whole. Research whose primary purpose is to meet "the health needs of the mother" can sometimes impose a difficult balancing decision on investigators. This is particularly true in cases where the health benefit to her is minimal and the risk to the fetus is high. IRB members are called on to determine just how much risk to the fetus is allowable to meet such needs. The very existence of this requirement, however, raises a larger question of whether the IRB is really the appropriate maker of this decision. Because a woman's health is at issue, some would ask why she should not have sole authority to determine the degree of risk to which both she and her fetus may be exposed.

Some have also questioned whether the fetal-protective nature of current regulations in this area does not evidence inherent discrimination and injustice. It has been pointed out, for example, that some substances have the potential to affect the genetic components of sperm and, through this, the health of any resulting child. Yet current regulations do not require investigators and IRBs to balance the health needs of fertile men involved in research against possible risks to their offspring.[5,6] It is also pointed out that current regulations have had a broad effect in reducing the amount of research done on women of childbearing age, preventing this group as a whole from benefiting from that research. The problem is compounded when drugs or procedures are then clinically utilized on women without the background of research results needed to test their efficacy or toxicity. Although members of IRBs must work within the framework of existing regulations, they should be aware of this ethical debate. They may also find that the debate impacts on their decision making when they must balance the requirement to protect potentially pregnant women while fulfilling the current federal mandate to include women in clinical trials and other studies.

A further complexity is posed by research aimed at improving our understanding of the process of pregnancy itself. Some studies in this area (e.g., a study of the physiological mechanisms initiating labor) are not directed at the health of either the mother or the fetus. Other studies, such as those examining the effects of maternal diabetes on a pregnancy, are directed at the health of both the mother and the fetus. In these cases, IRBs must determine how to categorize such research and which requirements apply. In general, unless the research is undertaken to meet the health problems of a pregnant woman or the fetus, the requirement of "minimal risk" to the fetus will apply, as will the paternal consent requirement (with its stipulated exceptions).

Fetal Tissue Transplantation Research

Once the fetus is dead, its cells, tissues, organs, or placental material may normally be used in research with the consent of the mother and in accordance with any applicable state or local laws regarding such activities.[2(Sec.210)] However, special regulations apply to fetal cells or tissues intended to be used in transplantation research. This is another reflection of our ongoing social debates about abortion.

The important healing and curative potential of fetal tissue was recognized as early as 1928 when fetal tissue was first transplanted into patients suffering from diabetes. More recently, fetal neural tissue has been used, with mixed results, in the treatment of Parkinson's disease and other neurological disorders as well as other conditions.[7] During the 1980s, there was substantial controversy about the ethical permissibility of such research. In 1988, a majority of the members of the Human Fetal Tissue Transplantation Research Panel concluded that permitting fetal tissue transplantation research under strict guidelines was "acceptable public policy."[8] However, because of resistance from then-president George Bush, this recommendation did not go into effect until 1993. In January of that year, President Clinton, in one of his first acts of office, issued an executive order permitting fetal tissue transplantation research. Subsequently, Congress passed this order into law in the provisions of the National Institutes of Health (NIH) Revitalization Act of 1993.[9]

In general, the relevant provisions of the NIH Revitalization Act seek to protect the donor of fetal tissue, ensure her free and informed consent, and reduce the likelihood that this research will offer her an incentive to abortion. The regulations also seek to prevent the emergence of a commercial market in cadaveric fetal tissues. To achieve these purposes, the act requires formal statements of consent or disclosure from the female donor, her attending physician, the researcher using fetal tissue, and the recipient of such tissue (donee). For example, the woman donating human fetal tissue must sign a statement declaring that the tissue is being donated for therapeutic transplantation research, the donation is being made without any restriction regarding the identity of individuals who may be the recipients of transplantations of the tissue, and the donation is being made without her (the donor) having been informed of the identity of those individuals who may be the recipients.

The attending physician must sign a statement declaring that the tissue has been obtained in accord with the donor's signed statement and that full disclosure has been made to her of: (a) the attending physician's interest, if any, in the research to be conducted with the tissue; and (b) any known medical risks to the donor or risks to her privacy that might be associated with the donation of the tissue and are in addition to the risks associated with the woman's medical care. In the case of tissue obtained as a result of an induced abortion, the attending physician's statement must also declare that the consent of the woman for the abortion was obtained before requesting or obtaining consent for donation, the abortion was conducted in accord with applicable state law, and no alteration of the timing, method, or procedures used to terminate the pregnancy was made solely for the purposes of obtaining the tissue.

The individual with the principal responsibility for conducting the research must sign a statement declaring that the individual is aware that the tissue is human fetal tissue donated for research purposes and may have been obtained as a result of a spontaneous or induced abortion or a stillbirth; that he or she has provided such information to other individuals with responsibilities regarding the research; that the researcher will require, before obtaining the consent of a person to be a recipient of a transplantation of the tissue, written acknowledgment of receipt of this information by the recipient; and that the researcher has had no part in any decisions as to the timing, method, or procedures used to terminate the pregnancy made solely for the purposes of the research.

Finally, an additional series of provisions of the NIH Revitalization Act declare it unlawful for anyone to solicit, acquire, receive, or transfer human fetal tissue for "valuable consideration" or as the result of a promise to the donating individual that the tissue will be transplanted into a recipient specified by such an individual or a relative of the donating individual.

It appears that these provisions, now in effect for over half a decade, have calmed the fears of some individuals concerned that fetal tissue transplantation research might legitimize or increase the incidence of abortion. One sign of this is the fact that during recent legislative debates about stem cells, Representative Jay Dickey (R-Arkansas), one of the most outspoken opponents of research using stem cells derived from spare embryos remaining from infertility procedures (ES cells), was willing, within the protections of existing fetal tissue transplantation regulations, to permit research using stem cells derived from the gonadal ridge of aborted fetuses (so called EG cells). However, it is not clear whether federally funded fetal tissue transplantation research or the use of cadaveric fetuses as a source of stem cells will continue to be permitted. In the first months of his administration, President George W. Bush has questioned any use of tissues from aborted fetuses in research.[10] Which direction his administration will move remains to be seen.

Human Embryo Research

If the history of fetal tissue transplantation research is convoluted, that of research on the preimplantation ex utero human embryo is even more so. With the advent of in vitro fertilization (IVF) during the 1970s, the ex utero human embryo became available as a subject of research. The need to increase the efficiency of IVF procedures also provided an incentive to increase federal support for such research.

In the late 1970s, a special body, the Ethics Advisory Board (EAB), was formed by an act of Congress to review and provide guidance for federally funded research on the human embryo. In late 1979, the EAB issued its report containing a broad permission for such research under federal auspices, subject to guidelines and limitations indicated in the report and to be implemented by the Board itself.[11] However, before the EAB's recommendations could be put into effect, there was a change in administrations. During the Reagan and Bush years, funding for the EAB and nominations to its membership were halted. The legal requirement of EAB approval of all such research and the absence of an EAB created a de facto moratorium on funding for embryo research in the United States. In 1993, the NIH Revitalization Act abrogated the requirement for EAB approval, freeing the NIH to support research in this area. To ensure ethical oversight, the NIH convened a special body, the NIH Human Embryo Research Panel, to provide recommendations for research guidelines. In September 1994, the panel issued its report, which was accepted by the Advisory Committee to the Director of NIH (ACD) in December of that year.[12]

Among the Human Embryo Research Panel's recommendations was permission for the deliberate creation of human embryos for research purposes under certain restricted circumstances. This included circumstances when the research "by its very nature cannot otherwise be validly conducted" (as in research whose end point is fertilization) and when such embryos are needed "for the validity of a study that is potentially of outstanding scientific and therapeutic value."[12(p.44–45)] Within hours of the acceptance of the Human Embryo Research Panel report by the ACD, President Clinton issued a statement rejecting this recommendation and limiting permissible research only to embryos remaining from infertility procedures. Subsequently, the provisions of the Dickey-Wicker Amendment, which prohibits any research involving the destruction of human embryos, revoked even this qualified permission. Where federally funded research is concerned, therefore, current U.S. regulations treat research on embryos as a form of fetal research. Because possibly conflicting maternal health considerations do not appear to apply to research on the ex utero embryo, this means that IRBs may approve such research only if it represents no more than "minimal risk" for the embryo.

One consequence of the prolonged absence of federal support for human embryo research is the relegation of this research to privately funded fertility clinics that lack sufficient resources for such research or large, multicenter studies. This has contributed to the inefficiency of IVF and related procedures and accounts, in part, for their cost, often amounting to tens of thousands of dollars per treatment course. It has slowed research on birth defects caused by failures in embryological development. Poorly researched infertility procedures also play a large role in the epidemic of premature births associated with current infertility treatments.[13]

Beyond the sphere of infertility medicine, the ban on federal funding for most human embryo research has recently become a source of controversy in other promising research areas. In November 1998, scientists at the University of Wisconsin and Johns Hopkins University announced the creation of the first immortalized pluripotent stem cell lines (hPSCs).[14,15] The Wisconsin team, headed by James Thomson, utilized spare embryos remaining from infertility procedures for this purpose. These em-

bryos were dissected; their inner cell mass of totipotent cells (capable of developing into virtually any bodily tissue) was removed and placed on a feeder layer to create a line of immortalized embryonic stem cells (ES cells). The Hopkins team, headed by John Gearhart, used tissues from the gonadal ridge of aborted fetuses (such stem cells are referred to as EG cells). Because the Thomson team's ES cell research required the destruction of embryos, it could not qualify for federal funding and was financed by private sources. The Gearhart team technically qualified for federal support because theirs was a form of fetal tissue research, but they did not seek it.

Many scientists view hPSCs as one of the most promising research areas in biomedicine today. These cells are undifferentiated, totipotent cells, and able to proliferate indefinitely in culture. Once techniques for growing and redifferentiating such cells are developed, stem cell lines may be used to replace damaged cardiac tissue after a heart attack or repair now irreversible spinal cord injuries. Parkinson's disease, Alzheimer's disease, and diabetes are among the long list of conditions that might be cured by the ability to produce new bodily tissues.

In December 1999, the NIH issued draft guidelines specifying the conditions and restrictions under which it would support research using hPSCs. These guidelines rested on an NIH-solicited legal opinion that hPSCs are not themselves "embryos" within the meaning of the Dickey-Wicker Amendment, and that research "utilizing" but not deriving hPSCs from human embryos does not constitute "research in which a human embryo or embryos are destroyed." This use-versus-derivation distinction has been subject to criticism both by friends and opponents of federally funded stem cell research according to a report by the National Bioethics Advisory Committee advocating a broad permission for federal funding of both the use and derivation of ES cells. After a period of public comment, the NIH issued revised but roughly similar final guidelines on August 25, 2000.[16]

The guidelines define hPSCs as "cells that are self-replicating, are derived from human embryos or human fetal tissue, and are known to develop into cells and tissues of the three primary germ layers." Research on such cells may be conducted "only if the cells were derived (without federal funds) from human embryos that were created for the purposes of fertility treatment and were in excess of the clinical need of the individuals seeking such treatment." The guidelines thus carry forth the prohibition begun with President Clinton's December 1994 intervention against any research using embryos that are deliberately created for research purposes. This prohibition will be relevant to broad areas of stem cell research, including research on human therapeutic cloning. This involves the use of somatic cell nuclear transfer (cloning) technology to activate enucleated oocytes, which can then be dissected to produce immunologically compatible stem cells for the original cell donor/patient.[17] Although Great Britain's Human Fertilisation and Embryology Authority has been authorized to support this research, it will remain off-limits for federal funding in this country even if the NIH guidelines go into effect. This is because the NIH guidelines prohibit research on stem cells derived from embryos deliberately created for that purpose and because the Dickey-Wicker Amendment defines even clonally activated eggs as "embryos."

The NIH guidelines also apply to this area restrictions found in fetal tissue research that were advanced to prevent the promise of research or its benefits from becoming an incentive abortion or embryo destruction. Thus, "no inducements, monetary or otherwise, [may be] offered for the donation of human embryos for research purposes." Fertility clinics and/or their affiliated laboratories must implement specific written policies against such inducements. There must be "a clear separation between the decision to create embryos for fertility treatment and the decision to donate human embryos in excess of clinical need for research purposes to derive pluripotent stem cells." To ensure that this is so by providing time for decision, only frozen embryos may be used as a stem cell source. Researchers or investigators proposing to derive or utilize human pluripotent stem cells in research should have no role in securing spare embryos for this research, and the attending physician for fertility treatment and researcher should not be one and the same person. As is true for fetal tissue for transplantation, donation of human embryos should be made "without any restriction or direction regarding the individual(s) who may be the recipients of transplantation of the cells derived from the embryo."

The guidelines specify that the consent for such research should include the following provisions: (a) a statement that the embryos will be used to derive human pluripotent stem cells for research that may include human transplantation research; (b) a statement that the donation is made without any restriction or direction regarding the individual(s) who may be the recipient(s) of transplantation of the cells derived from the embryo; (c) a statement as to whether information that could identify the donors of the embryos, directly or through identifiers linked to the donors, will be removed before the derivation or the use of human pluripotent stem cells; (d) a statement that derived cells and/or cell lines may be kept for many years; (e) disclosure of the possibility that the results of research on the human pluripotent stem cells may have commercial potential, and a statement that the donor will not receive financial or any other benefits from any such future commercial development; (f) a statement that the research is not intended to provide direct medical benefit to the donor; and (g) a statement that embryos donated will not be transferred to a woman's uterus and will not survive the human pluripotent stem cell derivation process.

Recognizing that the process of preparing stem cell lines may involve costs, the guidelines permit payment for cell lines using federal funding as long as payment "does not exceed the reasonable costs associated with the transportation, processing, preservation, quality control, and storage of the stem cells." An assurance to this effect is also a requirement of IRB review.

The guidelines specify a series of research directions that are ineligible for NIH funding. In addition to prohibitions on the derivation of stem cell lines, the use of embryos deliberately created for research purposes, and somatic cell nuclear transfer (therapeutic cloning), they include "research in which human pluripotent stem cells are utilized to create or contribute to a human embryo;" "research in which human pluripotent stem cells are combined with an animal embryo;" and "research in which human pluripotent stem cells are used in combination with somatic cell nuclear transfer for the purposes of reproductive cloning of a human."

Finally, the guidelines make provision for the establishment of a new high-level NIH review body, the NIH Human Pluripotent Stem Cell Review Group (HPSCRG). The HPSCRG must hold public meetings for each funding request to use a line of human pluripotent stem cells that has not been previously reviewed and approved by the HPSCRG. On an ongoing basis, the HPSCRG reviews documentation of compliance with the NIH guidelines. It compiles a yearly report on the number of applications and proposals reviewed and the titles of all awarded applications (including those for NIH intramural projects), and it serves as a resource for recommendations to the NIH with regard to any revisions to the guidelines.

On August 9, 2001, in a public address to the nation, President George W. Bush announced the adoption of a national policy on stem cell research. This permits federal funding for research on cell lines developed (under private auspices) previous to that date. He thus adopted a conservative version of the use-versus-derivation position articulated earlier by the NIH (although not one that would permit the use of cell lines from embryos destroyed following the August 9 date). In the same address, the President also announced formation of a council "to monitor stem cell research, to recommend appropriate guidelines and regulations and to consider all of the medical and ethical ramifications of biomedical innovation."[18]

As of this writing, many questions remain unanswered. Scientists have asked whether the cell lines existence at the time of the President's address will suffice for the needs of federally funded researchers.[19] It is also not clear whether those cell lines will be expected to conform to the conditions of derivation set by the previous NIH guidelines. IRBs should remain alert to developments in this rapidly evolving area.

Conclusion

Research involving fetuses and in vitro fertilization presents the IRB with a wide range of difficult regulatory and ethical questions. This chapter has presented the background information that IRB members, researchers, and institutional officials will need to establish policy related to this often complex and controversial area of research. Research involving stem cells is especially problematic as federal policy in this area is likely to undergo major changes over the next few years.

References

1. National Commission for the Protection of Human Subjects of Biomedical and Behavioral Research. Research on the fetus (DHEW (OS) 76–127) and Appendix: Research on the fetus (DHEW (OS) 76–128). 1975. Washington DC, Government Printing Office.

2. Code of Federal Regulations. Title 45A—Department of Health and Human Services; Part 46—Protection of Human Subjects. Updated 1 Oct 1997. Access date 18 Apr 2001. World Wide Web http://www4.law.cornell.edu/cfr/45p46.htm

3. 104th Congress. Making appropriations for fiscal year 1996 to make a downpayment toward a balanced budget, and for other purposes. Public Law 104–99, Section 128; 110 Stat 34. 26 Jan 1996.

4. 105th Congress. Omnibus consolidated and emergency appropriations for the fiscal year ending September 30, 1999, and for other purposes. Public Law 105–277; 112 Stat. 2681. 21 Oct 1998. Access date 24 Apr 2001. World Wide Web http://frwebgate.access.gpo.gov/cgi-bin/getdoc.cgi?dbname=105_cong_public_laws&docid=f:publ277.105.pdf

5. Merton V. The exclusion of pregnant, pregnable, and once-pregnable people (aka women) from biomedical research. *Am J Law Med* 19(4):369–451, 1993.

6. Charo R. A. Protecting us to death: Women, pregnancy, and clinical research trials. *St Louis Univ Law Journal* 38(1):135–187, 1993.

7. Freed C. R, Greene P. E, Breeze R. E, Tsai W. Y, DuMouchel W, Kao R, Dillon S, Winfield H, Culver S, Trojanowski J. Q, Eidelberg D, Fahn S. Transplantation of embryonic dopamine neurons for severe Parkinson's disease. *N Engl J Med* 344(10):710–719, 2001.

8. National Institutes of Health. Human fetal tissue transplantation research: Report of the Advisory Committee to the Director. Dec 1988. Washington D.C., The National Institutes of Health.

9. 103rd Congress. National Institutes of Health Revitalization Act of 1993, 10 Jun 1993, Access date 24 Apr 2001. World Wide Web http://ohrp.osophs.dhhs.gov/humansubjects/guidance/publiclaw103–43.htm

10. Weiss R. Fetal cell research funds are at risk: Scientists fear curbs over abortion. *Washington Post.* A3. Jan 26, 2001.

11. Ethics Advisory Board. Report and conclusions: HEW support of human in vitro fertilization and embryo transfer. *Fed Regist* 44:35033–35058, 18 Jun 1979.

12. National Institutes of Health. Report of the Human Embryo Research Panel, 27 Sep 1994. Bethesda, MD.

13. Green R. M. *The Human Embryo Research Debates: Bioethics in the Vortex of Controversy.* New York: Oxford University Press. 2001.

14. Thomson J. A, Itskovitz-Eldor J, Shapiro S. S, Waknitz M. A, Swiergiel J. J, Marshall V. S, Jones J. M. Embryonic stem cell lines derived from human blastocysts. *Science* 282(5391):1145–1147, 1998.

15. Shamblot M. J, Axelman J, Wang S, Bugg E. M, et al. Derivation of pluripotential stem cells from cultured human primordial germ cells. *Proceedings of the National Academy of Science* 95:13726–13731, 1998.

16. National Institutes of Health. NIH Guidelines for Research using Human Pluripotent Stem Cells. *Fed Regist* 65: 69951, 21 Nov 2000. Access date 7 May 2001. World Wide Web http://www.nih.gov/news/stemcell/stemcellguidelines.htm

17. Lanza R. P, Caplan A. L, Silver L. M, Cibelli J. B, West M. D, Green R. M. The ethical validity of using nuclear transfer in human transplantation. *JAMA* 284(24):3175–3179, 2000.

18. President's statement on funding stem cell research. *New York Times*, August 10, 2001.

19. Stolberg, SG. Scientists urge bigger supply of stem cells. *New York Times*, September 11, 2001.

Research Involving Pregnant Women

Angela J. Bowen

INTRODUCTION

Women have traditionally been protected from research risks, especially in early-phase studies. Women of childbearing potential were specifically excluded from participation in Phase I and II studies until new guidance was issued[1] that removed the need to preferentially exclude women of childbearing potential. This 1993 guidance also stressed the need for studies to be done to evaluate any sex- or gender-related differences in the response to study treatments. (These guidance documents unfortunately use *sex-related differences* and *gender-related differences* interchangeably, mirroring our cultural, political, and societal ambivalence in the use of these terms.) Later guidance documents to IRBs advised that they should "assure that women were not unreasonably excluded" from a protocol. This led many IRBs to try to devise systems to assure equal representation of women in all trials. The guidance did not anticipate that every protocol would have equal numbers of men and women, but simply aimed to assure that before approval some studies would be conducted in both sexes, thereby noting any differences of therapeutic significance.

The IRB process is ill equipped to determine whether enough women have been included in the evaluations of a new compound or device. The number of women already studied, or currently enrolled, is often not revealed in the protocol being reviewed, nor is the number planned into future studies. It is therefore appropriate that the study sponsor should assume the responsibility for determining if prior studies have adequately evaluated gender differences. From the standpoint of ethical standards, it makes no sense for the IRB to concentrate on the numbers of women enrolled in an individual trial.

Sex and Gender Differences

There are sometimes sex-dependent differences in pharmacokinetic and pharmacodynamics parameters. (*Sex dependent* denotes genetic, hormonal, reproductive, and physical differences.) There are likely to be gender differences in many areas of research, especially in the behavioral sciences. (*Gender differences* is the term used to describe the variability between men and women that is attributable to influences such as society, culture, or history.) These protocols should be carefully reviewed to ascertain whether one gender may have different risks, or receive different benefits, because of gender. Special protections may be necessary if increased risk or benefit is determined for one gender.

IRBs should recall that these guidance documents were developed in response to activist pressure to ensure that women had equal access to all things, and to the pressure from these and other groups to ensure that drugs, biologics, and devices were tested in all patient populations where they might be used. The historical practice had been to test compounds in normal young males through Phase II and, finally, in the general population, excluding pregnant women and children, in Phase III. After marketing, products were labeled with the indication that they had not been tested in pregnant women and, therefore, should be used with caution in this population. This system was imperfect but did have the advantage that, by the time the drug was marketed, it had been through animal testing and the teratologic and mutagenic tendencies were well documented. Considerable generalizable knowledge was also accumulated before marketing under this system, thereby reducing the relative risk to pregnant women and their fetuses.

The original guidance[2(Sec.207)] admonished that no pregnant woman could be involved as a research subject unless the purpose was to attend to health needs of the mother and the fetus was placed at risk only to the degree necessary to treat the mother. This is still sound advice and should be weighed by the IRB in review of such research. Although the FDA has urged IRBs to assist the agency in implementing changes and not to needlessly exclude pregnant women, the IRB's first responsibility is to the subject and not to social change.

Women of Childbearing Potential

One cannot discuss research in pregnant women without mentioning research in women of childbearing potential. It must be assumed that pregnancies will occur in this group regardless of the precautions advised. Thus, the IRB must evaluate the various safeguards that might be offered that would afford some increase in subject safety. Frequent pregnancy tests, "reliable" contraception, and abstinence are all recommended, with abstinence being the only choice one can really count on. Because reliable decision making in this age group is often not yet perfected, a strong warning about what to do in case unprotected intercourse occurs is highly recommended. The consent document should contain a clear warning about the possibility of birth defects if pregnancy should occur. In most cases, women of childbearing potential should not be included in trials if teratogenicity is likely. The risk of a malformed child far outweighs any possible societal benefit. Also note that the risks of teratogenic compounds may be transferable between the sexes. A mutagenic compound may be given to a man who may impregnate a woman who is unaware of the risk. Some caution should be extended by the IRB to known consorts, where possible. When new information regarding risk becomes available during the course of the study, the consent document should be revised, subjects may need to be contacted, and the IRB and investigator should consider narrowing the study inclusion criteria.

IRB Review of a Study Involving Pregnant Women

The investigator's brochure should be carefully reviewed by a physician IRB member to ascertain whether the appropriate animal studies have been completed and, if so, to evaluate the results. Look especially for fetal loss, deformities, low birth weight, and reduced survival, as well as any evidence of mutagenicity. If these studies have not been completed, research should not be commenced in pregnant women unless there is a clear therapeutic need or benefit to the mother or the fetus. In all cases, the risk to the fetus should be assessed and recorded in the minutes.

The protocol should be carefully reviewed for any opportunities to improve the risk/benefit ratio for both the mother and the fetus. In general, the later the term of the pregnancy, the less risk to the fetus. Therefore, if immediate intervention is not mandatory, delaying administration of the test article for as long as possible may be wise. The minutes of the IRB should clearly reflect that substantive thought and consultation, if necessary, has been given to protection of both mother and fetus. The protocol should be clear about what follow-up is planned for the pregnant woman up to and after delivery, although the research may be completed by then. Careful follow-up by the clinical investigator and consulting gynecologist can be recommended by the IRB. In no case should the investigator be the sole person to counsel or recommend termination of the pregnancy.

Be cautious in review that there is no added risk to the fetus as a consequence of the research and that, to the extent determinable, the possibility of survival of the fetus is enhanced by the research. Sometimes the research activity is directed at the fetus and not the mother. In such cases, the safety of the mother should be given primary attention.

The Consent Process

The consent document must clearly disclose all known risks of both the research article and research process, as well as how they compare with no intervention. When animal studies of reproductive toxicology and teratology have not been completed before initiation of clinical studies, the informed consent document becomes even more critical. The document must reveal, in simple terms, this lack of knowledge. If comparable compounds are available and are known or suspected to have deleterious effects on conception or fetal development, this should be included in the consent process and memorialized in the IRB minutes. Regular updates to the informed consent will be necessary as more complete information becomes available.

A considerable constituency believes that to exclude pregnant women from research until comprehensive reproductive toxicology testing is completed is to neglect them as a population. In any case, the pregnant woman must be fully informed regarding any reasonably foreseeable impact of the research on the fetus. As always, these controverted issues and their full discussion should be adequately recorded in the IRB minutes. If the father is known and available, his involvement in the decision should be encouraged, but not required.

The risks to the fetus and to the mother should be discussed individually so that it is clear who is at risk for what. If the father is available, he should be included in the consent process if the risk to the fetus is increased. If the mother's welfare is the primary concern, only her written consent should be required; however, having the father's agreement on behalf of the fetus is prudent. It is important to remember that the IRB can recommend and require additional protections beyond those already provided by the protocol. Consultation outside the research team can be beneficial to all parties.

Regulatory Issues

The Department of Health and Human Services (DHHS) amended its human-subjects protection regulations in January 2001.[2] The final rule was published in the *Federal Register* on January 17, 2001, to become effective March 19, 2001. The rule supports all special protections for pregnant women and fetuses involved in research that have been in force since 1975. The rule aims to promote a policy of presumed inclusion for pregnant women in research. This inclusion will be accomplished by allowing the woman to be the sole decision maker to participate in research. This particular change replaces the old policy of presumed exclusion.

Paternal consent had been necessary under the previous regulations. This provision led to the exclusion of many women from protocols that were expected to have direct benefit to the pregnant woman. Fathers were often not known or were unavailable to give consent. Rape victims were an especially vulnerable class. The new regulation provides for autonomy in these situations.

It should be noted that these changes in the regulations must be adhered to in the ongoing review of continuing projects funded under assurances with OHRP; therefore, changes to consents and/or protocols may be necessary. DHHS regulations require that certain conditions be met before IRB approval when the research involves pregnant women.[2(Sec.203,204)] These regulations require that, when the board considers such research, it should ensure that all of the following conditions are met:

1. Where scientifically appropriate, preclinical studies, including studies on pregnant animals, and clinical studies, including studies on nonpregnant women, have been conducted and provide data for assessing potential risks to pregnant women and fetuses

2. The risk to the fetus is not greater than minimal, or any risk to the fetus that is greater than minimal is caused solely by interventions or procedures that hold out the prospect of direct benefit for the woman or the fetus

3. Any risk is the least possible for achieving the objectives of the research

4. The woman's consent or the consent of her legally authorized representative is obtained in accord with the informed consent provisions of 45 CFR 46, subpart A, unless legally altered or waived[2(Sec.101(i)],2(Sec.116(c),(d)]

5. The woman or her legally authorized representative, as appropriate, is fully informed regarding the reasonably foreseeable impact of the research on the fetus or resultant child

6. For children[2(Sec.402(a)]] who are pregnant, assent and permission are obtained in accord with the provisions of 45 CFR 46, subpart D

7. No inducements, monetary or otherwise, will be offered to terminate a pregnancy

8. Individuals engaged in the research will have no part in any decisions as to the timing, method, or procedures used to terminate a pregnancy

9. Individuals engaged in the research will have no part in determining the viability of a fetus

The IRB should note that federal rules[2(Sec..202(e)]] define pregnancy as follows.

Pregnancy encompasses the period of time from the implantation until delivery. A woman shall be assumed to be pregnant if she exhibits any of the pertinent presumptive signs of pregnancy, such as missed menses, until the results of a pregnancy test are negative or until delivery.

Conclusion

Research involving pregnant women raises multiple important ethical and regulatory issues. Pregnant women are often vulnerable to exploitation and therefore require extra protections to ensure that research is conducted in an environment that allows all subjects to make informed and voluntary decisions about initial and ongoing research participation. This chapter explains the rationale for excluding pregnant women from research and the situations where the inclusion of this class of subjects may be appropriate. It is important for IRB members to understand the difference, in terms of criteria for IRB approval of research, between research that involves pregnant women and research that excludes women of childbearing potential.

References

1. Food and Drug Administration. Guidelines for the study and evaluation of gender differences in the clinical evaluation of drugs. *Fed Regist* 58(139):39406–39416, 22 Jul 1993.

2. Code of Federal Regulations. Title 45A—Department of Health and Human Services; Part 46—Protection of Human Subjects. Updated 1 Oct 1997. Access date 18 Apr 2001. World Wide Web http://www4.law.cornell.edu/cfr/45p46.htm

Research Involving Children

Robert M. Nelson

INTRODUCTION

Research involving children requires careful attention to the additional regulatory provisions[1(Subpart D)] that are intended to protect children from being enrolled in research that exceeds a level of justified risk. The National Commission in *The Belmont Report* wrote about the "special provisions" for children that respect for persons requires, including "the opportunity to choose to the extent they are able" (i.e., assent), honoring dissent "unless the research entails providing them a therapy unavailable elsewhere," and "seeking the permission of other parties [e.g., parents] in order to protect the subjects from harm."[2] In addition, the National Commission also established "an order of preference in the selection of classes of subjects (e.g., adults before children)" as "a matter of social justice" based on the judgment that children ought not to bear the burdens of research unless absolutely necessary. Finally, the National Commission discussed the scope of parental authority in enrolling a child in research, arguing that such decisions are morally justified if either the research may directly benefit the child[1(Sec.405)] or the risks of participation in the research "are equivalent to normal risks of childhood" (i.e., the concept of minimal risk).[1(Secs.404,406)] The concepts of minimal risk, prospect of direct benefit, assent, and permission are the basis for the special protections for children.[1(Subpart D)] This basis rests on the moral foundation of respect for children, justice, and the scope of parental authority.

This chapter will review the issues that should be considered when an IRB reviews research involving children, starting with the composition of the IRB and the general aspects of IRB review.

IRB Membership

Regulations[1(Sec.107),3(Sec.107)] require that if "an IRB regularly reviews research that involves a vulnerable category of subjects, such as children. . ., consideration shall be given to the inclusion of one or more individuals who are knowledgeable about and experienced in working with these subjects." Given that an IRB should also be "sufficiently qualified through the experience and expertise of its members," the simple addition of a pediatrician to an adult-oriented IRB does not create an IRB capable of reviewing pediatric research. In keeping with this concern, the National Bioethics Advisory Commission (NBAC) notes that "research involving special ethical considerations, such as. . .research involving individuals with vulnerabilities, should be reviewed by an IRB that has more expertise and experience in these special issues than a local IRB is likely to have."[4] The International Conference on Harmonisation (ICH) draft document on pediatric research (E11) requires that "there should be IRB/IEC members or experts consulted by the IRB/IEC who are knowledgeable in pediatric ethical, clinical, and psychosocial issues."[5]

Exempt Research

Research involving children can be considered exempt from further IRB review in accord with the pertinent regulations.[1[Sec.101(b)(1),(b)(3)-(b)(6)]] However, the exemption for "research involving the use of educational tests (cognitive, diagnostic, aptitude, achievement), survey procedures, interview procedures, or observation of public behavior"[1[Sec.101(b)(2)]] cannot be used for research involving children unless the research involves only the "observation of public behavior when the investigator(s) do not participate in the activities being observed."[1[Sec.401(b)]] An IRB should have a review process for determining exemptions that includes individuals with sufficient expertise in pediatrics to evaluate, for example, the normal educational practices that are used in "established or commonly accepted educational settings" for children.

General Criteria for IRB Approval

The Minimization of Risk

The special protections afforded to children found in 45 CFR 46, Subpart D, are in addition to the general criteria for IRB approval. First, the risks to children in the protocol must be minimized.[1(Sec.111(a)(1))] The IRB should consider the risks from the perspective of a child and not simply focus on the physical and economic risks. For example, the research area should be "child friendly" with an adequate play area and space for parents to remain with the child. Study-related laboratory samples should be obtained at the time of diagnostic testing whenever possible. With the growing number of pediatric drug studies, the IRB should be familiar with the various research design methods that minimize risk to the child. Examples include limiting research under some circumstances to pharmacokinetic and safety data, combining this approach with pharmacodynamic data, and minimizing the volume of blood withdrawn through the use of sensitive assays, pediatric-enabled laboratories, and population pharmacokinetic approaches.

A detailed explanation of these examples is provided in the ICH E11 draft guidance document.[5] First, "those conducting the study should be properly trained and experienced in studying the pediatric population, including the evaluation and management of potential pediatric adverse events." Second, "every attempt should be made to minimize the number of participants and of procedures, consistent with good study design." Third, data monitoring "mechanisms should be in place to ensure that a study can be rapidly terminated should an unexpected hazard be noted." The ICH E11 document presents a number of practical considerations "to minimize discomfort and distress." These include "personnel knowledgeable and skilled in dealing with the pediatric population and its age-appropriate needs, including skill in performing pediatric procedures; a physical setting with furniture, play equipment, activities, and food appropriate for age; . . . a familiar environment such as the hospital or clinic where participants normally receive their care; approaches to minimize discomfort of procedures, such as topical anesthesia . . . ; indwelling catheters rather than repeated venipunctures for blood sampling; [and] collection of some protocol-specified blood samples when routine clinical samples are obtained." Finally, given the difficulty at times of obtaining blood samples or placing an indwelling catheter, the IRB should consider limits on the number of "attempt[s] to obtain blood samples for a protocol and ensure a clear understanding of procedures if an indwelling catheter fails to function over time."

Selection of Subjects

The IRB is required to assure that the selection of subjects is equitable, taking into account the "purposes of the research and the setting in which the research will be conducted."[1(Sec.111(a)(3)),6(Sec.111)] Children are at risk of being a population of convenience, especially for researchers recruiting from within their own places of employment and from their own colleagues. An IRB should have sufficient expertise to consider the risks of either coercion or undue influence from the perspective of a child, given the setting in which recruitment takes place.

General Assessment of Risks

Before considering the special protections for children based on the category of risk and/or benefit, an IRB must first consider whether the "risks to subjects are reasonable in relation to anticipated benefits, if any, to subjects, as well as the importance of the knowledge that may reasonably be expected to result." As we shall see, Subpart D adds further specification to the reasonableness of risk by requiring that the risks and benefits of participating in the research are commensurate with the nonresearch alternatives. However, even minimal-risk research must be held to the standard of either anticipated benefits or knowledge gained in order to be approved by an IRB. In addition, the IRB should evaluate "only those risks and benefits that may result from the research" rather than the overall risks and benefits of therapies included in the research that the "subjects would receive even if not participating in the research." Although not explicitly stated in the federal regulations, one could interpret this requirement as calling for a "component analysis" of risks and benefits, and allow for a protocol that combines treatment and research to be judged as "minimal risk" based on the research component alone. These issues are discussed further below.

Research Design

An IRB must evaluate the experimental design of a research protocol, including the sample size justification, in order to minimize risks and determine the reasonableness of the risks with respect to the knowledge to be gained. A protocol that cannot answer the research question posed should not be approved. A sample size that exceeds the number of children necessary to answer the research question exposes additional children to unnecessary risk. As explained in the ICH E11 guidance document,[5] a pediatric trial requires different efficacy endpoints based on considerations of the age and development of the subjects. In addition, a pediatric trial may need to evaluate any adverse impact on "physical and cognitive growth and development" along with "possible effects on skeletal, behavioral, cognitive, sexual, and immune maturation and development." An IRB that reviews research involving children must have the necessary expertise and experience to evaluate the unique (and necessary) features of pediatric research.

Expedited Review

Expedited review of research involving children can be conducted by an IRB in accord with the regulations.[1(Sec.110),6(Sec.110)] The only difference is in category 2 concerning the volume and frequency of blood draws that can be considered under expedited review procedures. For children, "the amount drawn may not exceed the lesser of 50 mL or 3 mL per kg in an eight week period and collection may not occur more frequently than two times per week." This volume and frequency of blood draws does not establish an upper limit to what an IRB may approve using full-committee review. Neither does it establish an upper limit to what an

IRB may consider minimal risk depending on the age, weight, and health of the child.

Special Protections for Children in Research

The regulations[1(Sec.111(b))] require "additional safeguards . . . to protect the rights and welfare" of children involved in research as they are "vulnerable to coercion and undue influence." These special protections, found in Subpart D of 45 CFR 46, apply to all research subjects "who have not attained the legal age for consent to treatments or procedures involved in the research, under the applicable law of the jurisdiction in which the research will be conducted."[1(Sec.111(a)(2)),6(Sec.111)] The Food and Drug Administration (FDA) regulations found in 21 CFR 56[6(Sec.111)] also specify that additional safeguards should be considered by an IRB when children are involved in research. The Children's Health Act of 2000 requires that all research (including the FDA) "involving children that is conducted, supported, or regulated by the Department of Health and Human Services (DHHS) be in compliance" with Subpart D of 45 CFR 46 by April 17, 2001. The FDA adopted the provisions of Subpart D, with the exception of Sec. 46.408(c), effective April 30, 2001.[7]

The additional safeguards of Subpart D involve an additional determination by the IRB of the level of risk and the prospect of direct benefit presented by the proposed research. The IRB can approve research involving children only if it falls into one of three categories, provided that all of the criteria found in 45 CFR 46.111 are also fulfilled. The three categories are as follows.

1. Research presenting "no greater than minimal risk to children"[1(Sec.404)]

2. Research involving an intervention or procedure presenting more than minimal risk to children that offers the "prospect of direct benefit" or may "contribute to the . . . well-being" of the individual child[1(Sec.405)]

3. Research involving an intervention or procedure that presents only a "minor increase over minimal risk," yet does not offer any "prospect of direct benefit" or "contribute to the well-being" of the child[1(Sec.406)]

If an IRB cannot fit the research into one of these three categories, it must either disapprove the research or refer it to the Secretary of the DHHS. This is provided that "the research presents a reasonable opportunity to further the understanding, prevention, or alleviation of a serious problem affecting the health or welfare of children."[1(Sec.407)]

Sections 405 and 406 can be considered a breakdown of the stipulation in 45 CFR 46.111 that the "risks to subjects are reasonable in relation to anticipated benefits, if any, to subjects, and the importance of the knowledge that may reasonably be expected to result." Research that presents greater than minimal risk (to be defined later) can

only be approved if "the risk is justified by the anticipated benefit to the subjects"[1(Sec.405)] or the risk involved is only a "minor increase over minimal risk," and, as well, "the intervention or procedure is likely to yield generalizable knowledge about the subjects' disorder or condition which is of vital importance for the understanding or amelioration of the subjects' disorder or condition."[1(Sec.406)] For research to be approvable under §46.405, not only must there be a justifiable balance of risk and anticipated benefit, but "the relation of the anticipated benefit to the risk [must be] at least as favorable to the subjects as that presented by available alternative approaches." In effect, there must be "research equipoise" between two (or more) arms of a concurrently controlled trial (assuming one arm represents currently accepted practice), or between a single arm trial and the alternatives available outside of the research. Whether one can consider a placebo arm under this category will be discussed later.

As explained in Chapter 3 of the recent NBAC report, the concept of *research equipoise* refers to "the state in which there is 'an honest, professional disagreement' among experts about whether the proposed study interventions—both experimental and control interventions (including placebos)—should be the preferred treatment or practice. In other words, neither the experimental nor control intervention is preferred; there is genuine uncertainty about which intervention is better." Existence of research equipoise "does not require numeric equality of intervention risks or potential benefits. Rather, research equipoise requires approximate equality in the risk/ potential benefit ratios of the study and control interventions." A Phase 1 pediatric oncology trial is usually considered under this section, as the standard alternatives have been exhausted and the only remaining prospect for direct benefit may be the experimental intervention. "An experimental intervention may pose more risk to participants than accepted practice, as long as it also offers the prospect of greater direct benefit to the participant, and the relation between the risks and potential benefits falls within a range of equivalency to accepted practice." Although a parent's decision to enroll a child in a Phase 1 oncology trial is difficult, many believe the decision may be justified provided that the alternatives of no further experimental treatment and palliative care are presented.

The provision for IRB review and approval of research that does not offer the prospect of direct benefit was one of the more controversial aspects of the national commission's deliberations. One commissioner objected to the category, arguing that it unjustly exposed children with a "disorder or condition" to a level of risk, however minor, that was above that of a healthy child. Nevertheless, 45 CFR 46[1(Sec.406)] allows for research that does not offer the prospect of direct benefit to the individual child enrolled in the research, provided that it is only a "minor increase over minimal risk" and, additionally, the knowledge gained is of vital importance to understanding or ameliorating the child's disorder or condition. The ICH Good Clinical Practice

Guidelines also allows for nontherapeutic trials in children provided that the following conditions are met:

1. "Consent of a legally acceptable representative" is obtained.
2. The research objectives cannot be met using subjects capable of giving informed consent
3. The "foreseeable risks to the subjects are low"
4. The "negative impact on the subject's well-being is minimized and low"
5. The "trial is not prohibited by law"
6. The IRB has approved in writing the inclusion of such children
7. The research "should be conducted in patients having a disease or condition for which the investigational product is intended," unless otherwise justified

It is a matter of interpretation whether a "minor increase over minimal risk" is the same standard as "the foreseeable risks . . . are low." In addition, Subpart D does not allow IRB approval of research presenting greater than minimal risk to healthy child volunteers (i.e., without a disorder or condition).[1(Sec. 406)]

Interpretation of *Minimal Risk*

Key to the interpretation of Subpart D is the definition of *minimal risk,* as it establishes the level of risk to which children without a disorder or condition may be exposed during the course of research. *Minimal risk* is defined as "the probability and magnitude of harm or discomfort anticipated in the research are not greater in and of themselves than those ordinarily encountered in daily life or during the performance of routine physical or psychological examinations or tests."[1(Sec.102(i)),6(Sec.102(i))] The National Commission initially stipulated that this standard should be indexed to the lives "of healthy children." More recently, NBAC argued "that the standard for minimal risk should be an *absolute* standard and should be related to the risks of daily life that are familiar to all of us in the general population." Even so, reasonable differences of opinion exist about the interpretation of minimal risk according to an absolute standard. For example, if we interpret minimal risk to include all the risks that children ordinarily encounter, should a single radiograph of the hand and wrist be considered minimal risk given the frequency with which this routine examination is performed on healthy children?

The definition found in the current regulations does not include the phrase "of healthy children" out of concern that this may inappropriately restrict the types of research that could otherwise be performed. For example, could one perform a bone marrow aspiration to obtain research information as part of an oncology treatment protocol if there was no prospect of direct benefit (i.e., no clinically relevant information obtained at that same time)? Some would consider the overall risk and benefit of the protocol and find the research justified under 45 CFR 46;[1(Sec.405)] others would evaluate the risks and potential benefit of the bone marrow aspiration independently of the overall treatment protocol using a so-called compo-

nent analysis. As such, "the risks associated with components offering the prospect of direct benefits are judged and must be justified in relation to their potential to benefit the participant [i.e., 45 CFR §46.405]. Additionally, those of components designed solely to answer the research question are judged and must be justified in relation to their potential to generate knowledge [i.e., 45 CFR §46.406]." The NBAC's recent recommendations would not allow a child with a disorder or condition to be exposed to even a minor increase over minimal risk to pursue generalizable knowledge of vital importance in understanding or ameliorating that child's condition. Accepting the argument in favor of an absolute standard of minimal risk, one could still allow a relative standard of a minor increase over minimal risk provided that the research "intervention or procedure presents experiences . . . that are reasonably commensurate with those inherent in [the child's] actual or expected . . . situations." In effect, only those interventions or procedures that are reasonably commensurate with a particular child's experience could be considered as a minor increase over minimal risk. "In evaluating whether a given procedure or intervention qualifies as 'minimal risk,' an IRB should consider whether the risks presented are comparable to the risks that parents may ordinarily allow their children to experience in the course of their everyday lives."

Permission of the Parent(s)/Assent of the Child

The National Commission considered the commensurability of the research experience with a child's "actual or expected medical, dental, psychological, social, or educational" experience as establishing a child's ability to assent to the research. This requirement was explicitly added to the section referring to research presenting a minor increase over minimal risk (§46.405), as the commensurability of the research and nonresearch experience is implicit in the definition of minimal risk. A requirement that is common to all four categories of research (§46.404–407) is that "adequate provisions are made for soliciting the assent of the children and permission of their parents or guardians."

Parental Permission

Parental permission is treated in much the same way as informed consent, apart from some additional provisions found in §46.408. A *parent* (defined as "a child's biological or adoptive parent") or *guardian* (defined as "an individual who is authorized under applicable state or local law to consent on behalf of a child to general medical care") must agree to (i.e., permit) the child's participation in research.

All of the requirements of §46.116 of Subpart A concerning informed consent apply to parental permission, including the general and required elements. Similarly, the elements of informed parental permission can be modified or waived entirely in accord with §46.116(d). Documentation of parental permission is determined according to

§46.117 of Subpart A. There are some additional documentation and waiver requirements in Subpart D. "Where research is covered by §46.406 and §46.407 and permission is to be obtained from parents, both parents must give their permission unless one parent is deceased, unknown, incompetent, or not reasonably available, or when only one parent has legal responsibility for the care and custody of the child."[1[408(b)]] In addition, "if the IRB determines that a research protocol is designed for conditions or for a subject population for which . . . permission is not a reasonable requirement to protect the subjects (for example, neglected or abused children), it may waive the consent requirements. . ., provided an appropriate mechanism for protecting the children who will participate as subjects in the research is substituted, and provided further that the waiver is not inconsistent with federal, state, or local law." For example, many pediatric IRBs will waive the requirement for parental permission for research using adolescent subjects that involves medical procedures and treatment that the adolescent can consent to without parental knowledge, such as the use of contraceptives, treatment of sexually transmitted disease, treatment of alcohol and drug abuse, and so forth. The FDA did not adopt this provision for waiver of parent or guardian permission.[7]

Child Assent

Assent is defined as "a child's affirmative agreement to participate in research."[1[Sec.402(b)]] A child's passive resignation to submit to an intervention or procedure must not be considered assent. The federal regulations do not specify any of the elements of informed assent and do not indicate an age at which assent ought to be possible. Clearly, assent needs to be "tailored to the level of comprehension of the prospective participants." An IRB is granted wide discretion in determining whether a child is capable of assenting and can waive the requirement for child assent if a child is not capable of assent; if the research offers a prospect of direct benefit not available outside of the research (thus falling under the scope of parental authority in overriding a child's desires); or given the same conditions under which parental permission can be waived. An IRB is granted wide discretion in determining whether and how a child's assent is documented. As of April 30, 2001, the FDA is required to conduct research using children in accord with the special protections of Subpart D as incorporated into 21 CFR 50 and 56. Finally, as a matter of both justice and respect for persons, efforts should be made to conduct research using children capable of assent before enrolling those less able to assent.

Choice of Control Group (Placebo Controls)

An algorithm for evaluating the ethics of placebo control is presented in Chapter 10-10. The circumstances under which a placebo control is appropriate is a matter of controversy. The recent revision to the Declaration of Helsinki states that "the benefits, risks, burdens, and ef-fectiveness of a new method should be tested against those of the best current prophylactic, diagnostic, and therapeutic methods."[8] "This does not exclude the use of placebo, or no treatment, in studies where no proven prophylactic, diagnostic, or therapeutic method exists." The ICH document on the choice of control group (E10)[9] argues that one can use a placebo control if the withholding of the known effective therapy would not result in "serious harm, such as death or irreversible morbidity in the study population." The ICH E11[5] document on pediatric trials did not discuss placebo controls. Dr. Robert Temple of the FDA indicated in a recent public meeting that the threshold of irreversible morbidity or death contained in ICH E10 presumed informed consent and should not be applied to children. The presence of a placebo arm in a clinical trial does not preclude the research from being considered under 45 CFR 46[1(Sec.405)] as offering the prospect of direct benefit. An IRB should consider the risks and potential benefits of the research from the perspective of the subject, and evaluate the prospect of direct benefit without assuming the success or failure of the study intervention.

Approval by Federal Review Panel

Subpart D allows for the review and approval of research that is not otherwise approvable by an IRB under 45 CFR 46[1(Secs.404,405,406)] provided that "the research presents a reasonable opportunity to further the understanding, prevention, or alleviation of a serious problem affecting the health or welfare of children" and "the research will be conducted in accordance with sound ethical principles."[1(Sec.407)] An IRB may appeal to the Secretary of DHHS who, upon the advice of a "panel of experts" and after "opportunity for public review and comment," may issue an approval for the research. Clearly, such a review panel can only discharge this responsibility if the referring IRB (a) has already determined that the research fails to qualify under 45 CFR 46;[1(Secs.404,405,406)] (b) has determined that the research is potentially approvable under 45 CFR 46;[1(Sec.407)] and (c) has provided the underlying documentation and rationale for both determinations. A similar provision for appeal to the Commissioner of the FDA and expert consultation was adopted by the FDA.

Children's Health Act of 2000

A major concern of those interested in both supporting pediatric research and protecting the children who are involved as subjects in that research is the establishment of an effective and uniform set of protections. Toward this end, the Children's Health Act of 2000 was passed on October 17, 2000.[10] There are two aspects of this act that should be highlighted. First, the DHHS and thus the FDA were required to adopt by April 17, 2001, Subpart D of 45 CFR 46 as the uniform standard for the protection of children involved in research. The FDA adopted the provisions of Subpart D, with the exception of Sec.46.408(c), effective April 30, 2001. Second, the Secretary of DHHS is required to review Subpart D, "consider any modifications necessary to ensure the adequate and appropriate protection of children participating in research, and report the findings of the Secretary to Congress." In addition to a broad and in-depth review of the existing regulations, the Secretary is to review and report on the adequacy of IRB oversight of clinical trials involving children. The report is on whether "data and safety monitoring boards or other mechanisms" should be established to review the adverse events associated with ongoing research trials.

Conclusion

An IRB that reviews research involving children needs to possess sufficient experience and expertise, needs to be familiar with the special protections afforded pediatric research subjects by Subpart D, and needs to be capable of both ethical, scientific, and regulatory analysis of research trials from a pediatric perspective. Just as it is inappropriate for an investigator to conduct research involving children without sufficient pediatric expertise, an IRB that does not have the necessary knowledge and skill to analyze a pediatric research trial according to the "sound ethical principles" embodied in Subpart D is not in compliance with existing guidance regulations.

References

1. Code of Federal Regulations. Title 45A—Department of Health and Human Services; Part 46—Protection of Human Subjects. Updated 1 Oct 1997. Access date 18 Apr 2001. World Wide Web http://www4.law.cornell.edu/cfr/45p46.htm

2. National Commission for the Protection of Human Subjects of Biomedical and Behavioral Research. *The Belmont Report: Ethical principles and guidelines for the protection of human subjects of research,* 18 Apr 1979. Access date 22 Mar 2001. World Wide Web http://ohsr.od.nih.gov/mpa/belmont.php3

3. Code of Federal Regulations. Title 21, Chapter 1—Food and Drug Administration, DHHS; Part 50—Protection of Human Subjects. Updated 1 Apr 1999. Access date 18 Apr 2001. World Wide Web http://www4.law.cornell.edu/cfr/21p50.htm

4. National Bioethics Advisory Commission. Report on Institutional Review Boards, Vol 1, Dec 1998. Access date 29 Mar 2001. World Wide Web http://bioethics.gov/capacity/TOC.htm

5. Food and Drug Administration. International Conference on Harmonisation: E11 Clinical investigation of medicinal products in the pediatric population, 20 Jul 2000. World Wide Web http://www.ifpma.org/pdfifpma/E11step4.pdf

6. Code of Federal Regulations. Title 21, Chapter 1—Food and Drug Administration, DHHS; Part 56—Institutional Review Boards. Updated 1 Apr 1999. Access date 27 Mar 2001. World Wide Web http://www4.law.cornell.edu/cfr/21p56.htm

7. Food and Drug Administration, DHHS. Additional safeguards for children in clinical investigations of FDA-regulated products. *Fed Regist* 66(79):20589-20600, 2001. World Wide Web http:frwebgate.access.gpo.gov/cgi-bin/getdoc.cgi?dbname=2001_register&docid=fr24ap01-4

8. World Medical Association. *Declaration of Helsinki: Ethical Principles for Medical Research Involving Human Subjects.* World Medical Association, Inc.: WMA Policy. First adopted in Helsinki, Finland, in 1964. Updated 10 Jul 2000. Access date 20 Mar 2001. World Wide Web http://www.wma.net/e/policy/17-c_e.html

9. Food and Drug Administration. International Conference on Harmonisation: E10 Choice of control group and related issues in clinical trials. *Fed Regist* 64(185): 51767–51780, 24 Sep 1999. World Wide Web http://www.ifpma.org/pdfifpma/e10step4.pdf

10. 106th Congress. Children's Health Act of 2000, 9 May 2000. Access date 14 May 2001. World Wide Web http://frwebgate.access.gpo.gov/cgi-bin/getdoc.cgi?dbname=106_cong_public_laws&docid=cr09my00-78

Research Involving Adults with Decisional Impairment

Susan J. Delano

INTRODUCTION

Research involving adults with decisional impairment is not currently the subject of specific federal regulatory guidance. Federal research regulations provide that if an IRB regularly reviews research involving a vulnerable category of subjects, the membership should include "one or more individuals who are knowledgeable about and experienced in working with these subjects."[1][Sec.107(a)] The regulations also provide that "when some or all of the subjects are likely to be vulnerable to coercion or undue influence, such as children, prisoners, pregnant women, mentally disabled persons, or economically or educationally disadvantaged persons, additional safeguards have been included in the study to protect the rights and welfare of these subjects."[1][Sec.111(b)]

Based on the work of the National Commission for the Protection of Human Subjects of Biomedical and Behavioral Research, which was created in 1974, the then Department of Health, Education, and Welfare proposed specific additional regulations for research. These, in 1978, involved the "institutionalized mentally infirm" and they were never adopted.[2(Chap.11)] Research involving subjects with decisional impairment has recently been the subject of extensive debate at the state and national level.[3–5]

Who Are Adults with Decisional Impairment?

Adults who are decisionally impaired suffer from many different conditions that potentially affect their ability to reason and make sound choices. In the research context, this is most often considered in the context of a person's capacity to provide valid consent. The ability to provide initial or ongoing consent to research may be limited by a variety of problems associated with memory, understanding, and reasoning. For some, the impairment may be stable with little variation over time. For others, the level of impairment may fluctuate over time (e.g., a person with schizophrenia), or may progressively change over time (e.g., a person with Alzheimer's disease). It is also important to understand that capacity must be determined in relation to the specific task or decision-making circumstance. For example, a person may be capable of consenting to an interview but lack sufficient capacity to consent to a drug study.

The inclusion of decisionally impaired adults in research is an area of intense debate.[6] This is because, at the milder levels, these adults may be more vulnerable to coercion, and at more severe levels, they lack the capacity to provide informed consent, a basic legal and ethical requirement. For many, the issue of institutionalization is also a factor. Broad ethical concerns of justice, respect for persons, and beneficence are raised by the inclusion of decisionally impaired adults in research.

Protections for the Decisionally Impaired

The protections for this vulnerable population should be broadly applied to all decisionally impaired persons, regardless of the source of their impairment. A person impaired by a stroke, brain injury, or delirium secondary to renal failure or diabetes is entitled to the same level of protections as a person similarly impaired as a result of a mental illness such as schizophrenia or depression. With all such populations, however, care should be taken to distinguish between persons who are impaired and persons who have a condition that may cause impairment. For example, if a study involves persons with schizophrenia, the IRB should consider additional protections, as described in the following section. However, it would be incorrect to assume that all of the subjects will lack sufficient capacity to provide consent.

Issues That IRBs Should Consider

IRB Membership

If your IRB regularly reviews research involving adults with decisional impairment, your membership must include persons familiar with the nature of the disorders creating the decisional impairment and the concerns of the population. If your IRB does not regularly review this type of research, you must involve a consultant who has this expertise.[1(Sec.107)] Depending on the amount and type of research you conduct with decisionally impaired subjects, multiple representatives may be appropriate.

Types of Expertise to Consider

1. **Scientific/clinical expertise**—Such expertise provides an understanding of the scientific/clinical aspects of the protocol and an understanding of the subject population (what burdens their condition imposes, what the treatment of their condition entails, what their living conditions are likely to be) and how the research is likely to impact them.

2. **Patient/consumer representative(s)**—These individuals will provide an understanding of the subject population and how the research is likely to impact them. These persons can also help tailor recruitment procedures to minimize coercion and enhance the consent process and content to maximize understanding and free choice.

3. **Family member(s)**—Family members can provide an understanding of the subject population and how the research is likely to impact them. These persons may act as advocates for the role of family members/friends (when approved by the proposed subject) in providing support to subjects in their decision making and monitoring research participation.

4. **Advocacy group member(s)**—These people can provide an understanding of the subject population and how the research is likely to impact them. They may also bring a broader perspective, e.g., National Alliance for the Mentally Ill.

Limits on the Inclusion of Incapable Subjects

Necessity of Involving Subjects Who Lack Capacity. A generally agreed-upon principle is that incapable subjects (persons who do not have sufficient capacity to consent) should not be involved in research that could be conducted with capable subjects. An exception to this principle is that an IRB may permit incapable subjects to participate in such research when it provides access to an important potential benefit, particularly one that is not otherwise available to the subjects. For example, the IRB may decide that it is appropriate to permit inclusion of incapable subjects in a study of a new drug if the subjects are intolerant of, or have not responded to, standard medications.

Debate Over Participation in Research That Does Not Offer a Prospect of Direct Benefit. This is the most intense area of debate, with the focus being on research that is more than minimal risk but not high risk. It is widely accepted that in the absence of a specific advance directive, authorizing participation in this type of research *and* surrogate consent, no incapable person should be involved in research that involves moderate or high risk. When the research is not expected to benefit the person directly. Similarly, there is little debate about the authority of surrogates to consent to research involving no more than minimal risk. The remaining category, which generally equates to the "minor increase over minimal risk" category (e.g., MRI with sedation, indwelling catheters for a short duration) in the children's regulations, has been directly endorsed, with surrogate consent and appropriate protections, by many groups such as the New York State Department of Health Advisory Work Group on Human Subject Research Involving the Protected Classes, the Attorney General's Research Working Group of the Office of the Maryland Attorney General, and Expert Panel Report to the National Institutes of Health: Research Involving Individuals with Questionable Capacity to Consent. The National Bioethics Advisory Commission's report on adults with decisional impairments includes recommendations that prohibit research involving more than minimal risk and no expected benefit except when the subject has previously created a specific advance directive, or the research is approved by a special federal panel.

Capacity

Capacity to provide consent is an essential component of valid consent.

Assessment of Capacity. For all research, regardless of the study population, the person who obtains the subject's consent must determine that the person has sufficient capacity to give it. In most cases, this assessment occurs as part of the discussion with the proposed subject about the study. The person obtaining consent evaluates the questions raised by the subject and the answers given to questions asked. The consent interviewer may only seek consent when he or she is satisfied that the person is capable of making the decision. Capacity is documented by the signature on the consent form of the person obtaining consent. (Note: the person who obtains consent also documents, by his or her signature, lack of coercion and full disclosure.) When subjects are patients, a note should be written in the progress notes of their charts.

Based on the risk/benefit ratio of the study and the nature of the subject population, the IRB should consider the need for an independent assessment of capacity. The IRB may set qualifications for the person making the assessment, such as requiring a licensed clinical psychologist, psychiatric social worker, psychiatrist, or gerontologist. Generally, as the risks increase, the benefits decrease, the potential vulnerability of the subjects increases, and/or the likelihood increases that a person's capacity or lack of capacity will not be obvious, the requirements should become more stringent. The independent assessment of capacity should be documented by a formal note that is signed and dated. (A sample statement is shown in Figure 9.4.1.) When subjects are patients, a note should be written in the progress notes of their charts.

Standards for Capacity. The level of capacity required to consent varies according to the type and complexity of the decisions that are to be made. As the complexity and risks of the procedures increase, the required level of capacity should also increase. For example, the level of capacity needed to consent to a study involving a blood draw is less than the capacity required to consent to a placebo-controlled drug study. There are four commonly used standards of capacity:[7]

"I examined _____(name)_____ on ___(date)___ for the purpose of determining whether he/she is capable of understanding the purpose, nature, risks, benefits, and alternatives (including nonparticipation) of the research, making a decision about participation, and understanding that the decision about participation in the research will involve no penalty or loss of benefits to which the patient is otherwise entitled, for _____(investigator name)_____ 's research project _____(title of project)_____.

On the basis of this examination I have arrived at the conclusion that:

    (a)   this patient has this capacity at this time   [ ]

or   (b)   there is a doubt about this patient's capacity at this time   [ ]

or   (c)   this patient clearly lacks this capacity at this time   [ ]

     [Statement must be signed and dated.]

Figure 9.4.1   Sample Language for Documentation of Capacity

1. The ability to evidence a choice; that is, to communicate a yes or no decision. This standard is applicable to all risk/benefit levels.

2. The ability to understand relevant information, that is, the person can tell you what the research procedures involve and what the consent information includes; e.g., a right to withdraw. This standard is also applicable to all risk/benefit levels.

3. The ability to appreciate the situation and its likely consequences. The person can understand what research participation involves for him or her and what the likely outcomes are. He or she can apply the information to his or her own situation. This standard generally applies to all research involving more than minimal risk.

4. The ability to manipulate information rationally. This standard focuses on process, not outcome. For example, are decisions consistent with the religious, moral, and other beliefs of the person? This standard is critical at the most unfavorable risk/benefit levels.

Enhancing Comprehension. Enhancing comprehension increases the likelihood that a person will have the capacity to consent or to give a maximally informed assent. The process should be tailored to the specific population. Consider videotapes, photographs, breaking down information into more easily understood components, repetition, and involving a family member, friend, or peer counselor. The IRB should also consider ways of ensuring that information about the study is provided to the subjects during study participation.

As part of the consent process, prospective subjects should be asked questions about the research to determine whether they recall and understand what has been explained.[8] Questions should be open-ended; for example:

1. Can you tell me what will happen if you agree to take part in this study?

2. Will this study help you?

3. Can you tell me about the possible side-effects of the study drug?

4. Do you have to be in this study?

5. Can you leave this study once it begins?

6. What will happen if you decide not to be in this study?

Education of the subject can occur during this process and should continue until the person understands the information and is able to provide correct answers.

Studies Involving Persons Who Lack Sufficient Capacity to Consent

If your IRB determines that it is appropriate to involve subjects who do not have sufficient capacity to consent, additional concerns arise.

Notifications to an Incapable Subject. To the extent possible, do each of the following:

1. Inform the subject about the study and seek his or her agreement to participate

2. Notify the subject that he or she retains the right to object and can leave the study at any time

3. Notify the subject in a sensitive way that he or she lacks the sufficient capacity to consent and provide an opportunity for the subject to contest the decision

4. Explain surrogate consent procedures and options

Surrogate Consent.   Consider the proposed subject population. If it is likely that subjects will lose capacity during a study, they should be encouraged at the beginning of the study to appoint a surrogate. The surrogate will have the authority to consent to continuing participation, amendments to the study, and withdrawal from the study if the subject loses capacity.

For subjects found to lack sufficient capacity to consent, you should check with your legal counsel because the determination of who can provide surrogate consent for research is a matter of state law and varies from state to state. Although surrogate consent is routinely employed in research, as it is in clinical practice, the legal basis is often not clear.

Classes of Possible Surrogates.
  1. *Surrogate appointed by the subject when fully capable (durable power of attorney, research advance directive, health care proxy).* Although these surrogates are widely accepted, they have limited applicability, and such documents are rarely executed.

  2. *Court or court-appointed guardian with authority to consent to research.* These are also widely accepted, but of limited use. Research is not generally contemplated when guardians are appointed. Unless the purpose of the research is to provide access to an experimental treatment, the stress and stigma associated with a court determination of a lack of capacity are seldom justified for research purposes.

  3. *Surrogate chosen by the subject when incapable of consenting but capable of choosing a surrogate.* Individuals may lack sufficient capacity to consent to a complex study. However, they may have sufficient capacity to choose their spouse, adult child, friend, or trusted advisor to make decisions for them. The subject's capacity to choose a surrogate should be evaluated by an appropriately qualified person. The choice of a surrogate should be documented. (At least one witness who is independent of the research is recommended.) The surrogate should not be affiliated with the research or the institution. (This restriction should not apply if the surrogate is related to the subject by blood, marriage, or adoption.) Subject-chosen surrogates are generally accepted.

  4. *Family member (parent, spouse, adult child, adult sibling).* This class of surrogates is used in practice every day, but with some legal uncertainty. Consent by family members is generally accepted for minimal-risk research and for research that offers a prospect of direct benefit. Family members are generally not permitted to consent to research involving higher risk and no expected benefit. Some disagreement exists about the appropriateness of family members as surrogates for research with no expected benefit and a minor increase over minimal risk.

  5. *Close friend.* This class of surrogates recognizes nontraditional relationships. The use of close friends as surrogates has limited acceptance. In most states, there is currently no clear legal basis for their authority to consent to research.

Basis of Surrogate Decision Making.   Research surrogates need to be informed about the study, its implications for the individual, and their role in providing initial and ongoing consent. Research surrogates also need to be in-

formed about their responsibility for withdrawing a subject from participation when continuing participation is no longer consistent with the subject's known wishes or is no longer in the best interests of the subject.

The decisions of surrogates may be based on the preferred standard of substituted judgment, reflecting the views of the individual when he or she was capable. (The surrogate should consider known preferences, beliefs, and prior decisions about research.) Surrogate decisions can also be based on the best interests of the subject, when the views of the individual are not known.

Conclusion

Consent is an ongoing process. The research team should discuss participation with the subject, explaining procedures and obtaining continued agreement to participate as the study continues. Surrogates and, when appropriate, family members or friends should be kept informed about the subject's participation in the study. Note: The subject should be asked for permission to involve family members or friends, and may choose not to have them involved.

The IRB may add consent auditors to the consent process.[1][Sec.109(e)] Their use is encouraged when the level of risk is high or when vulnerable subjects are involved in more-than-minimal-risk research, particularly when there is no expected benefit to subjects. The IRB may also determine that a medical monitor should be appointed to review each subject's participation and recommend withdrawal from the study when clinically indicated. An expanded role has been proposed for data safety monitoring boards to provide information to IRBs during the course of a study.

The topics covered in this chapter and many other related topics are addressed in more detail in *Ethics in Psychiatric Research: A Resource Manual for Human Subjects Protection,* edited by Pincus, Lieberman, and Ferris.[9]

References

  1. Code of Federal Regulations. Title 45A—Department of Health and Human Services; Part 46—Protection of Human Subjects. Updated 1 Oct 1997. Access date 18 Apr 2001. World Wide Web http://www4.law.cornell.edu/cfr/45p46.htm

  2. Levine R J. *Ethics and Regulation of Clinical Research,* Ed 2. Baltimore, MD: Urban and Schwarzenberg. 1986.

  3. National Bioethics Advisory Commission. Research involving persons with mental disorders that may affect decisionmaking capacity: report and recommendations, Dec 1998. Access date 29 Mar 2001. World Wide Web http://bioethics.gov/capacity/TOC.htm

  4. National Institutes of Health. Research involving individuals with questionable capacity to consent: Points to consider, 5 Jan 2001. Access date 29 Mar 2001. World Wide Web http://grants.nih.gov/grants/policy/questionablecapacity.htm

  5. New York State Department of Health. Report of the Advisory Work Group to the Commissioner of the Department of Health. Human Subject Research Involving the Protected Classes. December 1998. New York.

6. Michels R. Are research ethics bad for our mental health? *N Engl J Med* 340(18):1427–1430, 1999.

7. Applebaum P S, Grisso T. The MacArthur Treatment Competence Study: Mental illness and competence to consent to treatment. *Law Hum Behav* 19:105–126, 1995.

8. Wirshing D A, Wirshing W C, Marder S R, Liberman R P, Mintz J. Informed consent: Assessment of comprehension. *Am J Psychiatry* 155(11):1508–1511, 1998.

9. Pincus H A, Lieberman J A, Ferris S. *Ethics in Psychiatric Research: A Resource Manual for Human Subjects Protection,* Ed 1. Washington, DC: American Psychiatric Association. 1999.

Research Involving Prisoners

Emest D. Prentice, Bruce G. Gordon, Christopher J. Kratochvil, and Gail D. Kotulak

INTRODUCTION

Prisoners are considered a vulnerable subject population in need of additional protections. Institutional Review Boards (IRBs) involved in the review of research involving prisoners should be familiar with the different federal and state regulations that apply to research to be conducted under their approval. Requirements may vary for the research conducted in a federal prison versus a state facility and according to the source of funding. For the purpose of this chapter, however, only the Department of Health and Human Services (DHHS) regulations for the protection of human subjects who are prisoners will be addressed. Although no precise figures are available, it is likely that most of the research involving prisoners conducted in the United States is subject to DHHS regulation 45 CFR 46.[1] This includes a subpart providing additional protections for prisoners who participate in research. It should also be mentioned that in 1978 the Food and Drug Administration (FDA) issued special regulations for research involving prisoners, but they were withdrawn. Thus, the current FDA regulations for the protection of human subjects, codified at 21 CFR 50, 56,[2,3] do not include any specific additional protections for research subjects who are prisoners. The FDA does consider prisoners to be a vulnerable subject population for which the IRB must include additional safeguards.[3][Sec.111(b)]

Historical Overview

Although medical experiments involving prisoners in the United States date back at least to the beginning of the twentieth century, World War II was the impetus for a dramatic increase in the number of experiments performed in prisons.[4] With the war raging in both Europe and the Pacific, medical endeavors to protect the lives of millions of American soldiers became an overriding goal. Society in general espoused the view that prisoners owed their country nothing less than participation in these worthy endeavors. Participation in research was cast as the prisoner's contribution to the war effort. Therefore, with little public scrutiny and, in many cases, willing cooperation of the inmates, the research proceeded apace. Prisoners participated in a wide range of experiments, including research on dengue fever, sandfly fever, gonorrhea, scurvy, malaria, gas gangrene, and studies of alternative sources of plasma.[5]

Some of the best known of these wartime prison experiments were the malaria studies conducted at Stateville Penitentiary in Illinois, which continued for two years and involved 400 prisoners.[6] During the 1946 Nuremberg doctors' trial, German physicians, accused of experimenting on concentration camp prisoners, offered the Stateville research as an example of similar experimentation in the United States.[7] Prominent American researcher and the prosecution's chief witness on American medical ethics,

Andrew Ivy, defended the U.S. prison research program, stating that no American prisoner had ever been experimented upon against his will. He also refused to concede that coercion was necessarily inherent in a prison environment. According to Ivy, as long as the consent of the subject was obtained, the research was based on animal experimentation, and was directed by qualified persons, experimentation on prisoners was acceptable.[7] Indeed, the American Medical Association in 1948 endorsed these three principles.[8]

After the war, experimentation on prisoners in the U.S. continued unabated. Indeed, the United States was one of a few countries in the world that persisted in using prisoners for research. In the 1960s, after the FDA mandated tests of new drugs on humans, large pharmaceutical companies turned to the penal system for a seemingly inexhaustible supply of "stable, long-term" subjects who were particularly valuable in Phase I drug and cosmetic testing.[9] The number of these subjects that fell ill or died as a direct result of these experiments was not insignificant.

In the late 1960s and early 1970s, as the public became aware of a series of ethically questionable studies, human subject research, in general, became an area of concern and distrust. In 1972, details of the then 40-year-long Tuskegee syphilis study were revealed in an exposé in the *Washington Star* and subsequently in the *New York Times*.[10] Public outcry, largely mirrored in political circles, was immediate; it expanded to encompass concern over all research, especially that involving vulnerable populations like prisoners. Both state and federal legislation were introduced to limit the use of inmates as research subjects, and state prison research programs were terminated in a large majority of the states. By 1976, the federal government announced the end of research in federal prisons.[11]

The Commissioner's Report

In 1978, the National Commission for the Protection of Human Subjects of Biomedical and Behavioral Research produced recommendations on prisoner research.[12] The commissioners' report formed the basis for 45 CFR 46 Subpart C—Additional DHHS Protections Pertaining to Biomedical and Behavioral Research Involving Prisoners as Subjects.[1] Under these regulations, prisoner research continued, though clearly on a much reduced scale, particularly in the area of medical research. As a matter of fact, in the preamble to Subpart C, it is noted that most testimony before the commission opposed the use of prisoners in any medical research that did not offer direct benefit to the individual prisoner.[13] Clearly, the regulations were intended to provide a high level of protection. Recent events, however, have called into question the adequacy of these additional protections and the extent to which they are being utilized. In May 2000, the Office of Protection from Research Risks (OPRR) issued guidance in interpreting the regulations in Subpart C.[14] In July and August 2000, OPRR demanded the suspension of prisoner research at the University of Texas Medical Branch at Galveston and the University of Miami because it did not appear that Subpart C regulations were being followed.[15] Whether these suspensions will lead to further guidance or regulations remains to be seen.

Definition of *Prisoner*

According to 45 CFR 46,[1][Sec.303(c)] "'prisoner' means any individual involuntarily confined or detained in a penal institution. The term is intended to encompass individuals sentenced to such an institution under a criminal or civil statute as well as individuals detained in other facilities by virtue of statutes or commitment procedures which provide alternatives to criminal prosecution or incarceration in a penal institution, and individuals detained pending arraignment, trial, or sentencing." This includes situations where a human subject becomes a prisoner after the research has commenced.

Composition of the IRB

The IRB reviewing prisoner research must be specially constituted.[1][Sec.304(a),(b)] The board must include at least one member who is a prisoner or a prisoner representative with the appropriate background and experience to serve in that capacity. Most IRBs, for obvious practical and lo-

gistical reasons, do not have prisoners as IRB members and, therefore, elect to use a prisoner representative. The representative should have a close working knowledge of prison conditions and the life of a prisoner. Suitable candidates are former prisoners, prison chaplains, and prison psychologists or social workers who deal with prisoners or the families of prisoners. Individuals who are prisoner advocates also qualify. The IRB must be so constituted for all reviews of research involving prisoners, including initial review, continuing review, protocol amendments, and review of adverse events. If a human subject participating in an IRB-approved protocol becomes a prisoner after the research has begun, the protocol and consent document would need to be reviewed by the IRB again, with a prisoner representative present. Unless the IRB reapproves the research for inclusion of the prisoner(s), the newly incarcerated individual must be withdrawn from the study.

Type of IRB Review

Per the requirements of 45 CFR 46,[1][Sec.101(i)] research involving prisoners may not be exempted under Section 46.101(b). In addition, OPRR (now the Office for Human Research Subject Protections [OHRP]) recommends that all prisoner research, even if technically expeditable under Section 46.110, should be reviewed by the full IRB with a prisoner or prisoner representative present at a convened meeting. This is because prisoners are a vulnerable subject population, and therefore review by the full IRB is warranted from an ethical standpoint.

Types of Research Permitted

Only certain types of research are permitted under 45 CFR 46, Subpart C. There are four categories (A, B, C, D) listed in 45 CFR 46.[1][Sec.306(a)(2)]

Categories A and B

Research that is not greater than minimal risk may be allowable[1][Sec.306(a)(2)(A),(B)] if it consists solely of the following:

(A) Study of the possible causes, effects, and processes of incarceration, and of criminal behavior, provided that the study presents no more than minimal risk and no more than inconvenience to the subjects; or
(B) Study of prisons as institutional structures or of prisoners as incarcerated persons, provided that the study presents no more than minimal risk and no more than inconvenience to the subjects.

Categories C and D

Research may be allowable under 45 CFR 46[1][Sec.306(a)(2)(C),(D)] if it consists solely of the following:

(C) Research on conditions particularly affecting prisoners as a class (for example, vaccine trials and other research on hepatitis which is much more prevalent in prisons than elsewhere; and research on social and psychological problems such as alcoholism, drug addiction, and sexual assaults) provided that the study may proceed only after the Secretary has consulted with appropriate experts including experts in penology, medicine, and ethics, and published notice, in the *Federal Register*, of his intent to approve such research; or

(D) Research on practices, both innovative and accepted, which have the intent and reasonable probability of improving the health or well-being of the subject. In cases in which those studies require the assignment of prisoners in a manner consistent with protocols approved by the IRB to control groups which may not benefit from the research, the study may proceed only after the Secretary has consulted with appropriate experts, including experts in penology, medicine, and ethics, and published notice, in the *Federal Register*, of his intent to approve such research.

IRB Classification of Research Under Subpart C

In the first two categories, (A) or (B), the prospect of direct subject benefit is unlikely. The research, therefore, must present no more than minimal risk to the subjects. Research that falls within the second two categories, (C) or (D), has a higher prospect of offering the prisoner direct benefit. Thus, studies involving greater than minimal risk are permitted but may include a requirement for approval by the Secretary of the DHHS after consultation with appropriate experts in penology, medicine, and ethics and after publication of a notice of intent to approve in the *Federal Register*.

In deciding which category of research under Subpart C is applicable, it is important for the IRB to recognize that the definition of minimal risk in Subpart C differs from that in Subpart A. *Minimal risk* is defined in Subpart C[1][Sec.303(d)] as "the probability and magnitude of physical or psychological harm that is normally encountered in the daily lives, or in the routine medical, dental, or psychological examination of healthy persons." This definition differs from that found in Subpart A[1][Sec.102(i)] in two respects. First, "harms" are specifically described as "physical or psychological." In nonprisoner research, IRBs consider a wide range of risks, representing the possibility of physical, psychological, social, economic, or legal harms. In Subpart C, however, only "physical or psychological harm" is mentioned. The reason for this limitation is not explained in the regulations. It is, therefore, unclear whether the implication is that only physical or psychological harms are relevant to prisoner research when deciding whether or not the risk is minimal. Certainly, social, legal, and economic risks are associated with some kinds of research involving prisoners and obviously must be assessed by the IRB. Indeed, such risks may be significant. Second, Subpart C specifies that the risk of harm must be relative to the "daily lives" of "healthy persons." Although the regulations offer no clarification, certainly the standard of minimal risk should not be based on the daily life of a healthy prisoner, for significant risk is often present within the prison environment. The reference to a healthy person implies an absolute standard, and IRBs should accordingly adopt a very conservative interpretation and application of the definition of minimal risk. Therefore, in the opinion of the authors, the threshold of minimal risk should be based on the daily lives of healthy, nonincarcerated individuals.

It should be noted that all category (C) as well as category (D) studies that involve assignment of subjects to control groups that may not benefit from the research require additional review at the level of the Secretary of the DHHS. Unlike nonprisoner research, the IRB cannot consider a "prerandomization" benefit, i.e., the chance of being assigned to the active arm, in determining the risk/benefit relationship in a category (D) study. Subpart C is more restrictive on this point. Each arm must, therefore, be analyzed separately in determining the prospect for direct subject benefit. This represents an additional protection for prisoners who participate in studies involving control groups where there may be little prospect of direct subject benefit, such as a randomized clinical trial that utilizes a placebo control.

IRB Approval Criteria for Prisoner Research

As with all other types of research, prisoner research must comply with the requirements of 45 CFR 46.[1][Sec.111] Those requirements are as follows: the risks to subjects must be minimized; risks to subjects are reasonable in relation to anticipated benefits; the selection of subjects is equitable; informed consent is obtained and appropriately documented; the research plan makes adequate provision for monitoring the data collected to ensure the safety of subjects; and there are adequate provisions to protect the privacy of subjects and to maintain the confidentiality of data.

In addition to these general requirements, Subpart C provides additional protections for prisoners as research subjects by setting further conditions that must all be satisfied before the IRB can approve the study. These seven requirements, which include appropriate categorization of the research, take into account the special circumstances of prisoners. They serve to further minimize the risks to subjects, help ensure that the prisoner will be able to give valid *informed* consent, and assure equitable subject selection. The following are the requirements specified:[1][Sec.305(a)]

(1) The research under review represents one of the categories of research permissible under 46.306(a)(2).

(2) Any possible advantages accruing to the prisoner through his or her participation in the research, when compared to the general living conditions, medical care, quality of food, amenities and opportunity for earnings in the prison, are not of such a magnitude that his or her ability to weigh the risks of the research against the value of such advantages in the limited choice environment of the prison is impaired.

(3) The risks involved in the research are commensurate with risks that would be accepted by non-prisoner volunteers.

(4) Procedures for the selection of subjects within the prison are fair to all prisoners and immune from arbitrary intervention by

prison authorities or prisoners. Unless the principal investigator provides to the Board justification in writing for following some other procedures, control subjects must be selected randomly from the group of available prisoners who meet the characteristics needed for that particular research project.

(5) The information is presented in language which is understandable to the subject population.

(6) Adequate assurance exists that parole boards will not take into account a prisoner's participation in the research in making decisions regarding parole, and each prisoner is clearly informed in advance that participation in the research will have no effect on his or her parole.

(7) Where the Board finds there may be a need for follow-up examination or care of participants after the end of their participation, adequate provision has been made for such examination or care, taking into account the varying lengths of individual prisoners' sentences, and for informing participants of this fact.

It should be noted that requirement (7)[1][Sec.305(a)] is unclear in terms of how and to what extent the investigator, institution, or sponsor is responsible for providing care to both prisoners and parolees after their participation in research. Interpretation of this requirement is particularly problematic in clinical research on life-threatening illnesses such as cancer or AIDS where the patient is likely to need continued treatment, perhaps for a prolonged period and at considerable expense. For example, what does "adequate provision . . . for . . . care" mean? Does it mean that the prisoner or former prisoner who participated in the research must be provided free care for as long as necessary? In the absence of guidance from OHRP, it seems reasonable for an IRB to ensure adequate provisions are made for the care of subjects who suffer a research-related injury but not to extend the provision for treatment of an illness that predates the beginning of the study or is unrelated to the study.

Participation in Research of Prisoners Who Are Minors

IRBs should recognize that, when a research subject is both a prisoner and a minor, in addition to 45 CFR 46, Subpart C, the board must also consider Subpart D—Additional DHHS Protections for Children Involved as Subjects in Research. Clearly, a minor who is also a prisoner is a highly vulnerable subject. Therefore, Subparts C and D apply. However, if the minor is tried, convicted, and sentenced as an adult, then, depending on state law, the prisoner may be constructively emancipated and can legally consent to participate in research. Therefore, IRBs that choose to recognize constructive emancipation of an incarcerated minor should do so only after careful review of all considerations. This includes vulnerability of the minor, developmental age, and the fact that the rights of the minor's parents to direct the child's activities have been involuntarily subjugated to the state department of corrections. Clearly, involvement in research of such subjects can be very problematic.

Protection at the Expense of Justice

Subpart C of 45 CFR 46 is obviously designed to protect the rights and welfare of prisoners who participate in research. Clearly, additional protection is needed. It is ironic, however, that while Subpart C protects the rights of prisoners, it also significantly restricts their right to participate in research. Although this population is vulnerable, it is of concern that the pendulum may have swung too far. The result may be a paternalistic set of regulations that limit a prisoner's autonomy to decide to participate in and benefit from taking part in research. The principle of justice requires that both the benefits and burdens of research be distributed fairly. Similarly, by denying prisoners the ability to make a decision as to whether they want to participate in research, or by limiting their access to research, the basic principle of respect for persons may be violated. Thus, it is important to consider these principles if and when future regulations are established to "protect" prisoners from the risks of research.

DHHS Certification

After the IRB reviews prisoner research that is supported by the DHHS, the IRB must notify OHRP and: (a) provide the name and qualifications of the prisoner representative, (b) provide a reasonably detailed description of the research, (c) document the category of research (A, B, C, or D per 45 CFR 46.306), and (d) document the additional seven protections required per 45 CFR 46.305. Research involving prisoners may not proceed until OHRP has reviewed the IRB's determination in accordance with 45 CFR 46, Subpart C, and concurs. When a category (C) or (D) study requires the Secretary of the DHHS to consult with a panel of experts before deciding whether a study is approvable, the OHRP acts on behalf of the Secretary to convene the required panel. OHRP has a standing panel to accommodate requests from institutions. If the research involving prisoners is not funded by the DHHS, the IRB need not notify OHRP, but should document in the record that the research has met all requirements of Subpart C. This may include, as necessary, appointment of a local review panel of appropriate experts to advise the IRB when the study is classified as category (C) or (D).

Conclusion

Prisoners are considered a vulnerable subject population in need of additional protections. Historically, these protections have not been available and, more recently, though available, are not consistently utilized. At the same time, however, because of the stringency of federal requirements, particularly when clinical research is conducted, prisoners are often denied the opportunity to participate in research. Clearly, this denial becomes an issue of justice. Therefore, investigators and IRBs should work together to formulate important research that can benefit prisoners individually and prisoners as a group while affording them the special protections they require.

References

1. Code of Federal Regulations. Title 45A—Department of Health and Human Services; Part 46—Protection of Human Subjects. Updated 1 Oct 1997. Access date 18 Apr 2001. World Wide Web http://www4.law.cornell.edu/cfr/45p46.htm

2. Code of Federal Regulations. Title 21, Chapter 1—Food and Drug Administration, DHHS; Part 50—Protection of Human Subjects. Updated 1 Apr 1999. Access date 18 Apr 2001. World Wide Web http://www4.law.cornell.edu/cfr/21p50.htm

3. Code of Federal Regulations. Title 21, Chapter 1—Food and Drug Administration, DHHS; Part 56—Institutional Review Boards. Updated 1 Apr 1999. Access date 27 Mar 2001. World Wide Web http://www4.law.cornell.edu/cfr/21p56.htm

4. Hornblum A M. They were cheap and available: Prisoners as research subjects in twentieth century America. *Br Med J* 315:1437–1441, 1997.

5. Mitford J. *Kind and Unusual Punishments*. New York: Vintage Books. 1973.

6. Leopold N F. *Life Plus 99 Years*. Garden City, N.Y.: Doubleday. 1958.

7. The Medical Case. Chapters 1–15. *Trials of War Criminals Before the Nuernberg Military Tribunals Under Control Council Law No. 10, Vols. 1 and 2*. Washington, DC: US Government Printing Office. 1949.

8. Supplementary Report of the Judicial Council. *JAMA* 132(17):1090, 1946.

9. Hornblum A M. *Acres of Skin: Human Experiments at Holmesburg Prison*. New York: Routledge. 1998.

10. Jones J H. *Bad Blood: The Tuskegee Syphilis Experiment*. New York: Free Press. 1981.

11. Robinson R J. Memorandum to the Office of the Commissioner (Food and Drug Administration document obtained via the Freedom of Information Act). 30 Jun 1976.

12. National Commission for the Protection of Human Subjects of Biomedical and Behavioral Research. Report and recommendations: Research involving prisoners (DHEW (OS) 76–131). 1976. Washington, DC, Government Printing Office.

13. Department of Health, Education and Welfare. Additional protections pertaining to biomedical and behavioral research involving prisoners as subjects. *Fed Regist* 43(222):53652–53655, 1978.

14. Office for Protection From Research Risks. OPRR guidance on approving research involving prisoners, 23 Jun 2000. Access date 3 Apr 2001. World Wide Web http://ohrp.osophs.dhhs.gov/humansubjects/guidance/prison.htm

15. Office for Human Research Protections. Compliance determination letters, 20 Mar 2001. Access date 30 Mar 2001. World Wide Web http://ohrp.osophs.dhhs.gov/detrm_letrs/jan2001.htm

Research Involving College Students

Jennifer J. Tickle and Todd F. Heatherton

INTRODUCTION

Given that much research takes place in college and university settings, it is not surprising that college students are often participants in research studies. Indeed, some fields, such as psychological science, rely on college students as their primary research participants. Students are convenient, easy to recruit, and relatively inexpensive when compared with nonstudents. Although many of the issues related to research participation are the same for college students as other populations, there are two issues deserving special mention with regard to their research participation.

Coercion

College students are typically given the opportunity to participate in research in one of several ways: in exchange for course credit as part of a course requirement, in exchange for extra credit in a course, or in exchange for payment on a voluntary basis after recruitment. The Code of Federal Regulations[1(Sec.116)] states that an investigator should seek consent "only under circumstances that provide the prospective subject . . . sufficient opportunity to consider whether to participate and that minimize the possibility of coercion or undue influence." The central controversy about college student participation involves whether participation for course credit is considered coercive. For instance, in cases where participation is linked to course requirements or credit, students may feel as if they have to participate in order to please the course professor. They may believe that their grades, potential letters of recommendation, or other opportunities in the department may be compromised if they do not participate in the research studies.[2(Chap.6)]

At the same time, research participation can be viewed as valuable for both the researcher and student participants. Research participation is a way for students to become involved in the learning process and to learn first-hand about the process of scientific research. Active learning by way of involvement is an effective way for students to acquire information. Therefore, the educational benefit of student participation in research should not be discounted.

Alternatives to Course-Required Research Participation

To decrease the potential for coercion with research participation for course credit, research departments can provide alternatives to participation that are comparable in time, effort, and fulfillment of course requirements. For instance, Gamble[3] and Cohen[4] have suggested such options as research papers (which can be comparable in time expenditure and educational benefit) or attendance at research talks given by department faculty (comparable in time, effort, and educational benefit) as alternatives to research participation. If alternative options cannot be offered, participants can at least be given a choice of studies in which to participate. Of course, as per federal standards,[1(Sec.116)] participants must be able to withdraw from participation in any study at any point without penalty. This means that even those participants who withdraw from a research study must receive full course-credit for research participation. When evaluating research that involves course credit, the IRB should understand how course-related participation in a given department is structured and whether comparable options are offered in the place of research participation to help ensure the voluntary nature of that participation.[2(Chap. 6)]

Recruitment Practices

Aside from actual course credit for participation, recruitment into research can be made less coercive with attention to the recruitment process itself. For instance, faculty and researchers can solicit participants more broadly, using sign-up sheets or general announcements rather than direct invitations to particular students. This reduces the likelihood of "undue coercion" by decreasing the influence of the faculty–student relationship and making the request less direct. IRBs should review all recruitment material to be sure the risks and benefits are not misrepresented and to be sure that participation for course credit is not presented in a way that is likely to be coercive.[2(Chap. 6)]

Paying Students to Participate in Research

Rather than offering course credit for research participation, some researchers have funds to pay participants for their time. Paying research participants is discussed in several other chapters in this book. Payment, in the form of money, gifts, privileges, or other resources, can only be offered as a recruitment incentive, not as a benefit of participation. Therefore, payment for research participation must be commensurate with the time, effort, and discomfort involved in the research, as well as the risk of participating. Payment should not be so extreme as to unduly influence people to participate without considering the risks. Although explicit standards for the amount of incentive do not exist, IRBs should use reason when considering whether an investigator's plans for recruitment incentives seem excessive for a given study.[2(Chap. 3)]

Some College Students Are Minors

One additional concern about using college students, particularly college freshmen, involves the age of the consent giver.[1(Sec.408)] Some college freshmen may be legal minors for whom parental consent is still needed. This is an issue to consider, especially if a college allows high school students to take its courses. IRBs should remind researchers about the regulations and law that relate to the need for surrogate (parental) consent to participate in research. IRB approval of research that targets college students should explicitly address the need for surrogate consent when appropriate.

Confidentiality

The second major concern of using college students as research participants, besides coercion, involves confidentiality. A variety of sensitive measures may be taken by researchers, ranging from medical information to ratings of self-esteem, depression, drug use, and so forth. Because of the close nature of many college environments, extra care must be taken to ensure participant confidentiality. For instance, data should be stored where access is restricted. If undergraduate research assistants are used for data collection, data coding, or data entry, they must understand the importance of the confidentiality of the data with which they are working. To help ensure confiden-

tiality, all appropriate measures must be taken to keep participant names separate from data at all stages of the research process. IRBs should monitor this by requesting information about the process of data storage. Where possible, investigators should be encouraged to use code numbers to identify participants in the place of other more identifying information.[2(Chap.3)]

Conclusion

College students are not usually defined as a separate class of research participants from the standpoint of ethical standards or regulatory compliance. However, since research often takes place on college campuses and some categories of research specifically target the student population, it is useful to review the issues that IRB members, researchers, and institutional officials should consider when evaluating research projects that are likely to enroll college students. In this setting, coercion and confidentiality are the two most common areas of concern. This chapter discusses ways to minimize problems in each of these areas. An additional issue that is often overlooked is that some college students are minors. Research involving minors must comply with federal regulations and, often, state law that does not apply to research limited to adult participants.

References

1. Code of Federal Regulations. Title 45A—Department of Health and Human Services; Part 46—Protection of Human Subjects. Updated 1 Oct 1997. Access date 18 Apr 2001. World Wide Web http://www4.law.cornell.edu/cfr/45p46.htm

2. Penslar R L, Porter J P, Office for Human Research Protections. *Institutional Review Board Guidebook*, ed. 2. 6 Feb 2001. Access date 29 Mar 2001. World Wide Web http://ohrp.osophs.dhhs.gov/irb/irb_guidebook.htm

3. Gamble H F. Case study: Students, grades and informed consent. *IRB: A Review of Human Subjects Research* 4(5):7–10, 1982.

4. Cohen J M. Extra credit for research subjects. *IRB: A Review of Human Subjects Research* 4(8):10–11, 1982.

PART 10

IRB Issues Based on Study Design or Category

Qualitative Social Science Research

Dean R. Gallant

INTRODUCTION

Not all research in the social sciences is laboratory-based experimental work. There is a long tradition of *qualitative research* by anthropologists, ethnographers, sociologists, survey researchers, psychologists, and others whose observations are typically conducted outside the laboratory. The purpose of their research is often to develop hypotheses rather than to test and validate them in controlled studies. Methods include observation (including participant observation), questionnaires or surveys, interviewing, or review and analysis of existing data. Because of the potential range of activities involved, qualitative research in the social sciences can present special problems for institutional review boards (IRBs), for investigators, and for the subjects themselves.

When Does Qualitative Research Require IRB Review?

Some regulatory guidance is available—but not much. Because the Common Rule focuses largely on quantitative procedures (experimental protocols, hypothesis testing, controlled studies) and primarily in the biomedical area, many aspects of the regulations are a poor fit for the circumstances of qualitative research. It is no surprise that IRBs struggle as they try to apply these regulations to ethnographic studies, focus groups, or oral histories.

The Common Rule[1][Sec.102(d)] defines research as "a systematic investigation . . . designed to develop or contribute to generalizable knowledge." How can IRBs decide when qualitative research meets this test? Criteria for defining research intent are the subject of Chapter 4-3. The key is to focus on the *intent* of the researcher. Collecting information for a biography would not warrant IRB review because the intent is to assemble information particular to a specific individual. Contrast this with, say, the participant–observer who travels for a year with a nomadic community to study their way of life. Here the intent is to study and illuminate the common—that is, generalizable—aspects of their behavior. In general, IRB review may be required if human subjects are involved and the researcher's intent is to generate insights about *phenomena that are themselves the actual topic of inquiry* (i.e., generalizable, as opposed to person-specific, knowledge).

With that being said, some research is exempt.[1][Sec.101.b(2)]

[Research is exempt if the only procedures involve] the use of . . . survey procedures, interview procedures or observation of public behavior, unless:

(i) Information obtained is recorded in such a manner that human subjects can be identified, directly or through identifiers linked to the subjects; *and*
(ii) Any disclosure of the human subjects' responses outside the research could reasonably place the subjects at risk of criminal or civil liability or be damaging to the subjects' financial standing, employability, or reputation.

Because much research will be exempt if identifiers (or identifying details) are not recorded, or if participation is judged to present no risk, and other research of not more than minimal risk will be eligible for expedited review, a primary consideration for the IRB is the risk that participation may present to subjects.

Types of Risk

Participants in medical protocols can risk death or disabling injury. Not so in qualitative social science research, where the risks are typically of a different order of magnitude. Most subjects in such research are healthy volunteers, but they nevertheless can face real risks, and it is the investigator's responsibility to ensure that those risks are minimized. Possible risks include the following:

1. Breach of confidentiality, whether actual or potential

2. Violation of privacy, even when confidentiality is assured

3. Validation of inappropriate or undesirable behaviors of subjects, perhaps based on misunderstanding of the researcher's intent

4. Presentation of results in a way that does not respect (or agree with) the subjects' interests

5. Possible harm to individuals not directly involved in the research, but about whom data are obtained indirectly

(*secondary subjects*), or who belong to the class or group from which subjects were selected

6. Harm to subjects' dignity, self-image, or innocence as a result of indiscreet or age-inappropriate questions in an interview or questionnaire

In practice, of course, many of these risks overlap, and disentangling them into separate categories must be done somewhat arbitrarily. Note that, with the exception of the last item above, the risks faced by subjects *during* participation are ordinarily negligible. They are simply being observed or asked to talk about their everyday lives much as they might do with a friend over a cup of coffee or a glass of beer. It is more likely that risks will emerge *after* participation is completed. Let us consider some examples.

Breach of Confidentiality

Subjects routinely share the stories of their daily lives with friends and colleagues. But, typically, a researcher collects information with the hope of publishing the results—if not necessarily attributing the subjects' comments directly (as a reporter might do), then at least revealing the cumulative knowledge gained from the research inquiry. If identities are poorly disguised, whether from others or from the participants themselves, subjects can risk embarrassment or more serious harms.

A classic example is *Small Town in Mass Society*[2], in which Arthur J. Vidich and Joseph Bensman report in great detail on the private lives of citizens of a small town in upstate New York. One of the authors lived in "Springdale" for two years and collected extensive information about the townspeople's public and private lives. Names were disguised in the book, but individuals' identities were all too obvious to the subjects themselves—and their neighbors—and the hard feelings and debate that followed the book's publication testify to the problems of conducting clandestine participant observation.

Data need not be revealed to cause problems. Even if their participation was voluntary, subjects may have second thoughts or worry about possible release of sensitive personal information, as in the case below.

Violation of Privacy

Privacy refers to a state of being free from unsanctioned intrusion. Ordinarily, individuals have a right to privacy; that is, control over the extent, timing, and circumstances of sharing information about themselves with others. Violation of this right, although not necessarily a direct harm, contradicts the *Belmont Report's* principle of respect for persons.

In the mid-1960s, Laud Humphreys, a sociology graduate student at Washington University, conducted a study of men who frequented "tearooms" (public restrooms where strangers met for impersonal sex). Most of his subjects had no idea that he was a researcher. Humphreys served as a "watchqueen" and would cough or otherwise signal to warn participants of the approach of police or others. He secretly noted the license plate numbers of many subjects and through the Registry of Motor Vehicles

obtained their names and addresses. A year later he arranged for these subjects to be added to a city-wide health survey and, in disguise, visited their homes to collect extensive personal information about them.

His 1970 book, *Tearoom Trade,*[3] won the C. Wright Mills Award from the Society for the Study of Social Problems. Nevertheless, many colleagues and members of the press roundly criticized Humphreys for violating the privacy of his subjects, despite the acknowledged fact that the subjects' behavior took place in a public space, and even though Humphreys (who was sympathetic toward his subjects) took scrupulous pains to keep identifiers separate from his data and destroyed all names soon after his data collection was complete.

Validation of Bad Behavior

Some research may unintentionally reinforce undesirable characteristics of research subjects. An investigator interviewing members of clandestine militant groups in a war-torn country worried about his ability to collect good data, thinking that subjects would be unwilling to reveal their "secrets." But to his surprise, and perhaps dismay, subjects reported that this interest from a faculty member at a major research institution gave an imprimatur of legitimacy to their anarchistic efforts! Another investigator studying recreational drug use among teens quickly learned it was necessary to develop a relationship of trust with his subjects, including being able to talk with them without criticizing their drug-taking behavior. A nonjudgmental relationship like this, with a senior researcher at a prominent university, can have the unhappy effect of persuading subjects that their behavior is acceptable—if not fascinating—to wise adults. In such cases, it may be appropriate for the IRB to discuss its concerns with the investigator to help narrow the gap between strict scientific objectivity and responsible social values.

Presentation of Results

A sociologist studying a multilevel marketing organization, although frank with his subjects about his role as a researcher, came to unflattering conclusions about the company's techniques and its effects on recruits. How should he balance his personal obligations to those who shared their experiences with him with his professional responsibilities as a social scientist to report the truth as he observed it? Did he owe his subjects any special consideration if publication of his results—while neither a violation of confidentiality nor libelous—reflected poorly on individuals associated with the organization? At what point does "objectivity" cross the line to "betrayal" and how can the IRB help the investigator steer away from that line? Some researchers allow their subjects to review portions of research reports that refer to them directly, but this is not always practical (or even possible if results are aggregated).

Risk of Harm to Others

Federal regulations specifically enjoin the IRB from considering the potential harmful effects of research results on *society*.

The IRB should not consider possible long-range effects of applying knowledge gained in the research (for example, the possible effects of the research on public policy) as among those research risks that fall within the purview of its responsibility.[1][Sec..111(a)(2)]

Nevertheless, when research deals with controversial topics, discussion of such risks will inevitably surface at IRB meetings, and members may feel strongly that legitimate knowledge to be gained from a study could be interpreted wrongly or be publicized with mischievous intent. In such cases, it may be appropriate for one of the investigator's colleagues on the IRB to mention, off-line, the concerns that were raised, but it is *not* proper for such concerns to affect IRB deliberations. Interestingly, there is no parallel prohibition from consideration of research benefits; investigators and IRBs routinely consider the value of new knowledge to society when balancing risks and benefits.

Are possible harms to *secondary research subjects*—that is, individuals who do not themselves participate in the study, but about whom the investigator obtains information via interview or other hearsay means—an appropriate area of concern for the IRB? In December 1999, OPRR cited failure to obtain informed consent from secondary subjects as a finding in a letter of suspension of IRB authority.[4] Oral historians and genetics researchers, among others, reacted promptly, insisting that extension of this regulatory interpretation would effectively halt much of their research, as they could not possibly obtain informed consent from everybody about whom they indirectly received information. As of this writing, the question is unresolved, but OPRR (now OHRP) has not rescinded its interpretation, so IRBs should at least consider whether special consideration should be given to secondary subjects in studies where primary informants provide information about others.

Direct Harm to Subjects

A researcher asking youngsters questions about a range of sexual behaviors, or use of inhalants or illicit drugs, will likely encounter parents who insist the research is "robbing the children of their innocence." Unfortunately, if the survey is not sensitively designed, the parents may be right. Harms from inappropriate instruments are not limited to children. Interviews of adults that include a range of questions about illegal or immoral behaviors may be demeaning or insulting. The IRB should ensure that the researcher understands enough about the potential subject population to minimize the chance of harming or needlessly offending them. Administering surveys in person allows investigators to judge whether certain avenues of questioning are appropriate for an individual subject. Reviewing surveys and questionnaires with representative community members (or parents, for surveys of children) may reveal sensitive or problem areas that can easily be fixed before the survey goes out to the field.

Special Considerations

There are several other issues for IRBs to attend to when reviewing qualitative research.

Respect for Subjects' Privacy

As many of the previous cases indicate, respect for subjects' privacy is essential, yet this simple advice is not always easy to follow. Humphreys' tearoom research demonstrated that public spaces can be the site of very private behaviors. Another example is Internet chatrooms, which often operate with the expectation of privacy even though they are accessible to anybody with a computer and a connection to the Web. Is the right to privacy absolute even when behaviors are only *relatively* private? Should a *false* sense of privacy be respected? These are thorny issues for investigators and IRBs, and the answers are not at all obvious. See the thoughtful paper on ethical issues raised by research in cyberspace, based on a 1999 conference sponsored by the American Association for the Advancement of Science.[5]

Informed Consent

Although the content and issues may differ, informed consent is no less important in qualitative research than it is in clinical research. However, much qualitative research is exploratory, and the areas of inquiry may not be apparent even to the research team. How, then, can subjects truly be informed? Prior information about risks, insofar as they are known or can be anticipated, cannot be withheld. But if the range of possible risks is potentially very large, how can an investigator present accurate information about the study in a manner that will not simply frighten subjects away? One strategy is to sustain the consent process throughout the course of a subject's participation. As new data are acquired and the researcher's overall knowledge of risks expands, subjects can be reminded that participation is voluntary, and their understanding of the risks and benefits of participation can be refreshed. This process should not be used to mask risks or to lure subjects into a relationship with the investigator before they fully understand the consequences, but it can help them develop an understanding of the research and the context of their role in it. Their continued participation is then based on active awareness of emerging developments.

Distortion of Subjects' Behavior

The simple presence of participant observers may lead to distortion of subjects' behavior. (This can be considered a more general expression of the *experimenter effect*, where the actions of the experimenter inadvertently influence subjects' performance on a task.) In *When Prophecy Fails* (1956),[6] a small group of people who believed that the end of the world was at hand eventually had to acknowledge the uneventful passing of the doomsday hour. The group of believers was infiltrated by several observers who, merely by their interest, reinforced the authenticity of the group's cataclysmic expectations. The authors (Festinger, Riecken, and Schachter) discuss at length how the research team's presence did not contaminate the validity of their observations, but nevertheless admit that their actions were not without effect on the believers. Even straightforward observation or interviewing can prompt subjects to behave unnaturally—and occasionally to their detriment—if they try to mold their behavior to what they imagine to be the researcher's expectations. This is especially likely when the researcher is viewed as a higher-status individual or when subjects are children. Minimizing the possibility of such distortions while maintaining an ethically defensible position on the boundary between unobtrusive and surreptitious can be a challenge. Chapter 6-5 is devoted to a discussion of research in which subjects are intentionally deceived in order to study human behavior.

Reportable Situations

Much qualitative research deals with sensitive topics and looks deeply into subjects' daily lives. As a result, investigators can encounter reportable situations such as evidence of child or elder abuse or neglect or the likely prospect of harm to self or others. In most states, investigators have a legal obligation to report such situations to appropriate authorities. Researchers who are at all likely to uncover reportable situations must be prepared for that possibility. Appropriate consultation should be available if the researcher is not a trained clinician with relevant clinical experience. A strategy for alerting subjects to the need for reporting is essential; depending on the nature of the study and the subject population, this can involve mention of the reporting requirement as part of the informed consent process, or a more ad hoc procedure when the likelihood of reportable situations is small. The IRB should consider the adequacy of the investigator's plans and may want to seek counsel from experts in the field.

Certificate of Confidentiality

Whether or not a researcher is studying behaviors likely to yield information about reportable situations, subjects' reputations, relationships, employability, or legal status may be threatened by disclosure of identifiable information. The law does not recognize any automatic privilege for social science researchers; data are vulnerable to subpoena or other official inquiry. If identifiers must be retained (for longitudinal studies, or where subjects are videotaped or audiotaped), and if the research deals with very sensitive topics, it may be appropriate to seek a certificate of confidentiality to protect against compelled disclosure—by federal, state, or local authorities—of identifying information. Certificates of confidentiality can be granted by the federal funding agency upon application, and are also available to investigators without federal funding. These certificates do not prohibit the investigator from disclosing information (and, in some states, confidentiality certificate protections are overridden by mandated reporting requirements), but they do provide a measure of protection for research subjects that would not otherwise be available.

Conclusion

Despite the many concerns detailed here, we should not forget that most research subjects are competent, autonomous adults and—absent willful deception by the investigator—can usually judge for themselves the degree to which they choose to reveal information about their personal lives and actions. It is not the IRB's responsibility to eliminate risk, which is often an inherent component of research on sensitive topics. However, the IRB may and should counsel the investigator on how to present the purpose and methods of the research to subjects in such a way that they can understand why they might want to participate in the study, and can make an informed, intelligent decision about any risk that their participation may entail. Qualitative research is, in essence, a kind of dialogue with its own special vocabulary; like all dialogues, it depends in large measure on shared understanding and common courtesy.

References

1. Code of Federal Regulations. Title 45A—Department of Health and Human Services; Part 46—Protection of Human Subjects. Updated 1 Oct 1997. Access date 18 Apr 2001. World Wide Web http://www4.law.cornell.edu/cfr/45p46.htm

2. Vidich AJ, Bensman J. *Small Town in Mass Society; Class, Power, and Religion in a Rural Community.* Garden City: Doubleday. 1960.

3. Humphreys L. *Tearoom Trade: Impersonal Sex in Public Places.* Chicago: Aldin Publishing Co. 1975.

4. Office for Human Research Protections. Dear Colleague Letters, 20 Mar 2001. Access date 30 Mar 2001. World Wide Web http://ohrp.osophs.dhhs.gov/dearcoll.htm

5. American Association for the Advancement of Science. Access date May 2001. World Wide Web http://www.aaas.org/

6. Festinger L, Riecken HW, Schachter S. *When Prophecy Fails.* Minneapolis: University of Minnesota Press. 1956.

Ethnographic Research

Elisabeth Smith Parrott

INTRODUCTION

There is no question that the authors of the Nuremberg Code, *The Belmont Report,* the Declaration of Helsinki, and, indeed, the federal regulations did not have ethnography in mind when they composed guidelines to govern the conduct of human subjects research. Although ethnography is one of the oldest qualitative methods of gathering data,[1] it has only recently come to be examined under the bright light of Institutional Review Board (IRB) review. Researchers have been guided by the ethics statements of professional organizations, such as the American Anthropological Association.[2] Traditionally, the ethics review of ethnographic studies has come in the form of funding sources and departmental review. Although these sources of review are not impartial, in this discipline such reviewers are probably more aware of the overall state of being of research participants than many other research fields. Compulsive self-examination is a feature of most ethnographers, even today, and though IRB review is new to this research environment, the values of beneficence and respect for persons have been an important part of many ethnographies. Although the worth of IRB review is indisputable, applying regulations that mainly refer to medical procedures and behavioral interventions to the ethnographic process can be a bewildering task.

Rooted in the social sciences—particularly anthropology and sociology—ethnography concerns itself with the lived experience of a population. As Hammersley and Atkinson write,

> In its most characteristic form [ethnography] involves the ethnographer participating, overtly or covertly, in people's daily lives for an extended period of time. They are watching what happens, listening to what is said, asking questions—in fact, collecting whatever data are available to throw light on the issues that are the focus of the research.[1]

In recent years, ethnography has sprouted up as the investigative method of choice in an ever-widening array of fields: medicine, education, geography, music, and other fields beyond the more traditional applications in the social sciences. In medical settings, particularly psychiatry, it is used to create a broader understanding of the impact of illness and subsequent medical intervention than usually supplied by formal outcomes analysis. Ethnography is employed by researchers at all levels and disciplines, from students (both in fulfillment of classroom assignments and independently) to health care practitioners, public health officials, educators, and social scientists.

Given the varied application of the technique, as well as the diversity in the backgrounds of ethnographic researchers, it is not surprising that IRB review of ethnographic research presents a unique set of challenges. It is not always immediately clear what path the course of approval should follow for ethnography research. Depending on the focus of the research and the plans for reporting the data, the study might be eligible for exemption or might best be examined in the setting of the expedited committee. In rare cases, ethnographic proposals require the rigors of full-committee review. It takes skill, experience, and, most importantly, unhurried dialogue with the researcher to determine the appropriate level of review.

The first section of this chapter will examine various institutional approaches to ethnography review. Then we will discuss methods for preparing ethnographers for IRB review, assessing risk in ethnographic proposals, and determining the review status of a study. Next will come a discussion of the three categories of ethnography review:

exempt, expedited, and full-committee review. From there we will examine the review process and the role of advisors and consultants. We will end the chapter with discussions of variations to the informed consent process, the use of audiotaping, videotaping, and still photography, the review of research involving vulnerable populations, and, finally, international research.

Institutional Approaches to Ethnography Review

Perhaps the greatest obstacle to painless review of ethnographic research is the lack of familiarity that most IRBs have with this type of research. Some institutions create IRBs dedicated to social science research that become very familiar with the issues surrounding ethnographic fieldwork. Many institutions, however, see few ethnographic proposals and approach them with uncertainty. Such institutions often rely on consultants on a case-by-case basis for help and advice in examining the unique ethical issues surrounding ethnography review.

The very decision to review ethnographic research can be confusing. Sometimes ethnographic proposals do not seem to describe a formal examination of a population with the intent to publish. Such studies may lead the IRB to reason that the federal definition of research, ". . . a systematic investigation, including research development, testing and evaluation, designed to develop or contribute to generalizable knowledge,"[3][Sec.102(d)] will not be met. Using this argument, some institutions have decided that most undergraduate projects do not meet the criteria for research and therefore fall outside the purview of the IRB. However, before reaching this conclusion, the institution must carefully assess its mission and the institutional agreement with the Office for Human Research Protections (OHRP).

Other institutions acknowledge that, although some undergraduate ethnography research may not meet the federal definition of research, the process of IRB review is educational to students and worthwhile in that it prepares future researchers for the ethical conduct of research. A policy of reviewing all undergraduate research also enables an institution to monitor student research and ensure that harmful proposals do not move forward.

At all levels of review, it is the role of the IRB to ensure that risks to subjects are minimized: "(i) by using procedures which are consistent with sound research design and which do not unnecessarily expose subjects to risk. . . ."[3][Sec.111(a)(1)] The message here is that risks should not be undertaken lightly, for the sake of curiosity, or for the fulfillment of an academic exercise, no matter how advanced the level. The typical ethnographic proposal does not purport to change public policy or even change the lives of the ethnographer's participants, although this may be an unintended consequence of the research. Rather, the goal of such research is to gather information about the human condition in order to better understand the complex ways in which people and populations function. Ethnography often functions as the equivalent of basic science: studying human behavior for the sake of knowledge itself.

However fundamental a social science ethnography is, there are situations where proposed research is clearly legitimate and others where the research design clearly does not warrant intrusion on participants' lives. For example, an ethnographic project evaluating the impact of a job-training program for individuals with severe mental illness could clearly benefit participants and society as a whole. In contrast, an undergraduate proposal seeking to document the sexual habits of fellow students in order to fulfill a classroom assignment probably introduces more risk than it is worth. A submission such as this presents a good opportunity to educate researchers about sensitivity in social science research and provide guidance in developing a less sensitive proposal for review.

Advising Ethnographers

The review process for such seemingly innocuous studies often involves a great deal of researcher education about the need for IRB review, the rationale for and methods of removing identifiers from data, and the process of obtaining appropriate informed consent. Because the data collection process associated with ethnography meets the federal definition of minimal risk—that is, the ethnographer himself has no plans to intervene with life as it happens—it may appear that IRB review is of little value. However, the risks associated with recording data and writing the ethnography may be significant. Ethnographers, particularly undergraduates and those working in fields that do not routinely interact with the IRB, often need to be educated about these risks and the role of IRB review in planning and implementing ethnography.

The process of determining review status often begins with the informal submission of a research protocol or summary. However, even before considering individual proposals, it is essential that the IRB educates the research community-at-large about the need for ethics review for all research involving human subjects. Researchers must also understand that the IRB has the authority to make the final decision regarding the review status of a project.

Providing researchers with a detailed list of questions, including definitions for such key terms as *anonymous, confidential, identifiable information,* can help prevent misunderstandings in the review process. Responding to a set of core questions relevant to ethics review may be helpful to ethnographers and the IRB alike. Points to cover include the following:

1. **Methods for the identification and contact of potential participants.** Researchers should describe how potential participants might refuse participation. If appropriate, contact letters, advertisements, or phone scripts should be written and submitted for IRB review.

2. **A description of the topics under investigation.** The researcher should assess the sensitivity of the inquiry and explain whether participants' answers may be embarrassing or put them at risk for criminal prosecution. Surveys, questionnaires, telephone or interview scripts, and letters must be reviewed prior to use.

3. **Methods for recording data.** This should include plans for recording or removing participants' identifiers and for protecting the confidentiality of participants.

4. **Plans for obtaining informed consent.**

5. **Plans for the participation of minors, if appropriate.** In addition, plans for obtaining parental consent and the consent of relevant institutional authorities, such as school principals and teachers, should be considered.

Planning for informed consent is often a fruitful way both to gather information about the research project and educate researchers about their project's risks. Training researchers about the required elements of informed consent is essential. The IRB may supply a template for consent documents and information sheets as well as samples of such documents for ethnographic projects. Researchers should be encouraged to submit draft documents to the IRB for feedback and informal review prior to comprehensive IRB review of the study as time allows.

These aspects of study participation are of particular importance to participants of any population:

1. The purpose of the research

2. A description of what participation will entail and the duration of the study

3. A description of the risks and benefits of participation

4. An explanation of how data will be recorded and information about the use and preservation of audio or video tapes

5. A lay discussion of the anonymity or confidentiality of data, including measures to safeguard data, publish data, etc.

6. A description of any financial considerations, including costs and/or payments to participants

7. Contact information, including the title and institutional affiliation of the researcher and his or her advisor (if appropriate)

Finally, it is important to emphasize to researchers, particularly inexperienced researchers and students, that anything can happen in the field. Researchers should bring concerns, complaints, and adverse events to the attention of the project advisor and the IRB immediately.

Assessing Risk

As with any research proposal, the first task at hand is to determine risk status. The federal regulations state, "minimal risk means that the probability and magnitude of harm or discomfort anticipated in the research are not greater in and of themselves than those ordinarily encountered in daily life or during the performance of routine physical or psychological examinations or tests."[3][Sec.102(i)]

At first glance, it may seem that all ethnographic research meets this definition for minimal risk, as by definition ethnography observes life as it happens, with no planned interventions and few interruptions. IRBs, particularly those that mainly review biomedical research, come to expect that risk to participants is introduced in the process of collecting data during procedures such as the administration of an experimental drug or a surgical procedure. In contrast, although the data collection phase of ethnography may present risks to participants, such as when a conversation becomes emotionally difficult for a participant or institutional authority figures request access to field notes, for the most part the risks of data collection are minimal (Frederick Erickson, Ph.D., personal communication dated October 17, 2000).

It is worth noting that study termination is one period of the data collection phase that presents considerable risk in many research settings (Hoyt Alverson, Ph.D., personal communication dated July 25, 2001). If participation observation has been successful, then by definition the departure of the ethnographer generates feelings of loss in the community. In many cases participants lose a trusted friend, someone who listened to them, treated them impartially and respectfully, participated in daily life, and perhaps even supplied money, food, transportation, or labor to the community. From the very beginning, ethnographers need to plan ahead for the termination of research, taking into account the characteristics and needs of the study community. Moreover, plans for ending the research should be discussed with participants at the initiation of the study and regularly throughout the period of data collection.

Perhaps the most widely recognized risks of ethnography are encountered when the researcher writes and publishes the data. It is in this situation, when an ethnographer reports back to the research participants (which in the case of applied institutional ethnography may involve hospitals, schools, or other fixtures of community life), that the potential arises for wider-reaching harms. Potential harms range from embarrassment to administrative or even legal action in response to data that have been revealed. Therefore it is important that, in their review of proposals and their education of investigators, IRBs focus on this aspect of the research plan (Frederick Erickson, Ph.D., personal communication dated October 17, 2000).

The other characteristic of ethnography that affects its potential for harm is that, by definition, ethnographic techniques prohibit the researcher from controlling what happens in the field. Because the ethnographer's role is to observe rather than direct or limit the actions or narrative of the participant, it is critical that the ethnographer consider every aspect of life that could possibly be affected in the field. Thus the emotional, social, and political ramifications of asking questions, reporting observations, and sharing conclusions with others outside of the research population must be examined comprehensively at the time of initial review.

The impact of reading an ethnographic account of oneself should not be underestimated. Individuals, or in fact whole communities, may be disturbed by the way they are represented in ethnographies. After publishing her ethnography of psychiatric clients, anthropologist Sue Estroff recalls being called in the middle of the night by a former research participant.

> The voice I heard was almost chanting in rage and anguish. There was ridicule too, and precision cuts at my fast-fading concepts of myself as a kind, careful, and just ethnographer. She had asked for a copy of the book I had written about her and the others. I gave it to her as a gift. She had just read what I had written about her ten years before. She was wounded by images of herself in the past—psychotic, rambling, wise, and charming. I had exploited her, used her, misunderstood everything, and was unmasked now, she said. Not the bright, "liberal," sympathetic researcher I claimed to be, but worse than the others for my self and other deception. Furthered my career, made a name for myself, all at her expense. How could you? (By now I was asking this silently, along with her.) How could you come see me again, spend the whole day with me, like a friend, pretending to understand, to like me?
>
> The facts were not in dispute—their public presence and meaning, and my commentary were. Seeing the now non-sensical notes she wrote when psychotic, seeing herself at that bewildered time on the printed page were somehow intolerable. She chanted on in howling pain and anger; nothing I said made any difference. I was shaking by now, desperate to intervene, to break the grip of the agony now swallowing both of us. Could we meet and talk it over? No. I never want to talk to you again. Could I please explain what I had written, place it in the broader concept of the book? Had she read the rest of it? No. No. Was there anything I could say or do to help? No. Please, would she accept my apology? No. She hung up. I called back. Don't ever bother me again. I apologized once more. She hung up again.[4]

Although she had signed a consent document, participated in the research freely, was not identified in the publication, and was aware that Estroff intended to publish, the participant did not anticipate how disturbing it would be to read an intimate, public account of her mental illness.[4] Responses such as these are to some degree unavoidable. However, the example teaches us that the way ethnography is reported and shared with the research community allows for harm to the research participants for an almost indefinite period of time.

In this way, ethnography review teaches us to think broadly. For example, if presented with a proposal to elicit family histories from a community of people, we may find ourselves asking a range of tough questions: Is it likely that this research format will lead the participant to reveal intimate details of family life unanticipated by the researcher? If so, how can reliving difficult memories affect the participant? Is the researcher prepared to respond sensitively to a distraught informant? Will the researcher be able to maintain professionalism should informants reveal unanticipated information that may be shocking or dis-

turbing? How will risks to confidentiality and reputation be minimized? When researchers propose to observe cultural activities, we find ourselves asking how the presence of an outsider could inhibit or harm the participants. What happens if participants feel ashamed, humiliated, or violated by the presence of an observer? Who provides consent for the researcher to observe a group? If an individual refuses to participate in the research, should the project be canceled, or is it possible to work around one member of a group?

Revisions to the Research Plan

To complicate matters, it is not uncommon for an ethnographic project to change direction during the data collection process.[1] In fact, researchers may approach the IRB for approval of a study with very little idea of what the ultimate research focus will be. They may simply wish to find an interesting population and see where the process of participant observation takes them. Although it is natural for ethnography to evolve in the field, IRBs should require researchers to define their field questions and research methods as specifically as possible at the time of initial review, including plans for adapting to changes in the field setting (Frederick Erickson, Ph.D., personal communication dated October 17, 2000).

Of course, once the research is underway, researchers should communicate with the IRB about revisions to the research environment, the focus of the project, or the study procedures.

Category of Review

Designation of Exemption

Once we determine that a study meets the definition of minimal risk, how do we determine which level of review is appropriate? Studies involving minimal risk face two options: (1) designation that they are exempt from further IRB review, or (2) review by expedited committee. Despite the wide and varied application of ethnographic techniques, much of this type of research meets the criteria for exemption.[3][Sec.101(b)(2)]

> Research involving the use of educational tests (cognitive, diagnostic, aptitude, achievement), survey procedures, interview procedures, or observation of public behavior, unless: (i) information obtained is recorded in such a manner that human subjects can be identified, directly or indirectly through identifiers linked to the subjects; and (ii) any disclosure of the human subjects' responses outside the research could reasonably place the subjects at risk of criminal or civil liability or be damaging to the subjects' financial standing, employability, or reputation.

These criteria allow for the exemption of innocuous studies, that is, studies in which participants are to be interviewed about or observed doing things that are not sensitive or potentially damaging. Such studies may be designated exempt regardless of whether identifiers are recorded. Presumably this regulation also allows for the exemption of studies in which some sensitive topics may arise but in which absolutely no identifiers are recorded (i.e., the information is anonymous).

It should be noted that ethnographic studies including minors cannot be designated exempt except in cases that would have to be called "nonparticipant observation," a rare situation in ethnography.

> . . . the exemption at 46.101(b)(2) for research involving survey or interview procedures or observations of public behavior does not apply to research covered by this subpart [concerning the participation of minors], except for research involving observation of public behavior when the investigator(s) do not participate in the activities being observed.[3][Sec.401(b)]

The determination of exemption requires a careful and forward-thinking process. If researchers describe their data as anonymous, we must be sure that identifying information will not be recorded at any time over the course of the study. For these purposes, a researcher who writes down the names of participants during the data collection phase of the research or keeps a list of participants' addresses for the purpose of following up with them, but then creates aliases in the writing and publishing phase of the study, does not meet these criteria for anonymous data. Although not foolproof, one extra step in confirming the minimal-risk status of a study is to cite the federal exemption to the researcher and ask her or him (and the advisor, as appropriate) to confirm that the project meets the federal criteria.

As discussed above, ethnographic research often evolves in the field. Sometimes changes are made to the research that affect its exempt status. When notifying a researcher (and in the case of student researchers, the advisor as well) that a project has been designated exempt, it is best to explain the reason and conditions for the exemption (citing the federal regulation and providing a lay translation, if needed). At this time, the researcher should also be informed that if changes are made to the project that affect its exempt status, prospective IRB review and approval of the revisions is required.

Finally, it is also important to be mindful of topics that are not sensitive themselves, but might be closely affiliated with or lead to sensitive disclosures. When there is any doubt about the sensitive nature of the study, expedited review is the best option.

Expedited Review

The benefit of expedited review to the IRB is that thorough review of a study can take place without sending the study to the full committee. The idea behind expedited review is that two or three IRB members (regular members and/or alternates) who are familiar with the field of study and the ethnographic method may conduct a detailed review of the proposal. They will confer about it informally (in person, by phone, or by e-mail) and make a decision regarding approval. The reviewers often include the IRB Chair and/or IRB administrator, if he or she is a voting member of the committee. Consultants may be used at this level to assess the adequacy of the research design and provide the IRB with detailed information about the re-

search setting. At the reviewers' discretion, the study may be sent to the full committee for further review. The expedited process saves time for researchers, as the wait for review is usually shortened, and for the IRB as a whole, as the full-committee workload is reduced.

Ethnographic research very clearly falls under expedited review.[3][Sec.110 (a)(7)]

> Research on individual or group characteristics or behavior (including, but not limited to, research on perception, cognition, motivation, identity, language, communication, cultural beliefs or practices, and social behavior) or research employing survey, interview, oral history, focus group, program evaluation, human factors evaluation, or quality assurance methodologies.

Like the exempt category, expedited review is appropriate for studies that meet the federal definition of minimal risk. In terms of ethnographic research, the distinction between the categories of exempt and expedited review lies in the way research data are recorded and in other peripheral factors, such as the inclusion of minors. The expedited review regulation[5] allows for the recording of information that could identify a participant (such as name, address, voice or video recording, or still photography), unless "identification of subjects and/or their responses would reasonably place them at risk of criminal or civil liability or be damaging to subjects' financial standing, employability, insurability, reputation, or be stigmatizing, unless reasonable and appropriate protections will be implemented so that risks related to invasion of privacy and breach of confidentiality are no greater than minimal" (i.e., no greater than those encountered in daily life).

Full-Committee Review

Where there are significant risks (i.e., risks that exceed those encountered in daily life) involved, such as when the purpose of a study is to study illegal activities, full-committee review is needed. At this point, risk/benefit ratios may be difficult to assess. By definition, ethnography is a largely observational process; the main potential benefits to a participant are the possible psychological benefits associated with "telling one's story." The potential benefits to society may also be somewhat vague, or at least not as clear as for some of the intervention-based studies that IRBs usually consider.

IRBs are required to determine that

> Risks to subjects are reasonable in relation to anticipated benefits, if any, to subjects, and the importance of the knowledge that may reasonably be expected to result. In evaluating risks and benefits, the IRB should consider only those risks and benefits that may result from the research. . . . The IRB should not consider possible long-range effects of applying knowledge gained in the research (for example, the possible effects of the research on public policy) as among those research risks that fall within the purview of its responsibility.[3][Sec.111(a)(2)]

The instructions not to consider the long-term ramifications of the research simplify the review of ethnographic risks but complicate the review of potential benefits. It is reassuring that we are not being asked to assess every possible negative effect a study might have in the distant future. This guidance, however, also instructs us not to count as benefits the long-range potential improvement in public policy that may result from ethnographic research.

The risks of this research method may be subtle. Remember that ethnography generally does not place participants at risk during the data collection phase. Rather, risks are introduced as the data are shared, with the participants themselves as well as with outsiders (Frederick Erickson, Ph.D., personal communication dated October 17, 2000).

The potential breach of privacy associated with this process is the most pressing review issue. Therefore, ethnographic research on certain topics, such as communities of illegal drug users, introduces significant risk. Participants who use illegal drugs may not do or say anything in the presence of the ethnographer that they would not do or say otherwise. And, of course, they are at risk of being arrested by virtue of their behavior at any time, regardless of the ethnographer's involvement. However, the fact that their illegal behavior is documented does present risks additional to those they face in ordinary life.

Even when an IRB is well prepared to review ethnography, the consideration of a study involving significant risk can be a difficult and controversial process. Ultimately, a decision regarding approval will rest on the scientific validity of the study and the protections to participants built into the data collection process, the informed consent process, and the training and preparation of the researcher.

The Review Process

The key to reviewing ethnographic research is to ask for complete study information from researchers. It is critical that the IRB receive comprehensive descriptions of the following five aspects of the research plan:

1. The training and preparation of the researcher

2. The research environment

3. The participants' background

4. The questions that will be asked of participants or the general structure for gathering information

5. Plans for analyzing, storing, sharing, and publishing data

Of equal importance to the review process is the expertise of the IRB and the availability of appropriate advisors; thus, the IRB's understanding of its own capabilities is also critical.

In addition to submitting a response to core IRB questions outlined above, it is useful for researchers to submit comprehensive research protocols (such as those submitted for funding) if they exist. Reviewing the full protocol enables the IRB to check for discrepancies and confirm that the project designated "exempt" or "approved" by the IRB is identical to the funded project. Occasionally a researcher will state that a project does not record identifiers, for example, but then describe plans for photographing participants in the research plan. Educating researchers before the submission of proposals will help

prevent misunderstandings in the review process, and a comprehensive review of project materials will enable the IRB to pick up on any persistent discrepancies.

Use of Advisors and Consultants

At our institution, we have learned that the key to appropriate review is bringing in not only the expertise of the IRB, but also the expertise of advisors to the researchers and consultants to the IRB in the researcher's field of study. As with all review, the trick is to combine the regulatory knowledge of the IRB staff with the field expertise of IRB reviewers. We accomplish this in two ways: first by relying on researchers' advisors to prepare students for the field, and second by seeking out the review of experts to supplement IRB review when needed.

For example, when requesting a research summary from an undergraduate, we ask the student's advisor to confirm that the advisor has discussed the ethical issues surrounding human subjects research in the proposed research setting with the student researcher. We also routinely cite the federal regulation permitting the exemption or expedited approval of a study to the student and advisor. Their confirmation that the proposed research satisfies the regulations, although not sufficient for approval, helps to ensure that we have all understood the risks of the research in the same way.

At institutions where the emphasis of review is on biomedical research, administrators may need to look beyond the usual circles of reference in order to obtain expert ethnographic review. Social scientists experienced in ethnographic research are best able to guide the IRB in conducting a comprehensive review. Provided that an institution has social science departments, the chairpersons of the anthropology or sociology departments are often willing to help an IRB locate an appropriate consultant. When social scientists are unavailable, such as when ethnography is proposed in a medical setting, representatives from psychiatry may be well suited to work with the IRB in identifying special areas of concern.

Variations to the Informed Consent Process

As the saying goes, "Informed consent is a process, not a form." The process of informed consent refers to the discussions, review of written study materials (including consent documents and information sheets), and any other means by which the potential participant learns about the research setting. The term *informed consent* does not refer to the consent document alone. In fact, it rejects the notion that it is possible to obtain true informed consent simply by providing informants with a written statement about the research.

Here, too, in preparation for informed consent, ethnography tends to buck IRB convention. Researchers routinely balk at being asked to provide consent documents to people they plan to observe over the course of daily life, in large part because asking for signed consent emphasizes the ethnographer's outsider status, a feature that ethnographers actively try to minimize (Frederick Erickson,

Ph.D., personal communication dated October 17, 2000.)[1] It makes the casual conversation with a policeman on the street, the chance interview with the jazz singer in a club at 3 AM, and the playful game of hide-and-seek with a child on an oncology unit into a formal research experience requiring federal oversight.

Federal regulations allow for the modification of standard consent procedures under certain circumstances. The waiver of signed consent is the variation to the informed consent process most readily permitted. Documentation of informed consent may be waived when the IRB finds:

> (1) That the only record linking the subject and the research would be the consent document and the principal risk would be potential harm resulting from a breach of confidentiality. Each subject will be asked whether the subject wants documentation linking the subject with the research, and the subject's wishes will govern; or (2) That the research presents no more than minimal risk of harm to subjects and involves no procedures for which written consent is normally required outside of the research context.[3[Sec.117(d)]]

This section of the regulations addresses two situations where documentation of consent may be waived. The first is when identifying information will not be recorded and the participant wishes not to be linked to the research. The second is when the research meets the criteria for minimal risk and does not involve any activities for which someone would ordinarily be required to sign a consent form. It is this second case that waives the requirement for documentation of informed consent for many ethnographers.

From time to time researchers request that the requirement for informed consent itself be waived in full or in part. Sometimes it is impossible for ethnographers to obtain informed consent from each participant, particularly when participant observation, as opposed to interviewing, is the main source of data. The federal regulations permit the waiver of informed consent as follows.

> An IRB may approve a consent procedure which does not include, or which alters, some or all of the elements of informed consent or waive the requirements to obtain informed consent provided the IRB finds and documents that: (1) the research involves no more than minimal risk to the subjects; (2) the waiver or alteration will not adversely affect the rights and welfare of the subjects; (3) the research could not practicably be carried out without the waiver or alteration; and (4) whenever appropriate, the subjects will be provided with additional pertinent information after participation.[3[Sec.116(d)]]

Though a bit more complicated to document, the criteria outlined above are widely applicable to minimal-risk ethnography. Indeed, the third criterion addresses the impracticality of obtaining consent in the setting of participant observation. When considering a waiver of this kind, the IRB documents that the researcher has met the federal criteria for a waiver. This documentation may be included in the reviewer's notes. It may also be helpful to document the researcher's confirmation of the criteria allowing a waiver.

Audiotaping, Videotaping, and Still Photography

Ethnography often makes use of audiotaping, photography, and videotaping technology. Researchers' plans for recording data should receive prospective IRB review and be included in the informed consent process. Plans to destroy, share, or archive the recordings should also be discussed with the IRB and with study participants. If a researcher chooses to archive recordings but obscure the identities of participants in publication (as is often the case), then plans for protecting the confidentiality of the original study records must also be addressed.

Occasionally, although researchers prefer to record or photograph participants, they state that they could carry out their research without such recordings. In these cases, participants should be provided with an opportunity to consent or decline to consent to recordings. This may be assured by providing separate signature sections or check boxes within the consent document for participants to consent or decline the recording.

Vulnerable Populations

Populations that are considered protected in the federal regulations, including prisoners, mentally incompetent persons, pregnant women, and children (including wards of the state), regularly participate in ethnographic research. The review of research involving prisoners should be conducted in compliance with the special protections outlined for this group.[3(SubpartC)] Regulations also explain how to obtain informed consent for the participation of mentally incompetent persons.[3[Sec.102(c)]] Pregnant women are permitted to participate in ethnography research with no additional protections:[3[Sec.207(a)(2)]] "No pregnant woman may be involved as a subject in an activity covered by this subpart unless . . . the risk to the fetus is minimal." Even when there may be significant risks to the pregnant participant, such as when the topic of the research is illegal behavior, the risk of ethnography to the fetus is minimal.

Children. Although children are not often the focus of ethnographic research, it is not unusual for them to be included in studies, particularly those originating in the social sciences or other disciplines where a cultural group of diverse ages is to be examined. Even when a study simply proposes participation observation that may include minors, it is important to remember that the federal regulations regarding the participation of minors apply.[3(SubpartD)] For these purposes, children are defined as "persons who have not attained the legal age for consent to treatments or procedures involved in the research, under the applicable law of the jurisdiction in which the research will be conducted." Subpart D requires parental consent until the participant reaches the legal age to consent personally, as specified by local law. Waivers to the documentation of informed consent and the informed consent process itself are permitted as described above.

From time to time, ethnography is proposed for use among a population of children. Such studies require the consent of a parent and the consent of the institutional authority. In a setting such as a school or hospital unit, teachers and health care providers may also need to provide consent. In addition, the IRB is instructed to ". . . determine that adequate provisions are made for soliciting the assent of the children, when in the judgment of the IRB the children are capable of providing assent. . . ."[3][Sec.408(a)]

With a description of the research setting and the age and maturity of the minor participants, the IRB can determine whether or not it is appropriate to obtain assent. If the IRB chooses to require minor assent, it must also specify how such assent is to be documented.[3][Sec.408(e)]

Research in Foreign Countries

Research proposed to take place in foreign countries can generate additional questions during IRB review. Assurance that the appropriate foreign authorities have reviewed the project and that the informed consent process is conducted appropriately, given the foreign population, is critical. Many times in international research, obtaining a signature for a consent document can be problematic, if not impossible. When researchers work with populations of illiterate persons, even a brief information sheet may be useless. In such cases, the IRB must focus on the training of the researcher and the plans for obtaining informed consent orally. As Frederick Erickson of UCLA explains, ". . . In cross-cultural research—especially overseas but also here in U.S.—the cultural notion of individual volition and consent may not apply in the setting being studied. Thus, written consent from village elders and oral assent from others may be more culturally appropriate than elaborate written consent documents for everybody. And if an IRB is willing to be true to the 'spirit of the law' that is fine, but if they are hung up on the 'letter of the law' they can impose consent conditions that are unreasonable" (Frederick Erickson, Ph.D., personal communication on October 17, 2000).

If an IRB sets out to review international research without knowledge of the region where the research will take place, consultants can provide invaluable help. A brief summary proposing participation observation in a mining town in rural South America, for example, may appear innocuous to the IRB, but put the researcher and study participants in grave danger due to the political issues surrounding a mining community. A reviewer with expertise in the cultural and political issues of the region will be able to spot potential risks far more comprehensively than the average IRB.

Finally, in addition to helping the IRB understand issues specific to the region of study, consultants can verify that consent documents and information sheets have been accurately translated.

Conclusion

An IRB is most effective when it maintains an open dialogue with the research community and works with researchers to facilitate the conduct of ethical research. At times, ethnography can stretch the system, requiring thoughtful consideration of the intent of the federal regulations and the use of consultants in order to make sense of the ethical issues raised by each unique study. Because ethnographic research involves so much face-to-face, unstructured interaction between researchers and participants, the review process offers a unique opportunity not only to monitor and modify this type of qualitative interaction but, more importantly, to teach researchers how to estimate the risks of their work and understand the impact of their work on the participant community. Becoming aware of these issues is a central part of good ethnography regardless of the specific field of study. In this way, the IRB steps into the larger research process to benefit the community of ethnographers as well as the community of participants.

References

1. Hammersley M, Atkinson P. *Ethnography: Principles in Practice,* Ed 2. London: Routledge. 1995.

2. American Anthropological Association. Access date 27 Aug 2001. World Wide Web http://www.aaanet.org/

3. Code of Federal Regulations. Title 45A—Department of Health and Human Services; Part 46—Protection of Human Subjects. Updated 1 Oct 1997. Access date 18 Apr 2001. World Wide Web http://www4.law.cornell.edu/cfr/45p46.htm

4. Estroff SE. Whose story is it anyway? Authority, voice, and responsibility in narratives of chronic illness. In: Toombs SK, Barnard D, Carson RA (eds). *Chronic Illness: From Experience to Policy (Medical Ethics Series).* Bloomington IN: Indiana University Press. 1995: 78–104.

5. Office for Protection from Research Risks, NIH. Protection of human subjects: Categories of research that may be reviewed by the Institutional Review Board (IRB) through an expedited review procedure. *Fed Regist* 63(216):60364-60367, 9 Nov 1998. World Wide Web http://ohrp.osophs.dhhs.gov/humansubjects/guidance/63fr60364.htm

Oral History Research

Alan Bliss

INTRODUCTION

EXAMPLE 1. *On a June morning, an Army retiree and veteran of the 1944 Normandy invasion answers his phone. The caller is a newspaper reporter, asking the veteran for comment about the remarks he made in his oral history interview, excerpts from which are to run in the next day's paper—part of an article commemorating the Allied invasion of Europe. The veteran is surprised by the call, and when the reporter reads a quote to him from the interview, he is disturbed. He doesn't recall saying that, he replies, and asks to hear more. After doing so, the veteran becomes angry, and denies saying any of those things. He has been misquoted, he informs the reporter. Maybe the oral history interviewer made a mistake, but in any event, the transcript is wrong.*

EXAMPLE 2. *A college president is being interviewed for her oral history. When a question comes up concerning a thorny relationship with an influential college trustee, the president answers guardedly. Sensing hesitation, the interviewer skillfully follows up by commenting that the trustee under discussion is famous for adversarial behavior. The president agrees, then declares that she will say nothing more concerning that individual. The interviewer confirms that the president is free to speak or not speak to any of the matters the interview raises, and notes that, because the interview eventually will become public, discretion is appropriate. Later during the interview, however, the president impulsively returns to the subject and offers baldly critical judgments of the trustee.*

Both of the scenarios outlined above have the potential to make an oral history administrator, and a host institution, uncomfortable. In the first case, an interviewee announces that he has been misquoted, a decidedly unwelcome and damaging charge. In the second, the interviewee has allowed herself to utter judgments that she clearly regards as sensitive, and that could cause bad feelings among other members of the institution's leadership. The least that each situation threatens is an interview subject who is unhappy after the fact with her or his contribution to the project. It is not hard to see how more serious recriminations might result.

An oral history program that remains faithful to certain basic professional practices need not be anxious about either of these situations, or about any of its interviews. Broadly, a program that subscribes to the standards of practice of the Oral History Association (OHA)[1] shows that it recognizes and accepts its responsibility to interviewees and to the other parties in its constellation of relationships. The institution that sponsors an oral history program shares those responsibilities. That is why the Institutional Review Board (IRB) is properly concerned that the conduct of its organization in oral history practice reflects the highest standards in the profession.

Oral History

Oral history is relatively youthful as a subdiscipline of historical practice; however, it has changed and evolved steadily. Its first institutional appearance was in 1948, at Columbia University in New York, as part of a diplomatic history project. As technology improved, awareness grew. By the early 1960s, many historians and researchers were concerned with examining history from the bottom up, learning about how events rose out of (or affected) the conditions and actions of typical peoples' lives rather than focusing on politicians, generals, and bureaucrats. In such an endeavor, oral history was an ideal technique—perhaps the only practical way to capture the experience of those participants in history who sometimes have no other voice or leave no other testimony. As historians turned their focus toward society's most marginalized people, oral history offered itself as a medium perfectly suited to the times. Those times also saw the introduction of the inexpensive cassette recorder, making the technology for compiling oral histories broadly accessible. An increasing number of institutions began to organize and archive their interviews, and the visibility of oral history practitioners continued to grow. In 1967, some of them founded the OHA, which issued its first goals and guidelines the following year. In

1979, the OHA produced a set of evaluation guidelines, organized as a checklist for practitioners to follow in collecting, processing, and archiving oral histories. At its 1990 annual meeting, after a two-year process of reevaluation of the previous standards, the OHA adopted the present "Principles and Standards."[2]

Oral History Association Standards

With respect to the obligations that an oral history program has to its interview subjects, the OHA lists ten specific responsibilities to interviewees:

1. Interviewees should be informed of the purposes and procedures of oral history in general and of the aims and anticipated uses of the particular projects to which they are making their contributions.

2. Interviewees should be informed of the mutual rights in the oral history process, such as editing, access restrictions, copyrights, prior use, royalties, and the expected disposition and dissemination of all forms of the record, including the potential for electronic distribution.

Author's note: Those mutual rights should be spelled out in writing.[3] The place to do so is in the document that the interviewee signs consenting to the interview. Some oral history projects employ a "deed of gift" in which the interviewee "gives" the interview to the oral history program in consideration for a copy of the transcript. Should your IRB also choose to employ an informed consent document, this is also the time to get the interviewee's approval of the document's conditions, which typically would include a specific description of the interviewee's rights. More discussion of electronic distribution appears below, following standard of practice No. 9.

3. Interviewees should be informed that they will be asked to sign a legal release. Interviews should remain confidential until interviewees have given permission for their use.

Author's note: This standard of practice addresses one of the means by which the oral history program may ultimately defend itself from the charges of someone such as the fictional Army veteran described earlier. That is not the only measure on which the program should rely. A successful program can hardly exist with a corps of disaffected interviewees who claim to have been misquoted and have no recourse. Other practices that may be useful in such a situation appear later, such as standard of practice No. 7 (explaining to the interviewee his or her right to edit or restrict the interview), and standard of practice No. 8 (ensuring that the oral history process yields an accurate record of the interview).

A signed release or deed of gift is best obtained before the interview. When preparing for an interview when there is any uncertainty about the subject's willingness to execute the deed of gift, mail it to the subject in advance with a letter explaining the purpose of the release. Invite the subject to contact you before the interview if there are any questions. The same applies to the IRB form. Upon arrival for the interview, obtain the required signatures on the consent or release form before unpacking and setting up the recorder. If any aspects of the legal release or the IRB forms require discussion, that should take place in an unhurried atmosphere without the subtle intimidation of having equipment set up and ready to record. The interviewer must remain prepared to politely offer to reschedule at a time when the subject is comfortable with proceeding, and to leave without protest. This is in the interviewer's practical self-interest as well: an interview that lacks a formal release or deed of gift is equally as unusable as if there had been no interview at all.

4. Interviewers should guard against making promises to interviewees that the interviewers may not be able to fulfill, such as guarantees of publication and control over the use of interviews after they have been made public. In all future uses, however, good-faith efforts should be made to honor the spirit of the interviewee's agreement.

5. Interviews should be conducted in accord with any prior agreements made with the interviewee, and such agreements should be documented for the record.

Author's note: While it is appropriate to discuss with the interviewee the possible uses for the interview, any agreements must be in writing.

6. Interviewers should work to achieve a balance between the objectives of the project and the perspectives of the interviewees. They should be sensitive to the diversity of social and cultural experiences and to the implications of race, gender, class, ethnicity, age, religion, and sexual orientation. They should encourage interviewees to respond in their own style and language and to address issues that reflect their concerns. Interviewers should fully explore all appropriate areas of inquiry with the interviewee and not be satisfied with superficial responses.

7. Interviewers should guard against possible exploitation of interviewees and be sensitive to the ways in which their interviews might be used. Interviewers must respect the rights of interviewees to refuse to discuss certain subjects, to restrict access to the interview, or, under extreme circumstances, even to choose anonymity. Interviewers should clearly explain these options to all interviewees.

Author's note: The preceding two standards are relevant to the fictional college president in the introduction. The oral history interviewer has a duty to draw out his or her subject, and to facilitate recall or stimulate reflection. On the other hand, it is not the purpose of the interview to build a file of previously hidden testimony or to obtain secrets. If the interviewee shows apprehension or concern about a sensitive answer, the interviewer should be responsive to that concern, perhaps turning off the recorder while the matter is discussed and an alternative approach developed. Once all parties are satisfied, the interview may continue, and a useable record may be produced. In the final analysis, the interviewee must be reminded that he or she will have an opportunity to strike responses from the transcript. The latter is not as desirable, as a redacted transcript is less historical than one that is faithful to the tape. Further, a recording of the original remarks will continue to exist, unless the oral history program acts to erase part of the tape, an awkward procedure at best. In every instance in which the interviewee makes changes to the draft of a transcript, the program ought properly to archive the copy of the transcript on which those edit marks appear. That copy then becomes the copy stored in the rough draft file, and it is the version from which the final transcript is prepared. The draft is not accessible to the public; however, it represents the oral history archivist's evidence of the interviewee's expressed wishes regarding the transcript.

An oral history archive must decide carefully whether to accept an interview that was granted under restrictive conditions. There are certain situations when it might represent the only way to secure a valuable addition to the collection, one that will inure to the benefit of future generations of archivists and researchers. Such holdings come at a price, however. A restricted interview requires cautious documentation, stating the duration of limitation, and the ways through which the limitation may be removed. It may be prudent to append some explanation as to the reasons for which the restriction on the interview is necessary or desirable. Once the materials have been received into the archive, their custody requires exceptional measures to ensure that changing staff members or relocation to new facilities does not result in the restricted material's being inadvertently comingled with the open access holdings of the collection.

8. Interviewers should use the best recording equipment within their means to accurately reproduce the interviewee's voice and, if appropriate, other sounds as well as visual images.

Author's note: Oral history interviews are always recorded, and the value of such recordings extends beyond merely being sure that an accurate record exists. Linguists use the audio portion of oral histories to analyze the speech of persons representative of particular regions or backgrounds. For such researchers, the content of a transcript is of no value.

In every instance, the recording of an interview must be duplicated immediately upon receipt of the tape. This is a simple recognition of the value of the work that has been done by the interviewer as well as the interviewee. Without a tape, there can be no hope of producing an accurate transcript, nor of documenting (in any dispute) precisely what was said. Without a backup copy of the audio part of the interview, the project is perpetually hostage to one piece of tape.

With respect to duplication of tapes, a responsible oral history program must be alert to developing technologies for the preservation of its audio archive. Magnetic audio and video tape becomes brittle with age; the recordings that were made in the 1960s and 1970s, when many programs were initially formed, are approaching obsolescence. Moreover, magnetic tape is vulnerable to data loss through proximity to electromagnetic fields that may be present near machinery of any kind. The potential for the permanent loss of archival material is great and increasing rapidly. Digital recordings and re-recordings are one answer, although we are still learning about the life expectancy of the digital compact disk. The long-term solution to this issue will remain dynamic and will require multiple copies of both the audio portions as well as the digitized texts of interviews. The copies should be stored in multiple formats and locations, using media that will allow for convenient periodic backups, and migration of the data to new storage formats as superior technologies become available. Such a system is presently under development at the University of Florida.

9. Given the rapid development of new technologies, interviewees should be informed of the wide range of potential uses of their interviews.

Author's note: This standard of practice introduces a developing area of concern to oral history programs, namely, Internet access to the oral history archive. To state that an interview's contents may be posted on the World Wide Web is to say that one has no control over access to the document. As a practical legal matter, this is readily addressed in the language of the deed of gift or the release and consent document. In terms of the interviewee's understanding of whose property the interview is to become, the matter often must be elaborated. A useful analogy is the situation of a book, magazine, or journal on a library shelf. Not everyone will read it, but it is available to everyone who cares to look at it. The same applies to documents on the Web, except that the universe of potential readers is considerably larger.

Some historians raise concerns about the possibility of abuse of the Web-based interview, by misquoting or using its contents out of context. The hazard is equally present with conventional library holdings. Digitization technology offers certain means through which the electronic text may be rendered as safe from abuse as the paper-and-ink version. These means include secure-formatting of text using software such as Adobe's Acrobat program. Using such programs, a reader must possess a copy of the program in order to read documents posted in the format. Other programs allow the electronic library to require positive identification of the user in order to allow access to the collection. Under such a condition, it is possible to restrict access to Web-based users whose identity matches certain criteria that the library has mandated, i.e., the user must be a student or faculty member at the institution that owns the archive being accessed. That is the means by which university libraries already control access to their databases and to online electronic journals (such as the widely-used digital journal library, JSTOR).

10. Good faith efforts should be made to ensure that the uses of recordings and transcripts comply with both the letter and spirit of the interviewee's agreement.

Conclusion

The increasing use of the methodology of oral history is contributing to the advancement and value of research in a variety of disciplines. Improvements in the technology available for oral history projects and programs are occurring almost constantly, making the medium more reliable and accessible than ever. The human element, however, will always make oral history a practice that requires sensitivity, rigorous adherence to unique archival measures, and thorough documentation. This chapter has outlined some of the issues that a typical oral history program should plan to encounter, and the basis for the responses that members of the OHA recommend.

By remaining attentive to the spirit of the standards discussed here, the institution that sponsors an oral history program may feel confident that it has in place a responsible, rational administrative structure. Such a program will allow research to continue and its product to be widely disseminated with ample protection for every party. The result is an invaluable resource that will benefit generations of researchers in ways that we can only imagine.

References

1. Oral History Association. Updated 7 May 2001. Access date: 30 Aug 2001. World Wide Web http://www.dickinson.edu/organizations/oha/

2. Oral History Association. Oral History Evaluation Guidelines. Revised Sep 2000. Access date: 30 Aug 2001. World Wide Web http://www.dickinson.edu/organizations/oha/EvaluationGuidelines.html

3. Neuenschwander JA. *Oral History and the Law.* Carlisle, PA: Oral History Association, 1993.

Health Services Research

Ann Barry Flood

INTRODUCTION

Health services research involves the development of new knowledge and the application of existing knowledge for the improvement of health care and its delivery. While much of this research focuses on care delivered in organizational settings, this field also embraces the need to look at the health care for regions, market areas, and the population as a whole—that is, for users and nonusers of health care—in order to examine and improve access, quality, and efficiency.

Most would agree that *health services research* is not a discipline. In recent years, academic programs have emerged to offer graduate-level training specifically in health services research, outcomes research, or the evaluative clinical sciences. Nevertheless, the majority of researchers in this field have had disciplinary-based training in the social sciences (principally economics, political science, psychology, public health, and sociology) and/or clinical training (principally medicine or nursing).

The field has emerged over the past three decades, shaped by two aspects of the multidisciplinary nature of the research. First, because of the diverse nature of the training of most practitioners in this broad field of research, many perspectives have developed regarding the most appropriate methods and most important questions. Second, because of the complexity and breadth of the basic content area and the array of methodological approaches and problem-solving that have evolved, better communication across disciplines and cross-disciplinary approaches are widely recognized to be of value.

The premier professional organization for this field, the Academy of Health Services Research and Health Policy,[1] and the lead federal agency charged with supporting this research, the Agency for Healthcare Research and Quality (AHRQ),[2] have similar visions of this field. Basically, it is to improve health care by conducting or sponsoring research designed to improve the quality of health care, reduce its cost, improve patient safety, decrease medical errors, and broaden access to essential services. AHRQ defines this research to include generating evidence-based information on health care outcomes (quality and cost, use, and access) with the intent to help health care decision-makers make better-informed decisions and improve the quality of health care services.[2]

Why Health Services Research Challenges the IRB

The multidisciplinary nature of health services research, the focus on groups or systems rather than individuals, and the pragmatic intent to inform policy makers often make it difficult for IRBs to determine how best to evaluate and monitor health services research projects. The overlap in methods with the social sciences, public health, and epidemiology is such that many issues related to human subjects protection are described elsewhere in this book. Similarly, health services research can involve international comparisons and can necessitate deception in informed consent (such as when studying the impact of placebos or compliance with therapeutic recommendations, where the subjects' behavior or outcomes of interest may be negated by true informed consent). These categories are also addressed in Chapters 6-5 and 10-10, but the reader is reminded that they may apply to health services research as well.

In the remainder of this chapter, we will focus on issues related to health services research that are especially impacted by the multidisciplinary and long-term nature of the work, its frequent location within organizational settings, its dependence on clinical data sources, and its pragmatic intent to improve health care. In this discussion, we focus on four key areas related to human subjects protection in its broadest interpretation: (1) issues of safety and balance between risks and benefits of participating in research; (2) the right to privacy and confidentiality of records of health and health care that are not generated by and for research; (3) the right to confidentiality of records generated solely as a consequence of participating in research; and (4) the right to choose to participate in research.

Group Risk

Given the importance of health services research for policy making, how should IRBs protect vulnerable populations of particular concern for policy makers? When subgroups are particularly targeted for research and researchers are enjoined to include them in sufficient numbers, these subgroups may bear an unusually high burden for participating in research. How should their overall burden as a class of research subjects be balanced against the intent to help them by providing policy-relevant evidence?

Given that the primary goal of health services research is to improve health care, a large number of studies are conducted to identify new or modified strategies for delivering cost-effective care. Some are designed to improve care by formulating guidelines that may result in less care. While health services research has indeed provided considerable evidence to suggest that less care may well be better, how should IRBs assess the risk and harm to individual subjects in studies that may reduce the level of their care?

Quality assurance for the benefit of a specific organization. Many studies in health services research are conducted with the express purpose of demonstrating quality assurance or cost-effectiveness and may be designed to apply to only one organization or system of care. The principal beneficiaries of such studies may not be society in general, but the individual provider organization or an insurance company with a vested interest in the results. Such studies raise three issues: Is this research at all if it is focused on one setting? How should the harms and benefits for an individual in this research be assessed? How and whose conflicts of interest should be addressed in assessing harms and benefits?

Multisite research. Another issue for health services research involves studies conducted in multiple settings, all of which must approve the protocol and informed consent forms. In a recent article, the investigators reported on informed consent processes involved in conducting a large clinical trial.[3] This trial was designed to improve information about prognosis of critically ill patients with the ultimate goal of improving decision-making regarding their care.

In all, 55 institutions responded to the investigators' call to participate. As a part of this process, numerous IRBs commented on the same design, protocol, and forms for participation in the study. This article reports on the large variation and inconsistencies in the process and decision outcomes by IRBs, particularly regarding the issue of written informed consent and the assessment of risk of research.

Aside from noting marked variation in how and how much information must be provided to patients, one important implication of this report is the lack of the IRB members' understanding of issues regarding studies designed to improve care. The investigators argued that many IRBs discounted or ignored the potential benefits of quality assurance or improved care, and in some cases created arguably unnecessary obstacles to "merely" improving care.

Organizations may be the real "subjects" of health services research. The authors of the paper previously discussed also noted the virtual disregard by IRBs of any issues related to protection for providers or for the institutions that were the true subjects of human research. For the most part, the IRBs did not address or challenge the investigators' and institutions' responsibilities for ethical conduct and human protection outside of the narrow issue of informed consent of the patients.

This report, coupled with recent reports from the Institute of Medicine and others, suggests that the paradigm for protection of human subjects does not fit the sort of health services research in which the true subject of research is the organization and system of care. In such situations, insisting on consent from each patient may be unnecessary and harmful to both the research and, ironically, to the patients themselves.

Although perhaps less critical an issue, this report also serves to illustrate the need to coordinate across IRBs for studies involving multiple institutions. The difficulty of coordinating and addressing inconsistent requests from IRBs is a process in need of improvement itself.

We turn next to formal design issues in health services research and their implications for human subject protection.

Health Services Research as a "Social Experiment"

The notion of conducting a systematic experiment in health-services research, where a defined population is randomly (or at least systematically) assigned to receive alternative treatments for purposes of informing policy, sounds so radical that one might think it to be politically unfeasible in the United States. Yet, to a large degree, such experimentation is carried out in many guises all the time.

Medicare offers multiple examples. The initial implementation of the program, coupled with mechanisms to provide additional support for poor elderly, created profound changes in our health care system, not only with respect to enhancing access to care, but also fundamentally altering the payment sources for medical education and helping to ensure that medical education would be hospital-based in its orientation. Since then, numerous modifications such as the implementation of a prospective, lump-sum payment system for hospitals in the 1980s, a resource-based form of reimbursement for services by physicians in the early 1990s, and a major reduction in payments for home health care in the late 1990s were all social experiments that affected hundreds of health care organizations, thousands of providers, and millions of beneficiaries. Likewise, nearly every state has a waiver from the federal agency that administers Medicare to carry out variations in services provided or payment mechanisms and to conduct and evaluate demonstrations of implementing innovative policy changes.

Similarly, states are encouraged by the federal government to serve as laboratories to implement major social policies such as universal coverage for health care or solving the problem of high out-of-pocket costs for prescription benefits. Major funding foundations such as the Robert Wood Johnson Foundation regularly solicit proposals for demonstrations and evaluations of new policy initiatives such as strengthening hospital nursing or implementing medical home models for children with special needs.

Despite the importance of these changes and the vast numbers of people involved, many of these social experiments do not fall under the purview of IRBs unless they are funded by grants and/or performed by people other than those employed by the government or the organizations charged with implementation.

When should human subjects protection be addressed formally in such social experiments and what are the special considerations? For purposes of illustrating the particular issues of concern for IRBs, we next discuss five types of social experiments in health services research: (1) the "true" social experiment; (2) the "natural" experiment; (3) research for follow-up of patients who refuse to be randomized in randomized clinical trials; (4) feasibility and demonstration studies of health-services tools; and (5) management/quality improvement efforts in health care organizations or systems.

The True Social Experiment

The true social experiment is a research project with a design that involves explicit and voluntary enrollment of people into an experiment with randomized or systematic assignment to experimental models. In health services research, these alternative models generally require subjects to agree to be assigned to different types of payment or organizational systems for a substantial period of time and to comply fully with the requirements to remain enrolled and as assigned during the study. As with randomized clinical trials, these experimental models assume that there is no evidence to confirm that one model is substantially superior to another. However, in the social experiment, there is no definitive treatment protocol and no mechanism to try to control for differences in routine provision of care in the alternatives.

The RAND Health Insurance Experiment is a classic example of this type of research.[4(Chap.12)] Conducted in the 1970s, it involved the assignment of approximately 2000 nonelderly families to insurance plans that varied in the price of health services which the individual families would subsequently experience. A primary research goal was to examine the impact of financial incentives for the patient on health care utilization and outcomes. There

were several key human protection issues faced in the course of designing and evaluating this study:

1. *In informing prospective subjects to be recruited into the study, how should the long-term potential advantages and disadvantages of participation be framed?* In this particular study, participation—irrespective of which program they were assigned to—appeared to be advantageous financially for all participants and offered them a guarantee for several years of a minimum level of insurance that was not otherwise available. Here, the financial incentives that were integrally important to the experimental design were also seen as potentially coercive for inducing participation because the offer tended to sound "too good to be true." The researchers used three techniques to address these concerns. First, they created statements about insurance alternatives that were substantially clearer and simpler than all those available in the market. Second, they offered a variety of local contacts for information and to legitimize the research effort. Third, they pledged confidentiality of all data, including questionnaires and utilization.

2. *How can incidental and unintended impact be anticipated and minimized?* For a variety of design issues, the researchers chose to enroll a family unit rather than an individual. One of the subsequent complex set of issues was what to do with family units that changed over the course of the study. One issue was how to handle the database for families that divided into smaller units. Ironically, the experiment also became a kind of endowment for enrollees in the study to use to allow access to the experiment to their new spouses.

3. *Confidentiality of data.* Because of the numbers of types of data, the length of the study, and the requirement for the data to be linked, confidentiality of data was difficult to ensure. The researchers used subcontractors to maintain a list of current addresses and names, to monitor changes in addresses or family composition, and to carry out linkages. The RAND researchers had a separate set of identifiers for their database but did not have names and addresses. When the RAND group needed to link other databases to their own, the subcontractor, who did not have access to all datasets, performed the linkages.

4. *Burdens of participation.* The RAND group monitored the burdens of enrollees, both to try to minimize drop-out through corrective responses and to learn what enrollees disliked most. Interestingly, among the 15% who considered dropping out, the most frequent issue named was the complexity and difficulty of filling out forms. However, the most sensitive and disagreeable information to provide was not related to health or mental health; people were most reluctant to provide financial disclosures to the researchers.

The Natural Experiment

The natural or administrative experiment is a design that is commonly used when it is impractical for scientific, political, and/or economic reasons to conduct a true social experiment. Basically, the design calls for taking advantage of naturally occurring administrative or policy changes in order to study their impact. Examples of this in health services research include these studies of the following: (a) mortality in hospitals after a physician strike; (b) practice style changes after a major redesign of financial incentives for physicians in a group practice; and (c) financial and health impact following closures of hospitals.

In many cases, the databases to be used for the research are collected for other purposes, and the research involves historical or case-control comparisons of secondary datasets. Here, the issues of human subjects protection are primarily whether researchers should have access to the data and whether the data can be provided so that it is without identifying information.

However, these experiments can be designed so as to involve prospectively collected data and survey data. In these situations, the issue for human subjects is *not* whether they are offered a choice to participate or have any harms or benefits associated with being in the natural experiment (as that is occurring outside of the context of research). Instead, it is whether they are at risk for being evaluated systematically for changes in their performance or behavior. Here, humans to be considered in the research database typically include patients, individual providers, and staff responsible for organizational performance.

Preference-Based Trials: Research for Follow-up of Patients Who Refuse to Be Randomized in Randomized Clinical Trials

In randomized control trials, patients must agree to be randomized into one of the treatment arms being evaluated. Typically, an important issue is to control for any differences in quality of care by instituting strong protocols for what actions should be taken, with little or no room for negotiating variations based on patient preferences.

Example

In an on-going study being conducted in several hospitals, patients are being told about two basically equivalent alternatives for treatment of low back pain, one involving surgery and one essentially without an active intervention. Subjects are invited to join the randomized arm, but if they refuse because they would prefer to exercise a choice, they are invited to participate in the preference-based arm of the study instead. Such patients have follow-up in the same way as patients in the randomized arm.

The primary reason for follow-up of patients who do not agree to be randomized is to examine whether choice appears to influence outcomes. The human subjects issues for this type of trial are essentially identical to those involved in a randomized control trial. However, this design raises an interesting issue for human subjects protection. If patients' willingness to participate in randomized control trials is intricately tied to their basic willingness to forego choice, it suggests that there may be a serious bias in recruitment of patients to randomized control trials. It also suggests that the basic design of the gold-standard clinical experiment prevents many people from participating in clinical research who would otherwise like to do so. Is there a right to participate in such research?

Feasibility and Demonstration Studies of Health Services Tools

With the increased attention to evidence-based medicine and systematic collection of data for monitoring outcomes comes the development of a variety of health services research tools such as the SF-36 health outcomes survey,[5] patient acuity measures such as the APACHE scores for intensive care, and mortality prediction scores for surgical patients. Many of these measures have undergone or will undergo rigorous research to examine their reliability and validity under a variety of circumstances. At the same time, whether for-profit or not, many of these tools are copyrighted and some are not open for scrutiny by the scientific community of the assumptions and evidence on which they are based.

In regard to human subjects protection, these developments, paralleling issues raised with respect to profit-based firms like the drug industry or durable medical equipment companies, raise issues about the importance of financial disclosure regarding the current and future intended uses of the tools. Although the issues may be far more controversial and potentially profitable for research in genetic engineering and clinical product development, health services research has parallel conflicts of interest. It shares a need to address a fundamental issue for human subjects: When the research for which people are volunteering is primarily intended to fine-tune a tool for proprietary use, should there be a different standard of risks and benefits and disclosure for subjects?

Management/Quality Improvement Efforts in Health Care Organizations or Systems

This issue has already been touched upon in the context of discussing health-services research conducted in multiple settings. It is mentioned again in this context because of its fundamental importance to the issues of human subjects protection in health services research. When and how should human subjects issues be raised when the research efforts are primarily aimed at improving the system of care, and may or may not be designed to be generalized or reported outside of an institution?

The most recent federal directive to the AHRQ is to study the systems of care that have given rise to an alarming number of medical errors and issues regarding patient safety. These concerns, coupled with increased attention to quality improvement techniques in health care, underscore the importance for IRB members and the processes of human protection to become better informed about who and what needs protecting. Defining issues too narrowly can defeat some of the most important charges to the IRB: to protect patients from ill-considered projects, to ensure that safety and risk-benefit ratios are monitored and appropriate—but not to undermine efforts to improve quality of care and hold institutions and systems accountable for ensuring it.

Conclusion

This chapter has explained why health services research often challenges the IRB system. Health services research projects are often multidisciplinary in nature, focus on groups or systems rather than individuals, and are conducted with the pragmatic intent to inform policy makers. Health services research can involve international comparisons and can necessitate deception in informed consent (such as when studying the impact of placebos or compliance with therapeutic recommendations, where the subjects' behavior or outcomes of interest may be negated by true informed consent). In most cases, the main issue for the IRB to evaluate for a health services research project is confidentiality of the medical record and other forms of health information. The information presented in this chapter helps IRBs, researchers, and institutional officials to make informed decisions about ethical standards for the design and regulation of health services research projects.

References

1. Alpha Center, Assoc. for Health Services Research. Academy of Health Services Research and Health Policy. Access date 14 May 2001. World Wide Web http://www.academyhealth.org/

2. Department of Health and Human Services. Agency for Healthcare Research and Quality. Access date 14 May 2001. World Wide Web http://www.ahcpr.gov/

3. Lynn J, Johnson J, Levine RJ. The ethical conduct of health services research: A case study of 55 institutions' applications to the SUPPORT project. *Clin Res* 42(1):3–10, 1994.

4. Newhouse JP, Insurance Experiment Group. *Free for All? Lessons from the RAND Health Insurance Experiment.* Cambridge, MA: Harvard University Press. 1993.

5. Medical Outcomes Trust. SF-36 health outcome survey. Access date 14 May 2001. World Wide Web http://www.outcomes-trust.org/catalog/sf36.htm

Epidemiology/Public Health Research

Marjorie A. Speers

INTRODUCTION

Public health research spans the spectrum of scientific study. It includes scientific questions directed at understanding biological processes, behavior, and social interactions, as well as a wide range of interventions. Likewise, the methods used in public health research are as wide ranging as research questions. Because ethical issues of concern to institutional review boards (IRBs) regarding specific methods, such as the use of existing data or surveys, are covered in other chapters, the focus here will be on a few key issues of importance to IRBs when they consider public health research, specifically epidemiological research.

Research Versus Practice

One of the more confusing, and sometimes time-consuming, issues facing IRBs regarding studies addressing a public health problem is whether the activities described in the study are public health research or public health practice. Making this research determination is important for both moral and practical reasons. First, if the activity is research, then it must be reviewed by the IRB to ensure that the individuals participating in the research are adequately protected, the research is ethically justifiable, and it meets all the federal requirements for human research. On the other hand, if the activity is not research, then the IRB has no legal or regulatory authority to direct the activity. Second, given that IRBs are heavily burdened by the huge volume of studies that are research, they should not unnecessarily spend their time reviewing and monitoring activities that are not research and often for which there are other systems of protection (i.e., state laws regarding confidentiality protection or informed consent).

Definition of Research

Criteria for identifying research intent are the subject of Chapter 4-3. The definition of research in the federal regulations is "a systematic investigation, including research development, testing, and evaluation, designed to develop or contribute to generalizable knowledge."[1][Sec.102(d)] Deciding whether a public health activity is research or practice is not easy because systematically collecting and analyzing data from individuals are essential functions of routine public health practice. In addition, scientific methodologies are often used in public health practice, adding to the confusion about whether the activity is research or practice. Moreover, because the profession of public health deals with populations, the distinction between using individuals or groups is also not helpful in deciding whether an activity is practice or research.

There is limited guidance and scientific literature addressing the difficulties in classifying public health activities as research or practice. In 1997, the Centers for Disease Control and Prevention (CDC) developed a document, *"Guidelines for defining public health research and public health non-research,"* that provides guidance in classifying public health activities as research or practice.[2] In addition, in its report *Ethical and Policy Issues in the Oversight of Research Involving Human Participants* (2001), the National Bioethics Advisory Commission (NBAC) suggests that not all public health activities are research.[3] However, it is important for public health activities to be accurately classified as research or nonresearch. NBAC describes four characteristics of research. First, the intent of the activity is to generate new knowledge, facts, principles, or theories or information that revises or improves upon an existing principle, theory, or knowledge. Second the anticipated results have validity in that what is learned about the particular scientific problem can be justifiably claimed to be true for all like scientific problems or facts. Third, it is a systematic collection and/or analysis of data. Fourth, the nature of the relationship between the researcher and the participants is such that the participants are used by the researchers to achieve the goals of the research. These are always intended to be of benefit to the researcher, personally, and may or may not be of benefit to the participants.[3]

Data Collection Techniques

Looking at methods or data collection techniques is instructive to the IRB that must decide whether the activity is research because public health practice and public health research activities both rely on the use of the same systematic procedures. For example, a case-control study design can be used to determine the risk factors in an outbreak investigation whose sole purpose is to bring the disease under control, but this is not research. Yet, the case-control design is routinely used in epidemiology to study disease etiology, and the study is research.

Thus, the IRB is forced to look at the researcher's intent in conducting the activity. Public health practice activities are carried out with the primary intention of preventing or controlling disease or injury and improving health, or improving a public health program or service. These activities are generally undertaken in such a manner that were some type of action necessary it could be initiated. Many argue that it is difficult to determine intent; however, several questions can be posed by the IRB to the researcher that will help in making the determination. The IRB can ask the researcher directly whether the activity is intended to generate new knowledge that will contribute to the scientific literature (i.e., that revises or improves upon an existing principle, theory, or knowledge). In addition, the IRB might ask whether the activity is intended to directly benefit a population or group of individuals. Quite frequently, researchers will state exactly what their intentions are. The IRB can ask the researcher how the data will be used. Specifically, is there an intention to publish or present the results to the scientific community? Intention to publish or present results does not always imply that the activity is research. As part of their civic responsibilities, federal, state, or local government officials will be obliged to publish results in government documents or share results with other public officials. This type of publication or presentation of data is not considered to be research. Perhaps another way to frame this question to the researcher is to ask whether the study would be conducted if the results could not be published in a scientific journal. If the answer is no, then the activity should be considered to be research from the IRB standpoint. Ask about the expected validity of the data or look at the protocol. Often, data collected for public health practice purposes have limited validity or generalizability beyond the population being studied. For example, prevalence of disease is estimated for a county. That prevalence estimate is meaningful to and has validity for that county, but it is not necessarily meaningful or valid for other counties either in that state or nationwide. Data generated from research activities should have validity that relates to our general understanding of a problem or situation.

Determining Research Intent

Often, a local IRB is not alone in making a determination about whether an activity is research. Sponsoring agencies will, and under federal regulations should, make a determination of whether an activity is research.[1(Sec.101)] Unfortunately, sponsoring agencies are not consistent in their interpretation of the regulations: the same activity will be classified as research by one agency and as nonresearch by

another. Moreover, more than one local institution may be involved in the research, in which case each IRB wants to weigh into the decision of whether the activity is research. In the latter case, it becomes important for IRBs to talk to each other and resolve IRB issues up front.

Classifying a study as research or nonresearch becomes even more challenging when the study involves multiple components. For example, an evaluation component might be added to a disease reporting system (e.g., cancer registry) to determine how completely the reporting system is identifying cases. In this case, the on-going disease reporting system is not research, but the evaluation component may be. When studies involve multiple components, IRBs should make an individual determination for each component regarding whether it is research.[2]

Privacy and Confidentiality

Much of the research conducted in public health does not involve invasive procedures. Instead, it involves the use of existing data (e.g., analysis of tissue samples, medical records, secondary analysis of databases) or surveys (or interviews) of individuals. Harms that may occur as a result of the research are mostly related to threats to privacy and breaches in confidentiality. Far too often these types of risks are overlooked by researchers and IRBs. Regulatory guidance regarding privacy and confidentiality is limited to the directive that IRBs may approve a research study only when they have judged that the study contains adequate protections for privacy and maintains confidentiality.[1(Sec.111(a)(7))] As the protection of privacy and confidentiality is such a broad and complex subject, IRBs will benefit from specific guidance from federal advisors on the implementation of this directive.

Clearly, IRBs can do more to address privacy and confidentiality issues in research studies. IRBs need to fully understand the concepts of privacy and confidentiality and their applications in research. Privacy and confidentiality are often incorrectly believed to be the same thing. Although the concepts are related, they address different issues. Privacy refers to a state of being of individuals. Individuals have information about themselves, and privacy refers to the ways in which researchers access information from individuals.[4] Privacy is influenced by culture, individuals' particular social situations, and the nature and context of the research.

Threats to Privacy

An individual's privacy is respected when the researcher seeks informed consent, but informed consent alone does not ensure that one's privacy interests are protected. To avoid threats to privacy, IRBs should consider all the factors involved and procedures intended to be used to obtain information from the research participant. While it is not possible to list all the factors and procedures here, the IRB should at least look at the following:

1. What types of harms are likely to result from participating in the study? Examples of harm might include worry, irritation, fear, embarrassment or self-doubt, arrest, stigmatization, or unemployment.

2. What type of information is being gathered? Is it sensitive or associated with a stigmatizing condition (e.g., drug addiction)? Are there cultural norms that may influence participants' willingness to share the information?

3. How will the information be gathered? What procedures will be used? Do the procedures reduce risk of embarrassment or other psychological or social risk if the information is sensitive (e.g., using a written questionnaire as opposed to a face-to-face interview if the questions are sensitive)?

4. What procedures will be used to ensure that participants can refuse to participate in general or refuse to answer a question?

5. In surveys, are interviewers of the same ethnicity, gender, socioeconomic status, or age as participants?

Confidentiality Protection

Confidentiality protection relates to the way in which data that can be linked to individuals are handled and used. Protection of confidentiality begins with the understanding between the research participant and the researcher about how the participant's data will be handled and with whom it will be shared.[5] In this sense, confidentiality is related to privacy because it involves informing the participants about how the data will be managed and shared and seeking their approval during the informed consent process. Thus, there are two aspects to confidentiality: how the data will be managed and with whom the data will be shared.

IRBs should carefully review the data-management plan for the study, and determine whether any of the proposed procedures might cause a breach in confidentiality. Such procedures include transmitting data, creating or eliminating linkages between the data and identifiers, data storage, and plans for long-term use or destruction.

IRBs should also review other study procedures that might influence confidentiality, such as the method by which participants will be paid or recontacted for follow-up. For example, using checks to reimburse participants for costs associated with participating in the study may create an unnecessary link between the participants and the study.

Finally, IRBs should review the study to determine with whom identifiable data will be shared and whether this information is clearly communicated to the prospective participants during the informed consent process. The review should include consideration of voluntary disclosures to others as well as the potential for compulsory disclosures. IRBs need to be aware of state and local privacy and confidentiality laws regarding mandatory reporting requirements (e.g., reports of child abuse) as well as federal reporting requirements (e.g., FDA regulations related to the use of investigational new drugs). Local IRBs should consult with their institutions' general counsel or contact their state attorney general's office regarding relevant state law.

Informed Consent

In some cases, applying the federal regulatory requirements[1(Sec.116,117)] for seeking informed consent and documentation of the informed consent process can be problematic in public health research. In surveys, the requirement that documentation of the informed consent process is a signed written consent form sometimes seems inappropriate (e.g., written consent for a telephone survey) or overly burdensome (e.g., a survey involves no more than minimal risk and the consent form is longer than the list of survey questions). The federal regulations do not provide much flexibility to IRBs in determining the type of documentation or the need for it. A signed written consent form is the only form of acceptable documentation.[1(Sec.117)] Yet, there are other forms of documentation that could serve the same purpose as a signed written consent form, such as using a witness, audiotaping or videotaping the consent process, using an audit process, or randomly recontacting a sample of the participants.

The federal regulations allow the documentation requirement to be waived if one of two criteria can be met: (1) the only record linking the participant to the research is the consent form, and the principal risk is breach in confidentiality, or (2) the research presents no more than minimal risk of harm and involves no procedures for which written consent is normally required outside the research context. Whereas the application of the first criterion is straightforward, the application of the second criterion to surveys is unclear. IRBs are often reluctant to waive the requirement for a signed written consent form. IRBs should work with researchers to waive the requirement for signed written consent forms when another method of documentation that is more appropriate to the research context can be used.

Using Existing Data

The other challenging area related to informed consent involves studies using existing data. Although the federal regulations make provisions for waiving the requirement for an informed consent process,[1[Sec.116(d)]] the requirements are often difficult to apply. Assuming IRBs can make a determination that the proposed study involves no more than minimal risk, they must also determine that the rights and welfare of the participants will not be adversely affected if the waiver is granted. In addition, the research could not practicably be carried out without the waiver. The fourth criterion—whenever appropriate, the participants will be provided with additional pertinent information after participating—is not relevant in studies involving the use of existing data with no subject contact. IRBs often do not know how to interpret the criterion related to practicability because the legal definition of that term means it would be impossible to conduct the research, which is rarely the case. Thus, IRBs are often advised not to consider time and costs of obtaining informed consent as relevant factors affecting practicability.

New pending medical privacy regulations (Health Insurance Portability and Accountability Act of 1996)[6] might greatly influence IRBs' decisions in this area. However, IRBs should feel more comfortable in waiving the informed consent requirement for such studies when there is an adequate plan to protect the confidentiality of the data and an adequate plan for contacting participants with information derived from the research, should the need arise.

Conclusion

Epidemiological and public health research can raise some special issues for IRBs. IRBs that review a substantial amount of public health research should consider having public health professionals as members. It may also be useful to the IRB to have a member from either the state or local health department or to build a relationship with the health department for consultative purposes.

References

1. Code of Federal Regulations. Title 45A—Department of Health and Human Services; Part 46—Protection of Human Subjects. Updated 1 Oct 1997. Access date 18 Apr 2001. World Wide Web http://www4.law.cornell.edu/cfr/45p46.htm

2. Centers for Disease Control and Prevention. Human subjects research: Guidelines for defining public health research and public health non-research, 14 Mar 2001. Access date 20 Mar 2001. World Wide Web http://www.cdc.gov/od/ads/opspoll1.htm

3. National Bioethics Advisory Commission. Ethical and Policy Issues in Research Involving Human Participants (draft report). Bethesda, MD, U.S. Government Printing Office. Updated 19 Dec 2000. Access date 20 Mar 2001. World Wide Web http://bioethics.gov/pubs.html

4. Boruch RF, Cecil JS. *Assuring the Confidentiality of Social Research Data*. Philadelphia, PA: University of Pennsylvania Press. 1979.

5. Institute of Medicine, Committee on the Role of Institutional Review Boards in Health Services Research Data Privacy Protection. Protecting data privacy in health services research. Washington, DC, National Academy Press, 2000. Access date 20 Mar 2001. World Wide Web http://www.nap.edu/html/data_privacy/

6. 104th Congress. *Health Insurance Portability and Accountability Act of 1996*. Public Law 104-191. 1996. World Wide Web http://frwebgate.access.gpo.gov/cgi-bin/getdoc.cgi?dbname=104_cong_public_laws&docid=f:publ191.104.pdf

Survey Research

J. Michael Oakes

INTRODUCTION

This chapter considers human subject protection issues in biomedical, biobehavioral, and public health surveys (hereinafter called health surveys). Surveys are the most common method of data collection, used in both clinical trials and observational epidemiologic investigations. They are too often viewed as benign, posing no or only minimal risk, by both survey researchers and Institutional Review Boards (IRBs). This view is incorrect. The risks associated with information that may be discovered in survey studies may be every bit as serious as the physical risks associated with an investigational drug or medical device.

In most cases, the risks posed by survey research involve privacy and/or confidentiality. Two distinguished survey researchers write, "When all the rationales and justifications for its use have been stripped away, the . . . survey is ultimately an intrusion into the private lives of individuals."[1] Included are the risks of harm or loss (e.g., disclosure of private medical problems or sexual preference), inconvenience (e.g., boredom, frustration), psychological risk (e.g., insult, trauma), and social (e.g., embarrassment, rejection), economic (e.g., loss of job, credit, insurance), and legal (e.g., subpoena, fine) risk.

The objective of this chapter is straightforward. I aim to help IRB Chairs, administrators, and members improve their reviews of health survey research protocols. To this end, a brief background is given to put the method in perspective, and the federal regulations regarding survey research are highlighted. The unique aspects of survey research an IRB may wish to consider are sketched, including the use of real-world examples from the IRB I serve. Finally, specific and practical recommendations for reviewing and monitoring survey research are offered.

Background

Because there are many variations on the theme, it is important to be clear on what a survey is. The *IRB Guidebook* defines *survey studies* as those designed to obtain information from a large number of respondents through written questionnaires, telephone interviews, door-to-door canvassing, or similar procedures.[2]

In other words, a research health survey involves a systematic and standardized approach to data collection through questioning a sample of individuals, households, or organizations. This definition includes in-person, mail, telephone, Internet, and other such surveys. Excluded are related techniques of focus groups, semistructured interviews, and observational analysis, although many of the issues discussed herein apply.

DHHS Regulations Related to Survey Research

General IRB responsibilities related to privacy and confidentiality are addressed in 45 CFR 46.

1. Criteria for IRB approval of research[3[Sec.111(a)(7)]] "When appropriate, there are adequate provisions to protect the privacy of subjects and maintain the confidentiality of data."

2. General requirements for informed consent[3[Sec.116(a)(5)]] "a statement describing the extent, if any, to which confidentiality of records identifying the subject will be maintained."

3. Revised criteria for expedited review of research[4] "Research not meeting these criteria must undergo full board review."

The word *survey* is mentioned four times in 45 CFR 46, twice under the exemption clause (§46.101), once in a footnote referring to the children's section (i.e., Subpart D), and once in the exemptions section of the children's section itself.

In 45 CFR 46,[3(Sec.101)] which outlines what research is and is not covered by the statute, Subsection (b) reads as follows:

(b) Unless otherwise required by Department or Agency heads, research activities in which the only involvement of human subjects will be in one or more of the following categories are exempt from this policy: . . .

2) Research involving the use of educational tests (cognitive, diagnostic, aptitude, achievement), survey procedures, interview procedures or observation of public behavior, unless:

(i) information obtained is recorded in such a manner that human subjects can be identified, directly or through identifiers linked to the subjects; and

(ii) any disclosure of the human subjects' responses outside the research could reasonably place the subjects at risk of criminal or civil liability or be damaging to the subjects' financial standing, employability, or reputation.

3) Research involving the use of educational tests (cognitive, diagnostic, aptitude, achievement), survey procedures, interview procedures, or observation of public behavior that is not exempt under paragraph (b)(2) of this section, if:

(i) the human subjects are elected or appointed public officials or candidates for public office; or

(ii) Federal statute(s) require(s) without exception that the confidentiality of the personally identifiable information will be maintained throughout the research and thereafter.

The most important section[3][Sec.401(b)(2)] means that survey research is exempt from IRB oversight unless identifying information is collected and the disclosure of such information may cause harm to the subjects. Some distinguished commentators suggest the "and" preceding point (ii) means that most survey research is beyond the scope of IRB review. Shelton, for example, argues that it is not enough that risk is hypothetically possible, but that risks from survey information must be readily significant and appreciable for research to be covered by an IRB.[5] But Shelton discounts the ease with which links between databases can increase risk. It no longer takes much effort to merge databases from any number of sources and discover new information about subjects, placing them at risk. This is especially true when researchers recruit subjects from the same neighborhoods, clinics, or businesses, as is typically the case. Subject protections will be maximized by placing less weight on the risks from disclosure and more on whether the data are identifiable. Although de-emphasizing the requirement of "appreciable risks from disclosure" means that few health surveys will enjoy exemption status, as noted below, this should not inhibit the conduct of survey research to a meaningful degree.

Subpart (b)(3) goes on to say that research on elected officials and research that enjoys strict federal confidentiality protections are both exempt from IRB review. Also exempt are surveys on groups, organizations, and associations, which are called *establishment surveys*. The reason for this is that organizations are not human subjects and thus 45 CFR 46 does not apply. IRBs should be aware, however, that in order to learn who filled out the questionnaire, many establishment surveys query the characteristics of the respondent himself or herself. Such questions may preclude the exemption. Except for the footnote referring to it, the other place the word survey appears is in Subpart D, "Additional Protections for Children." Here the regulations[3(Sec.401)] say that the survey research exemption applicable to adults does not apply to children.

Research Design

Just as with other research designs and methodologies, IRBs must evaluate the quality of the design of survey studies. A poorly designed survey study will yield little useful information and thus poses (minimal) risks without benefits, rendering the proposal unworthy of IRB approval.

There are many design issues specific to survey studies; in fact, too many to comprehensively discuss here. Interested readers are encouraged to review Bickman and Rog,[6] Aday,[7] Rossi, Wright, and Anderson,[8] McDowell and Newell,[9] Dillman,[10] Fink,[11] Fowler,[12] Lehtonen and Pahkinen,[13] and Henry.[14] In addition to these texts, major journals publish methodological articles on survey research.

Response Rates

To assess the quality of a survey protocol, IRBs must have a general understanding of the term *response rate*. *Response rate* refers to the proportion of potential participants who complete the survey after being contacted about enrolling in the study.[7] If a survey contacts 402 eligible respondents but only 376 complete the questionnaire, the response rate is 94%. Response rates are important to survey studies because a low response rate means that many targeted subjects refused to participate. This is troublesome because it is unlikely that those who refused are statistically identical to those who participated, and this bias may render the entire study useless.

There is no hard rule on what constitutes an acceptable response rate, but the closer to 100% the better. Expected rates vary by survey mode (in-person, mail-back, and telephone), with in-person achieving the highest. While it seems that many survey researchers hold out 70% as a target value, mail-back studies of physicians may be as low as 40% while studies of a rare cancer may require 90% response to be meaningful. Response rates for federally funded national health surveys conducted in person have ranged from 85% to 95%.[7] Remember: to avoid bias, nonrespondents must not be systematically different from respondents in terms of characteristics that are important to the study.

Sampling and Coverage Errors

Sampling errors result from collecting data on only a subset of subjects on a sampling frame, which is merely a list of potential subjects. Although related to response rate, sampling errors can be precisely calculated with statistical formulas and may be of interest to IRB members or consultants with statistical experience. Coverage error results from excluding potential subjects from a sampling frame. IRBs may look at whether investigators convincingly show that the group of potential subjects who are targeted are the same as the individuals in the list that will be used to contact them. It may be useful for the IRB to inquire whether those eligible subjects who refuse to participate in the survey are not expected to be systematically different from those that agree to participate. Again, this is no minor detail, as poorly executed sampling plans have indirectly harmed thousands through the promulgation of poorly evaluated health policies.[15] A related IRB issue is the probable equitable recruitment of underrepresented members of society, such as racial minorities, women, and, in some cases, children.

Recruitment

The recruitment of subjects for survey research is no less important than any other aspect of study design. It is important for IRBs to remember that a study that involves a no-risk survey is still unethical if the recruitment practices violate the IRB's ethical standards.[2]

Consider this real-world example. While some would consider it standard operating procedure to contact a list of subjects that a physician-group or laboratory identifies as having elevated cholesterol, others would take issue with this proxy consent and consider the contact an invasion of privacy that was potentially burdensome and coercive to subjects. Experience suggests that problems will occur if potential subjects receive recruitment letters when (a) subjects have not explicitly given their physician-group permission to release information about them for research purposes, or (b) subjects are not aware of the condition that caused them to be contacted—hypercholesterolemia in this example. While many more troubling cases may be imagined, more mundane cases must not be overlooked. The point is that just because a survey protocol appears benign does not mean its recruitment procedures do not harm human subjects.

A related recruitment issue stems from efforts to get a disposition on each subject. Survey researchers define *disposition* as a code indicating whether the survey has been completed, whether the subject actively refused (i.e., saying, "I do not want to be in the study and do not call me again"), whether the subject simply refused (i.e., saying, "I am too busy now"), or whether the subject was never contacted. In this era of mass marketing, survey study designers may plan to make 10 calls to a given telephone number or send three or four questionnaires to a house before coding the subjects as "unavailable." Moreover, subjects who hem and haw before saying no may be recontacted and converted to completing the survey by more experienced interviewers. That skilled interviewers ably convince subjects to participate raises the potential for coercion. IRBs must balance the needs of survey researchers, who want to generate credible results, and the needs of the subjects, who deserve privacy and freedom from harassing phone calls and mailings.

Call scripts document how study representatives interact with subjects, and they are the first item to review if there is a question of coercion or harassment. One mechanism to prevent recruitment problems is to temporally separate the announcement of a study and recruitment for it. Providing a mechanism (800-number or self-addressed postcard) for prospective subjects to say that they do not want to be contacted may be appropriate is some cases. The active versus passive consent issue is the subject of Chapter 6-7.

Informed Consent

Standards for informed consent in survey research are no different than for research that does not involve a survey.[3][Sec.116 (a),(b)] In many cases, researchers will request IRB approval with the understanding that informed consent will be obtained but not be documented in writing. DHHS regulations provide for the waiver of documentation of informed consent in two situations that frequently apply to survey research.[3][Sec.117(c)]

An IRB may waive the requirement for the investigator to obtain a signed consent form for some or all subjects if it finds either:
(1) That the only record linking the subject and the research would be the consent document and the principal risk would be potential harm resulting from a breach of confidentiality. Each subject will be asked whether the subject wants documentation linking the subject with the research, and the subject's wishes will govern; or
(2) That the research presents no more than minimal risk of harm to subjects and involves no procedures for which written consent is normally required outside of the research context.
In cases in which the documentation requirement is waived, the IRB may require the investigator to provide subjects with a written statement regarding the research.

It is important that researchers understand that the above waiver does not mean that subjects may be enrolled in research without giving full and voluntary informed consent. It simply means that written documentation of consent is not required. It may be useful for IRBs to remind survey researchers of the evidence that fully informed subjects respond to questions with the most candor.[16,17]

Surrogate Surveys

An ethically challenging aspect of survey research concerns surrogate, proxy, or what others might call "indirect" surveys. Surrogate surveys elicit information from one person about another. Classic examples include husbands reporting information about their wives, adult children surveyed about their aging parents, or teachers about their students. It is essential that IRBs and researchers understand that there are often two subjects in these kinds of studies: the person responding to the survey and the person who is the subject of the survey. The full level of ethical protections and consent requirements applies to both subjects.

Botkin[18] reads 45 CFR 46 narrowly and argues that the person who is the primary subject of the survey (e.g., the wife in a study where the husband provides personal information about his wife) is a research subject only if names and other identifying information are collected. He goes on to say that even if an IRB determines that the primary subject is a research subject, a waiver of consent (not just documentation of consent) is usually justified. Botkin correctly recites the justifications for a waiver, but his arguments do not apply to many situations.[18]

In my experience, most health survey questions are sensitive to someone. Although small compared with other medical interventions, the degree of risk should be determined by each subject, not the researcher. Being an experienced survey statistician, I believe information coded for the "father" or "daughter" of an identified (primary) subject makes the surrogate data identifiable. If an employer gets unauthorized access to the survey data of an employee and then, through coded and linked data, discovers her husband is HIV positive, it is not a big leap to infer that the primary subject herself is at least at greater risk for HIV, if not positive herself.

As a result of the above concerns, the IRB that I serve on is more conservative than Botkin, and insists that investigators get informed consent from both primary and surrogate subjects when a breach in confidentiality could result in meaningful harm. In some cases, it is impractical or impossible to get consent from all subjects who are at risk from survey information. Survey projects that do not meet the appropriate ethical standards should not be approved by the IRB.

Psychological and Social Harm

A January 2001 query of IRB professionals via the Web-based IRB Forum (formerly MCWIRB) revealed several cases where survey questions, in and of themselves, appeared to harm study subjects.

1. Three weeks after answering the questionnaire for a cancer study, a man in his early 20s committed suicide, leaving a note stating that until he answered the questionnaire he did not really realize all of the experiences he had missed.

2. A survey researcher was investigating attitudes towards rape. When filling out the questionnaire, several subjects became visibly emotionally distressed and asked the investigator for help.

3. A study involving adolescents with emotional difficulties included a few questions about sexual preference. One subject interpreted the questions as if the researcher were suggesting she or he was a homosexual. The subject became very upset, attacked the researcher, and had to be restrained.

It is common for health surveys to include items about mental health status (e.g., depression), previous sexual abuses, illicit and prescription drug use, and physical disabilities. These questions are of a sensitive nature, and they may: (a) provoke emotional responses by subjects and (b) place respondents at risk for discrimination, recrimination, or other harms—even physical ones. IRBs must balance the need to study difficult questions in vulnerable populations with their mandate to ensure the protection of human subjects.

Arguments that subjects are aware of the risks and thus a review of questions is not necessary may not withstand empirical scrutiny. Survey researchers are well trained to ask easy, noninvasive questions first in order to build rapport with subjects. Then, often gently, the more difficult questions are asked. This funneling technique is useful for survey researchers because respondents become more and more willing to answer tough questions after rapport is built. The problem is that once subjects begin to express their feelings, attitudes, and opinions—and because talk-ing about oneself can be therapeutic, they often do—their ability to withdraw at any time may be practically forestalled. People want to appear consistent and cooperative and will thus continue to answer questions when they otherwise would not. Although IRBs must be sure not to cripple the research enterprise, the ultimate definition of *sensitive* rests with the subject, not the investigators.

Even more generally, sensitive questions may be difficult to recognize. Health surveys will typically include questions on income, age, race, and gender. Although ostensibly benign, when coupled with responses about drug use, sexual behavior, or, say, mental illness, these linked responses may result in inappropriate stigmatizations of groups of individuals. For example, a survey study that finds Hispanic or Asian men to have a greater propensity for domestic violence may inappropriately create a social stigma that affects the entire Hispanic-American or Asian-American community. The point is that even seemingly benign questions may pose critical risks and thus deserve close IRB scrutiny. In focusing strictly on protecting human subjects, IRBs should ensure that subjects understand the potential for social risks prior to participation.

Privacy and Confidentiality

Confidentiality is different from privacy. Survey data deserves as much attention to confidentiality as any other data, including genetic markers. Rights to confidentiality may be distinguished from rights to privacy by noting that *confidentiality* implies that consented surrendered information must be used only in the negotiated and disclosed manner, whereas *privacy* implies that no consent for information is granted. Beauchamp and Childress make the point:

> An infringement of X's right to confidentiality occurs only if the person to whom X disclosed information in confidence fails to protect the information or deliberately discloses it to someone without X's consent. By contrast, a person who without authorization enters a hospital record room or computer data bank [and views or records information] violates rights of privacy. . . .[19]

Assuming that researchers have been authorized to collect and use a subject's information, survey research raises several more or less unique confidentiality issues. The *Institutional Review Board Guidebook* makes the point:

> In most research, assuring confidentiality is only a matter of following some routine practices: substituting codes for identifiers, removing face sheets (containing such items as names and addresses) from survey instruments containing data, properly disposing of computer sheets and other papers, limiting access to identified data, impressing on the research staff the importance of confidentiality, and storing research records in locked cabinets. . . .[2]

Because research suggests most respondents do not believe their answers will be kept confidential, it is incumbent on researchers and IRBs to regain or establish this trust. Pursuant to trust, the most important IRB issue with respect to nonanonymous (survey) data is the linking file.[20] A linking file is usually an electronic data file that contains each respondent's identifying information and the respondent's unique study identification number. Unless there are special reasons not to—such as when investigators are using computer-aided telephone interviewing (CATI/CAPI) computer systems to collect the data—this file should be the only place where subject identifying information is stored. Access to this file should be limited to only those who literally need access. The IRB should insist that the data file is encrypted, as computers may be hacked or physically stolen. All data files containing survey responses or any other information should be expunged of identifying information. Only the unique study identification number should be used. If CATI/CAPI systems are used to collect data, appropriate file deletion procedures should be enforced when the collection is complete.

Cryptic identifiers are easy for statisticians and computer programmers to assign to each person. They may simply be some combination of first and last name letters, birth dates, and, say, zipcodes. Jane Smith, born on July 6, 1967, and living in Longmeadow, MA, may thus have the code JASM766701106, which will almost certainly be unique for linking and analytic purposes. More advanced methods are also easily implemented.

Compensation

The tension between the need to recruit and retain research subjects and the obligation to protect them from coercive interests makes compensation one of the most difficult and debated topics in applied bioethics. The *Institutional Review Board Guidebook* points out:

> Federal regulations governing research with human subjects contain no specific guidance for IRB review of payment practices. One of the primary responsibilities of IRBs, however, is to ensure that a subject's decision to participate in research will be truly voluntary, and that consent will be sought "only under circumstances that provide the prospective subject . . . sufficient opportunity to consider whether or not to participate and that minimize the possibility of coercion or undue influence" [Federal Policy §46.116; 21 CFR 50.20].[2]

Dickert and Grady sketch four objections to monetary compensation: (1) that the promise of money leads to undue inducement; (2) that only the economically disadvantaged will participate, rendering unequal benefits to the wealthy; (3) that paid subjects may care only about money and not about credible scientific results; and (4) that subject payment changes the investigator–subject relationship into a commercial one.[21] But the authors admit that payment is probably here to stay and may be ethically justified. Accordingly, they go on to outline three approaches to payment: (1) the market model, where subjects are paid so as to attract and keep them; (2) the wage-payment model, where subjects are paid a standardized (unskilled labor) wage for participating; and (3) the reimbursement model, where subjects are reimbursed for expenses. Dickert and Grady ultimately advocate for the wage-payment model on the grounds that it is most egalitarian and should yield the least chance for coercion.[21]

Because the level of risk and effort is generally less than that encountered in biomedical studies, the question of compensation for health surveys is often overlooked in the bioethical literature. But health surveys do raise some more or less unique questions about compensation. For example, how much compensation, if any, should an investigator offer in a study of homeless drug or alcohol addicts who will only be interviewed once? What form should the compensation take: cash, food, or clothing? Anonymity is breached if payment is by check. When should the payment be made? Before or after completion of the survey? Must all questions be answered to receive a "completion bonus"?

In an effort to improve response rates, survey researchers have worked on the compensation problem. IRBs may use empirically generated survey research results in their deliberations about respondent compensation. Clearly, the potential for coercion is reduced when between $1 and $5 is included up front, as opposed to promises of payment when some task is complete. Evidence suggests, however, that this may be sufficient to gain the required response rates.

Conclusion

This chapter argues for continued, if not more vigorous, IRB review of health survey protocols. IRBs must balance the demand for research and the advancement of knowledge with the risks surveys pose. Although usually not the same level of risk posed by surgical, pharmacological or device trials, because surveys are ubiquitous, even marginal ethical infractions can cause aggregate harm. When reviewing survey research studies, IRBs should obviously consider all the regulations and obligations of 45 CFR 46, as well as those found in *The Belmont Report*, the Nuremberg Code, and the Declaration of Helsinki. Concerns raised in other kinds of reviews should also generally apply to survey research protocols. In addition, IRBs may consider the following unordered summary points:

1. All survey protocols should be reviewed by an IRB official to determine exemption or expedite status. Proper assessment requires reviewing the entire protocol, including recruitment, contact, and analysis procedures.

2. Though it offers the maximum protection, few health surveys can be anonymous.

3. Survey research involves identifying information if subjects may be identified at any point in the study, including the recruitment of subjects or payment by check.

4. Surveys of children, prisoners, and other vulnerable populations must be reviewed by the full IRB.

5. Reviewing recruitment protocols and scripts is integral to the protection of subjects.

6. Written consent documents may not be necessary, but the informed consent process is.

7. With projects that involve primary and surrogate subjects, the IRB should require that all subjects are afforded the full level of protections.

8. Nonresponse bias must be minimized or eliminated.

9. High response rates often require multiple subject contacts, but subjects should be protected from harassment.

10. The formatting and layout of the questionnaire influences response rates in a small way.

11. Pretests are almost essential, and good ones require significant resources.

12. Compensation is helpful, but evidence suggests sending $1 to $5 before the questionnaire is sent is sufficient and unlikely to be coercive.

13. Evidence suggests lotteries do little to improve survey response rates.

14. Linking files should be kept separate from response data and protected by limited access and encrypted methods.

15. Unless they gather information about respondents (i.e., human subjects), establishment (i.e., organizational) surveys are exempt.

16. IRBs should consider how survey studies are concluded. After expressing experiences and emotions, subjects are particularly vulnerable and deserve continued protection and sensitivity.

Acknowledgments

This paper was improved by the comments and criticisms of several colleagues and friends. I thank Cheryl Caswell, Samantha Dunn, Kevin Smith, Joan Sieber, and Andre Araujo, as well as the entire Institutional Review Board at the New England Research Institutes. Special thanks to members of the MCWIRB.ORG listserve who willingly shared their thoughts and opinions. I remain indebted to Professors Peter H. Rossi and Andy B. Anderson for their detailed comments on this paper, as well as their training more generally. The usual caveats apply.

References

1. Fox JA, Tracy PE. *Randomized Response: A Method for Sensitive Surveys*. Beverly Hills: Sage Publications. 1986.

2. Penslar RL, Porter JP, Office for Human Research Protections. *Institutional Review Board Guidebook*, 6 Feb 2001. Access date 29 Mar 2001. World Wide Web http://ohrp.osophs.dhhs.gov/irb/irb_guidebook.htm

3. Code of Federal Regulations. Title 45A—Department of Health and Human Services; Part 46—Protection of Human Subjects. Updated 1 Oct 1997. Access date 18 Apr 2001. World Wide Web http://www4.law.cornell.edu/cfr/45p46.htm

4. National Institutes of Health. Protection of human subjects: Categories of research that may be reviewed by the Institutional Review Board (IRB) through an expedited review procedure. *Fed Regist* 63(216):60364–60367, 1998.

5. Shelton JD. How to interpret the federal policy for the protection of human subjects or "Common Rule" (Part A). *IRB: A Review of Human Subjects Research* 21(6):6–9, 1999.

6. Bickman L, Rog DJ. *Handbook of Applied Social Research Methods*. Thousand Oaks: Sage Publications. 1998.

7. Aday LA. *Designing and Conducting Health Surveys: A Comprehensive Guide*, Ed 2. San Francisco: Jossey-Bass Publishers. 1996.

8. Rossi PH, Wright JD, Anderson AB. *Handbook of Survey Research*. Orlando: Academic Press. 1983.

9. McDowell I, Newell C. *Measuring Health: A Guide to Rating Scales and Questionnaires*, Ed 2. New York: Oxford University Press. 1996.

10. Dillman DA. *Mail and Internet Surveys: The Tailored Design Method*, Ed 2. New York: John Wiley & Sons, Inc. 2000.

11. Fink A. *The Survey Handbook*. Thousand Oaks: Sage Publications. 1995.

12. Fowler FJ. *Improving Survey Questions: Design and Evaluation*. Thousand Oaks: Sage Publications. 1995.

13. Lehtonen R, Pahkinen EJ. *Practical Methods for Design and Analysis of Complex Surveys*, Ed Revised. New York: John Wiley & Sons, Inc. 1996.

14. Henry GT. *Practical Sampling*. Newbury Park: Sage Publications. 1990.

15. Hartley SF. Sampling strategies and the threat to privacy. In: Sieber JE (ed). *The Ethics of Social Research: Surveys and Experiments*. New York: Springer-Verlag. 1982: 167–189.

16. Singer E. Informed consent: Consequences for response rate and response quality in social surveys. *American Sociological Review* 43(12):144–162, 1978.

17. Loo CM. Vulnerable populations: Case studies in crowding research. In: Sieber JE (ed). *The Ethics of Social Research: Surveys and Experiments*. New York: Springer-Verlag. 1982: 105-126.

18. Botkin JR. Protecting the privacy of family members in survey and pedigree research. *JAMA* 285(2):207–211, 2001.

19. Beauchamp TL, Childress JF. *Principles of Biomedical Ethics*, Ed 4. New York, NY: Oxford University Press. 1994.

20. Turner AG. What subjects of survey research believe about confidentiality. In: Sieber JE (ed). *The Ethics of Social Research: Surveys and Experiments*. New York: Springer-Verlag. 1982.

21. Dickert N, Grady C. What's the price of a research subject? Approaches to payment for research participation. *N Engl J Med* 341(3):198–203, 1999.

Research Involving a Medical Device

Erica J. Heath

INTRODUCTION

Although charms and talismans to prevent or cure disease have been used from ancient times, there was rarely any more than anecdotal proof as to their safety or efficacy. Along with other machinery, by the mid-1900s it became easier and cheaper to manufacture, distribute, and advertise devices on a large scale. After a brief history, this chapter describes the major components that distinguish the device regulations from the drug regulations, issues raised in clinical investigations of devices, and finally, the very critical and central role that IRBs play in the regulation of medical devices.

History

One good review of the history of device regulations is the 1976 Report by the House Committee on Interstate and Foreign Commerce;[1] it can be found in a 1976 Food and Drug Law Institute publication.[2]

A second resource, which is far more fun, is the Museum of Questionable Medical Devices in Minneapolis. Many of the devices on display in the museum can be seen at their Web site.[3]

The House report gives one of the best histories leading up to development of the device regulations. Among the scandals cited are lead poisoning of infants from lead nipple shields, women harmed by pessaries that punctured the uterus, and various prophylactics that failed. Several publicized scandals led Congress, in 1938, to grant to the FDA the authority to seize misbranded devices to protect people from "fraudulent claims." Multiple seizures were made, but little could be accomplished because of the very limited mandate from Congress. For example, in the late 1940s, Dr. Dinshah Ghadiali sold the Spectrochrome, a 1000-watt lamp in a cabinet with colored glass slides, purported to cure diabetes, cancer, tuberculosis, and syphilis. It sold for $90 with much literature. FDA action resulted in multiple seizures and criminal actions. In the mid-1960s, the FDA began an action to seize the Diapulse, a heat-generating device marked for 121 therapeutic claims with no data for any. The court case was lengthy, with an injunction being issued in 1972.

By the late 1960s, the FDA was concentrating on the safety of medical devices, but without any additional mandate beyond seizure for misbranding, their task was difficult. In fact, in several cases they successfully argued that substances including a nylon ligature[4] and a cardboard antibiotic sensitivity test[5] were drugs. As drugs, they could be regulated by the FDA. But for other devices, such as the Dalkon shield, intraocular lenses, and cardiac pacemakers with serious defects, such arguments were unsuccessful, and the devices could not be regulated.

In 1969, the Department of Health, Education, and Welfare (now the Department of Health and Human Services) formed a medical device study group chaired by Dr. Theodore Cooper. The Cooper Committee studied the problems, the range of kinds of devices, and the medical device business environment and published their findings and recommendations. Among the recommendations they proposed were: (a) the classification of devices according to the amount of regulation needed, (b) peer review of new devices with a specific view toward protection of potential patient users, and (c) review efforts in proportion to potential harms.

The next FDA commissioner, the same Dr. Cooper, had little trouble implementing the Cooper Committee recommendations, culminating in the Medical Devices Amendments of 1976.[6] A new unit called the Bureau of Devices [now known as the Center for Devices and Radiologic Health (CDRH)] was formed within the FDA. Concepts forged for regulation of devices differ significantly from drug regulations that were their precursor:

1. Devices were defined and distinguished from drugs.
2. Three classes of devices were identified based on the need for regulatory control.
3. Several routes to market were defined.
4. Several types of exemption were allowed for investigational devices.
5. Decisions external to the FDA were allowed concerning which devices posed enough risk to merit submission to the FDA for prior review.

Components of the Device Regulations

All the regulations about medical devices are found in the Code of Federal Regulations, Title 21, Part 800 through Part 1050.[7-9] In many ways, the device regulations are similar to the drug regulations. However, because of their uniqueness and their history, several important distinctions are made.

Definition of a Medical Device

An elementary feature distinguishing drugs from medical devices is that one can interact chemically with the body whereas the other cannot. This, however, leaves a large intermediate territory. The second element is that a medical device is a device that is being studied or promoted for a medical purpose.

1. Combination devices such as pumps or patches delivering drugs might be classified as either drugs or devices depending on which part is investigational. An ombudsman within the FDA makes this decision. As this decision makes a substantial difference in the requirements that must be met to go on the market, it is a core element in sponsor planning.

2. In vitro diagnostic test kits are medical devices.[7(Sec.809)] Their regulatory status depends on their intended use. When they are used for a medical diagnosis, it is of IRB interest. Nonmedical laboratory use generally is not of IRB interest.

3. Radiologic products that introduce energy are regulated as devices.[9]

Classification of Devices[7(Secs. 862,892)]

In 1976, the FDA identified about 1,100 device manufacturers responsible for about 8,000 devices on the market, none of which had been reviewed for safety or effectiveness. Although most of those devices were not known to have caused any harm, a literature search for the Cooper Committee found 10,000 injuries over 10 years with 751 fatalities.

The Medical Device Amendment of 1976[6] established three classes for devices.[7] *Not* intended to be a risk classification, the classes were instead a measure of the level of regulation required to establish that a device was "safe and effective" and the control required to maintain this assurance. In practice, the level of risk and the level of control are generally equivalent.

Over the next decade, all of the 8000 or so devices that had been on the market as of May 26, 1976, were classified by advisory panels into class I, II, or III. The classifications are arranged by discipline.[7(Sec.862,892)] The classifications were redefined slightly in 1992.

Class I—general controls.   Many devices need very little regulation to assure that they are safe and effective. Basic controls such as those on manufacturing and claims were expected to be sufficient. (Examples include crutches, band-aids, cast components.)

Class II—special controls.   The largest device category, this encompasses those device types that could be considered to be safe and effective if they met class I restrictions and if there were some additional standards according to the kind of device. (Examples include magnetic resonance imager, methyl methacrylate for cranioplasty.)[7(Sec. 882.5300)]

Class III—premarket application.   Class III devices are the most interesting ones for IRBs. These are devices about which there is insufficient information to determine that they are safe and effective. Any "new" devices (i.e., they are not substantially equivalent to any prior device) about which there are few or no data are automatically class III.

Preamendment devices that were determined to be in class III were allowed to remain on the market without demonstrating safety or efficacy with the caveat that, at any time, the FDA could ask for a submission of clinical data. This has been done in several cases. Because data on intraocular lenses (IOLs) were requested before the final device regulations were published, they had their own regulation. Silicone gel breast implant data were requested in April 1991, causing manufacturers to create large adjunct and core studies to gather information on a product already being marketed.

Registration and Listing[7(Sec.807)]

Device manufacturers must register all their manufacturing facilities. This registration allows the FDA to conduct manufacturing inspections. Manufacturers must also submit a complete product list annually. This registration and listing make it possible for the FDA to inspect facilities and devices; failure to register or list has resulted in at least one criminal conviction. For example, in one case in 1994,[10] failure to properly register, concealment of adverse patient information, making product changes without FDA permission, and illegally testing products on humans resulted in criminal action against the manufacturer.

Tracking[7(Sec.821)]

The FDA imposes additional requirements on manufacturers of some devices, most of which are implants. It is thought to be necessary to track patients so that they can be contacted in the event of a recall. In the investigational setting, IRBs may find they disagree with sponsors about how much private identifying data must be retained.

Quality Systems[7(Sec.820)]

Manufacturers of devices must meet general quality standards to produce their devices. The systems must be thoroughly documented in master files. FDA inspections of registered manufacturing sites are conducted under this section. Compliance is required for the manufacture of investigational devices as well and is a part of the FDA decision about marketing.

Routes to Market[7(Sec.814)]

As with drugs, before a medical device can be shipped in interstate commerce, it must be cleared for market by the FDA. Unlike drugs, however, devices can come to market by way of multiple regulatory routes. Although Congress and the Cooper Committee agreed that the drug IND-to-NDA (investigational new drug to new drug application) model was appropriate for higher risk devices, it was thought to be too cumbersome and expensive for less risky devices that were often manufactured by very small companies without the resources for a long regulatory process.

Although there are other routes, there are three that manufacturers use most often and several that are less common.

Premarket approval (PMA). This is the device equivalent of the NDA following clinical trials to determine safety and efficacy.

Substantial equivalence.[6(Sec.510K)] Between the long trip through clinical studies and minimal regulation, there is a wide gap. In the 1976 law passed by Congress, a company could make a claim (now known as "510K") to the FDA, indicating that its device was "substantially equivalent" to a device that was on the market as of the enactment date (May 1976). As 1976 had receded into history, substantial equivalence claims have been made to newer predicate devices. If such a claim is accepted by the CDRH, the new device can join the predicate device already on the market. A device cleared by the FDA under a 510K can be sold without demonstration of safety or efficacy.

Extension of a product line. If a company extends its product line (e.g., different sizes of a product), it is allowed to add that new form of the product to its catalog. These become part of the complete product list required in the manufacturer's annual report.

Reclassification. A brand new device (i.e., not substantially equivalent to another predicate device) is automatically in class III. The sponsor may request that the FDA reclassify it as a class II device.

Humanitarian use. Similar to an orphan drug, the humanitarian use device (HUD) was added to the regulations in 1996.[7(Sec.814.100)] To qualify for HUD designation, the indication must be for a disease or condition that affects fewer than 4,000 people in the United States per year. An HUD designation allows marketing approval "notwithstanding the absence of reasonable assurance of effectiveness that would otherwise be required. . . ." The HUD is the subject of a separate chapter in this book.

Clinical Investigation of a Medical Device

A medical device may not enter into interstate commerce until it receives FDA clearance for marketing. Interstate commerce is presumed in the case of medical devices. How can a device be shipped across state lines for use by investigators before it is cleared? Regulation 21 CFR 812 allows an investigational device exception (IDE) exempting the device from this rule.[7] No medical device can be shipped in interstate commerce without (a) being cleared for market or (b) obtaining an exemption from the ban on interstate shipment. An investigational device exemption (IDE) exempts the device so that it can be shipped.

Studies involving humans are required for gathering data to be submitted with a PMA. Although no clinical data to substantiate a 510K (substantial equivalence) claim were required originally, more recently, a number of other kinds of preclearance (or postclearance) studies, such as ergonomic, feasibility, preference, and acceptability, have been required.

A common point of confusion between companies and IRBs occurs when there is no agreement as to the regulatory definitions used. An IRB that follows the Common Rule, as well as the FDA rules, would need submission of research to the local IRB. Institutional rules take precedence in the institution. Because the Common Rule definition of research is broader than the FDA definition, sponsors relying on the FDA regulations may fail to consider the activity to be research. For instance, under 21 CFR 56,[11] the term *research subject* has little to do with the identifiability of samples. If the device is not cleared for market and is being shipped, it likely needs IRB review.

In many of these instances, defining a study (as defined in 45 CFR 46[12]) is difficult. Device engineers are renowned for "tweaking" the device; it may not be the same for two tests in a row, so there is no generalizable information. A test of an in vitro diagnostic kit by a research laboratory may be seen as having no subjects because there are no humans receiving a test article or being a control.

Investigational Exemptions[7(Sec.812)]

As recommended by the Cooper Committee, the degree of regulation for investigational devices was designed to be in proportion to their perceived risks. Thus, there are three levels of IDE, which are dependent on the perceived level of risk. Several other exemptions are made for specific situations.

Investigational device exemption (SR IDE).[7(Sec. 812, Subparts B,C,D)] Any device found to pose a significant risk of harm by the sponsor, by any reviewing IRB, or by the FDA must have an IDE. The IDE may be requested either before or after submission to the IRB; thus, IRB approval contingent on receipt of the FDA's IDE letter is not unusual. As this list is considered to contain trade secrets, the FDA does not publish it and cannot discuss any aspect of an IDE with the IRB. (As of March 2001, there is discussion that this may change.)

Exemption from an IDE.[7[Sec. 812.2(c)]] A device can be exempt from the IDE requirements. (An exemption from an exemption?) A claim that the device is exempt should be justified through reference to the exemption category being claimed. The exemption most commonly claimed is for diagnostic devices.[7[Sec. 812.2(c)(3)]]

An exemption from the IDE requirement of Part 812 is *not* an exemption from IRB review (Part 56) or informed consent (Part 50). Studies of devices that are IDE-exempt may be eligible for expedited review (category 1, which includes no device for which an IDE is required) by the IRB and, perhaps, for waiver of informed consent, but these are questions for the IRB to consider.

Abbreviated IDE (NSR).[7[Sec. 812.2(b)]] An abbreviated IDE is "considered to have an approved application for an IDE." Of seven sponsor requirements, the second affects the IRB: "sponsor obtains IRB approval of the investigation after presenting the reviewing IRB with a brief explanation of why the device is not a significant risk device, and maintains such approval."[7[Sec. 812.2(b)(ii)]] Risk designation (significant versus nonsignificant risk) is discussed later in this chapter.

HDE (humanitarian device exemption).[7(Sec. 812.104)] For a device to be marketed as a humanitarian device, an HDE must be granted by the FDA. The HDE holder is responsible for obtaining IRB approval;[7(Sec.812.124)] it is an amalgam of an approved device needing an exemption! As the device is considered to be marketed, its use may be therapeutic, and there may not be any sort of study or research involved.

Emergency exception: treatment use of an investigational device.[7(Sec.812.36)] Very similar to an emergency use of an investigational drug, a device may be used for a serious or life-threatening condition where there is no appropriate alternative. Investigators and sponsors must comply with parts 50 and 56,[7[Sec. 812.36(e)]] although there is little guidance concerning IRB evaluation of such an application.

Charging for an investigational medical device.[7[Sec. 812.7(b)]]

Unlike drug companies, device companies may recover costs by charging subjects or investigators a price no larger than that necessary to recover costs of manufacture, research, development, and handling of a device. This price should be made clear to the IRB and indicated on the consent document. It is possible that Medicare will cover the costs of an investigational device. The FDA will categorize each IDE as an A or B. Category B devices are investigational but not experimental; they may be class I or II devices or may be NSR devices.[13]

Role of the Institutional Review Board

The reviewing IRB must apply each of the three parts of the FDA regulations—21 CFR 50, 56, and 812—individually. The use of 21 CFR 50 and 56 is routine for IRBs; the application of 21 CFR 812 is considerably more difficult.

The type of IDE being used is often, but not always, linked to the classification of the device or the route to market being taken. A 510K application may claim substantial equivalence to a quite risky device already being marketed. A completely new device is a class III device although it may be intuitively clear that there are no conceivable harms. Although a PMA or reclassification route to market is necessary, the IRB may be able to determine that there is no significant risk. A company wishing to seek reclassification of a device from class III to class II might conduct a safety evaluation to support its request. Almost any of the forms of IDE could be sought for shipping the device for this trial.

Step 1. Is the Study Approvable,[11] and Are the Consent Form and Process Approvable?[14]

The primary purpose of any IRB is to protect the rights and welfare of the human subject. Thus, the primary IRB question remains whether the criteria for approval in the regulations and in the IRB's own written policies have been met. If the review criteria cannot be met, the study cannot be approved, and further work by the IRB (aside from assistance to the investigator) is not justified.

Occasionally IRBs have had difficulty with the risk/benefit evaluation because of the design of the device trial. Although there are well-controlled studies of devices, a greater number of activities are more developmental in nature and are designed and run by technical instead of clinical personnel. Instead of making a drug and progressing through set stages, many device trials are done to learn more about whether the instructions are understandable, whether the ergonomics are correct, or whether the device does what it was intended to do. Therefore, the range of designs is much broader for studies of medical devices than for drugs.

The FDA has the opportunity to impose postapproval requirements.[7(Sec. 814.80)] Often these are for continuing evaluation of the safety, effectiveness, or reliability of the device for the intended use. These are often mistaken for marketing or seeding studies rather than mandated requirements. The requirements and the reasons for them should be included with the FDA's approval letter. The IRB may request the PMA or 510K letter.

Under 21 CFR 50 and the Common Rule, the IRB determines if the consent form is appropriate. Under 21 CFR 812, however, the documents to be used to inform subjects are a part of the IDE request submitted to the FDA.[7(Sec. 812.20(b)(11))] Many sponsors contend, incorrectly, that this means the consent materials cannot be changed by the IRB. They can be.

Step 2. Is the Regulatory Status Clear?

A drug study requires an IND; a device study requires an IDE or an exemption from the IDE. It is the applicant's responsibility—with assistance from the sponsor—to make the regulatory status of the device clear. The sponsor has access to strategic information, decisions by other IRBs, and previous FDA decisions and should be able to clearly state the intended route to market and the type of investigational exemption being sought.

The various exemptions were previously discussed; IRB actions differ depending on the type of IDE sought. Knowing the regulatory status dictates the action an IRB must take.

Significant risk (SR) IDE. A sponsor may decide that a device poses a serious risk of harm and elect to file for an IDE. Alternatively, if *any* IRB determines that the device poses a significant risk, it must be submitted to the FDA for an IDE. Making an SR decision has the potential to have a substantial impact on the sponsor. If an IDE is claimed, an IDE letter from CDRH referencing the device and the indication should be submitted before final IRB approval.

Abbreviated IDE—nonsignificant risk (NSR).[7[Sec.812.2(b)]] Central to an abbreviated IDE application is the need for the IRB to agree with the applicant's NSR contention.

Sponsors may believe—reasonably or not—that the device does not pose a serious risk of harm to subjects. In this case, they may elect to seek an abbreviated IDE. If the claim is acceptable to the IRB *and* the study is approvable, the study may be approved and conducted. No report to FDA is required until the data are submitted.

The IRB may, however, decide that the claim is not justified and ask for a better justification. Just as study disapproval should not occur without presenting the investigator with written reasons, the IRB should not make a final SR determination without presenting the rationale and reviewing the response.

As the difference in development time can be substantial, sponsors have a major interest in obtaining the abbreviated IDE. However, at the end of a study the data must be presented to the FDA, and should the FDA disagree with the NSR decision, the agency could ask for more or different data. The risk of an inappropriate decision is primarily an economic risk borne by the sponsor.

Exemption from the IDE.[7[Sec.812.3]]   Sponsors claiming an exemption should be asked to clearly state which exemption is being claimed: the humanitarian or the emergency.

A humanitarian device exemption request presented to an IRB is often a cause for confusion, as generally no study is included. The device is "cleared for market" without information about effectiveness. The IRB is asked to determine that the rights and welfare of the patient are protected and the informed consent is appropriate.

In an emergency, as with other individual emergencies, a physician wishing to use an investigational device outside the parameters of a protocol may do so. The IRB should be consulted before, if time permits. Most IRBs have written policies regarding emergency use of an investigational drug, which can be extended to devices.

Step 3. If Such a Decision is Requested, Is It a Nonsignificant Risk Device?

If the sponsor believes that an abbreviated IDE is justified and it is willing to meet all seven elements, it should provide the IRB with a statement saying that it contends[7[Sec.812.2(b)]] that the device, as it is to be used in the context of the named protocol, poses a nonsignificant risk of harm to the subjects. The sponsor should then back up this claim. The documentation could be (a) an NSR determination made by the FDA, (b) inclusion on an FDA list of NSR devices (in their Information Sheets[15] in the section titled "Significant risk and nonsignificant risk—medical device studies"), or (c) a thorough risk analysis and a request for an IRB determination of NSR.

The congressional rationale for the abbreviated IDE was that there should be a lower level of regulatory structure for devices that pose less risk. Having the IRB act as the triage or decision point would lessen the FDA workload and speed the time to approval. This provides a constant tension between IRBs, sponsors, and the FDA. If the IRB agrees with the sponsor's NSR contention, the study

can proceed without any further notice to the FDA. No information (other than registering the manufacturing establishment and listing marketed devices) needs to go to the FDA. If the IRB disagrees with the contention and determines that the device is an SR device, the study may not start at that (or any other) site until the FDA has reviewed and either granted the IDE or determined that the device is, in fact, NSR.

The NSR determination is thus critical to the sponsor; it is a major point on a critical path, and it can substantially alter development time. Sponsors tend to seek the speediest and least restrictive route to market, and the FDA tends to seek the most protective route. In any case, early input from FDA reviewers may result in design of a trial that is more likely to answer questions that reviewers might later pose; this avoids a waste of the sponsor's time and money and the subject's time and risk.

Making the NSR Decision

Four elements are contained in the definition of an SR device.[7[Sec.812.3(m)]] Each element is modified by the phrase, "*and* presents a potential for serious risk to the health, safety or welfare of a subject." Grammatically, if it presents a serious risk of harm under any circumstance, it is an SR device; that is, an SR device is one that presents a serious risk of harm.

Significant Risk Device Determination:
If an IRB determines that an investigation . . . involves a significant risk device. . . .[7[(812.66)]]

'Significant risk device' means an investigational device that:

(1) Is intended as an implant *and* presents a potential for serious risk to the health, safety, or welfare of a subject;

(2) Is purported or represented to be for use in supporting or sustaining human life *and* presents a potential for serious risk to the health, safety, or welfare of a subject;

(3) Is for a use of substantial importance in diagnosing, curing, mitigating, or treating disease, or otherwise preventing impairment of human health *and* presents a potential for serious risk to the health, safety, or welfare of a subject; *or*

(4) Otherwise presents a potential for serious risk to the health, safety, or welfare of a subject. . . .[7[Sec.812.3(m)]]

The first step in making the decision is to understand all of the possible harms in terms of their potential frequency, their severity, and their permanence. Theoretical risks should be included. The second step is to examine the source of each potential harm. Is the possible harm due to the underlying disease, the baseline patient care, procedures required by protocol to evaluate the effects of the device, the device itself, or the modification made that makes it investigational? With this risk analysis ready, the IRB must then decide if those risks constitute a serious or significant risk to the subject. This is a judgment left to the IRB. Each IRB must have its own written policies and procedures for making this decision.

A crucial question is which risks to factor into the evaluation. Although the regulations define an SR device, the

FDA guidance[16] alters the language in an important manner. It refers to a "significant risk device study." The distinction is important. Should the risks in the risk analysis be limited to one, two, or all of the following?

1. Risks from the investigational form of the device
2. Risk of the entire device
3. Risks from tests done to evaluate research results
4. Risks of the treatment of the patient
5. Underlying condition

The position stated in the FDA guidance is the more conservative view: all of the study risks must be considered. This could result in an SR decision for a study of a non-risky device within the context of a very risky study.

The example used in the FDA guidance is instructive. A patient needs a pacemaker, consents to placement of a pacemaker, and has surgery (with its attendant risks) with insertion of the marketed pacemaker (with its attendant risks). This certainly yields a very serious risk of harm to the patient. However, if the pacemaker is altered sufficiently that it becomes an investigational device, should the IRB consider the risks of the investigational device in the context of the given study (e.g., the harms due to the alteration), or should it consider all of the risks of the device and the study (the altered device and the added monitoring), or should it consider all potential harms including the patient risks? Again, the more conservative and FDA-requested decision is to call this device SR. However, with documented procedures and risk analysis, the IRB may be able to support an NSR decision.

Should It Have Been SR Rather Than NSR?

An ongoing concern is what happens if the NSR decision is wrong. Generally this is unknown until after the study is underway. One of three things may occur.

1. The FDA learns of the decision and disagrees. This may occur through the sponsor's submission of data; through an IRB, investigator, or sponsor audit; or in other conversation. If the IRB has made a decision in good faith, according to written policies, and with good documentation, there is little likelihood of being found to be wrong—only incorrect.

2. The same set of conditions is presented to another IRB, which determines that the device (or device study) is SR rather than NSR. In this case, the SR decision is of higher rank and the study must be submitted to the FDA. If a study hiatus might harm enrolled subjects, it is best to halt enrollment (although not follow-up or continued necessary treatment) and to call the FDA for a rapid consultation.

3. Experience suggests that there is harm. Should significant new information show up in the form of an adverse effect, the sponsor and the IRB have an obligation to reexamine the decision. The IRB may decide to change the decision from NSR to SR based on the significant new information.

Conduct of an Investigational Device Study

Once the IRB finds that the study is approvable and that the regulatory requirements have been met, the study may proceed. The postapproval requirements are, again, based on the investigational drug requirements but are slightly different.

Responsibilities of the Sponsor[7(Sec.812.40)]

Instead of an FD 1572, the sponsor must obtain a signed investigator's agreement. Although the elements are dictated[7(Sec.812.43)] some of the responsibilities are different and financial disclosure is included. Because of the presence of financial information, some sponsors claim that this agreement is confidential.

Because there is no section on transfer of responsibilities to a contractor, the use of contract research organizations is less common, although involvement of clinical or regulatory consultants is more common.

Instead of preparing an investigator's brochure as for an IND, the sponsor must prepare a report of prior investigations for the IDE. Because a report of prior investigations is not required in the device regulations for submission of a 510K, an IRB may need to ask for the information.

Responsibilities of the Investigator[7(Sec.812.100)]

An investigator may speak with potential subjects to determine interest, but may not request their written consent or start any procedures before IRB approval. Responsibilities are set out in the investigator's agreement rather than the FD 1572.

Adverse Device Effects[7[(Secs.812.3(s),46(b),150(a)(1)])]

Instead of an adverse event, devices may have an unanticipated adverse device effect. As noted by the NBAC report[17] and the OIG report,[18] the difficulty in applying different standards makes assessment of safety issues difficult. Instead of safety reports from sponsors via the investigator, device sponsors are asked to report evaluation of "unanticipated adverse device effects" directly to the reviewing IRBs within 10 working days of their receipt of the information. Should an IRB determine that the new information gained in the adverse effect reports changes their risk assessment, the IRB has the ability to reconsider its prior NSR decision and ask for FDA review.

Final Reports[7[Sec.812.150(a)(6)]]

Unlike drug investigators, device investigators must submit a final report to the IRB within three months of termination or completion of the study.

Conclusion

When reviewing a device protocol, the IRB should ask two questions.

1. Is this device study approvable using the standard IRB review criteria found in the Common Rule and in 21 CFR 56, and the institutional policies?
2. What is the regulatory status of the device?

The investigational device regulations are all contained in Title 21, Code of Federal Regulations, Part 812. Sections 812.2 and 812.3 are most important for IRB review.

To understand the structure of the device regulations, it is helpful to know some of the history and rationale behind them.

Unlike drugs, a device may follow one of several paths to FDA market clearance. The SR/NSR decision is a critical factor to sponsors because it makes a considerable difference in the time and money necessary to develop the device. The IRB must have written policies and procedures for rendering the NSR/SR decision.

References

1. 94th Congress. Report No. 94-853 by the House Committee on Interstate and Foreign Commerce (to accompany HR 11124), 29 Feb 1976.

2. O'Keefe DF, Spiegel RA, Murphy EG. *An Analytical Legislative History of the Medical Device Amendment of 1976: An Amendment to the Federal Food, Drug, and Cosmetic Act.* Washington, DC: Food and Drug Law Institute. 1976.

3. Museum of Questionable Medical Devices. Updated 20 Jan 2001. Access date 18 Apr 2001. World Wide Web http://www.mtn.org/quack/

4. U.S. Court of Appeals for the 2nd Circuit. *AMP Inc v. John W. Gardner, Secretary of HEW, and James L. Goddard, Commissioner of Food and Drugs* (389 F.2d 825). 1968. Affirmed.

5. U.S. Supreme Court. *United States v. Bacto-Unidisk* (394 US 784). 1969. Reversed.

6. 94th Congress. Medical Devices Amendments of 1976. Public Law No. 94-295. 1976.

7. Code of Federal Regulations. Title 21, Chapter 1—Food and Drug Administration, DHHS; Subchapter H—Medical Devices; Parts 800 through 898. Updated 1 Apr 1999. Access date 18 Apr 2001. World Wide Web http://www4.law.cornell.edu/cfr/21p800.htm

8. Code of Federal Regulations. Title 21, Chapter 1—Food and Drug Administration, DHHS; Subchapter I—Mammography Quality Standards Act; Part 900. Updated 1 Apr 1999. Access date 18 Apr 2001. World Wide Web http://www4.law.cornell.edu/cfr/21p900.htm

9. Code of Federal Regulations. Title 21, Chapter 1—Food and Drug Administration, DHHS; Subchapter J—Radiological Health; Parts 1000 through 1050. Updated 1 Apr 1999. Access date 18 Apr 2001. World Wide Web http://www4.law.cornell.edu/cfr/21p1000.htm

10. U.S. Supreme Court. *United States v. C.R. Bard, Inc.* (848 F.Supp.287). 1994.

11. Code of Federal Regulations. Title 21, Chapter 1—Food and Drug Administration, DHHS; Part 56—Institutional Review Boards. Updated 1 Apr 1999. Access date 27 Mar 2001. World Wide Web http://www4.law.cornell.edu/cfr/21p56.htm

12. Code of Federal Regulations. Title 45A—Department of Health and Human Services; Part 46—Protection of Human Subjects. Updated 1 Oct 1997. Access date 18 Apr 2001. World Wide Web http://www4.law.cornell.edu/cfr/45p46.htm

13. Food and Drug Administration. Advice on medical devices, 7 Mar 2001. World Wide Web http://www.fda.gov/chrh/devadvice/ide/textonly/faq.shtml#reimbursement

14. Code of Federal Regulations. Title 21, Chapter 1—Food and Drug Administration, DHHS; Part 50—Protection of Human Subjects. Updated 1 Apr 1999. Access date 18 Apr 2001. World Wide Web http://www4.law.cornell.edu/cfr/21p50.htm

15. Food and Drug Administration. Information sheets: Guidance for institutional review boards and clinical investigators, Sep 1998. Access date 9 Apr 2001. World Wide Web http://www.fda.gov/oc/oha/IRB/toc.html

16. Food and Drug Administration. Guidance sheets: Significant risk and nonsignificant risk medical device studies, Sep 1998. World Wide Web http://www.fda.gov/oc/oha/IRB/toc.html

17. National Bioethics Advisory Commission. Ethical and policy issues in research involving human participants. Report and recommendations, 20 Aug 2001. Access date 31 Aug 2001. World Wide Web http://bioethics.gov/human/overvol1.html

18. Office of Inspector General, DHHS. Protecting human research subjects: Status of recommendations (OEI-01-97-00197), Apr 2000. Access date 31 Aug 2001. World Wide Web http://oig.hhs.govoei/reports/a447.pdf

Humanitarian Use Devices

Robert J. Amdur

INTRODUCTION

In 1996, the Food and Drug Administration (FDA) finalized regulations regarding humanitarian use devices (HUD). The purpose of the HUD classification is to encourage the development of devices to treat or diagnose conditions that occur infrequently. When the market potential of a medical device is limited, the expense associated with extensive clinical testing is likely to discourage product development. HUD regulations are to medical devices what orphan drugs laws are to medications. The HUD classification gives sponsors a mechanism for making beneficial devices available for general use without the level of testing that is required for FDA approval by other mechanisms. The process for FDA approval of a medical device is the subject of Chapter 10-7.

The HUD Classification

Information on the regulations related to HUDs may be obtained by contacting the FDA Center for Devices and Radiological Health. The specific Website for HUDs is http://www.fda.gov/cdrh/ode/hdeinfo.html. All information presented in this chapter is taken from the information presented on their Web site on February 1, 2001.

An HUD is a device intended to benefit patients by treating or diagnosing a disease that affects fewer than 4,000 individuals in the United States per year. To be considered for HUD status, a device sponsor must complete a humanitarian device exemption (HDE) application. The HDE is similar to an FDA premarket approval application with the exception that an HDE application is not required to present evidence of effectiveness to the degree that is required for FDA approval under other conditions. Specifically, an HDE application is not required to contain the results of appropriately conducted clinical investigations. However, an HDE application must contain sufficient information for the FDA to determine that the device does not present an unreasonable risk of illness or injury and the probable benefit from its use justifies the potential risks. In considering an HDE application, the FDA is required to consider the risk/benefit profile of alternative forms of management that are currently available for the condition. The applicant must demonstrate that no comparable devices are available for the use intended for the device in question and that the applicant device could not be brought to market without the conditions of the HDE.

Conditions for Use of an HUD

An approved HDE application authorizes the applicant to market the HUD. The labeling for the HUD must state that the device is an HUD and that the effectiveness of the device has not been demonstrated. FDA regulations require that a local IRB operating in compliance with FDA regulations approve the use of the HUD to treat or diagnose a medical condition as specified in the HDE application.

Longevity of an Approved HDE

An approved HDE application is valid for as long as the use of the device continues to meet the conditions of the HDE application. HDE applications do not have to be renewed. Once an HDE application has been approved, there is no regular correspondence between the applicant and the FDA. The applicant is not required to inform the FDA of use of the device, the outcome of patients treated with the device, or IRB decisions regarding the device.

A Unique Assignment for the IRB

It is important for the IRB, institutional officials, the device sponsor, and local users of the HUD to understand the unique role of the IRB in this setting. This is the only situation where federal regulations require the IRB to approve and monitor an activity that is clearly not research. An approved HDE application authorizes the applicant to market the device and local physicians to use the device to treat or diagnose a medical condition. Research is not required for use of an HUD. As all IRB regulations and guidance documents are written from the point of view of research regulation, the HUD puts the IRB in a position where it must operate without the level of guidance that is the hallmark of the federal IRB system. When evaluating a request to use an HUD for medical treatment or diagnosis outside the setting of a research protocol, each IRB is free to establish its own criteria for IRB approval. Regulatory requirements and issues to consider are listed here.

1. FDA regulations require local IRB approval before use of an HUD.

2. A local IRB may defer to another IRB that has agreed to assume responsibility for reviewing the use of the HUD in the

setting in question. All inter-IRB agreements must be documented in writing.

3. The holder of the HDE is responsible for ensuring that the HUD is used only at facilities that have established an IRB that operates in compliance with FDA regulations.

4. The regulations do not require the facility where the HUD is used, the local IRB, or the local user to document that an approved HDE application exists or that the device is to be used as specified in the HDE application. However, I recommend that IRB approval of the use of an HUD be contingent on IRB review of a letter or document from the device sponsor that documents the following 10 items.

   a. the generic and trade name of the device

   b. the FDA HDE number (this is a 6 digit number preceded by the letter H)

   c. the date of HUD designation

   d. indications for use of the device

   e. a description of the device

   f. contraindications, warnings, and precautions for use of the device

   g. adverse effects of the device on health

   h. alternative practices and procedures

   i. marketing history

   j. summary of studies using the device

   The HDE application contains these basic sections, and it is routine for the sponsor of an HUD to send a document with this information to local IRBs. Therefore, there should never be a situation where an IRB is pressured into approving the use of an HUD without this level of documentation.

5. Although it is not the IRB's responsibility to check HUD information directly with FDA files, the Web site referenced in the early part of this chapter contains a list of all approved HDEs with most of the information in the above list.

6. There is no time limit on the FDA approval of an HDE.

7. The IRB does not have to approve each individual use of an HUD. The IRB has the discretion to determine the conditions of HUD use. The IRB may approve the use of the device in general, in a specific number of patients, only under specific circumstances, etc. A local IRB may limit the use of the HUD based on any criteria that it deems appropriate.

8. The regulations require that an IRB conduct both initial and continuing review of an HUD. HUD regulations do not specify the interval of continuing review, but it is prudent to assume that this would be interpreted to be at least annually.

9. The regulations do not require informed consent to use an HUD outside the setting of a research protocol. The regulations do not discourage an IRB from requiring informed consent in any situation that it deems appropriate, and decisions of this kind on the part of local IRBs are certainly within the spirit of HUD rules.

10. The IRB should specifically ask for a statement from the local user that the HUD is not being used as part of a research project or clinical investigation designed to collect data to support an FDA premarket approval application. If the HUD is being used in research or a clinical investigation, the IRB must comply with all of the FDA regulations related to IRB review of research. The criteria for IRB approval and informed consent would be as discussed in the other chapters of this book.

Conclusion

Most IRBs have no experience reviewing the use of HUDs. The University of Florida IRB has approved the use of several different HUDs over the past year. I have discussed HUD review with IRB directors at several other institutions that have HUD experience. Most IRB members are uncomfortable approving the use of an HUD outside the setting of a research protocol. When an activity does not involve the research paradigm, the IRB is basically inventing the wheel regarding the standards for IRB approval and the endpoints for determining compliance. All of the IRB directors that I spoke with approved the use of HUDs based on the documentation listed above, a requirement for written informed consent stating the unproven status of the device, and a supporting opinion from a local physician who is familiar with the setting in which the device will be used.

Banking of Biological Materials for Research

Karen M. Hansen, Robert J. Amdur, and Elizabeth A. Bankert

INTRODUCTION

Research involving biological materials is essential to develop better methods for disease prevention, diagnosis, and treatment. The potential for gaining knowledge in the areas of research using biological materials is vast; equally important safeguards must be taken to protect the rights and welfare of the individuals whose material is being studied. The purpose of this chapter is to present basic guidance that the IRB should consider when reviewing a request to bank biologic materials for research. When reviewing research with biologic materials, it is often important for the IRB to consider issues related to genetic testing and the plan to inform subjects of research results. These issues are discussed in Chapters 10-14 and 6-10, respectively. The focus of this chapter is the situation where a study asks for permission to bank (store) blood or tissue samples for *future* research. Template wording for the consent document for two different scenarios is included at the end of the chapter.

Guidelines for IRB Review

Determine If Tissue Banking Activity Should Be Considered Research Involving Human Subjects

In some situations, the IRB must determine if IRB review of tissue banking activities is required. To make this decision, the IRB must determine if the tissue banking activity should be considered research involving human subjects. Defining research intent is a difficult problem for IRBs in many different settings. The chapters in Part 4 of this book that deal with project triage and the identification of research intent are applicable to activities that involve the banking of biologic material. A useful Web site for helping investigators gain a baseline understanding of the use of human biological materials in research was developed by the National Cancer Institute: "Research on human specimens: Are you conducting research using human subjects?"[1] Additional information about professional societies' expectations and/or policies for use of biological materials can be found in Appendix C of the 1999 report of the National Bioethics Advisory Commission.[2]

Identify Tissue Banking Facilities

Clinical diagnostic laboratories, pathology departments, tumor registries, individual research investigators, industry sponsors, and cooperative oncology groups may bank biological specimens for research. Identify researchers or activities within your organization that may store residual clinical specimens and/or prospectively collected research specimens. Educate these individuals or departments about IRB responsibilities for reviewing repositories of human biological specimens that are used in research. Ask the departments or investigators to complete an IRB application for review that describes the banking activity and oversight of banked materials.

Use a Consent Document Template

Create a model tissue collection consent template that conforms to your IRB and institutional requirements. When creating the template, consider any state, federal, or international regulations or policies that may influence the content of the consent document and/or process. Sample consent document templates are appended to this chapter.

OHRP Guidance

Both the IRB and the individuals or departments that direct tissue banking activities should review the federal guidance document[3] that is most applicable to the general topic of IRB review of research involving stored biologic material.

OPRR: Issues to Consider in the Research Use of Stored Data or Tissues (Nov 7, 1997)[3]
Human Tissue Repositories collect, store, and distribute human tissue materials for research purposes. Repository activities involve three components: (i) the collectors of tissue samples;

(ii) the repository storage and data management center; and (iii) the recipient investigators. . . .

If supported by the Department of Health and Human Services (HHS), each component must satisfy certain regulatory requirements. . . .

Operation of the repository and its data management center should be subject to oversight by an institutional review board (IRB). The IRB should review and approve a protocol specifying the conditions under which data and specimens may be accepted and shared, and ensuring adequate provisions to protect the privacy of subjects and maintain the confidentiality of data. The IRB should also review and approve a sample collection protocol and informed consent document for distribution to tissue collectors and their local IRBs. A certificate of confidentiality should be obtained to protect confidentiality of repository specimens and data. . . .

OPRR: Operation of Human Cell Repositiories Under HHS Regulations at 45 CFR 46(Aug. 19, 1996)[4]

OPRR offers the following guidance concerning operation of human cell repositories under DHHS regulations for the protection of human subjects.[5] The guidance assumes that repository activities include nonexempt human subjects research as defined under HHS regulations.

1. The operation of any HHS-supported human cell repository and its data management center should be subject to oversight by an IRB convened under an applicable OPRR-approved assurance of compliance. This IRB should set the conditions under which data and specimens may be accepted and shared. OPRR strongly recommends that one such condition stipulate that recipient-investigators not be provided access to the identities of donor-subjects or to information through which the identities of donor-subjects may readily be ascertained

2. Collection of data and specimens should be subject to oversight by local IRBs convened under applicable OPRR-approved assurances

3. Written informed consent should be obtained from each donor-subject in accordance with HHS regulations.[4] Included among the basic elements of informed consent should be a clear description of (i) the operation of the cell repository; (ii) the specific types of research to be conducted; (iii) the conditions under which data and specimens will be released to recipient-investigators; and (iv) procedures for protecting the privacy of subjects and maintaining the confidentiality of data

4. Informed consent information describing the nature and purposes of the research should be as specific as possible

5. Where human genetic research is anticipated, informed consent information should include information about the consequences of DNA typing (e.g., regarding possible paternity determinations)

6. Informed consent documents may not include any exculpatory language through which subjects are made to waive or appear to waive any legal rights

7. OPRR recommends that the cell repository develop a sample collection protocol and informed consent document for distribution to collector-investigators and their local IRBs

8. A written submittal agreement for collector-investigators should require written informed consent of the donor-subjects utilizing an informed consent document approved by the local IRB. It should also contain an acknowledgment that collector-investigators are prohibited from providing recipient-investigators with access to the identities of donor-subjects or to information through which the identities of donor-subjects may readily be ascertained.

9. A written usage agreement for recipient-investigators should include the following: "Recipient acknowledges that the conditions for use of this research material are governed by the cell repository Institutional Review Board (IRB) in accordance with Department of Health and Human Services regulations at 45 CFR 46. Recipient agrees to comply fully with all such conditions and to report promptly to the cell repository any proposed changes in the research project and any unanticipated problems involving risks to subjects or others. Recipient remains subject to applicable State or local laws or regulations and institutional policies which provide additional protections for human subjects. This research material may only be utilized in accordance with the conditions stipulated by the cell repository IRB. Any additional use of this material requires prior review and approval by the cell repository IRB and, where appropriate, by an IRB at the recipient site, which must be convened under an applicable OPRR-approved Assurance."

10. OPRR recommends that a certificate of confidentiality be obtained to protect confidentiality of human cell repository specimens and data

Use of Local Tissue Banks by Commercial Organizations

The IRB may be asked about a situation where a commercial organization not connected with the IRB's organization plans to acquire specimens from a local tissue bank with a goal of making them available for research in the future. This is a complex problem for the IRB and one for which there currently is no federal guidance. The first thing to do is to speak to your institutional officials to determine if they would allow such access and identify their expectations before proceeding to IRB review. The institution and in-house investigators may have opposing interests or contractual arrangements that prohibit any possibility of access by outside users. Alternatively, the administration may permit collaboration and access. In the latter case, the IRB could then review the research activity and make the final determination about approval of the access before the research materials are released from the repository.

Two Sample Consent Templates

The IRB is likely to encounter two different scenarios that involve a request to collect or store a person's blood or tissue for research. In one scenario, the investigator wants to ask for permission to perform certain tests as an add-on study that is being done in addition to the primary study. For example, a person is asked to participate in a cancer treatment study in which subjects receive an investigational medication. In addition to this primary study, the investigators would like to conduct genetic tests on certain blood cells to see if the expression of a gene called P-53 correlates with response to the study medication. The request for participation in the primary cancer treatment study and the request for tissue testing will be presented as two separate decisions. A subject may elect to participate in the cancer treatment study but decide not to participate in the genetic testing study. With this kind of add-on study, the request for consent for the secondary study appears as a section within the consent document for the primary study. The first sample template is used for this scenario (Appendix 1). Please note that this scenario is not an example of a request to bank tissue for future research because the tests that will be done on the tissue are already known and planned. We include this consent template in this chapter because it does not fit well with other chapters.

The second scenario is the main subject of this chapter: namely, a request to bank blood or tissue for *future* research. In this situation, the specific tests or evaluations that will be done on the banked material are not known at the time that the subject is asked to consent to tissue banking. In this situation, the consent document must ask the subject to donate biologic material for future research (Appendix 2). A request for the banking of biologic material for future research may be made as a stand-alone study with a separate consent document or as an add-on study. When a request to bank tissue for future research is presented as an add-on study, the template consent document language pertaining to tissue banking will appear as a section in the consent document for the primary study.

References

1. National Cancer Institute. Research on human specimens: Are you conducting research using human subjects? Updated 2001. World Wide Web http://www-cdp.ims.nci.nih.gov/policy.html

2. National Bioethics Advisory Commission. Research involving human biological materials: Ethical issues and policy guidance, Aug 1999. Access date 31 Aug 2001. World Wide Web http://bioethics.gov/hbm.pdf

3. Office for Protection from Research Risks. Issues to consider in the research use of stored data or tissues, 7 Nov 1997. Access date 28 Aug 2001. World Wide Web http://ohrp.osophs.dhhs.gov/humansubjects/guidance/reposit.htm.

4. Office for Protection from Research Risks. Operation of human cell repositories under HHS regulations at 45 CFR 46, 19 Aug 1996. Access date 28 Sep 2001. World Wide Web http://ohrp.osophs.dhhs.gov/humansubjects/guidance/reposit.htm.

5. Code of Federal Regulations. Title 45A—Department of Health and Human Services; Part 46—Protection of Human Subjects. Updated 1 Oct 1997. Access date 18 Apr 2001. World Wide Web http://www4.law.cornell.edu/cfr/45p46.htm

Appendix 1

Template Consent Language for an Add-On Study Involving Biologic Material
(Note: In this scenario, the type of testing that is to be done on the material is known and described in the consent document. Do not use this template for consent to donate biologic material for future research.)

We ask your permission to test your blood or tissue for research.

This study includes laboratory tests that will analyze samples of your blood or tissues. [If additional procedures, such as blood draws or biopsies, will be needed for this study then describe them here, including risks]. Blood or tissue samples will be sent to a laboratory where research tests will be performed. The purpose of testing your blood or tissue is to determine [complete this sentence].

Will you be given the results of research tests?

The results from these tests will not be sent to you or your doctor, and will not be used in planning your care. You will not be able to find out the results of these tests even if you ask for them. These tests are only for research purposes. [If this is not the case then explain the conditions under which subjects or their physicians will have access to these results. If the subject or his or her physician will have access to test results, you must explain the potential risks and implications of this disclosure. When applicable, discuss the need for genetic or psychological counseling before or after the study.]

Do you give us permission to test your blood or tissue?

Please indicate if you agree to participate by circling your response below. You do not have to give permission to use your blood or tissue for research to participate in the other parts of this study. If you do not want your blood or tissue to be tested in this part of the study it will not affect your care at this institution or the ability to receive treatment as part of this study. Please ask questions if you do not understand why we are asking for your permission to use your blood or tissue for research or if you would like more information about any part of this study.

I agree to participate in the part of the study that involves testing of my blood or tissue as described above: please circle YES or NO

Yes   No

Please print and sign your name here after you circle your answer.

Your name: _____

Your signature: _____ Date: _____

Appendix 2

Template Consent Language to Bank Biologic Material for Future Research

We are asking you to donate your blood or tissue for future research.
We are requesting your permission to donate some of your blood or tissue for future research. The blood or tissue samples that will be stored are left over from specimens that were taken, or will be taken, as part of your routine medical care [or as part of this study (if the tissue banking request is an add-on study within a primary study)]. [If additional procedures, such as blood draws or biopsies, will be done to procure the specimens that will be stored, this must be explained along with any associated risks.]

Will the blood or tissue that you donate be tested for diseases?
Some people may be worried about their blood or tissue being tested for things that indicate they have a particular disease or medical condition such as AIDS. Others may have concerns about genetic testing for a disease or condition in the genes of their family such as breast cancer or the gene for a disease called Huntington's chorea. At this time there is no plan to test your blood or tissue for things that indicate that you or your biologic relatives have a disease or medical condition. [If this is not the case then describe the relevant tests and the potential implications, benefits, and risks. When applicable, discuss the need for genetic or psychological counseling before or after the study.]

Will you or your doctor be given research results?
It is very important that you understand that the results from tests that are done on the blood or tissue that you donate for future research will not be given to you or your doctor, even if you ask that this be done. The results of tests that are done on the blood or tissue that you donate for future research will not be sent to your hospital medical record. These tests will be done only for research purposes. [If the subject or his or her physician will have access to research results, then describe the circumstances of this access and the potential implications, benefits, and risks. When applicable, discuss the need for genetic or psychological counseling before or after the study.]

What research studies will be done on the blood or tissue that you donate?
At this time it is impossible to name all of the kinds of studies that researchers may want to use your blood or tissue for. Any future research done on your stored blood or tissue must be approved by a committee called an Institutional Review Board (IRB). The IRB is a group of people who review research studies in order to protect the rights and welfare of research subjects like you. The IRB will determine that the research is done according to accepted standards. They will also determine if we need to contact you and ask your consent for specific future research studies using your stored specimens.

Will the blood or tissue that you donate be sold in the future?
Your blood or tissue will be used only for research and will not be sold.

Will you be paid for donating blood or tissue for future research?
No. You will not be paid for the blood or tissue that you are now being asked to donate for future research. In the future it is possible that the research that is done on your blood and tissue may help to develop something that is commercially valuable—meaning something that makes a lot of money for somebody. You will not receive payment for commercial activity that results from research with your blood or tissues.

Will you be penalized if you decide not to donate blood or tissue for research?
No. You will not be penalized in any way for not donating blood or tissue for future research. If you decide not to donate blood or tissue for future research it will not affect your medical care [or your ability to participate in the treatment part of this study (if tissue storage is being requested as an add-on study within a primary study)].

Why would you donate your blood or tissue for future research?
Research with your blood or tissue may lead to discoveries that will help people in the future.

Are there risks to donating your blood or tissue for future research?
Donating your blood or tissue for future research may have no risk. However, a serious risk that should be considered is the possibility that someone will learn things about you that you don't want them to know. It is difficult to estimate if this is a possibility in your case because we don't know exactly what studies may be done on your blood or tissue in the future. However, all reasonable efforts will be made to protect the confidentiality of information that can in any way be connected to you. As in many other kinds of research, certain authorities do have the right to review your research file. In addition to research directors, the people that may have access to your research information are representatives from the U.S. Food and Drug Administration and the Institutional Review Board. The Institutional Review Board is a committee that is set up to determine that research is done according to accepted standards as well as federal and state law.

Do you have any additional questions?

If you have questions about your rights as a research participant, please call _____.

If you have questions about specimen and/or data storage, please call _____.

If you have questions about your medical treatment or emergency care, please call _____.

Making your choice

Please put an X in the boxes below that indicate if you want to donate your blood or tissue for future research.

☐ Yes, I will donate my blood or tissue for future research. Please also check one of these boxes:

    ☐ There are no restrictions on the kind of research that may be done with my blood or tissue.

    OR

    ☐ You may use my blood or tissue for future research as long as the only kind of research that is done is research to improve the understanding or treatment of [name specific diseases or conditions].

☐ No, I do not want to donate my blood or tissue for future research.

Please print and sign your name here:

Your name: _____

Your signature: _____ Date: _____

The Placebo-Controlled Clinical Trial

Robert J. Amdur and C. J. Biddle

INTRODUCTION

The use of placebo in clinical research studies is currently a topic of active debate in the medical literature.[1,2] High-profile articles appear at regular intervals that criticize the use of placebo in particular patient populations.[1,3-9] At one end of the spectrum is the argument that the current use of placebo is often unethical because alternate study designs would produce results that are of similar value to society with less risk to individual research participants. The counterargument is that current policy regarding the use of placebo is essential to protect society from the harm that would result from the widespread use of ineffective medical treatments. In view of the range of scientific and ethical issues that influence the use of placebo in clinical research, both research investigators and regulatory authorities need better guidelines to determine when placebo therapy is or is not acceptable. This chapter presents a decision algorithm to help interested members of the research community evaluate the ethics of a clinical research trial that involves concomitant placebo control. The algorithm is shown as Figure 10.10.1. The chapter presents (a) concepts and issues related to each major decision point in the algorithm, and (b) case discussions to illustrate use of the algorithm in evaluating a wide range of placebo-controlled trials.

Basic Concepts

Formal definitions of *placebo* are referenced in a 1994 review of the placebo issue by Clark and Leaverton.[10] Basically, a placebo is any medical treatment (or component of a medical treatment) that is inactive for the condition being evaluated other than the effect that may result from a person's thinking that he or she may be receiving an active treatment. Placebo is frequently used as the control group in research studies that are designed to evaluate the efficacy of new medical treatments. The purpose of a control group in a clinical trial is to give the study the ability to distinguish between treatment-specific and treatment-nonspecific effects. The placebo effect, fluctuations in the natural history of the disease over time, and the influence of the study environment are examples of nonspecific treatment effects that may lead to false conclusions about the efficacy of a study treatment. To distribute nonspecific treatment factors equally between study groups, pa-

tients in medical trials are often assigned to a treatment group by a process called *randomization,* which means assignment to a treatment group by a process that involves chance.

The Use of Placebo in Place of Standard Therapy

The first step in evaluating the ethics of a placebo-controlled trial is to decide if placebo is being used in place of standard therapy. Standard therapy may be a type of active treatment (for example, a medication with treatment-specific activity); supportive care, meaning treatment designed to alleviate symptoms but without specific activity for the underlying medical condition; or no treatment. From the ethical standpoint, the potential problem with placebo therapy is that it exposes patients to a treatment that has no specific activity for their disease. When an available therapy is considered to be beneficial, the use of placebo *instead of* accepted therapy may be unethical. However, when placebo is being used *in addition to* standard therapy, as is done in add-on and sequential treatment study designs,[11] there is no ethical tension related to the use of treatment without disease-specific activity.

Adapted version of a contribution to a forthcoming issue of the *Radiation Oncology Investigations* ©2001 Wiley-Liss, Inc. Used by permission of Wiley-Liss, Inc., a subsidiary of John Wiley & Sons, Inc.

Figure 10.10.1 An Algorithm for Evaluating Studies That Use Placebo Control

The Efficacy of Standard Therapy

The second decision point is to determine if standard therapy is considered to be effective. With medical conditions for which there are no good treatment options, there may be legitimate controversy about the value of standard therapy. When standard therapy does not meaningfully improve length or quality of life, it is ethical to enroll informed subjects in research that uses placebo in place of standard treatment. However, when standard therapy is clearly effective in the study population, additional issues must be evaluated to determine if it is ethical to use placebo in place of standard therapy.

Evaluating the efficacy of standard therapy may not be straightforward because controversy often exists regarding the treatment-specific activity of treatments that are commonly recommended. In the absence of overwhelming evidence, some experts will question the efficacy of treatment that is considered to be beneficial by other segments of the medical community. From the ethical standpoint a lack of consensus within the overall medical community is less important than the opinion of the local physicians who will be asking patients to participate in research. The practice of medicine is based on the judgment of individual physicians taking care of specific patients. The evidence that a given medical treatment will or will not be effective in a specific patient is often not definitive. For this reason, the efficacy of standard therapy in any given community is best evaluated by asking local physicians how they would manage a patient who decides not to participate in research.

The Toxicity of Standard Treatment

The potential problem with the use of placebo in medical research is that subjects will be denied beneficial treatment. When evaluating the potential benefit of a medical treatment, it is important to consider both efficacy and toxicity. If the toxicity of available treatments is such that patients routinely refuse therapy that is known to have direct activity against their disease process, then it is ethical to conduct research that treats informed subjects with placebo in place of standard therapy. However, when standard treatment is both effective and well tolerated, other factors must be evaluated to determine the ethics of a placebo-controlled medical research trial.

As with treatment efficacy, there may be disagreement within the medical community about the level of toxicity of a given medical treatment in a specific patient population. Opinions about the overall effect of medical treatment are appropriately influenced to a large degree by personal values and individual experience. As discussed previously, from the ethical standpoint the important question is how the physicians who will be enrolling subjects in research view the risk/benefit profile of standard therapy. Again, the way a physician manages patients outside the setting of a research protocol is likely to be a useful indicator of opinion about the value of alternate therapies.

Temporary Discomfort Versus Irreversible Harm

Much of the recent literature on ethical requirements for the use of placebo has emphasized the importance of making a distinction between the use of placebo in a setting that increases the risk of temporary discomfort and use of placebo in a way that increases the risk of severe morbidity or irreversible health problems.[8,9,11] This distinction is not discussed in federal research regulations or in ethical guidelines like the Nuremberg Code, Declaration of Helsinki, or *Belmont* report.[12] The basic concept is that protections that recognize the inherent vulnerability of medical research subjects and the limitations of the informed consent process are needed when the risk associated with placebo treatment is high.[13] In practical terms, this means that the fact that a subject enrolls in a study with a process that complies with the standard requirements for informed consent does not mean that the study is ethical.

Concern about the quality and circumstances of informed consent is not unique to research that involves placebo. An extensive body of literature now supports the view that, in many medical situations, it is not possible to obtain the type of informed consent that is considered to be a requirement for ethical research.[1,5,13,14] When the risk of research participation is high, any imperfection in the consent process has a major effect on research ethics. When the use of placebo carries a risk of irreversible and serious harm, the ethics of research will hinge on the ability of alternate study designs to provide valuable information on the study question with less risk to research subjects.[15,16[Sec.111(a)(1)]]

At the other extreme is the situation where the risk of placebo is limited to minor, temporary discomfort. In this setting, it is appropriate that research standards rely on the informed consent process to create an environment where subjects understand the main implications of their decision to participate in research and important decisions are made without coercion.[8,9,11]

Considering Alternative Study Designs

A fundamental ethical standard is that research should be designed so that the risks to subjects are minimized and reasonable in relation to anticipated benefits.[17] A major element of the placebo controversy is debate over the implications of using alternate study designs to evaluate the efficacy of new medical treatments.[1,3] This is a complex topic without definitive answers to several important questions.

The factors that influence the choice of control group in a clinical trial are discussed in detail in a recent FDA guidance document.[11] The two main characteristics of a control group are the type of treatment received and the relationship of the control group to the present study population. In terms of the type of treatment received, the main options are: (a) active control, meaning the control group is treated with a therapy that is known to have specific activity in the study setting, (b) placebo, and (c) no treatment.

In terms of the relationship of the control group to the present study population, the basic options are to have a control group that is chosen from the study population (concomitant control) or from an external database. Concomitant control groups are usually selected by a randomization process with blinding of subject and/or healthcare providers to treatment group. External control groups are usually chosen from previously conducted trials of the study medication in circumstances similar to those of the current study. A control group that is chosen from studies that were completed in the past is called a *historical control group*.

As a society, we want to design clinical trials to minimize the chance of a false-positive result. The scientific quality of a clinical trial refers to the aspects of the study that influence the credibility and persuasiveness of research results. The remainder of this section will summarize the main arguments that have been made to support the use of placebo control to evaluate the efficacy of medical treatments. When applicable, a point/counterpoint approach is used to explain the different schools of thought on a given subject.

Evaluating Efficacy with Concomitant Active Control

The Value of a Positive Result in a Trial with Placebo versus Active Control

Point: *Scientific quality is superior with a study design that involves concomitant placebo control because it is usually not possible to accurately determine important statistical parameters in a trial that compares a study treatment with an active control. This is especially true in medical conditions where variability in the placebo response rate is known to be high.*

The fundamental question is different in a trial with active control than in a trial with placebo control. Trials that randomize subjects between study treatment and placebo use a study design that directly evaluates efficacy. Trials that use active treatment control are classified as *noninferiority trials* because the goal is to show that the study drug is not less effective than the control by more than a defined amount. A fundamental assumption of a noninferiority trial with active control is that noninferiority is evidence of equivalence.

A major argument against using a noninferiority (equivalence) trial to draw conclusions about treatment efficacy is that there is no accepted way to estimate some of the important statistical parameters needed to minimize the chance of a false positive result.[11] The main problem is that a noninferiority trial requires an estimate of a parameter called the *noninferiority margin,* which describes the degree of inferiority of the study medication (compared with active control) that the trial will attempt to exclude statistically. The value of the noninferiority margin is usually based on past experience in placebo-controlled trials, but clinical judgment also plays a role.

Estimating the noninferiority margin is especially difficult when there is variability in the placebo response rate between trials. For this reason, support for trials with concomitant placebo control is generally strongest in medical conditions where variability in the placebo response rate is likely to be large. There are many medical conditions for which medications that are considered to be effective cannot regularly be shown to be superior to placebo in well-designed clinical trials.[3,11,17,18]

Uncertainty in the design of a clinical trial compromises the credibility of study results. Lack of confidence in the scientific quality of an active-control trial is such that much of the scientific community, including some FDA officials, view a noninferiority trial using active control as a crude tool for evaluating the efficacy of unproven therapy in a wide range of medical conditions.[11,17] People with this point of view argue that trials with concurrent placebo control are essential to protect society from the harm that will result from approving new medical therapies based on false positive results from noninferiority studies.[4,6,11,17]

Counterpoint: *This is an example of a situation where many of the experts are mistaken. The scientific quality of results from placebo-controlled trials is overrated. The value of results from a noninferiority trial with active control is often underrated. Society would not be worse off if the FDA approval of new medical treatments were based on the results of noninferiority trials with comparison to standard therapy (concomitant active control) in many of the situations where concomitant placebo control is currently required.*

Arguments that support the use of placebo control in ethically controversial situations frequently include dogmatic statements about placebo-controlled trials being the "gold standard" for evaluating the efficacy of new medical treatments.[19] These kinds of statements imply that a placebo-controlled trial is unquestionably the most accurate way to evaluate treatment efficacy. Critics argue that there is no convincing evidence to support this concept. For example, in a recent review of studies used to support FDA approval of antidepressant medications—a prime example of a situation where experts argue that the large variability in placebo response rate demands the use of placebo control—Michels[3] concluded, "We can see from the data presented that standard therapy is almost always superior to placebo and similar in effectiveness to the investigational drugs that later gained market approval. Thus, therapeutic equivalence trials would have led to the same conclusions regarding effectiveness of the investigational medications as placebo-controlled trials. So why withhold effective treatment that is likely to benefit patients?" And, in a 1994 article in the *New England Journal of Medicine,* Rothman and Michels[1] commented on statements about the superiority of placebo control that are frequently found in FDA documents and research textbooks: "Without justification, such statements confer on placebo control a stature that ranks it with double blinding and randomization as a hallmark of good science. . . . No scientific principle, however, requires the comparison in a trial to involve a placebo instead of, or in addition to, an active treatment."

Quality Control

Point: *In a trial with placebo control, there is a built-in incentive to conduct the study as planned that is not present in a noninferiority study with active control.*

A positive result in an efficacy trial with concomitant placebo control means that the outcome is better with the study treatment than with placebo. When the goal of a trial is to detect a *difference* in outcome, a built-in incentive exists for the sponsor of the trial to work hard to see that the study is conducted according to the highest level of quality. This means careful screening of subjects based on eligibility criteria, rigorous monitoring to be sure that treatment is delivered as required by the protocol, selecting and supporting subjects so that the dropout rate is as low as possible, and so forth.

In contrast to a direct efficacy trial, in a noninferiority trial with active control, a positive result is the *lack of a difference* in outcome between study groups. In this situation, the sponsor of the trial has less incentive to enforce compliance with study guidelines because study errors usually act to blur any difference that exists between treatment groups and thus increase the chance of a positive result.[11] As with the other factors mentioned in this section, concern about the value of the results of a trial that compares a study treatment with active control biases many in the research community in favor of efficacy trials with concomitant placebo control.

Counterpoint: *Multiple factors determine the overall quality of the results of a clinical research trial. Although a placebo-control design may promote an environment that encourages compliance with the study protocol, other factors favor a study design that compares study treatment with active therapy.*

Study Size

Point: *A noninferiority trial with active control requires a larger study population than does a trial that directly evaluates efficacy with concomitant placebo control.*

Study design and a variety of statistical parameters determine the number of subjects that are required for a trial to detect important differences in the activity of study therapy. Because of variability in the placebo response, the number of subjects required to minimize the possibility of a false positive result is usually much larger for a noninferiority trial with active control compared to an efficacy study with concomitant placebo control.[11,20] A larger study population may be a negative factor for two reasons. First, the cost of a noninferiority trial may discourage researchers from evaluating new medical treatments; second, a larger study population increases the number of people who may be treated with inferior therapy.[4,11] Although increased risk is often an argument against placebo-controlled studies, it is important to remember that the study treatment in a noninferiority trial may indeed be inferior to standard therapy.

Counterpoint: *Medical progress will not be compromised by the use of active treatment control in clinical trials that evaluate the efficacy of medical treatments.*

The factors that serve to decrease the value of results from trials with concomitant placebo control were discussed previously. Several aspects of these arguments suggest that larger clinical trials will meaningfully improve the quality of the treatment evaluation process. Specifically, a larger study population will increase the applicability of study results to the general population and increase the persuasiveness of study results, either positive or negative. There is also the argument that noninferiority trials ask a more important question, from the standpoint of practical value to society and stimulation of medical progress, than do comparisons of study treatment with placebo.[21]

Evaluating Efficacy with Historical Placebo Control

Historical placebo control means that efficacy is evaluated by comparing the results of a study treatment with the results from patients treated with placebo in a previously completed trial. For comparison with historical control to be meaningful, the study population and study conditions must be similar for the trial that evaluates the study treatment and the study that generated the results with placebo control.

The main problem with historical placebo control is the problem common to all studies that attempt to make conclusions based on comparison with the outcome of a group of subjects who were treated under different study conditions: namely, the difficulty in balancing the effect of important nonspecific treatment effects between the current study and the historical control group. The fact that subjects in the study and control group are treated over different time periods (often separated by years or decades) introduces the potential for differences in selection factors, placebo response rate, and study environment to affect subject outcome independent of the direct activity of the study treatment. With the exception of some well-defined situations, the FDA will not approve an application to market a new medication or medical device based on comparison with historical control.[11]

Evaluating the Credibility of Altruism

Probably the most controversial aspect of the placebo debate concerns the tradeoff between the welfare of the in-

dividuals who will be the subjects of research and the welfare of people in the future who may benefit from research results.[1,5,6,8] Obviously, this tension exists in other areas of research, but the importance of the "individual-versus-society" issue to the placebo debate cannot be overemphasized. In a biomedical research study where the use of placebo increases the risk of irreversible harm, the only way to justify the use of placebo is to argue that it is ethical to increase risk to current subjects to produce information that may benefit people in the future. A major problem with this argument is that it appears to violate fundamental principles of accepted ethical guidelines. For example, the Declaration of Helsinki contains several sections that directly address the individual versus society issue.[22]

Part I (Basic principles), point 5: "Every biomedical research project involving human subjects should be preceded by careful assessment of predictable risks in comparison with foreseeable benefits to the subject or to others. Concern for the interests of the subject must always prevail over the interests of science and society."

Part II, point 3: "In any medical study, every patient—including those of the control group, if any—should be assured of the best proven diagnostic and therapeutic method."

Part III (Nonclinical research), point 4: "In research on man, the interest of science and society should never take precedence over considerations related to the well-being of the subject."

A recent *JAMA* article discusses the limitations of published ethical guidelines, including the Declaration of Helsinki.[12] Altruism may be an acceptable reason for a person to participate in research, regardless of the potential for increased risk. However, to accept the altruism argument, one must assume full and voluntary informed consent. When considering this argument, it is important to understand that an extensive body of literature now exists supporting the view that, in many medical situations, the researcher cannot obtain the type of informed consent considered to be a requirement for ethical research.[13,14] The documentation of informed consent is not credible when the nature of the study is such that reasonable people would not volunteer to participate in the research if they had a clear understanding of the implications of their decision.[1,5,13]

No definitive formula can be used to determine when a trade-off between the welfare of individual subjects and future patients is acceptable. Baruch Brody[5] has discussed a "reasonable person" standard for evaluating the ethics of clinical trials. In the context of the placebo discussion, the reasonable person standard says that a randomized, placebo-controlled trial is justified only if (a) the subjects have validly consented to being randomized, and (b) a reasonable person of an average degree of altruism and risk-aversiveness might consent to being randomized. This "reasonable person" standard articulates the criteria that should be used to evaluate the ethics of placebo in the final decision point of the placebo algorithm.

Case Discussions

Use of Placebo When Standard Treatment Is Supportive Care

Proposed study: *A randomized, placebo-controlled study of a new chemotherapy agent for patients with terminal cancer. Cancer has progressed despite use of all standard treatment options. Subjects are randomized between the study medication and placebo. All subjects get the best supportive care.*

Discussion: There is no ethical controversy about the use of placebo in this example. Placebo does not risk denying subjects effective therapy because no treatment is known to be effective in this situation.

Use of Placebo in Addition to Active Treatment

Proposed study: *A randomized, placebo-controlled trial of a new medication to relieve pain in patients with chronic pain from diabetic neuropathy. Standard therapy in this patient population is a narcotic analgesic and an antidepressant medication. The study randomizes subjects to treatment with standard therapy plus placebo or standard therapy plus the study medication.*

Discussion: There is no ethical controversy about the use of placebo in this example. The use of placebo does not deny subjects effective therapy because placebo is used in addition to—not in place of—standard treatment.

Use of Placebo When Doubt Exists About the Efficacy of Standard Therapy

Proposed study: *A randomized, placebo-controlled trial of an investigational gene therapy for patients with an extremely aggressive type of brain tumor called glioblastoma multiforme. The trial randomizes patients between the study treatment and placebo. Standard therapy in this patient population is either radiotherapy or supportive care. Published studies have shown that radiotherapy delays tumor progression, but patient outcome is uniformly poor. Legitimate controversy exists as to the ability of radiotherapy to meaningfully improve the length or quality of life in this setting. Some experts recommend radiotherapy as standard treatment for patients with glioblastoma multiforme, whereas other experts recommend supportive care. This trial excludes patients who have previously received radiotherapy.*

Discussion: Placebo is being used in this study in place of standard therapy. If radiotherapy is considered to be effective in this setting, there may be ethical problems with using placebo in patients who have not received radiotherapy. The study may be ethical in some communities and unethical in others. To investigate local standards it is necessary to ask the local physicians who would be enrolling subjects in this trial for their opinion about the benefit of radiotherapy. If managing physicians think radiotherapy is ineffective in this setting, then the trial is without ethical controversy. However, if local physicians routinely recommend radiotherapy for patients with this tumor because they think it improves the length or qual-ity of life, then additional issues must be evaluated to determine if placebo is ethically acceptable.

Use of Placebo When the Toxicity of Standard Therapy Is High

Proposed study: *A randomized, placebo-controlled trial of a new medication for patients with multiple sclerosis (MS). The study medication is the only FDA-approved treatment that has been shown to decrease the chance of debilitating problems from MS. Only 20% of patients have a positive response to the study treatment, but in the patients who do respond, there is no question that the use of the study medication prevents or delays the progression of debilitating problems. Patients in the proposed trial will not have been treated with the study medication.*

Discussion: This trial uses placebo in place of therapy that has been shown to prevent, or delay the progression of, debilitating problems. An important question to consider when evaluating the ethics of this study is the toxicity of alternative treatments. In this situation, the toxicity of the study medication is high, and many patients elect not to be treated with it. To investigate local standards, it is necessary to ask local physicians about the use of the drug in their practice. If the local physicians who would be asking patients to participate in research routinely recommend the study drug, then the study is ethical only for subjects who refuse the drug treatment with a clear understanding that it is the treatment recommended by their doctor. However, if local physicians do not recommend the study medication because they consider it to have an unfavorable risk/benefit profile, it is ethical to enroll subjects in a placebo-controlled trial without such eligibility restrictions.

Temporary Discomfort versus Irreversible Harm

Consider two proposed studies: *Study A is a randomized, placebo-controlled trial of a new medication for relief of a moderately severe tension-type headache. Study B is a randomized, placebo-controlled trial of a new antibiotic as first-line therapy for pneumonia. In both studies, placebo is used in place of standard therapy that is well tolerated and likely to be effective.*

Discussion: From the ethical standpoint, the critical difference between these two studies is the nature of the risk of placebo. In Study A, the risk of placebo is temporary discomfort from a condition that is familiar to potential research subjects. The level of discomfort is not severe. The period of discomfort is temporary. In view of these factors, the standard informed consent process is sufficient ethical justification for the use of placebo. Subjects are likely to understand the implications of their decision to participate in research because they will know from past experience how it feels to have a headache for the duration of the study. The nature of this study is such that coercion is unlikely. For these reasons, additional protection from the possibility of coercion and incomplete informed consent is not necessary. The use of placebo is ethical.

In contrast to Study A, Study B involves a medical condition that will cause serious, irreversible health problems if patients are not given effective treatment within a short period of time from diagnosis. Standard therapy in this setting has a favorable risk/benefit profile and is therefore recommended by local physicians. A study with concomitant placebo control is clearly the most definitive way to evaluate efficacy of the study medication. One could argue that there are patients who would participate in this study based on altruism because an additional effective antibiotic would benefit people in the future. Altruism and informed consent would be the ethical justification for this study.

In view of the risk of irreversible, serious harm in Study B, ethical research requires a demanding standard for a study design that minimizes risk. For the sake of this discussion, let us assume that a study with concomitant placebo control is the only credible way to evaluate efficacy in this setting. Given this assumption, the final step is to evaluate the credibility of altruism (as this is the main reason that an informed subject would participate in this type of study) with the "reasonable person" standard. In the absence of coercion, it is difficult to imagine an informed person volunteering for this study. Therefore, the use of concomitant placebo control in this study is unethical.

Severe Suffering
Proposed study: *A randomized, placebo-controlled trial of a new medication to prevent nausea and vomiting from chemotherapy. In the absence of effective antinausea medication, the patients in this study are expected to experience moderate nausea and vomiting for approximately three days. A variety of different medications are approved for use in this setting and are considered standard therapy by local physicians. Standard therapy is, without question, highly effective at preventing or decreasing chemotherapy-related nausea and vomiting. In this study, placebo is being used in place of standard therapy.*

Discussion: This is a situation where the risk of placebo is temporary suffering with little risk of irreversible physical harm. One could argue that this study is acceptable because the risk of placebo is temporary discomfort, which is something that an informed subject should be able to accept.[9] Another view would be that, at some point, temporary suffering and irreversible harm have the same ethical implications. One could argue that severe temporary physical suffering is likely to cause long-term psychological harm. No accepted guideline or formula identifies the situation where temporary physical suffering may result in irreversible psychological harm. Personal values and individual judgment will play a major role in deciding if this study is ethical.

Considering Alternative Study Designs
Consider two examples, one with little controversy regarding the quality of a study design that does not use concomitant placebo control and one where the use of alternate study designs are currently a topic of major debate.
Proposed study one: *The first example is that of Study B as presented in the previous discussion of temporary discomfort versus irreversible harm. In the case of first-line*

antibiotic therapy for pneumonia, there is little variability in the placebo response rate. Specifically, in patients who would be included in this trial, it is rare for pneumonia to resolve within the timeframe of the study without effective antibiotic treatment.

Discussion: When it is possible to estimate the placebo response rate with a reasonable degree of accuracy, study designs with historical placebo control or concomitant active control are likely to yield credible results. As pneumonia is a condition that may lead to serious and permanent health problems, it is unethical to conduct a trial with concomitant placebo control in this patient population.

Proposed study two: *The second example is that of a randomized, placebo-controlled trial of a new medication for major depression. The trial targets patients who have not been treated with approved medications that are considered standard therapy for this condition. Standard therapy, without question, has disease-specific activity in this patient population that results in meaningful benefit for many patients. The toxicity of standard medications is significant but manageable, and standard treatment is recommended by local physicians and tolerated by most patients. Major depression is a condition that causes severe suffering and irreversible health problems. From previous trials with concomitant placebo control, it is clear that variability in the placebo response rate for short-term treatment endpoints is likely to be as large as the expected effect of the study treatment.*

Discussion: The use of concomitant placebo control in place of standard therapy in studies of first-line therapy for major depression is a topic of major controversy in the research community. The April 2000 issue of the journal *Archives of General Psychiatry* contains a series of articles that present both sides of this debate. The fundamental arguments presented in these papers were discussed earlier in this chapter. Basically, some experts argue that it is feasible to conduct the kind of noninferiority trials that would produce valuable and persuasive results about the efficacy of new antidepressants without the risk of placebo. The counterargument is that the quality of the results from antidepressant studies that do not use concomitant placebo control is so low that society will be harmed by the routine use of medications that are not active in this medical condition.

Credible Altruism
It is difficult to find a real-life example where a reasonable and informed person would volunteer to be randomized in a study where placebo is being used in place of standard therapy that is known to be effective for a medical condition that may cause serious, irreversible harm. This is the basis for much of the current debate regarding the use of placebo in clinical trials. The principle of credible altruism is best illustrated with a study that randomizes subjects between a major surgical procedure and symptomatic treatment.
Proposed study: *A randomized trial of a major surgical procedure called radical prostatectomy for prostate can-*

cer. This procedure has been used for many years and is considered standard therapy by local physicians. In spite of previous studies, legitimate controversy remains about the efficacy of radical prostatectomy in terms of improvement in length or quality of life. Alternative therapies are commonly used to treat prostate cancer, but none are clearly beneficial. The study under consideration randomizes patients with a curable stage of prostate cancer to either radical prostatectomy or observation (no active treatment). Both study groups will receive standard palliative therapy (treatment designed to alleviate symptoms) if cancer progresses in the future. In most of the local communities where this study would take place, observation is rarely recommended by physicians, or chosen by patients who would be eligible for this study.

Discussion: In this study, the control group does not receive potentially curative therapy. "Observation with palliative treatment as needed" is being used in place of a standard therapy that is considered to be beneficial by local physicians. The risk of treatment in the control group is severe: permanent harm (cancer progression). Although the toxicity of radical prostatectomy is significant, patients routinely choose this therapy and recommend it to other patients. Determining the effect of radical prostatectomy on length and quality of life has major implications for a large number of future prostate cancer patients. This question can only be answered by means of a large-scale clinical trial with a concomitant "symptomatic treatment" control arm. Ethical justification for this study requires that it meet the "reasonable person" standard.

In many communities there are likely to be patients who will understand that there is legitimate controversy regarding the efficacy of radical prostatectomy, even though this is the therapy commonly recommended for their condition. In this situation, the value of study results to society may be extremely high, as the study could change the treatment recommendation for large numbers of future patients. Although the risk of the control arm of this study is high, the risk of standard therapy is significant. For these reasons, it is reasonable to conclude that a reasonable person, with an average degree of altruism and risk-aversiveness, would consent to being randomized in this trial.

References

1. Rothman KJ, Michels KB. The continuing unethical use of placebo controls. (Letter). *N Engl J Med* 331:394–7, 1994.

2. Marquis D. How to resolve an ethical dilemma concerning randomized clinical trials. (Letter). *N Engl J Med* 341:691–3, 1999.

3. Michels KB. The placebo problem remains. (Commentary). *Arch Gen Psychiatry* 57:321–2, 2000.

4. Addington D. The use of placebos in clinical trials for acute schizophrenia. *Can J Psychiatry* 40:171–6, 1995.

5. Brody BA. When are placebo-controlled trials no longer appropriate? *Control Clin Trials* 18:602–12, 1997.

6. Freeman TB, Vawter DE, Leaverton PE, Godbold JH, Hauser RA, Goetz CG, et al. Use of placebo surgery in controlled trials of a cellular-based therapy for Parkinson's disease. *N Engl J Med* 341:988–92, 1999.

7. Markman M. When regulatory requirements conflict with ethical study design: The case of oral ondansetron. *Cancer Invest* 12:654–6, 1994.

8. Stein CM, Pincus T. Placebo-controlled studies in rheumatoid arthritis: Ethical issues. *Lancet* 353:400–3, 1999.

9. Temple RJ. When are clinical trials of a given agent vs. placebo no longer appropriate or feasible? *Control Clin Trials* 18:613–20, 1997.

10. Clark PI, Leaverton PE. Scientific and ethical issues in the use of placebo controls in clinical trials. *Annu Rev Public Health* 15:19–38, 1994.

11. Food and Drug Administration. International Conference on Harmonisation: Choice of control group in clinical trials. Docket No. 99D-3082. Report number 64. Sep 24 1999: 51767–80. World Wide Web http://www.fda.gov/OHRMS/ DOCKETS/98fr/092499a.pdf.

12. Emanuel EJ, Wendler D, Grady C. What makes clinical research ethical? *JAMA* 283:2701–11, 2000.

13. Pullman D. General provisional proxy consent to research: Redefining the role of the local research ethics board. IRB: A Review of Human Subjects Research 21:1–9, 1999.

14. Daugherty CK, Banik DM, Janisch L, Ratain MJ. Quantitative analysis of ethical issues in Phase 1 trials: A survey interview study of 144 advanced cancer patients. *IRB: A Review of Human Subjects Research* 22(3): 6–14, 2000.

15. Ott L, Larson RF, Rexroat C, Mendenhall W. *Statistics: A Tool for the Social Sciences,* Ed. 5. Boston: PWS-Kent, 1992.

16. Code of Federal Regulations. Title 45A—Department of Health and Human Services; Part 46—Protection of Human Subjects. Updated 1 Oct 1997. Access date 18 Apr 2001. World Wide Web http://www4.law.cornell.edu/cfr/45p46.htm

17. Leber P. Placebo controls. No news is good news. (Commentary). *Arch Gen Psychiatry* 57:319–20, 2000.

18. Mcquay H, Moore A. Placebo mania. Placebos are essential when extent and variability of placebo response are unknown. (Letter). *Br Med J* 313:1008, 1996.

19. Kahn A, Warner HA, Brown WA. Symptom reduction and suicide risk in patients treated with placebo in antidepressant clinical trials. An analysis of the Food and Drug Administration database. *Arch Gen Psychiatry* 57:311–7, 2000.

20. Leon AC. Placebo protects subjects from nonresponse. A paradox of power. (Commentary). *Arch Gen Psychiatry* 57:329–30, 2000.

21. Kraemer HC. Statistical analysis to settle ethical issues? *Arch Gen Psychiatry* 57:327–8, 2000.

22. World Medical Association. Declaration of Helsinki: Ethical Principles for Medical Research Involving Human Subjects. First adopted in Helsinki, Finland, in 1964. Updated 10 Jul 2000. Access date 2 Sep 2001. World Wide Web http://www.wma.net/e/policy/17-c_e.html

Research Involving Sham Surgery

Robert M. Zwolak

INTRODUCTION

Performance of high-quality scientific research requires inclusion of appropriate controls. In the context of human research, it is always difficult to design control groups that do not expose volunteer subjects to unnecessary risk. In the realm of medication trials, a difficult decision is always posed between placebo controls versus the best medical therapy. When evaluating new surgical treatments, however, the decision regarding appropriate controls becomes increasingly complex as one considers that there may be nonspecific placebo effects of simply "undergoing surgery." Is that possible, and if so, is it ever ethical to consider an experimental control group of humans undergoing sham surgery? At first the concept sounds absurd, but sham surgery in humans has been used as a research tool intermittently for many years. In 1939, an Italian surgeon named Fieschi reasoned that ligation of the internal mammary arteries would increase bloodflow to the heart and thus relieve the symptoms of angina.[1] Fieschi reported excellent results with a procedure that involved ligating these arteries through two small chest incisions. This treatment approach was evaluated by Cobb[2] in 1959 in a National Institutes of Health (NIH) sponsored trial. Eight patients underwent internal mammary artery ligation, and nine underwent sham surgery limited to anesthesia with skin incisions. The sham surgery patients did just as well as those undergoing arterial ligation, thereby ending 20 years of enthusiasm for what in retrospect is a treatment that would be unlikely to work based on our current knowledge of the underlying disease process. In this case, sham surgery created risks for the research subjects, but it answered an important scientific question.

Sham surgery was used little throughout the 1970s and 1980s, but reappeared in the 1990s as researchers attempted to evaluate the efficacy of injecting fetal cells into the brains of Parkinson's disease patients. Several researchers and the NIH believed that appropriate consideration must be given to a placebo effect of surgery, and sham surgery was thought to be the only means to control for this effect. This chapter will review existing literature on this topic and will provide a framework for an IRB to consider sham surgery as a scientifically appropriate and ethically acceptable control.

When Do We Need To Consider Sham Surgery?

The good news is that in most surgical trials a sham surgery control group is scientifically unnecessary. For example, in situations where an accepted surgical treatment already exists, the control group would undergo the best surgical treatment and the experimental group would receive the investigational operation. Scientific rigor would be best served by randomly assigning subjects to investigational versus control surgery arms, and potential subjects would undergo an informed consent process outlining the risks of the new surgical treatment over and above those of the established surgery. For instance, if one were to devise an operation to repair inguinal hernias using a newly invented synthetic inguinal ligament, the appropriate control group would include patients undergoing hernia repair using currently accepted techniques. As part of the informed consent process, potential subjects would need to understand that the additional risks involved in the experimental arm would include migration or infection of the synthetic device plus the possibility that hernia recurrence could be more likely with the investigational treatment compared with standard surgery. Because effective standard surgical treatment exists for inguinal hernia, it would be scientifically unnecessary and ethically unacceptable to include a sham surgery control.

Another circumstance making it unnecessary to control with a sham surgery group is the ability to measure hard scientific endpoints that could not possibly be achieved by placebo effect. If a new operation is devised to treat a disorder that carries a high natural history risk of mortality, it would be inconceivable that the placebo effect of sham surgery could alter the incidence of that endpoint. The new operation might be tested against best medical therapy, be it pharmacological, radiation, etc., but a sham surgery control would be unnecessary.

So when is sham surgery an important control? The concept of sham surgery involving humans may well represent a conflict between the highest standard of research design and the ethical considerations of exposing human subjects to unnecessary risk. Nevertheless, a recent article by Freeman et al.[3] focused attention on a situation where the need for definitive scientific rigor apparently justified the risk to subjects in the eyes of the IRB and the NIH. These authors set out to undertake a definitive scientific evaluation of fetal nigral transplantation for treatment of Parkinson's disease. This disorder is one in which symptoms wax and wane in severity. Improvement in symptoms after fetal cell implantation could be due to the natural history of the patient's condition or to a placebo effect. A sham surgery control group was planned to help identify treatment-specific effects related to the study procedure.

Fetal tissue treatment requires general anesthesia, making scalp incisions, drilling holes through the skull, and implanting donor tissue in the patient's brain. Although these authors and others had previously demonstrated clinical benefits of this therapy in open trials, they were concerned that these benefits might be due to placebo effect or investigator bias. They proposed a control group wherein subjects would undergo the same anesthesia, scalp incisions, and burr holes, but without placement of fetal tissue. They reasoned that determining the value of fetal cell treatment in this setting was important enough to demand a rigorously controlled experiment, and that they could not collect reliable data in the absence of this sham surgery group. Following appropriate power calculations, they proposed an analysis in which 36 competent adults with advanced Parkinson's disease refractory to medical therapy would be randomized to active treatment with fetal tissue transplantation versus sham surgery. As noted in their article, the authors' local IRB and the National Institutes of Health (NIH) agreed that the risks of participation were "reasonable" in relation to the possible benefits. The trial was allowed to proceed as designed.

What Are the Risks and Benefits of Sham Surgery?

In a placebo-controlled drug trial, the inert substance used in the placebo group has no identifiable adverse effects. Risk of harm to subjects is minimized during the research as long as placebo-taking subjects are not exposed to the risk of progressive disease by withholding potentially effective medical therapy.[4] In contrast, sham surgery always involves risk. In the article by Freeman et al.,[3] sham surgery control subjects underwent placement of a large stereotactic frame on their head, general anesthesia administered by laryngeal mask airway, a surgical incision in their scalp, burr holes augured partway through their skull by an electric or air-driven drill, intravenous antibiotics, low-dose cyclosporine, and radioisotopes used for PET scans. Each of these steps is associated with considerable risks. Catastrophic complications are possible whenever general anesthesia is induced or when one human being approaches another with scalpel or power drill. The cumulative consideration of these risks led Macklin[5] to conclude, in an article published adjacent to Freeman's, that "sham surgery is ethically unacceptable as a placebo-control in trials of fetal-cell transplantation in patients with Parkinson's disease."

Are there benefits of sham surgery? From the IRB's perspective, benefit may be measured from two perspectives, that derived by the subject and that derived by society. Is there any benefit to a prospective subject from participating in sham surgery? The answer is no. Although some subtle benefit may accrue from the added attention derived by being a study participant, this is not readily measurable. Similarly, it is incorrect to conclude that subjects may benefit from being in a sham surgery trial because they have a 50% chance of receiving active therapy. The trial could be redesigned so that every subject gets active treatment.

The only valid argument for approving a trial that involves sham surgery is that the potential benefit of the information gained from the study for people in the future is so great that it justifies the discomfort and risk that sham surgery will clearly have for current research participants. As in many other areas of IRB practice, there is no cookbook formula for making this evaluation. Each IRB member will have to use personal judgement to decide if the tradeoff between current risk and potential future benefit justifies the conduct of a study involving sham surgery. One commentator argued that "Medical paternalism, in which physicians decide what risks to expose patients to, is ethically unacceptable. A medical maternalism in which research subjects are protected from all risks and from the autonomous exercise of the right to choose is no better."[6]

Can Investigators Provide Objective Information About Sham Surgery?

Another issue in this debate involves the objectivity of informed consent. Enthusiastic investigators may not accurately explain the risks of sham surgery, or the possibility of evaluating the study therapy with a trial that does not involve sham surgery. As explained in Chapter 10–13 by Miller on Phase I oncology trials, the behavior of both research subjects and physician investigators is frequently motivated by a type of misunderstanding or self-denial that has been called the *therapeutic misconception*. Subjects often assume that their physicians are primarily interested in their best medical outcome, uninfluenced by the excitement of developing a new, potentially effective treatment for some difficult medical problem. Medical investigators often deny the potential problems with the research treatments they advocate and the research studies they help to direct. Macklin[5] highlighted the defective nature of the informed consent process as part of her conclusion that sham surgery was ethically unacceptable. Horisberger[7] suggested that all potential subjects for a sham surgery-controlled trial be offered the new experimental treatment outside the randomization as another clinical option. This would force investigators to be objective about the potential fallibility of the new treatment in order to convince subjects to undergo randomization. This suggestion is intellectually intriguing, but it would create its own set of ethical and operational problems.

Should IRBs Approve Protocols with Sham Surgery?

In general, the answer is no. Sham surgery creates discomfort and risk with no potential for direct long-term benefit to research subjects. It is extremely rare to have a situation where there is likely to be a major difference in the persuasiveness of the data that will result from a study involving sham surgery compared with research that compares the study procedure with active treatment or historical control. When study endpoints are so labile or subjective that the placebo effect becomes an important consideration, it is difficult to imagine that a clinical trial will yield definitive results regardless of the form of the control group. In most situations, standard surgical therapy should be used as the control arm in studies that evaluate new surgical procedures. Having said this, there may be situations where a well-informed IRB will approve studies that involve sham surgery. At the present time, it is difficult to identify a situation where such an approval would be without major controversy. The guidelines noted previously will provide an IRB asked to review a study involving sham surgery with a framework for thoughtful discussion.

References

1. Stolberg SG. Sham surgery returns as a research tool. *New York Times*. Wk 3. 25 Apr 1999. New York City.

2. Cobb LA, Thomas GI, Dillard DH. An evaluation of internal-mammary-artery ligation by a double-blinded technic. *N Engl J Med* 260:1115–1118, 1959.

3. Freeman TB, Vawter DE, Leaverton PE, Godbold JH, Hauser RA, Goetz CG, Olanow CW. Use of placebo surgery in controlled trials of a cellular-based therapy for Parkinson's disease. *N Engl J Med* 341(13):988–992, 1999.

4. Code of Federal Regulations. Title 45A—Department of Health and Human Services; Part 46—Protection of Human Subjects. Updated 1 Oct 1997. Access date 18 Apr 2001. World Wide Web http://www4.law.cornell.edu/cfr/45p46.htm

5. Macklin R. The ethical problems with sham surgery in clinical research. *N Engl J Med* 341(13):992–996, 1999.

6. Burris JF. Correspondence Re: Placebo surgery in trials of therapy for Parkinson's disease. *N Engl J Med* 342:353, 2000.

7. Horisberger J. Correspondence Re: Placebo surgery in trials of therapy for Parkinson's disease. *N Engl J Med* 342:354, 2000.

Treatment-Withholding Studies in Psychiatry

Richard B. Ferrell

INTRODUCTION

The purpose of this chapter is to consider ethical questions raised by studies that involve withdrawal or discontinuation of current psychiatric treatment. There is overlap between the issues of treatment withdrawal and placebo control because in both of these situations there is a period of time when participants receive no active therapy. IRB management of studies involving placebo control is discussed in Chapter 10-10. This chapter will focus on the specific class of psychiatric drug studies in which active treatment is withheld for a period of time that may have an important effect on disease status. *Washout, withdrawal,* and *withholding* are other terms that refer to not giving active treatment. I will use the word *withholding* to refer to all studies of this type.

Treatment withholding is not unique to psychiatric research. For patients with psychiatric problems, there is often a question about the judgment or competence of the participants, but this question, while important, is also not the topic of this chapter. With psychiatric disorders there are a number of factors that make ethical evaluation of treatment-withholding studies difficult. The effects of some psychiatric illnesses, such as schizophrenia, bipolar disorder, and severe depression, can be extremely devastating, but other psychiatric illnesses can be less dangerous. There is a wide range of severity for the same psychiatric disorder across patients, and there may be large fluctuations in the severity of a condition in the same patient over time. With few exceptions, psychiatric treatments are not curative, but all carry significant risk. A significant problem is a lack of methods to definitively measure the effect of a given treatment in a patient. Experts do not always agree in their assessments of risks and benefits for treatment of a particular disorder. In view of this background, IRBs should expect to exercise a considerable degree of individual judgment when evaluating the ethics of a study in this category.

Ethical Guidance Documents

The Nuremburg Code, the World Medical Association Declaration of Helsinki, *The Belmont Report,* and the Code of Federal Regulations, Title 45, Part 46, of the Department of Health and Human Services are included in the reference section of this book and discussed in detail in other chapters. These guidelines all emphasize that the characteristics of ethical research are that the risks to subjects are minimized, the potential benefit of the research justifies potential risks, and that the research is not designed with the knowledge that research participation will harm the subject. None of these guidelines specifically discuss the withholding of treatment in psychiatric or other fields of research.

The "Statement of principles of ethical conduct for neuropsychopharmacologic research in human subjects" of the American College of Neuropsychopharmacology gives guidelines regarding ethical research design.[1] It discusses the importance of comparison with placebo in the evaluation of new psychiatric drugs. It does advocate careful review by the investigator and the IRB of "the use of placebo in severely ill patients, such as very disturbed and/or severely deteriorated schizophrenic patients who present gross thought disorders and hallucinations. . . ." This document does not specifically mention research in which existing treatment is to be stopped.

A Selective Literature Review

The National Alliance for the Mentally Ill (NAMI) has published standards designed to protect the welfare of psychiatric research participants.[2] Although NAMI has taken no official position on withholding treatment, prominent advocates from this organization have expressed concern about studies that do so:[3] "Many NAMI members now feel that a placebo is not acceptable, because we view schizophrenia and other psychotic disorders and affective illness as life-threatening diseases."[3] Hall and Flynn argue persuasively that studies involving withholding medication and placebo control in severe mental illness might not be ethical: "Indeed, NAMI has serious question about whether placebo-controlled studies are still necessary in this era. Researchers conducting such studies must be incredibly vigilant about these issues in their informed consent process, ongoing communication with families and patients, and follow-up to the research."[3]

Irving and Shamoo[4] and Shamoo and Keay[5] have seriously questioned the ethics of "washout" studies in schizophrenia. They assert that such studies cause unnecessary relapses in schizophrenic patients. Haas et al.[6] argued that delayed treatment of schizophrenia causes negative long-term effects. It is indeed hard to imagine how one could argue that delaying treatment could benefit a sick individual, unless one maintains that treatment is more likely to do harm than good. Nothing in my clinical experience in treating people with severe mental illness suggests to me that this is the case.

Persons with psychiatric illnesses have been stigmatized and treated with prejudice throughout history. Some would argue that informed consent is all that is needed to protect research participants and that additional protection perpetuates stigma. Others believe that people with psychiatric illness need special protection from research risk. Manschreck[7] discussed these countervailing points of view. He argued that scientific merit should not outweigh ethical concerns, and that efforts must be made to limit risks in schizophrenia studies involving placebo. Keeping the time when active treatment is not given as short as possible and having ". . . strict criteria for deciding when a patient should be withdrawn for failure to respond" are two ways of reducing risks.

One should not assume that withholding treatment could only cause harm. Cohen-Mansfield and colleagues[8] reported a study involving withdrawing treatment with haloperidol, thioridazine, and lorazepam from nursing home residents. This was a double-blind crossover study with a seven-week period of drug abstinence. The drugs had no clear beneficial effect.

One reason that psychiatric treatment research protocols might be controversial is that two ideals can be in conflict. The first ideal is the desire to find more effective and safe treatments for psychiatric illnesses and the second is the goal of protecting those afflicted with such illnesses from the risk of inadequate treatment. It is important to remember that advances in psychiatric treatment that derive from clinical research have been of tremendous help to many people. Such research is extremely important for current and future patients, but the welfare of individuals who may be participants in psychiatric research is highly important also.

Guidelines for IRB Review

Recognize the criteria that apply for IRB approval of research involving placebo are equally relevant to research involving withholding of active treatment. The IRB should use the placebo control algorithm presented in Chapter 10-10 to evaluate the ethics of trials that withhold treatment in psychiatric research. The main issues to consider are the nature of the patient's condition, the value of standard therapy in the study population, and rescue plans:

1. Is the purpose of the study to learn about the natural history of the disease or to find out if a study treatment is effective?

2. How effective is the treatment being withdrawn? Does it significantly alter the natural history of the disease, or greatly reduce symptoms and suffering?

3. How serious is the disease; what are its manifestations and consequences? If relapse occurs is there likely to be permanent harm or injury? If illness recurs is there likely to be a risk of suicide or risk of dangerous behavior toward others?

4. What is the tendency to relapse without treatment? If illness recurs, how likely is it that resumption of treatment will result in full recovery?

5. Is the period without active treatment as short as possible to answer the study question?

6. Are there possible advantages to withdrawing current treatment such as significant side effects or toxicity that might be reduced or eliminated?

7. What are the provisions in the study for timely rescue if symptoms *worsen*?

Do not hesitate to ask for the opinion of an unbiased expert regarding the questions that the IRB needs to answer to make a decision about approving the protocol. Consider making voluntary hospitalization or very close and careful outpatient care during the period of highest risk a requirement for IRB approval.

Case Discussions

Example 1

A proposed study would compare two dosage schedules of an investigational antipsychotic drug for treatment of schizophrenia. Previous studies with this drug over the dose range in this study suggest a favorable risk/benefit profile. Subjects whose symptoms are not optimally controlled on standard medications will have a seven-day washout period during which they receive no medication. The clinician–investigator has the option of reducing this period to three days, depending upon clinical judgment about the participant's condition. The study requires close monitoring of participants throughout the study with plans for immediate rescue treatment and/or hospitalization if symptoms worsen.

Withholding treatment is ethical in this study primarily because the period without treatment is brief and flexible depending on the severity of illness. Symptom control was suboptimal on standard therapy, and the study provides for close monitoring with appropriate rescue. The IRB should approve the study.

EXAMPLE 2

A study would investigate treatment of attention-deficit/hyperactivity disorder (ADHD) in children with a new long-acting formulation of methylphenidate (Ritalin) that is only taken once a day. An inclusion criterion is that patients are currently well controlled on the standard form of methylphenidate, which is given multiple times per day. The study requires a two-week washout period when all subjects will be given placebo. Subjects who do well on placebo (minimal symptoms of ADHD) are excluded from the remainder of the study. Subjects who deteriorate on placebo are then randomized to treatment with the new formulation of methylphenidate or placebo for a four-week study period.

The purpose of the washout period in this study is to identify subjects who are benefiting from methylphenidate treatment. The study is designed with a goal of producing symptom deterioration in a subgroup of study subjects. Consultation with several people who had experience with uncontrolled ADHD children in the classroom stressed that even a few weeks of symptom deterioration may be a serious problem for the child with ADHD and other children in the classroom. My IRB did not approve a study similar to this.

Conclusion

The IRB should understand that the withdrawal of active treatment is both ethical and necessary in many research settings. To evaluate a specific study, the IRB should use the guidelines discussed in this chapter and the placebo control algorithm presented in Chapter 10-10. In my experience, most disagreements among committee members have to do with understanding the facts differently, or with simply not enough facts being known. It is important for committee members to have as much information as possible. Prognosis is usually the greatest uncertainty and the most common source of dispute about a particular protocol.

If we knew that not treating a major illness such as schizophrenia for some period of time would result in a greater chance of neuronal injury or permanent disability, or decrease the chances of successful treatment when treatment is eventually begun, then any protocol that withheld treatment would be unethical. This would be even more the case if it were clinically evident that the illness was likely to cause much suffering and anguish. Although there is disagreement on this point, I do not think that it is currently ethical to withhold drug treatment from persons with schizophrenia for substantial time periods. This is especially true if the individual is currently receiving treatment that is improving his or her condition. This same argument might also be made for persons with severe forms of bipolar disorder, depression, anxiety disorders, and obsessive-compulsive disorder.

All psychiatric disorders cannot be lumped together. For some illnesses, the long-term consequences are clearly bad, and treatment for some illnesses is better than for others. Special attention must be paid to the risks of discontinuing treatment if the disease or disorder in question causes psychotic symptoms, produces deterioration of intellectual or social function, or is at all likely to result in dangerous behavior. If the facts are not clear, the IRB should get a consultant. For psychiatric studies involving treatment discontinuation, an actively practicing psychiatrist who regularly treats patients afflicted by the disease or disorder in question would be a good choice. A member of NAMI would also be a good choice if one is not already a member of the IRB committee. In either or both cases, a helpful consultant will have knowledge about psychiatric illness and the suffering of those afflicted. He or she will have a balanced view about the welfare of patients and the great importance of developing treatments better than those we now have.

Treatment of severe psychiatric illness is not easy. It is seldom simply a matter of correcting a "chemical imbalance" with a particular medicine. If a successful treatment is stopped and relapse occurs, restarting the medicine at a later time often will not return the person to health quickly, if at all. Not only is the prognosis for repeat recovery uncertain, during the period of illness the afflicted person is suffering from symptoms and also from the effects of illness on their social, emotional, family, and vocational life. Severe psychiatric illness also carries a risk of complications including concomitant illness and suicide. For example, persons with severe depression have a higher rate of death from causes other than suicide than people who are not depressed.

It is hard to imagine that a person who has suffered from severe mental illness and has recovered or significantly improved would want to take a chance of experiencing relapse or recurrence of symptoms for any reason, including altruism, if such recurrence could be avoided.

It is the job of researchers to design studies that attempt to answer important research questions, while at the same time not jeopardizing the health of those persons who volunteer to participate in the research. It is the job of IRBs to carefully examine research proposals regarding their ethical merit. Psychiatric studies that include any discontinuation of current treatment present a special challenge for IRBs. Knowledge, careful thought, and circumspect ethical judgment are necessary for making our best possible decisions.

References

1. American College of Neuropsychopharmacology. Statement of principles of ethical conduct for neuropsychopharmacologic research in human subjects. *Directory of Members.* 1996: 195–208.

2. Shamoo AE, Johnson JR, Honberg R, Flynn L. National Alliance for the Mentally Ill's standards for protection of individuals with severe mental illnesses who participate as human subjects in research. In: Shamoo AE (ed). *Ethics in Neurobiological Research with Human Subjects: The Baltimore Conference on Ethics.* Amsterdam: Gordon and Breach Publisher OPA. 1997: 325–328.

3. Hall LL, Flynn L. Consumer and family concerns about research involving human subjects. In: Pincus HA, Lieberman JA, Ferris S (eds). *Ethics in Psychiatric Research: A Resource Manual for Human Subjects Protection*. Washington, D.C.: American Psychiatric Assn. 1999: 219–238.

4. Irving DN, Shamoo AE. Washouts/relapses in patients participating in neurobiological research studies in schizophrenia. In: Shamoo AE (ed). *Ethics in Neurobiological Research with Human Subjects: The Baltimore Conference of Ethics*. Amsterdam: Gordon and Breach Publisher OPA. 1997: 119–127.

5. Shamoo AE, Keay TJ. Ethical concerns about relapse studies. *Camb Q Healthc Ethics* 5(3):373–386, 1996.

6. Haas GL, Keshavan MS, Sweeney JA. Delay to first medication in schizophrenia: Evidence for a possible negative impact of exposure to psychosis. (Abstract). *Proceedings of the 33rd Annual Meeting of the American College of Neuropsychopharmacology, San Juan, Puerto Rico.* 1994: 171.

7. Manschreck TC. Placebo studies: Lessons from psychiatric research. *Psychiatric Annals* 31(2):130–136, 2001.

8. Cohen-Mansfield J, Lipson S, Werner P, Billig N, Taylor L, Woosley R. Withdrawal of haloperidol, thioridazine, and lorazepam in the nursing home: A controlled double-blind study. *Archives of Internal Medicine* 159(15):1733–1740, 1999.

Phase I Oncology Trials

Matthew Miller

INTRODUCTION

A fundamental tension in human experimentation on patients arises from the inherent conflict between the goals of science and those of clinical care. Phase I cancer trials embody this conflict in perhaps its purest and most intense form because the subjects in these trials are terminally ill patients with advanced and incurable malignancies and the scientific goal is to effect toxicity, not cure, remission, or palliation.[1] This presents special challenges to IRB review, especially in light of empirical evidence that patients overwhelmingly enroll in these trials seeking physical benefit.[2-11] Benjamin Freedman summarized the fundamental issue:

> A Phase I study of drug X is often said to be a study of X's safety and efficacy. Calling a toxicity study a study of safety seems harmless, and perhaps even reflects a laudably optimistic view of the world. Calling it a study of efficacy is, however, simply false; although to be sure, were there no hope of this drug's working it would not be tested.[1]

This chapter begins with an overview of Phase I trials, touching on the dominant dose-escalation scheme employed, historical response rates, eligibility requirements, and the special vulnerabilities of trial participants. The following section focuses on the empirical evidence that suggests most patients currently enrolled in Phase I cancer trials fail to comprehend critically important elements about the nature of the sacrifice they are being asked to make. Against this background, I explore the possibility that patient misunderstanding may be shared and reinforced by virtue of a tendency among physician–investigators to view their role as investigator as serving patients' therapeutic interests. Problematic aspects of traditional and prevailing dosing regimens are explored by contrasting them with innovative but infrequently employed designs that are in less obvious conflict with patients' expectations. Finally, suggestions are made regarding what IRB members can do to protect patients' basic right of self-determination and freedom from unwarranted harms. These suggestions focus on: (a) structural elements of Phase I trials that must be disclosed clearly to patients and justified explicitly to the IRB (especially those elements that embody the conflict between the interests of science and those of personal care); and (b) accountability (beyond disclosure) for ensuring comprehending decision-making by prospective patient–subjects. Throughout this chapter, I will supplement findings from the empirical literature with descriptions of the difficulties I experienced navigating the tensions between research and patient care during my tenure as acting director of Phase I cancer trials at the Dana-Farber Cancer Institute in Boston.

Background

In the course of developing new anticancer compounds, agents that have demonstrated promise in cell culture and animal models must at some time be tested in human subjects. In these initial or *Phase I* human trials, compounds

Note: An abbreviated version of this chapter is published in *The Hastings Center Report,* Vol. 30, No. 4, 2000: 34–42. Used with permission.

are administered to terminally ill cancer patients in an attempt to estimate the highest dose human beings can tolerate.[6,12-17] Evaluating a drug's anticancer effect in human cancers—a primary objective of subsequent Phase II and III trials—is not a defined goal in Phase I studies.[15,17] Unlike Phase II and III trials, Phase I studies do not test hypotheses (such as whether new drug X is at least Y% effective in disease Z, or whether new drug X is better than old drug Y);[12] most drugs administered in Phase I trials go on to Phase II evaluation, independent of an antitumor effect in

Phase I. Indeed, if a partial tumor response were the basis of proceeding to Phase II trials, fewer than 5% of drugs would proceed; if a complete response were required, fewer than 0.5% would proceed.[18]

Subjects in noncancer Phase I (dose-toxicity) studies are usually healthy volunteers.[19] Because Phase I cancer trials use drugs that are selected for their ability to kill (tumor) cells and because these agents often produce their effects by causing damage to DNA, with attendant concerns about long-term carcinogenic consequences, subjects in Phase I cancer trials are never healthy volunteers.

To be considered for Phase I cancer trials, patients must have exhausted all known therapeutic options and generally have a life expectancy of at least three to four months. Typically, patients are referred by their primary oncologist to a major cancer program where a physician–investigator from the cancer center performs a physical examination, takes a medical history, and then invites eligible patients to enroll. For the duration of enrollment, a physician–investigator at the cancer center usually assumes substantial responsibility for monitoring and caring for each patient.

Phase I dose-toxicity information is usually gathered by administering increasing doses of a new drug (or of novel combinations of known agents) to successive cohorts of three to six patients. Once serious but reversible toxic effects are produced in a fixed proportion of patients (often one third of the patients in the highest-dose cohort), the trial ends.[6,20-26] Examples of ill effects severe enough to be considered dose-limiting include gross hemorrhage, nausea to the point that there is no significant intake of food or fluid, and painful mouth and throat sores that make eating impossible. Unless extremely severe, irreversible toxicities are observed in Phase I trials, agents generally go on to Phase II studies, independent of whether tumor responses were observed.

Because most responses occur at 80% to 120% of the maximum tolerated dose,[6,23] subjects enrolled in the earliest cohorts have the least risk of severe toxicity but also the least likelihood of a clinical response. It has been estimated that the traditional and prevailing cohort-specific dosing strategies subject approximately 60% to 80% of patients to doses that, based on preclinical models, are thought less likely to produce a response than higher, achievable levels.[6] Thus the predominant cohort-specific dose escalation schemes are at odds with what patients generally assume about the primacy of their interests, such as that *each* patient will receive a dose that attempts to maximize the chance for anticancer effect. Despite this significant departure from usual clinical practice, there are no formal requirements specifying that physician–investigators must share this information with patients.

Based on the long-standing rationale that the optimal therapeutic dose (of classical cytotoxic agents) is the highest safely achievable dose, the maximum tolerated dose determined from Phase I trials is usually recommended as the dose for subsequent Phase II studies.[27,28] The adoption of a therapeutic goal for Phase II trials is also reflected in patient characteristics. Patients in Phase II studies must have measurable disease (to assess response), usually have

a malignancy that is thought among the most likely to respond to the agent under investigation, and often have not received extensive chemotherapy or radiotherapy in the past.[15] In contradistinction, Phase I patients need not have measurable disease and can generally have any tumor type, even types that animal models do not suggest will respond to the agent in question. Over 90% of patients eligible for Phase I trials have been extensively pretreated.[29]

Planned Toxicity and No Direct Benefit

As mentioned above, Phase I oncology studies are not designed to benefit the patients who participate in the trials. The nontherapeutic objective of Phase I studies is supported by empiric data. One comprehensive review of Phase I cancer trials published between 1972 and 1987 found an overall response rate among the 6,639 patients of 4.5%. There were 23 complete remissions (0.3%) and 31 toxic deaths (0.5%).[18] Of the few complete remissions, most occurred in tumor types traditionally held to be the most responsive (hematological malignancies). When agents were classified by response rate, 9% produced an overall (i.e., partial and complete) response rate of 10% or higher and 1% produced a response rate of at least 20%. In a simulation study of 100 Phase I trials using a traditional dosing design, roughly half of all patients experienced at least mild toxicity, and approximately 20% experienced severe but reversible toxicity (grades 3 and 4 toxicity).[30] Other reviews of Phase I trials document similar response and toxicity rates.[6,20,31-34] As mentioned, patients in Phase I trials survive, on average, six months from the date of enrollment.[35] Among the few who achieve a complete response, half relapse within six months; partial responses last approximately three months.[28] It is also unknown whether the few patient–subjects who responded actually lived any longer or better as a result.[4]

The predominant structure of Phase I trials embodies peculiarly contrasting tensions at opposing ends of the dosing spectrum: at one extreme, requiring that at least one patient suffer severe (but reversible) toxicity;[12] at the other, subjecting 60% to 80% of patients to doses that, based on preclinical models, are a priori expected to prove less likely to produce a response than higher achievable levels.[6] Given a remission rate of under 1% and a comparable rate of death due to drug toxicity,[18] few would claim any aggregate survival advantage for participants. In fact, consent documents state that Phase I cancer trials are primarily toxicity studies and that response is neither intended nor expected.[6] Yet, when asked, patients enrolled in these trials overwhelmingly cite hope of physical benefit (rarely altruism) as their primary motivation for enrolling.[3-5,9,11]

Therapeutic Misconceptions of Subjects

This section explores the empirical evidence suggesting that Phase I cancer patients agree to participate in these trials largely in hope of physical benefit and generally assume that the structure of the trial itself serves their personal therapeutic goal. These beliefs reflect a profound trust patients have in the doctor–patient relationship and an underlying assumption about the immutability of this trusting relationship even in the face of the demands of science. This misunderstanding, whereby patients do not fully recognize the way that science sometimes deprives them of care chosen solely out of concern for their well being (what Fried[36] calls the right of "personal care"), has been called the "therapeutic misconception."[37] After reviewing evidence that suggests Phase I cancer patients are particularly susceptible to the therapeutic misconception, I explored the possibility that physician–investigators share elements of the therapeutic misconception. Lastly, I argue that this shared misconception has moral consequences for these trials, resulting in mutually reinforcing behaviors that are inimical to attaining truly informed consent.

Empirical studies of patient comprehension in Phase I cancer trials consistently suggest that patients participating in Phase I oncology trials are primarily motivated by the hope that they will derive physical benefit. Making a contribution to generalizable knowledge or to future patients appears to play an inconsequential and greatly subordinate role.[2-11] Although cancer patients participating in Phase I trials appear to have adequate knowledge of the risks of the investigational agents,[3] seldom do they understand that the purpose of Phase I studies is not to produce a tumor response or to palliate human suffering, but rather to establish a relationship between dose and toxicity.[2-6]

In 1995, a prominent team of ethicists and oncologists at the University of Chicago published one of the first empirical studies to explore the motivations and perceptions of cancer patients enrolled in Phase I trials.[3] Thirty consecutive cancer patients enrolled in Phase I trials were surveyed. Although 93% of patients said that they understood most of the information given them, only 33% were able to state that the purpose of the trial in which they were subjects was to determine toxicities, tolerability, or the safest dose of the administered agents. Fewer than one third said that the option of no treatment was discussed. Eighty-five percent decided to participate for reasons of possible therapeutic benefit, 11% because of advice or trust in a physician, and 4% because of family pressure. No one identified altruism as the primary motivation for participating. Of note, patients who were unable to state the purpose of Phase I trials were more likely to believe that they would derive benefit from the study. These findings are consistent with previous expectations: 94% of Phase I investigators and 85% of IRB Chairs believe that patients enroll in these trials for physical benefit, not for altruistic reasons.[38]

Other studies reveal similar deficiencies in what terminally ill patients generally comprehend about clinical trials.[2,4,7-10,39] These studies consistently find that patients enroll in research primarily motivated by a hope for improving their condition and that, frequently, therapeutic misconceptions are wedded to despair.[39] One comparative study of patient understanding in clinical trials found that

the therapeutic misconception is particularly strong among Phase I cancer trial subjects.[11] In this study, 127 subjects enrolled in four types of research protocols (three groups of ill subjects—Phase I and II cancer patients, Phase III HIV-positive symptom-free patients—and one group of healthy volunteers). *All* Phase I subjects stated that their study's goal (as distinct from their hopes) was related both to treatment and research; a majority considered that cure or remission was a benefit of participating. Patients held these beliefs despite the written consent document, which states that the purpose of their trial was "to determine the side effects of Ormaplatin in patients with cancer and to determine the highest safe dose that can be used in future patients." Eighty percent of Phase II subjects and 60% of Phase III subjects described their study as both research and treatment. Ninety-one percent of the healthy volunteers responded that they believed their study was mostly research, versus 35% of Phase III subjects and 8% of Phase II subjects. Significantly more subjects in the diagnosed groups than healthy volunteers reported that the consent document itself had no effect on their decision to participate in the study. In addition, responses were inversely related to health status: the greatest percentage of subjects reporting no effect were enrolled in the Phase I study (50%), followed by Phase II (42%), Phase III (23%), and healthy volunteers (17%). The two factors reported most frequently by both Phase I and II subjects for deciding to participate in a research study were: (1) "hope for control of disease" and (2) "present medical condition." In contrast, healthier Phase III subjects reported "NIH reputation" and "hope others benefit" most frequently. Healthy volunteers reported "hope others benefit" and "payment for participation in the study."

A particularly innovative study of the perceptions of patient–subjects enrolled in Phase I trials assessed the feasibility of a clinical trial design that uses an interactive informed-consent process in which patient–subjects can choose to become directly involved in decisions of dose escalation.[4] Subjects were patients with advanced cancer who were eligible to participate in a Phase I trial. These subjects underwent a three-step informed-consent process that used cohort-specific consent and allowed them the option to choose their own doses of the chemotherapeutic agents under study within predetermined limits. The agents in this Phase I study were known drugs, but the combination of the two drugs was novel. (In this way the trial differed from the more problematic nature of trials that use untried agents.) Participants in this study were surveyed, and the survey results were compared with a similar survey of a matched control population of subjects who participated in other concurrently active, conventional Phase I trials at the same institution. Almost all the subjects in both the cohort-specific and the matched control groups claimed that they understood all or most of what was told to them. Respondents felt that having been given cohort-specific information and the option to choose a dose within predetermined ranges made them feel better informed. Nevertheless, there were no statistically significant improvements in objective measures of the informed consent process in this group.

Therapeutic Misconceptions of Physicians

My experience as acting director of Phase I trials at the Dana-Farber Cancer Institute is consistent with the empirical literature. I found that patients in Phase I cancer trials agree to participate almost exclusively in hopes of physical benefit. Moreover, before our first meeting, almost every patient assumed that the imperatives of ordinary patient-centered care would prevail over any protocol constraints. They were wrong.

When patients came to see me, they did not appreciate critical aspects of Phase I trial design—aspects that were absolutely necessary for them to grasp if they were to have anything approaching an adequate understanding of the nature of the sacrifice they were being asked to consider. For example, patient–subjects did not have the faintest expectation that the drug upon which their hopes were pinned would be administered at doses that depended on contingencies unrelated to maximizing the likelihood of antitumor effect. They did not expect that the dosing structure was designed around parameters of toxicity, not effectiveness. They did not expect that the fixed dose they would receive depended on, for example, what day of the week they enrolled relative to others. In addition, few had been told by their primary oncologist that these trials historically have a partial response rate of <5% and a complete response rate equal to that of acute toxic death (0.5%). Few understood that these trials aim to induce grade 3 or 4 toxicity in at least one subject or that the trial would end as soon as that endpoint was reached. None had imagined possible the reality that moved one leading figure in modern oncology to write: "It is reasonably certain that if the full reality of subtherapeutic dosing were getting through to patients and families, very few would volunteer for Phase I studies." [6]

The direction our conversation took and, it turned out, the likelihood patients would enroll depended largely on whether, and the extent to which, we discussed the particular ways in which the protocol offered opposed customary assumptions about medical practice and physician loyalty. Yet, because terminally ill patients rarely if ever initiate such a discussion, no conversation was more tempting or easier to avoid.

Telling patients that they are unlikely to respond favorably is an inference drawn from historical data and reflects, apart from any research agenda, the limitations of medicine's capabilities in the face of advanced malignancy. It is a conversation familiar to anyone who has cared for sick patients and is peculiar neither to oncology nor to the Phase I setting. Telling a patient that his or her chance of responding will not necessarily be maximized is, however, less familiar and more difficult because this limitation is imposed by a particular methodology. In the one case, there is no need, per se, to redefine the doctor–patient relationship in ways that distinguish research from usual patient care; in the other, the distinction is inescapable.

One strategy to avoid discussing the way a patient's interests yield before those of protocol is to conflate the limitations inherent in medicine's capabilities with those that are imposed by protocol. My reluctance to distinguish between medicine's limitations and those imposed by protocol stemmed, in part, from an impulse to protect my patients. I was reluctant to further debilitate a patient's hope. But I was also reluctant to acknowledge (to myself and to my patients) the extent to which my clinical authority was undercut by protocol, and to examine the extent to which I had already been complicit in maintaining the status quo.

Another way to avoid making clear the therapy versus research distinction is to adopt a sweeping and undifferentiated concept of the uncertainty inherent in the proposed trial. To say, for example, one never knows when the next breakthrough drug will come along is to allow a vague conceptualization of uncertainty to devour the morally relevant little we do know, such as the fact that no one has ever been cured in a Phase I trial. Even the essential premise of the underlying design could be overshadowed—for what does the monotonicity of dose-response have to do with the advent of the miraculous? Cohort-specific dose escalation is, in fact, rarely a part of the consent form. So rare that even though more than a decade has passed since the late Benjamin Freedman argued persuasively that it is morally necessary to include a specific and clear explanation of the cohort-specific nature of the dosing design, few institutions have adopted his suggestion. [40]

In addition to unwitting strategies of avoidance, physician–investigators, by virtue of being physicians, tend to reinforce expectations patients have about the primacy of their individual therapeutic interests. [39,41-43] Katz has written: [41]

> Investigators who appear before patient–subjects as physicians in white coats create confusion. Patients come to hospitals with the trusting expectation that their doctor will care for them. They will view an invitation to participate in research as a professional recommendation that is intended to serve their individual interests.

What, after all, is a patient supposed to assume about a clinical trial proposed as an untried but promising new "therapy" or "treatment"? Add to this that the invitation is extended in a hospital clinic by a doctor who has just finished performing a history and physical examination—an act that is powerfully symbolic and intimate, one customarily the privilege and almost exclusive province of the personal physician. Unless explicitly and particularly addressed, why would a dying patient ever think that the dose she or he would be given is based on contingencies unrelated to maximizing the response?

There are many ways in which the language physicians use when speaking about these trials may reinforce the tendency among patients to distort those elements of experimental investigation that threaten to undermine hope of clinical benefit. [2,41,43,44] For example, speaking of these trials as offering experimental "therapy" or using consent forms that refer to investigational interventions as novel "treatments" lends misleading credibility to the proposed project as one designed to promote patients' interests. Even factually accurate information in a particular juxtaposition can mislead. Saying to a patient on the one hand that the probability of remission is slight, and on the other that one never knows when a miracle drug will come along, gives equal rhetorical weight to clinical success and failure.

More importantly, it is a formulation of the trial that omits specific reference to potential harms, to how the needs of science trump those of medicine, to the absence of intra-patient (individualized) dose-escalation, and to the uncertainty that even the rare responder benefits at all.

It took far longer for me to appreciate that these same words and surroundings performed a similar function for me, preserving the illusion that what I was engaged in was an extension of usual clinical practice. This, in turn, made it easier for me to assume that my patient's interests were not in conflict with those of protocol, nor with my own interests for career advancement. Viewing these trials as an extension of medical practice makes it harder for physicians (and therefore for our patients) to identify the troubling ways in which patients' interests yield to those of protocol, or the additional responsibilities of disclosure in human experimentation.

Physicians, it seems to me, do not adopt the oxymoronic language of "therapeutic research" in order to deceive subjects into thinking that they are patients. Rather, we do so unwittingly and in order that we may continue to see ourselves as compassionate physicians even as we perform duties in service of dispassionate science. It is not that we disingenuously hide from patients information we deem relevant; rather, it is that we are so adept at hiding it from ourselves. It is an accommodation that allows us to take comfort in our own good intentions. Unfortunately, it also makes it easier to characterize these trials wrongly, if inadvertently, as serving patients' interests.

Little empirical attention has been paid to the possibility that physicians, too, are susceptible to the therapeutic misconception. A few empirical findings indirectly hint at such a misconception among physicians. In one study of 144 patients enrolled in Phase I, II, and III trials at three cancer centers, virtually all of the 68 oncologists thought their patients would benefit from the investigational agents being tested. Moreover, 43% of physicians said they had "no doubts at all about benefits of treatment" despite a statement in the consent form that benefit could not be assured.[45]

In another study of exclusively Phase I cancer patients, 18 oncologists who had primary responsibility for enrolling and caring for Phase I patients were asked to estimate the likelihood of risks and benefit. Overall, physicians tended to overestimate both the likelihood of severe and fatal toxicity and the likelihood of anticancer effect. For example, approximately half of these physicians thought that the frequency of fatal toxicity was at least 5% (historically it is 0.5%) and that the chance of antitumor response (partial plus complete) was 15% (historically it is approximately 5%). These data may be superficially seen as consistent with physicians presenting to patients relatively more bias of ill effects than of benefits, by virtue of the greater exaggeration of the likelihood of ill-effects (ten-fold) than of likely benefits (three-fold). To me, however, the exaggerations of response (and toxicity) indicate that physician–investigators are *thinking* about untried agents the way that they would view a tried and powerfully successful agent if it were administered at the maximum tolerated dose to each patient. These exagger-ated estimates may represent ignorance, itself a worrisome finding as the physicians in this study were the ones to invite patients to participate. Yet physicians generally are quite skillful at knowing the response rates for given agents in specific diseases. Such wildly exaggerated projections, anchored as they appear to be to estimates of response and toxicity rates for proven chemotherapeutics in advanced disease, suggest another possibility: that these projections reflect a heuristic that physician–investigators adopt to avoid acknowledging to themselves the trade-off they are asking patient–subjects to make. In any event, these physician–investigators are attributing to untried agents a degree of effectiveness that, whatever else it betrays, makes it easier for them to see themselves as caring physicians rather than dispassionate researchers. To the extent that both patient–subjects and physician–investigators share the perspective that these trials provide dying patients with a venue in which to pursue their best chance for clinical benefit, their perspectives will be mutually reinforcing. For patients, the belief that their interests come first reflects a profound trust that patients have in the doctor–patient relationship. For physicians, it reflects the socializing force of clinical training steeped in the long-standing Hippocratic tradition of beneficence. As Katz has written:

> It is that belief, that trust, which physician-investigators must vigorously challenge so that patient subjects appreciate that in research, unlike therapy, the research question comes first. This takes time and is difficult to convey. It can be conveyed to patient subjects only if physician-investigators are willing to challenge the misperceptions that many patients bring to the invitation.[41]

This challenge is a difficult one because physicians, too, may have deep-seated, not fully recognized needs that these trials serve. Which is to say that the challenge is difficult because it is not strictly a matter of volition, but one of self-discovery and acknowledgement of complicity, however well intended. To meet this challenge successfully requires that physician–investigators repudiate *intention-based* definitions of what constitutes therapy. It asks that we acknowledge fundamental and irreducible conflicts between the role of researcher and that of clinician, an acknowledgment that conflicts with our identity as caregiver before all else. Ironically, if physician–investigators did not care so deeply about the well-being of their patients they would be less susceptible to this therapeutic misconception. In my experience, physician–investigators are susceptible precisely because they care and because they are drawn to search for new, more effective treatments out of a deep frustration with medicine's present capabilities and out of a painful awareness of their patients' suffering.

Alternatives to the Standard Phase I Dosing Strategy

IRB members and researchers should recognize that there are methodologically acceptable alternatives to the dosing schedules currently used in Phase I studies. This section examines one such alternative—intrapatient dose escalation—and contrasts it with the dominant cohort-specific dosing schema described earlier in the background section of this chapter. Intrapatient dose escalation is chosen as an example of innovative dosing strategies because it is precisely the proscription of individualized (i.e., within-patient) dose adjustments that most clearly demonstrated to my patients how research interests trump their medical interests. These trials are also of interest because the rarity with which they are employed throughout the United States illustrates a cultural refractoriness to change that stems from deep-seated but dimly acknowledged needs of patients, physicians, and the medical community as a whole. After reviewing the mechanics of intrapatient dose escalation, I discuss why the reasons most commonly offered in rejecting this dosing scheme do not hold up to scrutiny.

Intrapatient dose escalation is a dosing scheme that allows patients to be given successively higher doses of an experimental drug (within certain safety parameters) if the initial dose administered proves to be well tolerated but unable to shrink the tumor. Intrapatient dose escalation is based on the rationale that typical anticancer agents have the best chance of killing cancer cells when administered at the highest safely achievable dose. For more than 10 years, trial strategies (such as, and in addition to, intrapatient dose escalation) have been proposed that avoid consigning the bulk of patients to doses that animal data suggest do not maximize the chance for response.[6,12,16,21,30,33,46-55] Yet, fewer than 15% of Phase I cancer trials in the United States employ these innovative approaches.[20,28]

The initial interdiction of intrapatient dose escalation in Phase I trials occurred in the early 1960s, following clinical studies with nitrosoureas that resulted in delayed toxicity.[6,56] Although the movement away from intrapatient dose escalation is linked historically to the misfortune with nitrosoureas, there is no scientific justification for the persistence of this avoidance. In reviewing the National Cancer Institute's Phase I database, an expert panel concluded that cumulative toxicity does not appear to be a valid reason to prohibit intrapatient dose escalation:[28] where intrapatient dose escalation was used, there was no evidence that it had a negative impact on the trial or on individual patients. In fact, comparing conventional dosing schemes with these innovative designs[6,30,49] suggests that innovative individualized approaches (e.g., intrapatient dose escalation) effectively reduce the number of patients treated at doses substantially less than that recommended for Phase II trials and speed the completion of the trials.

Changing the dosing strategy does not, unfortunately, change the nature of a patient's incurable disease. It is unlikely, therefore, that any foreseeable technical modification (including intrapatient dose escalation) will greatly improve clinically meaningful Phase I trial response rates. Nevertheless, dosing schemes that attempt to maximize the response that each patient can expect, small as that chance may remain, bring into closer alignment what patients expect from their doctors and what protocol allows doctors to provide. Because of this, a critical impediment to open dialogue between doctor and patient is, if not removed, made less formidable. Similarly, if eligibility for Phase I trials resembled eligibility for Phase II trials, where tumor types that appear most likely to respond to the agent under investigation are the tumor types admitted, patients enrolled would at least be given a drug that has a specific anticancer rationale for their particular disease.

There are, however, dangers in an overly zealous attachment to making technical changes if such attachments serve to divert attention from the more fundamental issue of using persons as the means for other's ends. Perhaps intrapatient dose escalation (and like modifications) will unintentionally reinforce patients' and physicians' expectations that Phase I trials are therapy when, in fact, the gain under this regimen may be so slight as to be indistinguishable from that under more traditional approaches. If so, the specter of clinical benefit might obscure questions about what else is risked, who is most likely to benefit, and how the trial itself is still configured in service of science, not medicine. In addition, if these structural modifications encourage physicians to see these trials as enterprises that are therapeutic, the standards of disclosure in purely therapeutic doctor–patient encounters risk becoming, and thereby lowering, the standards for these trials. The admonition inherent in these critiques does not excuse inaction that would maintain a clearly suboptimal status quo. Rather, it warns us to be alert to the likely influence of proposed changes, to the conflicts of interest that remain, and to the particular susceptibility of some patients to choose harm.

Among some of my oncology colleagues not directly involved in Phase I trials, these initial human trials were viewed as ethically untenable, and consequently they rarely, if ever, referred patients for Phase I trials. Among physicians involved in Phase I studies, some stated that they prefer innovative designs but that costs and the level of sophistication required to coordinate and conduct such trials were impediments to employing them more commonly. Many, however, offered explanations that sustained current practice.

The most common explanations put forward by defenders of current practice fit into one of four groups. First, intrapatient dose escalation is not a workable Phase I strategy because it vitiates determination of the agents' acute and chronic toxicities. Although I accepted this explanation as creditable when I first heard it, upon further investigation it became clear that this view is not supported by the literature.[6,28,30,49] Second, newer anticancer agents were unlike the old chemotoxic drugs in that tumor response is not assumed to be roughly proportionate to drug dosage and that, therefore, the problem of predictably undertreating so many patients was soon to be a concern of the past. Although some of the newer agents, such as angiogenesis inhibitors, have anticancer effects at nontoxic levels, arguments regarding noncytotoxic agents do not apply to most of today's Phase I cancer trials. Third, because of our profound ignorance about these new agents, any dose can be considered (equally) potentially therapeutic. Although we are indeed profoundly ignorant about these agents, the little we do know from pre-clinical models is not generally being used in designing and implementing dosing strategies in most of today's trials.[6,20,28,57] Fourth, someone would have already made these changes if they were technically possible. Indeed, this last explanation was what I assumed when I first agreed to become a member of the Phase I clinical team.

What is striking about these explanations (offered by deeply committed and thoughtful professionals) is the way that the perception of technical necessity (to use traditional design) served to abruptly arrest attempts to think through the ethical imperatives in human experimentation. This perception may serve an important function within the Phase I community (or within the broader oncology community), an adverting rationalization that distracts ethical inquiry, looks to a monolithic notion of uncertainty as a way to avoid discussing the morally relevant little we do know, and maintains the status quo. Indeed, the status quo may be resistant to change because of the deeply embedded cultural and psychological function these trials, in their long-standing incarnation, serve. One of these deeply embedded functions may be as an instrument of affect management, as the magic card that referring physicians, physician–investigators, and patients can play together to keep in abeyance difficult and uncomfortable discussions that loom when therapeutic options have been exhausted. Referring physicians can rationalize putting off these difficult matters because the physician–investigator is offering one last hope. Physician–investigators, in a compromised state to speak about the lack of therapeutic options because they have not had the chance to earn the trust of a new recruit, can focus instead on the possibility of benefit to both society and patients. And patients, perhaps in the most compromised position of all to raise difficult questions about their fears and about possible conflicts of interest, can acquiesce in this avoidance and misunderstanding as a way of preserving a desperate hope.

Recommendations for IRB Review

With all these misperceptions, is anything approaching truly informed decision-making possible? As others have noted, many investigators have maintained that truly informed consent is a more difficult problem in clinical research than in usual clinical practice because patient–subjects are even less capable of understanding the additional scientific complexities that a clinical trial seeks to resolve.[41] These investigators are right that it is more difficult to achieve truly informed decision-making in clinical research than in clinical practice, but for the wrong reasons. It is not the recondite nature of scientific complexities that stymies understanding. Indeed, morally relevant information is too readily obscured by an overwhelming amount of unnecessary scientific minutiae. Rather, it is that physician–investigators are susceptible to unwittingly obscure the distinction between their roles as physician and as investigator.

As has been noted, given how little we know about the way fear and illness, being thought incompetent, and being kept ignorant limit a patient's capacity for reflective thought, it would be irresponsible to reach any conclusive judgments about what patients can and cannot understand.[41] This does not, of course, excuse trading on patients' desperate hopes. Perhaps Phase I cancer trials will accrue far more slowly if informed and uncoerced consent is even partially achieved; but that is a price that IRBs are obliged to insist upon in the name of protecting potential subjects' right to self-determination and the inviolability of their bodies. To this end, what can IRBs do? At the very least, IRBs can insist on clarity with regard to two critical aspects of Phase I trials: (1) the dosing strategy proposed, and (2) how investigators plan to assure that participating subjects understand the nature of the sacrifice they are being asked to make. What follows are some specific suggestions.

Require Investigators to Explain and Justify the Dose Schedule

IRBs should require that investigators explicitly justify to the committee whatever dosing schema they propose to use. Investigators should be required to explain why a drug that showed promise in an animal model of a particular cancer (e.g., breast cancer) is to be administered to subjects with cancers unrelated to the animal model in question (e.g., brain tumors). IRBs should reject the use of traditional schemata if the justification rests on any of the fallacious rationalizations laid out in the previous section.

Determine If the Study Agent Is Being Evaluated Simultaneously in Other Centers

IRBs should require that investigators report whether the agent proposed for study is being simultaneously studied in other Phase I centers and, if so, in what way information already known about the agent is going to be incorporated into the current proposal. Phase I research studies that seek to repeat other Phase I trials or are contemporaneous with other trials of the same agent must justify the rationale for repetition and must demonstrate, in the case of contemporaneous trials, how the centers will coordinate their dosing strategies based on daily exchange of shared data. As Katz[41] has written, we must not seek truth when it is already known or progress when it is already a reality.

Reject Justifications for a Phase I Protocol That Are Based on Adjunctive Elements Unrelated to the Research Question

Arguments that the general quality of the medical care that they receive will be higher if they participate in a research study should never offset ethical compromises in research design. Subjects should not participate in a Phase I trial because they benefit from "close follow-up" or have access to "free medical care."

Make Clear the Distinction Between Research and Patient Care

IRBs should reject in all written forms and should discourage, in the consenting dialogue itself, the use of oxymoronic language that serves to blur the distinction between the enterprise of research and the activity of patient-centered care. As Annas[43] has written: "Research is research, designed to test a hypothesis and performed based on the rules of the protocol; treatment is something else, designed to benefit a patient, and subject to change whenever change is seen in the patient's best interest. Confusing research with treatment confuses both the researcher and subject and permits self-interested self-deception by both of them." Examples of words that are likely to compromise the informed consent process include "experimental therapy" and "novel treatment."

Require a Cohort-Specific Consent Document

If cohort-specific escalation is employed, so too should a cohort-specific consenting process and cohort-specific consent form be used. This is based on the broadly agreed-upon notion that subjects of research are entitled to relevant information about purpose and consequent design of the study.[19] Benjamin Freedman has provided a template for such a cohort-specific consent form and for the way the invitation ought to be extended.[40] Freedman's template attempts to clearly explain the structure of the study and where a particular patient–subject fits into that structure—specifically, into which cohort he or she would be enrolled. It attempts to make clear how an individual's dose is cohort-specific. To this I would add the explicit statement that the dose administered is not chosen to maximize the chance of antitumor effect and that, in this way, it differs from alternatives such as second- or third-line chemotherapy. The invitation to participate must, as Freedman urges, make clear to patients that individuals enrolled in the earliest group are least likely to experience severe toxicity (but may nonetheless) and are also least likely to get a dose that is potent against their cancer. His template notes that it is often, but not always, true that the higher the dose, the more powerful are the effects against cancer, but also the more likely to produce unacceptable reactions. Lastly, patients are to be explicitly told that if they agree to enroll, they will be assigned to the *nth* group

of subjects, and told as well what is known about the responses and toxicities experienced by subjects previously enrolled.

Require a Commitment to Eliminating Misconceptions About Risks and Benefits

The principle of respect for persons requires that potential subjects understand the important implications of their decision to participate in research. This principle emphasizes the need to clarify the goals of Phase I trials to the people who are being asked to participate in them. Specifically, potential subjects should be told that Phase I trials are designed to determine toxicity, that severe toxicity is a planned event for a subset of subjects, and that direct benefit is both not intended and extremely unlikely.

As others have cautioned, this fact must not be disguised by drafting a protocol as a combined Phase I/II trial and calling it one of effectiveness and safety on the basis that the endpoint of the second, Phase II component.[40] The President's Commission's comments on Phase I cancer trials emphasize that it is "important that patients who are asked to participate in tests of new anticancer drugs not be misled about the likelihood (or remoteness) of any therapeutic benefit they might derive." In accordance with this emphasis, patients should be told that historically only 1 of 20 subjects has a partial response and that the complete response rate is roughly equal to that of fatal toxicity, 0.5%. Furthermore, patients should also be told that even if their cancer responds to the experimental agent, no one has ever been cured in a Phase I trial, and that any response is expected to be temporary, with most cancers recurring within three to six months. Patients must also be told that although it is possible that response correlates with physical benefit, it is also possible that even the few patient–subjects whose disease responds may not actually derive any benefit either in terms of prolonging life or in improving the quality of life. The recommended standard wording for the consent document in all Phase I studies is presented in Figure 10.13.1.

Purpose: The purpose of this study is to find the highest dose of _____ that people can tolerate without getting extremely ill.

Risks: In this study, the dose of _____ will be increased until people get extremely sick. It is impossible to predict the side-effects that you will experience.

Benefits: This study is not being done to treat your cancer. Based on prior experience, the chance that you will feel better or live longer as a result of participating in this study is almost zero. This study is being done in the hope that it will provide information that will improve the treatment of people in the future.

Figure 10.13.1   Recommended Standard Wording for Consent Document in Phase I Oncology Studies

Evaluate the Quality of Informed Consent

Telling patients what they need to know is not enough. Institutions and researchers must be held accountable not merely for a signature on a consent form, but for some minimal level of patient comprehension. Mandating that specific steps are taken is one approach to improving the consent process. There is, however, a drawback to an *overly* specified series of required steps: it introduces rigidity and diverts attention from creative approaches to achieving informed decision-making. An approach that may prove more effective (especially once fundamental inputs are identified) is to make physicians and institutions accountable not merely for incorporating a limited number of prespecified actions (important as these requirements are), but also for achieving some minimal threshold of patient understanding. Creative efforts will be stimulated, offering the best hope of amelioration, precisely because attention to the consenting *process* is demanded by the challenge to bring about the desired end: adequate patient comprehension.

IRBs ideally should insist on an objective assessment of patient understanding, with a special emphasis on the requirement that patients understand the ways in which their therapeutic interests are possibly opposed by the structure of the trial. The assessment of comprehending consent cannot rest on the signature of the consent form or the good intentions of the informing physician–investigator. To this end, IRBs should require the use (or development) of a validated instrument that assesses patient comprehension, such as the MacArthur Competence Assessment Tool for Clinical Research (MacCAT-CR)[58] or others in the literature.[59] In demanding higher standards of informed consent in clinical research compared with clinical practice, it should be remembered that respect for the subject's right to self-determination requires that he or she know the decision to participate entails making a gift for the sake of others. It is not an act of enlightened self-interest, not a quid pro quo, for these untried agents offer no more objective likelihood of effective anticancer effect than do existing agents that have been deemed unlikely to avail.

It is worth noting that research suggests that informed, uncoerced, voluntary, and understanding decision-making may not be a quixotic goal. Researchers have demonstrated that patients can be taught to recognize that research sometimes conflicts with the goals of ordinary treatment.[60] A technique that proved particularly helpful was to have a third party supplement what investigators disclose to subjects with a "preconsent disclosure." This discussion was led by a third party, distinct from the Phase I team, who was trained to teach potential subjects about critical methodological aspects of the protocol, especially those that might conflict with the principle of personal, individualized care. The authors of this study concluded that there is no reason to think that subjects will refuse to hear clear-cut efforts to dispel the therapeutic misconception. In my experience, patients could recognize that the requirements of Phase I trials were those of science, not of medicine, but only if and when we discussed the way the particular protocol offered undermined fundamental assumptions they held about the doctor–patient relationship. This, however, very often discouraged participation: patients wanted to be given a dose adjusted according to their own needs, as in intrapatient dose escalation schemes, or at least one predicted to have maximal anticancer effect.

References

1. Freedman B. The ethical analysis of clinical trials: New lessons for and from cancer research. In: Vanderpool HY (ed) *The Ethics of Research Involving Human Subjects: Facing the 21st century* (Chapter 13). Frederick, Maryland: Univ. Publishing Group, Inc. 1996: 319–338.

2. Miller M. Phase I cancer trials: A collusion of misunderstanding. *Hastings Cent Rep* 30(4):34–43, 2000.

3. Daugherty C, Ratain MJ, Grochowski E, Stocking C, Kodish E, Mick R, Siegler M. Perceptions of cancer patients and their physicians involved in Phase I trials [published erratum appears in *J Clin Oncol* 1995 Sep;13(9):2476]. *J Clin Oncol* 13(5):1062–1072, 1995.

4. Daugherty CK, Ratain MJ, Minami H, Banik DM, Vogelzang NJ, Stadler W.M., Siegler M. Study of cohort-specific consent and patient control in Phase I cancer trials. *J Clin Oncol* 16(7):2305–2312, 1998.

5. Daugherty CK. Informed consent, the cancer patient, and Phase I clinical trials. *Cancer Treat Res* 102(1):77–89, 2000.

6. Frei E. Clinical trials of antitumor agents: Experimental design and timeline considerations. *Cancer J* 3(3):127–136, 1997.

7. Tomamichel M, Sessa C, Herzig S, de Jong J, Pagani O, Willems Y, Cavalli F. Informed consent for Phase I studies: Evaluation of quantity and quality of information provided to patients. *Ann Oncol* 6(4):363–369, 1995.

8. Yoder LH, O'Rourke TJ, Etnyre A, Spears DT, Brown TD. Expectations and experiences of patients with cancer participating in Phase I clinical trials. *Oncol Nurs Forum* 24(5):891–896, 1997.

9. Rodenhuis S, Van Den Heuvel WJ, Annyas AA, Koops HS, Sleijfer DT, Mulder NH. Patient motivation and informed consent in a Phase I study of an anticancer agent. *Eur J Cancer Clin Oncol* 20(4):457–462, 1984.

10. Willems Y, Sessa C. Informing patients about Phase I trials—How should it be done? *Acta Oncol* 28(1):106–107, 1989.

11. Schaeffer MH, Krantz DS, Wichman A, Masur H, Reed E, Vinicky JK. The impact of disease severity on the informed consent process in clinical research. *Am J Med* 100(3):261–268, 1996.

12. Ratain MJ, Mick R, Schilsky RL, Siegler M. Statistical and ethical issues in the design and conduct of Phase I and II clinical trials of new anticancer agents. *J Natl Cancer Inst* 85(20):1637–1643, 1993.

13. Storer B, DeMets D. Current Phase I/II designs: Are they adequate? *J Clin Res Drug Devel* 1:121–130, 1987.

14. Gordon NH, Wilson JK. Using toxicity grades in the design and analysis of cancer Phase I clinical trials. *Stat Med* 11(16):2063–2075, 1992.

15. Fisher B. Clinical trials for the evaluation of cancer therapy. *Cancer* 54(11 Suppl):2609–2617, 1984.

16. Hawkins MJ. Early cancer clinical trials: safety, numbers, and consent (editorial comment). *J Natl Cancer Inst* 85(20):1618–1619, 1993.

17. Freedman B. A response to a purported ethical difficulty with randomized clinical trials involving cancer patients. *J Clin Ethics* 3(3):231–234, 1992.

18. Decoster G, Stein G, Holdener EE. Responses and toxic deaths in Phase I clinical trials. *Ann Oncol* 1(3):175–181, 1990.

19. Levine RJ. *Ethics and Regulation of Clinical Research,* Ed 2. Baltimore, MD: Urban and Schwarzenberg. 1986.

20. Dent SF, Eisenhauer EA. Phase I trial design: Are new methodologies being put into practice? *Ann Oncol* 7(6):561–566, 1996.

21. Gatsonis C, Greenhouse JB. Bayesian methods for Phase I clinical trials. *Stat Med* 11(10):1377–1389, 1992.

22. Storer BE. Design and analysis of Phase I clinical trials. *Biometrics* 45(3):925–937, 1989.

23. Van Hoff D, Kuh J, Clark G. Design and conduct of Phase I trials. In: Buyse M, Staquet M, Sylvester R (eds). *Cancer Clinical Trials: Methods and Practice.* Oxford: Oxford University Press. 1984.

24. EORTC New Drug Development Committee, Rozencweig M, Staquet M, Hansen H, et al. EORTC guidelines for Phase I trials with single agents in adults. *Eur J Cancer Clin Oncol* 21(9):1005–1007, 1985.

25. Geller NL. Design of Phase I and II clinical trials in cancer: A statistician's view. *Cancer Invest* 2(6):483–491, 1984.

26. Carter SK, Selawry O, Slavik M. Phase I clinical trials. *Natl Cancer Inst Monogr* 45:75–80, 1977.

27. *Cancer: Principles and Practice of Oncology,* Ed 5th. Philadelphia, PA: Lippincott-Raven. 1997.

28. Von Hoff DD. Is response in Phase I trials a useful predictor for the future clinical activity of a new agent? (Abstract). *Ann Oncol* 7(suppl 1): 14, 1996.

29. Decoster G, Cavalli F. Design of Phase I and II clinical trials in cancer: A statisticcian's view. *Cancer Invest* 5(6):649–650, 1987.

30. Mick R, Ratain MJ. Model-guided determination of maximum tolerated dose in Phase I clinical trials: Evidence for increased precision. *J Natl Cancer Inst* 85(3):217–223, 1993.

31. Von Hoff DD, Turner J. Response rates, duration of response, and dose response effects in Phase I studies of antineoplastics. *Invest new Drugs* 9(1):115–122, 1991.

32. Estey E, Hoth D, Wittes R, Marsoni S, Simon R, Leyland-Jones B. Therapeutic response in Phase I trials of antineoplastic agents. *Cancer Treat Rep* 70(9):1105–1115, 1986.

33. Penta JS, Rosner GL, Trump DL. Choice of starting dose and escalation for Phase I studies of antitumor agents. *Cancer Chemother Pharmacol* 31(3):247–250, 1992.

34. Smith TL, Lee JJ, Kantarjian HM, Legha SS, Raber MN. Design and results of Phase I cancer clinical trials: Three-year experience at M.D. Anderson Cancer Center. *J Clin Oncol* 14(1):287–295, 1996.

35. Janisch L, Mick R, Schilsky RL, Vogelzang NJ, O'Brien S, Kut M, Ratain MJ. Prognostic factors for survival in patients treated in Phase I clinical trials. *Cancer* 74(7):1965–1973, 1994.

36. Fried C. *Medical Experimentation: Personal Integrity and Social Policy.* New York: American Elsevier. 1974.

37. Appelbaum PS, Roth LH, Lidz C. The therapeutic misconception: Informed consent in psychiatric research. *Int J Law Psychiatry* 5(3-4):319–329, 1982.

38. Kodish E, Stocking C, Ratain MJ, Kohrman A, Siegler M. Ethical issues in Phase I oncology research: A comparison of investigators and institutional review board chairpersons. *J Clin Oncol* 10(11):1810–1816, 1992.

39. Kass NE, Sugarman J, Faden R, Schoch-Spana M. Trust, the fragile foundation of contemporary biomedical research. *Hastings Cent Rep* 26(5):25–29, 1996.

40. Freedman B. Cohort-specific consent: An honest approach to Phase I clinical cancer studies. *IRB: A Review of Human Subjects Research* 12(1):5–7, 1990.

41. Katz J. Human experimentation and human rights. *St Louis Univ Law Journal* 38:7–54, 1993.

42. Katz JM. "Ethics and clinical research" revisited. A tribute to Henry K. Beecher. *Hastings Cent Rep* 23(5):31–39, 1993.

43. Annas GJ. Questing for grails: Duplicity, betrayal, and self-deception in postmodern medical research. *J Contemp Health Law & Policy* 12(2):297–324, 1996.

44. Katz J. Informed consent—must it remain a fairy tale? *J Contemp Health Law Policy* 10:69–91, 1994.

45. Penman DT, Holland JC, Bahna GF, Morrow G, Schmale AH, Derogatis LR, Carnrike CL, Cherry R. Informed consent for investigational chemotherapy: Patients' and physicians' perceptions. *J Clin Oncol* 2(7):849–855, 1984.

46. O'Quigley J. Sequential design and analysis of dose finding studies in patients with life threatening disease. *Fundam Clin Pharmacol* 4(Suppl 2):81s–91s, 1990.

47. O'Quigley J, Pepe M, Fisher L. Continual reassessment method: A practical design for Phase I clinical trials in cancer. *Biometrics* 46(1):33–48, 1990.

48. O'Quigley J, Chevret S. Methods for dose finding studies in cancer clinical trials: A review and results of a Monte Carlo study. *Stat Med* 10(11):1647–1664, 1991.

49. O'Quigley J. Estimating the probability of toxicity at the recommended dose following a Phase I clinical trial in cancer [Published erratum appears in Biometrics 1994 March;50(1):322]. *Biometrics* 48(3):853–862, 1992.

50. Piantadosi S, Liu G. Improved designs for dose escalation studies using pharmacokinetic measurements. *Stat Med* 15(15):1605–1618, 1996.

51. Mick R, Lane N, Daugherty C, Ratain MJ. Physician-determined patient risk of toxic effects: Impact on enrollment and decision making in Phase I cancer trials. *J Natl Cancer Inst* 86(22):1685–1693, 1994.

52. Moller S. An extension of the continual reassessment methods using a preliminary up-and-down design in a dose finding study in cancer patients, in order to investigate a greater range of doses. *Stat Med* 14(9-10):911–922, 1995.

53. Eichhorn BH, Zacks S. Sequential search for an optimal dosage. *J Am Stat Assoc* 68(343):594–598, 1973.

54. Goodman SN, Zahurak ML, Piantadosi S. Some practical improvements in the continual reassessment method for Phase I studies. *Stat Med* 14(11):1149–1161, 1995.

55. Faries D. Practical modifications of the continual reassessment method for Phase I cancer clinical trials. *J Biopharm Stat* 4(2):147–164, 1994.

56. Hansen HH, Selawry OS, Muggia FM, Walker MD. Clinical studies with 1-(2-chloroethyl)-3-cyclohexyl-1-nitrosourea (NSC 79037). *Cancer Res* 31(3):223–227, 1971.

57. Eisenhauer EA. Phase I and II trials of novel anti-cancer agents: Endpoints, efficacy and existentialism. *Ann Oncol* 9(10):1047–1052, 1998.

58. Applebaum PS, Grisso T. The MacArthur Treatment Competence Study: Mental illness and competence to consent to treatment. *Law Hum Behav* 19:105–126, 1995.

59. Joffe S, Cook EF, Cleary PD, Clark JW, Weeks JC. Quality of informed consent: A new measure of understanding among research subjects. *J Natl Cancer Inst* 93(2):139–147, 2001.

60. Appelbaum PS, Roth LH, Lidz CW, Benson P, Winslade W. False hopes and best data: Consent to research and the therapeutic misconception. *Hastings Cent Rep* 17(2):20–24, 1987.

Research Involving Genetic Testing

Eric C. Larsen

INTRODUCTION

The rapid pace of genetic research creates unique challenges to the IRB review process. The dramatic progress in our understanding of the genetic basis of health and disease raises a number of key regulatory issues.[1-5] This chapter focuses on the issues that are important to consider when the IRB reviews genetic research studies.

When discussing genetic research, it is important to understand the difference between the study of *constitutional* (also called *host*) genes, meaning the genes common to all normal tissues in the body, and the study of genetic material from the pathologic tissue of humans, such as malignancies. Research on constitutional genes is likely to involve sensitive information about research participants and demand careful IRB review. An example of this type of research is the determination of the expression of certain genes that result in the subsequent development of a serious medical illness. The information collected in such a study clearly has potential for psychological and financial harm to research participants. In contrast, genetic research involving pathologic human tissue rarely poses risk to participants because genetic abnormalities in this setting are usually not representative of the subject's underlying genetic makeup. An example of genetic research with pathologic tissue is the study of the relationship between gene expression in tumor tissue with clinical outcome. This type of research poses almost no risk (and no direct benefit) to the participant.

Genetic research typically presents risks of social and psychological harm to participants rather than risks of physical harm. There are several areas in genetic research that pose challenges to the IRB process, including selection of participants, confidentiality, disclosure of information, storage of data and samples, and participant withdrawal.

Selection of Participants

Certain genetic research studies involve the investigations of individuals within a certain family pedigree or a certain social or ethnic group. The design of these studies may place undue influence on an individual's decision to participate in the study. An example of this is the analysis of the types of mutations of the Von Willebrand gene in large kindred affected by severe clinical bleeding. There will be an attempt to include all family members because the more complete the pedigree is, the more useful the resulting information will be. Family members who are not interested in participating will likely experience pressure to participate in order to enhance the quality of the study. At this point, the decision not to participate affects more than just the individual. The federal regulations provide little guidance in this situation: "Selection of subjects is equitable."[6[Sec.111(a)(3)]] "An investigator shall seek such consent only under circumstances that provide the prospective subject or the representative sufficient opportunity to consider whether or not to participate and that minimize the possibility of coercion or undue influence."[6(Sec.116)] The IRB review of pedigree studies must take into account the potential coercion of family members and be aware of alternative recruitment strategies.

Confidentiality and Privacy

Privacy and confidentiality issues are perhaps the most challenging regulatory aspects of genetic research. Because of the sensitive nature of the information that may be generated from genetic research studies, it is critical that investigators establish a method to secure information in a highly confidential manner. Studies that have the potential to ultimately predict the likelihood of subsequent serious illness could place participants at high risk for psychological and social harm. This type of sensitive information could adversely affect an individual's future insurability and employability as well as have significant impact on his or her psychological well being. For example, consider the study of the expression of a particular gene that places individuals at a very high risk of developing colon cancer at a young age. Personal knowledge of this finding presents a psychological burden on the individual, and disclosure of this information could affect one's ability to obtain medical insurance and/or employment. The regulation[6][Sec.111(a)(6)] states, "When appropriate, the research plan makes adequate provisions to protect the privacy of subjects and to maintain the confidentiality of data." Whereas confidentiality of research data is important in all studies, it is particularly crucial in genetic research studies because of the sensitivity of the data. Thus, IRB review must be scrupulous in assuring that privacy and confidentiality are always maintained.

Disclosure of Information

As genetic research may yield information of the most private nature, the IRB and potential research subject must understand exactly who will have access to study information and under what circumstances. This issue of disclosing research results to the subject should be explicitly addressed in the protocol application and consent document. This topic is the subject of Chapter 6–10. Investigators and IRBs have to weigh the risks and benefits of giving a subject access to research results. There are many different scenarios to consider. Something that may be overlooked is the possibility that the disclosure of unanticipated or incidental information may harm the subject. A common example of an incidental finding in genetic research that may have serious consequences is the finding that family members are not biologically related. During the informed consent process, potential participants should always be given the opportunity not to receive information, if they so desire.

An additional important consideration is the potential need for genetic counseling. There are situations in which genetic counseling is appropriate for participants involved in genetic research studies. It is impossible to clearly define the situations for which counseling is indicated, but IRBs should consider the potential benefits of genetic counseling to participants in these studies.

Secure Storage of Data and Tissue Samples

Genetic studies often involve the use of tissue or cell banks that may involve the long-term storage of biological materials.[7,8] In some studies, the precise nature of subsequent experiments on banked samples is not clear and/or not disclosed to the participant at the time of banking. Because the results of these studies may pose harm to individuals as outlined above, it is crucial that participants be fully informed about their subsequent knowledge of research results. For example, a study banks tissue on participants as an optional part of the study; in the future, these samples are screened for the expression of a gene that predicts for alcoholism. Clearly, the results of this subsequent study, which is conceived and carried out long after the actual collection of samples, carries substantial social and financial risk to the participants. Whenever possible, genetic test results should be stored in a secure manner. When participants are informed, there is really no way to make genetic samples completely anonymous. During the informed consent process, it is critical that participants understand both the inherent risk of this type of research and, if it is the case, that they will not be informed of the results of subsequent studies performed on their tissue. IRB management of studies that involve the storage of tissue for future research is the subject of Chapter 10-9.

Participant Withdrawal

Ethical research requires that subjects have the right to withdraw from research participation at any point in the study. In genetic research, there is the potential for continuation of individual risk after withdrawal from the study when there is long-term storage of tissue. For this reason, it is important to determine if the research plan provides for the destruction of all stored data and tissue if the subject wants this to be done. If the research plan does not provide for tissue or data destruction, the study may still be ethical as long as participants understand this limitation.

IRB Evaluation of Genetic Research Studies

A critical first step in the IRB review process of genetic studies is the determination of the predictive value of the study results. This determination should be made through an interactive dialogue between the IRB and the investigator. If there is reasonable scientific evidence that the expression of certain genetic markers within a study accurately predicts for a particular disease or condition, then participants are at risk, and the IRB must know the answers to a detailed list of questions before a determination can be made (see Appendix). Alternatively, if there is no clear evidence that a particular marker has predictive value, then there is virtually no risk to participants. At Dartmouth, questions about genetic testing are included as an attachment to the general IRB application package. When a study involves genetic testing, the principal investigator is first asked to make a determination about the predictive value of the genetic tests that will be done as part of the project. An investigator who thinks that the genetic testing is clinically useful in predicting the development of disease (answer "b" in the first section of the Appendix.) is required to go on to the second part of the Appendix, which is a detailed list of questions related to the risk of research participation. This list of questions is adapted from the OHRP *IRB Guidebook*.[3(Chap. 5H)] The third section of the appendix guides both the investigator and IRB in identifying the information that must be included in the consent document when research involves tests for markers that clearly predict the development of disease.

References

1. Allen HJ. Genetic protocols review by institutional review boards at National Cancer Institute-designated Cancer Centers. *Genetic Testing* 2(4):329–335, 1998.

2. American Society of Human Genetics. Statement on informed consent for genetic research. *Am J Hum Genet* 59(2):471–474, 1996.

3. Penslar RL, Porter JP, Office for Human Research Protections. *Institutional Review Board Guidebook,* ed. 2. Updated 6 Feb 2001. Access date 29 Mar 2001. World Wide Web http://ohrp.osophs.dhhs.gov/irb irb_guidebook.htm

4. Reilly PR, Boshar MF, Holtzman SH. Ethical issues in genetic research: Disclosure and informed consent. *Nature Genetics* 15(4):16–20, 1997.

5. Weir RF, Horton JR. Genetic research, adolescents, and informed consent. *Theoretical Medicine* 16(4):347–373, 1995.

6. Code of Federal Regulations. Title 45A—Department of Health and Human Services; Part 46—Protection of Human Subjects. Updated 1 Oct 1997. Access date 18 Apr 2001. World Wide Web http:www4.law.cornell.edu/cfr/45p46.htm

7. Clayton EW, Steinberg KK, Khoury MJ, Thomson E, Andrews L, Kahn MS, Kopelman LM, Weiss JD. Informed consent for genetic research on stored tissue samples. *JAMA* 274(22):1786–1792, 1995.

8. Knoppers BM, Laberge CM. Research and stored tissues: Persons as sources, samples as persons: *JAMA* 274(2):1806–1807, 1995.

Appendix

A Questionnaire For Research Involving Genetic Testing

For research studies involving genetic testing, the IRB has developed two basic categories to assist in the determination of further review. The researcher should determine if the research falls into category (a) or (b) as described below. If the research falls into category (a), indicate by circling below, and add comments as appropriate to this project. If the research falls into category (b), please respond to questions that follow.

(a) The study is looking for an association between a genetic marker and a specific disease or condition, but at this point it is not clear if the genetic marker has predictive value. The uncertainty regarding the predictive value of the genetic marker is such that studies in this category will not involve genetic counseling of participants.

COMMENT:

(b) The study is based on the premise that a link between a genetic marker and a specific disease or condition is such that the marker *is* clinically useful in predicting the development of that specific disease or condition (e.g., the gene that predicts the development of Huntington's Chorea). Respond to the questions on the list entitled "Human Genetic Research Questions for IRB Review."

Human Genetic Research Questions for IRB Review

For studies involving genetic testing, the PI must respond to the following items. If an item is not applicable to the study, please write "NA".

1. Are clear guidelines established for disclosure to participants of interim or inconclusive research results?
2. Will participants be informed of research results (and their meaning) at each point in the research? If not, is this clearly explained to them in the consent document?
3. If information is discovered about the participant that may have implications for biologic family members, what are the plans to protect confidentiality?
4. Will limits on such protections be clearly communicated to participants, including obtaining advance consent to such disclosures (e.g., when family members will be warned about health risks)?
5. Will the possible psychological and social risks of genetic research be adequately considered in the consent process?
6. Will appropriate counseling be provided, both as part of the consent process and when communicating test or other research results to participants?
7. Will participants be informed about the possibility of important incidental findings such as paternity, disease, or conditions other than the one(s) that is/are the focus of the study?
8. Will the data be protected from disclosure to third parties, such as employers and insurance companies?
9. Will the participant be told about the potential consequences if a third party, such as employer or insurance company, becomes aware of the study findings?
10. Will the data be stored in a secure manner?
11. Will the data be coded so as to protect the identity of subjects?
12. Is a request for a certificate of confidentiality appropriate?
13. Does the investigator plan to disclose research findings to subjects' physicians for clinical use? Are such plans appropriate?

(Continued)

14. Will the possibility of such disclosures be discussed in the consent process with prospective participants?

15. Will vulnerable populations (e.g., children, persons with impaired mental capacities) be adequately protected?

16. Under what circumstances can a research participant give permission to involve a minor or an adult who lacks decision-making capacity in an aspect of this study?

17. What are the provisions for protecting the confidentiality of tissue samples?

18. What procedures will be used to get the subjects' permission to store tissue or data for additional research in the future or for nonresearch medical practice?

19. What will happen to research data and tissue if a subject elects to withdraw from the study? Do subjects have the option of having all data and tissue related to this study destroyed?

20. Are the implications of study withdrawal in terms of destruction or use of established data or tissue clearly explained in the consent document?

21. Do the plans to publish or present data from this study threaten the privacy or confidentiality of participants?

22. If research may involve family members:

    (a) Is the strategy for recruiting family members sensitive to privacy and confidentiality issues?

    (b) Will information be obtained from the medical records of family members?

    (c) If so, should consent be obtained from the family members to access this information?

Information to Be Included in the Consent Document

- Clearly explain whether the subjects will have access to information obtained as part of this study. Explain what information they will be given whether they ask for it or not.

- Explain if subjects may learn things about themselves or their family that they do not want to know, or that they may be uncomfortable knowing.

- Explain if family members may learn about information generated in this study and the potential implications of this knowledge.

- Explain if participation in this study may compromise the subjects' insurability.

- Explain if participation in the study may prompt the subject to take actions that may incur unanticipated costs or expose the subject to additional risks. For example, genetic counseling may be expensive. If participation in the study creates the need for the subject to seek genetic counseling, this may be a financial hardship, and submitting a claim for these costs to an insurance company may compromise insurability.

- Accurately describe the limitations of protection of privacy and confidentiality.

- Explain what it means to withdraw from this study in terms of the destruction or use of data or tissue related to the study.

- Include an appropriately detailed explanation of all costs that are likely to be incurred by the subject or family members as a result of participation in the study. Address both the costs of procedures required by the study and costs, like genetic counseling, additional genetic testing, or psychological counseling, that the subject or family may be advised to pay based on study results.

International Research

David A. Borasky

INTRODUCTION

It is currently not unusual for Institutional Review Boards (IRBs) to review research proposed for international settings. Much of the new research is in less developed countries, where investigators have limited experience with U.S. sponsored studies, potential research participants are unfamiliar with concepts such as informed consent, and institutions have not established strong human-subjects protection programs. In addition, some studies, such as the placebo-controlled HIV prevention trials in Sub-Saharan Africa, sparked a firestorm of criticism both within the research community and among IRBs. As a result, international research is the focus of a great deal of scrutiny. IRBs must be continuously vigilant when reviewing research intended for international settings.

Because of these heightened sensitivities, mechanisms for the protection of international research subjects have been strengthened. The Declaration of Helsinki was revised in 2000, and the National Bioethics Advisory Commission (NBAC) in April 2001 completed a report on issues in international research.[1] A copy of the Declaration of Helsinki[2] is included in Part 11 of this book. More recently, the Office for Human Research Protections (OHRP) has revised the assurance process, replacing the single-project assurance with a federalwide assurance (FWA) that allows foreign research institutions to rely on procedural standards other than 45 CFR 46.[3] This chapter is intended to guide IRBs through the process of reviewing international research, beginning before IRB review and following through the review process to the end of the study.

Before IRB Review

For an IRB that has received its first international research proposal, there can be feelings of trepidation on the part of the staff and membership. Before the first reviewer receives the proposal, there are several questions that should be answered up front. Taking correct steps in the beginning will save time and effort in the long run. The following questions will help steer the IRB in the right direction.

Does Your Institution Hold a Multiple-Project Assurance or FWA?

If the answer is yes, then the proposed research site(s) will most likely need to file an FWA application. Instructions and templates are available on the OHRP Registration and Assurance Filing Web page.[3]

Does a U.S. Department or Agency Fund the Research?

If the answer is yes, then it is probable that the institution will need to file a FWA. Check with the funding officer for the project and/or contact the OHRP assurance manager for your geographic region. Assurance coordinator assignments are listed on the OHRP Web page.[3]

Is Your IRB Qualified to Review the Proposal?

This question is particularly important if your IRB will be the only one reviewing the proposal. An FWA requires an institution to name a designated IRB. OHRP expects the designated IRB to have knowledge of the local research context.[4] This is important because the local research environment and the characteristics of the subjects being enrolled can vary greatly. The level of local knowledge required by OHRP is based in part on the degree of risk presented by the research. For example, if the research involves minimal risk to subjects, the IRB should demonstrate that it has obtained necessary information about the local research context through written materials or discussions with appropriate consultants. As the level of risk increases, the steps an IRB must take to demonstrate local knowledge also increase. Additional steps might include adding a consultant to the IRB who is familiar with the research location, or sending IRB members on regular visits to the research site.

Local IRBs

In many cases, it is required that a local IRB review the proposal. This may be due to policies of the host institution or local regulations, or a requirement of OHRP or the research sponsor. In more experienced institutions, there will be an established review system in place, but if you are working with an independent investigator or a smaller institution, you may have to search for an appropriate local IRB. (Note that the term "IRB" is not widely used outside the United States In foreign countries, the IRB may be known as the Ethics Committee, the Research Ethics Committee, the Ethical Review Committee, etc.) If you are having trouble finding a local IRB, you might look at nearby universities or research centers, government agencies such as the local ministry of health, or U.S. agencies with international experience (such as OHRP). Be aware that the infrastructure for ethical review can vary greatly, and the quality of review may vary as well.

Reviewing the Proposal

When reviewing the proposal, the IRB must be aware of local conditions and situations that may impact the design and implementation of the research. For example, local regulations governing research with minors can vary from country to country (just as they can vary by state in the United States). Also, local social and political conditions may distort the way informed consent documents are viewed by foreign participants, and a request for a subject's signature may be viewed with suspicion. Also, offering monetary compensation or access to health care may be coercive in certain research settings. The IRB should be prepared to bring in a consultant if sufficient knowledge of the local context is lacking. In addition, the IRB must be sure that all of its questions are satisfactorily answered before granting approval. Finally, the IRB is encouraged to review informed consent document translations for accuracy. The original approved English version and the back-translation should be compared, and major discrepancies should be addressed.

Monitoring Approved Research

Once research is approved, IRBs that are responsible for international projects need effective mechanisms for ongoing review of research. IRB administrators should work closely with their own research staff to assure reliable access to collaborating investigators in the field. Regular correspondence between the field investigator and the IRB should be maintained. Because many foreign IRBs do not have continuing review requirements, foreign investigators should be informed of this requirement and any other related responsibilities. In addition, adverse event reporting requirements should be made clear so that IRBs receive required information in a timely manner. Any problems encountered with a foreign investigator should be reported to the study sponsor, relevant regulatory bodies, and, when applicable, to all reviewing IRBs for the project.

Conclusion

Reviewing international research is a challenge for any IRB. Problems that are considered routine for domestic IRBs can become much more complicated when encountered in an international setting. One example is the new education and training requirement for investigators and research staff, which may be difficult to implement in less-developed countries where access to on-line resources is limited or where English is not the primary language. IRBs should move forward with caution, and should take advantage of resources such as ARENA and the IRB Forum (formerly MCWIRB) when looking for answers to difficult questions.

References

1. National Bioethics Advisory Commission. Ethical and policy issues in international research: Clinical trials in developing countries. Updated 18 Apr 2001. Access date 3 Sep 2001. World Wide Web http:bioethics.gov/clinical/Vol1.pdf

2. World Medical Association. *Declaration of Helsinki: Ethical Principles for Medical Research Involving Human Subjects.* First adopted in Helsinki, Finland, in 1964. Updated 10 Jul 2000. Access date 2 Sep 2001. World Wide Web http://www.wma.net/e/policy/17-c_e.html

3. Office for Human Research Protections. Procedures for registering institutional review boards and filing federalwide assurances of protection for human subjects (FWAs). Updated 22 Aug 2001. Access date 3 Sep 2001. World Wide Web http://ohrp.osophs.dhhs.gov/polasur.htm

4. Office for Protection from Research Risks. Knowledge of local research context. Updated 27 Aug 1998. Access date 3 Sep 2001. World Wide Web http://ohrp.osophs.dhhs.gov/humansubjects/guidance/local.htm

Alternative Medicine Research

Timothy Callahan

INTRODUCTION

In this chapter, I will briefly survey the terrain of complementary and alternative medicine, indicating some areas of contemporary discussion and disagreement as to what constitutes the parameters of the field. As complementary and alternative medical practices become more popular in the United States and are being used by an increasing percentage of the population, they are coming under greater scrutiny. The American public is demanding unfettered access to insurance reimbursement for therapies whose safety and effectiveness may be as yet unknown. Evaluation of these practices has begun to move from collections of anecdotes and testimonials to established methods of scientific inquiry, including controlled research studies involving the use of human subjects. As more medical professionals begin to practice in an "integrative" fashion, there is an increased need for focused research on alternative therapies and modalities.

With the establishment of the National Center for Complementary and Alternative Medicine (NCCAM) at the National Institutes of Health (NIH) in 1998,[1] the federal government is supporting examination of alternative medical practices through an increased budget for competitive research proposals. From a research budget of $2 million in 1992 under the Office of Alternative Medicine to an FY 2000 budget of $68.3 million under NCCAM, efforts have grown exponentially in the past decade. These efforts are being used to investigate various practices that Americans are seeking out and using in record numbers. According to a widely publicized 1998 study, as many as 42% of Americans currently use one or more medical practices labeled as "alternative" by the medical establishment.[2] As more research institutions compete for available funds, their Institutional Review Boards (IRBs) will have to consider the safety of these interventions, modalities, and practices along with risks and benefits to subjects and society. This task is complicated by a relative lack of information available to IRBs about many alternative treatment modalities and substances. I will not attempt to provide definitive answers to questions of safety regarding particular interventions, such as acupuncture or bodywork, or ingestible substances, such as herbs or vitamins. However, I will attempt to provide a framework for IRB members to approach their task of evaluating complementary and alternative medical research proposals.

The Present Scope of Complementary and Alternative Medicine

The field of complementary and alternative medicine, often referred to as CAM, is a somewhat nebulous area of medicine. Medical practices labeled "alternative" are generally those that are not accepted or practiced by adherents of the allopathic model currently dominant in Western medicine. Many such alternative modalities have been practiced for centuries, such as traditional Chinese medicine (China, Japan, Korea), Ayurvedic medicine (India, Sri Lanka, Nepal), and Tibetan medicine (Tibet). Alternative medical practices generally do not fit into the standard Western biomedical model. Many practices are labeled as folk medicine, unproven, controversial, fraudulent, quackery, unscientific, and questionable by conventional medical practitioners.[3]

There is considerable disagreement in the literature as to what practices comprise the field of CAM. Some have noted that "alternative medicine is defined as consisting of medical interventions not taught widely at U.S. medical schools or generally available at U.S. hospitals."[4] Others have claimed, "There is no alternative medicine. There is only scientifically proven, evidence-based medicine supported by solid data or unproven medicine, for which scientific evidence is lacking."[5] No widespread agreement exists as to what actually constitutes the area of alternative medicine. Clearly, numerous practices and modalities ranging from acupuncture, massage, yoga, and chiropractic to distance healing, biofeedback, and therapeutic touch have practitioners and adherents worldwide. Nevertheless, these practices are not embraced or even accepted by the dominant Western medical orthodoxy. Although CAM practitioners practice a wide range of healing modalities that encompass incredible diversity, most practitioners do hold some common beliefs. These include the belief that the human body possesses innate healing powers; that religious and spiritual values are important determinants of health; and that physical, mental, emotional, and psychosocial aspects of an individual must be considered in the context of the whole individual and his or her particular condition or illness.[3]

Current Research Projects

Current NCCAM-supported research projects include investigation of acupuncture in the treatment of dental pain, back pain, depression, fibromyalgia, and hypertension. Also funded are investigations of the role of ginseng in the treatment of diabetes, melatonin for sleep disorders, high dose vitamin E for atherosclerosis, and St. John's wort for juvenile depression. There are also numerous other funded centers dedicated to investigation of a broad variety of alternative interventions into specific populations such as women, children, the elderly, and HIV-positive individuals. Individual investigators with a wide variety of backgrounds and levels of experience perform most federally funded CAM research at conventional medical institutions, although some funding has been awarded to colleges and universities specializing in CAM.

CAM Research and the IRB Process

Although CAM research presents the opportunity for IRB members to review many new and perhaps unfamiliar conceptual issues in medical research, the IRB process itself does not have to be modified to meet the demands of reviewing proposals intending to use human subjects in studies of various CAM therapies. At Bastyr University, the largest accredited, science-based, natural medicine university in the country, our IRB has had the opportunity to review a wide variety of CAM proposals. Our review process adheres to the regulations established in 45 CFR 46 and is thus the same as at any medical research institution that receives federal funding. The IRB is constituted according to the regulatory guidelines and meets regularly to consider full proposals, renewals, and reports on expedited reviews.

We have, however, added a few more steps to make the human-subjects review process more robust and meaningful in the context of our institution. For example, we have instituted a research seminar in which prospective principal investigators have an opportunity to present their research ideas to the community in a collegial fashion. They can get feedback, form collaborations, and generate discussion of possible future research agendas. In addition, we have instituted a scientific review committee that is charged with evaluating the scientific merit of proposals before they are sent out to granting agencies. Research proposals are generated both in response to NCCAM funding cycles as well as industry-sponsored research agendas, and we found that the IRB required additional support and expertise in evaluating the scientific merit of proposed research. These two stages of research seminar presentation and focused scientific merit review support the work of the IRB as the committee strives to determine the risks and benefits of participation for potential subjects.

Review of Proposals Involving Substances Not Controlled by the Food and Drug Administration

Many substances commonly used in complementary and alternative medicine, such as herbs and other botanicals, vitamins, minerals, and amino acids, are not regulated by the Food and Drug Administration (FDA). They are considered to be dietary supplements, as determined by the 1990 Nutrition Labeling and Education Act and further defined by the 1994 Dietary Supplement Health and Education Act. Under these acts, herbal and other dietary supplement manufacturers cannot make specific health claims regarding the ability of the supplement to treat or cure a specific disease in most cases. However, the product label may indicate "the supplement's effects on 'structure or function' of the body or the 'well-being' achieved by consuming the dietary ingredient."[6] Manufacturers must be able to substantiate the truth of any such statements and specifically state that the FDA has not evaluated any such claims. However, specific health claims may be made on product labels in certain cases, if previously approved by the FDA, as is the case with the claim that the use of calcium may reduce the risk of osteoporosis.

IRB committees that are more familiar with evaluating the use of investigational new drug applications (INDs) in studies sponsored by pharmaceutical companies may be unsure how to approach the evaluation of products that are not required to undergo comprehensive testing by the FDA. Package inserts are not necessarily available for most herbs and nutritional supplements. IRB members at conventional research institutions may have had no experience with evaluating homeopathic medicines or ultrahigh dilutions of FDA-approved drugs such as interleukin-2.

Steps Preceding Evaluation

In the absence of recognized expertise on the IRB, the committee should perhaps take a few preliminary steps before evaluating any such proposals. First, it should make sure that the investigator has done the appropriate background research to ascertain whether the study substance in question is indeed subject to FDA regulation. If it is, FDA procedures should be followed. If it is not, the investigator should be asked to provide available evidence of use of that substance in humans and/or animals in previous research studies. If there is no available evidence for the safety of a herbal product, for example, perhaps the committee should look carefully at the scale of the trial. This is to determine whether a pilot study may be more appropriate to investigate the substance in question. In the case of Chinese herbal medicines, they are usually purchased in bulk from a Chinese herbal dispensary, and the IRB may rightly have concerns about the purity, consistency, and potency of the herbs. The investigator should be responsible for providing evidence regarding methods of cultivating and processing the herbs in question. It may be helpful to consult with a pharmacologist and/or pharmacist to obtain the needed expertise if the IRB has questions about potential drug–herb interactions.

Perhaps a research forum could be organized to provide the scientific community, including the IRB, with relevant background information to familiarize the community with the proposed new area of research. If a separate scientific review committee is utilized to support the work of the IRB, that group may wish to hear from experts in the field of study under consideration. If the IRB approaches unfamiliar areas of proposed research with an openness to learning about different or perhaps unfamiliar medical paradigms, they may find their human subjects review experience to be more rewarding than frustrating. There are several good references available on complementary and alternative medicine that can help to educate and inform IRB members.[7-12]

Conclusion

Complementary and alternative medicine practices have become quite popular with the American public in the past decade. Some practitioners have begun to move toward an integrative model whereby CAM practices that have been shown to be efficacious are being adopted into mainstream medicine. As more research is initiated on CAM therapies at major medical institutions, IRB members face new challenges in evaluating the risks and benefits of proposed research studies. In the absence of FDA jurisdiction over many of the substances used in CAM therapies, IRB mem-

bers need to become educated about the nature of the proposed interventions. They will also need to work closely with principal investigators to gain the appropriate information required to make an informed judgment about the potential impact on human subjects of participation in the proposed study. This is part of the ongoing effort to protect human subjects of research from harm.

References

1. National Institutes of Health. National Center for Complementary and Alternative Medicine. Updated 4 May 2001. Access date 15 May 2001. World Wide Web http://nccam.nih.gov/

2. Eisenberg DM, Davis RB, Ettner SL, Appel S, Wilkey S, VanRompay M, Kessler RC. Trends in alternative medicine use in the United States, 1990–1997: Results of a follow-up national survey. *JAMA* 280(18):1569–1575, 1998.

3. Patel V. Understanding the integration of alternative modalities into an emerging healthcare model in the United States. In: Humber JM, Almeder RF (eds). *Alternative Medicine and Ethics*. Totowa, NJ: Humana Press. 1998: 46–48.

4. Eisenberg DM, Kessler RC, Foster C, Norlock FE, Calkins DR, Delbanco TL. Unconventional medicine in the United States: Prevalence, costs, and patterns of use. *N Engl J Med* 328(4):246–252, 1993.

5. Fontanarosa PB, Lundberg GD. Alternative medicine meets science. *JAMA* 280(18):1618–1619, 1998.

6. Food and Drug Administration. The Dietary Supplement Health and Education Act of 1994. Updated 27 Nov 2000. Access date 27 Mar 2001. World Wide Web http://vm.cfsan.fda.gov/~dms/dietsupp.html

7. Murray M, Pizzorno J. *Encyclopedia of Natural Medicine*. Rocklin, CA: Prima Publishing. 1990.

8. Collinge W. *The American Holistic Health Association Complete Guide to Alternative Medicine*. New York: Warner Books. 1996.

9. Humber JM, Almeder RF (eds). *Alternative Medicine and Ethics*. Totowa, NJ: Humana Press. 1998.

10. Spencer J. (ed). *Complementary Medicine: An Integrated Approach*. St. Louis: Mosby Year Books. 1999.

11. Spencer JW, Jacobs JJ. *Complementary/Alternative Medicine: An Evidence-Based Approach*. St. Louis: Mosby. 1999.

12. Cohen MH. *Complementary and Alternative Medicine: Legal Boundaries and Regulatory Perspectives*. Baltimore: Johns Hopkins University Press. 1998.

PART 11

Reference Material and Contact Information*

*Compiled by Elizabeth Bankert with assistance from the office of Public Responsibility and Medicine in Research (PRIMR) and Applied Research Ethics National Association (ARENA)

Ethical Codes

The Nuremberg Code
Web site: http://ohrp.osophs.dhhs.gov/irb/irb_appendices.htm
Note: Full text attached

The Belmont Report
Ethical Principles and Guidelines for the Protection of Human Subjects of Research
The National Commission for the Protection of Human Subjects of Biomedical and Behavioral Research. April 18, 1979
Web site: http://ohrp.osophs.dhhs.gov/humansubjects/guidance/belmont.htm
Note: Full text attached

The World Medical Association Declaration of Helsinki
Web site: http://www.wma.net/e/policy/17-c_e.html
Note: Full text attached

The Nuremberg Code

[From Trials of War Criminals before the Nuremberg Military Tribunals under Control Council Law No. 10. Vol. 2, Nuremberg, October 1946–April 1949. Washington D.C.: U.S. G.P.O., 1949–1953. pp. 181-182.]

Permissible Medical Experiments

The great weight of the evidence before us is to the effect that certain types of medical experiments on human beings, when kept within reasonably well-defined bounds, conform to the ethics of the medical profession generally. The protagonists of the practice of human experimentation justify their views on the basis that such experiments yield results for the good of society that are unprocurable by other methods or means of study. All agree, however, that certain basic principles must be observed in order to satisfy moral, ethical and legal concepts:

1. The voluntary consent of the human subject is absolutely essential.

   This means that the person involved should have legal capacity to give consent; should be so situated as to be able to exercise free power of choice, without the intervention of any element of force, fraud, deceit, duress, over-reaching, or other ulterior form of constraint or coercion; and should have sufficient knowledge and comprehension of the elements of the subject matter involved as to enable him to make an understanding and enlightened decision. This latter element requires that before the acceptance of an affirmative decision by the experimental subject there should be made known to him the nature, duration, and purpose of the experiment; the method and means by which it is to be conducted; all inconveniences and hazards reasonably to be expected; and the effects upon his health or person which may possibly come from his participation in the experiment.

   The duty and responsibility for ascertaining the quality of the consent rests upon each individual who initiates, directs or engages in the experiment. It is a personal duty and responsibility which may not be delegated to another with impunity.

2. The experiment should be such as to yield fruitful results for the good of society, unprocurable by other methods or means of study, and not random and unnecessary in nature.

3. The experiment should be so designed and based on the results of animal experimentation and a knowledge of the natural history of the disease or other problem under study that the anticipated results will justify the performance of the experiment.

4. The experiment should be so conducted as to avoid all unnecessary physical and mental suffering and injury.

5. No experiment should be conducted where there is an a priori reason to believe that death or disabling injury will occur; except, perhaps, in those experiments where the experimental physicians also serve as subjects.

6. The degree of risk to be taken should never exceed that determined by the humanitarian importance of the problem to be solved by the experiment.

7. Proper preparations should be made and adequate facilities provided to protect the experimental subject against even remote possibilities of injury, disability, or death.

8. The experiment should be conducted only by scientifically qualified persons. The highest degree of skill and care should be required through all stages of the experiment of those who conduct or engage in the experiment.

9. During the course of the experiment the human subject should be at liberty to bring the experiment to an end if he has reached the physical or mental state where continuation of the experiment seems to him to be impossible.

10. During the course of the experiment the scientist in charge must be prepared to terminate the experiment at any stage, if he has probably cause to believe, in the exercise of the good faith, superior skill and careful judgment required of him that a continuation of the experiment is likely to result in injury, disability, or death to the experimental subject.

Of the ten principles which have been enumerated our judicial concern, of course, is with those requirements which are purely legal in nature—or which at least are so clearly related to matters legal that they assist us in determining criminal culpability and punishment. To go beyond that point would lead us into a field that would be beyond our sphere of competence. However, the point need not be labored. We find from the evidence that in the medical experiments which have been proved, these ten principles were much more frequently honored in their breach than in their observance. Many of the concentration camp inmates who were the victims of these atrocities were citizens of countries other than the German Reich. They were non-German nationals, including Jews and "asocial persons", both prisoners of war and civilians, who had been imprisoned and forced to submit to these tortures and barbarities without so much as a semblance of trial. In every single instance appearing in the record, subjects were used who did not consent to the experiments; indeed, as to some of the experiments, it is not even contended by the defendants that the subjects occupied the status of volunteers. In no case was the experimental subject at liberty of his own free choice to withdraw from any experiment. In many cases experiments were performed by unqualified persons; were conducted at random for no adequate scientific reason, and under revolting physical conditions. All of the experiments were conducted with unnecessary suffering and injury and but very little, if any, precautions were taken to protect or safeguard the human subjects from the possibilities of injury, disability, or death. In every one of the experiments the subjects experienced extreme pain or torture, and in most of them they suffered permanent injury, mutilation, or death, either as a direct result of the experiments or because of lack of adequate follow-up care.

Obviously all of these experiments involving brutalities, tortures, disabling injury, and death were performed in complete disregard of international conventions, the laws and customs of war, the general principles of criminal law as derived from the criminal laws of all civilized nations, and Control Council Law No. 10. Manifestly human experiments under such conditions are contrary to "the principles of the law of nations as they result from the usages established among civilized peoples, from the laws of humanity, and from the dictates of public conscience."

The Belmont Report

OFFICE OF THE SECRETARY
ETHICAL PRINCIPLES AND GUIDELINES
FOR THE PROTECTION OF HUMAN
SUBJECTS OF RESEARCH
THE NATIONAL COMMISSION FOR THE PROTECTION
OF HUMAN SUBJECTS
OF BIOMEDICAL AND BEHAVIORAL RESEARCH
APRIL 18, 1979

AGENCY: Department of Health, Education, and Welfare.

SUMMARY: On July 12, 1974, the National Research Act (Pub. L. 93-348) was signed into law, there-by creating the National Commission for the Protection of Human Subjects of Biomedical and Behavioral Research. One of the charges to the Commission was to identify the basic ethical principles that should underlie the conduct of biomedical and behavioral research involving human subjects. To develop guidelines that should be followed to assure that such research is conducted in accordance with those principles. In carrying out the above, the Commission was directed to consider: (i) the boundaries between biomedical and behavioral research and the accepted and routine practice of medicine, (ii) the role of assessment of the risk-benefit criteria in the determination of the appropriateness of research involving human subjects, (iii) appropriate guidelines for the selection of human subjects for participation in such research and (iv) the nature and definition of informed consent in various research settings.

The Belmont Report attempts to summarize the basic ethical principles identified by the Commission in the course of its deliberations. It is the outgrowth of an intensive four-day period of discussions that were held in February 1976 at the Smithsonian Institution's Belmont Conference Center supplemented by the monthly deliberations of the Commission that were held over a period of nearly four years. It is a statement of basic ethical principles and guidelines that should assist in resolving the ethical problems that surround the conduct of research with human subjects. By publishing the Report in the Federal Register, and providing reprints upon request, the Secretary intends that it may be made readily available to scientists, members of Institutional Review Boards, and Federal employees. The two-volume Appendix, containing the lengthy reports of experts and specialists who assisted the Commission in fulfilling this part of its charge, is available as DHEW Publication No. (OS) 78-0013 and No. (OS) 78-0014, for sale by the Superintendent of Documents, U.S. Government Printing Office, Washington, D.C. 20402.

Unlike most other reports of the Commission, the Belmont Report does not make specific recommendations for administrative action by the Secretary of Health, Education, and Welfare. Rather, the Commission recommended that the Belmont Report be adopted in its entirety, as a statement of the Department's policy. The Department requests public comment on this recommendation.

National Commission for the Protection of Human Subjects of Biomedical
and Behavioral Research

Members of the Commission

Kenneth John Ryan, M.D., Chairman, Chief of Staff, Boston Hospital for Women
Joseph V. Brady, Ph.D., Professor of Behavioral Biology, Johns Hopkins University

Table of Contents

Ethical Principles and Guidelines for Research Involving Human Subjects

Scientific research has produced substantial social benefits. It has also posed some troubling ethical questions. Public attention was drawn to these questions by reported abuses of human subjects in biomedical experiments, especially during the Second World War. During the Nuremberg War Crime Trials, the Nuremberg code was drafted as a set of standards for judging physicians and scientists who had conducted biomedical experiments on concentration camp prisoners. This code became the prototype of many later codes (1) intended to assure that research involving human subjects would be carried out in an ethical manner.

The codes consist of rules, some general, others specific, that guide the investigators or the reviewers of research in their work. Such rules often are inadequate to cover complex situations; at times they come into conflict, and they are frequently difficult to interpret or apply. Broader ethical principles will provide a basis on which specific rules may be formulated, criticized and interpreted.

Three principles, or general prescriptive judgments, that are relevant to research involving human subjects are identified in this statement. Other principles may also be relevant. These three are comprehensive, however, and are stated at a level of generalization that should assist scien-

tists, subjects, reviewers and interested citizens to understand the ethical issues inherent in research involving human subjects. These principles cannot always be applied so as to resolve beyond dispute particular ethical problems. The objective is to provide an analytical framework that will guide the resolution of ethical problems arising from research involving human subjects.

This statement consists of a distinction between research and practice, a discussion of the three basic ethical principles, and remarks about the application of these principles.

Part A: Boundaries Between Practice & Research

It is important to distinguish between biomedical and behavioral research on the one hand, and the practice of accepted therapy on the other, in order to know what activities ought to undergo review for the protection of human subjects of research. The distinction between research and practice is blurred partly because both often occur together (as in research designed to evaluate a therapy) and partly because notable departures from standard practice are often called "experimental" when the terms "experimental" and "research" are not carefully defined. For the most part, the term "practice" refers to interventions that are designed solely to enhance the well-being of an individual patient or client and that have a reasonable expectation of success. The purpose of medical or behavioral practice is to provide diagnosis, preventive treatment or therapy to particular individuals. (2) By contrast, the term "research" designates an activity designed to test an hypothesis, permit conclusions to be drawn, and thereby to develop or contribute to generalizable knowledge (expressed, for example, in theories, principles, and statements of relationships). Research is usually described in a formal protocol that sets forth an objective and a set of procedures designed to reach that objective.

When a clinician departs in a significant way from standard or accepted practice, the innovation does not, in and of itself, constitute research. The fact that a procedure is "experimental," in the sense of new, untested or different, does not automatically place it in the category of research. Radically new procedures of this description should, however, be made the object of formal research at an early stage in order to determine whether they are safe and effective. Thus, it is the responsibility of medical practice committees, for example, to insist that a major innovation be incorporated into a formal research project.(3)

Research and practice may be carried on together when research is designed to evaluate the safety and efficacy of a therapy. This need not cause any confusion regarding whether or not the activity requires review; the general rule is that if there is any element of research in an activity, that activity should undergo review for the protection of human subjects.

Part B: Basic Ethical Principles

The expression "basic ethical principles" refers to those general judgments that serve as a basic justification for the many particular ethical prescriptions and evaluations of human actions. Three basic principles, among those generally accepted in our cultural tradition, are particularly relevant to the ethics of research involving human subjects: the principles of respect of persons, beneficence and justice.

1. Respect for Persons.—

Respect for persons incorporates at least two ethical convictions: first, that individuals should be treated as autonomous agents, and second, that persons with diminished autonomy are entitled to protection. The principle of respect for persons thus divides into two separate moral requirements: the requirement to acknowledge autonomy and the requirement to protect those with diminished autonomy.

An autonomous person is an individual capable of deliberation about personal goals and of acting under the direction of such deliberation. To respect autonomy is to give weight to autonomous persons' considered opinions and choices while refraining from obstructing their actions unless they are clearly detrimental to others. To show lack of respect for an autonomous agent is to repudiate that person's considered judgments, to deny an individual the freedom to act on those considered judgments, or to withhold information necessary to make a considered judgment, when there are no compelling reasons to do so.

However, not every human being is capable of self-determination. The capacity for self-determination matures during an individual's life, and some individuals lose this capacity wholly or in part because of illness, mental disability, or circumstances that severely restrict liberty. Respect for the immature and the incapacitated may require protecting them as they mature or while they are incapacitated.

Some persons are in need of extensive protection, even to the point of excluding them from activities which may harm them; other persons require little protection beyond making sure they undertake activities freely and with awareness of possible adverse consequence. The extent of protection afforded should depend upon the risk of harm and the likelihood of benefit. The judgment that any individual lacks autonomy should be periodically reevaluated and will vary in different situations.

In most cases of research involving human subjects, respect for persons demands that subjects enter the research voluntarily and with adequate information. In some situations, however, application of the principle is not obvious. The involvement of prisoners as subjects of research provides an instructive example. On the one hand, it would seem that the principle of respect for persons requires that prisoners not be deprived of the opportunity to volunteer for research. On the other hand, under prison conditions they may be subtly coerced or unduly influenced to engage in research activities for which they would not otherwise volunteer. Respect for persons would then dictate that prisoners be protected. Whether to allow prisoners to "volunteer" or to "protect" them presents a dilemma. Respecting persons, in most hard cases, is often a matter of balancing competing claims urged by the principle of respect itself.

2. Beneficence.—

Persons are treated in an ethical manner not only by respecting their decisions and protecting them from harm, but also by making efforts to secure their well-being. Such treatment falls under the principle of beneficence. The term "beneficence" is often understood to cover acts of kindness or charity that go beyond strict obligation. In this document, beneficence is understood in a stronger sense, as an obligation. Two general rules have been formulated as complementary expressions of beneficent actions in this sense: (1) do not harm and (2) maximize possible benefits and minimize possible harms.

The Hippocratic maxim "do no harm" has long been a fundamental principle of medical ethics. Claude Bernard extended it to the realm of research, saying that one should not injure one person regardless of the benefits that might come to others. However, even avoiding harm requires learning what is harmful; and, in the process of obtaining this information, persons may be exposed to risk of harm. Further, the Hippocratic Oath requires physicians to benefit their patients "according to their best judgment." Learning what will in fact benefit may require exposing persons to risk. The problem posed by these imperatives is to decide when it is justifiable to seek certain benefits despite the risks involved, and when the benefits should be foregone because of the risks.

The obligations of beneficence affect both individual investigators and society at large, because they extend both to particular research projects and to the entire enterprise of research. In the case of particular projects, investigators and members of their institutions are obliged to give forethought to the maximization of benefits and the reduction of risk that might occur from the research investigation. In the case of scientific research in general, members of the larger society are obliged to recognize the longer term benefits and risks that may result from the improvement of knowledge and from the development of novel medical, psychotherapeutic, and social procedures.

The principle of beneficence often occupies a well-defined justifying role in many areas of research involving human subjects. An example is found in research involving children. Effective ways of treating childhood diseases and fostering healthy development are benefits that serve to justify research involving children—even when individual research subjects are not direct beneficiaries. Research also makes it possible to avoid the harm that may result from the application of previously accepted routine practices that on closer investigation turn out to be dangerous. But the role of the principle of beneficence is not always so unambiguous. A difficult ethical problem remains, for example, about research that presents more than minimal risk without immediate prospect of direct benefit to the children involved. Some have argued that such research is inadmissible, while others have pointed out that this limit would rule out much research promising great benefit to children in the future. Here again, as with all hard cases, the different claims covered by the principle of beneficence may come into conflict and force difficult choices.

3. Justice.—

Who ought to receive the benefits of research and bear its burdens? This is a question of justice, in the sense of "fairness in distribution" or "what is deserved." An injustice occurs when some benefit to which a person is entitled is denied without good reason or a burden is imposed unduly. Another way of conceiving the principle of justice is that equals ought to be treated equally. However, this statement requires explication. Who is equal and unequal? What considerations justify departure from equal distribution? Almost all commentators allow that distinctions based on experience, age, deprivation, competence, merit and position do sometimes constitute criteria justifying differential treatment for certain purposes. It is necessary, then, to explain in what respects people should be treated equally. There are several widely accepted formulations of just ways to distribute burdens and benefits. Each formulation mentions some relevant property on the basis of which burdens and benefits should be distributed. These formulations are (1) to each person an equal share; (2) to each person according to individual need; (3) to each person according to individual effort; (4) to each person according to societal contribution; and (5) to each person according to merit.

Questions of justice have long been associated with social practices such as punishment, taxation, and political representation. Until recently these questions have not generally been associated with scientific research. However, they are foreshadowed even in the earliest reflections on the ethics of research involving human subjects. For example, during the 19th and early 20th centuries the burdens of serving as research subjects fell largely upon poor ward patients, while the benefits of improved medical care flowed primarily to private patients. Subsequently, the exploitation of unwilling prisoners as research subjects in Nazi concentration camps was condemned as a particularly flagrant injustice. In this country, in the 1940's, the Tuskegee syphilis study used disadvantaged, rural black men to study the untreated course of a disease that is by no means confined to that population. These subjects were deprived of demonstrably effective treatment in or-

der not to interrupt the project, long after such treatment became generally available.

Against this historical background, it can be seen how conceptions of justice are relevant to research involving human subjects. For example, the selection of research subjects needs to be scrutinized in order to determine whether some classes (e.g., welfare patients, particular racial and ethnic minorities, or persons confined to institutions) are being systematically selected simply because of their easy availability, to their compromised position, or their manipulability, rather than for reasons directly related to the problem being studied. Finally, whenever research supported by public funds leads to the development of therapeutic devices and procedures, justice demands that these not provide advantages only to those who can afford them and that such research should not unduly involve persons from groups unlikely to be among the beneficiaries of subsequent applications of the research.

Part C: Applications

C. Applications

Applications of the general principles to the conduct of research leads to consideration of the following requirements: informed consent, risk/benefit assessment, and the selection of subjects of research.

1. Informed Consent.—

Respect for persons requires that subjects, to the degree that they are capable, be given the opportunity to choose what shall or shall not happen to them. This opportunity is provided when adequate standards for informed consent are satisfied.

While the importance of informed consent is unquestioned, controversy prevails over the nature and possibility of an informed consent. Nonetheless, there is widespread agreement that the consent process can be analyzed as containing three elements: information, comprehension, and voluntariness.

Information

Most codes of research establish specific items for disclosure intended to assure that subjects are given sufficient information. These items generally include: the research procedure, their purposes, risks and anticipated benefits, alternative procedures (where therapy is involved), and a statement offering the subject the opportunity to ask questions and to withdraw at any time from the research. Additional items have been proposed, including how subjects are selected, the person responsible for the research, etc.

However, a simple listing of items does not answer the question of what the standard should be for judging how much and what sort of information should be provided. One standard frequently invoked in medical practice, namely the information commonly provided by practitioners in the field or in the locale, is inadequate since research takes place precisely when a common understanding does not exist. Another standard, currently popular in malpractice law, requires the practitioner to reveal the information that reasonable persons would wish to know in order to make a decision regarding their care. This, too, seems insufficient since the research subject, being in essence a volunteer, may wish to know considerably more about risks gratuitously undertaken than do patients who deliver themselves into the hand of a clinician for needed care. It may be that a standard of "the reasonable volunteer" should be proposed: the extent and nature of information should be such that persons, knowing that the procedure is neither necessary for their care nor perhaps fully understood, can decide whether they wish to participate in the furthering of knowledge. Even when some direct benefit to them is anticipated, the subjects should understand clearly the range of risk and the voluntary nature of participation.

A special problem of consent arises where informing subjects of some pertinent aspect of the research is likely to impair the validity of the research. In many cases, it is sufficient to indicate to subjects that they are being invited to participate in research of which some features will not be revealed until the research is concluded. In all cases of research involving incomplete disclosure, such research is justified only if it is clear that (1) incomplete disclosure is truly necessary to accomplish the goals of the research, (2) there are no undisclosed risks to subjects that are more than minimal, and (3) there is an adequate plan for debriefing subjects, when appropriate, and for dissemination of research results to them. Information about risks should never be withheld for eliciting the cooperation of subjects, and truthful answers should always be given to direct questions about the research. Care should be taken to distinguish cases in which disclosure would destroy or invalidate the research from cases in which disclosure would simply inconvenience the investigator.

Comprehension

The manner and context in which information is conveyed is as important as the information itself. For example, presenting information in a disorganized and rapid fashion, allowing too little time for consideration or curtailing opportunities for questioning, all may adversely affect a subject's ability to make an informed choice.

Because the subject's ability to understand is a function of intelligence, rationality, maturity, and language, it is necessary to adapt the presentation of the information to the subject's capacities. Investigators are responsible for ascertaining that the subject has comprehended the information. While there is always an obligation to ascertain that the information about risk to subjects is complete and adequately comprehended, when the risks are more serious, that obligation increases. On occasion, it may be suitable to give some oral or written tests of comprehension.

Special provision may need to be made when comprehension is severely limited—for example, by conditions of immaturity or mental disability. Each class of subjects that one might consider as incompetent (e.g., infants and young children, mentally disabled patients, the terminally ill, and the comatose) should be considered on its own terms. Even for these persons, however, respect requires giving them the opportunity to choose to the extent that they are able, whether to participate in research. The objections of these subjects to involvement should be honored, unless the research entails providing them a therapy unavailable elsewhere. Respect for persons also requires seeking the permission of other parties in order to protect the subjects from harm. Such persons are thus respected both by acknowledging their own wishes and by the use of third parties to protect them from harm.

The third parties chosen should be those who are most likely to understand the incompetent subject's situation and to act in that person's best interest. The person authorized to act on behalf of the subject should be given an opportunity to observe the research as it proceeds in order to be able to withdraw the subject from the research, if such action appears in the subject's best interest.

Voluntariness

An agreement to participate in research constitutes a valid consent only if voluntarily given. This element of informed consent requires conditions free of coercion and undue influence. Coercion occurs when an overt threat of harm is intentionally presented by one person to another in order to obtain compliance. Undue influence, by contrast, occurs through an offer of an excessive, unwarranted, inappropriate, or improper reward or other overture in order to obtain compliance. Also, inducements that would ordinarily be acceptable may become undue influences if the subject is especially vulnerable.

Unjustifiable pressures usually occur when persons in positions of authority or commanding influence—especially where possible sanctions are involved—urge a course of action for a subject. A continuum of such influencing factors exists, however, and it is impossible to state precisely where justifiable persuasion ends and undue influence begins. But undue influence would include actions such as manipulating a person's choice through the controlling influence of a close relative and threatening to withdraw health services to which an individual would otherwise be entitled.

2. Assessment of Risks and Benefits.—

The assessment of risks and benefits requires a careful array of relevant data, including, in some cases, alternative ways of obtaining the benefits sought in the research. Thus, the assessment presents both an opportunity and a responsibility to gather systematic and comprehensive information about proposed research. For the investigator, it is a means to examine whether the proposed research is properly designed. For a review committee, it is a method for determining whether the risks that will be presented to subjects are justified. For prospective subjects, the assessment will assist the determination whether or not to participate.

The Nature and Scope of Risks and Benefits

The requirement that research be justified on the basis of a favorable risk/benefit assessment bears a close relation to the principle of beneficence, just as the moral requirement that informed consent be obtained is derived primarily from the principle of respect for persons. The term "risk" refers to a possibility that harm may occur. However, when expressions such as "small risk" or "high risk" are used, they usually refer (often ambiguously) both to the chance (probability) of experiencing a harm and the severity (magnitude) of the envisioned harm.

The term "benefit" is used in the research context to refer to something of positive value related to health or welfare. Unlike "risk," "benefit" is not a term that expresses probabilities. Risk is properly contrasted to probability of benefits, and benefits are properly contrasted with harms rather than risks of harm. Accordingly, so-called risk/benefit assessments are concerned with the probabilities and magnitudes of possible harm and anticipated benefits. Many kinds of possible harms and benefits need to be taken into account. There are, for example, risks of psychological harm, physical harm, legal harm, social harm, and economic harm, and the corresponding benefits. While the most likely types of harms to research subjects are those of psychological or physical pain or injury, other possible kinds should not be overlooked.

Risks and benefits of research may affect the individual subjects, the families of the individual subjects, and society at large (or special groups of subjects in society). Previous codes and Federal regulations have required that risks to subjects be outweighed by the sum of both the anticipated benefit to the subject, if any, and the anticipated benefit to society in the form of knowledge to be gained from the research. In balancing these different elements, the risks and benefits affecting the immediate research subject will normally carry special weight. On the other hand, interests other than those of the subject may on occasion be sufficient by themselves to justify the risks involved in the research, so long as the subjects' rights have been protected. Beneficence thus requires that we protect against risk of harm to subjects and that we be concerned about the loss of the substantial benefits that might be gained from research.

The Systematic Assessment of Risks and Benefits

It is commonly said that benefits and risks must be "balanced" and shown to be "in a favorable ratio." The metaphorical character of these terms draws attention to the difficulty of making precise judgments. Only on rare occasions will quantitative techniques be available for the scrutiny of research protocols. However, the idea of systematic, nonarbitrary analysis of risks and benefits should be emulated insofar as possible. This ideal requires those making decisions about the justifiability of research to be thorough in the accumulation and assessment of information about all aspects of the research, and to consider alternatives systematically. This procedure renders the assessment of research more rigorous and precise, while making communication between review board members and investigators less subject to misinterpretation, misinformation, and conflicting judgments. Thus, there should first be a determination of the validity of the presuppositions of the research; then the nature, probability, and magnitude of risk should be distinguished with as much clarity as possible. The method of ascertaining risks should be explicit, especially where there is no alternative to the use of such vague categories as small or slight risk. It should also be determined whether an investigator's estimates of the probability of harm or benefits are reasonable, as judged by known facts or other available studies.

Finally, assessment of the justifiability of research should reflect at least the following considerations: (i) Brutal or inhumane treatment of human subjects is never morally justified. (ii) Risks should be reduced to those necessary to achieve the research objective. It should be determined whether it is in fact necessary to use human subjects at all. Risk perhaps can never entirely be eliminated, but it can often be reduced by careful attention to alternative procedures. (iii) When research involves significant risk of serious impairment, review committees should be extraordinarily insistent on the justification of the risk (looking at the likelihood of benefit to the subject—or, in some rare cases, to the manifest voluntariness of the participation). (iv) When vulnerable populations are involved in research, the appropriateness of involving them should itself be demonstrated. A number of variables go into such judgments, including the nature and degree of risk, the condition of the particular population involved, and the nature and level of the anticipated benefits. (v) Relevant risks and benefits must be thoroughly arrayed in documents and procedures used in the informed consent process.

3. Selection of Subjects.—

Just as the principle of respect for persons finds expression in the requirements for consent, and the principle of beneficence in risk/benefit assessment, the principle of justice gives rise to moral requirements that there be fair procedures and outcomes in the selection of research subjects.

Justice is relevant to the selection of subjects of research at two levels: the social and the individual. Individual justice in the selection of subjects would require that researchers exhibit fairness: thus, they should not offer potentially beneficial research only to some patients who are in their favor or select only "undesirable" persons for risky research. Social justice requires that distinction be drawn between classes of subjects that ought, and ought not, to participate in any particular kind of research, based on the ability of members of that class to bear burdens and on the appropriateness of placing further burdens on already burdened persons. Thus, it can be considered a matter of social justice that there is an order of preference in the selection of classes of subjects (e.g., adults before children) and that some classes of potential subjects (e.g., the institutionalized mentally infirm or prisoners) that may be involved as research subjects, if at all, only on certain conditions.

Injustice may appear in the selection of subjects, even if individual subjects are selected fairly by investigators and treated fairly in the course of research. Injustice arises from social, racial, sexual, and cultural biases institutionalized in society. Thus, even if individual researchers are treating their research subjects fairly, and the IRBs are taking care to assure that subjects are selected fairly within a particular institution, unjust social patterns may nevertheless appear in the overall distribution of the burdens and benefits of research. Although individual institutions or investigators may not be able to resolve a problem that is pervasive in their social setting, they can consider distributive justice in selecting research subjects.

Some populations, especially institutionalized ones, are already burdened in many ways by their infirmities and environments. When research is proposed that involves risks and does not include a therapeutic component, other less burdened classes of persons should be called upon first to accept these risks of research, except where the research is directly related to the specific conditions of the class involved. Also, even though public funds for research may often flow in the same directions as public funds for health care, it seems unfair that populations dependent on public health care constitute a pool of preferred research subjects, especially when more advantaged populations are likely to be the recipients of the benefits.

One special instance of injustice results from the involvement of vulnerable subjects. Certain groups, such as racial minorities, the economically disadvantaged, the very sick, and the institutionalized, may continually be sought as research subjects, owing to their ready availability in settings where research is conducted. Given their dependent status and their frequently compromised capacity for free consent, they should be protected against the danger of being involved in research solely for administrative convenience, or because they are easy to manipulate as a result of their illness or socioeconomic condition.

---

(1) Since 1945, various codes for the proper and responsible conduct of human experimentation in medical research have been adopted by different organizations. The best known codes are the Nuremberg Code of 1947, the Helsinki Declaration of 1964 (revised in 1975), and the 1971 Guidelines (codified into Federal Regulations in 1974) issued by the U.S. Department of Health, Education, and Welfare Codes for the conduct of social and behavioral research have also been adopted, the best known being that of the American Psychological Association, published in 1973.

(2) Although practice usually involves interventions designed solely to enhance the well-being of a particular individual, interventions are sometimes applied to one individual for the enhancement of the well-being of another (e.g., blood donation, skin grafts, organ transplants) or an intervention may have the dual purpose of enhancing the well-being of a particular individual, and, at the same time, providing some benefit to others (e.g., vaccination, which protects both the person who is vaccinated and society generally). The fact that some forms of practice have elements other than immediate benefit to the individual receiving an intervention, however, should not confuse the general distinction between research and practice. Even when a procedure applied in practice may benefit some other person, it remains an intervention designed to enhance the well-being of a particular individual or groups of individuals; thus, it is practice and need not be reviewed as research.

(3) Because the problems related to social experimentation may differ substantially from those of biomedical and behavioral research, the Commission specifically declines to make any policy determination regarding such research at this time. Rather, the Commission believes that the problem ought to be addressed by one of its successor bodies.

National Institutes of Health, Bethesda, Maryland 20892

World Medical Association Declaration of Helsinki

Ethical Principles for Medical Research Involving Human Subjects

Adopted by the 18th WMA General Assembly
Helsinki, Finland, June 1964
and amended by :
29th WMA General Assembly, Tokyo, Japan,
October 1975
35th WMA General Assembly, Venice, Italy,
October 1983
41st WMA General Assembly, Hong Kong,
September 1989
48th WMA General Assembly, Somerset West,
Republic of South Africa, October 1996
and the
52nd WMA General Assembly, Edinburgh, Scotland,
October 2000

A. Introduction

1. The World Medical Association has developed the Declaration of Helsinki as a statement of ethical principles to provide guidance to physicians and other participants in medical research involving human subjects. Medical research involving human subjects includes research on identifiable human material or identifiable data.

2. It is the duty of the physician to promote and safeguard the health of the people. The physician's knowledge and conscience are dedicated to the fulfillment of this duty.

3. The Declaration of Geneva of the World Medical Association binds the physician with the words, "The health of my patient will be my first consideration," and the International Code of Medical Ethics declares that, "A physician shall act only in the patient's interest when providing medical care which might have the effect of weakening the physical and mental condition of the patient."

4. Medical progress is based on research which ultimately must rest in part on experimentation involving human subjects.

5. In medical research on human subjects, considerations related to the well-being of the human subject should take precedence over the interests of science and society.

6. The primary purpose of medical research involving human subjects is to improve prophylactic, diagnostic, and therapeutic procedures and the understanding of the aetiology and pathogenesis of disease. Even the best proven prophylactic, diagnostic, and therapeutic methods must continuously be challenged through research for their effectiveness, efficiency, accessibility, and quality.

7. In current medical practice and in medical research, most prophylactic, diagnostic, and therapeutic procedures involve risks and burdens.

8. Medical research is subject to ethical standards that promote respect for all human beings and protect their health and rights. Some research populations are vulnerable and need special protection. The particular needs of the economically and medically disadvantaged must be recognized. Special attention is also required for those who cannot give or refuse consent for themselves, for those who may be subject to giving consent under duress, for those who will not benefit personally from the research and for those for whom the research is combined with care.

9. Research Investigators should be aware of the ethical, legal and regulatory requirements for research on human subjects in their own countries as well as applicable international requirements. No national ethical, legal or regulatory requirement should be allowed to reduce or eliminate any of the protections for human subjects set forth in this Declaration.

B. Basic Principles for All Medical Research

10. It is the duty of the physician in medical research to protect the life, health, privacy, and dignity of the human subject.

11. Medical research involving human subjects must conform to generally accepted scientific principles, be based on a thorough knowledge of the scientific literature, other relevant sources of information, and on adequate laboratory and, where appropriate, animal experimentation.

12. Appropriate caution must be exercised in the conduct of research which may affect the environment, and the welfare of animals used for research must be respected.

13. The design and performance of each experimental procedure involving human subjects should be clearly formulated in an experimental protocol. This protocol should be submitted for consideration, comment, guidance, and where appropriate, approval to a specially appointed ethical review committee, which must be independent of the investigator, the sponsor, or any other kind of undue influence. This independent committee should be in conformity with the laws and regulations of the country in which the research experiment is performed. The committee has the right to monitor ongoing trials. The researcher has the obligation to provide monitoring information to the committee, especially any serious adverse events. The researcher should also submit to the committee, for review, information regarding funding, sponsors, institutional affiliations, other potential conflicts of interest, and incentives for subjects.

14. The research protocol should always contain a statement of the ethical considerations involved and should indicate that there is compliance with the principles enunciated in this Declaration.

15. Medical research involving human subjects should be conducted only by scientifically qualified persons and under the supervision of a clinically competent medical person. The responsibility for the human subject must always rest with a medically qualified person and never rest on the subject of the research, even though the subject has given consent.

16. Every medical research project involving human subjects should be preceded by careful assessment of predictable risks and burdens in comparison with foreseeable benefits to the subject or to others. This does not preclude the participation of healthy volunteers in medical research. The design of all studies should be publicly available.

17. Physicians should abstain from engaging in research projects involving human subjects unless they are confident that the risks involved have been adequately assessed and can be satisfactorily managed. Physicians should cease any investigation if the risks are found to outweigh the potential benefits or if there is conclusive proof of positive and beneficial results.

18. Medical research involving human subjects should only be conducted if the importance of the objective outweighs the inherent risks and burdens to the subject. This is especially important when the human subjects are healthy volunteers.

19. Medical research is only justified if there is a reasonable likelihood that the populations in which the research is carried out stand to benefit from the results of the research.

20. The subjects must be volunteers and informed participants in the research project.

21. The right of research subjects to safeguard their integrity must always be respected. Every precaution should be taken to respect the privacy of the subject, the confidentiality of the patient's information and to minimize the impact of the study on the subject's physical and mental integrity and on the personality of the subject.

22. In any research on human beings, each potential subject must be adequately informed of the aims, methods, sources of funding, any possible conflicts of interest, institutional affiliations of the researcher, the anticipated benefits and potential risks of the study, and the discomfort it may entail. The subject should be informed of the right to abstain from participation in the study or to withdraw consent to participate at any time without reprisal. After ensuring that the subject has understood the information, the physician should then obtain the subject's freely-given informed consent, preferably in writing. If the consent cannot be obtained in writing, the non-written consent must be formally documented and witnessed.

23. When obtaining informed consent for the research project, the physician should be particularly cautious if the subject is in a dependent relationship with the physician or may consent under duress. In that case, the informed consent should be obtained by a well-informed physician who is not engaged in the investigation and who is completely independent of this relationship.

24. For a research subject who is legally incompetent, physically or mentally incapable of giving consent, or is a legally incompetent minor, the investigator must obtain informed consent from the legally authorized representative in accordance with applicable law. These groups should not be included in research unless the research is necessary to promote the health of the population represented and this re-search cannot instead be performed on legally competent persons.

25. When a subject deemed legally incompetent, such as a minor child, is able to give assent to decisions about participation in research, the investigator must obtain that assent in addition to the consent of the legally authorized representative.

26. Research on individuals from whom it is not possible to obtain consent, including proxy or advance consent, should be done only if the physical/mental condition that prevents obtaining informed consent is a necessary characteristic of the research population. The specific reasons for involving research subjects with a condition that renders them unable to give informed consent should be stated in the experimental protocol for consideration and approval of the review committee. The protocol should state that consent to remain in the research should be obtained as soon as possible from the individual or a legally authorized surrogate.

27. Both authors and publishers have ethical obligations. In publication of the results of research, the investigators are obliged to preserve the accuracy of the results. Negative as well as positive results should be published or otherwise publicly available. Sources of funding, institutional affiliations, and any possible conflicts of interest should be declared in the publication. Reports of experimentation not in accordance with the principles laid down in this Declaration should not be accepted for publication.

C. Additional Principles for Medical Research Combined with Medical Care

28. The physician may combine medical research with medical care, only to the extent that the research is justified by its potential prophylactic, diagnostic or therapeutic value. When medical research is combined with medical care, additional standards apply to protect the patients who are research subjects.

29. The benefits, risks, burdens and effectiveness of a new method should be tested against those of the best current prophylactic, diagnostic, and therapeutic methods. This does not exclude the use of placebo, or no treatment, in studies where no proven prophylactic, diagnostic or therapeutic method exists.

30. At the conclusion of the study, every patient entered into the study should be assured of access to the best proven prophylactic, diagnostic and therapeutic methods identified by the study.

31. The physician should fully inform the patient which aspects of the care are related to the research. The refusal of a patient to participate in a study must never interfere with the patient-physician relationship.

32. In the treatment of a patient, where proven prophylactic, diagnostic and therapeutic methods do not exist or have been ineffective, the physician, with informed consent from the patient, must be free to use unproven or new prophylactic, diagnostic and therapeutic measures, if in the physician's judgement it offers hope of saving life, re-establishing health or alleviating suffering. Where possible, these measures should be made the object of research, designed to evaluate their safety and efficacy. In all cases, new information should be recorded and, where appropriate, published. The other relevant guidelines of this Declaration should be followed.

Selected U.S. Government Regulations

Department of Health and Human Services

Office for Human Research Protections (OHRP)
Web site: http://ohrp.osophs.dhhs.gov/

Protection of Human Subjects
45 Code of Federal Regulations Part 46
Web site: http://ohrp.osophs.dhhs.gov/humansubjects/guidance/45cfr46.htm
Note: Full text attached

Revised Expedited Review Criteria (1998)
Web site: http://ohrp.osophs.dhhs.gov/humansubjects/guidance/expedited98.htm
Note: Full text attached

Food and Drug Administration (FDA)
Web site: http://www.fda.gov/

Protection of Human Subjects
21 Code of Federal Regulations Part 50
Web site: http://www.access.gpo.gov/nara/cfr/waisidx_00/21cfr50_00.html
Note: Full text attached

Institutional Review Boards
21 Code of Federal Regulations Part 56
Web site: http://www.access.gpo.gov/nara/cfr/waisidx_00/21cfr56_00.html
Includes:
Appendix A: A List of Selected FDA Regulations Relating to the Protection of Human Subjects
Appendix B: Significant Differences in FDA and HHS Regulations for Protection of Human Subjects
Note: Full text attached

Financial Disclosure by Clinical Investigators
21 Code of Federal Regulations Part 54
Web site: http://www.access.gpo.gov/nara/cfr/waisidx_00/21cfr54_00.html

Biologic Products: General
21 Code of Federal Regulations Part 600
Web site: http://www.access.gpo.gov/nara/cfr/waisidx_00/21cfr600_00.html

Investigational New Drug Application
21 Code of Federal Regulations Part 312
Web site: http://www.access.gpo.gov/nara/cfr/waisidx_00/21cfr312_00.html

Investigational Device Exemptions
21 Code of Federal Regulations Part 812
Web site: http://www.access.gpo.gov/nara/cfr/waisidx_00/21cfr812_00.html

Health Insurance Portability and Accountability Act (HIPAA)
Web site: http://aspe.hhs.gov/admnsimp/

Code of Federal Regulations: Title 45, Part 46

**CODE OF FEDERAL REGULATIONS: TITLE 45, PUBLIC WELFARE
PARTMENT OF HEALTH AND HUMAN SERVICES
NATIONAL INSTITUTES OF HEALTH
OFFICE FOR PROTECTION FROM RESEARCH RISKS**

**PART 46
PROTECTION OF HUMAN SUBJECTS**

* * *

Revised June 18, 1991
Effective August 19, 1991

* * *

Authority: 5 U.S.C. 301; Sec. 474(a), 88 Stat. 352 (42 U.S.C. 2891-3(a))

Note: As revised, Subpart A of the DHHS regulations incorporates the Common Rule (Federal Policy) for the Protection of Human Subjects (56 FR 28003). Subpart D of the HHS regulations has been amended at Section 46.401(b) to reference the revised Subpart A

The Common Rule (Federal Policy) is also codified at:

7 CFR Part 1c	Department of Agriculture
10 CFR Part 745	Department of Energy
14 CFR Part 1230	National Aeronautics and Space Administration
15 CFR Part 27	Department of Commerce
16 CFR Part 1028	Consumer Product Safety Commission
22 CFR Part 225	International Development Cooperation Agency, Agency for International Development
24 CFR Part 60	Department of Housing and Urban Development
28 CFR Part 46	Department of Justice
32 CFR Part 219	Department of Defense
34 CFR Part 97	Department of Education
38 CFR Part 16	Department of Veterans Affairs
40 CFR Part 26	Environmental Protection Agency
45 CFR Part 690	National Science Foundation
49 CFR Part 11	Department of Transportation

Title 45
Code of Federal Regulations

Part 46
Protection of Human Subjects

* * *

Revised June 18, 1991
Effective August 19, 1991

* * *

Subpart A

Federal Policy for the Protection of Human Subjects (Basic DHHS Policy for Protection of Human Research Subjects)
Source: 56 FR 28003, June 18, 1991.

§46.101 To what does this policy apply?

(a) Except as provided in paragraph (b) of this section, this policy applies to all research involving human subjects conducted, supported or otherwise subject to regulation by any federal department or agency which takes appropriate administrative action to make the policy applicable to such research. This includes research conducted by federal civilian employees or military personnel, except that each department or agency head may adopt such procedural modifications as may be appropriate from an administrative standpoint. It also includes research conducted, supported, or otherwise subject to regulation by the federal government outside the United States.

(1) Research that is conducted or supported by a federal department or agency, whether or not it is regulated as defined in §46.102(e), must comply with all sections of this policy.

(2) Research that is neither conducted nor supported by a federal department or agency but is subject to regulation as defined in §46.102(e) must be reviewed and approved, in compliance with §46.101, §46.102, and §46.107 through §46.117 of this policy, by an institutional review board (IRB) that operates in accordance with the pertinent requirements of this policy.

(b) Unless otherwise required by department or agency heads, research activities in which the only involvement of human subjects will be in one or more of the following categories are exempt from this policy:

(1) Research conducted in established or commonly accepted educational settings, involving normal educational practices, such as (i) research on regular and special education instructional strategies, or (ii) research on the effectiveness of or the comparison among instructional techniques, curricula, or classroom management methods.

(2) Research involving the use of educational tests (cognitive, diagnostic, aptitude, achievement), survey procedures, interview procedures or observation of public behavior, unless:

(i) information obtained is recorded in such a manner that human subjects can be identified, directly or through identifiers linked to the subjects; and

(ii) any disclosure of the human subjects' responses outside the research could reasonably place the subjects at risk of criminal or civil liability or be damaging to the subjects' financial standing, employability, or reputation.

(3) Research involving the use of educational tests (cognitive, diagnostic, aptitude, achievement), survey procedures, interview procedures, or observation of public behavior that is not exempt under paragraph (b)(2) of this section, if:

(i) the human subjects are elected or appointed public officials or candidates for public office; or

(ii) Federal statute(s) require(s) without exception that the confidentiality of the personally identifiable information will be maintained throughout the research and thereafter.

(4) Research involving the collection or study of existing data, documents, records, pathological specimens, or diagnostic specimens, if these sources are publicly available or if the information is recorded by the investigator in such a manner that subjects cannot be identified, directly or through identifiers linked to the subjects.

(5) Research and demonstration projects which are conducted by or subject to the approval of department or agency heads, and which are designed to study, evaluate, or otherwise examine:

(i) Public benefit or service programs; (ii) procedures for obtaining benefits or services under those programs; (iii) possible changes in or alternatives to those programs or procedures; or (iv) possible changes in methods or levels of payment for benefits or services under those programs.

(6) Taste and food quality evaluation and consumer acceptance studies, (i) if wholesome foods without additives are consumed or (ii) if a food is consumed that contains a food ingredient at or below the level and for a use found to be safe, or agricultural chemical or environmental contaminant at or below the level found to be safe, by the Food and Drug Administration or approved by the Environmental Protection Agency or the Food Safety and Inspection Service of the U.S. Department of Agriculture.

(c) Department or agency heads retain final judgment as to whether a particular activity is covered by this policy.

(d) Department or agency heads may require that specific research activities or classes of research activities conducted, supported, or otherwise subject to regulation by the department or agency but not otherwise covered by this policy, comply with some or all of the requirements of this policy.

(e) Compliance with this policy requires compliance with pertinent federal laws or regulations which provide additional protections for human subjects.

(f) This policy does not affect any state or local laws or regulations which may otherwise be applicable and which provide additional protections for human subjects.

(g) This policy does not affect any foreign laws or regulations which may otherwise be applicable and which provide additional protections to human subjects of research.

(h) When research covered by this policy takes place in foreign countries, procedures normally followed in the foreign countries to protect human subjects may differ from those set forth in this policy. [An example is a foreign institution which complies with guidelines consistent with the World Medical Assembly Declaration (Declaration of Helsinki amended 1989) issued either by sovereign states or by an organization whose function for the protection of human research subjects is internationally recognized.] In these circumstances, if a department or agency head determines that the procedures prescribed by the institution afford protections that are at least equivalent to those provided in this policy, the department or agency head may approve the substitution of the foreign procedures in lieu of the procedural requirements provided in this policy. Except when otherwise required by statute, Executive Order, or the department or agency head, notices of these actions as they occur will be published in the Federal Register or will be otherwise published as provided in department or agency procedures.

(i) Unless otherwise required by law, department or agency heads may waive the applicability of some or all of the provisions of this policy to specific research activities or classes or research activities otherwise covered by this policy. Except when otherwise required by statute or Executive Order, the department or agency head shall forward advance notices of these actions to the Office for Protection from Research Risks, National Institutes of Health, Department of Health and Human Services (DHHS), and shall also publish them in the Federal Register or in such other manner as provided in department or agency procedures.[1]

Institutions with DHHS-approved assurances on file will abide by provisions of title 45 CFR part 46 subparts A-D. Some of the other departments and agencies have incorporated all provisions of title 45 CFR part 46 into their policies and procedures as well. However, the exemptions at 45 CFR 46.101(b) do not apply to research involving prisoners, fetuses, pregnant women, or human in vitro fertilization, subparts B and C. The exemption at 45 CFR 46.101(b)(2), for research involving survey or interview procedures or observation of public behavior, does not apply to research with children, subpart D, except for research involving observations of public behavior when the investigator(s) do not participate in the activities being observed.

§46.102 Definitions

(a) Department or agency head means the head of any federal department or agency and any other officer or employee of any department or agency to whom authority has been delegated.

(b) Institution means any public or private entity or agency (including federal, state, and other agencies).

(c) Legally authorized representative means an individual or judicial or other body authorized under applicable law to consent on behalf of a prospective subject to the subject's participation in the procedure(s) involved in the research.

(d) Research means a systematic investigation, including research development, testing and evaluation, designed to develop or contribute to generalizable knowledge. Activities which meet this definition constitute research for purposes of this policy, whether or not they are conducted or supported under a program which is considered research for other purposes. For example, some demonstration and service programs may include research activities.

(e) Research subject to regulation, and similar terms are intended to encompass those research activities for which a federal department or agency has specific responsibility for regulating as a research activity, (for example, Investigational New Drug requirements administered by the Food and Drug Administration). It does not include research activities which are incidentally regulated by a federal department or agency solely as part of the department's or agency's broader responsibility to regulate certain types of activities whether research or non-research in nature (for example, Wage and Hour requirements administered by the Department of Labor).

(f) Human subject means a living individual about whom an investigator (whether professional or student) conducting research obtains

(1) Data through intervention or interaction with the individual, or

(2) Identifiable private information.

Intervention includes both physical procedures by which data are gathered (for example, venipuncture) and manipulations of the subject or the subject's environment that are performed for research purposes. Interaction includes communication or interpersonal contact between investigator and subject. Private information includes information about behavior that occurs in a context in which an individual can reasonably expect that no observation or recording is taking place, and information which has been provided for specific purposes by an individual and which the individual can reasonably expect will not be made public (for example, a medical record). Private information must be individually identifiable (i.e., the identity of the subject is or may readily be ascertained by the investigator or associated with the information) in order for obtaining the information to constitute research involving human subjects.

(g) IRB means an institutional review board established in accord with and for the purposes expressed in this policy.

(h) IRB approval means the determination of the IRB that the research has been reviewed and may be conducted at an institution within the constraints set forth by the IRB and by other institutional and federal requirements.

(i) Minimal risk means that the probability and magnitude of harm or discomfort anticipated in the research are not greater in and of themselves than those ordinarily encountered in daily life or during the performance of routine physical or psychological examinations or tests.

(j) Certification means the official notification by the institution to the supporting department or agency, in accordance with the requirements of this policy, that a research project or activity involving human subjects has been reviewed and approved by an IRB in accordance with an approved assurance.

§46.103 Assuring compliance with this policy—research conducted or supported by any federal department or agency

(a) Each institution engaged in research which is covered by this policy and which is conducted or supported by a federal department or agency shall provide written assurance satisfactory to the department or agency head that it will comply with the requirements set forth in this policy. In lieu of requiring submission of an assurance, individual department or agency heads shall accept the existence of a current assurance, appropriate for the research in question, on file with the Office for Protection from Research Risks, National Institutes Health, DHHS, and approved for federal wide use by that office. When the existence of an DHHS-approved assurance is accepted in lieu of requiring submission of an assurance, reports (except certification) required by this policy to be made to department and agency heads shall also be made to the Office for Protection from Research Risks, National Institutes of Health, DHHS.

(b) Departments and agencies will conduct or support research covered by this policy only if the institution has an assurance approved as provided in this section, and only if the institution has certified to the department or agency head that the research has been reviewed and approved by an IRB provided for in the assurance, and will be subject to continuing review by the IRB. Assurances applicable to federally supported or conducted research shall at a minimum include:

(1) A statement of principles governing the institution in the discharge of its responsibilities for protecting the rights and welfare of human subjects of research conducted at or sponsored by the institution, regardless of whether the research is subject to federal regulation. This may include an appropriate existing code, declaration, or statement of ethical principles, or a statement formulated by the institution itself. This requirement does not preempt provisions of this policy applicable to department- or agency-supported or regulated research and need not be applicable to any research exempted or waived under §46.101 (b) or (i).

(2) Designation of one or more IRBs established in accordance with the requirements of this policy, and for which provisions are made for meeting space and sufficient staff to support the IRB's review and record keeping duties.

(3) A list of IRB members identified by name; earned degrees; representative capacity; indications of experience such as board certifications, licenses, etc., sufficient to describe each member's chief anticipated contributions to IRB deliberations; and any employment or other relationship between each member and the institution; for example: full-time employee, part-time employee, member of governing panel or board, stockholder, paid or unpaid consultant. Changes in IRB membership shall be reported to the department or agency head, unless in accord with §46.103(a) of this policy, the existence of a DHHS-approved assurance is accepted. In this case, change in IRB membership shall be reported to the Office for Protection from Research Risks, National Institutes of Health, DHHS.

(4) Written procedures which the IRB will follow (i) for conducting its initial and continuing review of research and for reporting its findings and actions to the investigator and the institution; (ii) for determining which projects require review more often than annually and which projects need verification from sources other than the investigators that no material changes have occurred since previous IRB review; and (iii) for ensuring prompt reporting to the IRB of proposed changes in a research activity, and for ensuring that such changes in approved research, during the period for which IRB approval has already been given, may not be initiated without IRB review and approval except when necessary to eliminate apparent immediate hazards to the subject.

(5) Written procedures for ensuring prompt reporting to the IRB, appropriate institutional officials, and the department or agency head of (i) any unanticipated problems involving risks to subjects or others or any serious or continuing noncompliance with this policy or the requirements or determinations of the IRB; and (ii) any suspension or termination of IRB approval.

(c) The assurance shall be executed by an individual authorized to act for the institution and to assume on behalf of the institution the obligations imposed by this policy and shall be filed in such form and manner as the department or agency head prescribes.

(d) The department or agency head will evaluate all assurances submitted in accordance with this policy through such officers and employees of the department or agency and such experts or consultants engaged for this purpose as the department or agency head determines to be appropriate. The department or agency head's evaluation will take into consideration the adequacy of the proposed IRB in light of the anticipated scope of the institution's research activities and the types of subject populations likely to be involved, the appropriateness of the proposed initial and continuing review procedures in light of the probable risks, and the size and complexity of the institution.

(e) On the basis of this evaluation, the department or agency head may approve or disapprove the assurance, or enter into negotiations to develop an approvable one. The department or agency head may limit the period during which any particular approved assurance or class of approved assurances shall remain effective or otherwise condition or restrict approval.

(f) Certification is required when the research is supported by a federal department or agency and not otherwise exempted or waived under §46.101 (b) or (i). An institution with an approved assurance shall certify that each application or proposal for research covered by the assurance and by §46.103 of this policy has been reviewed and approved by the IRB. Such certification must be submitted with the application or proposal or by such later date as may be prescribed by the department or agency to which the application or proposal is submitted. Under no condition shall research covered by §46.103 of the policy be supported prior to receipt of the certification that the research has been reviewed and approved by the IRB. Institutions without an approved assurance covering the research shall certify within 30 days after receipt of a request for such a certification from the department or agency, that the application or proposal has been approved by the IRB. If the certification is not submitted within these time limits, the application or proposal may be returned to the institution.

(Approved by the Office of Management and Budget under Control Number 9999-0020.)

§§46.104—46.106 [Reserved]

§46.107 IRB membership

(a) Each IRB shall have at least five members, with varying backgrounds to promote complete and adequate review of research activities commonly conducted by the institution. The IRB shall be sufficiently qualified through the experience and expertise of its members, and the diversity of the members, including consideration of race, gender, and cultural backgrounds and sensitivity to such issues as community attitudes, to promote respect for its advice and counsel in safeguarding the rights and welfare of human subjects. In addition to possessing the professional competence necessary to review specific research activities, the IRB shall be able to ascertain the acceptability of proposed research in terms of institutional commitments and regulations, applicable law, and standards of professional conduct and practice. The IRB shall therefore include persons knowledgeable in these areas. If an IRB regularly reviews research that involves a vulnerable category of subjects, such as children, prisoners, pregnant women, or handicapped or mentally disabled persons, consideration shall be given to the inclusion of one or more individuals who are knowledgeable about and experienced in working with these subjects.

(b) Every nondiscriminatory effort will be made to ensure that no IRB consists entirely of men or entirely of women, including the institution's consideration of qualified persons of both sexes, so long as no selection is made to the IRB on the basis of gender. No IRB may consist entirely of members of one profession.

(c) Each IRB shall include at least one member whose primary concerns are in scientific areas and at least one member whose primary concerns are in nonscientific areas.

(d) Each IRB shall include at least one member who is not otherwise affiliated with the institution and who is not part of the immediate family of a person who is affiliated with the institution.

(e) No IRB may have a member participate in the IRB's initial or continuing review of any project in which the member has a conflicting interest, except to provide information requested by the IRB.

(f) An IRB may, in its discretion, invite individuals with competence in special areas to assist in the review of issues which require expertise beyond or in addition to that available on the IRB. These individuals may not vote with the IRB.

§46.108 IRB functions and operations

In order to fulfill the requirements of this policy each IRB shall:

(a) Follow written procedures in the same detail as described in §46.103(b)(4) and to the extent required by §46.103(b)(5).

(b) Except when an expedited review procedure is used (see §46.110), review proposed research at convened meetings at which a majority of the members of the IRB are present, including at least one member whose primary concerns are in nonscientific areas. In order for the research to be approved, it shall receive the approval of a majority of those members present at the meeting

§46.109 IRB review of research

(a) An IRB shall review and have authority to approve, require modifications in (to secure approval), or disapprove all research activities covered by this policy.

(b) An IRB shall require that information given to subjects as part of informed consent is in accordance with §46.116. The IRB may require that information, in addition to that specifically mentioned in §46.116, be given to the subjects when in the IRB's judgment the information would meaningfully add to the protection of the rights and welfare of subjects.

(c) An IRB shall require documentation of informed consent or may waive documentation in accordance with §46.117.

(d) An IRB shall notify investigators and the institution in writing of its decision to approve or disapprove the proposed research activity, or of modifications required to secure IRB approval of the research activity. If the IRB decides to disapprove a research activity, it shall include in its written notification a statement of the reasons for its decision and give the investigator an opportunity to respond in person or in writing.

(e) An IRB shall conduct continuing review of research covered by this policy at intervals appropriate to the degree of risk, but not less than once per year, and shall have authority to observe or have a third party observe the consent process and the research.

(Approved by the Office of Management and Budget under Control Number 9999-0020.)

§46.110 Expedited review procedures for certain kinds of research involving no more than minimal risk, and for minor changes in approved research

(a) The Secretary, HHS, has established, and published as a Notice in the Federal Register, a list of categories of research that may be reviewed by the IRB through an expedited review procedure. The list will be amended, as appropriate, after consultation with other departments and agencies, through periodic republication by the Secretary, HHS, in the Federal Register. A copy of the list is available from the Office for Protection from Research Risks, National Institutes of Health, DHHS, Bethesda, Maryland 20892.

(b) An IRB may use the expedited review procedure to review either or both of the following:

(1) Some or all of the research appearing on the list and found by the reviewer(s) to involve no more than minimal risk,

(2) Minor changes in previously approved research during the period (of one year or less) for which approval is authorized.

Under an expedited review procedure, the review may be carried out by the IRB chairperson or by one or more experienced reviewers designated by the chairperson from among members of the IRB. In reviewing the research, the reviewers may exercise all of the authorities of the IRB except that the reviewers may not disapprove the research. A research activity may be disapproved only after review in accordance with the non-expedited procedure set forth in §46.108(b).

(c) Each IRB which uses an expedited review procedure shall adopt a method for keeping all members advised of research proposals which have been approved under the procedure.

(d) The department or agency head may restrict, suspend, terminate, or choose not to authorize an institution's or IRB's use of the expedited review procedure.

§46.111 *Criteria for IRB approval of research*

(a) In order to approve research covered by this policy the IRB shall determine that all of the following requirements are satisfied:

(1) Risks to subjects are minimized: (i) By using procedures which are consistent with sound research design and which do not unnecessarily expose subjects to risk, and (ii) whenever appropriate, by using procedures already being performed on the subjects for diagnostic or treatment purposes.

(2) Risks to subjects are reasonable in relation to anticipated benefits, if any, to subjects, and the importance of the knowledge that may reasonably be expected to result. In evaluating risks and benefits, the IRB should consider only those risks and benefits that may result from the research (as distinguished from risks and benefits of therapies subjects would receive even if not participating in the research). The IRB should not consider possible long-range effects of applying knowledge gained in the research (for example, the possible effects of the research on public policy) as among those research risks that fall within the purview of its responsibility.

(3) Selection of subjects is equitable. In making this assessment the IRB should take into account the purposes of the research and the setting in which the research will be conducted and should be particularly cognizant of the special problems of research involving vulnerable populations, such as children, prisoners, pregnant women, mentally disabled persons, or economically or educationally disadvantaged persons.

(4) Informed consent will be sought from each prospective subject or the subject's legally authorized representative, in accordance with, and to the extent required by §46.116.

(5) Informed consent will be appropriately documented, in accordance with, and to the extent required by §46.117.

(6) When appropriate, the research plan makes adequate provision for monitoring the data collected to ensure the safety of subjects.

(7) When appropriate, there are adequate provisions to protect the privacy of subjects and to maintain the confidentiality of data.

(b) When some or all of the subjects are likely to be vulnerable to coercion or undue influence, such as children, prisoners, pregnant women, mentally disabled persons, or economically or educationally disadvantaged persons, additional safeguards have been included in the study to protect the rights and welfare of these subjects.

§46.112 *Review by institution*

Research covered by this policy that has been approved by an IRB may be subject to further appropriate review and approval or disapproval by officials of the institution. However, those officials may not approve the research if it has not been approved by an IRB.

§46.113 *Suspension or termination of IRB approval of research*

An IRB shall have authority to suspend or terminate approval of research that is not being conducted in accordance with the IRB's requirements or that has been associated with unexpected serious harm to subjects. Any suspension or termination or approval shall include a statement of the reasons for the IRB's action and shall be reported promptly to the investigator, appropriate institutional officials, and the department or agency head.

(Approved by the Office of Management and Budget under Control Number 9999-0020.)

§46.114 *Cooperative research*

Cooperative research projects are those projects covered by this policy which involve more than one institution. In the conduct of cooperative research projects, each institution is responsible for safeguarding the rights and welfare of human subjects and for complying with this policy. With the approval of the department or agency head, an institution participating in a cooperative project may enter into a joint review arrangement, rely upon the review of another qualified IRB, or make similar arrangements for avoiding duplication of effort.

§46.115 *IRB records*

(a) An institution, or when appropriate an IRB, shall prepare and maintain adequate documentation of IRB activities, including the following:

(1) Copies of all research proposals reviewed, scientific evaluations, if any, that accompany the proposals, approved sample consent documents, progress reports submitted by investigators, and reports of injuries to subjects.

(2) Minutes of IRB meetings which shall be in sufficient detail to show attendance at the meetings; actions taken by the IRB; the vote on these actions including the number of members voting for, against, and abstaining; the basis for requiring changes in or disapproving research; and a written summary of the discussion of controverted issues and their resolution.

(3) Records of continuing review activities.

(4) Copies of all correspondence between the IRB and the investigators.

(5) A list of IRB members in the same detail as described in §46.103(b)(3).

(6) Written procedures for the IRB in the same detail as described in §46.103(b)(4) and §46.103(b)(5).

(7) Statements of significant new findings provided to subjects, as required by §46.116(b)(5).

(b) The records required by this policy shall be retained for at least 3 years, and records relating to research which is conducted shall be retained for at least 3 years after completion of the research. All records shall be accessible

for inspection and copying by authorized representatives of the department or agency at reasonable times and in a reasonable manner.
(Approved by the Office of Management and Budget under Control Number 9999-0020.)

§46.116 General requirements for informed consent

Except as provided elsewhere in this policy, no investigator may involve a human being as a subject in research covered by this policy unless the investigator has obtained the legally effective informed consent of the subject or the subject's legally authorized representative. An investigator shall seek such consent only under circumstances that provide the prospective subject or the representative sufficient opportunity to consider whether or not to participate and that minimize the possibility of coercion or undue influence. The information that is given to the subject or the representative shall be in language understandable to the subject or the representative. No informed consent, whether oral or written, may include any exculpatory language through which the subject or the representative is made to waive or appear to waive any of the subject's legal rights, or releases or appears to release the investigator, the sponsor, the institution or its agents from liability for negligence.

(a) Basic elements of informed consent. Except as provided in paragraph (c) or (d) of this section, in seeking informed consent the following information shall be provided to each subject:

(1) A statement that the study involves research, an explanation of the purposes of the research and the expected duration of the subject's participation, a description of the procedures to be followed, and identification of any procedures which are experimental;

(2) A description of any reasonably foreseeable risks or discomforts to the subject;

(3) A description of any benefits to the subject or to others which may reasonably be expected from the research;

(4) A disclosure of appropriate alternative procedures or courses of treatment, if any, that might be advantageous to the subject;

(5) A statement describing the extent, if any, to which confidentiality of records identifying the subject will be maintained;

(6) For research involving more than minimal risk, an explanation as to whether any compensation and an explanation as to whether any medical treatments are available if injury occurs and, if so, what they consist of, or where further information may be obtained;

(7) An explanation of whom to contact for answers to pertinent questions about the research and research subjects' rights, and whom to contact in the event of a research-related injury to the subject; and

(8) A statement that participation is voluntary, refusal to participate will involve no penalty or loss of benefits to which the subject is otherwise entitled, and the subject may discontinue participation at any time without penalty or loss of benefits to which the subject is otherwise entitled.

(b) Additional elements of informed consent. When appropriate, one or more of the following elements of information shall also be provided to each subject:

(1) A statement that the particular treatment or procedure may involve risks to the subject (or to the embryo or fetus, if the subject is or may become pregnant) which are currently unforeseeable;

(2) Anticipated circumstances under which the subject's participation may be terminated by the investigator without regard to the subject's consent;

(3) Any additional costs to the subject that may result from participation in the research;

(4) The consequences of a subject's decision to withdraw from the research and procedures for orderly termination of participation by the subject;

(5) A statement that significant new findings developed during the course of the research which may relate to the subject's willingness to continue participation will be provided to the subject; and

(6) The approximate number of subjects involved in the study.

(c) An IRB may approve a consent procedure which does not include, or which alters, some or all of the elements of informed consent set forth above, or waive the requirement to obtain informed consent provided the IRB finds and documents that:

(1) The research or demonstration project is to be conducted by or subject to the approval of state or local government officials and is designed to study, evaluate, or otherwise examine: (i) public benefit or service programs; (ii) procedures for obtaining benefits or services under those programs; (iii) possible changes in or alternatives to those programs or procedures; or (iv) possible changes in methods or levels of payment for benefits or services under those programs; and

(2) the research could not practicably be carried out without the waiver or alteration.

(d) An IRB may approve a consent procedure which does not include, or which alters, some or all of the elements of informed consent set forth in this section, or waive the requirements to obtain informed consent provided the IRB finds and documents that:

(1) The research involves no more than minimal risk to the subjects;

(2) The waiver or alteration will not adversely affect the rights and welfare of the subjects;

(3) The research could not practicably be carried out without the waiver or alteration; and

(4) Whenever appropriate, the subjects will be provided with additional pertinent information after participation.

(e) The informed consent requirements in this policy are not intended to preempt any applicable federal, state, or local laws which require additional information to be disclosed in order for informed consent to be legally effective.

(f) Nothing in this policy is intended to limit the authority of a physician to provide emergency medical care, to the extent the physician is permitted to do so under applicable federal, state, or local law.

(Approved by the Office of Management and Budget under Control Number 9999-0020.)

§46.117 Documentation of informed consent

(a) Except as provided in paragraph (c) of this section, informed consent shall be documented by the use of a written consent form approved by the IRB and signed by the subject or the subject's legally authorized representative. A copy shall be given to the person signing the form.

(b) Except as provided in paragraph (c) of this section, the consent form may be either of the following:

(1) A written consent document that embodies the elements of informed consent required by §46.116. This form may be read to the subject or the subject's legally authorized representative, but in any event, the investigator shall give either the subject or the representative adequate opportunity to read it before it is signed; or

(2) A short form written consent document stating that the elements of informed consent required by §46.116 have been presented orally to the subject or the subject's legally authorized representative. When this method is used, there shall be a witness to the oral presentation. Also, the IRB shall approve a written summary of what is to be said to the subject or the representative. Only the short form itself is to be signed by the subject or the representative. However, the witness shall sign both the short form and a copy of the summary, and the person actually obtaining consent shall sign a copy of the summary. A copy of the summary shall be given to the subject or the representative, in addition to a copy of the short form.

(c) IRB may waive the requirement for the investigator to obtain a signed consent form for some or all subjects if it finds either:

(1) That the only record linking the subject and the research would be the consent document and the principal risk would be potential harm resulting from a breach of confidentiality. Each subject will be asked whether the subject wants documentation linking the subject with the research, and the subject's wishes will govern; or

(2) That the research presents no more than minimal risk of harm to subjects and involves no procedures for which written consent is normally required outside of the research context.

In cases in which the documentation requirement is waived, the IRB may require the investigator to provide subjects with a written statement regarding the research. (Approved by the Office of Management and Budget under Control Number 9999-0020.)

§46.118 Applications and proposals lacking definite plans for involvement of human subjects

Certain types of applications for grants, cooperative agreements, or contracts are submitted to departments or agencies with the knowledge that subjects may be involved within the period of support, but definite plans would not normally be set forth in the application or proposal. These include activities such as institutional type grants when selection of specific projects is the institution's responsibility; research training grants in which the activities involving subjects remain to be selected; and projects in which human subjects' involvement will depend upon completion of instruments, prior animal studies, or purification of compounds. These applications need not be reviewed by an IRB before an award may be made. However, except for research exempted or waived under §46.101 (b) or (i), no human subjects may be in-

volved in any project supported by these awards until the project has been reviewed and approved by the IRB, as provided in this policy, and certification submitted, by the institution, to the department or agency.

§46.119 Research undertaken without the intention of involving human subjects

In the event research is undertaken without the intention of involving human subjects, but it is later proposed to involve human subjects in the research, the research shall first be reviewed and approved by an IRB, as provided in this policy, a certification submitted, by the institution, to the department or agency, and final approval given to the proposed change by the department or agency.

§46.120 Evaluation and disposition of applications and proposals for research to be conducted or supported by a federal department or agency.

(a) The department or agency head will evaluate all applications and proposals involving human subjects submitted to the department or agency through such officers and employees of the department or agency and such experts and consultants as the department or agency head determines to be appropriate. This evaluation will take into consideration the risks to the subjects, the adequacy of protection against these risks, the potential benefits of the research to the subjects and others, and the importance of the knowledge gained or to be gained.

(b) On the basis of this evaluation, the department or agency head may approve or disapprove the application or proposal, or enter into negotiations to develop an approvable one.

§46.121 [Reserved]

§46.122 Use of federal funds

Federal funds administered by a department or agency may not be expended for research involving human subjects unless the requirements of this policy have been satisfied.

§46.123 Early termination of research support: Evaluation of applications and proposals

(a) The department or agency head may require that department or agency support for any project be terminated or suspended in the manner prescribed in applicable program requirements, when the department or agency head finds an institution has materially failed to comply with the terms of this policy.

(b) In making decisions about supporting or approving applications or proposals covered by this policy the department or agency head may take into account, in addition to all other eligibility requirements and program criteria, factors such as whether the applicant has been subject to a termination or suspension under paragraph (a) of this section and whether the applicant or the person or persons who would direct or has/have directed the scientific and technical aspects of an activity has/have, in the judgment of the department or agency head, materially failed to discharge responsibility for the protection of the rights and welfare of human subjects (whether or not the research was subject to federal regulation).

§46.124 Conditions

With respect to any research project or any class of research projects the department or agency head may impose additional conditions prior to or at the time of approval when in the judgment of the department or agency head additional conditions are necessary for the protection of human subjects.

Subpart B
Additional DHHS Protections Pertaining to Research, Development, and Related Activities Involving Fetuses, Pregnant Women, and Human In Vitro Fertilization

Source: 40 FR 33528, Aug. 8, 1975; 43 FR 1758, January 11, 1978;
43 FR 51559, November 3, 1978.

§46.201 Applicability

(a) The regulations in this subpart are applicable to all Department of Health and Human Services grants and contracts supporting research, development, and related activities involving: (1) the fetus, (2) pregnant women, and (3) human in vitro fertilization.

(b) Nothing in this subpart shall be construed as indicating that compliance with the procedures set forth herein will in any way render inapplicable pertinent State or local laws bearing upon activities covered by this subpart.

(c) The requirements of this subpart are in addition to those imposed under the other subparts of this part.

§46.202 Purpose

It is the purpose of this subpart to provide additional safeguards in reviewing activities to which this subpart is applicable to assure that they conform to appropriate ethical standards and relate to important societal needs.

§46.203 Definitions

As used in this subpart:

(a) Secretary means the Secretary of Health and Human Services and any other officer or employee of the Department of Health and Human Services (DHHS) to whom authority has been delegated.

(b) Pregnancy encompasses the period of time from confirmation of implantation (through any of the presumptive signs of pregnancy, such as missed menses, or by a medically acceptable pregnancy test), until expulsion or extraction of the fetus.

(c) Fetus means the product of conception from the time of implantation (as evidenced by any of the presumptive signs of pregnancy, such as missed menses, or a medically acceptable pregnancy test), until a determination is made, following expulsion or extraction of the fetus, that it is viable.

(d) Viable as it pertains to the fetus means being able, after either spontaneous or induced delivery, to survive (given the benefit of available medical therapy) to the point of independently maintaining heart beat and respiration. The Secretary may from time to time, taking into account medical advances, publish in the Federal Register guidelines to assist in determining whether a fetus is viable for purposes of this subpart. If a fetus is viable after delivery, it is a premature infant.

(e) Nonviable fetus means a fetus ex utero which, although living, is not viable.

(f) Dead fetus means a fetus ex utero which exhibits neither heartbeat, spontaneous respiratory activity, spontaneous movement of voluntary muscles, nor pulsation of the umbilical cord (if still attached).

(g) In vitro fertilization means any fertilization of human ova which occurs outside the body of a female, either through admixture of donor human sperm and ova or by any other means.

§46.204 Ethical Advisory Boards

(a) One or more Ethical Advisory Boards shall be established by the Secretary. Members of these board(s) shall be so selected that the board(s) will be competent to deal with medical, legal, social, ethical, and related issues and may include, for example, research scientists, physicians, psychologists, sociologists, educators, lawyers, and ethicists, as well as representatives of the general public. No board member may be a regular, full-time employee of the Department of Health and Human Services.

(b) At the request of the Secretary, the Ethical Advisory Board shall render advice consistent with the policies and requirements of this part as to ethical issues, involving activities covered by this subpart, raised by individual applications or proposals. In addition, upon request by the Secretary, the Board shall render advice as to classes of applications or proposals and general policies, guidelines, and procedures.

(c) A Board may establish, with the approval of the Secretary, classes of applications or proposals which: (1) Must be submitted to the Board, or (2) Need not be submitted to the Board. Where the Board so establishes a class of applications or proposals which must be submitted, no application or proposal within the class may be funded by the department or any component thereof until the application or proposal has been reviewed by the Board and the Board has rendered advice as to its acceptability from an ethical standpoint.

(d) [Nullified under Public Law 103-43, June 10, 1993]

§46.205 Additional duties of the Institutional Review Boards in connection with activities involving fetuses, pregnant women, or human in vitro fertilization

(a) In addition to the responsibilities prescribed for Institutional Review Boards under Subpart A of this part, the applicant's or offeror's Board shall, with respect to activities covered by this subpart, carry out the following additional duties:

(1) Determine that all aspects of the activity meet the requirements of this subpart;

(2) Determine that adequate consideration has been given to the manner in which potential subjects will be selected, and adequate provision has been made by the applicant or offeror for monitoring the actual informed consent process (e.g., through such mechanisms, when appropriate, as participation by the Institutional Review Board or subject advocates in: (i) Overseeing the actual process by which individual consents required by this subpart are secured either by approving induction of each individual into the activity or verifying, perhaps through sampling, that approved

procedures for induction of individuals into the activity are being followed, and (ii) monitoring the progress of the activity and intervening as necessary through such steps as visits to the activity site and continuing evaluation to determine if any unanticipated risks have arisen);

(3) Carry out such other responsibilities as may be assigned by the Secretary.

(b) No award may be issued until the applicant or offeror has certified to the Secretary that the Institutional Review Board has made the determinations required under paragraph (a) of this section and the Secretary has approved these determinations, as provided in §46.120 of Subpart A of this part.

(c) Applicants or offerors seeking support for activities covered by this subpart must provide for the designation of an Institutional Review Board, subject to approval by the Secretary, where no such Board has been established under Subpart A of this part.

§46.206 General limitations

(a) No activity to which this subpart is applicable may be undertaken unless:

(1) Appropriate studies on animals and nonpregnant individuals have been completed;

(2) Except where the purpose of the activity is to meet the health needs of the mother or the particular fetus, the risk to the fetus is minimal and, in all cases, is the least possible risk for achieving the objectives of the activity;

(3) Individuals engaged in the activity will have no part in: (i) Any decisions as to the timing, method, and procedures used to terminate the pregnancy, and (ii) determining the viability of the fetus at the termination of the pregnancy; and

(4) No procedural changes which may cause greater than minimal risk to the fetus or the pregnant woman will be introduced into the procedure for terminating the pregnancy solely in the interest of the activity.

(b) No inducements, monetary or otherwise, may be offered to terminate pregnancy for purposes of the activity. Source: 40 FR 33528, Aug. 8, 1975, as amended at 40 FR 51638, Nov. 6, 1975.

§46.207 Activities directed toward pregnant women as subjects

(a) No pregnant woman may be involved as a subject in an activity covered by this subpart unless: (1) The purpose of the activity is to meet the health needs of the mother and the fetus will be placed at risk only to the minimum extent necessary to meet such needs, or (2) the risk to the fetus is minimal.

(b) An activity permitted under paragraph (a) of this section may be conducted only if the mother and father are legally competent and have given their informed consent after having been fully informed regarding possible impact on the fetus, except that the father's informed consent need not be secured if: (1) The purpose of the activity is to meet the health needs of the mother; (2) his identity or whereabouts cannot reasonably be ascertained; (3) he is not reasonably available; or (4) the pregnancy resulted from rape.

§46.208 Activities directed toward fetuses in utero as subjects

(a) No fetus in utero may be involved as a subject in any activity covered by this subpart unless: (1) The purpose of the activity is to meet the health needs of the particular fetus and the fetus will be placed at risk only to the minimum extent necessary to meet such needs, or (2) the risk to the fetus imposed by the research is minimal and the purpose of the activity is the development of important biomedical knowledge which cannot be obtained by other means.

(b) An activity permitted under paragraph (a) of this section may be conducted only if the mother and father are legally competent and have given their informed consent, except that the father's consent need not be secured if: (1) His identity or whereabouts cannot reasonably be ascertained, (2) he is not reasonably available, or (3) the pregnancy resulted from rape.

§46.209 Activities directed toward fetuses ex utero, including nonviable fetuses, as subjects

(a) Until it has been ascertained whether or not a fetus ex utero is viable, a fetus ex utero may not be involved as a subject in an activity covered by this subpart unless:

(1) There will be no added risk to the fetus resulting from the activity, and the purpose of the activity is the development of important biomedical knowledge which cannot be obtained by other means, or

(2) The purpose of the activity is to enhance the possibility of survival of the particular fetus to the point of viability.

(b) No nonviable fetus may be involved as a subject in an activity covered by this subpart unless:

(1) Vital functions of the fetus will not be artificially maintained,

(2) Experimental activities which of themselves would terminate the heartbeat or respiration of the fetus will not be employed, and

(3) The purpose of the activity is the development of important biomedical knowledge which cannot be obtained by other means.

(c) In the event the fetus ex utero is found to be viable, it may be included as a subject in the activity only to the extent permitted by and in accordance with the requirements of other subparts of this part.

(d) An activity permitted under paragraph (a) or (b) of this section may be conducted only if the mother and father are legally competent and have given their informed consent, except that the father's informed consent need not be secured if: (1) His identity or whereabouts cannot reasonably be ascertained, (2) he is not reasonably available, or (3) the pregnancy resulted from rape.

§46.210 Activities involving the dead fetus, fetal material, or the placenta

Activities involving the dead fetus, mascerated fetal material, or cells, tissue, or organs excised from a dead fetus shall be conducted only in accordance with any applicable State or local laws regarding such activities.

§46.211 Modification or waiver of specific requirements

Upon the request of an applicant or offeror (with the approval of its Institutional Review Board), the Secretary may modify or waive specific requirements of this subpart, with the approval of the Ethical Advisory Board after such opportunity for public comment as the Ethical Advisory Board considers appropriate in the particular instance. In making such decisions, the Secretary will consider whether the risks to the subject are so outweighed by the sum of the benefit to the subject and the importance of the knowledge to be gained as to warrant such modification or waiver and that such benefits cannot be gained except through a modification or waiver. Any such modifications or waivers will be published as notices in the Federal Register.

Subpart C

Additional DHHS Protections Pertaining to Biomedical and Behavioral Research Involving Prisoners as Subjects

Source: 43 FR 53655, Nov. 16, 1978.

§46.301 Applicability

(a) The regulations in this subpart are applicable to all biomedical and behavioral research conducted or supported by the Department of Health and Human Services involving prisoners as subjects.

(b) Nothing in this subpart shall be construed as indicating that compliance with the procedures set forth herein will authorize research involving prisoners as subjects, to the extent such research is limited or barred by applicable State or local law.

(c) The requirements of this subpart are in addition to those imposed under the other subparts of this part.

§46.302 Purpose

Inasmuch as prisoners may be under constraints because of their incarceration which could affect their ability to make a truly voluntary and uncoerced decision whether or not to participate as subjects in research, it is the purpose of this subpart to provide additional safeguards for the protection of prisoners involved in activities to which this subpart is applicable.

§46.303 Definitions

As used in this subpart:

(a) Secretary means the Secretary of Health and Human Services and any other officer or employee of the Department of Health and Human Services to whom authority has been delegated.

(b) DHHS means the Department of Health and Human Services.

(c) Prisoner means any individual involuntarily confined or detained in a penal institution. The term is intended to encompass individuals sentenced to such an institution under a criminal or civil statute, individuals detained in other facilities by virtue of statutes or commitment procedures which provide alternatives to criminal prosecution or incarceration in a penal institution, and individuals detained pending arraignment, trial, or sentencing.

(d) Minimal risk is the probability and magnitude of physical or psychological harm that is normally encountered in the daily lives, or in the routine medical, dental, or psychological examination of healthy persons.

§46.304 Composition of Institutional Review Boards where prisoners are involved

In addition to satisfying the requirements in §46.107 of this part, an Institutional Review Board, carrying out responsibilities under this part with respect to research covered by this subpart, shall also meet the following specific requirements:

(a) A majority of the Board (exclusive of prisoner members) shall have no association with the prison(s) involved, apart from their membership on the Board.

(b) At least one member of the Board shall be a prisoner, or a prisoner representative with appropriate background and experience to serve in that capacity, except that where a particular research project is reviewed by more than one Board only one Board need satisfy this requirement.

§46.305 Additional duties of the Institutional Review Boards where prisoners are involved

(a) In addition to all other responsibilities prescribed for Institutional Review Boards under this part, the Board shall review research covered by this subpart and approve such research only if it finds that:

(1) The research under review represents one of the categories of research permissible under §46.306(a)(2);

(2) Any possible advantages accruing to the prisoner through his or her participation in the research, when compared to the general living conditions, medical care, quality of food, amenities and opportunity for earnings in the prison, are not of such a magnitude that his or her ability to weigh the risks of the research against the value of such advantages in the limited choice environment of the prison is impaired;

(3) The risks involved in the research are commensurate with risks that would be accepted by nonprisoner volunteers;

(4) Procedures for the selection of subjects within the prison are fair to all prisoners and immune from arbitrary intervention by prison authorities or prisoners. Unless the principal investigator provides to the Board justification in writing for following some other procedures, control subjects must be selected randomly from the group of available prisoners who meet the characteristics needed for that particular research project;

(5) The information is presented in language which is understandable to the subject population;

(6) Adequate assurance exists that parole boards will not take into account a prisoner's participation in the research in making decisions regarding parole, and each prisoner is clearly informed in advance that participation in the research will have no effect on his or her parole; and

(7) Where the Board finds there may be a need for follow-up examination or care of participants after the end of their participation, adequate provision has been made for such examination or care, taking into account the varying lengths

of individual prisoners' sentences, and for informing participants of this fact.

(b) The Board shall carry out such other duties as may be assigned by the Secretary.

(c) The institution shall certify to the Secretary, in such form and manner as the Secretary may require, that the duties of the Board under this section have been fulfilled.

§46.306 Permitted research involving prisoners

(a) Biomedical or behavioral research conducted or supported by DHHS may involve prisoners as subjects only if:

(1) The institution responsible for the conduct of the research has certified to the Secretary that the Institutional Review Board has approved the research under §46.305 of this subpart; and

(2) In the judgment of the Secretary the proposed research involves solely the following:

(i) Study of the possible causes, effects, and processes of incarceration, and of criminal behavior, provided that the study presents no more than minimal risk and no more than inconvenience to the subjects;

(ii) Study of prisons as institutional structures or of prisoners as incarcerated persons, provided that the study presents no more than minimal risk and no more than inconvenience to the subjects;

(iii) Research on conditions particularly affecting prisoners as a class (for example, vaccine trials and other research on hepatitis which is much more prevalent in prisons than elsewhere; and research on social and psychological problems such as alcoholism, drug addiction, and sexual assaults) provided that the study may proceed only after the Secretary has consulted with appropriate experts including experts in penology, medicine, and ethics, and published notice, in the Federal Register, of his intent to approve such research; or

(iv) Research on practices, both innovative and accepted, which have the intent and reasonable probability of improving the health or well-being of the subject. In cases in which those studies require the assignment of prisoners in a manner consistent with protocols approved by the IRB to control groups which may not benefit from the research, the study may proceed only after the Secretary has consulted with appropriate experts, including experts in penology, medicine, and ethics, and published notice, in the Federal Register, of the intent to approve such research.

(b) Except as provided in paragraph (a) of this section, biomedical or behavioral research conducted or supported by DHHS shall not involve prisoners as subjects.

Subpart D

Additional DHHS Protections for Children Involved as Subjects in Research

Source: 48 FR 9818, March 8, 1983; 56 FR 28032, June 18, 1991.

§46.401 To what do these regulations apply?

(a) This subpart applies to all research involving children as subjects, conducted or supported by the Department of Health and Human Services.

(1) This includes research conducted by Department employees, except that each head of an Operating Division of the Department may adopt such nonsubstantive, procedural modifications as may be appropriate from an administrative standpoint.

(2) It also includes research conducted or supported by the Department of Health and Human Services outside the United States, but in appropriate circumstances, the Secretary may, under paragraph (i) of §46.101 of Subpart A, waive the applicability of some or all of the requirements of these regulations for research of this type.

(b) Exemptions at §46.101(b)(1) and (b)(3) through (b)(6) are applicable to this subpart. The exemption at §46.101(b)(2) regarding educational tests is also applicable to this subpart. However, the exemption at §46.101(b)(2) for research involving survey or interview procedures or observations of public behavior does not apply to research covered by this subpart, except for research involving observation of public behavior when the investigator(s) do not participate in the activities being observed.

(c) The exceptions, additions, and provisions for waiver as they appear in paragraphs (c) through (i) of §46.101 of Subpart A are applicable to this subpart.

§46.402 Definitions

The definitions in §46.102 of Subpart A shall be applicable to this subpart as well. In addition, as used in this subpart:

(a) Children are persons who have not attained the legal age for consent to treatments or procedures involved in the research, under the applicable law of the jurisdiction in which the research will be conducted.

(b) Assent means a child's affirmative agreement to participate in research. Mere failure to object should not, absent affirmative agreement, be construed as assent.

(c) Permission means the agreement of parent(s) or guardian to the participation of their child or ward in research.

(d) Parent means a child's biological or adoptive parent.

(e) Guardian means an individual who is authorized under applicable State or local law to consent on behalf of a child to general medical care.

§46.403 IRB duties

In addition to other responsibilities assigned to IRBs under this part, each IRB shall review research covered by this subpart and approve only research which satisfies the conditions of all applicable sections of this subpart.

§46.404 Research not involving greater than minimal risk

DHHS will conduct or fund research in which the IRB finds that no greater than minimal risk to children is presented, only if the IRB finds that adequate provisions are made for soliciting the assent of the children and the permission of their parents or guardians, as set forth in §46.408.

§46.405 Research involving greater than minimal risk but presenting the prospect of direct benefit to the individual subjects

DHHS will conduct or fund research in which the IRB finds that more than minimal risk to children is presented by an intervention or procedure that holds out the prospect of direct benefit for the individual subject, or by a monitoring procedure that is likely to contribute to the subject's well-being, only if the IRB finds that:

(a) The risk is justified by the anticipated benefit to the subjects;

(b) The relation of the anticipated benefit to the risk is at least as favorable to the subjects as that presented by available alternative approaches; and

(c) Adequate provisions are made for soliciting the assent of the children and permission of their parents or guardians, as set forth in §46.408.

§46.406 Research involving greater than minimal risk and no prospect of direct benefit to individual subjects, but likely to yield generalizable knowledge about the subject's disorder or condition

DHHS will conduct or fund research in which the IRB finds that more than minimal risk to children is presented by an intervention or procedure that does not hold out the prospect of direct benefit for the individual subject, or by a monitoring procedure which is not likely to contribute to the well-being of the subject, only if the IRB finds that:

(a) The risk represents a minor increase over minimal risk;

(b) The intervention or procedure presents experiences to subjects that are reasonably commensurate with those inherent in their actual or expected medical, dental, psychological, social, or educational situations;

(c) The intervention or procedure is likely to yield generalizable knowledge about the subjects' disorder or condition which is of vital importance for the understanding or amelioration of the subjects' disorder or condition; and

(d) Adequate provisions are made for soliciting assent of the children and permission of their parents or guardians, as set forth in §46.408.

§46.407 Research not otherwise approvable which presents an opportunity to understand, prevent, or alleviate a serious problem affecting the health or welfare of children

DHHS will conduct or fund research that the IRB does not believe meets the requirements of §46.404, §46.405, or §46.406 only if:

(a) The IRB finds that the research presents a reasonable opportunity to further the understanding, prevention, or alleviation of a serious problem affecting the health or welfare of children; and

(b) The Secretary, after consultation with a panel of experts in pertinent disciplines (for example: science, medicine, education, ethics, law) and following opportunity for public review and comment, has determined either:

(1) That the research in fact satisfies the conditions of §46.404, §46.405, or §46.406, as applicable, or

(2) the following:

(i) The research presents a reasonable opportunity to further the understanding, prevention, or alleviation of a serious problem affecting the health or welfare of children;

(ii) The research will be conducted in accordance with sound ethical principles;

(iii) Adequate provisions are made for soliciting the assent of children and the permission of their parents or guardians, as set forth in §46.408.

§46.408 Requirements for permission by parents or guardians and for assent by children

(a) In addition to the determinations required under other applicable sections of this subpart, the IRB shall determine that adequate provisions are made for soliciting the assent of the children, when in the judgment of the IRB the children are capable of providing assent. In determining whether children are capable of assenting, the IRB shall take into account the ages, maturity, and psychological state of the children involved. This judgment may be made for all children to be involved in research under a particular protocol, or for each child, as the IRB deems appropriate. If the IRB determines that the capability of some or all of the children is so limited that they cannot reasonably be consulted or that the intervention or procedure involved in the research holds out a prospect of direct benefit that is important to the health or well-being of the children and is available only in the context of the research, the assent of the children is not a necessary condition for proceeding with the research. Even where the IRB determines that the subjects are capable of assenting, the IRB may still waive the assent requirement under circumstances in which consent may be waived in accord with §46.116 of Subpart A.

(b) In addition to the determinations required under other applicable sections of this subpart, the IRB shall determine, in accordance with and to the extent that consent is required by §46.116 of Subpart A, that adequate provisions are made for soliciting the permission of each child's parents or guardian. Where parental permission is to be obtained, the IRB may find that the permission of one parent is sufficient for research to be conducted under §46.404 or §46.405. Where research is covered by §46.406 and §46.407 and permission is to be obtained from parents, both parents must give their permission unless one parent is deceased, unknown, incompetent, or not reasonably available, or when only one parent has legal responsibility for the care and custody of the child.

(c) In addition to the provisions for waiver contained in §46.116 of Subpart A, if the IRB determines that a research protocol is designed for conditions or for a subject population for which parental or guardian permission is not a reasonable requirement to protect the subjects (for example, neglected or abused children), it may waive the consent requirements in Subpart A of this part and paragraph (b) of this section, provided an appropriate mechanism for protecting the children who will participate as subjects in the research is substituted, and provided further that the waiver is not inconsistent with Federal, State, or local law. The choice of an appropriate mechanism would depend upon the nature and purpose of the activities described in the protocol, the risk and anticipated benefit to the research subjects, and their age, maturity, status, and condition.

(d) Permission by parents or guardians shall be documented in accordance with and to the extent required by §46.117 of Subpart A.

(e) When the IRB determines that assent is required, it shall also determine whether and how assent must be documented.

§46.409 Wards

(a) Children who are wards of the State or any other agency, institution, or entity can be included in research approved under §46.406 or §46.407 only if such research is:

(1) Related to their status as wards; or

(2) Conducted in schools, camps, hospitals, institutions, or similar settings in which the majority of children involved as subjects are not wards.

(b) If the research is approved under paragraph (a) of this section, the IRB shall require appointment of an advocate for each child who is a ward, in addition to any other individual acting on behalf of the child as guardian or in loco parentis. One individual may serve as advocate for more than one child. The advocate shall be an individual who has the background and experience to act in, and agrees to act in, the best interests of the child for the duration of the child's participation in the research and who is not associated in any way (except in the role as advocate or member of the IRB) with the research, the investigator(s), or the guardian organization.

Code of Federal Regulations: Title 21, Part 50

21 CFR Part 50—Protection of Human Subjects—Food and Drug Administration

Subpart A—General Provisions

§ 50.1 Scope

(a) This part applies to all clinical investigations regulated by the Food and Drug Administration under sections 505(i) and 520(g) of the Federal Food, Drug, and Cosmetic Act, as well as clinical investigations that support applications for research or marketing permits for products by the Food and Drug Administration, including food and color additives, drugs for human use, medical devices for human use, biological products for human use, and electronic products. Additional specific obligations and commitments of, and standards of conduct for, persons who sponsor or monitor clinical investigations involving particular test articles may also be found in other parts (e.g., 21 CFR parts 312 and 812). Compliance with these parts is intended to protect the rights and safety of subjects involved in investigations filed with the Food and Drug Administration pursuant to sections 406, 409, 502, 503, 505, 506, 507, 510, 513-516, 518, 520, 706, and 801 of the Federal Food, Drug and Cosmetic Act and sections 351 and 354-360F of the Public Health Service Act.

(b) References in this part to regulatory sections of the Code of Federal Regulations are to chapter I of title 21, unless otherwise noted.

[45 FR 36390, May 30, 1980; 46 FR 8979, Jan. 27, 1981]

§ 50.3 Definitions
As used in this part:

(a) Act means the Federal Food, Drug, and Cosmetic Act, as amended (secs. 201-902, 52 Stat. 1040 et seq. as amended (21 U.S.C. 321-392)).

(b) Application for research or marketing permit includes:

(1) A color additive petition, described in part 71.

(2) A food additive petition, described in parts 171 and 571.

(3) Data and information about a substance submitted as part of the procedures for establishing that the substance is generally recognized as safe for use that results or may reasonably be expected to result, directly or indirectly, in its becoming a component or otherwise affecting the characteristics of any food, described in §§ 170.30 and 570.30.

(4) Data and information about a food additive submitted as part of the procedures for food additives permitted to be used on an interim basis pending additional study, described in § 180.1.

(5) Data and information about a substance submitted as part of the procedures for establishing a tolerance for unavoidable contaminants in food and food-packaging materials described in section 406 of the act.

(6) An investigational new drug application described in part 312 of this chapter.

(7) A new drug application described in part 314.

(8) Data and information about the bio-availability or bio-equivalence of drugs for human use submitted as part of the procedures for issuing, amending, or repealing a bio-equivalence requirement, described in part 320.

(9) Data and information about an over-the-counter drug for human use submitted as part of the procedures for classifying these drugs as generally recognized as safe and effective and not misbranded, described in part 330.

(10) Data and information about a prescription drug for human use submitted as part of the procedures for classifying these drugs as generally recognized as safe and effective and not misbranded, described in this chapter.

(11) Data and information about an antibiotic drug submitted as part of the procedures for issuing, amending or repealing regulations for these drugs, described in § 314.300 of this chapter.

(12) An application for a biological product license, described in part 601.

(13) Data and information about a biological product submitted as part of the procedures for determining that licensed biological products are safe and effective and not misbranded, described in part 601.

(14) Data and information about an in vitro diagnostic product submitted as part of the procedures for establishing, amending, or repealing a standard for these products, described in part 809.

(15) An Application for an Investigational Device Exemption, described in part 812.

(16) Data and information about a medical device submitted as part of the procedures for classifying these devices, described in section 513.

(17) Data and information about a medical device submitted as part of the procedures for establishing, amending, or repealing a standard for these devices, described in section 514.

(18) An application for premarket approval of a medical device, described in section 515.

(19) A product development protocol for a medical device, described in section 515.

(20) Data and information about an electronic product submitted as part of the procedures for establishing, amending or repealing a standard for these products, described in section 358 of the Public Health Service Act.

(21) Data and information about an electronic product submitted as part of the procedures for obtaining a variance from any electronic product performance standard, as described in § 1010.4.

(22) Data and information about an electronic product submitted as part of the procedures for granting amending, or extending an exemption from a radiation safety performance standard, as described in § 1010.5.

(c) Clinical investigation means any experiment that involves a test article and one or more human subjects and that either is subject to requirements for prior submission to the Food and Drug Administration under section 505(i), or 520(g) of the act, or is not subject to requirements for prior submission to the Food and Drug Administration under these sections of the act, but the results of which are intended to be submitted later to, or held for inspection by, the Food and Drug Administration as part of an application for a research or marketing permit. The term does not include experiments that are subject to the provisions of part 58 of this chapter, regarding nonclinical laboratory studies.

(d) Investigator means an individual who actually conducts a clinical investigation, i.e., under whose immediate direction the test article is administered or dispensed to or used involving, a subject, or, in the event of an investigation conducted by a team of individuals, is the responsible leader of that team.

(e) Sponsor means a person who initiates a clinical investigation, but who does not actually conduct the investigation, i.e., the test article is administered or dispensed to or used involving, a subject under the immediate direction of another individual. A person other than an individual (e.g., corporation or agency) that uses one or more of its own employees to conduct a clinical investigation it has initiated is considered to be a sponsor (not a sponsor-investigator) and the employees are considered to be investigators.

(f) Sponsor-investigator means an individual who both initiates and actually conducts, alone or with others a clinical investigation, i.e., under whose immediate direction the test article is administered or dispensed to, or used involving, a subject. The term does not include any person other than an individual, e.g., corporation or agency.

(g) Human subject means an individual who is or becomes a participant in research, either as a recipient of the test article as a control. A subject may be either a healthy human or a patient.

(h) Institution means any public or private entity or Agency (including Federal, State, and other agencies). The word facility as used in section 520(g) of the act is deemed to be synonymous with the term institution for purposes of this part.

(i) Institutional review board (IRB) means any board, committee, or other group formally designated by an institution to review biomedical research involving humans as subjects, to approve the initiation of and conduct periodic review of such research. The term has the same meaning as the phrase institutional review committee as used in section 520(g) of the act.

(j) Test article means any drug (including a biological product for human use), medical device for human use, human food additive, color additive, electronic product, or any other article subject to regulation under the act or under sections 351 and 354-360F of the Public Health Service Act (42 U.S.C. 262 and 263b-263n).

(k) Minimal risk means that the probability and magnitude of harm or discomfort anticipated in the research are not greater in and of themselves than those ordinarily encountered in daily life or during the performance of routine physical or psychological examinations or tests.

(l) Legally authorized representative means an individual or judicial or other body authorized under applicable law to consent on behalf of a prospective subject to the subject's participation in the procedure(s) involved in the research.

(m) Family member means any one of the following legally competent persons: Spouse; parents; children (including adopted children); brothers and sisters; and any individual related by blood or affinity whose close association with the subject is the equivalent of a family relationship.

[45 FR 36390, May 30, 1980, as amended at 46 FR 8950 Jan. 27,1981; 54 FR 9038, Mar. 3, 1989; 56 FR 28028, June 18, 1991; 61 FR 51497, Oct. 2, 1996; 62 FR 39440, July 23, 1997]

Subpart B—Informed Consent of Human Subjects
Source: 46 FR 8951, Jan. 27, 1981, unless otherwise noted.

Sec. 50.20 General requirements for informed consent
Except as provided in Secs. 50.23 and 50.24, no investigator may involve a human being as a subject in research covered by these regulations unless the investigator has obtained the legally effective informed consent of the subject or the subject's legally authorized representative. An investigator shall seek such consent only under circumstances that provide the prospective subject or the representative sufficient opportunity to consider whether or not to participate and that minimize the possibility of coercion or undue influence. The information that is given to the subject or the representative shall be in language understandable to the subject or the representative. No informed consent, whether oral or written, may include any exculpatory language through which the subject or the representative is made to waive or appear to waive any of the subject's legal rights, or releases or appears to release

the investigator, the sponsor, the institution, or its agents from liability for negligence.

[46 FR 8951, Jan. 27, 1981, as amended at 64 FR 10942, Mar. 8, 1999]

Sec. 50.23 Exception from general requirements

(a) The obtaining of informed consent shall be deemed feasible unless, before use of the test article (except as provided in paragraph (b) of this section), both the investigator and a physician who is not otherwise participating in the clinical investigation certify in writing all of the following:

(1) The human subject is confronted by a life-threatening situation necessitating the use of the test article.

(2) Informed consent cannot be obtained from the subject because of an inability to communicate with, or obtain legally effective consent from, the subject.

(3) Time is not sufficient to obtain consent from the subject's legal representative.

(4) There is available no alternative method of approved or generally recognized therapy that provides an equal or greater likelihood of saving the life of the subject.

(b) If immediate use of the test article is, in the investigator's opinion, required to preserve the life of the subject, and time is not sufficient to obtain the independent determination required in paragraph (a) of this section in advance of using the test article, the determinations of the clinical investigator shall be made and, within 5 working days after the use of the article, be reviewed and evaluated in writing by a physician who is not participating in the clinical investigation.

(c) The documentation required in paragraph (a) or (b) of this section shall be submitted to the IRB within 5 working days after the use of the test article.

(d)(1) Under 10 U.S.C. 1107(f) the President may waive the prior consent requirement for the administration of an investigational new drug to a member of the armed forces in connection with the member's participation in a particular military operation. The statute specifies that only the President may waive informed consent in this connection and the President may grant such a waiver only if the President determines in writing that obtaining consent: Is not feasible; is contrary to the best interests of the military member; or is not in the interests of national security. The statute further provides that in making a determination to waive prior informed consent on the ground that it is not feasible or the ground that it is contrary to the best interests of the military members involved, the President shall apply the standards and criteria that are set forth in the relevant FDA regulations for a waiver of the prior informed consent requirements of section 505(i)(4) of the Federal Food, Drug, and Cosmetic Act (21 U.S.C. 355(i)(4)). Before such a determination may be made that obtaining informed consent from military personnel prior to the use of an investigational drug (including an antibiotic or biological product) in a specific protocol under an investigational new drug application (IND) sponsored by the Department of Defense (DOD) and limited to specific military personnel involved in a particular military operation is not feasible or is contrary to the best interests of the military members involved the Secretary of Defense must first request such a determination from the President, and certify and document to the President that the following standards and criteria contained in paragraphs (d)(1) through (d)(4) of this section have been met.

(i) The extent and strength of evidence of the safety and effectiveness of the investigational new drug in relation to the medical risk that could be encountered during the military operation supports the drug's administration under an IND.

(ii) The military operation presents a substantial risk that military personnel may be subject to a chemical, biological, nuclear, or other exposure likely to produce death or serious or life-threatening injury or illness.

(iii) There is no available satisfactory alternative therapeutic or preventive treatment in relation to the intended use of the investigational new drug.

(iv) Conditioning use of the investigational new drug on the voluntary participation of each member could significantly risk the safety and health of any individual member who would decline its use, the safety of other military personnel, and the accomplishment of the military mission.

(v) A duly constituted institutional review board (IRB) established and operated in accordance with the requirements of paragraphs (d)(2) and (d)(3) of this section, responsible for review of the study, has reviewed and approved the investigational new drug protocol and the administration of the investigational new drug without informed consent. DOD's request is to include the documentation required by 56.115(a)(2) of this chapter.

(vi) DOD has explained:

(A) The context in which the investigational drug will be administered, e.g., the setting or whether it will be self-administered or it will be administered by a health professional;

(B) The nature of the disease or condition for which the preventive or therapeutic treatment is intended; and

(C) To the extent there are existing data or information available, information on conditions that could alter the effects of the investigational drug.

(vii) DOD's record keeping system is capable of tracking and will be used to track the proposed treatment from supplier to the individual recipient.

(viii) Each member involved in the military operation will be given, prior to the administration of the investigational new drug, a specific written information sheet (including information required by 10 U.S.C. 1107(d)) concerning the investigational new drug, the risks and benefits of its use, potential side effects, and other pertinent information about the appropriate use of the product.

(ix) Medical records of members involved in the military operation will accurately document the receipt by members of the notification required by paragraph (d)(1)(viii) of this section.

(x) Medical records of members involved in the military operation will accurately document the receipt

(xi) DOD will provide adequate follow-up to assess whether there are beneficial or adverse health consequences that result from the use of the investigational product.

(xii) DOD is pursuing drug development, including a time line, and marketing approval with due diligence.

(xiii) FDA has concluded that the investigational new drug protocol may proceed subject to a decision by the President on the informed consent waiver request.

(xiv) DOD will provide training to the appropriate medical personnel and potential recipients on the specific investigational new drug to be administered prior to its use.

(xv) DOD has stated and justified the time period for which the waiver is needed, not to exceed one year, unless separately renewed under these standards and criteria.

(xvi) DOD shall have a continuing obligation to report to the FDA and to the President any changed circumstances relating to these standards and criteria (including the time period referred to in paragraph (d)(1)(xv) of this section) or that otherwise might affect the determination to use an investigational new drug without informed consent.

(xvii) DOD is to provide public notice as soon as practicable and consistent with classification requirements through notice in the Federal Register describing each waiver of informed consent determination, a summary of the most updated scientific information on the products used, and other pertinent information.

(xviii) Use of the investigational drug without informed consent otherwise conforms with applicable law.

(xix) The duly constituted institutional review board, described in paragraph (d)(1)(v) of this section, must include at least 3 nonaffiliated members who shall not be employees or officers of the Federal Government (other than for purposes of membership on the IRB) and shall be required to obtain any necessary security clearances. This IRB shall review the proposed IND protocol at a convened meeting at which a majority of the members are present including at least one member whose primary concerns are in nonscientific areas and, if feasible, including a majority of the nonaffiliated members. The information required by Sec. 56.115(a)(2) of this chapter is to be provided to the Secretary of Defense for further review.

(3) The duly constituted institutional review board, described in paragraph (d)(1)(v) of this section, must review and approve:

(i) The required information sheet;

(ii) The adequacy of the plan to disseminate information, including distribution of the information sheet to potential recipients, on the investigational product (e.g., in forms other than written);

(iii) The adequacy of the information and plans for its dissemination to health care providers including potential side effects, contraindications, potential interactions, and other pertinent considerations; and

(iv) An informed consent form as required by part 50 of this chapter, in those circumstances in which DOD determines that informed consent may be obtained from some or all personnel involved.

(4) DOD is to submit to FDA summaries of institutional review board meetings at which the proposed protocol has been reviewed.

(5) Nothing in these criteria or standards is intended to preempt or limit FDA's and DOD's authority or obligations under applicable statutes and regulations.

[46 FR 8951, Jan. 27, 1981, as amended at 55 FR 52817, Dec. 21, 1990; 64 FR 399, Jan. 5, 1999; 64 FR 54188, Oct. 5, 1999]

Sec. 50.24 Exception from informed consent requirements for emergency research

(a) The IRB responsible for the review, approval, and continuing review of the clinical investigation described in this section may approve that investigation without requiring that informed consent of all research subjects be obtained if the IRB (with the concurrence of a licensed physician who is a member of or consultant to the IRB and who is not otherwise participating in the clinical investigation) finds and documents each of the following:

(1) The human subjects are in a life-threatening situation, available treatments are unproven or unsatisfactory, and the collection of valid scientific evidence, which may include evidence obtained through randomized placebo-controlled investigations, is necessary to determine the safety and effectiveness of particular interventions.

(2) Obtaining informed consent is not feasible because:

(i) The subjects will not be able to give their informed consent as a result of their medical condition;

(ii) The intervention under investigation must be administered before consent from the subjects' legally authorized representatives is feasible; and

(iii) There is no reasonable way to identify prospectively the individuals likely to become eligible for participation in the clinical investigation.

(3) Participation in the research holds out the prospect of direct benefit to the subjects because:

(i) Subjects are facing a life-threatening situation that necessitates intervention;

(ii) Appropriate animal and other preclinical studies have been conducted, and the information derived from those studies and related evidence support the potential for the intervention to provide a direct benefit to the individual subjects; and

(iii) Risks associated with the investigation are reasonable in relation to what is known about the medical condition of the potential class of subjects, the risks and benefits of standard therapy, if any, and what is known about the risks and benefits of the proposed intervention or activity.

(4) The clinical investigation could not practically be carried out without the waiver.

(5) The proposed investigational plan defines the length of the potential therapeutic window based on scientific evidence, and the investigator has committed to attempting to contact a legally authorized representative for each subject within that window of time and, if feasible, to asking the legally authorized representative contacted for consent within that window rather than proceeding without consent. The investigator will summarize efforts made to contact legally authorized representatives and make this information available to the IRB at the time of continuing review.

(6) The IRB has reviewed and approved informed consent procedures and an informed consent document consistent with Sec. 50.25. These procedures and the informed consent document are to be used with subjects or their legally authorized representatives in situations where use of such procedures and documents is feasible. The IRB has reviewed and approved procedures and information to be used when providing an opportunity for a family member to object to a subject's participation in the clinical investigation consistent with paragraph (a)(7)(v) of this section.

(7) Additional protections of the rights and welfare of the subjects will be provided, including, at least:

  (i) Consultation (including, where appropriate, consultation carried out by the IRB) with representatives of the communities in which the clinical investigation will be conducted and from which the subjects be drawn;

  (ii) Public disclosure to the communities in which the clinical investigation will be conducted and from which the subjects will be drawn, prior to initiation of the clinical investigation, of plans for the investigation and its risks and expected benefits;

  (iii) Public disclosure of sufficient information following completion of the clinical investigation to apprise the community and researchers of the study, including the demographic characteristics of the research population, and its results;

  (iv) Establishment of an independent data monitoring committee to exercise oversight of the clinical investigation; and

  (v) If obtaining informed consent is not feasible and a legally authorized representative is not reasonably available, the investigator has committed, if feasible, to attempting to contact within the therapeutic window the subject's family member who is not a legally authorized representative, and asking whether he or she objects to the subject's participation in the clinical investigation. The investigator summarize efforts made to contact family members and make this information available to the IRB at the time of continuing review.

(b) The IRB is responsible for ensuring that procedures are in place to inform, at the earliest feasible opportunity, each subject, or if the subject remains incapacitated, a legally authorized representative of the subject, or if such a representative is not reasonably available, a family member, of the subject's inclusion in the clinical investigation, the details of the investigation and other information contained in the informed consent document. The IRB shall also ensure that there is a procedure to inform the subject, or if the subject remains incapacitated, a legally authorized representative of the subject, or if such a representative is not reasonably available, a family member, that he or she may discontinue the subject's participation at any time without penalty or loss of benefits to which the subject is otherwise entitled. If a legally authorized representative or family member is told about the clinical investigation and the subject's condition improves, the subject is also to be informed as soon as feasible. If a subject is into a clinical investigation with waived consent and the subject dies before a legally authorized representative or family member can be contacted, information about the clinical investigation is to be provided to the subject's legally authorized representative or family member, if feasible.

(c) The IRB determinations required by paragraph (a) of this section and the documentation required by paragraph (e) of this section are to be retained by the IRB for at least 3 years after completion of the clinical investigation, and the records shall be accessible for inspection and copying by FDA in accordance with Sec. 56.115(b) of this chapter.

(d) Protocols involving an exception to the informed consent requirement under this section must be performed under a separate investigational new drug application (IND) or investigational device exemption (IDE) that clearly identifies such protocols as protocols that may include subjects who are unable to consent. The submission of those protocols in a separate IND/IDE is required even if an IND for the same drug product or an IDE for the same device already exists. Applications for investigations under this section may not be submitted as amendments under Secs. 312.30 or 812.35 of this chapter.

(e) If an IRB determines that it cannot approve a clinical investigation because the investigation does not meet the criteria in the exception provided under paragraph (a) of this section or because of other relevant ethical concerns, the IRB must document its findings and provide these findings promptly in writing to the clinical investigator and to the sponsor of the clinical investigation. The sponsor of the clinical investigation must promptly disclose this information to FDA and to the sponsor's clinical investigators who are participating or are asked to participate in this or a substantially equivalent clinical investigation of the sponsor, and to other IRB's that have been, or are, asked to review this or a substantially equivalent investigation by that sponsor.

[61 FR 51528, Oct. 2, 1996]

Sec. 50.25 Elements of informed consent

(a) Basic elements of informed consent. In seeking informed consent, the following information shall be provided to each subject:

(1) A statement that the study involves research, an explanation of the purposes of the research and the expected duration of the subject's participation, a description of the procedures to be followed, and identification of any procedures which are experimental.

(2) A description of any reasonably foreseeable risks or discomforts to the subject.

(3) A description of any benefits to the subject or to others which may reasonably be expected from the research.

(4) A disclosure of appropriate alternative procedures or courses of treatment, if any, that might be advantageous to the subject.

(5) A statement describing the extent, if any, to which confidentiality of records identifying the subject will be maintained and that notes the possibility that the Food and Drug Administration may inspect the records.

(6) For research involving more than minimal risk, an explanation as to whether any compensation and an explanation as to whether any medical treatments are available if injury occurs and, if so, what they consist of, or where further information may be obtained.

(7) An explanation of whom to contact for answers to pertinent questions about the research and research subjects' rights, and whom to contact in the event of a research-related injury to the subject.

(8) A statement that participation is voluntary, that refusal to participate will involve no penalty or loss of benefits to which the subject is otherwise entitled, and that the subject may discontinue participation at any time without penalty or loss of benefits to which the subject is otherwise entitled.

(b) Additional elements of informed consent. When appropriate, one or more of the following elements of information shall also be provided to each subject:

(1) A statement that the particular treatment or procedure may involve risks to the subject (or to the embryo or fetus, if the subject is or may become pregnant) which are currently unforeseeable.

(2) Anticipated circumstances under which the subject's participation may be terminated by the investigator without regard to the subject's consent.

(3) Any additional costs to the subject that may result from participation in the research.

(4) The consequences of a subject's decision to withdraw from the research and procedures for orderly termination of participation by the subject.

(5) A statement that significant new findings developed during the course of the research which may relate to the subject's willingness to continue participation will be provided to the subject.

(6) The approximate number of subjects involved in the study.

(c) The informed consent requirements in these regulations are not intended to preempt any applicable Federal, State, or local laws which require additional information to be disclosed for informed consent to be legally effective.

(d) Nothing in these regulations is intended to limit the authority of a physician to provide emergency medical care to the extent the physician is permitted to do so under applicable Federal, State, or local law.

Sec. 50.27 *Documentation of informed consent*

(a) Except as provided in Sec. 56.109(c), informed consent shall be documented by the use of a written consent form approved by the IRB and signed and dated by the subject or the subject's legally authorized representative at the time of consent. A copy shall be given to the person signing the form.

(b) Except as provided in Sec. 56.109(c), the consent form may be either of the following:

(1) A written consent document that embodies the elements of informed consent required by Sec. 50.25. This form may be read to the subject or the subject's legally authorized representative, but, in any event, the investigator shall give either the subject or the representative adequate opportunity to read it before it is signed.

(2) A short form written consent document stating that the elements of informed consent required by Sec. 50.25 have been presented orally to the subject or the subject's legally authorized representative. When this method is used, there shall be a witness to the oral presentation. Also, the IRB shall approve a written summary of what is to be said to the subject or the representative. Only the short form itself is to be signed by the subject or the representative. However, the witness shall sign both the short form and a copy of the summary, and the person actually obtaining the consent shall sign a copy of the summary. A copy of the summary shall be given to the subject or the representative in addition to a copy of the short form.

[46 FR 8951, Jan. 27, 1981, as amended at 61 FR 57280, Nov. 5, 1996]

[61FR 51497, October 2, 1996]

Code of Federal Regulations: Title 21, Part 56

21 CFR Part 56—Institutional Review Boards—Food and Drug Administration

[Source: 46 FR 8975, Jan 27, 1981, unless otherwise noted.]

Subpart A—General Provisions

§ 56.101 Scope

(a) This part contains the general standards for the composition operation, and responsibility of an Institutional Review Board (IRB) that reviews clinical investigations regulated by the Food and Drug Administration under sections 505(i) and 520(g) of the act, as well as clinical that support applications for research or marketing permits for products regulated by the Food and Drug Administration including food and color additives, drugs for human use medical devices for human use, biological products for human use, and electronic products. Compliance with this part is intended to protect the rights and welfare of human subjects involved in such investigations.

(b) References in this part to regulatory sections of the Code of Federal Regulations are to chapter I of title 21, unless otherwise noted.

§ 56.102 Definitions

As used in this part:

(a) Act means the Federal Food, Drug, and Cosmetic Act, as amended (secs. 201-902, 52 Stat. 1040 et seq., as amended (21 U.S.C. 321-392)).

(b) Application for research or marketing permit includes:

(1) A color additive petition, described in part 71.

(2) Data and information regarding a substance submitted as part of the procedures for establishing that a substance is generally recognized as safe for a use which results or may reasonably be expected to result, directly or indirectly, in its becoming a component or otherwise affecting the characteristics of any food, described in § 170.35.

(3) A food additive petition, described in part 171.

(4) Data and information regarding a food additive submitted as part of the procedures regarding food additives permitted to be used on an interim basis pending additional study, described in § 180.1.

(5) Data and information regarding a substance submitted as part of the procedures for establishing a tolerance for unavoidable contaminants in food and food-packaging materials described in section 406 of the act.

(6) An investigational new drug application, described in part 312 of this chapter.

(7) A new drug application, described in part 314.

(8) Data and information regarding the bioavailability or bioequivalence of drugs for human use submitted as part of the procedures for issuing, amending, or repealing a bioequivalence requirement, described in part 320.

(9) Data and information regarding an over-the-counter drug for human use submitted as part of the procedures for classifying such drugs as generally recognized as safe and effective and not misbranded, described in part 330.

(10) An application for a biological product license, described in part 601.

(11) Data and information regarding a biological product submitted as part of the procedures for determining that licensed biological products are safe and effective and not misbranded, as described in part 601.

(12) An Application for an Investigational Device Exemption, described in parts 812 and 813.

(13) Data and information regarding a medical device for human use submitted as part of the procedures for classifying such devices, described in part 860.

(14) Data and information regarding a medical device for human use submitted as part of the procedures for establishing, amending, or repealing a standard for such device, described in part 861.

(15) An application for premarket approval of a medical device for human use, described in section 515 of the act.

(16) A product development protocol for a medical device for human use, described in section 515 of the act.

(17) Data and information regarding an electronic product submitted as part of the procedures for establishing, amending, or repealing a standard for such products, described in section 358 of the Public Health Service Act.

(18) Data and information regarding an electronic product submitted as part of the procedures for obtaining a variance from any electronic product performance standard, as described in § 1010.4.

(19) Data and information regarding an electronic product submitted as part of the procedures for granting, amending, or extending an exemption from a radiation safety performance standard as described in § 1010.5.

(20) Data and information regarding an electronic product submitted as part of the procedures for obtaining an exemption from notification of a radiation safety defect or failure of compliance with a radiation safety performance standard, described in subpart D of part 1003.

(c) Clinical investigation means any experiment that involves a test article and one or more human subjects, and that either must meet the requirements for prior submission to the Food and Drug Administration under section 505(i), or 520(g) of the act, or need not meet the requirements for prior submission to the Food and Drug Administration under these sections of the act, but the results of which are intended to be later submitted to, or held for inspection by, the Food and Drug Administration as part of an application for a research or marketing permit. The term does not include experiments that must meet the provisions of part 58, regarding nonclinical laboratory studies. The terms research, clinical research, clinical study, study, and clinical investigation are deemed to be synonymous for purposes of this part.

(d) Emergency use means the use of a test article on a human subject in a life-threatening situation in which no standard acceptable treatment is available, and in which there is not sufficient time to obtain IRB approval.

(e) Human subject means an individual who is or becomes a participant in research, either as a recipient of the test article or as a control. A subject may be either a healthy individual or a patient.

(f) Institution means any public or private entity or Agency (including Federal, State, and other agencies). The term facility as used in section 520(g) of the act is deemed to be synonymous with the term institution for purposes of this part.

(g) Institutional Review Board (IRB) means any board committee, or other group formally designated by an institution to review, to approve the initiation of, and to conduct periodic review of, biomedical research involving human subjects. The primary purpose of such review is to assure the protection of the rights and welfare of the hu-

man subjects. The term has the same meaning as the phrase institutional review committee as used in section 520(g) of the act.

(h) Investigator means an individual who actually conducts a clinical investigation (i.e., under whose immediate direction the test article is administered or dispensed to or used involving, a subject) or, in the event of an investigation conducted by a team of individuals, is the responsible leader of that team.

(i) Minimal risk means that the probability and magnitude of harm or discomfort anticipated in the research are not greater in and of themselves than those ordinarily encountered in daily life or during the performance of routine physical or psychological examinations or tests.

(j) Sponsor means a person or other entity that initiates a clinical investigation, but that does not actually conduct the investigation, i.e., the test article is administered or dispensed to, or used involving, a subject under the immediate direction of another individual. A person other than an individual (e.g., a corporation or agency) that uses one or more of its own employees to conduct an investigation that it has initiated is considered to be a sponsor (not a sponsor-investigator) and the employees are considered to be investigators.

(k) Sponsor-investigator means an individual who both initiates and actually conducts, alone or with others a clinical investigation, i.e., under whose immediate direction the test article is administered or dispensed to, or used involving, a subject. The term does not include any person other than an individual, e.g., it does not include a corporation or agency. The obligations of a sponsor-investigator under this part include both those of a sponsor and those of an investigator.

(l) Test article means any drug for human use, biological product for human use, medical device for human use, human food additive, color additive, electronic product, or any other article subject to regulation under the act or under sections 351 or 354-360F of the Public Health Service Act.

(m) IRB approval means the determination of the IRB that the clinical investigation has been reviewed and may be conducted at an institution within the constraints set forth by the IRB and by other institutional and Federal requirements.

[46 FR 8975, Jan. 27, 1981, as amended at 54 FR 9038 Mar. 3, 1989; 56 FR 28028, June 18, 1991; 64 FR 399, Jan. 5, 1999; 64 FR 56448, Oct. 20, 1999; 65 FR 52302, Aug. 29, 2000]

§ 56.103 Circumstances in which IRB review is required

(a) Except as provided in §§ 56.104 and 56.105, any clinical investigation which must meet the requirements for prior submission (as required in parts 312, 812, and 813) to the Food and Drug Administration shall not be initiated unless that investigation has been reviewed and approved by, and remains subject to continuing review by, an IRB meeting the requirements of this part.

(b) Except as provided in §§ 56.104 and 56.105, the Food and Drug Administration may decide not to consider in support of an application for research or marketing permit any data or information that has been derived from a clinical investigation that has not been approved by, and that was not subject to initial and continuing review by, an IRB meeting the requirements of this part. The determination that a clinical investigation may not be considered in support of an application for a research or marketing permit does not, however, relieve the applicant for such a permit of any obligation under any other applicable regulations to submit the results of the investigation to the Food and Drug Administration.

(c) Compliance with these regulations will in no way render inapplicable pertinent Federal, State, or local laws or regulations.

[46 FR 8975, Jan. 27, 1981; 46 FR 14340, Feb. 27, 1981]

§ 56.104 Exemptions from IRB requirement

The following categories of clinical investigations are exempt from the requirements of this part for IRB review:

(a) Any investigation which commenced before July 27, 1981 and was subject to requirements for IRB review under FDA regulations before that date, provided that the investigation remains subject to review of an IRB which meets the FDA requirements in effect before July 27, 1981.

(b) Any investigation commenced before July 27, 1981 and was not otherwise subject to requirements for IRB review under Food and Drug Administration regulations before that date.

(c) Emergency use of a test article, provided that such emergency use is reported to the IRB within 5 working days. Any subsequent use of the test article at the institution is subject to IRB review.

(d) Taste and food quality evaluations and consumer acceptance studies, if wholesome foods without additives are consumed or if a food is consumed that contains a food ingredient at or below the level and for a use found to be safe, or agricultural, chemical, or environmental contaminant at or below the level found to be safe, by the Food and Drug Administration or approved by the Environmental Protection Agency or the Food Safety and Inspection Service of the U.S. Department of Agriculture.

[46 FR 8975, Jan. 27 1981, as amended at 56 FR 28028, June 18, 1991]

§ 56.105 Waiver of IRB requirement

On the application of a sponsor or sponsor-investigator, the Food and Drug Administration may waive any of the requirements contained in these regulations including the requirements for IRB review, for specific research activities or for classes of research activities otherwise covered by these regulations.

Subpart B—Organization and Personnel

§ 56.107 IRB membership

(a) Each IRB shall have at least five members, with varying backgrounds to promote complete and adequate review of research activities commonly conducted by the institution. The IRB shall be sufficiently qualified through the experience and expertise of its members and the diversity of the members, including consideration of race, gender, cultural backgrounds, and sensitivity to such issues as community attitudes, to promote respect for its advice and counsel in safeguarding the rights and welfare of human subjects. In addition to possessing the professional competence necessary to review the specific research activities, the IRB shall be able to ascertain the acceptability of proposed research in terms of institutional commitments and regulations applicable law, and standards of professional conduct and practice. The IRB shall therefore include persons knowledgeable in these areas. If an IRB regularly reviews research that involves a vulnerable category of subjects, such as children, prisoners, pregnant women, or handicapped or mentally disabled persons, consideration shall be given to the inclusion of one or more individuals who are knowledgeable about and experienced in working with those subjects.

(b) Every nondiscriminatory effort will be made to ensure that no IRB consists entirely of men or entirely of women, including the institution's consideration of qualified persons of both sexes, so long as no selection is made to the IRB on the basis of gender. No IRB may consist entirely of members of one profession.

(c) Each IRB shall include at least one member whose primary concerns are in the scientific area and at least one member whose primary concerns are in nonscientific areas.

(d) Each IRB shall include at least one member who is not otherwise affiliated with the institution and who is not part of the immediate family of a person who is affiliated with the institution.

(e) No IRB may have a member participate in the IRB's initial or continuing review of any project in which the member has a conflicting interest, except to provide information requested by the IRB.

(f) An IRB may, in its discretion, invite individuals with competence in special areas to assist in the review of complex issues which require expertise beyond or in addition to that available on the IRB. These individuals may not vote with the IRB.

[46 FR 8975, Jan 27, 1981, as amended at 56 FR 28028, June 18, 1991; 56 FR 29756 June 28, 1991]

Subpart C—IRB Functions and Operations

§ 56.108 IRB functions and operations

In order to fulfill the requirements of these regulations, each IRB shall:

(a) Follow written procedures: (1) For conducting its initial and continuing review of research and for reporting its findings and actions to the investigator and the institution; (2) for determining which projects require review more often than annually and which projects need verification from sources other than the investigator that no material changes have occurred since previous IRB review; (3) for ensuring prompt reporting to the IRB of changes in research activity; and (4) for ensuring that changes in approved research, during the period for which

IRB approval has already been given may not be initiated without IRB review and approval except where necessary to eliminate apparent immediate hazards to the human subjects.

(b) Follow written procedures for ensuring prompt reporting to the IRB, appropriate institutional officials, and the Food and Drug Administration of: (1) Any unanticipated problems involving risks to human subjects or others; (2) any instance of serious or continuing noncompliance with these or the requirements or determinations of the IRB; or (3) any suspension or termination of IRB approval.

(c) Except when an expedited review procedure is used (see § 56.110), review proposed research at convened meetings at which a majority of the members of the IRB are present including at least one member whose primary concerns are in nonscientific areas. In order for the research to be approved it shall receive the approval of a majority of those members present at the meeting.
[46 FR 8975, Jan. 27, 1981, as amended at 56 FR 28028, June 18, 1991]

§ 56.109 IRB review of research

(a) An IRB shall review and have authority to approve, require modifications in (to secure approval), or disapprove all research activities covered by these regulations.

(b) An IRB shall require that information given to subjects as part of informed consent is in accordance with § 50.25. The IRB may require that information in addition to that specifically mentioned in § 50.25, be given to the subjects when in the IRB's judgment the information would meaningfully add to the protection of the rights and welfare of subjects.

(c) An IRB shall require documentation of informed consent in accordance with Sec. 50.27 of this chapter, except as follows:

(1) The IRB may, for some or all subjects, waive the requirement that the subject, or the subject's legally authorized representative, sign a written consent form if it finds that the research presents no more than minimal risk of harm to subjects and involves no procedures for which written consent is normally required outside the research context; or

(2) The IRB may, for some or all, find that the requirements in Sec. 50.24 of this chapter for an exception from informed consent for emergency research are met.

(d) In cases where the documentation requirement is waived under paragraph (c)(1) of this section, the IRB may require the investigator to provide subjects with a written statement regarding the research.

(e) An IRB shall notify investigators and the institution in writing of its decision to approve or disapprove the proposed research activity, or of modifications required to secure IRB approval of the research activity. If the IRB decides to disapprove a research activity, it shall include in its written notification a statement of the reasons for its

decision and give the investigator an opportunity to respond in person or in writing. For investigations involving an exception to informed consent under Sec. 50.24 of this chapter, an IRB shall promptly notify in writing the investigator and the sponsor of the research when an IRB determines that it cannot approve the research because it does not meet the criteria in the exception provided under Sec. 50.24(a) of this chapter or because of other relevant ethical concerns. The written notification shall include a statement of the reasons for the IRB's determination.

(f) An IRB shall conduct continuing review of research covered by these regulations at intervals appropriate to the degree of risk, but not less than once per year, and shall have authority to observe or have a third party observe the consent process and the research.

(g) An IRB shall provide in writing to the sponsor of research involving an exception to informed consent under Sec. 50.24 of this chapter a copy of information that has been publicly disclosed under Sec. 50.24(a)(7)(ii) and (a)(7)(iii) of this chapter. The IRB shall provide this information to the sponsor promptly so that the sponsor is aware that such disclosure has occurred. Upon receipt, the sponsor shall provide copies of the information disclosed to FDA.
[46 FR 8975, Jan. 27, 1981, as amended at 56 FR 28028, June 18, 1991, and at 61 FR 51497, Oct. 2, 1996]

§ 56.110 Expedited review procedures for certain kinds of research involving no more than minimal risk, and for minor changes in approved research

(a) The Food and Drug Administration has established, and published in the Federal Register, a list of categories of research that may be reviewed by the IRB through an expedited review procedure. The list will be amended, as appropriate through periodic republication in the Federal Register.

(b) An IRB may use the expedited review procedure to review either or both of the following: (1) Some or all of the research appearing on the list and found by the reviewer(s) to involve no more than minimal risk, (2) minor changes in previously approved research during the period (of 1 year or less) for which approval is authorized. Under an expedited review procedure the review may be carried out by the IRB chairperson or by one or more experienced reviewers designated by the IRB chairperson from among the members of the IRB. In reviewing the research, the reviewers may exercise all of the authorities of the IRB except that the reviewers may not disapprove the research. A research activity may be disapproved only after review in accordance with the non-expedited review procedure set forth in § 56.108(c).

(c) Each IRB which uses an expedited review procedure shall adopt a method for keeping all members advised of research proposals which have been approved under the procedure.

(d) The Food and Drug Administration may restrict, suspend, or terminate an institution's or IRB's use of the expedited review procedure when necessary to protect the rights or welfare of subjects.
[46 FR 8975, Jan. 27, 1981, as amended at 56 FR 28029, June 18, 1991]

§ 56.111 *Criteria for IRB approval of research*

(a) In order to approve research covered by these regulations the IRB shall determine that all of the following requirements are satisfied:

(1) Risks to subjects are minimized: (i) By using procedures which are consistent with sound research design and which do not unnecessarily expose subjects to risk, and (ii) whenever appropriate, by using procedures already being performed on the subjects for diagnostic or treatment purposes.

(2) Risks to subjects are reasonable in relation to anticipated benefits, if any, to subjects and the importance of the knowledge that may be expected to result. In evaluating risks and benefits, the IRB should consider only those risks and benefits that may result from the research (as distinguished from risks and benefits therapies that subjects would receive even if not participating in the research). The IRB should not consider possible long-range effects of applying knowledge gained in the research (for example, the possible effects of the research on public policy) as among those research risks that fall within the purview of its responsibility.

(3) Selection of subjects is equitable. In making this assessment the IRB should take into account the purposes of the research and the setting in which the research will be conducted and should be particularly cognizant of the special problems of research involving vulnerable populations, such as children, prisoners, pregnant women, handicapped, or mentally disabled persons, or economically or educationally disadvantaged persons.

(4) Informed consent will be sought from each prospective subject or the subject's legally authorized representative, in accordance with and to the extent required by part 50.

(5) Informed consent will be appropriately documented, in accordance with and to the extent required by § 50.27.

(6) Where appropriate, the research plan makes adequate provision for monitoring the data collected to ensure the safety of subjects.

(7) Where appropriate, there are adequate provisions to protect the privacy of subjects and to maintain the confidentiality of data.

(b) When some or all of the subjects, such as children, prisoners, pregnant women, handicapped, or mentally disabled persons, or economically or educationally disadvantaged persons, are likely to be vulnerable to coercion or undue influence additional safeguards have been included in the study to protect the rights and welfare of these subjects.
[46 FR 8975, Jan. 27, 1981, as amended at 56 FR 28029, June 18, 1991]

§ 56.112 *Review by institution*

Research covered by these regulations that has been approved by an IRB may be subject to further appropriate review and approval or disapproval by officials of the institution. However, those officials may not approve the research if it has not been approved by an IRB.

§ 56.113 *Suspension or termination of IRB approval of research*

An IRB shall have authority to suspend or terminate approval of research that is not being conducted in accordance with the IRB's requirements or that has been associated with unexpected serious harm to subjects. Any suspension or termination of approval shall include a statement of the reasons for the IRB's action and shall be reported promptly to the investigator appropriate institutional officials, and the Food and Drug Administration.

§ 56.114 *Cooperative research*

In complying with these regulations, institutions involved in multi-institutional studies may use joint review, reliance upon the review of another qualified IRB, or similar arrangements aimed at avoidance of duplication of effort.

Subpart D—Records and Reports

§ 56.115 IRB records

(a) An institution, or where appropriate an IRB, shall prepare and maintain adequate documentation of IRB activities including the following:

(1) Copies of all research proposals reviewed, scientific evaluations, if any, that accompany the proposals, approved sample consent documents progress reports submitted by investigators, and reports of injuries to subjects.

(2) Minutes of IRB meetings which shall be in sufficient detail to show attendance at the meetings; actions taken by the IRB; the vote on these actions including the number of members voting for, against and abstaining; the basis for requiring changes in or disapproving research; and a written summary of the discussion of controverted issues and their resolution.

(3) Records of continuing review activities.

(4) Copies of all correspondence between the IRB and the investigators.

(5) A list of IRB members identified by name; earned degrees; representative capacity; indications of experience such as board certifications licenses, etc., sufficient to describe each member's chief anticipated contributions to IRB deliberations; and any employment or other relationship between each member and the institution; for example: full-time employee, part-time employee, a member of governing panel or board, stockholder, paid or unpaid consultant.

(6) Written procedures for the IRB as required by § 56.108(a) and (b).

(7) Statements of significant new findings provided to subjects, as required by § 50.25.

(b) The records required by this regulation shall be retained for at least 3 years after completion of the research, and the records shall be accessible for inspection and copying by authorized representatives of the Food and Drug Administration at reasonable times and in a reasonable manner.

(c) The Food and Drug Administration may refuse to consider a clinical investigation in support of an application for a research or marketing permit if the institution or the IRB that reviewed the investigation refuses to allow an inspection under this section.
(Information collection requirements in this section were approved by the Office of Management and Budget (OMB) and assigned OMB control number 0910-0130)
[46 FR 8975, Jan. 27, 1981, as amended at 56 FR 28029, June 18, 1991]

Subpart E—Administrative Actions for Noncompliance

§ 56.120 Lesser administrative actions

(a) If apparent noncompliance with these regulations in the operation of an IRB is observed by an FDA investigator during an inspection, the inspector will present an oral or written summary of observations to an appropriate representative of the IRB. The Food and Drug Administration may subsequently send a letter describing the noncompliance to the IRB and to the parent institution. The agency will require that the IRB or the parent institution respond to this letter within a time period specified by FDA and describe the corrective actions that will be taken by the IRB, the institution, or both to achieve compliance with these regulations.

(b) On the basis of the IRB's or the institution's response FDA may schedule a reinspection to confirm the adequacy of corrective actions. In addition, until the IRB or the parent institution takes appropriate corrective action, the agency may:

(1) Withhold approval of new studies subject to the requirements of this part that are conducted at the institution or reviewed by the IRB;

(2) Direct that no new subjects be added to ongoing studies subject to this part;

(3) Terminate ongoing studies subject to this part when doing so would not endanger the subjects; or

(4) When the apparent noncompliance creates a significant threat to the rights and welfare of human subjects notify relevant State and Federal regulatory agencies and other parties with a direct interest in the agency's action of the deficiencies in the operation of the IRB.

(c) The parent institution is presumed to be responsible for the operation of an IRB, and the Food and Drug Administration will ordinarily direct any administrative action under this subpart against the institution. However, depending on the evidence of responsibility for deficiencies, determined during the investigation, the Food and Drug Administration may restrict its administrative actions to the IRB or to a component of the parent institution determined to be responsible for formal designation of the IRB.

§ 56.121 Disqualification of an IRB or an institution

(a) Whenever the IRB or the institution has failed to take adequate steps to correct the noncompliance stated in the letter sent by the agency under § 56.120(a), and the Commissioner of Food and Drugs determines that this noncompliance may justify the disqualification of the IRB or of the parent, the Commissioner will institute proceedings in accordance with the requirements for a regulatory hearing set forth in part 16.

(b) The Commissioner may disqualify an IRB or the parent if the Commissioner determines that:

(1) The IRB has refused or repeatedly failed to comply with any of the regulations set forth in this part, and;

(2) The noncompliance adversely affects the rights or welfare of the human subjects in a clinical investigation.

(c) If the Commissioner determines that disqualification is appropriate, the Commissioner will issue an order that explains the basis for the determination and that prescribes any actions to be taken with regard to ongoing clinical research conducted under the review of the IRB. The Food and Drug Administration will send notice of the disqualification to the IRB and the parent institution. Other parties with a direct interest, such as sponsors and clinical investigators, may also be sent a notice of the disqualification. In addition, the agency may elect to publish a notice of its action in the Federal Register.

(d) The Food and Drug Administration will not approve an application for a research permit for a clinical investigation that is to be under the review of a disqualified IRB or that is to be conducted at a disqualified institution, and it may refuse to consider in support of a marketing permit the data from a clinical investigation that was reviewed by a disqualified IRB as conducted at a disqualified institution unless the IRB or the parent institution is reinstated as provided in § 56.123.

§ 56.122 Public disclosure of information regarding revocation

A determination that the Food and Drug Administration has disqualified an institution and the administrative record regarding that determination are disclosable to the public under part 20.

§ 56.123 Reinstatement of an IRB or an institution

An IRB or an institution may be reinstated if the Commissioner determines upon an evaluation of a written submission from the IRB or institution that explains the corrective action that the institution or IRB plans to take, that the IRB or institution has provided adequate assurance that it will operate in compliance with the standards set forth in this part. Notification of reinstatement shall be provided to all persons notified under § 56.121(c).

§ 56.124 Actions alternative or additional to disqualification

Disqualification of an IRB or of an institution is independent of, and neither in lieu of nor a precondition to, other proceedings or actions authorized by the act. The Food and Drug Administration may at any time, through the Department of Justice institute any appropriate judicial proceedings (civil or criminal) and any other appropriate regulatory action, in addition to or in lieu of, and before, at the time of, or after, disqualification. The Agency may also refer pertinent matters to another Federal, State, or local government Agency for any action that Agency determines to be appropriate.

Appendix A: List of Selected FDA Regulations Relating to the Protection of Human Subjects

This list contains Food and Drug Administration (FDA) regulations that specifically relate to the protection of human subjects in clinical investigations. The citations selected below are only a few of the FDA regulations (contained in nine volumes) that apply to clinical investigations and govern the development and approval of drugs, biologics, and devices. The regulations are contained in Title 21 of the Code of Federal Regulations (CFR), which can be purchased from the Superintendent of Documents, Attn: New Orders, P.O. Box 371954, Pittsburgh, PA 15250-7954; (202-512-1800, fax: 202-512-2233)

I. FDA HUMAN SUBJECT PROTECTIONS

Part 50—Protection of Human Subjects (Informed Consent)

Part 56—Institutional Review Boards

II. SUBSTANCES AND ARTICLES REGULATED BY FDA

Foods

Part 71—Color Additives

Part 171—Food Additive Petitions

Part 180—Food Additives (Interim)

Drugs

Part 312—Investigational New Drug Application

Part 314—New Drug Applications

Part 320—Bioavailability and Bioequivalence Requirements

Part 330—Over-the-Counter Human Drugs Part

361.1—Radioactive Drugs for Certain Research Uses

Biologics

Part 312—Investigational New Drug Application

Part 601—Licensing

Part 630—Additional Standards for Viral Vaccines

Medical Devices

Part 812—Investigational Device Exemptions

Part 814—Premarket Approval of Medical Devices

Radiological Health

Part 361.1—Radioactive Drugs for Certain Research Uses

Part 1010—Performance Standards for Electronic Products

III. RELATED FDA PROCEDURES

Part 10—General Agency Administrative Procedures

Part 16—Regulatory Hearings before the FDA

Part 20—Public Information

IV. STATUTES PROVIDING AUTHORITY FOR REGULATIONS LISTED ABOVE:

Biological Control Act of 1902/Virus, Serum and Toxin Act of 1902

Food, Drug and Cosmetic Act of 1938 (as amended)

Public Health Service Act of 1944 (as amended)

Food Additive Amendments of 1958

Color Additives Amendment of 1960

New Drug Amendments of 1962

Radiation Control for Public Health and Safety Act of 1968

National Research Act of 1974

Medical Device Amendments of 1976

Safe Medical Devices Act of 1990

Device Amendments of 1992

FDA Modernization Act of 1997

Appendix B: Significant Differences in FDA and HHS Regulations for Protection of Human Subjects

The Department of Health and Human Services (HHS) regulations [45 CFR part 46] apply to research involving human subjects conducted by the HHS or funded in whole or in part by the HHS. The Food and Drug Administration (FDA) regulations [21 CFR parts 50 and 56] apply to research involving products regulated by the FDA. Federal support is not necessary for the FDA regulations to be applicable. When research involving products regulated by the FDA is funded, supported or conducted by FDA and/or HHS, both the HHS and FDA regulations apply.

IRB Regulations

§ 56.102 (FDA)	FDA definitions are included for terms
§ 46.102 (HHS)	specific to the type of research covered by the FDA regulations (test article, application for research or marketing permit, clinical investigation). A definition for emergency use is provided in the FDA regulations.
§ 56.104 (FDA)	FDA provides exemption from the prospective
§ 46.116 (HHS)	IRB review requirement for "emergency use" of test article in specific situations. HHS regulations state that they are not intended to limit the provision of emergency medical care.
§ 56.105 (FDA)	FDA provides for sponsors and sponsor-investigators to request a waiver of IRB review requirements (but not informed consent requirements).
§ 46.101 (HHS)	HHS exempts certain categories of research and provides for a Secretarial waiver.
§ 56.109 (FDA)	Unlike HHS, FDA does not provide that an IRB
§ 46.109 (HHS)	may waive the requirement for signed consent
§ 46.117(c)(HHS)	when the principal risk is a breach of confidentiality because FDA does not regulate studies which would fall into that category of research. (Both regulations allow for IRB waiver of documentation of informed consent in instances of minimal risk.)
§ 56.110 (FDA)	The FDA list of investigations eligible for
§ 46.110 (HHS)	expedited review (published in the Federal Register) does not include the studies described in category 9 of the HHS list because these types of studies are not regulated by FDA
§ 56.114 (FDA)	FDA does not discuss administrative matters
§ 46.114 (HHS)	dealing with grants and contracts because they are irrelevant to the scope of the Agency's regulation. (Both regulations make allowances for review of multi-institutional studies.)
§ 56.115 (FDA)	FDA has neither an assurance mechanism nor
§ 46.115 (HHS)	files of IRB membership. Therefore, FDA does not require the IRB or institution to report changes in membership whereas HHS does require such notification.
§ 56.115(c) (FDA)	FDA may refuse to consider a study in support of a research or marketing permit if the IRB or the institution refuses to allow FDA to inspect IRB records. HHS has no such provision because it does not

§ 56.120—
§ 56.124 (FDA)

issue research or marketing permits.

FDA regulations provide sanctions for non-compliance with regulations.

Informed Consent Regulations

§ 50.23 (FDA)

FDA, but not HHS, provides for an exception from the informed consent requirements in emergency situations. The provision is based on the Medical Device Amendments of 1976, but may be used in investigations involving drugs, devices, and other FDA regulated products in situations described in § 50.23.

§ 46.116(c)&(d)

HHS provides for waiving or altering elements (HHS) of informed consent under certain conditions. FDA has no such provision because the types of studies which would qualify for such waivers are either not regulated by FDA or are covered by the emergency treatment provisions (§ 50.23).

§ 50.25(a)(5) (FDA)
§ 46.116(a)(5) (HHS)

FDA explicitly requires that subjects be informed that FDA may inspect the records of the study because FDA may occasionally examine a subject's medical records when they pertain to the study. While HHS has the right to inspect records of studies it funds, it does not impose that same informed consent requirement.

§ 50.27(a)

FDA explicitly requires that consent forms be dated as well as signed by the subject or the subject's legally authorized representative. The HHS regulations do not explicitly require consent forms to be dated.

IRB Expedited Review Criteria

Dept. of Health and Human Services, National Institutes of Health, Office for Protection from Research Risks

Categories of Research That May Be Reviewed by the Institutional Review Board (IRB) through an Expedited Review Procedure*
63 FR 60364-60367, November 9, 1998

Applicability

(A) Research activities that (1) present no more than minimal risk to human subjects, and (2) involve only procedures listed in one or more of the following categories, may be reviewed by the IRB through the expedited review procedure authorized by 45 CFR 46.110 and 21 CFR 56.110. The activities listed should not be deemed to be of minimal risk simply because they are included on this list. Inclusion on this list merely means that the activity is eligible for review through the expedited review procedure when the specific circumstances of the proposed research involve no more than minimal risk to human subjects.

(B) The categories in this list apply regardless of the age of subjects, except as noted.

(C) The expedited review procedure may not be used where identification of the subjects and/or their responses would reasonably place them at risk of criminal or civil liability. Nor may it be damaging to the subjects financial standing, employability, insurability, reputation, or be stigmatizing. Unless reasonable and appropriate protections will be implemented so that risks related to invasion of privacy and breach of confidentiality are no greater than minimal.

(D) The expedited review procedure may not be used for classified research involving human subjects.

(E) IRBs are reminded that the standard requirements for informed consent (or its waiver, alteration, or exception) apply regardless of the type of review—expedited or convened—utilized by the IRB.

(F) Categories one (1) through seven (7) pertain to both initial and continuing IRB review.

Research Categories

(1) Clinical studies of drugs and medical devices only when condition (a) or (b) is met.

(a) Research on drugs for which an investigational new drug application (21 CFR Part 312) is not required. (Note: Research on marketed drugs that significantly increases the risks or decreases the acceptability of the risks associated with the use of the product is not eligible for expedited review.)

(b) Research on medical devices for which (i) an investigational device exemption application (21 CFR Part 812) is not required; or (ii) the medical device is cleared/approved for marketing and the medical device is being used in accordance with its cleared/approved labeling.

(2) Collection of blood samples by finger stick, heel stick, ear stick, or venipuncture as follows:

(a) from healthy, nonpregnant adults who weigh at least 110 pounds. For these subjects, the amounts drawn may not exceed 550 ml in an 8 week period and collection may not occur more frequently than 2 times per week; or

(b) from other adults and children**, considering the age, weight, and health of the subjects, the collection procedure, the amount of blood to be collected, and the frequency with which it will be collected. For these subjects, the amount drawn may not exceed the lesser of 50 ml or 3 ml per kg in an 8 week period and collection may not occur more frequently than 2 times per week.

(3) Prospective collection of biological specimens for research purposes by noninvasive means.

Examples:

(a) hair and nail clippings in a nondisfiguring manner; (b) deciduous teeth at time of exfoliation or if routine patient care indicates a need for extraction; (c) permanent teeth if routine patient care indicates a need for extraction; (d) excreta and external secretions (including sweat); (e) uncannulated saliva collected either in an unstimulated fashion or stimulated by chewing gumbase orwax or by applying a dilute citric solution to the tongue; (f) placenta removed at delivery; (g) amniotic fluid obtained at the time of rupture of the membrane prior to or during labor; (h) supra-and subgingival dental plaque and calculus, provided the collection procedure is not more invasive than routine prophylactic scaling of the teeth and the process is accomplished in accordance with accepted prophylactic techniques; (i) mucosal and skin cells collected by buccal scraping or swab, skin swab, or mouth washings; (j) sputum collected after saline mist nebulization.

(4) Collection of data through noninvasive procedures (not involving general anesthesia or sedation) routinely employed in clinical practice, excluding procedures involving x-rays or microwaves. Where medical devices are employed, they must be cleared/approved for marketing. (Studies intended to evaluate the safety and effectiveness of the medical device are not generally eligible for expedited review, including studies of cleared medical devices for new indications.)

Examples:

(a) physical sensors that are applied either to the surface of the body or at a distance and do not involve input of significant amounts of energy into the subject or an invasion of the subjects privacy; (b) weighing or testing sensory acuity; (c) magnetic resonance imaging; (d) electrocardiography, electroencephalography, thermography, detection of naturally occurring radioactivity, electroretinography, ultrasound, diagnostic infrared imaging, doppler blood flow, and echocardiography; (e) moderate exercise, muscular strength testing, body composition assessment, and flexibility testing where appropriate given the age, weight, and health of the individual.

(5) Research involving materials (data, documents, records, or specimens) that have been collected, or will be collected solely for nonresearch purposes (such as medical treatment or diagnosis). (NOTE: Some research in this category may be exempt from the HHS regulations for the protection of human subjects. 45 CFR 46.101(b)(4). This listing refers only to research that is not exempt.)

(6) Collection of data from voice, video, digital, or image recordings made for research purposes.

(7) Research on individual or group characteristics or behavior (including, but not limited to, research on perception, cognition, motivation, identity, language, communication, cultural beliefs or practices, and social behavior) or research employing survey, interview, oral history, focus group, program evaluation, human factors evaluation, or quality assurance methodologies. (NOTE: Some research in this category may be exempt from the HHS regulations for the protection of human subjects. 45 CFR 46.101(b)(2) and (b)(3). This listing refers only to research that is not exempt.)

(8) Continuing review of research previously approved by the convened IRB as follows:

(a) where (i) the research is permanently closed to the enrollment of new subjects; (ii) all subjects have completed all research-related interventions; and (iii) the research remains active only for long-term follow-up of subjects; or

(b) where no subjects have been enrolled and no additional risks have been identified; or

(c) where the remaining research activities are limited to data analysis.

(9) Continuing review of research, not conducted under an investigational new drug application or investigational device exemption where categories two (2) through eight (8) do not apply but the IRB has determined and documented at a convened meeting that the research involves no greater than minimal risk and no additional risks have been identified.

* An expedited review procedure consists of a review of research involving human subjects by the IRB chairperson or by one or more experienced reviewers designated by the chairperson from among members of the IRB in accordance with the requirements set forth in 45 CFR 46.110.

** Children are defined in the HHS regulations as "persons who have not attained the legal age for consent to treatments or procedures involved in the research, under the applicable law of the jurisdiction in which the research will be conducted." 45 CFR 46.402(a).

U.S. Government Guidance and Resources

Office for Human Research Protections (OHRP): Dear Colleague Letters
Web site: http://ohrp.osophs.dhhs.gov/dearcoll.htm

Office for Human Research Protections (OHRP): Guidance Topics by Subject
Web site: http://ohrp.osophs.dhhs.gov/g-topics.htm

OHRP Compliance Activities: Common Findings and Guidance
Web site: http://ohrp.osophs.gov/compovr.htm

FDA Information Sheets (1998 edition)
Guidance for Institutional Review Boards and Clinical Investigators
Web site: http://www.fda.gov/oc/oha/IRB/toc.html

FDA Clinical Trials/ Human Subjects Protection
Information for Health Professionals
Web site: http://www.fda.gov/oc/oha/default.htm#clinical

National Bioethics Advisory Commission
Web site: http://bioethics.gov/nbac.html

Office of Research Integrity
Web site: http://ori.dhhs.gov/

Health Care Financing Administration (HCFA)
Medicare Coverage Policy—Clinical Trials
Web site: http://www.hcfa.gov/coverage/8d2.htm

Bioethics Resources on the Web—National Institutes of Health
Web site: http://www.nih.gov/sigs/bioethics/

National Human Genome Research Institute
Ethical, Legal and Social Implications of Human Genetics Research
Web site: http://www.nhgri.nih.gov/ELSI/

National Reference Center for Bioethics Literature— Kennedy Institute
Web site: http://www.georgetown.edu/research/nrcbl/

Office of Biotechnology Activities—NIH
Web site: http://www.nih.gov/od/oba/index.htm

International Guidelines

International Committee on Harmonisation (ICH)
Good Clinical Practice Guidelines
Web site: www.ifpma.org/ich5e.html

Council for International Organizations of Medical Sciences (CIOMS)
International Ethical Guidelines for Biomedical Research
Web site: http://www.who.int/ina-ngo/ngo/ngo011.htm

Canadian Institutes of Health Research
Web site: http://www.nserc.ca/programs/ethics.htm

National Council on Ethics in Human Research— Canada
Web site: http://www.ncehr-cnerh.org/english/mstr_frm.html

Danish Council on Ethics
Web site: http://www.etiskraad.dk/english/about_the_council.html

French National Consultative Committee on Ethics
Web site: http://www.ccne-ethique.org/

National Committee for Medical Research Ethics— Norway
Web site: http://www.etikkom.no/E/index.htm

Selected Books

Office for Protection from Research Risks. OPRR Guidebook (1993). Updated 23 Jun 2001. Access date 27 Mar 2001. World Wide Web http://ohrp.osophs.dhhs.gov/irb/irb_guidebook.htm

Beauchamp T L, Childress J F. *Principles of Biomedical Ethics*, Ed 4. New York: Oxford University Press, 1994.

Beauchamp T L, Faden R R, Wallace R J, Jr, and Walters L, eds. *Ethical Issues in Social Science Research*. Baltimore, MD: Johns Hopkins University Press, 1982.

Beauchamp T L, Childress J F. *Principles of Biomedical Ethics*, Ed 3. New York: Oxford University Press, 1989.

Beecher H K. *Research and the Individual: Human Studies*. Boston: Little, Brown and Company, 1970.

Brody BA. *The Ethics of Biomedical Research: An International Perspective*. New York: Oxford University Press, 1998.

Dunn C, Chadwick G. *Protecting Study Volunteers in Research: A Manual for Investigative Sites*. Boston: Center Watch, 1999.

Faden R, ed. *The Human Radiation Experiments*. New York: Oxford University Press, 1996.

Faden R R, Beauchamp T L. *A History of Theory of Informed Consent*. New York: Oxford University Press, 1986.

Freund P A, ed. *Experimentation with Human Subjects*. New York: George Braziller, 1970.

Jonsen A R, Veach R M, Walters L. *Source Book in Bioethics: A Documentary History*. Washington, DC: Georgetown University Press, 1998.

Katz J. *Experimentation with Human Beings: The Authority of the Investigator, Subject, Professions, and State in the Human Experimentation Process*. New York: Russell Sage Foundation, 1972.

Levine R J. *The Ethics and Regulation of Clinical Research* Ed. 2. New Haven: Yale University Press, 1988.

Penslar R L. *Research Ethics: Cases and Materials*. Indianapolis, Indiana: Bloomington and Indiana University Press, 1995.

Russell-Einhorn M, ed. *IRB Reference Book*. Washington, DC: Price Waterhouse Coopers, LLP, 2000.

Sieber J E. *Planning Ethically Responsible Research: A Guide for Students and Internal Review Boards*. Applied Social Research Methods Series, vol. 31. Newbury Park, CA: Sage Publications, 1992.

Sieber J E, ed. *The Ethics of Social Research: Surveys and Experiments*. New York: Springer-Verlag, 1982.

Sieber J E, ed. *The Ethics of Social Research: Fieldwork, Regulation, and Publication*. New York: Springer-Verlag, 1982.

Sugarman J, Mastroianni A C, Kahn. J P. *Ethics of Research with Human Subjects: Selected Policies and References*. Frederick, MD: University Publishing Group, 1998.

Vanderpool H Y. *The Ethics of Research Involving Human Subjects*. Frederick, MD: University Publishing Group, 1996.

Veatch R M. *Medical Ethics*. Boston: Jones and Bartlett Publishers, 1989.

Periodicals and IRB Forum

ARENA Newsletter
Applied Research Ethics in Medicine and Research
http://140.239.168.132/arena.html

Bulletin of Medical Ethics
Dr. Richard Nicholson, Editor
Email: bulletin_of_medical_ethics@compuserve.com

The Hastings Center
Web site: http://www.thehastingscenter.org/

Hastings Center Report
Web site:
    http://www.thehastingscenter.org/publications.htm

IRB: A Review of Human Subjects Research
Web site:
    http://www.thehastingscenter.org/publications.htm

Human Research Report
Web site: http://www.humansubjects.com/

Kennedy Institute of Ethics Journal
Web site:
    http://muse.jhu.edu/journals/kennedy_institute_of_
    ethics_journal/

The IRB Forum (previously MCWIRB)
Web site: http://www.irbforum.org/
The IRB Forum promotes the discussion of ethical,
    regulatory, and policy concerns with human subjects
    research.

Research Practitioner
Web site:
    http://www.researchpractice.com/rp_about.shtml

Video Recordings

Columbia University Seminars on Media and Society, in association with WNET New York. *The Human Experiment.* Produced by Betsy Miller and Martha Elliot. Annenberg: CPB Project, 1989.

National Library of Medicine. *Evolving Concern: Protection of Human Subjects.* Produced for the U.S. National Institutes of Health and the U.S. Food and Drug Administration. Bethesda, MD: National Institutes of Health, Office for Protection from Research Risks, 1986.

National Library of Medicine. *The Belmont Report: Basic Ethical Principles and Their Application.* Produced for the U.S. National Institutes of Health and the U.S. Food and Drug Administration. Bethesda, MD: National Institutes of Health, Office for Protection from Research Risks, 1986.

National Library of Medicine. *Balancing Society's Mandates: IRB Review Criteria.* Produced for the U.S. National Institutes of Health and the U.S. Food and Drug Administration. Bethesda, MD: National Institutes of Health, Office for Protection from Research Risks, 1986.

Selected Organizations

American Medical Association (AMA)
Web site: http://www.ama-assn.org

American Psychiatric Association
Web site: http://www.psych.org/

American Psychological Association
Web site: http://www.apa.org/

American Society of Law, Medicine, and Ethics
(ASLME)
Web site: http://www.aslme.org/

Applied Research Ethics National Association (ARENA)
Web site: http://140.239.168.132/arena.html

Association of American Medical Colleges (AAMC)
Web site: http://www.aamc.org

Association of Clinical Research Professionals (ACRP)
Web site: http://www.acrpnet.org/

Center for Clinical Research Practice (CCRP)
Web site: http://www.ccrp.com/index.shtlm

CenterWatch Clinical Trials
http://www.centerwatch.com

Drug Information Association (DIA)
Web site: http://www.diahome.org

National Association of IRB Managers (NIAM)
Web site: http://www.naim.org

National Council of University Research Administrators
(NCURA)
Web site: http://www.ncura.edu

Oral History Association (OHA)
Web site: http://omega.dickinson.edu/organizations/oha

Public Responsibility in Medicine and Research
(PRIM&R)
Web site: http://www.primr.org

World Medical Association (WMA)
Web site: http://www.wma.net

Standardized IRB Forms

Elizabeth A. Bankert

INTRODUCTION

In this section, we have included examples of most of the standardized forms used in the Dartmouth IRB office. We do not imply these are the best or the only ones to use; rather, we provide these as samples for you to enhance and improve as you wish. Over the past few years, federal agencies have provided increased guidance about IRB documentation. This information has resulted in many institutions' revising their internal forms. Our forms include information obtained directly from Food and Drug Administration (FDA) and the Office For Human Research Protections (OHRP) publications. We revise our forms as needed and try to update our forms on our Web site, http://www.dartmouth.edu/~cphs/.

1. **Full Committee IRB submission:** 1a-1d include the forms that we require for a full Committee IRB review.

   1a. **Submission Checklist:** This is a simple list describing each item needed in order for IRB review to proceed.

   1b. **Human Subjects Review Form:** This is a summary form that collects information for the IRB database and includes space to record the vote of each IRB reviewer.

   1c. **IRB Protocol Summary:** Based on federal research regulations, this form asks for the information that the IRB will need to conduct a thorough review of a research of a research protocol.

   1d. **Departmental Scientific Review Form:** We require that the protocol undergo a formal review by peers of the researcher prior to IRB review. The Department Scientific Review Form serves to document this level of peer review and must accompany each full Committee submission.

   1e. **Consent Form Template:** A standardized consent form template is based on the essential elements of informed consent listed in federal research regulations.

2. **Continuing Review Forms:** We found it very useful to create forms specifically geared toward the aspects of continuing review that the IRB office receives on a daily basis. These forms are attached to the applicable documents to provide a summary of the information needed for appropriate IRB review.

   2a. **Revision Request Form**

   2b. **Adverse Event Form**

   2c. **Continuing Review Form**

   2d. **Noncompliance / Complaint Form**

3. **Expedited Review Summary Form**

4. **Requirements for Review of Undergraduate Student Research Form**

5. **Primary Reviewer Template**

6. **Minutes Template:** A standardized template for the IRB minutes is based on the criteria for IRB approval of research listed in federal research regulations and on recent OHRP compliance oversight reports.

7. **Agenda Template:** A standardized template for the agenda of the IRB full committee meeting.

Appendix

Checklist for Full Committee Review Submission

---

1. [ ] **Human Subjects Review Form**
   Please fill out entirely and obtain original signatures as indicated.

2. [ ] **Departmental Scientific Review Form**
   Circle the appropriate responses and obtain signatures as indicated. The IRB views the report by the departmental review committee as a recommendation to approve the protocol. An independent review of all aspects of the study will be carried out by the IRB.

3. [ ] **IRB Protocol 2000**
   The IRB protocol is in addition to the sponsor supplied protocol and must follow the format in the template available from the IRB office.

4. [ ] **Consent Form**
   The consent form must follow the format as shown in consent form template. The IRB office will "pre-review" the consent form.

5. [ ] **Sponsor Protocol**
   If the study sponsor supplies the investigator with a protocol, please include **4 copies**, *double sided,* **3 hole punched.** *For NIH-sponsored studies, include 2 copies, double sided, 3 hole punched of the full NIH protocol.*

6. [ ] **Clinical Trial Agreement**
   For studies with an agreement with a pharmaceutical company or sponsor, please submit *one copy of the contract agreement* (specifically indemnification clause / participant injury information / insurance).

7. [ ] **Relevant Materials**
   Include all recruitment advertisements, questionnaires, statements read to the participants, letters to participants, information sheets, etc.

8. [ ] **Site Agreement/Federal Wide Assurance (FWA)**
   For studies taking place off-site, an Agreement is required to ensure other sites are aware of protections for human subjects. Contact the IRB office and be sure to list all sites as requested in the IRB protocol.

9. [ ] **IRB Fee**
   Non-federal, externally sponsored research will receive an invoice of $1,000 for the IRB review fee. The office of Grants & Contracts will send invoice to the PI.

Include Deadline Information
Contact Information
Address of IRB Office

HUMAN SUBJECTS REVIEW FORM

DARTMOUTH COLLEGE / DARTMOUTH-HITCHCOCK MEDICAL CENTER

PLEASE TYPE

CPHS USE ONLY
STUDY # _____

PRINCIPAL INVESTIGATOR: _____ DEPT: _____ PHONE: _____

CO-INVESTIGATOR: _____ DEPT: _____ PHONE: _____

CO-INVESTIGATOR: _____ DEPT: _____ PHONE: _____

CONTACT NAME: _____

STUDY TITLE (match title submitted to funding source): _____

_____

POTENTIAL FUNDING SOURCE(S): _____

LIST ALL SITES WHERE STUDY WILL TAKE PLACE: _____

[ ] NEW PROJECT   PROPOSED PROJECT DATES: _____

[ ] RENEWAL (check as applicable)   DATE STUDY *FIRST* APPROVED: _____
    [ ] There are *no revisions* in the enclosed protocol or consent form since last CPHS review (e.g., all revisions have rec'd CPHS approval)
    [ ] There *are protocol revisions* since last CPHS review (describe in Continuing Review Form: #2)
    [ ] There *are consent form revisions* since last CPHS review (describe in Continuing Review Form: #2)

RESEARCH MAY INVOLVE:
    [ ] Minors
    [ ] Fetuses
    [ ] Abortuses
    [ ] Pregnant Women
    [ ] Potentially Incompetent to Consent
    [ ] Prisoners

SUBJECT(S) WILL BE:
A. [ ] Paid [ ] Unpaid
B. [ ] Outpatients [ ] Inpatients [ ] Nonpatients (e.g., healthy volunteers, students)
C. Estimated Age Range of Subjects: _____ To _____
D. Estimated Number of Subjects:
    _____ Male _____ Female
    _____

E. [ ] Full Committee Review [ ] Expedited Review

KEY WORDS
Disease: _____
Condition: _____
Drug Name: _____
Drug Class: _____
Radioisotopes: _____
Biologic: _____
Other: _____
_____

DEPARTMENTS INVOLVED   **PERSONNEL NOTIFIED:**
[ ] Pharmacy   _____
Will there be increased patient costs relative to standard care? [ ] Yes [ ] No
How will subjects be notified?   _____
[ ] Nursing   _____
[ ] Radiation Safety Committee   _____
[ ] Environmental Health & Safety   _____
[ ] Other   _____

_____   DATE: _____
Principal Investigator signature   Printed name

_____   DATE: _____
Department Chairperson signature   Printed name

FOR CPHS USE ONLY - STUDY IS: Study Review Date: CPHS _____

[ ] Approved   [ ] Not Approved   [ ] Abstain   [ ] Conditionally Approved

Reviewer's Signature: _____ DATE: _____

Protocol Summary

Content Requirements for Full Committee Review

The following information is required for IRB review. Read through each section and respond to each item. Please also review the CHECKLIST for Full Committee Submission.

1. **Purpose:** A brief statement of the purpose of the research project. This should include the hypothesis to be tested.

2. **Introduction:** (a) Explain the background of this project so that we will understand why it is important to perform this research project. (b) Summarize previously published data and pilot studies. Be sure to include a discussion of any data that does not support the study hypothesis. If a study similar to the one being proposed has already been completed, explain why the proposed study is necessary. (c) For studies designed to compare or evaluate therapies, there should be a statement of the relative advantages or disadvantages of alternative modes of therapy. (d) If not obvious, explain why human subjects are necessary. *Include references for all published data cited.*

3. **Design, procedures, materials, and methods:** Use a level of detail similar to what would be used when submitting an article for publication in a peer reviewed journal. Another investigator should be able to replicate this study from the information provided in this section. Explain the study procedures and data collection and analysis process. Please define terms and explain concepts that might be confusing to reviewers who are not experts in this area.

   Location of study: List *all* sites where research will take place.

4. **List all Alliance Hospitals, Clinics, VA:**

5. **List all 'off site' locations:** where research will take place or circle *N/A*

   For studies taking place 'off-site', a Site Agreement may be required to ensure awareness of federal regulations for human subject research. A template Site Agreement is available from the IRB office.

   Financial Considerations: An area of importance in the enrollment of a research participant in a study is the potential for additional costs to the participant.

6. **List all tests/procedures to be performed for research purposes only** (i.e., those that fall outside the standard of care and would therefore not be billable to third party payers such as Medicare):

7. **Responsibility for costs of research:**

   Will the sponsor be responsible for all patient care related research costs?

   Yes or No

   If no, include an explanation as to who will be responsible:

   Note: Third party payers will *not* be billed for research related costs falling outside the standard of care and/or already covered by sponsor dollars. Therefore, either the department or the participant will be deemed responsible for research related costs not paid for by the sponsor. If the participant will be responsible for any research costs, this information needs to be clearly indicated here and in the consent form including approximation of costs to be incurred:

8. **Responsibility for costs of injury or illness related to research:**

   Will the sponsor be responsible for costs of injury or illness related to the research? Yes or No

   If no, include an explanation as to who is responsible:

9. **Timetables:**

   a) Indicate length of participant involvement in the study:

   b) Estimate how long it will take to enroll enough patients to complete this study:

(Continued)

10. **Medical Device:** Respond to items below   or circle   *N/A*

Is this device approved by the FDA? Yes or No

If no,

Provide IDE# (Investigational Device Exemption #): _____

or

Respond to *Medical Device Attachment A:*

11. **Investigational Drug:** Respond to items below   or circle   *N/A*

Are these drug(s) approved by the FDA? Yes or No

If no, provide IND # (Investigational New Drug): _____

12. **Placebo/Standard Care: If any part of the study involves placebo or procedures which may be considered less than the standard of care:**

Respond to *Placebo Attachment B*   or circle   *N/A*

13. **Genetics:** Respond to *Genetics Attachment C*   or circle   *N/A*

14. **Participant Population:** Certain populations are vulnerable and require special protections when asked to participate in a research study. If any of the following populations will be eligible to participate:

Prisoners, fetuses, human embryos, elderly persons, mentally disabled persons (also see #17 below), economically disadvantaged persons, educationally disadvantaged persons.

Refer to: Students, Employees *Attachment D*

Illiterate Subjects *Attachment E*

List vulnerable groups:

Describe special protections: or circle   *N/A*

15. **Children:** Are children eligible for enrollment into this study? Yes or No

If yes, respond to *Children Attachment F*

If no, present an acceptable justification for the exclusion:

Note: Effective October 1, 1998, NIH guidelines require that research involving human participation include children unless there is appropriate justification for their exclusion. All proposals for human subjects research must include a description of plans for including children. If children will be excluded from the research, the proposal must present an acceptable justification for the exclusion. The investigator should address the rationale for selecting or excluding a specific age range of child, or an explanation of the reason(s) for excluding children as participants in the research. When children are included, the plan must also include a description of the expertise of the investigative team for dealing with children at the ages included, of the appropriateness of the available facilities to accommodate the children, and the inclusion of a sufficient number of children to contribute to a meaningful analysis relative to the purpose of the study.

16. **Pregnancy:**

Are *pregnant women* eligible for enrollment into this study? Yes or No

If yes, justify and include potential harm to unborn fetus:

Note: Pregnant women may not be involved as participants in a Biomedical research study unless (1) the purpose of the activity is to meet the health needs of the mother, and the fetus will be placed at risk only to the minimum extent necessary to meet such needs or (2) the risk to the fetus is minimal.

If no, explain and include the process for determination of pregnancy status.

If a pregnancy test is required, note who will pay:

17. Women of child bearing capability:

Are women of *child bearing capability* eligible for enrollment into this study? Yes or No

If yes, describe potential harm to unborn fetus and process for determination of pregnancy. If a pregnancy test is required, note who will pay. If there is potential harm to an unborn fetus the investigator should review with each man/woman his/her plans to avoid pregnancy. If the investigator regards these contraceptive plans as inadequate, the man/woman should be advised on how to make them adequate or should be excluded from the study.

If no, explain and include process for determination of pregnancy. If a pregnancy test is required, note who will pay:

18. Competency:

Will participants potentially incompetent to provide informed consent be eligible to enroll in this study? Yes or No

If yes, respond to attached *Incompetent Participants Attachment G*

19. Gender and Racial/Ethnic distribution: NIH guidelines require that research involving human participation include minorities and both genders.

Note: If one gender and/or minorities are excluded or are inadequately represented in this research, particularly in proposed population-based studies, a clear compelling rationale for exclusion or inadequate representation should be provided.

Will eligibility into the study be based on gender and/or racial /ethnic group?
If yes, explain:

20. Inclusion/Exclusion Criteria: Please provide detailed description of inclusion/exclusion criteria:

21. Recruitment: Explain the process for recruiting participants.

Also include any advertisements and any process involving "finder fees" or incentives (bonus payment, gift certificate, etc.) to study personnel for enrollment of participants.

Note: Advertising should not use terms such as "new treatment," "new medication," or "new drug" without explaining that the test article is investigational. A phrase such as "receive new treatments" implies that all research participants will be receiving newly marketed products of proven worth.

Advertisements should not promise "free medical treatment," when the intent is only to say participants will not be charged for taking part in the investigation. The IRB will determine if the promise of treatment without charge is coercive to financially constrained participants. Advertisement may state that participants will be paid, but should not emphasize the payment or the amount to be paid.

The advertisement should include the name and address of clinical investigator and/or research facility; the condition under study and/or the purpose of the research; in summary form, the criteria that will be used to determine eligibility for the study; a brief list of participation benefits, if any (e.g., a no cost health examination); the time or other commitment required of the participants; and the location of the research and the person or office to contact for further information.

(Continued)

22. **Consent Process:** The *Principal Investigator* (PI) is responsible for ensuring that all participants enrolling in this study have *provided informed consent*. The PI may authorize other appropriately trained individuals to obtain informed consent. Please ensure the consent form is filed in the circulating medical record of the research participant.

    Summarize the planned consent process. Specifically include *when* consent will be obtained and *who* has been authorized by the PI to obtain consent:

23. **Risks:** Describe any potential risks (physical, psychological, social, legal, financial, or other) and assess their likelihood and seriousness. Describe the procedure for protecting against or minimizing any potential risks, including risks to confidentiality, and assess their likely effectiveness. Please list risks from most severe/likely to least severe/unlikely.

24. **Risk/Benefit analysis:** Describe why the risks to subjects are reasonable in relation to the anticipated benefits to participants and/or society, and in relation to the importance of the knowledge that may reasonably be expected to result, thereby falling in favor of performing the study.

25. **Confidentiality:** Describe methods of maintaining patient data confidentiality:

    Note: Under certain circumstances, an invasion of privacy or breach of confidentiality may present a risk of serious harm to subjects (e.g., as when the research obtains information about subjects that would, if disclosed by the researcher, jeopardize jobs or lead to prosecution for criminal behavior). Under other circumstances, an invasion of privacy or breach of confidentiality can be a moral wrong, or at least in theory, provide cause for legal action against a researcher or institution. *It is the responsibility of the researcher to be sensitive to the issues involved with privacy and confidentiality and to consider them appropriately in designing the study.*

26. **Data and Safety Monitoring:** Describe plans for data and safety monitoring. As described in federal regulations "... a variety of types of monitoring may be anticipated depending on the nature, size, and complexity of the trial. In many cases, the principal investigator would be expected to perform the monitoring function." This will include monitoring to determine:

    Note: The progress of the trial, including periodic assessments of data quality and timeliness, participant recruitment, accrual and retention, participant risk versus benefit, and other factors that can affect study outcome. Monitoring should also consider factors external to the study when interpreting the data, such as scientific or therapeutic developments that may have an impact on the safety of the participants or the ethics of the study.

27. **Statistical Methods and Review Statement:** Justify the sample size used with a power analysis. If applicable, briefly describe the study endpoint(s) and the criteria to determine a positive result. A statement documenting statistical review by a college or faculty member may facilitate review.

28. **Potential Conflict of Interest for Investigator:** Please explain any potential conflict of interest which could possibly occur now, or in the future, as a result of the investigator or other study personnel being involved in conducting this study. If there is no potential conflict of interest, make a statement to that effect. The Public Health Service (PHS) describes "significant financial interests" of the investigator that would reasonably appear to be directly and significantly affected by the research funded; examples are: "... ownership of stock, stock options, or any equity, debt, security, capital holding, salary or other remuneration, or financial consideration, or thing of value for services as an employee, consultant, officer, or board member. ..." NIH GUIDE, Volume 23, Number 25, July 1, 1994. If a conflict of interest is designated, the study will receive review from appropriate authorities to determine its status.

Medical Device Attachment A

1. The IRB protocol requires a description of the "FDA status" of the medical device. This information should include **non-significant risk (NSR)** or a **significant risk (SR)** designation by the sponsor, and the filing date if a 510K or IDE has been applied for from the FDA.

2. The IRB will decide if the sponsor designation is appropriate. The IRB may ask the manufacturer/sponsor for further information regarding the classification. The sponsor will provide an explanation of why the study is NSR, and other supporting information, e.g., reports of prior investigations. The sponsor will also inform the IRB if the FDA or any other IRB has determined the study to be SR or NSR.

3. A **significant risk** medical device is a device that "presents a potential for serious risk to the health, safety, or welfare of the subject." Risk level will be based on the seriousness of the harm that could result from the use of the device alone, or the conduct of the investigational protocol as a whole, relative to "everyday activities." Risk category will NOT be based on a comparison with alternate devices or therapies, including "standard therapy."

4. Protocols that involve a **significant risk** medical device are not permitted by federal regulations to enroll participants until the study has been approved by both the IRB and the FDA. The IRB will not approve a "significant risk" medical device study without written documentation that the study has been approved by the FDA. FDA approval means that the device has been granted "substantial equivalence" under the 501(k) section of the Food, Drug, and Cosmetic Act or have been given an Investigational Device Exemption (IDE) number. After a protocol has been approved by the FDA, the IRB will review all aspects of the protocol including the informed consent and it will determine the risk/benefit ratio for human subjects, as per the standard review process. A protocol that has been approved by the FDA may be approved, conditionally approved, or not approved by the IRB.

5. Protocols that involve **non-significant risk** medical devices do not require FDA approval (or FDA review) to enroll patients. The IRB will review all aspects of the protocol to determine the risk/benefit ratio for human subjects and render a decision to approve, conditionally approve, or not approve the protocol.

6. The IRB may agree or disagree with the sponsor's initial NSR assessment. If the IRB agrees, the investigation may begin without FDA review. If the IRB disagrees, the study can only be conducted as a SR investigation and the sponsor must notify the FDA that a SR determination has been made (whether or not the sponsor ultimately conducts the study at this institution).

References:

1. OPRR/NIH Protecting Human Research Subjects: Institutional Review Board Guidebook 1993 , Chapter 5 pages 18-22
2. Article: Medical Devices Significant vs. Nonsignificant Risk
3. Sherertz, RJ, Streed, SA. JAMA, 28 Sept., 1994 - Vol 272, No.12
4. FDA list of significant and nonsignificant devices
5. Oral communication (11/16/94) with FDA official Gary Chadwick (301-594-1026)
6. FDA IRB Information Sheets pp. 60-61

Placebo Attachment B

Discuss the ethical implications of using placebo instead of "standard of care" therapy in this situation. Specifically, explain what "standard of care" therapy is for this patient population and how the use of placebo therapy affects risks for participants. Also specifically address:

a. The safety and efficacy of other available therapies (if any)

b. The maximum total length of time a participant may receive placebo on study

c. The greatest potential harm that may come to a participant as a result of not receiving effective therapy (immediate or delayed onset)

d. Protocols in place to safeguard participants receiving placebo

Genetic Research Attachment C

For research studies involving genetic testing, the IRB has developed two basic categories to assist in the determination of further review. The researcher should determine if the research falls into category (a) or (b) as described below. If the research falls into category (a) indicate by circling below and add comments as appropriate to this project. If the research falls into category (b) please respond to questions that follow.

a. The study is looking for an association between a genetic marker and a specific disease or condition, but at this point it is not clear if the genetic marker has predictive value. The uncertainty regarding the predictive value of the genetic marker is such that studies in this category will not involve participant counseling.

COMMENT:

b. The study is based on the premise that a link between a genetic marker and a specific disease or condition is such that the marker is clinically useful in predicting the development of that specific disease or condition. Respond to the items below:

Human Genetic Research Questions for IRB Review

For studies involving genetic testing, the PI must respond to the following items (if an item is not applicable to the study, please write "NA.")

1. Are clear guidelines established for disclosure of information, including interim or inconclusive research results to the participants?
2. Will participants be informed of research results (and their meaning) at each point in the research?
3. Will family members be protected against disclosure of medical or other personal information about themselves to other family members?
4. Will they be given the option not to receive information about themselves?
5. Will limits on such protections be clearly communicated to participants, including obtaining advance consent to such disclosures (e.g., when family members will be warned about health risks)?
6. Will the possible psychological and social risks of genetic research be adequately considered in the consent process?
7. Will appropriate counseling be provided, both as part of the consent process and when communicating test or other research results to participants?
8. Will participants be informed about the possibility of important incidental findings such as paternity, disease, or conditions other than the one(s) that are the focus of the study?
9. Will the data be protected from disclosure to third parties, such as employers and insurance companies?
10. Will the participant be told about the potential consequences of a third party, such as employer or insurance company, becoming aware of the study findings?
11. Will the data be stored in a secure manner?
12. Will the data be coded to protect the identity of subjects?
13. Is a request for a certificate of confidentiality appropriate?
14. Does the investigator plan to disclose research findings to subjects' physicians for clinical use?
15. Are such plans appropriate?
16. Will the possibility of such disclosures be discussed in the consent process with prospective participants?
17. Will vulnerable populations (e.g., children, persons with impaired mental capacities) be adequately protected?
18. Under what circumstances can a research participant give permission to involve a minor or an adult who lacks decision-making capacity in an aspect of this study?
19. What are the provisions for protecting the confidentiality of tissue samples?
20. What procedures will be used to get the subjects' permission to store tissue or data for additional research in the future or for non-research medical practice?
21. What will happen to research data and tissue if a subject elects to withdraw from the study? Do subjects have the option of having all data and tissue related to this study destroyed?
22. Are the implications of study withdrawal, in terms of destruction or use of established data or tissue, clearly explained in the consent document?
23. Do the plans to publish or present data from this study threaten the privacy or confidentially of participants?
24. If research may involve family members:
24a. Is the strategy for recruiting family members sensitive to privacy and confidentiality issues?
24b. Will information be obtained from the medical records of family members?
24c. If so, should consent be obtained from the family member to access their information?

Information for Consent Document

1. Clearly explain what information the subjects have access to regarding information obtained as part of this study. Explain what information they will be given whether they ask for it or not, what information they must ask for to receive, and what information they will not be given under any circumstances.

2. Explain if subjects may learn things about themselves or their family that they do not want to know, or that they may be uncomfortable knowing.

3. Explain if family members may learn about information generated in this study and the potential implications of this knowledge.

4. Explain if participation in this study may compromise their insurability.

5. Explain if participation in the study may prompt the subject to take actions that may incur unanticipated costs or expose the subject to additional risks. For example, genetic counseling may be expensive. If participation in the study creates the need for the subject to seek genetic counseling this may be a financial hardship and submitting a claim for these costs to an insurance company may compromise insurability.

6. Accurately describe the limitations of protection of privacy and confidentiality.

7. Explain what it means to withdraw from this study in terms of the destruction or use of data or tissue related to the study.

8. Include an appropriately detailed explanation of all costs that are likely to be incurred by the subject or family members as a result of participation in the study. Address both the costs of procedures required by the study and costs, like genetic counseling, additional genetic testing, and psychological counseling that the subject or their family may be advised to pay based on study results.

Employees and Students Attachment D

One of the primary responsibilities of the IRB is to ensure that a participant's decision to participate in research will be voluntary and that consent will be sought "only under circumstances that provide the prospective subject . . . sufficient opportunity to consider whether to participate and that minimize the possibility of coercion or undue influence." Students and employees may be vulnerable to "subtle inducements to participate."

The researcher who plans to recruit either population must define clearly the participants to be enrolled and the rationale for their participation. In addition, the mode and timing of recruitment must be explained.

Another special consideration for employee and student populations is the issue of confidentiality of research data. Depending on the nature of the research and the data collected, a break of confidentiality could affect a person's employment, career path, educational plans, or social relationship with the hospital/academic community. Therefore, the researcher should document carefully the methods to protect the subjects' identity and research data (e.g., coding, storage of research files, limits of accessibility to research data, etc.).

Illiterate Subjects Attachment E

Subjects who are unable to read should not be excluded from research on the grounds of illiteracy. If a subject is unable to read or if a legally acceptable representative is unable to read, an impartial witness should be present during the entire informed consent discussion. After the written consent form and any other written information to be provided to subjects is read and explained to the subject or the subject's legally acceptable representative, and after the subject or the subject's legally acceptable representative has orally consented to the subject's participation in the trial, and, if capable of doing so, has signed and personally dated the consent form, the witness should sign and personally date the consent form. By signing the consent form, the witness attests that the information in the consent form and any other written information was accurately explained to, and apparently understood by, the subject or the subject's legally acceptable representative, and that informed consent was freely given by the subject or the subject's legally acceptable representative.

Children Attachment F

If a study involves minors (in NH < 18yrs) please complete sections 1, 2, and 3 below:

Section 1. Designation Risk / Benefit: Check the risk designation as you deem appropriate:

[ ] 1. Research not involving greater than minimal risk [45 CFR 46.404].

Minimal risk means that the probability and magnitude of harm or discomfort anticipated in the research are not greater in and of themselves than those ordinarily encountered in daily life or during the performance of routine physical or psychological examinations or tests.

[ ] 2. Research involving greater than minimal risk but presenting the prospect of direct benefit to the individual participants will be approved by the IRB only if

    a. The risk is justified by the anticipated benefit to the subjects;

    b. The relation of the anticipated benefits to the risk is at least as favorable to the subjects as that presented by available alternative approaches [45 CFR 46.405].

[ ] 3. Research involving greater than minimal risk and no prospect of direct benefit to individual participants, but likely to yield generalizable knowledge about the participant's condition, will be approved only if

    a. The risk represents a minor increase over minimal risk

    b. The intervention or procedure presents experiences to participants that are reasonably commensurate with those inherent in their actual or expected medical, dental, psychological, social, or educational situations;

    c. Intervention or procedure is likely to yield generalizable knowledge about the subjects' disorder or condition that is of vital importance for the understanding of the participants' condition [45 CFR 46.406].

[ ] 4. Research that is otherwise not approvable, but which presents an opportunity to understand, prevent, or alleviate a serious problem affecting the health or welfare of children. Research that is not approvable under numbers 1, 2, and 3, above, may be conducted, provided that IRB, after consultation with a panel of experts, finds that the research presents a reasonable opportunity to further the understanding, prevention, or alleviation of a significant problem affecting the health and welfare of children. The panel of experts must also find that the research will be conducted in accordance with sound ethical principles [45 CFR 46.407].

Section 2. Parental Consent
Please circle a or b as you deem appropriate for this study:

    a. Active parental consent required (one parent)

    b. Parental consent waived

Section 3. Assent of Minor
It is important the PI includes the minor in all aspects of the research as appropriate for his/her maturity level. The Assent signature line may be included on all consent forms where minors may be enrolled. However, the requirement for obtaining a signature is determined on the nature of the study. Please indicate below your view of the requirement of assent for this study:

    a. **Assent signature required:** This study does not involve interventions likely to be of benefit to minors nor can they comprehend and appreciate what it means to be a volunteer for the benefit of others.

    b. **Assent signature not required:** The inclusion of the minor in all aspects of the research will be conducted as appropriate. However, the possibility of direct benefit that is important to the health or well-being of the minor is available only in the context of this research and/or the minor is unlikely to understand the situation well enough to give meaningful assent.

Incompetent Participant Form Attachment G

When a subject is not competent to give informed consent federal regulations state that the investigator must obtain written permission from a **legally authorized representative** prior to enrolling the subject in a research study. Federal regulations define **legally authorized representative** as an "individual or judicial or other body authorized under applicable law to consent on behalf of a prospective subject to the subject's participation in the procedure(s) involved in the research" (45 CFR 46.102(c)). Neither federal regulations nor New Hampshire State Law provide specific information about who may, or may not, qualify as a **legally authorized representative** in a research setting. For the purposes of this policy statement, the options of defining a legally authorized representative include:

a. Durable power of attorney for health care (DPAHC)

b. Court appointed legal guardian

c. Next-of-kin

A strict interpretation of NH state law does not provide for the use of Next-of-kin as a surrogate decision maker for investigational activity. The argument for allowing next-of-kin to consent to participation in research activity for an incompetent individual is that, without such an option, it is often impractical or impossible to conduct important medical research on conditions where results with the best current therapy are suboptimal. When investigational therapy represents the best treatment option or when risks to the subject are small in relation to the potential benefit of research to society, a policy which creates a major obstacle to the conduct of important research activity is ethically unsound. With the above issues in mind, the IRB has established the following policy for research studies that may involve adult subjects who are not competent to give informed consent to participation in a research study:

1. When initially submitting a protocol for review by the IRB, the investigator will inform the IRB in the appropriate section of the IRB protocol document if the study may involve subjects who are NOT competent to give informed consent to participate in the study being proposed.

2. When a study may involve subjects who are not competent to give informed consent, the investigator will inform the IRB if they plan to allow an agent other than a DPAHC or court appointed legal guardian to consent to participation in the research study. Specifically, the investigator will inform the IRB if they would like to consider a next-of-kin as the legally authorized representative with the ability to provide permission for an incompetent individual to participate in research study.

3. When an investigator would like to use next-of-kin to consent to a research study involving a subject who is not competent to give informed consent, the investigator will answer the following questions as part of the IRB application material:

(a) Could the subject receive the same management that they will receive in the research study outside the setting of a research protocol?

(b) Will participation in the study increase the risk of harm or discomfort compared to what is expected with the management that the subject will receive if they do not participate in the research study?

(c) Will participating in the study increase the chance that the subject will experience a favorable outcome compared to what is expected with the management that the subject will receive if they do not participate in the research study?

(d) What is the magnitude of the benefit that future patients, or society in general, may experience as a result of the subject participating in this study?

(e) The process of appointing a legal guardian may take several months. Would this type of delay compromise patient care?

4. The IRB will focus on the questions described above when reviewing a protocol that may involve subjects who are not competent to give informed consent.

(a) Even with the permission of a DPAHC, or court appointed legal guardian, the IRB will not permit a subject who is not competent (to give informed consent) to participate in a research study that offers little chance of *direct benefit* to the research subject over what they could receive outside the research setting, and involves a meaningful increase in the risk of harm or discomfort, regardless of the potential gain to future subjects or society in general.

(b) When there is a meaningful chance of *direct benefit* to the research subject over what they could receive outside the research setting, the IRB will make a judgment decision about who may consent to participation in the study. The options include: DPAHC, court appointed legal guardian, and a properly motivated next-of-kin.

5. Below is the signature line to use when incompetent participants may be enrolled into a research study. As described above, use of the next-of-kin option requires special IRB approval:

_____

Participant Signature and Date   Printed Name

(Continued)

If participant is not competent to provide informed consent, sign below as appropriate:

_____

Durable Power of Attorney of Health Care and Date   Printed Name
or

_____

Court Appointed Legal Guardian and Date   Printed Name
or

_____

Next-of-kin and Date   Printed Name

Contact IRB Office:

☐ If requesting a waiver for obtaining informed consent respond to:
Waiver of Consent Attachment H.

☐ If requesting a waiver for obtaining a signed consent form respond to:
Waiver of Signed Consent Form Attachment I.

Waiver of Consent Attachment H

If you are requesting the waiver for participant consent, the following items must be addressed and deemed appropriate by the IRB.

(I) An IRB may approve a consent procedure which does not include, or which alters, some or all of the elements of informed consent set forth in this section, or waive the requirements to obtain informed consent provided the IRB finds and documents that:

1. The research involves no more than minimal risk to the subjects;

2. The waiver or alteration will not adversely affect the rights and welfare of the subjects;

3. The research could not practically be carried out without the waiver or alteration; and

4. Whenever appropriate, the subjects will be provided with additional pertinent information after participation.

Waiver of Signed Consent Form Attachment I

If you are requesting the waiver of the requirement for a signed consent form, the following items must be addressed and deemed appropriate by the IRB.

(I) An IRB may waive the requirement for the investigator to obtain a signed consent form for some or all subjects if it finds either:

1. That the only record linking the subject and the research would be the consent document and the principal risk would be potential harm resulting from a breach of confidentiality. Each subject will be asked whether the subject wants documentation linking the subject with the research, and the subject's wishes will govern; or

2. That the research presents no more than minimal risk of harm to subjects and involves no procedures for which written consent is normally required outside of the research context.

In cases in which the documentation requirement is waived, the IRB may require the investigator to provide subjects with a written statement regarding the research.

Departmental Scientific Review of Research Protocols Involving Human Subjects

Principal Investigator _____

Project Title _____

_____

_____

_____

    All protocols must undergo scientific review by a departmental research group or other designated authority prior to submission to the IRB. The review must involve individuals qualified to evaluate the scientific merit of the study being proposed. If the departmental research review group does not include individuals who are capable of evaluating the scientific merit of a particular proposal, it is the responsibility of the department chair or designated representative to have the protocol reviewed by an appropriate authority not involved in the study in question.

<u>Approval Checklist</u>

This protocol has been reviewed by the departmental research group . . . . .YES   NO

        Other (specify) _____

_____

_____

a. The scientific questions addressed in this protocol have adequate merit to justify experimentation involving

    human subjects . . . . .YES   NO

b. The potential risks of this study have been accurately and fully described . . . . .YES   NO

c. The study design is adequate to answer the questions being asked . . . . .YES   NO

(Please attach a brief summary of the discussion of the study design including issues that you think could be raised by the IRB)

d. Prior animal or *in vitro* studies are adequate to support human trials . . . . .YES   NO

e. Is there a method to investigate this scientific problem without
    human subjects? . . . . .YES   NO

(If **YES**, then please explain, on the back of this form, why human subjects are to be employed.)

f. The principal investigator and co-investigator(s) have adequate experience
    to conduct the study . . . . .YES   NO

Please identify a member of the review team (NOT an investigator involved in the study) who will be responsible for discussing this protocol with members of the IRB if necessary.

_____ Phone _____

_____ Date _____

Signature of Departmental Research Group Chair or other cognizant authority

Consent Form Template

General Instructions: The consent form is part of an ongoing dialog between researchers and participant. Please describe the consent process in item #22 of the IRB protocol.

• *The consent form should be written at an eighth grade level. Avoid dense paragraphs using lengthy sentences. Use 'bullets' and tables to clearly explain topics. We have provided suggested wording below.*

• *For medical studies, the signed consent form must be filed in the general circulation medical record and a copy must be given to the participant.*

• *The pages must be numbered and the footer must contain the most current version of the consent form.*

• *The IRB office will 'pre-review' a consent form at anytime via email.*

CONSENT TO PARTICIPATE IN RESEARCH

Name of Institution

Study title:

Introduction: You are being asked to participate in a *research study*. Your participation is *voluntary*.

Note: If the study includes minors, add the sentence: "You" in this study may refer to your child being enrolled in the study. If the study involves minors only use "Your child" throughout the consent form.

Your decision whether or not to participate will have no effect on the *quality of your medical care, academic standing, job status, etc. (whatever phrase is appropriate)*. Please ask questions if there is anything you do not understand.

What is the purpose of this study?
The purpose of the study is to learn about . . . *explanation (in lay language) of the basic purpose of the study.*

Suggested conclusion wording if applicable:
In order to learn about xxxxx, half the participants in this study will receive xxxx and half the participants in this study will receive a placebo (no medication).

Are there any benefits from participating in this study?
First sentence as appropriate to the specific study: choose one of the following:
You will not benefit from being in this research study.
There is almost no chance that you will benefit from being in this research study.
There is little chance you will benefit from being in this research study.
You may not benefit from being in this research study.

Second sentence, if applicable:
We hope to gather information that may help people in the future.

What does this study involve?
Include a sentence indicating length of time of study for participation:

Your participation in this study may last up to _____. You will be asked to return to the clinic _____ times.

Briefly explain (in lay language) the tasks, procedures, therapies, tests, etc., involved in this study. When applicable, clearly describe:
• *whether or not the drugs or devices are being used in ways that are not FDA approved*
• *the use of placebo*
• *whether or not all participants will receive the same therapy,*
• *and the process of randomization.*

Use tables and/or charts to simplify procedures. If there are multiple study groups, clarify this by listing the groups as follows:

If you decide to enroll into this research study you will be assigned *by chance* to one of the following groups:

Group A - receives xxx
Group B - receives xxx

Neither you nor your doctor can determine or will know into which group you will be assigned.

How is this different from what will happen if you do not participate in this study?
Explain alternatives in lay language.
Explain whether or not the research therapy can be obtained off study:
The therapy offered in this research project is available to you without enrolling in this study.
Because it is experimental, this therapy is only available to you in the context of a research study.

Include a list of the Tests/Procedures to be performed for research purposes only:
If you enroll in this study the following *additional* tests or procedures will be performed: *(this information should correspond to item #6 in IRB protocol)*

What are the risks involved with being enrolled in this study?
Do not list every possible side-effect or complication that could occur. Comprehension is usually inversely related to the amount of information presented so include only the things that you think are important for a potential participant to remember.

With drug studies involving a multi-drug regimen, list the problems associated with the entire regimen rather than providing separate information for each individual medication. Whenever possible, you should estimate the probability that a problem will occur. Words such as "common," "unlikely," "occasionally," or "rare" may be used when it is not desirable to use numerical estimates. Whenever possible, use a table format to summarize risk information.
Be sure to include risks of being in a placebo or observation group.
Note: When research involves therapy or procedures that would be recommended if medical care is delivered outside the setting of a research protocol, it is appropriate to explain that the risks associated with such therapy will not be avoided by electing not to participate in the study.

Sample wording:
We cannot be sure how your body may respond to the (medications or procedures) used in this study. The researchers will discuss possible difficulties and the chances that they will happen. Unknown problems may happen. Problems may range from a minor inconvenience or may be so severe as to result in death *(indicate highest severity level if death is not applicable)*. You should report any problems to your doctor or to the director of this study: *(PI name and phone number)*

Example of table format:

DRUG(S)	PROBLEM	CHANCE IT WILL HAPPEN TO YOU
		% chance (common, unlikely, occasionally, rare)

Risk of placebo:

If applicable include the following section, (include suggested wording as appropriate):

Pregnancy:
The risks of *name of drug* to an unborn child are unknown. Pregnant women may not take part in this research study. Pregnancy tests will be conducted on all women of child-bearing potential . . . every . . . xxx . . . The sponsor or your insurance company (indicate which one) will pay for pregnancy tests.

All *women of child-bearing potential* are required to use a medically approved method of birth control (diaphragm, IUD, progesterone implants or injections, or double barrier method) in order to take part in this research study. Please discuss these options with the researcher.

If you or your partner become pregnant, you should notify *(name to notify)* immediately.

Other important items you should know:

• **Withdrawal from the study:** You may choose to stop your participation in this study at any time. *{If withdrawal could affect medical treatment describe how, here.}* Your decision to stop your participation will have no effect on the *quality of medical care, academic standing, job status, etc. (whatever phrase is appropriate)*.

(Continued)

• *If applicable add here information about the possibility of termination by investigator without participant consent.*

• *If applicable add here information about the consequences of a participant's decision to withdraw from the research and procedures for orderly termination of participation.*

• **New Information:** To the best of our ability, any significant new findings during this research study will be made known to you. You can then decide if you want to continue in this study.

• **Confidentiality:** Every effort will be taken to protect the names of the participants in this study. *(describe methods to be used: coding, grant of confidentiality, etc.)* However, there is no guarantee that the information cannot be obtained by legal process or court order. Institutional authorities and certain federal agencies such as the Food and Drug Administration, the *National Cancer Institute, and Cancer and Leukemia Group B and the sponsor of this study, XYZ Co.,* will have access to records related to this research.

• **Funding:** [Name of institution] and the researcher conducting this project have been provided funding from [name of sponsor].

Use this section to describe potential conflicts of interest.

• **Number of participants:** We expect (## of) participants to enroll in this study here and (##) nationwide.

Who should you call with questions about this study?

Questions about this study may be directed to your doctor or to the researcher in charge of this study: Dr. xxx at (603) 555-1234 during normal business hours.

If Dr. xxx is not available, other members of the section of xxxxx will be available to answer your questions during normal business hours.

If you have general questions about being a research participant, you may call the IRB office at (123-4567) during normal business hours.

What about the costs of this study?

Clearly explain the costs which may be charged to the participant / insurance co. versus the charges which will be paid for by the sponsor. This information should correspond with items # 6 and #7 in the IRB protocol. Use suggested wording as appropriate:

The (study medication) will be supplied by (sponsor name) free of charge. Any tests, examinations, or other procedures that are done solely for research purposes as previously described will be paid for by the sponsor of this study (sponsor name). Insurance companies or other third party payers will not be billed for research procedures.

The rest of the medical care that you will receive in this study is considered standard care for your situation and thus would be recommended regardless of your decision to participate in research. These costs will be billed to you or your insurance carrier.

Will you be paid to participate in this study?

yes or no. If yes describe payment schedule / travel reimbursement etc.

What happens if you get sick or hurt from participating in this study?

Sponsor (Sponsor Name) Policy: The sponsor of this research is XYZ Company. If you develop an illness or an injury happens because you are in this research study the XYZ Company will . . . *enter the appropriate information regarding the level of liability the sponsor will assume in case of research related injury or illness.*

Institution Policy: It is the Institution policy that if you are injured or become ill as a result of research procedures, medical treatment will be provided to you but Institution will not pay for this treatment.

If you have any questions about the legal responsibility, please call the Office of Risk Management at (555-5555) between the hours of 8:00 A.M. and 5:00 P.M. on Monday through Friday. At all other times call 603-555-5000 and ask for Beeper #(777).

CONSENT

I have read the above information about *(name of study)* and have been given an opportunity to ask questions. I agree to participate in this study and I have been given a copy of this consent document for my own records.

SIGNATURE OPTIONS (choose one block) - Note: The *Principal Investigator* is responsible for ensuring all participants enrolling in this study have *provided informed consent.* The PI may authorize other appropriately trained individuals to obtain informed consent and sign as "designee." These individuals must be listed in the IRB protocol (item #22). The individual signing below should be the individual obtaining consent.

===**Option 1** *If study includes* competent participants only ================

_____

Participant's Signature and Date   PRINTED NAME

_____

Researcher or Designee Signature and Date   PRINTED NAME

===**Option 2** *If study may include* incompetent *participants* ==============

If your study receives IRB approval to include incompetent participants, include the following lines to signature section as the IRB has indicated is appropriate. IRB approval is required to add next-of-kin option - complete item #18 in IRB protocol

_____/_____

Participant's Signature and Date   PRINTED NAME

If participant is not competent to provide informed consent, please sign as appropriate:

_____

Durable Power of Attorney for Health Care /   PRINTED NAME
or

_____

Legally Court-Appointed Guardian   PRINTED NAME
or

_____

Next-of-kin   PRINTED NAME

_____

Researcher or Designee Signature and Date   PRINTED NAME

===**Option 3** *If study may include minors* ===========================
If study may include minors add the signature line for assent. The parent or legal guardian should sign as Legally Authorized Representative and the minor should sign the Assent line.

I have explained to this child what participating in this study will involve and have answered any questions that he or she has asked.

_____

Researcher or Designee Signature and Date   PRINTED NAME

_____

Assent of minor (age 7 - 17)   PRINTED NAME

_____

Legally Authorized Representative and Date   PRINTED NAME

Storing Blood or Tissue For Additional Studies

This study includes laboratory tests that will analyze samples of blood and specific blood cells. The blood samples will be collected by inserting a needle in your arm and drawing blood out into a tube. The blood cells will be sent to a laboratory where tests will be performed. Researchers will be performing these tests in order to understand your specific type of leukemia. They will also look at your blood cells to see if there are any left over leukemia cells after treatment. They hope this will help them better understand your type of cancer. The results from these tests will not be sent to you or your doctor, and will not be used in planning your care. These tests are only for research purposes.

Please indicate if you agree to participate by circling your response in the box below. You do not have to take part in the scientific laboratory tests. Your decision not to participate will have no effect on your care at this institution. You can still participate in the treatment part of the study without taking part in the additional research studies.

I agree to participate in the scientific laboratory tests that are being done as a part of this study.
Yes   No

Please print and sign your name here after you circle your answer.

Your name: _____

Your signature: _____ Date: _____

Will any of the samples (blood, bone marrow) taken from me be used for other research studies?

As part of this study, you are going to have some blood and bone marrow collected as part of your treatment and/or to do some tests. We would like to keep some of the blood and bone marrow that is left over for future research. If you agree, this blood and bone marrow will be kept and may be used in research to learn more about cancer and other diseases. This blood and bone marrow will only be given to researchers approved by the Eastern Cooperative Oncology Group (ECOG). Any research done on the bone marrow must also be approved by the researcher's Institutional Review Board (IRB).

Your blood and bone marrow may be helpful for research whether you do or do not have cancer. The research that may be done with your blood and bone marrow probably will not help you. It might help people who have cancer and other diseases in the future.

Reports about research done with your blood and bone marrow will not be given to you or your doctor. These reports will not be put in your health record. The research will not have an effect on your care.

Things to Think About

The choice to let us keep the leftover blood and bone marrow for future research is up to you. No matter what you decide to do, it will not affect your care and you may still take part in the (sponsor) treatment study.

If you decide now that your blood and bone marrow can be kept for research, you can change your mind at any time. Just contact your study doctor and let him or her know that you do not want us to use your blood and bone marrow. Then the blood and bone marrow will no longer be used for research.

In the future, people who do research may need to know more about your health. When the (sponsor) gives them reports about your health, they will not give them your name.

Sometimes blood and bone marrow is used for genetic research (about diseases that are passed on in families). Even if your blood and bone marrow is used for this kind of research, the results will not be put in your health records.

Your blood and bone marrow will be used only for research and will not be sold. You will not be paid for allowing your leftover bone marrow to be used in research even though the research done with your blood and bone marrow may help to develop new products in the future. Similarly there will be no cost to you for any blood and bone marrow collected and stored by the (sponsor).

It is possible that at some time in the future, that as part of deciding on what therapy to give you, a new test might be available that could be done on some of the blood and bone marrow that is now thought of as leftover. This situation is unusual, but it could happen. In order to see that not all of this leftover blood and bone marrow is used up, the (sponsor) will take care to see that some of your cancer blood and bone marrow is stored for 10 years so that it is available should it be needed by you or your doctors. This will depend upon the amount of leftover blood and bone marrow that is submitted for this study; however, there may not be any left over blood and bone marrow to store.

Benefits

The benefits of research using blood and bone marrow include learning about what causes cancer and other diseases, how to prevent them, how to treat them, and how to cure them.

Risks

There are very few risks to you. The greatest risk is the release of information from your health records. The ECOG will protect your records so that your name will be kept private. The chance that this information will be given to someone else is very small.

Making your choice

Please indicate if you agree to participate by circling your response in the box below. You do not have to take part in the scientific laboratory tests. Your decision not to participate will have no effect on your care at this institution. You can still participate in the treatment part of the study without taking part in the additional research studies.

---

1) My blood and bone marrow may be kept for use in research to learn about, prevent, treat, or cure cancer.

   Yes   **No**

2) My blood and bone marrow may be kept for research about other health problems (for example: causes of diabetes, Alzheimer's disease, and heart disease).

   Yes   **No**

3) My doctor or someone from the (sponsor) may contact me in the future to ask me to take part in more research.

   Yes   **No**

Please print and sign your name here after you circle your answer.

Your name: _____

Your signature: _____ Date: _____

Institution Name
IRB
Request For Revision Form

Principal Investigator: _____ IRB #: _____

Study Title: _____

1. Revision Description (check all as appropriate):
_____ Revision to currently approved *protocol*
_____ Revision to currently approved *consent*
_____ Other - (e.g., advertisement).

2. Check one:
_____ This revision *does not* increase risks to participants enrolled in the study.
_____ This revision *does* increase risks to participants enrolled in the study (include explanation in revision description and Department Chairperson signature is required).

3. Describe revision request:

4. Attach *revised* protocol and/or consent (Highlight all revisions)

Signature of PI: _____ Date: _____

Signature of Section Chief or Department Chairperson: _____
(Required if risks to patients are *increased*.)

TO:

[ ] Approved: *This signifies notification of IRB APPROVAL of the revision descibed above.*

Note to IRB reviewer(s): Please contact the IRB office with comments for follow-up on other options:
[ ] Not Approved   [ ] Abstain   [ ] Conditionally Approved

IRB REVIEWER'S SIGNATURE: _____ DATE: _____

Institution Name
IRB
ADVERSE EVENT REPORTING FORM

Is the event being reported SERIOUS AND UNEXPECTED?
        YES   NO   (circle one)

Serious: *Death, a life-threatening adverse drug experience, inpatient hospitalization or prolongation of existing hospitalization, a persistent or significant disability/incapacity, or a congenital anomaly/birth defect.*
Unexpected: *Any adverse drug experience, the specificity or severity of which is not consistent with the current investigator brochure or consent form.*

If yes, complete this form and forward with appropriate attachments to the IRB office.
If no, do not forward to the IRB office.
        Report to the sponsor and/or FDA as required.

Date: _____   IRB #: _____

Investigator: _____

Study Title: _____

_____

1. Study is: **Multi Site**   **Onsite only**

2. Is this a follow-up report?   YES   NO

3. **Describe Adverse Event:** _____
Indicate seriousness:
        a. Serious but not fatal
        b. Fatal
Provide a summary describing the circumstances of the event. Indicate if prolonged hospitalization or medical treatment was required. Include a copy of all notifications and/or letter of adverse event from the study sponsor or other sites. *INCLUDE A STATEMENT IN YOUR WORDS REGARDING THIS ADVERSE EVENT AND RELATION TO THE STUDY / PATIENTS AT THIS INSTITUTION:*

4. In your judgment, was the event caused by the therapy or procedures associated with this protocol?
        Possibly   Probably   Definitely related

5. Is the risk of this AE contained in the current consent form?   YES   NO
6. Is the risk of this AE contained in the investigator's brochure? YES   NO

7. Should the consent form or any portion of the study be revised as a result of this event?
    YES   NO   If yes, please enclose revised documents with all revisions in bold print or highlighted.

8. Will currently enrolled individuals be notified of this event?   YES   NO
        If yes, describe method of notification:

Signed : _____   Date: _____
                (Principal Investigator)
*********************************** For IRB use only ***********************************

Review by IRB chairperson: (initials) _____ Date: _____

IRB Continuing Review Form

Principal Investigator: _____ IRB #: _____

Study Title:_____

_____

Study Status:
_____ Active.
_____ Enrollment closed. Participants *are receiving study treatment.*
_____ Enrollment closed. Participants are *not receiving study treatment.* Follow-up involves procedures that would not
      be done if the pt. is followed off-protocol. Explain below.
_____ Enrollment closed. Participants are *not receiving study treatment.* Follow-up procedures are the same for pa-
      tients managed on or off protocol. *Study will be terminated.*
_____ Other (Explain).

Number of enrollees in *past year* at Institution name: Female _____   Male _____   Total _____
Total number of participants since starting study:

   Institution name   Female _____   Male _____   Total _____

   All sites (if multi-center)   Female _____   Male _____   Total _____

**Respond to following questions in detail sufficient for appropriate review (use additional pages as needed). If study is
being terminated provide a final summary:**

1. Summarize revisions previously reviewed and approved by IRB:

2. Summarize revisions not yet reviewed by IRB:

3. Synopsis of activities to date (include the progress of the study as compared to the hypothesis):

4. Have unexpected events, toxicities, or complications occurred that may indicate a need for a change in the protocol
   or consent?
   Yes   or   No   If yes, please explain:

5. Has information (publications, presentations, etc.) become available since starting this study that indicate a need to
   modify this study?
   Yes   or   No   If yes, please explain:

6. Were any grievances or complaints received about this study?
   Yes   or   No   If yes, please explain:

Signature of PI: _____   Date: _____

IRB: Noncompliance / Complaint Process

Upon notification to IRB office of noncompliance or complaint:

1. IRB Director will determine if immediate suspension of participant enrollment is required for project in question as well as for other projects with the same PI. This initial decision will be based on preliminary information and the seriousness of the situation. Consults and/or receipt of further information in conjunction with continuation of noncompliance process will determine length of time of suspension. If applicable, the sponsor contract or grant award notice will be reviewed to determine notification to sponsor requirements.

2. IRB Director will consult with IRB Chair to confirm categorization of:

   Suspension or Nonsuspension.

   a. **Suspension not merited:** If IRB Director and IRB Chair agree that suspension is not merited, the issue will be resolved between any combination of the following individuals: IRB Director, IRB Chairman, PI, PI Dept. Chair. All communication will be documented.

   b. **Suspension is merited:**

Notice of suspension effective immediately will be sent to: PI, Co-PIs, Dept. Chair, Grants & Contracts, IRB Institutional Official, IRB Chair.

Within 2 days a meeting will be called of any combination of the following individuals: IRB Director, IRB Chair, PI, and/or PI Dept. Chair to discuss the nature of the situation and to determine if the situation merits a designation of serious or continuing non-compliance.

In order to make the determination of serious or continuing noncompliance it may be necessary to perform an audit of study records. The PI will be required to produce:

All signed consent forms

All data related to study project

i. **Nonserious and Noncontinuing:** If the incident appears to be isolated and in essence is a miscommunication or misunderstanding of a nonserious and noncontinuing nature, the incident will remain internal. A letter from the IRB office to the PI describing a summary of the audit will be written. A response from the PI describing corrective actions is also required. This will be considered the final step if the incident is considered to be nonserious and noncontinuing. Suspension of patient enrollment will be lifted.

ii. **Serious or Continuing:** If the audit indicates noncompliance which is serious or continuing the Office for Human Research Protection (OHRP) will be notified. This will be a phone call to OHRP to apprise the office of the incident of noncompliance and will be followed with a letter. The initial letter to OHRP will briefly describe the incident, the preliminary steps, and an indication of the time frame for full audit. In addition, a full report will follow, including corrective actions for this specific incident and for the research program in general at [name of institution] to ensure incidents will not occur again.

IRB Expedited Review Study Form
Institution name

IRB #: _____(assigned at IRB office)

PRINCIPAL INVESTIGATOR: _____ DEPT: _____

CO-INVESTIGATOR: _____ DEPT: _____

STUDY TITLE: _____

SPONSOR: _____

SIGNATURES: _____ DATE: _____
Principal Investigator

_____ DATE: _____
Department Chairperson

*Department Chairperson signature indicates: a) the scientific questions addressed in this study have adequate merit to justify experimentation involving human subjects, b) the potential risks of this study have been accurately and fully described, and c) the study design is adequate to answer the questions being asked.

FOR NEW STUDIES, PLEASE ATTACH THE FOLLOWING INFORMATION:

Institution: Explain the study procedures, data collection and analysis process. Estimate study dates and number of subjects.

Location of study: List other locations. Describe procedures for obtaining approval (schools: letter of approval from principal, etc.)

Participants: List inclusion and exclusion criteria. Explain the rationale for the involvement of special classes of subject such as students, employees, pregnant women, children, incompetent individuals, prisoners, or other institutionalized individuals, or others who are likely to be vulnerable.

Describe any financial aspects related to participant involvement in study.

Note: Special classes may require full committee review; contact IRB for further information.

Explain the process for recruiting participants, in particular students and employees.

Risks: Describe any potential risks (physical, psychological, social, legal, or other) and assess their likelihood and seriousness. Describe the procedure for protecting against or minimizing any potential risks, including risks to confidentiality, and assess their likely effectiveness.

INFORMED CONSENT: Explain how informed consent will be obtained. Attach copies of consent form or information sheet if applicable. Please contact IRB office for sample consent form if signed consent is to be obtained.

Please submit 2 copies to the IRB office:

IRB office address.

For IRB USE ONLY: To Expedited Review Committee:

[ ] Approved   [ ] Not Approved   [ ] Abstain   [ ] Conditionally Approved

COMMENTS:

REVIEWER'S SIGNATURE: _____ DATE: _____
Expedited category:

IRB
Requirements for Review of Undergraduate Social Science Research
(Contact:)

STUDENT RESEARCHER: _____   PHONE: _____

FACULTY ADVISOR: _____   DEPT: _____

PHONE: _____

STUDY TITLE: _____

SIGNATURES: _____   DATE: _____
Student Researcher

_____   DATE: _____
Faculty Advisor*

* Faculty Advisor's signature or email message indicates that the advisor has discussed the ethical issues surrounding human subjects research in the proposed research setting with the student researcher.
An email message from the advisor may replace a signature on this form.

PLEASE ATTACH THE FOLLOWING INFORMATION:

Introduction: Explain the study procedures, data collection, and analysis process. If surveys will be conducted, explain if they are anonymous or linked by any identifiers to the subjects. Estimate study dates and number of participants (if possible).

Location of study: List locations where the research will take place. Describe procedures for obtaining approval if applicable (e.g., schools: letter of approval from principal, etc.). *Further information may be required if minors are involved.*

Participants: Explain the process for selecting and contacting participants. Describe any special feature of the study population (e.g., language barriers).

Risks: Describe any potential risks (physical, psychological, social, legal, or other) and assess their likelihood and seriousness. Describe the procedure for protecting against or minimizing any potential risks, including risks to confidentiality, and assess their likely effectiveness.

Informed Consent: Explain how informed consent will be obtained. Attach copies of consent form or information sheet if applicable. Please contact CPHS office for sample consent form if signed consent is to be obtained.

Addenda: Include copies of any questionnaires, cover letters, survey scripts, or other documents to be used with study participants.

For IRB USE ONLY   TO: _____

[ ] Exempt   [ ] Expedited, approved   [ ] Additional information required

COMMENTS:

REVIEWER'S SIGNATURE: _____   DATE: _____

IRB-01 PRIMARY REVIEWER TEMPLATE: STUDY #_____

Summarize the study (2 minutes):
The purpose of the study is to:

Study population:

Summary (background, # arms, controls, different from nonresearch alternative, IND/IDE):

Sponsor:

Investigator: (Name, Dept, qualified?, COI)

Vulnerability: (Children, incompetent adults, employees, students, prisoner)

Informed consent: (Required, Written, Surrogate)

Birth control:

Subject recruitment: (Who, Where, How, Advertise?) Subject selection is likely to be equitable.

Genetic testing/tissue repository:

Cost relative to nonresearch :

Payment or reimbursements: (coercive?)

Risks (relative to nonresearch alternative):

Potential benefit: (Direct for subject, altruism, state the benefit to the sponsor/PI)

Risk/Benefit analysis: Risks are minimized by study design and reasonable in view of potential benefits

Confidentiality: Provisions to protect the privacy of subjects and the confidentiality of data are adequate

Data oversight: (DSMB, stopping rules):

Consent document:

IRB Minutes Template
Name of Institution
Minutes
Date and Time
Location of meeting

IRB MEMBERS PRESENT:

STAFF PRESENT:

Guests:

CONTINUING EDUCATION:
Articles distributed prior to meeting:
Discussion items:
The committee discussed these items with specific emphasis on the implications for future IRB practice.

ITEMS:
1) The minutes from last months meeting (or give date) were reviewed. There were no controversial entries or objections.
2) The next meeting will be held on meeting (or give date) in (the location) beginning at (TIME).
3) Announcements:

Previously NOT APPROVED (date)
1) PI NAME   #IRB   Title:
                      Sponsor
                      VOTE:
                      Discussion items: Discussion followed outline as required in summary protocol. Summary of controverted issues and resolutions:

NEW PROTOCOLS:
2) PI NAME   #IRB   Title:
                      Sponsor:
                      VOTE:
                      Discussion items: Discussion followed outline as required in summary protocol. Summary of controverted issues and resolutions:

(Continued)

REVISIONS REQUESTS
3) PI NAME   #IRB   Title:
                          Sponsor:
                          VOTE:
                          Discussion items: Discussion followed outline as required in summary protocol. Summary of controverted issues and resolutions:

RENEWALS
4) PI NAME   #IRB   Title:
                          Sponsor:
                          VOTE:
                          Discussion items: Discussion followed outline as required in summary protocol. Summary of controverted issues and resolutions:

Expedited Review
*The following studies were approved by the **Expedited Review Committee** in (PROVIDE DATE RANGE):*

NEW PROTOCOLS
PI NAME   #IRB   Title:

RENEWALS
PI NAME   #IRB   Title:

REVISIONS - MINOR CHANGES APPROVED
PI NAME   #IRB   Title:

STUDIES DESIGNATED EXEMPT FROM FURTHER IRB REVIEW
PI NAME   #IRB   Title:

STUDIES VOTED CONDITIONALLY APPROVED AT FULL COMMITTEE MEETING
PI NAME   #IRB   Title:

Respectfully submitted,
Name
Director, IRB

Institutional Review Board
Name of Institution

Agenda
September 21, 2000 8:00 A.M.
Location

ITEMS:

1. Continuing Education:

2. Articles:

3. Review the minutes of the (previous date) meeting.

4. The next meeting will be held on (date) in (location) at (time)

NOT APPROVED on DATE /RE-REVIEW
1) PI NAME   #IRB   Title:
                                                 Sponsor:

NEW PROTOCOLS
2) PI NAME   #IRB   Title:
                                                 Sponsor:

REVISIONS
3) PI NAME   #IRB   Title:
                                                 Sponsor:

RENEWALS
4) PI NAME   #IRB   Title:
                                                 Sponsor:

Index